FRIENDS, FOLLOWERS, AND FACTIONS

Friends, Followers, and Factions

A READER IN POLITICAL CLIENTELISM

Edited by
STEFFEN W. SCHMIDT, LAURA GUASTI,
CARL H. LANDÉ and JAMES C. SCOTT

UNIVERSITY OF CALIFORNIA PRESS

Berkeley   Los Angeles   London

University of California Press
Berkeley and Los Angeles, California

University of California Press, Ltd.
London, England

Copyright © 1977 by
The Regents of the University of California

ISBN 0-520-02696-9
Library of Congress Catalog Card Number: 73-93060
Printed in the United States of America

CONTENTS

50689

PART III. Application: Clientelism in Traditional Settings

PART IV. Application: Clientelism in Local Perspective

*PART V. Application: Clientelism--Middle-Level Perspectives
    (Brokerage)*

PART VI. Application: Clientelism—National Perspectives

PART VII. Clientelism Theory and Development

PART VIII. Appendix

PREFACE

POLITICAL SCIENTISTS, anthropologists, and sociologists have long known that people act together on the basis of friendship, deference, and informal bonds. The mafioso boss has his kin and henchmen, the religious teacher his disciples, the ward-heeler his grateful retainers, the feudal lord his entourage of vassals and serfs, the landlord his tenants. In much of politics and social action such clusters of leaders and followers are the key units of action. When they occur at the elite level, they are often called cliques, at the local level they have been variously called "vote-banks," patron-client networks, or local factions. Many national parties or movements (e.g., the Christian Democrats in Italy, much of the Congress Party in India) are composed of pyramids of such leader-follower clusters.

While class, ethnic, and religious cleavage may often explain a portion of the contest for power, clientelism often illuminates a vast range of political life which is not easily reducible to such categorical groupings. Clientelism may, in addition, be instrumental to the study of, say, class issues, whether as a barrier to class consciousness or as the very structure of internal class organization.

Over the past ten years there has been something of a boom in both the theoretical and practical attention to clientelist structures. In sociology this has found expression in the growing use of exchange theory. In anthropology, the study of factional systems and the structure of local leadership has led to a host of new concepts. In political science the study of political middlemen or brokers, systems of patronage, and party factionalism has contributed to the study of clientelism. Although much of this new work grew from the study of third-world politics, the analysis of clientelism has proven useful in dealing with European politics, in explaining factional politics in socialist systems such as China, and in tracing the historical transition from feudal to class politics. These spreading ripples are a measure of the scope and wide applicability of clientelism as a theory. Given the recent explosion of work in this area, one expects that more and more research will systematically turn to this model of politics and that much of the best work on the third world will make use of its conceptual leverage.

We felt that the time was ripe to assemble a collection of the very best theoretical and case-study material on clientelism for students and colleagues in the social sciences. Following a theoretical introduction, the selections which follow move from theories of dependence and reciprocity to very tangible rural *caciques*. They move from anthropology, to sociology, to political science; from village to nation; from theory to case study. In assembling this reader, we have self-consciously tried to maximize its appeal across disciplines and subject areas. Working under the draconian constraints of the publishing industry we have nevertheless attempted to retain the scope and coverage which would make the reader valuable to a wide audience. It is our hope that this volume will find a place in many upper-division undergraduate and graduate courses in sociology, anthropology, and political science. The reader concludes with a lengthy bibliographical essay and a listing of relevant works by geographical area.

We would like, frankly, to congratulate ourselves for having survived, more or less intact, a collaboration that in retrospect has assumed the proportions of an epic struggle; one having more in common with the perils of Pauline than with The Odyssey. Nearly four years ago when we conceived of this project we assumed lightheartedly that, between the four of us, it would prove a relatively simple undertaking. The gestation period alone boggles the mind and we had ample opportunity to recall Pogo's injunction: "From here on down it's uphill all the way." Nor does the gestation metaphor, implying steady ontological growth, quite do justice to the nature of our collaboration which proceeded by fits and starts of hectic activity interrupted by long periods of silence and abandonment.

Constraints on size made it impossible to include a number of selections which we had hoped to reprint. We hope that the bibliographic essay to some degree makes up for these omissions. We would like to acknowledge the advice and help of Crawford Young, Herbert Lewis, William Foltz, and Fred Bailey in choosing selections and preparing the bibliographic essay. We thank Jeannie Hoyt who typed most of the manuscript and we hope nothing like this ever befalls her again.

Steffen Schmidt
Laura Guasti
Carl Landé
Jim Scott

ACKNOWLEDGMENTS

WE WISH TO THANK the following for permission to reproduce material in this book:

Sidney W. Mintz and Eric R. Wolf, "An Analysis of Ritual Co-Parenthood (Compadrazgo)," *Southwestern Journal of Anthropology*, Vol. 6, No. 4, Winter 1950, pp. 341-368.

George M. Foster, "The Dyadic Contract: A Model for the Social Structure of a Mexican Peasant Village," *American Anthropologist*, vol. 63, No. 6, December 1961, pp. 1173-1192. (Permission also granted by The American Anthropological Association).

Alvin Gouldner, "The Norm of Reciprocity: A Preliminary Statement," *American Sociological Review*, Vol. 25, No. 2, 1960, pp. 161-178. (Permission also granted by The American Sociological Association.)

Adrian C. Mayer, "The Significance of Quasi-groups in the Study of Complex Societies," *in* Michael Banton, ed., *The Social Anthropology of Complex Societies*. London: Tavistock Publications, 1966. (Permission also granted by the Associated Book Publishers Ltd.)

Ralph W. Nicholas, "Factions: A Comparative Analysis," *in* Max Gluckman and Fred Eggan, *Political Systems and the Distribution of Power*. London: Travistock Publications, 1965, pp. 21-61. (Permission also granted by the Associated Book Publishers Ltd.)

Carl H. Landé, "Networks and Groups in Southeast Asia: Some Observations on the Group Theory of Politics," *American Political Science Review*, LXVII, No. 1, March, 1973, pp. 103-127.

René Lemarchand, "Political Clientelism and Ethnicity in Tropical Africa: Competing Solidarities in Nation-Building," *American Political Science Review*, LXVI, No. 1, March, 1972, pp. 68-90.

James C. Scott, "Patron-Client Politics and Political Change in Southeast Asia," *American Political Science Review*, LXVI, March, 1972, pp. 91-113.

John Duncan Powell, "Peasant Society and Clientelist Politics," *American Political Science Review*, LXIV, No. 2, June, 1970, pp. 411-425.

Lucien M. Hanks, "The Corporation and the Entourage: A Comparison of Thai and American Social Organization," *Catalyst*, Sum., 1966, pp. 55-63.

Eric R. Wolf, "Kinship, Friendship and Patron-Client Relations in Complex Societies," *in* Michael Banton, ed., *The Social Anthropology of Complex Societies*. New York Frederick A. Praeger, Publisher, 1966, pp. 1-22.

Lilly Ross Taylor, *Party Politics in the Age of Ceasar*, Berkeley: University of California Press, 1961, pp. 25-49.

Marc Bloch, *Feudal Society*, Vol. 1, translated by L. A. Manyon. Chicago: University of Chicago Press, 1961, pp. 219-225, 241-251.

Lucy P. Mair, "Clientship in East Africa," *Cahiers D'Etudes Africaines*, II, No. 6, 1961, pp. 315-326. (Permission also granted by Edicom N. V. Contracts & Subsidiary Rights Department.)

Frederick Barth, *Political Leadership Among the Swat Pathans*, London School of Economics, Monographs on Social Anthropology, No. 19. London: The Athlone Press, 1965, pp. 42-50, 71-81.

Marshall D. Sahlins, "Poor Man, Rich Man, Big-Man, Chief: Political Types in Melanesia and Polynesia," *Comparative Studies in Society and History*, Vol. V, No. 3, April 1963, pp. 285-303.

Abner Cohen, "The Social Organization of Credit in a West African Cattle Market," *Africa*, 35, 1965, pp. 8-20. (Permission also granted by the International African Institute, who publish the journal *Africa*.)

J. K. Campbell, *Honour, Family and Patronage: A Study of Institutions and Moral Values in a Greek Mountain Community.*© Oxford University Press, 1964, by Permission of the Oxford University Press, Oxford.

Paul Friedrich, "The Legitimacy of a Cacique," *in* Marc J. Swartz, ed., *Local Level*

Politics: Social and Cultural Perspectives. Chicago, Aldine Publishing Co., 1968, pp. 243 -269. (Permission also granted by publisher.)

Jeremy Boissevain, "Factions, Parties, and Politics in a Maltese Village," *American Anthropologist*, 66, No. 6, December, 1964, pp. 1275-1287.

H. A. Gould, "The Hindu Jajmani System: A Case of Economic Particularism," *Southwest Journal of Anthropology*, 14, 1958.

Sydel F. Silverman, "Patronage and Community-National Relationships in Central Italy," *Ethnology*, 4, No. 2, April, 1965, pp. 172-189. (Permission also granted by the editor of *Ethnology*.)

Steffen W. Schmidt, "The Transformation of Clientelism in Rural Colombia," paper presented at the 1974 annual meeting of the American Political Science Association, ©APSA, 1974.

Alex Weingrod, "Patrons, Patronage, and Political Parties," *Comparative Studies in Society and History*, 10, July, 1968, pp. 377-400.

Wayne Cornelius, "Leaders, followers and official Patrons in Urban Mexico," a revised version of a piece appearing in Robert Kern, ed., *The Caciques: Oligarchial Politics and the System of Caciquismo in the Luso-Hispanic World*, Albuquerque, New Mexico: University of New Mexico Press, 1973. This paper is an abridgement of a chapter from the book *Politics and the Migrant Poor in Mexico City*, Stanford U. Press.

Michael Kenny, "Patterns of Patronage in Spain," *Anthropological Quarterly*, 33, No. 1, January, 1960, pp. 14-23.

Luigi Graziano, "Patron-Client Relationships in Southern Italy," reprinted from *European Journal of Political Research*, Vol. 1, No. 1 (1973), pp. 3-34, with permission of Elsevier Scientific Publishing Company, Amsterdam.

Nobutaka Ike, *Japanese Politics: Patron Client Democracy*, New York, Alfred Knopf, 1972, pp. 12-20.

Andrew J. Nathan, "A Factionalism Model for CCP Politics," *The China Quarterly*, January-March, 1973, pp. 34-66.

Douglas A. Chalmers, "Parties and Society in Latin America," *Studies in Comparative International Development*, VII, No. 2, Summer, 1972, pp. 102-128. (Published by permission of Transaction, Inc.)

James C. Scott and Benedict J. Kerkvliet, "How Traditional Rural Patrons Lose Legitimacy—A Theory with Special Reference to Southeast Asia," *Cultures et Developpment*, 5:3, 1973, pp. 327-339. (Permission granted by A. Lecointre, Redacteur en chef, *Cultures et Developpment.*)

W. F. Wertheim, "From Alirian Towards Class Struggle in the Countryside of Java," *Pacific Viewpoint*, No. 10, September, 1969, pp. 1-17. (Permission also granted by the editor, *Pacific Viewpoint.*)

Edward Hansen, Peter Schneider, and Jane Schneider, "Modernization and Development: The Role of Regional Elites and Non-Corporate Groups in the European Mediterranean," *Comparative Studies in Society and History*, June, 1972, pp. 328-350.

Carl H. Landé, "Group Politics and Dyadic Politics: Notes for a Theory," *Leaders, Factions and Parties: The Structure of Philippine Politics,* Yale Southeast Asia Monograph Series, No. 6. New Haven: Yale University Southeast Asia Studies, 1965, pp. 141-148. (Permission also granted by the publisher.)

Anthony Hall, "Patron-Client Relations: Concepts and Terms" *Journal of Peasant Studies*, Vol. 1, No. 4, July, 1974, pp. 506-509.

INTRODUCTION:

THE DYADIC BASIS OF CLIENTELISM
CARL H. LANDÉ

THIS VOLUME brings together a selection of writings dealing with a type of social and political organization that over the past two decades has attracted the attention of a growing number of scholars engaged in the study of the "developing" societies. In many such societies, these scholars have found, personal relationships play a more important part in the organization of political activity than do organized groups based on shared class identification, occupation, or ideological affinity. Even where groups of the latter type appear to exist, they often operate less as disciplined collectivities than as clusters of personal relationships. This observation has led a number of students of the politics of developing countries to examine and learn from a body of anthropological literature dealing with interpersonal relationships.

Among the terms used to denote interpersonal relationships and combinations of such relationships of varying degrees of complexity and magnitude are "dyadic relationship," "dyadic noncorporate group," and "social network." Dyadic relationships are composed of only two individuals, and thus are micro-level entities. Dyadic non-corporate groups, such as patron-client systems or clienteles, which are the main subject of this book of readings, are middle-level combinations consisting of sets of dyadic relationships linked together for limited purposes over limited periods of time. Social networks are the totality of dyadic relationships, or of significant dyadic relationships, to be found within a social field. There is some disagreement among scholars interested in these types

of structures concerning their exact nature, degree of distinctiveness, varieties, boundaries, the conditions which bring them into prominence, and the consequences of their presence for the political process. This introduction to the present collection will be devoted to a brief discussion of dyadic structures of these three differing degrees of magnitude, beginning with the smallest and simplest and ending with the largest and most complex, as well as to a consideration of their significance for political analysis.

DYADIC RELATIONSHIPS

A dyadic relationship, in its social science sense, is a direct relationship involving some form of interaction between two individuals.

The key word in this definition is *direct*. It connotes personal attachment. It distinguishes a dyadic relationship from a relationship in which two actors are connected with each other indirectly as a consequence of the fact that they occupy offices or positions which are interconnected, or because they are members of the same group.

In practice two individuals may be engaged simultaneously in both a dyadic and a nondyadic relationships. This can make it difficult, under stable conditions, to distinguish the two. The difference between them becomes clear however under conditions of change or conflict when a choice must be made between one or the other.

Imagine two officials, each of whom has a subordinate. The first official, A, is transferred laterally to a different office. His subordinate B moves with him. A rises to a higher post, and secures a better position for B as well. A is demoted and B follows him into disgrace. A dies or is dismissed and B gives up or loses his job as well. Official C also has a subordinate, D. C moves laterally, upwards, downwards, or out. But D remains in place. Or D moves while C remains in place. Observing these two sets of superordinates and subordinates we may infer that A and B regard themselves—or are regarded by higher authorities who make or approve job assignments—as members of a dyadic relationship that has precedence over their attachment to their posts. The reverse may be inferred in the case of C and D.

A second example will illustrate the distinction further. Imagine a person E who has two friends, F and G. All three are members of an association. E is expelled from the association, whereupon F resigns out of loyalty to E. We may infer that for F the dyadic relationship with E was more important than his organizational membership, while for G the opposite appears to have been the case.

Various patterned relationships, observable in diverse societies and in different historical periods, can be described as being dyadic or non-dyadic to varying degrees. A man who takes up arms to come to the aid of a friend is involved in a dyadic relationship. The vassal of a medieval king, the serf of that vassal, and the client of a pre-modern Thai official are involved in relationships which rely heavily upon personal attachment, i.e. dyadic linkage, for their stability and effectiveness. The enlistee in a modern army, the Weberian bureaucrat, and the factory worker who takes orders from his foreman and works in harness with his neighbor on the assembly line are involved in relationships which in the first instance are non-dyadic. Personal ties may develop subsequently, and may help or impede the operation of the non-dyadic connections. But they are not essential to the latter.

A dyadic relationship as it has been defined here can be wholly voluntary or can be obligatory for one or both members. It can be diffuse, and entail merely a mutual undertaking to be helpful to each other or it can involve clearly specified obligations for each member. It can exist between two persons of equal socio-economic status or between persons whose status is unequal. It can be of relatively short duration, last a lifetime, or be carried on from generation to generation by the descendants of those who created the original dyad. The only element essential to the definition is that the relationship must connect two individuals with each other by a direct personal tie.

Nevertheless, the distinctions between voluntary and obligatory dyadic relationships on the one hand, and between those with diffuse and with specific obligations on the other are important for an understanding of the nature of dyadic relationships. In a sense, the purest dyadic relationships are those which are voluntary and diffuse. For they reflect the free choices of their participants and depend for their endurance upon the reaction of each member to the inducements offered by the other. Even relationships that are imposed and that involve clearly delineated obligations are likely to be more acceptable to their participants and thus more active and durable to the extent that they conform to the content and style of voluntary and diffuse dyadic relationships. George Foster calls such relationships "implicit dyadic contracts."[1] As an alternative I suggest the term "dyadic alliances." Dyadic alliances are of two types, those between persons of equal status and those between persons of unequal status, i.e. those which are "horizontal" and those which are "vertical." They differ in various ways and must be examined separately. I shall begin with a discussion of horizontal dyadic alliances and will discuss vertical alliances subsequently.

HORIZONTAL DYADIC ALLIANCES

A dyadic alliance is a voluntary agreement between two individuals to exchange favors and to come to each other's aid in time of need. A consideration of the several elements of this definition, and of some of their implications for horizontal dyadic alliances follows.

The Mutual Assurance of Aid in Time of Need

The obligations to exchange favors and to come to each other's aid in time of need are not the same, and must be considered separately. I shall deal with the latter first, for it is the more important of the two.

The words "to come to each other's aid in time of need" suggests two of the distinctive characteristics of dyadic alliances. First, they suggest the genuinely dyadic nature of such alliances. The obligations of the two allies are to *each other*, not to any higher body of which one or both are members. Second, they suggest that the obligations of each ally depend on the *other's needs*. Each is expected to have a genuine concern for the other's welfare and to do what he can to promote the other's welfare without too precise a reckoning of his own costs. In particular, each is expected to help the other in extreme emergencies, i.e., when aid is most needed. Both allies, in short, are expected to display altruism towards each other. This expectation of altruism, and the diffuse obligations which are associated with it, most clearly distinguish a dyadic alliance from a contractual relationship in which the obligations of the contracting parties are clearly delimited and neither is expected to sacrifice his own interests for the benefit of the other beyond carrying out the specific terms of their contract.

The Exchange of Favors

Dyadic alliances involve the exchange of favors. A favor is something received on terms more advantageous than those that can be obtained by anyone on an *ad hoc* basis in the market place, or which cannot be obtained in the market place at all. Thus the superiority of a resource or service obtained through favoritism may lie in its lower-than-market price. It may lie in its availability to the recipient in quantity at a time when the item is generally in short supply or when he is in extreme need of it. Or it may lie in the fact that the benefit cannot be obtained through simple purchase at all.

The exchange of favors is one of the purposes of dyadic alliances. Favors are valuable in themselves. But the exchange of favors also serves as a *means* of maintaining a dyadic alliance and thus of achieving its other purpose: The binding together of two allies who can count on each other's help in time of need. Thus the exchange of favors allows each ally to demonstrate his interest in the alliance and his willingness to make sacrifices for his ally. It also serves as a public display of the alliance. Through such a display, the two publicly commit themselves to their alliance and invite social opprobrium if they fail to meet their mutual obligations. The conspicuous exchange of favors serves some additional functions. It shows each of the two to be a valuable ally and therefore attracts other would-be allies. And it puts their enemies on notice that each will come to the other's defense when asked to do so.

Because the exchange of favors serves as a means as well as an end in itself, exchanges may take place between allies even though neither ally needs the things that he receives in these exchanges. Thus dyadic alliances usually involve the giving of unwanted gifts and alternate hosting on ceremonial occasions.

The Narrow Objectives of Dyadic Exchange

Dyadic alliance building is especially well suited to the pursuit of particular private goals. In choosing this technique rather than, or in addition to, the alternative technique of working as a member of a group for objectives agreed upon by that group, an individual reserves for himself the right to set his own goals. But at the same time he commits himself to paying the full price for what he receives through dyadic exchange. His ally does the same. Hence neither is likely to seek through these exchanges more than he and his immediate dependents can use for themselves. Furthermore, as most ordinary individuals command but a limited stock of exchangeable resources, they usually cannot in fact offer more in trade than is needed to satisfy the private wants of an individual or family.

A further reason why dyadic exchange tends to be devoted to the pursuit of particular goals is that those engaged in dyadic trading often are individuals who in some important respect are un-alike. Each has sought out the other because the latter has something that he needs but lacks. Their dissimilarity may merely be quantitative and temporary. Both may have resources of the same type, but each has a shortage or excess of these at different points in time. Thus one peasant helps another in a time of emergency, and the other provides similar help in return at a later time. But their dissimilarity may also be of a qualitative sort: Each has much of one thing but none of the other, as in an alliance between a businessman and a politician, one of whom supplies the other with money while receiving the benefits of political influence in return. Finally the two may be dissimilar in that one has far more wealth or power than the other. This is so in the case of patron-client relationships, the main subject of this book.

When two allies are qualitatively dissimilar, it is unlikely that one person's self-interested desire to help his ally will take the broader form of a concern for the welfare of the occupational group or class to which that ally belongs. A tenant will do favors for his landlord, but is not likely to champion the interests of landowners in general. A landlord will extend loans to his tenant, but is not likely to concern himself with the collective needs of all tenants.

The Simplicity of Dyadic Alliance Building as a Technique

As will have become evident, dyadic alliance building is a simple technique. This is due to the small size of dyads, to the nature of the process of dyadic alliance building, and to the organizational characteristics of dyads. A dyad is composed of two individuals, which makes it the smallest of groups. The process of dyadic alliance building involves the simple trading of favors and not the more difficult task of furthering collective goals. A dyad, as Georg Simmel has noted, is not a super-individual entity with an existence above and independent of its members.[2] Therefore it has no organizational trappings of the sort found in even the simplest corporate group. It has no name, no agreed upon procedure for making collective decisions and selecting leaders, and no common commitment to obey such leaders and to act in unison in other specified ways. A dyadic alliance therefore is easy to create. Its formation can be proposed by either of its two prospective members through the offer or request of a favor with the implied understanding that the favor will be returned, that further exchanges will ensue, and that in general each can look to the other for help in time of need. The alliance becomes a reality and gains strength as the exchanges continue. It becomes strongest when help is given at some cost to the giver at a time of extreme need on the part of the recipient. When the exchanges cease and there is no intention of renewing them, or when an appeal for help in time of need is ignored, the alliance comes to an end.

Because of the simplicity of this technique, it is used in all societies. Children everywhere learn to assure themselves of favorable responses from persons on whom they must depend, first within the family and then outside it, by offering or returning favors to these individuals. As adults, they employ the same technique, in varying degrees, in diverse spheres of life. For this reason, as Jeremy Boissevain has pointed out, it is misleading to describe dyadic alliances or larger dyadic combinations as merely "interstitial," "supplementary," or "parallel," to corporate groups, as some writers have done.[3]

Indeed, dyadic alliance-building is an obvious strategy of first choice—and sometimes of last resort—for the lone individual as he pursues a variety of private interests or goals.

The technique is well suited for this purpose for several reasons: It allows an individual to give unequivocal priority to the pursuit of the objectives which he deems to be important. It requires of him to do no more for others than what is necessary as a *quid pro quo* for the achievement of his own aims. It allows him to be his own tactician, leaving him free to alter his system of alliances to suit changing power relationships and changes in his own interests and goals.

While advantageous from an egocentric point of view under the right conditions, the technique has serious limitations. It depends upon the willingness of others to ally themselves with that individual. Unless he can give something that is of value to another person, the latter cannot be expected to become his ally. Consequently persons who own or who have access to substantial resources have many would-be allies, and can afford to create alliances with many of them. The poor and the weak, on the other hand, may have few willing allies to choose from, and may find that they cannot afford to cultivate more than a few alliances in any case. Furthermore, as the maintenance of a dyadic alliance depends upon the willingness of both allies to maintain it, an individual may find himself losing allies at the time he is most in need of them, despite their earlier professions of a concern for his welfare, because they no longer find him to be useful from the point of view of their own interests. Finally, while well suited to the pursuit of private interest, dyadic alliance building is ill suited to the mobilization of large numbers of people for the pursuit of collective goals.

The Problem of Reliability

Dyadic alliances are voluntary relationships involving diffuse rather than clearly delineated obligations. Therefore they cannot be made dependent for their proper functioning and endurance upon legal sanctions. Indeed, dyadic alliance-building often is resorted to *because* of the absence of legal institutions capable of enforcing formal contracts, or because the individuals concerned prefer not to put their relationship on a contractual basis or to make it subject to legal oversight. The networks of alliances that exist in the criminal underworld illustrate this point.

Alliances are formed in the first instance because both allies expect them to be useful to themselves. But the needs and resources of individuals change with the passage of time. Allies of long standing may lose their attractiveness as potentially more useful allies appear on the scene. In the absence of legal impediments, one member of an alliance may be strongly tempted to let the alliance lapse, while the other still wishes to maintain it. Therefore the reliability of allies is often a matter of serious concern for those who engage in dyadic alliance building. To maximize the probability that obligations incurred through such alliances will be honored, various non-legal methods in addition to the exchange of favors must be employed.

One method is through the invocation of norms that support fidelity to alliances. One of these is what Alvin Gouldner calls the "norm of reciprocity." This norm, Gouldner states, "makes two minimal demands: (1) people should help those who have helped them, and (2) people should not injure those who have helped them." The important point about this norm is that it is internalized not only by those in a position of weakness but also by those who have the power to take without giving anything in return. This, Gouldner points out, accounts for the fact that the opportunity to exploit others is not normally used to its maximum advantage.[4] In the short run this norm, if respected, assures that unrepaid favors will be returned. But it does not require the indefinite continuance of a dyadic alliance unless the outstanding debts are so great that they cannot be discharged quickly. For this reason, a useful procedure for alliance-builders is to load an ally with an "unrepayable debt," i.e., a debt so great that it can never be fully repaid. An unrepayable debt is one given in time of extreme need or at great cost. Saving a life creates an unrepayable debt of course. In the Philippines, children often are reminded that they owe unrepayable debts to their parents and in particular to their mothers for the risks they took in giving them life.[5] This puts them under a continuing obligation to obey their parents and attend to them in their old age. Acknowledgement of the existence of such a debt means that the indebted ally cannot break the alliance, and must always be ready to respond to a call for aid, unless he can repay with a favor that is itself of such "unrepayable" magnitude that it cancels out the initial debt.

A somewhat different norm that can be used to buttress dyadic alliances, especially when these are of long standing, is the norm of personal loyalty. Personal loyalty helps to maintain an alliance in the face of the declining usefulness of one ally to the other. It requires that the latter respond favorably to requests for aid when the former has lost his ability to reciprocate even at the cost of foregoing the opportunity to forge a new alliance with a potentially more useful partner.

Both the norms of reciprocity and of personal loyalty are vulnerable, however, to a device which can be used to break off an alliance before outstanding debts have been repaid. This device, which is used sometimes in the Philippines, consists of the discovery or invention of a grievance, such as an affront to one's *amor proprio* or self esteem, of such weight that when thrown into the balance of reciprocity, it cancels out an outstanding debt.

Thus neither of these two norms is a wholly reliable guarantor that dyadic alliances will be maintained. There remains another mechanism which serves this purpose under some, though not all conditions. It will be discussed below.

Dyadic Alliances as Addenda

George Foster, in describing "implicit contracts," his term for what I have called dyadic alliances, contrasts them with what he calls "formal and explicit contracts."

Formal and explicit contracts "rest on governmental and religious law, are legally or ritually validated . . . and are enforceable through the authority of the particular system that validates them."[6] Examples of such formal, legal contracts are found in the mutual obligations assumed by marital partners, by parents and the godparents of their children, and by the buyers and sellers of goods. Their mutual obligations, which are conventional, are prescribed by the institutions of which these role-partnerships are a part, i.e., by the institutions of marriage, baptism and the market. And they may be enforced by the authorities which stand behind these institutions, i.e., by the Church or the state.

Yet, Foster notes, while the average peasant understands the conventional obligations required by these institutions, he recognizes:

That the way he fits into these institutions, does not, in fact, explain how his community works. He sees that, quite apart from conventional institutions, he is tied in another way to certain relatives, compadres, neighbors, and friends to the partial or complete exclusion of others occupying the same statuses vis à vis ego, who collectively make his world a workable world.[7]

This other way of being tied to *certain*—but *not all*—of these relatives, compadres, neighbors and friends is through "implicit contracts."

The distinction between, and coexistence of formal, explicit, institutionalized contracts on the one hand, and implicit contracts, or dyadic alliances, on the other, has important implications for an understanding of the nature and functions of dyadic alliances. Formal, explicit, institutionalized contracts, Foster suggests, do not offer an adequate explanation of the way a community works because they do not provide for all of the needs of a community or of the individuals who enter into such contracts. Some of these must be enlivened by the superimposition upon them of voluntary relationships of a more selective, flexible, intermittent and emotional sort that can give them a vigor not found in conventional institutionalized contracts when these stand alone. This need is met by the addition of dyadic alliances.

This argument may be reversed. Dyadic alliances, being selective, intermittent and voluntary, do not provide a sufficient basis for the organization of a society. Nor do they provide the guarantees of support that an individual needs to assure his survival. Dyadic alliances therefore ordinarily must be supported by a framework of institutionalized relationships, i.e. relationships which are continuing rather than intermittent, which are inclusive in that they do not permit the arbitrary exclusion of specific individuals, which are predictable in that they prescribe substantively and procedurally standardized patterns of interaction, and which are linked to other institutionalized relationships of society.

The interconnection between dyadic alliances and institutionalized relationships suggests the additional mechanism that promotes the reliability of dyadic alliances: The quality of one of these types of relationships inevitably affects the quality of the other. Furthermore, sanctions available through one type of relationship can be used to enforce the other. Thus two officemates who have established a close friendship outside their place of employment are likely to work especially well together while on the job. When such a double connection exists, the rupture of one connection is likely to threaten the other. If one individual breaks off the dyadic alliance he cannot simply walk away but must expect to be punished through institutional sanctions: The former friend is likely to become uncooperative on the job. If he happens to hold a supervisory position over his former friend, such uncooperativeness can have quite painful consequences. For this reason two dyadic allies who are also connected with each other through an institutionalized relationship can be expected to make special efforts to keep their alliance in good order. Each therefore can place some confidence in the reliability of the alliance even though that alliance as such contains *within itself* no very effective sanctions for its continuance.

While dyadic alliances and institutionalized relationships ordinarily are interrelated, it is important for purposes of analysis that the dividing line which separates them be kept clearly in mind. The failure to separate the two and to assume that both relationships together constitute the dyadic alliance accounts for much of the continuing lack of agreement concerning the distinctive features of dyadic alliances as a structural type. This lack of agreement is particularly marked with respect to vertical dyadic alliances as will be seen below. As the institutionalized

relationships to which dyadic alliances are attached in different societies and different historical periods are of various kinds and take diverse structural forms, the composite structures, i.e., institutionalized relationships plus their dyadic alliance addenda, also appear to take quite different forms. If the dividing lines between the addenda and their supporting structures is kept clearly in mind however, it becomes evident that dyadic alliances as such vary little in their characteristics regardless of the diversity of their institutional hosts, and that they affect these diverse institutions in rather similar ways.

The making of a clear distinction between dyadic alliances and the institutionalized relationships to which they are added is useful for another reason as well. This distinction offers insights into the strength and weakness of the institutions concerned. Dyadic alliances are added to institutionalized relationships because the latter fail to fulfill certain needs. Therefore if an institution is heavily overlaid with dyadic alliances, one may then inquire into the precise nature of the institutional inadequacies which invite the creation of a dyadic alliance as an addendum. On the other hand if one encounters institutions that are free of dyadic addenda, this may be attributed either to the perfection of the institution itself or to the presence of effective institutional prohibitions against the addition of dyadic alliances.

Some examples will illustrate this point: Gideon Sjoberg has noted that economic exchange in pre-industrial cities is characterized by a lack of clear standards. Fixed prices are rare. Prices are determined by haggling between buyers and sellers. Sorting by size, weight, and quality is uncommon. And products offered for sale may turn out to be spoiled or adulterated.[8] In short the institution of the pre-industrial market fails to protect an ordinary customer against the risk of paying a higher than necessary price for goods of lower than normal quality. This risk helps to explain why those who must make repeated purchases often make efforts to establish special relationships with particular sellers of the goods they need. By becoming what in the Philippines are called each others *suki*, customers are assured of a low price without a need for repeated haggling, and of the delivery of goods of the highest quality available. The sellers in turn are assured of steady customers.[9] Suki relationships, under different names, are found in the economies of many pre-industrial societies. They are far less common in modern industrial economies where fixed prices and products of standardized quality make them unnecessary. This explains the friendly neighborhood grocer's inability to compete with the faceless but lower-priced supermarket chain. An interesting exception is found in the sphere of auto repairing. There the fear that their ignorance of the complexities of auto mechanics subjects them to victimization in the form of unnecessary repairs at inflated prices leads many modern automobile owners to establish special relationships of steady patronage with garages or mechanics on whom they think they can rely for honest repairs and for preferentially speedy service when needed.

DYADIC NON-CORPORATE GROUPS

Dyadic relationships play an important part in binding together the members of certain types of non-corporate groups. The nature of such groups can best be understood by comparing them with corporate groups.

A corporate group is a discrete, multi-member aggregate having property, aims and duties which inhere in the group as such, and are distinct from those of its individual members. Each member has rights and duties with respect to the group. All members are bound together by virtue of their shared membership in the group and by their common obligation to protect its interests and fulfill its obligations. Some examples of corporate groups are families, lineages, clans, tribes, guilds, and in the modern world organized interest groups, political parties and nation states.

Non-corporate groups, as the term suggests form a residual category which includes all aggregates that can be called "groups" but that are not corporate groups. The term can be stretched, therefore, to include such unorganized and aimless aggregates as "the poor" or a leaderless mob.

The types of non-corporate groups under discussion here, however, do have organization of a sort, and perform tasks which are well understood by their participants. Thus they lie nearer to the somewhat fuzzy line which separates non-corporate from corporate groups. Non-corporate groups of this type will be referred to as "dyadic non-corporate groups." Examples include action sets, clusters of friends, political factions, and clienteles.

The non-corporateness of such groups lies in the fact that they lack the two distinguishing characteristics of fully corporate groups: Undivided common property, aims and duties, and uniform linkage through common membership in the group as such.

In dyadic non-corporate groups individual members are assisted in the protection of their private property, the advancement of their private interests, and the performance of their individual duties by other members of the group through reciprocal aid and parallel action. But the group as such does not have, to a significant degree, property, interests, or duties of its own, distinct from those of its members. If members have common property, aims or duties, at all, they have them for but brief periods of time. Thus property won through common action tends to be divided among those who helped in its acquistion soon after it has been acquired, or is appropriated by a leading member of the group who then permits other members to share in its use. Often however, the members of such groups have no common property even temporarily. Group action then is confined to helping individual members advance their individual interests and fulfil their individual obligations.

As members of dyadic non-corporate groups are bound together mainly or wholly by their interpersonal relationships of reciprocal aid, and only minimally if at all by a sense of common membership in a "group," individual members need not be linked equally to all members. Dyadic non-corporate groups vary from ones in which each member is linked directly, though not necessarily by ties of equal strength, to all other members—what J. A. Barnes has called a "cluster of maximum density," examples of which are a tight-knit group of friends, or a political faction whose members take turns running for public offices and campaigning for each other—to ones in which one central individual has many allies, but each of these is allied only with him—a structure which Barnes calls a "primary star."[10]

Various consequences flow from these two characteristics of dyadic non-corporate groups. Such groups, with the possible exception of those of maximal density, lack clear boundaries. Instead, they shade off gradually from those individuals at the center of a cluster who help and are helped by the greatest number of their fellows, to those at its periphery who give and receive aid from only one or a few other members. Political systems organized on the basis of such groups are likely to be characterized by a lack of clear dividing lines between political groups and a great deal of shifting and switching among peripheral group members. Examples of such shifting are to be found in Philippine politics and in factional politics in much of Southeast Asia, Latin America, and the Mediterranean region.

Among those members of a non-corporate group who give aid to one of their fellows, obligations of assistance may be unequal. The amount of aid given will depend upon the amount of aid the giver has received from the recipient in the past, or hopes to receive in the future. A cluster of this type therefore is a changing and amorphous group which alters its shape and size each time it is mobilized for action, depending upon which member of the group calls upon other members for aid. Even the same member will mobilize different allies within the cluster on different occasions. Thus it is unlikely that the whole or maximal cluster will be in action continuously. Seen over time rather than at a specific point in time, such a group resembles a smudge which results from the successive superimposition upon each other of a series of primary stars having different centers and different external dimensions.

A final consequence of the directly interpersonal nature of linkage in dyadic non-corporate groups is the important place occupied by intermediaries. In order to obtain the aid of other members of the group—or persons outside the group—with whom an individual has no direct personal ties, he may work through an intermediary aid-giver or aid-givers, thereby creating a dyadic chain. Such a chain involves the linking together of a set of dyads end to end. Thus A, in need of a favor from D with whom he has no direct connection asks B to ask C to ask D to do a favor for A. In return, A does a favor for B who does a favor for C who repays the favor to D. Jeremy Boissevain has provided a good description of the operation of such a horizontal chain.[11] An example of a vertical chain is provided by the downward flow of patronage and the upward flow of electoral support through a number of political leaders at successive levels of a political system.

Clienteles and Patron-Client Relationships

One type of primary star, which is the main subject of this volume, is a patron-client system or "clientele." Its constituent elements are patron-client relationships.

A patron-client relationship is a vertical dyadic alliance, i.e., an alliance between two persons of unequal status, power or resources each of whom finds it useful to have as an ally someone superior or inferior to himself. The superior member of such an alliance is called a patron. The inferior member is called his client.

Patron-client relationships share most of the characteristics of horizontal dyadic alliances. They involve the direct personal attachment of two individuals to each other. They exist for the purpose of exchanging favors and providing mutual assurances of aid. They are easy to create, but bring with them problems of reliability. At the same time, patron-client relationships have some distinctive features which set them off from alliances between persons of equal socioeconomic status.

In the patron-client relationships the benefits exchanged between patrons and clients almost always are different in kind. For the usefulness of patron and client to each other stems not so much from the fact that their needs occur at different points in time, but from the fact that each at almost any time can supply the other with benefits that the latter can never obtain by himself, or can obtain by himself only on rare occasions. This qualitative difference in the benefits exchanged applies both to the exchange of symbolic and substantive favors and to the mutual assurance of aid in time of need.

Typically, the favors which patrons do for their clients are material in kind, while those which clients do for their patrons involve the expenditure of labor or effort. Typically the assurances of aid which clients seek from their patrons involve economic assistance and physical protection in times of emergency, while those which patrons seek from their clients entail the risk of the latters' lives, health or reputations in the service of their patrons.

Most patrons, being by definition men of superior status and resources, are able to maintain alliances with numerous clients all of whom they supply with benefits in return for what each of the clients can supply to them. Indeed, the height of their status and the quantity of their resources tends to determine the number of clients they can maintain. Many patrons do maintain numerous clients with a view to securing the advantages that are to be derived from the support of a large, albeit individually poorly endowed, set of clients or followers. As a result, one often finds a set of vertical dyads extending upwards from various clients to a single shared patron who is the central individual of a vertical primary star.

As there are in any society more individuals of low than of high status, it is possible for a large part of a society to be organized into a relatively small number of clienteles, with most of the common people grouped under a small number of high status patrons. These clienteles may overlap, in the sense that one man may be the client of more than one patron.[12] But often clienteles are mutually exclusive. I.e., no client may have more than one patron. This is rarely the case with horizontal primary stars in which the central individual is of the same status as each of his allies. Such stars typically overlap with each other to form a continuous network of interlacing primary stars.

It is common for clienteles to be pyramided upon each other so that several patrons, each with their own sets of clients, are in turn the clients of a higher patron who in turn is the client of a patron even higher than himself. In such a pyramid, an individual may be both a patron and a client, but he is never both patron and client of the same individual. In a system of overlapping horizontal primary stars on the other hand, an individual who at one point in time organizes the efforts of all of the allies who come to his aid, will at other times place himself under the direction of each of them. I.e., he will at different times be leader and follower with respect to each of his horizontal allies.

When clienteles are mutually exclusive, they often develop a degree of discreteness and stability which, though less marked than in corporate groups, exceeds in strength that found in overlapping horizontal stars. They also may develop what appear to be collective goals, by making the private end-goals of the patron the intermediate goals of the clients. This is likely to happen when the prior achievement of his own goals by the patron is a precondition for the subsequent achievement of the private goals of the clients. Thus the election of a leader to public office may be a precondition for the channeling of patronage to his clients. His election therefore becomes the common intermediate goal of his clientele. In this sense, some of the goals pursued through patron-client relationships are less narrow than those typically pursued through horizontal dyadic alliances.

Patron-Client Relationships as Addenda

It was noted earlier that dyadic alliances often appear as additions to institutions whose deficiencies they remedy. This applies to patron-client relationships no less than to horizontal dyadic alliances. The institution of agricultural tenancy is a case in point. Under agricultural tenancy, an institution common to many traditional peasant societies, landless peasants cultivate land owned by prosperous landowners. Under a contractual arrangement which may or may not be written but which is clearly understood by both parties to the contract and which conforms to convention, the landlord provides the tenant with land and sometimes with certain other things needed in the process of agricultural production such as seed grain, plow animals, and nowadays, fertilizer. In return the tenant turns over a specified share of the harvest to the landowner and may be obliged to provide certain labor services as well. These mutual obligations are part of the institution of tenant farming as it has developed in a particular locality. They are predictable, continuing, apply to all landlords and tenants in that locality, and as they are contractual, may be enforced by the state.

But these institutional arrangements have limitations. They leave unsatisfied certain needs of rural people, rich and poor. They take no account of the fact that peasants may be in need of aid in various emergencies. They provide no guarantee of permanent tenure to the tenant. These are benefits that the landlord can provide to a tenant if he so desires, but he is not obligated to do so under the bare-bones landlord-tenant contract. If he does provide them, it constitutes a special favor. The tenant's contractual commitments for their part do not include an obligation to treat the landlord with special respect or affection. Yet it is important for members of the rural elite, especially if they aspire to local social and political leadership in their localities, that there are some among the common people who speak well of them and show them special respect. The best source to turn to for such status-support is, of course, among the landlord's own tenants. If some of these tenants provide such support this too constitutes a favor. The establishment of special relationships between a landowner and *some* of his tenants, and an assurance of conspicuous deference and loyalty to the landlord, constitutes the patron-client addendum to the institutionalized landlord-tenant relationship.

Patron-client addenda can also remedy the inadequacies of institutionalized relationships other than that of agricultural tenancy. Added to the legally sanctioned subordination of a slave to his master, a patron-client relationship protects a slave against the risks of being sold, killed or beaten, while giving the slave-owner some slaves whom he can trust. Attached to a bureaucracy it gives subordinate officials a better hope of attractive assignments and speedy promotion while giving their superiors groups of loyal subordinates who will support them in their intra-bureaucratic battles. Attached to business employment it gives some employees protection against dismissal while giving the owner some employees who will direct their loyalty to him rather than to a labor union. Attached to a voluntary association or to a state it protects an ordinary member or citizen against the risk of being left out during the distribution of particularistic benefits, while giving elected officials some voters who can be counted upon to support them in their efforts to remain in office.

While one can identify and abstract the patron-client addenda which are attached to the foregoing institutions, the institutions themselves appear to fall into two major groups which, when the addenda are attached, produce two distinctive types of combinations. The two types of institutions might be called ones of *personal subordination* and ones of *organizational subordination*.

Institutions of personal subordination include slavery, serfdom, agricultural tenancy and domestic service. These institutions consist of relationships that are, like their addenda, essentially dyadic. Subordinates are attached directly to individual slave-owners, lords, landowners, or householders, and rely on them for their subsistence in return for services provided to these individuals and their families. Patron-client relationships when added to these institutionalized relationships merge easily and naturally with the latter. A "good" slave, serf, tenant or household servant is almost by definition one who behaves like a good client. He makes himself personally amenable to his superior, and is entitled to personal consideration and loyalty in return.

On the other hand, in the case of institutions of organizational subordination which include modern bureaucracies, corporate business firms, and various types of modern voluntary associations, there is no such easy congruence between those relationships of superordination and subordination that are part of the institution and such patron-client relationships as may cling to them. While the addenda may be personally useful to the individuals concerned, and may even contribute to their ability to perform certain portions of their institutionalized roles, there is a continuing and unavoidable strain between the institutional requirements of impersonality and impartiality and the addendum's prescription of favored treatment for clients. In fact, if the institution is not to be subverted by its addenda, it must place clear limits upon the degree to which personal favoritism can be tolerated.

Because of the congruence between institutionalized relationships of personal subordination and patron-client relationships, much of the behavior characteristic of the latter may be incorporated into the former. That is to say, the dividing line between an institution and its addendum may shift its location over time. A pattern of behavior that is at first voluntary and is regarded as a special favor may become compulsory for all individuals who fill a given institutionalized role. In the course of this change it ceases to be an addendum and becomes an inseparable part of the institution itself. To give an example: A simple system of agricultural tenancy under which peasants are granted the use of land in return for the delivery of a share of the harvest to the landlord, accompanied in the case of *some* tenants by the performance of some extra and optional services to their landlords in return for various special favors, may grow and harden over time into a much broader set of clearly understood feudal obligations which are imposed upon all landless agriculturists as a condition for their access to arable land.

The dividing line may shift in the opposite direction as well. Various feudal obligations can be abolished by law without the simultaneous abolition of agricultural tenancy. However, some formerly compulsory or contractual interactions may continue on an optional basis as favors exchanged between those tenants and landowners who still find them to be to their mutual advantage. Other tenants may obtain the same benefits not from their landlords but from local political leaders, thereby preserving clientelism but separating it from the landlord-tenant relationship. Finally, patron-client relationships may disappear almost completely from the scene as needs that were once met through dyadic alliances are met through new non-clientelist institutions.

This happens when tenants are protected against emergencies and displacement by peasant associations or by the state, when slaves are emancipated or given legal protection, when bureaucratic tenure and promotion are regulated by strictly enforced civil service laws, when business employees have a strong and effective union, when the leaders of associations are subjected to strict supervision by the membership at large, and when governmental services become available to all on the basis of their qualifications under universalistic criteria rather than of their personal political connections.

When institutionalized relationships of personal subordination are heavily encrusted with patron-client addenda, or when such relationships make use of the patron-client model to such a degree that virtually all subordinates are expected to behave, and are entitled to be treated like clients, one may speak of a *clientelistic institution*. Thus feudalism is a clientelistic institution, and vassalage and serfdom are clientelistic relationships. The term "patron-client relationship" however should, I think, be preserved for the addendum alone.

Can patron-client relationships ever stand

alone? Can there be free-floating patron-client relationships outside the framework of any institution? I can think of no example of a patron-client relationship that exists in a total institutional vaccuum. The closest approximation is an alliance that ties together members of two hostile groups. But the hostility of groups is itself an institutionalized relationship, albeit a hostile one. And the need for such a cross-cutting alliance is likely to stem from this very fact of institutionalized hostility. Cross-cutting alliances of this sort are themselves likely to become institutionalized, as are the cross-regional trading partnerships and peace pacts of the pagan Kalingas of the Philippines.[13] In fact an institutional vaccuum, in which there exist nothing but vertical and horizontal dyadic alliances, is a virtual impossibility except as an extraordinary situation, and for a brief period of time. Horizontal dyadic alliances and patron-client relationships, it will be recalled, are selective intermittent and voluntary. They cannot by themselves perform the work of a society or provide the services upon which individuals depend for their survival from day to day. For this, regular interactions are necessary, and this means institutionalization.

The Rewards of Clientships

The analytical separation of patron-client relationships from the institutionalized relationships to which they may be attached makes it possible to explain why patron-client relationships are attractive to those who fill the roles of clients. Their special attractiveness stems from one of the features which distinguish patron-client relationships from many institutionalized vertical relationships; the fact that even though a patron-client relationship connects two persons of unequal status and power, it requires that they treat each other, and especially that the patron treat the client, equitably and with a special concern for each other's welfare. This point deserves elaboration: Many, indeed most traditional institutionalized relationships between persons of unequal power status and resources are highly exploitive in nature. This applies to such relationships as agricultural tenancy, feudal serfdom, indentured labor, and slavery. All of these relationships, by themselves, are harsh and impersonal. Many of them, furthermore, are relationships from which the subordinate knows he cannot in reality withdraw despite the fact that he may have a legal right to do so. The lack of alternative means or livelihood, continuous indebtedness to his superior, or legally enforced contractual relationships make withdrawal impractical. Yet while a man may be obliged to give up

his freedom and his dignity in exchange for a secure livelihood, he knows the relationship is inequitable. It may be assumed that he can distinguish what is "fair" or desirable from what he is obliged to do to survive. In any society or among any stratum of a society there are a set of normative standards governing "fair value" and justice that are distinct from the market price or the customary pattern of exchange which the relative bargaining power of unequals creates. Whenever the two diverge greatly, one can expect the weaker party to regard the situation as subjecting him to exploitation.

Under such conditions, there are several courses of action which the inferior member of a relationship may take to escape his condition of exploitation. One course is to find some way of withdrawing peacefully from the relationship. A second course is revolution. Both of these courses have become realistic options only in relatively recent times. The third option, which during most times in the past has been the only one open to a poor subordinate who feels he is being exploited is to induce his superior to voluntarily alter the terms of their relationship in the inferior's favor. The traditional way by which an inferior has sought to accomplish this has been by offering to become the superior's client, i.e., by making himself especially amenable to that superior, and doing various things that are not required of him, such as bringing him small gifts, performing more than the expected services, by spoiling the master's children, and in general by making himself useful and likeable to his master. These things the subordinate does voluntarily, in the expectation of receiving favors in return, i.e., benefits which those who do not make themselves extraordinarily useful and well liked do not receive. However, if these efforts to be ingratiating are not recognized and rewarded through reciprocal favors, no further efforts to ingratiate oneself are likely to be made. The attempt to add a dyadic alliance to the institutionalized relationship will be abandoned and only the latter will remain.

Not all tenants, serfs, servants or slaves are able to be clients. Those who enjoy the greatest opportunity for personal contact with their superior, house-slaves for example, have the best opportunity to become clients. Those who cultivate the most distant fields of their lord's estate have the least opportunity to do so. Hence the quantity of clientage that is added onto the underlying institutionalized relationship varies greatly between one class of subordinates and another. Among the ordinary field workers, the element of clientage may be minimal, even though various personal services are routinely expected of all of them and all may be entitled to some guarantee of special help in time of need.

Personal favors are favors only when there is favoritism, i.e., when the same benefits are not available to everyone. This means that the strength of the clientelist component of a vertical relationship, i.e., the quantity of clientage added onto the institutionalized relationship, differs not only between classes of subordinates but also between the members of each class. Granted that the benefits of clientelism may be greater and more widely distributed among household retainers than among field hands, still, some retainers will be favored above others, and will show greater loyalty in return. And the same applies to ordinary serfs. Such favoritism is functional. It rewards special loyalty, and encourages all clients and would-be clients to compete with each other for the favor of their patron. Thus clientelism is founded upon favoritism, within the clientele as well as between the clientele and those outside it.

The distinction between a patron-client relationship and the underlying relationship of economic superordination and subordination to which it is attached helps to explain what is frequently an ambivalent feeling of clients concerning their condition, and suggests some reasons why clientelistic institution may decline. A patron-client relationship creates some degree of equity, while the institutionalized relationship to which it is attached may be highly exploitive. Indeed, the same conditions which promote the establishment of patron-client relationships, i.e. extreme differences in wealth and power between members of different social strata, facilitate the harsh exploitation of those who are not given special protection of some patron. This may explain why clientelism may flourish, or be idealized, in societies which in other respects are harshly exploitative and where there prevails a general cynicism as to the possibility of genuinely selfless benevolence in the relations between different social classes. As a result a man who has been favored above his fellows, i.e., has enjoyed the benefits of client status, may still be impelled to revolt against a system of agricultural tenancy which he finds to be inequitable and thus, albeit reluctantly, joins other tenants in revolting against his lord. Having thus chosen to be disloyal to his benefactor instead of to his class, he will have forfeited the claim to be treated as a favored client thereafter, and thus will have contributed to the decline of clientelism. Conversely a man may reject the deferential role required of a client and may free himself of such an entangling alliance while being quite willing to remain a tenant. This may occur when the conditions of insecurity that made clientship attractive no longer exist, as for example when the state or a tenant's union provide protection against starvation and violence. It may occur also when alternative patrons, such as professional politicians, offer clientelist benefits more attractive than those which the tenant's landlord can supply.

The Sharing of Benefits

Various writers who have discussed horizontal and vertical dyadic alliances, have noted that such relationships rest on the expectations of reciprocity in the exchange of benefits between the two allies. The precise meaning of reciprocity remains a matter of some dispute, however.

Gouldner notes that there is a lack of agreement among scholars as to whether the norm of reciprocity "stipulates that the amount of return to be made is 'roughly equivalent' to what has been received," or whether it merely stipulates that something shall be given in return for things received, i.e., that "people should help those who have helped them" as Gouldner puts it.[14] The question is an important one. Clearly, dyadic alliances often are subject to considerable tension and sometimes disruption because one ally believes that the amount he has received, as compared with what he has given to his ally, is insufficient. At the same time, the determination of equivalence is a much more difficult undertaking in such complex relationships as dyadic alliances than in simple barter transactions.

The presence or absence of equivalence can be established fairly easily in one-time exchanges where the things exchanged are identical—as when one peasant gives a day of his labor to another peasant in return for a similar day of labor later on. Equivalence can also be ascertained when dissimilar things are exchanged but where both have a price in the market that is accepted by both parties to the exchange as being their real value for the purpose of their reckoning of equivalence. In such a case, two items having the same market price can be exchanged between two individuals. Neither will have made a cash profit from the transaction, but each now possesses something that is more useful to him than the thing he gave in exchange. It may be that the transaction has been of greater usefulness to one individual than to the other. But this fact is discounted as both have agreed to use the more objective measure of a market price as their test of equivalence.

In dyadic alliances, however, and especially

in vertical ones, it is harder if not impossible to determine reciprocity for several reasons: The things exchanged may not be alike, or may have no market price that makes them commensurable. They usually have a time dimension that complicates the task of measurement, and they combine different levels of interaction for which quite different types of measures are appropriate.

In horizontal alliances the things given by each ally to the other often are similar, making it possible to establish equivalence. But in vertical alliances this is rarely the case. The things that are exchanged often are intangible and unalike. Thus the protection which a patron gives to his client is something very different in kind from the support and deference which a client gives to his patron. Nor can these two types of benefits be subjected to a common standard of measurement. Neither of them ordinarily are purchasable for cash in the marketplace. To say that both are forms of help that require a certain amount of effort on the part of the giver does not make them commensurable, for help given by a person of power and status is more valuable from the point of view of an objective third party than the help given by a person of low status. But how many units of time or effort given by the latter balance off one unit given by the former is a question on which few would agree. If benefits of this type are exchanged their presumed equivalence, or non-equivalence, rests on custom and not on measurement by a common standard. If custom is observed, both parties are likely to accept the terms of the exchange in the ordinary course of events though to an outside observer from a distant place or time the terms of the exchange may seem highly inequitable.

In the absence of an impersonal standard of measurement that can be applied to a benefit and that is accepted by everyone, the focus of an observer must shift to the values given to that benefit by both the giver and the receiver. These values may be quite different. Indeed they must be different if there is to be a fruitful exchange. John Thibaut and Harold Kelley, two social psychologists, in their classic study of dyadic relationships have noted that such relationships are most likely to prosper if each member of the dyad can provide things highly rewarding to his partner at low cost to himself.[15] When this is the case, i.e., when each has low costs and receives high rewards, then both make a substantial gain from the relationship and have a strong incentive to maintain it. When on the other hand the costs for each are almost as high as his benefits, the

incentive to maintain the dyad is minimal. Finally, when one of the two members finds that his costs exceed his gains, it becomes in his interest to withdraw from the relationship if he has the freedom to do so.

One may add together the difference between costs and gains of both of the two allies, i.e., their individual profits, and think of the total as the total gains made possible by their relationship. In vertical alliances, these total gains tend to be rather large. An example is provided by a patron-client relationship between a lord and a serf in a feudal setting. Here the client receives things of which he is in desperate need: physical protection without which his life may be endangered, and material help in time of emergency, such as loans or gifts of grain or the like. In return he gives something of which he has a fair supply and on which he puts no great cash value: special labor service when needed by his lord, deference and unquestioned loyalty. From the serf's point of view, his special relationship with his lord yields him substantial gains. The lord for his part also has substantial gains. He receives some free labor. More important, he gains in status and power as a result of his ability to use the services of his clients in politics and war. The benefits which he gives to his clients in return are of no great cost to himself. He offers the client the protection of his arms, his castle, and his store of surplus grain. But offering these to the client adds little to the lord's costs for he maintains these resources mainly for his own security. In short, traditional feudal clientelism yielded substantial benefits for both patrons and clients, a fact which helps to account for the long endurance of this form of dyadic alliance.

When the total gains resulting from a dyadic relationship are large, it is possible for one member of the dyad to allow the other to make very substantial individual gains and still retain some gains for himself, i.e., something considerably short of exact reciprocity is tolerable to the less advantaged member of the dyad. On the other hand, when the total available gains are small, neither member can be allowed to have large individual gains for then little opportunity for gain would remain for the other, who would have slight reason to maintain the relationship. In short, the smaller the total gains produced by the relationship, the smaller the difference between the gains of the two partners that can be tolerated by the less advantaged of the two. Conversely, the larger the total gains, the larger the disparity in gains that can be tolerated.

The availability of large gains does not by itself mean that they will be divided unequally.

This will depend presumably upon the relative bargaining power of the two members of the dyad. In horizontal relationships, the bargaining power of the two is likely to be roughly equal, at least in the long run. And it is long run considerations that are uppermost in dyadic alliances. Hence an equal sharing of gains is likely to occur. In vertical alliances however, the bargaining power of the higher member of the dyad almost always exceeds that of his inferior ally. Equal bargaining power, or greater bargaining power in the hands of the lesser ally is exceptional and when it occurs tends to be a temporary condition. This would suggest that in vertical dyadic relationships the superior member of the dyad will be able to obtain a larger share of the total profits than the inferior member of the dyad. And in fact he usually does so, as Marx and many others have observed, unless there is some special consideration that leads him to decline such a larger share.[16] In every society there are a good many people who are ready and eager to maximize their own gains without much regard for the gains of those with whom they interact. Furthermore, in every society there are whole categories of people—slave owners, land owners, capitalists, or members of ruling bureaucracies who routinely maximize their gains at the expense of the gains of their inferiors though they may hide this fact from themselves. Nevertheless there are in even blatantly inequitable socio-economic systems certain related and socially recognized roles between persons known to be unequal in general status and power in which the cold-blooded, ruthless exploitation of superior bargaining power is regarded as improper. These related roles include those of parent and child, of friend and friend, and of patron and client. In such relationships there is invoked a norm of the same order as the norm of reciprocity, but one specifically applicable to dyadic alliances that produce a gain. This norm stipulates that when two persons are dyadic allies, whether that alliance be horizontal or vertical, any gains that result from their alliance shall be divided among them in a way that reflects their mutual obligation to show a concern for each other's welfare, i.e., to display altruism towards each other.

It was noted above that equivalence in dyadic alliances is hard if not impossible to measure with precision, in part because of the time dimension of most alliances and in part because they combine different levels of interaction to which different types of measurement are appropriate. These points require some elaboration.

A dyadic alliance, it will be recalled, was defined as a voluntary agreement between two individuals to exchange favors and to come to each other's aid in time of need. The two obligations—to exchange favors and to render mutual aid—were shown to be of a somewhat different nature. Furthermore, it was pointed out that the exchange of favors has two functions: Favors are valuable for their own sake. They may also be used as a means of maintaining a dyadic alliance. In fact it is often possible to classify a specific favor as being designed mainly for one of these two purposes, with the other purpose being served only incidentally. Thus small favors which are not desired by the recipient serve mainly the purpose of alliance-maintenance. Substantial favors which are asked for or really needed by the recipient are desired for their own sake, though incidentally they help to keep the alliance going. Thus it is possible to divide a complete dyadic alliance into three analytically distinctive types of exchange. Each of these types of exchange, furthermore, has somewhat different time dimensions. These differences result in different problems of benefit sharing at each level of a dyadic relationship.

Favors that are designed mainly to maintain an alliance tend to be small in substantive value, and often are not desired by the recipient. It is not therefore very important that they be of equal value. The concern here is with action, not with its value. More important is the timing of action. Favors must be given back and forth at intervals that are sufficiently short to prevent either ally from beginning to fear that the alliance has lapsed and sufficiently long to prevent him from thinking that the other ally is eager to rid himself of the obligation. Indeed, because the purpose of the exchange is to keep the alliance alive, the balancing out of favors at any one point in time is avoided, for this might be interpreted as being designed to bring the alliance to an end. Typically, each tries to over-repay the previous favor after a short interval so that at any point in time one of the two owes the other a favor. Over the long run, the total value of the favors given by each ally to the other may be close to equal, especially as the types of things exchanged for this purpose tend to be susceptible to monetary measurement. But this is of no great importance as the purpose of this pattern of exchange is a short run one: To keep the alliance going from one point in time to the next.

Favors that are exchanged for their own sake, i.e., favors that are desired and are of real value to the recipient, call for a different pattern of exchange. In the short run an effort may be made to avoid exact repayment of such favors since they serve the additional purpose of helping to maintain the alliance. But over a longer period of time it becomes important to maintain a rough balance in the values of the favors which each ally has done for the other. When favors are really valuable, neither ally will wish to fall very far behind in the total value of the benefits he has received for then it might be in the interest of the other party to break off the alliance while he is ahead. On the other hand, neither party, unless he has dishonorable intentions wants to fall too far behind in repaying substantial favors for this will put him in the psychologically painful position of being heavily in debt to the other and thus being in the other's power. Large favors however, bring with them difficult problems of measurement. The value of such favors consists not only of their monetary value but also of the fact that they were given when they were "really needed," or that they were given at great sacrifice to the giver. This intangible weight added to the substantive weight of *some* favors of this type makes much more difficult the task of measuring and achieving equivalence, unless by chance both allies at different points in time need favors of equal material value to the same degree, and make equal sacrifices to meet each others' needs. Because of this, disagreements about the relative weights of really valuable favors are common, and can be a serious source of stress in such relationships.

At another level of interaction, a major function of dyadic alliances is to provide each ally assurance of future aid in time of need. For the poor and the weak, in societies that lack institutional provisions for the protection of their physical safety and livelihood, this is perhaps the most important purpose of dyadic alliance-building. In horizontal dyadic alliances, when both allies are equally poor and weak, or equally rich and strong, the mutual promise of future aid represents equivalence. But in patron-client relationships this is clearly not the case. In these vertical relationships, patrons can give much more protection to their clients than the reverse. Furthermore, protection that is of great value to the client can be given at little cost to the patron. On the other hand even a very costly act by the client on the patron's behalf, e.g., the risking of his life in the patron's battles, is of relatively little value to the patron. There is thus, at this level of dyadic interaction, great difficulty in achieving equivalence. The client must attempt to pay part of his unrepayable debt in advance through a continuous display of affection, deference and obedience to his patron. Even then, it is made clear to him that he remains perpetually a debtor.

There is at this level of the relationship another complicating factor: A guarantee of future aid whenever it is needed is not the same thing as the actual receipt of aid. Whether aid will ever be needed and whether one's ally will then be alive and in a position to give it, cannot be predicted in advance. In this respect guarantees of future aid are like an insurance policy: Only the survivor will know, after his ally has died, whether he has come out ahead. If he has not, his premiums are not refundable. Even in horizontal dyadic alliances at this level, equivalence can only be measured subjectively i.e., in the continuing belief of each ally that he can count on the other. The moment either ally begins to have doubts about the other's good faith the alliance stands on the verge of dissolution, regardless of what lesser debts may remain unrepaid.

This dissection of a complete dyadic alliance into its parts with a view to looking for measures of equivalence suggests why any attempt to apply the test of equivalence to the alliance as a whole is fraught with such difficulty. The best one can say in this regard is that for an alliance to be created and to endure, there must be reciprocity in Gouldner's broadest sense: "people should help those who have helped them" i.e., benefits must move in both directions. Furthermore, each ally must remain convinced that his gains exceed his costs. At the same time if each ally displays a genuine concern for the other's welfare—which is one of the characteristics of dyadic alliances including patron-client relationships—then one can expect that both allies will show some self restraint in the claims they make on a share of the total gains made possible by their relationship.

Leadership and Followership in Clienteles

From the point of view of an individual client his vertical tie with his patron is likely to be among the most valuable of his dyadic alliances. In his horizontal alliances, i.e., those with his equals, he is expected to give as much as he receives. In a patron-client relationship, however, as has been noted, the patron by definition has more wealth, status and influence than the client, and gives more of these to the client than the latter can ever give him in return. Thus the tangible benefits received by the client—material help and protection—exceed his tangible costs. What the client gives to the patron in return is in large part intangible. Aside from some small token gifts which the client offers to his patron in recognition of his indebtedness, the client gives to his patron, in return for favors received or expected, his personal service, his loyalty and his acclaim. Still these are insufficient to balance what the client has received from his patron. The client therefore, must give something in addition: he accedes to the patron the preponderance of power to decide how the two of them shall interact and collaborate. That is to say, he gives leadership to the patron, and accepts followership for himself. This last gift, as will be seen, is of crucial importance for the structure of clienteles.

Variations in Patron-Client Relationships

While a separation of patron-client relationships from their institutionalized hosts reveals their general uniformity, some variations do exist among patron client addenda. These variations stem largely from differences in the substructures to which they are attached. This applies for example to the stability of clientelist role and status assignments. Thus both the occupancy by specific individuals of enduring roles of patronship or clientship, and the status of a given patron-client set in the larger hierarchy of power relationships of a society, may be fixed and unalterable, as is the case when patron client relationships exist within an established feudal order. On the other hand, patron and client may change places while the position of the patron-client set in society remains fixed, as in an outlaw band. Alternatively, assignment to roles of patron and client may remain fixed while the position of their patron-client set within a longer vertical chain changes, as in certain bueaucracies where ambitious officials rise with the help of their clients and these in turn are carried upward by their rising patron. Finally both role assignment and the position of the patron-client set may be unstable, as in the rough and tumble of electoral politics where a supporter may become a candidate and leap ahead of his leader, rising ultimately to a position much higher than his former patron.

Similarly, the endurance of the bond between patron and client varies with different settings. The tie may be unbreakable during the lifetime of the two partners, and may even be maintained for many generations, as is often the case where agricultural tenancy is well established. Here stability arises from the fact that the patron is secure in the possession of his resources while the client may be prevented by debts, a shortage of land, or serfdom, from quitting his patron.

Where on the other hand most patrons' access to resources is so unreliable that they cannot guarantee an enduring supply of benefits to their clients, as tends to be the case when patrons must depend on resources which are not their own, clients are likely to have the freedom to leave their old patrons when these no longer can support them. This is the case for example with patrons whose resources derive from their occupancy of offices in governmental or private organizations, or from the loot they can secure as leaders of bandit bands.

Finally, in settings where rival patrons are in active competition, and where success in their competition is closely related to the *relative* number of their clients, as in such zero-sum games as contests for elective public offices, patrons may be actively engaged in seeking to win away each other's clients, and clients may be able to play off other patrons against their own, giving their support temporarily to the highest bidder. In such settings, patron-client relationships may be highly unstable but may involve extraordinarily high short-term rewards.

Forms of clientelism differ, finally, in the degree to which all the clients of one patron act together in unison. Some patrons never find it necessary to call upon all of their clients to come together to work in a coordinated fashion. Thus for example, traditional landowners whose lands have been parcelled out to individual sharecroppers working separately, may ask nothing of their clients but that all of them repay favors received in whatever way they can whenever they can. A clientele of this type may never be seen to act as a group, and may not seem to be a group to its client members. There are other types of patrons, however, the achievement of whose goals depends upon their ability to mobilize all of their clients at specific points in time for massive efforts of coordinated action. Examples are war leaders, bandits, and candidates for elective offices.

Coordination, in cases of the latter type, may be initiated by the clients as well as by the leader. Thus when a group of clients perceive that their welfare as individuals—e.g., their lives, their access to the spoils of war or to governmental patronage—depends on the success of their patron in attaining his own goals, and that his success in this regard depends in turn upon the united support of his clients, the clients at their own initiative may apply strong group pressure upon the laggards in their midst to rally to their leader in his time of need. Sometimes such pressure is applied by a small core of subleaders who provide what in effect is a form of collective leadership for the clientele which may come close to supplanting the leadership of the patron. Whether or not this also occurs, a group of clients can display a degree of solidarity which, to an outside observer, is hard to distinguish from that to be expected from the members of a corporate group.

What then distinguishes such a cohesive clientele from a corporate group? The difference, which is a matter of degree rather than of kind, lies in the focal position occupied by the leader of a clientele which makes him more important to his combination than is the head of a corporate group. He is more important in three ways. First, he makes a greater personal contribution than does the head of a corporate group to the common effort of his organization. Thus he creates the clientele in the first instance. He provides many of the external connections and material resources used in the common effort. He may provide maintenance for his most needy followers. He has a special personal obligation to fulfill commitments that are made for the benefit of the clientele. Second, in return for his greater contribution he receives more discretionary power than does the head of a typical corporate group. He is entitled to decide who may be admitted to followership, and which followers will enjoy the most favored status. He is entitled to set many of the goals for which the clientele is mobilized and may include his private goals among them. If the goals are achieved, the credit and resulting prestige are largely his own. If spoils are obtained through the common effort of the clientele, the leader can distribute a portion of them among his followers in accordance with their services to him. Any undistributed porition remains to a high degree under his personal control. He can appropriate it wholly for himself, save it for later distribution, or pass it on to his heirs. It is in this sense that a clientele does not hold property continuously in a truly collective fashion, and thus is not a corporate group. All this in turn accounts for the third aspect of the leader's special prominence: His central position in the structure of the clientele. In view of his heavy contributions and broad discretionary power, his subordinates find greater security in their personal attachment to the leader than in their "membership" in the circle of their fellows. The opposite is the case in a corporate group. It is this fact that gives such prominence to the dyadic components of clientele structure, which makes it a primary star, centered on its leader.

By contrast, a combination is a corporate group insofar as the fruits of the group's activity, and any attendant duties, become for at least some length of time the collective possession or obligation of the group, of which the leader is simply the administrator. Typically in corporate groups cohesive action can be achieved for a broad range of truly collective policy or ideological goals that may have little connection with the personal goals of the group's head. This is unlikely to occur in a typical clientele. This does not mean that groups which are corporate do not also attend to particular private needs of their members. As Mancur Olson Jr. has shown, such attention often is necessary as an inducement to membership participation in voluntary associations of diverse types.[17] But it does mean that the presence of significant collective property, aims or duties is the distinguishing feature of corporate groups.

Traditional Rural Clientelism and Its Decline

Scholars interested in the rural sectors of medieval and early modern Europe and of offshoots of European society in Latin America were among the first to give serious attention to patron-client relationships. Much of the literature on this subject still deals with patron-client relationships between agricultural landowners and tenants in these parts of the world. The pattern described in these studies has been called "traditional rural clientelism." It has the following distinctive characteristics:

It involves both parties to the relationship in a broad spectrum of reciprocal obligations.

It is to a high degree a "face to face" relationship. Physical proximity and direct personal contact are of particular importance in maintaining such alliances in traditional societies where the narrow parochial scope of loyalties, and difficulties of transportation make it risky to place trust in individuals who are not readily accessible.[18]

Where the pattern of rural landholding is stable and hereditary, the rural patron client relationship tends to be stable and inherited as well. It also tends to be exclusive. This stems from the fact that for the client the relationship may entail an obligation to support his patron in his conflicts with other patrons, which means that the client cannot have similar obligations towards his patron's potential rivals.

The relationship ideally is one of affection and loyalty and, in societies where affection and loyalty ordinarily is confined to kinsmen, tends to imitate the relationship between parent and child, involving a display of paternalism on the part of the patron, and of deference on the part of the client. Often in such relationships kinship terminology is employed.

When rural society is organized in this fashion, the result is a highly oligarchical political structure. A certain number of rural landowning power figures are the real political actors and their dependent followings are their human political resources. The vertical structure of alliances inhibits the emergence of class loyalties or action among the subordinate client population. Although competition among rural patrons for land and power may be quite intense, the rules of competition among them generally serve to keep the existing class boundaries intact.

Traditional rural clientelism in its archtypical form tends to be prevalent in settings where subordinates are heavily dependent upon their superordinates, and where the latter are greatly in need of the support of loyal groups of personal dependents. The former is likely to be the case where those in positions of subordination are poor, uneducated, unskilled, legally underprivileged, forbidden to organize, and generally subject to victimization. The latter is likely to be the case where those in positions of superordination prey upon each other, and need private reserves of manpower for offense and defense. Both conditions exist in times and places that are to some degree anarchic. Thus the break-up of the Roman empire brought with it in Europe a period of near anarchy out of which grew the clientelistic institutions of feudalism. Thus too at a later time the expulsion of Spanish colonial rulers from Latin America resulted in a similar period of ineffective central government which created a vacuum that was filled by the clientelistic institution of *caudillaje*.[19] In both cases, the exposure of poor agriculturists to the dangers of pillage and penury, and the need of wealthy landholders for bodies of fighting men personally loyal to themselves, made men of both social strata extraordinarily dependent upon each other.

The personal dependence of superordinates and subordinates on each other is likely to be especially heavy when their relationships are not anchored in shared membership in corporate institutions, i.e., when the institutional relationships between them are ones of personal dependency, or when corporate institutions in which they share membership are weak. Under such conditions, individuals are likely to employ patron-client addenda as supplements to, or substitutes for their institutionalized relationships. Thus Carolingian monarchs, lacking effective bureaucratic sanctions to ensure the loyalty of their officials in the countryside, strengthened their control over some—and eventually all—of these officials by making them their personal vassals as well. The development of the rituals of homage and fealty, and the growth of a political culture which gave a high value to personal loyalty, supplied strong but non-legal sanctions to these vertical dyadic alliances.

What accounts for the decline of traditional rural clientelism? Most broadly, it would appear that relationships of this type break down when either those in superordinate positions or those in positions of subordination no longer are willing to fulfill their parts of the relationship. This may be the result of changes in material conditions which make such relationships no longer useful. It may also result from changes in ideology.

Thus one may see the breakdown of clientelism which accompanied the transition from feudalism to capitalism in Western Europe as a consequence of market forces which steadily undermined the economic and social guarantees which serfs had once enjoyed. This interpretation relies on the change in material relationships between patrons and clients as the major force undermining the practice of personal dependency. But the change may also be attributed to transformations in the realm of ideas. Thus it may be asked to what extent one can view the deterioration of feudal clientelism as a product of new ideas of personal freedom and autonomy embodied in town life which undermined the ideological hegemony of the feudal social order, and made personal dependency no longer legitimate. Presumably both material and ideological forces played parts in this transformation. In any event, accounting for the breakdown of traditional rural clientelism, and its relationship to other forms of social solidarity such as those of kinship, communalism, religion and class, remains a major analytical task in the study of clientelism.

Corporate Clientelism?

The question arises whether groups or other corporate entities can fill the roles of patrons or clients, or whether the clientelist model, and clientelist terminology, must be limited to relationships between individual persons. The question has been raised by the observations of Sydney Tarrow and Luigi Graziano in Southern Italy. There they have observed a pattern of politics in which entire local communities and entire peasant, workers, youth or professional associations deliver the votes of their members en bloc to specific politicans or political parties in return for various types of rewards for their members, including such indivisible rewards as local development projects and the results of various other "particularistic laws." Tarrow calls these "horizontal clienteles" and Graziano describes the pattern as "mass clientelism," or "corporate clientelism." It requires, he argues, a "corporative" kind of particularism which qualitatively is not different from the individual particularism of the interpersonal dyad. He calls this pattern "new clientelism" and suggests that it fits the patron client model.[20] This it does. But it is not a wholly new phenomenon. Similar types of corporate clientelism are found in various traditional settings. A common form of such clientelism has been reported in various unilineal societies where organized groups, including lineages of immigrants or other underprivledged individuals, have been attached to individuals or lineages of the dominant group. Examples are the *be* and *tomo* of ancient Japan, hereditary occupational corporations which were attached to members of the dominant Yamato clans, as well as the client lineages of the Mandari of the Sudan, and the immigrant Menangkabau lineages which were attached to ruling houses in peninsular Western Malaysia.[21]

It is certainly true that on a larger scale the new Italian clientelism displays the same structural features as traditional interpersonal clientelism. As in the latter, there is a trading arrangement between separate egos, one ego being the politician or party which fills the role of the patron, the other being the town or association which acts as a corporate client. Neither ego is part of the other, nor are they together part of a larger common group. As in the case of interpersonal clientelism, the corporate client demands and is satisfied with a particular reward: a specific local development project for itself, for which it competes against other corporate groups in other localities. It does not ask for a nation-wide development program seen from the point of view of the patron who stands outside the group, and of competing groups, the rewards given the group are particular. The fact that the members of the group may be alike, and that corporate spirit and solidaristic behavior are needed to give the new clientele its bargaining power does not alter the fact that the relationship between this client and its patron is essentially a dyadic alliance. The patron for his part can have such alliances with many local corporations who together constitute his clientele. It can be said therefore that the clientelist model can operate at any level ranging from the relationships between individual persons through that between sub-national groups to that between nation states.

Against this it can be argued that despite its structural similarities, the new corporate clientelism is sufficiently different from interpersonal clientelism to merit a separate niche in a typology of political structures. This point can be made first simply on the basis of the definition with which this essay began. There a dyadic relationship was defined as one between *individuals,* involving direct *personal* attachment. Most other discussions of dyadic relationships employ similar definitions. The choice of these words in turn reflects the observations of those who have described traditional clientelism that this relationship and other traditional dyadic relationships involve a highly individualistic style of interaction. Thus Foster reported that in his Mexican community no person shared his patron saint with other members of his own family.[22] To have a unique system of alliances seems to be a desideratum. Thus, it can be held, one does injury to the stylistic meaning of the old term by stretching it to include the rather rigid and impersonal loyalties which are imposed upon members of corporate groups by the alliance strategies of their leaders.

One can also argue on structural grounds that corporate clientelism represents a distinctive political tactic which from the point of view of the breadth of the goals towards which action is directed occupies an intermediate position between the individualistic particularism of interpersonal clientelist politics and the wholly nonlocalized categorical goals of class-oriented politics. The success of this tactic requires the use, in combination, of two techniques. Locally it requires the creation of local group solidarity through an appeal to local or trait consciousness. Externally it requires the traditional dyadic technique of clientelism. While each part of this dual operation represents a relatively pure form of what I have elsewhere described as two distinctive alternative techniques, their use in combination is, certainly, a half-way house, that deserves a separate place in a typology.[23]

Going beyond this static typology, it can be argued further that in specific countries or regions during specific periods of their history, corporate clientelism represents a historical stage in the transition from feudal personal clientelism to modern supra-local issue-oriented politics. This may be the case in Italy. There, as Tarrow and Graziano show, voters who once pursued their interests as lone individuals or families in the manner described by Edward Banfield, have learned the value of joining forces with their fellow townsmen, or with fellow workers in their own towns, so as to compete more effectively against similar groupings in other towns for benefits dispensed by the national government.[24] But they have not yet acquired a sense of supra-local class interest which when developed will lead them to settle for nothing less than programs designed to further the interests of all members of their class or occupational category throughout their nation. But this ordering of stages need not be universal. Thus in Japan, the corporate dependency of *be* and *tomo* upon specific clans preceded rather than followed the inter-personal clientelism of the feudal period.

In the Italian setting, power is held by relatively independent and non-ideologically oriented politians who are prepared to use their legislative powers to deliver concrete benefits of various types to any localized group whose leaders are able to deliver the votes of their followers en bloc in return. The presence at the center of government of power-holders of this type in turn reflects a lack of supra-local categorical consciousness among the electorate at large, i.e., it reflects a state of mind in which towns see themselves as being mainly in competition with other towns, and unions see their main competitors to be other unions. We see here in short a pattern of localistic group semi-particularism, less narrow than the particularism of purely personal interest, yet narrower than supra-local categorical groups.

Whether or not one decides to lump the two forms of clientelism together, the new Italian pattern is of considerable interest. It suggests that whether a group operates in the polity in clientelist fashion or in a more modern fashion will depend in part upon the character of those who hold power at the center of government, and that their character in turn will depend in part upon the expectation of the organized and unorganized electorate. The character of both, at a given point in time, presumably reflect traits of political culture shared by both members of the new dyad, as well as the state of social and economic development.

Factionalism and Feuding

A group, be it dyadic or corporate, may enjoy an organizational monopoly in its locale. Anyone who seeks the benefits of group membership in that place must join that group. Thus in a stable feudal system each lord has a monopoly of land and serfs in his domain. If any of these serfs wish to have a patron, they have little option but to become the clients of their lord. The lord therefore is assured of a stable clientele. There are other types of settings however where different groups compete actively for the allegiance of the same potential members or clients. When this is the case one speaks of inter-group, party, or factional competition.

The term "factionalism" is associated in particular with competiton between dyadic non corporate groups. This stems from the fact that this term has been used traditionally to denote groups engaged in political rivalry prior to the appearance of modern political parties in the West, and is used today to denote groups which compete for dominance *within* the confines of a political party. Both "factions" of the pre-party and intra-party type tend to be characterized by unstable membership, uncertain duration, personalistic leadership, a lack of formal organization, and by a greater concern with power and spoils than with ideology or policy, that is to say by a dearth of those characteristics usually associated with corporate groups. When dyadic non corporate groups are in competition, each group is commonly called a faction. I have summarized the distinctive characterisitics of competition between dyadically structured factions led by individual leaders elsewhere.[25] The subject is dealt with also in Marshall D. Sahlin's classic description of clientelist leadership in Melanesia.[26]

Factional rivalry creates both conflict and a sense of community. In the course of such rivalry, as Max Gluckman has noted, community-wide interests, and the legitimacy of community-wide offices, are affirmed, and the society is held more firmly together.[27] Yet the divisive aspects of factionalism must not be overlooked. One of the aims of each faction is to bring benefits to its leaders and adherents. To do so it must defeat efforts of rival factions to do the same. The losers in such zero-sum games are likely to be resentful, to hope for a turn-about in which they can "put down" their opponents as they have been put down themselves. This leads to the related subject of feuding.

Dyadic relationships can be ones of mutual hostility as well as of mutual aid. Injuries can be exchanged, as well as favors. The hostile form of reciprocity is expressed in the principle of vengeance. It is no accident that societies such as those of the Mediterranean region, which place a high value on favoritism and give it form through dyadic alliance building often are also described as societies characterized by strong feelings and expressions of distrust, envy and vindictiveness.[28] Many such societies institutionalize the spirit of vengeance through the development of clearly recognized rules concerning the right, duties, form, and proper participants in act of vengeance.[29]

The pursuit of vengeance, like the pursuit of private interest, may require the help of one or more individuals. Thus vengeance, like constructive cooperation in support of an ego, may require the creation of groups. However hostile reciprocity has organizational implications somewhat more complex than those which flow from reciprocity of a wholly benign sort. First, hostile exchanges necessarily lead to fragmentation i.e., to the alignment of members of a community into antagonistic camps of varying degrees of endurance. Cooperation for purely productive purposes does not necessarily lead to fragmentation. Secondly, in selecting individuals to help him in the execution of venegeance, an individual must consider not only whether another individual owes him support, but also whether that individual has conflicting obligations to support his enemy, and therefore may be entitled to claim exemption and the status of a neutral. Thirdly, the exaction of vengeance may create new and unintended victims whose own claims to vengeance may lead to the perpetuation and expansion of the conflict by continually involving new individuals.

In settings where individuals are divided into mutually exclusive corporate groups, such as lineages, clans, tribes, corporate local communities, and nation states, the organizational requirements of feuding are met in a straightforward fashion: The corporate group with its leader's permission serves as the feuding group, and provides collective support to its members. If a member of one group injures a member of another group, each group aligns itself en bloc behind the party to the conflict who belongs to that group. Conflicts of obligation do not arise: Individual members of either group know where their loyalties lie, and members of other groups have no obligation to involve themselves. When a balance of injuries has been attained between the two sides, the feud can be brought to an end, and individual compliance enforced by the leaders of the two groups.

But in settings where each victim of an injury becomes the leader of his own ad-hoc non corporate feuding group, feuds are more easily begun and harder to contain. An injury to any individual leads to the clustering around him of those upon whom he has claims for support, minus those who have conflicting obligations to the other side. A similar cluster forms around his opponent. The ensuing violence, in which others than the two primary rivals may suffer— especially if vengeance is inflicted on substitute victims—creates new persons with grievances and new support groups which may seek new victims long after the original victims have had their satisfaction, and the original support groups have been disbanded. In the absence of over-all leaders capable of imposing peace, the result, as R. F. Barton has shown in his detailed account of feuding among the tribal Kalingas of the highland Philippines, may be an endless succession of killings exchanged between shifting groups of partisans whose composition at any point in time depends upon the identity of the latest victim and the next victim to be.[30] This is what brings about what Bernard Siegel and Alan Beals call "pervasive factionalism," as distinguished from "schismatic factionalism."[31]

At the same time—and this helps to moderate the violence of dyadic feuding—each member of a dyadically structured feuding group attempts to limit his own participation to that required by his specific obligation to the group's leader, and to that not proscribed by his other alliances. Thus Thomas Kiefer, in his description of warfare among the Tausug of Sulu, notes that even in pitched battles between opposing groups, members of each group direct their fire with a careful concern for the nature of their personal ties or personal enmity towards each member of the opposing group.[32]

SOCIAL NETWORKS

Larger and more inclusive than dyadic relationships or dyadic non-corporate groups, are social networks. Networks have been defined as "matrices of social links" or as "social fields made up of relationships between people."[33] They include all individuals who find themselves in a given field, and who are within direct or indirect reach of each other. That is to say, they include all individuals who are connected directly with at least one other member of that network. Networks thus are not limited to individuals connected directly with the focal member of a given primary star, or those who participate in a specific coordinated action. Rather, networks include all individuals who are not totally isolated from each other, and serve as arenas for all of their interactions.

Various writers have noted the "unbounded," "infinite," and "everlasting" nature of the "total" network.[34] In order to be studied, however, networks must be of manageable size. In practice a scholar who wishes to examine a network must limit his attention to a finite number of individuals, i.e., to a network that is bounded in space and time. Thus he might confine himself to examining the dyadic relationships which exist among persons presently alive and to the inhabitants of a given territory. Doing so does not, however, absolve him from having to keep in mind that cross-boundary dyads exist, and that they affect dyadic relationships within a boundary. Similarly, he might restrict himself to examing those dyadic exchanges which are economic, religious or political in nature.

The question arises as to whether a temporally, spatially or functionally restricted portion of the total network should be called a network at all. Mayer is of the view that this term should be reserved for unbounded fields, and that bounded fields should be termed "sets."[35] Barnes, however, would allow at least functionally restricted portions of a network, to be called "partial networks." He defines a partial network as "any extract of the total network based on some criterion applicable throughout the whole network," and gives the partial networks of cognatic kinship, marriage, politics and religion as examples. The term partial network, he believes is appropriate "when some kind of social field is intended." It should "resemble the total network in structural form."[36] This criterion would seem to cover spatially or temporally delimited extracts of the total network as well. With this use of the term "partial network" I agree.

However, Barnes rejects the use of the term "partial network" for such ego-centric extracts of networks as primary stars. Because of their egocentric nature, these clearly are not social fields and do not resemble the total network in structural form. With this too I would agree.[37] But I would suggest the term "web" to describe Barnes' "primary star." The image of the outward-radiating strands of a spider's web contrasts nicely with that of the center-less strands of a fishing net. In addition, the concentric circles of strands of a spider's web suggest the direct connections between the focal individual's allies which enable them to work directly with each other in order to serve the focal individual's needs and which make it unnecessary for them to communicate with each other through him.

For purposes of network analysis, distinctions may be made among different partial networks on the basis of two closely related variables: Their density, measured as Barnes has suggested by the ratio of their direct links to the total number of theoretically possible direct links,[38] and the degree to which they are actually used. Most dense and least used is what might be called the *total conceivable network*. In such a network every individual in a field is linked to every other individual in that field, making for a density of 100 per cent. Norman Whitten and Alvin Wolfe have noted that no one has tried to make statements that apply to networks in this largest sense.[39] A network of this type has no resemblance to empirically useable networks except, as Barnes has noted, in small tribal societies where everyone is really connected directly with everyone else.[40] It has no heuristic value except as an ideal against which less dense but more useful networks can be measured. Less dense, and more useful both to its members and

to a network analyst is what may be termed a *realistically possible network*. Such a network consists of all links that individuals can realistically consider establishing given the impediments to interaction imposed by space, time, social class, ethnic or familial enmity, and the varying degrees of usefulness of individuals to each other. This realistically possible network, which differs in its configuration from society to society, reveals to an observer the probable lines of cooperation and of conflict within that society, and thus is of interest for its own sake. It also serves as a useful backdrop for an examination of the *actual network of dyadic interaction* which consists of all dyads that actually have been established. Specifically, a comparison of these two networks leads one to ask why some possible links were turned into actual links while others were not. The actual network of dyadic interaction in turn can be compared with the *network of most frequently used links*, an exercise which again suggests questions as to why certain dyads are used with greater frequency than others, and for what purposes.

J. A. Barnes, in an excellent recent survey of the subject, has noted that the two fundamental properties of networks are multiple interconnections and chain reactions.[41] A view of society as a network having these properties provides a useful approach to an understanding of some social processes that affect society as a whole.

Network analysis casts light on the basis of cohesion of societies. Thus it suggests how communities can be held together in the absence of strong governments or organized groups. Similarly it explains how class and other divisions within a society can be made tolerable by the presence of cross-cutting alliances. And it helps to explain how concensus within a community can emerge as the result of the exchange of opinions among individuals and how such concensus can contribute to the process of nation building.[42]

Network analysis also provides insight into the individual's relationship to and functioning within his society. Thus it leads one to note how a new member of a society, whether an infant or an adult immigrant, enmeshes himself in that society through interactions first with a few, and then—in part through their mediation—with an increasing number of its other members. This mode of analysis also alerts the observer to the fact that even long-time members of a society differ among themselves in the degrees of their social involvement. Thus some individuals may be deeply involved and extraordinarily influential in their society because of their many active links with other members. Others who have or desire few such connections may be virtual social isolates.

A network approach to the study of society sensitizes one to the society-wide effects of interpersonal conflict. It explains how what may have begun as a dispute between two individuals can expand, through the progressive involvement of persons directly or indirectly connected with the original antagonists, into a feud that eventually divides most of the community into two opposing camps. But it also explains how overlapping alliances, in which other individuals may be allied dyadically with both antagonists in a conflict, produce neutral mediators who work to abate the conflict.

Finally, network analysis contributes to an understanding of a society's communication system. A network model suggests how numerous radiating chains of linked individuals can pass a message originating with one of them quickly throughout a society without the aid of mass media. Similarly it shows how the receipt of the same message from diverse sources enables the receiver to assess its accuracy.

Social networks, as macro-level combinations, complete our survey of dyadic structures of different degrees of complexity and magnitude. Their analysis raises many interesting questions. But these are somewhat peripheral to the micro and middle level structures which are the main subjects of this volume. Therefore, they will not be dealt with further here.

THE APPLICATION OF DYADIC MODELS TO POLITICAL ANALYSIS

Because of the heavy reliance which political scientists traditionally have placed on group and class analysis, the most obvious contributions which dyadic, including clientelist models can make to the discipline lie in their ability to illuminate political behavior which is inconsistent with, or is not explained by, the Bentleyan group theory or by Marxist or non-Marxist class analysis.[43] From this point of view, three types of dyadic relationships mentioned by J. A. Barnes are of particular interest. They are relationships which cut across group and categorical limits, relationships within groups, and relationships that are established in the absence of groups.[44] To this one might add relationships between individuals so distant from each other that they could not interact effectively without the aid of dyadic links. A more detailed listing of the uses of dyadic analysis may be presented under these headings:

a. *Dyads which cross barriers between potentially hostile groups, thereby reducing the* *likelihood of conflicts between them and, in the case of unequal social strata, stabilizing their inequality.* Dyadic relationships of this type are most likely to have such consequences:

When they are exclusive, so that supportive exchanges in one direction preclude supportive exchanges in the perpendicular direction. An example of this is found in lower-class voting for upper-class candidates in single member districts, which prevents lower-class voting for lower-class candidates.

When supportive exchanges in one direction preclude hostile exchanges in the same direction. An example is the protection which a powerful patron gives to his weak client against being preyed upon by other powerful men.

When supportive exchanges provide sufficient gratification to significantly reduce the urge to engage in cross-cutting acts of solidarity or parallel acts of hostility. An example is found in the employees of paternalistic enterprises whose satisfaction with their terms of employment deters them from joining a trade union or voting for left-wing candidates.

Also of interest are cross-class or cross-occupational exchange systems which make possible occupational specialization and job security for low status persons. An example is found in the *jajmani* relationships between high and low caste persons in Northern India, under which two persons perform for each other services which, because of religious prohibitions, they cannot perform for themselves.

b. *Dyads which, through the mediation of brokers or chains of brokers, bridge the distance between persons so far removed from each other that they could not interact effectively otherwise.*

Brokers provide benefits for both of the individuals between whom they mediate, and in return for their services extract some rewards for themselves. In performing their tasks, brokers are able to influence the quality of the exchanges that take place between those for whom they serve as brokers. Their mediation can alter the meaning of issues and goals which seem salient to those at the center of power, while directing the aspirations of those at the periphery to needs which their mediating role as brokers enables them to supply. Typically, they favor goals which are likely to preserve their own freedom of action. Especially interesting to political scientists in this connection are brokers who provide linkage between weak central authorities and relatively independent local level leaders.

Gaps bridged by this method include those of space, culture, socio-economic level, legal status and authority. Examples of bridgers of spatial distance are rulers of tributary states on the fringes of empires, and noble vassals of feudal monarchs. Examples of bridgers of cultural distance are traditonal leaders in colonies under indirect rule, the semi-educated leaders of peasant followings mobilized in support of educated elites, and bi-cultural mediators between culturally distinct ethnic groups. Examples of bridgers of socio-economic status are elite or middle class patrons of peasant clienteles, and labor boss contractors of gangs of unskilled workers. Examples of bridgers of gaps of legal status are patricians or members of ruling tribes who offer legal protection to their plebeian or immigrant clients. Examples of bridgers of gaps of authority are traditional occupants of tribal offices in new states where newly created national offices lack legitimacy and their occupants lack personal authority.

c. *Intra-group dyads.* Dyadic relationships within classes, categories and organizations may contribute to their unity as well as to their internal division. Examples of dyads which strengthen—or substitute for—class or organizational loyalty are the "old boy network" within the British upper class, the clientelist relationships between leaders and followers within the Southern Italian and Indonesian Communist Parties which partly compensated for the weakness of class consciousness, and the loyalty to a respected officer which may unite a group of reluctant conscripts in the absence of loyalty to their unit or to the military service as a whole.

But personal loyalties to rival aspirants for leadership within a group may produce serious internal conflicts. Such rivalries often explain intra-group conflict where no ideological or policy differences are apparent, and may lead to the permanent division of such a group. This helps account for the proliferation of ideologically similar parties and trade unions in certain developing countries.

d. *Dyads which are created in the absence of effective corporate institutions or organizations.* Dyadically structured non-corporate groups may perform tasks which in other societies are performed by discrete entities. Insofar as they do this successfully, they lessen the need for the creation of such entities.

This can happen in the absence of government or of other corporate groups. Examples are the filling of the void, created by the collapse of a centralized state or empire or the withdrawal of a colonial authority, by the armed followings of isolated military commanders, robber barons, or armed landowners or ranchers.

It can occur, despite the existence of a government, when law is enforced irregularly and with partiality in return for favors supplied through personal connections. Examples of this kind of "corruption" are found in many old and new states.

It can occur when government withholds protection from, or victimizes, certain categories of people either because their activities are illegal or because they lack the ability to protect themselves. Examples are the private webs of alliances created by Mafia families, and the alliances found in certain new nations between "pariah capitalists" and government officials.

It can occur when the open establishment of voluntary associations is forbidden to some or all sectors of the population. As example is intra-party factionalism in ostensibly one-party states.

Finally, it can occur where there are patterns of shared interest or lines of cleavage which are at odds with those recognized by existing corporate groups. Examples are local-level factions which appear when local issues and local personal rivalries are ignored by national political parties.

NOTES

1. George M. Foster, "The Dyadic Contract: A Model for the Social Structure of a Mexican Peasant Village," *American Anthropologist*, 63 (December, 1961), 1174.

2. *The Sociology of Georg Simmel*, ed. & trans. Kurt H. Wolff (Glencoe, Ill.: The Free Press, 1950), p. 123.

3. Jeremy Boissevain, "The Place of Non-Groups in the Social Sciences," *Man*, new series, 3 (December, 1968), 544.

4. Alvin W. Gouldner, "The Norm of Reciprocity: A Preliminary Statement," *American Sociological Review*, 25 (April, 1960), 171, 174.

5. Charles Kaut, "*Utang na Loob*: A System of Contractual Obligation Among Tagalogs," *South-western Journal of Anthropology*, 17 (Autumn, 1961), 270; and Mary R. Hollnsteiner, "Reciprocity in the Lowland Philippines," in *Four Readings on Philippine Values*, ed. Frank Lynch, 2nd rev. ed. (Quezon City: Ateneo de Manila University Press, 1964), 31-33.

6. Foster, "The Dyadic Contract," p. 1175.

7. Foster, "The Dyadic Contract," p. 1176.

8. Gideon Sjoberg, "The Preindustrial City," *American Journal of Sociology*, 60 (March, 1955), 440.

9. James N. Anderson, "Buy-and-sell and Economic Personalism: Foundations for Philippine Entrepreneurship," *Asian Survey*, 9 (September, 1969), 652-658; Maria Christina Blanc Szanton, *A Right to*

Survive: Subsistence Marketing in a Lowland Philippine Town (University Park: Pennsylvania State University Press, 1972), pp. 97-111; and William G. Davis, *Social Relations in a Philippine Market: Self-Interest and Subjectivity* (Berkeley: University of California Press, 1973), pp. 216-234.

10. J. A. Barnes, "Networks and Political Process," in *Local Level Politics*, ed. Marc J. Swartz (Chicago: Aldine Publishing Co., 1968), pp. 112-113, 118-119.

11. Jeremy Boissevain, "Patronage in Sicily," *Man*, new series, 1 (March, 1966), 25-26.

12. During the classical age of feudalism, the practice of a vassal pledging homage to several lords came to be tolerated in some parts of Europe. See F. L. Ganshof, *Feudalism*, 3rd English ed. (New York: Harper & Row, 1964), pp. 102-103.

13. R. F. Barton, *The Kalingas: Their Institutions and Custom Law* (Chicago: University of Chicago Press, 1949), pp. 167-208.

14. Gouldner, 171, attributes the former views to Homans, Thurwald, Simmel and Malinowski.

15. John W. Thibaut and Harold H. Kelley, *The Social Psychology of Groups* (New York: John Wiley & Sons, 1959), p. 31.

16. Marx was quite aware of the vertical structures of loyalty which characterized feudal social orders, the basis for their origin, and the reasons for their decline. See his *Pre-Capitalist Economic Formations*, ed. E. J. Hobsbawm (New York: International Publishers, 1965).

17. Mancur Olson, Jr. *The Logic of Collective Action: Public Goods and the Theory of Groups* (Cambridge: Harvard University Press, 1965), pp. 132-167.

18. Thus as Marc Bloch notes, the feudal ritual of homage, whereby one individual became another's "man," began with the placing of the client's joined hands between those of his lord. And this could not be accomplished by proxy until the late middle ages when the old ceremony had lost much of its meaning. See Marc Bloch, *Feudal Society*, trans. L. A. Manyon (London: Routledge & Kegan Paul), p. 147.

19. *Feudalism in History*, ed. Rushton Coulborn (Princeton: Princeton University Press, 1956), pp. 188-214; and Eric R. Wolf and Edward C. Hansen, "Caudillo Politics: A Structural Analysis," *Comparative Studies in Society and History*, 9 (January, 1967), 168-179.

20. Sidney G. Tarrow, *Peasant Communism in Southern Italy* (New Haven: Yale University Press, 1967), pp. 331-342; and Luigi Graziano, "Patron-Client Relationships in Southern Italy," *European Journal of Political Research*, 1 (1973), 20-28.

21. For Japanese *be* and *tomo* see John Whitney Hall, *Government and Local Power in Japan 500 to 1700: A Study Based on Bizen Province* (Princeton: Princeton University Press, 1966), pp. 34-43, 46, 48, 89. For Mandari client lineages, see Jean Buxton, "'Clientship' Among the Mandari of the Southern Sudan," in *Comparative Political Systems: Studies in the Politics of Pre-Industrial Societies*, ed. Ronald Cohen and John Middleton (Garden City, N. Y.: The Natural History Press, 1967), pp. 229-241. For Men-

angkabau lineages see J. M. Gullick, *Indigenous Political Systems of Western Malaya* (London: The Athlone Press, 1958), pp. 37-42.

22. George M. Foster, "The Dyadic Contract in Tzintzuntzan, II: Patron-Client Relationships," *American Anthropologist*, 65 (December, 1963), 1287.

23. Carl H. Landé, "Networks and Groups in Southeast Asia: Some Observations on the Group Theory of Politics," *American Political Science Review*, 67 (March, 1974), 120-126.

24. Edward C. Banfield, *The Moral Basis of a Backward Society* (Glencoe, Ill.: The Free Press, 1958), pp. 85-127.

25. Landé, p. 122-126.

26. Marshall D. Sahlins, "Poor Man, Rich Man, Big-Man, Chief: Political Types in Melanesia and Polynesia," *Comparative Studies in Society and History*," 5 (April, 1963), 285-303.

27. Max Gluckman, *Custom and Conflict in Africa* (Oxford: Blackwell, 1943),pp. 45-47.

28. For excellent discussions of this aspect of Mediterranean behavior, see Banfield, pp. 121-122, and Jane Schneider, "Of Vigilance and Virgins: Honor, Shame and Access to Resources in Mediterranean Societies," *Ethnology*, 10 (January, 1971), 1-24.

29. Barton, pp. 218-255.

30. Barton, pp. 66-84.

31. Bernard J. Siegel and Alan R. Beals, "Pervasive Facionalism" *American Anthropologist*, 62 (June, 1960), 394-417.

32. Thomas M. Kiefer, *Tausug Armed Conflict: The Social Organization of Military Activity in a Philippine Moslem Society*, Philippine Studies Program, Department of Anthropology, University of Chicago, Research Series, No. 7 (Chicago: University of Chicago Philippine Studies Program, 1969), pp. 167-171.

33. Adrian C. Mayer, "The Significance of Quasi-Groups in the Study of Complex Societies," in *The Social Anthropology of Complex Societies*, ed. Michael Banton (New York: Praeger, 1966), p. 98.

34. Norman E. Whitten Jr. and Alvin W. Wolfe, "Network Analysis," in *Handbook of Social and Cultural Anthropology*, ed. John J. Honigmann (Chicago: Rand McNally, 1973), p. 725.

35. Mayer, p. 101.

36. Barnes, pp. 111-112.

37. Barnes, pp. 112-113.

38. Barnes, p. 117.

39. Whitten & Wolfe, p. 725.

40. Barnes, p. 127.

41. J. A. Barnes, *Social Networks*, Addison-Wesley Module in Anthropology (Reading, Mass.: Addison-Wesley Pub. Co., 1972).

42. The formation of public opinion through exchanges of opinion is discussed in C. Kadushin, "Power, influence and social circles: a new methodology for studying opinion makers," *American Sociological Review*, 33 (1968), 685-699.

43. Arthur F. Bentley, *The Process of Government* (Chicago: University of Chicago Press, 1908).

44. Barnes, "Networks and Political Process," p. 109.

PART I

Basic Theory: Reciprocity, Networks and Dyads

AN ANALYSIS OF RITUAL CO–PARENTHOOD (COMPADRAZGO)*

SIDNEY W. MINTZ · ERIC R. WOLF

AS ANTHROPOLOGISTS have been drawn into the study of Latin American cultures, they have gathered increasing amounts of material on the characteristic cultural mechanisms of *compadrazgo*. This term designates the particular complex of relationships set up between individuals primarily, though not always, through participation in the ritual of Catholic baptism.

This rite involves, among its various aspects, three individuals or groups of individuals. These are: first, an initiate, usually a child; secondly, the parents of the initiate; third, the ceremonial sponsor or sponsors of the initiate. It thus involves three sets of relationships. The first links parents and child, and is set up within the confines of the immediate biological family. The second links the child and his ceremonial sponsor, a person outside the limits of his immediate biological family. This relation is familiar to most Americans as the relation between godfather or godmother and godchild. The third set of relationships links the parents of the child to the child's ceremonial sponsors. In Spanish, these call each other *compadres* (Latin *compater-commater*, Spanish *compadre-comadre*, Italian *compare-commare*, French *compere-commere*, German *Gevatter-Gevatterin*, Russian *kum-kuma*, etc.), literally co-parents of the same child. The old English form of this term,

godsib, is so unfamiliar to most English-speaking people today that they even ignore its hidden survival in the noun "gossip" and in the verb "to gossip." In English, as in the Ecuadorian *compadrear*, the meaning of the term has narrowed to encompass just one, if perhaps a notable characteristic of *compadre* relations. Most other aspects of this relationship have, however, fallen by the wayside. In contrast, in Medieval Europe, the *compadre* mechanism was of considerable cultural importance, and in present-day Latin America, its cultural role is attested by its frequent extensions beyond the boundaries of baptismal sponsorship.

The thing itself is curious, and quite novel to an Englishman of the present day (wrote Edward B. Tylor in 1861[1]). The godfathers and godmothers of a child become, by their participation in the ceremony, relations to one another and to the priest who baptizes the child, and call one another ever afterwards *compadre* and *comadre*. In Mexico, this connexion obliges the *compadres* and *comadres* to hospitality and honesty and all sorts of good offices towards one another; and it is wonderful how conscientiously this obligation is kept to, even by people who have no conscience at all for the rest of the world. A man who will cheat his own father or his own son will keep faith with his *compadre*.

To such an extent does this influence become mixed up with all sorts of affairs, and so important is it, that it is necessary to count it among the things that tend to alter the course of justice in the country.

In this article, the writers hope to present some material dealing with the historical antecedents of the *compadre* mechanism, and to discuss some of its present-day functional correlates.

Emphasis in studies of *compadrazgo* to date has largely centered on attempts to identify a European or Indian background for its various component traits.[2] Other studies have dealt with the diffusion of the complex in certain parts of Latin America, and the diversity of functions which it has assumed.[3] A recent trend has been to consider the *compadre* system as a significant feature of a putative Criollo culture.[4]

The present writers hope to deal with the *compadre* system rather in terms of possible functional relationships to other aspects of culture, such as the family, the status system, the system of land ownership, the legal system, the role of the individual in culture, and so forth. We shall especially emphasize its functions in furthering social solidarity. We shall use the term "vertical" to indicate the direction it takes when tying together members of different classes. Finally, we hope to discuss *compadrazgo* not only in terms of the ethnographic present, but also in terms of its past functions, that is, in terms of its historical context.

I. HISTORICAL ANTECEDENTS

This section will deal with the historical development of *compadrazgo* and its functional implications in the past.

We have seen that in Catholic practice, a sponsor aids in the initiation of a new member into the Church. He must be an established member of the religious community. His presence and ministrations in effect testify that the new candidate is willing and able to receive the prescribed initiatory rite. In Catholic theory, this initiatory rite is regarded as a form of spiritual rebirth, and an analogy is drawn between the role of the biological father in the process of conception on the one hand and the role of the sponsor as a spiritual father on the other. This notion of spiritual affinity has in turn given rise to notions of spiritual kinship, and laid the basis for the formation of ritual kin relationships through the mechanism of sponsorship at baptism.

Each of these three ideas has a separate history. Each is made up in turn of strands derived from different cultural backgrounds. The notion of sponsorship finds no warrant in the New Testament, and Canon Law refers to "custom" as the judicial basis upon which the precept rests.[5] It may derive in part from Jewish practice at circumcision where a witness is required to hold the child undergoing the ritual. This witness is called by a term derived from the Greek.[6] In this connection, it is perhaps significant that the Eleusynian Mysteries of the Greeks also made use of sponsors.[7] The term "sponsor" itself represents an adaptation of a term current in Roman legal terminology where *sponsio* signified a contract enforced by religious rather than by legal sanctions.[8] Finally, we know that the primitive Church used sponsors to guard against the admission of untrustworthy individuals, clearly an important function in the early days of persecution. Hence the term *fidei iussores*, those who testified to the good faith of the applicant, by which sponsors were also known.

The second component, the notion of spiritual rebirth, may also represent the product of several divergent traditions. However, this aspect of the institution falls outside the province of the present article.

The aspect of ritual kinship derived from sponsorship at baptism underwent its own special development. During the period of St. Augustine (354-430 AD), parents usually acted as sponsors for their own children. This custom was so widespread that Bishop Boniface was of the opinion that no one but parents could act as sponsors for the child's baptism. In a letter to Bishop Boniface, St. Augustine discussed this point, and drew attention to cases in which the sponsors had not been the parents. Slave owners had acted as sponsors for children borne by their slaves; orphans had been baptized with the aid of unknown third persons who had consented to act as sponsors; and exposed children had been initiated under the sponsorship of religious women.[9]

Roughly a hundred years later, the Byzantine emperor Justinian, who ruled from 527-565 AD, first issued an edict prohibiting marriages between spiritual relatives. The terms *compater* and *commater* first appeared in 585 and 595 AD, within the confines of the Western Church. Thus we may note first that a separate set of sponsors tended to be a later development from a stage in which parents and sponsors were the same people; and secondly, that this separation must have been effected within both the Eastern and Western Empires roughly between the first quarter of the fifth century AD and the end of the sixth century. Nevertheless, full acceptance of this separation and consequent exogamy took place only gradually. From the evidence noted by the Byzantine historian Procopius, we may judge that in the beginning of this period, godparents still actually adopted their godchildren.[10] In 753 AD St. Boniface could still write:

The priests throughout Gaul and France maintain that for them a man who takes to wife a widow, to whose child he has acted as godfather, is guilty of a very serious crime. As to the nature of this sin, if it is a sin, I was entirely ignorant, nor have I ever seen it mentioned by the fathers, in the ancient canons, nor in the decree of the pope, nor by the apostles in their catalogue of sins.[11]

But the Council of Munich, held in 813 AD, prohibited parents from acting as sponsors for their own children altogether, and in the books of the Council of Metz of the same year, parents and sponsors are clearly referred to by separate sets of terms.

The next two hundred years witnessed a wider and wider extension of the ties of ritual kinship, and a concomitant growth of the exogamous group. A Council of Metz held in 888 AD attempted to restrict the development, but without effect. The incest group, biological as well as ritual, was extended to cover seven degrees of relationship. There was an increase in the number of ceremonials at which sponsors officiated, accompanied by an increase in the number of people executing distinctive roles at any one ceremony who could be included in the circle of kin. Finally, the number of sponsors executing any given function grew as well.

Where baptism and confirmation had originally been one set of rites, they grew apart and became two separate ceremonies, within the area dominated by the Western Church. This separation is documented for the Frankish kingdom in the eighth century, and was accompanied by the development of two different sets of sponsors, for baptism and for confirmation.[12] Since confirmation was looked upon as a completion of the baptismal act, confirmation sponsors similarly became ritual kin. In the Eastern Church, however, baptism and confirmation remained one rite, but different sets of sponsors and hence ritual relatives were added for a hair-cutting rite as well as for "wet" baptism.[13] The Western Church, in turn, added ritual kin relationships with a "catechismal" godfather, who was present at ceremonies and abjurations preceding the baptismal act. For a long time it was also believed that the sacrament of confession produced a bond of ritual kinship between the father confessor and the confessant, until Pope Boniface the Seventh abrogated this relationship in 1298 AD.

But as the number of ceremonies productive of ritual kin relations grew, so grew the number of people who were geared into kinship arrangements. First, the Western Church extended spiritual relationships to cover the officiating priest, the sponsors, the child, the child's parents, and their respective children. Thus we get spiritual fraternity as well as spiritual co-parenthood. In this context, we may recall that the final ban against priests' marriages and concubinage was not issued until the Council of Trent (1545-63 AD). Finally, the number of sponsors increased, until general custom admitted between one and thirty baptismal sponsors.[14] While Pope Boniface abrogated ritual kin relationships arising from the confessional, he decreed at the same time that all the sponsors who were present at any given ceremony entered into valid ritual kin relationships, and necessarily became part of the widening exogamic circles.

Despite the largely formal nature of the material that deals with the growth of ritual kin ties during this period, we may perhaps venture some guesses as to possible functional correlates of the mechanism, and attempt to delimit some of the factors in its formation.

Ecclesiastical legislation on the subject tends to center in two main periods: in the ninth century AD on the one hand, and in the period from about 1300 AD to the end of the sixteenth century on the other. The interim period witnessed the highest development of the feudal order. Its main cultural conditions may briefly be restated. Ownership of land was vested in the feudal lord. He also owned a share of the labor of the serfs who lived on his land. In return he granted the worker rights to use the land, ownership of certain tools, and the right to consume some of the agricultural and handicraft goods which he produced. The mutual obligations and services which made up this system were mained by custom, and this complex of custom operated largely through face-to-face relationships between its carriers. We hope to indicate that the *compadre* mechanism and its ritual kin correlates were a functioning part of the class system implicit in this basic relationship.

Many writers have suggested that the *compadre* mechanism superseded earlier relationships of a tribal character based on actual or fictitious ties of blood. Thus Kummer feels that "it subordinated the community of blood to the community of faith."[15] Tomasic notes that the *compadre* mechanism maintained itself within Dinaric society while blood brotherhood declined.[16] He sees some relationship between this phenomenon and "the strengthening of the power of the state," and states that the *compadre* mechanism "was transferred from the tribal to the state level." With the growth of the state and its formal institutions, *compadrazgo* thus served to manipulate the increasingly impersonal structure in terms of person-to-person relationships.

In more specific fashion, Dopsch has related some forms of artificial relationships and "brotherhood arrangements" among feudal tenants to changes in the pattern of inheritance.[17] When the power of the large landowners was at its peak during the declining phase of the Roman Empire and during the initial period of feudal consolidation, tenants inherited rights of tenure from their neighbors in the absence of descendants in the direct line. With changes away from the predominance of large landowners, and towards increased political centralization, this right of neighbor inheritance gave way to inheritance on the part of other relatives of the deceased, notably on the part of siblings. Blood or ritual brothers then became an asset in the struggle "to lighten the economic and social duties with which the landowners burdened their tenants."[18] During this period, inheritance of tenure on the manor within the same household became more secure, the greater the number of potential heirs and workers. Horizontally phrased mechanisms like the Latin *adfratatio* and the Visigoth *hermandad* kept the land within the group of ritual and blood brothers, and prevented its reversion to the lord's demesne. The Church, anxious to establish itself as an independent landowner in its own right, capitalized on this change in the process of inheritance to press its own claims. It accomplished this through the enforcement of religious rulings regarding exogamy.

The marriages within the kin group and within the group of affinal relatives heavily reinforced the weight of the old Germanic limitations on the right of the individual to dispose of property, and as a result put the Church in a disadvantageous position.[19]

These limitations were used against the Church by its main adversaries in the struggle over land, the lay aristocracy and feudal lords. When the Church prohibited marriage within seven degrees of relationship, it prohibited it among all persons who for any legal purpose could claim blood relationship with each other.[20] This struggle was won by the Church, which in the process acquired almost complete control over legislation covering the making and execution of testaments.

Thus we may trace the early increase in exogamy to three different, yet interdependent factors: the attempt of the serfs to maintain their economic status; the attempt of the people to manipulate the growing structure of the state and the growing number of formal institutions through the use of a mechanism with which they were familiar; and the attempt of the Church to establish itself as an independent owner of landed property. In the final analysis, all three factors are but facets of the growing centralization of the feudal structure. This process took place in the main at the expense of the lay aristocracy. In the struggle the Crown attempted to play off Church and serfs against the feudal barons; the Church supported Crown and serfs against its lay competitors; and the serfs looked to both Crown and Church in their effort to increase their rights on the estates of the lay aristocracy.

Just as the increase in ritual brotherhood and in the size of the exogamic group may relate to this early stage of development of feudal tenures, so the great increase in *compadre* relationships and ritual kin prohibitions connected with them appear to relate to later changes in the tenure of serfs in relationship to their feudal lords.

The outstanding characteristic of the *compadre* mechanism is its adaptiveness to different situations. As the structure of the situation changes, so we may expect to see the *compadre* mechanism serve different purposes. As tenure became increasingly fixed within individual households, these units were also drawn into individual vertical relationships to the manorial administration. These different relationships crystallized into different rules for different groups of people on the manor. Far from being homogeneous, manorial custom took clear note of this process of differentiation. Under feudal conditions, then, one of the main functions of the *compadre* relationship was to structure such individual or family relationships vertically between the members of different classes.

In medieval France, "parents attempted to win for the baptismal candidate material advantages through their choice of godparents."[21] In Germany, "poor people invited individuals of higher status to become godparents to their children .... The nobles reversed this custom and invited their subjects, or at least their subjects' representatives, as *compadres*."[22] Mercenaries asked nobles to serve as godparents; day laborers asked their employers or the service staff of the manor. Officials often asked the city council, and the city budgets of the time show that the outlays arising from these ceremonial duties were often charged to the city treasury.[23] A "luminous instance" of how the mechanism was manipulated in daily practice is furnished by Coulton.[24] Monks were not allowed to stand as godparents, for fear that increased material benefits thus derived might weaken the centralized structure of the Church. But in 1419, the abbot of a French monastery which had suffered grievously under the ravages of war petitioned the Holy See for a dispensation from this ruling. "Seeing that the favor of nobles and of other powerful folk is most necessary and opportune to the said monks for the preservation of their rights; seeing also that, in these parts, close friendships are contracted between those who stand as godparents and the parents of the children," he argued in favor of initiating *compadre* relationships with some forty nobles.

The second function of the mechanism was to solidify social relationships horizontally among members of the same rural neighborhood. It is expressed in linguistic terms in the widening of the meaning of the word *compadre* to include the term "neighbor." In Andalucia, for example, the term *compadre* is easily extended to cover any acquaintance and even strangers.[25] In the Tyrol, the word *Gevatterschaft* (*compadre* group) is used to draw a contrast to the *Freundschaft* (the group of relatives, from the old meaning of the word *Freund*=relative). Hence also the English word, "gossip," derived from *godsib*,[26] and the use which Robert Burns makes in his poetry of such Scottish terms as *cummer* and *kimmer* to designate any woman from the neighborhood, a gossip, or a witch.[27]

One of the outstanding functions of the neighborhood group during the period of the later Middle Ages was the struggle against prevailing forms of feudal tenure. The eleventh century saw the beginning of the fight to resist labor services on the lord's land "by a sort of passive resistance."[28] During the twelfth and the thirteenth centuries, tenants consolidated to their own advantage the various rights of tenure which they enjoyed. "Begun in the twelfth century, emancipation was mainly achieved ... by individual or collective acts of enfranchisement ... generally brought about through a revolt of the inhabitants of a seignorie."[29] This struggle was often carried on with the aid of Crown and Church, which supported the claims of serfs and tenants in order to undermine the position of the lay aristocracy. Not the least of these claims was directed against the feudal regulations governing marriage.

One of the most direct consequences of the extension of the exogamic group through ritual kin ties was to put pressure on existing provisions for a stable labor supply. Marriage off the manor meant the loss of property to one of the feudal lords, and he exacted compensation. A serf was not permitted to marry off the manor without payment of an indemnity variously known as *formariage*, *foris*, or *merchet*.[30] Extension of kinship ties through ceremonial sponsorship inevitably brought nearer the day when most of the inhabitants of a village would be ritually related, and yet unable to pay the fee required for marriages outside the estate. Conflicts might for a while be avoided through refusal to marry and baptize in church, through systematic choice of sponsors from one family.[31] The two last-named techniques are reported for modern Bulgar villages. Yet these devices proved temporary, especially in the smaller communities.[32] At first, lords tried to meet the situation of increasing migration and marriage off the manor by local agreements,[33] but in the thirteenth and fourteenth centuries, the payment of *merchet* fell into disuse altogether. Serfs acquired the right to marry off the manor when they took over their fathers' land, or bargained with their lords for the privilege of marrying without interference. When a bargain was struck, the serfs had the exemptions written down in the manorial rolls, to be certain of proof when the actual occasion arose.[34]

The special charters won by the peasantry during these times gave rise to a special kind of neighborhood solidarity, reflected, in terms of the present problem, in attempts to include all the members of the neighborhood within the *compadre* network. Thus we may note a Bosnian practice of including Muslim members of the community by making them sponsors on special occasions, until in 1676 the Holy Office issued a decree against "the admission of heretics as sponsors, even though the strongest reasons of friendship and familiarity prompted the choice of such a person."[35] Also, in some areas neighbors acquired special rights as witnesses in legal proceedings, surviving until recently in the right of the Serb *compadre* to defend his *kum* in court, and to act as witness for him.[36]

In passing we may mention that the pattern of sponsorship permitted of easy extension into other spheres of activity. Thus, the organizations of medieval journeymen used both the components of baptism and sponsorship in initiating apprentices to their ranks,[37] and knights who aided a candidate for initiation into knighthood went by godfather and *compadre* terms.[38]

Finally, we must mention the sanctions of the Church in the enforcement of exogamy. In setting new norms for its tenants, it acted in its own self-interest in competition with the lay aristocracy which jealously guarded and reinforced its position of immunity. In extending Canon Law, and at the same time stressing dispensations from it, the Church added a source of income. Canon Law is manmade law, and the Pope has the right, by virtue of his office, to change its stipulations at will. For sixteen groschen a commoner could marry his blood relatives of the fourth degree of relationship, not to speak of ritual kin relations,[39] and a price list for the years 1492-1513 specifically states that "in spiritual relationships paupers are not dispensed, and the composition is three hundred ducats; nevertheless, one hundred are commonly paid."[40] Coulton has pointed out that enforcement to the letter of Canon Law would have meant "papal dispensations . . . in almost every generation of almost every village in Europe,"[41] and the law was often honored in the breach. But punishment struck hard, as in the case of one John Howthon of Tonbridge who was whipped three times around market and church for having married a girl to whom his first wife had been godmother.[42]

As the Middle Ages draw to a close, we find an increasing number of local attempts to restrict the extension of exogamy through ritual kin ties, on the part of both Church and state. A number of synods, held between the years 1310 and 1512, tried to set limits to the number of sponsors at baptismal ceremonies, but failed.[43] In 1521 the German Estates petitioned the Pope for redress of a series of wrongs. Their complaint against ritual kinship derived from baptismal sponsorship heads a list of some sixty-odd complaints.[44] The German Reformation directed its attack against the custom. "This is the work of fools," Luther said.[45] "Because in this way one Christian could not take another one, because they are brother and sister among themselves. These are the money snares of the Pope." Luther declared that "love needs no laws whatsoever," and that "no man has the right to create such laws." He spoke out sharply against "these stupid barriers due to spiritual fatherhood, motherhood, brotherhood, sisterhood, and childhood. Who but Superstition has created these spiritual realtionships? . . . Behold, Christian freedom is suppressed due to the blindness of human superstition."[46] His collected proverbs stress the purely mundane and neighborly aspects of the *compadre* mechanism, and advocate that just as "good fences make good neighbors," so they also make for good relations among *compadres*.[47] As early as 1550, Saxony restricted the number of baptismal sponsors to between seven and nine for nobles, and to three for burghers. Under pressures from within and without, the Church also reformed its stand at the Council of Trent (1545-63). It restricted rit-

ual kin relationships to the baptizing priest, the child, the child's parents and the child's sponsors. But it put an end to spiritual fraternity, spiritual relationships between the sponsors themselves, and spiritual relationships arising from catechismal sponsorship. It restricted to one or to a maximum of two the number of sponsors at baptism, and the number of sponsors at confirmation to one. Again, state authorities followed suit, and the rules governing baptism issued by the Duke of Altenburg for the year 1681 are typical for a whole series of German cities. These rulings restricted the number of sponsors according to one's estate. Nobles were permitted more sponsors than burghers and artisans, burghers and artisans more than peasants.[48] The Austrian Emperor Joseph II restricted to only two or three the number of sponsors at Baptism, although a much larger number had been chosen in earlier times.[49]

The rationale for these restrictions emerges perhaps most clearly in rulings prohibiting peasants from seeking their *compadres* in the towns, and "since rich people were often selected as *compadres*," people were prevented from asking unknown persons for the service.[50] We may note that the bulk of the restrictions coincide with the period which witnessed the rise of Protestantism and the early beginnings of industrial civilization. The new ethic put a premium on the individual as an effective accumulator of capital and virtue, and was certain to discountenance the drain on individual resources and the restrictions on individual freedom implicit in the wide extension of ritual kin ties. As a result the *compadre* mechanism has disappeared almost completely from areas which witnessed the development of industrial capitalism, the rise of a strong middle class, and the disappearance of feudal or neo-feudal tenures. Within these areas *compadrazgo* has lost its function most completely within the classes in which the family no longer forms the primary unit of production. This would include the economically mobile upper and middle classes on the one hand, and the industrial wage-earning working class on the other. In both these segments, kinship mechanisms became increasingly non-functional, and tended to be replaced by more impersonal, institutionalized forms of organization. Within these same areas, however, kinship mechanisms have been retained most completely where peasants have not yet become farmers. This point of transition comes where production is still largely for immediate consumption rather than for accumulation, and where the familial unit still forms the active basis of economic life. In Europe, as a whole, it has been retained most completely in such areas as Spain, Italy, and the Balkan countries where the development of industrial capitalism, the rise of a middle class, and the disintegration of the feudal order has been less rapid. To this extent Robert Redfield is justified when he called *compadrazgo* a Southern European peasant custom.[51] It is from Southern Europe that the complex was transmitted to Latin America, along with the call to baptize the infidels and to bring them into the fold of the Christian community as an addition to the faith through baptism, and as an addition to the riches of the Spanish Empire through labor.

II. FUNCTIONAL ANALYSIS

The Catholic ceremonial complexes, when carried to the New World, were to develop under conditions very different from those of fifteenth-century Europe. Alienation of Indian lands through such devices as the *repartimiento* and the *encomienda* proceeded concurrently with the wholesale conversion of millions of native peoples to Catholicism. The functioning of such mechanisms as *compadrazgo* in Latin American communities is strongly colored by four hundred years of historical development within this new setting. Yet there is little material on the cultural significance and usages of the *compadre* mechanism during the Colonial period. Certainly considerable research needs to be carried out on the processes of acculturation following early contact. Analysis of the social functioning of *compadrazgo* in its American beginnings is but a minor aspect.

Historical sources attest that baptism of natives had proceeded from the time of first contact. Fray Toribio de Benavente writes that in the fifty-five year period between 1521 and 1576 more than four million souls were brought to the baptismal font.[52] The evidence is good that emphasis was not on prior instruction in the catechism, but rather on formal acceptance of the faith. Father Gante and an assistant, proselytizing in Mexico, claims to have baptized up to fourteen thousand Indians in a single day. In all, Gante and his companion stated that they baptized more than two hundred thousand souls in a single Mexican province.[53]

Baptism was a sacrament designed to remove the stigma of original sin. The acquisition of godparents purported to guarantee to the initiate religious guidance during the years following his baptism. Actually, Spaniards who were members of exploring parties frequently served as sponsors for Indian converts, and thus fulfilled but a formal ritual necessity.[54] We can assume that most of the social implications of the compadre mechanism developed but slowly at first, if for no other reason than this.

Yet the baptismal ceremony established an individual in the Catholic universe, and perhaps by virtue of its symbolic simplicity, it was readily accepted by many native populations. Redfield, Parsons, Foster, and Paul, among others, have sought to differentiate between aboriginal and Catholic elements in the modern Latin American ritual.[55] Parsons, Redfield, and Paul have felt further that certain derivations of the modern godparental ritual have come from the adaptation of this ceremonial form to pre-Columbian ceremonies and social patterns. The Maya of Yucatan possessed a native baptism so like the Catholic ritual that, according to one authority, some of our Spaniards have taken occasion to persuade themselves and believe that in times past some of the apostles or successors to them passed over the West Indies and that ultimately those Indian were preached to.[56]

The Aztecs also had a kind of baptism, and in addition, godparents of sorts were chosen in an indigenous Aztec ear-piercing ceremonial, according to Sahagun.[57] Paul feels there may even have been an aboriginal basis for the *compadre* aspect of the complex in the existence of various kinds of formal friendship among native peoples.[58]

But it is impossible to generalize about the ease with which aboriginal ceremonial procedure could be accommodated to the new sacrament, as endorsed by the Church. The most important modern social result of the baptismal ceremony in practice—the creation of a security network of ritual kin folk through ceremonial sponsorship—seems rather to be due to the institution's inherent flexibility and utility, than to any pre-existing pattern with which the new complex might be integrated. Present-day folklore concerning the fate of an unbaptized child[59] suggests that a strong emphasis on the moral necessity for baptism was made from the start. In modern practice, however, whether the people in a given culture will feel that baptism requires the official approval and participation of representatives of the Church varies considerably. The evidence is that once the secular utility of this sacred institution was established, the native populations could count on the fulfillment of those reciprocal obligations which godparentage and *compadrazgo* entailed, the Church might not even be consulted. Makeshift ceremonies, consummated without orthodox clerical approval, became so widespread as to be illegalized by ecclesiastical ruling in 1947, except in cases where the child's death seemed imminent before official baptism.

As has been indicated, the mechanism of godparenthood took shape originally as a means for guaranteeing religious education and guidance to the Catholic child. This aim was achieved through the ritual kinship established between the newborn infant, its parents, and its godparents, at the baptismal ceremony. The relationship frequently was reinforced, or extended with new sponsors, at other life crisis ceremonies, including confirmation and marriage.

From the original Catholic life crisis ceremonial sponsorship, godparenthood has been elaborated in various Latin American communities into the ceremonial sponsorship of houses, crosses, altars, or carnivals,[60] circumcision,[61] the future crop,[62] commercial dealings,[63] and so on. Gillin lists fourteen forms of *compadrazgo* for a single community.[64] In certain cases, it cannot be said with any certainty whether the new adaptation was developed locally, or constitutes a carry-over of some kind from some older European elaboration.

In general, ritual ties between contemporaries seem to have become more important than those between godparents and godchildren. This point is elaborated by Gillin in his discussion of the Peruvian community, Moche. He writes:

The essence of the system in Moche is an "artificial bond," resembling a kinship relationship, which is established between persons by means of a ceremony. The ceremony usually involves a sponsorship of a person or material object by one or more of the persons involved, and the ceremony itself may be rather informal. However in Moche it seems to be placing the wrong emphasis to label the whole system ... "ceremonial sponsorship." ... The emphasis in Moche is upon the relations between sponsors of an individual or thing, and between them and other persons—in other words, relations between adults rather than between adults and children or things.[65] While the custom derives primarily from a conception of spiritual parenthood, modern Latin American emphasis seems to be rather on ritual co-parenthood; the *compadre-compadre* relationship outweighs the godparent-godchild relationship.

The ritual complex has been demonstrated to be of so flexible and adaptable a nature that a wide group of individuals can be bound together ceremonially. Paul makes the points that the mechanism of *compadrazgo* may be used either to enlarge numerically and spatially the number of ritually related kin on the one hand, or to reinforce already existing blood or ritual ties on the other. These contrasting motives he calls "extension" and "intensification."[66] The authors of the present article feel that whether the *com-padre* mechanism will be used prevailingly to extend or to intensify a given set of relationships will be determined in a specific functional-historical context.

In modern Latin American communities, there is clear patterning of choice. *Compadres* may be chosen exclusively from within one's own family, or perhaps blood kin will be preferred to outsiders. In other communities, on the other hand, one pair of godparents may serve for all of one's children, or *compadres* chosen from outside one's own family may be rigidly preferred. The present writers are convinced that the rare usages of *compadrazgo* in inheritance indicate the lack of utility of this mechanism in dynamically affecting prevailing patterns of ownership. It is a mechanism that can be used to strengthen existing patterns, but not to change them. In the two cases in which *compadrazgo* plays any role in determining land inheritance, land is held by the village community, and all that is inherited is temporary right of use.[67] Marital impediment under Canon Law, a factor of continuing importance in much of the New World,[68] and the selection of *compadres* within the kin group or outside it, are also factors bound together functionally and historically. This problem lies beyond the scope of the present article.

Compadrazgo, once accepted by a social grouping, can be moulded into the community way of life by many means. It is a two-way system which sets up reciprocal relations of variable complexity and solemnity. By imposing automatically, and with a varying degree of sanctity, statuses and obligations of a fixed nature, on the people who participate, it makes the immediate social environment more stable, the participants more interdependent and more secure. In fact, it might be said that the baptismal rite (or corresponding event) may be the original basis for the mechanism, but no longer its sole motivating force. Some brief examples will demonstrate the institution's flexibility.

In Chimaltenango,[69] two *compadres* will lend each other maize or money ("as much as six dollars"). ... Two *comadres* should visit each other often and they may borrow small things readily from one another. When one is sick, or when one has just had another child, her *comadre* should come bringing tortillas for the family, and she should work in her comadre's house "like a sister."

In Peguche,[70] "white compadres are an asset for anyone who has business in Otovalo or Quito."

In Tzintzuntzan,[71] on the economic level, the

compadrazgo system forms a kind of social insurance. Few are the families which can meet all emergencies without outside help. Often this means manual help at the time of a fiesta, or the responsibility of a *carguero*. Sometimes it means lending money, which near blood relatives do not like to do, because of the tendency never to repay a debt. But *compadres* feel obliged to lend, and no one would have respect for a man who refused to repay a *compadre*.

In San Pedro de Laguna,[72] the practical purpose motivating the selection of Ladinas as *compadres* is the belief that they can cure infant illnesses and have access to the necessary medicines. The Indians store no medicine. But the Ladinas—by virtue of their cultural tradition and their greater income—customarily have on hand a number of drugstore preparations. The godparent bond imposes on the Ladina the responsibility of coming to the medical aid of her Indian godchild. The first year or two is correctly considered to be the most critical period of the infant's life. Hence the natives sacrifice long-run considerations in favor of providing a measure of medical protection during the infancy of the child ...

Evidence from studies of two communities in Puerto Rico suggests that the *compadre* relation may be invoked to forestall sexual aggressions.[73] Cases are mentioned where a man concerned about the attentions of a family friend to his wife, sought to avoid trouble by making his friend his *compadre*. Thus a new and more sacred relationship was established.

Among the Huichol,[74] the *compadre* relationship unquestionably strengthens Huichol social organization outside the family, which is not strong. Though *compadres* are not under economic bonds to each other, the injunction to be kind and friendly prevents drunken fights and brawls, which are the greatest source of weakness in Huichol society.

One form of *compadrazgo* is specifically organized to avoid aggression between two *compadres: "el compadrazgo de voluntad."* People say that where there are two bullies in the same *barrio*, they will conclude a "non-aggression pact" and make themselves *compadres de voluntad*, which means that they can no longer fight each other.[75]

The persistence of *compadrazgo* in very secularized contexts, and its existence in such cases even without the sponsorship of a person, object, or event, is evidence of its frequently high social and secular plasticity.

The formal basis for selecting godparents for one's children—religious guidance, and if nec-

essary, the adoption of orphaned children—is sometimes carried out. Gamio mentions this traditional usage in the Valley of Teotihuacan,[76], Redfield and Villa R. for Chan Kom,[77], Villa R. for Tusik,[78], Rojas Gonzales for the Mixe and Zoque,[79] and Wisdom for the Chorti.[80] Among the Chorti, the godfather often acts in every way as the actual father in the event of the latter's death. He gives his ward advice, gets him out of difficulties, sometimes trains him in a man's work, and may act as his parent when he marries. The same is done by the godmother for her female godchild. If both parents die, and the godchild is young, the godparent may receive the portion of the property which the child inherited, and put it to his own use, in return for which he must bring up the child as one of his own family. As soon as the young man or woman becomes eighteen years of age, his inheritance is made up to him by his godfather. Where there is more than one minor child, each godfather receives his ward's share out of the total property, each child going to live in the home of its own godfather, leaving the adult children at home.

This usage is of particular interest because the *compadre* mechanism can be seen here as a link in the process of inheritance. Yet final property rights in this society are vested in the village, and not in the individual. A single case of the same kind of usage is mentioned by Villa R. for the Maya Indian community of Tusik.[81] Yet *compadrazgo* cannot override the emphasis on group land tenure in either of these societies. The mechanism is flexible and adaptable specifically because it usually carries with it no legal obligations—particularly regarding inheritance. Paul makes this point clearly when he writes that, unlike the involuntary ties of kinship those of ritual sponsorship are formed on the basis of choice. This enables godparenthood to serve as the social link connecting divergent income groups, disparate social strata, and separated localities. Affinity too may cut across class and locality through the practices of hypergamy and intermarriage. But the frequency with which such irregular forms of marriage occur throughout the world is sharply limited by strong social pressures operating to keep the unions within the class or community. This is understandable in view of the fact that marriage is the means by which the in-group perpetuates itself. Because no such considerations of social recruitment impede the formation of godparent bonds between persons of different social strata, godparenthood more readily serves as a mechanism for intergroup integration.[82]

It may be fruitful to examine cases of *compadrazgo* as examples of mechanisms crosscutting socio-cultural or class affiliations, or as taking place within the socio-cultural confines of a single class. The authors believe such patternings will prove to be determined, not haphazard in character, nor determined solely along continuums of homogeneity-to-heterogeneity, or greater-to-lesser isolation. Rather they will depend on the amount of socio-cultural and economic mobility, *real and apparent*, available to an individual in a given situation. There is of course no clear-cut device for the measurement of such real or apparent mobility. Yet the utility of *compadrazgo* might profitably be examined in this light. The aim would be to assess whether the individual is seeking to strengthen his position in an homogeneous socio-cultural community with high stability and low mobility, or to strengthen certain crosscutting ties by alignment with persons of a higher socio-cultural stratum, via reciprocal-exploitative relationships manipulated through *compadrazgo*. Some examples may illuminate the problem.

The Maya Indian people of Tusik,[83] a community in east central Quintana Roo, Yucatan, are homogeneous in a tribal sense, rather than having a mono-class structure. Says Villa:

There are no classes here in the sense that different groups of people have different relations to the production and distribution of economic goods; in the sense that some people own land on which other people work, or that some people are engaged in producing goods while others are engaged in distributing them or in servicing the rest of the population. As we have already pointed out, everyone in the subtribe has the same relation to the land as everyone else; the land is commonly held by the subtribe, and a man's rights to a piece of land rests only on the right that he has put agricultural labor into the land and is entitled to the products of his labor. Every man makes *milpa*—even the sacred professionals earn their living as farmers—and since the secular division of labor is practically nonexistent, there are no merchants or artisans.

The economic life of the group centers about maize, and the people consume all that they produce. Labor for other men is rare, and when done, payment in kind prevails. The only cash commodity is chicle. Says Villa:

Apparently all the people of the subtribe enjoy the same economic circumstances. Nothing one observes in their ordinary, daily behavior suggests the existence of differences in accumulated wealth ... The acquisition of wealth is related directly to the personal ambition of the individual, for there are no differences in opportunity and no important differences in privilege. The principal source of wealth is the extraction of chicle, which is within the reach of all ... This equality of opportunity is a recent matter, for some years ago when the chiefs had greater authority, the lands of the bush were distributed by them and the best portion preserved for their own use. In some cases men were thus able to enrich themselves through special advantage.

Regarding *compadrazgo*, the grandparents of the child to be born, preferably the paternal ones, are chosen. If they are not alive, chiefs or *maestros cantores*, as persons of prestige and good character, are selected. It is noteworthy that no mention is made of any choice of travelling merchants as *compadres*, although the travelling merchants are the natives' main source of contact with the outer world. It is they who bring into the region ... the most important news from the city .... The arrival of the merchant is the occasion for the people to gather together and excitedly discuss the events he relates to them, and in this atmosphere the merchant's own friendly ties with the natives are strengthened. Chicle is sold, and commodities bought through these travellers, but apparently ritual kinship is not used to bind them with the community.

In marked contrast to the isolated, subsistence crop, tribal culture of Tusik, we may examine two communities which exhibit cultural homogeneity under completely different conditions. They are fully integrated economically, and to a great degree welded culturally into national cultures. The first of these is Poyal.[84]

Barrio Poyal is a rural community on the south coast of Puerto Rico, in an area of large-scale sugar cane production, with corporate ownership of land and mills. The lands are devoted exclusively to the production of the single cash crop. While the *barrio* working population forms what is practically a mono-class isolate, *compadres* could be selected among the foremen, administrators, public officials, store owners, and so forth. Instead, there is an overwhelming tendency to pick neighbors and fellow workers as *compadres*. A man who seeks a wealthy *compadre* in Poyal is held in some contempt by his fellows; a wealthy *compadre* would not visit him nor invite him to his house. People remember when the old hacienda owners were chosen as godparents to the workers' children, but this practice is totally outmoded now. A local landowning group no longer exists in Poyal.

Compadre relationships generally are treated reverentially; *compadres* are addressed with the polite *Usted*, even if they are family members, and the *compadre* relationship is utilized daily in getting help, borrowing money, dividing up available work opportunities, and so forth. However, as more and more Poyal workers migrate to the United States, the utility of many *compadre* ties is weakened.

Another example of the same category is Pascua,[85] a community of essentially landless, wage-earning Yaqui Indian immigrants who, with their descendants, form a village on the outskirts of Tucson, Arizona. The economic basis of Pascua life bears certain striking resemblances to *Barrio* Poyal: the almost total lack of subsistence activities, the emphasis on seasonal variation, the emphasis on wage-earning as opposed to payment in kind, and so on. Says Spicer:

Existence is wholly dependent on the establishment of relationships with individuals outside the village. If for any reason the economic relations of a Pascuan with outside persons are broken off for an extended period, it becomes necessary to depend upon other Pascuans who have maintained such relations.
While the economic linkages are exclusively with external sources of income and employment, the *compadre* structure is described as an all-pervasive network of relationships which takes into its web every person in the village. Certain parts of the network, here and there about the village, are composed of strong and well-knit fibers. Here the relationships between *compadres* are functioning constantly and effectively. Elsewhere there are weaker threads representing relationships which have never been strengthened by daily recognition of reciprocal obligations. These threads nevertheless exist and may from time to time be the channels of temporarily re-established *compadre* relationships.

Spicer notes that:

sometimes in Pascua sponsors are sought outside the village in Libre or Marana, or even among the Mexican population of Tucson. But everything suggests that the ritual kinship system here functions predominantly within the wage-earning, landless mono-class grouping of the Yaqui themselves.

Spicer's description of *compadrazgo* is probably the most complete in the literature today, and the Pascua system appears to be primarily between contemporaries in emphasis, and as in *Barrio* Poyal horizontal in character.

These three cases, Tusik, *Barrio* Poyal, and Pascua, illustrate the selective character of *compadrazgo* and some of its functionings, within small "homogeneous" groupings. The mechanism plainly has considerable importance and

utility and is treated reverentially in all three places. Yet while Tusik is isolated and lacks a class-character, *Barrio* Poyal and Pascua are both involved in wage-earning, cash crop, world market productive arrangements where the homogeneity is one of class membership only, and isolation is not characteristic.

In Tusik, *compadrazgo* is correlated with great internal stability, low economic mobility, ownership of land by the village, and the lack of a cash economy and class stratification. In *Barrio* Poyal and Pascua *compadrazgo* correlates with homogeneous class membership, landlessness, wage-earning, and an apparent growing identity of class interest.

An interesting contrast is provided by Gillin's study of Moche. This is a Peruvian coastal community which, according to the Foreword, is in the last stages of losing its identity as an Indian group and of being absorbed into Peruvian national life . . . . Surrounded by large, modern haciendas, Moche is "Indian" only in that its population is largely Indian in a racial sense, that it has retained much of its own lands, that it exists in a certain social isolation from surrounding peoples, retaining a community life organized on a modified kinship basis, mainly of Spanish derivation . . . . Its lands, however, are now owned individually, and they are being alienated through sale and litigation. It is on a cash rather than subsistence basis economically . . . . Many Mocheros even work outside the community for wages, and some are in professions . . . . Formal aspects of native social organization have disappeared, and contacts with the outside world are increasing.[86]

In Moche, the *compadre* system would expectably be subject to the same stresses as those suffered by any other local social institution. Yet the whole idea of this type of relationship has been carried to extremes in Moche. There are more types of *padrinazgo* (i.e. godfatherhood) in this community than in any other concerning which I have seen reports. This fact may be linked with the absence of spontaneous community organization and solidarity.

Gillin finds evidence for fourteen different kinds of *compadre* relations. As to the choice of *compadres*, Gillin says: Godparents may be blood relatives, but usually the attempt is made to secure persons who are not relatives of either of the parents. Not only Mocheros, but in these days, trusted *forasteros* (i.e. outsiders) are chosen. From the point of view of the parents it is desirable to choose godparents who are financially responsible, if not rich, and also persons who have "influence" and prestigeful social connections. The real function of godparents is to broaden, and, if possible, increase the social and economic resources of the child and his parents and by the same token to lower the anxieties of the parents on this score.

In a later section, however, Gillin states that he does not feel that socially defined classes as such exist in Moche.[87]

It is extremely noteworthy that the mechanism of *compadrazgo* has maintained itself here in the face of what appears to be progressively accelerating social change. We wonder whether the elaborations of the mechanism's forms may be part of the community's unconscious effort to answer new problems. It must increasingly face the insecurity of growing incorporation into the national structure and increasing local wage-based, cash crop competition. This may call forth an increased emphasis on techniques for maintaining and strengthening face-to-face relationships. Eggan's study of Cheyenne kinship terminology[88] suggests that the kinship structure is sensitive to rapid social change if the changing terminology reflects genuine structural modifications. Ritual kinship structures may react to the weakening of certain traditional obligations by spreading out to include new categories of contemporaries, and therefore potential competitors.

Other examples suggest that vertical phrasings of the *compadre* system may take place in situations where change has been slowed at some point, and relationships between two defined socio-cultural strata, or classes, are solidified. San Jose is a highland coffee and minor crop-producing community of Puerto Rico.[89] The frequency distribution of land shows a considerable scatter, with fifty-five percent of the landowners holding ten percent of the land at one extreme, and five percent holding forty-five percent of the land at the other. Thus, while Tusik people hold their land communally, *Barrio* Poyal and Pascua people are landless, and Moche people are largely small landowners with no farm over four acres, San Jose people are in large part landowners with great variability in the size of holdings. While a large part of the agricultural population is landless, agricultural laborers in San Jose may be paid partly in kind, and frequently will be given in addition a small plot of land for subsistence farming. Production for wages is largely of the main cash crop, coffee.

In the rural zones of this community, a prevailing number of the *compadre* relations tie agricultural workers to their landholding employers, or small landholders to larger ones.

Thus a large landowner may become *compadre* to twenty smaller landowners living around his farm. In isolated areas, where the "community" is defined entirely in familial terms, most *compadre* relationships take place within the family. Yet it must be recognized that members of the same family, and brothers of the same filial generation, may be variously landowners, sharecroppers (*medianeros*), and laborers.

Compadrazgo in San Jose may help in the stabilization of productive relations between large and small landholders, or between landholders and their sharecropping employees and laborers. Interesting in this connection is the fact that the economic basis in San Jose is much less exclusively cash than in Tusik, *Barrio* Poyal, or Pascua. The land tenure pattern in San Jose does not appear to be changing rapidly. *Compadrazgo* relations are phrased vertically, so as to crosscut class stratification, quite probably serving in this connection to solidify the relationships of people to the land. There is evidence of landowners getting free labor out of their laborer brothers who have been made *compadres*. Contrariwise, laborers bound by *compadrazgo* to their employers are accustomed to rely on this bond to secure them certain small privileges, such as the use of equipment, counsel and help, small loans, and so on.

The authors know of no fully documented study of *compadrazgo* in the context of an "old-style" plantation or hacienda. Siegel's material on the Guatemalan plantation community of San Juan Acatan indicates that the Indians often invite Ladinos with whom they come in contact to sponsor the baptisms of their children. But Siegel adds that the relationship in this community is "virtually meaningless."[90] The authors of the present article would in general predict that plantation laborers, either bound or very dependent on the plantation, with daily face-to-face contacts with the owner or *hacendado* would seek to establish a reciprocal coparental relationship with the owner. Historical material from old informants in *Barrio* Poyal offer evidence of this tradition, now markedly altered in the pure wage, absentee ownership context.

The mechanism may be contrasted, then, in several distinct contexts. In the first context are Tusik, *Barrio* Poyal, and Pascua. These communities are alike in their "homogeneity," and the horizontal structuring of the *compadre* system; yet they are markedly different in other respects. Tusik is tribal and essentially isolated from the world market, while *Barrio* Poyal and Pascua are incorporated into capitalistic world economies, and are fully formed working class strata.

In the second context is San Jose, with its varied land ownership pattern, its mixed (cash and subsistence) crop production and its several classes. Through the vertical phrasing of its *compadre* system, San Jose demonstrates a relatively stable reciprocity, economic and social, between the landed, large and small, and the sharecroppers and laborers.

In the third context is Moche. Land is held predominantly in small plots; the crops, as in San Jose, are both cash and subsistence, and while Gillin doubts the existence of classes, certainly the *compadre* system is described as a vertical structuring one. Here, too, the elaboration of face-to-face ceremonialism may help to slow the accelerated trend toward land concentration, a cash economy, and incorporation into the world market.

III. CONCLUSION

In the first section of this article, the writers traced the relationship between land tenure and the functioning of ritual kin ties under conditions of European feudalism. During this period, ritual kin ties gradually changed from bonds of blood brotherhood to those of *compadre* relationships. This accompanied a change from neighbor inheritance to the family inheritance of tenure. As these changes in the pattern of land tenure took place, the ritual ties were shifted correspondingly from a horizontal cementing of relationships to a vertical phrasing of artificial kinship at the height of feudalism.

With the breakdown of feudal land tenures and the increased assertion of peasant rights, such ritual ties were again rephrased horizontally to unite the peasant neighborhoods in their struggle against feudal dues.

Under conditions of advanced industrial development, mechanisms of social control based on biological or ritual kin affiliations tend to give way before more impersonal modes of organization. *Compadrazgo* survives most actively in present-day Europe within the areas of lesser industrial development. From one such area, Spain, *compadrazgo* was carried to the New World, and developed here in a new historical and functional context.

In the second section of this article, five modern communities with Latin American culture were analyzed to show the functional correlates of the *compadre* mechanism. In cases where the community is a self-contained class, or tribally homogeneous, *compadrazgo* is prevailingly horizontal (intra-class) in character. In cases where the community contains several interacting classes, *compadrazgo* will structure such relationships vertically (inter-class). Last, in a situation of rapid social change *compadre* mechanisms may multiply to meet the accelerated rate of change.

BIBLIOGRAPHY

Bamberger, M. L. 1923 *Aus meiner Minhagimsammelmappe* (Jahrbuch für Jüdische Volkskunde, vol. 1, pp. 320-332).

Bancroft, H. H. 1883 *History of Mexico* (San Francisco).

Beals, R.L. 1946 *Cherán: a Sierra Tarascan Village* (Publication, Institute of Social Anthropology, Smithsonian Institution, no. 2, Washington).

Bennett, H. S. 1938 *Life on the English Manor* (New York).

Boesch, H. 1900 *Kinderleben in der Deutschen Vergangenheit* (Monographien zur Deutschen Kulturgeschichte, vol. 5, Leipzig).

Boniface 1940 *The Letters of Saint Boniface* (Engl. transl., New York).

Committee on Latin American Anthropology, National Research Council 1949 *Research Needs in the Field of Modern Latin American Culture* (American Anthropologist, vol. 51, pp. 149-154).

Corblet, J. 1882 *Histoire Dogmatique, Liturgique et Archeologique du Sacrement de Baptème* (vol. 1, Geneva).

Coulton, C. G. 1926 *The Medieval Village* (Cambridge). 1936 *Five Centuries of Religion* (vol. 3, Cambridge).

Donadiny Puignan, D. D. no date *Diccionario de la lengua Castellana.* (vol. 1, Barcelona).

Dopsch, A. 1918-20 *Wirtschaftliche und Soziale Grundlagen der Europäischen Kulturentwicklung* (2 vols., Vienna).

Drews, P. 1907 *"Taufe, Liturg, Vollzug"* (in *Realenzyklopädie für Protestantische Theologie und Kirche*, vol. 19, Leipzig).

Durham, M. E. 1928 *Some Tribal Origins, Laws, and Customs of the Balkans* (London).

Eggan, F. 1937 "The Cheyenne and Arapaho Kinship System" (in *Social Anthropology of North American Tribes*, F. Eggan, ed., Chicago).

Erich, O. 1936 *Wörterbuch der Deutschen Volkskunde* (Leipzig).

Espinosa, J. M. 1942 *Crusaders of the Rio Grande* (Chicago).

Flick, A. 1936 *The Decline of the Medieval Church* (vol. 1, New York).

Foster, G. N. 1948 *Empire's Children: the People of Tzintzuntzan* (Publication, Institute of Social

Anthropology, Smithsonian Institution, no. 6, Washington).

Gamio, M. 1922 *La Población del Valle de Teotihuacán* (3 vols., Mexico).

Ganshof, F. L. 1941 "Medieval Agrarian Society in its Prime: France, the Low Countries, and Western Germany" (in *Cambridge Economic History of Europe from the Decline of the Roman Empire*, vol. 1, Cambridge).

Gillin, J. 1945 *Moche: a Peruvian Coastal Community*. (Publication, Institute of Social Anthropology, Smithsonian Institution, no. 3, Washington).

Handjieff, W. 1931 *Zur Sociologie des Bulgarischen Dorfes* (thesis Leipzig).

Heninger, E. 1891 *Sitten und Gebräuche bei der Taufe und Namengebung in der Altfranzösichen Dichtung* (thesis, Halle a. S.).

Herskovits, M. J. 1937 *Life in a Haitian Valley* (New York).

Howard, G. H. 1904 *A History of Matrimonial Institutions* (vol. 1, Chicago).

Kearney, R. J. 1925 *Sponsorship at Baptism According to the Code of Canon Law* (thesis, Catholic University of America).

Kummer, Bernhard 1931 "Gevatter" (in *Handwörterbuch des Deutschen Aberglaubens*, vol. 3, Berlin).

Landa, Diego de 1941 *Landa's Relación de las Cosas de Yucatan* (English transl., A. M. Tozzer, ed.: Papers, Peabody Museum of American Archaeology and Ethnology, Harvard University, vol. 18).

Laurin, F. 1866 *Die Geistliche Verwandtschaft in ihrer geschichtlichen Entwicklung* (Archiv für Katholisches Kirchenrecht, vol. 15, Mainz).

Lunt, W. E. 1934 *Papal Revenues in the Middle Ages* (vol. 2, New York).

Luther, M. 1520 "Von der bablonischen Gefangenschaft der Kirche: von der Ehe" (in *Reformatorische Schriften, Luthers' Werke*, vol. 2, 1924, Leipzig). 1539 "Tischreden: Anton Lauterbachs Tagebuch aufs Jahr 1539" (in *D. Martin Luthers Werke*, Kritische Gesamtausgabe, vol. 4, 1916, Weimar). 1900 *Sprichwörtersammlung* (Thiele, ed., Weimar).

Maitland, F. W. and (Sir) F. Pollock 1923 *History of English Law* (vol. 2, Cambridge).

Manners, R. A. 1950 *A Tobacco and Minor Crop Community in Puerto Rico* (manuscript).

Mintz, S. W. 1950 *A Sugar-Cane Community in Puerto Rico* (manuscript).

Münch, E. 1830 *Vollständige Sammlung aller älteren*

und neueren Konkordate (vol. 1, Leipzig).

Nabholz, H. 1941 "Medieval Agrarian Society in Transition" (in *Cambridge Economic History of Europe from the Decline of the Roman Empire*, vol. 1, Cambridge).

Parsons, E. C. 1936 *Mitla: Town of the Souls* (Chicago). 1945 *Peguche: a Study of Andean Indians* (Chicago).

Paul, B. D. 1942 *Ritual Kinship: with Special Reference to Godparenthood in Middle America* (Ph.D. thesis, University of Chicago).

Ploss, H. 1911 *Das Kind in Brauch und Sitte der Völker* (3rd ed., vol. 1, Leipzig).

Redfield, R. 1930 *Tepoztlan: a Mexican Village* (Chicago).

Redfield, R., and Alfonso Villa R. 1934 *Chan Kom: a Maya Village* (Publication, Carnegie Institution of Washington, no. 448, Washington).

Rojas Gonzales, F. 1943 *La Institucion del compadrazgo entre los indigenas de México* (Revista Méxicana de Sociologia, vol. 5, no. 1).

Sahagun, B. de 1932 *A History of Ancient Mexico*. (Engl. transl., Nashville).

Sanders, I. 1949 *Balkan Village* (Lexington).

Siemsen, R. 1942 *Germanengut im Zunftbrauch* (Berlin-Dahlem).

Spicer, E. 1940 *Pascua: a Yaqui Village in Arizona* (Chicago).

Tomasic, D. 1948 *Personality and Culture in Eastern European Politics* (New York).

Tuschen, A. 1936 *Die Taufe in der Altfranzösischen Literatur* (thesis, Bonn).

Tylor, E. B. 1861 *Anahuac* (London).

Villa R., A. 1945 *The Maya of East Central Quintana Roo* (Publication, Carnegie Institution of Washington, no. 559, Washington).

Wagley, Ch. 1949 *The Social and Religious Life of a Guatemalan Village* (Memoir, American Anthropological Association, no. 71).

Warrack, A. 1911 *A Scots Dialect Dictionary* (London).

Weekly, E. 1921 *An Etymological Dictionary of Modern English* (London).

Wisdom, Ch. 1940 *A Chorti Village in Guatemala* (Chicago).

Wolf, E. R. 1950 *A Coffee Growing Community in Puerto Rico* (manuscript).

Zingg, R. 1938 *Primitive Artists: the Huichols* (University of Denver Contributions to Ethnology, Denver).

NOTES

*All translations are by the authors unless otherwise indicated. The writers wish to thank the University of Puerto Rico and the Rockefeller Foundation for their sponsorship of the Puerto Rico Social Anthropology Project. Field data gathered by the authors and their colleagues on this project have been used in the present article.

1. Tylor, 1861, pp. 250-251.

2. Parsons, 1936, pp. 524-525; Redfield and Villa R., 1934, pp. 373-374; Foster, 1948, p. 264.

3. Paul, 1942.

4. Committee on Latin American Anthropology of the National Research Council, 1949, p. 152.

5. Kearney, 1925, p. 4.

6. Bamberger, 1923, p. 326.

7. Drews, 1907, p. 447.

8. Kearney, *op. cit.*, pp. 33-34.
9. Kearney, *op. cit.*, pp. 30-31.
10. Laurin, 1866, p. 220.
11. Boniface (English transl.), 1940, pp. 61-62.
12. Laurin, *op. cit.*, p. 220.
13. Durham, 1928, p. 304.
14. Tuschen, 1936, p. 61.
15. Kummer, 1931, p. 789.
16. Tomasic, 1948, p. 80.
17. Dopsch, 1918-20, vol. 1, p. 378.
18. *Ibid.*
19. Dopsch, 1918-20, vol. 2, p. 227.
20. Maitland and Pollock, 1923, pp. 387-388.
21. Henninger, 1891, p. 31.
22. Boesch, 1900, pp. 26-27.
23. *Ibid.*
24. Coulton, 1936, p. 264.
25. Donadin y Puignan, p. 863.
26. Weekly, 1921, p. 654.
27. Warrack, 1911, p. 117.
28. Ganshof, 1941, p. 295.
29. Ganshof, *op. cit.*, p. 319.
30. Boesch, *op. cit.*, p. 26.
31. Sanders, 1949, p. 129.
32. Laurin, *op. cit.*, p. 262. For parallels in modern Bulgaria, cf. Handjieff, 1931, pp. 36-37.
33. Nabholz, 1941, p. 506.
34. Bennett, 1938, pp. 241-242.
35. Kearney, *op. cit.*, p. 58.
36. Ploss, 1911, p. 325.
37. Erich, 1936, p. 275; Siemsen, 1942, pp. 61, 67.
38. Corblet, 1882, vol. 1, p. 180.
39. Flick, 1936, vol. 1, p. 122.
40. Lunt, 1934, vol. 2, pp. 525-526.
41. Coulton, 1926, p. 80.
42. Howard, 1904, p. 365.
43. Laurin, *op. cit.*, p. 263.
44. Münch, 1830, vol. 1, p. 344.
45. Luther, 1539, p. 301.
46. Luther, 1520, pp. 477-478.
47. Luther, 1900, p. 348.
48. Boesch, *op. cit.*, p. 32.
49. Ploss, *op. cit.*, p. 330.
50. Boesch, *op. cit.*, p. 32.
51. Redfield, 1930, p. 141.
52. Quoted in Rojas Gonzalez, 1943, p. 193.
53. Bancroft, 1883, p. 174.
54. Espinosa, 1942, p. 70 *passim*.
55. Redfield and Villa R., *loc. cit.*; Parsons, *loc. cit.*; Foster, *loc. cit.*; Paul, *op. cit.*, p. 79 *passim*.
56. Lopez Medel, quoted in Landa, 1941, p. 227.
57. Sahagun, 1932, pp. 34-35.
58. Paul, *op. cit.*, pp. 85-87.
59. Redfield and Villa R., *op. cit.*, p. 169; Parsons, 1945, p. 44; Paul, *op. cit.*
60. Gillin, 1945, p. 105.
61. Beals, 1946, p. 102.
62. Parsons, 1936, p. 228, n. 96.
63. Zingg, 1938, pp. 717-718.
64. Gillin, *loc. cit.*
65. Gillin, *op. cit.*, p. 104.
66. Paul, *op. cit.*, p. 57.
67. Wisdom, 1940; Villa R., 1945.
68. Herskovits, 1937, p. 98.
69. Wagley, 1949, p. 19.
70. Parsons, 1945, p. 45.
71. Foster, *op. cit.*, p. 264.
72. Paul, *op. cit.*, p. 92.
73. Wolf, 1950, ms.; Manners, 1950, ms.
74. Zingg, *op. cit.*, p. 57.
75. Wolf, *op. cit.*
76. Gamio, 1922, vol. 2, p. 243.
77. Redfield and Villa R., *op. cit.*, p. 250.
78. Villa R., *op. cit.*, p. 90.
79. Rojas Gonzales, *op cit*, pp. 204-205.
80. Wisdom, *op. cit.*, pp. 293-294.
81. Villa R., *op. cit.*, p. 90.
82. Paul, *op. cit.*, pp. 72-73.
83. Villa R., *op. cit.*
84. Mintz, 1950, ms.
85. Spicer, 1940.
86. Gillin, *op. cit.*; Foreword by Julian H. Steward.
87. Gillin, *op. cit.*, pp. 107, 113.
88. Eggan, 1937.
89. Wolf, *op. cit.*
90. Siegel, quoted in Paul, *op. cit.*, p. 72.

THE DYADIC CONTRACT:
A Model for the Social Structure of a Mexican Peasant Village[1]

GEORGE M. FOSTER

THE SOCIAL STRUCTURES of societies with unilineal descent groups are far better known than those of societies with bilateral kinship systems. And our conceptual models for dealing with them are much more sophisticated. The differences in our relative degrees of knowledge are particularly apparent when we compare African groups with what may be called "classic peasant society," of which the preindustrial European village is the type example.[2] By 1953, Fortes felt "we are now in a position to formulate a number of connected generalizations about the structure of the unilineal descent group, and its place in the total social system . . ." (1953:24). We are still unable to say as much about bilateral systems, as a class. As Fortes said about unilineal descent groups at that time.

Since Fortes wrote, Pitt-Rivers' account of a small Spanish town (1955) and Banfield's description of a poverty-striken Italian village (1958) have appeared. Both represent classic peasantry. Although the Spanish Alcalá and the Italian Montegrano differ from each other in many ways, and are described by the authors from distinct points of reference, it is clear that in social typology they fall together as compared to African corporate-unit groups. Most, and possibly all, non-Indian Latin American peasant communities, when better described, will be found to fall with the European Mediterranean type. This is important, since collectively the two areas, which share much common culture history and many social structural features, offer an excellent contrast to the African groups which have become the take-off point for so much structural-functional analysis.

This paper represents a preliminary attempt at a structural-functional analysis of the social organization of the Mexican peasant community of Tzintzuntzan. Specifically, I suggest a model —and describe part of the empirical data from which it is drawn—to reconcile the institutionalized roles which can be recognized and described with the underlying principle which gives the social system coherence. The model appears to account for the nature of interaction between people of the same socio-economic status, between people of differnet statuses, between fellow villagers, between villagers and outsiders, and perhaps between man and supernatural beings as well. Although my analysis deals only with Tzintzuntzan, I think the model will prove useful for other societies with similar structural features.

In Tzintzuntzan, as in Alcalá and Montegrano, the nuclear bilateral family is the basic social unit. And, as in these two communities, both villagers and the anthropologist recognize and think in terms of the institutions of the wider family, the godparenthood system (*compadrazgo*), neighborhoodship (to use Pitt-Rivers' term), and friendship. Yet a thorough description and a profound understanding of the workings of institutions which are evident enough to be named do not add up, by themselves, to a structural analysis of the social organization of the community. We need to know more than the totality of roles and attendant statuses that tradition recognizes in institutional frameworks.

It is not sufficient to conceive of the community as formed by a conventional arrangement of sociological constructs. What is needed is, at an intermediate level of analysis, an integrative principle—here reciprocity—which leads, at a higher level of analysis to a social model—here the dyadic contract.

Briefly, it is hypothesized that every adult organizes his societal contacts outside the nuclear family by means of a special form of contractual relationship. These contracts are informal, or implicit, since they lack ritual or legal basis. They are not based on any idea of law, and they are unenforceable through authority; they exist only at the pleasure of the contractants. The contracts are dyadic in that they occur only between two individuals; three or more people are not brought together. The contracts are noncorporate, since social units such as villages, *barrios*, or extended families are never bound. Even nuclear families cannot truly be said to enter contractual relations with other families, although spouses often honor the obligations inherent in each other's contracts.

The implicit dyadic contract is made between members of a family as close as siblings; it binds *compadres* (co-godparents) beyond the limits of the formally defined relationships of the institution; and it unites neighbors and friends. Contracts are found between social and economic equals within Tzintzuntzan or with similar people in other communities. And they are found between people (or beings) of different status and category, as on those few occasions when outside political leaders or economic patrons have ties with villagers and when a villager invokes the aid of the Virgin Mary or a saint.

It is clear that the contracts fall into two basic types: (1) those made between people of equal socio-economic status; and (2) those made between people (or beings) of differnet socio-economic statuses (or order of being). The first type of contract operates primarily within the village, but it also ties villagers to the inhabitants of adjacent peasant communities. The second type of contract operates almost exclusively between villagers and non-villagers (including supernatural beings), since socio-economic differences in Tzintzuntzan are nonfunctional.[3]

In both types the contract implies and is validated by reciprocal obligations. But here the structural similarity ends. The first type of contract can be called symmetrical, in that it binds people of equal status, and its associated reciprocal obligations can be called complementary since, averaged out over time, they are the same for both parties. By the same token, the second type of contract can be called asymmetrical, since it binds people of different statuses, and its associated reciprocal obligations are noncomplementary, since each partner owes the other different kinds of things. For example, in the symmetrical contract partners exchange similar goods and services of approximately equal value (measured in time and monetary terms) over a period of time. In the asymmetrical contract, partner A owes partner B something quite different from what he receives from the latter, and vice versa. Moreover, it is difficult and sometimes impossible to strike an equivalence in time and monetary values. To illustrate an asymmetrical, noncomplementary contract, a religious supplicant lights candles and hangs a votive offering before an image of the Virgin Mary, and perhaps promises to wear a special habit for a period of time and to crawl on her knees through the churchyard to the Virgin's image. In return, the Virgin is expected to grant the request that led to the supplicant's offering.

The model embraces both types of contract. In this paper, however, I am concerned descriptively only with the first, which, quantitatively at least, plays a far greater role in the lives of villagers and occupies much more of their time and thought. Relationships between villagers and outsiders of higher status, a client-patron contract for which the term *patronazgo* may be coined, are relatively rare, and my field data do not yet justify more complete analysis. The same is true with respect to the contract between a supplicant and the Virgin or a saint. At a later time when Tzintzuntzan is treated in monograph fashion, I hope to include these data.

In addition to implicit contracts, villagers also recognize formal and explicit contracts, represented by such acts as marriage, the establishment of the godparenthood relationship, and the buying and selling of property. These contracts rest on governmental and religious law, are legally or ritually validated through specific acts, are registered in writing, and are enforceable through the authority of the particular system that validates them. They may be dyadic, but often they bind several people, as when the baptism of an infant brings two parents, two godparents, and a godchild together. However, they are not to be thought of as corporate in nature.

These formal contracts may be but are not necessarily congruent with the dyadic contracts, since the latter cut across formal institutional boundaries and permeate all aspects of society. For example, two compadres are bound by a formal contract validated in a religious ceremony. This tie may be reinforced and made functional by an implicit dyadic contract, making the two relationships congruent. More often than not, however, compadre bonds are not backed up by implicit contracts.

In the absence of ritual or legal bases for implicit dyadic contracts, what justification is there for saying they exist? (The reader will remember that henceforth, unless otherwise specified, I speak only of the symmetrical, complementary contracts.) How can a villager be sure he is in fact tied to others, and that they similarly recognize the relationship? And what evidence can the anthropologist adduce to substantiate his construct? An outsider in Tzintzuntzan soon learns of an elaborate pattern of complementary reciprocity, almost entirely between pairs of individuals, in which goods and services are continually exchanged. Some of the exchanges are easily visible, as when plates of steaming food are carried by young children from one house to another. Other manifestations of the exchange pattern are not so readily seen, as when a compadre or friend speaks for another in a ceremonial act. But in its totality the system of complementary reciprocity validates, maintains, and gives substance to the implicit contractual networks. The symbolic meaning of exchanges (as contrasted to economic and other functions) is accepted without question by all villagers: as long as a person continues to give to and receive from a partner, he is assured that that particular relationship is in good order. When an exchange pattern between two people terminates, it is overt evidence to both that the contract is dead, regardless of the formal institutional ties or the religious validation which may, in theory, continue to bind the participants.

The implicit dyadic contract accounts for people's behavior to the satisfaction of the anthropologist: It provides him with a model of social structure abstracted from observed behavior. This model also very nearly coincides with the villager's understanding of how his personal world is organized. He is thoroughly conversant with the institutions of family, compadrazgo, neighborhoodship, and friendship, and he can describe the proper role behavior for the several statuses existing in each system. But not far below this level of awareness, he realizes that this picture by no means accounts for his actions, or for those of others. That is, the average Tzintzuntzeño, it seems to me, recognizes that the way he fits into these institutions does not, in fact, explain how his community works. He sees that, quite apart from conventional institutions, he is tied in another way to certain relatives, compadres, neighbors, and friends to the partial or complete exclusion of others occupying the same statuses vis à vis ego, who collectively make his world, the Tzintzuntzeño recognizes that these contractual ties are the glue that holds his society together and the grease that smooths its running.

Before further exploring the concept of dyadic contract and its validating reciprocity system, more of the characteristics of the village must be outlined. Tzintzuntzan, with 1,800 inhabitants, lies 250 miles west of Mexico City on the shores of Lake Pátzcuaro in Michoacán state. For many years it has been Spanish-speaking and mestizo in culture, but formerly it was Tarascan Indian and its nearest neighbor villages still are Tarascan. The nuclear bilateral family, as pointed out, is the basic social unit. A majority of families earn their living from pottery-making, but farming is important, and there is some fishing and day laboring on the highway or in the fields of the few farmers with more land than they can cultivate alone. Socially and economically the village is relatively homogeneous. Social classes are absent, and there are no families or individuals of disproportionate power and influence. The importance of the Catholic Church, and the complete absence of minority religious groups, further emphasize the homogeneous quality of the community. Tzintzuntzan is dependent economically on the local and national markets to sell pottery and fish and to purchase much food, clothing, and other staples. Its political and legal organizations, and its religious system, are directed from outside. In the classic sense of a peasantry, it is a part society existing in a symbiotic relationship with many facets of the nation of which it is a part.[4]

A peasant village of this type differs in many ways from the African lineage-based, segmental tribal societies which Fortes considers in his article on unilineal descent groups. Some of the major ways in which Tzintzuntzan contrasts with these societies are:

1) The primary social unit is based on locality, not descent. The basic, visible, identifiable segment is the village. It is there, a physical reality; it can be mapped; its inhabitants can be counted; one can walk around its limits. There is no question, as in the Balinese example recently described by Geertz (1959), of different planes of interaction which make difficult the isolation of the community.

In Tzintzuntzan there are no corporate, segmentary units. In the absence of lineages, functional extended families, and voluntary associations, the individual's only identification with and allegiance to a corporate body is to Tzint-

zuntzan itself, a legal entity granted a charter by King Charles V of Spain early in the 16th century. Membership, strictly speaking, stems from birth within the village, although in fact long residence confers legal equality on persons born elsewhere, even though it is always remembered they are not natives. As in Spain, outside the village a Tzintzuntzeño is identified in terms of his community and not as a member of a kinship-based corporate group.

2) As is characteristic of classic peasant societies, in the areas of political organization, of the administration of law and justice, and of religion, local and intervillage autonomy do not exist, and both policy and control rest in the hands of outsiders. The local political and legal systems are truncated, and do not have to cope with major problems. Religious activities are more elaborate than political activities, but they are planned, guided, and in most ways demanded by a hierarchy in no way indigenous to the community.

3) As a consequence of (2), there is little functional need for extended kin groups to play a major role in political, legal, juridical, and religious spheres. To state the matter in another way, much less is demanded of a kinship system in Tzintzuntzan than in many African societies, and a less rigid, more casually organized structure can do all that is required. There is no structural reason why unilineal descent groups could not exist in Tzintzuntzan. The village falls in the "middle range of relatively homogeneous, precapitalistic economies in which there is some degree of technological sophistication and value is attached to rights in durable property," where Fortes (1953:24) finds such groups most in evidence. But history has willed the community another form, one that works at least as well.

4) Tzintzuntzan, as a corporate entity, has no long-standing organic ties with other communities, and within the local area no villages recognize mutual corporate reciprocal obligations and rights.[5] Intervillage cooperative mechanisms, as in Alcalá (Pitt-Rivers 1953:32) are lacking. Quarrels involving communities as units occur only over the communally-owned lands belonging to the *Communidad Indígena*,[6] and the peace-making function for such disputes is vested in state or national law courts rather than with local authorities.

Similarly, there are no long-standing organic ties between groups of people in Tzintzuntzan and parallel groups in other villages. This is not to say there is no intervillage contact; there is a great deal. People marry in towns other than Tzintzuntzan, they form godparenthood bonds, they fight and litigate. The point is that all these contacts are carried out on an individual and not a corporate basis.

In the light of these four points, it is clear that the functional demands placed on a system of interpersonal relations in Tzintzuntzan will differ greatly from those placed on a corresponding system in Africa, where kinship looms so much more important. About all the Tzintzuntzéno asks from his system, and about all he gets, is a modicum of personal, economic, and emotional security which rests primarily on dyadic ties within the village and secondarily on similar ties with people outside the village.

The present analysis, while pointed toward the problem of a model for the total pattern of social ties in Tzintzuntzan, is limited descriptively to the symmetrical, dyadic contract and its validating complementary reciprocity patterns as expressed within the interlocking formal systems of family, compadrazgo, and neighborhoodship-friendship, which collectively provide the institutional framework for organizing most interpersonal relations within the village. Each of these systems, as will be seen, provides norms that define the ideal behavior appropriate to the settings in which people find themselves. With respect to ego, each offers ready-made rules governing his conduct with ever-widening circles of people. Toward all, as defined by the particular system concerned, he owes certain duties and from all he has specific expectations. Obligations toward and expectations from all individuals who stand in the same relation to him theoretically are equal.

But a catalogue of roles and statuses, as earlier pointed out, is not sufficient by itself to explain social structure, because real behavior deviates from ideal behavior. The dyadic contract, I hope to demonstrate, is the key to understanding the patterns found in these deviations. In this presentation the formal characteristics of family, compadrazgo, and neighborhoodship-friendship, and the ideal role behavior inherent in each will be described. The structural stresses and problems inhibiting ideal role behavior will then be considered, and the dyadic contracts and their validating exchanges will be examined.

Family—In structure and function the Tzintzuntzan family reflects the common Hispanic American particularistic pattern. The nuclear, bilateral unit is simultaneously the ideal and the most common household. Blood descent is traced equally through the father's and mother's lines, and this dual affiliation is expressed in the Spanish custom whereby a person's surname—always compound—is made up of the patronyms

of both parents. Thus Juan, the son of Pedro Morales Rendon and María Estrada Zavala, is Juan Morales Estrada. Patrilineality is evidenced by the priority of the father's patronym, and by the fact that with each new generation the parents' matronyms are sloughed off. But the system fulfills the function of identifying every individual in the eyes of the community as a full member of two family lines. The particularistic character of the kinship system is further emphasized by the fact that at marriage a woman does not merge her identity with that of her husband by assuming his patronym, as is done in Mexican cities. She remains María Estrada Zavala and does not become María Estrada de Morales, as she would in more elevated social circles. Throughout her life she continues to be called by her maiden name, and commonly she is identified as the daughter of so-and-so rather than as the wife of so-and-so. She inherits equally (in theory and often in fact) with male siblings; she may register property in her name; and she may buy, sell, or take court action without her husband's consent.

The extended family is noncorporate, highly informal, and rarely consists of more than three generations. Its most common form, as a residence group, is a married couple, their unmarried children, one or two married children, and grandchildren. More distant relatives in both paternal and maternal lines are recognized, although the degree of acknowledged relationship becomes fuzzier with increasing distance. Beyond *primos hermanos* (first cousins) and *tios* (parents' siblings), almost all relatives, depending on generation, are lumped as "cousins" or "uncles." People of the same surname do not form exogamous groups; marriage restrictions apply equally to both lines, and are set by the Church, which is the final arbiter in cases of doubt. A majority of marriages occur within the village, but there are few if any families not bound through the marriage of some members into other communities.

Theoretically, marriage is a family concern, in the sense that parents are supposed to have veto power over their children's choice of spouse. To some extent, then, marriage might be thought of as representing a contract between two nuclear families. Actually, elopement is the common marriage form, in itself a negation of the idea of a corporate contract between families. Marriage in fact boils down to a dyadic, if formal, contract uniting a man and a woman.

The potential structural chaos resulting from marriage by elopement is not realized, in part at least, because land-ownership is not a major function of the Tzintzuntzan family. Apart from house sites many families are landless, and many more have only small agricultural plots to supplement their major income from the sale of pottery. Most full-time farmers own only part of the land they till, sharecropping other fields to fill their time. Only a handful of men have sufficient land to produce a surplus for sale, and often these holdings have been built up by purchase by the farmer, rather than being inherited from parents. Obviously, in a community with very restricted total land holdings, the goal of keeping large farms together through judiciously planned marriages can scarcely loom large, and consequently elopement poses no threat to this aspect of economic life.

A newly married couple is expected to live in the home of the groom's family— less frequently of the bride's family—for a year or so or until the birth of the first child. After this the new family usually goes its own way. Married people's primary economic obligation is toward their spouses and above all toward their children. Provident parents work to leave separate homes for each married son, so that a great many new families become spatially independent early in their existence. Not uncommonly married siblings live in adjacent houses or next to the parents' home, but this pattern derives as much from the practice of the father's subdividing a large lot into inheritance shares as from feelings of fraternal warmth.

Except for obligations toward elderly parents, married couples feel little economic responsibility beyond the nuclear family toward relatives simply because they are relatives. Rather, beyond the nuclear family, the outer world, including relatives, is viewed with great reserve. Villagers, as in many other peasant communities, tend to distrust their neighbors, be suspicious of each other's motives, speak ill of one another, engage in back-biting and petty bickering, try to tear down those who get ahead, and be reluctant to join in cooperative enterprises of any kind.

The nuclear family as a social isolate is consonant with the demands of the productive system. In both pottery-making and farming this unit normally is adequate for all purposes. The father and older sons mine pottery clays and gather firewood which are brought on burro-back to the home where the mother and older girls prepare paste, mold pots, and grind glazes, perhaps with the help of the males. The father builds and tends the fire, and all family members help load and unload the kiln.

In agriculture, an able-bodied man is suffi-

cient for nearly all tasks, especially if he has a son or daughter 10 years of age or more, or a wife willing to help in planting. The lightweight Mediterranean wooden scratch plow is pulled by a single team of oxen and can be managed by one man. Cultivation and harvesting likewise require little or no help beyond that available within the nuclear family. Obviously, members of nuclear families, whether potting or farming, spend a large part of their time in each other's company; they must cooperate as a family group or face economic disaster.

On the other hand, there are relatively few economic activities in which extrafamilial cooperation is absolutely essential, or even desirable. Plow agriculture does not lend itself to cooperative work groups, like the African and West Indian Negro *dokpwe*, which are effective in hoe cultivation, and in the absence of pottery labor specialization beyond the elementary divisions described, more people working together simply bring confusion. Only in fishing, where a minimum crew of four or five able-bodied men is needed for the big nets and canoes, is there a functional demand for a work group, and in Tzintzuntzan there are only three or four such crews. The important point to note here is that there is no economic reason for cooperation involving groups larger than the nuclear family, and hence no premium is placed on social devices to provide such groups. Perhaps there is no other socio-technological level that permits such a high degree of family independence in normal daily pursuits. Among most simple hunting-fishing-gathering groups communal hunts or game drives are often essential to success. Among irrigation agriculturalists, canal systems force cooperative maintenance devices as well as juridical and legal interaction. At more advanced technological levels division of labor increasingly requires rationally integrated and cooperative organization of work. But Tzintzuntzan (and many other peasant societies) is at a particular technological point which maximizes the need for an effective nuclear family and minimizes the need for larger cooperative groups.

Ideal role behavior within the family is simply stated. The husband is dominant, owed obedience and respect by his wife and children even after the latter reach adulthood. The wife is faithful and submissive and recognizes her place in the home. Siblings are expected to display the fraternal virtues of mutual economic and moral support, both while they live under the same roof and after they set up independent households. Real patterns may deviate widely from these ideals. Children do not always show respect to their father, and wives may be far from submissive. Often children have migrated to cities or to the United States and their parents have lost all contact with them. Among those who remain in the village, friction is not uncommon, with quarrelling over inheritance a particular source of ill feeling. Incompatibility of sisters-and brothers-in-law may lead to tension when families occupy adjacent or joint dwellings, and a slackening off in relations between siblings is the result, often evidenced by one couple's selling its house or share and moving to a more distant location.

At least some of these tensions stem from the constraints inherent in the family institution. In the consanguineal line ego has no choice with respect to relatives. At birth he is presented with a ready-made extended family, with a multiplicity of expected rights and obligations stemming from his many statuses. Throughout his life he will continue to acquire relatives, with more obligations and rights, and still he has no choice in selection. Ego's only option is in picking a spouse, and, in an intensely Catholic society, once the decision is made it is as indissoluble as a blood relationship.

Ego's only real choice is in the degree to which he will in fact honor the obligations inherent in his several roles (and expect a corresponding return), and in the selection of the individuals with whom he will honor them. Thus, through selecting relatively few kinsmen from his total family toward whom he lives up to the behavior forms expected of him by virtue of his roles vis á vis theirs, ego in fact establishes dyadic contracts which determine his actual behavior. His family provides him a panel of candidates. He selects (and is selected by) relatively few with whom the significant working relationships are developed.

Compadrazgo —The importance of this institution in structuring social relations in Hispanic America is attested by descriptions found in nearly all studies dealing with the area. Tzintzuntzan follows the general pattern. A godfather and a godmother (rarely, only a godmother) sponsor the baptism of a child, thereby becoming spiritual parents. A single godparent of the same sex as the child is named for confirmation and first communion, and a pair of godparents, usually a married couple, is named for weddings. Godparents are responsible for moral advice to their godchildren, and for economic and physical care if necessary. Godchildren, in turn, are expected to show absolute obedience and respect to their godparents, if possible even in greater degree than toward parents. This is an asymmetrical relationship in that in the course of a lifetime godparents have greater tangible obligations toward their godchildren than the latter have toward them. In point of fact, however, the relationship between godparents and godchild's parents, who become co-parents, or *compadres* (a woman is a *comadre*), is the more important of the two. This is a symmetrical relationship in that the new obligations and expectations usually are between people of equal status and are essentially equal in form and quantity.

Behavior between new compadres becomes more formal. If perviously they addressed each other with the familiar second person "tu," now they use the third person formal "Usted." Simultaneously they abandon the use of personal names and address each other as compadre. The compadre relationship in theory is considered to be one of the most sacred of human ties. Compadres must help each other in every possible way, whatever the personal sacrifice and inconvenience may be. The compadrazgo is much like the family in that it has religious sanction, shares the same incest prohibitions, and once established is indissoluble.

These ideal patterns of behavior are expressed on a ritual and, curiously, a commercial level. Major ceremonial occasions in the life cycle are highlighted by the compadres' participation. When a family offers a ritual meal, compadres are the guests of honor who sit at the head of the table, are served the best food and drink, and are treated with exaggerated decorum. Members of the family, if not working in the kitchen, sit at the foot of the table or stand apart, and eat after the compadres are served. Again, if a person is to be honored on the occcasion of his saint's day, it is the job of the compadre to organize the early morning mañanitas serenade.

At the same time, the compadrazgo can cement commercial ties. In former years muleteers carried pottery on long journeys; they tried to establish compadre relationships in each town where they stayed so as to have a place to pass the night and a support in case of trouble with local authorities. Outsiders who come to Tzintzuntzan to buy often ask to baptize a new child of the man with whom they do business. Long-distance muleteering is past, but the pattern remains. Those who sell pottery wholesale in Pátzcuaro often sell to compadres who have been brought into the ceremonial relationship after establishing the commercial one. Within the village, pottery merchants who sell from stands on the highway buy much of their ware from compadres, and as in the Pátzcuaro example a developing commercial relationship often is bolstered by a baptism. Sometimes the relationship is frankly exploitive: the merchant hopes to obtain a slightly better price. In others, the potter hopes to assure an outlet for his production. In still others there appears to be a mutual feeling that a satisfactory commercial relationship is enhanced by a ceremonial tie. Whatever the reasons, the compadrazgo often strengthens commercial dealings.

As with the family, real compadrazgo behavior patterns often deviate greatly from ideal patterns. Far from being a close and sacred relationship, compadre ties often are routine in the extreme. They may become tenuous, and sometimes they are broken to the point where compadres do not even speak to one another! By middle age a man usually has acquired many more compadrazgo ties than he can fully maintain, but as with blood relatives, these are lifetime bonds which cannot formally be broken. The solution lies in ignoring completely a few compadres (if matters come to this point), in maintaining superficially correct ties with most, and in developing an effective working relationship with only a few.

The compadrazgo presents a curious anomaly. The relationship is initiated on the basis of an explicit, formal, contract in which two people agree to be compadres. Yet the system contributes to social stability only when the implicit contract follows—when compadres do in fact cooperate with each other through a system of continuing exchanges. It is clear that the compadrazgo can never be the basis for any kind of a group. No two people have the same combination of compadres. The system represents a net in which ego, represented by a knot, is formally linked to a great many other people, also represented by knots, but in only a few cases are the strands between the knots viable, capable of bearing the load theoretically placed on them by the ideal functioning of the institution.

Neighborhoodship-Friendship

The mere fact of geographical propinquity establishes ties between villagers and creates, if only on a low level, bonds of common interest. A suspicious character in the street is a matter of concern to all, as is a householder's vicious and dangerous dog, or an arroyo made impassable by a flash flood, thus preventing passage to a maize mill. Neighborhood interaction is often the basis for friendship, but not all neighbors are friends, and not all friends are found in ego's neighborhood. Lacking the formal structure and religious sanctions of family and compadrazgo, the institutions of neighborhoodship and friendship are of a somewhat different order. Only in the bonds between pairs of adolescent boys, and to a lesser extent girls, do we find as much as a

terminology to identify a relationship. Best friends refer to each other as *amigo carnal*, signifying that the friend is as close as a brother. An exchange of goods—knives, tops, or gadgets that post-adolescents treasure—usually marks the establishment of this friendship, and continuing exchanges occur as long as the ties are recognized. The relationship may last only a short time, or until one friend is married, at which time it may cease to be functional or, if the unmarried friend is asked to baptize the first child, it can be transformed into the compadrazgo.

Otherwise friendship and neighborhoodship are unstructured institutions. Two people begin to see they have interests in common and they like each other. They drop in at each other's homes; they offer food; they exchange favors. More often than not such ties are within the same sex line, but not infrequently, and with full propriety, they can cross sex lines. Whether between persons of the same or of opposite sexes, reservations seem always to be attached to friendship. It is not wise to reveal all of what one thinks and feels, to give of oneself completely. Even between amigos carnales it is doubtful that confidences are sufficiently complete to justify the word "buddies" to describe the pattern.

Friendship and neighborhoodship obligations are less specific than those of the other two institutions. Friends and neighbors are expected to help each other in time of need, to exchange favors, loan money, keep an eye on the temporarily vacant next-door house, and otherwise support those with whom the relationship is acknowledged. Friendship differs from the other systems in that a long-enduring gap between ideal and real behavior can hardly exist: when friends cease to be friendly, the institution dissolves. Neighbors remain neighbors, but neighborly behavior may, and often does, cease.

Friendship and neighborhoodship, as the most flexible of these institutions, fill the gaps left by the imperfections of the others. They flow into the nooks and crannies, fill the chinks, smooth out the rough points remaining in the social fabric. In a pinch they provide a mechanism for any situation normally provided for by the others, and in actual life they fill a good proportion of the functions theoretically assigned to them. Friends and neighbors help in the kitchen; they go with a young man's father to make peace with the girl's family; they sit at ceremonial tables; they engage in commercial transactions; and they enjoy the same degree of confidence as a relative or compadre. They may, of course, be taken into the latter institution, but surprisingly often they appear not to be. In a situation of increasingly rapid change, friendship is the most versatile of the institutions. It can do almost anything that can be accomplished within the framework of the others, but it makes possible the avoidance of long-range commitments. New friendships can easily be formed, and worn out ones can be dropped and forgotten. No messy ends are left, as when one ceases to speak to a man who continues to be a compadre.

The formal social institutions which structure the ideal behavior of Tzintzuntzeños have now been described. It is clear that the theoretical demands of each system far exceed the ability of an individual fully to comply with them. To solve the problem, ego chooses, and is chosen by, comparatively few people from within each system, with whom he develops and maintains implicit dyadic contracts. We will now examine the reciprocal exchange patterns which validate and give substance to these contracts.

Reciprocity is expressed in continuing exchanges of goods and services in ritual and nonritual contexts. The goods and services are tangibles; incorporeal values play little part in the system. Over the long term the reciprocity is complementary, because each partner owes the other the same kinds and quantities of things. Over the short term the exchanges are not necessarily complementary, because a material item or service offered to partner A by partner B does not require subsequent return of the same thing to cancel the obligation (and it may in fact require something different, as pointed out in the following paragraph). Rather, it is a question of long-range equivalence of value, not formally calculated yet somehow weighted so that in the end both partners balance contributions and receipts. In the usual situation each member of the dyad simultaneously counts a number of credits and debits which are kept, over time, in approximate balance.

Within the long-term complementary pattern there are short-term exchanges, often noncomplementary, in which a particular act elicits a particular return. For example, a friend fixes a bride's hair for the wedding; the friend must be invited to the wedding feast, or, if for any reason she cannot come, food must be sent her from the feast. One compadre organized a saint's day mañanitas predawn serenade for another compadre, providing guitar players, a chorus, and a tray, or "crown" of fruit and flowers. The honored compadre reciprocates by inviting the serenaders in for an alcoholic ponche and the hominy-like pork pozole expected at many ceremonial meals. But these specific, noncomplementary saint's day exchanges probably will be made complementary later in the year, when the second compadre returns the favor.

A functional requirement of the system is that an exactly even balance between two partners never be struck. This would jeopardize the whole relationship, since if all credits and debits somehow could be balanced off at a point in time, the contract would cease to exist. At the very least a new contract would have to be gotten under way, and this would involve uncertainty and possibly distress if one partner seemed reluctant to continue. The dyadic contract is effective precisely because partners are never quite sure of their relative positions at a given moment. As long as they know that goods and services are flowing both ways in roughly equal amounts over time, they know their relationship is solidly based.

For expository purposes the nature of exchanges can be considered in terms of services and goods offered and reciprocated in ritual and nonritual settings. It should be remembered, however, that these lines are not hard and fast in the minds of Tzintzuntzeños, and that a material return in a nonritual setting helps counterbalance a service previously offered in a ritual setting, and so on around the circle of logical possibilities.

Services in a Ritual Context

These services, which usually have material components as well, are associated with life crises such as baptism, confirmation, marriage, and death. A young man elopes with a girl, and his father must visit her father to ask pardon and arrange the wedding details. His compadre, the boy's baptismal godfather, accompanies him and speaks for him. Most of the other members of the small party which accompanies him will also be his compadres. At the home of the aggrieved father the group is met by *his* compadres, one of whom responds to the peace overtures in his name.

When a child dies young, as an *angelito*, the godfather not only supplies the casket, clothing, and rockets, but he makes the funeral arrangements, sets the time, and otherwise relieves the family of worry.

Goods in a Ritual Context

A marriage godfather pays most of the heavy costs of the wedding, and there are secondary exchanges as well, such as that in which the groom's baptismal godfather sends shoes to the bride. A mayordomo (here called *carguero*), faced with major fiesta expenses, visits the home of relatives, compadres, and friends with whom a dyadic contract exists, asking them to "accompany" him, that is, to contribute foodstuffs and money.[7] Emphasizing the ritual character of this transaction, foodstuffs equal to about half that given are returned following the fiesta. At ceremonial meals, such as saint's day fiestas, weddings, baptism, and funerals, guests bring pots in which they pour surplus food from the heaping dishes served them. This is taken home to be eaten the following day. At any festive meal some people invited are unable to come, and others not specifically invited must be remembered. After the guests have been served children are sent to their homes with plates of food.

Services in a Nonritual Context

These take an unlimited number of forms. One helps nurse a sick friend or relative, gives a hypodermic injection without the usual small charge, purchases something on request in Pátzcuaro, sews a dress or makes a picture frame without charge, lends a stud boar, or poses for the anthropologist's camera. Any one of thousands of helpful acts is considered, and remembered, as a service incurring some form of reciprocal obligation.

Goods in a Nonritual Context

Neighbors drop in constantly to borrow an egg, a few chiles, or some other food or household item immediately needed. When men go to the United States as *braceros* (indentured farm laborers) they often borrow money from friends and relatives, returning the money upon completing their contracts and adding as well some item such as nylon stockings or a shirt which serves to keep alive the exchange relationship. A person with heavy medical expenses expects to receive money outright or as a loan, thus simultaneously being repaid for earlier transactions and incurring new obligations.

The continuing informal exchange of food and drink is particularly important. Except on ceremonial occasions invitations to meals never occur. But when someone—a relative, neighbor, compadre, or friend— with whom the exchange pattern is fully developed drops in, he or she often is not allowed to leave without being offered whatever prepared food is available: a tortilla, perhaps with a fried egg or beans, a bit of candied sweet potato, a glass of warm milk, or fresh fruit. Men drinking at a bar feel obligated to invite any exchange partner who enters to drink with them; often but not always the late entrant then stands the next round. The nature of the food or drink is not important, but if they are offered they *must* be accepted. Failure

to accept food or drink seriously jeopardizes an exchange relationship, since it represents a denial of mutual understanding and friendly feelings, which are basic to the dyadic contract.

The food and drink exchange, important within all institutions, is especially so between friends and neighbors. Because they lack a formal structure, unlike the family and the compadrazgo, even greater attention to constant reaffirmation of the relationship is necessary. The offering of food and drink is the quintessence of this reaffirmation, and if someone professes friendship but fails in this informal exchange, he is said to be a "friend with his lips on the outside," that is, not a genuine friend.[8]

Food also tells us something else about dyadic contracts: they are of differing degrees of intensity; it is not a question of presence or absence. The situation is similar to that of American friendship patterns in which we see, visit, and interact more with some friends than with others, but the friends we see less often are still qualitatively different from mere acquaintances, since we do recognize obligations toward them. High-intensity contracts can be distinguished from low-intensity contracts by the role of food. If we see some people almost always being offered food when they come to a house, we may be sure that a high intensity dyadic contract is operating. If continuing exchanges of various types with other people are noted, but less thought is given to food, then we may be sure the contract is of lesser intensity.

The function and meaning of the goods and services which exchange in Tzintzuntzan cannot be understood if they are thought of as gifts. Disinterested gift-giving is foreign to the minds of Tzintzuntzeños and difficult for them to understand. Any favor, whatever its form, is part of a quid pro quo pattern, the terms of which are recognized and accepted by the participants. The favor or act simultaneously repays a past debt, incurs a furture obligation, and reaffirms the continuing validity of the contract binding the partners.

Both linguistic and behavior forms show why the word "gift" is inappropriate to describe the goods and services that exchange in Tzintzuntzan. In Anglo-Saxon society, a gift is thought of as something transferred from one person to another without measurable compensation. That it may, in fact, be part of a continuing exchange pattern is beside the point. A gift is accepted with thanks, verbally expressed, which symbolize something more than the courtesy thanks that accompany commercial transactions, since the words are recognized as striking a conceptual balance with the donor's thoughtfulness. In

Spanish, thanks are expressed in two distinct linguistic forms: *gracias* (literally the plural form of "grace"), usually translated into English as "thank you," and *Dios se le pague*, meaning "May God (re)pay you for it." The first form serves for casual, informal interchanges of no moment between persons of equal status, or equal status as far as the occasion that calls forth the word is concerned. But *Dios se le pague* is used in an entirely different sense, in which the thanker acknowledges the great difference in position and the fact that the object or service can never be reciprocated. Generally in Mexico, and in Spain too, beggars acknowledge alms with this expression. Only by asking God's favor can the beggar in any way repay the giver; neither expects any other balance. An item acknowledged with *Dios se le pague*, then, can properly be considered a gift in the Anglo-Saxon sense. An item or act acknowledged by *gracias* is something else, for the form is a courtesy and nothing more.

In Tzintzuntzan both forms are used. The anthropologist hears *Dios se le pague* when he has given something considered by the recipient to be far outside the normal patterns of friendship exchange, such as a substantial monetary contribution to help with unusual medical expenses. When he gives lesser items, such as a cut of cloth for a shirt or a dress—something within the normal range of exchanges—he hears *gracias*, and perhaps more often, nothing at all. He and the recipient know the item given will be reciprocated with pottery, a tule-reed figure, several fish, or something else commanded by the recipient; the cut of cloth is not a gift, nor are the pottery, the figure, or the fish.

Before I appreciated the nature of exchanges in Tzintzuntzan, I was puzzled by the usual absence of verbal thanks, and the near absence of emotional show of any kind when someone gave something to someone else. A "gift," it seemed to me, ought to be acknowledged with some degree of gratitude. But, to illustrate a common event, a tray of uncooked food would be sent, covered by a cloth, as a contribution to a mayordomo's fiesta. His wife would accept it unceremoniously at the door, carry it without looking under the cloth to the kitchen, unload the tray, and return tray and cloth to the donor with no more comment than accompanied normal passing the time of day. I was distressed, too, when my more modest "gifts" were accepted with an equal lack of enthusiasm; I feared I was not pleasing. Now, however, it is clear that the Tzintzuntzeño cannot express thanks on a level of verbal intensity equal to Anglo-Saxon practice, since to do so would be striking the balance which jeopardizes the contract. His way of showing he values the relationship is to accept the offering with minimum show of emotion. To express vehement thanks is the rudest thing he can do, since it suggests he is anxious to call it square and terminate the relationship.

The usual absence of verbal thanks and visible enthusiasm to accompany exchanges does not mean that the transactions are cold, calculated, and emotion-free. People do enjoy these transactions; it is satisfying to know one is living up to his obligations, and that one's partners continue to value the association. Some of the fundamental values of the culture are expressed in the exchange acts themselves, and people sense and appreciate this fact, even though they would have trouble in verbalizing it.

The functioning of dyadic contracts can now be briefly considered from another viewpoint: the real role behavior versus the ideal role behavior of a specific person in a specific situation. Faustino, aged 40, lives with his wife Pachita and their six children. He has two married brothers and two married sisters living in Tzintzuntzan; she has two married brothers, two married sisters, and both of her parents.

Faustino and Pachita have been godparents to the children of 10 fellow villagers so that, with the godparents of their own six children, they have "primary" compadrazgo ties with 16 couples. Of these 16, two are with Faustino's siblings and their spouses, two are with Pachita's siblings and their spouses, and one is with her father and mother, leaving 11 in categories other than that of close relatives. Faustino and Pachita have been marriage godparents only to his niece Chelo. They have also collected an unspecified number of "secondary" compadrazgo relations on the basis of confirmation, first communion, and a "scapulary" rite.

Faustino's home is on the edge of town in a small neighborhood slightly set off from the main grouping of village houses. Sixteen neighbor households lie within a block and a half, forming a recognizable unit. Primary compadres are found in four of these households, secondary compadres in two, while a seventh household is that of his married nephew Adolfo, with whom he shares a patio.

Both Faustino and Pachita also have additional friends, but there is no structural device that permits their easy identification. Thus, eliminating friends and the overlap in categories of primary compadres, neighbors, and close relatives, 30 households[9] with recognizable potential exchange relationships remain.

Which of these relationships are recognized and reaffirmed on the occasion of Faustino's saint's day predawn serenade and the subsequent pozole-and-ponche breakfast? As in previous years, in 1960 the serenade was organized by his compadre Eusebio, Pachita's brother-in-law, whose child they had baptized, and who lives outside the neighborhood area. Eusebio, exercising his prerogative, invited two of his friends, one of whom was accompanied by his wife. He also brought two guitar players, who by chance were nephews of Faustino. All these people were given food and drink. In addition, the other guests at this modest entertainment consisted of two of Faustino's four siblings and their spouses (the pairs who also are baptismal compadres), his niece goddaughter Chelo and her husband, the nephew and wife with whom he shares his patio, and the anthropologist.

When these people had been fed, plates of pozole were sent to the homes of 2 primary comadres, 2 secondary comadres, and 2 friends (all six in the neighborhood), and to the mother and to the batismal godmother of Chelo's husband (Faustino's marriage godson), to a sister and her husband, and to a friend, all living outside the neighborhood.

Thus, of the 30 households which could be placed in one or more of these institutional relationships to Faustino and Pachita, only 11 were invited to participate in his saint's day breakfast. Or, to look at the problem negatively, and not counting overlapping categories, of 16 primary godparenthood ties, only 6 were recognized; of 16 neighborhood ties, another 6 were recognized; and of 9 sibling-parent ties, 5 were recognized.

This particular example does not mean that only individuals in these households have dyadic contracts with Faustino, since in other settings ties with other people would be recognized and some of these might be overlooked. The illustration does show how the formal social institutions of Tzintzuntzan provide an individual with more potential associates than he can utilize. It would be very difficult for Faustino to live up to the ideal role behavior implicit in the 30 household relationships and impossible for him to do so in all the statuses he occupies in the community. His institutions provide him with outer limits for a circle of associates. By means of the dyadic contract, implemented through reciprocity, he patterns his real behavior.

In summary, the model outlined in the first pages of this paper may be restated. This model rests on the assumption of a structure in which critical social relationships inherent in all institutions beyond the nuclear family are contractual (hence selective) rather than ascribed (hence

nonselective). In the absence of corporate units, contracts can occur only between pairs of individuals; they must be dyadic. In the absence of legal or ritual validation, contracts must be considered informal or implicit. Informal or implicit contracts can be validated and maintained only by means of recognized reciprocal obligations, manifest by the continuing exchange of goods and services. The nature of these obligations will depend on the relative statuses of any two partners. When they are functionally equal— when the contract is symmetrical—the obligations and expectations must be complementary; otherwise there would be no purpose to the relationship. When the partners are functionally unequal—when the contract is asymmetrical— the obligations and expectations must be noncomplementary; otherwise there would be no purpose to this relationship. In neither instance can the goods and services which represent obligations and expectations be thought of as gifts. The contractual principle enables an individual to disentangle himself from the weight of ideal role behavior implicit in the totality of ascribed and achieved statuses he occupies in a society and to make functional such relationships as he deems necessary in everyday life.

Every incident of behavior in Tzintzuntzan, of course, does not fit this model. Friends and neighbors are not always given food when they drop in; neighbors may be unable or unwilling fully to comply with the obligations they recognize toward a particular person; guests outside a contractual relationship may turn up at ego's saint's day fiesta. But these, and similar examples, can be described *in terms of* the model, even though they do not fit it precisely. Again, the model may appear overly elaborate with respect to asymmetrical, noncomplementary type contracts in Tzintzuntzan, but this does not detract from its basic utility, since such behavior as does occur in these areas can be described in terms of the model.

Two final, more general questions may be asked about this model:

(1) To what extent, if any, does it help explain other aspects of Tzintzuntzan social structure and personal behavior not previously mentioned?

(2) To what extent, if any, does it serve for other Latin American communities, and perhaps peasant societies in general?

The model appears to account for two noteworthy characteristics of Tzintzuntzan: (a) There are no factions, as, for example, they have been described in India where longstanding, relatively permanent alliances of groups are pitted against each other. (b) Since the first "cultural missions" sent by the Mexican Government in the early 1930's, Tzintzuntzan has proved resistant to all outside attempts to stimulate cooperative action for community improvement. People consistently are reluctant to work with others toward group goals.

The model suggests that where a society is conceived as a network of social relations based on dyadic contracts, in which no two people have exactly the same ties, there can be no blocks to serve as the basis for either positive or negative action. Neither is there a unit to serve as base for feuding, nor a unit to serve as base for cooperative work for mutual goals. The model is consonant with the atomistic, or particularistic quality of society which an anthropologist feels so strongly when living in the village.

The second question, the applicability of the model to other societies, can only be answered impressionistically. I suspect it will prove useful in analyzing other Latin American communities. We know that in much of Latin America *patronazgo* patron-client type ties are more strongly developed than in Tzintzuntzan; the model covers these forms. Again, anthropologists speak of *personalism*, the relationship between people in which the individual distrusts the system and relies on personal ties, as a distinguishing characteristic of Latin American society. The model of the dyadic contract makes more precise this loose term, for *personalismo* is nothing more than a contractual tie between two people who feel they can help each other by ignoring in large measure the institutional context in which they meet.

With respect to the possible applicability of the model to other peasant societies, particularly those with bilateral kinship systems, again one can in large measure only speculate. In his description of the Spanish Alcalá, Pitt-Rivers sees the nature of conceptual equality leading to cooperation on the basis of reciprocal service much as I see it in Tzintzuntzan. It seems to me, too, that the Italian Montegrano, as portrayed by Banfield, in considerable degree fits the model drawn for Tzintzuntzan. Perhaps, also, potential for the use of the model in peasant studies lies in the area not described for Tzintzuntzan: relations between people of different statuses, and particularly those of villagers with outsiders. Redfield has pointed out that peasant villages may prove to be so incomplete as systems as to preclude their description as social structures (1956:37). He draws upon Barnes' "territorially-based social field," the "market," and the "network" to place the village in its larger social context. The model of the dyadic contract, it seems to me, offers a more precise way of interpreting these contacts. All of these are questions, however, which must be answered by those with intimate knowledge of peasant communities in other parts of Latin America and the world at large.

REFERENCES

Banfield, E. C.
  1958 The moral basis of a backward society. Glencoe, The Free Press.
Fortes, M.
  1953 The structure of unilineal descent groups. American Anthropologist 55: 17-41.
Foster, G. M.
  1948 Empire's children: the people of Tzintzuntzan. México, D. F., Imp. Neuvo Mundo. Smithsonian Institution, Institute of Social Anthropology Publication No. 6.
Geertz, C.
  1959 Form and variation in Balinese village structure. American Anthropologist 61:991-1012.
Kroeber, A. L.
  1948 Anthropology. New York, Harcourt, Brace & Company.
Pitt-Rivers, J. A.
  1955 The people of the sierra. London, Weidenfeld and Nicolson.
Redfield, R.
  1956 Peasant society and culture. Chicago, University of Chicago Press.

NOTES

1 The ideas here presented stem from field work made possible by a National Science Foundation Grant and a grant from the Research Committee of the University of California (Berkeley). I am indebted to May Diaz and Robert F. Murphy for critical comments which were helpful in determining the final form of this paper.

2 In Kroeber's oft-quoted definition, such villages form a class segment of a larger population usually containing urban centers; "they constitute part-societies with part cultures" (1948:284). Kroeber once told me that in writing these lines he had in mind only

European peasant communities and that he had not considered their possible applicability to agricultural communities of distinct historical antecedents and structural characteristics in other parts of the world.

3 In the sense that wealth differences and occupational distinctions have no bearing on the nature of interaction. The poor marry the less poor, the illegitimate marry the legitimate, the moderately well-to-do farmer and the poorest potter each accept identical *mayordomia* fiesta obligations.

4 A descriptive account of the village is found in Foster (1948).

5 Tzintzuntzan is the *cabecera*, the administrative head, of the *municipio* of the same name, composed of about 20 villages, ranches, and hamlets. People from other villages must come to Tzintzuntzan to register births, marriages, and deaths, and municipio taxes are collected from Tzintzuntzan. But municipio organization is arbitrary, often artificial, and in no sense represents an organic reciprocal union of neighboring communities.

6 The "Indigenous Community," a legal entity composed of all family heads, dates from colonial times, when all village lands were held by community title alone. Most lands now are individually owned, but the *Comunidad Indigena* still owns the higher hillsides, and in recent years it has bought pasture and marginal agricultural land from private owners outside the village.

7 The *mayordomia* is the only traditional, socially sanctioned way in which a person can compete for status. Success is achieved by the mayordomo who su-

pervises and finances an elaborate fiesta. It is noteworthy that he (and to a lesser extent his wife) alone receives credit for the effort. Unlike other societies in which the credit is shared with all who have contributed, the friends, relatives, and compadres who help do not bask in reflected glory. But they, in their turn, can expect an undiluted glory when, as mayordomo, they are helped in similar fashion.

8 An element of asymmetry obviously is present in food offerings, since, except under duress and in the absence of a woman in the house, a man does not cook. A man could offer fresh fruit or some other ready-to-eat food to a friend, but in practice he does not. Consequently, a woman offers food to both sexes but receives it from only one. Food exchanges therefore involve women more than men. This tendency is apparent, too, when on the occasion of a fiesta food is sent to another house, a woman usually is specified as the recipient. On the other hand, men, by offering alcoholic drinks, express the same thing women do in offering food. There is, however, an important limitation: men normally do not offer drinks to women in public places. But they may do so with full propriety at gatherings in private homes.

9 Viz., the nine close relatives; the 16 "primary" compadrazgo relationships which reduce to 11 because five of them are also close relatives; the one marriage godparenthood relationship; the 16 neighbor relationships which reduce to nine because four of them are also primary compadres, two are secondary compadres, and one is a nephew.

THE NORM OF RECIPROCITY:
A Preliminary Statement*
ALVIN W. GOULDNER

"THERE IS NO DUTY more indispensable than that of returning a kindness," says Cicero, adding that "all men distrust one forgetful of a benefit."—Men have been insisting on the importance of reciprocity for a long time. While many sociologists concur in this judgment, there are nonetheless few concepts in sociology which remain more obscure and ambiguous. Howard Becker, for example, has found this concept so important that he has titled one of his books *Man in Reciprocity* and has even spoken of man as *Homo reciprocus*, all without venturing to present a straightforward definition of reciprocity. Instead, Becker states, "I don't propose to furnish any definition of reciprocity; if you produce some, they will be your own achievements."[1]

Becker is not alone in failing to stipulate formally the meaning of reciprocity, while at the same time affirming its prime importance. Indeed, he is in very good company, agreeing with L. T. Hobhouse, who held that "reciprocity . . . is the vital principle of society,"[2] and is a key intervening variable through which shared social rules are enabled to yield social stability. Yet Hobhouse presents no systematic definition of reciprocity. While hardly any clearer than Hobhouse, Richard Thurnwald is equally certain of the central importance of the "principle of reciprocity": this principle is almost a primordial imperative which "pervades every relation of primitive life"[3] and is the basis on which the entire social and ethical life of primitive civilizations presumably rests.[4] Georg Simmel's comments go a step further, emphasizing the importance of reciprocity not only for primitive but for all societies. Simmel remarks that social equilibrium and cohesion could not exist without "the reciprocity of service and return service," and that "all contacts among men rest on the schema of giving and returning the equivalence."[5]

Were we confronted with only an obscure concept, which we had no reason to assume to be important, we might justifiably consign it to the Valhalla of intellectual history, there to consort eternally with the countless incunabula of sociological ingenuity. However convenient, such a disposition would be rash, for we can readily note the importance attributed to the concept of reciprocity by such scholars as George Homans, Claude Lévi-Strauss, and Raymond Firth,[6] as well as by such earlier writers as Durkheim, Marx, Mauss, Malinowski, and von Wiese, to name only a few masters.

Accordingly, the aims of this paper are: (1) to indicate the manner in which the concept of reciprocity is tacitly involved in but formally neglected by modern functional theory; (2) to clarify the concept and display some of its diverse intellectual contents, thus facilitating its theoretical employment and research utility; and (3) to suggest concretely ways in which the clarified concept provides new leverage for analysis of the central problems of sociological theory, namely accounting for stability and instability in social systems.

RECIPROCITY AND FUNCTIONAL THEORY

My concern with reciprocity developed initially from a critical reexamination of current functional theory, especially the work of Robert Merton and Talcott Parsons. The fullest ramifications of what follows can best be seen in this theoretical context. Merton's familiar paradigm of functionalism stresses that analysis must begin with the identification of some problematic pattern of human behavior, some institution, role, or shared pattern of belief. Merton stipulates clearly the basic functionalist assumption, the way in which the problematic pattern is to be understood: he holds that the "central orientation of functionalism" is "expressed in the practice of interpreting data by establishing their consequences for larger structures in which they are implicated."[7] The functionalist's emphasis upon studying the *existent* consequences, the ongoing functions or dysfunctions, of a social pattern may be better appreciated if it is remembered that this concern developed in a polemic against the earlier anthropological notion of a

"survival." The survival, of course, was regarded as a custom held to be unexplainable in terms of its existent consequences or utility and which, therefore, had to be understood with reference to its consequences for social arrangements no longer present.

Merton's posture toward the notion of a social survival is both pragmatic and sceptical. He asserts that the question of survivals is largely an empirical one; if the evidence demonstrates that a given social pattern is presently functionless then it simply has to be admitted provisionally to be a survival. Contrariwise, if no such evidence can be adduced "then the quarrel dwindles of its own accord."[8] It is in this sense that his position is pragmatic. It is also a sceptical position in that he holds that "even when such survivals are identified in contemporary literate societies, they seem to add little to our understanding of human behavior or the dynamics of social change . . ."[9] We are told, finally, that "the sociologist of literate societies may neglect survivals with no apparent loss."[10]

This resolution of the problem of survivals does not seem entirely satisfactory, for although vital empirical issues are involved there are also important questions that can only be clarified theoretically. Merton's discussion implies that certain patterns of human behavior are already known to be, or may in the future be shown to be, social survivals. How, then, can *these* be explained in terms of functional theory? Can functional theory ignore them on the grounds that they are not socially consequential? Consequential or not, such social survivals would in themselves entail patterns of behavior or belief which are no less in need of explanation than any other. More than that, their very existence, which Merton conceives possible, would seem to contradict the "central orientation" of functional theory.

Functionalism, to repeat, explains the persistence of social patterns in terms of their ongoing consequences for existent social systems. If social survivals, which by definition have no such consequences, are conceded to exist or to be possible, then it would seem that functionalism is by its own admission incapable of explaining them. To suggest that survivals do not help us to understand other patterns of social behavior is beside the mark. The decisive issue is whether existent versions of functional theory can explain social survivals, not whether specific social survivals can explain other social patterns.

It would seem that functionalists have but one of two choices: either they must dogmatically deny the existence or possibility of functionless patterns (survivals), and assert that all social behavior is explainable parsimoniously on the basis of the same fundamental functionalist assumption, that is, in terms of its consequences for surrounding social structures; or, more reasonably, they must concede that some social patterns are or may be survivals, admitting that existent functional theory fails to account for such instances. In the latter case, functionalists must develop further their basic assumptions on the generalized level required. I believe that one of the strategic ways in which such basic assumptions can be developed is by recognizing the manner in which the concept of *reciprocity* is tacitly involved in them, and by explicating the concept's implications for functional theory.

The tacit implication of the concept of reciprocity in functional theory can be illustrated in Merton's analysis of the latent functions of the political machine in the United States. Merton inquires how political machines continue to operate, despite the fact that they frequently run counter to both the mores and the law. The *general* form of his explanation is to identify the consequences of the machine for surrounding structures and to demonstrate that the machine performs "positive functions which are at the same time not adequately fulfilled by other existing patterns and structures."[11] It seems evident, however, that simply to establish its consequences for other social structures provides no answer to the question of the persistence of the political machine.[12] The explanation miscarries because no explicit analysis is made of the feedback through which the social structures or groups, whose needs are satisfied by the political machine, in turn "reciprocate" and repay the machine for the services received from it. In this case, the patterns of reciprocity, implied in the notion of the "corruption" of the machine, are well known and fully documented.

To state the issue generally: the demonstration that A is functional for B can help to account for A's persistence only if the functional theorist tacitly assumes some principle of reciprocity. It is in this sense that some concept of reciprocity apparently has been smuggled into the basic but unstated postulates of functional analysis. The demonstration that A is functional for B helps to account for A's own persistence and stability only on two related assumptions: (1) that B *reciprocates* A's services, and (2) that B's service to A is *contingent* upon A's performance of positive functions for B. The second assumption, indeed, is one implication of the definition of reciprocity as a transaction. Unless B's services to A are contingent upon the services provided by A, it is pointless to examine the latter if one wishes to account for the persistence of A.

It may be assumed, as a first approximation, that a social unit or group is more likely to contribute to another which provides it with benefits than to one which does not; nonetheless, there are certain general conditions under which one pattern may provide benefits for the other despite a *lack* of reciprocity. An important case of this situation is where power arrangements constrain the continuance of services. If B is considerably more powerful than A, B may force A to benefit it with little or no reciprocity. This social arrangement, to be sure, is less stable than one in which B's reciprocity *motivates* A to continue performing services for B, but it is hardly for this reason sociologically unimportant.

The problem can also be approached in terms of the functional autonomy[13] of two units relative to each other. For example, B may have many alternative sources for supplying the services that it normally receives from A. A, however, may be dependent upon B's services and have no, or comparatively few, alternatives. Consequently, the continued provision of benefits by one pattern,[14] A, for another, B, depends not only upon (1) the benefits which A in turn receives from B, but also on (2) the power which B possesses relative to A, and (3) the alternative sources of services accessible to each, beyond those provided by the other. In short, an explanation of the stability of a pattern, or of the relationship between A and B, requires investigation of mutually contingent benefits rendered and of the manner in which this mutual contingency is sustained. The latter, in turn, requires utilization of two different theoretical traditions and general orientations, one stressing the significance of power differences and the other emphasizing the degree of mutual dependence of the patterns or parties involved.

Functional theory, then, requires some assumption concerning reciprocity. It must, however, avoid the "Pollyanna Fallacy" which optimistically assumes that structures securing "satisfactions" from others will invariably be "grateful" and will always reciprocate. Therefore it cannot be merely hypostatized that reciprocity will operate in every case; its occurrence must, instead, be documented empirically. Although reciprocal relations stabilize patterns, it need not follow that a lack of reciprocity is socially impossible or invariably disruptive of the patterns involved. Relations with little or no reciprocity may, for example, occur when power disparities allow one party to coerce the other.

There may also be special mechanisms which compensate for or control the tensions which arise in the event of a breakdown in reciprocity. Among such compensatory mechanisms there may be culturally shared prescriptions of one-sided or unconditional generosity, such as the Christian notion of "turning the other cheek" or "walking the second mile," the feudal notion of *"noblesse oblige,"* or the Roman notion of "clemency." There may also be cultural prohibitions banning the examination of certain interchanges from the standpoint of their concrete reciprocity, as expressed by the cliché, "It's not the gift but the sentiment that counts." The major point here is that if empirical analysis fails to detect the existence of functional reciprocity, or finds that it has been disrupted, it becomes necessary to search out and analyze the compensatory arrangements that may provide means of controlling the resultant tensions, thereby enabling the problematic pattern to remain stable.

A RECONCEPTUALIZATION OF "SURVIVALS"

Thus far reciprocity has been discussed as a mutually contingent exchange of benefits between two or more units, as if it were an "all or none" matter. Once the problem is posed in this way, however, it is apparent that reciprocity is not merely present or absent but is, instead, quantitatively variable—or may be treated as such. The benefits exchanged, at one extreme, may be identical or equal. At the other logical extreme, one party may give nothing in return for the benefits it has received. Both of these extremes are probably rare in social relations and the intermediary case, in which one party gives something more or less than that received, is probably more common than either of the limiting cases.

Having cast the problem of reciprocity in these quantitative terms, there emerges an important implication for the question of social survivals. The quantitative view of reciprocity. These functionalists made the cogent of the *earlier* notion of a survival. It may now be seen that there a survival was tacitly treated as one of the limiting cases of reciprocity, that is, one in which a pattern provides *nothing* in exchange for the benefits given it.

The polemical opposition of the earlier functionalists to this view of a survival rests implicitly on an unqualified principle of reciprocity. These functionalists made the cogent assumption that a social pattern which persists must be securing satisfaction of its own needs from certain other patterns. What was further and more dubiously assumed, however, was that if this pattern continues to be "serviced" this could only be because it reciprocally provided *some* gratifications to its benefactors. In the course of the polemic, the question of the degree of such gratification—the relation between its output and input—became obscured. To the early functionalists, the empirical problem became one of unearthing the hidden contributions made by a seeming survival and, thereby, showing that it is not in fact functionless. In effect, this enjoined the functionalist to exert his ingenuity to search out the hidden reciprocities for it was assumed that there must be some reciprocities somewhere. This led, in certain cases, as Audrey Richards states, to "some far-fetched explanations . . ."[15]

If, however, it had been better understood that compensatory mechanisms might have been substituted for reciprocity, or that power disparities might have maintained the "survival" despite its lack of reciprocity, then many fruitful problems may well have emerged. Above all, the early functionalists neglected the fact that a survival is only the limiting case of a larger class of social phenomena, namely, relations between parties or patterns in which functional reciprocity is *not equal*. While the survival, defined as the extreme case of a *complete lack* of reciprocity, may be rare, the larger class of *unequal* exchanges, of which survivals are a part, is frequent. The tacit conception of survivals as entailing no reciprocity led the early functionalists to neglect the *larger class of unequal exchanges*. It is this problem which the functionalist polemic against survivals has obscured to the present day.

THE "EXPLOITATION" PROBLEM

It was, however, not only the functionalist polemic against the concept of survivals that obscured the significance and inhibited the study of unequal exchanges. A similar result is also produced by the suspicion with which many modern sociologists understandably regard the concept of "exploitation." This concept of course is central to the traditional socialist critique of modern capitalism. In the now nearly-forgotten language of political economy, "exploitation" refers to a relationship in which unearned income results from certain kinds of unequal exchange.

Starting perhaps with Sismondi's notion of "spoliation," and possibly even earlier with the physiocrat's critique of exchange as intrinsically unproductive, the concept of exploitation can be traced from the work of the Saint-Simonians to that of Marx and Proudhon.[16] It is also present in Veblen's notion of the Vested Interest which he characterizes as "the right to something for nothing" or, in other words, as *institutionalized* exploitation. Even after the emergence of sociology as a separate discipline the concept of exploitation appears in the works of E. A. Ross,[17] von Wiese, and Howard Becker.[18] As it passed into sociology, however, the concept was generalized beyond its original economic application. Ross and Becker-von Wiese, for example, speak of various types of exploitation: economic, to be sure, but also religious, "egotic," and sexual. However, just as the concept of exploitation was being generalized and made available for social analysis, it almost disappeared from sociological usage.

"*Almost* disappeared" because there remains one area in which unabashed, full-scale use of the concept is made by sociologists. This is in the study of sexual relations. As Kanin and Howard remark, "It has been the *practice* to speak of exploitation when males were found to have entered sexual liaisons with women of comparative lower status."[19] Kingsley Davis also uses the notion of exploitation implicitly in his discussion of the incest taboo, remarking that " . . . father-daughter incest would put the daughter in a position of subordination. While she was still immature the father could use his power to take advantage of her."[20] What Davis is saying is that one function of the incest taboo is to prevent sexual exploitation. He goes on to add that "legitimate sexual relations ordinarily involve a certain amount of reciprocity. Sex is exchanged for something equally valuable."[21] This is an interesting commentary, first, because Davis is quite clear about treating exploitation in the context of a discussion of reciprocity; and second, because he explicitly uses a notion of reciprocity in a strategic way even though it is not systematically explored elsewhere in his volume, once again illustrating the tendency to use the concept and to assume its analytic importance without giving it careful conceptualization.[22]

The continued use of the concept of exploitation in sociological analyses of sexual relations stems largely from the brilliant work of Willard Waller on the dynamics of courtship. Waller's ambivalent comments about the concept suggest why it has fallen into sociological disrepute. "The word exploitation is by no means a desirable one," explains Waller, "but we have not been able to find another which will do as well. The dictionary definition of exploitation as an 'unfair or unjust utilization of another' contains a value judgment, and this value judgment is really a part of the ordinary sociological meaning of the term."[23] In short, the concept of exploitation may have become disreputable because its value implications conflict with modern sociology's effort to place itself on a value-free basis, as well as because it is a concept commonly and correctly associated with the critique of modern society emphasized by the political left. But the concept *need* not be used in such an ideological manner; it can be employed simply to refer to certain transactions involving an exchange of things of unequal value. It is important to guarantee that the ordinary value implications of a term do not intrude upon its scientific use. It is also important, however, to prevent our distaste for the ideological implications of exploitation from inducing a compulsive and equally ideological neglect of its cognitive substance.

The unsavory implications of the concept of exploitation have *not* excluded it from studies of sexual relations, although almost all other specializations in sociology eschew it. Why this is so remains a tempting problem for the sociology of knowledge, but cannot be explored here. In the present context, the important implications are the following: If the possible sexual exploitation of daughters by fathers gives rise, as Davis suggests, to mechanisms that serve to prevent this, then it would seem that *other* types of exploitation may also be controlled by *other* kinds of mechanisms. These may be no less important and universal than the incest taboo. If the exploitation of women by men (or men by women) is worthy of sociological attention, then also worth studying is the exploitation of students by teachers, of workers by management or union leaders, of patients by doctors,[24] and so on. If the notion of exploitation, in a value-free sense, is useful for the analysis of sexual relations then it can be of similar aid in analyzing many other kinds of social relations.

Doubtless "exploitation" is by now so heavily charged with misleading ideological resonance that the term itself can scarcely be salvaged for purely scientific purposes and will, quite properly, be resisted by most American sociologists. This is unimportant. Perhaps a less emotionally freighted—if infelicitous—term such as "reciprocity imbalance" will suffice to direct attention once again to the crucial question of unequal exchanges.

In any event, the present analysis of reciprocity opens up long-neglected questions, yielding a new perspective on the relation between functional theory and the concepts of "survival" and "exploitation." In the latter case, moreover, intimations emerge of some of the ways in which two diverse theoretical traditions contain surprising convergences.

These two traditions are, first, that which is commonly if questionably[25] held to begin with Comte, was developed by Durkheim, and reaches its fullest current expression in the work of Parsons. The second tradition, while often ideologically distorted nevertheless retains significant sociological substance, derives from Marx and Engels, was developed by Kautsky, and ended in Bukharin. The latent convergence between these two schools involves the implicit stress that each gives to reciprocity, albeit to polar ends of its continuum.

The "Comteian" tradition, of course, approached reciprocity through its emphasis on the division of labor, viewed as a major source of social cohesion. Characteristically focusing on the problem of social instability and change, rather than stability and cohesion, the "Marxian" tradition emphasized the opposite end of reciprocity namely, exploitation. This, I suspect, is one of the major but overlooked convergences in the history of sociological theory.

This latent convergence becomes most evident in Durkheim's lectures on "Professional Ethics and Civic Morals."[26] Durkheim contends that the existence of social classes, characterized by significant inequalities, in principle makes it impossible for "just" contracts to be negotiated. This system of stratification, Durkheim argues, constrains to an unequal exchange of goods and services, thereby offending the moral expectations of people in industrial societies. The exploitation rendered possible by notable disparities of power among the contracting parties encourages a sense of injustice which has socially unstabilizing consequences. Thus both Durkheim and Marx use a concept of "exploitation" for analyzing social instabilities. Durkheim, however, adds an important element that was systematically neglected by Marx, namely, that unequal exchanges of goods and services are socially disruptive because they violate certain pervasive *values*. But the specific nature of this value element is never fully confronted and explored by Durkheim; we must here take as problematic what Durkheim took as given.

COMPLEMENTARITY AND RECIPROCITY

First, however, the question of the meaning of the concept of reciprocity should be reexamined. Consideration of some of the ways in which the reciprocity problem is treated by Parsons helps to distinguish reciprocity from other cognate concepts. "It is inherent in the nature of social interaction," writes Parsons, "that the gratification of ego's need-dispositions is contingent on alter's reaction and vice versa."[27] Presumably, therefore, if the gratification of either party's needs is not contingent upon the other's reactions, the stability of their relation is undermined. This, in turn, implies that if a social system is to be stable there must always be some "mutuality of gratification."[28] Social system stability, then, presumably depends in part on the mutually contingent exchange of gratifications, that is, on reciprocity as exchange.

This, however, remains an insight the implications of which are never systematically explored. For example, the implications of differences in the *degree* of mutuality or in the symmetry of reciprocity are neglected. Again, while the concept of "exploitation" assumes *central* importance in Parsons' commentary on the patient-doctor relation, it is never precisely defined, examined, and located in his *general* theory.

One reason for Parsons' neglect of reciprocity is that he, like some other sociologists, does not distinguish it from the concept of complementarity. Parsons uses the two concepts as if they are synonymous[29] and, for the most part, centers his analysis on complementarity to the systematic neglect of reciprocity rigorously construed. The term complementarity, however, is itself an ambiguous one and is not, in all of its meanings, synonymous with reciprocity. Complementarity has at least four distinct meanings:[30]

Complementarity₁ may mean that a right (x) of Ego against Alter implies a duty (—x) of Alter to Ego. Given the often vague use of the term "right," it is quite possible that this proposition, in one aspect, is only an expansion of some definition of the concept "right." To that degree, of course, this is simply an analytic proposition. The interesting sociological questions, however, arise only when issues of empirical substance rather than logical implication are raised. For example, where a group shares a belief that some status occupant has a certain right, say the right of a wife to receive support from her husband, does the group in fact also share a belief that the husband has an obligation to support the wife? Furthermore, even though rights may logically or empirically imply duties, it need not follow that the reverse is true. In other words, it does not follow that rights and duties are always transitive. This can be seen in a second meaning of complementarity.

Complementarity₂ may mean that what is a duty (—x) of Alter to Ego implies a right (x) of Ego against Alter. On the *empirical* level, while this is often true, of course, it is also sometimes false. For example, what may be regarded as a duty of charity or forebearance, say a duty to "turn the other cheek," need not be *socially* defined as the *right* of the recipient. While a man may be regarded as having an unconditional obligation to tell the truth to everyone, even to a confirmed liar, people in his group might not claim that the liar has a *right* to have the truth told him.

The other two meanings of complementarity differ substantially. Complementarity₃ may mean that a right (x) of Alter against Ego implies a duty (—y) of Alter to Ego. Similarly, complementarity₄ may mean that a duty (—x) of Ego to Alter implies a right (y) of Ego against Alter.

In these four implications of complementarity —sometimes called reciprocal rights and obligations—there are two distinctive types of cases. Properly speaking, *complementarity* refers only to the first two meanings sketched above, where what is a right of Ego implies an obligation of Alter, or where a duty of Alter to Ego implies a right of Ego against Alter. Only the other two meanings, however, involve true instances of *reciprocity*, for only in these does what one party receives from the other require some return, so that giving and receiving are mutually contingent.

In short, complementarity connotes that one's rights are another's obligations, and *vice versa*. Reciprocity, however, connotes that *each* party has rights *and* duties. This is more than an analytic distinction: it is an *empirical* generalization concerning role systems the importance of which as a datum is so elemental that it is commonly neglected and rarely made problematic. The English philosopher MacBeath suggests that this empirical generalization may be accounted for by the principle of reciprocity.[31] This would seem possible in several senses, one of which is that, were there only rights on the one side and duties on the other, there need be no exchange whatsoever. Stated differently, it would seem that there can be stable patterns of reciprocity *qua* exchange only insofar as *each* party has both rights and duties. In effect, then, reciprocity has its significance for *role systems* in that it tends to structure *each* role so as to include both rights and duties. It is now clear, at any rate, that reciprocity is by no means identical with complementarity and that the two are confused only at theoretic peril.

MALINOWSKI ON RECIPROCITY

Renewing the effort to clarify the diverse meanings of reciprocity, we turn to Malinowski's seminal contribution. This is most fully elaborated in his *Crime and Custom*,[32] which opens with the following question: Why is it that rules of conduct in a primitive society are obeyed, even though they are hard and irksome? Even under normal conditions, the savage's compliance with his moral code is at best partial, conditional, and evasive. These, says Malinowski, are the elementary facts of ethnography, and consequently we cannot assume that the savage's conformity is due only to his awe and reverence for traditional custom, or that he slavishly and spontaneously complies with its dictates.

Above all, Malinowski rejects the assumption that it is the sacred authority of the moral code, or the "collective conscience," which accounts for the conformity given it. It is to this anti-Durkheimian point that he directs the brunt of his polemic. Conformity, says Malinowski, is not sanctioned "by a mere psychological force, but by a definite social machinery . . . "[33] Thus Malinowski expressly rejects a psychological account of conformity and seeks instead a distinctively sociological explanation.[34] This he finds in the "principle of reciprocity."

One of Malinowski's central theses holds that people *owe obligations to each other* and that, therefore, conformity with norms is something they give *to each other*. He notes, for example, that almost every religious or ceremonial act is regarded as an obligation between groups and living individuals, and not only to the immortal gods. For Malinowski, therefore, one meaning of reciprocity refers to the interlocking status duties which people owe one another. Thus he speaks of reciprocity as taking place "within a standing partnership, or as associated with definite social ties or coupled with mutuality in noneconomic matters."[35]

Reciprocity also entails a "mutual dependence and (is) realized in the equivalent arrangement of reciprocal services . . . "[36] Here reciprocity is conceived as the complement to and fulfillment of the division of labor. It is the pattern of exchange through which the mutual dependence of people, brought about by the division of labor, is realized. Reciprocity, therefore, is a mutually gratifying pattern of exchanging goods and services.

As noted above, Malinowski speaks of reciprocity as involving an exchange of *equivalent* services; he further stresses this by insisting that "most if not all economic acts are found to belong to some chain of reciprocal gifts and counter-gifts, which in the long run balance, benefiting both sides equally."[37] For Malinowski, then, the exchange of goods and services is not only mutually gratifying but is equally so, "in the long run."

Speaking of the reciprocal exchange of vegetables and fish between inland communities and fishing villages, Malinowski remarks that there is a "system of mutual obligations which forces the fisherman to repay whenever he has received a gift from his inland partner, and vice versa. Neither partner can refuse, neither may stint, neither should delay."[38] This is seen to be related to the group's existential beliefs about reciprocity. That is, men are not regarded as blindly involving themselves in reciprocal transactions; they are viewed as having some presentiment of the consequences of reciprocity and of its breakdown. In this vein, Malinowski writes: "Though no native, however intelligent, can formulate this state of affairs in a general abstract manner, or present it as a sociological theory, yet everyone is well aware of its existence and in each concrete case he can foresee the consequences."[39] More specifically, it seems to be implied that people believe that (a) in the long run the mutual exchange of goods and services *will* balance out; or (b) if people do not aid those who helped them certain penalties will be imposed upon them; or (c) those whom they have helped *can* be expected to help them; or (d) some or all of these.

It is clear that two basically different elements were caught up in Malinowski's "principle of reciprocity." One of these is a set of sentiments or existential folk beliefs about reciprocity. The other is a mutually contingent exchange of benefits or gratifications. (The latter conception converges, though it is not completely identical, with the ecological concept of symbiosis.) There is, however, a third analytically distinct element which, if implicit in Malinowski, remained murky. This is a *value* element, the same value that Durkheim, as mentioned earlier, invoked but did not clarify. Like Durkheim, Malinowski never fully disentangles it from the other elements.

In the exchanges between the fishing and the inland villages, cited above, we may suggest that each side lives up to its obligations, not simply because of constraints imposed by the division of labor with its attendant mutual dependency, but also because the partners share the higher level *moral norm*: "You *should* give benefits to those who give you benefits." Note that this norm does not simply make it unconditionally imperative, say, for the fisherman to give the inland gardeners fish. I refer here not to the *specific* obligation to give fish but rather to a *general* obligation to repay benefits.

In sum, beyond reciprocity as a pattern of exchange and beyond folk beliefs about reciprocity as a fact of life, there is another element: a generalized moral norm of reciprocity which defines certain actions and *obiligations* as repayments for benefits received.

Malinowski frequently seems to confuse this general norm with the existence of complementary and concrete status rights and duties. It is theoretically necessary, however, to distinguish specific status duties from the general norm. Specific and complementary duties are owed by role partners to one another by virtue of the socially standardized roles they play. These may require an almost unconditional compliance in the sense that they are incumbent on all those in a given status simply by virtue of its occupancy. In contrast, the generalized norm of reciprocity evokes obligations toward others on the basis of their past behavior. In the first case, Ego's obligations to Alter depend upon Ego's status vis-à-vis Alter; in the second case, Ego's obligations toward Alter depend upon what Alter has done for Ego. There are certain duties that people owe one another, not as human beings, or as fellow members of a group, or even as occupants of social statuses within the group but, rather, because of their prior actions. We owe others certain things because of what they have previously done for us, because of the history of previous interaction we have had with them. It is this kind of obligation which is entailed by the generalized norm of reciprocity.

THE NORM OF RECIPROCITY

Contrary to some cultural relativists, it can be hypothesized that a norm of reciprocity is universal. As Westermarck stated, "To requite a benefit, or to be grateful to him who bestows it, is probably everywhere, at least under certain circumstances, regarded as a duty."[40] A norm of reciprocity is, I suspect, no less universal and important an element of culture than the incest taboo, although, similarly, its concrete formulations may vary with time and place.

Specifically, I suggest that a norm of reciprocity, in its universal form, makes two interrelated, minimal demands: (1) people should help those who have helped them, and (2) people should not injure those who have helped them. Generically, the norm of reciprocity may be conceived of as a dimension to be found in all value systems and, in particular, as one among a *number* of "Principal Components" universally present in moral codes. (The task of the sociologist, in this regard, parallels that of the physicist who seeks to identify the basic particles of matter, the conditions under which they vary, and their relations to one another.)

To suggest that a norm of reciprocity is universal is not, of course, to assert that it is unconditional. Unconditionality would, indeed, be at variance with the basic character of the reciprocity norm which imposes obligations only contingently, that is, in response to the benefits conferred by others. Moreover, such obligations of repayment are contingent upon the imputed *value* of the benefit received. The value of the benefit and hence the debt is in proportion to and varies with—among other things—the intensity of the recipient's need at the time the benefit was bestowed ("a friend in need . . . "), the resources of the donor ("he gave although he could ill afford it"), the motives imputed to the donor ("without thought of gain"), and the nature of the constraints which are perceived to exist or to be absent ("he gave of his own free will . . . "). Thus the obligations imposed by the norm of reciprocity may vary with the *status* of the participants within a society.

Similarly, this norm functions differently in some degree in different *cultures*. In the Philippines, for example, the *compadre* system cuts across and pervades the political, economic, and other institutional spheres. *Compadres* are bound by a norm of reciprocity. If one man pays his *compadre's* doctor's bill in time of need, for example, the latter may be obligated to help the former's son to get a government job. Here the tendency to govern all relations by the norm of reciprocity, thereby undermining bureaucratic impersonality, is relatively legitimate, hence overt and powerful. In the United States, however, such tendencies are weaker, in part because friendship relations are less institutionalized. Nonetheless, even in bureaucracies in this country such tendencies are endemic, albeit less legitimate and overt. Except in friendship, kinship, and neighborly relations, a norm of reciprocity is not imposed on Americans by the "dominant cultural profile," although it is commonly found in the latent or "substitute" culture structure in all institutional sectors, even the most rationalized, in the United States.

In otherwise contrasting discussions of the norm of reciprocity one emphasis is notable. Some scholars, especially Homans, Thurwald, Simmel, and Malinowski, assert or imply that the reciprocity norm stipulates that the amount of the return to be made is "roughly equivalent" to what had been received. The problem of equivalence is a difficult but important one. Whether in fact there is a reciprocity norm specifically requiring that returns for benefits received be *equivalent* is an empirical question. So, too, is

the problem of whether such a norm is part of or distinct from a more general norm which simply requires that one return some (unspecified) benefits to benefactors. Logically prior to such empirical problems, however, is the question of what the meaning of equivalence would be in the former norm of equivalent reciprocity.

Equivalence may have at least two forms, the sociological and psychodynamic significance of which are apt to be quite distinct. In the first case, heteromorphic reciprocity, equivalence may mean that the things exchanged may be concretely different but should be equal in *value*, as defined by the actors in the situation. In the second case, homeomorphic reciprocity, equivalence may mean that exchanges should be concretely alike, or identical in form, either with respect to the things exchanged or to the circumstances under which they are exchanged. In the former, equivalence calls for "tit for tat"; in the latter, equivalence calls for "tat for tat." Historically, the most important expression of homeomorphic reciprocity is found in the *negative* norms of reciprocity, that is, in sentiments of retaliation where the emphasis is placed not on the return of benefits but on the return of injuries, and is best exemplified by the *lex talionis*.[41]

Finally, it should be stressed that equivalence in the above cases refers to a definition of the exchangeables made by actors in the situation. This differs of course, from holding that the things exchanged by people, in the long run, will be *objectively* equal in value, as measured by economists or other social scientists. Here, again, the adequacy of these conceptual distinctions will be determined ultimately by empirical test. For example, can we find reciprocity norms which, in fact, require that returns be equivalent in value and are these empirically distinguishable from norms requiring that returns to be concretely alike? Are these uni-dimensional or multi-dimensional? Similarly, only research can resolve the question whether a norm of retaliation exists in any given group, is the polar side of the norm of reciprocity, or is a distinctive norm which may vary independently of the reciprocity norm. These conceptual distinctions only suggest a set of research possibilities and have value primarily as guides to investigation.[42]

RECIPROCITY AND SOCIAL SYSTEMS

As mentioned above, sociologists have sometimes confused the notion of complementarity with that of reciprocity and have recently tended to focus on the former. Presumably, the reason for this is because of the importance of complementarity in maintaining the stability of social systems. Clearly, if what one party deems his right is accepted by the other as his obligation, their relation will be more stable than if the latter fails to so define it. But if the group stabilizing consequences of complementarity are the basis of its theoretical significance, then the same consideration underwrites with equal potency the significance of reciprocity. For reciprocity has no less a role in maintaining the stability of social systems.

Note that there are at least two ways, not merely one, in which complementarity as such can break down. In the one case, Alter can refuse to acknowledge Ego's rights as his own duties. In the other case, however, Ego may not regard as rights that which Alter acknowledges as duties. The former is commonly viewed as the empirically more frequent and as the theoretically more significant case. That this often seems to be taken as a matter of course suggests the presence of certain tacit assumptions about basic human dispositions. It seems to assume, as Aristotle put it, that people are more ready to receive than to give benefits. In short, it premises a common tendency toward what used to be called "egoism," a salient (but not exclusive) concern with the satisfaction of one's own needs.

This or some cognate assumption appears to be eminently reasonable and empirically justified. There can be no adequate systematic sociological theory which boggles at the issue; indeed, it is one of the many virtues of Parsons' work that it confronts the egoism problem. His solution seems to be sidetracked, however, because his overwhelming focus on the problem of complementarity leads to the neglect of reciprocity. If assumptions about egoistic dispositions are valid, however, a complementarity of rights and obligations should be exposed to a persistent strain, in which each party is somewhat more actively concerned to defend or extend his own rights than those of others. There is nothing in complementarity as such which would seem able to control egoism.

One way out may be obtained by premising that socialization internalizes complementary rights and obligations in persons, before they fully assume responsible participation in a social system. Even if socialization were to work perfectly and so internalize such rights and obligations, there still remains the question as to what mechanism can sustain and reinforce these during full participation in the social system. The concept of complementarity takes mutually compatible expectations as given; it does not and cannot explain how they are maintained once established. For this we need to turn to the reciprocities processes because these, unlike pure complementarity, actually mobilize egoistic motivations and channel them into the maintenance of the social system. Benthamite utilitarianism has long understood that egoism can motivate one party to satisfy the expectations of the other, since by doing so he induces the latter to reciprocate and to satisfy his own. As Max Gluckman might put it with his penchant for Hegelian paradox, there is an altruism in egoism, made possible through reciprocity.

Furthermore, the existential belief in reciprocity says something like this, "People will usually help those who help them." Similarly, the *norm* of reciprocity holds that people should help those who help them and, therefore, those whom you have helped have an obligation to help you. The conclusion is clear: if you want to be helped by others you must help them; hence it is not only proper but also expedient to conform with the specific status rights of others and with the general norm. Both the existential belief in and the norm of reciprocity enlist egoistic motivations in the service of social system stability.[43]

A full analysis of the ways in which the whole reciprocities complex is involved in the maintenance of social systems would require consideration of the linkages between each of its various elements, and their relation to other general properties of social systems. There is no space for such consideration here. Instead, I examine only one part of the complex, namely, the generalized *norm* of reciprocity, and suggest some of the ways in which it contributes to social system stability.

If, following Parsons, we suppose that social systems are stable to the extent that Ego and Alter conform with one another's expectations, we are confronted with the problem of why men *reciprocate* gratifications. Parsons holds that once a stable relation of mutual gratification has been established the system is self-perpetuating; presumably, no special mechanisms are necessary to maintain it. Insofar as this is not simply postulated in analogy with the principle of inertia in physics, apparently reciprocity is accounted for by Parsons, and also by Homans, as a result of the development of a beneficent cycle of mutual reinforcement. That is, Ego's conformity with Alter's expectations reinforces Alter's conformity with Ego's expectations, and so on.

This explanation of reciprocity *qua* transaction is particularly strange in Parsons' case since he often stresses, but here neglects, the significance of shared values as a source of stability in social systems. So far as the question here is not simply the general one of why men conform with the expectations of others but, rather, the more specific problem of why they *reciprocate* benefits, part of the answer would seem to be that they have commonly internalized some general *moral norm*. In short, the suggestion is that the motivation for reciprocity stems not only from the sheer gratification which Alter receives from Ego but also from Alter's internalization of a specific norm of reciprocity which morally obliges him to give benefits to those from whom he has received them. In this respect, the *norm* of reciprocity is a concrete and special mechanism involved in the maintenance of any stable social system.

Why should such a norm be necessary? Why is it that expedient considerations do not suffice to mobilize motivations to comply with other's expectations, thereby inducing them to provide reciprocal compliances? One major line of analysis here would certainly indicate the disruptive potentialities of power differences. Given significant power differences, egoistic motivations may seek to get benefits without returning them. (It is notable that Parsons fails to define the power situation in his basic model of Ego-Alter equilibrium.) The situation is then ripe for the breakdown of reciprocity and for the development of system-disrupting exploitation. The norm of reciprocity, however, engenders motives for returning benefits even when power differences might invite exploitation. The norm thus safeguards powerful people against the temptations of their own status; it motivates and regulates reciprocity as an exchange pattern, serving to inhibit the emergence of exploitative relations which would undermine the social system and the very power arrangements which had made exploitation possible.[44]

As we have seen, Parsons stresses that the stability of social systems largely derives from the *conformity* of role partners to each other's expectations, particularly when they do their duty to one another. This formulation induces a focus on conformity and deviance, and the degrees and types of each. Presumably, the more that people pay their social debts the more stable the social system. But much more than conformity and deviance are involved here.

The idea of the reciprocities complex leads us to the historical or genetic dimension of social interaction. For example, Malinowski, in his discussion of the Kula Ring, carefully notes that the gifts given are not immediately returned and repayment may take as long as a year. What is the significance of this intervening time period?

It is a period governed by the norm of reciprocity in a double sense. First, the actor is accumulating, mobilizing, liquidating, or earmarking resources so that he can make a suitable repayment. Second, it is a period governed by the rule that you should not do harm to those who have done you a benefit. This is a time, then, when men are morally constrained to manifest their gratitude toward, or at least to maintain peace with, their benefactors.

Insofar as men live under such a rule of reciprocity, when one party benefits another, an obligation is generated. The recipient is now *indebted* to the donor, and he remains so until he repays. Once interaction is seen as taking place over time, we may note that the norm of reciprocity so structures social relations that, between the time of Ego's provision of a gratification and the time of Alter's repayment, falls the shadow of indebtedness. An adequate analysis of the dynamics of social interaction is thus required to go beyond the question of deviance from or conformity with the parties' obligations to one another. A second basic dimension needs to be examined systematically, namely, the time period when there is an obligation still to be performed, when commitments which have been made are yet to be fulfilled.

These outstanding obligations, no less than those already given compliance, contribute substantially to the stability of social systems. It is obviously inexpedient for creditors to break off relationships with those who have outstanding obligations to them. It may also be inexpedient for *debtors* to do so because their creditors may not again allow them to run up a bill of social indebtedness. In addition, it is *morally* improper, under the norm of reciprocity, to break off relations or to launch hostilities against those to whom you are still indebted.

If this conclusion is correct, then we should not only look for mechanisms which constrain or motivate men to do their duty and to pay off their debts. We should also expect to find mechanisms which induce people to *remain* socially indebted to each other and which *inhibit* their complete repayment. This suggests another function performed by the requirement of only *rough* equivalence of repayment that may be involved in one of the norms of reciprocity. For it induces a certain amount of ambiguity as to whether indebtedness has been repaid and, over time, generates uncertainty about who is in whose debt.[45] This all hinges, however, on a shared conception of the moral propriety of repayment, engendered by the norm of reciprocity.

Still another way in which the general norm

of reciprocity is implicated in the maintenance of social system stability is related to an important attribute of the norm, namely, its comparative indeterminancy. Unlike specific status duties and like other general norms, this norm does not require highly specific and uniform performances from people whose behavior it regulates. For example, unlike the status duties of American wives, it does not call upon them to cook and to take care of the children. Instead, the concrete demands it makes change substantially from situation to situation and vary with the benefits which one party receives from another.

This indeterminancy enables the norm of reciprocity to perform some of its most important system-stabilizing functions. Being indeterminate, the norm can be applied to countless *ad hoc* transactions, thus providing a flexible moral sanction for transactions which might not otherwise be regulated by specific status obligations. The norm, in this respect, is a kind of plastic filler, capable of being poured into the shifting crevices of social structures, and serving as a kind of all-purpose moral cement.

Not only does the norm of reciprocity play a stabilizing role in human relations in the *absence* of a well developed system of specific status duties, but it contributes to social stability even when these are *present* and well established. Status duties shape behavior because the status occupant believes them binding in their own right; they possess a kind of *prima facie* legitimacy for properly socialized group members. The general norm of reciprocity, however, is a second-order defense of stability; it provides a further source of motivation and an additional moral sanction for conforming with specific status obligations. For example, the employer may pay his workers not merely because he has contracted to do so; he may also feel that the workman has earned his wages. The housewife may take pains with her husband's meals not merely because cooking may be incumbent on her as a wife; she may also have a particularly considerate husband. In each case, the specific status duties are complied with not only because they are inherent in the status and are believed to be right in themselves, but also because each is further defined as a "*repayment*." In sum, the norm of reciprocity requires that if others have been fulfilling their status duties to you, you in turn have an additional or second-order obligation (repayment) to fulfill your status duties to them. In this manner, the sentiment of gratitude joins forces with the sentiment of rectitude and adds a safety-margin in the motivation to conformity.

The matter can be put differently from the standpoint of potential deviance or non-conformity. All status obligations are vulnerable to challenge and, at times, may have to be justified. If, for any reason, people refuse to do their duty, those demanding compliance may be required to justify their claims. Obviously, there are many standardized ways in which this might be done. Invoking the general norm of reciprocity is one way of justifying the more concrete demands of status obligations. Forced to the wall, the man demanding his "rights," may say, in effect, "Very well, if you won't do this simply because it is your duty, then remember all that I have done for you in the past and do it to repay your debt to me." The norm of reciprocity thus provides a second-order defense of the stability of social systems in that it can be used to overcome incipient deviance and to mobilize auxiliary motivations for conformity with existent status demands.[46]

STARTING MECHANISMS

Two distinct points have been made about the social functions of the norm of reciprocity. One is that this norm serves a group *stabilizing* function and thus is quite familiar in functional theory. The second point, however, is the view that the norm is not only in some sense a defense or stabilizing mechanism but is also what may be called a "starting mechanism." That is, it helps to initiate social interaction and is functional in the early phases of certain groups before they have developed a differentiated and customary set of status duties.

In speaking of the norm of reciprocity as a "starting mechanism," indeed in conceiving of starting mechanisms, we find ourselves outside the usual perspective of functional theory. Functional theory commonly focuses on already-established, on-going systems, and on the mechanisms by means of which an established social system is enabled to maintain itself. Although functional theory is concerned with the problems of how individual actors are prepared by socialization to play a role in social systems, its general theoretical models rarely, if ever, include systematic treatment of the beginnings of a social system as such and, consequently, do not formally raise the question of the nature of the mechanisms needed to start such a system.[47]

Every social system of course has a history, which means that it has had its beginnings even if these are shrouded in antiquity. Granted that the question of origins can readily bog down in a metaphysical morass, the fact is that many concrete social systems do have determinate beginnings. Marriages are not made in heaven, and whether they end in divorce or continue in bliss, they have some identifiable origins. Similarly, corporations, political parties, and all manner of groups have their beginnings. (Recent studies of friendship and other interpersonal relations in housing projects have begun to explore this problem.)

People are continually brought together in new juxtapositions and combinations, bringing with them the possibilities of new social systems. How are these possibilities realized? Is such realization entirely a random matter? These are the kinds of questions that were familiar to the earlier students of "collective behavior," who, in focusing on crowds, riots, and rumors, were often primarily concerned with investigating the development of groups in *statu nascendi*.[48] Although this perspective may at first seem somewhat alien to the functionalist, once it is put to him, he may suspect that certain kinds of mechanisms, conducive to the crystallization of social systems out of ephemeral contacts, will in some measure be institutionalized or otherwise patterned in any society. At this point he would be considering "starting mechanisms." In this way, I suggest, the norm of reciprocity provides one among many starting mechanisms.

From the standpoint of a purely economic or utilitarian model,[49] there are certain difficulties in accounting for the manner in which social interaction begins. Let us suppose two people or groups, Ego and Alter, each possesses valuables sought by the other. Suppose further that each feels that the only motive the other has to conduct an exchange is the anticipated gratification it will bring. Each may then feel that it would be advantageous to lay hold of the other's valuables without relinquishing his own. Furthermore, suppose that each party suspects the other of precisely such an intention, perhaps because of the operation of projective or empathic mechanisms. At least since Hobbes, it has been recognized that under such circumstances, each is likely to regard the impending exchange as dangerous and to view the other with some suspicion.[50] Each may then hesitate to part with his

valuables before the other has first turned his over. Like participants in a disarmament conference, each may say to other, "You first!" Thus the exchange may be delayed or altogether flounder and the relationship may be prevented from developing.

The norm of reciprocity may serve as a starting mechanism in such circumstances by preventing or enabling the parties to break out of this impasse. When internalized in both parties, the norm *obliges* the one who has first received a benefit to repay it at some time; it thus provides some realistic grounds for confidence, in the one who first parts with his valuables, that he will be repaid. Consequently, there may be less hesitancy in being the first and a greater facility with which the exchange and the social relation can get underway.

CONCLUSION

I have limited this discussion of the norm of reciprocity to its functions and its contribution to the stability of social systems, omitting examination of its dysfunctions and of the manner in which it induces tension and changes in social systems. That the norm commonly imposes obligations of reciprocity only "when the individual is able" to reciprocate does not guarantee agreement concerning the individual's "ability." Furthermore there may be occasions when questions as to whether the individual's return is appropriate or sufficient (apart from whether it is equivalent) that arise by virtue of the absence of common yardsticks in terms of which giving and returning may be compared. Moreover, the norm may lead individuals to establish relations only or primarily with those who can reciprocate, thus inducing neglect of the needs of those unable to do so. Clearly, the norm of reciprocity cannot apply with full force in relations with children, old people, or with those who are mentally or physically handicapped, and it is theoretically inferable that other, fundamentally different kinds of normative orientations will develop in moral codes. I hope to explore these and related problems in subsequent discussions.

NOTES

Sections of this paper were read at the annual meeting of the American Sociological Association, September, 1959. The author is indebted to Robert K. Merton, Howard S. Becker, John W. Bennett, Louis Schneider, and Gregory Stone for reading an earlier draft but knows of

no adequate "reciprocity" for their many valuable suggestions.

1 Howard Becker, *Man in Reciprocity*, New York: Prager, 1956, p. 1.

2 L. T. Hobhouse, *Morals in Evolution: A Study in Comparative Ethics*, London: Chapman & Hall,

1951, First edition, 1906, p. 12.

3 Richard Thurnwald, *Economics in Primitive Communities*, London: Oxford University Press, 1932, p. 106.

4 *Ibid.*, p. 137. See also, Richard Thurnwald, "Banaro Society: Social Organization and Kinship System of a Tribe in the Interior of New Guinea," *Memoirs of the American Anthropological Association*, 8, 1916; among other matters of relevance to the analysis of reciprocity, Thurnwald's discussion here (p. 275) opens the issue of the "exchange of women," which Lévi-Strauss later developed.

5 Georg Simmel, *The Sociology of Georg Simmel*, translated and edited by Kurt H. Wolff, Glencoe, Ill.: Free Press, 1950, p. 387.

6 See, respectively, George Homans, "Social Behavior as Exchange," *American Journal of Sociology*," 63 (May, 1958), pp. 597-606; C. Lévi-Strauss, *Les Structures élémentaires de la parenté*, Paris: Presses Universitaires, 1949; and Raymond Firth, *Primitive Polynesian Economy*, New York: Humanities Press, 1950.

7 R. K. Merton, *Social Theory and Social Structure*, Glencoe, Ill.: Free Press, 1957, pp. 46-47.

8 *Ibid.*, p. 33.

9 *Ibid.*, p. 34.

10 *Ibid.*

11 *Ibid.*, p. 73. Among the functions of the political machine to which Merton refers are: the organization and centralization of power so that it can be mobilized to satisfy the needs of different groups, provision of personalized forms of assistance for lowerclass groups, giving political privileges and aid to business groups, and granting protection for illicit rackets.

12 An initial statement of this point is to be found in A. W. Gouldner, "Reciprocity and Autonomy in Functional Theory," in L. Gross, editor, *Symposium on Sociological Theory*, Evanston, Ill.: Row, Peterson, 1959, pp. 241-270.

13 For fuller discussion of this concept, see Gouldner, *ibid*.

14 Use of terms such as "pattern" or "unit" is intended to indicate that the present discussion deliberately collapses distinctions between institutional, interpersonal, group, or role reciprocities, treating them here under a single rubric for reasons of space.

15 Raymond Firth, editor, *Man and Culture: An Evaluation of the Work of Bronislaw Malinowski*, New York: The Humanities Press, 1957, p. 19.

16 The views of these and other analysts of exploitation are ably summarized in C. Gide and C. Rist, *A History of Economic Doctrines*, translated by R. Richards, Boston: Heath, revised edition, 1918.

17 See, e.g., E. A. Ross, *New-Age Sociology*, New York: Appleton-Century, 1940, esp. Chapter 9.

18 Note von Wiese and Becker's comment: "The Marxians trace the social process of exploitation to the 'capitalistic' economic order; their thesis is that capitalism creates exploitation. We, on the other hand, do not deny the existence of capitalistic exploitation, but it is for us only one of the forms which are found among the phenomena of exploitation. The destruction of capitalism will not signalize the end of exploitation, but will merely prevent the appearance of some of its forms and will open up new opportunities for others." L. von Wiese and Howard Becker, *Systematic Sociology*, New York: Wiley, 1932, p. 700. It would seem that 20th century history amply confirms this view.

19 E. Kanin and D. H. Howard, "Postmarital Consequences of Premarital Sex Adjustments," *American Sociological Review*, 23 (October, 1958), p. 558. (My italics.)

20 Kingsley Davis, *Human Society*, New York: Macmillan, 1949, p. 403.

21 *Ibid.*, p. 404.

22 Note Davis's tendency to assume that legitimate sexual relations entail an exchange of *equal* values even though his previous sentence indicates that there may be no more than "a *certain amount* of reciprocity" involved. The latter is a way of talking about *unequal* exchanges and thus implies that these occur in institutionalized and not only in illicit relations. This is an important problem that cannot be developed here.

23 Willard Waller, *The Family: A Dynamic Interpretation*, revised by Reuben Hill, New York: Dryden, 1951, p. 163.

24 The point is not to stress, as Parsons does, the unique exploitability of the patient or the peculiar power of the physician, but to see this relationship as but one dramatic case of a larger class of phenomena of basic theoretic significance which should be explicitly dealt with in systematic theory rather than given only *ad hoc* treatment in specific empirical contexts. See Talcott Parsons, *The Social System*, Glencoe, Ill.: Free Press, 1951, p. 445.

25 The thesis that this is more mythological than real is developed in my introduction to Emile Durkheim, *Socialism and Saint-Simon*, translated by C. Sattler and edited by A. W. Gouldner, Yellow Springs: Antioch Press, 1958, esp. p. ix.

26 Emile Durkheim, *Professional Ethics and Civic Morals*, translated by C. Brookfield, Glencoe, Ill.: Free Press, 1958; see esp. pp. 209-214.

27 Parsons, *op. cit.*, p. 21.

28 Talcott Parsons and Edward A. Shils, editors, *Toward a General Theory of Action*, Cambridge: Harvard University Press, 1951, p. 107.

29 Parsons' tendency to equate complementarity and reciprocity may be illustrated by his comment that "Role expectations organize . . . the reciprocities, expectations, and responses to these expectations in the specific interaction systems of ego and one or more alters. This reciprocal aspect must be borne in mind since the expectations of an ego *always* imply the expectations of one or more alters. It is in this *reciprocity* or *complementarity* that sanctions enter . . . " *Ibid.*, pp. 190-191 (my italics); see also p. 105. The burden of Parsons' analysis attends to the conditions and consequences of complementarity, by which he means that a role player requires of himself what his role partner requires of him. It is precisely for this reason that Parsons emphasizes that values must be held in common by the actors, if their expectations are to be compatible. The equation of reciprocity with complementarity is not peculiar to Parsons. It is evident in the work of other sociologists who sometimes speak

of the rights and obligations in a pair of roles as "reciprocal" and other times as "complementary." And, like Parsons, others state that rights and duties, or role expectations, are *always* complementary.

30 The analysis here closely follows W. D. Ross, *The Right and the Good*, Oxford: Clarendon Press, 1950.

31 Alexander MacBeath, *Experiments in Living*, London: Macmillan, 1952; see esp. pp. 127 ff.

32 Bronislaw Malinowski, *Crime and Custom in Savage Society*, London: Paul, Trench, Trubner, 1932.

33 *Ibid.*, p. 55.

34 This, by the way, is why I cannot concur in Parsons' judgment that Malinowski never disentangled a social system level of analysis from an encyclopedic concept of culture. See Talcott Parsons, "Malinowski and the Theory of Social Systems," in *Man and Culture . . . , op. cit.*, pp. 53-70. Malinowski's *Crime and Custom* transcends a clinical case analysis of specific primitive societies and presents a generalized and basic contribution to the theory of social systems when it addresses itself to the problem of *reciprocity*. Parsons, however, does not mention the significance of reciprocity in Malinowski's work and is able to support his claim that it ignores social system analysis only by this noteworthy omission. Parsons' neglect of the principle of reciprocity in Malinowski's work, it would seem, is consistent with his own neglect of the distinction between reciprocity and complementarity.

35 Malinowski, *op. cit.*, p. 39.

36 *Ibid.*, p. 55.

37 *Ibid.*, p. 39.

38 *Ibid.*, p. 22.

39 *Ibid.*, p. 40. This is not to say, however, that Malinowski regards reciprocity *qua* transaction as *always* intended by all the actors or as something of which they are always aware. In brief—and I agree—there are both latent and manifest reciprocities.

40 Edward Westermarck, *The Origin and Development of the Moral Ideas*, London: Macmillan, 1908, Vol. 2, p. 154.

41 It is further indicative of our terminological difficulties in this area that this is often what Piaget spoke of as "reciprocity." For example, " . . . reciprocity stands so high in the eyes of the child that he will apply it even where to us it seems to border on crude vengeance." J. Piaget, *The Moral Judgment of the Child*, New York: Harcourt, Brace, 1932, p. 216.

43 I suppose that one can take two different attitudes toward this transmutation of the base metal of egoism. One can deplore the situation and say with Eliot:

"The last temptation is the greatest treason;
To do the right thing for the wrong reason."

Or one can adopt the older and perhaps sociologically wiser view that here, once more, "private vices make public benefits," and provide an indispensable basis for the *spontaneous self-regulation* of social systems.

44 This line of analysis is further strengthened if we consider the possibility that Ego's continued conformity with Alter's expectations may eventually lead Alter to take Ego's conformity for "granted" and thus lead Alter to reciprocate less for later acts of conformity by Ego. In short, the value of Ego's conformity

may undergo an inflationay spiral in which his later conforming actions are worth less than earlier ones, in terms of the reciprocities they yield. As reciprocities tend to decline, the social system may experience mounting strain, either collapsing in apathy or being disrupted by conflict. In this connection, the general norm of reciprocity may serve as a brake, slowing the rate at which reciprocities decline or preventing them from declining beyond a certain (unknown) level, and thus contributing to the stability of the system. This is more fully developed in A. W. Gouldner, "Organizational Analysis," in R. K. Merton *et al.*, editors, *Sociology Today*, New York: Basic Books, 1959, esp. pp. 423 ff.

45 An interesting case of a mechanism serving to create and maintain outstanding obligations is part of the Vartan Bhanji, a form of ritual gift exchange in Pakistan and other parts of India. Eglar's study of this pattern makes it clear that a fundamental rule of Vartan Bhanji is reciprocity, that a gift should be returned for a gift, and a favor for a favor. It is also notable that the system painstakingly prevents the total elimination of outstanding obligations. Thus, on the occasion of a marriage, departing guests are given gifts of sweets. In weighing them out, the hostess may say, "These five are yours," meaning "these are a repayment for what you formerly gave me," and she then adds an extra measure, saying, "These are mine." On the next occasion, she will receive these back along with an additional measure which she later returns, and so on. See Z. E. Eglar, *Vartan Bhanji: Institutionalized Reciprocity in a Changing Punjab Village*, Ph.D. thesis, Columbia University, 1958.

Other mechanisms for maintaining outstanding obligations may be found in cultural prescriptions which require men not to be overly eager to repay their social obligations. It still seems to be understood that there is a certain impropriety in this, even if we do not go as far as Seneca in holding that "a person who wants to repay a gift too quickly with a gift in return is an unwilling debtor and an ungrateful person."

46 A cogent illustration of this is provided by William F. Whyte: "When life in the group runs smoothly, the obligations binding members are not explicitly recognized . . . It is only when the relationship breaks down that the underlying obligations are brought to light. While Alec and Frank were friends I never heard either one of them discuss the services he was performing for the other, but when they had a falling out . . . each man complained to Doc that the other was not acting as he should in view of the services which had been done for him." *Street Corner Society*, Chicago: University of Chicago Press, 1945, p. 256.

47 Modern functionalism emerged in a world in which Newtonian mechanics was the overshadowing scientific achievement and a basic model for the development of social sicence. The Newtonian standpoint was not, of course, a cosmology concerned with the question of planetary origins but took the existent relations among planets as given. Today, however, two developments of global significance encourage and perhaps require a shift in social perspectives. In one, rocket engineering, the question is raised as to how

new, man-made, planets may be "shot" into stable orbits. Secondly, international politics require us to help "underdeveloped" countries to *begin* a beneficent cycle of capital accumulation which will be self-sustaining. In both instances, practical "engineering" problems forcefully direct attention to the question of "starting mechanisms" and would seem likely to heighten dissatisfaction with general sociological models that largely confine themselves to already established systems.

48 I am indebted to Howard S. Becker for this and

many other insights into what seemed to be the guiding impulses of the "Chicago School" of collective behavior.

49 Some indications of the utilitarian approach to this problem may be derived from the stimulating paper by T. C. Schelling, "An Essay on Bargaining," *American Economic Review*, 46 (June, 1956), pp. 281-306.

50 Cf. M. Deutsch, "A Study of Conditions Affecting Cooperation," New York: Research Center for Human Relations, 1955, p. 25, dittoed.

THE SIGNIFICANCE OF QUASI-GROUPS IN THE STUDY OF COMPLEX SOCIETIES

ADRIAN C. MAYER

TWO CONCEPTS of major importance for social anthropologists are those of group and association. Both have been defined in a number of ways. Even in the most inclusive view, however, both bodies are held to consist of a number of members with some form of expected interaction, if not rights and obligations, towards one another. Both the association and the group show an 'even spread' of the membership criteria on which this interaction is based, whether these are highly informal or whether they produce a corporate body. Much fruitful work has been carried out with the aid of these concepts. Nevertheless, they are inadequate for those situations involving another kind of collection of people, which may be termed the 'quasi-group'.

Quasi-groups can be divided into two types. The first can be termed that of the classificatory quasi-group. Here, the classification may be made in terms of the common interests which lie beneath what could also be called a 'potential group'. Ginsberg, for example, defines quasi-groups as entities without a 'recognizable structure, but whose members have certain interests or modes of behaviour in common which may at any time lead them to form themselves into definite groups'.[1] The classification may also be made by an individual in terms of his perceived status *vis-á-vis* others, as Barnes shows in his analysis of class mentioned below. I do not propose to deal with this type of quasi-group. Rather, I shall confine myself to quasi-groups of the second type. These possess a degree of organization, but are nevertheless not groups. They can be called interactive quasi-groups, for they are based on an interacting set of people.

These quasi-groups differ fundamentally from the group and the association. First, they are ego-centred, in the sense of depending for their very existence on a specific person as a central organizing focus; this is unlike a group, in which organization may be diffuse. Second, the actions of any member are relevant only in so far as they are interactions between him and ego or ego's intermediary. The membership criteria do not include interaction with other quasi-group members in general.

The interactions of this type of quasi-group occur in an action-set[2] or rather in a series of action-sets. I wish to examine the properties of the action-set by studying it in operation. This I shall do from data gathered in India. But first I must show what is meant by 'set' and how it is related to social network.

NETWORK AND SET

Sets are embedded in the matrices of social links contained in social fields, which have also been called networks. Recent use of the terms 'set' and 'network' has been somewhat confusing, and I will therefore try to clarify the distinction between them.

The term network was used by Radcliffe-Brown (1952, p. 190) when he characterized social structure as being a 'network of actually existing social relations' and maintained that this structure should be the object of the anthropologist's investigation. The relations making up the structure were maintained by a convergence of interests, or at least a 'limitation of conflicts that might arise from divergence of interests' (ibid., p. 199). In some cases, the structure could be defined by a single criterion, as for instance in an Australian tribe, where 'the whole social structure is based on a network of such relations of person to person, established through genealogical connections' (ibid., p. 191).

As Firth (1954, p. 4) points out, Radcliffe-Brown used network to express impressionistically 'what he felt by describing metaphorically what he saw' and it was left to Barnes to give the term a more precise definition.

Barnes saw a network as a social field made up of relations between people. These relations were defined by criteria underlying the field—in the case he cites, for instance, these were criteria of neighbourhood and friendship which might in turn subsume kinship and economic connections. The network was 'unbounded' (at least, by the local boundary of the parish studied)[3] and was without leadership or a coordinating organization. Any person had relations with a number of other people, who in turn were linked to further people.[4] The links might cluster in some parts of the network; but if the people concerned formed a group, their group linkages would exist apart from the network, since an extra criterion would have been added to the linkages defining the network.

The definition of network formed the first step in Barnes's analysis. The second was the identification of sets of people on the basis of linkages provided by the network. The set was different in form from the network. For it was centred on a single person (ego), and consisted of the people classified by him according to a certain criterion. These people thus formed only part of the network—that part which ego recognized as being contained in the set. Barnes's purpose was to use the network-set concept to analyse social class. For him, classes consisted of those people whom an ego identified, through his linkages with them, as comprising sets with statuses above, equal to, or below him. The set did not form a group; nor was ego its leader. But it was at that moment a bounded entity. Moreover, the connections which ego had with the various people he identified in the class context were along 'paths' which might consist of more than one link. It whould be noted that these sets lacked any purposive content, and can therefore be categorized as classificatory sets. Here, they differ from the interactive set of the type previously discussed by Chapple and Coon (1947, p. 283), with which I shall be concerned in this paper. Nevertheless, both types of set are similar in that they are ego-centred and may contain intermediaries between ego (the originator) and the terminal individuals.

The aspect of Barnes's analysis which has re-ceived most attention is his view of the network. Firth admits that the image it presents may be useful and vivid, and Nadel refers to it in his discussion of network. But neither writer considers the part played by the set in Barnes's scheme. For instance, Firth (1954, p. 4) sees Barnes's use of the network as 'a metaphor convenient to describe the personal sets of relationships[5] which characterize the particular structure of a Norwegian fishing community'. I would rather suggest that Barnes conceives of the network as important in so far as it is a *basis* for sets rather than as a means of describing them, and that the two are distinct.

In her study of urban families, Bott uses the term to cover both of Barnes's concepts. On the one hand, a family maintains relationships of friendship, kinship, and neighbourhood with a certain number of other families; these constitute the family's network. On the other hand, each of the other families has its relations with yet other families, many of which are not connected to the initial family at all. Viewed, therefore, from the central family, there is a finite number of relations based on its own interaction, beyond which stretch further links (unbounded from this central family's viewpoint) which have nothing to do with it. Both the bounded and the 'unbounded' entities are included under the rubric network by Bott (1957, p. 58), though it would have been clearer to call the former a set. The articulation between the set of an ego (individual or family) and the network (or social field) which stretches away on all sides is provided by the fact that the 'lateral' links between units other than ego in the set are at the same time elements in other sets centred on these units. Nevertheless, at any given time the component units of a set have a known boundary; it is not one of group membership, as I have pointed out, but of their common connection to the central ego. It is this common link which enables Bott to treat her networks as unit entities which can be analysed and compared.

A reason for Bott's lack of distinction between network and set may well be provided by an ambiguity in Barnes's article itself. On the one hand, Barnes uses the term 'set' in his definition of network, saying

. . . I find it convenient to talk of a social field of this kind as a *network*. The image I have is of a *set*[5] of points some of which are joined by lines. The points of the image are people, or sometimes groups, and the lines indicate which people interact with each other . . . A network of this kind has no external boundary (Barnes, 1954, p. 43, second italics mine).

Here, set is being used in an indefinite way, to

denote the links of a network in the metaphorical way noted by Firth. On the other hand, Barnes uses the term in a different way when he talks of an individual 'generating his set of cognatic kin' and later says ' . . . Thus for every individual A the whole of the network, *or at least that part of it of which he is aware*, is divided into three areas or sets of points' (Barnes, 1954, p. 46, my italics). Here, the set is bounded by ego's vision, and is centred on ego. This, I would maintain, is the more significant use of the word as far as analysis is concerned. But the fact that it is used differently in the two passages may have confused the distinction between the bounded and 'unbounded' entities.

Later writers have followed Bott rather than Barnes in their terminology. Thus, Epstein defines network with reference to a particular individual and the linkages he has with others, and goes on to make a distinction between different parts of this network according to the amount of interaction. Here, network is used in Barnes's sense of the set[6]. Again, Lancaster (1961, p. 326) briefly discusses network mainly in Bott's 'unbounded' sense of the word which, she notes, 'tends to interpret "network" in the Barnes manner'. After stressing the unsatisfactory analytical nature of such 'unbounded' entities, she advocates the use of a delimited unit 'such as the total set of Ego's recognized kin' and says that such a unit would be more suited to comparative analysis. This is, in fact, what I believe Barnes to have concluded; but it is not possible to know whether Lancaster was referring to his article here, since Barnes's use of set is not mentioned. Finally, I myself (Mayer, 1962, p. 275) have also referred to networks both as 'unbounded' as well as defined at a particular time (i.e. bounded); the latter I would now call sets.

It should be noted that Nadel also uses the term network, though in a rather different way. For he equates it to system, since he says that it is through 'abstracting from the concrete population and its behaviour the pattern or network (or "system") of relationships' (Nadel, 1957, p. 12) existing between role-playing actors that social structure is arrived at. Nadel notes that Barnes has used the term in a different sense but, though he recognizes the existence of 'open networks', he places his main emphasis on the systematic nature of the linkages between actors which form a network. The analysis of these kinds of linkages is crucial for Nadel in his building up of social structure on a basis of roles. For it is the interlocking of relationships— through the dichotomization of roles—which brings about an expansion of the areas of rela-

tionships into networks. These can be of an open-ended kind, similar to the fields envisaged by Barnes; or they can be into bounded sub-groups, whose systematic interrelation makes up the social structure. Nadel stresses that both kinds of network exist in a society, but he is more interested in the latter and therefore devotes little attention to the open-ended network.

To sum up: there has been an attempt by social anthropologists to put forward two concepts for dealing with social situations in which collections of people are found that do not form groups. One is the 'unbounded' network of relationships between pairs of people, making up a field of activity. The other is the finite set of linkages initiated by an ego, which forms part of such a network.[7] Despite some ambiguity over terminology, these two concepts are distinguished by both Barnes and Bott and by others. We can further distinguish between the classificatory set discussed by Barnes, and Bott's set (i.e. the 'network' of her analysis) which is based on interaction around an ego. The latter is made up of people brought into contact in a variety of situations and over a period of time. It is the sum, as it were, of the people involved in a series of purposive action-sets in specific contexts. To find out more about it, therefore, one must first inquire into the characteristics of the action-set. This I will do now, using my own material on political processes in India.

THE DEWAS ELECTORAL SITUATION

My data come from the Dewas District of Madhya Pradesh State in India.[8] The District has a population of 446,901 (1961) and is situated some 75 miles west of the State's capital of Bhopal, and 20 miles north-east of the industrial town of Indore. Part of it is prosperous farming country, in which cotton and wheat are major cash crops. Here is situated Dewas town, the District headquarters and only sizeable urban centre, with a population of 34,577 in 1961.

Until 1948, Dewas town was divided into halves, which were the capitals of the States of Dewas Senior and Dewas Junior. The town was politically united after the Princely States were merged into the Indian Union in that year, and a single Municipality was constituted. The Municipal Council has a degree of autonomy in civic affairs, and is elected by universal suffrage. There have been three elections, and I wish to focus my attention on the last one, which took place in April 1961.

I have already given a general description of this event elsewhere (Mayer, 1963). There, I considered the types of workers active in the campaign, and the bases on which they and their candidates solicited and attracted votes. The various political parties each had a core of full-time election 'workers' (the English word being used). These primary workers helped with the organization of the campaign—by arranging meetings, etc., and helping to recruit secondary workers. The latter were people who would at least commit themselves to the support of a party (by contrast to a large part of the electorate) and who would perhaps join in canvassing parties and undertake to get the vote out in their localities. There were about 250 primary workers of all parties in the town's 14 wards, and perhaps between two and three times as many secondary workers, out of a total electorate of 16,332.

These workers acted as links between the candidate and the electorate. Sometimes they did this for the advantages they calculated would accrue to them if the candidate were elected; sometimes they were acting because of party loyalty and friendships formed over the years without any thoughts of gain from the election itself; and at yet other times they were discharging specific obligations contracted at earlier times. In the same way, there was an attempt to reach voters on the basis of a past or future benefit. As one shrewd observer told me, 'Every man will bleed; it is a question of knowing which is the vein to open so that he will bleed most.' In consequence, a great deal of the electioneering was carried out by workers, who sought to influence those with whom they had some appropriate relationship. Besides this, the candidate himself canvassed voters, often as a formal duty towards those who wished to have been asked for their vote. Both the general ideological and the local urban policies of the parties, as expressed in public meetings, were also deemed to have played some part in influencing voters. I am less interested in these latter aspects than in the pattern of interpersonal contacts through which votes were said to have been recruited; for it is from these that we can abstract the action-set. To show this I will present the detailed situation in one candidate's campaign.

The ward in which this candidate fought provided one of the key contests of the election. In the previous election, the seat had been won by the Congress party in a triangular contest with the Praja Socialists (PSP) and an Independent. Sixty per cent of the 852 electors had voted, and the Congress (with 210 votes) had just beaten the Independent (205 votes), though the 90 votes gathered by the PSP meant that victory was gained on a minority vote. In the succeeding term of the Municipality, the victor was said to have paid little attention to the repair of his polit-

ical fences in the ward. He lived in another part of the town, and was a busy professional man. The Independent loser, on the other hand, was a resident of the ward. Over the years, he had built up strong support, partly through people's discontent with the sitting Councillor, and partly through the public and private work which he was sometimes able to do through intercession with officials and so forth.

At the 1961 election, then, the Independent stood again. This time he was an official Jan Sangh candidate. He himself did not appear to be an active party member, but received whatever support the rather sketchy Jan Sangh election organization was able to give him. He was opposed on Congress's behalf by another resident of the ward; this was a man who had recently retired from a senior government post, and who had previously held important appointments in the service of Dewas Senior, to which this part of the town had belonged. The candidate had not been a member of Congress before his retirement, and he too, therefore, was not part of the inner party organization; nevertheless, the support he received from Congress party leaders was considerably greater than that given to the Jan Sangh candidate. By contrast with his opponent, the Congress candidate had not built up any sort of ward support before being nominated, and had to start mobilizing followers there and then. The third candidate, representing the PSP, was a resident of the ward, but had little influence and received minimal support from PSP party leaders. The main contest was therefore between Congress and Jan Sangh.

Physically, economically, and socially, the ward is heterogeneous. Situated at the north-eastern end of the town, a large part of its people live in mud houses built along earthen streets in the same style as in the surrounding villages. Other people live in houses similar to those of wealthier villagers, with inside courtyards formed by house and cattle byres; and yet others reside in urban-style houses surrounded by gardens. Beyond them lie barracks housing a detachment of the State's Special Armed Police, many of whom are eligible to vote. Within the ward, there is no meeting square and few stores exist. People gather mainly within each street, at informal sitting-places under a tree or on the porch of a temple or teashop. This has an obvious effect on the kind of election campaign that can be organized and strengthens the tendency to stress individual contacts, rather than to rely on public meetings.

A survey shows the main occupations of the population to be as set out in Table 1.

TABLE 1*

Occupation	Per cent
Manual labour	38.2
Government officials	15.9
Farming and dairying	14.7
Pension	6.5
Construction: artisan and contractor	5.3
Commerce and hotel-keeping	5.3
Services: legal, domestic, medical, etc.	4.7
Other	9.4
Total	100.0

*These figures are compiled from a 20 per cent sample made on the basis of the 1957 voters' list: I doubt whether there have been great changes since then. The information was gathered from knowledgeable residents, rather than from a door-to-door inquiry, but is probably none the less accurate for that. The categories are those of the Dewas Census; where a woman's name appeared on the sample, her husband's occupation was taken.

As might be expected, occupations are to some extent correlated with the main castes represented in the ward. The same survey shows these to be as set out in Table 2.

TABLE 2

Caste	Per cent
Goali	17.1
Bagri	17.1
Lunia	10.0
Balai	9.4
Rajput	8.2
Northern (Rangre) Brahman	8.2
Maratha	6.5
Maharashtrian Brahman	5.9
Other	17.6
Total	100.0

The Brahmans and Marathas are mainly in government service, and many of the Rajputs farm land in the countryside beyond the ward boundaries. In this, they have Goali and Bagri farm labour; there are also a few Bagri policemen and government messengers, and a number of Goali dairymen. For the rest, the men of these castes are manual labourers, as are the Balais and Lunias—the latter specializing in the building trade. Hierarchically, below the Brahmans come Marathas and Rajputs, and Goali, Lunia and Bagri, and Balai follow.

It is clear that a candidate cannot be elected on the support of a single caste, or of a single occupational interest. Hence, pressure has to be brought on various sections of the electorate. This may be in terms of policy, or it may be through linkages stretching from each candidate directly or through intermediaries to the voter. The pattern of the Congress candidate's linkages, as they were described to me and as I observed them, is given in the diagram.

I must stress that the diagram shows the links

known to me.[9] Further study would possibly have revealed others; but this outline of the situation is, I believe, sufficient to indicate what the full pattern would look like. Moreover, it is probable that, at least where factions are involved, there are several further links before the voter is reached; but I do not know enough about these alignments to be able to show them diagrammatically. As I have pointed out, these are not the only contacts made by the candidate with the public; nor do they show all the reasons why people supported him. Some, for instance, may have done so because of his party's official policy; others may have voted for him because of the auspiciousness of his party's electoral symbol—the best example in the election of purely ideological support, which in other cases might underlie other reasons (e.g. support of a castemate is partly ideological and partly self-interested). But it is these links which are of interest, because I would maintain that they constitute an action-set in the context of this election. What are the characteristics of this action-set, and what is its relation to the underlying network?

CHARACTERISTICS OF A DEWAS
ELECTORAL ACTION-SET

One feature of this action-set is that a wide variety of bases for linkage are involved. Included as criteria are kinship, political party, religious sect, and so on. But the crucial point is that, whatever may be these 'outward' bases for the links which together make up the path from candidate to voter, the 'inward' content is always the same—namely political support of the candidate. Thus, action-sets of this kind are formed of links derived from many social fields; but because they are purposive creations by an ego, this purpose gives all the links a common feature, without which the action-set could not be classed under the quasi-group rubric. This results in an action-set whose structure may be similar to the classificatory set described by Barnes, but whose content is different. Rather, it is similar to the set envisaged by Chapple and Coon, at whose centre is an 'originator' of linkages.

A second feature of the action-set is that the links are sometimes, but not always, based on group membership. Many of the candidate's closest links were party-political ones, based on the primary group of active Congress workers which he joined upon his adoption as candidate. Other instances of primary group links are provided by membership of the same wrestling gymnasium, or of a group of religious worshippers.

THE PATTERN OF THE CONGRESS CANDIDATE'S LINKAGES

Examples of links through secondary group membership would be those based on distant kinship relations,[10] and also, perhaps, membership of the same village or trade union—though these latter might be primary group links. Yet further from primary membership were the ties evoked through common caste. A crucial linkage, for example, was made between a Rajput Congress worker and Bagri voters. Bagris, officially a Backward Class, can produce 'historical' evidence which they believe gives them Rajput status. But this is not generally accepted by the Rajputs of Malwa. Hence, when the Congress worker showed that he did not object to eating and drinking with Bagris in their homes, they were greatly attracted to the Congress candidate—particularly since the Rajput supporters

of the Jan Sangh were strongly conservative over such matters. More than mere sentiment was involved; for it was said that the Rajput had told the Bagris that they could become members of the newly instituted Dewas branch of the Rajput Parishad, a social organization restricted to Rajputs.[11] I shall return later to this transactional element in linkages.

Some links are not based on group membership at all, of course. Examples would include the economic links of employer-employee, creditor-debtor, storekeeper, customer, etc. Again, people with a history of service to the Maharaja did not form part of any group. The fact that some links are based on group relations does not affect the form of the action-set. For such groups are not contained within the action-set, nor are their aims necessarily relevant to the purpose of the latter. The action-set is a different kind of entity from a group, though it may include group relations in its 'outward' content of links.

A third feature is that (as Barnes shows) the action-set contains paths of linkages, and is thus a combination of relationships linking people directly to ego, and of those linking people to intermediaries who are themselves in direct contact with ego. In this it differs from the units of Bott's analysis, which contained linkages between people who were all directly linked to ego; and one might find it useful to distinguish between simple and complex action-sets on this basis.

Fourth, the action-set is a bounded entity. It is not a group, however. For the basis for membership is specific to each linkage, and there are no rights or obligations relating all those involved; even the common act of voting for ego does not bring members into relation with each other.[12] Moreover, the action-set could not exist without the ego around whom it is formed. Yet, it is different in quality from a category. For members are aware that they form part of a population recruited for a particular common purpose, and they know that there are other linkages similar to theirs—though they may not be able to identify all the other people involved.

Finally, the action-set is not a 'permanent' entity like the group. Although the 'outward' aspects are those of continuing role-relationships—e.g. those of Caste, etc.—the 'inward' aspect is that of a linkage based on a specific purposive impulse stemming from ego. This action-set thus exists only at ego's election. Any action-set constructed for a future election might contain a majority of the same people. But many of the linkages would have to be re-made since, as I shall suggest later, they are based on specific transactions. To the extent that the same linkages remain in use in successive contexts of activity, a quasi-group is formed, as I shall discuss later.

THE ACTION-SET IN COMPARATIVE STUDY

A major feature of the action-set is that by contrast with the 'unbounded' network it is limited in its membership and can therefore be used in comparative analysis and in the study of social change. Let me give a few examples from the Dewas electoral situation I have described.

One could compare, for instance, the patterns of linkage in the action-sets of the three candidates in the ward. I did not study in such detail the action-set centred on the Jan Sangh candidate, but it was clear that it differed from that of his Congress opponent. Partly this was because, as I have said, the Jan Sangh candidate had gathered support over the past three years. He therefore had an action-set in which he was generally directly in contact with voters, or at the most stood at one remove from them. By contrast the Congress candidate started to work less than a month before the election. He could therefore make only superficial contacts with most voters, and had to rely on recruiting primary workers, who would then construct their own linkages. There were thus more intermediaries, and longer paths, in the Congress action-set.

This kind of comparison is connected to the analysis of election strategies.[13] I have elsewhere (Mayer, 1963, p. 126) distinguished between 'hard' and 'soft' campaigns in the Dewas elections. In the former, support is lined up at the start, and any attacks on prepared positions are rebuffed by the candidate or his workers, who keep especially close watch on the opposing primary workers. In the latter, a drive at the end of the campaign is calculated to produce enough pressure to win, without the need for elaborate fence-mending among waverers and constant counter-bidding for those who sell their support in some way. In this ward, the Jan Sangh conducted the harder and the Congress the softer campaign. Now, it is possible to argue that an action-set with shorter paths will be more appropriate to a harder campaign. For any damage done by an opponent will be more quickly apparent to the candidate, who can then counteract it. The long-pathed set, on the other hand, would seem to be better for a softer campaign. For it involves a late drive by the largest number of supporters. Hence, whether by design or by their previous connection with the ward, the candidates' strategies and the pattern of their electoral action-sets can be correlated.

Another basis for comparison is the number of lateral links. By lateral link is meant a connection between intermediaries without reference to either ego or the terminal respondents. Lateral links are defined in terms of relevance to the criterion governing the formation of the action-set. In this case, then, only the lateral links connected with ego's election are relevant. This is not to deny, of course, that there are many lateral *network* ties linking people in the action-set, which are not used by ego or his intermediaries to achieve their ends. We must distinguish between the potential material of network links, and those links which are actually used in the action-set's constitution. The lateral linkage in an action-set does not indicate the complete pattern of interaction between members. For instance, in our diagram there is only one lateral linkage (between A and B) in terms of ego's recruitment of votes; yet, there would have been very many in terms of general interaction, notably those between all the people who were directly linked to the candidate as members of the Congress party. But these latter connections did not appear to recruit voters directly,[14] and so are not relevant to this action-set.

Lateral linkages can be contrasted with what might be called the multipronged linkage. This occurs when a respondent is linked to several intermediaries and possibly directly to ego as well. It differs from the lateral link, which is between intermediaries themselves. An example of a multipronged linkage in the action-set I have described would be the approach by several people to the Bagri voters (marked C). In terms of outward content, the lateral linkage brings several pressures to bear on an intermediary to approach the respondent, whereas the multipronged linkage brings several pressures to bear on the terminal respondent himself.

Clearly, the pattern of lateral and multipronged connections will reflect a difference in electoral campaigns. One might speculate, for example, that the part of the electorate at which the greatest number of prongs are pointed is the part which has the critical votes in the election. This would certainly be true as regards the Bagri vote in this ward, for it provided the balance of victory and was notoriously fickle. One might also suggest that the candidate with the action-set having the greatest number of lateral linkages is operating the strongest campaign, since intermediaries who might find a single inducement inadequate for their support are fortified by a second incentive coming to them laterally. The matter clearly needs further research; for one could also say that an action-set in which no lateral ties exist is one in which loyalties must be firm enough not to require reinforcement. Such an analysis of action-sets could help to examine these and similar hypotheses on the nature of the political process.

Another example of the comparative and explanatory value of the action-set comes from an investigation of the content of its linkages. This reveals that linkages exist because they carry transactions furthering in some way the interests of the parties concerned. The interest of the transactor is the same in each case—it is the interest of the ego around whom the action-set has formed (in my example, the interest of his election). The interest of the respondent can vary,

ranging from specific aims to be fulfilled immediately after the election (such as help in arranging a marriage), to a generalized interest of potential help of some sort in the future.

This transactional element distinguishes action-set linkage from network linkage. True, persons linked in a network may derive some benefit from their relationships; but this is not because of the very nature of the relationship, and many of these relationships have an only minimally interactional aspect, a fact which prompted Firth's (1954, p. 4) caution when considering their part in defining the network.

In the Dewas example, the transactional element distinguishes the linkages of the action-set from other contacts between candidate and electorate. As I have said, the candidate personally met most of the voters in the ward in the course of his canvassing tours. These meetings were, it is true, transactional in the widest sense of the word; for the candidate would ask for support in return for promises to improve the roads, the water supply, etc. But such appeals to the voter were made publicly, and were made in the same terms to *all* voters. The support given through the linkages in the diagram, on the other hand, were specific to an individual, or, at most, a few people. The campaign, therefore, contained activities at two levels: one was a public level, at which promises were given to the general electorate as part of the party's stated programme; the other was the private level, at which the promises given, and obligations encashed, were not necessarily connected with the party's programme for the Municipality. The first could be called diffusely and the second specifically transactional.

These two kinds of contact with electors can be used to distinguish different types of candidate and electoral campaign. In Dewas, for example, there were clear examples of both specifically and diffusely transactional candidates. The latter were mainly concerned with appealing to all sections of the electorate, and therefore phrased their campaign in non-partisan terms, promising to do their best for the ward. The former made no public speeches at all, as far as I could ascertain, and went on few canvassing expeditions in the ward. Instead, they concentrated on recruiting a number of allies who would each bring a few voters with him. The further analysis of why particular candidates operated a particular type of campaign will tell us more about small-town politics and politicians.

A study of action-set linkages in Dewas reveals two types of specific transaction, namely, those of patronage and brokerage. In the first, the transactor has the power to give some benefit which the respondent desires; upon fulfillment of the latter's part the benefit is made available. Examples of this would be the improvement of a road near the respondent's house, or the employment of the respondent (or his relative) in an office over which the transactor has control. The number and extent of such benefits naturally vary with the power of the transactor; but even the most influential is unlikely to be able to please everyone who comes to him, or who needs to be brought into the action-set. He must therefore husband these direct patronage transactions so that they produce linkages with key people who can bring followers with them.

Patronage resources are thus not unlimited; and patronage is an unambiguous transaction, in which the responsibility for any failure to redeem a promise can be clearly put down to the patron. The brokerage transaction differs somewhat in both these respects. A broker is a middle-man, and the transaction is one in which he promises to obtain favours for the respondent from a third person. Thus, brokers are intermediaries for the favours of government officials, or they have influence with powerful townsmen and are said to be able to expedite the business of the respondent. The ultimate responsibility for action rests not on the broker, however, but rather on the person to whom he has access. Clearly, the broker cannot maintain his reputation if too many of his efforts are unsuccessful; but at least some failures can be explained away by putting the blame on his contact. Hence, the broker can enter into more transactions, in relation to his resources of power, than can the patron. Both may make what turn out to be campaign promises at election time; but the broker has greater possibilities of doing so, since the patron will often be inhibited by unfulfilled promises of the past, or the fear of over-extending his activity.

Though these two types of transaction may overlap in practice, and though (as I have said) not all respondents have specific and immediate interests in mind, the distinction helps to explain the linkages of an action-set and their patterning. For instance, the patrons in an action-set may not deal directly through intermediary brokers. One may, therefore, expect to find action-sets with longer paths of linkages where there are the more powerful patrons—other things being equal. This may be a reason why the Congress action-set in the diagram had longer paths than did the Jan Sangh action-set in the same ward (as I have noted). For Congress, as the ruling party, held greater powers of patronage in its hands.

ACTION-SET AND QUASI-GROUPS

I believe that these examples show the value of the action-set concept in the study of political activities. How is it related to the concept of the quasi-group and what value does this approach have for the study of complex societies?

The action-set exists in a specific context which provides the terms of ego's purpose in forming linkages. When successive action-sets are centred on similar contexts of activity, personnel and linkages may also be similar. By 'superimposing' a series of action-sets, therefore, one may discern a number of people who are more often than not members of the action-sets, and others who are involved from time to time. Taken together, these people form a catchment for ego's action-sets based on this type of context. It is this potential membership which Bott calls a network; for all the people in any family's (or individual's) networks are not recruited on every occasion, but are possible members. Again, Epstein's network is of this sort, and he distinguishes between its effective and extended membership. I have already said why I do not consider network to be a very happy term here. Set is less confusing; it fits into Barnes's terminology and I have talked of classificatory and interactive sets at the start of this paper. But I think it may be well to adopt the word quasi-group, since this best expresses the sociological implications of this type of collection of people and suggests the qualitative difference between the quasi-group and the group.

The quasi-group, then, has the same pattern of linkages as the action-set, and exists through a series of contexts of activity without any formal basis for membership. The people who are more constantly involved in the successive action-sets need not be those closest to ego. It is possible to conceive of a supporter of a candidate in successive elections who is recruited through paths composed of different and transient intermediaries. However, when the more constant members *are* at the same time those directly linked to ego, one can characterize them as the 'core' of the quasi-group. This core may later crystallize into a formal group; in the example I have given, this might involve the starting of a ward branch of the Congress party, to which those core members resident in the ward would belong. If it does not become a formal group, it can be seen to be a clique. This is a body of informally linked people, having a high rate of interaction and with that 'even spread' of membership activities which I have said distinguishes the group from the quasi-group. Though possessing leaders, cliques are not ego-centered bodies.[15] Where there is a clique at the centre of the quasi-group, it is possible for different egos, as members of the clique, to evoke the same pattern of linkages in different action-sets having similar contexts, and even in different contexts. Thus, where the core becomes a formal group or a clique, it may be possible to take it, rather than an individual, as the central ego—as Bott takes the whole family, rather than any single member, as her central unit.

It is clear that quasi-groups can be found in many arenas of social activity. In politics, for instance, a succession of action-sets of the kind we have seen to exist in Dewas would add up to form a quasi-group which could be called a faction. For, according to one view,[16] factions are units of conflict activated on specific occasions rather than maintained by a formal organization. They are 'loosely ordered' and with 'structurally diverse' bases of recruitment, and they are made manifest through a linkage of personal authority between leader and follower.[17] They are also based more on transactions than on issues of principle (Mayer, 1961, pp. 135-136), and may have groups or cliques as cores.

One way to study factions is to analyse the action-sets which make them up, focusing on such features as the size of core and periphery, the nature of the outward content of linkages, and the lengths of paths in various situations. From this could be built up a picture of the developmental cycle of factions, since an analysis of the content and pattern of linkages and their correlation with rivalries may reveal to us more about the critical point at which factions split.[18] From such a study would come a greater understanding of political situations involving quasi-groups rather than organized political units.

Quasi-groups also exist in the economic sphere, as an example from Dewas shows. Each of the sub-district towns, and the headquarters of Dewas, is concerned with the purchase of crops and their export from the District. This is done in officially supervised markets, where crop dealers buy from farmers. How do these dealers recruit and maintain their customers? Here, again, we can see action-sets, with the dealer as the central ego. For it is he who recruits a following with an 'inward' linkage based in each case on economic advantage, but with an 'outward' linkage resting on many criteria, including those of locality and common subcaste. We cannot say that all farmers dealing with a particular trader form a group; but since each is aware that many others (some of whom he knows) deal with the same trader they form an action-set at each harvest. Over a succession

of harvests, there is some variation in the composition of the action-sets, since there is no compulsion to continue to deal with a particular trader. Nevertheless, there is also a continuity[19] within which a quasi-group is built up—one could call it a clientele. These clienteles can be studied in much the same way as I have suggested for political quasi-groups.

In the field of kinship, too, one can discern quasi-groups. In Central Indian peasant society, for example, a person has a number of kin whom he calls on for help in his affairs. I have called this the kindred of co-operation (Mayer, 1960, p. 4); one might characterize it as a quasi-group formed from a succession of action-sets centred on the individual or his household. Again, in talking of Iban society, Freeman distinguishes between the *de jure* kindred which constitutes a field of cognatic relations, and the *de facto* relationships of moral obligation which a man activates within this field and which form a major basis for recruitment to action-groups containing mainly cognatic kin though also including affines and friends (Freeman, 1961, pp. 202-211).[20] These action-groups sometimes appear to be organized groups (e.g. the travelling groups), but on other occasions seem to correspond to the action-sets I have described, and repeated recruitment might well produce a quasi-group.

The action-sets made up of kin are not mutually exclusive. Kindreds of cooperation form a series of overlapping collections of people and an individual belongs to many at once, as he would not belong to different political factions or clienteles—an exception to this would be where two kinsmen are in opposition and recruit kin as supporters. Again, the outward content of recruitment is always at least partly one of kinship and its entailed moral obligations, whatever other incentives there may be to support ego; hence the content of linkages is less heterogeneous than it is in other action-sets. Thus we should perhaps see the kin-based quasi-group as a special and more restricted form.

More study is needed of this question, as well as of many others. For instance, what are the circumstances surrounding the emergence of cores and the part they play in the operation of the quasi-group; or what are the influences of space and time on quasi-groups? Again, what are the possibilities of making action-sets more easily comparable? One could, for example, tabulate the content of the first, second, third, etc., links along paths; one could also distinguish paths with different numbers of links, and thereby attempt to present a picture of the action-set without a cumbersome diagram of the kind I have presented. Quantification must, however, adequately express the total configuration, rather than merely categorize the properties of single links and paths; if this can be done, action-sets and consequently quasi-groups can be more easily compared.

CONCLUSION

I have attempted in this paper to see whether certain concepts may not be fruitful for social anthropologists. The identification of the action-set and the quasi-group owes much, of course, to the sociometric approach; it is also connected to analyses of other informal collections of people, such as cliques. Again, the action-set can be seen in terms of status- and role-sets (Merton, 1957, p. 368 et seq.). For a person as an ego has a role-set composed of relations towards intermediaries and terminal respondents; and as an intermediary he has a role-set comprising roles towards ego, respondents and perhaps further intermediaries. At a different level, ego and his intermediaries, and the intermediaries and the respondents, are linked by roles chosen from their status-sets. That is, an ego or an intermediary in a Dewas election will choose roles from the role-sets of caste, party, trade union, or from other role-sets in his status-set to attract followers. These two levels are connected with the inward and outward content of action-set linkages respectively.

The title of this paper suggests that I should discuss to what extent these concepts have particular reference to the study of complex societies. But, quite apart from a reluctance to involve myself in an effort to distinguish between complex and simple societies, I suggest that the action-set and the quasi-group are concepts which may apply in *any* situation where no organized groups operate. It is therefore relatively unimportant to assess whether they are more useful in complex than in simple societies. If indeed there are action-sets among, say, the Iban, one clearly cannot restrict the discussion to complex societies. Yet if one defines simple and complex societies as more and less involute (Nadel, 1957, p. 68) systems of role-relations, one might expect social relations in simpler societies to be more likely to be those of common group membership than they are in societies where there is a greater scatter of roles. If this be so, then the organizing of people in a simpler society will be more likely to bring together people with common group membership;[21] thus, in a given context, a sub-group will be more likely to form than an action-set.

Whether or not this be true, I have myself found that an approach of the kind I have outlined presented itself to me in the 'complex situation' of the Dewas election. It may well be that, as social anthropologists become more interested in complex societies and as the simpler societies themselves become more complex, an increasing amount of work will be based on ego-centred entities such as action-sets and quasi-groups, rather than on groups and sub-groups. This paper, therefore, is an attempt to explore and clarify the concepts involved, by applying them to an actial situation.

REFERENCES

Barnes, J. A. 1954. Class and Committees in a Norwegian Island Parish. *Human Relations* 7:39-58.

Bott, E. 1957. *Family and Social Network*. London: Tavistock Publications.

Chapple, E. D. & Coon, C. C. S. 1947. *Principles of Anthropology*. London: Cape.

Epstein, A. L. 1961. The Network & Urban Social Organisation. *Rhodes-Livingstone Institute Journal* 29:29-62.

Firth, R. W. 1954. Social Organization & Social Change. *Journal of the Royal Anthropological Institute* 84:1-20.

1957. Factions in Indian & Overseas Indian Societies: Introduction. *British Journal of Sociology* 8:291-295.

Freeman, J. D. 1961. On the Concept of the Kindred. *Journal of the Royal Anthropological Institute* 91:192-200.

Ginsberg, M. 1934. *Sociology*. London: butterworth.

Lancaster, L. 1961. Some theoretical Problems in the Study of Family & Kin Ties in the British Isles. *British Journal of Sociology* 12:317-333.

Loomis, C. P. & Beegle, J. A. 1950. *Rural Social Systems*. New York: Prentice-Hall.

Mayer, A. C. 1960. *Caste & Kinship in Central India*. London: Routledge & Kegan Paul.

1961. *Peasants in the Pacific: A Study of Fiji Indian Rural Society*. London: Routledge & Kegan Paul.

1962. System & Network: An Approach to the Study of Political Process in Dewas. In T. N. Madan & G. Sarana (eds.), *Indian Anthropology*. Bombay: Asia.

1963. Municipal Elections: A Central Indian Case Study. In C. H. Philips (ed.), *Politics & Society in India*. London: Allen & Unwin.

Merton, R. K. 1957. *Social Theory & Social Structure* (Rev. Edn.). Glencoe, Ill.: Free Press.

Mitchell, W. E. 1963. Theoretical Problems in the Concept of Kindred. *American Anthropologist* 65:343-354.

54

Moreno, J. L. 1953. *Who Shall Survive? Foundations of Sociometry, Group Psychotherapy & Sociodrama*. Beacon: Beacon House.

Nadel, S. F. 1957. *The Theory of Social Structure*. London: Cohen & West.

Radcliffe-Brown, A. R. 1952. *Structure & Function in Primitive Society*. London: Cohen & West.

Siegel, B. J. & Beals, A. R. 1960. Conflict and Factional Dispute. *Journal of the Royal Anthropological Institute* 90:107-117.

Snyder, R. C. 1955. Game Theory & the Analysis of Political Behaviour. In S. K. Bailey *et al.*, *Research Frontiers In Politics & Government*. Washington: Brookings Institution.

Sower, C. *et al.* 1957. *Community Involvement: The Webs of Formal & Informal Ties That Make for Action*. Glencoe, Ill.: Free Press.

Truman, D. B. 1959. *The Congressional Party: A Case Study*. New York: Wiley.

Whyte, W. F. 1955. *Street Corner Society*. Chicago: Chicago University Press.

NOTES

1 Ginsberg (1934, p. 40). Such quasi-groups are noted in field research too (e.g. Sower, 1957, p. 276). See also the use of the term 'collectivity' in this connection (Merton, 1957, p. 299).

2 I am indebted to Dr. P. H. Gulliver for this term.

3 One must emphasize that a network is, of course, bounded by the total population which is being examined, or by the discontinuities in social relations produced by its own criteria. Hence, the 'unboundedness' is only relative.

4 Cf. the introduction of the term 'chain' by Moreno (1953, p. 720) as 'an open series of mutual choices on any criterion'.

5 A printer's error makes Bott (1957, p. 59) misquote Barnes as saying "The image I have is of a net of points . . . ".

6 In saying that Barnes calls it a network when a person 'is in touch with a number of people, some of whom may be in touch with each other, and some of whom may not', Epstein (1961, p. 56) takes only the first part of Barnes's characterization; but this continues, 'each person has a number of friends and these friends have their own friends; some of any one person's friends know each other, others do not' (Barnes, 1954, p. 43). The difference here is between a finite set and an 'unbounded' entity.

7 Cf. the matrix of interrelated pairs constructed by Truman from voting records in the U. S. Congress, within which can be discerned the clusters which he calls blocs (Truman, 1959).

8 Research was conducted in 1960-1961 with the generous aid of the School of Oriental and African Studies, University of London.

9 For simplicity's sake, I have not shown the direct influence people acting as intermediaries may have on voters, but have marked only their links with others in the path itself.

10 I have called all links based on common subcaste 'kin' ties, since the people involved were all more or less distantly related; they are distinct from ties based on the membership of two subcastes in a caste, which I have called 'caste' ties.

11 When asked whether this pledge would be redeemed after the election, another Congress supporter cynically remarked that the issue would never arise. For Bagris would forgo Rajput status if it were pointed out to them that the considerable benefits they now received as a Backward Class would cease forthwith.

12 As Bott (1957, p. 58) says, 'In an organized group, the component individuals make up a larger social whole with common aims, interdependent roles, and a distinctive sub-culture. In network formation on the other hand, only some, not all, of the component individuals have social relationships with one another.'

13 I use this word in its popular, rather than in its game theory, meaning (see Snyder, 1955, p. 79).

14 A large number of links in the diagram are based on statements made by the interested parties to me or to other people in my hearing. Others are the results of my own observations and inferences, and of third-person information. In both cases, there may be other reasons for the actions of people, since it is impossible to know whether motives have been adequately assessed.

15 One must distinguish between those cliques formally recognized by the people themselves (e.g. those dealt with in Whyte, 1955) and those which the observer isolates. Loomis & Beegle (1950, p. 141) provide an example of the latter, in which there is an almost comprehensive series of linkages between clique members and an almost complete discontinuity of relations with the outside.

16 For another approach, see Siegel and Beals (1960).

17 Firth (1957, p. 292), summing up the conclusions of a symposium on factions.

18 For instance, my diagram shows that one of ego's close supporters has almost as many radiating linkages as ego himself. How far can splits be predicted where the linkages of supporters outnumber those of ego?

19 This is due in part to the contracting of debts with the dealer; hence there is less mobility than might be the case were the action-set to rest solely on the price offered by the dealer.

20 Freeman limits the kindred to cognatic kin, excluding affines. I have myself included the latter in my definition (and see Mitchell, 1963, p. 351). The issue here is not a terminological one, however, but one of the constitution of the action-sets and quasi-groups formed from these ties.

21 As Merton (1957, p. 311) puts it, 'in less differentiated societies, group affiliation tends to engage a considerably larger share of each member's personality'.

FACTIONS:
A Comparative Analysis
RALPH W. NICHOLAS

COMPARATIVE POLITICS is a variety of research usually conducted by political scientists and aimed at comprehending structures and events of significance for the governments of entire nation states. Nowadays it is customary for students of this subject to include one or more non-Western governments in their comparisons. Local politics, another subdivision of political science, has remained largely a Western enterprise, practiced by Westerners on small-scale political arenas found in their own countries. Social anthropologists have a well-established concern with small-scale non-Western political institutions, but comparison (when it is admitted as a legitimate method) has been confined to similar and related tribal political systems, largely in Africa. By this means, the study of *institutional* politics, systems in which principles of recruitment and alignment are relatively clear, has progressed. Such studies generally place only as much emphasis upon political *process* as is consonant with an interest in political structure. My study of politics in some Indian peasant communities, however, and preliminary comparison with descriptions of politics in other peasant societies, suggest that social anthropologists may be able to make contributions to general political studies and comparative politics by elucidating small-scale, non-institutional political processes in non-Western societies. This paper deals with 'faction', one kind of political process which I found it necessary to understand in analyzing the politics of Indian peasant villages. In studying faction one must, as Professor Firth (1957, p. 294) says, leave 'the well-trodden ground of conventional structural analysis for a type of inquiry which is from the outset an examination of "dynamic phenomena"'. The faction is a troublesome form of social organization—troublesome because of the frequency with which it appears in primitive and peasant societies, and because it is so refractory to the usual analytic methods. Here, by comparing several different cases of factional development and conflict, I attempt to analyze factions as a special form of political organization. I have studied factional politics in two distinct kinds of society: the reservation society of the Six Nations' Iroquois Confederacy in Canada, and some peasant villages in India.[1] Most of what is said here about the social organization of factions and about the relationship between factionalism and political change derives from these societies. In order to determine the essential principles of factional organization—to give a sociological definition of 'faction'—I have drawn on published cases of factional politics in five different societies and social institutions. A number of social scientists have commented upon various aspects of factionalism, and I shall attempt to examine some of their views in one or another of the sections into which this paper is divided: (I) definition, (II) social organization, and (III) political change. Before taking up the sociological definition of the phenomenon, however, I would like to make clear two important assumptions.

Lasswell (1931, p. 51) points out that 'the term faction has been employed as an opprobrious epithet in the political field since Roman days . . . A faction seems to subordinate the public good to private gain, and thus the term takes its place in the dialectic of political struggle especially as a means of defense and counterattack by those in power'. It seems hardly necessary to indicate that, for present purposes, I shall use the word 'faction' in the most neutral sense possible. Some observers of factional politics, though their interests are scholarly, seem to have permitted the emotional load of the term to influence their thinking about factions. Thus, it is common to find factions connected with a 'breakdown' of social institutions, rather than treated as an expectable alignment of personnel in certain kinds of political fields, or regarded as one mode of organizing political relations under conditions of rapid social change.

There are, broadly speaking, two ways of approaching factions which lead to different though equally useful results: one approach focuses on the analysis of political conflict, the other on the analysis of political organization. Students of political organization, such as Oscar Lewis (1958, pp. 113-154), may count the number of factions present in a community, and explore the reasons for the persistence over many years of discrete, identifiable factions.[2] Those who are interested primarily in conflict place emphasis upon the transitory character of factions and assert with Scarlett Epstein (1962, p. 139) that 'it is not the number of factions that is important, but rather the way hostilities between opposing factions are expressed. In any one dispute there can be only two opposing factions and a neutral one'.[3] I disagree with Lewis's contention that factions may have important social functions outside politics; as Firth (1957, p. 292) says, factions 'operate for the most part in the political field or with political effects in other fields'. At the same time, my analysis aims primarily at an understanding of political organization rather than the nature of political conflict. Factions cannot, of course, be separated from conflict, but it is not conflict in which I am now most interested.

I. A SOCIOLOGICAL DEFINITION OF FACTION

I have tried to separate the distinctive from the incidental features of factional politics by comparing reported instances of factions from five different kinds of society and social institution. A brief sketch of each of these five cases is presented, followed by a set of five propositions, derived from analysis of the cases, which I consider to characterize factions and to distinguish them from other kinds of political grouping.

(i) *A wandering Pygmy band*. The BaMbuti, described by Turnbull (1961), is a Pygmy group living in wandering hunting and collecting bands in the Ituri Forest of the Eastern Congo. The band described consisted generally of about 100 persons, three patrilineal groups with a few affines attached to each. Turnbull relates three instances of conflict in the band. In one case the leader of the smallest of the three groups was threatened with the expulsion of his group from the band (pp. 99-100). In the second instance, the leaders of the two major kin groups divided their camps for a time (pp. 237-238). The third conflict, however, did not invite simple recruitment of supporters along kin lines because the disputants were brothers. The man who was originally wronged began, one day, to name friends and relatives who would support him in punishing his brother (pp. 107-109); immediately the band's censure shifted from the offender to his belligerent brother who 'was guilty of the much more serious crime of splitting the hunting band into opposing factions'.

(ii) *A village-dwelling African tribe*. The Ndembu, described by Turner (1957) live primarily by shifting cultivation and hunting. Villages, ordinarily groups of ten or eleven huts with two or three persons resident in each, may be composed of a headman, his brothers, their wives and children, the headman's sisters (with their children) returned to the village after divorce, and a miscellany of other persons attracted to the village by the influence of the headman. Although residence among the Ndembu is virilocal, descent is matrilineal, so that a village headman's sister's son might succeed him (pp. 76, 87-88). Under such a system many conflicts over succession developed, both between senior and junior claimants, and between established and aspiring political leaders. During the course of his work Turner witnessed several crisis situations during which 'the whole (village) group might be radically cloven into two factions' (p. 91). The distinctive feature of these factional conflicts, which sets them off from conflicts in a segmentary lineage system, is that the conflict groups changed in composition owing to 'transferences of persons from one faction to another, loss and replenishment in the followings of leading men' (p. 131). Here, clearly, is political recruitment and affiliation which could not be managed under only the principles of a kinship system.

(iii) *An overseas Indian community*. In areas such as Fiji to which large numbers of indentured Indians, drawn from the poorest rungs of Indian society, have been brought, there is virtually no indigenous authority system. Peasants were transplanted from several different cultural and linguistic regions of India and left to settle in politically 'decapitated' communities after the abolition of the indenture system in 1916.

When Mayer (1961) studied it in 1951, Vunioki was a village of 514 persons who were members of three cultural groups: Hindus descended from South Indians, largely members of a single kinship group; Muslims, most of them members of two kin groups; and Hindus descended from North Indians, comprising two principal kin groups and thirteen homesteads outside these groups (p. 36). These groups provided the raw material for recruitment to factions in Vunioki. The cleavage between Muslims and Hindus in India is customarily referred to as a 'communal' division, while that between speakers of different languages, on a broad scale, is known as 'linguistic regionalism'. Expectable conflicts of this kind are not so interesting here, since the organization of support follows a single clear principle, just as in the case of kin-group conflict in tribal societies. This does not mean that political recruitment in Vunioki does not follow the lines of cultural and kin groups, but conflict in the community is not about the differences between Hindus and Muslims, between speakers of Hindi and Tamil, or between kinship groups. The fact that political competition in the village is neither communal nor kin-based means that support may be recruited across these important lines of cleavage. Factions in Vunioki seem to radiate from an intense schism, cross-cutting kin lines, within the Southern cultural group. These factions developed originally over a land dispute between two brothers (pp. 122-125).

Mayer found a number of reasons for joining factions in Fiji Indian villages: an important factor was simply 'individual benefit, expressed in the repayment of obligations or the support given in anticipation of favours', either often strictly economic on both sides. Ties within the kin and cultural groups were multiple and strong, and could be used to bring fellow members into a faction. Balanced against the advantages of factional membership, however, were the disadvantages resulting from the hostility of opposing factions—which meant that there were some neutrals in every dispute. Of course, the merits of any case might place a man in one camp or another, 'but the recruiting power of the subject matter of a dispute, though considerable at any particular time, was less lasting than the motives of benefit' (pp. 135-136).

(iv) *An Indian peasant village*. The village of Namhalli in Mysore state had a population of 615 when Alan Beals (1959) studied it in 1952 and 1953. Namhalli had, in contrast to Vunioki, a plethora of leaders, both traditional and government-sponsored (pp. 429-432). Yet, like Vunioki, politics in Namhalli operated on the basis of factions, two or three of which seemed always to be present in the village (p. 433). There were seventeen different castes resident in the village, each of these being made up of several kin groups, but 'the basis of the faction cannot be established by reference to previously existing traditional groupings. The faction need not represent opposed castes, a conflict between progressives and conservatives, or a conflict between economic groups'.

Factions in Namhalli were built up from several 'cliques'. The most ordinary kind of clique was composed of a family, its affines, and its servants. Small, tight-knit caste groups might also act as cliques. Groups of friends who, for example, had been schoolmates might make up a clique. 'In nearly every case, cliques included relatives, friends, and persons bound together by economic ties, such as employee-employer or borrower-lender relationships' (pp. 433-434). Members of 'politically dominant cliques' were likely to enter into any village dispute and make it a context of factional struggle. The relations between two leading factions consisted 'of boycotting each other and of trying to create incidents which would cause some or all members of the other faction to lose money or property' (p. 436).

(v) *The Japanese political parties*. The Japanese Parliament consists of a Liberal Democratic majority and a Socialist opposition. Each of the parliamentary groups, however, is actually a federation of factions, of 'multiparties constantly in flux' according to a recent study by Scalapino and Masumi (1962, p. 81). The factions are 'leader-follower groups' in which roles are well defined: followers give their support to the leader in parliament and in intra-party struggles; 'the leader has the primary responsibility to provide positions, funds and other necessities of a good life'.

A faction leader utilizes old school connections, long-standing ties of friendship made in former offices, and mutual interests, to recruit members of his faction. Questions of ideology, policy, and mutual tactics enter into factional affiliation, and they do so to a greater extent among Socialists than among Conservatives. But at the bottom, all factional ties are personal between leader and follower and are based upon an assessment of mutual self-interest (p. 101). Political competition is primarily factional competition, and 'the activity and energies of the members are largely taken up in this struggle, because it determines the individual fortunes of the members . . . Factional loyalty becomes the primary loyalty . . . ' In a footnote to this, the authors observe that 'each faction is organized as a club'; each club has a name, and factional coalitions organize themselves similarly and take a name. The dominant coalition within either party is generally known as the Main Current group, and it is opposed by the anti-Main Current (pp. 79-80).

There are several other instances of factional politics which could have been treated here. I would like to have increased the range of social institutions represented to include, for example, factions in a bureaucracy and in a trade union. The five cases presented will, however, assist in getting a grasp of the fundamental nature of factional politics. By distinguishing the common features from the local peculiarities, it is possible to specify some of the essential characteristics of this political phenomenon. I state what I think these characteristics to be in the form of five propositions.

1. *Factions are conflict groups*. In all cases presented the conflict of factions is at least implicitly obvious. In fact, it is during social conflict that factions emerge out of a sociologically undefined background to give the observer a view of their personnel. Certainly, factions are visible more constantly in the Japanese political parties than in the peasant villages, and more

visible in the villages than in the tribal societies. Still, it is certain that factions would not exist in the Japanese parties without conflict, just as they would not in a BaMbuti band—conflict is the *raison d'etre* of factional membership. Conflict explains why there is no such thing as *one* faction in any political arena; obviously, there must always be at least two factions. I shall not attempt now to deal with the process of factional development, except to note that it seems to be through some kind of dialectical process that two or more factions can come about simultaneously in a field.

2. *Factions are political groups*. This proposition simply specifies the kind of conflict in which factions engage. If we regard politics as 'organized conflict about the use of public power' (Curtis, 1962, p. xxiii), then it is factions which organize this conflict in certain kinds of society and institution.[4]

3. *Factions are not corporate groups*. This negative criterion is important since it points out a basic difference between factional and other kinds of political conflict. Anthropologists are accustomed to deal with political conflicts between enduring corporate groups such as dual divisions, clans, or lineages; political scientists study conflicts between corporate political parties. Factions seem to lack the permanence of any of these kinds of group. Even in the extreme case of the Japanese parties, where factions are institutionalized in the form of clubs, it seems clear that the next generation of parliamentarians will not provide personnel for the same series of factions their seniors now possess. In fact, on the basis of the example provided by ex-Prime Minister Nobusuke Kishi's faction, it seems that one of these groupings may not outlive its leader (*The Times*, 2 November 1962). That factions are not corporate, that they are basically impermanent, does not mean that they may not persist for a long period of time; Beals traces the Namhalli factions back to 1920. The lifetime of factions among the Ndembu was limited by secession; the most extreme result of any factional struggle was the withdrawal of one faction to form a new village, which would then presumably lack factions for the time being. The only instance of factionalism in the BaMbuti band was very ephemeral indeed, being crushed in its incipient stage. There seems to be a regular gradation of societies along a scale of complexity according to the degree to which there is institutionalization of factions.

4. *Faction members are recruited by a leader*. Although such concepts as 'membership' and 'recruitment' must be under-

stood broadly when speaking of factions, they are matters of primary sociological importance here as in the study of institutional politics. Members can be connected to a faction only through the activity of a leader, since the unit has no corporate existence or clear single principle of recruitment. The leader who is responsible for organizing the personnel of a faction is ordinarily a man with more political power than any of his followers. He is not usually a leader with 'charisma', the Weberian 'gift of grace' which motivates political supporters on a level above narrow self-interest. To use Nadel's (1951, p. 99) term, the 'pointer relation' which marks a man as a member of a faction is an effective social display of allegiance to the leader —speaking or fighting on the leader's behalf, joining the leader's club, voting as the leader tells him, or whatever other functional political act is regarded as appropriate. Leadership may be provided not only by a politically powerful individual, but also, as Beals suggests, by a 'clique' based in an influential family. Another kind of clique might be composed of several leaders, each of whom has a modest following, but none of whom is individually capable of mobilizing an effective unit.

5. *Faction members are recruited on diverse principles*. A faction leader ordinarily has several different kinds of connections with his followers; he makes use of all possible ties to draw supporters into his faction. This proposition is closely related to Firth's (1957, p. 292) observation that the bases of recruitment to factions

. . . are usually structurally diverse—they may rest upon kin ties, patron-client relations, religious or politico-economic ties or any combination of these; they are mobilized and made effective through an authority structure of leader and henchman, whose roles are broadly defined and whose rewards in many cases depend upon the leader's discretion.

The importance of various kinds of connection binding members to the leader will become clearer in the next section.

II. THE SOCIAL ORGANIZATION OF FACTIONS

I turn abruptly now from comparison of the most general kind to detailed examination of factional politics in a single Indian peasant village. This case study is intended to clarify by concrete example the meaning of the five abstract criteria which I hold to be sociologically significant in defining factions and in distinguishing them from other kinds of political conflict group. Particular emphasis is placed here upon the continuity of conflict which keeps factions alive and maintains their personnel in surprisingly unchanging alignments over long periods of time. The social characteristics and roles of faction leaders, and the means by which supporters are recruited, are examined in some detail. To explain the dominant political cleavages leading to the pattern of factions I saw in this village in 1960 and 1961, I begin the story of social conflict about 1910 and bring it up to the time of the 1960 village council election. This election constituted a kind of political crisis, like the crises found by Turner (1957, p. 91) among the Ndembu, during which 'the pattern of current factional struggle' is revealed. At the time of the election the political alignment of almost every villager became apparent because each leader utilized every possible connection with other villagers to bring support to the candidates of his camp. Before sketching in the history of conflict in the village it will be useful to outline very briefly some of the principal characteristics of the village.

Govindapur Village

Govindapur village is located in the deltaic eastern portion of Midnapore District, West Bengal. It lies about sixty miles southwest of Calcutta, and is relatively inaccessible by road except during the dry season. Like most villages in the active portion of the Bengal delta, Govindapur is dispersed in settlement pattern. Houses are built along the raised banks of streams which criss-cross the countryside. Much of the land inside the inhabited area of the village is low-lying, filled with marsh grasses, bamboo, patches of jungle, and tanks from which earth has been removed for raising house platforms.

Most Govindapur families depend primarily upon agriculture for their livelihoods. Outside the inhabited area of the village virtually all land is employed in the cultivation of a single wet rice crop each year. A few plots which are near tanks may be used during the dry season to grow potatoes, pulses, or other minor crops. For almost twenty years now, however, most people in the Govindapur area have been engaged in the commercial cultivation of betel leaf, which involves only small plots of land, utilizes labor intensively, and brings a substantial cash income. The deltaic silt of the area is ideally suited to the cultivation of this leaf. Extremely high population density (over 1,500 persons per square mile) means that plots of rice land large enough to feed a family are scarce and very expensive. The village had a population of 677 in 1960.

There are representatives of eleven different castes in Govindapur, an unusually large number for a village in this area (see Nicholas & Mukhopadhyay, 1965), but most people (423 or 63 per cent) are members of the Mahisya cultivator caste. Households of this group held two-thirds (156 acres) of all land owned by Govindapur residents. The Mahisyas stand high in the local system of caste ranking, constitute a majority in virtually all the villages of Midnapore District, and otherwise qualify as the dominant caste of the village and the area. The only other castes which have substantial populations in Govindapur are the Potters (21 households, 86 persons owning 9 per cent of the land), Herdsmen (5 households, 32 persons owning 8 per cent of the land), and Brahmans (6 households, 30 persons owning 9 per cent of the land). Only the Herdsmen and Potters figure importantly *as caste groups* in Govindapur politics; political affairs in the village, on the whole, are *not* caste affairs.

Fifty Years of Social Conflict in Govindapur

About 1910 the fathers of many of the present leaders of Govindapur figured prominently in village affairs. The two leading rivals at that time were Siva Mukhya,[5] father of Hari the present headman, and Niranjan, father of a current oppositionist and village schoolmaster, Ram. Siva Mukhya built his center of influence largely on the east side of the canal which passes through the village; Niranjan held much property and had most supporters on the west side. About 1913, simultaneously it seems, Siva and Niranjan determined to construct temples. To construct a temple is meritorious and confers prestige upon the builder. Also, agricultural land attached to a temple as *devottar* property was not taxed, and a crafty owner could hold a good deal of land tax-free in this way. Siva Mukhya dedicated his temple to *Raghunāth;* he signed over about 100 acres of revenue-producing land and about thirty acres of sharecropped land to the deity. He continued to administer the land himself, however, and brought a Brahman family to live near the temple and perform daily worship there.

Niranjan dedicated his temple to two representations of *Krsna, Srīdhar Gopāl and Syām Sundar*. Though not so wealthy as Siva Mukhya, he gave land producing an annual revenue of Rs. 400 plus about ten acres of rice and raised garden land to the deities. In 1915 he handed over the affairs of the temple to a North Indian Brahman. The Brahman served the temple for about two years, then left for another part of the District taking the deeds to the temple property with him. About 1920 a Bihari *sādhu* named Krisnadas Mahanta, who was living in a nearby village, offered to take charge of the temple and recover the land. In fact, Niranjan had by then recovered the land through a technicality, but if Krisnadas Mahanta could induce the Brahman to relinquish his claim an expensive court session might be avoided. Therefore, Niranjan agreed and, eventually, Krisnadas was successful. Krisnadas became priest of the temple, but continued to live in another village, employing a Govindapur Brahman to perform daily worship in the temple. He believed he had control over the lands of the temple and apparently shared the proceeds amicably with Niranjan. Krisnadas inherited the property of a temple in the village where he lived and, in his aggressive style, soon began to diversify his economic operations to include lending money to cultivators. Because of his connection with Govindapur, many of his borrowers were residents of this village.

In 1940 Siva Mukhya died and his family suffered a temporary setback. Siva was twice married and father of twelve children. There was a distinct cleavage between the children of the two wives, probably related to the dissatisfaction of the second wife that her own eldest son would not succeed to the headmanship, and that her daughters had been married in other villages while the first wife's daughters were married to sons of important Govindapur families. When Hari became head of the family, his youngest half-brother, Nitai, decided to sell his share of the family property and move to an area where uncultivated land was available. The remaining three half-brothers decided that they too would partition the joint property. Had joint property been maintained—as Hari would have liked—the family would stand far above all others in economic power; with partition, there were four (later five, when Natai returned to Govindapur) moderately well-to-do families. And Hari, a younger and less wealthy man than Niranjan, was confronted with the problem of consolidating political power over the village.

Siva Mukhya had extended his influence in the portion of the village west of the canal through a series of marriages. His two eldest daughters were married to sons of two large, prosperous families in that neighborhood. A third wealthy family was allied to Siva's when his youngest son, Nitai, was married to a daughter from that group. In Bengal, as in much of North India, the relation between a man and his wife's brother is formally distant and frequently hostile. (In Bengali the most common term of

abuse is *śālā*, 'wife's brother'.) All three of these alliances turned to ashes in the hands of Hari when he succeeded to the headmanship, and these three families constituted the core of the anti-headman group among the Mahisya caste in 1960 Govindapur politics. To be sure, the rivalry between Hari Mukhya and his sisters' husbands was not merely an institutionalized kin conflict; after the division of Siva's property among five sons, political and economic rivalry between these families became a much more realistic possibility.

Faced with both the opposition of Niranjan's family and the formidable group of sisters' affines, Hari was anxious to gather support in whatever ways he could. Of course, his sharecroppers were supporters, as were the men who cultivated the *devottar* property of the common village temples—Hari personally collected 50 per cent of the produce of this land, in the name of the village, and paid the priests himself. He regularly employed the low-caste Toddy-tappers and several poor Mahisya men who lived near him as agricultural laborers, and he loaned several of them small amounts of money. He could count on their physical support, but poor men had no influence in village decision-making or in the settling of disputes. He needed not so much supporters as allies, and he needed them on the populous west side of the canal. He had to look for persons outside the principal families, and one of the first persons to whom he turned was Krisnadas Mahanta.

Krisnadas was still living in a nearby village and lending money in Govindapur and other areas. In 1950 he moved into Niranjan's temple and began to use it as a center of operations. During the next three years relations between Krisnadas and Niranjan became increasingly hostile, and Krisnadas became increasingly friendly with Hari Mukhya. In 1953 Niranjan and Krisnadas fought physically. Krisnadas left the temple to live in the house of a man named Arjun, an ally of the headman. Krisnadas still believed that he held title to the land attached to Niranjan's temple and appointed a village Brahman to perform worship there. During the next two years he was occupied in constructing a large, expensive temple dedicated to *Sitā* and *Rām* on a plot of land slightly outside the inhabited area of the village. In 1955 he moved into his new temple with his servant woman, a young Mahisya widow named Kalpana, and his disciple, a young Brahman from the family which served Hari Mukhya's temple.

In the meantime, old Niranjan died. His eldest son had preceded him, so the second son,

Ram, who was intended to be a schoolmaster, became head of the household. Ram's political position was weakened by joint family difficulties, as Hari Mukhya's had been fifteen years previous. Niranjan had maintained a joint family with his younger brother. The younger brother decided to partition the joint property and shortly thereafter began to suffer from asthma and heart disease; his fortunes declined as Niranjan's rose and his son, Kali, came into bitter conflict with Niranjan and later Ram over the property. When Ram discovered that his father had long ago recovered title to the family temple lands, he expelled Krisnadas' appointee and named a Brahman from another village to serve the temple. Kali lodged an unsuccessful claim to some of the proceeds from the temple lands.

Krisnadas Mahanta's affairs in the new Sita Ram temple were not going altogether smoothly either. He was a wealthy and successful man, but he was now quite old. Consequently, the young Brahman disciple had no difficulty in alienating the affections of Kalpana, the Mahanta's servant woman. Krisnadas promised Kalpana that he would leave her some land on his death if she remained with him in his declining years, and she agreed. The Brahman—to Hari Mukhya the obvious heir to the Mahanta and thus, potentially, an important and easily influenced ally—remained too, but kept his distance from Krisnadas. One day, only about a year before the old Mahanta's death, a young Bihari police officer came to visit him, having heard that there was a fellow Bihari in the area. The police officer, named Ramdas, flattered the old man, who then convinced him of the moral and material benefits of life as a Mahanta. Ramdas thus became Krisnadas' second disciple and, when he died, heir to a considerable fortune. The young Brahman was disowned despite Hari Mukhya's support.

Krisnadas died suddenly while Ramdas was away in another part of the District. It is widely believed that Hari Mukhya and Kalpana immediately seized several thousand rupees in cash which was hidden in the temple. Kalpana took the titles to the land which was promised her and went to live with the young Brahman and his family. Ramdas was in a rage when he discovered what had happened and subsequently spent much time and effort trying to reclaim both the money and the land. In pursuit of his claim against the headman, Ramdas was a natural ally of the opposition.

Hari Mukhya was himself still searching for allies to strengthen his position in the increasingly hostile west side of the village. He proved a very useful intermediary for men 'on their way up' in the world. A man who was rising economically inevitably had to fight many cases in government courts, pursuing tenuous claims to land, hoping weak opponents would give up easily rather than risk financial ruin in the courts. Hari Mukhya was a valuable ally for such a man because of his intimacy with the government bureaucracy. Among other positions, he was Union Welfare Officer, which meant he had control over distribution of money and food to the destitute of nine villages. In addition, he had arranged for his son to become tax collector for the Union. These positions gave Hari considerable power over some villagers as well as useful connections with the local government bureaucracy.

Arjun, the man with whom Krisnadas Mahanta lived after his fight with Niranjan, was one of the economically mobile villagers who found the headman's assistance valuable. Arjun began as a servant in the house of oppositionist Krisna's father. He eventually established a claim to some of the land on which he had worked and, using his first property skilfully, had become a prosperous cultivator of eight acres by 1960. Much of his land came from Krisna's family and, though he continued to live in their midst, the breach was never healed. This made him a natural ally of the headman, but as a lone figure without a large kin group, without share-croppers (he and his brother parsimoniously cultivated the eight acres themselves), he was not of much use to Hari.

Visnu was another man who pursued his fortune aggressively. His father was a moderately prosperous cultivator who left him about five acres of land. This Visnu immediately parcelled out to share-croppers, and he began to spend most of his time around the courts. He soon developed a special style of operation: he entered land litigation on behalf of the weaker claimant, bought the disputed plot from him at a low price, and fought the case in court himself. Several pleaders in town were obligated to Visnu for 'touting' or directing clients to them. Many friends in and around the courts helped him when he pursued a case of his own. Until about 1955 Visnu operated as a 'lone wolf' in village affairs; then he came into direct conflict with opposition leader Chandi, his nearest neighbor. Visnu had previously been close to Niranjan's faction, but its strength and importance seemed to be declining at the time, and also it was connected with Chandi's faction. He turned to Hari Mukhya, who was only too happy to have an aggressive, wealthy ally like Visnu on his weak western flank. Visnu found Hari's connection with the government bureaucracy valuable also. By 1960 Visnu had amassed over eleven acres of land and was in pursuit of more. This land was cultivated by fifteen men of different families, twelve in Govindapur and three in the neighboring village of Radhanagar. Visnu was 'tough' and demanded unquestioning loyalty from his sharecroppers.

The events related thus far have concerned almost exclusively the Mahisya caste. Some of the sustained conflicts in Govindapur have concerned minority castes also. Old Siva Mukhya did not bother the Govindapur Potter caste group a great deal. Until about 1920, when a group of outsiders moved in, all the Potters in Govindapur were descendants of a single man and they ran affairs in their neighborhood very much as a large extended family might. Several events which occurred after 1943 brought the Potters increasingly into village affairs. When Hari became headman one of the methods he employed to extend his control in the village was 'subordination'. If he intervened in small local disputes—which he might easily do in the neighborhoods of poor minority castes—and brought about a settlement, he might supersede the less powerful senior men in the locality. In this way he gained control over the low-ranking Toddy-tappers and in the mixed-caste neighborhood near his house, but many of these people were economically dependent upon him and thus under some pressure to accept his decisions anyway. The Potters lived in the politically important west side of the village and Hari determined to exert his authority over them. The Potters were acutely conscious of their inferior caste position in a Mahisya-dominated society, so when Hari Mukhya attempted to interfere in a dispute they rallied around their own headman, Durga Potter, against the outsider. But a new generation was succeeding the old one, and as the distance between the Potters and their common ancestor increased, so did the social distance between the various descent groups. One such group, headed by Suren Potter, was under heavy criticism because one of its members, Tapan, was 'behaving like a Mahisya': he was attempting to seize land by foreclosing in usufructuary mortgages. During the height of the tension, Suren arranged the marriage of his son without consulting the Potter headman or other members of the group. In the ensuing dispute Suren's descent group supported his action and the entire group was boycotted. Hari Mukhya supported Suren's group, in return for which they now support him in village affairs, as do the unrelated Potters.

The Govindapur Herdsman caste group was smaller and less closely tied by kinship and co-residence, but more prosperous than the Potters. The group was, however, unified and watchful of its interests under the vigorous leadership of seventy-year-old Rakhal Herdsman. Rakhal was head of the eastern Midnapore Herdsman caste organization. Like the Potters, the Herdsmen generally in Bengal rank higher than the Mahisyas but must accept their dominance in Midnapore. Rakhal and his group have always trod a cautious middle ground in village politics. Kanai, an aggressive and intelligent young man from one Herdsman household, allied himself with Hari Mukhya. Bhima, head of a large Herdsman joint family, was just as closely allied with the opposition. Kanai lives near the canal and thus near the headman's house; Bhima's nearest neighbors are oppositionists. Between these two families lives Rakhal whose stance in village affairs—like his residence—is squarely in the center. He associates with both groups and gets on equally well with Hari Mukhya and opposition leader Chandi.

The Panchayat Election

The election of members to the *grám panchayat* (village council) which was held in Govindapur in the autumn of 1959 brought about what I shall call, with thanks to Hugh Gray, a 'crystallization' of political alignments in the village. Political leaders canvassed villagers for support; they utilized every possible tie to bring out votes. Leaders discussed among themselves, organized coalitions, and jockeyed for position. During the pre-election period almost all relations of alliance and opposition between villagers became clear, and it is these relations which were reported to me at the end of 1960.

Under the Indian government scheme for the 'decentralization of administration' each revenue village was to elect a council with a number of members in proportion to its population. Each village panchayat was to send up one delegate, not a member of the panchayat, to the *anchal* or area panchayat which covered a group of fifteen to twenty villages. Eventually, power to levy and collect taxes for use in local development work was to be given to anchal panchayats. In preparation for the first panchayat election in Govindapur, an official from the Block Development Office responsible for the village visited Hari Mukhya and together they divided the village into two constituencies. The east side of the canal was joined with the northernmost portion of the village on the west side to make a constituency 'safe' for the headman's supporters. The opposition groups were almost entirely confined to the south constituency, where it was hoped they might defeat one another in triangular contests.

Workers from both Congress and Communist parties, who had canvassed the village during two national general elections, came to prepare their supporters for the panchayat election also. Hari Mukhya, like most village headmen in West Bengal, was strongly identified with the Congress party; this identification left the opposition little choice—they were Communists or nothing. The rearrangement of political conflict along partisan lines brought home to the opposition leaders the necessity of coalition. There were five distinct opposition factions in the village at the time of the election, but none of them, alone could muster a quarter of the voting strength commanded by Hari Mukhya. If each of these factions, or even two or three of them, offered its own slate of candidates, they all stood a very good chance of defeat.

Chandi and his matrilateral cross-cousin Krisna, with a comparatively large factional following, were joined by Ramdas Mahanta, who lacked followers but was wealthy and well-educated. Ramdas prevailed upon his friend Durga Potter who brought the large Potter vote-bloc into the coalition. Gopal, undisputed 'boss' of the isolated neighborhood on the extreme west side of the village, was unenthusiastic about the Communist party but willingly joined an alliance with his friends Chandi and Krisna against his wife's brother, Hari Mukhya. Govinda, the only prosperous cultivator outside the headman's kin group on the east side of the canal, also lent his small support to the coalition.

The alliance within the opposition structured very strongly the choices of Ram and Visnu. Ram and Ramdas Mahanta carried on the fight over the property of Ram's family temple. Ram saw that the Mahanta, without any political following, was being given a position of importance in the coalition. His struggle for precedence over the headman's family went on, and he would certainly vote against Hari Mukhya, but he could not join an alliance with Ramdas Mahanta. The opposition leaders regarded Ram's family as a declining force in the village, since it was internally divided and much less wealthy than it had been. Visnu had little choice, both because of his attachment to the headman and because of his bitter conflict with Chandi. Although Visnu's house was in the midst of the opposition neighborhood, his sharecroppers were located throughout the village. Facing a losing battle against the united opposition in his own locality, he could still bring out a number of important votes in the northern constituency.

Rakhal Herdsman went about the village in his usual way agreeing with everyone about what needed to be done. Young Kanai Herdsman, however, cultivated Hari Mukhya's friendship assiduously during the pre-election period. Bhima Herdsman was close to Gopal and promised the support of his family to the opposition. (When the election actually came, Rakhal voted Congress and his wife voted Communist—at least, that is what Rakhal told other villagers.)

The Congress and Communist coalitions each fielded four candidates, two from each of the constituencies, plus a candidate for the anchal panchayat to be elected by the new panchayat members. Since the candidate for the anchal could not be a member of the village panchayat, each group had to hold in reserve one strong candidate.

	Congress candidates	Communist candidates
North constituency	Kali* Kanai Herdsman*	Nitai Syama
South constituency	Visnu Arjun	Krisna* Durga Potter*
Anchal panchayat	Hari Mukhya*	Chandi

*=successful candidates

The choice of candidates by the two coalitions reflects some careful political calculation. The north constituency was predominantly under Hari Mukhya's control; the Congress candidates chosen were the ones who stood the greatest chance of winning marginal votes. Kali, Ram's disaffected classificatory brother, might win votes from his kinsmen, and Kanai Herdsman might ensure the support of his caste group. The opposition chose Hari Mukhya's half-brother Nitai in hopes of dividing the headman's kin group. Syama was a moderately prosperous grocer who lived just inside the north constituency boundary, well away from the headman's sphere of influence, which made him slightly stronger than Govinda, the other possible candidate.

The south constituency proved to be as 'safe' for the opposition as the north was for the Congress. Neither Krisna nor Durga Potter was a particularly wealthy or powerful leader. Krisna had a large kin group while Durga had the large group of loyal Potters. Much more important was that the combined forces of Chandi, Ramdas Mahanta, and Gopal were behind them. Thus, though they were opposed by two wealthy and powerful candidates, Visnu and Arjun, both won easily.

The two most powerful candidates, Hari Mukhya and Chandi, were held in reserve for the anchal panchayat election. Of course, with two votes for Chandi and two for the headman, the choice of an anchal member was at first a stand-off. Ultimately, Krisna and Durga Potter had to admit that it would not be proper for the village to send someone other than the headman to the anchal panchayat, so they agreed to elect Hari Mukhya.

It is not surprising that the men who, despite the election, continue to carry the most weight in the village, to make most of the decisions, or to prevent one another from making them, are Hari Mukhya, Visnu, and Chandi—none of them a member of the village panchayat. In practice, a panchayat meeting is still what it was before the election, a loose congregation of important men who gather whenever a village decision must be taken, a dispute settled, or a case decided and punishment meted out. Most of the affairs with which they deal are not the officially defined business of a village panchayat and, indeed, they do not pay much attention to their official business. Still, the election was seen as an important event which tested the strength of village factions. Further, villagers have been told that bursary functions will one day be handed over to panchayats, and no one wants to let funds be controlled by his enemies, since they would certainly be used to alienate his political followers.

Recruitment to factions

Throughout this account I have attempted to tell, wherever the question arose, what kind of link connected a faction leader and a follower. In Table I, I set down systematically the connections of adult villagers to faction leaders. This tabulation reflects information given primarily by Hari Mukhya, Chandi, Krisna, Durga Potter, and Visnu's nephew. Connections are not always clear and occasionally they are multiple, as in the case of some of Chandi's sharecroppers who are also relatives; the relation between them is observably one of 'affection' rather than 'subordination'. In this case I have charged half the votes to kinship and half to economic dependence, though the kin connection may be the primary tie between them.

I identified factions initially by villagers' references to *dal*, a word which in local usage means 'faction', 'party' (but not a political party), 'group', or 'band'. The term is used to describe a group of traveling performers, a band

of men who sing devotional songs, drinking companions, and village political factions. A political faction can be distinguished from other kinds of *dal* by the fact that the leader uses the expression 'I have a number of men in my hand'. Only faction leaders use such an expression, and other villagers may describe them as having such a group. If asked, Govindapur faction leaders may enumerate the adult men they could muster in a fight, though they usually exaggerate. Actual physical conflicts, known to the villagers as *mārāmāri* ('a beating affair'), are comparatively rare, but 'factional affairs' (*daladāli*) are not at all uncommon.

The most ordinary sort of conflict in the village, however, is *gālāgāli*, 'a shouting affair'. One man's bullock strays into another man's garden and eats some plants; the garden owner beats the bullock and drives him out. The bullock's owner abuses his neighbor for beating the animal. The mutual recriminations develop in intensity as they go on, and the first prominent man to hear the dispute is expected to appear and settle it. The only essential qualification for such a referee is that he should have some authority— i.e. he should be relatively wealthy—and that he should live within shouting distance of the disputants. In a dispersed village like Govindapur, authority for settling *gālāgāli* disputes must also be dispersed. (In general usage, the village is divided into four wards, each with its own leaders.) Authority expressed in this way, though it appears not to amount to a great deal, proved to be important for political recruitment in Govindapur. In the table it is seen that 62 votes were decided by the influence of the neighborhood headman, either because there was an element of subordination in their relationship, because the headman had recently decided disputes in favor of his supporter's household, or because the supporter hoped to win favor. Offended parties, however, were likely to support an opposed faction. Hari Mukhya collected the votes of several households which felt they had been wronged in one dispute or another.

Analysis

If I were to analyze the case just presented *in vacuo* I would would doubtless be able to derive from it the five criteria which I believe define 'faction'. I might at the same time erroneously decide that factions almost always persist over comparatively long periods of time, that this variety of factional activity is peculiar to peasant societies, or that some other inessential characteristic is fundamental. By framing beforehand a set of criteria, based upon a wide-ranging com-

TABLE 1

Factional alignments of all possible voters in Govindapur[a]

Faction leader	Party	Possible voters supporting by basis of support					Total
		Kinship	Factors related to caste	Eonomic dependence	Leader is neighborhood headman	Leader opposes mutual enemy	
Hari Mukhya	Congress	13	12	57	18	26	126
Visnu	Congress	9	-	16	13	3	41
Rakhal Herdsman	Independent (pro-Congress)	3	12	-	9	-	24[b]
Ram	Independent (pro-Communist)	7	-	5	-	-	12[c]
Chandi & Krisna	Communist	24	-	4	8	-	36
Durga Potter	Communist	7	24	-	-	-	31
Gopal	Communist	17	-	1	11	-	29
Govinda	Communist	14	-	-	3	2	19
Ramdas Mahanta	Communist	1	-	5	-	-	6
		95	48	88	62	31	324

[a]Data included in Table 2 of Nicholas and Mukhopadhyay 1965 have here been reanalyzed to show possible voters rather than only households. By 'possible voters' is meant members of village households whose ages were reported to me as 21 years or above; this does not tell how many persons were registered as voters. Votes from faction leaders' own households are included in the category 'kinship'.
[b]Includes 17 Congress and 7 Communist votes.
[c]Includes 10 Communist and 2 Congress votes.

parison of related social phenomena, I am able, figuratively speaking, to 'read' the events in Govindapur directly in sociological terms. Posterior analysis is undoubtedly most productive of coherent structures; it is less useful, however, in getting a grasp of 'dynamic phenomena'. I shall briefly recapitulate the elements in the definition to see what light they shed on Govindapur politics.

1. *Factions are conflict groups*. There was a great deal of obvious conflict in the village both prior to and during the panchayat election. Factions appeared as groups (or, perhaps better, as quasi-groups) only during conflict. But, curiously, there are several instances of factions cooperating with one another, of factional 'coalitions' or 'alliances'. If the criterion of conflict is observed, there seems to be no way of accommodating alliances. Looked at over time, however, factions may be seen moving from alliance to opposition; factions do not lose their separate identities in an alliance. This objection will be dealt with further under Item 4 below.

2. *Factions are political groups*. In citing a definition of politics, I directed attention to 'the use of public power'. Following Bailey (1960, p. 10), I conceive of power as command over resources and control over men. Analyzing politics in a small society, it is not always clear how much socially recognized power is to be thought of as 'public' and how much as 'private'. Commonly owned resources, such as the land attached to the Govindapur village temples, certainly belong to the public arena; the headman had command over this resource and, thereby, control over the men who utilized it. The governments of the Indian Union and the State of West Bengal have intervened in the village to define an area of public power—the business of the new panchayat—and the means by which that power should be disposed—universal adult franchise election. Given this definition of the situation, Govindapur political leaders immediately converted their 'private power', such as control over share-croppers, debtors, kinsmen, neighbors, etc., into public, political power in the form of votes.

3. *Factions are not corporate groups*. A student of tribal societies examining an Indian peasant community might reasonably expect to find that the obvious corporate segments of the society, castes, would provide the structure for village political relations as they do for economic relations. Although two minority caste groups in Govindapur, Potters and Herdsmen, appear as more or less united political groups, describ-

tion of inter-caste conflict would not come close to describing Govindapur politics. Analyzing caste in purely abstract, structural terms, Bailey (1963, p. 118) points out that the system, ideally, permits only cooperative and never competitive relations between castes. 'Only the dominant caste has an autonomous political existence, not as a corporate political group, but as a field for political competition. Certainly no subordinate caste is a corporate political group.' Within the dominant Mahisya caste of Govindapur there is no single principle which organizes political relations. Among certain Jat and Thakur dominant caste groups in some North Indian villages, as in the case of Rampur described by Lewis (1958), segments of a unilineal descent group or clans may organize political conflict (see Note 2, p. 124). In Govindapur, however, no such divisions are reckoned within the dominant caste and, to a great extent, it is 'every man for himself' in village politics.

4. *Faction members are recruited by a leader*. The essential position of the leader in organizing a Govindapur faction is obvious without further analysis here; there is neither structural principle nor common interest to hold together faction members in the absence of the leader. Certain factions, particularly those based upon large extended kinship groups, may have 'clique' leadership like that described by Beals (1959, p. 433). The faction based among some west ward Mahisya families and led by Chandi and Krisna is an example of clique leadership. To return to the question of factional coalitions mentioned above, it was seen that separate factions continue to be distinct from one another even when they are in alliance. The fundamental reason for this is that two faction leaders can never have identical interests; with resources as scarce as they are in Govindapur, men powerful enough to be faction leaders are always at least potentially in conflict.

5. *Faction members are recruited on diverse principles*. An analysis of the bases upon which Govindapur voters supported their faction leaders during the 1960 panchayat election shows that 29 per cent were kinsmen and 27 per cent were economic dependents of their leaders; 19 per cent of the voters backed their neighborhood headman, 15 per cent gave their support on grounds related to caste, and 10 per cent endorsed leaders in hopes of defeating a mutual enemy. In other villages, grounds for support might appear to be dramatically different, but they are invariably diverse (cf. Benedict, 1957, p. 340).

III. FACTIONS AND POLITICAL CHANGE

In the preceding sections which defined faction and analyzed the social organization of factions in a concrete instance, the question of 'origin' was studiously avoided. Obviously there are cases in which the genesis of factions is recorded and may be sociologically analyzed without recourse to conjectural history. The persistent connection of factionalism with social change suggests that, in at least one context, it may be possible to discuss this political process in greater time depth than is permitted by functional analysis.

Where communities, like the Fiji Indian village discussed in Section I, have been deprived of political authority, factions seem to arise unbidden to organize the personnel in disputes. Siegel and Beals (1960, p. 399) assert that factionalism of the kind described in the preceding pages 'is essentially a phenomenon of socio-cultural change'. And as a definition they offer: 'Factionalism is overt conflict in a group which leads to increasing abandonment of cooperative activities'. This definition suggests that factions may eventually 'work themselves out' when all cooperative activity in a community has been abandoned. Such a conclusion does not fit well with the long lifetimes of factions in some societies. With Siegel and Beals, I find factionalism frequently connected with change in political structure, but I think factions, in the absence of conventional political divisions, perform necessary functions in organizing conflict. The example of the Iroquois will help to show what I mean.

Aboriginal Iroquois politics

By careful study of Lewis Henry Morgan's *League of the Iroquois* (1901) and other historical works, and by comparison with better-analyzed segmentary political systems, it is possible to discover a good deal about the precontact political system of the Iroquois. They were semi-sedentary cultivators and hunters living in what is now upper New York State. The name 'Iroquois' actually covers five—and later six—tribes which formed a Confederation or League including the Mohawk, Onondaga, Oneida, Seneca, and Cayuga tribes which speak related, mutually unintelligible languages. The sixth tribe, the Tuscaroras, lived in the area of what is now Delaware. Driven out of their homelands by white settlement, they joined the League over a period between 1715 and 1722, but never occupied full status on the Council (Morgan, 1928, p. 16).

According to traditional Iroquois history, the Confederation was founded—perhaps late in the sixteenth century—by one Deganawidah, who is said to have been troubled by strife between the component tribes (Scott *et al.*, 1911). Each of the original five tribes (with minor exceptions) was made up of a series of like-named matriclans. The brotherhood of fellow clansmen in different tribes seems to have been an important cross-tying principle in what was otherwise a loose political alliance (Morgan, 1901, I, pp. 77-78). The clans were divided into two ritually and socially opposed moieties. Members of opposite moieties (called by Morgan 'phratries') occupied the two ends of the 'Longhouse' in which ceremonies were held. All of the gambling and athletic events in Iroquois life symbolized one of the levels of social segmentation. As Morgan (1901, I, p. 281) wrote:

There were strifes between nation and nation (i.e. tribes), village and village, or tribes and tribes (i.e. clans), in a word, parties against parties, and not champion against champion. The prize contended for was that of victory; and it belonged, not to triumphant players, but to the party which sent them forth to the contest.

Morgan (1881, pp. 12-14) noted other functions of Iroquois dual divisions. When a murderer and his victim were of opposite moieties, a moiety council would be called and negotiations for reparation would be conducted between the moieties. If both murderer and victim were members of the same division, discussion would be carried on by representatives of their respective clans. At the funeral of a particularly important person the body would be addressed by members of the opposite moiety. The body would then be carried to the grave by members of the opposite moiety followed, in order, by the family of the deceased, members of his clan, other clans of his moiety, and finally members of the opposite moiety. The directly political functions of Iroquois dual divisions are best seen in the fact that the appointment of a new chief had to be approved first by his own moiety—which rarely objected—then by the opposite moiety—which rarely failed to object to an appointment.

Morgan could not be expected to see that Iroquois clans were composed of a number of matrilineages, one or occasionally two of which were politically dominant and responsible for the appointment of chiefs. He did notice, however, that a new chief was frequently 'a son of one of the deceased ruler's sisters' or 'one of his brothers' (Morgan, 1901, I, p. 84). Golden-weiser (1915, pp. 366-367) said the power to name a chief resided with the senior woman of what he called the 'maternal family'. Recent research by Merlin Myers has revealed that Goldenweiser's 'maternal family' is, in fact, a corporate matrilineage. Morgan (1901), I, pp. 60-61) identified fifty named chiefships ('sachemships') which composed the Council of the Confederacy. They admitted to their discussions some 'Pinetree Chiefs', men who had distinguished themselves as leaders without being appointed to named chiefships. Such positions died with their holders. The Council dealt, of course, only with affairs of common concern, and local matters were handled by the chiefs of each tribe or clan. Tribes occupied their own territories and land seems to have been held by the clan under the primary control of the dominant lineage.

Early Contact Political Cleavages

The nice balance of equal, opposed, 'nesting' social segments was disturbed early in the eighteenth century by a cleavage within the League between supporters of the English and supporters of the French in North America (Fenton, 1955, p. 338). Partisans of the French, many of them Mohawks, but members of other tribes also, were converted to Roman Catholicism and led to new settlements in Quebec by Jesuit missionaries. The second major schism in the League was created by the American Revolution, some members of all tribes supporting the British and others the colonists.

In 1784 Frederick Haldimand, Governor of Quebec and its adjacent territories, signed a deed giving to the Mohawk Indians and 'others of the Six Nations who have either lost their settlement within the territory of the American States, or wish to retire from them to the British', a strip of land six miles wide on either side of the Grand River from the source to the mouth. Joseph Brant, a Mohawk Pinetree Chief, had sought and won this grant in order to bring the tribes of the Confederacy into one area, thereby preventing the complete dissolution of the alliance and loss of its political and military power. Many of the Iroquois who had fought on the side of the colonists or been neutrals remained in New York. Some of the Mohawks who had fought on the British side had already taken up new territory along the Bay of Quinte on a strip of land granted by the British shortly after the conclusion of the Revolution. The Senecas were urging other member tribes

to move into the Genesee valley where they held land. The League was losing its unity and power. When Brant pulled together the remnants of the Six Nations on the Grand River Reserve it was apparently with an eye to salvaging whatever bargaining power he still had with the British. With members of all six tribes of the Confederacy living within the confines of a single reserved area, functions of local government seem to have gone automatically into the hands of the Council of Chiefs. Of the fifty named Iroquois chiefships, thirty-nine remained on the Grand River Reserve at the end of the nineteenth century (Chadwick, 1897, pp. 86-97).

The Reservation Period

Both of the early schisms in the Iroquois Confederacy, the French vs. British and British vs. colonist, cut across all six tribes. There is no way of knowing the structural bases of these divisions, so it is not possible to tell if they were fundamentally factional. Something is known, however, about a religious cleavage which became apparent in Iroquois society during the nineteenth century. Many supporters of the British cause were or became Protestant Christians, largely Anglicans. The group which migrated to the Grand River Reserve included both Christians and followers of traditional Iroquois religion. Early in the nineteenth century a Seneca preacher named Handsome Lake began to propagate a syncretic revivalist religion known as the 'Good Message'. It was quickly accepted by the non-Christians in both the United States and Canada, but it was not successful in the reconversion of the Christians (Noon, 1949, p. 19). The faith taught by Handsome Lake is still an integral part of the aboriginal social system wherever it is found, and is generally known as the 'Longhouse Religion', since followers carry on their ceremonies in traditional long wooden buildings which were, in origin, lineage dwellings. The vigor of the Longhouse revival apparently deepened the religious schism, so that by Morgan's time there was a group which he described (1901, II, pp. 112-113) as a 'Christian Party' among the Iroquois in New York. The cleavage between Christians and non-Christians goes very deep, as examination of contemporary factions on the Grand River Reserve will show.

Early in the present century the Canadian government resolved to rid itself of the Indian problem by encouraging the assimilation of Indians. In line with this policy, the government in 1924 eagerly responded to the wishes of a number of Six Nations men who sought to replace the hereditary Council of the League with an elective council. The installation of the elective council divided the people, already split along religious lines, into factions according to their support for or opposition to the elective system. This cleavage has persisted to the present, so that the two basic issues of religion and representation provide the basic political divisions on the Six Nations Reserve today.

Contemporary Factional Politics

In March 1959, the hereditary chiefs of the Six Nations, supported by several hundred young men, marched into the old council house and forcibly expelled the elective council. They issued a proclamation declaring themselves the legal government of the 'independent Indian nation of Grand River'. In 1924 many of the same hereditary chiefs had themselves been ejected from the council house by Royal Canadian Mounted Police who had been dispatched by the government to support the elective council. By the end of March the hereditary chiefs had again been evicted from the council house by the R.C.M.P., but they continued to hold meetings as they always had, and to receive at least passive support from a majority of the Reserve's 6,385 inhabitants. Behind this incident lies a complex of political action based ostensibly upon the cleavages created by religion and by views on election as a method of selecting a government. These two cross-cutting cleavages gave four principal factions on the Reserve when I studied it in 1958.

(i) *The 'Progressive' faction.* The men who originally petitioned the Canadian government to displace the Council of the League with an elective council form the basis of the 'progressive'[6] group. Since 1924 they have attracted many ambitious young men into their camp. All members of this group are Christians and many of them are among the hardest-working and most prosperous farmers. They have ambitions for large houses and automobiles, and encourage their children to continue their education off the Reserve. They often comment unfavorably on the behavior of the Longhouse people. They attempt to maintain white friends and occasionally encourage their children to marry whites.

The Progressive faction depicts the hereditary council as 'primitive' and 'unprogressive'; something which, like the Longhouse religion, gives Indians low social status in white eyes. Underlying the views of the leaders of this faction, however, seems to be the fact that, to my knowledge, none of them is a member of a chiefly lineage. In other words, the political aspirations of socially successful and economically mobile individuals had, before 1924, been frustrated by hereditary government. For the Progressives there was no course to political power other than changing the system.

(ii) *The Longhouse faction.* It is somewhat misleading to speak of the followers of the Longhouse religion as a 'faction', since they constitute a social group for purposes other than politics. Since this group functions as a faction in relation to other Reserve factions, however, I feel justified in treating it as such. It is significant, moreover, that there are four Longhouses on the Reserve; these are culturally distinct, originally meeting the needs of different tribes, and one of the key aspects of their recent association with one another has been political. Members of all Longhouses may go to hear a visiting preacher in one Longhouse, but their annual ceremonies are separate. The four Longhouses at Grand River are the Sour Spring or Upper Cayuga, Seneca, Onondaga, and Lower Cayuga. The Lower Cayuga Longhouse is, politically, a special case and will be treated separately below.

In 1954 there were 1,260 followers of the Longhouse religion on the Reserve, that is, about 20 per cent of the total population. They did not oppose 'progress' in principle; they were quite willing to take advantage of tractors, power tools, automobiles, and automatic appliances. On the whole, however, they were not prosperous and did not encourage their children to seek much education. Many Longhouse children attended only elementary school, which was offered on the Reserve by Indian teachers. The Longhouse people were localized in the southeast quarter of the Reserve, and the few Christians resident in the area were socially isolated.

The Longhouse group held a majority on the hereditary council, partially because they retained to a greater extent than other groups the recollection of the lineage. The investiture of a chief was a Longhouse ceremony and the naming of a new chief required action on the part of a lineage matron, the eldest female of a chiefly lineage, action less likely to be taken by a Christian than a Longhouse woman. Since the Canadian government deprived the hereditary council of its right to decide on the economic and civil affairs of the Reserve, this group has had fewer functions. Yet it continued to hold regular meetings and to take decisions which were widely respected on the Reserve. One of the most important decisions of the traditional council was its interdiction of voting in elections. The chiefs said in 1924 that election was not a suitable means for Indians to select a government. Consequently, most people on the Reserve have never voted for members of the elective council.

(iii) *The Lower Cayuga Longhouse*. In 1957, to the surprise of all the factions, members of the Lower Cayuga Longhouse voted in the council election. There are, of course, sound reasons for this unexpected behavior. The Lower Cayugas had recently come under strong criticism from other Longhouses for 'not picking their chiefs correctly', that is, for either not knowing or failing to follow the order of succession in the matrilineage correctly. They betrayed certain 'modernist' tendencies and had even discussed wiring their Longhouse for electricity. Equally important seems to be the fact that, by their united action, the Lower Cayuga group actually elected the chief councilor in 1957.

There were several competitors for the office of chief councilor, all but one of them important figures in the Progressive faction. One elderly man with poor control over English, little education, and little evidence of prosperity was elected, it is said, by the united vote of the Lower Cayuga group. Too many candidates stood for the election and so divided the small number of voters that the comparatively small bloc vote of the Lower Cayuga Longhouse was sufficient to elect the chief councilor. Members of the Lower Cayuga group refer to the chief councilor as 'more of an Indian than most Christians'.

While the Lower Cayuga Longhouse is declining in prestige among the Longhouse people, it has become an important factor in the politics of the Reserve as a whole. Apparently the group made a straightforward political calculation and determined that their interest would best be served by rejecting the most important ruling of the hereditary council.

(iv) *The Mohawk Workers*. The 'Mohawk Workers' are not all workers nor wholly Mohawks. Many men from this group have, at one time or another, worked in high steel construction and been members of trade unions. But not all men who had been thus employed were members of this faction. The group was founded at about the time of the 1924 political crisis by non-Longhouse people who opposed the installation of the elective council. In fact, the leadership of the Mohawk Workers is provided by men of Christian families who claim membership in the hereditary council.

In the political rhetoric of Grand River the Progressives placed primary emphasis upon 'progress' while the Mohawk Workers emphasized 'rights'. Every step taken by the Canadian government in Indian affairs was interpreted by the Mohawk Workers with respect to how it affected their rights. They are particularly concerned with the rights stemming from their original land grant, most of which has passed into white hands by a variety of means until all that now remains is an area seven miles wide and ten miles long. 'No Indian,' said the Mohawk Workers, 'has ever had the right to sell the land granted to all of us; and no white man has the right to take Indian land.' They believe that Iroquois land tenure was once communal and that the Grand River lands belonged to all equally. In 1930 a group of Mohawk Workers was sent to London in a vain attempt to get a ruling from parliament on their right to the alienated land.

In the late 1940s the Mohawk Workers sent a delegation to the United Nations in hopes that they might be recognized as an independent nationality by the world body. The issue of independent nationality is important to many Reserve people who are not necessarily members of this faction. Indians have the right to unhampered border crossing between the U.S. and Canada in recognition of the aboriginal absence of this boundary. Preachers of the Good Message frequently perform marriage ceremonies (though such marriages are not legally recognized in Canada), and they believe that their right to do so derives from their independent nationality.

Mohawk Workers frequently refer to members of the elective council as 'traitors' to the Indians. They employ the term 'loyalist council' to distinguish the elected body from the hereditary council. They frequently assert that members of the elective council 'buy all their votes' with 'bribes' of the welfare money, which they administer. In fact, it is very difficult for a supporter of the Mohawk Workers—or for any non-voter—to receive welfare benefits, while recipients have been observed to build new houses while living on welfare funds. In order to teach school on the Reserve an Indian must sign an oath of loyalty to the government of Canada. The Mohawk Workers regard assent to this oath as 'taking a bribe', that is, signing away Indian 'nationality' for the sake of a monthly wage.

It would be a mistake to think of the Mohawk Workers as a clearly structured group. Leadership seems to be diffuse except in crisis situations, when it comes from members of the hereditary council. Thus also, there are stronger and weaker supporters of the faction. The Progressive faction also lacks clear leadership, though a few members of this group who are more prosperous and better educated are treated as spokesmen for the faction. Only the Longhouse people have any kind of formal organization, based upon their recognition of the primacy of the chiefs and lineage matrons, and their affiliation with one or another Longhouse. Any member of Reserve society, however, can easily identify the factional affiliation of any other person, whether he is politically active or not. The two diacritical phenomena, religion and voting or non-voting, can be applied to any member of the society to determine his place in the system of political alignments.

Factions and Social Change

My principal intention in dealing with factional politics among the Iroquois is to elucidate the relation between factions and social change. American Indian societies, particularly those with aboriginal acephalous political systems, have suffered the most intense external pressure. The fact that so many of these societies, subjected to similar forces, have factioned suggests a regularity, noted over twenty-five years ago by Linton (1936, p. 229):

Among American Indians the pattern of factions is certainly deep-seated. In some cases two factions have survived for generations, changing leaders and the bases of their disputes and winning some individuals from each other . . . Opposition seems to be the main reason for their existence, their policies and declared grounds for opposition shifting with the circumstances. In some cases any cause which is espoused by one will immediately be resisted by the other.

The first band of Iroquois which migrated to Canada after the American Revolution was made up of Christian Mohawks who settled at Tayendenaga on the Bay of Quinte. There was no religious cleavage to provide an initial organizing principle, yet when the Canadian government introduced the elective system on this Reserve, an anti-government faction immediately rose to oppose the change. This group, known as the 'Longhairs' soon began to participate in the elections, however, and about 1958 this faction controlled the Reserve council.

Fenton (1955, p. 338) has reported similar factions among Iroquois on the Tonawanda and Onondaga Reservations in New York, while he says 'true political parties' operate among the New York Senecas. Wallace (1952, p. 33) has described the strong factional tendencies he found among the New York Tuscaroras. At Taos Pueblo in New Mexico (Fenton 1957, pp. 317-318, 335) there are the out-of-power 'People's Party', which resembles the Mohawk Workers in ideology and action, and the in-power pro-government faction. Fenton (1955, p. 330) has observed similar factions elsewhere in the U.S. among the Klamath and Blackfoot.

Siegel and Beals (1960) are also concerned with the regularity and widespread occurrence of factions. Independently, Siegel observed the factions at Taos, while Beals found a similar pattern in the Indian village of Namhalli described briefly above. They distinguished three varieties of factionalism: party, schismatic, and pervasive factionalism;[7] of these they are primarily concerned with the pervasive form which they assert is common to Taos Pueblo and Namhalli (p. 394), and 'is essentially a phenomenon of socio-cultural change' (p. 399). Such factionalism is the result of 'a complicated interaction between internal strains and external pressures' (p. 414).

The definition of factionalism offered by Siegel and Beals (p. 399) and discussed at the beginning of this section — 'Factionalism is overt conflict within a group which leads to increasing abandonment of cooperative activities' — is related to the authors' view that 'the main incentive for joining a faction appeared to be hostility toward some members of the opposing faction'. I have attempted here to show that individuals align themselves politically with one another primarily out of self-interest; this interest may in some cases be primarily hostility, but obviously hostility alone cannot explain the factional alignments of all the persons in any political arena. Further, I have attempted to show that factions are conflict groups which perform essential political functions. A factional system is not the political 'state of nature' of any of the societies I have examined. The fact that factions are so often found in rapidly changed or changing societies and institutions has no doubt drawn the attention of Siegel and Beals as well as other observers to the disruptive features of factional politics. If we distinguish between the social disruption brought about by social change and the social order brought about by almost any kind of political system, our attention will be drawn to the functions of factions.

Iroquois lineages certainly had multiple functions during the pre-contact and early contact periods. In addition to being the fundamental political segments of Iroquois society, lineages were residential and ceremonial groups. Part of the breakdown of the lineage structure was no doubt due to the inability of white administrators and military personnel to cope with an acephalous political system. They saw chiefs and made a series of assumptions about social inequality and the primacy of certain individuals over others. This factor alone would not have been sufficient to bring about a breakdown of the lineage system, however. But the disruption of lineage landholding and hence of residence pattern brought on by Reserve settlement and sedentary agricultural pursuits, and the disruption of lineage ceremonial functions brought on by Christianity, were probably sufficient severely to weaken the structure. The collapse of the economic and ceremonial functions of lineages was, in turn, responsible for their partial loss of political function.

A society cannot exist without a political system, but political systems can be largely destroyed or rendered ineffective. The view of the Canadian government must have been that the political system at Grand River had either been destroyed by social change or should be rendered ineffective. The government wanted to substitute a new bit of social structure based upon elective representation for an old 'undemocratic' feature based upon hereditary lineage representation. Their assumption that a hereditary government is 'undemocratic' is justified to an extent; the question of 'democracy' does not arise in acephalous societies with general economic equality. But during the Reservation period economic inequality gradually developed; a man farmed his own fields and did not share his produce with other members of his matrilineage or clan. Persons successful under the new economic system did not need to accept the assumptions of the traditional political system if it did not suit them—if they had no hereditary right to membership on the council. Thus, about 1924, the Six Nations people were confronted with a pair of alternative political structures: an elective council, made up of the prosperous minority, and the traditional hereditary council, disrupted as it was by the collapse of lineage functions. Whether because of the remaining functions of the old social structure, or because the hereditary council has never conceded the right of the elective council to decide on Reserve affairs, most people still give at least tacit support to the traditional system by refusing to vote. The recent acceptance of the electoral system by the Lower Cayuga Longhouse may represent the 'wave of the future'. It would be a mistake, however, to see contemporary factional politics as merely a phase in the transition from one political structure to another. These factions have existed, with minor changes, since 1924, and are based upon much older cleavages in Reserve society. Even if, in the next generation, the elective system is accepted by a majority, the character of the new political system will be strongly colored by the present factional system. The implication of this is that the contemporary system has been strongly affected by the previous acephalous system with its institutionalized moiety conflicts and absence of strong, consistent leadership roles.

NOTES

1 The material contained in this paper was presented originally in the South Asia Seminar of the School of Oriental and African Studies while the author was Research Fellow in the Department of Anthropology and Sociology there. I am grateful to the participants in the seminar, particularly Prof. C. von Fürer-Haimendorf, Dr. F. G. Bailey, Dr. Adrian C. Mayer, Dr. P. H. Gulliver, and Mr. Hugh Gray for penetrating criticism and stimulating discussion. Fieldwork in Govindapur village from October 1960, through April 1961, was made possible by a Ford Foundation Foreign Area Training Fellowship; work among the Grand River Iroquois from June through September 1958, was financed by a grant from the Lichtstern Fund of the Department of Anthropology at the University of Chicago. I have taken advantage of the discussion following the presentation of this paper at the Cambridge A.S.A. Conference to strengthen it at a few points.

2 Together with a number of others who have read Lewis's account of factions in Rampur, I think what he treats as factions might more profitably be regarded as Jat descent groups with clients and other appendages. Therefore, in identifying myself as a student of political organization like Lewis, I do not mean that I define faction as he does.

3 The idea of a 'neutral faction' does not fit well into the system I propose here, since I hold that factions appear only during conflict; otherwise, they may be regarded as something like 'latent social organization'.

4 In a discussion after the presentation of this paper Professor Firth argued convincingly that this definition of politics is too narrow, since it cannot easily take account of political events about which all participants are in agreement. I have—perhaps only temporarily— solved this dilemma by relegating events of this kind to the sphere of 'government'. In utilizing this definition, however, it is essential to regard what is ordinarily spoken of as 'competition' as a species of conflict, and, in general, to interpret conflict very widely.

5 All the names used in this section—including the name of the village—are pseudonyms. I have used a different name for each actor identified in this account, and I have distinguished them by titles wherever possible. Thus, Siva and Hari are identified as 'Mukhya', the local term for a village headman; Krisnadas and Ramdas are called 'Mahanta', abbott of a temple'. I have added caste names for members of minority castes; persons not thus identified are members of the dominant Mahisya cultivating caste.

6 The term 'Progressive' is not usually employed on the Reserve to identify this faction. Looking for a convenient label to use in talking about them, I chose 'progress' because it figures so importantly in their rhetoric.

7 The distinction proposed by Siegel and Beals, under the definition I employ here, confuses some non-factional kinds of social conflict with factionalism, and misses what might be a very useful distinction between schismatic and pervasive factionalism. The term 'schismatic' might well be applied to situations, like that among the Ndembu, in which prolonged conflict leads to the fission of the local community; but if the division is between corporate groups, as in lineage fission, I would not apply the term 'factional' to the conflict.

REFERENCES

Bailey, F. G. 1960. *Tribe, Caste, and Nation: a Study of Political Activity and Political Change in Highland Orissa.* Manchester: Manchester University Press.

——— 1963. Closed Social Stratification in India. *Archives of European Sociology* 4:107-124.

Beals, Alan. 1959. Leadership in a Mysore Village. In Richard L. Park & Irene Tinker (eds.), *Leadership and Political Institutions in India.* Princeton: Princeton University Press. Pp. 427-437.

Benedict, Burton. 1957. Factionalism in Mauritian Villages. *British Journal of Sociology* 8:328-342.

Chadwick, E. M. 1897. *People of the Longhouse.* Toronto: Church of England Publishing Company.

Curtis, Michael. 1962. Introduction. In M. Curtis (ed.), *The Nature of Politics.* New York: Avon Books. Pp. xxi-xxx.

Epstein, T. Scarlett. 1962. *Economic Development and Social Change in South India.* Manchester: Manchester University Press.

Fenton, W. N. 1955. Factionalism in American Indian Society. Vienna. *Actes* du IVe Congrés International des Sciences Anthropologiques et Ethnologiques, 1952. Vol. II:330-340.

——— 1957. Factionalism at Taos Pueblo, New Mexico. Washington: Bureau of American Ethnology, Bulletin 164:297-344.

Firth, Raymond. 1957. Introduction to Factions in Indian and Overseas Indian Societies. *British Journal of Sociology* 8:291-295.

Goldenweiser, A. A. 1915. Social Organization of the North American Indians. In *Anthropology in North America.* New York: G. E. Stechert & Co.

Lasswell, Harold. 1931. Faction. *Encyclopaedia of the Social Sciences.* New York: The Macmillan Company. Vol. V:49-51.

Lewis, Oscar. 1958. *Village Life in Northern India: studies in a Delhi Village.* Urbana, Ill.: University of Illinois Press.

Linton, Ralph. 1936. *The Study of Man.* New York: D. Appleton-Century Company.

Mayer, Adrian C. 1961. *Peasants in the Pacific: A study of Fiji Indian Rural Society.* London: Routledge & Kegan Paul.

Morgan, Lewis Henry, 1881. *Houses and House Life of the American Aborigines.* Washington: U.S. Geographical and Geological Survey.

——— 1901. *League of the Ho-de-no-Sau-nee or Iroquois.* Dodd Mead edition of 1901, reprinted 1954. New Haven: Human Relations Area Files, 2 vols.

——— 1928. *Government and Institutions of the Iroquois.* Ed. by Arthur C. Parker. Rochester: Researches and Transactions of the New York State Archaeological Society.

Nadel, S. F. 1951. *The Foundations of Social Anthropology.* Glencoe, Ill.: The Free Press.

Nicholas, Ralph W. 1963. Village Factions and Political Parties in Rural West Bengal. *Journal of Commonwealth Political Studies* 2:17-32.

Nicholas, Ralph W. & Mukhopadhyay, Tarasish. 1965. Politics and Law in Two West Bengal Villages. *Bulletin of the Anthropological Survey of India* (Forthcoming).

Noon, John A. 1949. *Law and Government of the Grand River Iroquois.* New York: Viking Fund Publications in Anthropology, No. 12.

Scalapino, Robert A. & Masumi, Junnosuke. 1962. *Parties and Politics in Contemporary Japan.* Berkeley: University of California Press.

Scott, D. C., *et al.* 1911. Constitution of the Six Nations Iroquois Confederacy; Laws of Dekanawidah; Kane-kon-kets-kwa-se-rah (Condolence Ceremony). MS. on file in the Department of Anthropology, University of Chicago.

Siegel, Bernard J. & Beals, Alan. 1960. Pervasive Factionalism. *American Anthropologist* 62:394-417.

Turnbull, Colin. 1961. *The Forest People.* London: Chatto & Windus.

Turner, V. W. 1957. *Schism and Continuity in an African Society: a Study of Ndembu Village Life.* Manchester: Manchester University Press.

Wallace, A. F. C. 1952. The Modal Personality Structure of the Tuscarora Indians as revealed by the Rorschach Test. Washington: Bureau of American Ethnology, Bulletin No. 150.

PART II

Theories of Clientelism

NETWORKS AND GROUPS IN SOUTHEAST ASIA:
Some Observations on the Group Theory of Politics

CARL H. LANDÉ

FIFTEEN YEARS AGO the Committee on Comparative Politics, in the course of its grand design for the cross-national study of politics along the lines outlined in Gabriel Almond's classic introductory essay in *The Politics of the Developing Areas*, commissioned a series of investigations of "Interest Groups and the Political Process." I was one of the Committee's grantees.

One of our main tasks was to perform censuses of interest groups and to describe their work. On the whole the results were disappointing. The conclusion of most of those who examined developing polities was that "interest groups" do not play as important a part in the political process as had been expected. This conclusion is reflected in the fact that the Princeton series of Studies in Political Development, the major compilation of the product of the Committee and its grantees, includes as yet no volume on "Interest Groups and Political Development." And it seems unlikely that such a volume will appear in the near future.

But if Almond's list of conversion functions remains sound, and I think it does, then "interest articulation" must take place in any political system in which political decision making is a specialized task, and there must be structures to perform it. Almond and Powell, in their 1966 work, amended the theory to take account of the disappointing performance of the four types of groups listed in Almond's 1960 essay, i.e., institutional, non-associational, anomic, and associational interest groups, by drawing attention to the importance of individuals as "articulators of their own interests."[1] But they added that individual self-representation is "commonly cast in the guise of the articulation of more general societal or group interests." This missed a crucial point: That in many developing polities the great bulk of individual self-representation is self-representation pure and simple, without any pretense of a concern for the categorical interests of any collectivity, be it society as a whole or a subgroup within it. The purpose of this paper is to explore the structural basis and the consequences of pure and impure self-representation in several Southeast Asian political systems, and to suggest some propositions and models which, it is hoped, will explain some of their peculiar features.

At the outset, it may be useful to review the essentials of the "group theory" of politics, as well as some criticism of that theory. Stated in its broadest terms, the theory assumes that individuals act in politics largely as members of groups. A group is a set of individuals who share an attitude. They act together because they perceive that by doing so they are most likely to attain objectives consistent with the attitude which they share, and thus to gain similar individual rewards. Groups often, though not invariably, consist of persons whose common attitude stems from the fact that they have some similar "background" characteristic such as sex, age, religion, occupation or social class. For this reason, much theorizing and research by political scientists in modern Western countries has focused on the assumed interrelationship among the socioeconomic background attributes of political actors, their political attitudes, and their political behavior.

The American version of the group theory comes to us from Arthur Bentley by way of David Truman and Earl Latham.[2] Marxist theory makes a similar assumption, that men who have something in common, in this case social class, will and should act in unison in their collective interest. The now largely forgotten theorists of the fascist corporate state also maintained that individuals who are alike do and should act in unison, though in their view the various "corporations" composed in each case of a functionally specialized sector of the economy should not clash but, like the organs of a living organism, work in harmony for the higher purposes of the corporate state.[3]

In all versions of the theory, individuals who become aware of their similar attitudes and/or background are assumed to find it to their advantage to create formal organizations of some sort, the better to advance their shared goals or interests, or to perform their organic functions. But formal organization is not essential to the theory in its broadest form. The essential feature is that individuals who are alike in some respect are more likely to act together than individuals who are not.

As a prescription for self-interested action, the group theory has grave shortcomings. Mancur Olson, an economist, has pointed out that if the purpose of group action is merely to achieve categorical goals through which all members of a category will derive benefits, an individual member has no great incentive to contribute to the common effort. For even if he does not, he can expect to share in the fruits of that effort simply by being a member of that category.[4] The theory has another serious weakness: It assumes that governmental action must take a categorical form: that government, or at least modern government, proceeds according to the rule of law, that is, that laws will be *enforced* rigidly

and impersonally whatever their content, and that individuals can benefit only through the operation of laws which provide similar benefits for all others similar to themselves. Only if this is assumed—and in many developing countries it is a highly dubious assumption—need individuals resort to the cumbersome method of advancing their private interests by working for the similar interests of countless others. These criticisms of the group theory lead to some alternative conceptualizations of political structure, including interest articulation structure: those of the dyad and the dyadically structured system.[5]

THE NATURE OF DYADS

A standard anthropological dictionary defines a "dyadic group" as "a pair of human beings in a social relationship."[6] This simple definition fits almost any two-person group. For the purposes of this discussion, however, some distinctions between different types of dyads are needed.

First, it is useful to distinguish between *corporate dyads* and *exchange dyads*. The former consist of two persons who, in matters that interest the analyst, behave as one. The latter consist of two persons who maintain their separate identities, but are engaged in relationships of exchange. Typically in exchange dyads the two members give or lend property to each other. But its ownership at any point in time, is individual, not joint.

Exchange dyads in turn can be subdivided into *supportive* and *antagonistic* ones. In the former, the two members trade things of value. In the latter they trade injuries.

In actual dyadic relationships, of course, these analytically distinct forms can be mixed. The relationship between the United States and the Soviet Union, for example, now involves both supportive and antagonistic exchanges. And a marriage involves both the pooling and the exchange of resources.

For political scientists, exchange dyads, especially supportive ones, are of primary interest. In the remainder of this paper, when I use the term "dyad" I shall mean supportive exchange dyads unless another type is specified. Some characteristics of dyads, other than those mentioned above, follow:

Dyads may bind together persons who are alike or unalike. The ease with which dyads cut across occupational and class lines makes them of particular importance to political scientists interested in the processes of national integration and conflict resolution.

Benefits obtained through dyadic exchanges tend to be particular rather than categorical. Each partner must reward the other, but need not support the goals of the whole category to which the other belongs.

Dyadic exchanges tend to involve some degree of reciprocity, but need not achieve exact reciprocity. Reciprocity is most likely to be approximated when the relationship is voluntary for both partners, when both must compete freely with other suppliers of the same rewards, when both control resources of roughly equal value, and when the relationship involves a minimum of antagonism. The achievement of exact reciprocity at any point in time, however, facilitates the termination of the dyad, and thus may be avoided.

Dyads usually are linked to other dyads in larger structures, or are capable of being so linked. All the dyadic ties within a society or subsociety constitute its dyadic *network*.

Each member of a dyadically structured system has a personal combination of dyadic partners which is uniquely his own. The personal alliance systems of different individuals may overlap and intersect, but are rarely identical. An individual's personal set of dyadic relationships constitutes his dyadic *web*. As in a spider web, the structurally most important strands are those which extend outward from the central individual by whom or in whose behalf various of his allies, plus some of *their* allies, are brought into action. As in a spider web, the concentric circles of connecting links are of less importance. They represent the cooperation among the central individual's allies that takes place in their common effort to assist him. Insofar as a system is structured dyadically, i.e., as a network, organized action involving many persons tends to begin with the effort of one individual to mobilize members of his web, and then of their webs, in support of what he regards as desirable goals.

Personal webs, like individual dyads, can be subdivided analytically into vertically and horizontally structured ones. *Vertical webs* are those whose central individual has greater status, resources or power than his various dyadic partners have. As a general designation for most vertical webs of a political nature, I suggest the term "personal following." A specific subtype of this general type are patron-client systems. The distinguishing feature of archetypal patron-client relationships is a broad but imprecise spectrum of mutual obligations consistent with the belief that the patron should display an almost parental concern for and responsiveness to the needs of his client, and that the latter should display almost filial loyalty to his patron—beliefs reflected by the tendency for familial appellations to be employed in the relationship. The operation of patron-client systems in politics has been the subject of three recent articles in the *American Political Science Review*. They are characteristic of traditional societies, and appear to be on the decline. Other types of personal followings, however, are likely to be with us for some time to come.

Horizontal webs are those whose central individual has status, resources or power roughly equal to those of his various partners. For these, when they are political, the term "personal alliance system" seems appropriate. An example is an individual congressman's log-rolling arrangements with various of his fellows. All the log-rolling arrangements in Congress constitute a network.

The various dyadic ties within an individual's web may differ in the quality and quantity of their exchanges. Where this is the case, graded favoritism in the treatment of different partners usually is made explicit.

The dyadic webs of individuals may differ in size. The number of one's alliances tends to be limited by one's material resources, and to be positively related to one's status and power.

Dyadic structures tend to be most important, or most noticeable, where discrete structures are in short supply. That is to say, in systems which are small and premodern. Anthropologists therefore have been interested in them for some time. But political scientists, whose models are mainly of modern Western derivation, until recently have given them little attention.[7]

With a view to exploring various forms which dyadic structure can take and various tasks which they can perform, I shall describe certain elements of four Southeast Asian political systems, each at a different point along a rough scale of modernization, and each imbedded in a different religious tradition. These systems are: the pagan Kalinga of Northern Luzon in the Philippines; the Tausug, a Muslim society in the Southern Philippines; the Theravada Buddhist monarchy of Thailand during the Ayudhya and Bangkok periods; and the predominantly Catholic Republic of the Philippines.

THE KALINGA

The first and most "primitive" example of a Southeast Asian polity is that of the Kalinga, one among several pagan peoples who inhabit the mountain region of Northern Luzon. During the period of American colonial rule, the Kalinga, or at least those of them who live near the several roads which have been built through the mountains by the colonial administration, have come increasingly under the influence of the outside world. But many of their traditional institutions survive, or survived long enough to be observed by anthropologists.

The following description of Kalinga political structure is based on studies by Roy Franklin Barton and Edward P. Dozier.[8] From them one learns that like many primitive societies, Kalinga society until recently was organized almost wholly on the basis of kinship ties. Kalinga kinship structure, like that of the other Southeast Asian societies described here, as well as of those of Northern Europe, is a type which anthropologists call "cognatic" or "bilateral."

The interesting characteristic of cognatic kinship, from the point of view of this paper, is that outside the bounds of the immediate or "conjugal" family, its structure is essentially dyadic. In cognatic systems each individual, when he looks beyond his conjugal family, finds himself surrounded by a circle of relatives, a collection of individuals whom anthropologists call the "personal kindred." It is made up of the descendants of all his ancestors of a certain earlier generation without regard to sex or the side of his family tree. In Kalinga, the personal kindred consists for each individual, of all descendants of his eight pairs of great-grandparents.

The main features of cognatic kindreds in Kalinga and elsewhere are as follows: .

Kindreds are individual-centered. That is to say, each individual's kindred is defined with reference to himself, and exists primarily to serve his needs. After his death, it disappears as a distinctive entity.

Kindreds lack discrete external boundaries. Like the ripples from a stone dropped into a pool, the strength of kinship ties gradually declines as the genealogical and affective distance of kinsmen from ego increases.

The size and precise membership of each kindred depends largely upon the person at its core. It does so because he alone can decide how wide a circle of kinsmen he will attempt to cultivate, and which specific kinsmen he wishes to include among the functioning (as distinguished from purely nominal) members of his kindred. It does not depend exclusively upon his wishes, however, for each of those kinsmen with whom he wishes to maintain active ties must in turn be willing to maintain ties with him, i.e., must wish to count him as a member of his own personal kindred.

No two individuals other than siblings have identical kindreds. The kindreds of close relatives other than siblings overlap, but do not coincide. Further, as the kinsmen with whom an individual maintains effective ties depend in large part upon his choice, the effective kindreds of even siblings are not necessarily identical.

Thus a person's kindred is an outwardly radiating collection of dyads with one individual at its core. A community so structured—and this is the case with Kalinga communities—may be conceived of as a dyadic network of what George Peter Murdock describes as "interlacing and overlapping" kinship ties.[9]

Kalinga political culture is of a sort appropriate to an essentially anarchic society characterized by endemic feuding. Fighting skill and bellicosity are highly valued among men, being essential to survival. Contentiousness in litigation, a major preoccupation of the Kalinga, provides less dangerous opportunities for the display of truculence. Egocentrism and family centrism are characteristic of the society, being modified only by the personal loyalty to more distant kinsmen that is necessary for personal survival in a dangerous environment. Similar cultural traits will be noted in connection with some of the other Southeast Asian societies. Because there were in the Kalinga region until American times no "public" functionaries charged with the punishment of murderers or other offenders, the most important function of the kindred was, and to a large degree still is, to support the individual in conflicts over property or personal affronts which might lead to killing, or in case of actual killing to take vengeance through counter-killing against the killer or one of his kinsmen.[10]

While rallying to his support or avenging his death, the personal kindred of an individual, is in a sense, a "group." But it is an ephemeral group, and the willingness of an individual kinsman to participate depends largely upon the way he has been treated in the past by the individual at the kindred's core. In short it depends upon dyadic reciprocity.

It may be asked whether traditional Kalinga society contains any discrete groups of a corporate type. There are a few. One such group, found among the Kalinga as among other peoples, is the conjugal family consisting of a set of parents and their unmarried children. But the family is a temporary group, which disappears with the death of the parents and is replaced by the separate newly formed conjugal families of the children. Furthermore, the Kalinga family begins as a rather uncertain alliance, subject to fission under the stress of rival claims for loyalty from the parental families of each marital partner. Only with the birth of the first child—i.e., with the appearance of an individual related by blood to both parental kindreds, does the marriage become a really stable one.

Among some neighboring and otherwise similar tribes, the people of Sagada and the Ifugao, there are to be found in addition to conjugal families and personal kindreds some cognatic descent groups. These consist of all the descendants, through both male and female links, of some prominent founding ancestor.[11] Such groups, sometimes called "conical clans," are discrete. Their usefulness for the organization of society is limited, however, by the fact that, unlike unilineal descent groups, they overlap so that an individual, through different ancestral lines, may be a member of many such groups. In Sagada, conical clans since the introduction of electoral politics in American times, form the bases of political factions. In addition there are in Sagada clearly demarcated "wards" within which councils of old men settle disputes and organize rituals. But neither of these types of discrete structure are present to a significant degree in Kalinga. They are mentioned here because they remind one of the advantages which lie in discrete groups, and show how discrete groups can be created in simple cognatic societies.

The nature of the terrain inhabited by the Kalinga divides them geographically into a number of distinct settlements. These however had little that could be called local government prior to that which is now imposed by the lowland state. Nowhere in Kalinga, even in very small settlements where all regarded each other as kinsmen, was there a single identifiable "headman." Nowhere was there a body whose members separately or collectively had authority over all inhabitants of the settlement. What existed was not authority but personal leadership. There were and are in every Kalinga settlement some individuals whose exeptional prowess in combat or whose superior wealth or wisdom gave them influence not only over their immediate family members but over many of their more distant kinsmen as well. When one of these self-made leaders decided upon some course of action, a cluster of persons made up of his family and of these more distant kinsmen-followers were likely to support him. And when all of the leaders of substantial personal followings could agree on some course of action—a rare occurrence in any case—a large proportion of the settlement could be mobilized into action—but not the entire settlement. For while not everyone could be a leader, no one was obliged to be a follower. There was always the option of being an independent individual who neither led nor followed any man, and it was the presence of

such individuals, as well as frequent disagreement among leaders, that made communitywide action extremely hard to achieve.

Further, community action was of an extremely limited sort, being concerned mainly with such matters as defense against raiding parties from other settlements. It fell far short of "government." There was no law making, no tax collection, no arresting of accused persons by policemen, no courts, and no public executioner. Killing and other wrongs were torts against individuals and their kindreds, not crimes against the community, and they were dealt with by individuals with the assistance of their kinsmen, and the help of neutral mediators. Under such conditions justice varied, depending upon the relative ferocity of the two antagonists and the size of the kindred which each could mobilize in his support.

While the Kalinga lacked territorial authority, even at the local level, they at least recognized the existence of discrete geographic boundaries between neighboring settlements. Not so the Ifugao, another pagan tribe living nearby. Among the Ifugao, Barton reports, geographic boundaries were vague and shifting. Each "region" or settlement was viewed by its inhabitants as the center of a series of concentric rings which Barton calls respectively the "home region," the "feudist zone," and the "war zone," terms which suggest the decreasing restraints upon violence toward people who live at increasing distances from one's home. The Ifugao had no common conception of a larger territory subdivided into districts or similar units. Zones structured territory as the kindred structured people: in terms of distance from ego or ego's place of residence. Barton, citing Henry Sumner Maine, assumed the absence of discrete territorial boundaries to be a fairly primitive trait. But as will be noted in several of the later cases, a dearth of discrete boundaries or of organization based upon such boundaries, is characteristic of some more advanced polities as well and seems to be consistent with their preference for dyadic structures.

Because the Kalinga, in contrast to the Ifugao, recognized discrete territorial boundaries, they were able to create an interregional network of "peace pacts" which, though essentially dyadic, had some relationship to territory. Until recent times the absence of roads, the virtual restriction of marriage to members of the same locality, and the danger of being killed if one ventured far from one's home region served as a strong deterrent to interregional travel. With the construction of roads through the mountains by the lowland colonial government during the

nineteenth and twentieth centuries, travel between regions became easier while the possibility of profit making through interregional trade
provided incentives for such travel. To assure
their safety when visiting each others' regions,
pairs of native traders established trading partnerships through which each partner gave food
and lodging to the other and, more important,
promised to avenge him as he would avenge his
own kinsmen should the other be killed by someone in that region. During the latter part of the
nineteenth century, this institution which initially had given protection only to the two partners, became transformed into a more elaborate
system under which two "pact holders" living
in different regions undertook each in his own
region to avenge *any* traveler from the other's
region who met violence while visiting there. Individual protection thus became blanket protection, but was still anchored in individuals. It was
the pact holder assisted by his personal kindred,
and not the region, which offered protection. It
was the pact holder who paid compensation if
he failed to avenge, and who collected compensation if the other pact holder failed to do so.
And if a pact holder died, and no one else came
forth to take his place, the pact lapsed and with
it the possibility of safe travel between the two
regions. Furthermore, each two of the many regions of Kalinga had—or did *not* have—their
separate pacts with each other, and for each pact
affecting a region the pact-holder might be a different individual. The complex of pacts thus was
a network, not an association. Finally, whenever a new pact was negotiated, any individual
in either pact holder's region who had an unsettled blood-debt to avenge in the other region
could assert the right to be excluded from the
coverage of the pact.

Thus the Kalinga were never able to devise
what to foreigners might seem a much more logical, effective, and categorical solution to the
problem of individual security: the establishment of a Kalinga-wide confederation guaranteeing everyone protection everywhere. The
system was as primitive, and as dyadic in structure, as was the international community of
powers prior to the establishment of the League
of Nations.

THE TAUSUG

The second Southeast Asian political system
is that of the Tausug, a Moslem ethno-linguistic
group of some 325,000 persons who live in the
Sulu island chain which links the main Southern
Philippine island of Mindanao with Northern

Borneo. Roughly half of the Tausug reside on
the largest of the Sulu islands, Jolo. The Tausug
have a cognatic kinship system with a slight
patrilineal bias which is attributable to the influence of Islam. Most of them live in scattered
upland settlements where they engage in intensive dry rice farming. The description and explanation of Tausug political institutions presented
here is taken entirely from the studies of Thomas
M. Kiefer, an anthropologist.[12]

Unlike the rest of the territory of the present
Republic, the Southern extremities of the Philippine archipelago, including Sulu, never came
under the effective rule of the Spanish colonial
regime. Foreign military subjugation of its
"Moro" inhabitants was accomplished only
during the American colonial period. Even now
the authority of the national government in this
region is uncertain. The Tausug continue to deal
with their own affairs, and in particular to settle
their own disputes, largely through traditional
political institutions. Thus the Tausug, though
nominally Filipinos, retain a political culture
and a largely autonomous political system which
are premodern in nature and which have more
in common with the culture and polity of traditional Moslem Indonesia and Eastern Malaysia
than with those of the long Christianized majority of the Philippines.

Except for some now moribund functions of
the sultan, Kiefer's description is of Tausug political institutions as they function today. These
institutions are of interest here because, as
Kiefer observes:

Corporate groups on all planes of society except
the ultimate level of the *sultan*, are distinctly
secondary to dyadic social relationships.[13]

and:

The Tausug seem to have taken the pervasive
Philippine indigenous institution of dyadic
ritualized friendship and used it as a major
foundation for the establishment of a state based
on islamic models, without having developed
the geographically defined units of . . . more
politically centralized societies.[14]

In contrast to the Kalinga, the Tausug, prior
to the imposition of American colonial rule during the second decade of this century succeeded
in creating an incipient state. They shared a conception of a supralocal community with a common body of law and a collection of offices differing in their dignity and the spatial extent of
their authority. These offices reached their apex
in the office of the sultan.

This community, its law, and its offices survive today. The sultan in recent years has lost

many of his old duties. Not so the local head-men-leaders who are the main subjects of Kiefer's study, and are of special interest from the point of view of the dyadic model. These functionaries continue to play a number of important roles—the nature of which can be explained in part by certain features of Tausug culture.

Like the political culture of the Kalinga, that of the Tausug places a high value upon the personal defense of honor and property. This encourages a high incidence of both violence and litigation. Vengeance killing in the pursuit of private feuds is endemic. The obvious parallels with Kalinga feuding suggest that this is a pre-Islamic element of Tausug political culture. At the same time, Kiefer notes, the Tausug seek order and a sense of community through their common acceptance of a Tausug version of Islamic law.

Out of these contrasting values arises a need for figures of superordination who are adept both at peacekeeping through the enforcement of the law, and at the type of violent action demanded by feuding. Both tasks are performed by men whom Kiefer describes variously as headmen or as leaders.

That part of Tausug ideology which the Tausug themselves believe to be Islamic in derivation requires that every Tausug be subject to the law. More precisely, it requires that he be subject to an *individual* capable of acting as "the law," a person who has the authority to adjudicate, arbitrate or mediate, and the physical means to see to it that the outcomes of such legal actions are obeyed. The substance of this law is laid down in written form by each reigning sultan. The authority to enforce it, i.e., to act as "the law" is also bestowed by the sultan through the awarding of one of a variety of ranked secular or religious titles, though this function of the sultan now is performed less frequently than formerly.

But subjection of individuals to specific superordinates qualified to act as "the law" involves a substantial element of individual consent. While some titles are claimed through inheritance, they are in practice awarded only to those who have been able to gain acceptance as leaders. Furthermore, a headman's authority when it has been given formal sanction by the sultan, remains confined to those who are willing to be subject to it. This means that headmanship is not, strictly speaking, territorial. Receipt of a title, Kiefer reports, "does not necessarily guarantee to the holder any particular territory which is exclusively his own and distinct from that of any other office holder."[15] It has more the character of a license to practice law then of judicial authority over a specified bailiwick. Yet it does have a limited spatial aspect: Usually in any local settlement there will be found but one title holder. In the general vicinity of his domicile, his authority, legal and otherwise, is strong and nearly exclusive. The requirement that every Tausug be subject to *some* title holder qualified to act as the law, and the awesome proximity of a popular headman would seem to encourage acceptance. But with increasing distance from his place of residence, the proportion of individuals who decline to accept his authority in legal matters or who divide their allegiance between him and the headman of a neighboring settlement increases. Furthermore, his power to adjudicate declines with increasing distance, and only the ability to arbitrate or mediate remains. Finally, the range of his authority and influence may expand and contract during the course of his lifetime, and differ markedly from that of previous headmen who had the same place of residence.[16]

When disputes arise between the subjects of different headmen, they usually can be arbitrated by a higher title holder. But many disputes, it appears, are not settled through such peaceful means. Often disputes lead to violence which may turn into large scale warfare. And then Tausug headmen, especially the younger among them, assume different and more partisan roles as leaders of small bands of men of fighting age whose function is to support their members in their private feuds with non-members. Indeed, it is leadership of such armed bands that gives them the raw power needed to qualify as agents of the law in the Tausug state.[17] These armed followings in turn are but elements of larger fighting alliances which are made necessary by the Tausug dedication to feuding and to war.

Kiefer examines this system of fighting alliances in detail. In describing its structure he begins with simple dyadic relationships of friendship and of leadership and followership. For this purpose he employs a formal model of dyadic interaction based upon a model I had presented in an earlier publication.[18] Alliances for mutual aid between leaders of personal followings in turn are used to create *ad hoc* combinations of increasing size, culminating in maximal alliances which may stretch across an area spanning the whole Sulu archipelago, and pit themselves against equally extensive opposing alliances. At all levels except that of the sultanate itself, Kiefer finds "dyadism" to be the most striking structural feature of the system. Indeed, dyadism manifests itself even in the heat of battle, where each combatant directs his fire with a due regard for the nature of his connection with, and the degree of his enmity toward each member of the opposing side.[19]

While using the same structural devices as the Kalingas, the Tausug in their alliances are able to mobilize much larger numbers of fighting men for individual engagements. The reason for this is clear. The Kalinga, in pursuing what remain purely private feuds, rely for support upon a relatively small number of actual kinsmen. The only exception to this rule is the peace pact, a recent invention which through the establishment of compacts between unrelated pact holders in different regions offers protection to individual travelers far from home. The Tausug have moved to a higher stage of both integration and conflict. Sharing a sense of membership in an incipient state, which brings with it a general interest and involvement in the power struggles of great men, and being far more mobile than the mountain-bound Kalinga, the Tausug have created large alliances for the pursuit of civil and external war. For this, ties between kinsmen are not enough. Therefore, they have learned to make extensive use of interpersonal alliances of friendship and ritual kinship formalized through the common Muslim Filipino custom of swearing together on the Koran.

To sum up, in a society where discrete descent groups, voluntary associations, and territorial units are lacking, relationships of superordination and subordination are highly personal, and to a large degree voluntary. The span of a superordinate's authority has no clear cut boundaries either in terms of territory or population groups. Thus as in Kalinga, dyadic structure is superimposed upon both space and society.

THE MONARCHY OF PREMODERN THAILAND

The next example of a Southeast Asian political system is that of a fully developed monarchy. The case employed for this purpose is the absolute monarchy of Thailand from the beginning of the reign of King Trailokanat (1448 AD) in the latter part of the Ayudhya period, until the accession of King Chulalongkorn (1873) which marked the end of the early Bangkok period. This monarchy had a strong ruler, and performed a wide variety of administrative tasks. Nonetheless it relied heavily upon dyadic structure in performing them.

The institutions of the monarchy underwent many changes during the four centuries from which information is drawn. But the features to which I call attention retained their essential character throughout most of this time. My main sources are two historical reconstructions, one focusing upon the Ayudhya period and based largely on legal texts, by H. G. Quaritch-Wales, the second dealing with the early Bangkok period, and based on a broader spectrum of contemporary records by a Thai scholar, Akin Rabibhadana.[20]

Like almost all of Southeast Asia prior to the twentieth century, premodern Thailand had a population much smaller than that which could be supported by the available land. This was especially the case because the population of Thailand, like most of lowland Southeast Asia, cultivated irrigated rice, a grain which produces a very high yield for a given amount of land. The surplus of land meant that most of premodern Southeast Asia, in the words of Georges Condominas, consisted of a scattering of cultivated islands of population set in an empty but potentially cultivable jungle. As a result, Rabibhadana argues, manpower was more in demand than land. This had important political consequences. One of these consequences was that in mainland Southeast Asia the main purpose of warfare was the capture of populations with a view to settling them on uncultivated land in the environs of the conqueror's capital, rather than the acquisition of new terrain in distant places. This meant in turn that from a ruler's point of view the effective mobilization of his own subjects for attack and defense in time of war was essential to the survival of his realm, while the demarcation of precise jungle boundaries between his and the neighboring realm was of less importance.[21]

This favorable ratio of men to land may have encouraged the growth of structural and normative patterns useful for the maintenance of control over people: Patron-client ties imposed by the state, obedience, deference, the repayment of favors on the part of those subject to the power of others, and the possession and conspicuous display of large personal retinues on the part of the powerful.[22]

Students of Thai history are in some disagreement as to the structure of the Thai political system during the first century of the Ayudhya period and the Sukhothai period which preceded it. As early as the time of King Trailokanat, however, most of the realm was under direct royal administration through governors appointed by the king, though some outlying areas were in the early part of the period under the largely independent but non-hereditary control of certain princely kinsmen of the king. In the capital there were established a number of departments of government called *krom*. During the early portion of the period these *krom* with few exceptions were under the effective or titular headship of high ranking princes or princesses. Commoner officials staffed their lower levels, and during the Bangkok period often rose to *krom* headships. Nonetheless, the princes and princesses as a group maintained their positions of privilege well into the present century. Indeed resentment of these privileges by Western-educated commoner officials was one of the causes of the palace revolt of 1932 which ushered in the present system of government.

The main administrative tasks of the premodern Thai monarchy consisted in peacetime, of public works construction, and in wartime of the organization of large scale military activity. The labor involved in these efforts was provided by the mass of the king's subjects. It is the manner in which this labor was mobilized and directed that is of special interest here, for it was managed through an elaborate system of patron-client arrangements which endured with but minor modifications from the fourteenth to the nineteenth century.

The earliest references to such a system are for the year 1356, when by a royal command everyone was required to register under a leader. Those who failed to do so were to be registered directly under the king.[23] It was under such leaders or patrons *(nai)* that service to the king was to be performed by those who were registered as their clients *(phrai)*. The *nai* were thus in effect officials of the state, and this soon came to mean that for those who were not princes or princesses, and thus were not entitled to have clients as a matter of right, an appointment to an official post became a prerequisite—and a license—for the enlistment of clients.

The system was actually a pyramidal one. Lesser officials who had clients of their own were in their turn the clients of higher officials, and all officials above a certain grade, whether they were princes or not, were the direct clients of the king to whom they pledged personal allegiance.

Although this officially created patron-client tie entailed quite specific government-related duties, it appears to have included a broader, more diffuse set of mutual obligations as well. Aside from service to the state and the patron's legal responsibility to deliver his client to the courts and defend him there if he was charged with a crime, it involved, as do patron-client relationships in most premodern societies, a broad range of supervisory and protection responsibilities on the part of the patron who in turn could dispose of substantially more of his clients' time than that which they owed the state.

Eventually the system became quite complex. For those outside the ranks of the *nai*, three distinctive alternative forms of subordination were recognized by law. All of these involved attachment to a specific superordinate. Some clients were attached for their government service directly to a princely or bureaucratic superior. Others were attached directly to the king. He in turn assigned them to perform their service under specific officials who thus had both direct and royal clients working under their direction. Finally, a substantial number of Thai, estimated by a nineteenth-century European observer to comprise one-fourth of the population, were bound to specific members of the princely and bureaucratic elite not as government service clients but as private debt bondsmen.[24]

The subordination system described here is thus a classic example of vertical dyadic structure.[25] As might be expected in a system so organized, conflict between the king and the lesser power-holders of his realm took the form of a struggle over the right to control and make use of manpower more than over the possession of land.[26] In this struggle the *nai*, led by the great princes were for a time the stronger. As royal clients were wholly the king's men, their annual periods of *corvée* service were longer than those which could be demanded of direct clients of officials, a portion of whose time belonged to the latter for their private disposal in lieu of what in modern times would have been their salaries, or of debt bondsmen who had the heaviest nonofficial demands on their time. As many commoners had at least some choice in determining their own status, their patrons encouraged them to choose direct clientage or, ideally, debt bondage. The patrons did this by securing for their direct clients or debt bondsmen increased (and sometimes total) exemption from government service, and by making private service less onerous than government service.[27] This alienation of royal clients during the latter years of the Ayudhya period contributed, in the opinion of Rabibhadana, to the weakening and defeat of the state at the hands of the Burmese. Subsequent rulers at Bangkok reversed the trend and increased their control of manpower by lessening the burdens of royal clients while decreasing the exemptions from *corvée* service of private clients and debt bondsmen, and by requiring that all clients be tatooed with the names of their patrons and their towns of residence.[28]

One aspect of the traditional Thai system has

special importance for an understanding of the functioning of dyadic structures and of the conditions under which they can be expected to be prominent: A question on which Thai specialists have been in some disagreement is whether the *krom* of premodern Thailand were territorial units, functionally specialized units, or a mixture of the two. The historical materials presented by H. G. Quaritch-Wales suggested to him and to others who have accepted his interpretation, including Vella, Mosel, and Siffin, that an earlier "feudalistic" territorial form of organization was replaced in King Trailokanat's time by a system of centrally directed *krom* that in the words of Mosel, "tended to have both territorial and functional responsibilities, which in time led to considerable confounding and overlap."[29]

Fred Riggs, drawing on Heine-Geldern, has attempted to account for this apparent structural confusion by suggesting that late Ayudhya *krom* were designed to be neither territorial nor functionally specialized entities but rather to be "cosmological and topological" units which would conform to the requirement, derived from Indian religious belief, that the realm, like the palace at its center, be arranged in accordance with the directions of the compass. Territorial or functional responsibilities or both were then assigned to these units, Riggs argues, as convenience dictated.[30] Riggs' suggestion that *krom* were designed to be something other than territorial or functional units seems reasonable, but a cosmological explanation of this fact seems unconvincing as more than a partial explanation. I find more persuasive the interpretation of Rabibhadana, which was foreshadowed by Hanks, that the *krom* were intended primarily to be units of manpower.[31] If this interpretation is correct, then the aim of the monarch in establishing the *krom* would appear to have been a dual one: to attain tight control over a maximum number of his subjects, and to make use of, but at the same time limit, the power of his princely kinsmen. Given the man-land ratio of premodern Thailand and the values and forms of organization which this encouraged, as well as the rule of declining princely descent, the most efficient method of achieving these overarching goals was to attach individuals to individuals in a great pyramid of centrally controlled nonhereditary patron-client arrangements.[32] The assignment to such units of designations which satisfied cosmological, functional, or territorial needs would have been a matter of little difficulty.

Some evidence that supports this interpretation, presented by Rabibhadana, includes his finding that new *krom* frequently were created to provide positions and clients for specific princes and princesses, and conversely that on the death of a prince his clients often were transformed into royal clients and the *krom* as a whole, consisting of both clients and lesser officials, converted into a sub-*krom* and attached to another major *krom*.[33]

But the contrary interpretation, that *krom* were more than transitory unspecialized aggregations of manpower, is supported by the fact that various *krom* did have names indicative of specific functions. And further ambiguity is added because during some periods at least, when a high personage lost his *krom*, his direct clients remained with him and could be inherited by his descendants, while his royal clients stayed with the *krom*.[34]

It appears, then, that there is no single way of describing a *krom* in premodern Thailand. It seems to have been a catchall term used to describe various kinds of units including the personal retinue of a prince, a troop of soldiers under an appointive nonprincely commander, and a rough territorial jurisdiction defined as much by its inhabitants as by precise geographic boundaries. In later years it came to mean a functionally specific department of the central government. But clearly even in quite recent times, many *krom* were designed at least in part to provide support groups and a living for the great men and women of the realm.

The advantages of a system of administration employing movable entourages is obvious. The leader with his clients can be shifted about without being allowed to develop the strength that is to be derived from a fixed territorial base. Yet he is made a useful agent of the king by being given a body of men personally loyal to himself —an essential ingredient of effective administration in premodern societies. If he proves his loyalty to the king, he can be allowed to increase the size of his following. If his loyalty is in doubt, his retinue can be decreased or taken from him, or he can be made subordinate to a more trusted leader, or sent off with his men to some distant place. This type of organization is possible, however, only in a state which can dispense with complex and stable territorial organization, and one in which the need for a high degree of functional specialization at the center has not yet developed. This, it appears, was the case in premodern Thailand.

Patron-client relationships described here for the late Ayudhya and early Bangkok periods, continue to be among the main building blocks of the Thai society and polity today. David Wilson has given us the classic description of how great personal followings serve as the support groups of individual members of governing "coup groups" both in the Thai bureaucracy, military and civilian, and in Parliament. Fred Riggs has examined the same subject further, and in addition has explored patron-client relationships between high Thai officials and Chinese pariah capitalists on the one hand, and those between such officials and the organizers of various voluntary associations on the other. William Siffin has explored the same subject in the sphere of administration. Finally, various non-political scientists, aside from Hanks and Rabibhadana, including James Mosel and Herbert Phillips, have noted the importance of personal alliances in nonpolitical spheres of contemporary Thai society.[35] Their findings will not be summarized, for Thailand is employed here as the example of a premodern monarchy.

THE MODERN PHILIPPINES

For analysis of a modern system which makes much use of dyadic structures and techniques, a society with yet another religious tradition may be examined: that of the predominantly Christian, Hispanicized, and Americanized Republic of the Philippines.

The Philippine case is based upon my own past and ongoing research. A more detailed discussion of Philippine politics may be found elsewhere.[36] The Philippine political system is set within a political culture which may be described as follows: The individual sees himself in an unpredictable, competitive world in which his first concern must be with his own welfare and that of his immediate family. In the pursuit of self and family interest he finds himself in conflict with others. This leads to mistrust and envy. It also leads to the placing of a high value upon the achievement of power and dominance, which places him beyond the reach of the envious and allows him to advance his interests with a minimum of external interference.[37]

The individual and his family need not, however, face the competitive world alone. They can form alliances with others for the purpose of mutual aid. Power and wealth are useful in the building of such alliances. The ideal is to have many allies which maximizes one's security. Alliances are built not only for the dyadic exchange of aid but also for the establishment of a common front against outsiders which allows a successful combination to appropriate a disproportionate share of the available benefits. Combinations can vary in size, expanding or contracting in accordance with the size of the arena and the size of the largest opposing combination. Old allies can quickly become opponents in a struggle over the allotment of the rewards of their earlier collaboration. In such a setting a high value is placed upon the redistribution, among followers and allies of any member of a combination, of benefits which he may obtain.

Though Philippine society is highly competitive, there exists, nonetheless, an awareness of a broader community-wide interest and a yearning for community-wide harmony. While skeptical of the practicality of achieving a general increase in wealth through collective action, and dubious about the possibility of achieving exact justice through the equalization of benefits, Filipinos realize that no important individual or group will accept permanent exclusion from access to benefits, and that peace within the community requires that none be permanently excluded. Inclusion is achieved not through equalizing policies but through the rotation of benefits over time. Letting other people "have their chance," like redistributive sharing, is thus seen to be essential to social harmony.

Philippine political culture thus has some similarities with those of the earlier political systems, but it differs from them as well. Though "individualistic" to the point of disorder, it is not anarchic to the same degree as those of the Kalinga and Tausug. Though highly inegalitarian, it lacks the harsh authoritarianism of premodern Thailand. Finally, while it provides a setting appropriate for a heavy reliance on dyadic action, it also offers hope to aspirations for collective action for the common good.

Structurally, the Philippine political system viewed from the top downward, appears to be composed mainly of discrete entities: There are a wide variety of occupationally specialized voluntary associations. There are two nation-wide political parties which biennially run slates of candidates for a wide variety of elective offices. There is a Congress, both of whose houses usually though not invariably organize themselves at the beginning of each session on party lines. There are departments and agencies of government staffed largely by those who have passed civil service examinations. And there is a system of courts. All of these political and governmental structures function in part at least as do their American counterparts.

But in other ways, which seem puzzling to American observers, these structures operate in a manner not easily explained by the group theory of politics. Associational and institutional interest groups account for only a small part of the totality of interest articulation. The two major parties are identical in their social composition and do not present distinctive or

---

even distinguishable programs to the electorate. Party switching is endemic, as are cross-party alliances for control of the government. Two presidents of the Republic, since Independence, switched parties shortly before being elected. Repeatedly in the House of Representatives disloyal members of one party have helped to overthrow their party's speaker by joining with the opposite party to install one of the latter's members in this powerful post. Twice in recent years members of one party helped the opposite party retain the speakership with the tacit support of their own party's chief executive. Members of the bureaucracy, on the whole, show but limited regard for formally established lines of authority, while judges often are suspected of deciding cases with less than strict impartiality.

Some reasons why this system operates quite differently from the American one, whose macro-structures it seems at first sight to duplicate, begin to appear when one examines the Philippine political system not from the top downward but from the bottom upward. One then discovers that it makes as much use of non-discrete as of discrete structures. For the performance of certain tasks it relies heavily, though not of course exclusively, upon a great net of dyadic alliances, some of them horizontal but more of them vertical, leading inward and upward from the villages to the national government, from "little people" to "big people," and from those who have favors to ask or demands to make to those who have the power to grant them. This network of alliances often shows little regard for the boundaries which separate discrete structures, whether they be interest groups, parties, or the various instrumentalities of government. And in performing its various tasks, the Philippine political system proceeds as much through particular decisions affecting specific individuals, and based on the principles of favoritism and the *quid pro quo*, as through categorical decisions applied impersonally and impartially in accordance with the law. In short, the Philippine political system makes use of both discrete and dyadic structures in a mix which contains a substantially larger component of dyadic structure than does its American counterpart.

The nature of this Philippine mixture can be seen in the way the system performs two major tasks: the election of public officials and the processing of the public's demands for governmental outputs. I shall discuss each of these two tasks and the structures which perform them separately.

The most striking feature of elections in the Philippines is the strong disposition of the mass of ordinary citizens to vote for "personalities" rather than political parties. Clear evidence of this was found in the course of analyzing the contents of a large number of ballots taken from ballot boxes in ten sample precincts of a typical province after the off-year elections of 1963. These showed that in the average precinct, 74 per cent of the ballots were cross-party ones, i.e., contained votes for candidates of more than one party.[38]

The cross-party voting habits of the electorate have their counterpart in the campaign techniques of candidates for elective offices. These find it necessary to build what are essentially personal campaign organizations. In this they seek the help of lower level political leaders who have personal followings whose votes they can deliver, and of candidates for even higher offices who are willing to help finance the candidate's campaign in exchange for aid in their own search for votes. In both cases, their main concern is to find strong allies, without much regard for their party identification. Thus many such alliances cut across party lines.

Formally, each party is an association composed of those who have become party members. In practice each party, at any point in time, is a multi-tiered pyramid of personal followings, one heaped upon the other. Each link in the chain of vertical dyads is based upon personal assurances of support and conditional upon the downward flow of patronage and spoils. But even this description of a party exaggerates its coherence. For as has been noted, political leaders wander into and out of parties with their personal followers in tow, feeling no strong obligation, and being under no real pressure, to support their party mates. Party membership is not a category but a matter of degree.[39]

If one wishes to discover the real framework upon which election campaigns are built, one must turn away from political parties and focus one's attention upon individual candidates and the vertical chains of leadership and followership into which they arrange themselves at any given point in time. While tending to tie together persons who claim the same party label, these chains must in fact be viewed as independent structures resembling a network of strong vines which variously cling to or twist back and forth between two great but hollow trees.

The personal basis of political loyalty helps to account for the types of individuals who win elections. Victory tends to go to those with the greatest personal wealth, to those with the most flamboyant campaign styles, and to those who are thought most likely to be able to win and thus to have access to patronage and other rewards of office. A candidate's position on questions of ideology or his loyal support of such as there is of party policy appears to be of minimal importance.

When one inquires into the way the public's demands for governmental outputs are processed in the Philippines, one finds that less use is made of the "primary" ties of kinship and patronship-clientship than was the case in the contesting of elections, and more use is made of ties arising out of considerations of specialized economic interest. But such arrangements insofar as they are employed, also are in large part dyadic.

In Almond's reworking of the "group theory" of politics into the framework of a political systems model, the demands of individual citizens, in a more developed polity are satisfied through a series of consecutive "conversion processes," performed by a number of specialized structures. Conversion as it goes through its several stages involves the progressive transformation of the particular into the categorical, and then into the particular once again. In the end, the individual citizen gets what he wants, or a portion of it, but only as a result of a lengthy process that is designed to assure that all who are like himself will receive the same benefits or be subjected to the same deprivations.

Almond's model of this process fits the Philippines only to a limited degree. Private goals may be attained in disregard of the law by members of all social strata. The powerful, the rich, and the well connected, can obtain favored treatment through personal office holding, through the use or threat of force, or by offering material rewards to bureaucratic decision makers. The weak and the poor often can hope to obtain leniency either by becoming the clients of persons in positions of power or, in the case of those who lack such connections, through appeals for *awa* (pity)—an appeal which carries much weight in Philippine culture. For those who can obtain governmental favors or exemption from law for themselves, and this includes most of the politically adept members of society, there is little incentive to work for the passage of general legislation. This helps to account for the relatively small part which is played in the interest articulation process by organized interest groups.

The argument should not be overstated. There are in the Philippines many voluntary associations which to some degree resemble American pressure groups, and their number is growing rapidly.[40] With a few exceptions, however,

notably that of the sugar industry, for whose political effectiveness there is a special historical explanation, these groups are small, subject to fission, and fairly short lived. While they do press for general legislation, major portions of their leaders' efforts are devoted to interceding with public officials on behalf of specific individuals and firms. As a result, many such associations are widely thought to be the personal instruments of their leaders whose private interests receive first attention. Ordinary members of the category for which an association professes to speak usually have little to gain through membership unless they have personal ties with the leaders sufficiently close to justify the hope that special efforts at intervention will be made in their behalf. Most individuals find it more to their advantage to cultivate whatever personal connections they may have with any politician who is willing to help them obtain favors.

The nature of Philippine political structure also affects the outcome of the interest aggregation process. Specifically, it prevents the two major parties from offering the electorate a choice between two reasonably coherent and distinctive party programs. The reason for this appears to be as follows: According to Almond's schema, which fits most modern democracies, individual political parties, while representing broader slices of society than do individual interest groups, still seek support mainly from one or another part of the whole spectrum of interests. This permits each party to devise a program that is at least to some degree distinctive and coherent. In the Philippines, however, both major political parties are what Maurice Duverger called "cadre parties," led by members of the elite who in each province and town compete with each other in seeking electoral support from members of all social strata.[41] They are able to win such support largely through the massive distribution of a broad spectrum of particular rewards appropriate to the private needs of members of all sectors of society. At the same time, leaders in both parties compete with each other in trying to satisfy to some degree at least the broader legislative demands of virtually all articulate interest groups.

This makes both major parties excellent compromisers but poor instruments for the formulation of distinctive and consistent programs. Such programs, insofar as they exist at all in the Philippines, are the creations not of parties but of individuals. Each new president when he takes office begins to create his own program. In doing so, he is guided by his personal views, the views of his advisers, and by a variety of pressures from diverse sources which no president can ignore. Each member of the Congress does roughly the same, though many members of both parties respond in some degree to pressure or persuasion from the incumbent president. Thus, the legislative output of the Philippine government is the resultant of the individual decisions of numerous legislators, guided to some degree by the president, rather than the handiwork of the dominant political party as such.

However legislation in any case is a less important aspect of the governmental process in the Philippines than in countries where laws are strictly enforced. More important from the point of view of most voters and therefore of most legislators is the way law is enforced—or not enforced—with respect to specific individuals, firms, and localities by administrators.

Members of the Congress influence administrative decisions by threatening to cut departmental appropriations or block promotions, as well as by placing their own proteges in various departments and agencies. One finds therefore a complex network of personal alliances which cut across the formal boundaries between the branches of government. This is the case, of course, in all political systems to some degree, but in the Philippines the pattern is especially marked.

This system of alliances has consequences for the informal operation of the executive branch. Since the proteges of members of Congress are more dependent for their advancement upon the intervention of their extradepartmental patrons than upon the good will of their immediate superiors, bureaucratic discipline is uncertain. Saddled with many uncontrollable subordinates, the wise official responds by attempting to create a personal following of his own among those of his subordinates who show a willingness to give him their primary loyalty in return for the receipt of special favors, and by refusing to delegate authority to any but his personal clients.[42]

To summarize: Together with a multistage conversion process, performed by a succession of specialized structures, one finds in the Philippines a much more simple process of favor seeking and favor giving between members of the public and administrative decision makers. This process is carried on through chains of dyadic ties that bypass interest groups, parties and the lawmaking structures, and therefore lessen the part they play in the country's governance.

A number of consequences follow from this heavy reliance upon dyadic methods of goal attainment:

(1) It provides specific benefits for some members of all sectors of society, thereby minimizing intercategorical, including interclass, hostility, and reducing the bitterness of conflict between the political parties as well as between other organized groups. At the same time, it produces dissatisfaction among those other members of all sectors of society who have not received their share of specific rewards.

(2) By permitting favoritism to undermine the impersonal administration of justice, it contributes to the near anarchy which presently prevails in many parts of the Philippines, and it erodes public confidence in the system of government.

(3) It causes changes in governmental policy to be secular rather than cyclical, for it makes change depend not upon the alternation in power of the two political parties but mainly upon long-term changes in the constellation of forces in Philippine society, as well as upon the accident of an individual president's personal views.

(4) It produces a system whose responsive and distributive capabilities are quite high, but whose extractive and regulative capabilities are exceedingly low.

(5) It makes the mobilization of political support immensely costly both in money and effort. An added cost is the growing conviction among many Filipino intellectuals that holding these highly expensive periodic elections is too high a price to pay for the advantages of democracy.

(6) Finally, it leads to that preoccupation with personalities, offices, and spoils, and that lack of interest in policy or ideology, which is so strikingly characteristic of Philippine politics.

THE FOUR SYSTEMS COMPARED

Four Southeast Asian political systems, imbedded in different political traditions and representing different stages of political modernization, have illustrated the tasks which can be performed by dyadic structures composed variously of ties of kinship, friendship, patronship-clientship and interpersonal political alliances.

It may be asked why these Southeast Asian societies show such a marked tendency to employ dyadic structures in preference to discrete ones. Several possible explanations suggest themselves: One is that the peoples of these societies find models of dyadic structure in their cognatic kinship systems, and therefore are inclined to favor dyadic devices when they build larger structures that embrace nonkinsmen. If this is true, then peoples that have unilineal descent systems, which divide society into discrete clans and lineages, should favor those nonkinship structures that are discrete. I have discussed some cases which illustrate such a transfer of structural principles from the kinship to the nonkinship sphere elsewhere.[43] And there is statistical evidence of a strong association between the presence or absence of these two types of kinship and that of some other political institutions.[44] But the argument must not be pressed too far. A growing body of anthropological research shows that peoples with unilineal systems of descent employ various types of dyadic structures alongside discrete descent groups and voluntary associations. In such societies, dyads are used especially to build alliances across the boundaries which separate descent groups so as to free rulers and others from an exclusive dependence upon their lineage and clan mates.[45] And peoples with cognatic systems of kinship in Southeast Asia and elsewhere, as they become more modern, do of course make an increasing use of discrete structures.

There are other possible explanations for the proliferation of dyadic structures of the type described here in these four societies, which are not inconsistent with the previous one. The shortage of manpower in relationship to available land, which prevailed in most of Southeast Asia until quite recently, may have encouraged the development of a variety of simple but effective dyadic devices, ranging from compulsory clientage through debt bondage to slavery, which allow individuals to exploit the labor of other individuals for their private advantage. (In regions where land is scarce the impetus for the creation of patron-client ties probably is more likely to come from below, i.e., from tenants who seek to ensure their access to land.)

The endemic nature of private violence, encouraged by a conception of honor which requires that personal affronts and injuries be avenged by force, may have also encouraged the extension of webs of alliances suitable for defense and offense in private warfare. The steady growth of private armies under the control of warlord-politicians, a neo-feudal development which has characterized the Philippines since independence and is one of the underlying causes

of the current crisis in that country, illustrates this point.

Finally, all four societies share a "limited good," "constant pie," or "zero sum" view of the resources available in a community in the sense in which these terms have been applied by George Foster in Mexico and James Scott in Malaya.[46] Such a view, which perceives anyone else's gain to be one's own loss, would seem to encourage a strategy for self advancement that leads the individual to concentrate upon seeking concrete benefits for himself and his family, to reward others only on the basis of a quid pro quo, and to try to convert others into exploitable dependents.

It may be asked how it was possible for these four systems to operate with so little reliance on discrete structures. The answer would seem to lie in the fact that the particular needs of individuals can be met fairly effectively through dyadic interactions, and that discrete structures, general laws, and their impersonal enforcement are necessary only when categorical or collective goals are sought.

Barton's and Kiefer's descriptions of Kalinga and Tausug political life suggest that the traditional political process in these societies consists mainly of tasks that can be performed separately for various individuals, and in a decentralized fashion, i.e., of the *adjudication* of private disputes. Deliberate *legislation* does not occur in Kalinga where custom is the basis of law. In the Tausug state, law codes are formulated by the sultan, without the aid of a council or similar body. *Administration*, Kiefer reports, does not exist in the Tausug state as something separate from adjudication and the same may be said of Kalinga.[47]

The tasks of the Thai monarchy were more diverse and therefore required more complicated structures. To perform them, the monarchy established an elaborate system of administration. But that system lacked the structural stability and functional specificity found in the modern state. Tasks appear to have been assigned as much to individuals as to localities or departments. Governmental departments were subject to dissolution when their heads died or lost royal favor. Officialdom as a whole thus was unable to develop the cohesion and strength of a full-fledged Weberian bureaucracy. Finally, the Thai monarch, like other traditional Southeast Asian rulers, and unlike the monarchs of Europe, governed without a parliament. Legislation was the prerogative of the king, who usually ruled in a fairly arbitrary fashion. The Thai thus lacked the experience, so crucial to the evolution of the modern democratic *rechtsstaat*, of observing open debates on legislation by representatives of different social orders or points of view, taking the form of conflicting categorical demands that were resolved categorically. All this helps to explain why the king and the massive network of clients and subclients who staffed his government appear more prominent than the corporate structures of the premodern Thai state.

There remains the most nearly modern of the four Southeast Asian political systems, the Republic of the Philippines. Like other postcolonial states it has the usual functionally specialized branches of government patterned closely upon the model of its colonial tutor. And it has a growing number of formally organized voluntary associations including political parties which attempt to perform what Almond calls the articulation and aggregation of interests. Yet to a considerable degree, the interests of individuals in the Philippines are satisfied individually through direct dyadic arrangements of exchange between them and specific officeholders in the bureaucracy or the judiciary. Insofar as this occurs, the conversion of particular demands into categorical prescriptions becomes unnecessary, and the specialized associational and governmental conversion structures are bypassed.

A TYPOLOGY OF ACTION GROUPS

The main argument of this article has been that dyadic structures perform tasks differently than do groups of the type described by the

"group theory" of politics. If the argument is valid, then it should be possible to devise a set of models to describe these and perhaps other structural types and their modes of performance.

I propose to do this at two different levels of what Giovanni Sartori has called the "ladder of abstraction."[48] I shall begin with a set of three very simple types, arrived at deductively, cast at a very high level of abstraction; and designed to be very broadly applicable. As suggested by Sartori the number of attributes of each highly abstract type will be kept to a minimum. Then, at a lower level of abstraction, which permits the filling in of more detail, I shall outline, with the help of a set of paired propositions, two contrasting types which, though they are in principle less broadly applicable, do fit, I believe, a large number of real institutions found in developing and more developed countries.

Each of the first three highly abstract types consists of three principles which, I suggest, are linked in each type. The principles are those of *composition, action pattern* and *task*. They are linked in that they are logically most suited to each other. By "most suited" I mean that the inner logic of each of the three is such that if one principle is chosen, the acceptance also of the other two provides logically the most efficient means (though *not* the only means) of goal achievement.

The three types are named "trait group," "web" and "collectivity." Each designates a distinctive type of action group. Their features are outlined in Table 1.

TABLE 1.
A Partial Typology of Action Groups
Three Types at High Levels of Abstraction

	Types of Action Groups		
Structure	"Trait group"	"Web"	"Collectivity"
Composition	Shared trait	Shared ally or leader	Shares membership in a bounded community
Action pattern	Like action	Exchange of aid	Division of common tasks
Task	Narrow spectrum categorical goal attainment	Disparate individual goal attainment	Broad spectrum collective goal attainment
Examples	Interest groups, ideological groups, classes	Personal alliance systems, personal followings	Families, lineages, corporations, states

I shall not discuss the principles which comprise each type here. To elaborate on the characteristics of trait groups and webs would repeat arguments made elsewhere in this article. To discuss collectivities would greatly expand the

article's scope. I have included the last type in the table simply in order to suggest how another basic type of action group might be described in terms of a few interrelated principles.

The structural elements of each type, that is

to say *composition* and *action pattern*, have been listed first for the following reason: Structure can be a cause as well as a consequence of other elements of a system. Ancient institutions often display an ability to survive which may be hard to explain on functional grounds, and by their presence may discourage the growth of new institutions and the performance of new tasks. A similar conservative bias applies, I think, to structural *principles*. A society accustomed to certain of these is likely to make use of them even in those new institutions which it creates to replace old ones that have fallen into decline. If it is true, as I have argued here, that certain principles of composition, action and task are linked, then a society's addiction to given principles of structure will limit to some extent the types of goals it will be able to pursue. Conversely, if a society's leaders commit themselves to pursuing wholly new types of goals, they must create not merely new institutions, but institutions based on the structural principles appropriate to these new types of goals.

The types suggest an approach to one of the problems of structural-functional analysis: The disjunction between those strategies for analysis that begin with structures and those that begin with functions. Perhaps it will be possible to move back and forth between structural and functional analyses more easily at the level of their underlying principles. A concern with such principles also may help one to connect micro-, macro- and middle-level analysis, a point previously made by René Lemarchand.[49]

It may be useful now to descend the ladder of abstraction a rung or two and to examine two further types which are subtypes of two of the types described in the previous table. Because the new types are less general than the previous ones, they can be outlined in greater detail. The trait group now takes the more specific form of a "trait association," with some degree of organization and a head. The web takes the form of a vertical web or "personal following." It need not be given a head for a web is inconceivable without a central figure. Both types, furthermore, are described as they operate in a setting where group attachment is voluntary and there is at least some competition among rival groups. Thus the types do not fit either a one-party state or a feudal fief.

In many but not in all of their characteristics these two types are polar ones, whose distinctive features can be placed at opposite ends of the same continua. For this reason, I shall describe the two types together, with the help of a set of paired propositions. These are the result of (a) deduction from simple structural concepts; (b) current theory concerning networks and dyads, especially that formulated by Robert Pehrson, George Foster, John Thibaut and Harold Kelley, Norman Whitten and Alvin Wolfe, and myself; and (c) a growing body of empirical research conducted in certain geographic regions where networks have attracted particular scholarly attention.

TABLE 2.

Trait Associations and Personal Followings
A Set of Paired Propositions

DEFINITIONS

A *trait association* is an organized group of persons united by the fact that they believe themselves to share a distinguishing trait, or fall into a distinguishing category. It has a head.

A *personal following* is a vertical dyadic web, bound together by the fact that the followers have a common leader.

CONDITIONS

The following propositions concerning the structure and performance of trait associations and personal followings assume a setting charaterized by *voluntary membership* in, and a measure of *competition* between groups.

PROPOSITIONS
Group Configuration
Genesis

TRAIT ASSOCIATIONS:
Tend to grow out of pre-existing trait groups. (Recognition of the possession of a shared trait tends to precede organization and the selection of a head.)

PERSONAL FOLLOWINGS:
Tend to be the creations of their leaders. (A would-be leader by winning the adherence of various individuals, creates a following. Only then does a sense of community appear.)

Reason for Appearance

Tend to appear when there are objects of common interest which can be attained through collective action.	Tend to appear when there are opportunities for mutually advantageous exchanges between leaders and followers.
Are especially likely to appear when such objects cannot be attained through individual action.	Are especially likely to appear when leaders and followers can provide large gains to each other at small costs to themselves.

Methods of Maintenance

Tend to be maintained by emphasizing shared needs and shared dangers, and by the demonstration of gains resulting from past collective action.	Tend to be maintained by periodic exchanges of favors between leaders and followers. (Such favors may be either substantial or symbolic. Thus they may be the ends or the means of group cohesion.)

Size

Size tends to be closely related to:	Size tends to be limited by:
The number of persons who share the trait.	The number of followers with whom the leader can maintain face-to-face relationships.
The presence of parallel groups with similar traits and interests with which fusion can take place.	The resources for distribution available to the leader.
The presence of rival groups with conflicting traits and interests which can serve as stimuli for counter-organization.	

Stability and Endurance

Tend to be stable and enduring.	Tend to be unstable and of short endurance.
For the group to endure, gains for participants need not equal or exceed costs in the short run but must promise to do so in the long run.	For the group to endure, gains for participants must equal or exceed costs in the short run.
Endurance is threatened by indications that individual or group goals cannot be attained through collective action.	Personal followings are highly vulnerable to fragmentation, shrinkage, disintegration, or dissolution if:
	The leader loses his access to distributable resources.
	The leader is challenged by rival leaders with greater resources.
	The leader dies without being replaced at once by a suitable successor with equal resources.

Roles of Superordination and Subordination
Group Headship

Heads tend to be "officers," entrusted with authority to act by their groups.	Heads tend to be "leaders" who act on their own initiative.
Their official acts tend to be enforced by sanctions imposed by the group.	Group sanctions to compel obedience to leaders tend to be rare.
Such sanctions tend to be most effective when groups are multi-functional or mutually exclusive, or both.	Individual compliance with the leaders' commands tends to depend heavily upon the consent of each follower.

Group Membership

The rank and file tend to regard themselves as "members" having rights and obligations towards the group.	The rank and file tend to regard themselves as "followers," having claims upon and owing favors to their leader.

Criteria for Headship

The primary criterion for officership tends to be that the officer share the traits which distinguish the group.	The primary criterion for leadership tends to be that the leader have status or resources superior to those of his individual followers.

Responsibility or Responsiveness

Officers tend to a high degree to be responsible to their groups for actions taken in the group's behalf.	Leaders tend to a high degree to be responsive to the private demands of individual members.

Responsibility or Responsiveness (Continued)

Responsibility tends to be enforced by collective action involving the whole group or representatives of the group.

Responsiveness tends to be enforced through pressure from individual followers, rather than by collective action involving the whole group.

Responsibility tends to be highest on matters of general group policy.

Leaders tend to have considerable freedom to set broad goals and policies, as long as they satisfy the immediate private needs of their followers.

Officers tend to be relatively unresponsive to the private demands of individual members.

Prestige

Within the association, the prestige of the officer and of members tends to a high degree to depend on their services to the association.

Within the following and the larger community, the prestige of the leader tends to a high degree to depend on the size of his following.

In the larger community, the prestige of the officer and of members tends to a high degree to depend upon the prestige of the trait group as a whole.

Within the following and the larger community, the prestige of an individual follower tends to a high degree to depend on the prestige of the leader, and the follower's closeness to him.

(The distribution of prestige in the community resembles the top of a circus tent: The peaks, supported by the points where poles are placed, denote leaders whose prestige is their own. The sloping areas near the peaks represent the derivative prestige of close followers who are raised above the common mass by their leaders. The troughs denote the prestige of minor followers and the unattached.)

Goals and Goal Attainment
Types of Goals

Tend to focus upon a narrow spectrum of related categorical or ideological goals.

Tend to focus upon a broad spectrum of particular goals, which need not be related.

Agreement on Goals

Tend to require a high degree of agreement concerning specific goals.

Tend not to require a high degree of agreement concerning specific goals.

Alteration of Goals

Tend to find it difficult to alter specific goals.

Tend to find it easy to alter specific goals.

Participation in Rewards and Costs

Rewards tend to be of a kind that benefit all who share a trait, whether or not they are members of the trait association.

Rewards tend to be of a kind that can be restricted to members of the following:

Hence, trait-wide participation in the association or trait-wide contribution to its costs, will be sought.

Within the following, shares in the rewards tend to be closely related to the follower's value to the leader.

Equality within the group tends to be highly valued.

Favoritism tends to be valued and made explicit.

Methods of Goal Attainment

Tend to rely to a high degree upon collective action by the membership.

Tend to rely to a high degree upon the manipulative skill of the leader.

Frontal attacks against opposing groups are a favored tactic.

Among favored tactics are the following: Playing other actors off against each other; wooing away the allies of others; monopolizing access to distributors of resources.

Communication

Officers tend to communicate with members in broadcast fashion.

Leaders tend to communicate privately with each follower.

Messages tend to be categorical in content.

Messages tend to be particular in content.

A high value tends to be placed on confidential information, diverse sources of information, and direct access to originators of information.

Goals and Rewards of Headship

To a relatively high degree officers are obliged to focus their efforts upon the attainment of group goals.

The rewards received by officers tend to be relatively modest, and be set by the group.

To a relatively high degree, leaders are free to focus their efforts upon the attainment of their private goals.

The rewards received by leaders tend to be relatively large, and to be set by themselves.

The Interaction of Groups in the Polity
Similarities and Differences Between Groups

Rival associations tend to be dissimilar in their composition and goals.

Inter-association disputes tend to turn on categorical issues.

Rival followings tend to be similar in their composition and goals.

Inter-following disputes tend to turn on "personalities" and spoils.

Expansion and Consolidation of Groups

Associations tend to be expanded through the broadening of categories, and the "nesting" of narrower trait associations within more comprehensive ones.

This is made possible by broadening the spectrum goals.

Followings tend to be expanded through the "pyramiding" of leaders. Under this procedure several lesser leaders, each accompanied by those who remain his personal followers, become the followers of a higher leader.

This is made possible by supplying larger quantities of the same types of rewards. Consolidation through pyramiding tends to be limited by the resources available to the highest leader.

Changes in Individual Loyalties

Relatively few members shift their allegiance from one association to another.

The shifting of individual allegiance from one leader to another tends to be fairly common.

Changes in allegiance tend to be affected by the ability of rival leaders to provide individual rewards to their followers.

The Stability of Inter-Group Alliances

Alliances between associations tend to be relatively stable.

Two-directional reversals of alliances are very uncommon (i.e., AB vs CD may become ABC vs D or A vs BCD, but not AC vs BD).

Alliances between followings tend to be relatively unstable.

Two-directional reversals of alliances are not uncommon.

Omnibus Propositions
The Resolution of Conflict

Systems composed of trait associations tend to resolve conflicts by the following means:

Fostering an awareness among individuals and groups that they have in common higher interests which override their areas of disagreement.

Under certain conditions: By creating stable majorities which are able to impose solutions to conflicts.

Systems composed of personal followings tend to resolve conflicts by the following means:

Avoiding issues that are socially divisive.

Employing bargaining as a method of conflict-resolution.

Making rival groups open in their recruitment, heterogeneous in composition, syncretic in policy, and flexible in their alliances.

Providing opportunities for individual (as distinguished from group) social mobility, and thereby placating potential advocates of conflict.

Organization for Goal Achievement

Systems composed of trait associations tend to be better suited than systems composed of personal followings for the concentration of collective effort towards the achievement of clearly defined collective goals. Specifically, they are well suited for the following tasks:

Fusing scattered private goals into collective goals, devising long-range programs for their attainment, and mobilizing for such programs support which is massive, disciplined, and sustained.

Systems composed of personal followings tend to be better suited than systems composed of trait associations for the rapid attainment of the particular goals of individuals. Specifically, they are well suited for the following tasks:

Focusing attention upon goals which are concrete and quickly attainable.

Fostering mutual aid between dissimilar individuals in the pursuit of their private goals.

Organization for Goal Achievement (Continued)

Forcing clear-cut choices between incompatible goals.

Restraining individual and sub-group rivalries that jeopardize collective goals.

Creating officers who are committed to collective goals, maintaining group control over them, and enforcing compliance with their commands.

Creating leaders who are sensitive to the needs of individual followers, and able to intercede with power holders on their behalf.

Effects upon National Cohesion

National whose rival political groups are trait associations tend to avoid localistic politics.

Nations whose rival political groups are trait associations tend to be divided on lines of ideology or general policy.

Nations whose rival political groups are trait associations tend to achieve community-wide or nation-wide unity by broadening categories.

Nations whose rival political groups are personal followings tend to have localistic politics.

Nations whose rival political groups are personal followings tends to be divided by a simple struggle for power.

Nations whose rival political groups are personal followings tend to achieve community-wide or nation-wide unity by replacing particular goals with categorical or collective goals.

While the two types are meant to be quite broadly applicable, few institutions will conform to them exactly. Real institutions may combine different structural principles, or fall between the ends of a continuum. Or they may change their position on a continuum over time. Thus Adrian Mayer shows how the closest allies of the central member of an ego-centered web may over time form so tight a core that the central member becomes obscured by what has become a discrete multimember group.[50] Finally, the peculiar traditions of a specific culture may in various ways alter a case which in other ways would fit the type.

THE FUTURE OF DYADIC STRUCTURE

Dyadic arrangements for the advancement of self-interest seem natural to man. They satisfy the yearning for security, favored treatment, and power. They provide a simple means for the advancement of self-interest which require a minimum of elaborate organization, trust in a minimum number of people, and minimal delay in the achievement of private goals. Dyadic arrangements furthermore are extremely flexible and can be employed in diverse situations to mobilize a wide variety of individuals. But they have disadvantages as well: Stable dyads restrict their members' freedom to engage in more profitable exchanges. Vertical dyads can be demeaning for the subordinate partners, leave them in disadvantageous bargaining positions, and may deprive them of the advantages to be gained from class based organization. All concerned in a dyadic system may see as unjust the favoritism that usually characterizes dyadic interaction.

Under certain conditions, the disadvantages of dyadic political arrangements may seem to outweigh their benefits and lead to their abandonment. What are these conditions and why do they seem to be most common in modern societies? James Scott has explored this subject at length in two excellent papers.[51] I should like to add a few comments.

The conditions are not necessarily the same for the ruler and the ruled. From the point of view of the ruler the staffing of government with personal clients rather than with those who have most skill becomes unnecessary when he can count on the loyalty of all his subordinates as a matter of course. This is most likely to be the case when officials lack the ability to overthrow the ruler or influence the succession. Such was the case in the stable constitutional monarchies of nineteenth century Europe and is the case in modern democracies. It is not the case in many developing countries, particularly in embattled traditional monarchies where the ruler feels threatened by many of his own servants, or in such "bureaucratic polities" as contemporary Thailand, where the outcome of the struggle for control of the government is determined by the maneuvering of bureaucratic cliques and not by the results of popular elections.

From the point of view of the ruler also, the attachment of the common people to his officials or to a landholding nobility becomes unnecessary and need not be allowed when the ruler finds it possible to control his subjects and to extract taxes or services from them by other means. His ability to do the latter is likely to increase as population grows and labor shortage is replaced by land shortage. For then subjects are not likely to run away and *corvée* labor can be replaced by landless laborers and soldiers hired with taxes taken from the agricultural sector.

From the point of view of the common man, the protection of a patron ceases to be advantageous when he can expect to be secure in his life and property and count on equal treatment before the courts without the help of a powerful protector. This condition is likely to be achieved in a *rechtsstaat*, a state governed by the impersonal rule of law. Lacking this, it is likely to be achieved also where the individual has available to him membership in a discrete group which can offer him such protection.

Finally, from the point of view of both potential patrons and clients, these roles become unattractive when it begins to be in their interest to have freedom to shift their superordinates, subordinates, or trading partners at will. This, of course, is the case in a modern market economy. Where such an economy prevails, one can expect dyadic structures to deteriorate in the political sphere as well.

An apolitical bureaucracy, an easily taxable populace, a *rechtsstaat*, freedom of associational activity, and a market economy—these conditions are all characteristic of the modern democratic state. It is not surprising therefore that a political science which has devoted most of its attention to the study of modern Western democracies should have found little reason to interest itself in dyadic structures. As other societies achieve similar conditions, we may expect this to be the case there as well.

Still, in modern states where some of these conditions are absent, dyadic and other "traditional" structures may continue to be important. Thus, in the Soviet Union and China, the proscription against the creation of formally organized teams of would-be competitors for those in power, either outside or within the ruling party, has resulted in the emergence instead of informal cliques and personal followings reminiscent of those found in premodern polities.[52]

And even in modern democracies at certain levels of the political system dyadic structures flourish. Thus, while the mass of American citizens is accustomed to confining its political activity to membership in various voluntary associations and to the periodic casting of ballots, those who aspire to positions of high leadership in these associations organize themselves dyadically. The reason is simple: The benefits derived from general legislation can be shared by innumerable people. But high offices are in limited supply. If one hopes to be a presidential advisor, one had best attach oneself to a promising candidate early in the game.

To conclude: While traditional patron-client relationships appear to be breaking down in many peasant societies, other types of dyadic structures and techniques will continue to play a part in politics as long as political actors seek and are able to advance their interests particularistically. The study of the political process is deficient insofar as it fails to give attention to such structures.

NOTES

1 Gabriel A. Almond and G. Bingham Powell, Jr., *Comparative Politics: A Developmental Approach* (Boston: Little, Brown & Co., 1966), p. 75. For Almond's earlier formulation, see *The Politics of the Developing Areas*, ed. Gabriel A. Almond and James S. Coleman (Princeton: Princeton University Press, 1960), pp. 3-64. For the paper which guided the research of the Committee's grantees, see Gabriel A. Almond, "A Comparative Study of Interest Groups and the Political Process," *American Political Science Review*, 52 (March, 1958), 270-82.

2 Arthur F. Bentley, *The Process of Government* (Chicago: University of Chicago Press, 1908); David B. Truman, *The Governmental Process* (New York: Knopf, 1951); Earl Latham, *The Group Basis of Politics* Ithaca: Cornell University Press, 1952).

3 See Giovanni Gentile, "The Philosophical Basis of Fascism," and Alfredo Rocco, "The Political Doctrine of Fascism," in *Readings on Fascism and National Socialism*, Department of Philosophy, University of Chicago (Denver: Allan Swallow, n.d.).

For a discussion of the corporate state in practice, see Michael T. Florinsky, *Fascism and National Socialism: A Study of Economic and Social Policies of the Totalitarian State* (New York: Macmillan, 1938), pp. 86-100.

4 Mancur Olson, Jr., *The Logic of Collective Action* (Cambridge: Harvard University Press, 1965).

5 A more rudimentary version of the dyadic model, developed here, may be found in Carl H. Landé, *Leaders, Factions, and Parties: The Structure of Philippine Politics*, Yale Southeast Asia Studies Monograph Series, No. 6 (New Haven: Yale University Southeast Asia Studies, 1965), Appendix II, "Group Politics and Dyadic Politics: Notes for a Theory." An earlier statement is found in "Politics in the Philippines," Diss. Harvard University, 1958. The relationship between dyadic political structure and cognatic kinship is discussed at greater length in a paper, "Kinship and Politics in Pre-Modern and Non-Western Societies," which was submitted to the *American Political Science Review* in 1961. While not published at the

time, it now appears in *Southeast Asia: The Politics of National Integration*, ed. John T. McAlister, Jr. (New York: Random House, 1973), pp. 219-233. These writings owe a heavy debt to the late Robert N. Pehrson, whose classic study, *The Bilateral Network of Social Relationships in Könkämä Lapp District*, Indiana University Publications, Slavic and East European Series, Vol. 5 (Bloomington: Indiana University Research Center in Anthropology, Folklore, and Linguistics, 1957) introduced me to the peculiarities of dyadic structure.

6 Charles Winick. *Dictionary of Anthropology* (New York: Philosophical Library, 1956), p. 242.

7 There is a growing body of literature dealing with dyadic structures and in particular with patron-client relationships. Some seminal studies which are not mentioned elsewhere in this paper include the following: For *Southeast Asia*: James C. Scott, "Patron-Client Politics and Political Change in Southeast Asia," *American Political Science Review*, 66 (March, 1972), pp. 81-113. For *South Asia* see Frederik Barth, *Political Leadership among Swat Pathans*, London School of Economics Monographs on Social Anthropology No. 19 (London: The Athlone Press, 1965), pp. 71-126. For *Northern Europe* see Otto Blehr, "Action Groups in a Society with Bilateral Kinship: A Case Study of the Faroe Islands," *Ethnology*, 3 (July, 1963), 269-275. For the *Mediterranean* area see Jeremy Boissevain, "Factions, Parties and Politics in a Maltese Village," *American Anthropologist*, 66 (December, 1964), 1275-1287; and by the same author, "Patronage in Sicily," *Man*, New Series 1 (March, 1966), 18-33. For *Latin America* see George M. Foster, "The Dyadic Contract: A Model for the Social Structure of a Mexican Peasant Village," *American Anthropologist* 63 (December, 1961), 1142-1173; and by the same author "The Dyadic Contract in Tzintzuntzan, II: Patron-Client Relationship," *American Anthropologist* 65 (December, 1963), 1280-1294. For *Africa* see C. W. Gutkind, "Network Analysis and Urbanism in Africa: The Use of Micro and Macro Analysis," *Canadian Review of Sociology and Anthropology*, 2 (May, 1965), 123-131. For theoretical works which are not limited to specific countries or regions see John W. Thibaut and Harold H. Kelley, *The Social Psychology of Groups* (New York: Wiley, 1959), especially Part I, "Dyadic Relationships," pp. 9-187; John A. Barnes, "Networks and Political Process," in *Social Networks in Urban Situations*, ed. J. Clyde Mitchell (Manchester: Manchester University Press, 1969); John Duncan Powell, "Peasant Society and Clientist Politics," *American Political Science Review*, 64 (June, 1970), 411-425; René Lemarchand, and Keith Legg, "Political Clientelism and Development," *Comparative Politics*, 4 (January, 1972), 149-178; and Norman E. Whitten, Jr. and Alvin W. Wolfe, "Network Analysis," prepared for Chap. 3, *The Handbook of Social and Cultural Anthropology*, ed. John J. Honigmann (Chicago: Rand-McNally, in press) which includes an extensive bibliography.

8 Roy Franklin Barton, *The Kalingas: Their Institutions and Custom Law* (Chicago: University of Chi-

cago Press, 1949); and Edward P. Dozier, *Mountain Arbiters: The Changing Life of a Philippine Hill People* (Tucson: University of Arizona Press, 1966).

9 George Peter Murdock, *Social Structure* (New York: Macmillan, 1949), p. 60. For an excellent discussion of the nature of groups resulting from cognatic descent, see Robin Fox, Chap. 6, "Cognatic Descent and Ego-centered Groups," *Kinship and Marriage* (Baltimore: Penguin Books, 1967), pp. 146-174.

10 The personal kindred performed very similar tasks in early Europe. For an exploration of this subject see Bertha Surtees Phillpotts, *Kindred and Clan in the Middle Ages and After: A Study in the Sociology of the Teutonic Races* (Cambridge: Cambridge University Press, 1913).

11 Fred Eggan, "The Sagada Igorots of Northern Luzon," in *Social Structure in Southeast Asia*, ed. George Peter Murdock (Chicago: Quadrangle Books, 1960), pp. 27-30. Similar groups are found among the Muslim Maranao of the Southern Philippines, but not among the Christian peoples of the islands. See Melvin Mednick, *Encampment of the Lake: The Social Organization of a Moslem-Philippine (Moro) People*, Philippine Studies Program, Department of Anthropology, University of Chicago, Research Series No. 5 (Chicago: University of Chicago Philippine Studies Program, 1965).

12 Thomas M. Kiefer, "Institutionalized Friendship and Warfare among the Tausug of Jolo," *Ethnology* 7 (July, 1968), 225-244; and *Tausug Armed Conflict: The Social Organization of Military Activity in a Philippine Moslem Society*, Philippine Studies Program, Department of Anthropology, University of Chicago, Research Series, No. 7 (Chicago: University of Chicago Philippine Studies Program, 1969); *The Tausug: Violence and Law in a Philippine Moslem Society* (New York: Holt, Rinehart and Winston, 1972).

13 Kiefer, *Tausug Armed Conflict*, p. 189.

14 Kiefer, *Tausug Armed Conflict*, p. 192.

15 Kiefer, *Tausug Armed Conflict*, p. 36.

16 Kiefer concludes, "Territoriality . . . is not generally conceived in terms of boundaries which create discrete spatial units, but rather in terms of the space which vaguely surrounds a single point." Kiefer, *Tausug Armed Conflict*, p. 31.

17 Kiefer, *Tausug Armed Conflict*, p. 37.

18 Landé, *Leaders, Factions, and Parties*, pp. 141-148.

19 Kiefer, *Tausug Armed Conflict*, pp. 167-171.

20 H. G. Quaritch-Wales, *Ancient Siamese Government and Administration* (London: Bernard Quaritch, Ltd., 1934); and Akin Rabibhadana, *The Organization of Thai Society in the Early Bangkok Period, 1782-1873*, Cornell University Southeast Asia Program, Data Paper No. 74 (Ithaca: Cornell University Southeast Asia Program, Department of Asian Studies, 1969).

21 Rabibhadana, p. 53.

22 Rabibhadana notes, pp. 119-120, that the large volume of historical legal documents concerning disputes over the control of manpower contrasts sharply

with the dearth of similar documents dealing with disputes over land. For a discussion of Thai retinues today, see Lucien M. Hanks, Jr., "The Corporation and the Entourage: A Comparison of Thai and American Social Organization," *Catalyst* (Summer, 1966), pp. 53-63.

23 Rabibhadana, p. 20.

24 Debt bondage, which varied in its degree of unfreedom from merely nominal mortgaging of the debtor or a member of his family, through actual debt service, to hereditary slavery, was encouraged by the rule that a patron had a first right to extend loans to his government clients. If a debtor defaulted in his repayments, he could be transformed from a government client into the patron's private debt bondsman, the degree of his unfreedom depending upon the extent of this indebtedness.

25 Whether the obligation of clientage was confined to men, or applied to both men and women is unclear. Some comments by Wales suggest the latter. See his observation, p. 53 that "When the parents belonged to different *kroms*, or had different patrons in the same *krom*, their children, on reaching the age at which government service was required of them, were divided between the patrons of their parents." Other descriptions of Thai clientage make no reference to women. But women it appears, were sold into slavery. Almost all men, at least, of nonelite status were obliged to assume one of these roles of subordination, according to the observation of an early nineteenth-century foreign observer, mentioned by Rabibhadana, p. 81; this foreigner noted that free labor did not exist, for the labor of every individual was appropriated by one or another chief, without whose approval he could not work.

26 Rabibhadana, pp. 36-39, 56-59.

27 Under Ayudhya law, as reported by Wales, p. 5, commoners were entitled to choose and leave their patrons. That in practice this right was always preserved seems unlikely. A decree by King Rama II quoted by Rabibhadana, p. 88, which promised runaway clients that if they returned from the jungle "this time only they would not be punished and would be allowed to choose their new patrons," attests to this. On the other hand Rabibhadana reports, pp. 34-35, that it was fairly easy, prior to the institution of tatooing of clients, for a dissatisfied client to abscond and have himself secretly taken in by another patron, or find another patron who would buy him from his first master, or by lending him money convert him into his debt bondsman.

28 Rabibhadana, pp. 38, 59. The alienation of royal clients by princely patrons and the consequent weakening of royal authority recalls a somewhat similar development which took place in Japan during the several centuries which followed the first attempt to establish a centralized bureaucratic state in the seventh and eighth centuries. In the Japanese case however the development involved the control of land and only secondarily the enlistment of manpower. See George Sansom, *A History of Japan to 1334* (Stanford: Stanford University Press, 1958), pp. 83-89.

29 James N. Mosel, "Thai Administrative Behavior," in *Toward the Comparative Study of Public Administration*, ed. William J. Siffin, (Bloomington, Ind.: Indiana University Press, 1957), p. 287. Rabibhadana, pp. 29, 31, notes that, legally, towns were equated with *krom*, and that governors were equated with chiefs of *krom*.

30 Fred W. Riggs, *Thailand: The Modernization of a Bureaucratic Polity* (Honolulu: East-West Center Press, 1966), pp. 70-72, 79; and Robert Heine-Geldern, *Conceptions of State and Kingship in Southeast Asia*, Cornell University Southeast Asia Program Data Paper No. 18 (Ithaca: Cornell University Southeast Asia Program, Department of Far Eastern Studies, 1956), pp. 3-5.

31 Rabibhadana, p. 77. Hanks, who is quoted by Rabibhadana has described the premodern social order of Thailand as one "which resembles a military organization more than an occidental class type society." Lucien M. Hanks, Jr., "Merit and Power in the Thai Social Order," *American Anthropologist*, 64 (December, 1962), pp. 1247-1261; cited at 1252.

32 Under the rule of declining princely descent, a king's numerous male descendants by his many wives could pass on their rank to their descendants only in diminished form. The sixth generation became commoners. A king's female descendants could receive rank but could not transmit it even in diminished form. This would seem to have discouraged the creation of stable heritable princely clienteles.

33 Rabibhadana, pp. 31, 78.

34 Rabibhadana, pp. 30-31.

35 David A. Wilson, *Politics in Thailand* (Ithaca: Cornell University Press, 1962); Riggs, "Thailand"; William J. Siffin, *The Thai Bureaucracy: Institutional Change and Development* (Honolulu: East-West Center Press, 1966); Mosel, "Thai Administrative Behavior"; Herbert P. Phillips, *Thai Peasant Personality: The Patterning of Interpersonal Behavior in the Village of Bang Chan* (Berkeley: University of California Press, 1965).

36 Landé, *Leaders, Factions, and Parties*; and *Southern Tagalog Voting: Political Behavior in a Philippine Region*, A.I.D. Research Paper (January, 1972).

37 For excellent discussions of behavior and its structural basis in societies not very different from that of the Philippines, see Edward C. Banfield's classic *The Moral Basis of a Backward Society* (Glencoe: The Free Press, 1958); and more recently Jane Schneider, "Of Vigilance and Virgins: Honor, Shame and Access to Resources in Mediterranean Societies," *Ethnology*, 10 (January, 1971), 1-24.

38 For a report on the analysis of these ballots, see Carl H. Landé, "Parties and Politics in the Philippines," *Asian Survey*, 8 (September, 1968), pp. 242-247; and *Southern Tagalog Voting*, pp. 81-93.

39 For case studies of local and provincial politics which illustrate these points, see Mary R. Hollnsteiner, *The Dynamics of Power in a Philippine Municipality* (Quezon City: Community Development Research Council, University of the Philippines, 1963); Remigio E. Agpalo, *Pandanggo-Sa-Ilaw: The Politics of Occidental Mindoro*, Papers in Interna-

tional Studies, Southeast Asia Series, No. 9 (Athens, Ohio: Ohio University Center for International Studies, 1969); and Landé, *Leaders, Factions, and Parties*, pp. 132-140.

40 See Remigio E. Agpalo, *The Political Process and the Nationalization of the Retail Trade in the Philippines* (Quezon City: University of the Philippines, 1962); and Robert B. Stauffer, *The Development of an Interest Group: The Philippine Medical Association* (Manila: University of the Philippines Press, 1966).

41 Maurice Duverger, *Political Parties: Their Organization and Activity in the Modern State*, 2nd ed. (London: Methuen, 1959).

42 The Tagalog term for such a client is *bata* (literally, "child"). Modern organizations in the Philippines, both in the government and the private sector, are honeycombed with *bata* systems of the classic patron-client type. Equally widespread are *compadre* relationships of the type found in Latin America and medieval Europe. These may be either vertical or horizontal. A functionally equivalent tie among Filipino Muslims is that which results from swearing together on the Koran. Finally, in the economic sphere there are to be found *suki* relationships between buyers and sellers who deal with each other on the basis of favored treatment. The latter type of relationships has been described by James N. Anderson, in "Buy and Sell Economic Personalism: Foundations for Philippine Entrepreneurship," *Asian Survey*, 9 (September 1969), 641-668. The "compadre system" which in Latin America is called *compadrazgo*, has been described by numerous writers. The best comparative discussion is that of Sidney W. Mintz and Eric R. Wolf, "An Analysis of Ritual Co-Parenthood (Compadrazgo)," *Southwestern Journal of Anthropology*, 6 (Winter, 1950), 341-468. For an excellent survey of various relationships of this sort see Julian Pitt-Rivers, "Pseudo Kinship," in *The International Encyclopedia of the Social Sciences*, 8 (New York: Crowell, Collier and Macmillan, 1968), 408-431.

43 See Landé, "Kinship and Politics in Pre-Modern and Non-Western Societies."

44 Data from George Peter Murdock's "World Ethnographic Sample" were employed to test the hypothesis that cognatic societies are less likely than unilineal societies to assign positions of political leadership on a hereditary basis. This entailed the construction of a two-by-two table for unilineal versus bilateral (cognatic) descent and for hereditary versus non-hereditary political succession. The number of societies which fit into the table were 384. Unilineal societies tended to have hereditary political succession approximately four times as often as non-hereditary succession, while bilateral (cognatic) societies were almost equally divided between the two types of suc-

cession. The Phi coefficient was .32, indicating a relatively strong relationship in the hypothesized direction. The Chi square test indicated that the relationship would occur by chance in less than one out of 1,000 cases. Another two-by-two table was constructed for unilineal descent versus bilateral (cognatic) descent and for hereditary slavery versus the absence of hereditary slavery (slavery if present, being only temporary or non-hereditary). This time the number of societies in the table was 464. While 27 per cent of the unilineal societies had hereditary slavery, only 12 per cent of those with bilateral (cognatic) descent did so. The Phi coefficient was .18. The Chi square test again indicated the relationship would occur by chance in less than one out of 1,000 cases. The data were taken from George Peter Murdock, "World Ethnographic Sample," *American Anthropologist*, 59 (August, 1957), 664-687. I shall be glad to supply the tables on request.

45 See J. P. Singh Uberoi, *Politics of the Kula Ring: An Analysis of the Findings of Bronislaw Malinowski* (Manchester: Manchester University Press, 1962); and Franz Michael, *The Origins of Manchu Rule in China: Frontier and Bureaucracy as Interacting Forces in the Chinese Empire* (Baltimore: Johns Hopkins Press, 1942), especially pp. 80-98.

46 George M. Foster, "Peasant Society and the Image of Limited Good," *American Anthropologist*, 67 (April, 1965), 293-315; and James C. Scott, *Political Ideology in Malaysia: Reality and Beliefs of an Elite* (New Haven: Yale University Press, 1968), pp. 91-149. Foster, p. 296 associates the "image of limited good" with land shortage. But like clientage, it seems to be found also in peasant societies where land is not in short supply.

47 Kiefer, *Tausug Armed Conflict*, p. 194.

48 Giovanni Sartori, "Concept Misinformation in Comparative Politics," *American Political Science Review*, 64 (December, 1970), 1040-1046.

49 René Lemarchand, "Political Clientelism and Ethnicity in Tropical Africa: Competing Solidarities in Nation Building," *American Political Science Review*, 64 (March, 1972), p. 68.

50 Adrian C. Mayer, "The Significance of Quasi-Groups in the Study of Complex Societies," in *The Social Anthropology of Complex Societies*, ed. Michael Banton, ASA Monograph No. 4 (New York: Praeger, 1966), pp. 115-117.

51 James C. Scott, "The Weakening of Rural Patron-Client Ties in Colonial Southeast Asia," and "How Traditional Rural Patrons Lose Legitimacy," unpublished papers, 1971.

52 Andrew J. Nathan, "A Factionalism Model for Chinese Politics," *The China Quarterly*, 53 (January/March, 1973).

POLITICAL CLIENTELISM AND ETHNICITY IN TROPICAL AFRICA:*
Competing Solidarities in Nation-Building
RENÉ LEMARCHAND

THE ANALYSIS presented here is an attempt to follow up, qualify, and elaborate upon, some earlier hypotheses about the role of political clientelism in the light of empirical data from West and Central Africa.[1] More specifically, the aim is, first, to use the concept of clientelism as an auxiliary tool to elucidate some of the ambiguities surrounding the relationship between ethnicity and nation-building in contemporary Africa; and, second, to provide what appears to be a "missing link" between the micro- and macrosociological or system-centered theories that have dominated the field of developmental politics since the last decade. Succinctly stated, this "missing link" is to be found in the varieties of personal and institutional linkages and reciprocities which, depending on the circumstances, have bridged or accentuated ethnic and other discontinuities within traditional and modernizing pluralistic polities.

Because it cuts across both "traditional" and "modern" referents, political clientelism, as a concept, has a heuristic value generally missing from the conceptual arsenal of either "modern" or "traditional" polities; it directs attention to processes of adjustment between traditional and modern patterns of behavior, expectations, and normative orientations to politics which might otherwise go unnoticed. As an analytical concept, clientelism brings into focus units of analysis, political actors, and relationships which have thus far received scant attention from political scientists.[2] As a developmental construct, it suggests new perspectives from which to look at processes of nation-building in Africa: Viewed from the micropolitical perspective of traditional patterns of interaction among groups and individuals, nation-building becomes not so much an architectonic, voluntaristic model divorced from the environmental materials available; it becomes, rather, a matter of how best to extend to the national level the discrete vertical solidarities in existence at the local or regional levels. Seen through the prism of traditional forms of clientelism, the processes of integration and disintegration that have attended the growth and decline of historic African polities may give us additional clues to similar processes in contemporary Africa. Finally, looked at from the standpoint of the exchange processes involved in clientelism, patterns of resource allocation and distribution may yet emerge as among the most meaningful indicators of political development; at least they may provide a useful corrective to the current bias toward power accumulation as a presumed prerequisite of political modernization.

This said, two cautionary remarks are in order: One is that the empirical data available are still far too limited and unreliable to permit anything like a full-fledged theory of political development; although an attempt has been made in the latter part of this discussion to relate clientelism to current theories of development, the accent here is primarily on "national integration." What follows, then, is better seen as a series of tentative and piecemeal hypotheses awaiting further testing and systematization. Moreover, if many of the observable patterns of behavior in contemporary Africa are indeed reminiscent or expressive of traditional client-patron relationships, it does not follow that *all* such patterns are reducible to clientelism.[3] This kind of naive reductionism would make unduly short shrift of the emergent integrative mechanisms, norms, and symbols attendant upon the rise of nationalist sentiment and activity, and hence ascribe to clientelism more credit than it actually deserves.

CLIENTELISM, ETHNICITY, AND INTEGRATION

Although it would be too much to expect universal agreement on any single definition, for the purpose of this discussion political clientelism can be viewed as "a more or less personalized relationship between actors (i.e., patrons and clients), or sets of actors, commanding unequal wealth, status or influence, based on conditional loyalties and involving mutually beneficial transactions."[4] However vague, this definition has a dual advantage. First, it is broad enough to encompass synchronic and diachronic variations (i.e., the various kinds of microlevel solidarities associated with the operation of traditional forms of clientelism, as well as the broader, overarching solidarities characteristic of the machine pattern). Second, it suggests alternative means for integration where coercive power is not sufficiently coercive to command widespread compliance and where conceptions of legitimacy are as yet too weak or circumscribed to produce consensus.

This type of situation is clearly the rule rather than the exception in most of Africa. Equally plain is that, whatever virtues clientelism may have in bringing people together, a more prevalent type of integration is that which has taken place at the local or regional level through horizontal solidarities associated with kinship or ethnic ties, or the extension of such solidarities on a more inclusive scale—in short, through ethnicity.[5] It is less obvious, however, that clientelism and ethnicity have seldom operated independently of each other, particularly in recent times. Just as ethnicity has sometimes been credited with integrative properties that really belong to the realm of clientelism, so clientelism as an integrative mechanism has often developed out of the exigencies of ethnic fragmentation.

Aside from the conceptual vagueness attached to each term, analysis of the relationship between clientelism and ethnicity is rendered peculiarly arduous by the similarity of the processes to which they refer. For if ethnicity is a matter of self-definition, and if "its ultimate referent is necessarily subjective,"[6] the same can be said of patron-client relationships. Thus what from one standpoint might be regarded as an example of ethnicity in the sense in which Wallerstein uses the term—a redefinition of one's cultural identity through membership in a wider community, usually in the context of an urban situation[7]—might, from another angle, be viewed as a redefinition of rural clientelistic ties in an urban setting. Moreover, clientelism and ethnicity may have overlapping memberships, with some individuals solidly anchored in the ethnic substructure, and others acting as intermediary links between this substructure and the higher reaches of the clientelistic pyramid. What may be taken for a clear example of ethnicity at one level may be nothing more than the lower reticulations of a more extensive clientelistic network. A third source of confusion lies in the reciprocal processes of interaction which normally enter into the ethnicity-clientelism relationship. Rarely has this relationship been unidirectional or fixed. Just as clientelism may in some cases weaken the strength of ethnic identification, the latter may in turn affect the shape and stability of clientelistic networks.

If their contours are often blurred by the complexity of their interrelationships, clientelism and ethnicity are nonetheless analytically separable—and so are their relative contributions to national integration. The first thing to note in this connection is that although clientelism and ethnicity are both relational concepts, involving a subjective definition of the position of an individual or group in relation to another, clientelism incorporates a potentially wider range of social referents and thus offers *wider scope for integration*. Clientelism in M. G. Smith's terms, "incorporates such differentiating factors as ethnicity, occupational status, lineage, and rural-urban distinctions, and defines the boundaries of the political society . . . in functional terms"[8] or, one might add, if not always in the functional terms associated with traditional forms of clientelism, at least in terms of mutual interest. In the case of ethnicity, perceptions of mutual interest are dependent upon, and limited by, perceptions of cultural affinities; clientelism, on the other hand, extends these perceptions beyond the realm of primordial loyalties and establishes vertical links of reciprocity between ethnically or socially discrete entities.

This is not to argue that perceptions of mutual interest will necessarily prevail over ethnic loyalties and cause their extinction—though this possibility is by no means excluded. The mutations of ethnic loyalties entailed by the play of clientelism may range from extinction to dilution and accommodation, depending on the nature of the reciprocities involved and the level at which they operate.

Three possible types of situations suggest themselves: First, there may be a substitution of the client's original ethnic identity for that of his patron: A case in point is Gallais's description of the Bobo tribesman who, upon settling in Mopti (Mali), looks for a protector and having found one, becomes his client and through a kind of mimetic process, acquires not only the external behavioral patterns of his patron but his ethnic identity.[9]

Second, clientelism may cause a redefinition of one's original tribal identity by reference to a wider cultural focus. Though often conceptualized in terms of "super-tribalization"[10] or "ethnicity," much of this phenomenon is reducible to a quest for an alternative focus of security, in the form of clientelism, to that provided through clan or lineage affiliations. Thus, speaking of "associations founded by the urban tribal population" of Monrovia, Frankel notes that these associations "gain respectability from (the widespread custom of patronage), and the patrons, for their part, expect to be able to count on the support of their members for personal and political ends."[11]

Third, clientelism may provide the cement by which ethnic identities are amalgamated within the boundaries of a more inclusive political system. This phenomenon calls to mind two different types of situations: (1) those in which clientelism acts as the major "social adhesive"[12] of the traditional political system, in effect extending to the traditional political arena the principle of reciprocity operative at the level of interpersonal relations (as in the emirate system of Northern Nigeria), and (2) those in which clientelism operates within the context of a nation-wide political party and takes on the qualities of machine politics (as in the case of the *Parti Démocratique de la Cote d'Ivoire* (PDC) in the Ivory Coast). However different the processes and reciprocities involved, in each case the result has been to accommodate ethnic discontinuities to the requirements of a more or less integrated political community.

As the foregoing suggests, although clientelism and ethnicity—like integration—are relative concepts, implying varying degrees of cohesiveness and identification, clientelism denotes a *greater variety of possible types and levels of integration*.

In the perspective of the modern African state system, such integrative potentialities as may exist in clientelism operate essentially at two levels: Clientelism can be evaluated for its contribution to processes of unification among all or some of the parts of the ethnic subsystem, or to the adaptation of these parts to the central governmental and bureaucratic structures. In either case integration stems from the exchange of valued and presumably scarce resources, which in turn permits the attainment of individual or collective goals. Yet the kinds of resources, exchanges, and normative expectations involved are liable to differ significantly from one level to another, and so also will the implications for national integration.

By way of illustration one might compare the operation of traditional clientelism in Northern Nigeria with the machine form operative in Senegal. In his discussion of *bara*-ship in Nupe, Nadel calls attention to three different types of integrative responses elicited through the inducements of clientelism:[13] first, the type of personal identification that originates from the desire of an inferior to obtain the political protection of a superior; second, that which results from the efforts of "impecunious craftsmen to obtain a prosperous customer"; third, that which, "over and above securing material assistance, stems from attachment to a man of rank and influence," thereby offering the client a chance "of becoming somebody," "of being lifted from the ignominy of a commoner's life into the sphere of rank and importance." Whether the motive happens to be a quest for protection, for material assistance, or for social mobility, integration at this level stems from an exchange of psychological and material rewards between a *superior and a subordinate*; extended to the emirate system the relationship remains basically the same: "The crux of the clientage relationship in all the emirates," writes C. S. Whitaker, "is that patronage, economic security, and protection can be exchanged for personal loyalty and obedience."[14]

Rather different is the type of clientelism through which the interests of maraboutic elites of Senegal are aggregated within the *Union Progressiste Sénégalaise* (UPS). What W. Foltz describes as "a pyramiding of clan alliances in super patron-client relationships" involves, in addition to personal bonds of friendships between the national elites and the maraboutic notables, certain calculated reciprocities, in the form of policy outputs and votes, between the party leadership and the leaders of the Muslim brotherhoods. "The prerequisite of political action," according to Foltz, is "not that it be progressive, nationalist, or such, but that the spoils be fairly distributed. The parallels with American ethnic and urban politics are fairly close; as in American cities, long range planning is often sacrificed to short-run expediency."[15] Clientelism, in short, becomes an adaptive device through which the demands of the maraboutic patrons are channeled into the political system and converted into policy outputs in return for electoral support.

In one case, integration depends on reciprocities between superiors and subordinates; its scope is limited to and at the same time delineates boundaries of the subsystem; the payments include predominantly affective rewards, in the form of identifying with a superior or receiving deference from an inferior. In the other case, integration hinges on reciprocities between equals; its scope transcends the boundaries of the ethnic or cultural subsystem; and the transactions are invested with a high degree of instrumental rationality.

If the first of our examples retrospectively suggests the nature of the obstacles placed in the way of national integration through the operation of microlevel clientelistic solidarities, the second indicates a far greater area of compatibility among the different levels at which clientelism operates. In the case of Senegal, the contribution of clientelism to nation-building would seem to involve several different types of integrative mechanisms: First, insofar as it implies a normative commitment to certain "instrumentalities and procedures for the achievement of goals and resolving conflicts,"[16] clientelism may provide at least some of the ingredients which enter into processes of consensus formation at the national level. Second, to the extent that it creates functional reciprocities among otherwise unrelated ethnic groupings, it may also generate feelings of interdependence among them and help reduce the saliency of primordial loyalties. Third, through the vertical bonds it creates among hierarchically distinct groups and communities, clientelism may supply the critical links between rulers and ruled, and through the intervention of "brokers" help bridge the proverbial gap between the elites and the masses. These three types of integration can be refered to, respectively, as "subjective," "transactional," and "structural."

To emphasize the integrative potential of clientelism is not to deny the divisive tendencies inherent in the formation of factions and personal followings. Nadel's comments on the effects of factionalism in Nupe might apply to other contexts as well: "Rivalry and feuds between the leaders of local factions may throw the whole town, indeed the whole country, into a civil war . . . "[17] In specific situations, however, the mere existence of factionalism may reinforce rather than diminish popular allegiances to the system, and hence positively aid subjective integration at the national level. This is the core of the argument advanced by Gluckman in his discussion of "rebellion" (as distinct from "revolution") in a traditional monarchical context:

All sections struggle for the kingship and this unifies them. They seek to place their own prince on the throne; they do not try to become independent from the kingship . . . It is a historical fact that these struggles kept component sections of the nation united in a conflicting allegiance about the sacred kingship.[18]

Gluckman's hypothesis cannot be accepted unreservedly, if only because much of the outcome would seem to depend on the character and composition of the factions involved, and the environmental conditions under which competition takes place. Nevertheless, it does not suggest that competition among patrons could encourage the cohesiveness of different ethnic segments in the lower reaches of the clientelistic pyramid.

Finally, although clientelism and ethnicity both provide opportunities for manipulation and adaptation, clientelism offers a significantly *broader range of strategies for the achievement of national integration*. For purposes of analysis these strategies may be conceptualized in terms of (1) a pyramiding of patron-client ties, (2) a spillover of reciprocities, and (3) changing partnerships, each involving specific changes in the character and structure of clientelistic relationships. What these changes consist of, and how they may affect national integration, will be discussed at greater length in a subsequent section. Suffice it to note here that although these processes are induced and not spontaneously occurring, their viability depends in part on the environmental transformations arising from colonial rule and on the limitations imposed by the character of the ethnic and clientelistic subsystem.

Since political integration is often a function of the limitations and opportunities inherent in traditional clientelistic networks, it will be useful at this stage to take a brief look at some of the varieties of traditional dependency relationships encountered in Tropical Africa.

VARIETIES OF TRADITIONAL DEPENDENCY RELATIONSHIPS

For most anthropologists, clientelism—or "clientage"—refers to a specific type of interpersonal relationship, more often than not institutionalized in the form of a contractual agreement between a superior and an inferior.[19] Examples are the *bara*-ship of Nupe, the *buhake* in Rwanda, the *bugabire* in Burundi, the *okutoisha* in Ankole. Our concern here, however, is with the generic and the recurrent rather than the idiosyncratic or the unique. Taking as our criteria of differentiation (1) the occupancy of role sets, (2) the normative orientations of patrons and clients, (3) the types of transactions involved, and (4) the base values of differential control over resources, we find that at least four different types of political clientelism may be said to have guided social and political relationships in traditional Africa—the patrimonial, the feudal, the mercantile, and the "saintly" type (see typological chart).

Patrimonial clientelism is explicitly political in character. Historically associated with the emergence of archaic state systems in the Sudanic and Interlacustrine areas, it suggests a significant expansion in scale of the original community, along with an increasing differentiation of governmental structures. In Weber's terminology, it implies "(the transformation of the original community) into a stratum of aids to the ruler

TYPOLOGY OF DEPENDENCY RELATIONSHIPS IN TRADITIONAL AFRICA

Type of Clientelism	Occupancy of Role Sets	Normative Orientation	Type of Transaction	Base Values of Differential Control Over Resources
1. *Patrimonial* Example: Sudanic States; Interlacustrine States (Rwanda, Burundi, Ankole, Buganda)	King-chief; chief-subchief	Mutual trust and loyalty	Office (political or administrative) —service and support	Power
2. *Feudal* Example: Buhake (Rwanda) Bugabire (Burundi) Okutoisha (Ankole) Bara-ship (Nupe)	Notable or freeborn noble-serf or com- moner	Deference- Affection	Protection—service and prestige	Status
3. *Mercantile* Example: Diula-Diatigi; diulaba-diulade; dillali-mai gida	Trader (or middle- man)-associate or customer	Economic self- interest and mutual trust	Commercial exchange	Wealth
4. *"Saintly"* Example: Sheikh-talibé Murabit-tlamith	Religious leader (marabout)-follower (talibe)	Benevolence- Devotion	Salvation— Obedience and Service	Sanctity

NOTE: The categories included in the above typology are adapted from the process-model developed in Lemarchand and Legg, "Political Clientelism and Development: A Preliminary Analysis," *Comparative Politics*, Vol. 4, No. 2 (January, 1972); although the terms "patrimonial" and "feudal" are used in this article to denote a possible evolutionary sequence from one type of clientelism to another, in the present context they are merely intended to provide an analytic framework for distinguishing among types. This, however, is not meant as a counterargument to the evolutionary scheme formulated by Maquet in "In- stitutionalisation féodale des relations de dépendance dans quatre cultures interlacustres," *Cahiers d'Études Africaines* (1969), 402-414, in which the author suggests the possibility of an historical movement from "patrimonial" to "feudal" clientelism.

(and its dependence upon him) for maintenance through the usufruct of land, office fees, income in kind, salaries and hence through pre- bends."[20] A basic feature of this transformation is the recruitment of client-chiefs who stand in relation to the sovereign not unlike bureaucrats in relation to their superior, in the sense that "they (do) not claim their position by right of in- heritance or by virtue of any prior connexion with the area to which they were appointed."[21] The underlying values, however, are those of mutual trust and loyalty. The basic transaction consists in the doling out of offices in return for administrative and political benefits. The base value through which initial control over scarce resources is obtained is political power defined in terms of the ruler's capacity to make effective use of a coercive apparatus, but as status differ- ences emerge in consequence of differential suc- cess in military skills, exchange relations be- come increasingly differentiated from military ones, at which point, in Weber's terms, "princely prerogatives become patrimonial in character."

Unlike the foregoing, *feudal clientelism*, in the sense in which the term is here used, is not necessarily coextensive with the formal political hierarchy; it refers to the anthropologist's more circumscribed definition of "clientage"—i.e.,

to an interpersonal bond between a superior and a subordinate, as between a freeborn noble and a commoner, involving "an exchange of protec- tion, economic security and a position in the so- ciety in return for loyalty, obedience and service from the subordinate.[22] Often institutionalized in the form of a ceremonial gift by the patron (as in traditional Nupe, where "the offering of a turban and a sword by the patron to his hench- man sealed the pact"),[23] and involving contrac- tual elements, it partakes of the qualities of the feudal homage. Yet, as a departure from what some might consider the hallmark of feudal- ism,[24] the base value through which a patron lays claim to the allegiance of his client lies in the differential social prestige and influence which goes along with one's membership in a "dominant" ethnic or status group.

Mercantile clientelism, traceable to the incep- tion of the long-distance trans-Saharan trade, in the thirteenth or fourteenth centuries, has per- sisted in one form or another throughout and in- deed long after the Malinke diaspora. Although in this case the participants are essentially con- cerned with the buying, storing, transport, and selling of marketable goods, out of these com- mercial transactions have developed more or less personalized relationships not only between buyers and sellers but *within the trading commu-*

nity. The reciprocities which exist between the *diula* traders of Mali, Guinea, or Senegal and their hosts, the *diatigi*, are duplicated by similar relationships between the long-distance Hausa traders from up-country and their "landlords" in places like Kumasi, Freetown and Ibada, and, in Ibadan between landlords *(mai gida)* and middlemen *(dillali)*.[25] These reciprocities involve, besides material benefits, a sense of mutual trust between the parties. A landlord or a *diatigi* is one who not only has material resources at his disposal but who also enjoys a certain "credit rating" from his reputation of trustworthiness and reliability. Although the anthropological literature dealing with this type of clientelism is scarce and the political science literature virtually nonexistent, the basic principle of social interaction in this case is unquestionably that of patron-client relationships defined in terms of reciprocal economic benefits and mutual loyalties.

The fourth type, here labeled somewhat uncritically *"saintly" clientelism*, expresses itself most conspicuously within the context of the Sufi brotherhoods *(tariqas)* of Senegal but is also found in Mauretania, Mali, Niger, and Northern Nigeria.[26] Sometimes referred to as "maraboutism," this type of relationship emphasizes the blind submission of the *talibé* to his *sheikh* or *muqaddam*. At the root of this dependence lies the disciple's conviction that his salvation depends on the intercession of his marabout, and the latter's realization that his status in society depends on the personal devotion of his followers, as well as their contributions in kind or cash. The *sheikh-talibé* relationship among the Mourides of Senegal represents the most striking example of this type of reciprocity; but one might also cite as an example the nexus of mutual obligations which to this day links the maraboutic elites of Mauretania and their followers. Whether it expresses itself in a secular or religious context, this type of clientelism still provides the basic articulation of social and political processes among individuals and groups in the predominantly Islamicized areas of West Africa.

Like all classifications, the foregoing is unabashedly arbitrary. None of the above categories can be treated in isolation. As the case of prerevolutionary Rwanda suggests, the patrimonial and feudal types may coexist with and indeed reinforce each other, as seems to have happened in the case of the mercantile and patrimonial variants at particular junctures of the evolution of the Sudanic states.[27]

Moreover, although client-patron relations are here conceptualized in terms of dyadic relationships for purposes of clarity, this is not meant to exclude the possibility of middlemen or brokers. In prerevolutionary Rwanda, the chief was not only a client of the sovereign but also a broker between the sovereign and the subchief; in Senegal the *sheikh-talibé* relationship was and still is mediated by regional officers *(fode)* and assistants *(tamsirs)* who might also qualify as middlemen; in Mali the *diatigi* were almost by definition ("the stranger's master") cast in the role of brokers between the *diulas* and the host community, a function they still perform in many of the trading centers of West Africa.[28] Client-patron ties, in short, are not necessarily dyadic and unidirectional, but may involve networks of reciprocities which in turn produce reversible relationships among the parties. Depending upon their position in the society, one man's patron may act as another man's client. Finally, because of its somewhat static qualities, the above typology underplays possibilities of conflicting clientelistic solidarities, as well as the potential for conflict that may arise from the juxtaposition of vertical and horizontal solidarities. While suggesting too much in the way of an integrative potential, it may also suggest the wrong kind of potential for integration.[29]

Aside from illustrating the variety of traditional dependency relationships that might conceivably be subsumed under the rubric of political clientelism, this classification sketches out how one type of relationship can be distinguished from another, and how their projections into the political space of contemporary Africa can be analyzed. Presumably, before one can infer a set of causal relationships between traditional and modern forms of clientelism, one must ask certain preliminary questions about the variables determining each type: Who are the patrons, and who are the clients? How compatible are their status positions, normative orientations, and transactional roles with conditions of rapid social change? In what ways do various types of differential control over resources "fit" with the conditions of the colonial and postcolonial situations? The answers to these questions are likely to vary not only with the heritage of specific colonial policies but with the characteristics of each type of clientelism.

Along with these differences, however, we find certain basic uniformities about how, in Africa as elsewhere, power is organized and generated. Power is not so much a commodity that some just happen to possess by virtue of their privileged membership in any particular group as a relational phenomenon. Inherent in each of the clientelistic patterns noted above is a relationship of reciprocity between an individual (or group of individuals) whose influence stems from his ability to provide services, goods or values that are so desired by others as to induce them to reciprocate these gratifications in the form of alternative services, goods, and values.[30] And since the norm of reciprocity is by nature malleable and indeterminate in terms of the obligations it implies—being, in Gouldner's terms "like a kind of plastic filler, capable of being poured into the shifting crevices of social structures, serving as a kind of all-purpose moral cement"[31]—one can see why, as a role model, clientelism should have persisted over time, through adjustment and adaptation. Although social mobilization may lead to different partnerships, the role model may remain basically unaffected. The evidence on this score is indeed abundant. Far from evident, however, are the types of adjustment that have taken place over the years and the conditions that have caused one type of adjustment to occur rather than another.

Irrespective of the types of clientelism operative in the traditional society, three distinctive patterns of adjustment can be discerned: First and most prevalent has been the *spillover of clientelistic reciprocities* from one field of activity to another. Reciprocities that were once restricted to a specific type of exchange have thus led to cumulative or alternative exchanges among parties. A case in point is the transformation of "feudal" into "saintly" patron-client ties within the framework of the Muslim brotherhoods of Senegal, and the projection of both into the context of "clan politics."[32] Similarly, the patrimonial ties that once existed among the ruling aristocracy of Rwanda provided the foundation for the establishment of patron-client ties of a feudal variety between Hutu and Tutsi and for the extension of dependency relationships based on the appropriation of land to a dependency relationship based on the ownership of cattle.[33] A more recent example is the "spillover" of mercantile clientelism into the realm of local politics in Ibadan: "Of all the patrons," writes Abner Cohen, "the cattle landlords are the most powerful as they have dominated the (Hausa) Quarter politically ever since its foundation in 1916. The Chief of the Quarter has always been a cattle landlord and, since 1930, he has also been the chief of the cattle market."[34] In each of these cases a new type of relationship has been added to or substituted for a preexisting one, leading to a transactional integration at the national or regional level.

Second, clientelism can lead to a *pyramiding of client-patron ties*, and, through the recruitment of new brokers, to an expansion of local or regional reciprocities on a more inclusive scale. The appropriation of landed fiefs under the hegemony of a royal clan, accompanied by the appointment of client-chiefs, was indeed a critical feature of the twin processes of state-building and territorial aggrandizement that took place throughout the Interlacustrine zone.[35] Similarly, much of the structural integration conducted under the auspices of colonial powers can be viewed in terms of a pyramiding of patron-client ties.

Third, there may be a *substitution rather than an extension of patron-client relationships*, leading to a continuation of reciprocal exchanges but in a totally different partnership. Here again the evidence, both historical and contemporary, is considerable, though not always as conclusive as one might hope. Perhaps the most striking example of the phenomenon is offered by the Rwandese revolution of 1959-62, leading to the eviction of the Tutsi patrons and a redefinition of clientelistic partnerships within the Hutu stratum.[36]

Empirically, these types of adjustments are neither self-sustaining nor mutually reinforcing. Although the building-up of dominant parties sharing the qualities of political machines is in part traceable to the selective use of one or more of these adjustive mechanisms, their mere occurrence is no guarantee that the end result will be the creation of a nationwide political machine. Whether operating individually or in conjunction with each other, these processes may lead to widely different types of relationships between the clientelistic substructures and the center, as well as between the constituent segments of each substructure. Just as one may conceive of different types of machines operating alongside each other, one may also envisage the possibility of the party machine being superimposed upon, and in some ways tributary of, microlevel solidarities of a traditional type. Similarly, one may conceive of a machine being wholly centered upon the party structure (as in the Ivory Coast), or, on the contrary, revolving almost exclusively around bureaucratic structures of a traditional or neotraditional type (as in Ethiopia, or in Burundi until 1967). In short, before one can generalize about the effects of these internal adjustments on the political systems of contemporary Africa, it may be useful to consider the conditions which in recent times have reinforced, hampered, or altered the operation of traditional forms of clientelism.

These conditions can best be understood by

looking at (1) the processes of incorporation achieved through the imposition of colonial controls; (2) the alternative structures of opportunity made available through the introduction of new resources; and (3) the new competitive processes arising from the conjunction of (1) and (2). Only by taking each of these variables into account is it possible to gain a clear picture of the fourth and most crucial variable—ethnicity.

PATTERNS OF INCORPORATION, ALLOCATION, AND COMPETITIVENESS

Difficult though it may be to generalize about the effects of colonial rule upon traditional forms of clientelism, the weight of evidence suggests important areas of compatibility between the two. At the broadest level of generalization one might argue, first, that the colonial situation has created a psychological climate eminently congenial to the maintenance of a "dependence complex"[37] among Africans. Whether or not Mannoni's depiction of the personality structure of the Malagasy can be applied across the board to Africans in general, a convincing case can be made for the view that the homage of dependence sought by European colonizers through the projection of their own "Prospero complex" onto the African scene must have fostered similar dispositions on the part of traditional patrons toward their clients.[38] Second, the conditions of rapid social change generated through various transformative influences—economic, social, and political—probably intensified the clients' need for something or somebody to depend on; the heightened feelings of insecurity released by social change, along with the resultant quest for anxiety-reducing mechanisms, have operated to reinforce the strength of client–patron relationships. Third, for reasons of practicality or opportunism, European administrators have often been very tolerant toward existing forms of clientelism, and sometimes equally receptive to the creation of new ones. Where these expressed the structure of political relations—as in the case of patrimonial clientelism—and where their suppression would have entailed greater costs than seemed justifiable or tolerable, the tendency of European officials has been to use traditional clientelistic structures as instruments for mediating and legitimizing their rule.

Yet, if there are excellent reasons for viewing "The pyramiding of patron-client ties" as a byproduct of European rule, one can easily exaggerate the extent to which traditional African societies really lent themselves to this kind of manipulation. Not only can one discern major discontinuities in the overall distribution and extensiveness of clientelistic networks in any given territory (suggesting corresponding variations in the serviceability of the incorporated units); one can also perceive fundamental differences in the degree to which European policies proved compatible with the preservation of traditional forms of clientelism.

If the first type of discontinuity may clearly be attributed to the different patterns of incorporation achieved through the more or less erratic tracing of colonial boundaries, there are several possible explanations for the differential impact of colonial policies on traditional forms of clientelism.

One such explanation lies in the hypothesis advanced by Ronald Cohen that "given a similar incorporative experience differences in traditional African political structures will create significant differences in the way these systems and the people within them adapt to the modern nation-state."[39] Another possible explanation has to do with the official policies and practices of European powers, and in particular the extent to which the effective practice of indirect rule presupposed the retention of clientelism of a feudal variety. Where the preservation of "feudal clientelism" was more or less consistently regarded as a necessary adjunct of indirect rule (as in Northern Nigeria), feudal and patrimonial forms of clientelism have evidently reinforced each other, structurally or normatively.[40] But one must also note the persistence of clientelistic patterns where indirect rule was neither regarded as legitimate or systematically pursued, and where the social system made no allowance for the operation of feudal clientelism. Thus, drawing upon his personal experience as a former colonial administrator, Pierre Alexandre notes that in those parts of French-speaking West Africa that had a high rate of turnover among European officials, "African officials, shop clerks or cocoa brokers and catechists were, on the whole, permanent;" African "middlemen" were thus cast in the role of patrons in relation to the masses, with "clientelism cutting across tribal divisions, or, more widely, across traditional jural relationships."[41]

A third explanatory factor, operating independently of the formal assumptions underlying colonial policies, involves the variable assessments of the economic implications of client-patron relationships made by European administrators. Where traditional clientelism was found incompatible with the immediate or long-range economic objectives of the colonial authorities and accordingly done away with, as in Rwanda in the early 1950s, its suppression had profoundly destabilizing consequences for the internal cohesion of the community at large.

Economic motives may have precisely the opposite results, however, perpetuating or even accentuating the patron-client nexus at the community level. Here two different types of situations may be distinguished: One, most clearly suggested by the case of the Mouride brotherhoods of Senegal, involved a deliberate attempt by the European colonizer to draw maximum benefits from the manipulation of clientelistic relations. Although this may not have been the sole motive, the prospects of economic development offered by the marabouts' control over most of the peanut producing areas, and indeed their control of the labor force needed for agricultural development, were certainly instrumental in prompting the French to preserve by all possible means the "saintly" relationship which to this day links the *talibés* to their *sheikhs*—and in trying to establish a similar, though far less "saintly," relationship between themselves and the *sheikhs*.[42]

Recognition or reinforcement of clientelistic patterns may also occur in response to the economic demands of indigenous local communities. Meillassoux's discussion of the role of *diula* in the Ivory Coast provides a good illustration.[43] Although they were initially denied access to their original trading areas by the French army, supposedly because of the need to set up a "commercial blockade" to facilitate the subjugation of the local communities, the *diula* traders were subsequently allowed to resume their commercial activities after their former trading partners, the Gouro, repeatedly demanded that right for them. Writing in the early sixties, Meillassoux noted:

Diula relations with the Gouro compared to the precolonial period are apparently the same: In addition to kola—of which they largely control the trade today—they buy coffee and cocoa. They even improved their position in regard to their geographical extension . . . They are the only intermediaries at the first level in the coffee-buying process.[44]

In each of these two instances, then, economic considerations have tended not only to encourage existing clientelistic networks but also to facilitate the forging of new links between the center and the periphery. Thus, through their economic base in the Gouro milieux, the *diula* were able to capitalize upon the new opportunities opened by European commerce, and to establish themselves as intermediaries between

local producers and European firms; similarly, through their economic and religious influence in the countryside, the maraboutic elites of Senegal were able to provide the crucial connecting links between the rural communities and the central governmental-bureaucratic structures.

As the foregoing makes plain, the new allocative centers set up under the colonial powers have generated new resources and linkages. How these in turn have affected African societies can best be understood by reference to (1) the type of resources generated by the colonial environment, (2) the channels through which these resources have been allocated, and (3) the transaction flows attendant upon the emergence of new reciprocities.

Taking the term "resources" in its broadest sense, as Dahl does, to describe "anything that can be used to sway the specific choices or the strategies of another individual," we discover that each of the patterns of adjustment noted earlier are reducible to the adaptation of clientelistic strategies to different resources—or, if one takes the view that clientelism is itself a resource, to different combinations of resources. "Political resources," writes Dahl, "can be pyramided in much the same way that a man who starts out in business sometimes pyramids a small investment into a large corporate empire."[45] Just as the building up of corporate and African empires can be seen as one example of pyramiding of clientelistic and other resources, the fashioning of new political entities under imperial rule may be viewed in basically the same terms.

In the latter case, however, allowance has to be made for the introduction of new resources— in the form of wealth, education, technological skills, and the like—and new types of reciprocities. The result has been a shift of emphasis away from symbolic or affective rewards to expectations of material benefits, in turn leading to a sloughing off of the "mechanical" solidarities characteristic of feudal clientelism for a type of relationship, if not always based on "organic" solidarities in Durkheim's sense, at least much closer to those associated with "machine politics." Conceptualizing this transformation in terms of different perceptions of a patron's competence, one might argue with Colson[46] that the trend in recent times has been to dissociate political competence from traditional status distinctions and to identify it with the ability to manipulate technical and political resources effectively. European patrons were sought after not only because of their political "pull" but because they controlled the technical resources and know-how through which the demands of their clients could be met; by the time African "bosses" stepped into the shoes of the European patrons, however, political competence meant in essence the ability to keep in tow a reliable clientele through the dispensation of prebends. Political parties in many instances took on the qualities of political machines.

Thus, another way of looking at political change in colonial and independent Africa is from the standpoint of the new partnerships established at the center, first between Europeans and Africans, and later among Africans. But these new partnerships did not always exclude the maintenance of traditional clientelistic solidarities at the local level, or indeed, the reinforcement of such solidarities through a "spillover" effect.

Therefore the weakness of African political machines may be due not, as some have suggested,[47] to their operating at the national rather than the local level, but to their operating at cross-purposes with local machines rendered all the more powerful by their control of traditional and modern political resources.

For an example of how the "spillover" of reciprocities at the local or regional level may inhibit national integration one can do no better than quote C. S. Whitaker on the organization of the NPC in Northern Nigeria:[48]

The structure of the NPC fits conveniently into this structure of traditional (clientage) relationships in at least two important respects. First, by virtue of powers it exercised through control of the government, the party was a principal agency of patronage offices, loans, scholarships, contracts, and other opportunities sought by the upwardly mobile. This could be accomplished either directly and formally or indirectly and informally through the medium of the party or ex-party men who dominated the public boards, corporations, and commissions. Second (and of greater consequence in terms of winning mass support), the interlocking directorate of local administrative and party personnel inescapably bound humble persons to traditionally august figures in their capacity as party men. The dependency that derived from the vast network of clientage relationships inherent in the traditional society were transferred to the party. Loyalty to the NPC became a way of defraying traditional political obligations.

In the national context of Nigeria, the "traditionally august figures" of the Northern Region played the role of brokers or middlemen; poised between the national and regional cultures and communities, they became the manipulators of first- and second-order resources—i.e., of patronage offices, loans, scholarships, and contracts on the one hand, and of contacts and connections on the other.[49] Similar roles have been played, with greater or lesser degrees of success by the *ganwa* in Burundi, the *sheikhs* in Senegal, the *hassan* and *zawya* in Mauretania, the *saza* chiefs in Buganda, and some traditional chiefs in the Ivory Coast, Ghana, Niger, and Upper Volta.

The relative importance of traditional patrons in the mediating process, both before and after independence, must be seen in the light of the brokerage functions they once performed at the juncture of external and internal clientelistic channels, the latter operating within the African society and the former through the sponsorship of the European oligarchy. As brokers they were all in some degree concerned with the transmission of the same resource, namely to maintain and facilitate strategic contacts and communication with individuals holding direct access to political resources. They became, in Boissevain's words, "professional manipulators of people and information to bring about communication."[50] Following up Boissevain's thesis that "brokerage is a business (in which) a broker's *capital* consists of his personal network of relations with people, and his *credit* of what others think his capital to be," one could regard the passage from colonial to independent status as representing successive transfers of capital and credit from one set of brokers to another— presumably from "traditional" to modern brokers. Yet in many instances, traditional patrons (chiefs, subchiefs, landlords, etc.) managed to retain a high credit rating among their people even when their capital at the national level was low or nonexistent. Thus, in the early sixties, the traditional Tutsi chiefs of Rwanda had lost virtually all contacts with the Belgian administration; but in spite of their loss of capital, certain segments of the peasantry persisted in believing that they still enjoyed considerable influence in administrative spheres. Conversely, a transfer of political credit from the traditional patrons to the new recipients of wealth and influence did not necessarily imply a commensurate transfer of capital from one category to the other. Thus instead of speaking of "patron" and "mass" parties to characterize African political groups, it might be more useful to distinguish between different patron parties enjoying different credit ratings and capital assets in different circumstances and environments.[51]

That some traditional patron parties managed to keep relatively high credit ratings in times of high demand-inflation (as in Northern Nigeria,

Burundi, and even Ghana), while others did not, invites consideration of the different transaction flows generated through clientelistic structures.[52] The analysis of transaction flows between traditional patrons and clients can easily be distorted by the normative idiom in which these relationships are phrased. Where the notion of an opposition is ruled out by the nature of the relationship (as in Northern Nigeria),[53] one might all too easily assume the existence of mutually indulging transactions when in fact there is little more than grudging acquiescence on the part of clients. Yet transactions of a mutually rewarding type clearly did occur during and after the colonial period between, say, the *diula* traders of the Ivory Coast and their traditional "clients" (the Gouro); the "saintly" patrons of Senegal and their *talibés*; the traditional Emirs of Northern Nigeria and some of their subordinates. In exchange for salt, cattle and *sombe*, the Gouro gave the *diula* the kola, coffee and cocoa which enabled them to become wealthy middlemen; in exchange for a promise of salvation, marabouts received from the *talibés* the labor they needed to cultivate their fields; in return for the dispensation of psychological and material gratifications, the Fulani Emirs received deference, prestige, and services from their clients, and in time, they received the political support they needed to retain control over the provincial legislature. Because of the Emirs' control over the recruitment process, and because such control was regarded as the "natural" expression of their traditional prerogatives, "those elected became, by the same logic, the clients of the Emirs."[54]

In the case of Nigeria, restriction of the scope of mutually advantageous transactions to the northern region, coupled with the cultural differences between North and South, has undoubtedly stimulated feelings of regional particularism and even secessionist aspirations in the North. In both the Ivory Coast and Senegal, however, the expansion of reciprocities on a broad geographical and socioeconomic scale has tended to favor a similar extension of integrative bonds. The profits accumulated by the Ivoirien planters were also shared by the *diula* intermediaries and even by the chiefs as "some profited directly from the new crops and most benefited at least from the increased wealth of their kinsmen;"[55] similarly, while some of the marabouts of Senegal proved eminently useful in aggregating support for the UPS elites (in particular through the sale and distribution of party cards),[56] they also received substantial rewards from the party leadership, in hard cash as well

as in the form of policy outputs. In each country national integration was achieved through a widening of clientelistic ties accompanied by mutually rewarding transactions.

Clearly, mutually rewarding exchanges at one level can create basic incompatibilities at another; but one can also conceive of mutually rewarding exchanges deteriorating over time into mutually depriving ones, with similarly dysfunctional consequences for national integration. Consider the case of Mali: Initially the *diula* community shared a close identity of interest with the Union Soudanaise (US) elites, largely because of their "opposition to European commercial policies and interests."[57] They provided the US elites with strategic contacts along the Niger, among both rural and urbanized Africans, and in turn expected their contribution to the cause of Malian nationalism to be repaid in the form of new economic opportunities for themselves and their clientele.[58] Yet by the mid-sixties, the socialist options of the Keita regime had alienated a substantial number of *diula*, and the events of 1967 further intensified their sense of disaffection toward the regime.[59] The recent history of Guinea tells a somewhat similar story: The *diula* played a crucial role in the diffusion of the PDG ideology in the late 'fifties, but as in Mali, and for much the same reasons, their opposition has since become a source of major concern for the regime.

Implicit in the foregoing is that with the opening or closing off of political resources and the proliferation of new brokerage roles, competition is likely to set in among different clientelistic networks. Although the shape of competitive patterns and their implications for national integration can only be ascertained empirically, at least two generalizations suggest themselves: one is that competition is likely to take place at different levels depending on the time period considered; another is that the rate and character of clientelistic competition tends to vary with the nature of the resources made available at any given time.

A major consequence of the opening, and subsequent exhaustion, of the political resources released through the manipulation of nationalist ideology and propaganda has been to intensify clientelistic competition between African and European patrons and in time between different sets of African patrons. Each type of competition has tended to interact with and affect the outcome of the other. The history of Rwanda, for example, clearly shows the destabilizing consequences of competitive strivings between African and European patrons upon preexisting clientelistic networks. Already in the twenties, as a result of "their involvement in ever-widening spheres of African life, (the White Fathers) assumed more and more the character of patrons within the existing system . . . The Hutu accepted these new patrons, seeing in them an additional source of security."[60] The increments of security gained by Hutu clients inevitably meant a loss of social prestige for the Tutsi patrons; the adverse consequences which this implied for the application of indirect rule caused the administration to intervene and reverse the trend. By the late fifties and early sixties, however, the approach of independence raised the prospects of new political opportunities for the Hutu; and the ever-expanding involvement of the Church and the administration in the process of institutional transfer, while adding significantly to the rate of competition between Hutu and Tutsi elites, provided the Hutu elite with the resources which made possible the disengagement of the Hutu masses from the hold of their traditional patrons.

If the case of Rwanda shows an intensification of inter-African rivalries through European involvement, the history of the Ivory Coast in the late forties illustrates precisely the opposite. In Rwanda the conflict of interest between Hutu and Tutsi elites (which might be conceptualized in terms of competition between a presumptive and an incumbent set of brokers) was too fundamental not to supersede their common grievances against their European patrons; in the Ivory Coast the conflict of interest between African and European planters (also reducible to a competition between different sets of brokers) was too deep, and the economic deprivations it entailed for the Africans too widespread, not to supersede inter-African rivalries. Moreover, the concurrence of economic interests between traditional chiefs and African planters further diminished the possibilities of such rivalries.[61] This situation played directly into the hands of the nationalist elites, converting the indigenous Ivoirien planters into fervent PDCI militants, and providing at the same time the economic resources through which further support could be generated from below and new networks of clientelism activated. The significance of the contribution (economic and political) made by African planters to the cause of Ivoirien nationalism becomes all the more apparent when compared with the very different situation then confronting African planters in Ghana: "In Ghana there were no European planters and the African farmers were much less involved in nationalist activities."[62]

That the rate and character of clientelistic competition have tended to reflect the nature of the resources available is again nowhere better illustrated than in Rwanda:[63] Only with the opening of new political resources, through elections and constitutional reforms, did the conflict of interest between Hutu and Tutsi elites assert itself in any structured fashion; only when they realized the futility of attaining their political goals through electoral processes did the Hutu elites actively court the support of European patrons; and it was largely through the manipulation of violence that the Hutu elites were able to aggregate a solid political clientele. If violence made security a scarce resource, clientelism in turn provided the means by which security could be obtained.

In this case, the conjunction of electoral processes and violence provided the key resources through which a traditional form of clientelism reasserted itself—albeit in somewhat modified fashion—within an ethnically homogeneous stratum. Elsewhere, however, elections, with or without violence, provided the conditions for the emergence of a different type of clientelism, identified with dominant parties often sharing the characteristics of political machines. The irony is that the same forces that encouraged the birth of political machines also helped activate the ethnic solidarities which in many instances destroyed the machine as a form of political organization.

ETHNICITY AS AN INDEPENDENT VARIABLE

This brings us to a consideration of ethnicity as an independent variable: How does ethnicity —whether taken to refer to the "givens" or "assumed givens of social existence"[64]—affect the scope, stability, and functioning of clientelistic networks? The answer is anything but clear. At least three possible types of situation suggest themselves, each in some way contradicting the other: The activation of ethnic solidarities may lead to a rupture of client-patron ties (as in Rwanda); or it may set sharp cultural or geographical limitations (or both) on the scope of clientelistic networks (as in Nigeria); or it may coexist with or indeed foster clientelistic ties on a nationwide basis (as in the Ivory Coast, Liberia, and, in a qualified sense, Senegal).

What might otherwise seem like a thoroughly confusing situation becomes somewhat more comprehensible in the light of the following caveats: (1) Although clientelism and ethnicity are in many ways interrelated, they refer to basically different levels of solidarity; whereas clientelism describes a personalized relationship, ethnicity is fundamentally a group phenomenon;[65] hence, there is no compelling reason to expect concommitant variations between ethnic and client-patron solidarities. (2) Just as group solidarities can be activated at many different levels and with varying degrees of intensity, one must also expect wide variations in the extent to which ethnic solidarities can be said to conflict with or reinforce patron-client solidarities. Whether or not the activation of solidarities in one sphere leads to a weakening of such solidarities in the other is an empirical question that can only be answered in the light of specific situations. (3) Seldom has there been a direct relationship between ethnicity and clientelism; as our previous discussion makes clear, the relationship between the two can best be seen in the light of certain intervening variables, structural and conjunctural.

These intervening variables may conveniently be analyzed under the following three major headings: (1) the nature of the structural "fit" between ethnic or cultural boundaries on the one hand, and status differences between patron and clients on the other; (2) the actor's perceptions of the relative costs and benefits involved in the maintenance of particular patron-client sets; (3) the pattern of resource allocation prevailing at any given time.

"By itself," writes M. G. Smith, "clientage is unlikely to dissolve sectional boundaries wherever differences of culture, religion or race are prominent."[66] By the same token, where cultural cleavages not only are prominent but tend to coincide with patrons and clients, these cleavages may help break up the patron-client nexus. Thus, the greater the cultural differences between patrons and clients, and the more conspicuous the social distance between them, the greater the likelihood of violent ethnic strife in conditions of rapid social mobilization.[67] Rwanda is an obvious example: Just as the spread of egalitarian ideas among Westernized Hutu elements threatened the "premise of inequality" which underlay the traditional order, the emergence of this presumptive elite, together with the support they received from the European administration and the Church, provided the conditions through which a new category of patrons was able to displace the old, and a "new" and ethnically homogenized society substituted for the old pluralistic order. Although Burundi has tended toward a similar polarization of ethnic loyalties, the greater flexibility of its stratification system and the absence of a rigorous coincidence of ethnic and status distinctions

have significantly delayed ethnic conflict.

Yet, even where cultural or ethnic differences between patrons and clients might otherwise spell a lack of cohesiveness, preexistent clientelistic activities may reorient the actors' perceptions of their mutual interest so as to promote transactional integration among different ethnic segments, whether at the local or national levels. This phenomenon is perhaps best illustrated by the solidarities that have developed between the Hausa landlords of Ibadan and the predominantly Yoruba Action Group leaders of the Western Region of Nigeria; what initially began as a mutually advantageous economic transaction between cattle landlords and Yoruba butchers developed into similarly advantageous reciprocities between the Action Group leadership and the Hausa landlords:

When during the 1950's the butchers affiliated themselves within . . . the Action Group, which was until 1962 in power in the Western Region, the Hausa landlords reacted not only by joining the same party themselves, but also by dragging almost the whole Hausa Quarter with them in joining it, and in successive elections the Ibadan Hausa gave their votes to it. . . . (In return for their votes), the party not only prevented hostile action being taken against the cattle landlords, but even tried to prevent individual butchers from defaulting, by exerting pressure on these to honor their obligations, and sometimes by granting loans to those among them who did not have the cash to pay.[68]

Although integration in this case occurred partly because mercantile clientelism had spilled over into the political sphere, economic interests will not everywhere and inevitably assert their primacy and lead to political compromise. Moreover, compromise may also be due to several other contributory factors. It may be due to perceptions of external threats that may submerge perceptions of local antagonism, or—as in the case discussed above—to the relative smallness of the migrant community and its consequently weak political leverage regionally or nationally.

Where no prior transactional integration exists among groups, how does the allocation of new resources affect interethnic or intercommunal relations? The answer depends in part on the character of the resources available at any given time, and on the sources of control over these resources. Where politically significant resources tend to become the monopoly of a particular ethnic or communal group, the clientelistic solidarities arising from the exploitation of these sources may possibly reinforce ethnic or communal solidarities. Take the example of the

Eastern Region of Nigeria: The displacement of "strangers" (Sierra Leonians, Yoruba, etc.) in favor, first, of Onitsha Ibo, and then Owerri Ibo, has reflected basic changes in the political significance attached to specific resources (first education, then wealth, and finally "numbers"). But it has also tended to accentuate the communal bases of clientelistic politics among Ibo. Moreover, in time the preeminence of "numbers" at the national level has tended to relegate the Ibo as a group to a comparatively minor position in the federal superstructure, and hence has dissipated communal differences within the Ibo community while at the same time exacerbating ethnic and regional tensions between Ibo and non-Ibo.

But this is by no means the only conceivable pattern. Where ultimate control over financial and economic resources is vested in nationally oriented politicians, the distributive capacities of the system can be used to foster new patterns of reciprocity among groups, associated with the techniques of machine politics. What is involved here is the creation of new solidarities based on expectations of concrete, short-run benefits. Although the men in charge of running the machine may occasionally bolster their authority by charisma or by coercion, they can best be thought of as political entrepreneurs. Their job is to weld together disparate ethnic segments through the allocation of prebends.

Nowhere is this type of clientelism better illustrated than by the development of the PDCI in the Ivory Coast between 1952 and 1959. According to Zolberg,

the PDCI secured support by co-opting ethnic leaders into the organization by means of a major distributive effort, itself made possible by the sheer accident of prosperity stemming from high prices for tropical commodities during and immediately after the Korean war, a prosperity which was later bolstered by protectionist props extended by France toward its showcase colony . . . The entire system of communications between the center and the localities took the form of ethnic channels, through official representatives such as members of the Territorial (later National) Assembly, or other forms of ethnic clientship.[69]

Although the PDCI must certainly be regarded as the prototype of the African machine, elements of the machine pattern can also be detected in the UPS of Senegal, the True Whig party of Liberia, and, to a lesser extent, the Parmehutu of Rwanda. Several other parties shared at one time or another machine characteristics—the CPP in Ghana (at least until

1960), the SLPP in Sierra Leone, and each of the three major Nigerian parties in existence until 1959. That few of these "machines" were able to maintain themselves in power raises the question of the part played by ethnicity in hastening or precipitating their demise.

Two general answers have been suggested— one related to the character of the ethnic balance in any given state, and the other to the conditions affecting the enlistment of ethnic support. Arguing from a somewhat broader perspective, James Scott hypothesizes that where a single ethnic group held a dominant position, and provided the basis for the construction of a political machine, "the excluded ethnic groups . . . demanded at the very least more regional autonomy and launched secessionist revolts in some areas. The resulting threat to the territorial integrity of the state was commonly the occasion for military takeovers."[70] Moreover, the elimination of electoral processes, according to Scott, deprives the machine of the incentives it needs to hold its clientele. In the absence of electoral pressures, expectations of payoffs are bound to decline. The bonds of cohesion which initially tied ethnic segments to the machine are thus gradually loosened, introducing possibilities of ethnic strife or secession.

Formulated in these terms, neither hypothesis is entirely convincing. Can one really visualize (as Scott does) the ethnic map of Nigeria as being characterized by a "dominant ethnic group"? Could not the Baule of the Ivory Coast just as well qualify as a dominant ethnic group— or for that matter the Wolof of Senegal? And if one associates ethnic dominance not with numbers but with social status and power, would it not be legitimate to regard the Americo-Liberians of Liberia as "dominant"? Moreover, granting that in the American context electoral processes were instrumental in keeping political machines going, in Africa these processes have usually released those very centrifugal forces that spelled the defeat of the machine as a form of political organization. Pushing the logic of the argument a step further, one is entitled to wonder why American machines declined while electoral pressures did not. Much more relevant is Scott's contention that "the durability of the machine as a political form is maximized . . . where it is part of a larger growing economy that can afford its expensive habits, and where its bosses do not have a monopoly of coercive authority."[71] The crucial factor, however, lies in the pattern of resource allocation, in the extent to which resources (economic and political) are allowed either to move evenly from the center to the periphery, or to accrue exclusively to a particular region or ethnic group. The Ivory Coast provides the clearest example of the first pattern: except for the Agni of Sanwi, and, to a lesser extent, the Bete (two of the least favored groups), resources, whether in the form of jobs, material payoffs, sinecures of one kind or another, or social overhead capital, are fairly evenly distributed among the representatives of the various ethnic segments. This is not to deny the existence of gross disparities of income between the Ivoirien bureaucratic-planter oligarchy on the one hand and ordinary peasants on the other;[72] the only point here is that the oligarchy represents a fairly wide cross-section of the ethnic interests at stake.

In Nigeria, by contrast, resource allocation has tended to reflect and reinforce the fragmented pattern of cultural loyalties.

The parties themselves were part of rival business and financial structures which existed to make money for the individuals concerned and provide financial backing for the parties . . . Each regional government has gradually acquired a number of public boards by 1959 which could be used as means of dispensing patronage to party worthies.[73]

Not only did the machines reinforce the ethnic loyalties of their clientele; electoral processes offered new opportunities for the creation of satellite machines in regions other than those in which the parent organization operated. The effect has been to exacerbate communal tensions so that the stability of the entire federal structure is threatened.

In short, the higher the distributive capacity of the system, the more congenial the environment to the operation of machine-like clientelism; a high distributive capacity alone, however, is not a sufficient condition to ensure the stability of the system. Even more important is the capacity of the machine to strike an adequate balance of patronage along the vertical axis of class stratification and the horizontal dimension of ethnic cleavages. An exceedingly lopsided distribution of spoils on each of these dimensions may bring disaffection, revolt, or ethnic strife.

There is yet another factor to consider, perhaps the most elusive: the social context of machine politics. Drawing upon Kilson's insight that "the principle of reciprocity refers to a fundamental aspect of the traditional or neo-traditional patterns of political action (and hence) is the most effective way (for Africans) to maximize material and prestige benefits derived from politics, as well as to minimize the losses," one might look upon African machines as the em-

bodiment of at least one aspect of African tradition.[74] Not all African machines, however, exhibit the characteristics of traditional reciprocity patterns; even where the latter prevail there is still considerable room for variation in the way in which tradition and modernity combine and coalesce. Leaving aside those rare instances where the machine operates in the context of a no-party state and becomes synonymous with palace politics (as in Ethiopia or Burundi between 1962 and 1968), at least two different types of machines can be distinguished: the more orthodox, PDCI-type of machine, in which patronage becomes the essential source of cohesion; and the "neo-traditional machine," such as the UPS, in which exchange processes between the center and the periphery are mediated by, and contingent upon, the operation of traditional forms of clientelism at the local level. In the latter case, traditional micro-level solidarities provide the essential linkages between the party and the masses; the machine is superimposed upon, and in some ways tributary to, the clientelistic subsystem.

Furthermore, in the more orthodox type machine, ethnic segments are incorporated through a mixture of patronage and cooptation; vertical solidarities are maintained through material inducements; the party structure defines the organization of the machine, and is coextensive with its field of operation. The neo-traditional machine, on the other hand, seeks to enlist the support of micro-level clientelistic structures through bargaining with traditional patrons who act as brokers between the party elites and the masses; vertical solidarities are maintained in part through material inducements but mainly through perpetuation of deference patterns between the brokers and their traditional clientele; moreover, the party structure is not synonymous with the traditional clientelistic substructures but adjacent to it. The party structure in Senegal, for example, "remains separate from the brotherhoods"; and if the marabouts are in no position to control the party, there are, likewise, limits to how far the party can impose its policies upon the marabouts.[75]

The integrative action patterns (what Bailey refers to as "bridge-actions")[76] through which links are established between the subsystem and the macropolitical structure are likely to vary substantially from one type of machine-clientelism to the other. In each case subordinate political actors cast their lot with the central authorities because they expect certain rewards to accrue from this relationship. In the context of the more orthodox type of political machine (like the PDCI) expectations of patronage are paramount; the securing of material benefits becomes an end in itself. For traditional brokers operating in the context of a "neo-traditional" machine, however, expectations of material payoffs are only part of a larger complex of motivations. Material incentives may only serve the purely instrumental purpose, of maximizing the symbolic or affective rewards to which the brokers consider themselves entitled. Commenting on the motives which actuate "aspiring *samba linguers*" in Senegal, Foltz notes that "money is a major goal, but primarily because it can bring with it a greater following and thus increased prestige." This characterization applies equally well to the behavior of maraboutic elites. For some the resources of the political kingdom may yield handsome dividends in cash as well as other tangible rewards, but this merely strengthens their prestige as religious leaders since, as Foltz points out, "it is popularly felt that a marabout's potential for conferring grace and ultimate salvation is reflected in his personal wealth and magnificence."[77] Here the bridge-action by which the client-patron relationship is connected to the political system is really an attempt by traditional patrons to use the resources of modern politics to reaffirm a traditional relationship.

Not all African machines, therefore, are equally dependent upon the allocation of material resources. Whereas the PDCI and the TANU, for example, are both potentially vulnerable to what Bienen calls the "vicious circle of underdevelopment" (that is, "limited resources— weak organization—limited resources"),[78] this would seem less of a danger for a neo-traditional party machine such as the UPS, in which traditional reciprocity patterns provide alternative resources for the consolidation and manipulation of grass-roots support.

To return to the question raised earlier: the incorporation of ethnic loyalties into the framework of a political machine does not necessarily do away with the brokers' loyalty to their group of origin; it merely enlarges the scope of their loyalties at the same time that it redefines their conceptions of self-interest. In other words, the relationship between ethnicity and clientelism cannot be reduced to a zero-sum game, in which increments of clientelism augment a person's sense of self-interest in the same proportion that they diminish his loyalty to the tribe. Just as the building of modern states on the debris of the old often tends to require the adjustment of tradition to modernity, rather than the substitution of one for the other, integrative processes in Africa are more often than not dependent on a redefinition of individual conceptions of self-interest in the context of multiple group loyalties.

POLITICAL CLIENTELISM AND DEVELOPMENT

In trying to clarify the relationship between political clientelism and ethnicity, and the relationship of both to national integration, I have only touched upon one dimension of the developmental process. It may be useful, therefore, in conclusion, to shift to certain broader aspects of political development. Since there are almost as many definitions of political development as there are of clientelism, assessments of how one relates to the other will necessarily depend on one's conceptualization of each.

Political development can be looked at in one of two ways—as synonymous with the modernization historically experienced by the West, or, following Huntington's lead, as a process of institution building "independent of, although obviously affected by, the process of modernization."[79] The first of these approaches focuses on those forces of change leading to a dispersion of power; the second on the containment of such forces for purposes of power accumulation. In one case analysis centers upon such well-known facets of the "developmental syndrome" as (1) differentiation of political roles and structures; (2) equality as the "central operative ideal" of society; (3) capacity as "not only the logical imperative of system maintenance, but also the enhanced adaptive and innovative potentialities possessed by man for the management of his environment, human and nonhuman."[80] In the other the microscope is turned on "the institutionalization of organizations and procedures" as the absolute precondition of political development.

It takes no special gift of intuition to realize that the second of these approaches is clearly more compatible with our earlier characterization of machine-clientelism, and that neither is particularly congenial to traditional forms of clientelism. Indeed, in the light of the assumption which underlies the first of these approaches, the contribution of traditional clientelism to political development might seem negligible if not counterproductive: "Political development," writes Coleman, "can be regarded as the acquisition by a political system of a *consciously-sought*, and *qualitatively new and enhanced political capacity* as manifested in the successful institutionalization of (1) *new* patterns of integration . . . and (2) *new* patterns of participation and resource distribution . . ."[81] (my emphasis). Making due allowance for the variations noted earlier among different types of traditional clientelism, one might argue that the differentiation of political roles and structures along functional lines is hardly compatible with the dichotomous, particularistic basis of role-differentiation between patrons and clients; that the principle of equality is violated by the very definition of traditional clientelism; and that the distributive capacities of the political system are lessened rather than enhanced by the "prebendal" features of traditional clientelism and the subjective criteria it implies for allocating resources. Moreover, since traditional forms of clientelism have rarely been coextensive with the boundaries of the newly created states, "the institutionalization of political organizations and procedures" would seem to require rather different materials than those available from traditional clientelistic networks.

The trouble with this line of reasoning is, first, that it so reifies traditional forms of clientelism as to deny their adaptive capacities; and second, that it overstresses the compartmentalization between "traditional" and "modern" forms of clientelism, thus ignoring the contribution that one makes to the other. Each of these points requires elaboration.

The first point has already received partial substantiation from our previous discussion: That certain forms of traditional clientelism are more adaptable than others, and may lend themselves to innovation both on a horizontal and vertical plane can be explicitly inferred from our analysis of the "spillover" and "pyramiding" processes. Suffice it to note here that some of the specific features conventionally associated with modernization can just as well be identified with the operation of traditional clientelism; the patron-client relationship may contain, in germ as it were, the elements of a further hierarchical differentiation of political roles and structures; in spite of traditional status differences between patrons and clients, the reciprocities attendant upon this relationship may lead to an equalization of wealth among the parties; and the distributive capacities of the system may be enhanced as a result of the brokerage functions performed by local patrons and the control they exercise at the subsystem level.

That there may be limits to how far traditional patrons can be relied upon to accelerate processes of modernization is equally obvious; yet the very obstacles to mass political mobilizations that may be raised by traditional clientelism can be turned into major assets in the sphere of institution building. Traditional clientelism regulates political mobilization along traditional patron-client lines and maintains a measure of cohesion among ethnic segments, meanwhile permitting the accumulation of political and economic capital at the center. To the extent that it does these things, traditional clientelism releases those very resources that are needed for the "institutionalization of organizations and procedures," while at the same time insulating the ethnic subsystem from the disruptive impact of modernization. The main dilemma in this case is that those very forces that encourage the growth of political institutions at the center may in time generate their own destruction. The more power that is accumulated at the center, the greater the potential for initiating social and economic change, and hence also the greater the chances that modernization may sap the strength of traditional clientelistic networks.

Whether power accumulation at the center leads to a decay of traditional clientelism on the periphery, or, on the contrary, provides the support necessary for its continuation, depends in part on the balance of reciprocities between the central political institutions and the clientelistic subsystem. As long as exchange processes are seen as mutually satisfying by the machine politicians at the center and the traditional brokers in the countryside, the system retains its homeostatic qualities. Preservation of the system's equilibrium, however does not necessarily lead to political development. When the power asymmetry between patrons and clients is matched by gross disparities of wealth and income, and when the resources generated through this relationship become the privilege of a sybaritic class of political entrepreneurs, the chances for political development are slim. Liberia is a prime example: Although the True Whig party represents one of the most successful efforts at institutionalization in contemporary Africa (indeed to the point where it is now regarded as too successful by the incumbent elites), Liberia is hardly a showcase of successful political development. "Economic growth has not spread its benefits evenly but has tended to make the rich richer,"[82] meanwhile keeping the populations of the rural hinterland in a state of near stagnation. Economic choices in Liberia, as elsewhere in Africa, have paid relatively little attention to conventional criteria of long-range economic and political development; the volume and quality of immediate political and economic payoffs have been the only yardsticks for evaluating the soundness of social and economic policies. Although similar criticisms have been leveled against the Ivoirien plantocracy,[83] the evidence in this case suggests a far less lopsided pattern of exchange, as well as a more conscious attempt to de-emphasize short-run benefits for long-term developmental goals.

The next point is that the juxtaposition of modern and traditional value orientations at different levels of the clientelistic structure may meet the requirements of modern organizational forms at the center and yet impose serious handicaps on the system's capacity to innovate. What Powell describes as the "rural problem-solving system"[84]—whereby demands for goods and services in the rural sector are met by governmental agencies in return for voting support—is not a very widely accepted procedure in contemporary Africa; the least that can be said is that in specific instances the social context imposes major limitations on how far the local traditional patrons can tolerate reformist moves without at the same time destroying their own bases of support. The setbacks suffered by the "rural animation" program in Senegal illustrate the point: Having noted that "determined maraboutic opposition is reserved for those governmental ventures which have more than mere technical content, those inspired by theories of socialist development, which are designed not only to improve methods of cultivation but also to bring radical changes in the social structure of rural Senegal," Donal Cruise O'Brien goes on to observe that "rural animation . . . was the worst of all these schemes from a maraboutic point of view."[85] Only to the extent that exchange processes are perceived as mutually beneficial by government officials and rural patrons is there a reasonable chance of harnessing developmental goals to the clientelistic substructure. This is where the cooperative movement in Senegal, in contrast with rural animation schemes, offered genuine scope for innovation.[86]

Exchange processes are conditioned not only by perceptions of self-interest but by the overall availability of resources at the center. Thus where clientelism becomes a technique for neutralizing a political opposition absorbing at the same time the economic and financial resources needed for development, the result is evidently dysfunctional in terms of the developmental process.[87] Much, of course, depends on the overall volume of disposable resources, and the relative costs involved in the diversion of such resources. In an environment of scarcity, where the demands for jobs or sinecures become ever more pressing with every new generation of university graduates, clientelism as a preventive political technique may lose its instrumental value

for the achievement of long-range development goals.

Clearly, considerably more empirical data must be assembled before the patron-client model can serve as a general instrument for assessing developmental strategies. Much of what has been said in this section, therefore, must be seen as a starting point for further investigation rather than a conclusive formulation of the relationship of clientelism to development. At least three major avenues of inquiry suggest themselves:

(1) There is, first, the problem of determining the relationship of different types of clientelism to patterns of resource allocation. How effective, for example, is the party-institutionalized type of clientelism, as compared to the traditional or neo-traditional types, in promoting what Uphoff calls "political market integration" and "increases in factor endowments?"[88] What are the intervening variables that need to be taken into account in order to assess the relative advantages and disadvantages attendant upon each type of clientelism? What sorts of factors or circumstances are likely to bring about the conversion of one type of clientelism into another, and with what consequences for the political system? So far only the most speculative answers can be given to these questions.

(2) Closely related to the foregoing is the question of how new political resources are likely to affect the operation of preexisting patron-client networks, and, conversely, how new types of resources, whether defined in terms of status, wealth, authority or legitimacy, can be generated out of such networks. Passing reference must be made in this connection to the wealth of interesting insights to be gleaned from Ilchman and Uphoff's seminal work on *The Political Economy of Change*: Besides offering a much more rigorous conceptualization of "political resources" than has been attempted in this article, by emphasizing the productivity and convertibility of political resources made available through self-interested exchanges, the authors suggest new and theoretically significant perspectives from which to look at clientelistic reciprocities.[89]

(3) A third area of investigation concerns the relationship between external and internal forms of dependency. However much disagreement there may be among political scientists about the extent of economic, social, and political control exercised over their former dependencies by metropolitan powers, it is difficult not to recognize the reality of such control. How these external links of dependency may in turn affect the

operation of patron-client ties invites attention from students of African politics. If the domestic level has as yet received little it may be, however, that just as the international dimensions of clientelism can help us elucidate some of its domestic manifestations, the latter may in turn give us valuable insights into what Nkrumah once referred to, not inaccurately, as "clientele sovereignity." If nothing else, some of the phenomena currently lumped together under the convenient rubric of "neo-colonialism" may thus be brought into a universe of discourse more amenable to dispassionate inquiry.[90]

In view of what remains to be done to operationalize further the concept of clientelism, some may well feel that our claim to have identified the "missing link" in current theories of development is grossly exaggerated. Some ques-

tions may also arise about the universality of the phenomenon described, or the presumed generality of its manifestations. Certainly, the conclusions one may reach about the effect of clientelism on political conflict, or the absence of conflict, are bound to reflect the nature of the empirical data from which one seeks to generalize. That something does lie between "ethnicity" and "class" in contemporary Africa is nonetheless undeniable. Thus, whether referred to as "political clientelism," "the patron-client nexus," or "dependency relationships," the kind of interpersonal relationships described in this article may yet emerge as one of the central foci of inquiry in African scholarship. My hope, in the meantime, is that it can stimulate some fresh thinking on the part of those interested in political development.

NOTES

*For their searching comments and criticisms on an earlier version of this paper I should like to express my gratitude to the participants in the MIT-Harvard Joint Faculty Seminar on Political Development, as well as to Professor Norman Uphoff, Crawford Young, and Herbert Bergmann. For their assistance in proffering specific information on the countries discussed in this paper, I owe a similar debt to Yves Person, Pierre Verger, Alfred Gerteiny, and Richard Sklar. I alone, however, am responsible for the views expressed in this article.

1 See René Lemarchand & Keith Legg, "Political Clientelism and Development: A Preliminary Analysis," Comparative Politics, Vol. 4, No. 2 (Jan. 1972), 149-178.

2 A notable exception is William J. Foltz, "Social Structure and Political Behavior of Senegalese Elites," Yale Papers in Political Science No. 33; see also C. S. Whitaker's illuminating discussion of "clientage" phenomena in Northern Nigeria in The Politics of Tradition (Princeton: Princeton University Press, 1970), pp. 373-375. Nor is this neglect typical of political scientists alone, as can readily be inferred from a content analysis of a recent issue of the Canadian Journal of African Studies 1 (Winter, 1969) devoted to Rural Africa: Clientelism is conspicuously absent from the list of research priorities assigned to various cross-disciplinary subfields (Political Anthropology, Local Politics and Development Administration, Agricultural Economics, Rural Sociology and Communications, and Rural Geography).

3 Even where the evidence suggests the presence of clientelistic networks, these may in fact be so fluid and unstable as to defy analysis. Especially pertinent in this connection is Professor Young's query (in a personal communication): "Clientelism (in the Congo) is certainly crucial, but how can one deal with it when all is fluidity, when the networks are far more ephemeral, when mutual costs and benefits of mainte-

nance of particular patron-client sets are apparently recalculated very frequently, and on the basis of very short-run contingencies?" In such a spasmodic environment the analysis of clientelism is evidently a far more risky endeavor than in settings where client-patron relationships are more clearly institutionalized and offer a basis for relatively stable interactions among actors. If for no other reason, our analysis is restricted to the latter type of situation, as illustrated by Senegal, Mali, the Ivory Coast, Northern Nigeria, Rwanda, Burundi and Liberia. Among other states that might fit into this category but which are not specifically dealt with in this paper one might mention the Sudan, Chad, Upper Volta, Niger, Dahomey, Sierra Leone and Mauretania.

4 Lemarchand & Legg.

5 The case for ethnicity as a source of national integration is stated in Immanuel Wallerstein, "Ethnicity and National Integration in West Africa," Cahiers d'Etudes Africaines, 1 (October, 1960), 129-139; using "tribalism" in a very different sense from that which Wallerstein ascribes to the term, Richard Sklar makes a similar case in "The Contribution of Tribalism to Nationalism in Western Nigeria," Journal of Human Relations, 8 (Spring-Summer, 1960), 407-415. Unless otherwise specified, our use of the term ethnicity incorporates Wallerstein's notions of "tribe" (a reference group defined by its loyalty to a tribal government, in a rural setting) and "ethnicity" (denoting loyalty to a community detached from its traditional government, in an urban setting). Our assumption here is that the boundaries of ethnicity are inevitably self-ascriptive, regardless of the setting—a point persuasively argued by Paul Mercier, ("On the Meaning of Tribalism in Black Africa") in P. Van der Berghe, ed., Africa: Social Problems of Change and Conflict (San Francisco: Chandler Publishing Co., 1965), pp. 483-501.

6 See Aristide Zolberg, "Ethnicity and National

Integration," a paper prepared for delivery at the 1966 Annual Meeting of the African Studies Association, Bloomington, Indiana, p. 2.

7 Wallerstein.

8 Michael G. Smith, *Government in Zazzau* (London: Oxford University Press, 1960), p. 260.

9 Jean Gallais, "Signification du Groupe Ethnique au Mali," *L'Homme* 2 (May-August 1962), p. 122.

10 The term "super-tribalization." suggested by Jean Rouch in "Migrations au Ghana," *Journal de la Société des Africanistes* 26, Nos. 1-2 (1956), 163-164, has more restrictive implications than Wallerstein's use of the concept of ethnicity as it suggests common cultural affinities between the group from which an individual is detached and that in which he is incorporated. For Wallerstein, ethnicity does not presuppose preexisting cultural bonds. Regardless of this distinction, the process to which these terms refer occurs on a far wider scale than that involved in ethnic mutation through the identification of a client with his patron; one might say that the latter is an individual mutation and the former a collective one usually taking place within the context of ethnic associations.

11 Merran Fraenkel, *Tribe and Class in Monrovia* (London: Oxford University Press, 1964), p. 187.

12 The expression is borrowed from C. S. Whitaker, *Politics of Tradition*, p. 373.

13 Siegfried F. Nadel, *A Black Byzantium* (London: Oxford University Press, 1951), p. 123.

14 Whitaker, p. 374.

15 Foltz, "Social Structure and Political Behavior . . , " p. 153.

16 Myron Weiner, "Political Integration and Political Development," *Annals of the American Academy of Political and Social Science*, 358 (March, 1965). p. 53. The distinctions drawn in this paragraph lean heavily on Weiner's classification. For a somewhat different approach, see John N. Paden, "Conceptual Dimensions of National Integration Theory, with Special Reference to Inter-Ethnic (Horizontal) Integration," Internal Working Paper No. 2, Instability/Integration Project, Council for Intersocietal Studies, Northwestern University (January, 1968).

17 Nadel, *Black Byzantium*, p. 126.

18 Max Gluckman. *Custom and Conflict in Africa* (Oxford: Basil Blackwell, 1963), pp. 45-47.

19 For a further elaboration of this definition, see Georges Balandier, "Les Relations de Dépendence Personnelle: Présentation du Thème," in *Cahiers d'Etudes Africaines*, 9, 35 (1969), 345-349.

20 Cited in Hans H. Gerth and C. Wright Mills, eds., *From Max Weber: Essays in Sociology* (New York: Oxford University Press, 1958), p. 297.

21 Lucy Mair, *Primitive Government* (Baltimore: Penguin Books, 1962), p. 153.

22 Ronald Cohen, "The Dynamics of Feudalism in Bornu," *Boston University Papers on Africa*, Vol. II (Boston: Boston University Press, 1966), p. 91. For further characterizations of "feudal" clientelism, see Lucy Mair, "Clientship in East Africa," *Cahiers d'Etudes Africaines*, 2, 6 (1961), 315-326; Edward I. Steinhart, "Vassal and Fief in Three Interlacustrine Kingdoms," *Cahiers d'Etudes Africaines*, 7, 25 (1967), 606-624; Jacques J. Maquet, *The Premise of*

Inequality in Ruanda (London: Oxford University Press, 1961).

23 S. F. Nadel, *Black Byzantium*, p. 126.

24 For Fallers and Lombard, a feudal relationship can only obtain among equals (i.e., among nobles); a clientele relationship, on the other hand, establishes reciprocities between nobles and commoners. See Lloyd A. Fallers, *Bantu Bureaucracy* (London: Oxford University Press, 1956, and Jacques Lombard, "La Vie Politique dans une ancienne société de type féodal: Les Bariba du Dahomey," *Cahiers d'Etudes Africaines*, 1, 3 (1960), 5-45.

25 On the sociopolitical role of the *diula* in contemporary Bamako, see Claude Meillassoux, *Urbanization of an African Community* (Seattle and London: University of Washington Press, 1968), and his article on "The Social Structure of Modern Bamako," in *Africa*, 35, 2 (1965), 125-142. Cf. Majhemout Diop, *Histoire des classes sociales dans l'Afrique de l'Ouest* (Paris: 1971), pp. 148-152. For an excellent account of the *mai gida-dillali* relationship in contemporary West Africa, see Polly Hill, "Landlords and Brokers: A West African Trading System," *Cahiers d'Etudes Africaines*, 6, 23 (1966), 349-367; and her "Markets in Africa," *The Journal of Modern African Studies*, 1, 4 (1963), 441-455. See also, V. R. Dorjahn and C. Fyfe, "Landlord and Stranger: Change in Tenancy Relations in Sierra Leone," *Journal of African History*, 3, 3 (1962), 391-399. Perhaps the most illuminating discussion of this type of clientelism, from the standpoint of the political scientist, is Abner Cohen, "The Social Organization of Credit in a West African Cattle Market," *Africa*, 35, 1 (1965), 8-20. For an interesting discussion of the role of the *diatigi* in traditional African society, see in particular the contributions of J. L. Boutiller and J. L. Amselle in C. Meillassoux, ed., *The Development of Indigenous Trade and Markets in West Africa* (Oxford: 1971), pp. 240-252, 253-265.

26 For a detailed analysis of the sociopolitical role of the Mouride brotherhoods of Senegal, see Donal B. Cruise O'Brien, *The Murids of Senegal: The Socio-Economic Structure of an Islamic Order* (Ph.D. Thesis, University of London, 1969). See also Lucy Behrman, "The Political Influence of Muslim Brotherhoods in Senegal" (unpublished ms.), and "The Political Significance of the Wolof Adherence to Muslim Brotherhoods in the 19th Century," in *African Historical Studies* 1 (1968), pp. 60-78. For a broader perspective, see J. Spencer Trimingham, *The Influence of Islam upon Africa* (New York: Praeger, 1968).

27 Under what conditions a particular form of clientelism brings another into being is a question that lies beyond the scope of this paper. What seems clear, however, is that there is no logical relationship between forms of government and types of clientelism (except where governmental and clientelistic structure merely duplicate each other, as in the case of patrimonialism). If there is any common denominator to these forms of clientelism, it is to be found, in Ronald Cohen's words, "in conditions of personal insecurity, a lack of widespread use of payment for specific purposes, lack of adequate social control outside such (clientelistic) relationships, and the inability of the

kinship units to perform all the required and desired services for individuals." See Cohen, "The Dynamics of Feudalism in Bornu," p. 91. Given our ignorance, the most that can be said at this point is that the emergence of mercantile clientelism, as a historical phenomenon, has been dependent upon, as well as limited by, the growth of centralized state structures; conversely, the expansion of state structures has itself been conditioned by the economic and political resources made available through the development of regional trade circuits. For further evidence on this point, see J. Vansina, "Long-distance Trade Routes in Central Africa," *Journal of African History*, 3, 3 (1962), 375-388.

28 The brokerage function traditionally performed by the *diatigi* is described by Charles Monteil in the following terms: *"Dans les centres soudanais les étrangers sont pargués dans un quartier special. Les simples passagers doivent se présenter au chef de la localité et ce chef leur assigne un hote ou diatigi ("le maitre de l'étranger"). Cet hote est, à proprement parler, le répondant de l'étranger et celui-ci ne doit agir que par son intermédiaire . . . Souvent par leur nombre et leur richesse, non moins que par l'importance du personnel qu'ils emploient, les étrangers sont assez puissants pour jouir d'une indépendance relative, moyennant paiement de redevances. Voire meme ils arrivent à constituer un état dans l'état, et dominer les pouvoirs locaux."* Charles Monteil, "Les Empires du Mali," *Bulletin du Comité d'Etudes Histoiriques et Scientifiques de l'AOF*, 12, 3-4 (1929), 326. See also Félix Dubois, *Tombouctou la mystérieuse* (Paris, 1897), p. 295.

29 A further qualifier is that the above typology only deals with highly institutionalized forms of clientelism and thus excludes societies in which clientelism, though never firmly institutionalized, did in fact play a major role in the definition of traditional power relationships. Traditional Ibo society is a case in point:

As in the urban communities of Boston, New Haven, and New York, political survival in an Ibo community hinged fundamentally on the leader's ability to mould and maintain a personal following . . . In the Ibo context, as in the American, the politician acted as a broker of conflicting interests and personalities and as a provider of personal favors. His political success, in short, was a function both of his ability to resolve disputes and his generosity. (Howard E. Wolpe, "Port Harcourt: Ibo Politics in Microcosm," *The Journal of Modern African Studies*, 7 (1969), 475.)

Such noninstitutionalized forms of clientelism are obviously relevant to our discussion; their omission from our typology is only justified by the lack of relevant anthropological and historical data and the consequent difficulties involved in the task of classification and comparison.

30 The basic theoretical work on this theme is Peter M. Blau, *Exchange and Power in Social Life* (New York: John Wiley and Sons, 1967). The relevance of Blau's insights to an understanding of traditional African political structures is suggested by

Polanyi's description of reciprocity patterns in precolonial Dahomey; see Karl Polanyi, *Dahomey and the Slave Trade: An Analysis of an Archaic Economy* (Seattle & London: University of Washington Press, 1966), especially pp. 33-95.

31 Alvin W. Gouldner, "The Norm of Reciprocity: A Preliminary Statement," *American Sociological Review*, 15 (1960), 175.

32 Foltz, "Social Structure & Political Behavior of Senegalese Elites."

33 See Claudine Vidal, "Le Rwanda des Anthropologues ou le Fétichisme de la Vache," *Cahiers d'Etudes Africaines*, 9, 35 (1969), 384-401.

34 Abner Cohen, "The Social Organization of Credit . . . ," p. 12.

35 A very similar process appears to have taken place in Northern Nigeria; see, for example, M. G. Smith, *Government in Zazzau*, pp. 6-8.

36 See René Lemarchand, *Rwanda and Burundi* (London: The Pall Mall Press, 1970), and "Les relations de clientèle comme agent de contestation: Le cas du Rwanda," *Civilisations*, 18, 4 (1968), 553-573; see also Yves Person, *Samori: Une Révolution Diula*, *Mémoires de l'FAN*, No. 80 (Dakar, 1968); for another historical example of the same phenomenon, see Moussa Oumar Sy, "Le Dahomey: Le Coup d'Etat de 1818," *Folia Orientalia*, 6 (1965), 205-238.

37 The expression, borrowed from Dominique O. Mannoni, *Psychologie de la Colonisation* (Paris: Editions du Seuil, 1950), carries unfortunate connotations as it suggests a cultural "hang-up" of some sort or another, evenly distributed among all Africans, regardless of rank or status. I substantially agree with Professor Uphoff's objection (in a personal communication), to the effect that one is here dealing not so much with a "dependency complex" as with "more or less fruitful role relationships" (resource-exchange relationships) which a person having few resources seeks to establish. Creating a client-patron relationship is often the most fruitful. Has anybody found a "dependency complex" in a wealthy market-women, or a powerful chief, or even a clan head? I suggest that what Europeans have observed is a function of power (or powerlessness) rather than of "Africanness." What should be emphasized here is the persistence of certain psychological orientations to politics, which often tend to outlive the specific power relationships from which they originally stemmed. Externalization of the superego, leading to its identification with an outside authority or "patron" figure, is certainly a key characteristic of clientelistic orientations, a point persuasively argued by James Scott in *Political Ideology in Malaysia* (New Haven and London: Yale University Press, 1968), p. 80 ff. For a discussion of the affective component which enters into the patron-client nexus, see Abner Cohen, *Custom and Politics in Urban Africa* (Berkeley and Los Angeles: University of California Press, 1969), p. 91.

38 See Dominique O. Mannoni, *Psychologie de la Colonisation*; for further insights into the influence of the colonial framework upon the behavior and orientation of indigenous actors see J. P. Nettl and

Roland Robertson, *International Systems and the Modernization of Societies* (New York: Basic Books, 1968), esp. pp. 63-127. The notion of "inheritance situation" discussed by the authors provides a useful analytic framework for an understanding of the persistence of clientelistic norms after independence; see in particular their discussion of "Benefactor and Beneficiary as Their Reference Groups," pp. 72-81. Their analysis of the process of the "role-taking of the benefactor by the beneficiary" evokes some of the familiar dimensions explored by Mannoni in the work cited above.

39 Ronald Cohen, "Research Directions in Political Anthropology," *Canadian Journal of African Studies*, 3, 1 (1969), p. 27.

40 In Bornu, according to Cohen, "patron-client relationships continue to be of great importance . . . and people still utilize their associations with important superiors in the emirate, not the Nigerian, social system"—a statement that might also apply, *mutatis mutandis*, to contemporary Rwanda society within the context of an all-Hutu social system, and to Burundi within what threatens to become an all-Tutsi social system. (The above quotation is from Ronald Cohen's comments (p. 105) on Elizabeth Colson's article, "Competence and Incompetence in the context of Independence," *Current Anthropology*, 8, 1-2 (1967), 92-100. For a discussion of the transformations that have affected the operation of patron-client ties in contemporary Rwanda, see René Lemarchand, "Political Instability in Africa: The Case of Rwanda and Burundi," *Civilisations*, 16, 3 (1966), 319, and Lemarchand, *Rwanda and Burundi*.

41 From Alexandre's comments on Colson's article, p. 100.

42 Behrman, "The Political Influence of Muslim Brotherhoods in Senegal."

43 Claude Meillassoux, *Anthropologie Economique des Gouro de Cote d'Ivoire* (Paris: Mouton & Co., 1964), and "The Gouro-Peripheral Markets between the Forest and the Sudan," in Paul Bohannan and George Dalton, eds., *Markets in Africa* (Garden City: Anchor Books, 1965), pp. 67-92.

44 Bohannan and Dalton, p. 86.

45 Robert A. Dahl, *Who Governs?* (New Haven & London: Yale University Press, 1961), p. 226, 227.

46 Colson, "Competence and Incompetence in the Context of Independence."

47 See James C. Scott, "Corruption, Machine Politics, and Political Change," *American Political Science Review*, 63, 4 (1969), 1142-1158.

48 C. S. Whitaker, *The Politics of Tradition*, p. 375.

49 The distinction between first and second order resources is drawn from Jeremy Boissevain, "Patrons and Brokers," (unpublished ms.). According to Boissevain a broker differs from a patron in that the former has control over second-order resources (i.e., contacts and connections) and the latter over first order resources; although the distinction between types of resources holds important implications in the context of colonial and independent Africa, it has rela-

tively little utility for distinguishing between patrons and brokers. A more useful discussion of brokerage functions will be found in Marc J. Swartz, "The Political Middleman," in *Local-Level Politics: Social and Cultural Perspective*, ed. Marc. J. Swartz (Chicago: Aldine, 1968), pp. 199-204.

50 Boissevain, "Patrons and Brokers."

51 One might, for example, compare the different ways in which recruitment and patronage have affected the fortunes of the NCNC and the NPC in Nigeria. As Wolpe's study of Port Harcourt politics so plainly indicates, the growth of the NCNC has tended to reflect "profound alterations in the structures and criteria of political recruitment." With the opening of new resources at each stage of the NCNC's historical development, a new category of elites emerged, displacing the old, and assuring that wealth and numbers became the most significant political resources. At this stage "the wealthy businessmen and traders became party 'patrons,' the petty traders and contractors, party workers (or town councillors) . . . Simultaneously, the proportion of administrators and clerical functionaries on the one hand, and of professionals, educators and journalists, on the other, declined" (Wolpe, "Port Harcourt . . . " pp. 482-483). In the case of the NPC, by contrast, control over the party apparatus remained firmly in the hands of the emirs throughout the preindependence period and for some time thereafter; moreover, neither wealth nor numbers played a significant part in recruitment processes or patronage. Status, rather, was the key factor. Thus if the picture conveyed by Port Harcourt politics in the fifties reminds one of contemporary New Haven or New York, this could hardly be said of Kano or Zaria. In one case power belonged to what Dahl called the "ex-plebes," in the other to the "patricians." See Robert Dahl, *Who Governs*, pp. 11-24 and pp. 32-51.

52 The concept of transaction flow is here used to refer to the movement of commodities, persons, or messages within and between communities. See Karl Deutsch, "Transaction Flows as Indicators of Political Cohesion" in Phillip E. Jacob & James V. Toscano, eds., *The Integration of Political Communities* (Philadelphia & New York: Lippincott & Co., 1964), pp. 75-97.

53 See B. J. O. Dudley, "Traditionalism and Politics: A Case Study of Northern Nigeria," *Government and Opposition*, 2, 4 (1967), 516.

54 Dudley, p. 518.

55 Ruth Schachter Morgenthau, *Political Parties in West Africa* (Oxford: The Clarendon Press, 1964), p. 171.

56 Donal Cruise O'Brien, "The Murids of Senegal . . . .".

57 Thomas Hodgkin & Ruth Schachter Morgenthau, "Mali," in James S. Coleman and Carl G. Rosberg, *Political Parties and National Integration in Tropical Africa* (Berkeley & Los Angeles: University of California Press, 1964), p. 223.

58 These expectations were natural considering the tenor of the economic policies contemplated by the US leaders: "At its extraordinary congress of 1960, the

Union Soudanaise confirmed publicly some of its leaders' long-held economic views: The party resolved to launch 'immediately and vigorously' a program of economic decolonization; to create a new economic structure . . . to develop communications, intensify agricultural production, launch new industries, stress mineral exploration . . . ". Aristide Zolberg, "Political Revival in Mali," *Africa Report*, 10, 7 (1965), 18.

59 For an excellent discussion of Mali's socialist options under Modibo Keita, see John N. Hazard, "Marxian Socialism in Africa: The Case of Mali," *Comparative Politics*, 2, 1 (1969), 1-16. The political implications of Mali's decisions to reenter the franc zone, in 1967, are analyzed in Francis Snyder, "An Era ends in Mali," *Africa Report*, 14; 3, 4 (1969), 16-23.

60 Alison Des Forges, "Kings without Crowns: The White Fathers in Rwanda," in Daniel McCall, Norman R. Bennett, and Jeffrey Butler, eds., *Eastern African History*, Boston University Papers on Africa, Vol. III (New York: Praeger, 1969), p. 181.

61 Ruth Schachter Morgenthau, *Political Parties in French-Speaking West Africa*, p. 171. Equally worth emphasizing are the patron-client relationships which in many cases prevailed between migrant Mossi workers and Ivoirien planters; these relationships help explain why the Mossi minority resident in the Ivory Coast never (at least until recently) became the source of acute intergroup tensions. According to M. Dupire, *"l'attitude des immigrants Mossi envers les autochtones est faite de respect, de soumission et de crainte. Ils conservent souvent d'excellentes relations avec leurs anciens patrons, qu'ils assistent en reconnaissance des chances qu'ils leur ont offertes."* See M. Dupire, "Planteurs Autochtones et Étrangers en Basse Cote D'ivoire," *Etudes Eburnéennes*, 8 (1960), 50.

62 Morgenthau, p. 170. This is why the CPP in Ghana never developed the characteristics of a "machine" in the sense in which the term might apply to the PDCI in the Ivory Coast. Feit's description of CPP as a machine which "exists almost exclusively to stay in power" conveys an oversimplified view of both the CPP and machine politics and thus fails to bring out the essential differences between the CPP and the PDCI: the latter's original clientele was not made up of "verandah boys" but of rural workers; its resource base is still overwhelmingly dependent upon a plantation economy; and its "bosses" are themselves closely connected with the rural sector, most of them still owning large plantations. As of 1969, the *Bureau Politique* and *Comité Directeur* of the PDCI comprised, respectively, five and eight planters, and at least five of the members of the High Court of Justice and the State Security Court were planters. Cf. Edward Feit, "Military Coups and Political Development: Some Lessons from Ghana and Nigeria," *World Politics*, 20, 2 (1968), 179-194.

63 Further evidence of this phenomenon may also be found in Wolpe, "Port Harcourt: Ibo Politics in Microcosm," esp. pp. 478-485.

64 Clifford Geertz, "The Integrative Revolution," in Clifford Geertz, ed., *Old Societies and New States* (New York: The Free Press of Glencoe, 1963), p. 109.

65 I am grateful to Professor Crawford Young for forcefully reminding me of this fact.

66 M. G. Smith, "Institutional and Political Conditions of Pluralism," in L. Kuper and M. G. Smith, *Pluralism in Africa* (Berkeley and Los Angeles: University of California Press, 1969), p. 56.

67 This tends to confirm the more general hypothesis developed by Dahrendorf in his theory of social conflict: The more consistent the criteria of differentiation between groups—i.e., the more they tend to define and isolate groups from each other through cumulative cleavages—the greater the likelihood of violence among them. See Ralf Dahrendorf, *Essays in the Theory of Society* (Stanford: Stanford University Press, 1968).

68 Abner Cohen, "The Social Organization of Credit . . ." pp. 16-17; see also his *Custom and Politics in Urban Africa*.

69 Zolberg, "Ethnicity and National Integration," p. 7.

70 Scott, "Corruption, Machine Politics and Political Change," *American Political Science Review*, 63, 4 (1969), p. 1157.

71 Scott, p. 1158.

72 The point is persuasively argued in Basil Davidson, "The Outlook for Africa," *The Socialist Register 1966* (New York: Monthly Review Press, 1966).

73 Kenneth W. J. Post, *The Nigerian Federal Elections of 1959* (London: Oxford University Press, 1963), p. 58. The prime example of a machine-type clientelism is offered by the NCNC, between 1955 and 1959. The political fortunes of the NCNC were heavily (if not exclusively) dependent on the direct or indirect financial support it received from Marketing Board and Eastern Region Finance Corporation, (via the African Continental Bank). See Post, p. 56-58.

74 Martin Kilson, *Political Change in a West African State* (Cambridge: Harvard University Press, 1966), p. 268.

75 See Lucy Behrman, "The Political Influence of Muslim Brotherhoods in Senegal."

76 Frederick G. Bailey, *Tribe, Caste and Nation: A Study of Political Activity and Political Change In Highland Orissa* (Manchester: Manchester University Press, 1960), p. 248. In contrast with the types of strategy described earlier, usually originating from the center, a "bridge-action," in the context of this discussion, refers to the motives which cause the actors in the subsystem (whether patrons or clients) to establish a new type of relationship with another system.

77 Foltz, "Social Structure and Political Behavior . . ."

78 Henry Bienen, *Tanzania: Party Transformation and Economic Development* (Princeton: Princeton University Press, 1967), p. 412.

79 Samuel P. Huntington, "Political Development and Political Decay," *World Politics*, 17, 3 (1965), 393.

80 James S. Coleman, "Introduction" in James S. Coleman, ed., *Education and Political Development*

(Princeton: Princeton University Press, 1965), p. 15.

81 Coleman, p. 15.

82 See "Tubman Asks for Opposition," *West Africa*, January 3, 1970.

83 Samir Amin, *Le Développement du Capitalisme en Cote d'Ivoire* (Paris: Editions de Minuit, 1967).

84 John D. Powell, "Peasant Society and Clientelist Politics." *American Political Science Review*, 64 (June, 1970), 411-425.

85 O'Brien, *The Murids of Senegal* . . .

86 O'Brien.

87 Absorption of opposition elements (mainly student and trade-union leaders) through clientelistic techniques has been a standard procedure in both Senegal and the Ivory Coast; how far this technique can be used without posing a major threat to development goals remains to be seen. For further information on the sources and implications of the *mouvements contestataires* in each country, see *Le Monde* (Sélection Hebdomadaire), December 18-24, 1969.

88 See Norman T. Uphoff, "Ghana and Economic Assistance: Impetus and Ingredients for a Theory of Political Development," a paper prepared for delivery at the annual meeting of the American Political Science Association, Los Angeles, 1970.

89 Warren E. Ilchman and Norman T. Uphoff, *The Political Economy of Change* (Berkeley and Los Angeles: University of California Press, 1969). Other discussions of political exchange that might interest social scientists dealing with clientelist politics, include: Anthony Heath, "Exchange Theory," *British Journal of Political Science*, Vol. 1, Part 1 (January 1971), 91-119, and Georges Dupré and Pierre-Philippe Rey, "Réflexions sur la pertinence d'une théorie de l'histoire des échanges," *Cahiers Internationaux de Sociologie*, 46 (Jan.-June 1969), pp. 133-162.

90 These and other questions are tentatively dealt with in my unpublished manuscript "Political Exchange, Clientelism and Development in Tropical Africa," a paper presented for delivery at the annual meeting of the Southern Political Science Association, Atlanta, 1970.

PATRON-CLIENT POLITICS AND POLITICAL CHANGE IN SOUTHEAST ASIA

JAMES C. SCOTT

THE ANALYSIS presented here is an effort to elaborate the patron-client model of association, developed largely by anthropologists, and to demonstrate its applicability to political action in Southeast Asia. Inasmuch as patron-client structures are not unique to Southeast Asia but are much in evidence particularly in Latin America, in Africa and in the less developed portions of Europe, the analysis may possibly have more general value for an understanding of politics in less developed nations.

Western political scientists trying to come to grips with political experience in the Third World have by and large relied on either (or both) of two models of association and conflict. One model is the horizontal, class model of conflict represented most notably by Marxist thought. It has had some value in explaining conflict within the more modern sector of colonial nations and in analyzing special cases in which rural social change has been so cataclysmic as to grind out a dispossessed, revolutionary agrarian mass. By and large, however, its overall value is dubious in the typical nonindustrial situation where most political groupings cut vertically across class lines and where even nominally class-based organizations like trade unions operate within parochial boundaries of ethnicity or religion or are simply personal vehicles. In a wider sense, too, the fact that class categories are not prominent in either oral or written political discourse in the Third World damages their *a priori* explanatory value.

The second model, and one which comes much closer to matching the "real" categories subjectively used by the people being studied, emphasizes primordial sentiments (such as ethnicity, language, and religion), rather than horizontal class ties. Being more reflective of self-identification, the primordial model naturally helps to explain the tension and conflict that increasingly occurred as these isolated, ascriptive groups came into contact and competed for power. Like the class model, however—although less well developed theoretically—the primordial model is largely a conflict model and is of great value in analyzing hostilities between more or less corporate and ascriptive cultural groupings.[1] Important as such conflict has been, it hardly begins to exhaust the political patterns of Southeast Asia and Africa, let alone Latin America. If we are to account, say, for intra-ethnic politics or for patterns of cooperation and coalition building *among* primordial groups, then the primordial model cannot provide us with much analytical leverage.

The need to develop a conceptual structure that would help explain political activity that does not depend solely on horizontal or primordial sentiments is readily apparent in Southeast Asia.[2] In the Philippines, for example, class analysis can help us understand the recurrent agrarian movements in Central Luzon (e.g., Sakdalistas and Huks) among desperate tenants and plantation laborers; but it is of little help in explaining how Magsaysay succeeded in weaning many rebels away from the Huks, or, more important, in analyzing the normal patterns of political competition between Philippine parties. In Thailand, primordial demands may help us discern the basis of dissident movements in North and Northeast Thailand, but neither primordialism nor class analysis explains the intricate pattern of the personal factions and coalitions that are at the center of oligarchic Thai politics. The almost perpetual conflicts between the central Burman state and its separatist hill peoples and minorities are indeed primordial, communal issues, but communalism is of no use in accounting for the intra-Burman struggles between factions within the Anti-Fascist People's Freedom League (AFPFL) or, later, within the military regime. Ethnicity and class do carry us far in explaining racial hostilities and intra-Chinese conflict in Malaya, but they are less helpful when it comes to intra-Malay politics or to interracial cooperation at the top of the Alliance party.[3]

As these examples indicate, when we leave the realm of class conflict or communalism, we are likely to find ourselves in the realm of informal power groups, leadership-centered cliques and factions, and a whole panoply of more or less instrumental ties that characterize much of the political process in Southeast Asia. The structure and dynamics of such seemingly *ad hoc* groupings can, I believe, be best understood from the perspective of patron-client relations. The basic pattern is an informal cluster consisting of a power figure who is in a position to give security, inducements, or both, and his personal followers who, in return for such benefits, contribute their loyalty and personal assistance to the patron's designs. Such vertical patterns of patron-client linkages represent an important structural principle of Southeast Asian politics.

Until recently the use of patron-client analysis has been the province of anthropologists, who found it particularly useful in penetrating behind the often misleading formal arrangements in small local communities where interpersonal power relations were salient. Terms which are related to patron-client structures in the anthropological literature—including "clientelism," "dyadic contract," "personal network," "action-set"—reflect an attempt on the part of anthropologists to come to grips with the mosaic of nonprimordial divisions. Informal though such networks are, they are built, they are maintained, and they interact in ways that will permit generalization.

Although patron-client analysis provides a solid basis for comprehending the structure and dynamics of nonprimordial cleavages at the local level, its value is not limited to village studies. Nominally modern institutions such as bureaucracies and political parties in Southeast Asia are often thoroughly penetrated by informal patron-client networks that undermine the formal structure of authority. If we are to grasp why a bureaucrat's authority is likely to depend more on his personal following and extrabureaucratic connections than on his formal post, or why political parties seem more like *ad hoc* assemblages of notables together with their entourages than arenas in which established interests are aggregated, we must rely heavily on patron-client analysis. The dynamics of personal alliance networks are as crucial in the day-to-day realities of national institutions as in local politics; the main difference is simply that such networks are more elaborately disguised by formal facades in modern institutions.

In what follows, I attempt to clarify what patron-client ties are, how they affect political life, and how they may be applied to the dynamics of Southeast Asian politics. After 1) defining the nature of the patron-client link and distinguishing it from other social ties, the paper 2) discriminates among different varieties of patron-client bonds and thereby establishes some important dimensions of variation, and 3) examines both the survival of and the transformations in patron-client links in Southeast Asia since colonialism and the impact of major social changes (such as the growth of markets, the expanded role of the state, and so forth) on the content of these ties.

I. THE NATURE OF PATRON-CLIENT TIES

The Basis and Operation of Personal Exchange

While the actual use of the terms "patron" and "client" is largely confined to the Mediterranean and Latin American areas, comparable relationships can be found in most cultures and are most strikingly present in preindustrial nations. *The patron-client relationship—an ex-*

change relationship between roles—may be defined as a special case of dyadic (two-person) ties involving a largely instrumental friendship in which an individual of higher socioeconomic status (patron) uses his own influence and resources to provide protection or benefits, or both, for a person of lower status (client) who, for his part, reciprocates by offering general support and assistance, including personal services, to the patron.[4]

In the reciprocity demanded by the relationship each partner provides a service that is valued by the other. Although the balance of benefits may heavily favor the patron, some reciprocity is involved, and it is this quality which, as Powell notes, distinguishes patron-client dyads from relationships of pure coercion or formal authority that also may link individuals of different status.[5] A patron may have some coercive power and he may also hold an official position of authority. But if the force or authority at his command are alone sufficient to ensure the compliance of another, he has no need of patron-client ties which require some reciprocity. Typically, then, the patron operates in a context in which community norms and sanctions and the need for clients require at least a minimum of bargaining and reciprocity; the power imbalance is not so great as to permit a pure command relationship.

Three additional distinguishing features of patron-client links, implied by the definition, merit brief elaboration: their basis in inequality, their face-to-face character, and their diffuse flexibility. All three factors are most apparent in the ties between a high-status landlord and each of his tenants or sharecroppers in a traditional agrarian economy—a relationship that serves, in a sense, as the prototype of patron-client ties.[6]

First, there is an *imbalance in exchange between the two partners which expresses and reflects the disparity in their relative wealth, power, and status*. A client, in this sense, is someone who has entered an unequal exchange relation in which he is unable to reciprocate fully. A debt of obligation binds him to the patron.[7] How does this imbalance in reciprocity arise? It is based, as Peter Blau has shown in his work, *Exchange and Power in Social Life*,[8] on the fact that the patron often is in a position to supply unilaterally goods and services which the potential client and his family need for their survival and well being. A locally dominant landlord, for example, is frequently the major source of protection, of security, of employment, of access to arable land or to education, and of food in bad times. Such services could hardly be

more vital, and hence the demand for them tends to be highly inelastic; that is, an increase in their effective cost will not diminish demand proportionately. Being a monopolist, or at least an oligopolist, for critical needs, the patron is in an ideal position to demand compliance from those who wish to share in these scarce commodities.

Faced with someone who can supply or deprive him of basic wants, the potential client in theory has just four alternatives to becoming the patron's subject.[9] First he may reciprocate with a service that the patron needs badly enough to restore the balance of exchange. In special cases of religious, medical, or martial skills such reciprocation may be possible, but the resources of the client, given his position in the stratification, are normally inadequate to reestablish an equilibrium. A potential client may also try to secure the needed services elsewhere. If the need for clients is especially great, and if there is stiff competition among patron-suppliers, the cost of patron-controlled services will be less.[10] In most agrarian settings, substantial local autonomy tends to favor the growth of local power monopolies by officials or landed gentry. A third possibility is that clients may coerce the patron into providing services. Although the eventuality that his clients might turn on him may prompt a patron to meet at least the minimum normative standards of exchange,[11] the patron's local power and the absence of autonomous organization among his clients make this unlikely. Finally clients can theoretically do without a patron's services altogether. This alternative is remote, given the patron's control over vital services such as protection, land and employment.

Affiliating with a patron is neither a purely coerced decision nor is it the result of unrestricted choice. Exactly where a particular patron-client dyad falls on the continuum depends on the four factors mentioned. If the client has highly valued services to reciprocate with, if he can choose among competing patrons, if force is available to him, or if he can manage without the patron's help—then the balance will be more nearly equal. But if, as is generally the case, the client has few coercive or exchange resources to bring to bear against a monopolist-patron whose services he desperately needs, the dyad is more nearly a coercive one.[12]

The degree of compliance a client gives his patron is a direct function of the degree of imbalance in the exchange relationship—of how dependent the client is on his patron's services. An imbalance thus creates a sense of debt or obligation on the client's part *so long as it meets his basic subsistence needs* and represents, for the patron, a "'store of value'—social credit that . . . (the patron) can draw on to obtain advantages at a later time."[13] The patron's domination of needed services, enables him to build up savings of deference and compliance which enhance his status, and represents a capacity for mobilizing a group of supporters when he cares to. The larger a patron's clientele and the more dependent on him they are, the greater his latent capacity to organize group action. In the typical agrarian patron-client setting this capacity to mobilize a following is crucial in the competition among patrons for regional preeminence. As Blau describes the general situation,

The high-status members furnish instrumental assistance to the low-status ones in exchange for their respect and compliance, which help the high-status members in their competition for a dominant position in the group.[14]

A second distinguishing feature of the patron-client dyad is the *face-to-face*, personal quality of the relationship. The continuing pattern of reciprocity that establishes and solidifies a patron-client bond often creates trust and affection between the partners. When a client needs a small loan or someone to intercede for him with the authorities, he knows he can rely on his patron; the patron knows, in turn, that "his men" will assist him in his designs when he needs them.[15] Furthermore, the mutual expectations of the partners are backed by community values and ritual.

In most contexts the affection and obligation invested in this tie between nonrelatives is expressed by the use of terms of address between partners that are normally reserved for close kin. The tradition of choosing godparents in Catholic nations is often used by a family to create a fictive kinship tie with a patron—the father thereby becoming like a brother to the parents.[16] Whether the model of obligation established is father-son, uncle-nephew, or elder-younger brother, the intention is similar: to establish as firm a bond of affection and loyalty as that between close relatives. Thus while a patron and client are very definitely alive to the instrumental benefits of their association, it is not simply a neutral link of mutual advantage. On the contrary, it is often a durable bond of genuine mutual devotion that can survive severe testing.

The face-to-face quality of the patron-client dyad, as well as the size of the patron's resource base, limits the number of direct active ties a single patron can have.[17] Even with vast resources, the personal contact and friendship built into the

link make it highly unlikely that an active clientele could exceed, say, one hundred persons. The total following of a given patron may be much larger than this, but normally all except 20-30 clients would be linked to the patron through intermediaries. Since we are dealing with positive emotional ties (the ratio of "calculation" to affection may of course vary), a leader and his immediate entourage will be comparatively small.

The third distinctive quality of patron-client ties, one that reflects the affection involved, is that they are *diffuse, "whole-person" relationships rather than explicit, impersonal-contract bonds*. A landlord may, for example, have a client who is connected to him by tenancy, friendship, past exchanges of services, the past tie of the client's father to his father, and ritual coparenthood. Such a strong "multiplex" relation, as Adrian Mayer terms it,[18] covers a wide range of potential exchanges. The patron may very well ask the client's help in preparing a wedding, in winning an election campaign, or in finding out what his local rivals are up to; the client may approach the patron for help in paying his son's tuition, in filling out government forms, or in getting food or medicine when he falls on bad times. The link, then, is a very flexible one in which the needs and resources of the partners, and hence the nature of the exchange, may vary widely over time. Unlike explicit contractual relations, the very diffuseness of the patron-client linkage contributes to its survival even during rapid social change—it tends to persist so long as the two partners have something to offer one another.[19] Just as two brothers may assist each other in a host of ways, patron-client partners have a relationship that may also be invoked for almost any purpose; the chief differences are the greater calculation of benefits and the inequality that typifies patron-client exchange.

The Distinctiveness of the Patron—The role of patron ought to be distinguished from such role designations as "broker" or "middleman" or "boss" with which it is sometimes confounded. Acting as a "broker" or "middleman"—terms which I shall use interchangeably—means serving as an intermediary to arrange an exchange or transfer between two parties who are not in direct contact. The role of middleman, then, involves a three-party exchange in which the middleman functions as an agent and does not himself control the thing transferred. A patron, by contrast, is part of a two-person exchange and operates with resources he himself owns or directly controls.[20] Finally, the terms "middleman" and "broker" do not specify the relative status of the actor to others in the transaction, while a patron is by definition of superior rank to his client.

Important as this distinction is, it is easily lost sight of for two reasons. First, it is not always a simple task to determine if someone personally controls the resources he uses to advance himself. What of the case in which a civil servant distributed the subordinate posts in his jurisdiction to create an entourage? Here it would seem that he was acting as a patron, inasmuch as the jobs he gave out were meant as *personal* gifts from the store of scarce values he controlled and were intended to create a feeling of personal debt and obligation among recipients. The social assessment of the nature of the gift is thus crucial. If we were to find, on the other hand, that the civil servant was viewed as someone who had acted as an agent of jobseekers and put them in touch with a politician who controlled the jobs, then he would be acting as a broker. It is only natural that many an ambitious public official will seek to misrepresent acts of brokerage or simple adherence to the rules as personal acts of patronage, thereby building his following.[21] To the extent that he succeeds in representing his act as a personal act of generosity, he will call forth that sense of personal obligation that will bind his subordinates to him as clients.[22]

A second potential source of confusion in this distinction is that the terms designate roles and not persons, and thus it is quite possible for a single individual to act both as a broker and a patron. Such a role combination is not only possible, but is empirically quite common. When a local landowning patron, for example, becomes the head of his village's political party he is likely to become the middleman between many villagers and the resources controlled by higher party officials. In this case he may have clients for whom he also serves as broker. The diffuse claims of the patron-client tie actually make it normal for the patron to act as a broker for his clients when they must deal with powerful third parties—much as the patron saint in folk Catholicism who directly helps his devotees while also acting as their broker with the Lord.[23] If on the other hand, the political party simply gives the local patron direct control of its programs and grants in the area, it thereby enhances his resources for becoming a patron on a larger scale and eliminates the need for brokerage.

Patrons ought finally to be differentiated from other partly related terms for leadership such as "boss," "caudillo," or "cacique." "Boss" is a designation at once vague and richly connotative. Although a boss may often function as a patron, the term itself implies (a) that he is the most powerful man in the arena and (b) that his power rests more on the inducements and sanctions at his disposal than on affection or status. As distinct from a patron who may or may not be the supreme local leader and whose leadership rests at least partly on rank and affection, the boss is a secular leader *par excellence* who depends almost entirely on palpable inducements and threats to move people. As we shall show later, a settled agrarian environment with a recognized status hierarchy is a typical setting for leadership by patrons, while a more mobile, egalitarian environment is a typical setting for the rise of bosses. The final two terms, "caudillo" and "cacique" are most commonly used in Latin America to designate the regional—often rural—bosses. Again the implication is that coercion is a main pillar of power, and in the case of the *caudillo*, a personal following is common.[24] A "cacique" or "caudillo" may act as patron to a number of clients but he typically relies too heavily on force and lacks the traditional legitimacy to function mainly as a patron. At best, a *cacique* or *caudillo* may, like a boss, be a marginal special case of a patron, providing that a portion of his following is beneath him socially and bound to him in part by affective ties. Over time, however, a metamorphosis may occur. Just as the successful brewery owner of late 18th century England might well anticipate a peerage for his son, the *cacique* who today imposes his rule by force may do well enough to set his son up as a landowner, whose high status and legitimacy strengthens his role as patron.

Patron and Clients as Distinctive Groupings—
To this point, the discussion has centered on the nature of the single link between patron and client. If we are to broaden the analysis to include the larger structures that are related by the joining of many such links, a few new terms must be introduced. First, when we speak of a patron's immediate following—those clients who are directly tied to him—we will refer to a patron-client *cluster*. A second term, enlarging on the cluster but still focusing on one person and his vertical links is the patron-client *pyramid*. This is simply a vertical extension downward of the cluster in which linkages are introduced beyond the first-order.[25] Below are typical representations of such links. Although vertical ties are our main concern, we will occasionally want to analyze *horizontal dyadic ties*, say, between two patrons of comparable standing

PATRON-CLIENT CLUSTER

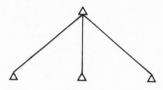

PATRON-CLIENT PYRAMID

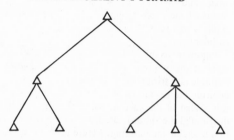

who have made an alliance. Such alliances often form the basis of *factional systems* in local politics. Finally, patron-client *networks* are not ego-focused but refer to the overall pattern of patron-client linkages (plus horizontal patron alliances) joining the actors in a given area or community.

Patron-client clusters are one of a number of ways in which people who are not close kin come to be associated. Most alternative forms of association involve organizing around categorical ties, both traditional—such as ethnicity, religion, or caste—and modern—such as occupation or class—which produce groups that are fundamentally different in structure and dynamics. The special character of patron-client clusters stems, I believe, from the fact that, unlike categorically-based organizations, such clusters a) have a basis of *membership that is specific to each link*,[26] and b) are *based on individual ties to a leader* rather than on shared characteristics or horizontal ties among followers.

Some other important distinctions between categorical and patron-client groupings follow from these particular principles of organization. Here I rely heavily on Carl Landé's more elaborate comparisons between dyadic followings and categorical groups.[27]

1. *Members' Goals:* Clients have particularistic goals which depend on their personal ties to the leader, whereas categorical group members have common goals that derive from shared characteristics which distinguish them from members of other such groups.

2. *Autonomy of Leadership:* A patron has wide autonomy in making alliances and policy decisions as long as he provides for the basic material welfare of his clients, whereas the leader of a categorical group must generally respect the *collective* interest of the group he leads.

3. *Stability of Group:* A patron-client cluster,

being based on particularistic vertical links, is highly dependent on its leader's skills and tends to flourish or disintegrate depending on the resources of the leader and the satisfaction of individual client demands. A categorical group, by contrast, is rooted more firmly in horizontally shared qualities and is thus less dependent for its survival on the quality of its leadership and more durable in its pursuit of broader, collective (often policy) interests.

4. *Composition of Group:* Patron-client cluster, because of the way they are created, are likely to be more heterogeneous in class composition than categorical groups which are based on some distinctive quality which members share. By *definition*, patron-client pyramids join people of different status rankings while categorical groups *may or may not* be homogeneous in status.

5. *Corporateness of Group:* In a real sense a patron-client cluster is not a group at all but rather an "action-set" that exists because of the vertical links to a common leader—links which the leader may activate in whole or in part.[28] Followers are commonly not linked directly to one another and may, in fact, be unknown to each other. An organized categorical group, by contrast, is likely to have horizontal links that join members together so that it is possible to talk of a group existence independent of the leader.

Although this listing is not exhaustive, it does illustrate the special character of patron-client networks. Bearing in mind the generic qualities of these ties, we now turn to the range of variation within the genus.

II. VARIATION IN PATRON-CLIENT TIES

One could potentially make almost limitless distinctions among patron-client relationships.

The dimensions of variation considered here are selected because they seem particularly relevant to our analytical goal of assessing the central changes in such ties within Southeast Asia. Similar distinctions should be germane to the analysis of other preindustrial nations as well.

The Resource Base of Patronage—A potential patron assembles clients on the basis of his ability to assist them. For his investment of assets, the patron expects a return in human resources— in the form of the strength of obligation and the number of clients obligated to him. The resource base or nature of the assets a patron has at his disposal can vary widely. One useful basis for distinguishing among resources is the directness with which they are controlled. Patrons may, in this sense, rely on a) their own knowledge and skills, b) direct control of personal real property, or c) indirect control of the property or authority of others (often the public). The resources of *skill and knowledge* are most recognizable in the roles of lawyer, doctor, *literatus,* local military chief, teacher—religious or secular. Those equipped with these skills control scarce resources than can enhance the social status, health, or material well being of another. Inasmuch as such resources rest on knowledge, they are less perishable than more material sources—although the *time* of the expert *is* limited—and can be used again and again without being diminished. Such resources are relatively, but not entirely, secure. In the case of lawyers and literati, for example, the exchange price of their services depends respectively on the continued existence of a court system and the veneration of a particular literary tradition, both of which are subject to change. The value of a local military chief's protection is similarly vulnerable to devaluation once the nation state has established local law and order.

Reliance on *direct control of real property* is a second common means of building a clientele. Traditionally, the typical patron controlled scarce land. Those he permitted to farm it as sharecroppers or tenants became permanently obligated to him for providing the means of their subsistence. Any businessman is in a similar position; as the owner of a tobacco factory, a rice mill, or a small store he is able to obligate many of those of lower status whom he employs, to whom he extends credit, or with whom he does business. This kind of resource, in general, is more perishable than personal skills. A landlord has only so many arable acres, a businessman only so many jobs, a shopkeeper so much ready cash, and each must carefully invest those resources to bring the maximum return. Like any real property, moreover, private real property is subject to seizure or restrictions on its use.

A third resource base available to the potential patron is what might be called *indirect, office-based property.* Here we refer to patrons who build a clientele on the strength of their freedom to dispense rewards placed in their trust by some third party (parties). A village headman who uses his authority over the distribution of communal land to the poor or the distribution of *corvée* labor and taxation burdens in order to extend his *personal* clientele would be a typical example of traditional office-based patronship. One can classify similarly office-holders in colonial or contemporary settings whose discretionary powers over employment, promotion, assistance, welfare, licensing, permits, and other scarce values can serve as the basis of a network of personally obligated followers. Politicians and administrators who exploit their office in this way to reward clients while violating the formal norms of public conduct are, of course, acting corruptly. Finally, we should add private-sector office-holders such as plantation managers, purchasing agents, and hiring bosses, who may also use their discretionary authority to nurture a clientele.

Indirect, office-based property is least secure in many respects, as its availability depends on continuity in a position that is ultimately given or withdrawn by third parties. A landlord will usually retain his local base whereas an office-holder is likely to be swept out by a new victor at the polls or simply by a power struggle within the ruling group. In spite of the risks involved, these posts are attractive because the resources connected with many of them are far greater than those which an individual can amass directly.

The categories of resources just discussed are not mutually exclusive. It is common, for example, for a patron to have a client who is obligated to him by being a tenant on his land and also by having secured an agricultural loan through his patron's chairmanship of the ruling party's local branch. The resources that cement a dyadic tie may thus be multiple—it is often a question of deciding which is the predominant resource. Much the same analysis can be made of a patron-client cluster or network, since a patron may have clients who are bound to him by quite different resources, and it is often important to determine what the main resource is that holds the cluster together.

Resource Base of Clientage—As the other member of a reciprocating pair, the client is called upon to provide assistance and services when the patron requires them. The variation in the nature of such assistance is another means of distinguishing one patron-client dyad from another. Here one might want to differentiate: (1) *labor services and economic support*, as provided by a rent-paying tenant or employee, (2) *military or fighting duties*, such as those performed by members of a bandit group for their chief, and (3) *political services* such as canvassing or otherwise acting as an agent of a politician. Within the "political service" category one may wish to separate electoral services from nonelectoral political help. I should add here that the term "clients" can refer to those who are in the middle of a patron-client pyramid—being a client to someone higher up and a patron to those below. In this case a superior patron will be interested in his client's potential services, but those services will include the size, skills, assets, and status of the client's own subordinate following.

Just as a patron-client dyad can be distinguished by the main resource base of clientage so can a patron-client cluster be categorized by the modal pattern of client services for the cluster or pyramid as a whole.

Balance of Affective and Instrumental Ties:— By definition, instrumental ties play a major role in the patron-client dyad. It is nonetheless possible to classify such dyads by the extent to which affective bonds are also involved in the relationship. At one end of this continuum one might place patron-client bonds which, in addition to their instrumental character, are reinforced by affective links growing, say, from the patron and the client having been schoolmates, coming from the same village, being distant relatives, or simply from mutual love. Comparable affective rewards may also spring from the exchange of deference on the one hand and *noblesse oblige* on the other in a settled agrarian status network—rewards that have value beyond the material exchanges they often involve.[29] At the other end of the spectrum lies a dyadic tie much closer to an almost neutral exchange of goods and services. The more purely coercive the relationship is and the less traditional legitimacy it has, the more likely that affective bonds will be minimal.

This distinction has obvious analytical value. If we were to look at a patron's entire following, we would be able to classify each vertical bond according to the ratio of affective to instrumental rewards involved. (One could, of course, do the same for horizontal alliances.) Using this criterion we could identify a set of followers among whom the ratio of affective to instrumental ties was relatively high, reflecting perhaps distant kinship, old village or neighborhood ties, or comparable bonds. The loyalty of this set of followers would be less dependent upon a continued flow of material benefits, simply because their loyalty is partly based on nonmaterial exchanges. As we move beyond this partly affective following to a patron's other supporters, the weight of instrumental, usually material, ties becomes relatively more important. The nature of a man's following—the balance of affective to instrumental ties obligating his clients to him—can tell us something about its stability under different conditions. When a patron increases his material resource base, it is his instrumental following that will tend to grow rapidly, and when he is in decline, that same following will shrink rapidly, as clients look for a more promising leader. The degree of dependence on material incentives within a following is, in principle, a quality one could measure by establishing how much more than their present material rewards a rival patron would have to offer to detach a given number of another's clients.

The affective-instrumental distinction just made leads to a similar, but not identical, distinction between the *core* and *periphery* of a man's following. These categories actually are distributed along a continuum; at the *periphery* of a man's following are those clients who are relatively easy to detach while at the *core* are followers who are more firmly bound to him. The periphery is composed of clients bound largely by instrumental rewards, while the core is composed of clients linked by strong affective ties, *as well as* clients who are attracted to a patron by such strong instrumental ties that they seem unbreakable.[30] This amounts, in effect, to a distinction between a man's virtually irreducible following and his more or less fluctuating, "fair-weather" following. Patrons can then be differentiated by the size of their core-following relative to their peripheral-following. A landlord or a businessman will generally have a sizable core group composed both of his friends, kin, etc., and of his tenants or employees. This nucleus is his initial following; his clientele may grow larger, but it is unlikely to contract further than this durable core. A politician or bureaucrat, on the other hand, unless he is privately wealthy, is likely to have a comparatively smaller core group composed mostly of those with whom he has strong affective ties and, hence, a relatively large proportion of "fair-weather" clients. The blows of fortune such a politician or administrator suffers are more likely to be instantly and fully reflected in a reduction of the size of his clientele, which is largely a calculating one. Politicians, and bureaucrats, because they have smaller core followings and because they can, through their office, often tap vast resources, are apt to have meteoric qualities as patrons; the landholder by contrast, is likely to cast a steadier, if dimmer, light.

Balance of Voluntarism and Coercion—There are obvious and important differences in the degree of coercion involved in a patron-client bond. At one end are the clients with virtually no choice but to follow the patron who directly controls their means of subsistence. Here one might place a tenant whose landlord provides his physical security, his land, his implements and seed, in a society where land is scarce and insecurity rife. Nearer the middle of this continuum would perhaps be the bonds between independent smallholders who depend on a landlord for the milling and marketing of their crops, for small loans, and for assistance with the police and administration. Such bonds are still based on inequality, but the client, because he has some bargaining power, is not simply putty in his patron's hands. Finally, let us assume that an electoral system has given clients a new resource and has spurred competition among patrons for followings that can swing the election to them. In this case the inequality in bargaining power is further reduced, and the client emerges as more nearly an independent political actor whose demands will receive a full hearing from his patron.

In general, the oppression of the client is greater when the patron's services are vital, when he exercises a monopoly over their distribution, and when he has little need for clients himself. The freedom of the client is enhanced most when there are many patrons whose services are not vital and who compete with one another to assemble a large clientele—say for electoral purposes.

The greater the coercive power of the patron vis-à-vis his client, the fewer rewards he must supply to retain him. A patron in a strong position is more likely to employ *sanctions*—threats to punish the client or to withdraw benefits he currently enjoys—whereas a relatively weaker patron is more likely to offer inducements—promises to reward a client with benefits he does not now enjoy.[31] In each instance, superior control over resources is used to gain the compliance of followers, but the use of sanctions indicates a higher order of power than the use of inducements. Assessment of the coercive balance and of the ratio of sanctions to inducements can be made not only for a dyad but also for a patron-client cluster or pyramid. The cluster of a local baron with a private army may be held intact by a mix of deference and sanctions, while a campaigning politician may build a cluster simply with favors if he has no coercive power or traditional legitimacy. Each cluster or pyramid has its special vulnerability. The coercive cluster will be jeopardized by a breach of the patron's local power monopoly, and a cluster based on inducements will be in danger if its leader's income or access to public funds is cut off.

Durability Over Time—Patron-client dyads may be rather ephemeral, or they may persist for long periods.[32] In a traditional setting they are likely to last until one of the partners has died. Knowing how durable such ties are can also tell us something about the structure of competition over time. Where dyads are persistent they tend to produce persistent factional structures with some continuity in personnel over time, at least stable clusters or pyramids that may recombine in a variety of ways but are constructed from the same components. Where dyads are fragile, personal alignments may undergo an almost total reordering within a decade.

Since patron-client clusters are based ultimately on power relations, they will endure best in a stable setting that preserves existing power positions. A particular patron will thus retain his clients as long as he continues to dominate the supply of services they need. A patron is also likely to keep his followers if the scope of reciprocity that binds them is greater. That is, the more of the client's vital needs a patron can meet (i.e., if he can supply not only land and security but also influence with the administration, help in arranging mortgages or schooling, and so forth), the greater the tendency for the tie to be invoked frequently and to endure over long periods. Compared with patrons who can provide only legal services, only financial help, or only educational advantages, the *multiplex* bond between patron and client is a solid linkage that serves many needs; since it is more of a whole-person tie, it will be called into action often.

Homogeneity of Following—A patron may have a heterogeneous set of followers drawn from all walks of life, or he may have a following composed, say, of only his poor sharecroppers or only clerical subordinates in his office.[33] The proportion of a man's supporters who share social characteristics and the salience of those social characteristics to them constitute a measure of how homogeneous a following is. Since a patron, by definition, occupies a higher social station than his clients, the greater the homogeneity in a following, the greater the latent shared interests among followers that might threaten the relationship. When a landed patron whose clients are his tenants, for example, sells off what had been common pasture land, all his tenants are equally affected. Their shared situation and the common experiences it provides create a potential for horizontal ties, whereas a heterogeneous clientele lacks this potential.

Field Variables—Occasionally, we will want to describe and contrast configurations of patron-client clusters within a political arena rather than dealing with a single cluster or dyad. Four particularly useful distinctions in this respect are a) the degree of monopoly over local resources by a single patron, b) the degree of monopoly over links to other structures by a single patron, c) the *density* of patron-client linkages in the population,[34] and d) the extent of differentiation between different pyramids and clusters. The first two variables are self-explanatory and measure the degree of dominance exercised by a patron over local and supralocal resources. "Density" refers to the proportion of a given population that is a part of the patron-client network. In some situations, for example, a large part of the lower classes may not actually have any vertical links of clientage to a patron. To gauge accurately the explanatory power of patron-client politics in a political field requires that we know for how much of the population such ties are effective. Finally, the degree of differentiation among clusters is a means of discerning whether one cluster looks pretty much like the next one or whether many clusters are socioeconomically distinct. In the classical feudal situation, the pyramidal structure of one lord's small domain was similar to that of his neighbor—the social structure of the landscape resembled a repetitive wallpaper pattern—and competition was thus between almost identical units. In other circumstances, pyramids may be differentiated by predominant occupation, by institutional affiliation, and so forth, so that the seeds of a distinctive and perhaps durable *interest* have been sown.

III. SURVIVAL AND DEVELOPMENT OF PATRON-CLIENT
TIES IN SOUTHEAST ASIA

A. Conditions for Survival

As units of political structure, patron-client clusters not only typify both local and national politics in Southeast Asia, they are also as characteristic of the area's contemporary politics as of its traditional politics. In one sense, the "style" of the patron-client link, regardless of its context, is distinctively traditional. It is particularistic where (following Parons) modern links are universal; it is diffuse and informal where modern ties are specific or contractual; and it produces vertically-integrated groups with shifting interests rather than horizontally-integrated groups with durable interests. Despite their traditional style, however, patron-client clusters both serve as mechanisms for bringing together individuals who are not kinsmen and as the building-blocks for elaborate networks of vertical integration. They cannot, therefore, be merely dismissed as vestigial remains of archaic structures but must be analyzed as a type of social bond that may be dominant in some contexts and marginal in others.

In my view, most of traditional and contemporary Southeast Asia has met three necessary conditions for the continued vitality of patron-client structures: (1) *the persistence of marked inequalities in the control of wealth, status, and power which have been accepted (until recently) as more or less legitimate;* (2) *the relative absence of firm, impersonal guarantees of physical security, status and position, or wealth, and* (3) *the inability of the kinship unit to serve as an effective vehicle for personal security or advancement.*

The first condition is more or less self-evident. A client affiliates with a patron by virtue of the patron's superior access to important goods and services. This inequality is an expression of a stratification system which serves as the basis for vertical exchange. Classically in Southeast Asia, the patron has depended more on the local organization of force and access to office as the sinews of his leadership than upon hereditary status or land ownership. Inequalities were thus marked, but elite circulation tended to be comparatively high. With the penetration of colonial government and commercialization of the economy, land ownership made its appearance (especially in the Philippines and Vietnam) as a major basis of patronage. At the same time access to colonial office replaced to some extent victory in the previously more fluid local power contests as the criterion for local patronage. Although land ownership and bureaucratic office have remained two significant bases of patronship in postcolonial Southeast Asia, they have been joined—and sometimes eclipsed as patronage resources—by office in political parties or military rank.

If inequities in access to vital goods were alone sufficient to promote the expansion of patron-client ties, such structures would predominate almost everywhere. A second, and more significant, condition of patron-client politics is the absence of institutional guarantees for an individual's security, status, or wealth. Where consensus has produced an institutionalized means of indirect exchange—one that is legally based, uniformly enforced, and effective—impersonal contractual arrangements tend to usurp the place of personal reciprocity. A patron-client dyad, by contrast, is a *personal* security mechanism and is resorted to most often when personal security is frequently in jeopardy and when impersonal social controls are unreliable. In this context, direct personal ties based on reciprocity substitute for law, shared values, and strong institutions. As Eric Wolf has noted, "The clearest gain from such a (patron-client) relation . . . is in situations where public law cannot guarantee adequate protection against breaches of non-kin contracts."[35]

It is important to recognize the unenviable situation of the typical client in less developed nations. Since he lives in an environment of scarcity, competition for wealth and power is seen as a zero-sum contest in which his losses are another's gain and vice-versa.[36] His very survival is constantly threatened by the caprice of nature and by social forces beyond his control. In such an environment, where subsistence needs are paramount and physical security uncertain, a modicum of protection and insurance can often be gained only by depending on a superior who undertakes personally to provide for his own clients. Operating with such a slim margin, the client prefers to minimize his losses —at the cost of his independence—rather than to maximize his gains by taking risks he cannot afford. When one's physical security and means of livelihood are problematic, and when recourse to law is unavailable or unreliable, the social value of a personal defender is maximized.

The growth of strong, institutional orders that reduce the need for personal alliances was a rare occurrence—the Roman and Chinese imperial orders being the most notable exceptions—until the 19th and 20th centuries, when modern nation-states developed the technical means to impose their will throughout their territory. Before that, however, the existence of a fair degree of local autonomy was inevitable, given the limited power available to most traditional kingdoms. The greater that autonomy, or what might be called the *localization* of power, the more decisive patron-client linkages were likely to be. In settings as diverse as much of Latin America, feudal Europe, and precolonial Southeast Asia, the localization of power was pervasive and gave rise to networks of patron-client bonds. From time to time in Southeast Asia a centralizing kingdom managed to extend its power over wide areas, but seldom for very long or with a uniform system of authority. A typical Southeast Asian kingdom's authority weakened steadily with increasing distance from the capital city. Beyond the immediate environs of the court, the ruler was normally reduced to choosing which of a number of competing petty chiefs with local power bases he would prefer to back.[37] Such chiefs retained their own personal following; their relationship to the ruler was one of bargaining as well as deference; and they might back a rival claimant to the throne or simply defy demands of the court when they were dissatisfied with their patron's behavior. Thus, the political structure of traditional Southeast Asia favored the growth of patron-client links, inasmuch as it was necessary for peasants to accommodate themselves to the continuing reality of autonomous personal authority at almost all levels.

The localization of power is in many senses as striking a characteristic of contemporary as of traditional Southeast Asia. As Huntington aptly expressed it, "The most important political distinction among countries concerns not their form of government but their degree of government."[38] Many of the outlying areas of Southeast Asian nations, particularly the upland regions of slash-and-burn agriculturalists, are only intermittently subject to central government control and continue to operate with much autonomy. By far the most important manifestation of the localization of power, however, has occurred within the very bureaucratic and political institutions that are associated with a central state. The modern institutional framework is a relatively recent import in Southeast Asia; it finds minimal support from indigenous social values and receives only sporadic legal enforcement. With the exception of North Vietnam and Singapore, where a portion of the intelligentsia with modernizing ideologies and popular backing have taken power, these new institutions do not command wide loyalty and must therefore fight for survival in a hostile environment. The net effect of this fragile institutional order is to promote the growth of personal spheres of influence within ministries, administrative agencies, and parties. Sometimes the vertical links are strong (e.g., Thailand) and sometimes a high degree of decentralization or "sub-infeudation" occurs (as in parliamentary Burma from 1955 to 1958). In either case, what replaces the institution are elaborate networks of personal patron-client ties that carry on more or less traditional factional struggles rather than operate as agents of a hierarchial organization. Patron-client politics are thus as much a characteristic of faction-ridden central institutions as of the geographical periphery in these nations.

The third condition under which patron-client bonds remain prominent relates directly to the capacity of such ties to foster cooperation among nonkin. As a mechanism for protection or for advancement, patron-client dyads will flourish when kinship bonds alone become inadequate for these purposes.

Although kinship bonds are seldom completely adequate as structures of protection and advancement even in the simplest societies, they may perform these functions well enough to minimize the need for nonkin structures. Such is the case among small isolated bands of hunters and gatherers, among self-sufficient, corporate lineages and within corporate villages.[39] None of these conditions, however, is particularly applicable to Southeast Asian societies. The highland areas are inhabited by poorly integrated minorities but only rarely are these minorities so isolated as to lack economic and political ties with the larger society. Corporate lineages, outside traditional Vietnam, are uncommon in low-land Southeast Asia where bilateral kinship systems lead to overlapping kindreds rather than mutually exclusive lineages. Finally, corporate village structures (except in Java and perhaps Vietnam's Red River delta) are not typical of Southeast Asia. The scope for nonkin ties in general, and patron-client links in particular, has thus been quite wide throughout the region.

Even when government did not impinge much on their activities, villagers in traditional Southeast Asia still had need of extrakin and extravillage contacts. They needed to secure marriage partners, to assure themselves protection and contacts for the limited but vital trade carried on between villages, and finally to establish an outside alliance in case a village quarrel forced them to seek land and employment elsewhere.[40] If vertical dyadic ties were of some value in the traditional context, they assumed a more decisive role in the colonial and postcolonial periods. First, the commercialization of the economy and the growth of markets enhanced the value of cooperative arrangements among nonkin. Both corporate kin groups and corporate village structures had depended on a certain level of economic autarky for their vitality—an

autarchy which colonial economic policy quickly eroded. These corporate structures (where they existed) tended "to lose their monopoly over resources and personnel in situations where land and labor became free commodities."[41] As the communal land controlled by the village dwindled, as outsiders came increasingly to own land in the village, and as villagers increasingly worked for nonkin, the value of patron-client links increased for all concerned.

In traditional Southeast Asia, as in feudal Europe, then, the inability of kindreds to provide adequate protection and security fostered the growth of patron-client structures. The limited effectiveness of kindreds as units of cooperation and security was further reduced by the new structures and uncertainties of the colonial economy. Within this new economy, the goals of wealth, protection, power, and status could not be realized without outside links to nonkin (and often nonvillagers), and the establishment of these links, for the most part, followed the patron-client model.

The relative decline in the protective capacity of kindreds (which, given the absence of strong, predictable new institutions would widen the scope of patron-client ties) accelerated the *political* transformation of the colonial and postcolonial period as well. Both administration and electoral politics created new political units that did not generally coincide with the kindred or with the traditional village. As Gallin has shown for electoral politics in Taiwan, the political vitality of the corporate lineage is sapped by changes in the governing unit which no longer permit a single lineage to dominate. The lineage thus loses much of the material basis of its previous solidarity, and new dyadic ties become the means by which winning coalitions are built in the new unit.[42] Political consolidation, like economic consolidation, beyond minimal kin and village units can thus enlarge the potential role of such nonkin structures as patron-client clusters.

Considering all three criteria, Southeast Asian states, like most traditional nations, satisfy most conditions for the survival of patron-client structures as a common means of cooperation. First, the disparities in power and status that form the basis of this kind of exchange have, if anything, become more marked since the colonial period. Second, nonkin structures of cooperation have always been important in the complex societies of Southeast Asia and have become more significant because of the new economic and political dependencies introduced by colonialism and nationhood. Finally, with the possible exceptions of Singapore and North Vietnam, the nations of Southeast Asia have not developed strong modern institutions which would begin to undermine purely personal alliance systems with impersonal guarantees and loyalties.

At this point in the argument, it is essential to show how patron-client structures, as one form of vertical cleavage, coexist with communalism, another form of vertical cleavage, in Southeast Asia. If loyalty to an ethnic or religious group is particularly strong it will mean that the only possible partners in most patron-client dyads will be other members of the same community. Since the community is a categorical group which excludes some possible dyadic partnerships, it represents a different form of cleavage from patron-client links. Vertical dyadic bonds can, nonetheless, coexist with communal cleav-

age in at least three ways: 1) as intercommunal patron-client ties above corporate communities; 2) as intercommunal patron-client ties above factionalized communities, and, 3) as intracommunal patron-client structures. First, when communal groups do deal corporately with the outside—as quite a few small, highland tribes do in Southeast Asia—we may get patron-client ties that join their leaders, as clients, to regional or national leaders. If two distinct corporate communities were linked through their leaders who were clients of an outside leader, the structure could look like that in Figure A. More often in Southeast Asia, however, the second situation prevails in which a number of *patrons with separate followings within the same communal group* compete for the most advantageous links to the outside. A simple representation of this pattern is presented in Figure B, in which two patrons

FIGURE A

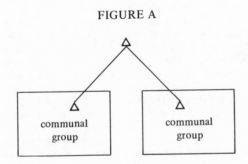

FIGURE B

are linked as clients to an outside patron and thereby have established a working alliance against a third patron in the same communal group who is linked to a different outside leader. Here, the communal group is rent by factionalism and has multiple ties to the outside world.[43] The vertical links outside the communal group, however, are likely to be somewhat weaker or more tentative than links within the community. This is so because all competing subordinate patrons and their clientele fall within a communal unit which shares a potentially strong interest; if the communal group as a whole were threatened, the shared parochial links would serve as the basis for a unity that might supersede any exterior patron-client links. The situation described in Figure B is only likely to arise, then, if there are no salient collective threats to the communal group as a whole.

The mixture of communalism and patron-client structures portrayed in Figures A and B focuses on the extracommunal patron-client links that achieve a measure, however weak, of intercommunal integration. A third mixture of communal and dyadic association focuses instead on intracommunal politics alone. This would be represented by just the boxed portion of Figure B, which indicates that, even if communal conflict is widespread, it may well be that the *intra*communal politics of each contending group is best described by the patron-client model.

The salience of communal feeling, especially in Malaysia, Burma, and Laos, but also in Indonesia and Vietnam makes such mixtures of communalism and patron-client politics common. Except at the apex of the political structure where a leader may have leaders of smaller communal groups as his clients, most patrons have followings that are almost exclusively drawn from their own community. Intercommunal integration tends to take place near the apex of the political structure with the base of each communal pyramid remaining largely separate. The links that represent this integration tend, moreover, to be fragile and to disintegrate in the face of a communitywide threat. Both communalism and patron-client links share the political stage, but patron-client structures are most prominent in periods of peace and stability. In addition, the process of politics *within* each communal group —in effect holding communal affiliation constant—is usually best analyzed along patron-client lines. In nations such as Thailand, the Philippines, and Cambodia, which are comparatively homogeneous culturally, there are few communal barriers to the proliferation of patron-

client linkages. Thus, the patron-client model can be applied to those nations in its "pure" form since communal affiliation is not important in creating discontinuous patron-client networks.

B. THE TRANSFORMATION OF TRADITIONAL PATRON-CLIENT TIES

1. The General Trend—The typical patron in traditional Southeast Asia was a petty local leader. Unlike the representative of a corporate kin group or a corporate village structure (rare outside Vietnam and Java, respectively), the local patron owed his local leadership to his personal skills, his wealth, and occasionally to his connections with regional leaders—all of which enhanced his capacity to build a personal following. The fortunes of such petty leaders waxed or waned depending on the continuing availability of resources and spoils which served to knit together a following. Perhaps the most striking feature of local patron leadership in Southeast Asia was its fluidity and instability, which contributed to a relatively high rate of local elite circulation. In contrast to India, where hereditary office-holding and landholding provided somewhat greater continuity, the typical local leader in Southeast Asia had put together many of the necessary resources of wealth, force, connections, and status on his own and could probably only promise his son a slight advantage in the next round. Two important reasons for this oscillation in local power are a) the weakness of the central state, which lacked either the force or durability to sustain and guarantee the continuation of local power elites, and b) the relative ease with which clients in a slash-and-burn economy could, if dissatisfied simply move to another area, thus undermining their ex-patron's basis of power.[44]

Patron-client systems have survived—even flourished—in both colonial and postindependence Southeast Asia. There have been important changes, however. New resources for patronage, such as party connections, development programs, nationalized enterprises, and bureaucratic power have been created. Patron-client structures are now more closely linked to the national level with jobs, cash, and petty favors flowing down the network, and votes or support flowing upward. In the midst of this change, old style patrons still thrive. Highland leaders, for example, still operate in a personal capacity as patron/brokers for their people with lowland leaders. Landowners in the Philippines and elsewhere have used their traditional control

TABLE 1

Secular Trends in the Nature of Patron-Client Ties in Southeast Asia

Quality	Traditional	Contemporary
1. Duration of bond	more persistent	less persistent
2. Scope of exchange	multiplex	(increasingly) simplex
3. Resource base	local, personal	external links, office-based
4. Affective/instrumental balance	higher ratio of affective to instrumental ties	lower ratio of affective to instrumental ties
5. Local resource control	more local monopoly	less local monopoly
6. Differentiation between clusters	less differentiation	more differentiation
7. Density of coverage	greater density	less density

of land and the tenants who farm it to win positions of local or regional party leadership. Whatever the particular form they take, patron-client networks still function as the main basis of alliance systems among nonkin throughout Southeast Asia.

The nature of patron-client bonds within Southeast Asia has varied sharply from one period to the next and from one location to another. Different resources have risen or plummeted in value as a basis of patronage depending upon the nature of the political system: The capacity to mobilize an armed following was particularly valuable in the precolonial era; access to colonial office was a surer basis of patronage than armed force in the colonial period; and the ability to win electoral contests often became the central resource with the advent of independence. Not only have resource bases proved mercurial over time, but the nature of patron-client ties in the indirectly ruled highland areas has remained substantially different from lowland patterns. Amidst this variety and change, it is nevertheless possible to discern a number of secular trends in the character of patron-client bonds. Such trends are far more pronounced in some areas than others, but they do represent directions of change that are important for our analysis.

(1) In comparison with more bureaucratic empires, patron-client bonds in precolonial Southeast Asia were not, as I have pointed out, markedly persistent. With the quickening of social change brought about by the commercialization of the economy and the penetration of the colonial state into local affairs, however, a patron's resource base became even more vulnerable to the actions of outside forces over which he had little or no control. It was an ingenious patron indeed who could survive the creation of the colonial state, the export boom, the depression of the 1930s, the Japanese occupation, and independence with his resources and his clien-

tele intact. The major exception to this trend was the colonial period in indirectly ruled areas where colonial military and financial backing of traditional rulers, if anything, brought a stability or stagnation—to political systems that had been more chaotic. Elsewhere, patron-client links tended to become more fragile and less persistant.

(2) With the differentiation of the economy and its effects on the social structure, the scope of exchange between patron and client tended to narrow somewhat. Where traditional patrons could generally serve as all-purpose protectors, the newer patron's effectiveness tended to be more specialized in areas such as political influence, modern sector employment, or administrative influence. Although patron-client ties remained flexible and personal, the more limited capacities of the patron tended to make relationships less than comprehensive and hence less stable.[45]

(3) The traditional patron for the most part operated with personally controlled local resources. One effect of the colonial period—and independence as well—was to increase radically the importance of external resources for local patronage. A following based on purely local office or landholding was seldom sufficient to sustain a patron in a new environment where schools, agricultural services, regional banks, and public employment represented competing sources of patronage. The growing role of outside resources, in most cases, thus led to competition among patrons, each of whom recruited followings with the particular resources at his command.[46] In addition, since those who controlled the new resources were generally office-holders subject to transfers or political changes at the center, the new patrons were less secure than older patrons and probably more inclined to maximize their gains over the short run.

(4) Because the new patron-client ties were weaker and less comprehensive, and because the new patrons were often from outside the local

community, the instrumental nature of the exchange became more prominent. A relationship that had always involved some calculations of advantage lost some of its traditional legitimacy and grew more profane. Patron-client exchanges became more monetized, calculations more explicit, and concern centered more on the rate of return from the relationship rather than on its durability. This trend meant that newer patron-client clusters were likely to have a comparatively large "fair-weather" periphery, a comparatively small core-following, and a less "constant" patron as well.

(5) The breakdown of local patron monopolies follows logically from most of the changes we have already discussed. Where one local landowner or traditional leader had once dominated he now faced competitors who might be local administrators of state welfare and loan programs, teachers in new secular schools, a local trader or businessman, or the resident manager of a foreign-owned plantation. Factional strife which reflects this competition was most common in villages where socioeconomic change and government penetration had been far-reaching, and less common in more traditional areas.[47]

(6) As differentiation occurred within the local societies, they gave rise to patron-client clusters that were distinct. A bureaucrat might have a following primarily within his agency, a businessman among his laborers, and a landowner among his tenants. This process of differentiation among clusters provided the potential basis for durable group interests inasmuch as many clusters now had an institutional distinctiveness.

(7) While the changes we have examined may have assisted the vertical integration of patron-client pyramids, they tended to reduce the universality of coverage. That is, more and more people in the new market towns and cities, on plantations, and on small plots they rented from absentee landlords were no longer attached—or were very weakly attached—to patrons. These new elements of the population varied greatly in their interests and their levels of organization, but, in any event, they fell outside the older patron-client network.

While some long run trends in patron-client ties seem clear, it is difficult to say anything about the balance between voluntarism and coercion over time. On the one hand, changes in the economy have made clients less autonomous and more dependent on patrons for protection against a fall in world prices, for cash advances before the harvest, and so forth. Also contributing to a decline in the client's bargaining position is the imported legal system of property guarantees which allow a wealthy man, if he so chooses, to resist pressures for redistribution that operated in a traditional setting. On the other hand, the breakdown of local patronly monopolies and the exchange resources that electoral systems often place in the hands of clients work in the opposite direction. Given these contradictory tendencies, one can draw the tentative conclusion that patron coerciveness has declined only where extralocal resources *and* competitive elections are common and has elsewhere either increased or remained the same.

In general, patron-client ties have tended to become more instrumental, less comprehensive, and hence less resilient. They still represent diffuse personal bonds of affection when compared to the impersonal, contractual ties of the marketplace, but the direction of change is eroding their more traditional characteristics. Even this supple traditional protective mechanism has had to pay a certain price to survive in the midst of a nation-state with a commercialized economy. The durability and legitimacy of the patron-client tie was best served when all of a client's dependencies were focused on a single patron. But, as Godfrey and Monica Wilson have shown, this situation is less and less likely since the process of modernization tends to create multiple dependencies—each of less intensity—rather than concentrating dependence on one person.[48] The slowly weakening comprehensiveness of the link is, ultimately, what undermines its sanctity and legitimacy for the client.

2. *The Dynamics of the Transformation*—The engine behind the shift in patron-client ties was largely provided by the penetration of the local arena by an intrusive national economy and national political system. This penetration wrought two major changes that transformed patron-client links: a) during the colonial period, especially, it impaired the effectiveness of local redistributive pressures and b) particularly after independence it "nationalized" access to patronly resources, thus creating new bases of patronage and devaluating old ones.

Traditional peasant societies, operating in an economy of great scarcity in which one family's gain is another's loss, have generally developed a variety of social control mechanisms that guarantee a measure of security to each family and temper the centrifugal forces generated by the struggle for subsistence.[49] These mechanisms commonly involve forcing anyone who has accumulated considerable wealth to redistribute a portion of it. A wealthy man is pressed to assume expensive ceremonial offices, to make large religious contributions, to give loans and donations, and so forth. He trades his wealth for prestige, and, by so providing for at least the minimum well-being of others, he becomes a legitimate patron with a personal entourage of those obligated to him.

The central fact about these redistributive mechanisms, however, is that they operate by virtue of a local power situation. That is, the wealthy man in a peasant village can seldom rely on outside force or law to protect him; instead, his wealth and position are ultimately validated by the legitimacy he acquires in the local community. Unless a wealthy individual can persuade most of the community that his wealth is no threat to them or can win enough personal allies to sustain his position, he is in danger. Colonialism, however, broke the relative autonomy of the local arena and hence weakened many of the community's redistributive pressures. Supported in effect by the power of the colonial regime to enforce its notion of law, the patron could increasingly ignore local levelling pressures. If he lost much of the social approval he previously enjoyed, he had gained an outside ally with the power to guarantee his local position. The colonial power situation thus offered the *older* patron new leverage in the local arena —leverage which was further strengthened by the growing complexity of colonial society. As Blau has explained,

Social approval has a less pervasive significance as a restraining force in complex societies than in simpler ones, because the multiplicity of groups and the possible mobility between them in complex societies allows deviants of nearly all sorts to escape from the impact of community disapproval by finding a sub-group of likeminded persons . . .[50]

Absentee landlords, the new urban wealthy, and minority communities (who were relatively impervious to local social approval so long as they had colonial backing) were *new* elements in colonial society which could escape patronly obligations. The colonial system thus tended to allow existing patrons greater latitude for exploitation while producing a class of wealthy nonpatrons.

If the intrusion of external power could strengthen the hand of an existing patron, it could also create a resource base for the rise of the new patrons. The activities of the colonial regime included the hiring, firing, and promotion of public employees, the dispensing of contracts, and the granting of licenses and permits, all of which could be used to create a personal following. With independence, not only did local leaders take over responsibility for all these decisions, but the scope of government activity and regulation was generally expanded into new areas such as community development. The survival or demise of a local patron often depended, as Geertz has shown, on how successful he was in tapping these new bases of power.[51]

Except for the rare local patrons—especially in indirectly ruled areas —who were able to monopolize these external resources, the new situation produced more competition and mobility among patrons. Many potential clients quickly discovered that their needs were best served by a patron who had access to the institutions which controlled the use of these external resources. In any local context this shift could be measured by the rise of new patrons who were wholly or partly based in these new structures. Studying the incorporation of Sardinia into the Italian nation-state in the 20th century, Alex Weingrod has documented the growing importance of such externally based patrons.[62] The proportion of outsiders asked to be godparents, for example, increased dramatically from 1920 to 1960, and patrons with links to the ruling party and the state bureaucracy had increased their followings at the expense of traditional landholders. A similar process has occurred in Southeast Asia as the integration of villages into a national economy and political system tended to produce a number of more specialized local patrons who often became factional leaders.

Most of the transformations in patron-client bonds that we have been discussing apply with greatest force to the directly ruled, lowland areas of Southeast Asia where the colonial impact was both swift and far-reaching, and where colonial officials more thoroughly replaced indigenous leaders. In the indirectly ruled areas—such as highland Burma, the Unfederated States of Malaya, most of Indonesia's Outer Islands, Cambodia, Laos (and perhaps Thailand belongs here as a limiting case of indirect colonial influence) —these generalizations must be qualified. To ease the financial and administrative burden of colonial rule in these areas, the colonizers generally kept local rulers in place and used them as agents. Since these were by and large peripheral areas of marginal commercial interest, the pace of economic change tended to be slower as well.

The effects of this policy on patrons, in contrast to the directly ruled regions, were twofold. First, local patron/leaders tended to be strengthened by colonial backing and the new powers given to them. What had probably been a fairly unstable and minimal chieftaincy now became a local regime stabilized and extended by the colonial power. Secondly, the sanction of colonial authority permitted many such leaders to broaden the resource base of their authority.[53] It is true of course that a local patron's new source of strength entailed some threat to his legitimacy, but since the colonial regime demanded little beyond the maintenance of law and order in those areas, it was seldom crippling. On the other hand, the annointed patron now had the means to eclipse his rival patrons. He not only had his traditional authority and the discretionary administrative powers given him by the colonial regime, but he could use his power to purchase land, control local trade, and act as the commissioned agent of private firms. Frequently, then, the local ruler gained a new lease on political life as the dominant local figure owing to his wealth, his administrative power, and a measure of traditional legitimacy. Given the slower pace of economic change and state penetration in these regions, the local leader had to contend less with new competitors who flourished amidst such changes. The strength many patrons achieved under indirect rule is nowhere more apparent than in postcolonial elections in which they often could deliver most of their region's vote.

3. Electoral Politics and Patron-Client Ties— Most Southeast Asian states have had functioning electoral systems at one time since their independence. Although only the Philippines retains a parliamentary system, the electoral studies that do exist can tell us much about the effects of party competition on patron-client bonds and, beyond that, highlight some of the unstable features of patron-client democracies.

The dynamics of electoral competition transformed patron-client relations in at least four important ways: (1) it improved the client's bargaining position with a patron by adding to his resources; (2) it promoted the vertical integration of patron-client structures from the hamlet level to the central government; (3) it led to the creation of new patron-client pyramids and the politicization of old ones; and (4) it contributed to the survival of opposition patron-client pyramids at the local level.

First, with popular elections the client gained a new political resource, since the mere giving or withholding of his vote affected the fortunes of aspirants for office. Nor were voters slow to realize that this resource could be turned to good account. Even someone with no other services of value to offer a patron found that the votes of his immediate family were often sufficient to secure the continuous assistance of a local politician. This pattern could be found throughout Southeast Asia in electoral situations but is most striking in the Philippines, where most patron-client ties are centered around landholding and elections. The Filipino politician, as Wurfel points out, does favors *individually* rather than collectively because he wishes to create a personal obligation of clientship.[54] The voter, for his part, asks that his patron/politician favor him because of a personal obligation to reciprocate.

In one sense, popular elections can be seen as a reestablishment of the redistributive mechanisms of the traditional setting. Once again a patron's position becomes somewhat more dependent on the social approval of his community—a social approval that is now backed by the power to defeat him or his candidate at the polls. Unable to depend on outright coercion, and faced with competitors, the electoral patron knows he must (unless his local economic power is decisive) generally offer his clients better terms than his rivals if he hopes to maintain his local power.

Second, nationwide elections make it necessary for a national party to establish a network of links extending down to the local level. For the most part a party does this by taking advantage of existing patron-client clusters and incorporating them into its structure. The competitive struggle of Indonesian parties to forge such links in Java during the 1950s is apparent in the accounts Feith and Geertz give of electoral campaigns.[55] They agree that effective campaigning in the village took the form of activating and politicizing preexisting personal links rather than mass meetings or policy stands. The campaign was, as Feith says,

. . . a race for a foothold in these villages . . . a foothold involving allegiance of as many as possible of their influential people. Here the first step was to secure the support of those whose authority was accepted by the village prominents. Thus the parties struggled with one another for influence with the bupatis, the wedanas, and the tjamats . . . with the local military commanders and the heads of local offices of Religion, Information, and Mass Education, kijaijis, ulamas, heads of clans, old guerrilla leaders . . .[56]

As elsewhere in Southeast Asia, a party succeeded best at the polls by securing the adhesion of the important local patrons, who would deliver their clients as a matter of course. Working on voters individually or by class affiliation made little sense when most of the electorate was divided into patron-client clusters. The affiliation of patrons was often gained by making them candidates, by promising them jobs or other patronage, or even by cash payments. It is clear, however, that, in comparison with those parties who had to create new links to village leaders, parties such as the Nahdatul Ulama which could rely on bonds that antedated the election, were in a stronger position. Nash's account of the 1960 election in upper Burma reveals a similar pattern of patron mobilization. When a local patron was approached to join U Nu's faction of the AFPFL on the promise of later patronage, he was able to get thirty-nine others—his relatives and those who owed him money or for whom he had done favors, i.e., his clients—to join as well.[57]

The nature of the new exchange relationship that gives vitality to this patron-client pyramid is similar in most electoral systems. The local patrons and their clients provide votes at election time, hopefully carrying the village, while the party undertakes to help its local adherents (through their patron) with jobs, help in dealing with the bureaucracy, providing public works, and so forth. Since the winning party can generally offer more support to local allies than the opposition can, local patrons are likely to display a "bandwagon effect," switching allegiance to a probable winner. In addition, the party's need for a powerful local base is likely to lead to a certain localization of power. In return for delivering local votes for its list, the party is likely to give its local patron a wide discretion in administrative and development decisions affecting the locality. Thus many local patrons are able to entrench themselves further as dominant figures.

A third consequence of elections for the patron-client structure is to promote the expansion of patron-client ties and the politicization of existing bonds. Knowing that an electoral victory is important, a local patron with a modest following will probably try to obligate more clients to him in order to strengthen his electoral position. Patrons who have previously been politically inactive would "immediately convert their private power such as control over sharecroppers, debtors, kinsmen, neighbors, etc., into public political power in the form of votes."[58] Given these tendencies, the patron-client structures in a given community are most evident immediately before an election, especially a hotly contested one, when the contestants attempt to activate any links that might advance their cause.

A final point about the impact of elections on patron-client structures is that they tend to heighten factionalism and unless one cohesive party completely dominates, to promote the survival of local opposition factions. In most traditional settings, patron rivalry was largely limited to the local arena so as not to invite external intervention. An electoral system, by contrast, creates rival national or regional parties which need allies at the local level. A weak faction that might previously have been forced to compose its differences with a dominant faction, can now appeal for external support. Many of these external allies are able to provide their local adherents with patronage, cash, or other favors so as to maintain a local foothold. The net effect of electoral competition is thus to exacerbate many of the latent factional differences among patron-client clusters and occasionally to buttress weak patrons whose position would otherwise have disintegrated.

The effects we have attributed to elections can be compared to the situation in Thailand, where elections have only rarely been any more than a device to legitimate self-selected rulers. There the local client's vote is not important enough to materially improve his bargaining position with a patron, and the vertical integration of patron-client clusters had not gone very far beyond the central institutions of the bureaucracy and armed forces. In Thai villages unlike the electoral settings of Java in the 1950s, or the Philippines, many patron-client clusters are of purely local significance and are not highly politicized. Local factional conflict, as a result, is much less striking in Thailand than where competitive elections have helped to subsidize it.

To this point we have focused on the general influence of elections on patron-client structures. Depending on the region and the party in question, however, there has been a noteworthy variation in the connection between party and patron-client structures. The essential distinction is one between a party that has created its own network of patron-client linkages from the center and a party that relies on preexisting patron-client bonds and merely incorporates them into its organization. This corresponds to René Lemarchand's distinction between types of party machines in Africa.

In situations where micro-level clientelistic structures provide the essential linkages between the party machine and the masses ... the machine is superimposed upon, and in some ways tributary of, the clientelistic subsystem. A distinction must therefore be drawn between the more orthodox types of machine ... in which patronage becomes the essential source of cohesion, and what one might call the neo-traditional machine, in which exchange processes between the center and periphery are mediated by, and contingent upon, the operation of traditional forms of clientelism.[59]

As Lemarchand adds, the "orthodox" machine is more dependent on material inducements since its linkages are of more recent origin and hence more instrumental. "Neo-traditional" machines, by contrast, can rely somewhat more heavily on established patterns of deference, though they must bargain with nearly autonomous local patrons. This distinction has validity in Southeast Asia as well, both in accounting for the different styles of politics in the indirectly ruled, more traditional areas as compared to the directly ruled, heavily commercialized areas and also in explaining the structural differences between the more traditionalist as compared to more modern parties. In the indirectly ruled areas, political parties confronted fairly stable constellations of local patron power which would have been difficult to destroy. It was simpler to come to terms with local leaders rather than to try to circumvent them, even though this accommodation tended to divide the party into a coalition of political fiefdoms. In directly ruled areas where competition among patrons and heavily instrumental ties were more common, a party had a greater opportunity to create new linkages but at perhaps greater expense in favors and patronage. Throughout Southeast Asia all parties had to adapt themselves to these differences in social structure in different regions of the country: the PNI of Indonesia operated differently in Central Java than in the Outer Islands; U Nu's AFPFL faction could not win the support of the hill tribes in the same way they won the vote of the lowland Burmese, and the Nationalists in the Philippines campaigned differently in Central Luzon than in Mindanao.

There were also systematic differences between the neo-traditionalist and modernist parties within a given area. In Java, for example, the Nahdatul Ulama incorporated more traditional patron-client ties than did the PNI, which could rely more on its access to material rewards and local administration. On the East Coast of Malaya, the Islamic PMIP appealed most to the more traditional peasantry while the ruling UMNO concentrated on the town population and those dependent on federal funds. One would also guess that the Ba Swe faction of the AFPFL had a more instrumental base in towns and the modern sector, while U Nu's faction was more frequently based on existing patron-client links in the countryside. Simply knowing the kind of patron-client bonds a party had created or incorporated could reveal a great deal about the party's cohesiveness, the nature of its local base, and the extent of its reliance on material inducement.

4. The Inflationary Character of "Patron-Client Democracy—The introduction of competitive elections in Southeast Asia increased the pressures on regimes for the downward distribution of tangible benefits. In return for votes flowing up the vertical chain of patron-client structures, each patron depended upon the downward distribution of patronage in the form of administrative favors, land grants, public employment, and so on, in order to keep his own pyramid of followers intact. Elections, by themselves, had shifted the balance of exchange so that it favored the client somewhat more than before. The consequence of this shift in exchange terms was a greater flow of material benefits toward the base of the patron-client network.

The strength of the downward distributive pressures generated by electoral procedures in Southeast Asia depended primarily on four variables which are stated below in contrasting terms. (See Table 2 next page.)

Each of these four variables related to the strength of incentives impelling a party to maximize its clientele and the degree to which that clientele will depend on concrete material incentives rather than ties of affection or deference. The first and obvious requirement for distributive pressures is that elections be important in the selection of an elite. Secondly, a shaky regime or party will be in a less advantageous position to resist client demands than a strong one, since an election is an all or nothing affair and uncertainty over the outcome will raise costs; when the race is close, the party in its recruitment efforts knows that the marginal value of the extra dollar, patronage job, or development grant is all the greater. That is one reason why distributive pressures were greater in 1955 in Indonesia when an election fraught with uncertainty would determine which parties would form a coalition, than in Malaysia in 1964 when the question was not whether the Alliance would win but whether or not it would take two-thirds of the seats.

The importance of social change (item three) is based on the observation that patron-client ties in less traditional areas typically require the patron to deliver more in the way of instrumental, material rewards. The maintenance of a loyal patron-client network in a traditional area where deference is strong, will, I assume, cost a party somewhat less in material rewards and favors than will a network of the same size in a built-up

TABLE 2

Distributive Pressures of Elections

A. Strongest when	B. Weakest when
1. Elections determine powerholders	1. Elections have marginal significance
2. Regime is weak, unstable regime	2. Regime is strong, stable regime
3. Socioeconomic change is extensive (direct rule, lowland areas)	3. Socioeconomic change is less extensive (indirect rule, highland areas)
4. Party is modernist, secular.	4. Party is traditionalist, religious.

Examples of Strong Distributive Pressure (A): Indonesia (until 1955); Burma (until 1959 at least), the Philippines.
Examples of Weaker Distributive Pressures (B): Thailand, and perhaps Malaysia (until 1967).

area where traditional patron-client bonds have eroded. Finally, a neo-traditionalist party such as UMNO in Malaysia can, in part, rely upon the traditional legitimacy of many of its leaders while a party of "new men" such as the PNI in Indonesia or the AFPFL in Burma has to rely more often on highly instrumental ties. Thus a weak party led by "new men" and relying on votes from among an uprooted population is likely to develop a patchword patron-client structure that is very expensive to maintain. It is indicative of just how much financial backing such structures require that only a ruling party with access to the public till can generally afford the construction costs.[60]

The distributive pressures experienced by such regimes manifest themselves in familiar ways. Government budgets, and of course deficits, swell quickly with expenditures on education, growing public employment, community development projects, agricultural loans, and so forth. Particularly since votes in Southeast Asia are to be found in the countryside, one would expect that regimes with strong electoral pressures would spend more in the grass-roots rural areas than would regimes without such pressures. Given such pressures, local expenditure is also arranged as much as possible so that benefits can be distributed individually since that arrangement is more appropriate to patron-client exchange patterns. Even with pork-barrel programs a local party leader will claim personal responsibility for the gift and personally help distribute whatever employment or subcontracting it includes. The capacity of the regime to keep its network intact and win elections depends on its capacity to provide rewards for the lower tiers of its structure at a constant or even expanding rate.

A regime that is dependent on its particularistic distributive capacity is also unlikely to solve its financial dilemmas either by structural reform or by tapping new sources of revenue. Most conceivable structural reforms, such as land redistribution, would strike at the resource base of many patrons and are thus unacceptable

to parties whose *policy* interests coincide with the desires of its dominant patrons. Such regimes also have a most difficult time raising revenue from internal taxation. A rise in direct taxation would threaten their base of support; and, in fact, they are notorious for the undercollection of revenues due them, since favors to their clients often take the form of either leaving them off local tax rolls or ignoring debts they owe the government. The Burmese peasants connected to U Nu's faction of the AFPFL, for example, were almost universally in default on agricultural loans they had received as party supporters. They assumed the loan was a gift for clientship and knew that a government dependent on their votes could scarcely press matters.

If this analysis is correct, regimes under intense distributive pressures will characteristically resort to budget deficits, especially in election years, to finance their networks of adherents. Their reliance on heavily instrumental and highly monetized patron-client ties will also make it difficult for them to avoid running down their foreign exchange reserves to maintain their strength at the polls. The division of expenditures within the budgets of such regimes should also reveal a heavy emphasis on distributive expenses at the local level. Empirical studies of budget distribution, budget deficits, and foreign exchange expenditures over time in parliamentary Burma, Indonesia, and the Philippines, when compared with similar statistics for nonparliamentary periods in these same countries, or say, with statistics from Thailand and Malaysia should confirm this prediction.[61]

Democratic regimes which must cater to the strong distributive pressures generated by their electoral clientele are thus particularly vulnerable to the vagaries of world prices for primary products on which their budgets depend. As long as the economy expanded and world prices were buoyant, they could afford the costs in public jobs, pork-barrel projects and loan programs to solidify and expand their huge patron-client network. But a stagnating economy or declining world prices threatened the entire structure they had pieced together, since it relied so heavily on material inducements and relatively little on affective ties. In this context it may be that the collapse of Korean warboom prices for primary exports was the crucial blow to democracy in Indonesia and Burma. The Philippines may narrowly have escaped a similar fate by virtue of their longer and more legitimate democratic tradition, as well as by their not having suffered as proportionately large a loss in foreign exchange. Malaysia was less vulnerable, since she had just become independent and her strong government faced only moderate distributive pressures, while the Thai military elite was even less reliant on its distributive performance. The political stability or instability of parliamentary forms in these nations in the late 1950s was thus strongly affected by the strength of distributive pressures fostered by these political systems in the mid 1950s.

NOTES

1 Two influential anthropologists who employ this mode of analysis are: Clifford Geertz, "The Integrative Revolution," in Geertz, ed., *Old Societies and New States* (New York: The Free Press of Glencoe, 1963); and Max Gluckman *(Custom and Conflict in Africa* (Oxford: Basil and Blackwell, 1963).

2 A number of political studies of Southeast Asia have dealt with factionalism or patron-client ties. The most outstanding is Carl Landé's *Leaders, Factions, and Parties: the Structure of Philippine Politics,* Monograph No. 6 (New Haven: Yale University— Southeast Asia Studies, 1964). For the Thai political system, Fred W. Riggs' *Thailand: The Modernization of a Bureaucratic Polity* (Honolulu: East-West Center Press, 1966) and David A. Wilson's *Politics in Thailand* (Ithaca: Cornell University Press, 1962) pursue a similar line of analysis; and for Burma, see Lucian W. Pye, *Politics, Personality, and Nation-Building: Burma's Search for Identity* (New Haven: Yale University Press, 1962). Some notable attempts to do comparable studies outside Southeast Asia are: Colin Leys, *Politicians and Policies: An Essay on Politics in Acholi Uganda 1962-1965* (Nairobi: East Africa Publishing House, 1967); Myron Weiner, *Party-Building in a New Nation: The Indian National Congress* (Chicago: University of Chicago Press, 1967); Paul R. Brass, *Factional Politics in an Indian State* (Berkeley and Los Angeles: University of California Press, 1965); Frederick G. Bailey, *Politics and Social Change: Orissa in 1959* (Berkeley and Los Angeles: University of California Press, 1963).

3 Class as well as ethnicity is relevant to Malay-Chinese conflict, since the different economic structure of each community places them in conflict. Many a rural Malay experiences the Chinese not only as pork-eating infidels but as middlemen, money lenders, shopkeepers, etc.—as the cutting edge of the capitalist penetration of the countryside.

4 There is an extensive anthropological literature dealing with patron-client bonds which I have relied on in constructing this definition. Some of the most useful sources are: George M. Foster, "The Dyadic Contract in Tzintzuntzan: Patron-Client Relationship," *American Anthropologist*, 65 (1963), 1280-1294; Eric Wolf, "Kinship, Friendship, and Patron-Client Relations," in Michael Banton, ed., *The Social Anthropology of Complex Societies*, Association of Applied Social Anthropology Monograph #4

(London: Tavistock Publications, 1966), pp. 1-22; J. Campbell, *Honour, Family, and Patronage* (Oxford: Clarendon Press, 1964); John Duncan Powell, "Peasant Society . . . ," p. 412, Carl Landé, *Leaders, Factions and Parties . . . ,"* Alex Weingrod, "Patrons, Patronage, and Political Parties," *Comparative Studies in Society and History*, 10 (July, 1968), pp. 1142-1158.

5 Powell, "Peasant Society and Clientelist Politics," *American Political Science Review*, 64 (June, 1970), 412.

6 Another comparable model, of course, is the lord-vassal link of high feudalism, except in this relationship the mutual rights and obligations were of an almost formal, contractual nature. Most patron-client ties we will discuss involve tacit, even diffuse standards of reciprocity. Cf. Rushton Coulborn, ed., *Feudalism in History*, (Princeton: Princeton University Press, 1956).

7 In most communities this sense of obligation is a strong moral force, backed by informal community sanctions that help bind the client to the patron. A good account of how such feelings of debt reinforce social bonds in the Philippines is Frank Lynch's description of *utang na loob* in *Four Readings in Philippine Values*, Institute of Philippine Culture Papers, No. 2 (Quezon City: Ateneo de Manila Press, 1964).

8 Peter M. Blau, *Exchange and Power in Social Life* (New York: Wiley, 1964), pp. 21-22. Blau's discussion of unbalanced exchange and the disparities in power and deference such imbalance fosters is directly relevant to the basis of patron-client relationships.

9 These general alternatives are deduced by Blau (p. 118) and are intended to be exhaustive.

10 Later, we will examine certain conditions under which this may actually occur.

11 There is little doubt that this last resort usually acts as a brake on oppression. The proximate causes for many peasant uprisings in medieval Europe during hard times often involved revocation of small rights granted serfs by their lords—e.g., gleaning rights, use of the commons for pasturage, hunting and fishing privileges, reduction of dues in bad crop years—rights which offered a margin of security. Such revolts, even though they generally failed, served as an object lesson to neighboring patrons. Cf. Friedrich Engels, *The Peasant War in Germany* (New York: International Publishers, 1966); Norman Cohn, *The Pursuit of the*

Millennium (New York: Harper, 1961); and E. B. Hobsbawm, *Primitive Rebels* (New York: Norton, 1959).

12 Blau, *Exchange and Power in Social Life*, pp. 119-120, makes this point somewhat differently: "The degree of dependence of individuals on a person who supplies valued services is a function of the difference between their value and that of the second best alternative open to them." The patron may, of course, be dependent himself on having a large number of clients, but his dependence upon any *one* client is much less than the dependence of any one client upon him. In this sense the total dependence of patron and client are similar, but almost all the client's dependence is focused on one individual, whereas the patron's dependence is thinly spread (like that of an insurance company—Blau, p. 137) across many clients. Cf. Godfrey and Monica Wilson, *The Analysis of Social Change; Based on Observations in Central Africa* (Cambridge: The University Press, 1945), pp. 28, 40.

13 Blau, p. 269.

14 Blau, p. 127.

15 The classic analysis of the functions of gift-giving (prestation) in creating alliances, demonstrating superiority, and renewing obligations, is Marcel Mauss, *The Gift*: *Forms and Functions of Exchange in Archaic Societies* (Glencoe, Illinois: The Free Press of Glencoe, 1954).

16 See Sidney Mintz and Eric Wolf, "An Analysis of Ritual Co-Parenthood (Compadrazgo)," *Southwestern Journal of Anthropology* 6 (Winter, 1948) pp. 425-437.

17 Carl Landé, "Networks and Groups in Southeast Asia: Some Observations on the Group Theory of Politics," Unpublished manuscript (March, 1970), p. 6.

18 Adrian C. Mayer, "The Significance of Quasi-Groups in the Study of Complex Societies," in Michael Banton, ed., *The Social Anthropology of Complex Societies*, pp. 97-122. Mayer would call a short-term, contractual interaction that was limited in scope a *simplex* tie.

19 In another sense the patron-client dyad is fragile. Since it is a diffuse, noncontractual bond, each partner is continually on guard against the possibility that the other will make excessive demands on him, thus exploiting the friendship. A patron may, for example, prefer to hire an outsider for an important job because he can then contractually insist that the work be of top quality. With a client, it would be a delicate matter to criticize the work. As in friendship, "the diffuseness of the (patron-client) obligation places a corresponding demand for self-restraint on the parties if the relationship is to be maintained." William A. Gamson, *Power and Discontent* (Homewood, Illinois: Dorsey, 1968), p. 167.

20 A *broker* does, in a real sense *have a resource*: namely, *connections*. That is, the broker's power—his capacity to help people—is predicated on his ties with third parties.

21 U.S. Congressmen spend a good portion of their time trying to seize personal credit for decisions which benefit their constituents whether or not they had anything to do with the decision—as broker or pa-tron. For similar reasons, cabinet ministers in Malaysia and elsewhere have travelled about the country with government checks in hand, making grants to mosques, temples, and charitable groups in a way that will dramatize the largesse as an act of personal patronage. Every government decision that benefits someone represents an opportunity for someone to use that act to enlarge the circle of those personally obligated to him.

22 And it naturally follows that in underdeveloped countries, where the patrimonial view of office is especially strong, a public post could be a client-creating resource.

23 Foster, "The Dyadic Contract in Tzintzuntzan," pp. 1280-1294.

24 For good descriptions of both types of leadership, see Eric R. Wolf and E. C. Hansen, "Caudillo Politics: A Structural Analysis," *Comparative Studies in Society and History*, 9, 2 (January, 1967), 168-179 and Paul Friedrich, "The Legitimacy of a Cacique," in Marc J. Swartz, ed., *Local Level Politics: Social and Cultural Perspectives* (Chicago: Aldine 1968), pp. 243-269.

25 The terms "cluster," "network," and "first" and "second" orders are adapted from a somewhat similar usage by J. A. Barnes, "Networks and Political Processes," in Swartz, ed., pp. 107-130.

26 Mayer, "The Significance of Quasi-Groups . . ." p. 109.

27 Landé, "Networks and Groups . . ." (unpublished manuscript), pp. 6-12.

28 Mayer, p. 110.

29 There is no contradiction, I believe, in holding that a patron-client link originates in a power relationship and also holding that genuine affective ties reinforce that link. Affective ties often help legitimate a relationship that is rooted in inequality. For an argument that, in contrast, begins with the assumption that some cultures engender a psychological need for dependence, see Dominique O. Mannoni, *Prospero and Caliban: The Psychology of Colonization* (New York: Praeger, 1964).

30 F. G. Bailey uses the terms "core" and "support" in much the same fashion: see his "Parapolitical Systems," in Swartz, ed., *Local-Level Politics*, pp. 281-294.

31 Here I follow the distinctions made in Blau, *Exchange and Power in Social Life*, pp. 115-118. Other power theorists have made the same distinction.

32 Both J. A. Barnes, "Networks and Political Process," in Swartz, pp. 107-130, and Powell, *Peasant Society . . .*, p. 413, discuss this variable.

33 This variable thus relates not to a dyad but to the following in a cluster or pyramid.

34 My use of the term is adapted from Barnes, p. 117.

35 Wolf, "Kinship, Friendship, and Patron-Client Relations . . . ," p. 10.

36 In this connection, see my *Political Ideology in Malaysia* (New Haven: Yale University Press, 1968), chapter 6; and for zero-sum conceptions among peasants, see George M. Foster, "Peasant Society and the Image of Limited Good," *American Anthropologist*, 65 (April, 1965), 293-315.

37 See, for example, Edmund R. Leach, "The Frontiers of Burma," *Comparative Studies in Society and History*, 3 (October, 1960), 49-68.

38 Samuel P. Huntington, *Political Order in Changing Societies* (New Haven: Yale University Press, 1968), p. 3.

39 Corporate villages are included here since they generally stress shared kinship links to a common ancestor. Part of the corporate character of the Javanese village was perhaps further reinforced as a consequence of the collective exactions required by Dutch colonial policy. "Sanctioned reciprocity" is probably a better term for village structures in Java and Tonkin than "corporate."

40 Richard Downs, "A Kelantanese Village of Malaya," in Julian H. Steward, ed., *Contemporary Change in Traditional Societies*, Vol. II: *Asian Rural Societies* (Champaign-Urbana, Illinois: University of Illinois Press, 1967), p. 147.

41 Wolf, "Kinship, Friendship, and Patron-Client Relations . . . ," p. 5. For a brilliant account of the same process in England, see Karl Polanyi, *The Great Transformation* (Boston: Beacon Press, 1957).

42 Bernard Gallin, "Political Factionalism and Its Impact on Chinese Village School Organization in Taiwan," in Swartz, ed., pp. 377-400.

43 A combination of situations one and two would occur when the tacit rules within a communal group allowed patron-client conflict but forbade the losing or weaker patrons within the communal group from maintaining ties to outside leaders.

44 See, for example, Edmund R. Leach, *The Political Systems of Highland Burma* (Cambridge: Harvard University Press, 1954), and J. M. Gullick, *Indigenous Political Systems of Western Malaya*, London School of Economics Monographs on Social Anthropology #17 (London: University of London/Athlone Press, 1958).

45 Again, indirectly ruled areas were often exceptions in that local rulers tended to take on new powers under the colonial regime and thus became more comprehensive patrons than in the past.

46 For Malaysia, M. G. Swift, *Malay Peasant Society in Jelebu* (London: University of London, 1965), pp. 158-60, captures this shift in local power. A general treatment of such changes is contained in Ralph W. Nicholas, "Factions: A Comparative Analysis," in M. Banton, general ed., *Political Systems and the Distribution of Power*, Association of Applied Social Anthropology Monograph #2 (London: Tavistock Publications, 1965), pp. 21-61.

47 In his study of politics in an Indonesian town, Clifford Geertz has shown that the more traditional hamlets were more likely to be united under a particular leader than were hamlets which had changed more; *The Social History of an Indonesian Town* (Cambridge: M.I.T. Press, 1965), Chapter 6. This finding is corroborated by Feith's study of the 1955 Indonesian elections; Herbert Feith, *The Indonesian Elections of 1955*, Interim Report Series, Modern Indonesia Project (Ithaca: Cornell University, 1961), pp. 28-30. A comparative study of two Burmese villages also supports this conclusion: Cf. Manning Nash, *The*

Golden Road to Modernity (New York: Wiley, 1965). In this context, directly ruled areas (especially high-land areas) more frequently retained some unity behind a single patron who remained their broker with the outside world.

48 G. and M. Wilson, *The Analysis of Social Change*, pp. 28, 40.

49 For a description of such mechanisms see Clifford Geertz, *Agricultural Involution* (Berkeley: University of California Press, 1963); George M. Foster, "Peasant Society and the Image of Limited Good," *American Anthropologist* 67, 2 (April, 1965), pp. 293-315; Swift, *Malay Peasant Society . . .* , and Mary B. Hollnsteiner, "Social Control and Filipino Personality," *Symposium on the Filipino Personality* (Makati: Psychological Association of the Philippines, 1965), p. 24.

50 Blau, *Exchange and Power in Social Life*, p. 114.

51 Geertz shows how local leaders often managed to become agents of the local sugar mills—buying crops, renting land, and recruiting labor and thereby enlarging their power in the community. *The Social History . . .* , p. 57.

52 Alex Weingrod, "Patrons, Patronage, and Political Parties," pp. 388-397.

53 Similar assessments of the effects of indirect rule can be found in M. G. Swift, pp. 148-149; Harry J. Benda and John Bastin, *A History of Modern Southeast Asia* (Englewood Cliffs, N.J.: Prentice-Hall, 1968), pp. 75-122. The best accounts of the pattern, however, come from India. Cf. Bailey, *Politics and Social Change*, Chapter 4, and Paul R. Brass, *Factional Politics in an Indian State* (Los Angeles and Berkeley: University of California Press, 1965), Chapter 4.

54 David Wurfel, "The Philippines," in *Comparative Studies in Political Finance: A Symposium, Journal of Politics*, 25 (November, 1963), 757-773.

55 Feith, *The Indonesian Elections of 1955*; Geertz, *The Social History of an Indonesian Town*.

56 Feith, p. 79.

57 Manning Nash, "Party Building in Upper Burma," *Asian Survey*, 3 (April, 1963), pp. 196-202.

58 Nicholas, "Factions . . . ," p. 45.

59 René Lemarchand, "Political Clientelism and Ethnicity: Competing Solidarities in Nation-Building," *American Political Science Review*, 66 (March, 1972).

60 Adrian C. Mayer seems to have this distinction in mind, in his study of an Indian town comparing the "hard" campaign of the Jan Sangh, which relied on durable social ties and tried to prevent defections, and the local Congress Party, which ran a "soft" campaign of short-term links by promising favors and benefits to intermediaries. See Mayer, "The Significance of Quasi-Groups in the Study of Complex Societies," p. 106.

61 Many of these data are not in a form that permits easy comparisons. Although budget deficit and foreign exchange figures seem to fit this pattern, statistical confirmation will have to await further research.

PEASANT SOCIETY AND*
CLIENTELIST POLITICS
JOHN DUNCAN POWELL

I. ELEMENTS OF THE PATRON-CLIENT RELATIONSHIP

THE BASIC SOCIAL relations of peasant life are directly related to an environment characterized by extreme scarcity. The major factor of productive wealth in agriculture is land, to which the peasant has little or no free access. Labor—his own, and that of his family members—is available to the peasant, but this relatively unproductive factor must be applied to land in order to generate wealth. Few other outlets for productive labor employment are available to him. When the peasant is able to combine land and labor in a wealth-generating endeavor, his productivity is likely to be extremely low, due to limiting factors such as technology, capital, marketing information, and credit. All of these life aspects combine to hold down the peasant's income and preclude savings. He is, in a word, poor.

Furthermore, the peasant is powerless against many threats which abound in his environment. There are disease, accident, and death, among the natural threats. There are violence, exploitation, and injustice at the hands of the powerful, among the human threats. The peasant knows that this environmental constellation is dangerous. He also knows that there is relatively little he can do about his situation, and, accordingly, his culture often features themes of vulnerability, calamity, and misfortune.[1] As George Foster has neatly summarized it, the outlook this situation engenders in the peasant is the "Image of the Limited Good." Within this image: peasants view their social, economic, and natural universes—their total environment—as one in which all of the desired things in life such as land, wealth, health, friendship and love, manliness and honor, respect and status, power and influence, security and safety, *exist in finite quantity* and are *always in short supply* as far as the peasant is concerned. Not only do these and all other "good things" exist in finite and limited quantities, but in addition *there is no way directly within peasant power to increase the available quantities.*[2]

But there are basic patterns of social relations which develop in peasant societies in order to cope with these realities. They are, in general, anxiety-reduction behaviors by which the peasant attempts to build some security in the face

of his perceived environmental threats, or at least to make life more tolerable within a basically threatening context.[3] These social arrangements are adaptive means for increasing the peasant's access to the "good things" in life, and, as Foster implies, they are, of necessity, indirect. One basic set of such arrangements is found in the various kinship systems—nuclear families, extended families and clan organizations.[4] An extension of such arrangements may be found in the fictive kinship relationships present in many peasant societies.[5] Finally, there are a number of typical peasant social mechanisms which function to "equalize poverty" by means of individual, group, or even institutional actions—the latter, typically, through rituals of conspicuous consumption.[6]

One of these patterns of cooperative social arrangement I wish to treat in detail: *the extended patron-client relationship, or clientele system.* Such a relationship, involving an interchange of noncomparable goods and services between actors of unequal socioeconomic ranks, is of profound importance when extended beyond the confines of the peasant community. An extended patron-client network, or clientele system, is important in two distinct ways: one, in its consequences for the political system in which it concretely manifests itself; and two, as an heuristic device for the understanding of a wide range of political behavior which political scientists, in the main, consider to be either pathological, deviant, or of minor import. I refer to patterns of political behavior such as nepotism, personalism, or favoritism; and political structures such as cliques, factions, machines, and patronage groups, or "followings." A fuller understanding of clientele systems, I believe, will render such phenomena more intelligible and significant.[7]

At the core of the patron-client relationship lie three basic factors which at once define and differentiate it from other power relationships which occur between individuals or groups. First, *the patron-client tie develops between two parties unequal in status, wealth and influence;* hence the most apt description by Pitt-Rivers, who called the patron-client bond a "lopsided friendship."[8] Second, *the formation and maintenance of the relationship depends on reciprocity in the exchange of goods and services.* Such mutual exchanges involve noncomparable goods and services, however. In a typical transaction, the low-status actor (client) will receive material goods and services intended to reduce or ameliorate his environmental threats; while the high-status actor (patron) receives less tangible rewards, such as personal services, indications of esteem, deference or loyalty, or services of a directly political nature such as voting. Third, *the development and maintenance of a patron-client relationship rests heavily on face-to-face contact between the two parties*; the exchanges encompassed in the relationship, being somewhat intimate and highly particularistic, depend upon such proximity. These three characteristics of the patron-client pattern—unequal status, reciprocity and proximity—hold whether the parties are individuals, which is often the case, or kinship groups, extended kinship groups, informal or formal voluntary groups, or even institutions. *It is important to note that patron-client ties clearly are different from other ties which might bind parties unequal in status and proximate in time and space, but which do not rest on the reciprocal exchange of mutually valued goods and services—such as relationships based on coercion, authority, manipulation, and so forth.* Such elements may be present in the patron-client pattern, but if they come to be dominant, the tie is no longer a patron-client relationship.[9]

Within many rural communities the patron status is highly correlated with land-ownership and the client status with poor cultivators dependent upon the patron's land for their livelihood. Here is how one anthropologist describes such a "traditional" relationship between landlord and sharecropper:

A peasant might approach the landlord to ask a favor, perhaps a loan of money or help in some trouble with the law, or the lanrdlord might offer his aid knowing of a problem. If the favor were granted or accepted, further favors were likely to be asked or offered at some later time. The peasant would reciprocate—at a time and in a context different from that of the acceptance of the favor, in order to de-emphasize the material self-interest of the reciprocative action—by bringing the landlord especially choice offerings from the farm produce, or by sending some member of the peasant family to perform services in the landlord's home, by refraining from cheating the landlord, or merely by speaking well of him in public and professing devotion to him.[10]

Silverman also found, in the same Italian community, that similar patron-client relationships could be established by persons who were not personally linked to a powerful figure through the agricultural system, but were merely lower-status persons who lived in the community: "The potential client would approach one of the *signori* with a request, or he might attempt to establish the relationship first by presenting him with some small gift or by making himself available to run errands or help out in various ways."[11] An important aspect of these relationships is that the needs of the client tend to be critical—for example, a peasant may need more land to farm in order to feed his growing family —while the needs of the patron, while important to him, tend to be marginal. Not only can a large landowner get along without the esteem or loyalty of an individual peasant and his family, but there are many more peasant families with needs than there are patrons with assets. The bargaining power of the patron is by definition greater than that of the client.

Several aspects of the patron-client relationship are fixed—such as unequal status, reciprocity and proximity—and some are variable. We should take note of these variables in the relationship before proceeding to the extension of these relationships beyond the confines of the peasant community. The first variable is the origin of the initiative to establish the relationship. Either patron or client may take the initiative. This is less important in enduring relationships than in *ad hoc* or periodic patron-client ties. Duration or persistence over time, then, is a second variable. Third, the scope of the relationship may vary. A patron-client tie may cover the full range of the client's needs, if he is fortunate— from the cradle to the grave, as it were. Other relationships may be defined by the very narrow range of goods and services which are exchanged. Finally, the patron-client tie may vary in its intensity. Affect, feelings of loyalty, obligation, and satisfaction with the benefits of the relationship may be strong or weak. These variables, furthermore, tend to cluster together in distinct patterns. In a "traditional" village— isolated, with few market-network or governmental ties with the outside—patron-client relationships tend to be enduring, extensive and intense. In a more integrated, differentiated village context, patron-client relationships tend to be periodic, defined by special, narrow interests, and casual.

II. LINKAGES WITH THE LARGER SYSTEM

This brings us to a most crucial point in the analysis—the linking of the "little community" with the larger socio-economic system in which it exists. Two underlying processes are largely responsible for the establishment of these linkages: state centralization and market expansion.[12] Each involves differentiation and specialization of roles and the elaboration of networks of interdependent parts, or more simply put, transaction systems. At the boundary of the little community stands the "gatekeeper" —the landed patron.[13] As the twin processes of state and market penetration of the peasant village occur, the patron becomes transformed into a broker, mediating the impact of the larger society on peasant society.

As a result of increased attention to the interpenetration of present-day peasant cultures and national cultures over the past twenty years or so, the anthropological community has become increasingly aware of these brokers, "hinge groups," "mediators" or "buffers," as they have been portrayed in the literature. Eric Wolf's original definition of brokers will serve us nicely:

. . . they stand guard over the critical junctures and synapses of relationships which connect the local system to the larger whole. *Their basic function is to relate community-oriented individuals who want to stabilize or improve their life chances, but who lack economic security and political connections, with nation-oriented individuals who operate primarily in terms of complex cultural forms standardized as national institutions, but whose success in these operations depends on the size and strength of their personal following.*[14]

While they vary in cultural forms, Wolf provides as examples of such brokerage systems, the *compadrazgo* system in Latin America, the Chinese *kan ch'ing*, and the Japanese *oyabunkobun*; to which I would add *clientela* in Italy and Sicily, the *jajmani* system in India, and the patron-client system in the Philippines.[15] I would hypothesize that such clientele systems might be encountered in any developing country in which kinship systems are unable to perform linkage functions between persons of low and high status, or between the community and the nation. Where kinship systems can perform these linkage functions at all, as in Greece (and under certain conditions in Italy), they are likely to be responsive to only a limited range of needs, leaving low-status clients to rely on non-kinship clientele systems as well.[16]

Of great importance is the manner in which these extended clientele systems change over time. Traditional, land-owning patrons may become brokers, but additional brokers may appear to compete with them for followings on the local level. Power holders on the national level may or may not consolidate and formalize some of these clientele systems, playing off one network of brokers against another in the process. These processes of change, and their significance for political development, will be more understandable if we consider some concrete historic examples.

Sydel Silverman, in "The Community-Nation Mediator in Traditional Central Italy," focuses precisely on such changes over time.[17] According to her, prior to Italian national unification, the patron-client system was almost the exclusive domain of the great landlords, who acted in the main as direct benefactors, but also as links with the larger, Church-dominated society of central Italy. As far as commercial ties were concerned, they too were guarded by the landlords, but extended only to provincial market towns. Following unification in the 1860-1861 period, nation-community contacts grew, and landlords added to their functions as direct benefactors (loans, employment, land-access, dowry gifts, medicines) those of brokerage services. When a peasant client had dealings with bureaucracies—taxes, credits, etc.—or with the police in the area, the patron acted as broker. The role of broker, in fact, became generalized in peasant dealings with "outsiders," and the "letters of recommendation" became more highly valued in many instances than direct patronage benefits. Such letters were considered imperative when undertaking an arrangement with a distant merchant, or in seeking public employment. As outside relationships became more important over time, says Silverman, "the most valuable patron was neither the wealthiest nor the most generous, but the one with the best connections."[18]

In addition to the changes of function of the traditional patrons (the large landowners), which transformed them into brokers, other local people with "outside connections" also began to assume brokerage functions—bourgeois landowners, schoolteachers, physicians and pharmacists, priests, tax collectors and other local officials. Some of these "new" brokers had connections with the marketing system, and some with the political system, but all were intermediate in socio-economic status. They were, in other words, those whom one writer has recently characterized as the "small intellectuals" of society, whose status and role functions place them in the "strategic middle" of the social structure.[19] The Italian case clearly suggests the impact of state centralization in the little community, transforming traditional patrons into brokers (i.e., governmental agents) on the periphery of the peasant society. Similarly, the penetration of market networks, with its resultant differentiation and specialization of new roles, further enlarged the pool of potential brokers. These twin forces for change may be seen in another historic case, that of Mexico.

Eric Wolf specifically undertook a diachronic analysis of brokerage groups in rural Mexico in his seminal article, "Aspects of Group Relationships in a Complex Society: Mexico."[20] First, he traced the entry of the Spaniards into the previously autonomous Indian communities, and the establishment of landed power-holding by representatives of the Crown. This was accomplished through the *encomienda* system, and in agriculture as well as mining, enclaves of primary production were established and linked into a rudimentary trade system with the mother country. In addition to the landholdings producing for international trade, landed powerholders, encroaching on the communal lands of the Indians, established autonomous, self-sufficient holdings in the manorial or patrimonial style.[21] Both types of holding provided bases of manpower and wealth for a highly decentralized system of political power. In time, the struggle by Spain for the recapture of its political power and monopoly in the trading system precipitated the War of Independence by the New World landed elites. During this period of Mexican land history, the same kind of "traditional" patron behavior described for Italy by Silverman, characterized Mexican landlord-peasant relationships, exaggerated by cultural and linguistic differences.

According to Wolf, a byproduct of the trade systems established under the Crown had been a group of "marginals"—small storekeepers, middlemen, casual farmers and specialized workers located in the villages and entrepreneurial communities near mines, *haciendas*, or mills. With the destruction of the ties to Spain, the legal devices which had until that time granted a small measure of protection to the Indian communities were swept aside, and a long period of land-grabbing began. Communal property-holding dissolved into "land as a commodity," and the best remaining Indian lands were taken over by large landlords, or invaded by the upward-striving "marginals." From these processes grew the classic *hacienda* system, the epitome of autonomous, self-sufficient localism.

The Revolution of 1910 had, as one of its major consequences, the recapture of local political power by the central authorities. Violent peasant upheavals eliminated some of the local,

landed powerholders, and agents of government were dispatched into the rural areas to foster the business of the "outside" authorities. As in Italy, many of the remaining landowners, more likely to be bourgeois than "aristocratic" in standing, became transformed from direct benefactors (patrons) into brokers. With the greater flow of goods and services into the rural areas which characterized post-revolutionary Mexican governments, not only did local representatives of the national government proliferate and increase in importance as brokers, but the local "small intellectuals" found increasing employment for their specific mediating skills, thereby gaining for themselves a useful channel of socioeconomic mobility and influence.

III. THE CLIENTELIST STATE

Small-scale patrons, we have seen, may become transformed into brokers in the course of state and market centralization. This implies that the patron-client pattern is replicated on a higher level of organization; and indeed this is found to be the case. Thus, in discussing the Thai bureaucracy, Shor observed that:

. . . The personal clique, based on a feudal-like system of personal obligation, provides the principle focus on bureaucratic loyalty and identification. Bonds of reciprocal obligation, reminiscent of earlier patron-client structures in the traditional social system, informally align a number of dependent subordinates with individual political and administrative leaders in more or less cohesive informal structures.[22]

And in commenting on Rustow's study of the Turkish bureaucracy, Guenther Roth points out that there exists "what is imprecisely known as 'corruption': 'connections' count, favoritism prevails, and for the few there is abundant profit in real-estate dealings."[23] There are probably few countries in which such forms of behavior cannot be encountered; the important difference lying in the fact that in some—for example, contemporary South Vietnam—these forms dominate the organization of the polity. What we have then is a variation on Weber's Patrimonial State. As Guenther Roth has said of this variation, "The second type of patrimonialism is personal rulership on the basis of loyalties that do not require any belief in the ruler's unique personal qualifications, but are inextricably linked to material incentives and rewards."[24] I propose that we call this model the Clientelist State.

The utility of the clientelist notion is not limited to personalist, primitive polities. As Roth quite rightly points out, "in terms of traditional political theory, some of these new states may not be states at all but merely private governments of those powerful enough to rule" . . . but, on the other hand," . . . personal rulership . . . is an ineradicable component of the public and private bureaucracies of highly industrialized countries."[25] I should now like to turn to the impact of clientelist politics in the national electoral process of many developing countries. The client-broker-patron network, we shall find, is of key importance as the electoral process reaches the level of the peasant village. I do not intend to digress for the moment to analyze the historic processes by which peasant voters— usually illiterate—become enfranchised, nor the processes by which elections come to play a central role in the distribution and transfer of political authority. Let us simply acknowledge the observable fact that in many countries today, including Italy, Venezuela, India, Turkey, the Philippines, and others, peasants do vote and elections are determinative. Patron-client patterns of behavior become significant for such countries in the periodic mobilization of peasant voters. At the level of the village, we find competition among brokers and potential brokers for peasant votes which can be delivered to a particular political patron or potential patron. Such competition, which has been described as "factionalism" in village politics, is an essential ingredient in the process of aggregating clienteles into a widespread network, and linking them to vertical patronage structures in the political system.[26]

National or regional political leaders recruit local political leaders from among the competing patrons and brokers. Local brokers and patrons recruit subleaders, or political workers, in turn; and these workers recruit or assemble small followings from among their kin, caste brothers, occupational colleagues, or voluntary group associates. Mayer calls such a cross-cutting electoral aggregate an "action-set," assembled for a particular action fixed in time and space (i.e., an election). In all essential details, it appears to be an aggregation of clienteles:

These workers acted as links between the candidate and the electorate. Sometimes they did this for the advantages they calculated would accrue to them if the candidate were elected; sometimes they were acting because of party loyalty and friendships formed over the years without any thoughts of gain from the election itself; and at yet other times they were discharging specific obligations contracted at earlier times. *In the same way, there was an attempt to reach voters on the basis of a past or future benefit . . . In consequence, a great deal of the electioneering was carried out by workers, who sought to influence those with whom they had some appropriate relationship.*[27]

The exact nature of the "appropriate" relationship is a significant question. A local political worker may pull together voters on the basis of kinship ties, fictive kinship or caste ties, or through a variety of relationships, including patron-client ties. The worker who pulls such electoral bloclets together assumes the role of broker for that group with a patron group or institution, in this case a political party. Furthermore, there is some evidence which suggests that the "appropriate relationship" for pulling in peasant voters may be distinctly different from one party to another. Table 1 below is a re-arrangement of data presented by Ralph Nicholas from his study of factional politics in Govindapur, West Bengal, in which he analyzed the basis for membership in nine village factions, each with a leader linked to a particular political party.

The data in Table 1 leads me to the following tentative hypothesis. The exact nature of the ties to peasant voters which are activated in mobilizing an electoral turnout depends on two related factors: the particular needs of the client, and the relationship of the potential patron's political party to the government. In this Indian case, all parties tended to succeed in mobilizing followings based on neighborhood ties—the headman worked well for the Congress, the Independents, and the Communists were heavily dependent on utilizing kinship and caste ties to assemble their clienteles. This suggests that the brokerage functions which they performed for

TABLE 1

Factional Alignments of All Possible Voters in Govindapur, West Bengal

Factional Leader No.	Party affiliation of leaders	Basis of membership support (per cent)					
		Kinship	Caste	Economic dependence	Neighborhood headman	Mutual enemy	Total
1 & 2	Congress	13%	7	44	17	19	100%
3 & 4	Independent	28%	33	14	25	0	100%
5 - 9	Communist	52%	20	7	20	1	100%

Source: Adapted from Ralph Nicholas, "Factions: A Comparative Analysis," in *Political Systems and the Distribution of Power* (New York: Praeger, 1965), edited by Gluckman and Eggan. Table 1, page 42.

their clients were essentially defensive in nature —insuring that their relatives and caste brothers received equitable treatment at the hands of governmental representatives such as tax collectors, credit and extension agents, and the police. This is the other side of the coin of the functions mostly likely performed by the Congress party brokerage system which involved preferential treatment. This might include access to and influence in the making and administration of economic programs and policies which affected rural enterprises (and the people dependent on them); and in addition, knowledge of and influence in the judicial and police systems for the purpose of dealing with mutual enemies.

IV. CLIENTELIST POLITICS AND POLITICAL PARTIES

We need now to examine more broadly the impact of clientele politics on political parties; and further, to project our analysis into the realm of national politics. This can be economically accomplished by comparing two striking cases which have been rather fully documented and analyzed: Italy and Venezuela.[28] While many of the elements of clientelist politics—with a peasant mass base—can be encountered in the recent or current political history of India, Mexico, Bolivia, Chile, Brazil, Peru, and the Philippines, and to a lesser degree in Indonesia, France, Guatemala, Spain, and Turkey, the cases of Venezuela and Italy are not only well-documented, but seem to represent the upper limits, or fullest development, of which such transaction systems are capable.

Both countries are multiparty electoral democracies in which more than one political party has competed for a peasant base of support through the elaboration of clientele systems. The degree to which the various parties depend on the peasant vote varies, of course, but it is very substantial for the Communist Party (PCI) in Italy, and for the Democratic Action (AD) and Social Christian (COPEI) parties in Venezuela. The Italian Christian Democratic Party (PDC) also receives significant support from peasant constituencies in the south. In both cases, peasant clienteles have been organized into a peasant union movement, which interpenetrates the party system at the local, regional, and national levels. In each country, there has been an extensive agrarian reform program which has provided land and a flow of governmental goods and services downward through the same clientele system which channels votes upward from the peasant base. What we have, in essence, is a transaction system with reciprocal, but unequal, flows of goods and services— votes for agrarian reform benefits. Figure 1 illustrates the Venezuelan system (which I have called the "rural problem-solving system") from the point of view of the peasant. Working through such a network is one of the new instrumental ways in which the peasant can counter his environmental threats.[29] The Italian clientele system, while somewhat more complex, functions in exactly the same manner. An important factor, obviously, is whether or not a particular party is included in a coalition government— and which portfolios or ministries it can influence. In general, the brokerage function is performed by all parties, but those parties outside the government tend to focus on the defense of peasant clients, and the government parties focus on influencing the flow of patronage for their clients. This is a strong tendency, not an absolute distinction.

I wish to emphasize at this point the explicit argument that *peasant clientele systems are built upon, incorporate, and recapitulate the interpersonal patterns of behavior known as clientelism.* Unlike simple patron-client relations, or primitive clientele systems, the Italian and Venezuelan networks have been purposively organized from above, endure in institutionalized form, exchange a wide range of goods and services, and provide quite lengthy chains of linkages—from the peasant to the President or Prime Minister. They are, in a quite specific sense, politically representative. How did such networks come into being, and what effect have they had on national politics in these countries?

In both cases, an urban-based political elite group undertook the organization of the peasantry as a way to mobilize the political capital needed to break into a traditional, elite-dominated inner circle of power in national politics. In Italy, it was the Communist Party which succeeded in organizing the peasantry in the postwar period. In Venezuela, it was the Democratic Action Party (struggling simultaneously to establish a meaningful electoral process and to break the hold of the entrenched, traditional elites on governmental power) which began to organize the peasantry during the 1930s. The responsiveness of the peasantry in both cases rested in part on two factors: a history of bourgeois encroachments on lands formerly available for peasant use; and a recent period of prolonged, serious dislocation of commercial agriculture. In Italy the theme of land *irredenta*, according to Tarrow, originated in the massive take-over of Church and State lands by the bourgeoisie following the national unification in

1861. In Venezuela, there were twin strands of peasant land irredentism: broken promises of land for military service in the armies which fought the War of Independence and the Federal Wars of the nineteenth century; and the encroachment of the bourgeoisie on public lands during the extended, personalistic regime of the dictator, Gómez (1908-1935). The encroachments of the bourgeoisie signalled a "commoditization" of the land, and a subsequent reduction in free land use by the peasantry, often drawing them into a tenancy relationship with the new owners.[30] Dislocations in both commercial and peasant agriculture occurred during the depression in both countries, and were further exacerbated in Italy by World War II. In short, the peasants' status in the prevailing land tenure situation was precarious to begin with, and grew worse prior to their mobilization.

Both AD and the PCI, then, turned to the organization of a discontented peasantry as a way of mobilizing political capital. In the initial stages, before either was in a position to control a government patronage network, their efforts focussed on direct action at the community level, often involving the invasion of farm properties.

FIG. 1. The rural problem-solving system.

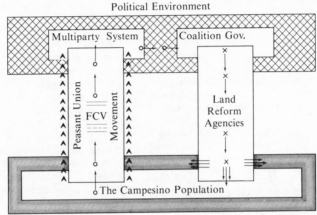

MAJOR TRANSACTIONAL FLOWS:

Inputs.

○——→ ○——→ demands for goods and services

＞＞＞＞＞＞＞＞＞ voting support

Outputs:

×——→ ×——→ budget-making & programming

⟹——→ ⟹——→ field projects

This was especially true in the case of Italy, where the land invasions of the early 1950s were closely related to the efforts of the PCI to shape and capitalize on peasant discontent. In Venezuela, AD's opportunity to open up lands to peasant access followed its participation in the *coup d' état* of October 1945. Dominating the subsequent Revolutionary Government, AD initiated a *de facto* agrarian reform, granting (by decree) access to governmental and private farms to peasant unions organized by the party. The ability to reward followers with land—whether by invasion, as in Italy, or by governmental action, as in Venezuela—quickly expanded the networks of peasant unions, which were actual or aspiring clienteles of the parties. Within a period of two or three years, the PCI in the early 1950s, and the AD in the mid-1940s, established solid positions in the rural areas.

At this point, the parallels between Italy and Venezuela broke down. AD had established a rudimentary version of its clientele system during the three-year period from 1945-1948, when it was dislodged by a counter-revolutionary coup. When the dictatorship of Pérez Jimenéz fell in 1958, and AD was successful in gaining the presidency and dominating a decade of subsequent coalition governments, then the system illustrated in Figure 1 reached fruition, with a well-financed *de jure* agrarian reform program providing a flow of goods and services into the rural areas. In response to AD's successful building of a peasant base of electoral support, the Social Christian (COPEI) party began its own program of organizing peasant unions. For six years, COPEI was included in the coalition government, providing it some direct access to agrarian reform patronage. After leaving the co-alition government, the COPEI peasant unions still maintained indirect access to governmental decision-making (though less effectively than before) through their participation in the multi-partisan Federation of Venezuelan Peasants.[31]

In Italy, however, the Christian Democrats, and not the Communists, were in control of the government when the *de jure* agrarian reform program was established. As a result, many of the local leaders and peasant clients organized by the PCI for the purpose of obtaining land (by invasions) were drawn into the Christian Demo-cratic peasant-union-party structure when land and other benefits could be had through the agrarian reform program. As Tarrow describes the resulting dilemma of the Communists:

. . . the Catholic Confederation of Direct Culti-vators is really a corporate arm of the govern-ment which dispenses patronage to peasants through a complicated system of interlocking di-rectorates with the provincial agricultural syndi-cates . . . The chain of causation is revealing. In leading the struggle for the land, the Commu-nists forced the Agrarian Reform; but in the achievements of the Reform, many peasants be-came dependents of the Christian Democrats and of the state.[32]

With the successful establishment of a state-supported clientele system which provided land, credit, extension services, infrastructure and marketing services to peasant clients, the peas-antry became "demobilized" in Tarrow's phrase. That is, land invasions and threats of vi-olence subsided. In an important sense, how-ever, the electoral mobilization of the peasantry was not a phenomenon which faded away, but one which was in fact stabilized and institu-tionalized through the same clientele system which provided the agrarian reform benefits. In short, the notion that peasants will lapse into po-litical inactivity once they obtain a piece of land seems to be a myth. A piece of land is only a necessary, but not sufficient, condition to allow the peasant to escape the world of *la miseria*. He also needs financial, technological, and marketing assistance to significantly improve his standard of living. There is a continuing need for a patron, or patronage system, which

can respond to increasingly sophisticated and complex demands, and thus peasant dependency and peasant mobilization become institutionally linked.

Both the Christian Democrats in Italy and Democratic Action in Venezuela have achieved the necessary transactional equilibrium within their peasant clientele systems to stabilize a de-pendable base of legitimizing electoral support. From the point of view of the party leaders at the national level, a clientele system based on peas-ants rather than on other societal groups seems to be a sound investment. The peasant is an eco-nomical client. His range of needs tends to be narrower and more fixed than that of comparable urban clients. And in meeting the needs of peas-ants for more land to farm, technological and fi-nancial assistance in farm operations, public health and sanitation projects, and finally, mar-keting assistance, governmental decision-mak-ers are acting in a manner not only compatible with, but prescribed by the logic of economic development. This is not the case in responding to the needs of potential urban client groups, where the costs of improving the quality of the urban environment are high, the gestation peri-ods long, and the returns on capital investment indirect. But the support of such an electorally-legitimizing clientele system has its disadvanta-ges as well as its advantages in the national polit-ical arena.

In analyzing the assets and liabilities of a peasant clientele system for a political party in governmental power, I would like to leave aside the Italian case, in which peasant support is rela-tively marginal to the position of the Christian Democrats, and consider, in addition to Venezu-ela, the cases of Bolivia and Mexico.[33] In the latter two cases, peasant clientele support is, or has been, of much more critical import than in the Italian case. In Bolivia and Mexico, as in the other two countries, the peasantry had lost land to an encroaching bourgeoisie. And both countries had experienced a prolonged period of economic dislocation, which was both a con-tributing cause and a partial effect of the Mexi-can Revolution of 1910 and the Bolivian Revo-lution of 1952. In neither of these two cases had a political party seeking to break into the ranks of the traditional elites originally organized a po-litical base among the peasantry as a part of that effort. In Mexico and in Bolivia, governmental parties which grew out of the revolution incorpo-rated embryonic peasant organizations and trans-formed them into a supportive clientele network as part of their consolidation of political power. As in Venezuela and Italy, an agrarian reform program was the patronage vehicle, partly consolidating and ratifying *de facto* changes brought about by peasant land invasions, and partly distributing land and other goods and services throughout the areas of peasant concentration. While the Bolivian, Mexican, and Venezuelan cases differ in detail and circumstances, one can state that governmental parties, supported by peasant clientele systems, successfully governed for extended periods of time—in Bolivia from 1952 through 1964; in Mexico, from the mid-1930s to the present; and in Venezuela from 1958 to at least 1968. There is reason to believe that the government which replaced the original sponsor of the Bolivian Revolution (the MNR) in 1964 has continued to rely on the peasant clientele system established by its predecessor.

One of the salient characteristics of governments based on peasant clientele systems has been their capacity to withstand challenges from groups on both extremes of the political spectrum. In Mexico and Bolivia, where the traditional military establishments were eliminated, worker and peasant militias were used to resist the overthrow of the revolutionary governments by right-wing violence. Obregón, with the help of agrarian unions, successfully defended his government in 1923 against the attack by General de la Huerta. In Bolivia miner and peasant militias were instrumental in resisting the overthrow of the Revolutionary government until 1964. In Venezuela, where the professional armed forces were co-opted into the governmental clientele system rather than destroyed, armed peasant and labor militias were never formed, but mass peasant demonstrations were organized in Caracas on several occasions when the threat of a right-wing or dissident military *coup* seemed imminent, as in 1960. We might characterize such a capacity of resistance as stability against the recapture of political power by the traditional elites who were earlier displaced by the parties in government.

A peasant clientele base has been effective in meeting destabilizing challenges from the left, also. In Bolivia and Mexico, one-party states during the period under consideration, this amounted to resistance by the peasant branch, to a left-wing challenge from the labor branch of the party. In Mexico, in 1940, insurrection within the party by the leader of the left-wing labor sector, Lombardo Toledano, was resisted partly through the intervention of the peasant unions. In Bolivia, Juan Lechín, the leader of the miners' unions, made a similar attempt in 1964 to capture his party's presidential nomination, and was resisted by the peasant branch of the

party. In Venezuela, the violent opposition of the Communists and left-wing splinter groups, and guerilla efforts have been unsuccessful partly because of the disinclination of the peasants—who are clients of the government—to join in an attack on the source of their patronage. The characterization of all of these efforts as "left-wing" probably needs some qualification. In all three of these cases, the longer a peasant-based party has remained in governmental power, the more centrist, pragmatic, and moderate its policies have become. In other words, the drift away from earlier doctrinal positions has been toward the "right." Attacks from the "left," therefore, may also be accurately described in many cases as attacks from party loyalists who are unwilling to make compromises for the sake of maintaining governmental legitimacy among other groups in the political system.

Whatever the ideological implications of these events—and perhaps ideological references are more confusing than helpful in this context—rural-based parties have been able to withstand the destabilizing challenges of a number of urban-based, competing elites. As Samuel P. Huntington sees this phenomenon (which he describes as the result of a "ruralizing election"):

. . . the party which was strong in the countryside normally secured control of the national government and inaugurated a regime characterized by a high degree of political stability. Where no party had a clear base of support in the countryside, some form of instability was the result. In some instances, urban revolts may overturn rural-based governments, but in general governments which are strong in the countryside are able to withstand, if not to reduce or eliminate, the continuing opposition they confront in the cities.[34]

The use of peasant clients for purposes of political combat outside of the electoral realm has its limitations, obviously. But a clientelist base of support is also quite advantageous in political struggle and accommodation short of combat. Since the nature of the "contract" struck between the government (patron) and the peasantry (client) is concerned, really, with the flow of a rather mundane range of pay-offs—small amounts of land, credit, technological and marketing assistance—there is little or no ideological or programmatic content in the "contract" which might entangle a political elite with dissidents within or without its own party. As a result, peasant-based parties enjoy an amazing degree of flexibility in questions of policy, doctrine, and dogma. They are able to accommodate many divergent points of view within their own parties, and to deal pragmatically with opposition points of view without stirring up internal resistances. They are "pragmatic parties" *par excellence*.

But these very advantages of clientelist bases of support suggest the limitations of such systems. First, a clientelist base of support tends to erode the ideological coherence and program content with which the leaders of these parties come to power. This is less true in a revolutionary situation, as in Bolivia and Mexico, where the parties which came to power had no ideological coherence to begin with. But Democratic Action, and to an even greater extent, the Italian Christian Democrats, did attach some importance to doctrine and ideology. The Italian case is especially striking, for both the Communists and the Christian Democrats were frustrated by the manner in which their policy and doctrinal preferences were thwarted by the clientelist mentality. The power of the peasant culture in this respect was clearly noted by Tarrow:

. . . social groups remain chaotic, and political organization normally resides latently in the clientele ties between landholder and agricultural worker, lawyer and client, and bureaucrat and favor seeker. Local and parochial loyalties suffuse politics. Politics has very little ideological content, and popular imagery recognizes only two basic social groups: peasants and non-peasants.[35]

The result has been internally traumatic for the Italian Communist Party, which operates in a distinctly different milieu in the north. "Party leaders," notes Tarrow, "complain that southern members cluster around dominant personalities and neglect the day-to-day tasks of organization and proselytism," and "critics maintain that the evidence points to the PCI's being a typical southern party of clienteles."[36]

Ideological erosion in the southern clientelist milieu has equally dismayed the leaders of the Christian Democratic Party, despite the fact that electoral support is derived therefrom:

Fanfani called for the *political*, and not simply the economic, development of the South. "Above all," he said, "we must create active and efficient party sections and organizations in southern Italy, if we want to create a politics of facts and ideas instead of a politics of agitation and macaroni" . . . terms that epitomized the traditional tools of southern Italian politics: the generic protest, the patronage appointment, the

letter of recommendation, the sack of pasta on election day—in other words, the clientele system.[37]

In short, one of the limitations of clientelist politics is the strain it places on coherent ideologies. This may manifest itself in several important ways. Ideological parties may find it so difficult to reconcile discrepancies in ideas and reality that they will be either unable to build a clientelist base to begin with, or to maintain one if they do. Therefore, other, more pragmatic, parties may outdo them in competition for the peasant vote. Similarly, within parties, the stretching of ideology to encompass and legitimate clientelism may work in one of two ways: either the majority of the party leadership accepts the erosion of ideology, in which case the ideological pursuits among the leadership may leave the party; or the leadership majority may resist the erosion of ideology, in which case the peasant clients may leave or be lured away from the party. In either case, the party is weakened.

A second general limitation of clientelist politics is that it seems to be a transitional phenomenon—or, better put, appropriate and successful only under certain conditions, and then for a limited period of time. As Huntington has analyzed this situation in his book, *Political Order in Changing Societies*, political modernization involves several alternative cycles of change in urban-rural power and stability.[38] The mobilization of a peasant base of support by an urban-based political party is one form of what Huntington calls the "Green Uprising." Eventually, in the course of overall modernization, the growth of the city becomes a destabilizing phenomenon; in some cases, an urban elite group can form an alliance with the peasantry, surrounding, as it were, the unstable city with the stable countryside by bringing the two into an interdependent relationship. The resulting period of governmental stability may then be used to perform many of the necessary modernizing tasks of government in the course of development. Success, however, brings with it a decreasing relevance and effectiveness of the original peasant base of support:

If revolution is avoided, in due course the urban middle class changes significantly; it becomes more conservative as it becomes larger. The urban working class also begins to participate in politics, but it is usually either too weak to challenge the middle class or too conservative to want to do so. Thus, as urbanization proceeds, the city comes to play a more effective role in the politics of the country, and the city itself becomes more conservative. The political system and the government come to depend more upon the support of the city than upon that of the countryside. Indeed, it now becomes the turn of the countryside to react against the prospect of domination by the city.[39]

In terms of a peasant-based clientele system, such as Venezuela's, the end of this cycle is marked by a gradual tapering off of governmental support for the agrarian reform program, as growing urban-based clientele groups exert increasing influence on internal party politics. The budgetary priorities problem may provoke splintering within the party, as brokers in the peasant clientele system find their ability to deliver the goods downward gradually eroded. These party subleaders in many cases demand a "reradicalization" of the agrarian reform—that is, a resumption of larger flows of land and other agrarian reform benefits—and may even try to reinstate the land invasion tactic. In Venezuela and in Mexico, such internal dissension has resulted in brokerage leaders identified with the peasant branch either leaving the party for a more radical alternative, or being purged; and the occasional establishment of new peasant union splinter movements.

The general pattern, then, seems to be a cyclical one—the rise and fall of peasant-based clientelist politics. Where the political culture is a carrier of patron-client patterns of behavior, the disintegration of peasant clientelist politics does not mark the demise of the generic pattern. To the contrary, urban-based clientelist politics may proliferate. They may be more subtle and complex, but function in essentially the same manner. The agrarian reform, often begun with an initial burst of distributive activities, is slowed down, or consolidated, into a bureaucratic program of gradually receding importance. It may be succeeded by vast programs in workers' housing construction, or public works projects to improve the nature of life for the urban masses. These and other signs may indicate that the cycle described by Huntington is nearing its end.

V. CONCLUSION

It seems appropriate to conclude this discussion of clientelist politics by placing the concept in perspective: what claims are made for it as an heuristic tool, and what are its limitations? The concept, I believe, helps to illuminate the political behavior of low-status actors, particularly peasants, as they are incorporated, recruited, mobilized, or inducted into the national political process. Inasmuch as the induction of the peasantry into this process has in fact not yet occurred in many of the developing countries, an understanding of clientelist politics may be useful in a predictive sense. And while clientelist behavior may be most visible in the political cultures of Mediterranean extraction, there is much—although scattered—evidence that it can be encountered in political cultures in many parts of the world. This is not a prediction that clientele systems of the type found in Italy or Venezuela are to be anticipated elsewhere, but that clientelist patterns of interpersonal behavior may be a significant factor in the process of peasant politicization everywhere.

Clientele systems clearly differ from other forms of politically representative systems in several ways. In clientelism, there is an almost complete dependency on face-to-face relationships in the building and maintenance of the system. Impersonal communications between persons low and high in the system hierarchy are as ineffective as they are rare.[40] A low-status participant may, on occasion, personally approach a high-status participant in the same clientele system, but normally he depends on a series of linkages with intermediate brokers. This norm-dependency on personal contact—derives from the nature of the patron-client contract.

The dyadic contract between patron and client—or broker and patron—is a private, unwritten, informal agreement, and highly personalistic in content. There is no public scrutiny of the terms of such agreements. There is no public entity which functions as an enforcement authority concerning such agreements. There is, in short, no process by which either partner of the agreement can go "outside" the dyadic relationship for enforcement of the contract, or to bring sanctions for noncompliance. Enforcement, compliance, and performance are bound up in, and limited to, the face-to-face relationship between the client and broker, or the broker and patron.

This stands in sharp contrast to the relationship between citizen and representative, or even party member and party leader, in modern systems of political transactions. In essence, the patron-client pattern occurs in the realm of private accountability, the modern pattern in the realm of public accountability. In fact, such a distinction is what makes patron-client ties functional in the first place. As Eric Wolf has put it, in a slightly different context:

The clearest gain from such a relation should therefore appear in situations where public law cannot guarantee adequate protection against breaches of non-kin contracts. This can occur where public law is weak, or where no cultural patterns of cooperation between non-kin exist to guide the required relationship. It can also occur in dealings which border on the illegal or the extra-processual.[41]

The most obvious difference that the private-public distinction makes is in the degree of power asymmetry between superior and subordinate. Superiors in a clientele system are relatively free to behave in an arbitrary and highly personalistic manner in dealing with their subordinates. Subordinates in a clientele system have relatively little recourse in such a situation. Theoretically, clients could improve their bargaining position relative to patrons through the formation of horizontal organizations, such as peasant unions. In practice, this seems difficult for at least two reasons. First, the power asymmetry between client and broker, or patron, on the local level works against the formation of such independent organizations. Organizers, potential local leaders, and prospective members are all relatively vulnerable to the negative sanctions available to the local broker or patron, who often enjoys the cooperation of other local authorities. Second, clientelist patterns of behavior frequently exist in the relationship between peasant union leader and follower.[42] For both of these reasons, peasant unions tend to be part of a clientele system organized from above rather than a bargaining organization initiated from below.

The burden of this essay has been to explain the transformation of patron-client ties from a strictly local, landlord-peasant relationship of a traditional kind, into a complex, relatively modernized national transaction system. The main point has been that clientelist patterns of behavior persist in modern organizational form, and that an explanation of interpersonal or institutional behavior will be significantly enhanced by understanding the nature of clientelist politics. The fact that achievement criteria become more important in filling patron and brokerage roles is not inconsistent with the maintenance of traditional values embodied in the ascriptive-oriented traditional forms of clientelism. In fact, just as a relatively high power asymmetry promotes stability within clientele systems, the combination of traditional and modern value orientations in the "new" clientelism may function to perpetuate old forms in a manner quite consistent with modern organizational requirements. Seymour Martin Lipset, in discussing ways in which the Japanese have maintained particularistic and ascriptive traits while at the same time combining universalistic and achievement patterns into the elite recruitment process, illustrates how such a combination can function in a highly successful manner.[43] The example of Japanese industry, in fact, suggests that traditional patterns of behavior can be consistent with the requirements of a highly competitive environment. The implication which might flow from this would be that peasant-based transaction systems successfully perform in a competitive, modernizing political environment because of, not in spite of, the functionality of traditional practices and values.

The argument can be carried one step further. I would submit the proposition that certain traditional elements of the political culture, such as clientelism, become more, not less, important as modernizing changes take place in a peasant-based society. Evidence relevant to this proposition has been turned up repeatedly by social anthropologists studying the adaptation of peasant cultures to the stresses and tensions associated with socio-economic change. As Mintz and Wolf suggest in their analysis of *compadrazgo* (a fictive kinship tie) in Hispanic America:

It is extremely noteworthy that the mechanism of *compadrazgo* has maintained itself here in the face of what appears to be progressively accelerating social change. We wonder whether the elaborations of the mechanism's forms may be part of the community's unconscious effort to answer new problems. It must increasingly face the insecurity of growing incorporation into the national structure and increasing local wage-based, cash crop competition. This may call forth an increased emphasis on techniques for maintaining and strengthening face-to-face relationships.[44]

Further evidence that change increases reliance on certain traditional practices was found by Wolf in Mexico. In his study of the changing intergroup relations of Mexican Indian communities, he took note of the "tendency of new group relationships to contribute to the preservation of traditional cultural forms."[45] Myron Weiner's findings in India were also consistent with the proposition advanced above. In *The Politics of Scarcity*, he noted the strong tendency of post-independence political change to bring about marked increases in the activities of traditional community associations of various kinds. These associations were relied on to link village interests with the emerging structures of a modern nation-state.[46]

In short, modernizing transformations in

peasant societies may well make the study and analysis of clientelist politics more relevant than ever before.[47] While scholars generally acknowledge the importance of patrimonial-type behavior in traditional politics, both at the mass and at the elite levels, there may be insufficient appreciation of the fact that such behavior may survive, quite functionally, very late into the developmental process. Much of the evidence presented here has concerned the nature of such behavior in local politics, but I have also tried to demonstrate the importance of clientelist politics as an organizing principle at all levels of developing polities. Whether or not, and to what degree clientelism exists; whether it functions at the level of the village or throughout the polity; and what impact such behavior has on the course and pace of political development are significant, if not critical, empirical questions in the study of politics in peasant-based societies.

NOTES

*I am grateful for the support of the Center for International Affairs, Harvard University, during the development of this analysis; and I wish to thank the many individuals who were helpful at various stages of its preparation, including Professors James Kurth, Joan Nelson, Samuel Huntington, and various members of the joint Harvard-MIT faculty Seminar on Political Development to whom the original version was presented in 1968. An intermediate version of this essay was presented at the convention of the American Political Science Association in New York, September, 1969.

1 Consider the interesting results of Thematic Apperception Tests given to peasant respondents in Southern Italy, reported in Edward Banfield, *The Moral Basis of a Backward Society* (New York: Free Press, 1958), ch. 6.

2 George Foster, "Peasant Society and the Image of the Limited Good," in *Peasant Society: A Reader* (Boston: Little, Brown, 1967), edited by Potter, Diaz, and Foster, p. 304. This is a very useful collection of materials.

3 On anxiety-reduction as the most powerful organizer of behavior, see Harry Stack Sullivan's *The Interpersonal Theory of Psychiatry*, as applied by Robert Presthus in *The Organizational Society*(New York: A. Knopf, 1962), esp. ch. 4.

4 See, among others, C. K. Yang, *A Chinese Village in Early Communist Transition* (Cambridge: MIT Press, 1959), ch. 6.

5 *Peasant Society, op. cit.*, contains reprints of several good articles dealing with fictive kinship systems and their effects, including Sidney Mintz and Eric Wolf, "An Analysis of Ritual Co-Parenthood *(Compadrazgo)*," pp. 174-199, and Mary Hollensteiner, "Social Structure and Power in a Philippine Municipality," pp. 200-212.

6 Foster, "Image of the Limited Good," *op. cit.*, p. 316. Also, see Eric Wolf, "Closed Corporate Peasant Communities in Mesoamerica and Central Java," pp. 230-246 in the same volume; and Mehmet Bequiraj, *Peasantry in Revolution* (Ithaca: Cornell Center for International Studies, 1966).

7 Two exceptional treatments of the phenomenon in question are found in Alex Weingrod, "Patrons, Patronage and Political Parties," *Comparative Studies in Society and History*, Vol. 10 (July 1968), pp. 376-400; and James C. Scott, "Corruption, Machine Politics, and Political Change," this *Review*, LXII (December, 1969), 1142-1158.

8 Julian Pitt-Rivers, *The People of the Sierra* (New York: Criterion Books, 1954), p. 140.

9 For an elegant and fascinating exploration of the varieties of power relationships, see Frederick W. Frey, "Concepts of Development Administration and Strategy Implications for Behavioral Change," unpublished ms, Department of Political Science, MIT.

10 Sydel Silverman, "The Community-Nation Mediator in Traditional Central Italy," in *Peasant Society, op. cit.*, p. 284.

11 *Ibid.*, p. 285.

12 These processes are illuminated and applied with excellent effect by Charles Tilly in *The Vendée* (Cambridge: Harvard University Press, 1964), especially ch. 2.

13 "Gatekeepers," as described by Kenny, "largely dominate the paths linking the local infrastructure of the village to the superstructure of the outside urban world." See his article "Patterns of Patronage in Spain," in the *Anthropological Quarterly*, 33 (January 1960), pp. 14-23.

14 Eric Wolf, "Aspects of Group Relations in a Complex Society: Mexico," in *Contemporary Cultures and Societies of Latin America* (New York: Random House, 1965), edited by Dwight Heath and Richard Adams, p. 97. (Italics added)

15 Latin America, China, and Japan cited by Wolf, *ibid*. A full treatment of *clientela* in Italy is given by Sidney Tarrow, *Peasant Communism in Southern Italy* (New Haven: Yale, 1967). For India, see Lewis and Barnouw, "Caste and the Jajmani System in a North Indian Village," in *Peasant Society, op. cit.*, pp. 110-134. The Philippine materials are presented by Carl Landé in *Leaders, Factions and Parties—The Structure of Philippine Politics* (New Haven: Yale University Southeast Asian Studies, 1965), Monograph No. 6.

16 Ernestine Friedl, "The Role of Kinship in the Transmission of National Culture to Rural Villages in Mainland Greece," *American Anthropologist*, 61 (Feb. 1959), 30-38; and Joseph Lopreato, *Peasants*

No More (San Francisco: Chandler, 1967), Part Two.

17 In *Peasant Society*, op. cit., pp. 279-293.

18 *Ibid.*, p. 289.

19 Belden Paulson, "The Role of the Small Intellectual as an Agent of Political Change: Brazil, Italy, and Wisconsin," paper delivered at the American Political Science Association annual meeting in Chicago, September, 1967.

20 Originally published in the *American Anthropologist*, 58 (December, 1956), 1065-1078.

21 See Eric Wolf, *Peasants* (Englewood Cliffs: Prentice-Hall, 1966), especially "Types of Domain," pp. 50-59.

22 Edgar Shor, "The Thai Bureaucracy," *Administrative Science Quarterly*, 5 (June, 1960), pp. 70, 77, 80, as cited in Guenther Roth, "Personal Rulership, Patrimonialism, and Empire-Building in the New States," *World Politics* 20 (January, 1968), p. 202.

23 Roth, *ibid.*, p. 203.

24 *Ibid.*, p. 196. For vestiges of such behavior in complex societies, see Eric Wolf, "Kinship, Friendship, and Patron-Client Relations in Complex Societies," in *The Social Anthropology of Complex Societies* (New York: Praeger, 1966), edited by Michael Banton, pp. 1-22. An excellent study of clientelist politics in administration is Anthony Leeds, "Brazilian Careers and Social Structures: An Evolutionary Model and Case History," reprinted in Heath & Adams, *Contemporary Cultures, op. cit.*, pp. 379-404.

25 Roth, *op. cit.*, p. 196.

26 It would be a mistake, however, to assume that inter-broker competition automatically increases the power of the client in relation to the broker or patron. Individual brokers and/or patrons tend to control different resources, not to have differential control over the same resources. Furthermore, competition may occur in terms of the number of peasant votes, but not necessarily for the votes of the same peasants. Each broker tends to mobilize the votes of the peasants over whom he has some kind of critical leverage. Indeed, inter-broker competition may lead to less bargaining power for the client, rather than more, as for example the case of a peasant who finds himself within the power domain of a landlord, a moneylender, and a storekeeper, all of whom pressure him to vote in accord with their particular preferences. In short, the degree of power asymmetry between patron and client or broker, and client is a matter for empirical enquiry; and if there is no asymmetry, the relationship in question is not clientelism.

27 Adrian Mayer, "The Significance of Quasi-Groups in the Study of Complex Societies," in *The Social Anthropology of Complex Societies, op. cit.*, p. 103. (emphasis added). Note that at this point we might break down brokers into at least three types, or specialists: one, a grass-roots mobilizer, or "ward-heeler"; two, a pure broker, of the kind found on the floor of a stock exchange; and three, a high level influence peddler. The mobilizer can turn out the bodies for any particular purpose, the influence peddler locates political patrons who desire mass political services, and the pure broker brings them together in the political market place. Note also the cross-class–cutting nature of this process. In a significant sense, it functions to integrate actors high and low in the social hierarchy, thereby serving as a potential buffer to inter-class conflict.

28 See Sidney Tarrow, *op. cit.*; and John Duncan Powell, *Peasant Mobilization and Agrarian Reform in Venezuela* (Cambridge: Harvard University Press, forthcoming).

29 See John Duncan Powell, "Venezuela: The Peasant Union Movement," in *Latin American Peasant Movements* (Ithaca: Cornell University Press, 1969), edited by Henry Landsberger, pp. 62-100.

30 For the proposition that the degree of tenancy correlates positively—and highly—with radical or revolutionary action on the part of the peasantry, see Arthur Stinchcombe, "Agricultural Enterprise and Rural Class Relations," reprinted in *Political Development and Social Change (New York: Wiley, 1966), edited by Finkle and Gable, pp. 485-497*. The same point is made by Bruce Russett in "Inequality and Instability: The Relation of Land Tenure to Politics," in *World Politics*, 16 (April, 1964), p. 452, when tenancy is combined with a high degree of inequality in landholdings.

31 In the December 1968 elections COPEI won the presidency and hence control over the formation of a subsequent coalition government from which AD was excluded. As of this date, therefore, access of the two parties is the reverse of the 1964-1968 situation.

32 Tarrow, *Peasant Communism, op. cit.*, p. 364.

33 See Peter P. Lord, "The Peasantry as an Emerging Political Factor in Mexico, Bolivia, and Venezuela," (Madison: University of Wisconsin Land Tenure Center, 1965), Research Paper No. 35 (mimeo.); and Charles Erasmus, "Upper Limits of Peasantry and Agrarian Reform: Bolivia, Venezuela, and Mexico Compared," in *Ethnology*, 6 (October, 1967), 349-380.

34 Samuel P. Huntington, *Political Order in Changing Societies* (New Haven: Yale University Press, 1968), p. 437.

35 Tarrow, *Peasant Communism, op. cit.*, p. 261.

36 *Ibid.*, p. 270.

37 *Ibid.*, pp. 308-309.

38 Huntington, *op. cit.*, especially the first and last chapters.

39 *Ibid.*, p. 77.

40 In my study of local peasant union leaders in Venezuela, it was found that 79.9% of all contacts between local and state leaders were in the nature of personal visits. Even contacts with national level peasant union leaders were predominantly in the nature of personal visits (33.1%), rather than through correspondence (11.9%) or other means.

41 Wolf, "Kinship, Friendship, and Patron-Client Relations in Complex Societies," in *The Social Anthropology of Complex Societies, op. cit.*, p. 10.

42 For a concise picture of such relationships in the Brazilian Peasant Leagues, see Benno Galjart, "Class and 'Following' in Rural Brazil," *America Latina*, 7 (July-September, 1964), 3-23.

43 Seymour Martin Lipset and Aldo Solari (eds.), *Elites in Latin America* (New York: Oxford University Press, 1967), pp.42-44. See also Anthony Leeds. "*Brazilian Careers . . .*" *op. cit.*, and Charles Wagley, "Luso-Brazilian Kinship Patterns: The Persistence of a Cultural Tradition," in *Politics of Change in Latin America* (New York: Praeger, 1964), edited by Maier and Weatherhead, pp. 174-189.

44 Sidney Mintz and Eric Wolf, "An Analysis of Ritual Co-Parenthood *(Compadrazgo)*," in *Peasant Society, op. cit.*, p. 194.

45 Eric Wolf, "Aspects of Group Relations in a Complex Society: Mexico," in *Contemporary Cultures and Societies of Latin America, op. cit.*, p. 96.

46 Myron Weiner, *The Politics of Scarcity* (Chicago: The University of Chicago Press, 1962), especially pp. 36-72.

47 In fact, such a literature seems about to emerge. For example, Professors René Lemarchand and Keith Legg of the University of Florida presented an excellent comparative study, "Clientelism and Politics: A Preliminary Analysis," to the members of the joint Harvard-MIT faculty Seminar on Political Development in February, 1970. The paper is planned for early publication.

THE CORPORATION AND THE ENTOURAGE:
A Comparison of Thai and American Social Organization
L. M. HANKS

IN 1957 a mission from the International Bank of Reconstruction and Development surveyed Thailand in order to launch a program of economic development. A broad report followed from which I quote the following:

Government administration presents its own additional problems. Predominance of political considerations over those of efficiency and economy is not, of course, peculiar to Thailand. But there is also a tenacious adherence in the administration to traditional practices and to status relationships which tend to diffuse authority and responsibility, to de-emphasize the need for special training and competence, and to prevent the establishment and exercise of efficient procedures . . .[1]

Further on the mission adds:

Good organization requires, that, as a general rule, where a particular function needs to be performed, a specific governmental unit be made responsible for it. Otherwise (unless the task in question is quite minor), either the work will not get done, or it will be intermingled with other tasks and be done half-heartedly. Thus we have already stressed the planning function, and recommended an organization to perform it.[2]

And

Establishing a well-designed agency to do a job, however, does not mean that it will be done properly. An 'agency' is simply a group of people with definite duties and responsibilities, and unless they are energetic rather than lazy, re-

sponsible instead of irresponsible, and competent as opposed to incompetent, their performance will be poor. Better recruitment practices can help remedy these defects.[3]

Thus runs a portion of the mission's observations about governmental management. The report pronounces its judgment in the carefully unoffending manner of a physician prescribing for his sick patient.

In this paper I am contending that the members of this mission were simply meeting for the first time an unfamiliar social arrangement. I can imagine that they, like any visiting westerners, expected the head bookkeepers in the ministry they were visiting to inform them on over-all income and expenditures. When the records were found to be imprecise and the directors knew little about the arrangements of the books, the mission was disconcerted. When no other source of information could help them, the mission was flabbergasted. Managerial responsibility and efficiency were being flouted on every side. How could a modern state keep operating thusly? Fortunately, despite the reservations in the mission's report, the board of governors of the Bank decided to advance the needed funds. Thailand's economic growth was one of the most substantial of Southeast Asia;[4] by now the additional funds at work over five years, have accelerated the upward movement of economic indices.[5]

No information about miraculous changes in the operation of Thai enterprises or governmental agencies has reached me, and were there any such reports, I would doubt their credibility. Thai social organization and hence governmental procedures work well but are not like ours. Thus it seems important to understand their mode of operation. I shall describe them, using the term *entourage*, instead of Wilson's *clique*.[6] Here is the Thai equivalent of our corporation, the building block of social activity, an ubiquitous arrangement which Wilson described only as the one "ruling clique." I shall first show the workings of an entourage, then describe it in its social setting, and finally develop the position that an entourage can operate in an industrial order.

TWO MODES OF ORGANIZATION

The American, and in fact, the occidental, corporation is a voluntary association of 'equals' banding together to accomplish some mutually desired end. However much their wealth or social position may tip the balance of equality, they are equals in their interest to further a common endeavor, perhaps also equals before the law and God. As individuals they could not have achieved their ends, whether keeping the peace in some territory, manufacturing airplanes, promoting fraternal love, or advancing the appreciation of archery. Within the corporation, authority must be vested in an individual or group. Then as the tasks are subdivided according to function, the group delegates limited authority to the treasurer, the secretary, the foreman, etc. Carrying out these functionally arranged tasks achieves the corporate end. So commonplace is this kind of organization to us that we assume it to occur everywhere.

Let us, however, now consider the entourage. It too, affirms that an individual cannot achieve as much as a group, but it binds together not equals in status but unequals. Thai see no advantage in associating people with identical resources: a landowner wishing to plant a crop should not seek out another landowner but some hungry waif willing to help. When this landowner has all the people working for him that he can support, his entourage is complete. His group has no necessary goal, unless it be contented living. Its activities vary from day to day, month to month, for living requires meeting a wide variety of circumstances. All members take their orders directly from the leader and may work quite independently of each other. Jobs are assigned roughly according to status, so that the more arduous and unpleasant tasks go to inferiors. In general such a mode of

organization suggests Louis XIV at Versailles, surrounded by princes, generals, musicians and mistresses; his entourage built palaces, fought wars, staged operas and *bals masqués*.

If we use the Thai version as our standard, King Louis' entourage diverged in several important features. Inevitably his was a corporation, and as much as it may have injured his dignity, Louis had to acknowledge that his power was derived and not of his own. All corporations derive their authority from above, be it the covenant made on Mount Sinai, a charter from Queen Elizabeth to trade in the Indies, or just a license from City Hall for selling plastic dolls on Main Street. The corporate world has grown sensitive to questions about due process in gaining authority, insists on clear definition of jurisdiction, and curtails appeals to alternative authorities. Our rich vocabulary of usurpers, imposters, pretenders, charlatans, quacks, fakers, etc., suggests our concern with legitimate authority as well as our uneasiness before it and our will to circumvent it. Indeed, we prefer to discuss *authority* rather than *power*, which tends to become bestial and unclad.

The Thai meet authority with much less tension than we do, though not because official wrath is pleasanter or justice more merciful. Thai speak forthrightly of power, saying it arises from virtue, or, to use the Buddhist term, *merit*. The higher the status in the social hierarchy, the greater the piety and wisdom.[7] Though misuse of power is as familiar as in any land, the Thai faith in cosmic retribution remains undisturbed. Cruel tyrants will be reborn as mangy dogs. Those who are trapped by tyranny are not martyrs but persons deserving of punishment because of misdeeds in previous existences. So power arises from unknowable sources, and effectiveness becomes the main criterion for judging its magnitude. All watch a rising young man to see how far he will go; the extent of his rise rather than a carefully marked jurisdiction, determines the limits of his power. The inscriptions from rediscovered southeast Asian kingdoms contain no hint of an authorization to rule.[8] Instead they testify solely to the strength, bravery, piety and capacity of the monarch to bring prosperity to the people.

Admission to a corporation takes place by being accepted to carry out a certain task for which the candidate must produce evidence of his competence. The employer then contracts to give specific services. If either party seriously violates the agreement, the contract is void.

Some one seeking to join an entourage is ordinarily introduced to the leader by a mutual acquaintance who seeks to match the interests of the two parties. The initial relationship may be contract-like and limited, to mend a plow in return for money, or to build a wharf in return for the use of a boat. If trust and affection grow from these beginnings, the liaison passes toward an uncalculable exchange of benefits, as if the two had become kinsmen. A business man told me of his chauffeur who, after several years in his employ, stole valuables. Instead of rebuking or dismissing the chauffeur, the business man quietly instructed the members of his household not to leave tempting valuables around. When mutual attraction continues, the liaison may endure much torment. However, should either party become convinced that mutual advantage has disappeared, he may end the relationship. Law offers no recourse for the offended.

As no one in an entourage contributes identically, each member occupies a special position and receives unique benefits. Indeed, the returns from living for mutual benefit, as between amiable spouses, are difficult to reduce to any single feature, nor are they constant, like wages and working conditions. This week's food, spending money, jokes and good times are never the same as those of last week. The general rule, nevertheless, applies that those who are more esteemed receive richer benefits, yet the coolie as well as the computer operator may petition for remedy of his grievance. Rivalry between members may provide back-stabbing intrigue until harmony has been restored, yet no one argues that because another enjoys a benefit, he should have it too.

Unlike their corporate counterparts, leaders of entourages cannot shunt responsibility to an underling. The initiator assumes full responsibility. Even when an underling negligently fails a specifically delegated task, a leader would be unwise to censure him. Anyone able to speak frankly may simply ask, "If you wished the job done well, why did you pick the man you just called stupid?" Failure raises awkward questions of the limits of a leader's power and wisdom. Praise may be used unstintingly but censure rarely, for the health of an entourage depends upon successful ventures.

Life has many long waits, and so an entourage need not function continuously. The presence of idle persons in an office disturbs no one. In fact the leader who continuously drives his members may find them disappearing. Yet an entourage must be able to demonstrate its vitality in an emergency. I was staying in a remote and sleepy governmental agency when the leader, after many days of absence, returned at 2 AM with the terrifying news of an impending visit by a very important dignitary. Since the leader's reputation was at stake, the entire personnel rose from bed to scrub, polish and ready the place. By 10 *AM*, when the distinguished visitor arrived, all stood smiling in their pressed uniforms ready to receive him. Without specific contracts to work a given number of hours per day or to receive extra pay for additional work, an entourage is ready any time for any kind of work.

The life of an entourage is limited by the life of its leader. Most entourages dwindle before a leader retires or his fortune ebbs. Succession is impossible. The member with the greatest resources may attempt to take over, but he must make his own arrangements with the members and probably he cannot hold them all. While some speak of royal succession, according to Wales[9] a law of succession, taken over from the Cambodians, was rarely used. Thai Kings tried to appoint their successors, yet the effectiveness of the royal wishes depended on the outcome of struggles between palace entourages. Perhaps it is a semantic as well as a metaphysical question whether a new kingdom appears at the beginning of each new reign. The palace and realm remained the same, and ordinarily the successor was of royal birth, but the list of new appointments was enormous. The lucky ones received a ministry, the less lucky, governorships of provinces, for it was men and the men they commanded, not land, that determined the strength of the new regime.

ENTOURAGES AND THEIR SETTINGS

It should now be easy to identify Thai entourages, whether in the coastal plains or the mountains. The leaders assume full responsibility, while members, acting independently of each other, work at no necessarily fixed task but with type of work limited by status. They are units of total living held together by a leader's acumen.

The architectural manifestation of an entourage is the compound. For instance, the Thai Tobacco monopoly is organized into compounds containing several hundred members, if we count dependents as well. This is a governmental agency which grows, buys, processes and sends tobacco to its main factory in Bangkok. A wall pierced by occasional gates encloses perhaps 10 to 20 acres of land. Within the wall, as in commercial enterprises the world over, are offices, warehouses, and garages. However, there are also houses for many of the office staff and workers. Between the buildings are fruit and shade trees as well as flower gardens. A little apart are guest houses for visitors. After hours the westernized office staff plays tennis, if there is a court, while the work force plays *takraw*, kicking around a rattan ball in the parking area.

At the guest house a custodian cares for the rooms, sees to the laundry and prepares the meals. For him this is a concession rather than a job. To be sure, he receives a wage for his work, but whenever he buys food or sends out clothes to be washed, he charges the visitors and takes his cut. During good months he may double or triple his wage. Knowing nothing about the entourage, a westerner might read corruption into these actions. The fact is that the manager has arranged the job to include these perquisites. Other employees enjoy, for example, the use of company automobiles after hours.

Out in the country a single family dwelling with parents, children, a nephew or two, or an aging grand parent forms a smaller and poorer entourage. All work together under the head of the household to raise a crop of rice and live jointly from the returns through the rest of the year. If hard times come, the man lowest on the status ladder will be regretfully asked to leave, and all the others must work harder to make up for his absence. A parent may place a child with some sister or brother in another household until good times return. Some may go off to earn wages, when the season is slack, and contribute their earnings to the leader of the entourage.

Anyone walking through the market of a town sees to right and left the stores that sell pots and pans, cloth and stationery. But these are not just shops. At night, when the shutters are closed, the shop is a bedroom, and, several times through the day, the dining room. So, too, the movie theatre is not just a functional theatre, but houses a few who tidy the premises before the next show, paint eye-trapping pictures of coming attractions, and drum them through the streets to draw the crowds. So the entourage forms its space for living, larger for a larger entourage.

Though the various gates, fences and walls enclose a group rather neatly, the precise functional boundaries of an entourage are more difficult to establish. A leader engages in intercourse with certain persons more frequently than with others. The warmth of affection and degree of mutual trust varies, so that one may speak of gradients of intercourse within an entourage. At the outer fringe stand perhaps the boat maker or the radio repairman with whom occasional, more or less contractual dealings take place. Yet these persons may become close members of an entourage, should circumstances change or they may move off. The entourage is continuously reknitting the loose outer fringe more tightly and releasing the claims on other members.

The tissue of Thai society is made by joining entourages together. The capitalist who constructs a market building brings together a dozen or more tiny entourages of shopkeepers together under his roof. The landowner constructs his entourage with the entourages of his tenants. If he so chooses, the possibly perfunctory relations of landlord to tenant can become affectionate and endearing. If the status differences between leader and follower are small, the newly formed entourage tends to be short-lived. In the early days of one agricultural community, a certain man organized a village by being the sole owner of a plow and water buffalo, but the village broke up a few years later when prosperity brought plows and buffaloes to others. Of course, many a rice crop is harvested by householders of equal resources exchanging days of work, but they are careful to give the owner of the field the special status of leader for the day. Then he does no field work but oversees the feeding of the workers. When prosperity comes, however, most seek to increase their own entourages, perhaps by hiring a hand, saying it is hard to criticize a neighbor. Criticism is unpalatable in any circumstance, as we have seen, but the leader likes to be able to select the best available man for the job.

It would be tempting to summarize Thai social synthesis by saying: The greater the status difference between two entourages, the better they mesh. In practice there seems to arise an optimal difference. A woodcutter from the forest seeking to join a prince would probably be rebuffed by some member of the immediate entourage. Ordinarily a lowly person must reach the high through one or more intermediaries, and then it would seem ridiculous that anything a woodcutter might need could not be handled as well by a less elevated personage. So the extremes rarely meet, and more effective connections lie a few short steps up or down the hierarchy.

By dint of such optimal differences, entourages interlock into many layers. Toward the top are the larger and wealthier ones: the single capitalist with interest in a bank, an export firm, a radio station, and a rice mill. The managers of these enterprises are in his entourage, and in turn each manager forms an entourage among his employees. The changes within each give freedom for personal mobility. Thereby the capitalist may promote the boy, who once unloaded sacks on the wharf, from a position he achieved in the rice mill to manager of the radio station.

At the summit of society lies the most complex and largest entourage, namely government. Its entourage character appears clearest in its old form of a century or more ago. Students have despaired at finding functional divisions of government. Instead they have found ministers with perplexing titles performing a variety of more or less overlapping tasks. Comparing one reign with another or searching back for the expected clarity of the original form only increases the mystery.[10] Some positions like the second king or *uparath* seemed to do nothing. On one point all agree: the titles were hierarchically arranged and carried varied degrees of honor. This is precisely the backbone of an entourage: a variety of statuses without predetermined duties.

With each title went a concession, the size of which was determined by rank. A member of the royal entourage received the right to collect revenues in a certain area or run an enterprise, thus enabling him to live in a manner befitting his rank. Each official then subdivided his concession among the members of his own entourage. As long as they continued to pass in some portion of their tax receipts and could maintain the local peace, the kingdom was governed.

Subsequent occidental reforms have increased the size of bureaucracy, centralized the administration, and multiplied the divisions of government. They have not, however, converted it into a set of functionally differentiated corporate units each performing a limited task. During the 1950s the police enjoyed tanks, planes and armed boats, becoming the fourth armed unit of the nation. Many ministries and departments operated their own radio and television stations, despite the existence of a Public Relations Department; others have their own communications systems despite postal and telegraph services. The mission from the International Bank was well aware of these and many other duplications when it said, "Too many ministries are trying to do the same thing . . ."[11] The mission further reported on the heads of ministries and departments: "A further cause of inefficiency in the public service is the habit of passing all questions upward for decision. This results in great delays . . ."[12] On questions of placement the mission noted the lack of functional definition of jobs: "As already noted, great stress is laid on foreign degrees as such, without much regard to the kind or quality of the training they represent. Job descriptions, which outline the responsibilities and qualifications of various positions, are virtually non-existent."[13]

Such observations reveal the entourage behind the facade of functional government. Each member of the governmental entourage has received his concession which he uses to support his own following. A casual observer might easily mistake what was going on for a western corporate kind of action. Only if he had been present at the inception, would he perhaps be aware that the undertaking had begun without authorization from a superior source. Yet even then, had it begun under formal order, it would have seemed very much like a corporate delegation of responsibility. Then the shape of the entourage might be apparent only from the assumption of total responsibility by the leader, the absence of job specifications, and the variety of collateral activities.

Entourages set the arrangement of towns and cities. Bangkok, for instance, appears shapeless and sprawling; there is no center, no factory, no shopping, nor clear residential section. Only after several months does one come to realize that the city falls into village-like sections. Around a market lie the residences of tailors, barbers, shoe makers, and whoever is needed to make a village complete. In some of these villages there still remains the house compound of the leader of an entourage who built the stores that now enclose his compound. Government never scrupled to clear away one or more of these villages to found a temple, and when the wave of occidentalization began, it ploughed through many to make streets, excised holes to build monuments, and cleared away others entirely for government buildings. So government entourages lie above and shape the entourages beneath them in the hierarchy.

At the center of Thai society all looks eventextured and finely knit. The village clusters, whether in the city or countryside, do not differentiate into public and private domains. They do not section into slums, factories or residential areas, for the poor, the workers, and the entrepreneur live together. So villages succeed each other, one after the other, thinning out gradually on approaching the borders of the kingdom. Even before the borders, at forest and hill, the government entourage radiates no farther, and the fringe of the country, like the fringe of an entourage, raggedly yields to scattered knots of ne'er do wells, brigands and alien people, who go their own way.

THE ENTOURAGE IN AN INDUSTRIAL SETTING

If the entourage is the building block of Thai society, will it not disappear with increased westernization and industrialization? In the American scene our cities and countryside contained units of living until well after the 1860s:

the family farm, the general store, the grist mill. Specialization, better transportation, and cost accounting have all contributed to the demise of these arrangements. May we not anticipate a repetition of this tale in Thailand?

In view of what has already been said, my answer must be "no." Nearly a century of western pressures on Thailand have not changed the entourage. Though America of a century ago resembles modern Thailand, the direction of development differs. America responded to industrialization by developing more specialized corporate units. Thailand, with its particular kind of culture, proliferated more entourages and built them into higher layers.

The essentials in the very process of industrialization, of course, remain uncertain. I assume that the diffusion of industrialization will be no more disturbing than was the spread of Christianity or Islam. Each society, maintaining its own type of organization, absorbs and gives a local style to the new, like the difference between fiestas of Spain and Mexico, between Ramadan in Egypt and Malaysia. Others, however, see in industrialization a revolution which will wipe away the entourage and replace it with new kinds of organization. The advocates of this view state that Thailand still has no less than 75% of its population engaged in agriculture and so has not felt the full brunt of the changes to come. There are other views as well. Nevertheless, I shall indicate within these limits some of the ways that entourages are adapting to industrialization.

Specialization of function seems to present no difficulties to an entourage. Thailand enjoys banks and bus lines, public utilities and factories conducting their affairs with dispatch. As I have already observed, they are not the lean functional institutions of the west, but units of living, where employees and employer may play badminton and celebrate the New Year together. The real head may not be present at all, having left the operation to a local manager. In fact the leader of this entourage may have as varied a range of enterprises as a mammoth American corporation forced to diversify before the threat of antitrust suits. The entourage is like a holding company, with its many operations, though it never keeps books. The financial soundness of the operations might be approximated by running through a dozen ledgers, for with extra capital always available from the pockets of the leader, each enterprise is not the isolatable unit that accountants must assume. So the ledgers, kept for other purposes, tell little about profit or loss, and on the basis of these records a western

accountant could probably not judge operational efficiency. We can best follow the local example in sizing up the success of an operation by the acumen of its leader.

More difficult for an entourage is the development of a steady supply of skilled workers, for the ordinary methods of training people in sufficient numbers do not work. Today the Thai educational system is grinding out hundreds of carpenters, electricians, engineers, etc., but these are statuses in an occupational ladder rather than occupational groupings. No one chooses his occupation but is sorted into it by examination. Those who pass all at the highest point become physicians; those next in line become engineers, and so on down to the left-overs who have to farm because they can do nothing else. As soon as they have gained access to work through their skills, all seek to improve their positions by abandoning the skill in which they were trained. Only the top of the hierarchy remains faithful to its training. So workers learn on the job to acquire the minimum skills for the next job. The skilled mechanic, rather than blacken his own hands, directs his entourage of assistants to assemble the newly repaired motor. Since no one harbors trade secrets in order to hold his job, some may become very competent, yet few apply their skills constantly enough to become *virtuosi*. Without many dependable skills a factory must improvise, and the quality of its output depends on morale and the leader's ability to make clear that the best efforts redound to the benefit of all.

Industrialization requires the careful coordination of many processes. Certainly today's factory is of western origin, designed by corporate hands for corporately oriented populations. The corporation assumes a constant output because the machines must pay for themselves, and the product be sold to pay the wages and profit. So a given number of carloads of raw materials comes daily to the plant to keep the machines running. If, however, continuous maximum output is not important, the coordination may be less precise. A Thai boss need not wring his hands nor send his men home because a machine cannot be operated. The men may work on some other job, and if they merely go fishing, having fresh fish for dinner in every house is also a gain for an entourage. The rate of output may vary widely, but no one need complain that men are being run by machines.

Inevitably questions of efficiency arise, and I have no doubt that a pair of entourage shoes picked at random from the pile will cost more and may be of poorer quality than my present corporate pair. Where artistry is concerned, the product may be better where workers pay no heed to time. Even appealing to unit cost, the corporately organized skills do not always prove more efficient. Compare the installation that once could be done reasonably well by a jack-of-all-trades with the same done today by the joint efforts of three or more highly paid skills. Functionally organized production may or may not reckon the cost of strikes and law suits that are necessary to keep production flowing. How much does it add to the cost of our products to maintain roads and vehicles so that we can distinguish between a place of work and a place of living? We have not shown in the balance sheet the many specialized institutions which our society must have to keep the factories running: the educational system that keeps children away from the factory; the homes for the aged that take care of the retired; the hospitals that care for the sick; the relief that cares for the unemployed, unemployables, and technologically displaced. Our measures of efficiency, like our measures of beauty, best fit the assumptions of a corporate system.

Despite all the borrowing of machines and institutions from the West, Thailand may never become a great industrial nation. It seems predetermined to organize itself for living rather than for functionally isolatable ends. Yet it may be able to produce abundance without blight. Perhaps it can capture the inventive imagination of Thais without dehumanizing them through monotony. Certainly it can arrange living beyond the threat of isolated loneliness, if industrialization is not the revolution that uproots a social order.

NOTES

1 International Bank for Reconstruction and Development, *A Public Development Program for Thailand; Report of a Mission Organized by the International Bank for Reconstruction and Development at the Request of the Government of Thailand*, (Baltimore: John Hopkins Press, 1959), p. 14.

2 *Ibid.*, p. 224.

3 *Loc. cit.*

4 See Douglas Paauw, "Economic Progress in Southeast Asia," *Journal of Asian Studies*, Vol. 23, (November 1963), pp. 69-92.

5 Economic Commission for Asia and Far East, *Economic Survey of Asia and the Far East 1962*, (New York: United Nations, 1963), pp. 82-88.

6 David Wilson, *Politics in Thailand*, (Ithaca, New York: Cornell University Press, 1962), pp. 116-117.

7 See L. M. Hanks, "Merit and Power in the Thai Social Order," *American Anthropologist*, Vol. 64, (1962), pp. 1247-1261.

8 See G. Coedés, *Receuil des Inscriptions du Siam Deuxième Partie*, (Bangkok: Siam Society, 1961).

9 M. G. Quaritch Wales, *Ancient Siamese Government and Administration*, (London: Bernard Quaritch, 1939), pp. 19-20.

10 See Walter F. Vella, *Siam Under Rama III*, (Locust Valley, New York: J. J. Augustin, 1957), pp. 14-15; Wales, *op. cit.*, pp. 84-87.

11 International Bank for Reconstruction and Development, *op. cit.*, p. 223.

12 *Ibid.*, p. 225.

13 *Ibid.*, p. 221.

KINSHIP, FRIENDSHIP, AND PATRON-CLIENT RELATIONS IN COMPLEX SOCIETIES

ERIC R. WOLF

CORE AND PERIPHERY IN COMPLEX SOCIETIES

THE ANTHROPOLOGIST'S study of complex societies receives its major justification from the fact that such societies are not as well organized and tightly knit as their spokesmen would on occasion like to make people believe. If we analyze their economic systems, we shall find in any one such society resources which are strategic to the system—and organizations set up to utilize these strategic resources—but we shall also find resources and organizations which are at best supplementary or wholly peripheral. If we drew these relations on a map, some areas would show strong concentrations of strategic resources and the accompanying core organizations; other areas would appear in grey or white, economic *terra incognita* from the point of view of the larger system. The same point may be made with regard to political control. There are political resources which are essential to the operation of the system, and the system will try to remain in control of these. But there are also resources and organizations which it would be either too costly or too difficult to bring under direct control, and in these cases the system yields its sovereignty to competitive groups that are allowed to function in its entrails. I shall argue that we must not confuse the theory of state sovereignty with the facts of political life. Many organizations within the state generate and distribute and control power, in competition with each other and with the sovereign power of the state. As examples one might cite the Teamsters' Union of the United States, the Mafia, or the American Medical Association. Thus we could also draw a map of political power for any complex society in which the key centers of control —Lenin's strategic heights—appeared in red— showing strong concentrations of sovereign power—while other political regions appeared as grey or white. We thus note that the formal framework of economic and political power exists alongside or intermingled with various other kinds of informal structure which are interstitial, supplementary, parallel to it. Even the study of major institutions, such as of the American and German armies during World War II, or of factories in Britain and the United States, or of bureaucratic organizations, has yielded statements about the functional importance of informal groups. Sometimes such informal groupings cling to the formal structure like barnacles to a rusty ship. At other times, informal social relations are responsible for the metabolic processes required to keep the formal institution operating, as in the case of armies locked in combat. In still other cases, we discover that the formal table of organization is elegant indeed, but fails to work, unless informal mechanisms are found for its direct contravention, as in the network of *blat* relationships among Soviet industrial managers.

The anthropologist has a professional license to study such interstitial, supplementary, and parallel structures in complex society and to expose their relation to the major strategic, overarching institutions. In this paper, I should like to focus on three sets of such parallel structures in complex societies: kinship, friendship, and patron-client relations. Since my fieldwork experience has been confined to Latin-America and to the European Mediterranean, my examples will be largely drawn from these areas, and my thinking will be based largely on these examples. I shall indicate where I think it could be extended to other areas, but I shall expect to hear that they cannot be applied universally.

We must not, of course, picture the structures of complex society as an ordered anarchy. The informal structures of which I have spoken are supplementary to the system: they operate and exist by virtue of its existence, which is logically, if not temporally, prior to them. Allow me to make use of Lewis Henry Morgan's dichotomy of *societas* and *civitas* to clarify my meaning. In *societas*, the principle of kinship embodies all or most strategic relations; in *civitas*, relations of political economy and ideology guide and curtail the functions of kinship. Let me caution that this is true more of kinship functions than of kinship form. Indeed we are learning a great deal about just how far or how little kinship mechanisms can be stretched and bent to accommodate different interests. Nevertheless we must recognize a polarity in function. Relations may still have kinship form, but no longer primarily kinship functions. Take, for example, the corporate patrilineages in pre-Communist Southeastern China, studied by Freedman (1958). These units combined a kinship dogma of organization with the functions of commercial corporate organizations.

CORPORATE KIN GROUPS IN COMPLEX SOCIETIES

We may, reasonably, at the outset of our discussion of kinship in complex societies, ask when it is that we might expect to find kinship units of a corporate kind. There are two such units. One is the shallow local landed descent group, usually associated with primogeniture, of the kind which recently drew my attention in my study of the South Tyrolese (Wolf, 1962). Using a hypothesis put forth by Marshall Sahlins for the occurrence of similar groups in Polynesia (1957, pp. 294-295), I should argue that such units are likely to persist where the successful conduct of the enterprise requires the control —within one economic unit—of a number of ecological resources. In the case of the South Tyrolese, these resources would be agricultural land, meadowland close enough to the homestead to receive additional sources of fertilizer, pasture on higher ground, and forest. Division of the property upon inheritance would, in such circumstances, tend to splinter the viable economic unit into fragments, none of which could be meaningfully exploited by itself.

The second kind of corporate kin unit for which we must account is the unilineal kinship corporation which transcends the local, three-or four-generation descent group. Thinking primarily of pre-Communist China and of the Near East, I would argue that such superlocal kinship corporations appear under two sets of conditions. The first of these concerns the mechanism regulating access to land. I would argue that where you gain access to land through paying rent, membership in a kinship coalition of the kind described would offer advantages in increasing one's ability to obtain and keep land, and to affect the terms of rent. Second, and equally important, membership in a kinship coalition would be advantageous in situations where the state delegated the taxing power and the execution of other demands to entities on the local level. Paying taxes through lineages or sub-lineages thus offers an opportunity to distribute the tax burden within the community on local terms, together with an ability to call on the protection and aid of these lineages. These two conditions, then, and perhaps also others which are not yet clear to me—the delegation of state fiscal power to entities lower down in the political hierarchy, coupled with the system which Hans Bobek (1962, pp. 233-240) has called 'rent-capitalism' —would favor the emergence of the large-scale kin coalitions which anthropologists call ranked unilineal corporate descent groups.

CORPORATE COMMUNITIES

I would invoke similar factors for the continued existence, in certain parts of the world, of what I have labeled elsewhere the closed corporate peasant community (Wolf, 1955, 1957). Such communities—and I am thinking here primarily of Middle America, but also of Central Java, the Russian mir, perhaps also the Near Eastern musha'a—occur in areas where the central power does not or cannot intervene in direct administration, but where certain collective tasks in taxation and corvée are imposed on the village as a whole, and where the local village retains or builds administrative devices of its own natural and social resources.

Both corporate kin groups and corporate peasant villages are growing fewer in the modern world. One is tempted to point out that historically the essential change in organizational forms leading from so-called traditional to modern societies lies in the elaboration—in the

Mediterranean world—of non-agricultural corporate units like the *maone* and *commenda* which—though originally commercial or artisan kinship organizations—developed the organizational potential of the corporate business structure.

Corporate kinship organization thus occurs where the groups involved have a patrimony to defend, and where the interests associated with this defense can best be served by the maintenance of such a coalition. Such groups, too, must restrict and regulate the affinal bond, in order to restrict the number of people who may have access to the patrimony through inheritance. Another function served by such restrictions and regulations of the affinal bond is to restrict the number of coalitions with other individuals that can be entered into by any one individual. The kinship coalition or the village coalition is thus made to override any coalitions which the individual may wish to form, by paying off affinal and consanguineal ties against each other.

INDIVIDUAL-CENTERED COALITIONS

In situations where land and labor become free commodities, such corporate kin coalitions tend to lose their monopolies over resources and personnel. Instead, the individual is 'freed' to enter into individual coalitions, to maximize his resources both in the economic field and in the marriage market. Increasing mobility, moreover, brings an increase in the number of possible combinations of resources, including varying combinations of knowledge and influence with access to goods or personnel. The theoretically unrestricted marriage market may thus be seen as offering increasingly wider choices of mates, thus providing the mechanisms for an increasing number of combinations of natural and social resources. In reality, however, the capacity to choose marriage mates is no more equal than the capacity to combine resources as commodities in the market. Theoretically, tycoon and beggarman may both have equal freedom to marry the king's daughter, just as both are free to sleep under the bridges of Paris. In actuality, however, we find that both access to resources and the capacity to maximize combinations through marriage relationships are unequally distributed throughout the social structure.

Different potentials for effecting combinations of resources will result in a different functional load for the marital tie and for the mobilization of kin, and hence also in different patterns of marriage. In the Creole areas of Latin-America, as among the inhabitants of urban slums, we may find a minimal capacity to effect resource combinations reflected in a predominant or co-dominant pattern of matrifocal family arrange-ments. Among personnel located at the apex of society and capable of great potential in making resource combinations, we shall find corporate-like restrictions upon marital alliances to mini-mize the outward and downward flow of re-sources. In between, we shall encounter a whole range of patterns, representing more or less sta-ble adjustments to possible combinations of goods, influence, knowledge, and power. Thus differential access to resources also leads to dif-ferences in the capacity for social maneuver, a differential capacity which is, in turn, reflected in differential patterns of marriage choice.

Seen from the perspective of resource distri-bution, the differential distribution of a popula-tion in terms of resources has been called the class system of a society. Seen from the perspec-tive of the anthropologist interested in kinship, overlapping circles of kin tend to cluster in what one might call kinship regions. To the extent that kinship bonds constitute one set of resources for an individual or a family, the distribution of kinship alliances forms one important criterion for demarcating the classes of a society. As Schumpeter has said, 'the family, not the physi-cal person, is the true unit of class and class theory' (1955, p. 113).

In this regard, anthropologists need to pay much more attention to the rise and fall of fami-lies than they have done in the past. The best material to date comes from China, where a number of studies show the rise of families to gentry status, as well as their subsequent decline (see, for instance, Fei, 1953; Hsu, 1948; Yang, 1945). Similarly, Pi-Sunyer has recently shown how in the Mexican town of Zamora a new elite of entrepreneurs, who rose by their bootstraps during the revolution to displace an older landed aristocracy, has nevertheless fathered a set of sons who—in the changed circumstances of their lives—model themselves on that older aris-tocracy, to the detriment of the parental enter-prises created by their self-educated and unpol-ished fathers (1962). I have, similarly, described how in Puerto Rico poor immigrants from Spain rose from rags to riches in the course of an ex-ploitative process, but how the sons of these im-migrants did not take up the parental enterprise. Instead, the father would send home to Spain for a poor young kinsman or youth from his home community, discipline him mercilessly in the tasks of business, turn him into a son-in-law, and pass the business on to him, rather than to the no-good sons (Wolf, 1956). Here, too, the anthropologist may follow Schumpeter's lead

and ask himself why and how some families rise and others fall, 'quite apart from accidents', as he says, 'to which we attribute a certain impor-tance but not the crucial role' (1955, p. 118).

PERSISTENT FUNCTIONS OF THE FAMILY

Nor is it at all self-evident, to this writer, why *families*—rather than some other kind of unit—should be the functional entities within kin circles and in connecting circles. If we do not regard the family as a natural group, then we must at least assay its functional capacity and range, to account for its continued persistence. One of its characteristics which continues to rec-ommend it is its ability effectively to unite a number of functions.

There are, of course, the usual functions of economic provisioning, socialization, the ex-change of sexual services, the bestowal of af-fect. Although each of these functions could be handled in segmented and institutionalized fash-ion by a separate institution, the family can per-form these multiple tasks in small units of output and in quick succession, with a relatively low cost and overhead. At any one time, the de-mands of a family represent only small-scale de-mands, for a quart of milk rather than for a rail-road car, a song rather than a jukebox, an aspirin rather than the output of Lever Brothers. More-over, these small-scale demands occur in quick succession, and involve a rapid shift of labor to meet them, a trip to the store to get a bottle for the baby when the old one breaks, followed by the preparation of peanut butter and jelly sand-wiches, followed by a game of chess. Maxi-mally efficient for the least amount of cost, therefore, the family is also maximally adaptive to changes in the conditions that define and cir-cumscribe its existence. This is especially im-portant, I believe, in families with meager re-sources where labor can be increased to meet variable demands—as when a man takes over an extra job to pay for a refrigerator or when the wife tends a sick baby all night—without incur-ring expenses other than the exploitation of self. Here we may also underline the fact that in its pursuit of multiple purposes, the family remains the multi-purpose organization *par excellence* in societies increasingly segmented into institu-tions with unitary purposes. As such it may have compensatory functions, in restoring to persons a wider sense of identity beyond that defined by unitary demands of the job, be this cutting cane on a Puerto Rican plantation or tightening nuts on bolts on an assembly line.

Let me make an additional point, however. It is notable that a relation continues to exist between the way in which a family carries out these multi-purpose tasks and the ways in which it is evaluated in the eyes of the larger community. The family not only performs all the tasks we have just described; it remains also, even where ties of kinship are highly diffuse, the bearer of virtue, and of its public reflection, reputation. Because the family involves the 'whole' man, public evaluations of a man are ultimately led back to considerations of his family. Moreover, any gross infringement of virtue by one of its members reflects on the amount of virtue held by the others. This virtue has two aspects, one horizontal, in relationship to class equals, one vertical or hierarchical, in relation to class groups above and below one's station. The horizontal aspect of virtue refers to the guarding of a family's reputation in equivalent relation to other people's reputations. Standards for evaluating reputations are culturally highly variable; yet in each society there exist vital indices for the relative ranking of reputations. These rankings define whom one can trust, whom one may marry. Invariably, they refer back to ways in which people handle their domestic affairs. Frequently, as in the European Mediterranean or among the Ladinos of Latin-America, reputation is tied to what is potentially its weakest link, the sexual behavior of one's womenfolk. The concept of honor, in its horizontal aspect, implies a fixed amount of reputation for each contestant in the game of honor, an amount which can be lessened or increased in competitive interaction with others. Such interaction establishes one's social credit rating, a rating in which intrafamilial behavior is the final referent. Moreover, past familiar behavior has important bearing on present and future evaluation. This element is sometimes missed in the discussion of societies characterized by bilateral kinship arrangements. The maintenance of a family 'name', the importance of family 'names', even in situations where genealogical reckoning is weak or shallow, make less sense when thought of in terms of patrilineal or matrilineal filiation than in terms of the storage and enlargement of virtue for each family. What has been said here of horizontal virtue holds with increased intensity for members of ranked class groups. The point is obvious and need not be labored in this context.

COOPERATION OF KIN IN NON-KIN SITUATIONS

Not only does filiation with a family define one's social credit rating. It also structures the nature of social resources at one's command in operations in the non-kin realm. Kin relations in such maneuvers possess two advantages over non-kin ties. First, they are the product of social synchronization achieved in the course of socialization. The private relation of trust may thus be translated into cooperation in the public realm. I would like to point here, for example, to the relations of uncles and nephews in Euramerican culture which gave rise to the concept of nepotism. It is interesting, parenthetically, that this relation is described in great detail in such sources as the French *chansons de geste*, including all the psychological attributes ascribed by Homans and Schneider to the relation of mother's brother and sister's son, in contrast to the relation between son and father, in the absence of known patterns of complementary filiation and matrilateral cross-cousin marriage. Moreover, such a relation between kinsmen can rely on the sanctions of the kin network, as well as on the sanctions of the public realm. Should one partner to the relationship fail in his performance, his alter can mobilize against him not only the immediate sanctions of the ego-alter tie, but all the other bonds that link ego and alter to other kin. It is obvious, of course, that such a reliance on kin may also entail liabilities to one or the other member of the partnership. Kinsmen may become parasitic upon one another, thus limiting the capacity of any one member to advance his wealth or power. The clearest gain from such a relation should therefore appear in situations where public law cannot guarantee adequate protection against breaches of non-kin contracts. This can occur where public law is weak, or where no cultural patterns of cooperation between non-kin exist to guide the required relationship. It can also occur in dealings which border on the illegal or extra-processual. Cooperation among kin, for example, is important in gangster organizations, even where non-kin relations may sometimes be forced at gun point, or in political hatchet-work, in which kin relations are employed privately to prune the political underbrush. It is finally useful for kin to cooperate where access to the law would entail such costs and complications as to leave the partners to a dispute economically or otherwise deprived after settlement. The relation of kin in non-kin operations, therefore, implies a clear balance of gains and costs, in which the gains outweigh the costs only when cooperation with non-kin is clearly more hazardous and disadvantageous.

KINDS OF FRIENDSHIP

At this point, the tie of kinship merges with the tie of friendship. In contrast to the kin tie, the primary bond in the friendship dyad is not forced in an ascribed situation; friendship is achieved. If we are to make headway in a sociological analysis of the friendship tie, we must, I believe, distinguish two kinds of friendship. I shall call the first expressive or emotional friendship, the second instrumental friendship. From the point of view of the friendship dyad, emotional friendship involves a relation between an ego and an alter in which each satisfies some emotional need in his opposite number. This is the obviously psychological aspect of the relation. Yet the very fact that the relation satisfies a deficit of some kind in each participant should alert us also to the social characteristics of the relation involved. It leads us to ask the question: under what kind of conditions can one expect to find an emotional deficit in two persons which draws them into the relation described? Here it is useful to look upon friendship as a countervailing force. We should, I think, expect to find emotional friendships primarily in social situations where the individual is strongly embedded in solidary groupings like communities and lineages, and where the set of social structure inhibits social and geographical mobility. In such situations, ego's access to resources—natural and social—is largely provided by the solidary units; and friendship can at best provide emotional release and catharsis from the strains and pressures of role-playing.

FRIENDSHIP: A MIDDLE-AMERICAN CASE

I think primarily here, for instance, in terms of my own experience, of the behavior of Indians in closed corporate communities in Middle America. The community is solidary towards outsiders and against the outside; it maintains a monopoly of resources—usually land—and defends the first rights of insiders against outside competition. Internally, it tends to level differences, evening out both the chances and the risks of life. This does not lead to the warm communal relations sometimes imputed to such a structure. Quite the contrary, we may note that envy and suspicion play an essential part in maintaining the rough equality of life chances. Friendship in such a community provides an escape from the press of life, but it does not in and of itself serve to alter the distribution of resources.

Ruben Reina has described how friendship works in such a community in Guatemala. 'For the Indians,' he says, 'it offers an amotional fulfillment and a means of assuring oneself that one will not be standing alone. Before marriage and after childhood, the *camarada* complex reaches

high emotional intensity—at that transition in life when a Chinautleco achieves adult status but has not acquired all its emotional rewards.' At the same time, the very intensity of the relation has a tendency to dissolve it. 'The explanation seems to lie in the fact that Indians seek extreme confidence *(confianza)* and this in itself endangers friendship. They demand reciprocal affection, and it is expected that the *camarada* will act only in a manner which will bring pleasure to his friend.' *Camaradas* are jealous of each other: 'once a high intensity of friendship was attained, scenes of jealousy and frustration could be expected and the cycle would end in a state of enmity'. Hence such emotional friendship is also ambivalent. As Reina says,

'they are proud of this relationship and affectionate in it, but from a practical viewpoint have mixed feelings. A *camarada* is a potential enemy when the *puesto* (prescribed role and status) is lost. A certain reserve on the part of the *camaradas* is therefore observed, especially in the realm of family secrets, plans, and amounts earned at work. Friendship is maintained not for economic, political, or practical purposes, but only an emotional fulfillment' (Reina, 1959).

Emotional friendship is thus self-limiting; its continuation is threatened from the inside. It is also subject to limitation from the outside. Here we may use Yehudi Cohen's observation that solidary groups feel cross-cutting friendship ties as a threat and hence will attempt to limit them. He advances this hypothesis to explain the institution of the inalienable friend in what he calls maximally solidary communities, characterized in the main by corporate kin groups (1961, p. 375).

In contrast to emotional friendship is what I have called instrumental friendship. Instrumental friendship may not have been entered into for the purpose of attaining access to resources—natural and social—but the striving for such access becomes vital in it. In contrast to emotional friendship, which restricts the relation to the dyad involved, in instrumental friendship each member of the dyad acts as a potential connecting link to other persons outside the dyad. Each participant is a sponsor for the other. In contrast to emotional friendship, which is associated with closure of the social circle, instrumental friendship reaches beyond the boundaries of existing sets, and seeks to establish beachheads in new sets.

Ruben Reina, whose Indian material I have described, contrasts the Indians in Chinautla with the Ladinos.

'To the Ladinos, friendship has practical utility in the realm of economic and political influence; this friendship is looked upon as a mechanism beneficial from the personal viewpoint. *Cuello*, a favorite expression among the Ladinos, indicates that a legal matter may be accelerated, or a job for which one is not totally qualified might be secured through the personal influence of an acquaintance who is in power or knows a third party who can be influenced. The *cuello* complex depends upon the strength of friendship established and is often measured in terms of the number of favors dispensed to each other. It finds its main support in the nature of a convenient social relationship defined as friendship. It follows that, for the Ladinos of Chinautla, the possession of a range of friends is most favorable' (Reina, 1959, pp. 44-45).

Despite the instrumental character of such relations, however, a minimal element of affect remains an important ingredient in the relation. If it is not present, it must be feigned. When the instrumental purposes of the relation clearly take the upper hand, the bond is in danger of disruption. One may speculate about the function of this emotional burden. The initial situation of friendship is one of reciprocity, not of the tit-for-tat kind which Marshall Sahlins has referred to as balanced reciprocity, but of more generalized reciprocity. The relation aims at a large and unspecified series of performances of mutual assistance. The charge of affect may thus be seen as a device for keeping the relationship a relation of open trust or open credit. Moreover, what may start out as a symmetrical reicprocal relationship between equal parties may, in the course of reciprocal services, develop into a relation in which one of the parties—through luck or skillful management—develops a position of strength, the other a position of weakness. The charge of affect which retains the character of balanced reciprocity between equals may be seen as a device to ensure the continuity of the relationship in the face of possible ensuing imbalance. Hence, too, the relation is threatened when one party is too clearly exploitative of the other (Pitt-Rivers, 1954, p. 139). Similarly, if a favor is not forthcoming, the relation is broken and the way is left open for a realignment of friendship bonds. The relation thus contains an element which provides sanctions internal to the relation itself. An imbalance in the relation automatically severs it.

CORPORATE GROUPS AND MIGRANT POPULATIONS

Just as the persistance of corporate groups in a society discourages the mobilization of friendship ties for mobility beyond the corporate group, so it also places a special restriction on the use of kin bonds to effect this crossing of social boundaries. I believe this to be characteristic of the closed corporate communities of Middle America. There the individual who wishes to move beyond the orbit of the community—or is pushed beyond that orbit—is frequently accused of actual or potential witchcraft, and thus defined as a deviant, against whom social sanctions may be invoked. This can be seen most clearly, of course in witchcraft accusation. Manning Nash has given us a remarkable and convincing picture of how witches in the corporate community of Amatenango are socially isolated, until their kinfolk abandon them to their ultimate fate of death (Nash, 1960). The records of the Chiapas project of the University of Chicago are full of cases of splinter groups which have left the villages of their origin under the onus of witchcraft accusations to settle elsewhere. When a person migrates from such a community, he is lost to it unless the corporate mechanisms break down and allow him to resume relations with kinfolk in the village, or further migrants seek his help in the greater outside. Similarly, in the South Tyrolese village I studied, the prevalent pattern of inheritance by one son breaks up the sibling group and causes the supernumary siblings, *die weichenden Erben*, the yielding heirs, to emigrate. In such cases, contact between remaining heir and migrants is cut and lost.

'OPEN' ORGANIZATION AND MIGRANT POPULATIONS

This is not, however, the case in 'open' communities where neither corporate communal organization nor/and corporate lineal groups divide potential stay-at-homes from potential migrants. There a person is free to mobilize both friendship and kinship ties to advance his mobility both inside and outside the community. Kinship ties with migrants are not lost—they become valuable assets for the transmission or distribution of goods and services. Thus, the Puerto Ricans of San José retain strong ties with their migrant kin in San Juan and in the United States. The people of Tret, the Italian community which I studied contrastively with St. Felix, the German South Tyrolese community, keep track of every relative who has gone to the United States, and keep in touch through letters and mutual gifts. And Ernestine Friedl has shown in her study of Vasilika in Boetia that 'the role of kinship ties as a mechanism for maintaining urban-rural connections is extensive and permeating. Nor does a change in social status from poorer to wealthier Greek peasant, or to any other more prestige-giving position, result in a rupture of kinship ties and obligations' (1959, p. 31).

Finally, it will have been noted that the instrumental friendships discussed above thrive best in social situations which are relatively open, and where friends may act as sponsors for each other in attempts to widen their spheres of social maneuver. The twentieth century has, however, also witnessed a new form of social closure, not this time on the level of the landed corporate group, but in the tendency of large-scale bureaucratic organizations to lessen the area of free maneuverability. In such large bureaucracies as industrial concerns or armies, instrumental friendship merges into the formation of cliques or similar informal groups.

CLIQUES

Compared to the type of situation discussed above, in which the friendship relation still covers the entire role repertoire of the two participants, clique friendship tends to involve primarily the set of roles associated with the particular job. Nevertheless, the clique still serves more purposes than are provided for in the formal table of organization of the institution. It is usually the carrier of an affective element, which may be used to counter-balance the formal demands of the organization, to render life within it more acceptable and more meaningful. Importantly, it may reduce the feeling of the individual that he is dominated by forces beyond himself, and serve to confirm the existence of his ego in the interplay of small-group chit-chat. But it also has important instrumental functions, in rendering an unpredictable situation more predictable, and in providing for mutual support against surprise upsets from within or without. This is especially true in situations characterized by a differential distribution of power. Power superiors and inferiors may enter into informal alliances to ensure the smooth prosecution of their relationship, to guard against unbidden inquiries from the outside or competition from the inside, to seek support for advancement and other demands. Prize examples of such informal alliances are provided by J. Berliner's discussion of familyness and *blat*, influence, among Soviet industrial managers (1957); but they can be had in any account of the functioning of a large bureaucratic organization. Indeed, paraphrasing a comment of Edward Shils, an interesting perspective on the study of such large organizations may be gained by looking upon them as organi-

zations of supply for the cliques they contain, rather than the other way round, by visualizing the clique group as a servant of the bureaucracy that provides its matrix.

PATRON-CLIENT RELATIONS

When instrumental friendship reaches a maximum point of imbalance so that one partner is clearly superior to the other in his capacity to grant goods and services, we approach the critical point where friendships give way to the patron-client tie. The relation between patron and client has been aptly described as 'lop-sided friendship' (Pitt-Rivers, 1954, p. 140). As in instrumental friendship, a minimal charge of affect invests the relation of patron and client, to form that trust which underwrites the promise of future mutual support. Like kinship and friendship, the patron-client tie involves multiple facets of the actors involved, not merely the segmental needs of the moment. At the back of the material advantages to be gained by the client, says Kenny of patron-client relations in Spain, 'there lies not only a striving to level out inequalities but also a fight against anonymity (especially in the urban setting) and a seeking out of primary personal relationships' (1962, p. 136).

The two partners to the patron-client contract, however, no longer exchange equivalent goods and services. The offerings of the patron are more immediately tangible. He provides economic aid and protection against both the legal and illegal exactions of authority. The client, in turn, pays back in more intangible assets. These are, first, demonstrations of esteem. 'The client has a strong sense of loyalty to his patron and voices this abroad. By doing so, he constantly stimulates the channels of loyalty, creates good will, adds to the name and fame of his patron and ensures him a species of immortality' (Kenny, 1962, p. 136). A second contribution by the client to his patron is offered in the form of information on the machinations of others. A third form of offering consists in the promise of political support. Here the element of power emerges which is otherwise masked by reciprocities. For the client not only promises his vote or strong arm in the political process, he also promises—in effect—to entertain no other patron than the one from whom he has received goods and credit. The client is duty-bound not merely to offer expressions of loyalty, but also to demonstrate that loyalty. He becomes a member of a faction which serves the competitive purposes of a faction leader. 'Crises,' says

Kenny, 'clearly reveal this when protestations of loyalty and support significantly show the alignment of different patronage forces.' It is this potential competition of patron with patron that offers the client his leverage, his ability to win support and to insist on its continuation. The relation remains reciprocal, each party investing in the other.

VARIATIONS IN PATRON-CLIENT TIES

We may, moreover, engage in some speculation as to the form which the patron-client relation will take in different circumstances. I should expect the relation here analyzed to occur where no corporate lineal group or corporate village intervenes between potential client and potential patron, but where the network of kin and friendship relations is sufficiently open for each seeker after support and each person capable of extending support to enter into independent, dyadic contracts (Foster, 1961). Moreover, such ties would prove especially functional in situations where the formal institutional structure of society is weak and unable to deliver a sufficiently steady supply of goods and services, especially at the terminal levels of the social order. Under such conditions, there would be customers for the social insurance offered by potential clients, while the formation of a body of clients would increase the ability of patrons to influence institutional operation. These considerations would lead one to predict further that patron-client relations would operate in markedly different ways in situations structured by corporate groups, or in situations in which the institutional framework is strong and ramifying. Among the South Tyrolese, there is no patron-client tie of the kind discussed here. Its place is taken by political party leadership which communicates hierarchically to the various lineal corporate units in the village. On the other hand, where you have superlocal unilineal descent groups, as in China and the Near East, we find the patron incorporated into the lineage, in the person or persons manning the executive 'gentry' positions in the lineage. Similarly, among corporately organized Indians in Middle America, the individual can approach a patron—hacienda owner or political power figure—only as a member of the group, and the patron then acts as power broker relating the entire group to the institutional framework outside it. On the other hand, where there are no corporate kin or village units of the type indicated, but where the institutional framework of society is far flung and solidly entrenched, patronage cannot lead to the formation of bodies of followers relatively independent of the formal structure. Rather, patronage will take the form of sponsorship, in which the patron provides connections (hence the Spanish *enchufe*—plug-in) with the institutional order. In such circumstances, his stock-in-trade consists less of the relatively independent allocation of goods and services than of the use of influence. Correspondingly, however, his hold on the client is weakened, and in place of solid patron-client blocks we may expect to encounter diffuse and cross-cutting ties between multiple sponsors and multiple clients, with clients often moving from one orbit of influence to another.

THE PROBLEM OF NATIONAL CHARACTER

I cannot refrain, at the end of this discussion, from pointing out a point of encounter with what has sometimes been called the national-character approach. When one examines the work of Benedict, Mead, and others who have devoted their attention to the problem of defining national character, one is struck by the fact that they have utilized—in the main—data on the interpersonal sets discussed in this paper, and on the etiquettes and social idioms governing them. Take, for instance—and picking at random—Geoffrey Gorer's account of the intricacies of mate selection involved in the American dating complex (1948), or Benedict's discussion of the circle of *on* and *giri* obligations between persons of different hierarchical status (1946), or Rhoda Métraux's analysis of the constitution of the French *foyer* (1954). There is no need to labor this point. It is obvious that such descriptions and analyses do not cope with the institutional features of national structure. Yet it is equally possible that complex societies in the modern world differ less in the formal organization of their economic or legal or political systems than in the character of their supplementary interpersonal sets. Using the strategy of social anthropology, moreover, we would say that information about these sets is less meaningful when organized in terms of a construct of homogeneous national character than when referred to the particular body of social relations and its function, partial or general, within the supplementary or parallel structure underlying the formal institutional framework.

If our argument is correct that these supplementary sets make possible the functioning of the great institutions, then it must also be true that these supplementary sets developed or changed character historically, as the great institutions developed historically. And with changes in these supplementary sets we should also expect to find changes in the norms governing these sets, and in the symbolic forms assumed by these norms. The integration of the great society requires the knitting of these interstitial relations. As the integration of society is promoted by certain groups who draw after them a variety of others, some groups moreover set the pace and tone in the formation of the new patterns, which draw in or influence the segmental patterns of other groups. The patterns of interpersonal etiquettes of one group are then recut and reshaped to fit the patterns of interpersonal etiquettes utilized by the tone-setting group. Put in terms of reference theory, we might say that the choice of behavioral etiquettes and the direction of their circulation reflect the degree of dominance of one or another reference group within the society. An example of downward circulation of such patterns would be the spread of courtly forms in France (Elias, 1939), the establishment and diffusion of public-school manners in Britain, the communication of urban forms to rural groups via the kinship network in Greece and Italy (Friedl, 1959; Wolf, 1962). But there can also be cases of upward circulation of behavioral models, reflecting changes in the distribution of power in a society, as when the etiquette governing the relation of traditional hacienda owner and agricultural worker in Puerto Rico was transferred to pattern the relation between the new island-wide political leadership and its mass following (Wolf, 1956, pp. 212-213), or when the behavioral etiquette of a despised interstitial group in Mexico became the behavior grammar standardizing interaction between power-seekers and followers (Wolf, 1959, ch. 11). Description and analysis of the supplementary interpersonal sets discussed in this paper thus not only reveal a great deal about the hidden mechanisms of complex society. Description and analysis of the origin and circulation of the models of etiquette structuring these sets also reveal much of the social dynamic, of the changing distribution of forces in the social body. If such studies do not lead us to definitions of national character, as this term has hitherto been employed, they nevertheless indicate the way in which the parallelogram of social forces in one society differs from that of another.

ACKNOWLEDGEMENT

Thanks are due to the Editor of the *American Anthropologist* for permission to quote a passage from 'Two Patterns of Friendship in a Guatemalan Community' by Ruben Reina.

REFERENCES

Benedict, Ruth F. 1946. *The Chrysanthemum and the Sword*. Boston: Houghton Mifflin.

Berliner, Joseph. 1957. *Factory and Manager in the U.S.S.R.* Cambridge, Mass.: Harvard University Press.

Bobek, Hans. 1962. The Main Stages in Socioeconomic Evolution from a Georgraphic Point of View. In Philip L. Wagner & Marvin W. Mikesell (eds.). *Readings in Cultural Georgraphy*. Chicago: University of Chicago Press, pp. 218-247.

Cohen, Yehudi. 1961. Patterns of Friendship. In Yehudi Cohen (ed.), *Social Structure and Personality: A Casebook*. New York: Holt, Rinehart & Winston, pp. 351-386.

Elias, Norbert. 1939. *Ueber den Prozess der Zivilisation: Soziogenetische und Psychogenetische Untersuchungen*, 2 vols. Basel: Verlag Haus zum Falken.

Fei, Hsiao-Tung. 1953. *China's Gentry*. Chicago: University of Chicago Press.

Foster, George M. 1961. The Dyadic Contract: A Model for the Social Structure of a Mexican Peasant Village. *American Anthropologist* 63:1173-1192.

Freedman, Maurice. 1958. *Lineage Organization in Southeastern China*. London School of Economics Monographs on Social Anthropology No. 18. London: Athlone Press.

Friedl, Ernestine. 1959. The Role of Kinship in the Transmission of National Culture to Rural Villages in Mainland Greece. *American Anthropologist* 61:30-38.

Gorer, Geoffrey. 1948. *The American People*. New York: Norton.

Hsu, Francis L. K. 1948. *Under the Ancestors' Shadow: Chinese Culture and Personality*. New York: Columbia University Press.

Kenny, Michael. 1962. *A Spanish Tapestry: Town and Country in Castile*. Bloomington: University of Indiana Press.

Métraux, Rhoda. 1954. Themes in French Culture. In Rhoda Métraux & Margaret Mead (eds.), *Themes in French Culture: A Preface to a Study of French Community*. Hoover Institute Series, D: Communities, No. 1. Stanford: Stanford University Press, pp. 1-65.

Nash, Manning. 1960. Witchcraft as Social Process in a Tzeltal Community. *América Indígena* 20:121-126.

Pi-Sunyer, Oriol. 1962. Personal communication.

Pitt-Rivers, Julian A. 1954. *The People of the Sierra*. New York: Criterion Books.

Reina, Ruben. 1959. Two Patterns of Friendship in a Guatemalan Community. *American Anthropologist* 61:44-50.

Sahlins, Marshall D. 1957. Differentiation by Adaptation in Polynesian Societies. *Journal of the Polynesian Society* 66:291-300.

Schumpeter, Joseph. 1955. *Social Classes. Imperialism: Two Essays*. New York: Meridian Books.

Wolf, Eric R. 1955. Types of Latin American Peasantry. *American Anthropologist* 57:452-471.

————. 1956. San José: Subcultures of a 'Traditional' Coffee Municipality. In Julian Steward (ed.). *The People of Puerto Rico*. Urbana: University of Illinois Press, pp. 171-264.

————. 1957. Closed Corporate Peasant Communities in Mesoamerica and Central Java. *Southwestern Journal of Anthropology* 13:1-18.

————. 1959. *Sons of the Shaking Earth*. Chicago: University of Chicago Press.

————. 1962. Cultural Dissonance in the Italian Alps. *Comparative Studies in Society and History* 5:1-14.

Yang, Martin C. 1945. *A Chinese Village: Taitou, Shantung Province*. New York: Columbia University Press.

Addendum

After completion of this paper, I encountered in an excellent discussion, based on African materials, many ideas on the subject of friendship which parallel my own. This is Gibbs, James L., Jr. 1962. Compensatory Blood-Brotherhood: A Comparative Analysis of Institutionalized Friendship in Two African Societies. *Proceedings of the Minnesota Academy of Science* 30:67-74.

PART III

Application: Clientelism in Traditional Settings

NOBLES, CLIENTS, AND PERSONAL ARMIES

LILY ROSS TAYLOR

THE DOMINANT FIGURES in Roman party politics and party organization were usually members of the hereditary noble or consular houses. By their traditions these houses kept alive the hallowed customs of old Rome, the *mos maiorum*.[1] The noble families considered it their right to provide the men who as magistrates and senators represented the people, the *res publica*. Particularly they held it to be their prerogative to supply the consuls; they passed the office "from hand to hand" and considered that the consulship was polluted if a new man was elected to it.[2] It is with the nobles that we are concerned in this chapter, their inheritance of politics as a profession, their training and experience, their marriages and friendships, their contacts with their clients, and, if they were generals, with their soldiers.

The Roman nobles have often been compared to the so-called British ruling class. There is some similarity in the way the profession of politics was passed down from father to son and in the recurrence of familiar names in high office. But the Roman nobility, unlike the British ruling class, did not constantly renew itself by the admission of new men and by marriages outside its own circle. A far better parallel for the exclusive inbred nobility of Rome is provided by the patriarchate of the Republic of Venice, the oligarchy which for more than five hundred years maintained its primacy, but maintained it by statute such as the Romans never enacted.

To understand the noble houses of Rome one should turn to the sixth book of the *Aeneid*, to the lines where Anchises foretells the glories of Aeneas' descendants and fires his son with love of fame to come *(incenditque animum famae venientis amore)*; or one should read the vivid pages on which Livy sets forth the deeds in war and in peace of the great republican heroes. There was a splendid tradition of sternness, discipline, courage, and patriotism, and every noble strove to keep it alive both by recalling constantly the distinctions of his ancestors and by striving himself to reach an equal eminence. The atrium of the city house was adorned with the wax images of the noble's ancestors, accompanied by emblems and inscriptions recording the consulships and the censorships, the priesthoods, and the triumphs they had held. In the magnificent pageantry of the public funerals of members of these great houses, these images were taken with the dead to the Rostra and were placed on descendants who were thought to resemble their ancestors. And in the funeral orations the achievements of these ancestors were lauded along with the deeds of the man who had died. Polybius, who had seen such funerals, is deeply impressed with the stimulus this "constant renewal of the good report of brave men" provides for the younger generation.[3]

Cicero, the new man, speaks with scorn of the "commendation of smoky wax images" through which an enemy reached high position, and makes fun of the defeated candidate who asks, "What shall I say to the images of my ancestors?";[4] but there is no doubt that he felt deeply all his life his exclusion from the traditions that belonged to the great noble houses. Even when he reached the consulship he was never really accepted, never in the inner circle of nobility. Sallust, another new man, who gave up a political career before he reached the highest office, felt it too, and comments more than once that the nobles considered themselves defiled if an outsider broke into their group.[5]

In the nobility, as everywhere in Roman society, there were classes within classes. The highest class was represented by the princes of the state, the men who could marshal on the Rostra for a family funeral the greatest array of masks with the emblems of the highest distinction. Among these the great patrician houses had a preëminent place, for they traced their ancestry back to the kingship and even sometimes to the expedition of Aeneas. Still prominent in the late republic were the Claudii, the Aemilii, and certain branches of the Cornelii and the Valerii. But the majority of the fourteen patrician houses still surviving from the fifty-odd patrician families whose names we know from the early republic[6] were no longer in the front ranks of the nobility. Cicero notes that the nobility of Servius Sulpicius Rufus, a patrician who expressed his wrath at being defeated for the consulship by a man of less distinguished name, had to be "dug out of ancient records."[7] The same thing was true in less degree of the family of Julius Caesar. Although a collateral branch of his house had reached the consulship in the middle of the second century, none of Caesar's ancestors had held the office for three hundred years, and few of them were really eminent. Vergil went back to the legendary past to provide a glorious tradition for the Julian House. The fortunes of Caesar's family had been improved by the marriage of his aunt with the new man Marius.

Of the patricians it may be noted that a surprising number, like Caesar, embraced popular programs in order to rise in the state. Marcus Aemilius Lepidus, Catiline, and Clodius are other examples. These men had a decided disadvantage if they wished to be *populares*, for they were ineligible for the tribunate unless, like Clodius and certain of his predecessors, they had themselves adopted into a plebian house. There were other disadvantages for patricians. Only one of them could be elected to the consulship in each year, and sometimes a man, who would otherwise have won, had to withdraw when another patrician had already been chosen.

On a level with the greatest patrician houses and far above the lesser families of the patriciate were certain illustrious houses of the plebeians, the Mucii Scaevolae, the Licinii, the Lutatii Catuli, the Domitii Ahenobarbi, ancestors of Nero, the Livii Drusi, ancestors of Augustus' wife, Livia, the related Poreii Catones, and the most eminent of all, the prolific and wealthy house of the Caecilii Metelii, related through marriage and adoption to many families of the patrician and plebian nobility.[8] On the Appian Way today a splendid tomb of a lady of this house, wife of Crassus' son, is still a monument of the princely position attained by the family. From these houses and not from the patriciate came the leaders of the optimate opposition to Pompey and Caesar—Catullus, Metellus Pius, Lucullus, Cato, and Domitius. In contrast to houses like these, Pompey, also a plebeian, was a newcomer, with his father his only forerunner in the consulship.

Along with the wealth that made it possible for him to engage in a lifework which at least in theory provided no means of gain, the noble inherited from his family the profession of politics and he was expected to pursue it. Late in his life Cicero, proud of the nobility which he had brought to his family, addressed to his son an essay, *De Officiis*, "On Duty," or perhaps more accurately, since the essay is filled with practical advice, "On propriety of conduct." In it Cicero outlines the obligation of the citizen. Although much that he says is of more general application, he is concerned particularly with the obligations of the young man whose birthright is participation in the state. His discussion is based, as he frankly says, on an essay of the Stoic Panaetius, who almost a century earlier wrote on the same subject for the noble circle of the younger Scipio; but Cicero writes in terms of the obligations and responsibilities that his own renown had conferred on the young Marcus. Men who have the natural endowments needed to conduct public affairs should he says, without hesitation seek office and take part in their conduct.[9] They should not be deterred by the toil and trouble of a political career or the fear of meeting defeat at the polls. They are justified in not going in for politics if they are too weak to undergo the strains of public life. Perhaps also, though here Cicero is doubtful, men devoted to learning may be excused from politics, but there is no excuse for those who, in order to secure tranquillity and ease, avoid the trouble of a political career.

It was, it may be noted, partly because the Epicureans recommended avoidance of politics that the Roman state was officially hostile to the sect. The Roman nobility could not countenance the view of the contemporary Epicurean poet Lucretius when he stood on the heights and looked down with pity and saw men

Certare ingenio, contendere nobilitate
noctes atque dies niti praestanti labore
ad summas emergere opes rerumque potiri.

Rivals in genius, or emulous in rank,
pressing through days and nights with hugest toil
for summits of power and mastery of the world.[10]

At least officially the nobles would have rejected the poet's description of public life, with its defeats, as hell on earth.

We have before our eyes
Here in this life also a Sisyphus
In him who seeketh of the populace
The rods, the axes fell, and ever more
Retires a beaten and a gloomy man.
For to seek after power—an empty name,
Nor given at all—and ever in the search
To endure a world of toil, O this it is
To shove with shoulder up the hill a stone
Which yet comes rolling back from off the top,
And headlong makes for levels of the plains.[11]

Lucretius might scorn the goals of politicians, but he was undoubtedly right about the incessant toil of public life. It was grueling even for the noblest, who were said to have been elected to the consulship in their cradles. The boy's entire education was planned for public life. The chief emphasis was on physical fitness, training of voice and diction, familiarity with public affairs, and the development of ready ease in speaking. To accomplish this last aim the boy had to store his mind, and that meant familiarity with Greek and Latin literature and with history and philosophy.

As the boy grew older, he had daily exercises in speaking under Greek rhetors, who were useful for technique but could of course teach their Roman masters nothing about statecraft. To learn that art, the boy was taken to the Forum to hear the public speeches and the orations in the law courts, and he sat at the feet of great Romans who had achieved renown in public affairs. At least by the time he was twenty the youth began to appear in court, perhaps as a character witness for a family friend. If he was good at speaking he would even assume the exacting role of prosecutor of a family enemy. Over and over again such public accusations were conducted by men in their youth, by the orator Crassus at nineteen, by Lucullus, Caesar, Calvus, and Asinius Pollio when they were not much older.[12]

Along with the young man's practice in speaking went his first military service, which began when he was about seventeen. The requirement of ten years' military service, which Polybius states as a prerequisite for a political career,[13] seems no longer to have been in force in the late republic, but some military experience was apparently demanded. After initial training at home, the young man often went out to serve in one of the provinces, perhaps as a *contubernalis* (tentmate) of a governor, who was very likely a family friend; later he often served as military tribune, a rank that corresponded to a lower commissioned officer in our army.

With his military training he frequently continued his practice in speaking, seeking out the great teachers of the Greek cities if he was in the East, or, if he was not sent to a center of traditional culture, taking a teacher along with him, as the young Augustus did.[14] Before the day came for his first candidacy—and he often held a minor office or an elective military tribunate before he sought for the quaestorship—the young noble had to make himself known to the electorate, perhaps to journey about Italy and become acquainted with the men of the municipalities, particularly with the richest men, who were most likely to come to Rome to vote.

At his house in Rome, which, Cicero emphasizes, should be a seemly mansion, with plenty of space in it,[15] he had to be ready in the morning to greet the family clients and retainers and friends who came for the daily *salutatio*, and in the Forum he had to appear with a retinue and to be always at the call of any friend who might need him in the courts. If he had good family traditions, he would have no difficulty in securing immediate election at the age of thirty to the office that admitted him to the senate,[16] the quaestorship, and then he would be engaged for a year as an aide to the chief magistrates, either in Italy or, more likely, in the provinces. At that time he might well have further experience in war.

The next obligatory office in the *cursus* was the praetorship, which could not be held until nine years after the quaestorship. In the intervening period the noble would probably seek election to one of the optional offices, the curule aedileship or, if he was a plebeian, the plebeian aedileship or the tribunate of the plebs. All these offices were a great help to the aspirant for the consulship. The aediles had to put on public theatrical and circus games and, if they had enough wealth, or, like Caesar, could borrow enough money, they could attract attention by making the games magnificent.[17] Sometimes the nobles made the aedileship the occasion of gladiatorial games in honor of a member of the family who had died. There was a tendency to postpone such celebrations until candidacy for the consulship was in view, so that the memory of the show would be fresh in the minds of voters. Thus Caesar in his aedileship gave a splendid gladiatorial show for his father, who had died nearly two decades earlier.[18] The tribune, especially after Pompey restored the full powers of the office, had great opportunities to gain popular favor by intervention for citizens under attack, vetoes of unpopular measures, addresses to the citizens, and bills proposed in the council of the plebs. Even though tribunes were not necessarily interested in the people, they claimed to be *populares* when in office.

This intervening period between quaestorship and praetorship was often spent in part in the provinces, usually as legate of a governor in command, and, though many such posts were mainly administrative, there was often opportunity of gaining further military experience under a tested commander like Lucullus or Pompey or Caesar.[19]

The praetorship also was usually secured by the nobles as soon as the law allowed, for, since there were eight of these officers, the competition was not too severe. After a year of service in this office as judge in the urban, peregrine, or criminal courts, the praetor normally went out, the following year, to a province. Although in general the provinces likely to be involved in war were saved for consular governors, the governor of praetorian rank sometimes, like Caesar in Further Spain, had opportunity for military exploits and might occasionally win a triumph. He always had a chance to enrich himself—a chance that was in part legitimate, for the state allowances were far in excess of necessary expenditures. He also had great opportunity for plunder. He returned with his mind completely on the consulship.

The consulship could be held three years after the praetorship, and every noble hoped to hold it in what he called "his year," the year he reached the age of forty-three. Here, since there were only two places and a number of candidates, the competition was intense. It was, moreover, fraught with personal danger, for rivals or their adherents were continually bringing suit in the courts in order to eliminate, through exile or removal from the senate, an opponent who seemed likely to win.[20] The favorite charge was extortion in the provinces, but embezzlement of public funds and treason against the state were also possible charges. With the elections (to be considered in the next chapter) the dangers of an accusation were not over, for, though the man was immune while in office, he could still be prosecuted in the interval between election and entrance into office. In such cases the usual charge was illegal canvassing, including bribery.[21]

After the consulship there was regularly another provincial governorship, again with opportunities for enrichment and new dangers of accusations. Often, too, there were chances to conduct a war, and if these came his way the noble's ambition was whetted again. He wished the senate to vote first a thanksgiving to the gods for any victories he had won, and then the great distinction of a triumph, which would enable him to array himself in the costume of Jupiter the Best and Greatest, drive with a splendid procession in a chariot along the Sacred Way, and lay his spoils at the feet of Jupiter on the Capitol. Cicero, a peaceful man, after his lieutenants won some victories, longed for that honor, and for years during the Civil War went about accompanied with the laurels he hoped to bestow on Capitoline Jupiter.

The man of consular rank might occasionally, after an interval of ten years, seek a second consulship, and repeated consulships were a great honor.[22] He might also seek the censorship, to which every five years two of the most eminent *consulares* were elected.[23] The censor's task of reviewing the list of senators and overseeing the enrollment of citizens enabled him to eliminate his enemies from the senate and to make alterations to the advantage of his associates in the registration of citizens. But the office was even more valued for the honor which the censor, resplendent in the purple toga that belonged to this office alone, conferred on the family. The other great distinction of Rome, coveted by all the high nobility and limited almost exclusively to them, was membership in the great colleges of priests. This distinction might be achieved at any time after the noble took the toga of manhood, and men of the most distinguished houses were apt to be chosen when they were very young.[24]

Even if he fell short of the distinction of a triumph or a second consulship or a censorship or a priesthood, the ordinary *consularis*, with an influential place in the body that was, for purposes of empire at least, the ruling body of the state, was in a position of great prestige. It was in no sense a position of leisure, for now he had to think of the maintenance of his *dignitas*, his rank, and he also had to concern himself with his family and particularly his sons, who must achieve a career like his own. And that meant that he had to keep powerful friends and make new ones, that had in fact to be a candidate all over again, this time for the younger generation.

To carry on the traditions of the house the noble counted on having a son to succeed him, but he rarely had a large family; he did not wish the responsibility of a number of sons who had to be brought to the consulship and of several daughters for whom he had to find noble or consular husbands. The family of Metellus Macedonicus, which consisted of four sons, all of whom reached the consulship, and two daughters, who married into families of the high nobility, was exceptional. So also was the family of Appius Claudius Pulcher, consul in 79, who died and left in relative poverty three sons and three daughters. Through the interest of relatives and friends these children prospered. One of the sons reached the consulship, and two others, one of whom was Cicero's enemy Clodius, were on the way to the office when they died. The three daughters, one of whom gained immortality as the Lesbia of Catullus, all married husbands who reached the consulship. Another comparatively large family was that of the younger Cato, who had two sons and probably three daughters.[25] In contrast to these families, most of the other nobles about whom we have information either had no issue or small families of one, two, or three children. Thus Pompey had two sons and a daughter; Crassus, two sons; Caesar, one daughter; Catullus, probably two daughters; Lucius Domitius Ahenobarbus, one son; Metellus Scipio, one daughter; and Metellus Pius, no children.

It was through intermarriage and adoption from one family to another that the closest bonds between the noble houses were established. As Horace tells us, one of the questions asked about a candidate was whether people had heard of his mother.[26] The nobles considered carefully the political importance of the family connections, when arranging the marriages of their sons and daughters.[27] In consequence the princely houses were an inbred group, bound to one another by relationships going back for generations. The great family of the Caecilii Metelli intermarried with the patrician Aemilii, Claudii Pulchri, Cornelii Scipiones Nasicae, and Cornelii Sullae,

and with the plebeian Mucii, Servilii, Licinii Luculli, and Licinii Crassi. The relations of two houses joined by marriage frequently continued when, as often happened, there had been a divorce. Cicero maintained friendship with two former sons-in-law from whom his daughter Tullia was divorced. The attitude toward divorce is illustrated by the fact that Cato agreed to give up his wife Marcia to his friend Hortensius, and then, after Hortensius' death, married her again himself. According to Caesar, she came back to Cato much richer than she was before.[28]

To unite families, adoptions were as important as intermarriages.[29] A noble without an heir frequently adopted a son, and he regularly chose from a distinguished family the child, or often the full-grown man, whom he wished to carry on his name. Thus the conqueror of Macedonia, Lucius Aemilius Paullus, allowed two of his four sons to be adopted by the Cornelii Scipiones and the Fabii Maximi, two other great patrician houses; and then, tragically, his family became extinct through the death of the two remaining sons. Sometimes a noble who had no heir adopted in his will the son of a relative or friend. Caesar supplies an illustration, for he adopted his great-nephew, the young Gaius Octavius. By such adoptions the two houses were brought closely together, and the man adopted was thought to belong to both families. Thus the younger Scipio Africanus, son of Aemilius Paullus, the leading figure in Cicero's essay on the state, speaks of *both* his fathers, and is proud of the family tradition of both his houses.[30]

A remarkable example of such a double tradition in the days of Cicero was Publius Cornelius Scipio Nasica. He belonged to a line of the Scipios that was collateral to the Africani, and he could trace his house back for at least eleven generations in which all his paternal ancestors except two, who had probably died too young, had reached the consulship; some of them had been censors and had triumphed. His inheritance had been enriched by intermarriages of his ancestors with the line of the elder Africanus, the Caecilii Metelli, the Licinii Crassi, the Mucii Scaevolae, and the Laelii, all great consular families. He himself married Lepida, daughter of Mamercus Aemilius Lepidus Livianus, a relative of Cato (whom she jilted for Nasica), by birth an heiress to the traditions of the noble plebeian Livii, the family of Augustus' wife, and by adoption to the glories of the patrician Aemilii. To this splendid heritage from patrician and plebeian nobility Scipio Nasica added glories by accepting testamentary adoption from Quintus Metellus Pius, *pontifex maximus*, consul, and *triumphator*. By this adoption he gained another direct line of six consular ancestors. His atrium, with the wax masks of two long lines of consular ancestors and with many more added from the female side, must have been a showplace of Rome. His daughter, married first to a son of Crassus and later to Pompey, was the great catch of Rome.[31] In Lucan's epic on the Civil War Pompey addresses her as femina *tantorum titulis insignis avorum*.[32]

The noble's family, with his connections by marriage and adoption, was strengthened into a party grouping by his bonds of friendship with other noble houses.[33] We have already seen that *amicitia* was the time-honored substitute for party. Friendships were often passed down from one generation to another. The strength of inherited friendship is illustrated by the array of counsel and character witnesses that rallied to the defense when the son of the first man of the senate of Marius' time, Marcus Aemilius Scaurus, was accused in 54. Party rivalry, then strong between the "triumvirs" and the *optimates*, was laid aside, and among the nine men of consular rank who appeared were Pompey and Crassus and some of their strongest opponents. In the group also were the two fierce rivals, Milo and Clodius, whose adherents were busy murdering each other at the time.[34]

Nobles in politics not only inherited friends; they constantly made new friends. They also inherited personal enemies *(inimici)* and, as a result of their political activities, acquired new enemies; from time to time, too, they made their peace with former enemies. The news of fresh alliances of friendship, of enmities, and of reconciliations looms large in the political gossip of the Ciceronian collection of *Letters*.

Obligations of friendship often led to conflict with other friends, but it was accepted procedure that a man should pay his personal obligations, whatever the conflict. Thus, after Milo had risked his life to bring Cicero back from exile, Cicero had to pay his debts, though at the time he was in the orbit of Pompey, who had clashed with Milo. Cicero gave vigorous support to Milo's candidacy for the consulship, which was opposed by Pompey, and in court defended Milo against the charge of violence. Cicero later acknowledged Pompey's understanding attitude on this occasion.[35] When the Civil War came and Cicero was debating his own course, the fact that Pompey had also helped to bring Cicero back from exile was the deciding factor in leading him to join Pompey. As Cicero puts it, *ingrati animi crimen horreo*.[36]

"Friends," as we saw in the first chapter,

often joined together in closely knit cliques. The short-term unions of candidates, *coitiones*, designed to shut out competitors, will be considered in the next chapter. Long-term combinations, "bad friendships," were known by the invidious term *factio*. We have seen that the word came to mean oligarchy or to suggest oligarchical designs, and that it was applied to Caesar's enemies in the senate and one occasion to Caesar's deal with Pompey and Crassus.

There were also various associations of men of the senatorial class which had political importance. Among these were the colleges of priests, in our period made up of nobles, and the brotherhoods like the *Luperci* and the *sodales Titii*.[37] We hear also of *sodalitates* that functioned in the law courts, apparently for both prosecution and defense. Quintus Cicero, in writing to Marcus, speaks of such groups, which were committed to support Marcus' candidacy because he had taken their cases in the courts.[38] But at Rome such *sodalitates* seem to have been less important than the Athenian clubs which played a major role in politics and in the courts.[39]

Occasionally there was a revolutionary organization of prominent men bound together, as the members of the Athenian clubs often were, by a joint oath. That may have been true of the senators who were accused of having conspired with Marcus Livius Drusus in 91 to obtain citizenship for the Italians,[40] a subject to be considered later in the discussion of clientage. The best-attested example of a *coniuratio* is the conspiracy of Catiline which included, with knights and disaffected city and country people, a number of senators, among them two men of eminent patrician ancestry. The steadfastness of the members in refusing to reveal the details of the conspiracy was taken as proof that the Catilinarians were living up to an oath they had taken.[41] The group of sixty-odd senators who united to murder Caesar was, we are explicitly told, not bound together by oath.

Political associations were also cultivated outside the nobility and the senate. Of first importance were the knights, men with property valued at 400,000 sesterces (about $25,000) or more. The knights included members of the senatorial class who had not yet entered upon a political career. Most senators' sons were enrolled in the eighteen centuries of knights with public horse, comprising men of the officer class in the army who looked forward to a political career. They voted as a separate unit in the major Roman assembly. They had great prestige with the electorate, for they were cultivating it in the hope of future advantage for themselves. Older men sought to enhance their prestige by having as many younger men as possible in their group of friends.[42] Cicero's fame in the law courts brought many young men of prominence into association with him, and he valued their support both in his elections and in maintaining his position in subsequent years.

Then there was the great body of knights, men theoretically eligible for office, who in general preferred to remain knights because they were not restricted, as senators were, in their business activities. Some of the knights, like Cicero's friend Atticus, while not engaging in political life, had enormous influence in a wide circle of friends among the nobles. Cicero considered Atticus' aid of great importance in his own candidacies and in his time of peril. As a group the knights did not, in the late republic, regain the full measure of political influence that they had wielded when they controlled the juries from the time of Gaius Gracchus to the dictatorship of Sulla, but their votes counted heavily in the assembly that elected consuls and praetors. Among the knights a particularly well organized group was composed of the public contractors who worked in societies in the various provinces and had their representatives at Rome. Every provincial governor became involved with these societies, and Cicero, who frequently handled the business of the publicans in the law courts, carried on an extensive correspondence in their interest.

The knights and the public contractors were, in large part, drawn from the aristocracy of Italian municipalities. With this aristocracy, the leaders of their communities, the Roman nobility often established rights of hospitality. Municipal leaders could be helpful in swinging the election districts for the noble and his friends, and the noble himself provided his *hospes* with a place to stay and with suitable entertainment when he came to the city. *Tesserae* recording such rights of hospitality between prominent Roman houses and municipal families have come to light in Italian excavations.[43]

An example of a municipal leader who had such ties with various Roman houses is provided by Sextus Roscius from an Umbrian town, of whom Cicero says: "By birth, descent, and fortune he was easily the chief man not only in his own town but also in the neighborhood, while his influence and relations of hospitality with those of the highest rank enhanced his reputation."[44] Cicero goes on to note his relations of hospitality with the Caecilii Metelli, the Servilii, and the Scipiones in Rome and to point out that, in the struggle between Marius and Sulla,

Roscius had favored the Sullan side, that is, the nobility, for "he thought it his duty to fight for the honour of those to whom he owed it that he was reckoned a most honourable man among his fellow citizens."[45] It is an indication of the close relationship of Rome to the municipal aristocracy that both in the Hannibalic and in the Social War, when their fellow townsmen revolted, the chief men of the Italian towns often maintained fealty to Rome.

The Roman nobility found in the municipal leaders the same conservatism that they themselves represented in Roman politics. Thus Cicero's grandfather, a leader of his native town, Arpinum, fought, and with more success than the nobles did at Rome, against the institution of the secret written ballot at Arpinum, an institution that curbed the influence of the aristocrats on the vote. According to Cicero, Marcus Aemilius Scaurus, the first man of the Roman senate in Cicero's grandfather's day, expressed regret that the elder Cicero had preferred to devote himself to his own town rather than to the Roman state.[46]

Sometimes Roman nobles, to strengthen their relations with municipal men, married their children into municipal houses. Such alliances were a good thing because they brought new blood into the nobility, but they were usually considered unworthy.[47] In spite of the use of the term *hospitius*, technically a designation of equality, to dignify the relationship, the Roman noble looked upon even the wealthiest man from a municipality as an inferior. That attitude was shown even toward men who secured high office, like Cicero. Catiline dubbed Cicero an *inquilinus*, an immigrant, and a patrician opponent in the courts called him a *peregrinus rex*.[48]

To maintain their contacts with their friends of their own class, with the knights and the municipal aristocracy, and with the inferior group of clients, to be considered later, the nobles had to have an elaborate organization. The Romans understood the need of organization in politics, but the organization was personal. It was in line with the "rugged individualism" that prevailed in the republic.

There was no police force, no postal or freight service, and, except in the treasury, practically no civil service. The nobles looked after their personal safety by keeping up bands of followers and attendants. They communicated with the cities of Italy and the provinces through personal messengers, using vehicles, horses, or ships which were their private property. They often made their means of communication available to their friends, but in doing so they were conferring a personal favor. Every important man had a staff of slaves and freedmen to aid in political activities. The staff included a secretariat to keep up the voluminous correspondence that was necessary.

Cato must have needed a number of aides to keep up his assiduous exchange of letters not only with the men in the provinces but with allied peoples in whose concerns he showed interest,[49] especially if there were any suggestion that they were being exploited. Cicero also was constantly writing to men in the provinces, recommending people to them, and assuring them that he was looking out for their prestige in Rome. When he was governor of Cilicia he carried on an immense correspondence, not only with Roman senators who, he hoped, would secure him a thanksgiving and a triumph, but with men who had special interests in his province. He exchanged many letters with the young Marcus Junius Brutus, future leader of Caesar's assassins, who kept recommending a certain Saufeius.[50] This man was trying by pressure and force to collect money at an exorbitant rate of interest from a city of Cyprus, and Cicero was appalled to learn that the money had really been lent by Brutus himself.

Cicero, as we know from the letters of introduction included in his correspondence, was involved through his own personal agents in the affairs of other provinces. He writes to one provincial officer about a slave of a certain Lucius Egnatius, a knight who often did business for him. "I commend him to you with no less warmth," Cicero says, "than if the business I commend to you were my very own."[51] To show Cicero's relations with a leading municipal man I quote a letter written to Brutus when he was governor of Cisalpine Gaul. "L. Castronius Paetus, by far the most important member of the municipality of Luca, is an honourable, sterling and most obliging man, a thoroughly good fellow, and graced not only with all the virtues but also, if that has anything to do with the matter, with a handsome fortune. Besides he is on very good terms with me, so much so indeed that there is no member of our order to whom he pays more particular attention. I therefore commend him to you as being both my friend and worthy of your friendship; and whatever you do to oblige him will assuredly give pleasure to yourself and in any case be a favor to me."[52]

Caesar's organization of his contacts at Rome through the loyal Balbus was remarkably efficient during his years of absence in Gaul. There was a steady stream of messengers between Rome and Gaul, and Caesar was informed of everything, *omnia minima maxima*.[53] Balbus, later aided by the equally efficient Oppius, did wonders in upholding Caesar's influence and seeing to it that the men whom Caesar supported lived up to their obligations.

In maintaining this great private organization, the noble aimed to keep up his own influence at Rome when he was away and in the provinces when he was at Rome; he was seeking, too, through patronage to add steadily to the group of men who had received favors which they might be expected to repay. When Cicero writes to a friend about some senator, public contractor, or provincial, he frequently adds, "Please tell him I wrote to you about this."

Particularly important for every noble was the organization of his contacts with the members of his own voting group or ward, his *tribules*, whom he counted on being able to carry for his own elections or those of his friends. This group will be discussed in the next chapter.

I turn now to the admittedly inferior group, the clients, for whom also the maintenance of organized contacts was essential.[54] These were the men for whom the noble, as *patronus*, a word related in origin to *pater*, was expected to take paternal responsibility. The clients, men said to be in the *fides* of their patron, provided the Roman politician with a basis in popular support. The institution of clientage went far back in Roman history. In a passage that seems to depend on a monograph of Caesar's time,[55] the Greek historian Dionysius of Halicarnassus attributes the institution to Romulus, who "placed the plebeians as a trust in the hands of the patricians by allowing every plebeian to choose for his patron any patrician whom he himself wished." The relationship of *fides*,[56] trust, loyalty, theoretically entered into voluntarily, was at the root of the institution. Dionysius describes the duties of both sides, the obligation of the patron to explain the law to his client, to look out for him and his family, to bring suit for him and defend him, and the client's responsibility to serve his patron in every way. The relation of mutual loyalty between patron and client (*fides* again) is further demonstrated in Dionysius' account. "For both patrons and clients alike," he says, "it was impious and unlawful to accuse each other in law suits, or to bear witness or to give their votes against each other or to be found in the number of each other's enemies; and whoever was convicted of doing any of these things was guilty of treason . . . The connections between the clients and patrons continued for many generations, differing in no wise from the ties of blood relationship, and being handed down to their children's children. And it was a matter of great praise to men of illustrious family to have as many clients as possible and not only to preserve the succession of hereditary patronage but also by their own merit to acquire others."

These clients had once been serfs in the power of their noble patrons, but that condition had ended several centuries before the age of Caesar. The relationship in our period is frequently not an exclusive one. A client could have a number of different patrons. We know more about the whole class under the empire, for Martial and Juvenal tell us a great deal about the inconveniences and difficulties of the morning *salutatio*, for which the poor man had to climb up the hills to the great houses of Rome. The class was equally strong under the republic, and more useful to the patron in the days of free elections.

To understand the importance of clients in the late republic, we have to go to a passage like the following in Cicero's speech for Murena: "Men of slender means have only one way of earning favors from our order or of paying us back and that is by helping us and following us about in our campaigns for office. For it is not possible and cannot be asked of men of our class and of the Roman knights that they should for entire days follow after their friends who are candidates. If they come in numbers to our houses and sometimes accompany us down to the Forum, if they deign to walk with us the length of a public hall, we think we are securing great attention and respect. It is the men of rather slender means, men with free time, who supply the steady attention that is regularly given to good men and to benefactors. Don't take from the lower class of men this fruit of their devotion. Let the men who hope for everything from us have something themselves to give us."

Cicero goes on to indicate that to have influence the men of lower station have to do something more than cast their ballots for their benefactors. "As they often say, they can't talk for us or make speeches or offer bail or invite us to their houses. These are all things they secure from us and they can make return only by their services."[57] In this passage Cicero appears to be protecting the humbler people from restrictions on electioneering, but he clearly shows the value the nobles places on the assiduous service of the client class. That value is also shown in Quintus Cicero's advice on Marcus' candidacy for the consulship.

Quintus classifies the clients who show attention to candidates for office into three groups,[58] the throngs that come to the morning *salutatio* and that often journey about from one candidate to another, the men who accompany the candidate down to the Forum, and the men who follow him about as he goes around asking for votes. The second class, the *deductores*, are apparently more respectable than the other two, and Quintus advises Marcus to go to the Forum at a regular hour every day, so that they will not be kept waiting.

Both Marcus and Quintus seem to be speaking mainly of the urban populace which provided most of the people that thronged the houses of the great and followed the leading men around, especially when they were candidates, but in smaller numbers also at other times. The urban plebs, especially after it had been increased by men evicted from their lands, by vagrants who came to the city to enjoy the games and to benefit from the grain dole, and by the steady manumission of slaves, had in it a large group of people who possessed no means of livelihood except what could be had from attachment to nobles of the great houses and to popular leaders like Caesar or Clodius—who, by advancing popular measures in the assemblies, were actually building a personal party.

Sallust, in a rather sweeping statement, says that every man of a people that was once sovereign has made private arrangements for slavery.[59] Plenty of them were actually hired out to individuals, and they could be used not only for legitimate campaigns, where they followed the candidate about, but also, as we shall see in the next chapter, for violence. It was easier to gather such men together because many of them, including slaves and freedmen, were, under the free right of association that prevailed at Rome, already organized in guilds or *collegia*, primarily burial colleges for men in the same trade or adherents of a common cult. There were also neighborhood guilds, centering about altars at the crossroads where annual games were celebrated in religious organizations. Such groups, made up of men associated in their trades and cults, or living in close proximity, could easily be brought together for political purposes.

Catiline seems to have used these guilds to terrorize his opponents, and it was apparently during his campaign for the consulship in 64 that the senate passed a decree disbanding all the guilds except such as contributed to the public welfare.[60] Clodius as tribune in 58 revived the guilds and even created new ones; he armed the members with sticks and stones and sometimes with swords, and employed them as a private army in politics. The senate attempted again to dissolve the guilds, but apparently without success.[61]

The client class went far beyond the bounds of the city. It included inhabitants of towns, and in fact of whole regions, over which the nobles assumed patronage because they or their ancestors had conquered them in war, or had aided them in obtaining citizenship and other advantages. Thus the descendants of the commissioners who had established Roman colonies—the city founders, who in Roman tradition functioned in groups and not individually—thought of themselves as the patrons of the towns their ancestors had established. As Rome's empire extended, the nobles conquered territory overseas—provincials and even peoples of client kingdoms.[62] The Claudii Marcelli, descendants of the conqueror of Syracuse, considered themselves the patrons of all Sicily. Lucius Domitius Ahenobarbus, grandson of one of the conquerors of Narbonese Gaul, thought that that region was in his care and for years looked with jealous eyes on Caesar's tenure of the province. Every man who had been a provincial governor strove to maintain relations with the people, and especially the "best" people, of the province he had administered. When Flaccus, who had governed Asia, was tried for extortion, many Asiatics were there to testify for him.[63]

All the great noble houses had great numbers of clients in their service. Crassus and Pompey each had a band so large that he could raise an army in Sulla's service. Crassus had built up his inherited riches by his policy of continually annexing more clients.[64] It is the fashion of modern historians to single Crassus out as the weakest of the three men in the so-called triumvirate, but it is noteworthy that both Caesar and Pompey thought he counted. The reason he counted is that in his great following clients he was a rival of the strongest of the nobles who combined against the three men.

Pompey's clients were perhaps more numerous than Crassus', but they were probably less well distributed in the voting districts. From his father, a leading general of the Social War, and a man who once threatened to take the state over by force, Pompey had inherited a large band of loyal veterans who had been richly rewarded by the elder Pompey; he had also inherited masses of clients in Picenum, where his father had vast estates, and in the Social War had managed to conciliate the richest elements in the population. In the elder Pompey's bodyguard, as we know from an inscription, was a group of young Picene officers,[65] and men from that region appear later in his son's entourage. One of them was Caesar's most trusted lieutenant in Gaul, Titus

Labienus, whose defection to Pompey at the beginning of the Civil War is to be explained by his Picene origin.[66] The elder Pompey had also won a large following both in the Gallic cities south of the Po and in the teeming and vigorous population north of the Po, where he had, under a consular law, bestowed Latin rights on the towns. He also had numerous clients in Spain, to many of whom he gave citizenship.

The younger Pompey himself increased his inherited clients through his enlistment of soldiers, his bestowal of citizenship, and his conciliation of many individuals and groups. His adherents were so numerous in Spain that his sons were able to make the peninsula a base of resistance not only against Caesar but later against Caesar's heir. Pompey's eastern conquests also added to his clients huge forces of allied peoples —barbarians, and not Romans, as the opposing side took care to point out.

Extension of citizenship was a favorite means of adding to one's clients. Gaius Gracchus had tried to give citizenship to the Latin communities (towns whose magistrates acquired Roman citizenship through election to local offices) and Latin rights to the other Italian people, and at the end of his career, when he was hard pressed by his enemies, he seems to have encouraged Latins and Italians to rally to his defense. His example was followed by the tribune Marcus Livius Drusus, who in 91 B.C. attempted to enfranchise all the Italians. We have an extraordinary document of Drusus' activity in an oath of fealty that the Italians took in Drusus' name. The text of the oath, quoted by the Greek historian of the Augustan Age, Diodorus Siculus, has generally been rejected because it was considered inconsistent with Roman religious formulae, but the recent discovery of an inscription has provided strong reason for believing it genuine.[67] It reads: "I swear by Jupiter Capitolinus and the Vesta of Rome and by Mars, the ancestral god of Rome, and by the Sun, the founder of the race *(Sol Indiges)*, and by earth, the benefactress of living and growing things, and by the demigods, who are the founders of Rome, and the heroes who have contributed to increase her domain that I will hold the friend and enemy of Drusus to be my friend and enemy and that I will not spare possessions or the life of my children or of my parents if it be to Drusus' advantage and to the advantage of those who have taken this oath. If I become a citizen by the law of Drusus I will hold Rome as my country and Drusus as my greatest benefactor, and I will share this oath with as many citizens as I can. And if I swear faithfully, may all good things come to me; if falsely, the reverse." If, as I believe, this oath is genuine, it is clear that Drusus was building a very powerful body of followers among the Italians, who were then more numerous by far than the Roman citizens. There was some basis for the nobles' fear that Drusus was striving for personal supremacy.[68] It was as swearers of a joint oath that, aroused by the murder of Drusus, the Italians rose in revolt in the Social War.[69]

When the Italians acquired citizenship after that war, the next group clamoring for the right was the Transpadane people, the inhabitants of the cities across the Po, the country of Catullus, Vergil, and Livy, the richest and most populous district of Italy. The Latin rights given them by the elder Pompey meant that the men elected to magistracies in the towns—that is, the richest inhabitants, like Catullus' father, for instance—already had such rights, but plenty of noncitizens remained, and there were men at Rome who wished for the credit of enrolling them with full franchise. Pompey was interested in them because of his father's benefactions, and so was Crassus, who tried to give them citizenship when he was censor, but failed because of the opposition of his colleague Catullus.

Caesar, who had shown his concern for the subject as early as the year 68, was able to make progress with the awards during his long Gallic proconsulship. Many of the men had acquired citizenship through enlistment in his army, and others through the colony he established at Novum Comum.[70] Sallust, in the letter to Caesar written in 51, urged Caesar to adopt a general policy of enfranchisement, acknowledging that the nobles would, as they subsequently did, oppose his policy bitterly.[71] Sallust supported the enrollment of new citizens as a means of purifying the state, but he did not deny that the awards would greatly strengthen Caesar's position. The Transpadane region was enfranchised in 49 under a law proposed by one of Caesar's praetors.

We do not know how usual it was for the client to swear allegiance to his patron, but the example of Livius Drusus may indicate that it was customary procedure for new citizens. The humbler followers of Catiline, as well as the senators and knights, took such an oath. They included a large group of the city plebs, hard pressed by misery and debt, and another in the country, where Sulla's veterans, who had not proved to be good farmers, and the men who had been dispossessed made common cause.

The most important group under oath to individuals was the personal army.[72] The Roman soldier, recruited in earlier times for a year's service under a consul who also functioned for a year, though the command might be prolonged, had regularly taken an oath of allegiance to his general. The relationship was a close one, but, since terms of service were often brief and generals constantly changed, the citizen soldiers had been distributed in military allegiance among various generals of the nobility. When Marius instituted the army of the proletariat, which remained under arms for years, the old military oath seems to have been administered for the entire period of service. The soldiers were turned into clients of the general; while they were in the army they looked to him for rewards, and after they were established in colonies with grants of land they continued as veterans to regard him as their patron, to look to him for aid, and to respond to his call in time of need. Certainly Caesar, and perhaps Sulla and Pompey before him, settled the veterans in colonies according to their military units so that it would be possible to call them out for renewed service in their old formations. And they had an advantage over other clients, for they already knew the art of war. They were the most important and decisive accretion to the personal party.

From 70 to 49, Pompey's veterans constituted a major factor in Roman politics. The union of Pompey, Crassus, and Caesar brought them into the service of the three men, where they were added to the strong forces of inherited clients belonging to Pompey and Crassus. Caesar, with an ancestry that had in recent generations been less distinguished, probably inherited no such large group of clients, but he had built his personal following out of the old Marians, both the upper classes, who had been debarred from public office by Sulla, and the populace, who revered the memory of Marius.[73] Caesar had also, by conciliating the urban plebs and sponsoring laws that looked out for their interests, added greatly to his adherents. These three men were opposed by the great mass of the nobility, men like Cato and his wealthy brother-in-law Lucius Domitius Ahenobarbus and the influential Cornelii Lentuli, all provided with inherited clients, of whose strength Sallust warns Caesar.[74] There were fewer trained soldiers in this group, but there were plenty of men available to provide armed bands to oppose the forces of the "triumvirs," and to keep the streets of Rome and the popular assemblies in a state of confusion for a decade.

When Pompey broke with Caesar, he united his clients and his veterans with the forces of the men who had been his enemies for years, the *optimates* of the senate. The combination made a strong party, but not strong enough to prevail against the party that Caesar had built for himself alone. That party included the urban plebs to whom Caesar and his tribunes had for years presented popular laws, but the plebs no longer counted when arms took the place of legislation. What did count was Caesar's army, ten legions, most of them tested by years of victorious fighting and devoted to their leader. And after he won the war, Caesar attempted to turn all Italy into a single unit bound in personal loyalty to him. He failed, but his successor Augustus, by administering an oath of fealty to himself, succeeded. That development, to be more fully discussed in the last chapter, was not clearly understood until a German, and, I feel confident, an anti-Nazi German, Anton von Premerstein, writing under the domination of a leader and a party which had become identified with the whole state, interpreted Roman politics in terms of the scene in which he was living and showed how the totalitarian party of the empire (which the Romans were not so illogical as to call a party) evolved from the personal parties of the old Roman nobility.

NOTES

1 Throughout this chapter, I am constantly under obligation to Gelzer's *Nobilität*; for a more general treatment, which follows Gelzer, see W. Knoll, *Die Kultur der ciceronischen Zeit* (Leipzig, 1933) 1.1-80.

2 Sall. *Iug*. 63.6-7 (of Marius): Consulatum nobilitas inter se per manus tradidit. novos nemo tam clarus neque tam egregius factis erat quin indignus eo honore et ⟨is⟩ quasi pollutus haberetur. Compare the similar statement on Cicero, Sall. *Catil*. 23.6. On new men see Gelzer, *op. cit*. 1-42, especially 40-42. For more recent bibliography and a discussion of the varying meaning of *novus homo* see Strasburger in RE. I have in general employed the term, as Cicero often does, for men of equestrian family who advanced all the way to the consulship.

3 6.54.2 (Paton's translation, Loeb text).

4 *Pis*. 1; *Planc*. 51. Cf. Sall. *Iug*. 4.5.

5 *Iug*. 4.7-8; cf. 73-7.

6 On the patrician families see Mommsen, *Röm. Forschungen* (Berlin, 1864) 1.71-127; for the patrician houses surviving in the late republic see 122.

7 *Mur*. 16. See Gelzer, *op. cit*. 25; on the patriciate in the time of Caesar see Syme, RR 68 f.

8 For the family tree of the Caecilii Metelli see Syme, RR table 1. For the kinsmen of Cato see table 11. Numerous genealogical tables are to be found in Münzer, RA (see n. 7 to chap. i, above), and in the biographical articles in RE.

9 *De off*. 1.71-73, with the succeeding discussion of the duties of the statesman. The *De Officiis* was written in 44 after the death of Caesar. For an earlier statement of Cicero on the duty of taking part in public affairs see *Rep*. 1.1-12.

10 *Lucretius* 2.11-13. This passage and the next are quoted in the translation of William Ellery Leonard.

11 3.995-1002.

12 Tac. *Dial*. 34; Quintil. *Inst*. Or. 12.6.1.

13 6.19.2.

14 Suet. *Aug*. 89.

15 For the house of the man of politics (and therefore of his son) see *Off*. 1.138. The emphasis on decorum in the passage that follows is important; on the unseemliness of certain trades and professions see 150-151.

16 On the age at which various offices could be held see Mommsen, *Römisches Staatsrecht* (3d ed., Leipzig, 1887) 1.563-572.

17 On extravagant aedileships see Cic. *Off*. 2.57. The passage that follows deals with all manner of liberality in public life.

18 Suet. *Iul*. 9. In Cicero's law on malpractice (passed in 63) candidates were forbidden to give such shows unless provision for them had been made in a will. See Mommsen, *Römisches Strafrecht* (Leipzig, 1899) 870 n.5.

19 Provincial governors regularly had *legati* under them; men entrusted with special commands might have a considerable number. Pompey had twenty-five in his war against the pirates, and Caesar about a dozen in Gaul, all of whom were provided with *imperium (legati pro praetore)*. See Drumann-Groebe, *Geschichte Roms* (Leipzig, 1899-1929) 4.420 ff.; 3.700 f.; cf. Mommsen, *Staafsrecht*, 3d ed., 2.696 ff. Caesar is conspicuous among men who eventually pursued a military career because, except for brief absences in Further Spain as quaestor and praetorian governor, he remained in the city during the entire interval between his quaestorship and his consulship. He held two special offices in the city in this period, that of road commissioner and that of *index quaestionis*. According to Plutarch, *Caes*. 5, he was curator of the Via Appia and spent large sums in repairing the road. On the political value of such a task for the candidate see Cic. *Att*. 1.1.2. The roads over which men traveled to vote were doubtless placarded with notices publicizing the benefactions of road commissioners.

20 The candidate himself should not, according to Cicero (*Mur*. 43-46), have his mind on a prosecution since it would divert him from the campaign. But there were always friends who could act for him. Such trials were particularly numerous in the year 54.

21 Under this charge *(ambitus)* the successful candidates for the consulship of 65 were prosecuted through the agency of their defeated competitors and were condemned. The defeated men then obtained the consulship.

22 Pompey and Crassus are the only men who attained a second consulship in the interval between the dictatorships of Sulla and Caesar. Cicero hoped for a second consulship after the death of Caesar.

23 The censorship was suspended by Sulla and revived by Pompey in 70. The five sets of censors chosen after that date (65, 64, 61, 55, and 50) did not

complete the *lustrum*. For Cicero's desire for the censorship see *Att.* 4.2.6.

24 See Sall. *Iug*. 31.10 (from the speech of the tribune C. Memmius): Sed incedunt ⟨pauci nobiles⟩ per ora vostra magnifici, sacerdotia et consulatus, pars triumphos suos ostentantes. On the priesthoods see chap. iv. Since the *lustrum* was completed only in 69, in our period, one of the greatest distinctions of the nobles, the honor of being *princeps senatus*, the first man on the census rolls, fell into disuse. That honor was regularly bestowed on a patrician, and, in every instance that we know, on a member of the *gentes maiores*, the Aemilii, Claudii, Cornelii, Fabii, and Valerii. It is probable that in the censorship of 70-69 it was conferred on Mamercus Aemilius Livianus, consul of 77 (Val. Max. 7.7.6), who seems not to have lived long after 69. On his career see Münzer, *RA* 312 f. On the *princeps senatus* see Mommsen, *Röm. Forsch.* 1.92-94.

25 For the evidence see Drumann-Groebe, *Geschichte Roms* 5.209 ff., esp. 213 n. 5.

26 *Serm.* 1.6.34-37.

Sic qui promittit civis, urbem sibi curae, Imperium fore et Italiam, delubra deorum, Quo patre sit natus, num ignota matre inhonestus Omnis mortalis curare et quaerere cogit.

27 Compare the numerous comments on the selection of Tullia's third husband in Cicero's correspondence of 51-50.

28 Plut. *Cato Min.* 52; cf. 25. Hortensius was not, as is sometimes asserted, childless, but he and Cato would be more closely bound together if they had children by the same mother. See Lucan, *Phars.* 2.332-333: sanguine matris permixtura domos. Thus Pompey and M. Aemilius Scaurus were considered to be united because they had children by the same mother. Cf. Ascon. pp. 19-20 C.

29 On adoptions as a method of uniting families see Münzer, *RA* 103 f. and *passim*.

30 *Rep*. 2.1. See also the *Somnium Scipionis* in Bk. 6, *passim*.

31 See Münzer, *RA* 314 ff. and *Hermes* 71 (1936) 222 ff.

32 *Phars.* 8.73.

33 Cicero's *De Amicitia*, a discussion put into the mouth of C. Laelius, whose friendship with Scipio Aemilianus was renowned, has significant material on friendship between men in politics.

34 Ascon. *In Scaur.*, pp. 20, 28 C.

35 *Fam.* 3.10.10 (to Appius Claudius, whose daughter had married Pompey's son): Qua denique ille facilitate, qua humanitate tulit contentionem meam pro Milone adversantem interdum actionibus suis?

36 *Att.* 9.2A.2. Cicero was not unaware that Pompey had deserted him when the bill for exile came up (*Att.* 8.3.3), and the Caesarians kept reminding Cicero of it to keep him from feeling obligation. See the letter of Mark Antony, *Att.* 10.8A.2 (of Pompey): ut beneficium daret prius iniuriam fecit.

37 Cic. *Cael.* 26; cf. L. Mitteis, *Römisches Privatrecht* (Leipzig, 1908) 1.390 f. See Pfaff s.v. "Sodalicius" and Ziebarth s.v. "Sodales" in *RE*; De Robertis, *Il Diritto Associativo Romano* (Bari, 1938). The

lex repetundarum (*CIL* 1.2 (2d ed.) 583, secs. 20 and 25) provides that a man who was a *cognatus*, *adfinis*, or *sodalis*, or a member of the same *collegium* as the accused should be ineligible for jury duty on the case.

38 *Comm. Pet.* 19: Nam hoc biennio quattuor sodalitates hominum ad ambitionem gratiosissimorum tibi obligasti C. Fundani Q. Galli C. *Corneli* C. Orcivi. Horum in causis ad te deferendis quid tibi eorum sodales receperint et confirmarint scio, nam interfui. *Factio* seems to be used in the same sense in Cic. *ad Q. Fr.*3.1.15. Gabinium tres ad huc factiones postulant; cf. *Brut.* 164. See Mommsen, *De Collegiis et Sodaliciis Romanorum* (Kiel, 1843) 41 f.

39 See G. M. Calhoun, *Athenian Clubs in Politics and Litigation* (Austin, Texas, 1913).

40 See the evidence for the trials under the *lex Varia* of 90, G. Niccolini, *I Fasti dei Tribuni della plebe* (Milan, 1934) 222 ff.

41 Cicero constantly uses *coniurare, coniuratio* of the conspiracy. See the story in Sallust, *Catil.* 22, for which however Sallust does not vouch. Premerstein, "Vom Werden und Wesen des Prinzipats," *Abh. bayer. Akad. der Wiss.*, phil.-hist. Abt., N.F. 15 (1937) 31 f. holds that, while the Athenian clubs (*éraipeiai* and *ouvwuooiai*) were associations of equals, the Roman *coniuratio* was usually made up of inferiors who swore allegiance to a leader. The evidence for the conspiracy of Catiline does not support his view. Certainly Lentulus, an ex-consul who boasted of his destiny, and probably Cethegus asserted leadership for themselves.

42 Cf. Q. Cicero, *Comm. Pet.* 33 on the equestrian centuries; 6 on noble youths. See nn. 33, 36, 38 to chap. iii below.

43 *CIL* 1.2, 2d ed., 1764, with references cited there. Cf. *ILS* 6993 ff. See also Münzer, *RA* 51 n. 1. On *hospitium* see Gelzer, *Nobilität* 52 ff., where he discusses *hospites* in association with the whole group of adherents in the *fides* of a noble.

44 *Rosc. Am.* 15, J. H. Freese's translation, Loeb text.

45 *Ibid.* 16. On Roscius' association with Roman nobles see 15, 77, 119, 149. On the relations of hospitality between M. Livius Drusus and Q. Pompaedius Silo, leader of the Italians, see Plutarch, *Cato Min.* 2.1.

46 *Leg.* 3.36.

47 Cf. Cic. *Phil.* 3.15-16. See Tac. *Ann.* 4.3 on the scorn felt for Livilla and her *municipalis adulter*, Sejanus.

48 Sall. *Catil.* 31.7; Cic. *Sulla* 22-25.

49 See Cicero's letters to Cato from Cilicia, *Fam.* 15.3 and 4. Cf. Plut. *Cato Min.* 19.2.

50 See Max Radin, *Marcus Brutus* (Oxford Univ. Press, 1939) 81 ff.

51 Cic. *Fam.* 13.45, W. G. Williams' translation, Loeb text. Cf. also 43, 44, 47. See Münzer s.v. "Egnatius" (35) *RE*.

52 *Fam.* 13.13, W. G. Williams' translation.

53 Cic. *ad Q. Fr.* 3.1.10.

54 There was no hard-and-fast distinction between *amici, hospites,* and *clientes* (see however Gell. 5.13). Seneca (*de benef.* 6.34) notes that is was an old custom for kinds to divide their friends into groups:

Apud nos primi omnium C. Gracchus et mox Livius Drusus instituerunt segregare turbam suam et alios in secretum recipere, alios cum pluribus, alios universos. See Fustel de Coulanges, *op. cit*. (in n. 13 to chap. i, above) 211 ff.

55 Dion. Hal. 2.9-11, E. Cary's translation, Loeb text. See M. Pohlenz, "Eine politische Tendenzschrift aus Caesars Zeit," *Hermes* 59 (1924) 157-189.

56 *Fides* between friends and inferiors is discussed by Gelzer, *op. cit*. 52 ff., and by R. Heinze, *Hermes* 64 (1929) 140-166 (reprinted in Heinze, *Vom Geist des Römertums* (Leipzig and Berlin, 1938) 25-58).

57 Cic. *Mur*. 71-72.

58 *Comm. Pet*. 34-38.

59 *R.P*. 2.5.4-5: Ita paulatim populus qui dominus erat ac cunctis gentibus imperitabat, dilapsus est et pro communi imperio privatim sibi of nobles, but the statement is equally applicable to the followers of the demagogic leaders.

60 Cic. Pis. 8, and Ascon. *ad loc*. p. 7 C; cf. M. Cary, *CAH* 9.484. For the complete evidence see Kornemann, s.v. "Collegium," *re* 405 ff.; De Robertis, *op. cit* (in n. 37 above) 74 ff.

61 Cic. *ad Q Fr*. 2.3.5 (in February, 56). On the interpretation of this passage see De Robertis, *op. cit*. 100 ff. Cf.n. 101 to chap. iii, below.

62 See Syme, *op. cit*. 73 ff.; *JRS* 34 (1944) 93; Premerstein, *op. cit*. (in n. 41 above) 16 ff.

63 See Cic. *Flacc*., *passim*.

64 Plut. *Crass*. 7. Crassus is quoted as saying that no man was really rich who could not support an army out of his revenues. Cf. Cic. *Parad*. 45; *Off*. 1.25; Plut. *Crass*. 2.7; Pliny, *N.WH*. 33.134.

65 *CIL* 1.2, 2d ed., 709, with *addenda* on p. 714 (*ILS* 8888). On the elder Pompey's influence on his son's career see Gelzer, *Abh. preuss. Ak. Wiss*., phil.-hist. Kl. 1941, 14.1-33.

66 See Syme, *JRS* 28 (1938) 113 ff.

67 Diodorus 37.11D (17B). See the discussion of Premerstein, *op. cit*. (in n. 41 above) 27 ff. Premerstein, though believing that an oath was taken on this occasion, did not accept Diodorus' version as the genuine text of the oath. But see the illuminating study of Carl Koch, *Gestirnverehrung im alten Italien* (Frankfurt, 1933) 89 ff. Through a newly discovered calendar fragment from Ostia (*CIL* 14, Suppl. 4547) it was possible for Koch to identify ρον γεναρχην Η lov of Diodorus' text with Sol Indiges and to show that there was an ancient cult of the god at Rome. Koch's investigation has provided evidence for believing that Diodorus' version is a translation of the oath actually taken.

68 Sall. *R.P*. 2.6.4-5.

69 See the *denarius* struck by Drusus' *hospes*, Q. Pompaedius Silo. On the reverse is represented a youth about to sacrifice a pig; eight warriors point their swords toward the victim. See H. A. Grueber, *Coins of the Roman Republic in the British Museum* (London, 1910) 2.329.

70 See Ascon. p. 3 C; Suet. *Iul*. 8; Dio 37.9.3; cf. Plut. *Crass*. 13.2. On Caesar's colony at Novum Comum and the attendant enfranchisements see T. Rice Holmes, *The Roman Republic* (Oxford, 1923) 1.326; 2.317-320.

71 *R.P*. 2.6. Sallust does not specifically mention the Transpadanes, but there can be no doubt that he has them in mind.

72 All soldiers, on entering military service, took the regular military oath. Premerstein, *op. cit*. 44 ff., 73 ff., distinguishes between it and the oath of fealty to the emperor taken by the soldiers. The latter oath, he believes, established a relationship like the old Roman bond between patron and client.

73 See L. R. Taylor, *CPh* 36 (1941) 113 ff.; *TAPhA* 73 (1942) 1 ff.

74 *R.P*. 2.11.3: Quippe cum illis maiorum virtus partam reliquerit gloriam dignitatem clientelas. Cf. *Iug*. 85.4.

FEUDAL SOCIETY

MARC BLOCH

1. The Lord's Estate

THE RELATIVELY HIGH social circles of which military homage was a characteristic feature were not the only ones where 'men' of other men were to be found. But at the lower level relationships of dependence found their natural setting in an arrangement which was much older than vassalage and which was for a long time to survive it. This was the manor (*seigneurie*). Neither the origins of the manorial régime nor its role in the economy fall within the scope of the present work: we are here concerned solely with its place in feudal society.

Whereas the authority deriving from vassal homage became a source of profit only belatedly and by an undoubted deviation from its original form, in the manor the economic aspect was of primary importance. There, from the beginning, the object—if not the exclusive, at least the principal object—of the powers enjoyed by the chief was to provide him with revenues by securing for him a portion of the produce of the soil. A manor was therefore first and foremost an estate (*terre*)—there was hardly any other word for it in spoken French—but an estate inhabited by the lord's subjects. As a rule the area thus delimited was in its turn divided into two closely interdependent parts. on the one hand there was the 'demesne', known also to historians as the 'reserve', all the produce of which was taken directly by the lord; on the other there were the tenements (*tenures*), small or medium-sized peasant holdings, which, in varying numbers, were grouped round the lord's 'court.' The superior real property right which the lord claimed over the cottage, the arable, and the meadow of the villein was expressed by his demand for a new investiture (rarely granted free of charge) every time they changed hands; by the right to appropriate them in case of default of heirs or by lawful confiscation; finally and above all, by the right to impose taxes and demand services. The latter consisted for the most part in agricultural labour services performed on the demesne. Thus, at least at the beginning of the feudal era, when these compulsory labour services were particularly heavy, the tenements not only added their contribution in produce or money to the revenues of the fields directly exploited by the master; they were in addition a source of manpower in the absence of which those fields must have lain fallow.

Needless to say, all manors were not of the same size. The largest, in the regions of nucleated settlements, covered the whole of the village territory. From the ninth century onward, however, this was probably not the most usual case; and in spite of some examples of successful concentration here and there it became in the course of time increasingly rare throughout Europe. No doubt this was a result of partitions amongst heirs; but it was also a result of the creation if fiefs. In order to pay his vassals for their services more than one chief had to parcel out his estates. Moreover, since it happened fairly often that—whether by gift or sale or as a result of one of those acts of territorial subjection, of which the mechanism will be described later—a powerful individual asserted his authority over a number of fairly widely-dispersed peasant farms, there were many manors which spread their tentacles over the lands of several villages at once, without coinciding exactly with any. In the twelfth century, manor and village were seldom any longer coterminous, except in the zones of recently cleared land where manors and villages had been founded together on virgin territory. The majority of peasants belonged therefore at one and the same time to two groups constantly out of step with each other; one of them composed of subjects of the same master, the other of members of the same village community. For the cultivators whose houses stood side by side and whose holdings were interspersed were perforce united—although they might be subject to different lords—by all manner of bonds of common interest, and indeed by submission to common agricultural practices.

This dualism was eventually to bring about a serious weakening of the lord's authority. As for the regions where families of patriarchal type lived either independently or two or three together in tiny hamlets, the manor there comprised as a rule a larger or smaller number of these little establishments; and this dispersion must have meant an appreciably looser structure.

2. The Extension of the Manorial System

How extensive was the manorial régime? And if it is true that small islands of independence always existed, what was the proportion of these to the manors at different times and places? These are extremely difficult problems. For only the manors kept archives (those of the Church at least did so), and fields without lords are fields without a history. If an independent field by chance figures in the texts, it is only at the moment of its disappearance, so to speak—at the moment when a written document records its final absorption in the complex of manorial rights. Therefore the more lasting the independence of such lands, the more irremediable our ignorance of them is likely to be. In order to clear up a little of this obscurity, we ought at least to distinguish carefully two forms of subjection: that which affected a man in his person, and that which affected him only as the holder of a certain piece of land. Undoubtedly, the two forms were closely related; so much so that one of them frequently involved the other. In the lower classes, however—in contrast with the world of vassalage and the fief—they were far from identical. Let us begin with dependence on the land or through the land, leaving for the next chapter the discussion of personal conditions.

In the countries where Roman institutions, themselves superimposed on ancient Italic or Celtic traditions, had left a deep impress on rural society, the manor had already under the early Carolingians assumed a very definite shape. For all that, it is not difficult to find evidence in the *villae* of Frankish Gaul or Italy of the various elements from which they had been formed. Among the tenements or—to employ the name given to the most important of them, which were characterized by their indivisibility—the *mansi*, a certain number were described as 'servile.' This epithet, like the heavier and more arbitrary obligations to which they were subjected, recalled the time when the masters had created them by allotting to their slaves, whom they were transforming into farmers, vast portions of their former *latifundia*, which had ceased to be profitable under direct exploitation. This process of parcelling out estates, having also attracted free cultivators, had given rise simultaneously to other types of grant destined to be placed in the general category of 'free' tenements, which term recalled the condition of personal freedom enjoyed by their original tenants. But among the very considerable number of tenements so described the majority were of very different origin. Far from originating in grants made in the process of whittling down a great estate, they had always been peasant farms, as old as agriculture itself. The rents and compulsory services with which they were burdened had been originally only the mark of the subordination of the occupants to a village chief, or the head of a tribe or clan, or a patron—masters who had been gradually transformed into lords in the true sense. Finally—just as in Mexico in recent times groups of peasant proprietors were to be found side by side with the *haciendas*—there still subsisted a substantial number of genuine rural allods, exempt from seignorial rule.

As for the truly Germanic regions—of which the purest type was unquestionably the Saxon plain between Rhine and Elbe—in these areas also many slaves, freedmen, and doubtless even free farmers were established on the estates of the powerful, in return for rents and services. But among the peasant body the distinction between manorial dependants and allodialists was much less clearly drawn because only the first indications of the manorial system itself had so far appeared. The stage had still hardly been passed in which a chief of a village or part of a village was in process of becoming a lord; the gifts he traditionally received—as Tacitus bears witness in the case of the German chiefs—were only beginning to be transmuted imperceptibly into rents.

Now, during the first feudal age, the evolution of the two sections of the Frankish empire followed the same course. There was a uniform tendency towards increasing manorialization. A more or less complete fusion of different kinds of tenure; the acquisition of new powers by the manors; above all the transference of many allods to the control of a powerful individual—this happened everywhere or almost everywhere. Furthermore, where at the outset the only relationships of territorial dependence that existed were still somewhat loose and unstable, these were gradually regularized, giving rise to genuine manors. Let us not imagine that these developments were uniformly spontaneous. They were subject to the play of particular influences, favoured by the circumstances of immigration or conquest. This was seen in Germany where, in the south, from before the Carolingian age, and then, during that period, in Saxony itself, the bishops, the abbots, and the other great men who had come from the Frankish kingdom helped to spread the social habits of their country among a native aristocracy ready to imitate them. It was seen still more clearly in England. So long as Anglo-Saxon or Scandinavian traditions predominated there, the network of territorial dependence remained singularly tangled and unstable; the demesne and the tenements were but imperfectly linked together. It was not till after 1066, under the brutal compulsion of foreign masters, that a manorial régime of exceptional rigour made its appearance.

In this triumphant progress of the manor the abuse of force had nowhere been a negligible factor. With good reason the official texts of the Carolingian period were already deploring the oppression of the 'poor' by the 'powerful.' The latter, as a rule, had little desire to deprive men of their land; for the soil without labour to till it was of little value. What they wanted was to assert their authority over the small cultivators along with their fields.

In the achievement of this object many of them found a valuable weapon in the administrative structure of the Frankish state. Whoever still enjoyed complete freedom from any seignorial authority was, in theory, directly dependent on the king; which meant, in practice, on his officials. The count or his representatives conducted these people to the king's army, presided over the courts which tried them, and levied on them such public taxes as remained—all this, of course, in the king's name. But was the distinction clearly appreciated by those who were subject to these obligations? At all events, it is certain that the royal officials were not slow to exact taxes or labour services, for their own benefit, from the free subjects thus committed to their care. This, admittedly, was done under the honourable name of a voluntary gift or service. But soon, as one capitulary declares, the abuse became 'custom.'[1] In Germany, where the old Carolingian edifice took a long time to disintegrate, at least the new rights sprung from this usurpation remained, in a considerable number of cases, linked to the office; and the count exercised them, as such, over men whose property had not been annexed to his manorial estates. Elsewhere, as a result of the dividing-up of the count's authority—amongst the heirs of the first holder of the office, or the count's subordinates or vassals—the former allodialist, henceforth subject to rents and labour services, ended by being merged completely in the mass of manorial subjects and his fields became tenements.

Moreover, it was not necessary to hold an office in order to exercise legitimately a portion of the public authority. By the operation of the Frankish 'immunity,' which will be studied later, the majority of ecclesiastical lords and a great number of lay potentates had acquired by delegation a fraction at least of the judicial powers of the state as well as the right to collect for their own profit certain of its revenues. This, of course, applied only to the estates which were already dependent on them or were to become so in the future. The immunity strengthened the lord's authority; it did not—at least in theory—create it. But these manors were only rarely all in one piece. Small allodial estates were often to be found in their midst, and to make contact with these became extremely inconvenient for the royal officials. Sometimes, it appears, the judicial and fiscal rights over them were abandoned to the holder of the immunity by the express decision of the sovereign. Much more often and much more quickly, the allods succumbed of their own accord to this inevitable attraction.

Finally, and this was not the least frequent case, downright violence was employed. About the beginning of the eleventh century, there was in Lorraine a widow living on her allodial estate. Since the death of her husband had left her without a protector, the agents of a neighbouring lord attempted to extort from her the payment of a quit-rent, as a sign of the dependent character of the estate. The attempt in this case failed because the woman placed herself under the protection of the monks.[2] How many similar claims, with no better foundation in law, were more successful! *Domesday Book*, which offers us two successive cross-sections, as it were, of English agrarian history, one immediately before the Norman Conquest, the other eight to ten years later, shows how during the intervening period many little independent estates had been unceremoniously 'attached' to the adjacent manors. A German or French *Domesday Book* of the tenth century, if there were one, would certainly record many plain 'attachments' of this sort.

Nevertheless manors expanded by another method, too, which, in appearance at least, was much less open to criticism—namely, by virtue of contracts. This was perhaps the most common method. The petty allodialist surrendered his land—sometimes, as we shall see, together with his person—to take it back subsequently in the form of a tenement, just like the knight who converted his allod into a fief, and with the same ostensible purpose of securing a protector. These agreements were invariably represented as being entirely voluntary. Were they so, in fact, everywhere and at all times? The adjective could be employed only with strong reservations. There were undoubtedly many ways of imposing one's protection on someone weaker than oneself; one would need only to begin by dunning him. Add to this the fact that the first agreement was not always respected. When the people of Wolen, in Alemannia, took a local landowner as their protector they promised him only a quit-rent; but soon, by assimilation to other tenants of the same powerful man, they were forced to perform labour services and denied the use of the neighbouring forest except on payment of rents.[3] Once get a finger trapped in the machine and your whole body may be drawn into it. Let us not imagine, however, that the situation of the lordless man appeared uniformly enviable. The peasant of Forez who, as late as 1280, transformed his allod into a villein tenement on condition of being henceforth 'protected, defended and warranted' (*gardé, défendu et garanti*) by the Hospitallers of Montbrison, his new lords, 'as are the other dependants of that house,' doubtless thought he was doing something to his advantage.[4] And yet this was a less troubled period than the first feudal age, Sometimes a whole village submitted itself in this way to a powerful man. It was an especially frequent occurrence in Germany, where, at the beginning of the evolution, there were still a large number of rural communities enjoying complete freedom from seignorial authority. In France and in Italy where, from the ninth century, the lord's power was much more developed, deeds of conveyance assumed as a rule an individual character. They were no less numerous on that account. About the year 900, as many as fourteen free men had burdened their own property with labour services in this way, in favour of an abbey at Brescia.[5]

Indeed, the most flagrant brutalities as well as the most genuinely spontaneous contracts proclaimed the influence of the same fundamental cause, namely, the weakness of the independent peasants. Let us not attempt to explain it as the result of economic adversity. That would be to forget that the expansion of the manorial régime was not confined to the country districts: even in a good many of the cities, few of which had known anything of the kind in Roman times, the system of the tenement, with its normal obligations, was introduced on the same lines as in the ancient rural *villa*. What is more, such an explanation would assume a contrast between farming methods in large and small landholdings respectively; a contrast which may hold good of other societies, but certainly not of this one. For the manor was first and foremost an agglomeration of small dependent farms; and on becoming a tenant the allodialist, though assuming new obligations, in no way changed his farming methods. He sought or submitted to a master only on account of the inadequacy of the other social arrangements—the kinship groups or the authority of the state. The case of the men of Wolen is significant. Victims of the most flagrant tyranny, they tried to make their complaint to the king, but finding themselves in the midst of a great court in full session they failed, with their rustic speech, even to make themselves understood. It is true that the lack of an effective government was partly due to the sluggishness of trade and monetary circulation. It is also true that the same factors, by depriving the cultivators of any reserve of cash, helped to undermine their capacity for resistance. But it was only in such indirect ways as this that economic conditions contributed to the social crisis of the peasantry. In the humble drama of rural life we recognize an aspect of the same development which, at a higher social level, impelled so many men to submit themselves to the ties of vassalage.

Moreover, in this connection it is enough to refer to the diversity of examples with which Europe presents us. The Middle Ages knew one extensively manorialized, but not feudalized, society—Sardinia. It is not surprising that, in this land long isolated from the great currents which swept the continent, an ancient system of rural chiefdoms, regularized during the Roman period, could be maintained without the power of the local aristocracies assuming the specific form of Frankish commendation. On the other hand, there were no countries without manors which were not at the same time countries without vassalage, as witness most of the Celtic societies of the British Isles; the Scandinavian peninsula; and finally, in Germania itself, the low-lying regions along the shores of the North Sea —Dithmarschen, beyond the estuary of the Elbe, and Frisia, from the Elbe to the Zuider-

zee. This applies to the last-named country till the fourteenth or fifteenth century, when certain dynasties of 'chiefs'—the word is an exact translation of the Frisian *hoveling*—raised themselves above the mass of free peasants. Strong in the possession of landed wealth accumulated from generation to generation, in the armed bands which they maintained and by their seizure of certain judicial functions, these petty village tyrants succeeded late in the day in creating for themselves what was really a manorial system in embryo. The fact was that at this time the old framework of Frisian society, based essentially on the ties of kinship, was beginning to crack. In the period when feudal institutions were at their height, these non-feudal societies on the fringes of the West were certainly not unfamiliar with the dependence of the small farmer (whether slave, freedman or free man) upon a richer man than himself, or the devotion of the companion to the prince or the leader of the warband. But they had nothing which recalled the vast, hierarchically organized system of peasant subjection and military vassalage to which we give the name of feudalism.

Shall we attribute the sole responsibility for this to the absence of any enduring Frankish influence—seeing that in Frisia itself the administrative organization which the Carolingians had for a time imposed collapsed at an early date? This factor is undoubtedly important; but it chiefly applies to the inability of companionage to transform itself into vassalage. The dominant facts went beyond questions of influence. Where every free man remained a warrior, liable to be constantly called to service and distinguished from the pick of the fighting-men by nothing essential in his equipment, the peasant had no difficulty in avoiding subjection to the manorial régime, while the groups of armed retainers failed to develop into a clearly recognized knightly class with a legal structure of its own. Where men of all ranks were able to rely for support on other forms of strength and solidarity than personal protection—kindred groups especially among the Frisians, the people of Dithmarschen and the Celts, kindred groups again among the Scandinavians, but also institutions of public law of the type common to the Germanic peoples—neither the relationships of dependence peculiar to territorial lordship, nor vassalage and the fief invaded the whole of social life.

Furthermore, just as was the case with the feudal system proper, the manorial régime was destined to reach a state of perfection only in the countries where it had been imported bag and baggage. In the England of the Norman kings there were no peasant allods any more than there were knightly ones. On the continent the peasant allod was much harder to eliminate. It is true that in France between the Meuse and the Loire, and in Burgundy, it had become extremely rare in the twelfth and thirteenth centuries; over wide areas it seems to have disappeared altogether. But there were peasant allods, in varying but always appreciable numbers, in south-western France, in certain provinces of central France like Forez, in Tuscany, and above all in Germany, where Saxony was their favourite soil. These were the very regions where, by striking parallelism, the allodial estates of the nobility survived—agglomerations of tenements, demesnes and political authority owing homage to no one. The manor was something much older than the institutions truly characteristic of the first feudal age. But its progress during this period, like its partial setbacks, is explained—everything points to this conclusion—by the same causes which contributed to, or militated against, the success of vassalage and the fief.

3. Lord and Tenants

Apart from contracts of individual subjection —and these were generally imprecise in their terms and quickly forgotten—the relations of the lord with the tenants were regulated only by 'the custom of the manor.' So true was this that in France the ordinary name for rents was simply 'customs' and that of the person who owed them 'customary man.' From the first appearance of a rudimentary form of manorial system —as far back as the Roman Empire, for example, or Anglo-Saxon England—it was this peculiar tradition which really defined each manor, as a human group, by distinguishing it from its neighbours. The precedents which thus governed the life of the community were themselves necessarily of a communal kind. That a tax has ceased to be paid by a particular holding almost since time immemorial makes no difference, says in effect a judgment of the Parlement of Paris in the reign of St. Louis; if the other holdings have paid it regularly all this time, it is compulsory also for the one which has so long evaded it.[6] This at least was the opinion of the jurists. Actual practice must often have been more elastic. In theory, everyone was required to observe these ancestral rules—the master as well as the dependants; but this professed respect for what had been done before was characteristically deceptive. For although they were

linked together through the ages by a supposedly unchanging custom nothing was less like the manor of the ninth century than the manor of the thirteenth.

The responsibility for this state of things cannot be ascribed to the defects of oral transmission. In the time of the Carolingians, many lords, after inquiry, had had the customs of their estates set down in writing, in the form of those detailed descriptions which were later called 'surveys' (*censiers*) or 'terriers.' But the pressure of local social conditions was stronger than respect for the past.

Through the innumerable conflicts of daily life legal memory was unceasingly stocked with new precedents. Above all, a custom could only be really binding where there was an impartial and effective judicial authority to enforce it. In the ninth century, in the Frankish state, the royal courts came to assume this role; and if the only decisions of these courts which are known to us are invariably unfavourable to the tenants the reason is perhaps simply that the ecclesiastical archives were not greatly concerned to preserve the others. Subsequently, the appropriation of judicial authority by the lords ruled out the possibility of recourse to the royal courts. The most scrupulous of lords did not hesitate to defy tradition when it interfered with their own interests or with those entrusted to them. Thus we find Abbot Suger, in his memoirs, congratulating himself on having been able to force the peasants of one of his estates to replace the quit-rent in money, which within living memory they had always paid, by a rent proportional to the harvest, from which more profit could be expected.[7] Almost the only forces that were now capable of counterbalancing (often very effectively, it is true) the abuses of power by the masters were the peasantry's remarkable capacity for passive resistance and, on the negative side, the inefficient management of the manors.

Nothing varied more from manor to manor according to locality, nothing exhibited more diversity, than the burdens of tenancy in the first feudal age. On certain days, the tenant brings the lord's steward perhaps a few small silver coins or, more often, sheaves of corn harvested on his fields, chickens from his farmyard, cakes of wax from his beehives or from the swarms of the neighbouring forest. At other times, he works on the arable or the meadows of the demesne. Or else we find him carting casks of wine or sacks of corn on behalf of the master to distant residences. His is the labour which repairs the walls or moats of the castle. If the master has guests the peasant strips his own bed to provide the necessary extra bed-clothes. When the hunting season comes round, he feeds the pack. If war breaks out he does duty as foot-soldier or orderly, under the leadership of the reeve of the village. The detailed study of these obligations belongs primarily to the study of the manor as an economic 'enterprise' and source of revenue. We shall confine ourselves here to stressing the facts of the evolution which most profoundly affected the human tie proper.

The dependence of the peasant farms on a common master was expressed by the payment of a sort of land rent. In this respect the work of the first feudal age was above all one of simplification. A fairly large number of dues which were paid separately in the Frankish period ended by being combined in a single quit-rent; and this in France, when it was paid in money, was generally known by the name *cens*. Now, among the earliest taxes, there were some which the manorial administrations had originally, in theory, levied only on behalf of the State. (An example is the purveyance formerly due to the royal army, or the payment which was substituted for it.) Their embodiment in an obligation which benefited only the lord and was conceived of as the expression of his superior rights over the soil attests with a peculiar clarity the preponderance acquired by the local power of the little chief of a group, at the expense of any higher social bond.

The problem of inheritance, one of the most delicate which the institution of the military fief had set, had almost no place in the history of rural tenements—at least during the feudal era. Almost universally, the peasants succeeded each other from generation to generation on the same fields. Occasionally, as will be explained later, collaterals were excluded when the tenant was of servile status; but the right of descendants was always respected, provided that they had not already deserted the family circle. The rules of succession were fixed by the old regional usages, without any interference from the lords, save for their efforts, at certain periods and in certain districts, to ensure the indivisibility of the property, which was considered necessary for the accurate levying of taxes. What is more, the hereditary succession of tenants seemed so much a matter of course that as a rule the texts, taking the principle as already established, did not trouble to mention it, except incidentally. Doubtless one reason for this was that with the majority of peasant farms, before the village chiefdoms transformed themselves into lordships, hereditary succession had been the imme-

morial custom; and it had gradually been extended to the holdings more recently carved out of the demesne. Moreover it was not in the interest of the lords to break with this practice. At this period, when land was more plentiful than men, when moreover economic conditions precluded the exploitation of excessively large demesnes with the help of hired labour or workers maintained in the lord's household, it was better for the lord instead of keeping all the plots of land in his own hands to have permanently at his disposal the labour and resources of dependants who were in a position to maintain themselves.

Of all the new 'exactions' imposed on the tenants, the most characteristic were the monopolies of many different kinds which the lord arrogated to himself at their expense. Sometimes he reserved for himself the right to sell wine or beer at certain times of year. Sometimes he claimed the sole right to provide, in return for payment, the services of bull or boar for stud purposes, or again to supply the horses which, in certain regions of southern France, were used to tread out the corn on the threshing-floor. More often he forced the peasants to grind their corn at his mill, to bake their bread in his oven, to make their wine in his wine-press. The very name of these exactions was significant. They were normally called *banalités*. Unknown in the Frankish period, their sole foundation was the lord's acknowledged power to give orders, signified by the old Germanic word *ban*. This was a power obviously inseparable from any authority exercised by a chief and therefore in itself, as a part of the lord's authority, of great antiquity; in the hands of petty local potentates, however, it had been greatly reinforced by their role as judges. The distribution of these *banalités*, by area, is no less instructive. France, where the weakening of governmental authority and the usurpation of judicial rights had been carried farthest, was their favourite soil. Yet even there they were chiefly exercised by those of the lords who held the highest form of judicial rights, known as *haute justice*. In Germany, where they did not extend to such a large number of activities, they seem frequently to have been retained by the direct heirs of the counts, those judges *par excellence* of the Frankish state. In England, they were introduced only by the Norman Conquest, and even then incompletely. Evidently the less effective the competition from the other *ban*—that of the king or his representatives— the more pervasive and profitable was the lord's authority.

The parish church was dependent almost everywhere on the local lord, or if there were several in the same parish, on one of them. Usually the church would have been built not long before by one of his predecessors on the demesne. But that condition was not necessary in order to justify an appropriation of this kind; for the idea prevailed at that time that the place of public worship belonged to the worshippers. Where, as in Frisia, the manor did not exist, the church belonged to the village community itself; in the rest of Europe the peasant group, having no legal existence, could be represented only by its chief or one of its chiefs. This right of ownership, as it was called before the Gregorian reform, or of 'patronage,' as it was later more modestly labelled, consisted primarily in the power to nominate or 'present' the priest in charge. But the lords also claimed to derive from it the right to take for their own benefit a part at least of the parish revenues. Of the latter the fees, though not negligible, scarcely amounted to a large sum. Tithe brought in much more. After having long been considered a purely moral duty, the payment of tithe had been rigorously imposed on all the faithful—in the Frankish state by the first Carolingians and in Britain, about the same time, by the Anglo-Saxon kings, their imitators. It was, in theory, a tax of one-tenth, collected in kind and levied on all forms of income, without exception. Actually it came very soon to be applied almost exclusively to agricultural produce. The appropriation of tithe by the lords was by no means complete. England was to a large extent free from this abuse owing to the tardy development there of the manorial system. Even on the continent the parish priest frequently, and the bishop occasionally, retained a certain proportion. Moreover, the religious revival born of the Gregorian reform quickly brought about the 'restitution' to the clergy (which in practice meant to the monasteries in most cases) of many tithes—together with a still greater number of churches—which had earlier fallen into lay hands. Nevertheless, the appropriation of this revenue of spiritual origin by eminently temporal masters, in the first feudal age, had been one of the most striking as well as one of the most profitable achievements of a power which certainly appeared to repudiate the right of anyone else to demand anything from its subjects.

The pecuniary aid or tallage (*taille*) required of the rural tenants arose, like the tallage of vassals and at about the same time, out of the general duty incumbent on every subordinate to give succour to his chief. Like the vassals' tallage it tended at first to masquerade as a gift, and this fiction was till the end commemorated in some of the names which it bore: in France, *demande* or *queste*, in Germany *Bede*, which means prayer. But it was also called, more frankly, *toulte* from the verb *tolir*, 'to take.' Its history, though it began at a later date, was not unlike that of the manorial monopolies. It was very widespread in France, and it was imported into England by the Norman conquerors; but in Germany it remained the privilege of a smaller number of lords—those who exercised the higher judicial powers, which were less divided up in that country than in France. (In the feudal era the most powerful individual was always the judge.) No more than the tallage of the vassals did the tallage of the peasants escape the regularizing influence of custom, though the results were perceptibly different. Since the peasant taxpayers were not as a rule strong enough to secure a strict definition of their obligations, the tax, which had at first been exceptional, was levied at more and more frequent intervals as the circulation of money increased. This process, moreover, was marked by great variations from manor to manor. In the Ile-de-France, about the year 1200, estates where tallage was collected annually or even biennially adjoined others where it was collected only at irregular intervals. The law almost everywhere was uncertain. This newest of manorial burdens was not only too recent to be incorporated easily in the fabric of 'good customs'; the irregularity with which it was collected and, even where its recurrence had been regularized, the uncertainty of the sum exacted on each occasion caused it to retain an arbitrary character. In Church circles, 'worthy people,' as a Parisian text says, questioned the legality of tallage, and it was particularly hateful to the peasants whom it frequently drove to active revolt. Half-crystallized in an age of monetary scarcity, the tradition of the manor did not lend itself easily to the needs of a new economy.

Thus the tenant at the end of the twelfth century paid tithe, tallage and the multifarious dues of the *banalités*—all exactions which, even in the countries where the manor had been in existence longest, his ancestor of the eighth century, for example, had not known. Unquestionably compulsory payments had become heavier, though not without—in certain regions, at least—some compensating reduction of compulsory labour services.

For—by a sort of prolongation of the process of dismemberment from which the Roman *latifundium* had formerly suffered—the lords in a great part of Europe began to parcel out vast portions of their demesnes. Sometimes they distributed them piece-meal to their old tenants; sometimes they carved them up into new tenements; occasionally they even formed them into little vassal fiefs, soon in their turn to be broken up into peasant holdings. Provoked mainly by economic causes which it is impossible for us to examine here, the movement seems to have started as early as the tenth and eleventh centuries in France and Lotharingia, as well as in Italy; it had reached trans-Rhenish Germany a little later and—more slowly still and not without some capricious regressions—England, where the manorial system itself was of more recent origin. Now a decline in the size of the demesne meant also, of necessity, abolition or reduction of compulsory labour services. Where the tenant under Charlemagne owed several days a week, in the France of Philip Augustus or St. Louis he no longer worked in the fields or meadows of the demesne more than a few days a year. The development of new 'exactions' not only varied from country to country, according to the extent

to which the right to issue orders had been taken over; it operated also in direct ratio to the lord's abandonment of personal exploitation of the estate. Having both more time and more land, the peasant could pay more. And the master, naturally, sought to recover on one side what he lost on the other. If in France the mill had not been the monopoly of the lord, how could it have continued to function once the supply of corn from the demesne had ceased? Nevertheless, by ceasing to exact labour from his subjects throughout the year, by transforming them into producers, heavily taxed certainly, but economically autonomous, by himself becoming a landed proprietor pure and simple, the lord, where this evolution was fully accomplished, inevitably allowed some small relaxation of the bond of human domination. Like the history of the fief, the history of the peasant holding was, in the long run, that of the transition from a social structure founded on service to a system of land rent.

NOTES

1 *Cap.*, I, no. 132, c. 5.

2 A. Lesort, *Chroniques et chartes . . . de Saint-Mihiel*, no. 33.

3 *Acta Murensia*, in *Quellen zur Schweizer Geschichte*, III, 2, p. 68, c. 22.

4 *Chartes du Forez antérieures au XIVe siècle*, no. 500 (t. IV).

5 *Monumenta Historiae Patriae*, XIII, col. 711.

6 *Olim.*, I, p. 661, no. III.

7 Suger, *De Rebus*, ed. Lecoy de la Marche, c X., p. 167.

VASSAL AND LORD

1. Aid and Protection

'To serve' or (as it was sometimes put) 'to aid,' and 'to protect'—it was in these very simple terms that the oldest texts summed up the mutual obligations of the armed retainer and his lord. Never was the bond felt to be stronger than in the period when its effects were thus stated in the vaguest and, consequently, the most comprehensive fashion. When we define something, do we not always impose limitations on it? It was inevitable, nevertheless, that the need to define the legal consequences of the contract of homage should be felt with increasing urgency, especially in so far as they affected the obligations of the subordinate. Once vassalage had emerged from the humble sphere of domestic loyalty,

what vassal thenceforth would have regarded it as compatible with his dignity if it had been frankly stated as in early times, that he was compelled 'to serve the lord in all manner of tasks which may be required of him'?[1] Furthermore, could the lord continue to expect to have always at his beck and call persons who thenceforward —since they were for the most part settled on fiefs—lived at a distance from their master?

In the gradual work of definition professional jurists played only a belated and, on the whole, insignificant part. It is true that, as early as about 1020, Bishop Fulbert of Chartres, whose study of the canon law had trained him in the methods of legal reflection, attempted an analysis of homage and its effects. But interesting though it was as a symptom of the penetration of jurisprudence into a sphere which had hitherto been alien to it, this endeavour scarcely succeeded in rising above the level of a rather barren scholastic exercise. The decisive influence, here as elsewhere, was that of custom, formed by precedents and progressively crystallized by the legal practice of courts attended by many vassals. More and more frequently, the practice was adopted of having these stipulations, which but a short while before had been purely traditional, included in the agreement itself. The oath of fealty, since it could be expanded at will, formed a better vehicle for the details of these conditions than the few words that accompanied the act of homage. Thus a detailed contract, carefully drawn up, replaced an unqualified submission. As a further precaution, which clearly testifies to the weakening of the tie, the vassal as a rule no longer promised merely to undertake not to injure him. In Flanders, from the beginning of the twelfth century, these negative clauses had assumed sufficient importance to give rise to a separate oath of 'security' which was sworn after fealty and apparently authorized the lord, in the event of the vassal's failure to observe it, to distrain on certain specified pledges. It goes without saying, however, that for a long time it was the positive obligations which continued to hold first place.

The primary duty was, by definition, military service. The 'man of mouth and hands' was bound, first and foremost, to serve in person, on horseback and with full equipment. Nevertheless he rarely appeared alone. Apart from the fact that his own vassals, if he had any, would naturally gather under his banner and share his privileges and his prestige, custom sometimes required him to be attended by at least one or two squires. On the other hand there were as a rule no foot-soldiers in his contingent. Their role in battle was considered so unimportant and the difficulty of feeding fairly large bodies of men was so great that the leader of the feudal host contented himself with the peasant infantry furnished by his own estates or those of the churches of which he had officially constituted himself the protector. Frequently the vassal was also required to garrison the lord's castle, either during hostilities only, or—for a fortress could not remain unguarded—at any time, in rotation with his fellow-vassals. If he had a fortified house of his own, he was obliged to throw it open to his lord.

Gradually differences in rank and power, the development of inevitably divergent traditions, special agreements, and even abuses transformed into rights introduced innumerable variations into these obligations. This, in the long run, almost invariably tended to lighten them.

A serious problem arose from the hierarchical organization of vassalage. Since the vassal was at once subject and master, he would often have vassals of his own. The duty which required him to render aid to his lord to the utmost of his ability might be thought to oblige him to join the lord's army, together with the entire body of his dependants. Custom, however, at an early date authorized him to bring with him only a stated number of followers; the figure was fixed once and for all, and might be much less than the number he employed in his own wars. Take the case, towards the end of the eleventh century, of the bishop of Bayeux. More than a hundred knights owed him military service, but he was bound to provide only twenty of them for the duke of Normandy, his immediate lord. Moreover, if the duke demanded the help of the prelate in the name of the king of France (of whom Normandy was held as a fief) the number was reduced to ten. This fining down of the military obligation towards the summit, which the Plantagenet kings of England in the twelfth century tried without much success to arrest, was undoubtedly one of the principal causes of the final failure of vassalage as a means of defense or conquest in the hands of governments.[2]

It was the chief desire of vassals both great and small not to be held to an indefinite period of military service. But neither the traditions of the Carolingian state nor the earliest usages of vassalage offered direct precedents for limiting its duration. Both the subject and the household warrior remained under arms as long as their presence seemed necessary to king or chief. The old Germanic customs, on the other hand, had widely employed a sort of standard period fixed at forty days or, as they said earlier, forty nights. This not only regulated many forms of procedure; Frankish military legislation itself had adopted forty days as the period of rest to which the levies were entitled between two mobilizations. This traditional period, which came naturally to mind, provided from the end of the eleventh century the normal standard for the obligation imposed on the vassals; on the expiration of forty days they were free to return home, usually for the rest of the year. It is true that they fairly frequently remained with the army, and certain 'customs' even sought to make this prolongation of the period of service compulsory, though only on condition that the lord bore the expense and paid wages to the vassal. The fief, once the stipend of the armed 'satellite,' had so far ceased to fulfil its original purpose that it was necessary to supplement it by other remuneration.

It was not only for war that the lord summoned his vassals. In peacetime, they constituted his 'court,' which he convoked in solemn session at more or less regular intervals, coinciding as a rule with the principal liturgical feasts. It was by turns a court of law, a council which the master was required by the political conceptions of the time to consult on all serious matters, and a ceremonial parade of rank and power. Could a chief have a more striking manifestation of his prestige or a more delightful way of reminding himself of it than to appear in public surrounded by a multitude of dependants, some of whom were themselves men of high rank, and to get them to perform publicly those gestures of deference—by acting as squire, cupbearer or steward—to which an age susceptible to visible things attached great symbolic value?

The splendour of these courts, 'full, marvellous and great,' has been naively exaggerated by the epic poems, in which they are frequent backgrounds to the action. While the glories of the ceremonial gatherings graced by the presence of crowned kings were greatly magnified, the poets even added gratuitous splendours to the modest courts convoked by barons of medium or lesser rank. Nevertheless, we know from the most reliable sources that much legal business was dealt with in these assemblies; that the most brilliant of them were marked by much ceremonial display and attracted—in addition to those who normally attended—a mixed crowd of adventurers, mountebanks and even pick-pockets; and that the lord was required by usage as well as by his acknowledged interest, to distribute to his men on these occasions those gifts of horses, arms, and vestments which were at once the guarantee of their fealty and the symbol of their subordination. We know, moreover, that the presence of the vassals—each, as the abbot of Saint-Riquier prescribed, 'carefully arrayed in accordance with his rank'—was always expressly required. According to the *Usages of Barcelona*, the count, when he holds court, must 'render justice . . . give help to the oppressed . . . announce mealtimes with trumpets so that nobles and others of lesser rank may participate; he must distribute cloaks to his chief vassals; make arrangements for the expedition which will harry the lands of Spain; and create

new knights.' At a lower level of the social hierarchy, a petty knight of Picardy, acknowledging himself in 1210 the liegeman of the vidame of Amiens, promised him, in the same breath, military aid for a period of six months and 'to come, when I am required to do so, to the feast given by the said vidame, staying there, with my wife, at my own expense, for eight days.'[3]

This last example (together with many others) shows how court service, like military service, was gradually regulated and limited—though it is true that the attitude of the vassals towards the two obligations was not altogether the same. Military service was an obligation and little else, but attendance at court carried with it many advantages: gifts from one's lord, a groaning board and a share in the exercise of authority. The vassals were, therefore, much less eager to be relieved of court service than of military service. Till the end of the feudal era these assemblies compensated in some measure for the separation of lord and vassal resulting from the grant of a fief; they helped to maintain the personal contact without which a human tie can scarcely exist.

The vassal was bound by his fealty to 'render aid' to his lord in all things, and it was taken for granted that this meant placing his sword and his counsel at his lord's disposal. But there came a time when he was expected to make his purse available as well. No institution reveals better than this financial obligation the deep-seated unity of the system of dependence on which feudal society was built. Whoever owed obedience was obliged to give financial help to his chief or master in case of need: the serf, the so-called 'free' tenant of a manor, the subject of a king, and finally the vassal. The very terms applied to the contributions which the lord was thus authorized to demand from his men were, at least in French feudal law, identical regardless of who paid them. People spoke simply of 'aid'; or again of *taille* (tallage), a vivid expression which was derived from the verb *tailler*, meaning literally to take from someone a part of his substance and, consequently, to tax him.[4] Naturally, in spite of this similarity of principle, the history of the obligation followed very different lines in different social groups. For the moment we are concerned only with the 'aid' or *taille* payable by vassals.

In its primitive form this tax appears simply as an occasional and more or less voluntary gift. In Germany and Lombardy it seems never to have passed beyond this stage; a significant passage of the *Sachsenspiegel* shows the vassal still 'bringing gifts to his lord.' In these countries the bond of vassalage was not strong enough to enable the lord who wanted additional help after the primary service had been duly performed, to demand it of right. It was otherwise in France. There, towards the end of the eleventh century or the beginning of the twelfth, conditions favoured the development of the *taille* as a feudal exaction. This was the moment when it was becoming more widespread in the form applied to the poor and when, altogether, the increasing circulation of money was tending to make the needs of the chiefs more urgent and the means of the taxpayers less limited. Custom was making the payments compulsory; but, by way of compensation, it also specified the occasions when they could be demanded. Thus in 1111 an Angevin fief was already subject to the 'four standard *tailles*': for the lord's ransom, if he were taken prisoner; for the knighting of his eldest son; for the marriage of his eldest daughter; and to enable the lord himself to make a purchase of land.[5] The last case was too arbitrary in its application and it quickly disappeared from most of the customs. The first three, on the other hand, were recognized almost everywhere. Others were sometimes added—the 'aid' for the crusade, in particular, or that which the lord levied when his superiors demanded one from him. Thus the money element, which we have already noted as present in the case of relief, gradually insinuated itself among the old relationships based on fealty and service.

It was to enter by yet another channel. Inevitably it happened from time to time that the obligation of military service was not carried out. The lord thereupon claimed a fine or compensation; occasionally the vassal offered it in advance. This was called 'service,' in conformity with the linguistic convention whereby the payment of compensation was frequently given the name of the obligation which it extinguished; in France it was sometimes known as *taille de l'ost*. These dispensations for a cash payment were not in fact widely practised except in the case of two categories of fiefs: those which had fallen into the hands of religious communities, who were unable to bear arms; and those held directly of the great monarchies, which were adept at turning to their own financial profit the inadequacies of the system of vassal recruitment. For the majority of feudal tenements, the duty of military service from the thirteenth century onward merely became less and less exacting, without any tax being imposed in its place. Even the pecuniary aids frequently fell into desuetude in the end. The fief had ceased to procure good servants: neither did it long remain a fruitful source of revenue.

Custom in most cases did not require of the lord any verbal or written agreement corresponding to the oath of the vassal. Such pledges on the lord's part appeared only at a later date and always remained exceptional. There was no opportunity, therefore, to define the obligations of the chief in as much detail as those of the subordinate. A duty of protection, moreover, did not lend itself so well as services to such precise definition. The vassal was to be defended by his lord 'towards and against all men who may live and die'; first and foremost in his person, but also in his property and more especially in his fiefs. Furthermore he expected from this protector—who had become, as we shall see, a judge—good and speedy justice. In addition, there were the imponderable but nevertheless precious advantages which accrued, rightly or wrongly, from the patronage of a powerful man in a highly anarchic society. All these advantages were prized; nevertheless in the long run the vassal's obligations outweighed the benefits he received. As remuneration for service, the fief had originally redressed the balance, but when by reason of its transformation into a patrimonial property its original function was lost sight of, the inequality of the obligations seemed all the more flagrant, and those who suffered from it were all the more anxious to limit their burden.

2. Vassalage as a Substitute for the Kinship Tie

Nevertheless, were we to concern ourselves only with this debit and credit balance we should gain but an emasculated impression of the essential nature of the tie of vassalage. The relationships of personal dependence had made their entry into history as a sort of substitute for, or complement to, the solidarity of the family, which had ceased to be fully effective. In the eyes of tenth-century Anglo-Saxon law, the lordless man is an outlaw unless his relatives are prepared to assume responsibility for him.[6] In relation to the lord, the vassal long remained a sort of supplementary relative, his duties as well as his rights being the same as those of relatives by blood. If an incendiary, declares Frederick Barbarossa in one of his peace ordinances, shall have sought asylum in a castle, the master of the fortress shall be compelled, if he does not wish to be regarded as an accomplice, to hand over the fugitive, 'provided, however, that the latter be not his lord, his vassal or his kinsman.' And it was no accident that the oldest Norman customary, in treating of the murder of a vassal by his lord or of a lord by his vassal, grouped these crimes indiscriminately in the same chapter with the most atrocious homicides committed within the family group. This quasi-family character of vassalage was responsible for several enduring features, in the legal rules as well as in the habits of feudal society.

The primary duty of the kinsman was vengeance. The same was true of the man who had done homage or received it. Was not the Latin *ultor*—avenger—simply translated, in an ancient German gloss, by the Old High German word *mundporo*, patron?[7] This equality of function between the kinship group and the tie of vassalage, which began in the blood-feud, continued to manifest itself in the courts of law. No one, declares a twelfth-century English customary, if he has not himself been present at the crime, may bring an accusation in a case of murder, unless he is a kinsman of the dead man, his lord, or his vassal. The obligation was equally binding on the lord in relation to his vassal and on the vassal in relation to his lord. A difference of degree was nevertheless noticeable, very much in conformity with the spirit of this relationship of subordination. If we are to believe the poem of *Beowulf*, the companions of the slain chieftain in ancient Germania were entitled to a share of the *wergild*. It was no longer so in Norman England. The lord shared in the compensation paid for the murder of the vassal; of that which was due for the murder of the lord the vassal received nothing. The loss of a servant was paid for; that of a master was not.

Only in rare instances was the knight's son brought up in his father's house. Custom decreed—and was obeyed so long as feudal *mores* retained some vitality—that his father entrust him, while still a child, to his lord or one of his lords. In the household of this chief the boy, while performing the duties of a page, received instruction in the arts of hunting and of war, and later in courtly manners. An historical example of this tradition was the young Arnulf of Guines in the household of Count Philip of Flanders; in legend, there was little Garnier of Nanteuil, who served Charlemagne so well:

When to the woods the king repairs, the child goes too; Sometimes his bow he bears, sometimes his stirrup holds. If wildfowl lure the king, Garnier is by his side. Oft on his wrist the hawk or keen-eyed falcon sits. And when to rest the king retires, Garnier is there, Beguiling him with song and old heroic lays.

In other medieval European societies similar practices prevailed, and there also they served to reinforce, through the agency of the young, ties which the physical separation of lord and vassal constantly threatened to stretch to breaking point. But the system of 'fosterage' practised in Ireland seems to have been used agove all to strengthen the link between the child and the maternal clan, and occasionally to establish the pedagogic prestige of a body of learned priests. Among the Scandinavians, it was the dependent's duty to bring up his master's children. So much was this the case that, when Harald of Norway wished to demonstrate to the world at large the overlordship which he claimed over King Aethelstan of England, he found no better means to this end, the Saga tells us, than to have his son set down unexpectedly on the knees of this involuntary foster-father. The feudal world reversed the obligation, and the vassal's son was brought up by the lord. The ties of respect and gratitude thus created were held to be very strong. All his life the little boy of earlier days remembered that he had been the *nourri* of the lord—the word, with what it stood for, dates in Gaul from the Frankish period and still recurs in the pages of Commynes.[8] Doubtless, in this case as in others, the facts were often at variance with the rules of honour. Nevertheless, this practice certainly served a purpose; for, while placing a precious hostage in the lord's hands, it enabled each generation of vassals to enjoy anew something of that participation in the overlord's intimate domestic life whence early vassalage had derived its deepest human value.

In a society where the individual was so little his own master, marriage (which, as we know already, was bound up with a great variety of interests) was very far from being considered an act of personal choice. The decision was first and foremost a matter for the father. 'He wishes to see his son take a wife while he is still alive; he therefore buys for him the daughter of a nobleman'—that is how the old *Poem of St. Alexis* puts it, with no beating about the bush. The relatives intervened in these matters, sometimes in association with the father, but especially when he was no longer alive. So too did the lord, when the orphan was the son of a vassal; and the vassals also occasionally had a say when the marriage of their lord was at issue. In this latter case, it is true, the rule never amounted to more than a mere formality; on all important matters the baron was bound to consult his men and hence in this. On the other side, the lord's rights in regard to the personal affairs of his vassal were much more clearly defined. The tradition went back to the remotest origins of vassalage. 'If a private warrior (*bucellarius*) leaves only a daughter,' declares a Visigothic law of the fifth century, 'she shall remain under the control of the master, who will find her a husband of the same social status. If, however, she herself shall choose a husband, against the wishes of the master, she shall be obliged to restore to the latter all the gifts which her father has received from him.'[9] The heritability of fiefs, already present in this text in a rudimentary form, furnished the lords with one or more reason, and a very cogent one, for keeping a close eye on marriages which, when the estate had passed to the distaff side, resulted in their acquiring a vassal who did not belong to the original line. Their control over marriages became absolute, however, only in France and Lotharingia, the true homelands of the system of vassalage, and in the countries of imported feudalism. It is true that families of knightly rank were not the only ones which had to submit to such interference in their personal affairs; for many others were subjected, through various ties, to an authority of seignorial character, and kings, in their capacity as sovereign, sometimes considered that they were entitled to dispose of the hands of their female subjects. But as applied to vassals—as sometimes to serfs, who also were personal dependants—a practice which was regarded as an abuse of power when applied to other types of subordinates was almost universally held to be lawful. 'We will not marry widows and daughters against their will,' Philip Augustus promises the people of Falaise and Caen, 'unless they hold of us, in whole or in part, a *fief de haubert*'—that is to say, a military fief characterized by service with coat of mail.[10]

The ideal procedure was that the lord should come to an agreement with the kinsfolk. Such collaboration was provided for in the thirteenth century, for example, by an Orleans 'custom,' and the arrangement is given prominence in a curious charter of Henry I of England.[11] When the lord was strong, however, he could overrule all opposition. In Plantagenet England this institution, derived from the principles of guardianship, degenerated in the end into blatant commercialism. Kings and barons—kings especially vied with each other in giving or selling the hands of orphan sons or daughters. Sometimes, threatened with the prospect of an unwelcome husband, a widow would pay in hard cash

for permission to refuse him. Despite the progressive loosening of the tie, it is clear that vassalage did not always avoid the other danger which threatens almost every system of personal protection—that of degenerating into a device for the exploitation of the weak by the strong.

3. Reciprocity and Breach of Engagements

The contract of vassalage bound together two men who were, by definition, on different social levels. Nothing shows this more strikingly than one of the provisions of the old Normal law. Both the lord who has killed his vassal and the vassal who has killed his lord are punished by death, but only the crime against the chief involves the dishonourable penalty of hanging.[12] Yet, whatever the inequalities between the obligations of the respective parties, those obligations were none the less mutual: the obedience of the vassal was conditional upon the scrupulous fulfilment of his engagements by the lord. This reciprocity in unequal obligations, which was emphasized by Fulbert of Chartres as early as the eleventh century and which was very strongly felt to the end, was the really distinctive feature of European vassalage. This characteristic distinguished it not only from ancient slavery but also, and very profoundly, from the forms of free dependence known to other civilizations, like that of Japan, and even to certain societies bordering on the feudal zone proper. The very ceremonies perfectly express the contrast. The 'prostration' of the Russian 'men of service' and the kissing of hands practised by the warriors of Castile contrast with the French form of homage which, by the gesture of hands closing upon hands and by the kiss on the mouth, made the lord no mere master with the sole function of receiving whatever was due to him, but a partner in a genuine contract. 'As much,' writes Beaumanoir, 'as the vassal owes his lord of fealty and loyalty by reason of his homage, so much the lord owes his vassal.'

The solemn act which had created the contract seemed so binding that even in face of the worst breaches its final rupture seemed to demand a sort of cancellation ceremony. Such at least was the practice in the old Frankish regions. In Lotharingia and northern France, a ceremony of breach of homage took shape, in which perhaps was revived the memory of the gestures used by the Salian Frank, in times gone by, to renounce his kindred. The procedure was adopted occasionally by the lord, but more often by the vassal. Declaring his intention to cast away from (*rejeter*) the 'felon' partner, with a violent gesture he hurled to the ground a twig—sometimes breaking it beforehand—or a thread from his cloak. But, in order that the ceremony should seem as decisive as the one whose effects it was to destroy, it was necessary that it should follow the pattern of homage by bringing the two individuals face to face. This proceeding was not without its dangers. Consequently, in preference to the gesture of throwing down the 'straw' (which before reaching the stage at which a usage becomes a rule fell into disuse) the practice developed of making a simple 'defiance' (*défi*)—in the etymological sense of the word, that is to say a renunciation of faith—by letters or by herald. The less scrupulous, who were not the least numerous, naturally began hostilities without any preliminary declaration.

But in the great majority of cases the personal tie had its counterpart in a real property tie. So once the vassalage was broken, what happened to the fief? When the fault lay with the vassal, there was no difficulty: the property reverted to the injured lord. This was what was called the *commise*, confiscation, of the fief. The 'disinheritance' of Duke Henry the Lion by Frederick Barbarossa and that of John Lackland by Philip Augustus are the most celebrated examples of this procedure. When the responsibility for the breach appeared to be the lord's the problem was more delicate. The fief, as the remuneration for services which were no longer to be rendered, would lose its *raison d'etre*. Yet it would be unfair that an innocent man should be thus dispossessed. The hierarchical arrangement of fealties permitted escape from this quandary. The rights of the unworthy lord passed to his own lord—just as if a chain should be re-united after the removal of a broken link. It is true that when the fief had been held directly of the king, the highest link, this solution was not feasible. But it seems to have been admitted that in relation to the king no renunciation of homage could be lasting. Italy alone steered a separate course. There, the vassal who had suffered from a seignorial felony merely had his fief changed into an allodial property—a feature symptomatic (among many others) of the weakness of the more strictly feudal conceptions south of the Alps.

Carolingian legislation had defined the felonies which were held to justify the abandonment of the lord by the vassal, and its principles were never quite forgotten. In the poem of *Raoul de Cambrai*, the 'foster-child' Bernier, despite many grounds for hatred, repudiates Raoul only when struck by him. Now the Carolingian capitulary had said: 'No one shall quit his lord after having received a shilling's worth from him . . . unless this lord has beaten him with a stick.' A little later this motive for the breach was invoked by a court romance, in the course of a curious discussion of feudal casuistry; it was still expressly retained in the thirteenth century by various French customaries, and at the beginning of the following century by the *Parlement* of the first Valois king.[13] Nevertheless, even the soundest of the legal rules of former days survived, in feudal times, only as parts of an indeterminate tradition. The arbitrary conduct which resulted from this transformation of a legal code into a vague collection of moral laws could have been combated by the influence of courts capable of establishing a standard of judicial practice and giving it authority. Indeed, certain tribunals were in theory available for such cases. There was in the first place the lord's court, composed in reality of the vassals themselves, who were considered the natural judges of law-suits between the lord, their master, and his man, their peer; next, at the level above, there was the court of the chief of more exalted rank to whom the lord in his turn had done homage. Also certain 'customs', committed to writing at an early date, like those of Bigorre, endeavoured to outline a procedure to which the vassal must conform before his 'departure' should be lawful.[14] But the great weakness of feudalism was precisely its inability to construct a really coherent and efficient judicial system. In practice, the individual who sustained what he considered or professed to consider an infringement of his rights would decide to break his engagement and the issue of the struggle would depend on the relative strength of the parties. It was as though a marriage were to be terminated by divorce, without the petitioner's case having been proved and without there being a judge to pronounce the decree.

NOTES

1 M.G.H., EE., V., p. 127, no. 34.

2 C. H. Haskins, *Norman Institutions*, 1918, p. 15; Round, *Family Origins*, 1930, p. 208; H. M. Chew, *The English Ecclesiastical Tenants-in-Chief*

and *Knight-Service*, Oxford, 1932; Gleason, *An Ecclesiastical Barony of the Middle Ages*, 1936; H. Navel, *L'Enquete de 1133*, 1935, p. 71.

3 Hariulf, *Chronique*, III, 3, ed. Lot, p. 97; *Us.*

Barc., c. CXXIV.; Du Cange, *Dissertations sur l'hist. de Saint Louis*, V, ed. Henschel, VII, p. 23.

4 In England, however, these terms were eventually assigned to different social levels. 'Aid' was reserved for vassals and 'tallage' for the more humble classes of dependants.

5 First cartulary of Saint-Serve (Marchegay's restoration). Arch. Maine-et-Loire, H., vol. 293. Naturally, the occasions were different on ecclesiastical fiefs; on those held of the bishop of Bayeux, for example, they were the bishop's journey to Rome, repairs to the cathedral, a fire at the bishop's palace (Gleason, *An Ecclesiastical Barony*, p. 50).

6 Cf. above, p. 182.

7 Steinmeyer and Sievers, *Althochdeutsche Glossen*, I, p. 268, 23.

8 Flodoard, *Hist. Remensis eccl.*, III, 26 in M.G.H., SS., XIII, p. 540; cf. already *Actus pontificum Cenomannensium*, pp. 134 and 135 (616: 'nu-

tritura'); Commynes, VI, 6 (ed. Mandrot, II, p. 50).

9 *Codex Euricianus*, c. 310. The vassal mentioned by the synod of Compiegne of 757, whose marriages were arranged by his two successive masters, is—in conformity with the original meaning of the word vassal—a mere slave, and we are not concerned with such cases here.

10 *Ordonnances*, XII, p. 275.

11 *Et. de Saint Louis*, I, c. 67; F. M. Stenton, *The First Century of English Feudalism* (1066-1166), 1932, pp. 33-34.

12 *Très ancien Countumier*. XXXV, 5.

13 *Le Roman de Thébes*, ed. L. Constans, I, v. 8041 *et seq.*—Arch. Nat. X IA, 6, fol. 185; cf. Olivier-Martin, *Histoire de la countume de la prévôté et vicomté de Paris*, 1922-30, I, p. 257, n. 7.

14 J. Fourgous and G. de Bezin, *Les Fors de Bigorre*, Bagnéres, 1901 (*Travaux sur l'histoire du droit méridional*, fasc. 1), c. 6.

POLITICAL LEADERSHIP AMONG SWAT PATHANS

FREDRIK BARTH

RELATIONS OF INEQUALITY AND AUTHORITY

ELSEWHERE I HAVE described a series of groupings and relationships which are basic to the social organization in Swat, but which do not have any explicit political content or significance. Membership in these groups is determined mainly by various aspects of kinship and residence, and none of them are characterized by any internal differentiations.

The groups that will be described here differ from the above in two ways: they are internally differentiated, and recruitment is by contractual agreement with a leader. These characteristics are connected in terms of Pathan ideas of differentiation and dominance. Any differentiation of functions between co-operating persons is regarded by Pathans as implying some degree of dominance. Such relations are conceived by Pathans as dyadic relations between one superordinate and one subordinate person. Even where the relation is apparently specific—e.g., a negotiated contract involving stipulated economic services and payments—it still implies a generalized inequality and dominance of one partner

over the other. Thus any differentiation of functions within a group is associated with a differentiation in authority; and internal relations within such groups are conceptualized as a series of individual contracts with a pivotal, dominant leader.

The main groups in Swat which are characterized by this kind of internal structure are: productive units, based on economic contracts; groups based on house tenancy contracts, and having certain administrative functions and serving as labour gangs; recreational groups, based on men's house membership; and religious groups, based on relations of tutelage to a Saint. Each such group is characterized by the presence of a single dominant leader, and membership in each is defined by a dyadic contractual relationship between the leader and each individual member.

I should emphasize that the contracts on which the groups are based are, with a few exceptions specified later, all voluntary. Not only is each individual free to choose his partner in any contract; he is also free to refrain entirely from making any particular kind of contract. In other words, a man may not only choose which men's house he wishes to visit or which religious teacher he desires to follow; he is also free to choose not to belong to any men's house, or to be no one's disciple.

In the case of economic contracts and house tenancy contracts, this argument may appear specious, since a person who has no land of his own is, in practice, forced to enter into a contract of some kind to obtain a house and make a living; but at all events he is free to take any kind of available contract he likes.

The importance of these groups to the present study should thus be evident. Since they are based on free contracts, and membership is not compulsory, they do not offer an all-embracing system which can serve directly as a political organization. But through their constituent contracts they define leaders and relations of dominance and submission, and these relations may be utilized by the leaders as a source of political authority. In the following, I shall attempt to describe these groups in some detail, with particular attention to the different rights and obligations of partners in the different types of contracts on which they are based, and to the direct or implicit political authority of the dominant partners in the contracts.

ECONOMIC CONTRACTS[1]

There is no native money of any kind in the Swat area, and the currency of the administered areas, the Pakistan rupee, though widely used, is not present in the required volume to serve as a medium for most exchanges in the Swat valley. Indeed, in the outlying villages with bad communications, rupee notes are rarely seen, and I was forced to import grain from the more sophisticated districts to barter in the more isolated areas for the necessities of life.

Currency is however unnecessary for the smooth functioning of the highly developed system of division of labour and production in Swat. The units exchanged in the economic system are not goods but services; and the economic activities in the villages are organized in a complex system of interlocking mutual services and/or compensations in kind. This system clearly constitutes a variant of the traditional Hindu Jajmani system (see e.g. Wiser, 1936).

Mutual relations of service and/or compensation are organized through a series of individual contracts, and the economic system is best described in terms of these relations. The more important of them fall into six main categories, to be described in the following order:

(a) land tenancy and agricultural labour contracts,

(b) relations between agriculturalists and specialists who supply tools, transport etc.,

(c) relations between a craftsman and private buyers or consumers,

(d) relations between performers of various personal services and their clientele,

(e) relations between a master and his private servant and, finally,

(f) in Swat State relations between the Ruler and his staff, particularly the Army, to be described elsewhere.

Of particular interest in the present context are (a) and (b), since the main productive groups are based on these contracts.

a. Land is held and leased in a variety of ways. The tenure system which was outlined elsewhere will be discussed later. A very marked concentration of land in relatively few hands is characteristic of nearly all parts of Swat. By far the largest area is held by members of the Pakhtun caste.[2]

Even among Pakhtun landowners land is usually concentrated in a few hands. The majority of Pakhtuns are a sort of yeomanry with only small holdings. Most of the land is thus held by a few persons who do not themselves engage in manual labour; they grant occupation rights for specified or unspecified periods to tenants and serfs, who support themselves on an agreed share of the total crop.

There are four types of contract, the holders of which are termed respectively:

(i) *ijaragar*—'rent-companion', who, for a specified period, pays a rent based on an estimate of the net productivity of the land. He assumes all risks on the crop, is free to organize cultivation and to sub-let at his own discretion. The rent is usually paid in kind.

(ii) *brakha-khor*—'sister-of-the-plot'. This type of tenant supplies seed, tools and draught animals, though usually not manure, and in return receives an agreed share of the crop. The share varies somewhat between localities in relation to the average productivity of the land; in the hilly areas such *tenants*, as I shall call this group, receive three-fifths (Parona) to a third (Nalkot); on fertile land the usual share is a quarter (Biha, Worejo, Babuzai). Shares are invariably paid in kind. The tenant may be expelled from the land at the owner's convenience as soon as the harvest is finished. There are traditional rules defining the rights of entry of the succeeding tenant before the crop has been harvested, such as his right to seed clover in the ripening rice fields.

(iii) *dehgan*—agricultural labourer, who is supplied by the landowner with a plot of land, tools, seed and animals. In return for his efforts, the labourer receives a fifth of the gross crop. Like the tenant, he can acquire no rights in the land, no matter how long the landowner may have chosen to assign the same plot to him.

(iv) *faqir*. This word is a wider term for dependent, but has the specific meaning of a poor man who works on the infertile, unirrigated marginal land of a landowner, and pays for this right in labour, or occasionally in money or clarified butter. Such a person is often called a 'servant' (*naukar*). These crofters usually occupy separate hamlets or villages in the hills or mountain areas (*sarkeli*=villages above or away; *band-a*=hill settlement). The occupation rights over particular fields tend to be inherited. The amount of service to be given is rarely stipulated, and depends upon the needs, and the coercive powers, of the landowner. It usually includes the obligation to husk the total maize crop of the landowner.

It should be noted, that tenants and labourers have a recognized right to assistance at the peak seasons of wheat harvest, rice transplantation and rice harvest. At such times the landowner is expected to mobilize all the dependants he controls, or—particularly for rice transplantation—to bring in outsiders and pay them out of his own funds. Such payments are traditionally stipulated in terms of shares of the crop: for harvesting, one fortieth; for shucking the maize cobs (woman's work), one fortieth; for transplanting rice, about one rupee (1 shilling) per day plus meals.

Tenancy and labour contracts for garden plots vary considerably, as the work is more skilled and specialized than that in the grain fields. Tenants working in fruit and vegetable gardens usually get a half or one third of the crop.

b. Agricultural production requires more than land and agricultural labour; a group of subsidiary specialists are necessary to produce tools and keep them in good repair, and to provide for the transportation of the crop. In the solution of these technical problems, the occupational aspects of Swat's caste system are used, and a complex set of relationships develops between the different producers and specialists. A single productive unit comprises as a minimum, *landowner, tenant* or *labourer, carpenter, blacksmith, roper-* and *thong-maker* and *muleteer*. In Swat, this productive unit maintains something like what industrial sociologists usually term a 'continuous flow pattern of work'—i.e. relations between any person and his supporting specialists are direct, so that the toolmakers respond directly to the specific requirements of other members of the productive unit. There are no intermediary agents, no shops and no storage of finished goods for eventual use by others. Payment of all members of the unit is also deferred until the whole productive cycle is completed, and is generally an agreed proportion of the total product.

The landowner holds the pivotal position in this system. It is through their contracts with him that the other persons become partners in the productive unit, and it is from him that the ultimate profits or reimbursements flow. In practice, the arrangement is usually as follows:

A craftsman specialist, for example a carpenter, makes a contract with a landowner or a group of landowners by which he commits himself to produce and maintain all implements or parts of implements traditionally made by carpenters which are required to maintain the agricultural production of the fields which his employers own. These fields are actually being farmed by tenants or labourers; it is their specific needs which the carpenter in fact supplies. Thus, when a plough is jammed between big stones and broken—whether it belongs to a tenant or landowner—it is taken to the carpenter and he is required to repair it. A similar contract exists with a smith, a rope- and thong-maker, and a muleteer who is responsible for transporting the crop to the appropriate storehouses. Although these services are not directly reciprocal (except between carpenter and blacksmith), the partners in the unit make no payments of any kind to each other. The tenant does not pay the carpenter to repair his plough, the muleteer claims nothing from the tenant for transporting the seed, and gives nothing to the blacksmith for having the mules shod.

At the completion of harvest and threshing, however, the tenant or labourer calls all partners to the *rasha*, the cleaned and dried grainpile beside the threshing ground out among the fields. In the simplest case, shares in the crop are then allotted under the supervision of the landowner to each in proportion to his traditional claim. The crop is usually laid out in long rows of small heaps of equal size. A special servant of the chief—his *naser* or estate overseer—then passes along the rows and allots one in every four to the tenant, one in every twenty to the muleteer, one each in every forty to the smith and the carpenter, and occasional heaps as alms to the poor. The rope- and thong-maker is usually paid by a set amount yearly. Thus, every member of the productive unit receives his share of the gross product, the remainder—the lion's share —going to the landowner.

The manner of payment—except to tenant and labourer—may vary considerably from this type. In Madyan, a group of landowners may allot fields to blacksmiths and carpenters in return for their services. Elsewhere they are paid a specified weight of grain, of the order of 100 to 300 lb., for every pair of bullocks working on the fields they have served (Thana, Nalkot). Not uncommonly, the smith or carpenter is given charge of a water-powered mill—which he must then man and keep in repair—in payment for his general services to the persons using it. He then collects the traditional one-twentieth share of all flour ground in the mill, which compensates him both for his work on the farm tools, and for his work in grinding the flour (Nalkot, Worejo). The muleteer may sometimes receive instead of a fixed share of the crop, an agreed quantity of grain per load transported (Thana). These various ways of arranging payment are regarded as alternative and essentially equivalent.

c. Arrangements of this kind usually apply only in the field of agriculture; the relations between professional specialists and private consumers are dyadic and involve direct payment. Thus, if a landowner or a tenant wants a new bed, he pays the carpenter in money or in kind. Wealthy persons may attach some craftsmen— in addition to carpenters, usually potters and tailors—to their household on a yearly basis, the craftsman receiving a stipulated weight of grain per annum. This type of arrangement is said to have been more common in the old days; today most such private business is done on a piece-work basis, with bargaining over the price.

d. On the other hand, relations between the performers of various personal services and their clientele take the form of long-term contracts. They may concern such specialists as washer-men and ferrymen, but invariably include the priest and the barber. There are usually only one Imam and one barber within convenient reach of any given customer; they are under a heredi-tary obligation to perform their traditional ser-vices, and receive in return a yearly payment.

An Imam receives either a land grant for the support of himself and his family (Thana, Nal-kot) or a fixed yearly weight of grain (about 80 lb.) per bullock pair working for his congrega-tion (Worejo). Thus in either case the burden of his support falls on the landowners of the group. In return he leads the congregation in prayer, and preaches on Fridays and other sacred days.

He is also bound, in return for a small considera-tion, to solemnize the major *rites de passage*: *bang*, the reciting of the call to prayer into the ear of every newborn child; *nike*, the ritual con-firming betrothal and marriage, and *talqin*, the prayers and recitations of the funeral ceremony. Like any other specialist, he also gives private services for a suitable payment. He recites for-mulae for the cure of specific pains; he writes amulets for cures or for protection against spirits and fairies; he cures insanity by extracting the insect in the head which causes it, and also dis-turbances caused by the evil eye.

The Imam holds his appointment for life, and the position is regarded as hereditary in the paternal line. The congregation, however, may reject a successor whom they consider incompe-tent; and where the incompetence is demonstra-ble and extreme, saintly mediators will confirm their decision. The position of Imam is, as far as I know, never held by persons of other than priestly caste; it ranks too low for the descend-ants of Saints. The general status of priests— usually referred to by the less distinguised term mullah—is low, with exceptions to be noted below (p. 61 ff); one of the favourite derogatory jeers of Swat Pathans is 'you wife of a mullah'.

The Imam is normally required to be present in the community at all times, but he may leave temporarily to negotiate settlements between warring groups, wherever they may be, or to travel on business, for the sale or barter of his yearly income, for a certain portion of every year. One of his assistants or pupils officiates in his absence.

A *barber* is usually employed communally by a group of households. He and his wife per-form a number of traditional services, and re-ceive an annual payment in grain, which is cal-culated either on the basis of the number of persons in the household served, at about 8-12 lb. per person (Nalkot, Parona, Thana), or on that of the number of pairs of bullocks employed on its land, at about 160 lb. per pair (Worejo). His duties fall mainly into two categories: shav-ing and hair-cutting, and duties connected with *rites de passage*. These two types of function may in some places be delegated to different in-dividuals (Thana). One male barber shaves the men of the household at a set rate per year, while an unrelated female barber serves the women of the household, and her husband is called in to perform ritual services.

The ritual services of the barber and his wife are as follows:

He announces every birth by drumming, his wife congratulates the mother, and they carry the news to relatives; for this they receive small gifts.

He cuts the child's hair ceremonially on the seventh or fortieth day (depending on its rate of growth) after informing all the relatives; for this he receives six to twenty rupees' worth in gifts. The hair is balanced on scales against gold-dust, which amount of gold is given as alms to the poor.

He performs the circumcision operation, informs relatives of the occasion, helps in the sacrifice of an animal, assists and joins in the feast —all accompanied by incessant drumming. For this he receives five rupees.

He and his wife are usually sent to arrange marriages, and assist in the many stages of negotiation and the reciprocal foodgiving which solemnize the contract. They organize the wedding procession and the serving of food at the wedding. After the meal, guests contribute gifts for the barber.

He informs all concerned about deaths, and receives a larger proportion of the alms than other attendants at the funeral.

He makes all necessary announcements of a public kind after calling for attention with his drum.

e. Finally we must consider the relation between a master (*naek*) and his private servant (*naukar*). To receive from any person a salary or any stipulated payment is to engage as the *servant* of that person; it implies a general subordination to him. The idea of a professional relationship like that between a Western doctor and his patient, in which the recipient of the service has no authority over the giver, is unknown in the traditional system of Swat. Characteristically, Western medical treatment is given only in two free hospitals supported by the Ruler, in the capital of Saidu Sharif; and the high status practitioners of Eastern medicine refuse to receive payments from their patients, but only accept unsolicited gifts.

Similarly, the idea that a particular role confers *limited* authority is unknown in Swat. A craftsman pursuing his trade in the temporary employment of a person is also expected to perform personal services for his employer; he will, if told, fetch a glass of water, or deliver a message. All persons employed by the State of Swat are the 'servants' of the Ruler (*da Badshah naukarān*); chiefs of high status refuse to enter into this type of relationship with anyone, and have therefore remained outside the growing administrative bureaucracy. My own position was a puzzle to many and a concern to my servant: I obviously claimed a politically autonomous status and acted, on occasion, as the equal of local chiefs; then why should I submit to the dishonour of being the servant of the King of Norway by receiving a salary from his University?

Anyone in Swat who receives an agreed remuneration has renounced his autonomy; he is acting at the command of another person, and is therefore inferior to that person. On the other hand, this frees him from full responsibility for his actions—it is the person who commands who has the responsibility. Thus, for example, if a chief hires a thug to commit a murder, the thug is in danger only while executing the murder. When it is done, all responsibility falls on the chief who paid the thug, and the honour for bravery goes to him as well. Similarly, the recipient of a bribe has renounced his autonomy, and the responsibility for his perjury or deception falls on the giver of the bribe.

The occupation of servant is the only one in Swat that is not associated with a single caste or a limited number of castes; it is regarded as appropriate for all but *Pakhtuns*. A person who employs servants is invariably the owner of considerable land. Servants are of various kinds. The highest rank is that of the estate overseer (*nāzer/kotwāl*), who, unless there are several servants under him, usually has more general household duties as well. The servant is expected to be continuously at the disposal of his master, fetching, delivering, carrying messages, cooking if the master's wives do not, carrying the meal to the men's house, massaging his master when tired, accompanying him everywhere and acting as his bodyguard. The tie between master and servant is usually an extremely close and intimate one—much more so than between brothers, friends, or even father and son—apparently by far the closest emotional tie between males that Pathans ever experience. Theirs is a symbiotic relationship: they are unequal and complementary, and the fate and career of the one depends to a very great extent on the actions of the other.

Larger, more prosperous households may also have female servants as nursemaids for the children, or servants for the women of the house. Such female servants often walk about unveiled, and have, as they reach older age, a highly privileged position in the household.

Servants are paid by the year, in kind; usually an agreed weight of grain, occasionally, in the case of overseers, a proportion of the gross crop. As they rarely have large storage-bins of their own, the payment is usually in practice a claim to a share of the grain in the master's storehouse.

In addition, they have their meals with or after their master, and receive occasional presents, particularly of clothes. They may also receive financial assistance for such special needs as the marriage of their sons. Sometimes they are in debt to their masters, but the reverse may also be the case. No interest is charged on such debts, and the relationship is usually too personal for the various aspects of debt bondage to become emphasized. As an alternative to a basic wage in grain, servants may be merely supplied with a house in their master's ward, and depend on his gifts for the sustenance of their family.

Finally, slaves (male: *andiwāl*; female: *andiwāla*) fall within the wider category of servants —they are found, though only rarely, in the households of wealthy, politically dominant persons in the Swat valley. They are mostly women, sold from, or arriving as refugees from, Dir and Bajaur. Chiefs may employ them as servants on more exclusive occasions in their men's houses, to add spice to the life of distinguished visitors, though their sexual services are apparently usually monopolized by their owners. Though in fact held captive, and less able than other female servants to resist the advances of their masters, their pattern of daily life does not differ greatly from that of free female servants. Male slaves are very rare; I have no reliable information on their role and position.

Except in the case of slaves, the relation between master and servant is contractual, and terminable at the will of either party.

The economic organization of the villages of Swat is thus very complex. It embraces a series of different kinds of contract, relating not only to land but also to services, between a wide variety of occupational specialists. This specialization derives from the caste system, and economic organization is to a very considerable extent a working out of the practical implications of caste.

Certain features of this system are of great importance for political organization.

As an essentially non-monetary system, it does not permit any considerable capital accumulation in other forms than in land. Rights in land are, however, essentially limited to members of locally dominant lineages of *Pakhtun* caste, and subsidiarily to Saints.

The great majority of economic relationships take the form of tenancy or occupational contracts of relatively long duration, in which payments are deferred or left outstanding in the form of claims on third persons.

In the main productive enterprise, agriculture, the landowner has a pivotal position as the co-ordinator of the many specialists engaged in production, and only through him do the partners in the enterprise receive their final shares in the product.

All such relationships between 'employer' and 'employee'—except for that between master and private servant—are formally purely economic in character and contractually delimited; no wider aspects of political dominance and submission are explicit in them. However, the person who gives the contract is superordinate to the person who sells his skill and labour, and as there is considerable population pressure in the area and far from full employment, the latter is in a weak bargaining position and is in fact eager to obtain and keep such contracts. The threat of discontinuing the contract is thus a strong sanction in the hand of the landowner, and gives him power which he may, if he so chooses, convert to political authority over his contract-holders.

HOUSE TENANCY CONTRACTS

The dwelling houses of the village (*kōta*) belong to landowners in numbers proportional to the area of land held by each. Most villagers thus reside in houses belonging to other persons. For this they pay the owner, while, by living on his property, they also become his political subjects, a relationship implied in the terms *faqir* and *kandari*. Thus, while economic relations and land tenancy contracts have no direct political implications, house tenancy contracts stipulate, as well as payments in goods and services, an administrative or political relationship between owner and tenant. These two aspects of house tenancy, the economic and the political, may be described separately.

In return for the right to occupy the house belonging to another person, a tenant must pay a rent (*kálang/kándar*). The nature of this rent depends somewhat on the position of the tenant; it may be in money, kind or labour. Persons not engaged in agriculture (i.e. members of craftsman or service castes) usually have some money income, and often pay a money rent. The majority of house tenants pay in labour or kind, or both. They provide some firewood from the hills—usually about one bundle a month—for the master's household; they are expected, in turn, to run errands for him. They must keep both their own and his house in good repair, and assist—either free of charge, or in return for a small compensation—in his fields in the peak seasons of agricultural activity. They are thus occasionally mobilized as labour gangs in construction work and in the fields. Finally, in most villages, they make regular monthly or yearly payments, usually in clarified butter, to the house-owner.

The house-owner has further rights over his tenants which emphasize the nature of their relationship. On the occasion of the marriage of a tenant's daughter—whether within or outside the community—the tenant gives a standard fee in money and kind to the house-owner (e.g. in Parona: six rupees, two pounds of clarified butter, ten pounds rice, one chicken). This fee, though given by the tenant to the owner, has in fact been expressly supplied by the groom and his father as a part of the brideprice. The house-owner also has the right to a third of any fine collected from his tenant by any judicial institution, from the village council to that of Swat State.

It should be emphasized that the group defined by common relations to a house-owner is rarely a territorially compact group. Pathan landowners usually hold a number of scattered plots of land; similarly, the houses they own may be in several different villages. Within each village, one man's houses are usually concentrated in one ward, but they may be scattered within that ward. Especially where the re-allotment system operates (see pp. 65 ff), so that the rights of particular landlords lapse periodically, the tenants who at any one time have obligations to the same landlord form a social group only by virtue of their relationship to him. They emerge as a corporate body only in so far as he is able and willing to mobilize them to joint action. Structurally, these groups are thus like the groups which engage in agricultural production, in that they are formed through a number of individual contracts with a single leader.

AUTHORITY AND FOLLOWING OF CHIEFS

General Discussion of Leadership

Pathans, when discussing political events or contemplating political action, are naturally aware of the existence of definite alignments of people who can be mobilized as corporate units in the event of conflicts. But Pathans were as unable as myself to see any simple principle for the recruitment of such groups. One does not hear reference to 'my descent group', 'my association', 'my caste' or even 'my men's house' in such contexts—the reference is always to 'the party of so and so'. The activities of groups are discussed in terms of the actions of their leaders. From Pathan descriptions of conflicts, one might think they were duels. One description, taken down verbatim through an interpreter, reads as follows:

'There were four Khans: Mohammed Awzel Khan, Taj Mohammed Khan, Amir Khan and Biha Malak. They invited the Nawab of Dir to invade upper Swat. He came and supported them, and they ruled the Sebujni and Shamizai. The other party was the Darmei Khan. He and the Badshah (later the founder of Swat State) were getting ready. When they invaded, Khan Bahadur Sahib, who was the brother's son of Taj Mohammed Khan, rebelled against his uncle and joined the Badshah—but this he only did after the Nawab had been driven out, and Taj Mohammed Khan had been weakened; he slowly took over one village after another, ate his way through the whole thing. The four old Khans fled to Dir, but some later returned. Their rifles were confiscated, their movable property taken, but their inherited land was returned to them, except that which was claimed by their relatives.'

As a matter of fact, these conflicts involved armies of the order of ten thousand soldiers, and scores of very prominent chiefs. None of the four old Khans ever returned to Swat, but hundreds of their followers did (though most of their followers did not accompany them on their flight in the first place), and the number of rifles confiscated ran into thousands.

When speaking of corporate groups, I shall be referring to groups capable of concerted action under the direction of a leader or a number of co-ordinating leaders. According to Maine's definition (Maine, 1861), corporate groups should persist in perpetuity, independently of the life and death of individuals. This is true of the groups in question, though not unequivocally so: a great turnover of personnel is possible through death or secession, but the death of the leader creates a crisis, since conflicts over succession to leadership frequently dissolve the group.

The criterion of common jural responsibility, applied by Fortes (1953, pp. 25-6) in his discussion of lineages as corporate groups, is also only roughly applicable. Since policy is determined predominantly by the leading members, responsibility too is allotted on a graded scale. Followers who are mere tools in a leader's hand have but little responsibility, even for their own actions. It is the part in the decision, not in the action, which confers responsibility; thus the members of groups share jural responsibility only in proportion to their authority.

There are fundamentally two kinds of political leaders among Pathans, which I have called respectively chiefs and Saints.

Chiefs may hold several different titles, but by far the most common is *Khān*. This title may be used as a term of address and respect to any landowner, and is occasionally also given as a personal name. When necessary, a chief in the political sense is distinguished from such chiefs-by-courtesy by the phrase *da tārne Khān*— 'chief of the fortress'. Alternatively, a chief may be known as *málak*. This title refers properly to a lineage headman, and is used extensively in other Pathan areas. In Swat it is going out of use, as has the office of lineage headmanship itself, though it is occasionally retained as a title. A *málak* should in general rank lower than a *khān*, but as a result of the wide use of khan as a courtesy title, this difference is not always clear, and the ranks may even be reversed. Finally, a chief of very great prominence and authority over a large area, or state, is known as *Nawāb*, as the Nawab of Dir, various lesser Nawabs of Bajaur, and the Nawab of the State of Amb. Common to all chiefs is their claim to some kind of lineal inheritance of the title, their membership in the Pakhtun caste, and their dominance in the region by virtue of their prominence as a *daftar*-holding landlord.

Saints also may hold one of several titles, usually *Pir, Bāba*, or *Pācha*. *Sāhib* is frequently used as a title of address and reference to all persons of holy descent, but also occasionally to chiefs or other prominent persons. The name of the grade of sainthood held, such as *Sayyid, Akhundzada, Mian*, may also be used as a title by a Saint. The ranking of these various titles is not agreed upon.

Politically corporate groups are created by the actions of leaders. Any such group consists of all the persons whom a leader is able to mobilize in the event of conflict. Its limits are undefined except in relation to the leader, and its solidarity derives from the latter's authority. This authority may be attained in various ways. Persons may be committed by previous arrangements to support a given leader. Their services may be bought by gifts and promises. Their support may be won by the leader's prestige and moral or ethical fitness. Or, finally, their support may be compelled by force.

Previous commitments of followers are mainly those arising from house tenancy or occupational contracts. In these relationships the leader is in a position to exercise control by threatening to withdraw benefits, and the follower, on the other hand, can expect to obtain advantages through his leader's success. The ability to give gifts depends on superior wealth, and so ultimately on the control of land. Direct force is of limited use in winning supporters, since it presupposes a strong following. Terrorism designed to cause secessions from the ranks of opponents is sometimes effective.

In most parts of Swat there is no necessary connexion between the different relationships that imply political submission. There is thus nothing to prevent the more peripheral members of one leader's following from having some commitments to another leader, particularly if the two are allies, or belong to the different categories of chief and Saint. Furthermore, there is nowhere any *a priori* reason why a man should attach himself to any particular leader. The position of a leader is thus never secure; his following may swell or shrink almost without warning. Since leaders are permanently in competition, the sources of their authority are most clearly exhibited in situations of conflict.

The objects of strife among Pathans are, according to a Pakhto proverb, *zin, zer, zamīn* —'women, gold, land'. *Zamīn*, land, is the ultimate source of livelihood for leader and follower alike; its acquisition and retention are in the interest of both. His ownership of land gives the leader power over those who depend on it. *Zer*, gold, stands for riches in general, which, utilized in making gifts or bribes, gives authority over others. Finally, *zin*, women, are a source of conflicts in so far as family honour is involved in the conduct of sisters and wives. Such conflicts are regarded as the ultimate tests of a man's honour, martial valour and ability to command.

In what follows I choose to look at these conflicts, not as disputes to be settled by recourse to law, but as political contests. This emphasis corresponds to the point of view generally adopted by my informants. It is also particularly suitable in the empirical situation, since the outcome of such conflicts is decisive for the political careers of leaders.

Followers seek those leaders who offer them the greatest advantages and the most security. With this aim they align themselves behind a rising leader who is successfully expanding his property and field of influence. In contrast, the followers of leaders who are on the defensive suffer constant annoyance from the members of the expanding groups. Under this pressure they tend to abandon their old leaders and seek protection and security elsewhere. Leaders are thus forced to engage in a competitive struggle. A position of authority can be maintained only through a constant successful struggle for the control of sources of authority.

THE CHIEF'S SOURCES OF AUTHORITY

The title of *Khān*, chief, even apart from its extended courtesy use, does not denote incumbency of any formal office. There is no recognised hierarchy of positions to be filled by successful pretenders. The title merely implies a claim to authority over others; it is a statement of a person's willingness to lead. Chiefs compete with each other for followers. The main sources of influence over followers are control of the sources of livelihood, the distribution of wealth, martial valour in defense of the family honour, and also in some areas, an organizational device known as the *telgeri* system.

Land forms the basis for the whole system of organization in Swat. Quite apart from the profits it supplies in the form of rent, its owner, by his mere possession, gains authority and control over numerous persons. The whole population of Swat is directly dependent on land in some form or other; and non-landowners can only gain access to it through agreements with landowners. The two important categories of land in the present context are dwellings and agricultural land. A dwelling in this sense is known as a *kota*, and consists of a house-site in the village area, and at least the four walls of the house structure. The roof-beams are private movable property, and are often removed if the dwelling changes hands. Every family must have a dwelling of this kind, and persons who do not own land obtain one through a house tenancy contract (pp. 50 ff). Such a contract places the tenant in a relation of dependence on the owner; it also gives the owner a certain political authority over the tenant, who becomes his client for administrative purposes. But the tie of clientage is not exclusive; the house tenant may seek other political patrons for protection against the house-owner. Nevertheless, the house-owner is in a clear position of political dominance over the tenant. The possession of agricultural land is a political asset in the same way. Though no political clientage is implied in land tenancy contracts (p. 44), the tenant depends on the land for his livelihood, and the power of eviction gives the landowner a hold on him.

The ownership of land is thus a direct source of political influence. An increase in land holdings implies an increase in such influence; indeed the possession of extensive lands is a basic requirement for any kind of security in a position of ascendancy. The competition between chiefs is thus largely for the control of land, and the acquisition of land is an important move in a political ascent. Land may be obtained in four ways: by inheritance, as a reward for political service, by purchase, or by violence or threats. These four methods merit some attention.

Real property passes in inheritance from a man to his closest agnatic relatives in the order: son, father, son's son, father's father, brother, father's brother, brother's son, father's brother's son. The presence of a person in any one category excludes the succeeding categories, so where there are one father's brother and four brother's sons, the father's brother takes the whole estate. Thus it is only groups of brothers who ever share an estate. In the division among them, each receives an equal share; there is no preference for the first- or last-born son.

Sometimes a descent group segment of Pakhtun landowners may recognize a single leader. In such cases, the chief may be vested with a certain area of land in return for his services as leader; such land is called *pargéi siri*. During his lifetime, it forms part of his private property. On his death, however, it is not divided between his heirs, but passes as a unit to his successor in the position of leader. Such *pargéi* estates form the nuclei in the formation of *khānates*, petty principalities, by preventing the fragmentation of property between multiple heirs. They are not, however, a regular feature of the tenure system in the Swat valley.

Land is a scarce resource in Swat and there are always eager prospective buyers; consequently the price, in cases of outright sale, is extremely high. But people hesitate to sell real property, since this is tantamount to renouncing all claim to high status. Nevertheless, chiefs occasionally find themselves in such great need of funds that they sell part of their land, hoping to be able to regain it later. The volume of such transfers is difficult to estimate, as both parties generally maintain a discreet silence.

Finally, land may be obtained by force or deception. There are various recognized methods.

Where there has been permanent settlement, a stronger landlord generally attempts to encroach on the land of his weaker neighbours by the slow but steady technique of ploughing the borderpath between the fields. These borders are marked by a low wall. In the irrigated rice-lands this is less than a foot wide, and serves as a retaining wall for irrigation water and a raised path for reaching the further paddy fields. In the natural-flow irrigation system, fields are usually very small, and the 'share' system makes for extreme fragmentation and dispersal of holdings. The total length along which one man's fields adjoin those of others is considerable, and the amount that can be gained by twice yearly adding one furrow along this whole length may be spectacular in the course of a generation. The strategic advantage of this technique is that there is no critical moment in its execution when dramatic counteraction is precipitated. Pathan landowners exercise constant vigilance against it.

As there is no survey or registration of land

holdings among Swat Pathans, all claims to land must be supported by witnesses and boundaries are delimited by the decision of mediators or assemblies. In the course of recent history considerable landed estates have been gained and lost, and there is a confusion of conflicting claims to many fields, which refer for their validation to different periods of time. This offers a fertile field for controversy, of which chiefs may take advantage by backing the claims of small landowners. The chief contracts to carry another man's case successfully through the assembly or to a mediator, and to protect the claimant against foul play by his more powerful opponents. In return for this service, the chief asks for a half share of the property concerned, to be discreetly passed on to him at a later date. The small claimant has nothing to lose and half a field to gain by this arrangement; he can moreover expect his relationship with the powerful chief to bear additional fruits in the future. An influential chief can thus use his influence directly to enlarge his own estate, as well as that of his followers. This technique is extensively used today.

Finally, powerful chiefs can frighten or force people to sell or abandon their claim to land. This method was apparently popular in the past, though under present conditions it is no longer prevalent. However, I was able to collect numerous examples. Almost inevitably, it leads to feud, since many small landowners are prepared to be killed in defense of their land rather than give it up. The simplest procedure was outright murder followed by occupation of the murdered man's estate. Less blatant is 'sale' under duress, or the quiet abandonment of rights. This technique requires secrecy, lest public opinion should rally in support of the weaker party. In the traditional re-allotment system it was difficult to maintain such secrecy. According to informants, one famous Khan, who amassed a great deal of land by this means, found a gentlemanly solution to this problem: he gave the other chiefs of his village first choice at each re-allotment, retaining what remained after they had all received their shares, so that his own share was never counted up.

Rights to land are thus the subject of considerable dispute. A conflict of this kind is known as *shar*. If, in such a situation, the weaker party refuses to give in, he can adopt either of two courses, both very dangerous to him; feud, which may lead to his own death, or the mobilization of support among other leaders, which may lead to total defeat. His decision and that of the leaders whose support he seeks, are political decisions and can only be explored in the

wider political setting described in Chapter 9. Apart from these controls, there is an upper limit to every chief's aggressiveness, since he must always keep the number of his enemies lower than the total force of his following.

Within these limits, chiefs are constantly engaged in attempts to increase their landed property. Conflicts over land have the advantage, from the chief's point of view, that they automatically involve the self-interest of many of his non-Pakhtun followers. If his title is threatened, their rights are threatened too; if his property is expanded, their potential profits are expanded as well. Conflicts over land mobilize all the tenants of the landowners concerned in groups based on common interest; they divide co-villagers and identify followers more closely with their leaders. They enable the landowner to cement the unity of his own following by leading them in activities where their common interest is clear.

Rights to land are thus an important direct source of political authority, but they are not the only such source. Land is also the basis of wealth, and Pathans see wealth as a second source of conflicts and thus, in this analysis, of authority.

The people of Swat, though till recently, and to a considerable extent still, living in a non-monetary economy, have long been familiar with coinage, and had access to a certain volume of exchange media. In the valley bottom, the farmer ploughing his fields often turns up Bactrian coins, and children and adults alike dream of finding vast hidden hoards. At least since the beginning of Moghul times, doles and bribes have been paid the tribesmen by the successive governments of the plains, and some external trade has augmented these sources. Gold-dust and coins have thus long been familiar as a measure of value and medium of exchange; however, in the proverb referred to earlier, 'gold' is taken to refer to any conveniently movable form of wealth.

The authority of a chief depends very directly on the manipulation of such wealth, and chiefs use their yearly income to support their position and assure themselves a following in several ways, by bribes, payments, gifts and hospitality. The cultural significance of these different kinds of transaction must be understood if their political role is to be understood.

Payment in return for services implies a relationship of inequality between the partners to the transaction, and responsibility on the part of him who pays for the actions of him who performs the service.

Gifts can be cancelled out by an equivalent

return, and do not imply any authority of the giver over the receiver. Gift giving is used to express relationships of friendliness and rough equality—never to shame the recipient. Unilateral gift-giving expresses a difference in status between the giver and the receiver, but does not effectively put the recipient under an obligation to respond to the command of the giver, as does the payment of bribes or salaries.

Hospitality is, in a sense, a special variety of gift-giving, with the added factor of commensality. Commensality implies solidarity, and the recipient of food is under an obligation to respect his host, and to support him in times of need. To abandon persons with whom one has shared a meal in case of trouble is dishonourable, to stick by them is meritorious. But no sanctions can be brought to bear on dishonourable persons, and the loyalty and solidarity that are expressed in commensality need not be very deep-seated.

It might seem from this that gifts and hospitality would be less important than bribes and payments in supporting claims to authority. As a matter of fact, the reverse is true. Bribes and payments create relationships which render them onerous or hazardous. Gifts and hospitality, on the other hand, are of prime importance in the building up of a political following. The reason for this is to be found in a consideration of the order of magnitude involved.

To show this we need to examine the sources and amount of a chief's income. The sources are diverse, and include income from the political position itself, from the outlying land and pasture areas controlled by the chief, and from his own agricultural land.

Of sources of income deriving from the position of chiefship, the following are important. Direct subsidies have long been paid by governments in the plains: two chiefs in Thana receive 1,500 rupees per year and a third 3,000. When this payment was instituted, before 1900, the importance of such a large outside source of money income for the chief was very considerable. Since Swat was officially recognized by British India in 1926, all external subsidies have been paid directly to its ruler, just as they were and are also paid to the Nawab of Dir, who receives 50,000 rupees a year. The ruler of Swat redistributes these and other funds in subsidies to the chiefs who support him. Each of these receives an annual grant which depends on his importance and influence; the amounts range from 300 to 2,000 rupees. These fixed subsidies have largely replaced the older system of claiming head-tax and protection money from caravans passing through the chief's demesne. For example, lumber merchants formerly had to pay the chiefs controlling the banks of the Swat river for the right to float timber, at the rate of 6,000 rupees yearly to the Aka-Maruf and Barat khel chiefs of Babuzai. Fines imposed on their subjects, in the traditional system as well as in Swat State, form another source of income. In the traditional system as it exists in present-day Thana, such fines are used for public or political purposes by the chiefs in power, while in Swat State chiefs receive a cut of every fine collected from their subjects.

The outlying land and pasture areas contribute a variable, but at times very important, amount to the chief's total income. Forests and mountains are a source of revenue, since nomadic herdsmen have to pay for the right to the pastures; they pay also for grazing rights in the stubble and embankments of the rice-fields after harvest. The fee is calculated in numbers of buffalo, on the equation 20 sheep=4 cows=1 buffalo. It is generally paid in clarified butter, though the nomads who visit administered districts and have money income in the winter often pay in Pakistan rupees. Such fees are generally shared by all landowners in proportion to the size of each one's *daftar*; in some areas, however, they are paid into a fund which is administered by the chief.

Finally, as one of the main landlords of his village, the chief collects the landowner's share of the crops from his own fields. Even a minor chief—and there are generally several in any one village—must be a landlord of some importance to be able successfully to claim authority: of the small chiefs with whom I came into contact, none had less than five labourers working in their fields and depending on these fields for their and their families' subsistence. As the agricultural labourer takes one fifth and the landowner four fifths of the crop, this implies a gross income for even the smallest chief, from his agricultural land alone, twenty times greater than that of the average tenant. Prominent chiefs own ten times as much land, and a few even more.

The difference in the yearly income from agriculture of a tenant and a prominent chief is truly spectacular, and at harvest-time staggering amounts of grain are deposited in the storehouses of a chief. Most of this wealth remains in the form of grain, which indeed serves as a medium of exchange and remuneration. But in parts of the Swat valley where communications have been developed an increasing quantity is sold to the grainmarkets of Peshawar. At the time of my visit, one of my acquaintances among the more prominent chiefs had an approximate income of 50,000 Pakistan rupees (then about £5,000) from the sale of grain. The average villager's income is about 300 rupees. But this development of exports is recent, and has not yet gone very far. Most of the agricultural produce of Swat circulates in an internal system of exchange, and is consumed in the area.

A prominent chief thus disposes of literally a hundred times the wealth, both perishable and imperishable, which is required to satisfy the reasonable needs of his own family.

Not so the majority of the village population. The Swat valley is densely populated, and pressure on land is great. A considerable proportion of the population lives near subsistence level. The birth rate is fairly high, but so is the child mortality rate. Pathan parents are aware that the high mortality among their children is due to insufficient or inappropriate food, and to the poverty that prevents them from procuring sufficient clothes, medicines and protective amulets. Wealthy families do not suffer these hardships, and the sibling groups among the wealthy are larger.

This picture is based on my own impressions and the statements of informants. In poor families one frequently sees small sibling groups spanning an age differential of twenty years. Where I was able to obtain the information, I found that in such cases there had been numerous conceptions and births, but a high rate of infant and child mortality. The larger sibling groups of wealthy people are in part the result of polygamy, but informants agreed that full sibling groups are also larger, mainly owing to their better diet.

In the idiom of Swat Pashto, the world is divided into two kinds of people: *mõr sarî*, 'satisfied men', and *wúge sarî*, 'hungry men'. The 'satisfied men' have enough food in their storehouses to feed the families of scores of 'hungry men' throughout the year. The chief, by his overwhelming wealth, is thus not only in a position to offer occasional gifts and hospitality; he can really make a substantial contribution to the subsistence of his followers. If offered such a contribution over a period of time, a poor man inevitably bases his domestic economy on it. The possibility of its being cut off becomes a major threat.

It is against this background that the importance of gifts and hospitality as a source of the chief's political authority must be understood. Gift-giving and hospitality are potent means of controlling others, not because of the debts they create, but because of the recipient's dependence on their continuation. A continuous flow of gifts creates needs and fosters dependence, and the threat of its being cut off becomes a powerful disciplinary device. In contrast to the giving of salaries and bribes, which places responsibility on the chief who pays, gifts and hospitality give a chief political control over followers without saddling him with responsibility for their actions.

The scene of most gift-giving and hospitality is the men's house. Here the efficacy of the gifts is enhanced by their public transfer; the chief's character as a lavish giver becomes known to outsiders, who are thus attracted to visit his men's house.[3]

Distributions of durable wealth are fairly rare today in the Swat men's houses, though the alms enjoined by the Koran are often given by the chief in his men's house, thereby contributing to his political, as well as his religious, merit. Gifts to individuals of some single valuable item are much more frequent. In the old days, according to informants, gift-giving in the men's house was much more lavish, and Jamroz Khan of Babuzai, for one, used to walk into his men's house with his shirt-front full of rupees, giving the money out in handfuls to all those present. Hospitality, on the other hand, is still maintained at a lavish level. Food is provided for all travellers, visitors and needy persons; feasts are given at which rice, chicken, clarified butter and soured milk are consumed from large flat trays by circles of hungry men. Around them hover the little boys, to descend on the remains and lick the trays when the men have finished. I was not able to collect any detailed figures on the economics of a chief's household and feast-giving in the men's house. But since the lack of transport facilities in most places prevents the export of grain on any scale, practically all the locally produced grain must be consumed in the village, and a large proportion of it in feasts in the men's houses.

The importance for chiefs of the bonds created by hospitality is best seen by their actions when under political pressure, or when their income falls short of its usual level. In such circumstances the hospitality offered in the men's house is intensified rather than reduced; and if a sale of real property can be negotiated without too much publicity, the amount realized will be expended so as to maintain this higher level.

This condition was exemplified by several chiefs at the time of my visit. One such chief is the senior son of a former leader of great importance. He is himself fairly prominent, but he is subject to irregular loss of land, and frequent fines by the Ruler of Swat. Through all this he maintains a higher level of hospitality than any of the other chiefs in the area; in the course of the last ten years he has sold extensive lands to feed the many visitors to his men's house. I discussed this policy with him, and he was fully aware that his actions were progressively reducing his yearly income and thus aggravating the crisis. 'On the other hand,' he said, 'if people stop sitting in my men's house, I shall lose the land even faster; only this constant show of force keeps the vultures at bay.' The substantial group of goldsmiths and muleteers living as landowners in the village of Worejo is another example. This group of small landowners has come into being because the Manki khel chiefs of the village have repeatedly sold land in order to finance hospitality, and have maintained their political position by living beyond their income.

The chief's hospitality in his men's house makes his followers dependent on him as a source of food—for very many of the regular visitors could not do without the numerous free meals provided there. The chief also establishes a reputation for lavishness, shows himself capable of profitable management of his estates, and in general gains prestige as a desirable leader. Followers flock to his men's house and his political influence increases. Through this influence he can expect to enlarge his lands and gain greater wealth, ever more followers and still greater influence. At the same time, his followers are welded into a group the solidarity of which is reinforced by commensality, which puts them all under a moral obligation to support one another. Persons without common interests, or even with opposed interests, such as tenant and herdsman, or shopkeeper and labourer, in this way become members of a viable unit under external pressure.

NOTES

1 In a politically autonomous population which is predominantly illiterate, none of these 'contracts' take the form of written documents; they are in fact not even formally made before witnesses, though where conflicts are brought for settlement to the village council or a mediator, witnesses are usually produced. Unless otherwise stated, 'contract' will in the following refer to any agreement made between two or more partners to cooperate in a specified way within a defined field of activity.

2 My only complete figures are from the Barat khel branch of the Babuzai, occupying the land adjoining about five miles of the Swat river, and stretching eastward from the river bank to the mountain ridge. In this area, the non-Pakhtun landowners are predominantly *Lalas* of high Saintly status, and control an area estimated to correspond to twenty shares, against the 160 shares of the local Pakhtuns. This appears on the basis of rough estimates from other areas to be a fairly representative situation for most of the main valley. The proportion of land held by Saints in the hilly districts is much higher.

3 This view of the connexion between the institution of the men's house and the political activities of chiefs is supported by the changes that have taken place in the neighbouring Peshawar District. In that area, which formerly had an economic and social system similar to that of Swat today (Elphinstone, 1839, vol. II, pp. 27-8), the registration of titles and establishment of a police system under British administration progressively guaranteed tenure and thus eliminated the necessity for landowners to maintain political supremacy. At the same time, the introduction of an effective monetary economy made possible the conversion of perishable wealth into cash. The result of these inter-connected changes was the disappearance from Peshawar District of the men's house. With improved communications and greater security, similar changes are taking place in Swat, though at the time of fieldwork they had not yet proceeded very far.

POOR MAN, RICH MAN, BIG-MAN, CHIEF:
Political Types in Melanesia and Polynesia*
MARSHALL D. SAHLINS

WITH AN EYE to their own life goals, the native peoples of Pacific Islands unwittingly present to anthropologists a generous scientific gift: an extended series of experiments in cultural adaptation and evolutionary development. They have compressed their institutions within the confines of infertile coral atolls, expanded them on volcanic islands, created with the means history gave them cultures adapted to the deserts of Australia, the mountains and warm coasts of New Guinea, the rain forests of the Solomon Islands. From the Australian Aborigines, whose hunting and gathering existence duplicates in outline the cultural life of the later Paleolithic, to the great chiefdoms of Hawaii, where society approached the formative levels of the old Fertile Cresture is exemplified.

Where culture so experiments, anthropology finds its laboratories—makes its comparisons.[1]

In the southern and eastern Pacific two contrasting cultural provinces have long evoked anthropological interest. *Melanesia*, including New Guinea, the Bismarcks, Solomons, and island groups east to Fiji; and *Polynesia*, consisting in its main portion of the triangular constellation of lands between New Zealand, Easter Island, and the Hawaiian Islands. In and around Fiji, Melanesia and Polynesia intergrade culturally, but west and east of their intersection the two provinces pose broad contrasts in several sectors: in religion, art, kinship groupings, economics, political organization. The differences are the more notable for the underlying similarities from which they emerge. Melanesia and Polynesia are both agricultural regions in which many of the same crops—such as yams, taro, breadfruit, bananas, and coconuts—have long been cultivated by many similar techniques. Some recently presented linguistic and archaeological studies indeed suggest that Polynesian cultures originated from an eastern Melanesian hearth during the first millenium B.C.[2] Yet in anthropological annals the Polynesians were to become famous for elaborate forms of rank and chieftainship, whereas most Melanesian societies broke off advance on this front at more rudimentary levels.

It is obviously imprecise, however, to make out the political contrast in broad culture-area terms. Within Polynesia, certain of the islands,

such as Hawaii, the Society Islands and Tonga, developed unparalleled political momentum. And not all Melanesian polities, on the other side, were constrained and truncated in their evolution. In New Guinea and nearby areas of western Melanesia, small and loosely ordered political groupings are numerous, but in eastern Melanesia, New Caledonia and Fiji for example, political approximations of the Polynesian condition become common. There is more of an upward west to east slope in political development in the southern Pacific than a step-like, quantum progression.[3] It is quite revealing, however, to compare the extremes of this continuum, the western Melanesian underdevelopment against the greater Polynesian chiefdoms. While such comparison does not exhaust the evolutionary variations, it fairly established the scope of overall political achievement in this Pacific phylum of cultures.

Measurable along several dimensions, the contrast between developed Polynesian and underdeveloped Melanesian polities is immediately striking for differences in scale. H. Ian Hogbin and Camilla Wedgwood concluded from a survey of Melanesian (mostly western Melanesian) societies that ordered, independent political bodies in the region typically include seventy to three hundred persons; more recent work in the New Guinea Highlands suggests political groupings of up to a thousand, occasionally a few thousand, people.[4] But in Polynesia sovereignties of two thousand or three thousand are run-of-the-mill, and the most advanced chiefdoms, as in Tonga or Hawaii, might claim ten thousand, even tens of thousands.[5] Varying step by step with such differences in size of the polity are differences in territorial extent: from a few square miles in western Melanesia to tens or even hundreds of square miles in Polynesia.

The Polynesian advance in political scale was supported by advance over Melanesia in political structure. Melanesia presents a great array of social-political forms: here political organization is based upon patrilineal descent groups, there on cognatic groups, or men's club-houses recruiting neighborhood memberships, on a secret ceremonial society, or perhaps on some combination of these structural principles. Yet a general plan can be discerned. The characteristic western Melanesian "tribe," that is, the ethnic-cultural entity, consists of many autonomous kinship-residential groups. Amounting on the ground to a small village or a local cluster of hamlets, each of these is a copy of the others in organization, each tends to be economically self-governing, and each is the equal of the others in political status. The tribal plan is one of politically unintegrated segments—segmental. But the political geometry in Polynesia is pyramidal. Local groups of the order of self-governing Melanesian communities appear in Polynesia as subdivisions of a more inclusive political body. Smaller units are integrated into larger through a system of intergroup ranking, and the network of representative chiefs of the subdivisions amounts to a coordinating political structure. So instead of the Melanesian scheme of small, separate, and equal political blocs, the Polynesian polity is an extensive pyramid of groups capped by the family and following of a paramount chief. (This Polynesian political upshot is often, although not always, facilitated by the development of ranked lineages. Called *conical clan* by Kirchhoff, at one time *ramage* by Firth and *status lineage* by Goldman, the Polynesian ranked lineage is the same in principle as the so-called *obok* system widely distributed in Central Asia, and it is at least analogous to the Scottish clan, the Chinese clan, certain Central African Bantu lineage systems, the house-groups of Northwest Coast Indians, perhaps even the "tribes" of the Israelites.[6] Genealogical ranking is its distinctive feature: members of the same descent unit are ranked by genealogical distance from the common ancestor; lines of the same group become senior and cadet branches on this principle; related corporate lineages are relatively ranked, again by genealogical priority.)

Here is another criterion of Polynesian political advance: historical performance. Almost all of the native peoples of the South Pacific were brought up against intense European cultural pressure in the late eighteenth and the nineteenth centuries. Yet only the Hawaiians, Tahitians, Tongans, and to a lesser extent the Fijians, successfully defended themselves by evolving countervailing, native-controlled states. Complete with public governments and public law, monarchs and taxes, ministers and minions, these nineteenth century states are testimony to the native Polynesian political genius, to the level and the potential of indigenous political accomplishments.

Embedded within the grand differences in political scale, structure and performance is a more

personal contrast, one in quality of leadership. An historically particular type of leader-figure, the "big-man" as he is often locally styled, appears in the underdeveloped settings of Melanesia. Another type, a chief properly so-called, is associated with the Polynesian advance.[7] Now these are distinct sociological types, that is to say, differences in the powers, privileges, rights, duties, and obligations of Melanesian big-men and Polynesian chiefs are given by the divergent societal contexts in which they operate. Yet the institutional distinctions cannot help but be manifest also in differences in bearing and character, appearance and manner—in a word, personality. It may be a good way to begin the more rigorous sociological comparison of leadership with a more impressionistic sketch of the contrast in the human dimension. Here I find it useful to apply characterizations—or is it caricature?—from our own history to big-men and chiefs, however much injustice this does to the historically incomparable backgrounds of the Melanesians and Polynesians. The Melanesian big-man seems so thoroughly bourgeois, so reminiscent of the free enterprising rugged individual of our own heritage. He combines with an ostensible interest in the general welfare a more profound measure of self-interested cunning and economic calculation. His gaze, as Veblen might have put it, is fixed unswervingly to the main chance. His every public action is designed to make a competitive and invidious comparison with others, to show a standing above the masses that is product of his own personal manufacture. The historical caricature of the Polynesian chief, however, is feudal rather than capitalist. His appearance, his bearing is almost regal; very likely he just *is* a big man—" 'Can't you see he is a chief? See how big he is?' "[8] In his every public action is a display of the refinements of breeding, in his manner always that *noblesse oblige* of true pedigree and an incontestable right of rule. With his standing not so much a personal achievement as a just social due, he can afford to be, and he is, every inch a chief.

In the several Melanesian tribes in which big-men have come under anthropological scrutiny, local cultural differences modify the expression of their personal powers.[9] But the indicative quality of big-man authority is everywhere the same: it is *personal* power. Big-men do not come to office; they do not succeed to, nor are they installed in, existing positions of leadership over political groups. The attainment of big-man status is rather the outcome of a series of acts which elevate a person above the common herd and attract about him a coterie of loyal, lesser men. It is not accurate to speak of "big-man" as a political title, for it is but an acknowledged standing in interpersonal relations—a "prince among men" so to speak as opposed to "The Prince of Danes". In particular Melanesian tribes the phrase might be "man of importance" or "man of renown", "generous richman", or "center-man", as well as "big-man".

A kind of two-sidedness in authority is implied in this series of phrases, a division of the big-man's field of influence into two distinct sectors. "Center-man" particularly connotes a cluster of followers gathered about an influential pivot. It socially implies the division of the tribe into political in-groups dominated by outstanding personalities. To the in-group, the big-man presents this sort of picture:

The place of the leader in the district group (in northern Malaita) is well summed up by his title, which might be translated as "centre-man" . . . He was like a banyan, the natives explain, which, though the biggest and tallest in the forest, is still a tree like the rest. But, just because it exceeds all others, the banyan gives support to more lianas and creepers, provides more food for the birds, and gives better protection against sun and rain.[10] But "man of renown" connotes a broader tribal field in which a man is not so much a leader as he is some sort of hero. This is the side of the big-man facing outward from his own faction, his status among some or all of the other political clusters of the tribe. The political sphere of the big-man divides itself into a small internal sector composed of his personal satellites—rarely over eighty men—and a much larger external sector, the tribal galaxy consisting of many similar constellations.

As it crosses over from the internal into the external sector, a big-man's power undergoes qualitative change. Within his faction a Melanesian leader has true command ability, outside of it only fame and indirect influence. It is not that the center-man rules his faction by physical force, but his followers do feel obliged to obey him, and he can usually get what he wants by haranguing them—public verbal suasion is indeed so often employed by center-men that they have been styled "harangue-utans". The orbits of outsiders, however, are set by their own center-men. ' "Do it yourself. I'm not *your* fool," ' would be the characteristic response to an order issued by a center-man to an outsider among the Siuai.[11] This fragmentation of true authority presents special political difficulties, particularly in organizing large masses of people for the prosecution of such collective ends as

warfare or ceremony. Big-men do instigate mass action, but only by establishing both extensive renown and special personal relations of compulsion or reciprocity with other center-men.

Politics is in the main personal politiking in these Melanesian societies, and the size of a leader's faction as well as the extent of his renown are normally set by competition with other ambitious men. Little or no authority is given by social ascription: leadership is a creation—a creation of followership. "Followers", as it is written of the Kapauku of New Guinea, "stand in various relations to the leader. Their obedience to the headman's decisions is caused by motivations which reflect their particular relations to the leader."[12] So a man must be prepared to demonstrate that he possesses the kinds of skills that command respect—magical powers, gardening prowess, mastery of oratorical style, perhaps bravery in war and feud.[13] Typically decisive is the deployment of one's skills and efforts in a certain direction: towards amassing goods, most often pigs, shell monies and vegetable foods, and distributing them in ways which build a name for cavalier generosity, if not for compassion. A faction is developed by informal private assistance to people of a locale. Tribal rank and renown are developed by great public giveaways sponsored by the rising big-man, often on behalf of his faction as well as himself. In different Melanesian tribes, the renown-making public distribution may appear as one side of a delayed exchange of pigs between corporate kinship groups; a marital consideration given a bride's kinfolk; a set of feasts connected with the erection of a big-man's dwelling, or of a clubhouse for himself and his faction, or with the purchase of higher grades of rank in secret societies; the sponsorship of a religious ceremony; a payment of subsidies and blood compensations to military allies; or perhaps the giveaway is a ceremonial challenge bestowed on another leader in the attempt to outgive and thus outrank him (a potlatch).

The making of the faction, however, is the true making of the Melanesian big-man. It is essential to establish relations of loyalty and obligation on the part of a number of people such that their production can be mobilized for renownbuilding external distribution. The bigger the faction the greater the renown; once momentum in external distribution has been generated the opposite can also be true. Any ambitious man who can gather a following can launch a societal career. The rising big-man necessarily depends initially on a small core of followers, principally his own household and his closest relatives. Upon these people he can prevail economically: he capitalizes in the first instance on kinship dues and by finessing the relation of reciprocity appropriate among close kinsmen. Often it becomes necessary at an early phase to enlarge one's household. The rising leader goes out of his way to incorporate within his family "strays" of various sorts, people without familial support themselves, such as widows and orphans. Additional wives are especially useful. The more wives a man has the more pigs he has. The relation here is functional, not identical: with more women gardening there will be more food for pigs and more swineherds. A Kiwai Papuan picturesquely put to an anthropologist in pidgin the advantages, economic and political, of polygamy: " 'Another woman go garden, another woman go take firewood, another woman go catch fish, another woman cook him—husband he sing out plenty people come kaikai (i.e., come to eat).' "[14] Each new marriage, incidentally, creates for the big-man an additional set of in-laws from whom he can exact economic favors. Finally, a leader's career sustains its upward climb when he is able to link other men and their families to his faction, harnessing their production to his ambition. This is done by calculated generosities, by placing others in gratitude and obligation through helping them in some big way. A common technique is payment of bridewealth on behalf of young men seeking wives.

The great Malinowski used a phrase in analyzing primitive political economy that felicitously describes just what the big-man is doing: amassing a "fund of power." A big-man is one who can create and use social relations which give him leverage on others' production and the ability to siphon off an excess product—or sometimes he can cut down their consumption in the interest of the siphon. Now although his attention may be given primarily to short-term personal interests, from an objective standpoint the leader acts to promote long-term societal interests. The fund of power provisions activities that involve other groups of the society at large. In the greater perspective of that society at large, big-men are indispensable means of creating supralocal organization: in tribes normally fragmented into small independent groups, big-men at least temporarily widen the sphere of ceremony, recreation and art, economic collaboration, of war too. Yet always this greater societal organization depends on the lesser factional organization, particularly on the ceilings on economic mobilization set by relations between center-men and followers. The limits and the weaknesses of the political order in general are the limits and weaknesses of the factional in-groups.

And the personal quality of subordination to a center-man is a serious weakness in factional structure. A personal loyalty has to be made and continually reinforced; if there is discontent it may well be severed. Merely to create a faction takes time and effort, and to hold it, still more effort. The potential rupture of personal links in the factional chain is at the heart of two broad evolutionary shortcomings of western Melanesian political orders. First, a comparative instability. Shifting dispositions and magnetisms of ambitious men in a region may induce fluctuations in factions, perhaps some overlapping of them, and fluctuations also in the extent of different renowns. The death of a center-man can become a regional political trauma: the death undermines the personally cemented faction, the group dissolves in whole or in part, and the people re-group finally around rising pivotal big-men. Although particular tribal structures in places cushion the disorganization, the big-man political system is generally unstable over short terms: in its superstructure it is a flux of rising and falling leaders, in its substructure of enlarging and contracting factions. Secondly, the personal political bond contributes to the containment of evolutionary advance. The possibility of their desertion, it is clear, often inhibits a leader's ability to forceably push up his followers' output, thereby placing constraints on higher political organization, but there is more to it than that. If it is to generate great momentum, a big-man's quest for the summits of renown is likely to bring out a contradiction in his relations to followers, so that he finds himself encouraging defection—or worse, an egalitarian rebellion—by encouraging production.

One side of the Melanesian contradiction is the initial economic reciprocity between a center-man and his followers. For his help they give their help, and for goods going out through his hands other goods (often from outside factions) flow back to his followers by the same path. The other side is that a cumulative build-up of renown forces center-men into economic extortion of the faction. Here it is important that not merely his own status, but the standing and perhaps the military security of his people depend on the big-man's achievements in public distribution. Established at the head of a sizeable faction, a center-man comes under increasing pressure to extract goods from his followers, to delay reciprocities owing them, and to deflect incoming goods back into external circulation.

Success in competition with other big-men particularly undermines internal-factional reciprocities: such success is precisely measurable by the ability to give outsiders more than they can possibly reciprocate. In well delineated big-man polities, we find leaders negating the reciprocal obligations upon which their following had been predicated. Substituting extraction for reciprocity, they must compel their people to "eat the leader's renown," as one Solomon Island group puts it, in return for productive efforts. Some center-men appear more able than others to dam the inevitable tide of discontent that mounts within their factions, perhaps because of charismatic personalities, perhaps because of the particular social organizations in which they operate.[15] But paradoxically the ultimate defense of the center-man's position is some slackening of his drive to enlarge the funds of power. The alternative is much worse. In the anthropological record there are not merely instances of big-man chicanery and of material deprivation of the faction in the interests of renown, but some also of overloading of social relations with followers: the generation of antagonisms, defections, and in extreme cases the violent liquidation of the center-man.[16] Developing internal constraints, the Melanesian big-man political order brakes evolutionary advance at a certain level. It sets ceilings on the intensification of political authority, on the intensification of household production by political means, and on the diversion of household outputs in support of wider political organization. But in Polynesia these constraints were breached and although Polynesian chiefdoms also found their developmental plateau, it was not before political evolution had been carried above the Melanesian ceilings. The fundamental defects of the Melanesian plan were overcome in Polynesia. The division between small internal and larger external political sectors, upon which all big-man politics hinged, was suppressed in Polynesia by the growth of an enclaving chiefdom-at-large. A chain of command subordinating lesser chiefs and groups to greater, on the basis of inherent societal rank, made local blocs or personal followings (such as were independent in Melanesia) merely dependent parts of the larger Polynesian chiefdom. So the nexus of the Polynesian chiefdom became an extensive set of offices, a pyramid of higher and lower chiefs holding sway over larger and smaller sections of the polity. Indeed the system of ranked and subdivided lineages (conical clan system), upon which the pyramid was characteristically established, might build up through several orders of inclusion and encom-

pass the whole of an island or group of islands. While the island or the archipelago would normally be divided into several independent chiefdoms, high-order lineage connections between them, as well as kinship ties between their paramount chiefs, provided structural avenues for at least temporary expansion of political scale, for consolidation of great into even greater chiefdoms.[17]

The pivotal paramount chief as well as the chieftains controlling parts of a chiefdom were true office holders and title holders. They were not, like Melanesian big-men, fishers of men: they held positions of authority over permanent groups. The honorifics of Polynesian chiefs likewise did not refer to a standing in interpersonal relations, but to their leadership of political divisions—here "The Prince of Danes" *not* "the prince among men." In western Melanesia the personal superiorities and inferiorities arising in the intercourse of particular men largely defined the political bodies. In Polynesia there emerged suprapersonal structures of leadership and followership, organizations that continued independently of the particular men who occupied positions in them for brief mortal spans.

And these Polynesian chiefs did not make their positions in society—they were installed in societal positions. In several of the islands, men did struggle to office against the will and stratagems of rival aspirants. But then they came *to* power. Power resided in the office; it was not made by the demonstration of personal superiority. In other islands, Tahiti was famous for it, succession to chieftainship was tightly controlled by inherent rank. The chiefly lineage ruled by virtue of its genealogical connections with divinity, and chiefs were succeeded by first sons, who carried "in the blood" the attributes of leadership. The important comparative point is this: the qualities of command that had to reside in men in Melanesia, that had to be personally demonstrated in order to attract loyal followers, were in Polynesia socially assigned to office and rank. In Polynesia, people of high rank and office *ipso facto* were leaders, and by the same token the qualities of leadership were automatically lacking—theirs was not to question why—among the underlying population. Magical powers such as a Melanesian big-man might acquire to sustain his position, a Polynesian high chief inherited by divine descent as the *mana* which sanctified his rule and protected his person against the hands of the commonalty. The productive ability the big-man laboriously had to demonstrate was effortlessly given Polynesian chiefs as religious control over agricultural fertility, and upon the ceremonial implementation of it the rest of the people were conceived dependent. Where a Melanesian leader had to master the compelling oratorical style, Polynesian paramounts often had trained "talking chiefs" whose voice was the chiefly command.

In the Polynesian view, a chiefly personage was in the nature of things powerful. But this merely implies the objective observation that his power was of the group rather than of himself. His authority came from the organization, from an organized acquiescence in his privileges and organized means of sustaining them. A kind of paradox resides in evolutionary developments which detach the exercise of authority from the necessity to demonstrate personal superiority: organizational power actually extends the role of personal decision and conscious planning, gives it greater scope, impact, and effectiveness. The growth of a political system such as the Polynesian constitutes advance over Melanesian orders of interpersonal dominance in the human control of human affairs. Especially significant for society at large were privileges accorded Polynesian chiefs which made them greater architects of funds of power than ever was any Melanesian big-man.

Masters of their people and "owners" in a titular sense of group resources, Polynesian chiefs had rights of call upon the labor and agricultural produce of households within their domains. Economic mobilization did not depend on, as it necessarily had for Melanesian big-men, the de novo creation by the leader of personal loyalties and economic obligations. A chief need not stoop to obligate this man or that man, need not by a series of individual acts of generosity induce others to support him, for economic leverage over a group was the inherent chiefly due. Consider the implications for the fund of power of the widespread chiefly privilege, related to titular "ownership" of land, of placing an interdiction, a tabu, on the harvest of some crop by way of reserving its use for a collective project. By means of the tabu the chief directs the course of production in a general way: households of his domain must turn to some other means of subsistence. He delivers a stimulus to household production: in the absence of the tabu further labors would not have been necessary. Most significantly, he has generated a politically utilizable agricultural surplus. A subsequent call on this surplus floats chieftainship as a going concern, capitalizes the fund of power. In certain islands, Polynesian chiefs controlled great storehouses which held the goods congealed by

chiefly pressures on the commonalty. Davis Malo, one of the great native custodians of old Hawaiian lore, felicitously catches the political significance of the chiefly magazine in his well-known *Hawaiian Antiquities*: It was the practice for kings (i.e., paramount chiefs of individual islands) to build store-houses in which to collect food, fish, tapas (bark cloth), malos (men's loin cloths), pa-us (women's loin skirts), and all sorts of goods. These store-houses were designed by the Kalaimoku (the chief's principal executive) as a means of keeping the people contented, so they would not desert the king. They were like the baskets that were used to entrap the *hinalea* fish. The *hinalea* thought there was something good within the basket, and he hung round the outside of it. In the same way the people thought there was food in the store-houses, and they kept their eyes on the king. As the rat will not desert the pantry . . . where he thinks food is, so the people will not desert the king while they think there is food in his store-house.[18] Redistribution of the fund of power was the supreme art of Polynesian politics. By well-planned *noblesse oblige* the large domain of a paramount chief was held together, organized at times for massive projects, protected against other chiefdoms, even further enriched. Uses of the chiefly fund included lavish hospitality and entertainments for outside chiefs and for the chief's own people, and succor of individuals or the underlying population at large in times of scarcities—bread and circuses. Chiefs subsidized craft production, promoting in Polynesia a division of technical labor unparalleled in extent and expertise in most of the Pacific. They supported also great technical construction, as of irrigation complexes, the further returns to which swelled the chiefly fund. They initiated large-scale religious construction too, subsidized the great ceremonies, and organized logistic support for extensive military campaigns. Larger and more easily replenished than their western Melanesian counterparts, Polynesian funds of power permitted greater political regulation of a greater range of social activities on greater scale.

In the most advanced Polynesian chiefdoms, as in Hawaii and Tahiti, a significant part of the chiefly fund was deflected away from general redistribution towards the upkeep of the institution of chieftainship. The fund was siphoned for the support of a permanent administrative establishment. In some measure, goods and services contributed by the people precipitated out as the grand houses, assembly places, and temple platforms of chiefly precincts. In another measure, they were appropriated for the livelihood of circles of retainers, many of them close kinsmen of the chief, who clustered about the powerful paramounts. These were not all useless hangers-on. They were political cadres: supervisors of the stores, talking chiefs, ceremonial attendants, high priests who were intimately involved in political rule, envoys to transmit directives through the chiefdom. There were men in these chiefly retinues—in Tahiti and perhaps Hawaii, specialized warrior corps—whose force could be directed internally as a buttress against fragmenting or rebellious elements of the chiefdom. A Tahitian or Hawaiian high chief had more compelling sanctions than the harangue. He controlled a ready physical force, an armed body of executioners, which gave him mastery particularly over the lesser people of the community. While it looks a lot like the big-man's faction again, the differences in functioning of the great Polynesian chief's retinue are more significant than the superficial similarities in appearance. The chief's coterie, for one thing, is economically dependent upon him rather than he upon them. And in deploying the cadres politically in various sections of the chiefdom, or against the lower orders, the great Polynesian chiefs sustained command where the Melanesian big-man, in his external sector, had at best renown.

This is not to say that the advanced Polynesian chiefdoms were free of internal defect, of potential or actual malfunctioning. The large political-military apparatus indicates something of the opposite. So does the recent work of Irving Goldman[19] on the intensity of "status rivalry" in Polynesia, especially when it is considered that much of the status rivalry in developed chiefdoms, as the Hawaiian, amounted to popular rebellion against chiefly despotism rather than mere contest for position within the ruling-stratum. This suggests that Polynesian chiefdoms, just as Melanesian big-man orders, generate along with evolutionary development countervailing anti-authority pressures, and that the weight of the latter may ultimately impede further development.

The Polynesian contradiction seems clear enough. On one side, chieftainship is never detached from kinship moorings and kinship economic ethics. Even the greatest Polynesian chiefs were conceived superior kinsmen to the masses, fathers of their people, and generosity was morally incumbent upon them. On the other side, the major Polynesian paramounts seemed inclined to "eat the power of the government too much," as the Tahitians put it, to divert an undue proportion of the general wealth toward the chiefly establishment.[20] The diversion could be accomplished by lowering the customary level of general redistribution, lessening the material returns of chieftainship to the community at large—tradition attributes the great rebellion of Mangarevan commoners to such cause.[21] Or the diversion might—and I suspect more commonly did—consist in greater and more forceful exactions from lesser chiefs and people, increasing returns to the chiefly apparatus without necessarily affecting the level of general redistribution. In either case, the well developed chiefdom creates for itself the dampening paradox of stoking rebellion by funding its authority.[22]

In Hawaii and other islands cycles of political centralization and decentralization may be abstracted from traditional histories. That is, larger chiefdoms periodically fragmented into smaller and then were later reconstituted. Here would be more evidence of a tendency to overtax the political structure. But how to explain the emergence of a developmental stymic, of an inability to sustain political advance beyond a certain level? To point to a chiefly propensity to consume or a Polynesian propensity to rebel is not enough: such propensities are promoted by the very advance of chiefdoms. There is reason to hazard instead that Parkinson's notable law is behind it all: that progressive expansion in political scale entailed more-than-proportionate accretion in the ruling apparatus, unbalancing the flow of wealth in favor of the apparatus. The ensuing unrest then curbs the chiefly impositions, sometimes by reducing chiefdom scale to the nadir of the periodic cycle. Comparison of the requirements of administration in small and large Polynesian chiefdoms helps make the point.

A lesser chiefdom, confined say as in the Marquesas Islands to a narrow valley, could be almost personally ruled by a headman in frequent contact with the relatively small population. Melville's partly romanticized—also for its ethnographic details, partly cribbed—account in *Typee* makes this clear enough.[23] But the great Polynesian chiefs had to rule much larger, spatially dispersed, internally organized populations. Hawaii, an island over four thousand square miles with an aboriginal population approaching one hundred thousand, was at times a single chiefdom, at other times divided into two to six independent chiefdoms, and at all times each chiefdom was composed of large subdivisions under powerful subchiefs. Sometimes a chiefdom in the Hawaiian group extended beyond the confines of one of the islands, incorporating part of another through conquest. Now, such extensive chiefdoms would have to be coordinated; they would have to be centrally tapped for a fund of power, buttressed against internal disruption, sometimes massed for distant, perhaps overseas, military engagements. All of this to be implemented by means of communication still at the level of word-of-mouth, and means of transportation consisting of human bodies and canoes. (The extent of certain larger chieftainships, coupled with the limitations of communication and transportation, incidentally suggests another possible source of political unrest: that the burden of provisioning the governing apparatus would tend to fall disproportionately on groups within easiest access of the paramount.)[24] A tendency for the developed chiefdom to proliferate in executive cadres, to grow top-heavy, seems in these circumstances altogether functional, even though the ensuing drain on wealth proves the chiefdom's undoing. Functional also, and likewise a material drain on the chiefdom at large, would be widening distinctions between chiefs and people in style of life. Palatial housing, ornamentation and luxury, finery and ceremony, in brief, conspicuous consumption, however much it seems mere self-interest always has a more decisive social significance. It creates those invidious distinctions between rulers and ruled so conducive to a passive—hence quite economical!—acceptance of authority. Throughout history, inherently more powerful political organizations than the Polynesian, with more assured logistics of rule, have turned to it—including in our time some ostensibly revolutionary and proletarian governments, despite every pre-revolutionary protestation of solidarity with the masses and equality for the classes.

In Polynesia then, as in Melanesia, political evolution is eventually short-circuited by an overload on the relations between leaders and their people. The Polynesian tragedy, however, was somewhat the opposite of the Melanesian. In Polynesia, the evolutionary ceiling was set by extraction from the population at large in favor of the chiefly faction, in Melanesia by extraction from the big-man's faction in favor of distribution to the population at large. Most importantly, the Polynesian ceiling was higher. Melanesian big-men and Polynesian chiefs not only reflect different varieties and levels of political evolution, they display in different degrees the capacity to generate and to sustain political progress.

Especially emerging from their juxtaposition is the more decisive impact of Polynesian chiefs on the economy, the chiefs' greater leverage on the output of the several households of society. The success of any primitive political organization is decided here, in the control that can be developed over household economies. For the household is not merely the principal productive unit in primitive societies, it is often quite capable of autonomous direction of its own production, and it is oriented towards production for its own, not societal consumption. The greater potential of Polynesian chieftainship is precisely the greater pressure it could exert on household output, its capacity both to generate a surplus and to deploy it out of the household towards a broader division of labor, cooperative construction, and massive ceremonial and military action. Polynesian chiefs were the more effective means of societal collaboration on economic, political, indeed all cultural fronts. Perhaps we have been too long accustomed to perceive rank and rule from the standpoint of the individuals involved, rather than from the perspective of the total society, as if the secret of the subordination of man to man lay in the personal satisfactions of power. And then the breakdowns too, or the evolutionary limits, have been searched out in men, in "weak" kings or megalomaniacal dictators—always, "who is the matter?" An excursion into the field of primitive politics suggests the more fruitful conception that the gains of political developments accrue more decisively to society than to individuals, and the failings as well are of structure not men.

REFERENCES

Bacon, Elizabeth E., *Obok*. (= *Viking Fund Publications in Anthropology* No. 25) (New York: The Wenner-Gren Foundation, 1958).

Barnes, J. A., "African Models in the New Guinea Highlands", *Man* 62(2):5-9 (1962).

Blackwood, Beatrice, *Both Sides of Buka Passage* (Oxford: Clarendon Press, 1935).

Bromley, M., "A Preliminary Report on Law Among the Grand Valley Dani of Netherlands New Guinea", *Nieuw Guinea Studien* 4:235-259 (1960).

Brown, Paula, "Chimbu Tribes: Political Organization in the Eastern Highlands of New Guinea", *Southwestern Journal of Anthropology* 16:22-35 (1960).

Buck, Sir Peter H., *Ethnology of Mangareva* (= *Bernice P. Bishop Mus. Bull.* 157) (Honolulu, 1938).

Bulmer, Ralph, "Political Aspects of the Moka Exchange System Among the Kyaka People of the Western Highlands of New Guinea", *Oceania* 31:1-13 (1960-61).

Burridge, Kenelm, Mambu: *A Melanesian Millenium* (London: Methuen & Co., 1960).

Conklin, Harold C., *Hanunoø Agriculture* = *FAO Forestry Development Paper* No. 12) (Rome: Food and Agricultural Organization of the United Nations, 1957).

Deacon, A. Bernard, *Malekula: A Vanishing People in the New Hebrides*. (C. H. Wedgwood, ed.) (London: Geo. Routledge and Sns, 1934).

Dyen, Isidore, Review of *The Position of the Polynesian Languages within the Austronesian (Malayo-Polynesian) Language Family* (by George W. Grace). *Journal of the Polynesian Society* 69:180-184 (1960).

Firth, Raymond, *Primitive Polynesian Economy* (New York: Humanities Press, 1950).

———, *We, the Tikopia*. Second ed. (London: Allen and Unwin, 1957).

Fornander, Abraham, *An Account of the Polynesian Race*. Vol. II (London: Trübner, 1880).

Freeman, J. D., *Iban Agriculture* (= *Colonial Research Studies* No. 18) (London: Her Majesty's Stationery Office, 1955).

Fried, Morton H., "The Classification of Corporate Unilineal Descent Groups". *Jour. of the Royal Anthrop*. Instit. 87:1-29 (1957).

Gifford, Edward Winslow, *Tongan Society* (= *Bernice P. Bishop Mus. Bull*. 61) (Honolulu, 1929).

Goldman, Irving, "Status Rivalry and Cultural Evolution in Polynesia", *American Anthropologist* 57:680-697 (1955).

———, "Variations in Polynesian Social Organization", *Journal of the Polynesian Society* 66:374-390 (1957).

———, "The Evolution of Polynesian Societies", *Culture and History* (S. Diamond, ed.) (New York: Columbia University Press, 1960).

Golson, Jack, "Polynesian Culture History", *Journal of the Polynesian Society*, 70:498-508 (1961).

Goodenough, Ward, "Oceania and the Problem of Controls in the Study of Cultural and Human Evolution", *Journal of the Polynesian Society* 66:146-155 (1957).

Grace, George, "Subgroupings of Malayo-Polynesian: A Report of Tentative Findings", *American Anthropologist* 57:337-39 (1955).

———, *The Position of the Polynesian Languages within the Austronesian (Malayo-Polynesian) Family* (= *Indiana University Publications in Anthropological Linguistics* 16) (1959).

Handy, E. S. Craighill, *The Native Culture in the Marquesas* (= *Bernice P. Bishop Museum Bull*. 9) (Honolulu, 1923).

———, *History and Culture in the Society Islands* (= *Bernice P. Bishop Mus. Bull*. 79) (Honolulu, 1930).

Held, G. J., *The Papuas of Waropen* (The Hague: Koninklijk Instituut Voor Taal-, Land- En Volkenkunde, 1957).

Henry, Teuira, *Ancient Tahiti* (= *Bernice P. Bishop Mus. Bull*. 48) (Honolulu, 1928).

Hogbin, H. Ian, "Culture Change in the Solomon Islands: Report of Field Work in Guadalcanal and Malaita", *Oceania* 4:233-267 (1933-34).

———, "Social Advancement in Guadalcanal, Solomon Islands", *Oceania* 8:289-305 (1937-38).

———, "The Hill People of North-eastern Guadalcanal", *Oceania* 8:62-89 (1937-38a).

———, *Experiments in Civilization* (London: Geo. Routledge and Sos, 1939).

———, "Native Councils and Courts in the Solomon Islands", *Oceania* 14:258-283.

———, *Transformation Scene: The Changing Culture of a New Guinea Village* (London: Routledge and Kegan Paul, 1951).

Hogbin, H. and Camilla H. Wedgwood, "Local Groupings in Melanesia", *Oceania* 23:241-276; 24:58-76 (1952-53, 1953-54).

Ivens, W. G., *Melanesians of the Southeast Solomon Islands* (London: Kegan, Paul, Trench, Trubner and Co., 1927).

Kaberry, Phyllis M., "The Abelam Tribe, Sepik District, New Guinea: a Preliminary Report", *Oceania* 11:233-258, 345-367 (1940-41).

———, "Law and Political Organization in the Abelam Tribe", *Oceania* 12:79-95, 209-225, 331-363 (1941-42).

Kirchhoff, Paul, "The Principles of Clanship in Human Society", *Davidson Anthropological Journal* 1:1-11 (1955).

Landtman, Gunnar, *The Kiwai Papuans of British New Guinea* (London: Macmillan, 1927).

Linton, Ralph, "Marguesan Culture", *The Individual and His Society* (Ralph Linton and A. Kardiner) (New York: Columbia University Press, 1939).

Malo, David, *Hawaiian Antiquities* (Honolulu: Hawaiian Gazette Co., 1903).

Mariner, William, *An Account of the Natives of the Tonga Islands* (John Martin, compiler) (Edinburgh: Constable & Co., 1827).

Mead, Margaret, "Kinship in the Admiralty Islands", *Amer. Mus. Nat. Hist. Anthrop. Papers* 34:181-358 (1934).

———, "The Manus of the Admiralty Islands", *Cooperation and Competition Among Primitive Peoples* (M. Mead, ed.) (New York and London: McGraw-Hill, 1937).

———, "The Arapesh of New Guinea", *Cooperation and Competition Among Primitive Peoples* (M. Mead, ed.) (New York and London: McGraw-Hill, 1937a).

———, "The Mountain Arapesh I. An Importing Culture", *Amer. Mus. Nat. Hist. Anthrop. Papers* 40:159-232 (1947).

Meggitt, Mervyn, "Enga Political Organization: A Preliminary Description", *Mankind* 5:133-137 (1957).

———, "The Enga of the New Guinea Highlands: Some Preliminary Observations", *Oceania* 28:253-330 (1957-58).

Oliver, Douglas, *A Solomon Islands Society* (Cambridge: Harvard University Press, 1955).

Pospisil, Leopold, *Kapauku Papuans and Their Law* (= *Yale University Publications in Anthropology*, No. 54.) (New Haven: Yale University Press, 1958).

——, "The Kapauku Papuans and their Kinship Organization", *Oceania* 30:188-205 (1958-59).

Powdermaker, Hortense, *Life in Lesu* (New York: W. W. Norton, 1933).

Powell, H. A., "Competitive Leadership in Trobriand Political Organization", *Jour. Royal Anthrop. Instit.* 90:118-145 (1960).

Read, K. E., "Social Organization in the Markham Valley, New Guinea", *Oceania* 17:93-118 (1946-47).

——, "The Political System of the Ngarawapum", *Oceania* 20:185-223 (1949-50).

——, "The Nama Cult of the Central Highlands, New Guinea", *Oceania* 23:1-25 (1952-53).

——, "Leadership and Consensus in a New Guinea Society", *American Anthropologist* 61:425-436 (1959).

Reay, Marie, *The Kuma* (Melbourne University Press, 1959).

Sahlins, Marshall D., *Social Stratification in Polynesia* (= *American Ethnological Society Monograph*) (Seattle: University of Washington Press, 1958).

——, "The Segmentary Lineage: An Organization of Predatory Expansion", *American Anthropologist* 63:322-345 (1961).

Service, Elman R., *Primitive Social Organization: An Evolutionary Perspective* (New York: Random House, in press).

Suggs, Robert C., *Ancient Civilizations of Polynesia* (New York: Mentor, 1960).

Thomson, Sir Basil, *The Diversions of a Prime Minister* (Edinburgh and London: William Blackwood & Sos, 1894).

Vayda, Andrew Peter, "Polynesian Cultural Distributions in New Perspective", *American Anthropologist* 61:817-828 (1959).

Wedgwood, Camilla H., "Report on Research in Manam Island, Mandated Territory of New Guinea", *Oceania* 4:373-403 (1933-34).

Williams, F. E., "Orokaiva Society" (Oxford University Press, London: Humphrey Milford, 1930).

——, *Drama of Orokolo* (Oxford: Clarendon Press, 1940).

Williamson, Robert W., *The Mafulu: Mountain People of British New Guinea* (London: Macmillan, 1912).

Worsley, Peter, *The Trumpet Shall Sound* (London: Macgibbon and Kee, 1957).

NOTES

*The present paper is preliminary to a wider and more detailed comparison of Melanesian and Polynesian polities and economies. I have merely abstracted here some of the more striking political differences in the two areas. The full study—which, incidentally, will include more documentation—has been promised the editors of *The Journal of the Polynesian Society*, and I intend to deliver it to them some day.

The comparative method so far followed in this research has involved reading the monographs and taking notes. I don't think I originated the method, but I would like to christen it—The Method of Uncontrolled Comparison. The description developed of two forms of leadership is a mental distillation from the method of uncontrolled comparison. The two forms are abstracted sociological types. Anyone conversant with the anthropological literature of the South Pacific knows there are important variants of the types, as well as exceptional political forms not fully treated here. All would agree that consideration of the variations and exceptions is necessary and desirable. Yet there is pleasure too, and some intellectual reward, in discovering the broad patterns. To (social-) scientifically justify my pleasure, I could have referred to the pictures drawn of Melanesian big-men and Polynesian chiefs as "models" or as "ideal types". If that is needed to confer respectability on the paper, may the reader have it this way.

I hope all of this has been sufficiently disarming. Or need it also be said that the hypotheses are provisional, subject to further research, etc.?

1 Since Rivers' day, the Pacific has provided ethnographic stimulus to virtually every major ethnological school and interest. From such great landmarks as Rivers' *History of Melanesian Society*, Radcliffe-Brown's *Social Organization of the Australian Tribes*, Malinowski's famous Trobriand studies, especially *Argonauts of the Western Pacific*, Raymond Firth's pathmaking *Primitive Economics of the New Zealand Maori*, his functionalist classic, *We, The Tikopia*, and Margaret Mead's, *Coming of Age in Samoa*, one can almost read off the history of ethnological theory in the earlier twentieth century. In addition to continuing to provision all these concerns, the Pacific has been the site of much recent evolutionist work (see, for example, Goldman 1955, 1960; Goodenough 1957; Sahlins 1958; Vayda 1959). There are also the outstanding monographs on special subjects ranging from tropical agriculture (Conklin 1957; Freeman 1955) to millenarianism (Worsley 1957).

2 This question, however, is presently in debate. See Grace 1955, 1959; Dyen 1960; Suggs 1960; Golson 1961.

3 There are notable bumps in the geographical gradient. The Trobriand chieftainships of eastern New Guinea will come to mind. But the Trobriand political development is clearly exceptional for western Melanesia.

4 Hogbin and Wedgwood 1952-53, 1953-54. On New Guinea Highland political scale see among others, Paula Brown 1960.

5 See the summary account in Sahlins 1958, especially pp. 132-33.

6 Kirchhoff 1955; Firth 1957; Bacon 1958; Fried 1957.

7 The big-man pattern is very widespread in western Melanesia, although its complete distribution is not yet clear to me. Anthropological descriptions of big-man leadership vary from mere hints of its existence, as among the Orokaiva (Williams 1930), Lesu (Powdermaker 1933) or the interior peoples of northeastern Guadalcanal (Hogbin 1937-1938a), to excellent, closely grained analyses, such as Douglas Oliver's account of the Siuai of Bougainville (Oliver 1955). Big-man leadership has been more or less extensively described for the Manus of the Admiralty Islands (Mead 1934, 1937); the To'ambaita of northern Malaita (Hogbin 1939, 1943-44); the Tangu of northeastern New Guinea (Burridge 1960); the Kapauku of Netherlands New Guinea (Pospisil 1958, 1959-60); the Kaoka of Guadalcanal (Hogbin 1933-34, 1937-38); the Seniang District of Malekula (Deacon 1934); the Gawa' of the Huon Gulf area, New Guinea (Hogbin 1951); the Abelam (Kaberry 1940-41, 1941-42) and the Arapesh (Mead 1937a, 1938, 1947) of the Sepik District, New Guinea; The Elema, Orokolo Bay, New Guinea (Williams 1940); the Ngarawapum of the Markham Valley, New Guinea (Read 1946-47, 1949-50); the Kiwai of the Fly estuary, New Guinea (Landtman 1927); and a number of other societies, including, in New Guinea Highlands, the Kuma (Reay 1959), the Gahuka-Gama (Read 1952-53, 1959), the Kyaka (Bulmer 1960-61), the Enga (Meggitt 1957, 1957-58), and others. (For an overview of the structural position of New Guinea Highlands' leaders see Barnes 1962.) A partial bibliography on Polynesian chieftainship can be found in Sahlins 1958. The outstanding ethnographic description of Polynesian chieftainship is, of course, Firth's for Tikopia (1950, 1957—Tikopia, however, is not typical of the more advanced Polynesian chiefdoms with which we are principally concerned here.

8 Gifford 1929:124.

9 Thus the enclavement of the big-man pattern within a segmented lineage organization in the New Guinea Highlands appears to limit the leader's political role and authority in comparison, say, with the Siuai. In the Highlands, intergroup relations are regulated in part by the segmented lineage structure; among the Siuai intergroup relations depend more on contractual arrangements between big-men, which throws these figures more into prominence. (Notable in this connection has been the greater viability of the Siuai big-man than the native Highlands leader in the face of colonial control.) Barnes' (1962) comparison of Highland social structure with the classic segmentary lineage systems of Africa suggests an inverse relation between the formality of the lineage system and the political significance of individual action. Now, if instances such as the Siuai be tacked on to the comparison, the generalization may be further supported and extended: among societies of the tribal level (cf. Sahlins 1961, Service in press), the greater the self-regulation of the political process through a lineage system, the less function that remains to big-men, and the less significant their political authority.

10 Hogbin 1943-44:258.

11 Oliver 1955:408. Compare with the parallel statement for the Kaoka of Guadalcanal in Hogbin 1937-38:305.

12 Pospisil 1958:81.

13 It is difficult to say just how important the military qualifications of leadership have been in Melanesia, since the ethnographic researches have typically been undertaken after pacification, sometimes long after. I may underestimate this factor. Compare Bromley 1960.

14 Landtman 1927:168.

15 Indeed it is the same people, the Siuai, who so explicitly discover themselves eating their leader's renown who also seem able to absorb a great deal of deprivation without violent reaction, at least until the leader's wave of fame has already crested (see Oliver 1955:362, 368, 387, 394).

16 "In the Paniai Lake region (of Netherlands New Guinea), the people go so far as to kill a selfish rich man because of his 'immorality'. His own sons or brothers are induced by the rest of the members of the community to dispatch the first deadly arrow. *'Aki to tonowi beu, inii idikima enadani kodo to niitou* (you should not be the only rich man, we should all be the same, therefore you only stay equal with us)' was the reason given by the Paniai people for killing Mote Juwopija of Madi, a *tonowi* (Kapauku for 'big-man') who was not generous enough". (Pospisil 1958:80, cf. pp. 108-110). On another egalitarian conspiracy, see Hogbin 1951:145, and for other aspects of the Melanesian contradiction note, for example, Hogbin 1939:81; Burridge 1960:18-19; and Reay 1959:110, 129-30.

17 Aside from the transitional developments in eastern Melanesia, several western Melanesian societies advanced to a structural position intermediate between underdeveloped Melanesian polities and Polynesian chiefdoms. In these western Melanesian protochiefdoms, an ascribed division of kinship groups (or segments thereof) into chiefly and nonchiefly ranks emerges—as in Sa'a (Ivens 1927), around Buka passage (Blackwood 1935), in Manam Island (Wedgwood 1933-34, 1958-59), Waropen (Held 1957), perhaps Mafulu (Williamson 1912), and several others. The rank system does not go beyond the broad dual division of groups into chiefly and nonchiefly: no pyramid of ranked social-political divisions along Polynesian lines is developed. The political unit remains near the average size of the western Melanesian autonomous community. Sway over the kin groups of such a local body falls automatically to a chiefly unit, but chiefs do not hold office title with stipulated rights over corporate sections of society, and further extension of chiefly authority, if any, must be achieved. The Trobriands, which carry this line of chiefly development to its highest point, remain under the same limitations, although it was ordinarily possible for powerful chiefs to integrate settlements of the external sector within their domains (cf. Powell 1960).

18 Malo 1903:257-58.

19 Goldman 1955; 1957; 1960.

20 The great Tahitian chiefs were traditionally enjoined not to eat the power of government too much, as well as to practice open-handedness towards the people (Handy 1930:41). Hawaiian high chiefs were given precisely the same advice by counselors (Malo 1903:255).

21 Buck 1938:70-77, 160, 165.

22 The Hawaiian traditions are very clear on the encouragement given rebellion by chiefly exactions—although one of our greatest sources of Hawaiian tradition, David Malo, provides the most sober caveat regarding this kind of evidence. "I do not suppose," he wrote in the preface to *Hawaiian Antiquities*, "the following history to be free from mistakes, in that material for it has come from oral traditions; consequently it is marred by errors of human judgment and does not approach the accuracy of the word of God." Malo (1903:258) noted that "Many kings have been put to death by the people because of their oppression of the *makaainana* (i.e., commoners)." He goes on to list several who "lost their lives on account of their cruel exactions," and follows the list with the statement "It was for this reason that some of the ancient kings had a wholesome fear of the people." The propensity of Hawaiian high chiefs for undue appropriation from commoners is a point made over and over again by Malo (see pp. 85, 87-88, 258, 267-68). In Fornander's reconstruction of Hawaiian history (from traditions and genealogies) internal rebellions are laid frequently, almost axiomatically, to chiefly extortion and niggardliness (Fornander 1880: 40-41, 76-78, 88, 149-150, 270-271). In addition, Fornander at times links appropriation of wealth and ensuing rebellion to the provisioning of the chiefly establishment, as in the following passage: "Scarcity of food, after a while, obliged *Kalaniopuu* (paramount chief of the island of Hawaii and half brother of Kamehameha I's father) to remove his court (from the Kona district) into the Kohala district, where his headquarters were fixed at Kapaau. Here the same extravagant, *laissez-faire*, eat and be merry policy continued that had been commenced at Kona, and much grumbling and discontent began to manifest itself among the resident chiefs and cultivators of the land, the 'Makaainana'. *Imakakaloa*, a great chief in the Puna district, and *Nuuampaahu*, a chief of Naalehu in the Kau district, became the heads and rallying-points of the discontented. The former resided on his lands in Puna (in the southeast, across the island from Kohala in the northwest), and openly resisted the orders of *Kalaniopuu* and his extravagant demands for contributions of all kinds of property; the latter was in attendance with the court of *Kalaniopuu* in Kohala, but was strongly suspected of favouring the growing discontent" (Fornander 1880:200). Aside from the Mangarevan uprising mentioned in the text, there is some evidence for similar revolts in Tonga (Mariner 1827i:80); Thomson 1894:294f) and in Tahiti (Henry 1928:195-196, 297).

23 Or see Handy 1923 and Linton 1939.

24 On the difficulty of provisioning the Hawaiian paramount's large establishment see the citation from Fornander above, and also Fornander 1880:100-101; Malo 1903:92-93, *et passim*. The Hawaiian great chiefs developed the practice of the circuit—like feudal monarchs—often leaving a train of penury behind as they moved in state from district to district of the chiefdom.

PART IV

Application: Clientelism in Local Perspective

THE SOCIAL ORGANIZATION OF CREDIT IN A WEST AFRICAN CATTLE MARKET[1]

ABNER COHEN

CREDIT IS A VITAL economic institution without which trade becomes very limited. In the industrial Western societies, where it is highly developed, it operates through formal, standardized arrangements and procedures by which the solvency of the debtor is closely assessed, securities against possible default are provided, and the conditions of the agreement are documented and endorsed by the parties concerned. Ultimately, these arrangements and procedures are upheld by legislated rules and sanctions administered by central, bureaucratized, fairly impartial, efficient, and effective courts and police. In West Africa, on the other hand, where long-distance trade has been fostered by varying ecological circumstances, such organization has not yet evolved, particularly for long-distance trade. Nevertheless extensive systems of credit have been developed.

I discuss in this paper the organization and operation of credit in one Nigerian market which I studied intensively. After a preliminary description of the formal organization of the market and of the credit by which it functions, I discuss some non-economic social relations which, while formally exterior to the market situation, are in practice built into the structure of the credit system in such a way that they make its functioning as a going concern possible.

Nearly 75,000[2] head of cattle are sold every year in the cattle market of Ibadan, capital of the Western Region of the Federation of Nigeria. The forest belt of West Africa, of which Ibadan is part, is infested with the disease-carrying tsetse fly which is fatal to cattle. The inhabitants depend for their beef supplies on herds of cattle brought from the savannah country, hundreds of miles to the north. These herds are collected mainly from the semi-nomadic Fulani by Hausa dealers from Northern Nigeria and are then brought south to be sold with the help of local Hausa middlemen. In the Ibadan market, which is locally known as 'Zango',[3] the buyers are Yoruba butchers and are total strangers to the Hausa dealers. Nevertheless, all sales are on credit and there is always an outstanding total amount of about a hundred thousand pounds current debt.[4] No documents are signed and no resort is made to the services of banks or to the official civil courts, and the whole organization, which has developed over the past sixty years, is entirely indigenous.

The cattle are brought to Ibadan either on foot or by train. In the market there is a sharp distinction between the two categories of cattle, not only in price but also in the organization and the scale of the business. After about five weeks of continuous travel, the foot cattle[5] arrive at the

233

market thin, weak, and already having been exposed, for many days, to the disease[6] as they penetrated the forest area. The maneuverability in selling them is therefore limited in both time and place and dealers are always eager to sell. This eagerness is further enhanced by the need of the dealers to release, as soon as possible, the capital invested in the herd in order to have a quicker business turn-over. In recent years, cattle have increasingly been brought south by train, but between thirty and forty per cent still come on foot, either because they are brought from districts which are remote from a railway line, or because no train wagons happen to be available at the time. The principal advantage of bringing cattle on foot is that part of the herd can be sold on the way to small towns and villages which are not served by the railways or which are not large enough to have cattle markets.[7]

Foot cattle are brought by smaller-scale Hausa dealers, each dealer making an average of four journeys to Ibadan in a year, bringing to the market each journey an average of seventy head of cattle.[8] The herd is driven by hired Fulani drovers, an average of one drover[9] for every twenty-five head. The herd owner walks with his cattle as far as Ilorin, where he usually parts with the caravan and starts a reconnaissance trip, by lorries and mammy wagons, along the ninety-five-mile route to Ibadan, stopping at the cattle markets in Ogbomosho and Oyo, and also at other, smaller towns, choosing the most advantageous place to sell. The more southerly place, the higher the price, but the greater the hazards to the health of the cattle and the longer the period in which the capital is engaged.

The train cattle[10] are either brought by smaller-scale dealers, who travel with the herd, or are sent by relatively larger-scale dealers to their permanent agents in Ibadan. The cattle are transported in special wagons, each wagon accommodating between twenty and thirty head.[11] The herd in each wagon is looked after by an attendant[12] whose main task is to guard the beasts against theft. The journey to Ibadan takes two to three days and the few cattle who show signs of sickness in the meantime are slaughtered and sold in the several intervening stations, where local butchers are always waiting for such opportunities.

According to men in the business, the life expectancy of cattle after arriving in Ibadan is about two weeks for those brought on foot and about two and a half months for those brought by train. Train cattle therefore fetch a higher price than foot cattle of the same size and qual-

ity, particularly because they are demanded by butchers, not only from Ibadan, but also from neighbouring towns and villages. Also, when prices in Ibadan are unfavourable train cattle can be taken south as far as Lagos.

Despite the sharp distinction in the market between the two categories of cattle, the organization of credit is essentially similar in both cases.

When the cattle dealer,[13] whether he is the owner of the herd or only an agent of the owner, is in Ibadan he lodges with his usual 'landlord' in the Hausa Quarter. The word 'landlord' is a literal translation of the Hausa term *mai gida*, but the *mai gida* plays several kinds of roles in the cattle business which are not denoted by the English translation and need to be analytically separated. In the first place, the *mai gida* is a house-owner, having, besides that in which he and his family live, at least one more house for the accommodation of his dealers from the north. Of the twelve cattle landlords who operated in Zango in 1963, one had six such houses, a second had four, two others had two houses each, and the rest had one each. The landlords usually own additional houses in which their assistants, clerks, servants, malams, and other men of their entourage are accommodated, free of charge. The landlord also provides three meals a day for his dealers and entertains them in the evenings, but this function as inn-keeper is by no means the most fundamental of his roles.

The landlord is also a middleman[14] who mediates between his dealers and the local butchers in the market. Each landlord has for this purpose a number of middlemen[15] working under him, but responsibility for their business conduct remains always with him. Thus, when the herd of the dealer arrives at the market, the landlord entrusts its sale to one of his middlemen. The dealer then accompanies the middleman in the market and remains with him until the whole herd is sold. But no transaction can be finally concluded without the approval of the landlord.

Here we come to the role of the landlord as insurer or risk-taker, which is the most crucial factor in the operation of the whole market. As sale is on credit, the landlord is the guarantor that the money will eventually be paid, and that if the buyer should default, he would pay the full amount to the dealer himself. This obligation means that he must be very well acquainted with the buyers, and it is only through long experience in the business that he comes to acquire the necessary knowledge. He has to know not only where a buyer slaughters the cattle, or where he has his shop or market stall, but also where he lives, who are his relatives and associates, what is the size of his business, and how honest and trustworthy he has proved himself to be in his dealings so far. In this way, every butcher in the market is informally graded by the landlords and their middlemen on a scale of credit-worthiness from nil up to about   1,000 of credit, for a period of up to four weeks. No sane landlord would give a butcher credit in excess of the latter's 'quota'. Misjudgment in this respect can ruin the business of the landlord. This actually happened early in 1963 to one of the landlords, when a number of butchers who had bought cattle through him defaulted, and he eventually failed to pay the money himself to the dealers. These stopped lodging with him and complained to the Chief of the Cattle Market. He finally sold his only house of strangers to meet his obligations and became an ordinary middleman.

Thus landlords need to have not only a precise assessment of the buyer's social background and of his business conduct in the past, but must also be continuously vigilant as to his day-to-day purchases in the market. For while a dealer is attached to one landlord at a time, the butcher is free to buy through any landlord, and he usually makes his purchases through many landlords. It is conceivable, therefore, that he may succeed in buying, within a short period of time, from several unsuspecting landlords in excess of the limits of his credit-worthiness. The only way in which the landlords can meet this potential danger is by the continuous exchange of business information. No formally institutionalized channels for such an exchange exist in the market, but the objective is nevertheless achieved through informal relations.

Landlords interact very intensively among themselves, since it is in the nature of their business both to compete and to cooperate. They compete fiercely over business, and countless disputes arise among them over what they describe as 'stealing of dealers'. Generally speaking, a dealer has one landlord to whom he is accustomed to entrust the sale of his cattle whenever he comes to Ibadan. This attachment of a dealer to one landlord usually holds for years and sometimes continues to hold between their sons when they die. Landlords do much to keep their dealers attached to them, offering them various services, some of which have little to do with the cattle business. When a dealer finally goes back to the north, after selling his cattle, his landlord gives him a present, the minimum standard being a bottle of French perfume costing (as in 1963) 18 shillings.[16] But some deal-

ers, particularly those of foot cattle who come to Ibadan only occasionally, *do* change their landlords, for one reason or another, and sometimes landlords send emissaries as far as Ilorin to meet such dealers, offer them presents, and direct them to lodge with their masters.

Disputes between landlords over dealers have often led to political crises within the Hausa Quarter. The basic principle of political grouping among the 5,000 Hausa of the Quarter is that of the client-patron relationship, which is essentially dyadic, holding between the patron and each client separately, without leading to the formation of corporate groups. A man's clients are his employees, attendants, and tenants. The patrons of the Quarter are the thirty landlords, in the various economic fields, who control much of the employment and of the housing of the rest of the population. Each one of them is the head of what may be described as a 'house of power'. Clients often 'change house', i.e. change their allegiance from one landlord to another, which often means literally moving from one house to another. Generally speaking, landlords are old residents in Ibadan while most of their clients are new migrants.[17]

The landlords and their clients pay allegiance to the Hausa Chief of the Quarter,[18] who mediates between them and the authorities, adjudicates—with the help of his advisers—in cases of disputes within the Quarter, and appoints men to titled positions who regulate communal affairs. One of these positions is that of the 'Chief of the Cattle Market',[19] who is responsible for keeping order in the market and who arbitrates in cases of disputes within it.

Of all the patrons, the cattle landlords are the most powerful as they have dominated the Quarter politically ever since its foundation in 1916. The Chief of the Quarter has always been a cattle landlord and, since 1930, he has also been the Chief of the Cattle Market.[20]

The cattle business is thus directly involved in the politics of the Quarter. The same men who meet in the cattle market as landlords confront each other in the Quarter as political leaders, and their behaviour in the one role affects their behaviour in the other. For example, one of the duties of the Chief of the Quarter is to give accommodation to any Hausa stranger who comes to him, and the Chief runs many houses for this specific purpose. When a new cattle dealer comes for the first time to Ibadan and lodges in one of these houses, as a stranger, it is only natural that he should eventually sell his cattle through the Chief, in the latter's role as cattle landlord.

Within the context of the Quarter, one major source of dispute between the landlords has been the struggle for the control over houses, since from the early 1930 these have become relatively scarce because of overcrowding. A man needs housing in the Quarter to secure membership of the community, to establish himself in business, to gather clients around him, to enlarge his family by marrying more wives, to foster the sons and daughters of his kin, and to accommodate malams whose services in the mystical world are indispensable to his success and well-being. Thus, command over housing is in no small measure command over economic and political power. When the Quarter was first established, the land, which had been allotted for the purpose by the city's native authority, was distributed in equal plots among the first settlers. But since then many changes have taken place in the ownership and distribution of houses and land. In 1963 only five of the many hundreds of houses of the Quarter were registered as deeds. There were no documents of any kind to establish ownership over the rest of the houses. Most of the original houses and plots have changed hands many times through sale or the death of their owners. The houses of persons who died without leaving heirs have been 'inherited' by the Chief of the Quarter, who is presumed to use them for the general welfare of the community. In this way the Chief has come to control scores of houses in which he accommodates, rent free, several hundreds of people who have in this way automatically become his clients. Landlords thus struggle over the ownership of houses in the Quarter because these are the means to political and economic power.

In the cattle market the landlords also compete over the buyers and each landlord has a number of young men who act as 'advertisers', trying to draw the attention of the butchers to the herds marketed through their employers. But landlords are at the same time forced to co-operate in the market in several respects, the most important being to present a united front vis-à-vis the butchers. These are very powerfully organized through an association which has played an important role within the Ibadan polity and only a strong landlords' front can keep the necessary balance in the market.

The market is held twice a day, once in the morning, between 9 and 10, and again in the afternoon, between 5 and 7. These official hours are enforced by the Chief of the Market.[21] But landlords come to the market about an hour before each session to sit informally together and 'joke', often very clumsily, and it is in the course of this joking that much of the vital information on the buyers is exchanged.

Another informal channel through which business information is exchanged is the interaction between the clerks. Every landlord has a clerk[22] whose main duty is the registration of sales and the collection of money from the debtors. As soon as a transaction is concluded, the middleman involved calls the clerk of his landlord to note down the details. These include the date of the transaction, name of dealer, name of middleman, name and address of buyer, the number of cattle sold, the price and total amount as well as the exact time and place of payment.[23] The clerk occupies a central position within the structure of the 'business house' because, while the middlemen and the other assistants are individually related to the landlord and are not formally related to each other, the clerk is formally related to everyone within the house, and thus knows about all the transactions concluded through the house. Being also the collector of substantial amounts of money, he is always a man who is fully trusted by the landlord. Of the twelve landlords in the Ibadan market, three have their own sons as clerks, two their 'fostered'[24] sons, and three perform the task themselves. The clerks are young, educated 'in Arabic',[25] and are Ibadan-born. They speak Yoruba as well as Hausa and belong to the same age-group. Sharing the same background, they belong to the same group whose members pray, eat, learn, and seek entertainment together.[26] They thus meet in various social situations every day and in the course of their interaction they exchange information about the solvency of the butchers, which they eventually pass on to their respective masters.

These exchanges of information, however, relate only to the behaviour of the butchers in the past and it is conceivable that a butcher may in one hour buy from several landlords who, in the pressure of business, may not realize that he is exceeding his limits. A protection against such a possibility is obtained through the informal activities of, and interaction among, the 'boys',[27] who perform various jobs in helping their landlord and his middlemen in the market, 'boys' can be seen everywhere in the market, and indeed the literal meaning of the Hausa word kankamba is 'going hither and thither'. Their tasks take them to many parts of the market and they mingle with the 'boys' of other landlords. When, in the course of their activities, they notice a butcher who, having already bought cattle in other corners of the market, comes to buy also from their landlord, then they alert the middlemen to the impending danger.[28]

Thus, joking and gossiping between the landlords, informal meetings among the clerks, and the activities of the 'boys' serve as means of disseminating business information and help to guard against the hazards of credit.

But the conflicting interests of the landlords are implicit even in this very fundamental issue of exchanging information about the butchers' purchases, and it sometimes happens, though not often, that a landlord tries to suppress information. I witnessed in 1963 a case of a butcher who failed to pay, on time, a debt of a few hundred pounds to a landlord, but promised to do so as soon as his business improved. The landlord withheld this news from the other landslords, since otherwise these would have refrained from selling cattle to the butcher, who would thus have been without business and would have failed to settle his original debt. An unsuspecting landlord eventually sold cattle to the butcher in question, who duly settled his debt to the first landlord but defaulted in payment to the second. When the first landlord was later blamed for his unethical conduct he replied that no one had asked him to give the information which he had withheld. The landlord who suffered in this case had himself acted as his own clerk and had therefore no means of knowing of the default of the butcher except from the first landlord. Landlords are thus sometimes in an invidious position about revealing information concerning their sales.

The credit is given for a period of two to four weeks.[29] Dealers in foot cattle usually remain during this period accommodated and fed by the landlord, and when the money is finally collected it is kept by the landlord until the dealer arranges transport for himself to go back to the north.[30] Dealers in train cattle often go back to the north as soon as their cattle are sold and collect the proceeds when they come back with the next herd.

The landlord receives no direct reward whatsoever from the buyer, in cash, on the conclusion of the sale. During 1963 the commission in Ibadan was 13 shillings on each head of cattle, irrespective of the price. From this amount the landlord pays 3 shillings to the middleman who arranged the transaction, about a shilling to the clerk and the 'boys', 2 shillings to the dealer himself, and retains the rest to cover his expenses and to remunerate himself for the financial risks he has taken in assuring the credit.[31]

This credit arrangement is not fool-proof and cases of default occur, but, barring political or economic upheavals, the risks are greatly reduced by a variety of factors.

In the first place a loss is always distributed among several individuals because a butcher is usually indebted not to one landlord but to many, and a dealer's herd is sold not to one butcher but to many butchers. Thus, if a butcher defaulted the loss would be shared by the several landlords who gave him credit. The incidence of the loss is spread still wider when the case is eventually arbitrated, and in nearly all the cases I have recorded the dealer was made to share in the loss even though the formal principle is that the whole loss should be borne by the landlord.[32] I am talking here of loss, but it nearly always happens that an arrangement is reached, as a result of arbitration, by which the butcher undertakes to pay his debt by installments over several months. During these months he is allowed to buy from the market but must pay in cash.

Unless a butcher is prepared to go out of the business altogether he is forced to abide by such an arrangement, since according to municipal rules he would forfeit his licence as a butcher if he did not slaughter at least one beast every week. This is a very important source of pressure on him because a licence is very difficult to obtain and is also very expensive. He cannot evade payment by buying cattle elsewhere. The Hausa throughout the region, indeed throughout southern Nigeria, monopolize the sale of cattle and control all cattle markets. These markets, together with the Hausa Quarters to which they are attached, constitute a widespread network of highly interrelated communities. In each of the three large cattle markets which are within a radius of sixty miles of Ibadan (Ogbomosho, Oyo, and Abeokuta) the Chief of the Cattle Market is himself the Chief of the Hausa Quarter, as well as being a cattle landlord. Thus, when the landlords in the Ibadan market decide not to sell to a defaulting butcher, they usually send a word to the neighbouring cattle markets about him and if he ever appeared there no one would sell to him even if he paid cash.

An equally important form of pressure on individual defaulters comes from the butchers themselves, who are organized in eight slaughter-houses, as well as within the overall occupational association. When one butcher defaults, the landlords are often forced to retaliate by declaring a temporary boycott of all the butchers within his slaughter-house. I witnessed one such case in 1963 when a butcher failed to pay a debt of about £700 which he owed to many landlords. In their gossiping time one day the landlords decided to refuse selling any cattle to the whole slaughter-house of the defaulting butcher in order to mobilize the pressure of his colleagues on him. This action was so effective that the butchers involved, together with the chief of the whole Association,[33] as well as the defaulting butcher, came to the Chief of the Hausa Quarter, in his capacity as Chief of the Cattle Market, on the same evening and an arrangement was made there and then to settle the matter. Indeed it happens sometimes that when a butcher shows signs of financial difficulties, some of his colleagues within the same slaughter-house will caution some of their trustworthy middlemen not to sell to him. Thus, the butchers on their part watch each other's conduct in business and can exert a great deal of pressure on potential defaulters.

The market is therefore not seriously disturbed by the occasional default of individual butchers. Indeed, from the study of cases seen against the background of the history of the market organization, it appears that occasional default (as crime in Durkheim's analysis)[34] has led to continual re-examination and retightening of the control mechanisms in the market and thus made the continuity of the credit system possible. The cattle landlords' main worry is not the individual defaulter but the sudden collapse of the market as a result of a concerted hostile action on the part of the butchers.[35] The position of the landlords is particularly vulnerable, since the pressure which they can exert on the butchers is limited in degree and is not without its dangers. This is because the cleavage in the market between buyer and seller, debtor and creditor, is also a cleavage between Yoruba and Hausa and, indeed, both sides describe their mutual relationships in tribalistic terms. The landlords often talk of the 'machinations' and the 'treachery' of the Yoruba and the butchers of the 'exploitation' and 'greed' of the Hausa. When the Ibadan cattle landlords appeal for support and solidarity from the cattle landlords in other markets in the region they actually do so not in the name of the profession but in the name of Hausa-ism, and the communication between the markets is effected through the respective Hausa chiefs, acting *as* Hausa chiefs, and not as chiefs of the cattle markets.

In the same way, the butchers confront the landlords as a tribal group and rely on the support of various other Yoruba groupings in this confrontation. The butchers resent the fact that it is they, and not the Hausa sellers, who are made to pay the commission to the landlords, and for years they have been agitating against it. In this agitation they have often succeeded in mobilizing support from the press and from the city's traditional chiefs, who on several occasions in the past reminded the Hausa that they were strangers, that the Quarter stood on the Olubadan's land, that if they did not behave they would be made to leave, and so on. The landlords are always afraid that the city council or the regional government may impose on them new taxes or new restrictions on the movement and sale of cattle, or that they will decide to remove the Hausa Quarter or to 'scrap' it altogether.

The cattle landlords have not been passive in the face of such threats. When during the 1950s the butchers affiliated themselves within the predominantly Yoruba Action Group Party, which was until 1962 in power in the Western Region, the Hausa landlords reacted not only by joining the same party themselves, but also by dragging almost the whole Hausa Quarter with them in joining it, and in successive elections the Ibadan Hausa gave their votes to it.[36] In the 1961 election for the Ibadan local council, 93 per cent of the votes in the Quarter went to the Action Group candidate. Within the party, the Hausa eventually formed a strong pressure group. According to the 1952 Census of Nigeria there were in the Western Region nearly 41,000 Hausa residents and even then it was realized that there were many more Hausa who for a variety of reasons had not registered themselves. In 1953 the chiefs of all Hausa communities in the Region formed a joint Hausa association[37] and unanimously elected the Ibadan Hausa Chief as their chairman. This occurred on the eve of the 1954 Federal Election and there is little doubt that the association played an important role in mobilizing Hausa support for the party chosen by their chiefs. At that time the Action Group was struggling to establish itself, not as a regional, but as a national, party which was to gain the support of the masses from the other tribes of the Federation of Nigeria. For that purpose the party fought particularly hard to gain a foothold in Hausaland in the north, as that region contained more than half the population of the Federation. A party with such objectives could not allow the persecution of a Hausa minority in its own capital. Thus, the party not only prevented hostile action being taken against the cattle landlords, but even tried to prevent individual butchers from defaulting, by exerting pressure on these to honour their obligations, and sometimes by granting loans to those among them who did not have the cash to pay.

The risks of the credit system have thus made it necessary for the cattle landlords to act politically within the Hausa network of communities, as well as within the Ibadan, the regional, and the national polities. To do so, they have had to act not on occupational but on tribal lines, and it has therefore been essential for them to control the Chieftaincy of the Hausa Quarter. Under the prevailing conditions it is only through the Chieftaincy that political interaction with other Hausa communities, on the one hand, and with the Yoruba, on the other, can be effected.

The cattle landlords are few in number and, together with all their middlemen, clerks, and assistants, constitute only 6 per cent of the working Hausa male population of the Quarter.[38] And yet they have always been so dominant that the history of the Quarter is to a great extent the history of the cattle trade in Ibadan. From the very beginning of Hausa settlement in Ibadan, at the beginning of the present century, until today, the Chief of the Quarter has always been a cattle landlord. And this is the case not only in Ibadan but also in the other Hausa communities in those Yoruba towns where a cattle market exists. Indeed it was initially this sociological problem, i.e. 'How is it that a handful of cattle landlords have come to dominate the whole Quarter politically?', which led me to study the organization of the cattle market.

There are various factors involved in this phenomenon, but it is beyond the limits of this paper to discuss them in detail. It is sufficient to point out that the landlords not only 'need' the Chieftaincy because of its role in the organization of credit, but also have the power and the organization to dominate the Quarter. They interact among themselves most intensively, as they meet in a relatively small place (the market) twice a day, seven days a week. In contrast, the kola landlords, for example, who run business on similar lines and who, as an occupational group, constitute nearly 18 per cent[39] of the working Hausa males in the Quarter, and certainly command greater wealth, do not have opportunities to interact so frequently and so intensively, since they have to leave the Quarter every morning and disperse in all directions within a radius of about forty miles in quest of supplies. They also operate mainly with cash and, since they are dealing in a local product for export from the area, whenever credit is involved, they are the debtors, not the creditors, and hence are not impelled to political action to the same degree as are the cattle landlords, who seem to be always beset by great anxieties over the thousands of pounds of credit which continuously weigh on their conscience. Another factor which should be taken into account is that of continuities from the past. The cattle landlords and middlemen were among the very first of the Hausa migrants to Ibadan. In a census taken in the Quarter in 1916, a few months after its establishment, 56 out of 261 (20 per cent) Hausa males were described as cattle traders, which

means that men working in the cattle trade constituted a much higher proportion of the working population in the past than today. On the other hand, the kola men came to the Quarter mainly during the past generation, since kola has been grown in the Western Region of Nigeria only in recent decades. For the cattle landlords, seniority in the Quarter has meant greater opportunities for acquiring houses, for rallying clients, and for establishing connexions with local sources of power and authority. These are advantages which help the cattle landlords, within the contemporary situation, to control the Quarter.

I am not arguing here that the majority of the Quarter blindly align themselves for political action behind the cattle landlords, to the latter's private interests. I am only suggesting that, because of their role in the cattle market, the cattle landlords are more politically active and better organized for political action than any other group within the Quarter. They are also the group most sensitive to any changes in Hausa-Yoruba relations. When the 1962 emergency situation in the Western Region of Nigeria came to an end, in January 1963, and the former Prime Minister, Chief Akintola, returned to his previous position in Ibadan, the cattle landlords and middlemen, who had been ardent Action Groupers until the emergency, went *en masse*, taking with them any Hausa they could mobilize, to greet the returning Premier and to express allegiance to him and to his party (at the time the UPP), which had emerged in opposition to the Action Group. They did this not as cattle men but as Hausa, representing the whole Hausa Quarter. It is significant, incidentally, that at the doors of the Premier they came face to face with another delegation who had also come to express their allegiance—it was the delegation of the Yoruba butchers.

The cattle landlords have very serious reservations about submitting their disputes with the butchers to the civil courts. There are many reasons for this attitude. When a butcher defaults he is usually indebted to many dealers from whom he has bought cattle. As these dealers are the legal creditors, it is they, not the landlords, who should apply to the courts for adjudication, which means that a number of dealers should act jointly in order to pursue their case against the defaulting butcher. But this is highly impracticable. The amount due to each dealer from the defaulting butcher is relatively small, while the expenses of adjudication are high. Furthermore, court procedure is long and the dealers, whose residence is usually far in the North, cannot wait in Ibadan indefinitely. There is also the problem of language and cultural differences. Furthermore, the landlords believe that court rulings in cases of this nature are not effective, since a butcher who pleads that he has no money can be asked to pay only a few pounds a month to his creditors until an amount of hundreds of pounds could be finally settled.[40]

Arbitration by the Chief of the Market, on the other hand, is prompt, convenient, and effective. It is performed by a Hausa, but in nearly all cases of dispute, the Chief of the Butchers, a Yoruba, participates in the arbitratory process. The ruling of the Chief of the Market is final and is nearly always honoured.[41] Thus the organization of credit in the market is ultimately upheld, not by the civil courts, but by what may be labelled as 'tribal politics'. In the market, debtors and creditors face each other as tribesmen as well as business men. This double cleavage is basic to the operation of the credit system. It is the product of a number of processes which have driven the Hausa out of the butchering business, on the one hand, and prevented the Yoruba from performing the functions of the cattle landlords, on the other. Until the early 1930s many of the butchers of Ibadan were Hausa, and the Quarter's Hausa 'Chief of the Butchers' was a very powerful man. But today there is only one Hausa butcher[42] in the city, and the title 'Chief

of the Butchers' within the Quarter has sunk into insignificance.[43] On the other hand, all the attempts that have been made every now and then by some ambitious Yoruba to act as cattle landlords or even as cattle dealers have completely failed.

I have attempted to show that in order to understand the operation of credit in the cattle market in Ibadan we need to consider such phenomena as informal gossiping and joking, age-grouping, and inter-tribal politics. These are essentially non-economic factors which seem to be exterior to the market situation. In considering credit in Western society, it is equally essential to take into account some non-economic factors, but because of the highly developed centralization, communication, and bureaucratization, these factors are fundamentally the same throughout the society and there is therefore one unitary system of credit. In his analysis, the economist can thus regard these factors as constant, take them for granted, and never mention them. In a pre-industrial society, on the other hand, there are many systems of credit, each having its own structure which consists of both formal and informal relations. This is why, in order to explain such a system, the economist has to rely much on anthropologists or become one himself.

NOTES

1 The material on which this paper is based was collected in the course of field study among Hausa migrants in the Western Region of Nigeria between September 1962 and November 1963. I am grateful to the School of Oriental and African Studies, University of London, for financing the project and to the Nigerian Institute of Social and Economic Research and the University of Ibadan for their invaluable help in carrying it out.

2 This is an approximate figure which is higher by about 12 per cent than that obtained from the records of the veterinary service offices.

3 Throughout the Western Region of Nigeria the cattle markets are locally known by the Hausa word Zango (literally meaning a camping place of caravan or lodging place of travellers), while the local Hausa quarter is known as Sabo, short for Sabon Gari. In Ghana, on the other hand, the word Zango, which is usually pronounced as Zongo, is used for the native strangers' quarter which is often predominantly Hausa.

4 This, again, is an approximate figure derived from the number of cattle sold in the market, the average price per head, and the average length of the period of credit.

5 Shanun kasa.

6 Trypanosomiasis.

7 According to figures from the veterinary service offices, for the years 1959 to 1962, 20 per cent, of all the cattle which started the journey from the North towards Ibadan as the final destination did not actually reach Ibadan, which means that they were sold on the way. As nearly all the cattle brought by train eventually arrive at Ibadan, this percentage represents the foot cattle which are sold on the way. This means that about 50 per cent of the foot cattle originally destined for Ibadan are sold on the way.

8 These figures are from a survey covering 118 dealers in foot cattle.

9 Dan kōre.

10 Shanun Jirgi.

11 Depending on the size of the animals. Usually the horns of the cattle are cut short before the journey so that more cattle can be accommodated in a wagon, and in the market, train cattle can usually be easily identified by their shorter horns.

12 Dan taragu, literally 'son of the wagon'.

13 Mai shānu.

14 Dillāli.

15 Between them, the twelve cattle landlords operating in Ibadan in 1963, had fifty-two middlemen working for them. The senior among these middlemen

had assistants under them, as they were usually given more cattle to sell than were the junior middlemen. Some of these senior middlemen provided food, cooked by their own wives, to the dealers who were 'allotted' to them, and they therefore received a greater proportion of the commission. There were a few middlemen in the market who were not attached to any particular landlord but who worked on a temporary basis for landlords who had more business on their hands than could be dealt with by their permanent middlemen.

16 It is customary for Hausa *men* to wear perfume.

17 According to census material which I collected in 1963, only 12 per cent of the Hausa migrants in the Quarter had been in Ibadan for twenty years or more.

18 Known as *Sarkin Hausāwa* and sometimes as *Sarkin Sābo*.

19 *Sarkin Zango*.

20 These two positions, the *Sarkin Sābo* and the *Sarkin Zango*, have become so involved in each other that in some situations it is difficult to separate them, even analytically.

21 The beginning and the ending of a session are announced by a whistle blown by one of the 'boys' of the Chief of the Market.

22 Known as *mālam*, in the sense of 'literate', not of 'religious functionary'.

23 The register in which these details are written down serves as a reminder, not a document. The details are neither checked nor ratified by the buyers.

24 Child fostering is very widespread among the Hausa.

25 All education in the Hausa Quarter is 'Arabic' education which consists mainly in learning to read the Kor'an and to write in Arabic.

26 The overwhelming majority of the Hausa in Sabo adhere to the Tijaniyya order which enjoins intensive collective ritualism and ties initiates to a ritual leader known as *mukaddam*. Groupings emerging in the course of ritual performance tend to become fraternities whose members co-operate in many social fields.

27 *Kankamba*.

28 The butchers are always under constant observation by the landlords and their subordinates. The absence of a butcher for three or four days in succession is always marked with suspicion in the market.

29 As the Hausa are Muslims, the dealers do not in principle charge interest for the credit they give to the butchers. But cash price is always lower than credit price by £1 to £3 for a head of cattle which is usually sold at £20 to £40.

30 Landlords often keep in their houses several

thousands of pounds, in cash, for their dealers. The money is kept in simple wooden chests which are protected from thieves by amulets prepared by the malams and are also watched night and day by trusted attendants.

31 There are slight variations in the distribution of the commission between foot cattle and train cattle.

32 A landlord would run the risk of losing all his dealers if he did not meet his obligations. The payment of compensation to the dealers is always by monthly installments, in accordance with the ruling of the Chief of the Market in the case.

33 The *Sarkin Pāwa*. The incumbent of the office is of course a Yoruba man.

34 See E. Durkheim, *The Rules of Sociological Method*, pp. 64-75, translated by S. A. Solovay and J. H. Mueller, and edited by G. E. G. Catlin, The Free Press, Glencoe, Illinois (1950).

35 Such an action is not unlikely to happen. It happened in 1963 in the Abeokuta cattle market, when the butchers stopped paying their debts to the dealers and completely paralyzed the market for about five weeks, until the two sides accepted arbitration by the Ibadan Hausa Chief. The dispute arose when some of the Hausa cattle landlords attempted to enter the butchering business by slaughtering a number of cattle and selling the meat to local retailers. The arbitrator eventually ruled that no slaughtering should be done by the landlords.

36 Men in the Quarter do not conceal the fact that in their political behaviour they follow the instructions of their patrons unquestionably.

37 The association was formally called 'The Federal Union of the Western Sarkis Hausawa'.

38 Ninety-seven out of a total of 1,570. The figures are from a general census which I took in Sabo with the help of local assistants.

39 285 out of a total of 1,570.

40 The landlords often skip over most of these factors and dismiss the case for submitting disputes to the courts by saying: 'After all these are *Yoruba* courts'.

41 One of the most striking phenomena I witnessed in this respect was the obedience which the Yoruba butchers showed towards the Hausa Chief, whose authority was so strong that he could send his messenger and summon any butcher to his office.

42 Besides this licensed butcher there are a few Hausa men who work as 'meat cutters', buying wholesale from Yoruba butchers and selling within the Quarter or in the neighbouring Mokola Quarter.

43 The case of dispute between the local Yoruba butchers and the Hausa cattle landlords mentioned in footnote 35, points in the same direction.

SOCIAL STRUCTURE AND POLITICAL
BEHAVIOR OF SENEGALESE ELITES

WILLIAM J. FOLTZ*

THIS PAPER will take the case of the West African country of Senegal to show in what ways traditional social structures and patterns of behavior, though much transformed, influence a contemporary political system.[1] Senegal provides a particularly interesting case, because the traditional political structures were almost completely destroyed or discredited even in rural areas soon after the beginning of the twentieth century, while modern representative political institutions were introduced in some urban areas, under the French policy of cultural and political assimilation of the African population, as early as the 1870s. "Traditional" influences have thus themselves undergone a certain amount of change, and the particular forms they take today reflect the rapid evolution of the Senegalese political system in the past twenty years.

This paper will use three words to designate three different social structures, their attendant patterns of behavior, and those individuals who fall within each rubric. By "traditional" I mean those structures or parts of society which have undergone no noticeable effects of European presence in the country. For our purpose the traditional element is of only historical interest, since the 5 - 10 per cent of Senegalese people who live in a purely traditional manner live almost entirely outside the contemporary political system. The great bulk of the general population and most of the current political elite in Senegal are characterized by a general pattern of social behavior, values, and expectations that I term "transitional." They integrate major aspects of both traditional African and modern European social forms in their lives. This broad category could in turn be broken down into subcategories, each having relatively a high traditional or a high modern component, but it is precise enough to illustrate many typical behavior and value patterns. Although the word "transitional" indicates an element of instability, this is so only in the long run; for the foreseeable future, transitional society is likely to remain the dominant element of Senegalese life.

Finally, by "modernist" I mean that part of Senegalese society which takes its inspiration primarily from European models, however imperfectly adapted, and which consciously rebels against transitional society. The modernist sector represents a maximum of 5 per cent of the Senegalese population, although its influence is disproportionately large; and it may be defined roughly as those who have had at least an advanced secondary school education through the *baccalauréat* level.

THE TRADITIONAL ELITE

To simplify matters, I shall discuss the traditional system of only the dominant Senegalese ethnic group, the Wolof, as it existed before colonial rule. Although the Wolof represent only about 35 per cent of the population, their social structure is closely related to that of the other Senegalese ethnic groups, except for the Diola of the Casamance and a few minor groups. The Wolof language is the unofficial lingua franca of Senegal, and Wolof society is constantly incorporating into itself members from other ethnic groups who have come to the city or lost contact with their traditional society in some other way. Wolof culture is considered the Senegalese common denominator, to the point where the terms "Wolof" and "Senegalese" are often used interchangeably by Africans.

Traditional Wolof society stratified its members by endogamous castes (Thiam 1949; Gamble 1957:44; Silla 1966). At the top were the nobles of great families, those with royal blood and hereditary access to roles of formal political leadership. Immediately below those of royal blood came two related castes of warriors and freeborn farmers, who were theoretically the equals of the first in almost every sense except the possession of royal blood. These three groups could intermarry with few restrictions, and together they made up about half of the population. Below this level came the artisan castes —blacksmiths, leather workers, weavers, and the like—most of whom might intermarry freely, but who were decidedly inferior to the first level. Next in rank came the *griots* (genealogists and praise-singers) and slaves. The major jump in the social hierarchy was that between the freeborn-noble ranks and everyone else. In everyday language, the privileged group today frequently speaks of itself as being "without" or "above" caste.

Although these castes were fixed by birth,

considerable possibility for distinction and achievement once existed within each caste. For the nobles and warriors, fighting and the search for booty provided frequent tests of valor and worth that could be easily recognized by the whole society and immortalized in the songs of the *griots*. Similarly, for the freeborn farmers, cooperative village work projects gave a chance to the zealous worker to show his capabilities and to "overfulfill his quota" in contributing to the common granary. The prestige that went with such distinctive feats meant much in the relatively simple life of the traditional Senegalese, and could in turn be translated into such concrete rewards as the ability to acquire additional wives (Ames 1959:234-37).

Somewhat outside the normal caste system in traditional Senegal were the Muslim religious leaders, or marabouts, who could obtain considerable economic, social, and occasionally political power. While most have been of noble caste (those with the greatest access to Arabic education), at least one important family, the Niasse of Kaolack, is of artisan origin.

The caste divisions, as is apparent from their names, had their origins in a functional division of work within the traditional community. These functional distinctions have now been almost destroyed by the pressures of a rapidly evolving monetary economy, but to a great extent the patterned relationships among the castes remain. Particularly important among these traditional relationships was that between patron and client, whereby a man of noble caste and some financial means took responsibility for the support of an informal household of hangers-on. These were primarily *griots* and slaves, but might include members of the artisan castes who worked for the noble's family, or even less fortunate nobles and members of the patron's extended family. The patron was expected to help clothe, house, and nourish his clients and sometimes to assist in raising bridewealth for a client. In return, his clients provided personal services to the household and, by their number and ostentatious devotion to the patron, gave public measure of his social distinction. The patron-client arrangement emphasized reciprocal obligations and benefits: the patron guaranteed his clients support and protection; the clients, in addition to whatever specific tasks they might perform, guaranteed their patron the most valuable of all commodities—the prestige of supporting a large and grateful household. The relationship between patron and client was also a very personal one, and a client would be proud to acknowledge that he was "so-and-so's man." The vertical solidarity implicit in the patron-client system provided the cement that held this stratified society together.

THE TRANSITIONAL ELITE

European conquest and rule greatly affected the traditional social hierarchy. By destroying the traditional political units and limiting warfare in Senegal, the French eliminated the distinctions among the noble-warrior-freeborn group, and this group collapsed into a signle caste, the *guer*, usually translated as "noble" or "freeborn." The base for recruitment into top elite roles was thus broadened to include half of Senegalese society, and competition for prestige became accordingly more fierce. At the same time, the elimination of local wars and the introduction of cash crops and new agricultural techniques in rural areas eliminated the traditional means of elite distinction by personal achievement. In small rural villages, elite status continued to be accorded by common recognition, largely on the basis of personal descent, but the determination of elite status in the relatively individualized and differentiated society of urban Senegal had to be made on new grounds—although a direct relationship to traditional society remains apparent. The goal toward which an ambitious transitional *guer* must aspire is to be known as a *samba linguer*, to be first among the nobles. The traditional referent is made clear in this passage from Ousmane Socé's novel about transitional urban Senegalese life, *Karim* (Socé 1948:23).

A *samba linguer*, in heroic times, would not flee before the enemy. When the *griots* sang his praises, he gave away all his possessions to them. He had a high concern for honor and executed anyone who gave him offense. In our own time, he knows his duty and fulfills it under all circumstances.

Without actual battle in which to prove his worth, the would-be *samba linguer* must manifest the secondary, outward signs of elite status to assure his reputation: he must be a successful patron, with a large entourage to proclaim his glories. In today's Senegal, this means that he must have and distribute money. Two aspects of the role of money in determining elite status in transitional society are of particular importance. First, money is not a reward or a by-product of attaining elite status, but a precondition for it. Second, money is important only as something to display or give away, not as anything to be sought for itself. This attitude toward money has nothing to do with conservative gentility or with the "Protestant Ethic." It is the spending or giving away of money that is highly valued, not just possessing or acquiring it. Only through spending it ostentatiously for public display or to increase the size of one's entourage of personal clients can it serve to enhance one's status. Money plays many other social roles of importance to the elite. Common ostentatious expenditure is a symbol of personal solidarity among elite members. Amatory success, in a polygynous society where there is intense competition for women and where bridewealth is expected, depends also on one's ability to pay (Ames 1953). In a culture which pays as much attention to sex as does the Wolof, this use for money is far from negligible.

The size of a person's clientship of poor relations and *griots* is likely to be directly proportional to his generosity and to his ability to further his clients' fortunes through influence in society. However—and the distinction is of great importance—a patron does not *buy* his clients' support and recognition. Rather, his generosity, particularly to members of lower castes, shows that he is an individual worthy of popular acclaim. Thus, public gift-giving is a patterned process, designed to ennoble the giver and reflect his "high concern for honor," not an underhanded and reprehensible attempt to buy support or status. As such, it is a particularly difficult pattern to extirpate, and one that is likely to continue to pervade many aspects of Senegalese life.

The activities of religious elites must also be understood in light of transitional patterns of behavior. As is readily apparent to any observer of the Senegalese scene, the great Senegalese marabouts signify and reinforce their elite status with the same elements of money, entourage, and personal honor as do the *samba linguers*. Competition for advancement and recognition within the families of the great caliphates is at least as intense as competition for elite status in secular society. The use of money by the religious elite is somewhat different, however. The fact that a marabout has the gift of grace, which he can dispense in unlimited quantities to his followers, absolves him from the normal requirements of dispensing monetary gifts to his clients. Accordingly, he can put his financial resources to work for his personal financial aggrandizement. Indeed, all conspires to make this a rational action on his part, for it is popularly felt that a marabout's potential for conferring grace and ultimate salvation is reflected in his personal wealth and magnificence—an inter-esting African twist on Calvinism. Since the colonial and independent Senegalese governments have contributed handsomely to the financial well-being of the marabouts, and since their followers *(talibeś)* reveal their devotion by the size of their annual gifts to the religious leaders, the marabouts' economic power is great. More than half of Senegal's single cash crop, peanuts, is produced on land controlled by marabouts.

A layman, too, can use religion to bolster his elite position. A Senegalese may save and borrow for years to make the pilgrimage to Mecca and to add the prestigious title "El Hadj" to his name. Whatever the spiritual rewards of the pilgrimage may be, it is usually a sound investment in worldly terms. A Hadji in trade may find his business greatly increased; he is sure to be considered a good match by young ladies and may be required to pay less bridewealth. Above all, his household is certain to attract numerous hangers-on, who can bask in the renown of their patron while they sing his temporal and religious virtues. It is not uncommon for a successful Senegalese to make the pilgrimage four or five times. Senegalese politicians are particularly given to repeated pilgrimages.

People of lower caste may under certain circumstances attain elite positions, although the fact that they are of lower caste is almost invariably a handicap of some sort. In traditional society, lower-caste people, particularly slaves of nobles and *griots*, sometimes attained positions of considerable behind-the-scenes influence as advisors to their patrons. They could be granted both influence and wealth by a patron since, like eunuchs in other African societies, they could not dream of supplanting their master. They have continued to hold such positions in transitional society, and some have attained positions of considerable importance by participating in the modern sector of the economy.

The Senegalese political system today strongly reflects transitional society. Even those successful political leaders who, like President Léopold Senghor, lead modern personal lives must operate in a political environment in which most of their colleagues and their audience accept transitional norms. Senegalese politics is dominated by one political party, the Union Progressiste Sénégalaise (UPS), members of which hold all elective offices in the country. Other parties are legal, but, through a combination of their own ineptitude and government pressure, they have no chance of winning an election. On paper, the UPS looks like a hierarchical, disciplined, and ideologically-oriented political party, much like the PDG or the Union Soudanaise of neighboring Guinea and Mali. In principle, major decisions are taken centrally by the party's political bureau and sent down to local committees for application. In fact, however, little central control is possible, discipline is nearly non-existent, and ideology consists of catch words that have little demonstrable effect on action. Particularly in the crucial field of economic development, reform measures which may threaten individual power bases are regularly blocked by local politicians, while the money appropriated for such purposes often finds its way into private pockets. Such regular "abnormalities" can be traced to the influence of transitional modes of behavior.

The basic unit of transitional Senegalese politics is the *clan*. The *clan*, which has nothing to do with the "clan" of formal anthropological terminology, is the extension of the patron-client relationship into the political arena. The regularity with which *clans* are denounced by national political leaders attests to their continued importance. The *clan* is a group of people united behind a single leader (or leading family) who expect to profit indirectly from any political success the leader may achieve (Senghor; 1966). The members of a *clan* may be aligned on the basis of lineage, ethnic group, religion, or other independent criterion, but most often simply reflect the diffuse clientele of a popular and successful individual. Most *clans* are locally based —on a group of villages, a rural town, or an urban district—and rare is the electoral district that does not have two or more competing, and often bitterly rival, *clan* leaders with their followings.

The close link between *clan* politics and the patron-client system in everyday life has had certain consequences for the conduct of Senegalese politics. First, it has meant that a political role is considered a natural extension of the social role of any member of the top elite and an additional source of prestige. Indeed, since the financial rewards of politics are likely to be considerable, it may well be necessary for an aspiring *samba linguer* to try his fortune in the political arena. His personal entourage of clients provides him with a ready-made campaign staff and, with their relatives, the beginning of an electoral following. Moreover, a patron's success in political life is expected to redound to the advantage of his followers—in very concrete financial terms. Extensive questioning of nonelite transitionals yields the almost unanimous expectation that the prime reason for anyone's going into politics is to make money. What is especially noteworthy, however, is that the respond-

ents were not expressing a negative judgment, since the successful politician must share his profits with his followers and in fact may well impoverish himself in doing so. Indeed, many successful politicians (like nonpolitical elites) live in homes scarcely distinguishable from those of their electors, but may spend half a month's salary on a Saturday night party for the faithful and more on gifts and "loans" to various hangers-on. Money is a major goal, but primarily because it can bring with it a greater following and thus increased prestige.

National politics requires a constant balancing among *clan* interests. The prime requisite of political action is not that it be "progressive," "nationalist," or such, but that the spoils be fairly distributed. The parallels with American urban and ethnic politics are fairly close; as in American cities, long-range planning is often sacrificed to short-range expediency.

Since competition among *clan* leaders is intensely personal and is closely linked with social as well as political standing, questions of honor and prestige take on great importance. As a result, leaders tend to prefer to make decisions behind the scenes, where more complicated forms of reward can be quietly arranged and where the clash of personalities is veiled, away from the public eye. All serious business of the National Assembly, which frequently indulges in ferocious wrangling, is carried out behind closed doors. Public meetings are all sweetness and light and invariably end with the unanimous vote of all present, although unhappy *clan* leaders may quietly sabotage the assembly decision once they get back home. This is also a very strong support for a one-party system, in which a privately engineered nomination replaces a public election, and the loser can be compensated with an ambassadorial post or a straight payoff.

Within the national party, *clan* alliances may be pyramided in super patron-client relationships. Thus, a major national leader will have as "clients" important regional *clan* leaders. Like local *clan* alignments, these larger alliances seldom have any firm ideological or programmatic base, though leaders are more likely to discuss issues publicly as if these programmatic differences did exist. Being nonideological, these vertical alignments can be kept sufficiently fluid for the basic *clan* quarrels at the lower end of the pyramid to remain undisturbed. Thus, if a village *clan* leader X allies himself with national leader A, his rival village *clan* leader, Y, can be expected to ally himself with A's national rival, B. If for any reason X should shift his allegiance to B, Y would probably discover a distant cousin in common with A, and shift his allegiance accordingly. In politically tranquil periods, these vertical alliances may not be much in evidence, but an election or a serious falling-out among national leaders (as in December 1962, when the President and the Prime Minister fought it out in Dakar) will bring the alliances to the fore. Nearly every local party committee will break out in opposing *clans*, or at least *tendances*, reflecting the split at the top. Only by closely following the shifting patterns of interelite personal relationships can one predict which local *clan* leader will follow which national leader, and even then, this writer must confess, one cannot be too sure.

The shifting pattern of vertical alignments works to distribute the political spoils to a reasonably large number of groups, since no local *clan* leader can count on guessing right every time the greats fall out. It also softens the penalties of losing, for there is usually some national leader who will try to pick up a defeated local *clan* leader for his own entourage and will protect him against overzealous reprisals by the victor. Where national alliances may change suddenly, where nobody wins all the time, and where ideology seldom rears its ugly head, it is to everyone's advantage to soften the blows of bad fortune against the time when today's loser rebuilds his *clan* and becomes tomorrow's *samba linguer* and useful ally.

The great marabouts occupy a crucial position in transitional politics, for in a sense they are the greatest of *clan* leaders. The Grand Khalifa of the Muridiyya brotherhood, for instance, can mobilize at least 400,000 assured votes, which in a country of 3,200,000 total population is not negligible. The spiritual mission of the marabouts, however, restrains their overt participation in politics, and their own rivalries for personal prestige and honor make a common maraboutic front unlikely. Such a common front was attempted in 1959 to slow down Senegal's march to independence, but the Conseil Supérieur des Chefs Religieux then created soon fell apart when the marabouts were unable to pick one of their number to speak for the group. The marabouts exert considerable pressure on political leaders from behind the scenes and are bought off handsomely by the government and by individual candidates at each election, but they lack any real power of initiative except in matters directly affecting their personal fortunes. Their influence—and their financial rewards—are maximized by a competitive political system wherein the votes they control can decide the winner. The establishment of de facto one-party rule has somewhat cramped their style of political action, but they manage to draw considerable benefit from intervening in and often exacerbating existing *clan* quarrels.

Men of lower caste have been able to play some elite roles in transitional Senegalese politics; however, with a few notable exceptions, such roles have been those of technical experts or behind-the-scenes manipulators—logical extensions of their roles in traditional society. It is surely significant that the two men used by President Senghor as his closest collaborators, Mamadou Dia from 1948 to 1962 and Doudou Thiam from 1963 to 1968, are both of inferior caste. In this way, the man at the top assures himself of some additional protection against his closest collaborator. This is not exclusively a Senegalese trait. In Mali, sensitive ministries and technical posts have gone to people of lower caste, and in pre-coup Nigeria the fact that the Federal Prime Minister was of slave origin provided insurance that he would not impinge on the regional powers of the leader of the Northern Region. In Senegalese party affairs, men of lower caste have played a considerable role as party organizers and lower party officials. Aside from the few who have exceptional educational qualifications and those who are semiofficial representatives of marabout patrons, there are virtually no lower-caste men in important elective positions. Perhaps half a dozen of the 80 National Assembly delegates are lower caste; the rest are all *samba linguers*. Contrary to what has happened in other caste-stratified societies, there exists no apparent lower-caste political solidarity. As one *griot* put it: "Me vote for a *griot*? Never! I know what crooks *griots* are!"

THE MODERNIST ELITE

Since the values and social pattern of the modernist elite are much closer to those of Western experience, they can be described quite briefly here. The modernist elite pattern their values on the European model, although the particular European norms that are most salient may vary greatly from individual to individual. These people reject out of hand any ascriptive distinctions based on caste, ethnic group, religion, or family as being "feudal" remnants. They attain status through achievement of the most formal sort—educational achievement. Among younger people, achieving the *baccalauréat* is the most obvious sign of entry into the modernist elite. However, in social life it may still be necessary to reckon with "feudal" prejudices.

Most lower-caste members of the modernist elite marry either métisses or Europeans, since few lower-caste girls are of their social or educational level, and since intercaste marriage is still virtually unknown even among the modernists.

Without an obvious ascriptive base to modernist elite status, such symbols as style of dress, possession of a car, a university diploma, and certain recreation patterns take on great importance. The instances in which members of the modernist elite have appropriate large sums of public money for private purposes have raised considerable scandal in Senegal. The scandal has come not because they necessarily took more from the coffers than have numerous transitions, but because they spent it on highly visible status purchases—like villas or cars—for themselves, instead of giving it away or throwing feasts for their clients.

Although there is a modernist elite, there are no modernist masses behind them. Modernist society is entirely an elite society, although of course it is only one of Senegal's elite societies. As a result, the vertical links of the patron-client variety that are of such great importance to the transitional elite are replaced by horizontal links among members of the modern elite. These horizontal links are based on—and reinforced by—common educational experiences and recreational habits. Cleavages of generation are accordingly felt considerably more sharply by the modernist elite than they are by members of the transitional elite, who lack these distinctive experiences and who are more closely linked with older and younger people by family and other traditional or transitional social institutions. It is a rare member of the modernist elite who has an extensive personal following. Some of the older members of the modernist elite, who received their advanced training as isolated individuals before the period when hundreds of young men achieved the *baccalauréat*, were obliged to make their peace quietly with transitional society. This is the case most notably of President Senghor, *agrégé ès lettres*, who has long been the recognized champion manipulator of *clan* politics. A younger individual, Valdiodio N'Diaye, former Minister of the Interior, successfully used his descent from one of Senegal's greatest traditional ruling families to build himself a *samba linguer's* personal clientele, despite his French law degree and generally modernist orientation. As the number of modernists has increased with the spread of education since the Second World War, fewer and fewer members of the modernist elite have found it to their taste to seek friendships or fol-lowings outside their own set. Thus, in recent years, the spread of advanced education has tended to exacerbate rather than soften clashes between the transitional and modernist ways of life.

The political ideal of the modernist elite is public service. But the public of the modernist elite is an undifferentiated mass, not a personal clientele. It is the nation as a whole, not a segment of it. Indeed, the nation may be too restricted a public—or rather it may have to be redefined to take in all of *la nation africaine* or, in Senghor's terms, *la nation nègro-herbére*. The fact that the modernist elite as a whole is not closely linked with any segment of the nation permits it to view affairs from this lofty perspective. This blurring of national identity is most apparent among those who have studied abroad (N'Diaye 1962:216-20).

A member of the modernist elite is in a difficult position. He is torn between his intellectual desire to be close to or at least to serve the transitional masses and his natural desire to remain above the sordid melee of transitional politics while maintaining the distinctive features of his elite status. In a similar manner, he may be torn between the European values he has assimilated and his awareness of and pride in his African identity. Men of Senghor's generation used the doctrine of *nègritude*, which emphasized the distinctiveness, unity, and high cultural content of "Black" civilization and values, to resolve these conflicts on an intellectual plane. This solution has few adherents among younger Senegalese. The method of resolving these conflicts determines in large part the form of the modernist elite's participation in political life.

The simplest response to these dilemmas has been to take a position of systematic left-wing opposition to all that the government undertakes. Until it collapsed under government harassment in 1967, the Parti Africain de l'Indépendance (PAI) was the opposition party with the greatest appeal to the young modernists. It was allied with the French Communist Party and espoused both scientific socialism and militant pan-African and pan-Islamic nationalism (Diop 1959, Traoré et al. 1966:91-99). Its single most telling programmatic plank was continual denunciation of the neocolonialist activities of the French in Senegal, with particularly violent attacks against the Frenchmen who served the government as technical assistants and the African "valets of imperialism" who held top government jobs. While their attacks were couched in Marxist and nationalist terminology, their viewpoint in many ways represented that of a solidly bourgeois interest group, seeking to oust other people from the jobs its members might hold. The PAI was signally ineffective in promoting the changes it wanted, and remained almost completely outside the effective Senegalese political arena. While this course of action proved politically sterile, it did permit the PAI to develop something approaching a systematic political doctrine, a hard core of dedicated modernist members, and a distinctive position above the "sordid" transitional politics of Senegal.

Members of a second group of modernists have made their peace with the regime, if not with all its supporters. These young men, a number of whom have received advanced technical or administrative training in France's Grandes Écoles, have chosen to serve the nation by working as "technicians" in the Senegalese civil service. They still maintain their distance from the regime, however, by not joining the government political party or seeking to participate directly in "political" as opposed to "administrative" activities. For most of these men, the ideal is one of public service, not very different from the ideals held up to the European colonial administrators whom the technicians have replaced. Many of the top government leaders have approved and even fostered this attitude on the part of the young modernists, for they have seen in these technicians a means of promoting dynamic and disinterested government action without the added complications of young men using their administrative positions as a means to further their political ambitions, as any *clan* leader would naturally do. Many of the younger transitional *clan* politicians were less than enchanted with the government's practice of giving administrative jobs on the basis of scholarly achievement rather than according to the spoils system, but the alternative possibility, that the modernists might join the party en masse and transform the rules of the game completely, convinced them to accept the technicians with a minimum of ill grace.

After independence, with the active support of Prime Minister Mamadou Dia, the technicians were given major responsibility for the regional administrative hierarchy of governors, *préfets*, and *commandants*, and were charged with implementing economic and social development schemes, reporting directly to Dia and his interior minister. The creation of this administrative hierarchy, which paralleled the communication links between the capital and local areas established by the party and the National Assembly deputies, led to friction between the technicians and the *clan* politicians. Neither side could agree on a firm dividing line between administrative and political matters, particularly when the economic or patronage interests of local *clan* leaders were involved. Perhaps inevitably, the nonpartisan position of the technicians became untenable, as was made perfectly clear when President Senghor and Prime Minister Dia came into open armed conflict in December 1962. Much to the distress of many of them, the technicians were immediately cast in the role of important members of the Prime Minister's *clan* by the transitional politicians. When the Prime Minister was removed from office, a number of important technicians lost their jobs, were demoted, or were exiled as representatives to international organizations, as if they had been patronage appointees. In the year after the Prime Minister's fall, the President slowly began to recall many of the deposed technicians, partly because they performed useful government functions, but also, as he admitted, because he did not want his political support to rest exclusively on the constellation of *clan* interests that supported him in his fight against the Prime Minister. Whether they wish it or not, the technicians have been assimilated as one more *clan* playing for the patronage and prestige rewards of transitional Senegalese politics.

WHAT NEXT?

In the short run, it seems unlikely that there will be any great internally generated change away from the transitional style of politics. Any further reconciliation of modernist and transitional patterns of behavior can take place in the near future only within the basically transitional society of the great majority of the Senegalese people. The continuation of this pattern of politics will mean that general economic and social development will be restrained, and that the government will continue to function with the inefficiency that so frustrates foreign aid missions and investment bankers in most underdeveloped countries. At the same time, the system should continue to assure a respectably high degree of popular participation in politics, a circulation of political elites, and a wide, if not equitable, distribution of the spoils of political power. While not negligible virtues, these will probably be insufficient to permit the government to solve the problems presented to it by the world outside its own *clan* politics.

In a longer perspective, one can foresee two lines of development under modernist control. The first (and, from this writer's perspective, the least useful) is a takeover by the radical left.

A disastrous fall in the world price for peanuts, a continued lessening of France's interest in Black Africa, and a lack of competent transitionalist leadership (which might result from President Senghor's loss of interest, senility, or removal from the scene) could together permit a dedicated band of modernist revolutionaries like the PAI to seize power. Without the habits of popular acquiescence and apathy built up in neighboring countries like Guinea and Mali, such a radical left regime in Senegal would probably be obliged to use extraordinary repressive techniques if it were successfully to put through the minimal structural reforms it would find necessary. Without extensive help from the outside, these reforms would probably not be forthcoming, and a stagnation of a new and far less agreeable sort would be the result.

A second possibility is a return of the technicians, quite possibly brought back to power by the army as a means of forestalling the radical left coup discussed above. Such a regime, while appealing to many foreign observers, would lack the crucial transitionalist political skills necessary to bring about cooperation from the population. In nearly every particular except color, such a regime would seem to the masses like a colonial administration, and would be plagued by many of the weaknesses of colonial administrations without falling heir to their advantages of technical talent and money. Such a regime would probably be inherently unstable and would be subject to capture by either transitionalist or radical modernist politicians if it did not adopt extreme repressive measures.

Each of these alternatives assumes that the split between Senegal's transitional and modernist cultures will persist, and that in one form or another one of the cultures will dominate the political system to the near exclusion of the other. At the present time, the discontinuities between transitional and modernist societies seem so great as to make this assumption plausible. Any stable progression toward both democracy and economic development would seem to require a more continuous political elite culture, which would mix some of the modernists' technical expertise and idealism with the transitionals' understanding of the masses and their problems. This would not at all require the development of a new homogeneous elite culture; on the contrary, diversity would be its essence. It would, however, require a greater interlocking of transitional and modernist approaches, which could come about only if a significant number of the political elite could incarnate aspects of both transitionalist and modernist values, i.e. if Senegalese society could create a dynamic middle elite sector capable of bridging the gap and putting both extremes to work.

While it is beyond the scope of this paper to set forth strategies for developing such a middle elite sector, it is worth pointing out the importance of a drastic shift in the education given to today's modernist elites. Senegalese education, based on the classical French curriculum, successfully isolates the student from the society around him and rewards him for maintaining and increasing this separation. A shift to a more concrete study of African problems and to practical work experience within the larger social environment would seem to be imperative if the social and cultural discontinuities between the intellectual and the transitional society are to be overcome.

Education alone is no panacea for political problems. It may already be too late, and the will may be lacking to put reforms into operation. However, without some major changes in elite culture, it is very difficult to see how Senegal will be able to produce any internally generated and continuous political and economic development that will not alienate or subjugate the vast majority of its citizens.

REFERENCES

Ames, David W. 1953 *Plural marriage among the Wolof in the Gambia,* unpublished doctoral dissertation, Evanston, Northwestern University. 1959 "Wolof co-operative work groups," in *Continuity and Change in African Cultures,* William R. Bascom and Melville J. Herskovits, eds., Chicago, University of Chicago Press: 224-37.

Diop, Majhemout 1959 *Contribution à l'étude des problémes politiques en Afrique noire,* Paris, Présence Africaine.

Foltz, William J. 1964 "Senegal," in *Political Parties and National Integration in Tropical Africa,* James S. Coleman and Carl G. Rosberg, Jr., eds., Berkeley and Los Angeles, University of California Press: 16-64. 1965 *From French West Africa to the Mali Federation,* New Haven, Yale University Press.

Gamble, David P. 1975 *The Wolof of Senegambia,* London, International African Institute.

Morgenthau, Ruth Schachter 1964 *Political parties in French-speaking West Africa,* Oxford, Clarendon Press.

N'Diaye, Jean Pierre 1962 *Enquete sur les étudiants noirs en France,* Paris, Réalités Africaines.

Senghor, Léopold S. 1966 *Rapport de politique générale*, Kaolack, 5éme Congrès de l'U.P.S. (mimeographed).

Silla, Ousmane 1966 "Persistance des castes dans la société Wolof contemporaine," *Institut Fondamental d'Afrique Noire, Bulletin, Série B* 28:731-70.

Socé, Ousmane 1948 *Karim*, 3. éd., Paris, Nouvelles Editions Latines.

Thiam, Bodiel 1949 "Hiérarchie de la société ouolove," *Notes Africaines* 41:12.

Traoré, Bakary, Mamadou Lo, and Jean-Louis Alibert 1966 *Forces politiques en Afrique noire*, Paris, Presses Universitaires de France.

Zuccarelli, Francois 1968 *Un parti politique africain: L'Union Progressiste Sénégalaise*, doctoral thesis, Dakar, Université, Faculté de Droit.

NOTES

1 Field research for this paper was made possible by a grant from the John Simon Guggenheim Foundation, which is in no way responsible for statements made herein. For general descriptions of the Senegalese political system, see Foltz 1964, 1965; Morgenthau 1964; and Zuccarelli 1968.

HONOUR, FAMILY AND PATRONAGE:
A Study of Institutions and Moral Values in a Greek Mountain Community
J. K. CAMPBELL

VILLAGE FRIENDSHIP AND PATRONAGE

IN THE VILLAGES authority rests in the hands of a council of five members. From its own number it elects a President and Vice-President while the choice of the council itself is the result of local elections which are held every four years. In these, all adult villagers of both sexes, and those shepherd families who possess citizenship rights in the village, are entitled to vote.

For electoral purposes any person may form a party providing he can present to the electorate a card with the names of seven candidates. In practice village elections seldom produce more than two parties, those who support the President in power because they are his friends, and those who want a change because they are not his friends. These parties are essentially personal followings, not corporate associations, and there is not necessarily any direct alignment with the parties of national politics. The citizens vote by handing in the party card of their choice with four crosses against those of the seven candidates who are preferred. The party which polls the greater number of cards wins the election. The four candidates of the successful party who record the largest aggregates of personal votes become members of the council. The person amongst the candidates of the defeated party or parties who claims the largest number of personal votes is also elected to the council as the representative of the defeated minority's interests. The five members of the new council then proceed to elect two of their number as President and Vice-President. These men hold office for two years, at the end of which period their authority may either be confirmed for the remaining two years of the council's term of office, or they may be replaced by the election of new officers.

The powers of this council are wide. By a simple majority vote it may institute any local by-law it pleases, providing this does not conflict with the letter or spirit of national legislation. Within statutory limits, it determines the local grazing charges to be levied on the flocks of pastoralists. And it draws up its own budget of future communal expenditure. These privileges are balanced by the discretionary power of veto over budgetary and taxation decisions which is possessed by the Nomarch, who is the provincial administrator appointed by the central Government.

The day-to-day administration of village affairs is the task of the President, who receives an allowance in compensation for the time he spends on community affairs. He is assisted in this work by a permanent salaried village secretary who keeps the registers up to date, deals with correspondence, and draws up a variety of returns which are required by different Government Ministries. Indeed, both these village officials act, not infrequently, for the central Government in matters of routine administration, instruction, and in the collection of information. Although in the decisions of the council the President's vote, of itself, carries no greater weight than that of any other member, his control over the administration of parochial affairs and his intimate relations with the Government bureaucracy, whether he is acting as a negotiator representing the interests of the villagers, or as an agent of the bureaucracy, give him in fact substantially greater power than other members of his council.

For these reasons it is generally with the President that the Sarakatsani must negotiate their affairs. In a number of important matters he has the power to affect their interests collectively or individually. In the first place, the council decides the scale of grazing charges. The village is permitted by law to charge, for summer grazing, up to two shillings a head for the first 150 animals and up to four shillings for the remainder of the flock. It may, however, charge less.[1] And it is noticeable that in those villages where the shepherd families are in a politically strategic position grazing charges tend to be lower than in other villages where this is not the case. Threepence or sixpence a head difference in a grazing charge does not represent a very large sum of money, but to men who are already deeply in debt to merchants or shopkeepers, it has significance. For them, debt implies a form of dependence which is a measure of weakness.

The Sarakatsani say that if a village President and council enforce all local laws without allowing some flexibility, it becomes impossible for a shepherd family to live. If, on the other hand, the President is willing to grant them various favours, which take into consideration the effect of the law on personal circumstances, their position may be, at least, not entirely hopeless. In practice, all Presidents with Sarakatsani on their citizenship rolls relax certain regulations for the shepherd families which support them. The political skill of a President, even an implacable opponent of the shepherds, is that he grants just a sufficient number of favours to a few Sarakatsan families to detach them from the ranks of the opposition at the time of the elections.

It is the President who decides each spring which area of the village grazing land shall be allotted to each family or cooperating 'company' of shepherds. At Skamneli, for instance, there are three main areas, Goura, Tsoumako, and Gyphtokambos. Goura has the best grass, Gyphtokambos the worst. It is the customary arrangement that each family goes to a different

area each year. Yet within each general area different sections are of different quality so that friends may still be rewarded and enemies punished in a way that touches them very closely through the milk yield and the condition of their animals.

The President is often able to influence the actions of the village agricultural guard and forester. Both these officials, although they belong to a Government service, are dependent in various ways on the goodwill of the President, and if he is displeased with their work it is relatively easy to have them exchanged. By regulation, if an agricultural guard discovers a trespass on village land, or the forester finds animals grazing in forbidden areas, they must issue a summons against the shepherd in charge of the offending animals. But if the President is able to have a word with the guard or forester before he writes the details of the case in his report book, and if no third person is present, he may be able to persuade him to ignore the matter.

The President has more direct control over the man who is employed by the village to regulate the flow of water to the village vegetable gardens. He is able to arrange matters so that a fair share of water is given to, or withheld from, a Sarakatsan family.

For a number of purposes the Sarakatsani require the signature of the President on forms, certificates, or passes. He may be able to cause considerable trouble to a shepherd through delay, or by finding technical irregularities in his documents. These powers of the President are particularly feared. Although some of the leaders of cooperating 'companies' of families are extremely able and alert men, the ordinary Sarakatsan head of family is completely bewildered by documents, printed forms, and regulations, most of which are written in an official language which he only half comprehends. A Sarakatsanos with a large family and only 60 sheep lost six of his animals through disease in the summer of 1955. He came to the village office to ask the President to sign a form for a loan from the Agricultural Bank to replace the dead animals. At the time he was in considerable difficulties, his family was short of flour, and on account of his poverty, small flock, and deep indebtedness, his cheese merchant would make no further advances of credit. There was no doubt about the authenticity of his claim. The agricultural guard had made a report that the animals belonged to this man and that they had the unmistakable symptoms of liver fluke. After ignoring the man's presence in the office for about three-quarters of an hour, the President suddenly pointed to one of the many conditional clauses in the regulations printed in small type. 'You understand that yours is a difficult case. It is only five days since you arrived here from the plains and this clause says that confirmation of the details of the case must be signed by the President of the village where the disease was contracted. Obviously they became sick in the plains or on the road; anyway, not here. Perhaps you must return to Philippiada to have this signed. However, I shall write to the Ministry of Agriculture in Jannina and we shall see.' The man haltingly explained his difficulties, referring to the plight of his family. The President spread his hands and smiled benignly, 'You know that I always try to help you tent-dwellers but in this case,' putting his thumb on the offending clause, 'what can I do?' After the man had left the office the President explained that he would sign the form in a few days. He was a man who loved honour, he added, but it was necessary that the men who had voted against him in the recent election should learn that their interests lay in supporting him and not that Communist cuckold (a reference to the leader of the opposition party).

The Agricultural Bank has been mentioned. Each year, the shepherd applies to the bank for an annual loan, the application form for which must carry the President's signature as a guarantee that the information given by the shepherd is accurate. Long-term loans are also available from this bank to assist families which have lost their stock through disease. In these cases, the shepherd must produce evidence that the animals in fact died of a particular disease, and were not sold, or given away as dowry. In addition, the application must be approved by the local officer of the Ministry of Agriculture; and this support will be hard to win if the village President has characterized the shepherd as spendthrift or inefficient.

Twice a year when the Sarakatsani leave the mountains, or the plains, the local village President must sign a clearance certificate which confirms that all their grazing charges have been paid. This is required by the police before they will issue the pass without which a family cannot move its flocks to another district. These moneys are not paid directly to the village council but into a treasury in Jannina, whose official collector arrives in the village some three weeks before the flocks are normally moved to their winter pastures in the plains. If, as frequently happens, a Sarakatsanos is unable to pay his dues, the collector may send a demand notice to the police, and if this is not met when it is presented, the shepherd is arrested. But in many cases the President intervenes and persuades the treasury to allow the defaulter six months' grace until he returns in the spring.

A man requires the President's signature on his identity card. He requires it when he applies for an allotment of free timber from village forest land for the repair of his house, and on other documents which it would be tedious to enumerate. In all these situations the President may be the helper who makes all things easy, or a deliberate and successful obstructionist.

There are other ways, less legal, in which the President may sometimes help Sarakatsan friends. When the sheep are mustered for counting each spring on their arrival at the village, it is relatively easy for the President to arrange that the total of animals is underestimated so that perhaps 350 instead of 400 is entered in the records for taxation purposes. Similarly, when milk, meat or wool are sold to a merchant a tax of 2 per cent is levied on the value of the sale. For a friend the President may mark down the price actually paid over for animals or the products they yield. With the connivance of the President and the schoolteacher, a family which is short of labour may sometimes take a child from school before the full term of its compulsory education is completed. It is also possible for the President to do some things to a Sarakatsanos which are strictly against law or custom, because the man may be frightened that if he takes the case to the courts, or the Nomarch, he may suffer worse injustices in the long run. After Theodoros voted against the President in the elections, his sheep were sent for the second year in succession to the worst area of village grazing land. Theodoros could have appealed to the Nomarch but decided it was more politic to settle his differences with the President by more indirect methods.

The strength of the President's position is apparent. In their efforts to come to terms with his authority and influence, the Sarakatsani attempt to draw him into some form of personal relationship that will introduce a moral element of mutual consideration. Three methods are in general practice: spiritual kinship, friendship, and gifts. The first of these has been discussed. The second possibility is that the Sarakatsanos may be able to align himself as the 'friend' and political supporter of the President, if he will accept him.

Here a brief digression is necessary to consider the nature of friendship in Zagori villages.[2] Between villagers ties of friendship relate persons who are, in principle, equals. All villagers, without discrimination, possess the same legal rights in the local polity. If a man is also honourable in his conduct, a good neighbour, and legitimately born of Zagori parents, he is entitled in the social life of the village to be treated with a degree of consideration that represents a recognition of his social personality. Persons who are equal in these respects must show some concern for each other's social sensibilities by avoiding public rudeness and by a careful and courteous exchange of greetings when they meet.

Friendship begins where one man accepts a favour from another. The person who gives the favour will assert that he expects no return; it would be insulting to suggest that his act of friendship had a motivation. It is, however, the very altruism of the act, whether this is simulated or not, which demands a counter favour. Default destroys the friendship and provokes accusations of ingratitude. Although liking and sympathy are alleged to be the premises on which friendship between village equals is based, it would be more true to say that villagers who are able to do each other reciprocal favours sometimes discover from this experience confidence in one another. From these beginnings there may grow a relationship of intimacy and warmth. But in essence friendship of this kind remains a contractual relation, a form of cooperation in which services of various kinds are exchanged and accounted.

The network of friendships of the President or of other influential villagers becomes in reality a system of patronage. Accountancy is then more difficult because the patron is able to do more material favours for his client than the latter is able to return. But although the character of the relationship is now, in effect, asymmetrical, patron and client, because they are interacting in the context of village community relations where all true villagers are in principle equals, they continue to treat one another as if they were equals in the situation of their friendship as well. Both patron and client claim publicly that the other 'is my friend'. The patron says that he helps his client simply because it pleases him to help those of his friends who are in difficulties. The client explains that he is the friend of the patron, not simply because he receives benefits from him, but because he is a good man. In short, their friendship exists within the field of village values where behaviour is evaluated against the ideals of independence and love of honour.

In the Sarakatsan community the situation is different. There is no cooperation between unrelated families and no established political authority in the shepherd community which might lead to relations of political friendship. A relationship which has many of the aspects of patronage exists between the dominant family and the other associated families in a cooperating 'company', but these connexions are based on the values of kinship, not friendship. When a Sarakatsanos says 'I have him as a friend', he generally means that he has established a relation of mutual advantage with a person outside the community who in most cases is in the superordinate position of patron. The use of the word 'friend' by the Sarakatsanos is not here encumbered with any theory of equality or disinterested motives. The fact that in terms of power he is the weaker partner in the majority of his relations of friendship is recognized by the Sarakatsanos but does not immediately concern his pride since these people stand outside his community. On the contrary, the more effective relationships of this kind that a man possesses, the greater his prestige in the community since it proves him to be an able protector of his family and his flocks.

It is by no means certain that a President will accept any Sarakatsanos as his political client. What the President has to offer will be clear enough from the earlier description of the ways in which he can help or hinder. The chief service the shepherd is able to pledge in return is his vote and those of his family and associated kinsmen. But to accept a man as a client commits the patron to protection instead of exploitation, and to that extent it is a restriction on the free exercise of his power. A President generally prefers to assume these obligations only to Sarakatsani with some influence. Naturally, more humble families have vicarious access to his patronage through their influential kinsmen, but the intermediate link which separates them from the President's beneficence makes it less likely that their affairs will be settled with the same despatch and satisfaction.

The extent to which a President needs to enter these commitments depends, of course, on the balance of the political groupings in his village. In one village the President commanded about three quarters of the village vote, but by his generally uncompromising hostility he had driven the Sarakatsani into the arms of the small opposition party. A month before the election it appeared that he had no Sarakatsan supporters and that his cause was lost. Conveniently the election was held in November, after the Sarakatsani had departed to the plains eighty miles away.

The opposition party chartered a lorry to transport, as they had calculated it, an adequate number of Sarakatsan voters to assure their victory. But, in the event, the President skillfully contrived a narrow majority by making secret agreements with two shepherd families. The five members of these families who returned from the plains, ironically enough in the lorry chartered by the opposition, were sufficient to give the President victory and a new term of office.

After the election the two families received a number of favours. In the spring the sheep of one family were short-counted by sixty and the flock of the other, which by right of the customary rotation of grazing areas ought to have gone to an area of indifferent grazing, spent a more profitable summer on the village's best grassland. In the face of the unusual solidarity of the local Sarakatsan group at the time of the election, the action of the two dissident families was described as treacherous. They were branded as 'The President's men', with an overtone of meaning which implied that they were puppets dancing at the command of the master, capable even of betraying their own people. Yet as passions cooled and the months passed, evaluations changed perceptibly. At first the members of these families were unequivocally 'traitors', but later they were considered merely 'cunning' (by no means an entirely pejorative judgment), and eventually one sometimes heard grudging admissions of their 'cleverness'. For it is recognized that each family is free to seek its own protection and the political friends who can provide it. Indeed, Sarakatsani believe that in the nature of the situation favours and concessions are to be won only by some, not all families. It is, therefore, the duty of each head of family to scheme and intrigue for his own security. Only in the case of a breach of faith between kinsmen is an accusation of treachery seriously considered.

But the friendship which a Sarakatsanos achieves with a village President, or indeed with any other influential person, involves more than the exchange of specific material favours; it establishes, also, an asymmetrical relation of sociability which enhances the prestige of both men. A Sarakatsanos who has friendship with the President boldly sits down with him at the same table when he enters the coffee-shop. The President offers him a drink, he stands him a drink in return. Meeting him in the village square, the shepherd stops to talk for a few minutes about this and that. Were they not patron and client, a curt 'Good day' from each side would be the extent of their social intercourse. However, it is not a relationship of equals. The shepherd belongs not only to a different community, but to a qualitatively inferior one. While the President will say of a villager who is similarly his client that this man is his friend, he will not say this of a shepherd. If an explanation in his presence is necessary, he may say, 'George is a good lad, I help him', but behind his back he will simply say, 'He is my man'. Yet, although they are his social inferiors, the President gains prestige by being seen publicly with his shepherd clients. If he drinks with other villagers who are his supporters, this is no cause for comment. He merely keeps company with those who are his social equals and natural companions. When he drinks with four or five shepherds it draws attention to his possession of power, to his ability to hold men who do not waste their time drinking with ordinary villagers whom as a class of persons they detest and despise. The Sarakatsanos accepts his position of inferiority in the relationship because he must. He does not, as most villagers would, address the President by his Christian name; but he is not subservient in his manner. He speaks to him courteously as 'President'. When another person of importance comes to speak to the President, and it is clear that he is dismissed, he moves to another table, or with a 'Good health, President', to which the latter replies, he leaves the shop. These are the conventional terms on which these unequal friendships are founded. What is important to the Sarakatsanos in these situations is that other shepherds who do not possess this valued link should see and envy him.

In asymmetrical friendship relations, since it is assumed that the patron has more favours to offer than the client can return, or that reciprocal favours are so dissimilar in quality that accountancy is difficult, there is often greater stability than in friendships between equals, which are very frequently bedevilled by accusations of ingratitude. Yet, even here, there are many complaints, the patron asserting that the client should be more vocal in his gratitude, the client complaining that the patron does very little in relation to the client's worth and needs, and the services he has rendered. In short, the patron wants more honour, the client more benefits.

The third widely practised method of placating or influencing the President is to present him with a gift of cheese, butter, or meat. Some families do this each spring as a matter of general policy without having in mind any particular favour. They hope that the gift may moderate his general attitude towards them in the coming months. More often, families wait until they face some specific difficulty. A gift of cheese or some other produce is delivered to the President's home and then, perhaps two days later, the gift-giver walks into the village office and makes his request. The President may be helpful or he may not. The assumptions of the giver and the recipient of the gift are not necessarily the same. The giver hopes that the gift will arouse some sense of obligation in the receiver. But the latter, if he chooses to feel that the gift was forced on him against his will, may decide that he is not obliged to feel grateful. If he intends not to grant the favour, the refusal is never direct. The many difficulties which stand in the way are elaborated at very great length. He explains that he will see what can be done, he will write to a friend in Jannina, he wants to help. In fact he will do nothing; and the original gift is not returned.

A gift is frequently offered to the President by a Sarakatsanos when he meets with legal troubles. Stratos and a number of his kinsmen were using 20 mules to transport wooden planks from a saw-mill to the road below the village where the wood was loaded on to lorries. The area for the grazing of Sarakatsan mules and horses is an hour's climb above the village and this was very inconvenient for Stratos and the other muleteers. They chanced their luck and grazed their animals at night in the little-frequented village orchards close to their loading-point. On the thirty-ninth night of their operations they were discovered by the agricultural guard who from his examination of the length of the grass and some damage to young apple trees was confident of a very successful case. Stratos was not able to claim that the President was his friend, but since he was a law-abiding careful man his relations with the President had been generally good. He begged for his assistance, explaining the extreme difficulty the group would have suffered if each night the mules had had to be released so far from the scene of operations. He managed also to mention that he would like to help the President in the current rebuilding of his house. It so happened that he had two loads of timber which he did not require. The next day, the President saw the agricultural guard and warned him that, in his opinion, it would only be reasonable to take into consideration the one night when he had actually seen the mules. For the rest, who could say? There had been high winds recently which often damaged trees, and he added that he had noticed one of

the agricultural guard's own goats straying one evening in the direction of the orchards. Accordingly, the President received his wood, Stratos and his kinsmen escaped with a small fine, and the agricultural guard's dream of a triumphant case came to nothing.

Two points must be stressed about this method of influencing the President. Gifts must be presented with finesse. A man of honour is not to be crudely bought by social inferiors if he does not wish to lose prestige in the community. The shepherd must give the lamb, butter, or cheese to the President as if it were merely an expression of friendly respect, and in no way tied to the favour he is about to request. Secondly, whether in relation to these gifts of produce, or to other perquisites of his office, the limited dishonesty and corruptibility of a President is not dishonourable. 'He eats money', others say with envy. But they concede that this is the right of his office. His allowance is not large, he too must live, he also has a family to support. If a favour, even where it is entirely legal, involves trouble beyond the ordinary routine duties of his office, why should he weary himself for a man to whom he is not related in any way, unless that man by a gift, or in some other way, demonstrates the esteem in which he holds him.

We have now discussed in the order of their effectiveness three ways in which the Sarakatsani attempt to influence the President of their summer village—spiritual kinship, friendship, and gifts. In principle, spiritual kinship binds a President to help the shepherd in all situations. Ideally it is a diffuse relation, there is nothing reasonable that cannot be requested, and the right to expect this assistance is sanctioned by the ritual link between godfather and godchild. Friendship of the kind established between a village President and a Sarakatsanos, is a patron-client relationship of some stability over time, and the range of favours which may be demanded is almost as extensive as that between spiritual kinsmen, but the atmosphere of calculation is more pronounced. Confidence which is ritually sanctioned in spiritual kinship is more easily destroyed in the relations of patron and client. Gifts given by a shepherd to the President generally have a specific object in view and each gift is effective for only a short period of time if, indeed, it is effective at all.

The President is not the only man with power or influence in a village; the other members of the council, the schoolmaster, the priest, other villagers of wealth or reputation may have these qualities in varying degree. When the President is particularly severe towards them, the shepherds attempt, by the same methods we have just considered, to attach themselves to other persons in the village who are known to have influence on the council, or personally over the President himself.

When the sheep of Theodoros were dispatched by the President to the poorest area of grazing for the second year because of his active opposition during the elections, Theodoros did not appeal to the Nomarch against this injustice. He went instead to Vlachopoulos. Vlachopoulos is the Vice-President of the village, and the President's closest friend. He also owns the older of the two village coffee-shops which is the one more generally patronized by the Sarakatsani both for social gatherings and for the many small purchases which they make. After the bitter feelings aroused by the autumn elections there was a spontaneous boycott of the Vlachopoulos shop by the Sarakatsani and at the time when Theodoros approached him two or three weeks after the shepherds had returned to the summer pasture, only a few Sarakatsan men were to be seen drinking in the old shop. For a week Theodoros assiduously made small purchases in the shop. Finding Vlachopoulos alone one day, he took the next step by remarking that he was not a man to dwell on old scores and that he thought his return to the shop proved this point. It seemed, however, that the President was still governed by his rage and spite. This was surely unjust, and he asked Vlachopoulos if he would not intercede with the President on his behalf. Vlachopoulos agreed to do this. It is a fair assumption that he was especially pleased to see Theodoros who leads a substantial cooperating 'company' and has many other kinsmen in the local group of shepherds. It was very probable that if Theodoros returned to his shop to drink, as well as to buy, the boycott would be over. This proved to be the case. Vlachopoulos persuaded the President to rearrange the grazing areas; and after a week or two of further delay to impress upon Theodoros the misguided nature of his opposition in the previous autumn, the President eventually effected the necessary changes.

A Zagori village and the local group of Sarakatsani that is linked to it through rights of citizenship, form a network of friendship relations, some of which are symmetrical and others of the patron-client variety. This network enables a man in many situations to obtain a measure of satisfaction from a person with whom he is in direct opposition. He achieves this by indirect pressure because he is a client, or friend, of the friend of his enemy. Villagers and shepherds are careful to maintain friendship links with opposed political factions and personages whenever this is possible. The implication is that there are often inherent limits on the way in which the President or other influential villagers may use their power against most individuals, since, very probably, in any particular act of victimization they are attacking the friend, or client, of one of their own friends. Only very poor villagers, or Sarakatsani with small flocks who are not attached to the cooperating 'company' of more powerful kinsmen, may be treated unjustly without encountering some responding pressure through the system of friendships; for these persons, having little to offer in return, may not have patrons. But in other cases to ignore the pressures received through the system of friendships may endanger important relationships on which a man's influence and prestige largely depend. It is not suggested, however, that a man with strategically aligned friendships is secure from all injustice. On the contrary, Theodoros suffered a considerable financial loss until his friendship with Vlachopoulos rescued him from further punishment.

In the Zagori villages, as in the Sarakatsan community, a dominant feature of the social system is the isolation of the family and its struggle against other families, whether in terms of the possibility of bare subsistence or of social prestige. The more important social obligations are particular to the individual's family, and these stand in direct conflict with the weaker and more general responsibilities of good neighbourliness. The notion of service to the community exists, and is honoured. But the service takes a form which honours the individual, his family and the community in equal degree as, for instance, in the foundation of a church or school. Such services are never anonymous. The idea of service to fellow citizens of the same community exists also, but it remains an ideal value which is not realized in a society where familiar obligations have an absolute priority. The President and councilors of the village are firstly heads of households and only secondly public servants. A President does not feel under the same moral obligation, even within the sphere of his formal duties, to help equally a close kinsman, a spiritual kinsman, a friend, and a man to whom he is linked only by common citizenship. It is suggested that in this absence, for the most part, of universally applicable values the system of village friendship and patronage in fact achieves a distribution of various facilities which, although it is never equitable, guards most families, even those of the hard-pressed Sarakatsani of Zagori, against complete exclusion. The system of friendship and patronage achieves this, not by upholding any general rights of citizenship, but, in a sense paradoxically, by an appeal to the individual and family interests of a person in authority. For without friends a man loses all power, influence, and social prestige.

NOTES

1 The minimum charge is 4½ d. a head.
2 Friendship in Epirote villages appears to be very similar to the parallel institution in Andalusia. Cf. Pitt-Rivers.

LAWYERS AND GOVERNMENT OFFICIALS

The Sarakatsani not only need to come to terms with the village authorities, they must also adapt themselves to the laws and regulations of the State, and attempt in their own interests to influence the administration of Government regulations so far as these affect their own affairs. This involves relations with civil servants at various levels in the hierarchy.

Some State regulations are administered through the structure of village authority which has been examined. In other instances the impact of State administration is direct. In the Zagori, as in other local districts, an agricultural officer of the Ministry of Agriculture has an office in the capital village of the district. Such matters as loans from the Agricultural Bank, permission to burn off grass, appeals against the various restrictions on grazing in forest areas, advice about animal disease, and free distribution of sprays to combat insect pests fall within this official's competence. But in these and other questions a shepherd is often referred to the provincial office at Jannina, or in winter at Igoumenitsa, Arta, and Preveza. The Greek police, a paramilitary organization, have a central station under the command of a captain in the capital village of each local district, but sections of police are also stationed in outlying areas of the district, each section serving three or four villages. It frequently happens that Sarakatsani are late in the payment of their grazing dues. Although these are assessed by the village, they are paid to the public treasury in the provincial centre. When the police are informed by the treasury that a payment has not been made, they must attempt to serve a demand notice. If payment is again withheld, the debtor is taken under escort to the public treasury and, if he is still unable to pay, from there to prison. But the circumstance that these demands for payment must be served on one individual in person, and not merely to his home or a member of his family, results in a perpetual pantomime of hide-and-seek between police and heads of shepherd families. This causes irritation and bad feeling on both sides. It is a common experience to find a man secreted under a blanket in the darker corner of a kinsman's hut when it is known that police are in the village.

Sarakatsani are sometimes involved in difficulties with the military authorities over conscription. A family with only one son, a physically handicapped father, and without sufficient resources to hire a shepherd, may submit a case for the postponement or abbreviation of the son's term of military service before a committee of appeal. This committee, however, is not thought to be very liberal in its decisions.

The Sarakatsani face the jurisdiction of the State in their frequent adventures in courts of law.[1] The laws that concern the Sarakatsani in their daily life do not generally favour them. The interests of shepherds tend to be opposed to those of peasants or townsmen. For instance, there are many civil suits between owners of private properties and Sarakatsani who claim a disputed right of protected lease for their grazing. And, sometimes, shepherds are plaintiffs in cases challenging the decisions of a village administration. The regulations of village life differ from the conventions of semi-nomads. And their adherence to the traditional code of honour necessarily conflicts with the laws of a modern State. They distrust legal procedures because their pleas are frequently unsuccessful and in many instances they regress into acts of violence which two generations ago would have been the general response to the interference of outside authority. Often a certain *naïveté* or simple ignorance about what is legal, and what is not, leads them into trouble. It is rare for a head of family not to be involved in some capacity in at least one suit each year. In 1955 George Carvounis, who was not exceptional in this respect, acted as a principal in two cases, one civil, one criminal. In the first he was sued for violent assault and defamation of character by a village woman, whom he had rough handled when she attempted to pull down a wall which she alleged had been set up by Carvounis on her land. In the second case he was charged with forgery, having found it innocently convenient to sign a document with the name of another member of his cooperating 'company'.

But the critical point of contact between the Sarakatsanos and the bureaucrat is in the situation where his winter grazing is in danger. Then, the leader of a stani must attempt to influence the highest State officials in the Epirus if he is to face, with confidence, the threat of exclusion from his winter pastures.

Gifts and money bribes are freely offered in making approaches to a minor State servant. Gifts of produce are generally made to the agricultural officer; for, even if he is not a native of the district, he becomes a member of the local village community where he occupies a respectable position in the system of village friendship; moreover, since he has some pretensions to education and culture it might be insulting to offer money. Gifts of produce are also preferred in dealing with a local police sergeant. Not all policemen are venal and it is a serious offense to offer bribes of money to a member of this force. Money bribes are often effective in preventing agricultural and forest guards from reporting the trespasses of animals, if the offense has not been observed by a third party. These guards belong, generally, to poor families of low prestige, and in the Zagori they are often villagers of gipsy origin. Such persons are despised by the Sarakatsani, and they themselves are generally prepared to accept money bribes without the least embarrassment.

To conduct business with minor public servants in the administrative offices at Jannina, Sarakatsani use small bribes. Often at the doorways of these buildings there is a desk staffed by two or three ushers. These men examine with a brusque lack of sympathy the forms which the shepherd has in his hand, or they demand to know his business, if only to ignore his explanation. He may wish to see a particular official to whom he has been recommended. He believes that a gratuity of five to ten shillings is essential if he is to find the right man. If he wishes to submit an application form in the general office of the same building, he hands it over the counter to the clerk with the equivalent of a ten shilling note on the underside. The shepherd hopes that this will at least ensure that the form

is filed; and perhaps nearer the top than the bottom of the pile. Here, the relationship between the shepherd and the junior official is temporary and anonymous. The reputation of the man of higher status, in the eyes of the man in the lower position, is not at stake. The bribe is small, not necessarily effective, and it is not discussed. It is passed secretly. And this saves each clerk from losing the esteem of his colleagues who are themselves engaged in the same practice.

But in affairs of great importance, which must reach the desk of senior officials, the shepherd leader generally feels unable to conduct his own affairs. It is difficult, in any case, for a humble shepherd to penetrate to the offices of senior officials. If he does reach this point, his rough clothes and awkward manners, alternating between obsequiousness and effrontery, make progress difficult. Sarakatsani say, with good reason, that in offices nobody pays the least attention to a man without a collar and tie. And they have little confidence in their own forensic abilities in this kind of situation. As one Sarakatsanos said of himself and his people, 'Shepherds hesitate. If I can make five points in a conversation, he (the official) can return twenty.'

Moreover, even the director of an office does not conduct business privately. His secretary and aides have desks in the same room. By the public transaction of affairs, and the display of his power, he emphasizes his status before the eyes of his subordinates and stresses their dependence in himself. To listen patiently to the incoherent ramblings of a Sarakatsanos, the name of whose very profession, shepherd, is a synonym for stupidity, much less to take trouble and thought over assisting him, would be to lose prestige and betray the status of his position, the validation of which lies in pride, not humility. Generally such officials are curt, rude, and unhelpful, or to indulge their attendants, use the shepherd for a show of witty mockery. Direct bribery is out of the question in the absence of secrecy, and it is also dangerous, since the corruptibility of officials grows less certain as the hierarchy is ascended.

Where he cannot reach or influence a high State official, the shepherd turns to his patron or, if he is a man without influence, to the patron of a more powerful kinsman. The patron may be a man of any profession with political influence in Jannina, a doctor, engineer, or merchant; but most frequently he is a lawyer. The lawyer in Greek rural society is not only the man who gives legal advice and attends a client in court, but he also acts as an intermediary between the peasant or shepherd and the State authorities. He acts in the general role of a professional 'fixer'.

Some of the difficulties which arise between the State and the Sarakatsan community have their origin in the necessarily general character of government legislation. Perhaps it is decided to protect the nation's forests. A law is passed which forbids the grazing of goats in forested areas. Incorporated within the general law are a number of conditional clauses relating to the definition of various kinds of forest, the priority for their protection, and the question of hardship to pastoralists which may lead to a relaxation of the restrictions in certain circumstances and in certain categories of forest. But the law-making assembly cannot legislate for all possible local contingencies. The administration and interpretation of the law lie in the hands of the public servants.

However, within the public service there exists a certain inertia and reluctance to delegate power. A senior official defines the unequivocal superiority of his status in the hierarchy by forcing his junior officers to refer to himself every case which involves the initiative of judgment and decision. In this manner he attaches junior officials to his own will since they cannot move without his approval, and he enhances his prestige because he is seen to be indispensable. At the same time, he secures his power and nourishes his self-regard. But the convergence of so many cases awaiting decision upon a limited number of senior officials in Jannina and Athens who cannot personally know the detailed circumstances of a case except through the exiguous details set out on printed forms, creates interminable delays and inhibits the equitable administration of government laws and regulations. In the Epirus, where many villagers and shepherds live on the margin of bare subsistence, these limitations of administration might prove disastrous for many families, were they not able to put their affairs into the hands of a lawyer or some other patron. For if, in the example we have chosen, a man cannot graze his goats in the one area where he has the right to do this, he must sell the animals which provide him with his living. The lawyer is able to bring a case to the direct notice of a senior official, to frame it to the best advantage; and sometimes, if he has considerable influence, to gain concessions for his client which are not strictly within the relevant law's terms of reference.

The significance of the lawyer's position is his ability to face in two directions. Because of the prestige and status of a successful lawyer in Greek society he may be able in a provincial town to number amongst his friends, judges, army officers, doctors, the Nomarch, and other senior officials of the Government bureaucracy. With these men he sits and drinks at the tables of the town's more fashionable coffee-shops and in the lounge of the best hotel. As a member of this professional élite he is able to recommend the affairs of his clients to the attention of various friends who may be able to help. They give this help because of their friendship for the lawyer; they are relatively indifferent to the worth of the client and the justice of his case. In return, a lawyer is able during local and national elections to promise the political support of his clients. He also assists his friends by legal advice in their own affairs and in the affairs of their kinsmen many of whom, often, are themselves villagers.

The Sarakatsani because of their many political difficulties and disabilities are critical assessors of the personal abilities of different lawyers. The profession is over-crowded and there is a wide range of choice. It is essential for the Sarakatsanos that his lawyer has influential affiliations with the leading political parties. It is not fortuitous that the Jannina lawyer with the largest Sarakatsan following in 1955 happened to be the secretary of the Epirus branch of the Government party. But the secretary to the Liberal party also has many clients. Although he supports an opposition party, Government servants do not lightly refuse his requests for they are anxious to avoid questions and 'revelations' in Parliament, and to secure some form of reinsurance against the day when the Government changes.

In general, it is to the advantage of both the lawyer and the Sarakatsan family head to make their association a personal relationship with diffuse mutual obligations. The lawyer becomes obliged to act as a general protector of the shepherd in all his affairs, the shepherd as a good client must show esteem and respect and give his patron the political support on which his power depends. It is not unusual for lawyers to become the godparents of their clients' children. Clients, whether or not they possess ties of spiritual kinship, cultivate the goodwill of their lawyer by periodic gifts of cheese and butter, and sometimes at Easter a lamb is presented. The nearer the relation between a Sarakatsanos and his lawyer approaches that of a patron and client friendship the more nominal the professional charges of the lawyer for legal services become. But in the nature of things it is easier for the leader of a substantial cooperating 'company' to establish an enduring friendship with his lawyer and to persuade him to win important concessions. He has more followers and more votes to offer. The lawyer does not lose prestige by attending to the affairs of simple men. This is his professional duty, and the more clients who throng his office and call out greetings to him as he walks along the street, the more political power he has, the more friends amongst the body of the provincial *élite*, and the more social prestige.

It would be tedious to present in detail examples of the many successful interventions by lawyer patrons. An over-zealous policeman in one village who made a speciality of arresting Sarakatsani for alleged disturbances of the peace was removed by the influence of a lawyer patron to a post in Mitylene. Another instance is the abbreviation of the military service of Christos Balatsos, an only son, whose family was handicapped by poverty and a father disabled by pleurisy. In this case the lawyer was a friend of the chairman of the appeal committee.

In the many court cases in which Sarakatsani figure the lawyers play a more strictly professional role. But there may still be scope on occasion for informal action, especially in civil suits which are heard before the bench without a jury. In a case concerning a disputed right of protected lease which threatened a Sarakatsanos with the loss of his winter pasture, the man in desperation asked his lawyer to approach the judge with a gift of 25. The lawyer took the money and the case was won. Without exception, villagers and shepherds assumed that at least half this money found its way into the 'judge's pocket. Villagers and shepherds have a simple faith that anybody, if he is approached in the right way and with the right sum, may be bought. In fact, there is no evidence that judges may be bribed. It may happen rarely. It probably happens more often that a lawyer friend is able to mention in conversation to a judge some aspect of a case which comes before him. And it certainly happens frequently that Sarakatsani put money into the hands of their lawyers which they believe will be used to bribe a judge or a senior Government official, but which remains, in fact, in the lawyer's pocket.

Yet there is no doubt about the genuine assistance the lawyer gives to the shepherd in his critical fight to retain his rights of winter grazing. For instance, in the example already mentioned in chapter four, a considerable 'company' of families that winter their sheep in Thesprotia were able to counter the refusal of the villagers to rent them grazing land by presenting their case, through the influence of two powerful lawyer patrons, directly to the Governor-General

of the Epirus. The lawyers pleaded that humanly and politically it was impossible to allow eighty men, women, and children, and two thousand sheep, to walk the roads. As individuals moving in the same social *élite*, they were able to present an argument immediately suggesting that the Governor-General's reputation for honour, and his political interests, were in danger.

The Member of Parliament for a provincial district plays in Athens a role very similar to that of the lawyer in the provincial centre. More members of the Greek Parliament belong to the legal profession than to any other. It is partly by possessing many clients, and many friends with clients, that a man is successful in national elections.

Since decisions of importance are rarely made by junior officials it frequently happens that a man must take action in Athens if he is to find a favourable solution to his problems. The friend or client of a Member may ask him to use his influence in the office of the Ministry which is handling his case. When the Member visits his constituency his political friends and clients of all social standings come to wait on him in his office, or to drink with him in the coffee-shops. On these occasions he carries a notebook in which he writes down the details of the favours he is asked to arrange.

We see that the Sarakatsanos in facing the hierarchy of Government confronts persons of higher social status who share with him no bond of kinship or community. As a rule only nationality and common humanity link them together. In Greek society this is not an adequate basis for the acceptance of social obligations other than the common duty to defend the nation against its external enemies. The indifference or hostility of very junior officials may be bought off. It is a simple *ad hoc* commercial transaction between persons almost entirely isolated from one another in terms of social relations or morality. But the indifference of senior officials cannot be directly countered with bribes, nor is it easy because of the social distance which separates them for a shepherd to approach successfully a senior official. These circumstances are also related to the public arrangement of business by senior Government servants and the need to assert their status and maintain their prestige before their colleagues and immediate subordinates.

The system of lawyer patronage, which is an extension of the more strictly legal practice of the lawyer, makes it possible for the affairs of villagers and shepherds to receive attention at that level of the administrative hierarchy where decision and execution are possible. A shepherd and a senior official are not directly linked to each other by social obligation or morality. A Government servant sees no reason why he should assist some illiterate shepherd and many reasons why he should not, such as loss of prestige before his professional colleagues. But the lawyer, as the intermediary who stands between them, is related by obligations of patronage to the first, and the duties of friendship to the second. In this manner the shepherd, because he is useful and necessary to his patron through the power and prestige which his political allegiance and social attentions confer on him, is never entirely powerless to resist those administrative actions of Government which threaten his way of life. The system of patronage introduces a flexibility into administrative machinery whose workings are very often directed by persons remote from the people whose fortunes they are affecting.

NOTES

1 I am not considering here the many cases of animal trespass which are heard in local agricultural courts.

CONCLUSION

It is evident that the form and function of patronage connexions are immediately related to the moral solidarity and isolation of the family, and to the reciprocal hostility and distrust that exist between families unrelated by kinship or marriage. In general, there are few circumstances where his own wishes, or public opinion, allow a Sarakatsanos to honour an obligation outside the family at the expense of an obligation within it. Moreover, with the assistance of some kinsmen or affines the economy of each family is generally self-sufficient, and working cooperation between unrelated men is seldom necessary or, indeed, practicable. Families, within the community, compete for social prestige in terms of values which underline the particularist obligations to the family honour. A man's work, affections, and moral obligations are almost exclusively contained within the one small group. The commitment of energy, physical resources, or deep affection to an unrelated person is a kind of betrayal. For these reasons men do not associate, even within the community, on the basis of any universal principle of fair dealing. Nepotism is an obligation not a moral fault; and honour is opposed to the canon of honesty.

Inhibitions against self-seeking conduct are yet more tenuous in the relations of men who do not share the common bonds of community. The Sarakatsanos expects to be exploited by the merchant and ignored by the government official. The bureaucrat or merchant not only stands outside the local community, he is divided from the villager or shepherd by his status as a member of the urban middle class. The shepherd is aware of the ill-concealed contempt of the 'civilized man' for country people and their ways; he knows of the official's meagre and insufficient salary, and something of his competitive struggle to win prestige symbols (houses, clothes, cars, radios) which validate the nuances of family status within this urban middle class. He does not believe in the existence of any ethic of professional bureaucratic service to the community. 'They are all "eaters"', he says in sweeping condemnation. It is thought that few officials will exert themselves over the affairs of a man of lower social status unless he is offered some inducement. And generally it is believed that concessions and facilities are seldom to be won on a broad front for the whole community but only as exceptional dispensations to favoured families. In these circumstances men consider it useless to conduct their business with the State on the ground of their general rights as citizens.

As I have already said, from his side a Government official sees no reason why he should assist some illiterate shepherd or villagers and many reasons why he should not, such as loss of prestige before his professional colleagues. Like the villager or shepherd he has the same primary and categorical obligation towards his own family and its status. He also owes a loyalty to his service and his colleagues; but this is shown by marking the distance between those who rule and those who are ruled, by the display of arrogance, not service.

There are other, less personal, reasons for the distrust between the bureaucrat and the villager or shepherd. One half of Greece is a society of small village communities dependent on agriculture or pastoralism. To administer and physically control these many discrete communities, and the small towns which serve them, the central Government in Athens has erected a complex and costly bureaucratic organization which links, in the formal sense, the simple village community to the central body which governs and legislates for the nation. This is not a structure which has developed even in part from the villages themselves; it is an organization which has been imposed from above by the Government. Moreover, Greece is not, by European standards, a rich country. For the greater part of her national history taxation has been almost wholly absorbed in paying for the luxury of maintaining the panoply of a modern state with its full quota of Ministries and portfolios and in supporting substantial armed forces. Under these conditions, the State and its agencies must always appear to the villager or shepherd as a body from which he is excluded, something threatening and hostile, which takes away from the family and returns nothing. It stands, therefore, in opposition to the nation, the community of Hellensim for which every Greek feels a deep and natural devotion.

Each family in a village, or in a shepherd community, therefore attempts to establish an exclusive and particular relationship with persons in power. As we have seen, decision or initiative is seldom possible at the lower levels of the Government service because of the reluctance of an official to delegate power. To reach that level at which his affairs can be effectively dealt with, he tries to discover a patron, generally a lawyer, who in return for a man's political allegiance, places his case before a friend in the right place. The lawyer, or other patron, bridges the gulf of hostility and indifference created by the absence of relationship and the difference in status. And he introduces some flexibility into the rigid and uncomprehending administration of village life by a centralized bureaucracy.

In effect, patronage converts impersonal and ephemeral connexions into permanent and personal relationships; for in Greek society it is, generally, only in established personal relationships, of which the archetypal forms are found in the family, that any considerable element of moral obligation exists. The initial motive is utilitarian, protection and assistance on the side of the client, political power and social prestige on the part of the patron. But when such a relationship endures for any length of time it takes on a strong moral quality. The patron feels obliged to assist and take a general interest in all the client's affairs, and in doing so he is able both to sense his superiority and approve his own compassionate generosity. The client is conscious of a duty to support his patron politically without undue concern about his protec-

tor's party allegiance, and to give free expression to his feelings of gratitude and indebtedness.

The role of patron is to give benefits; that of the client is to honour the patron by accepting dependence. In a society where the concept of honour is intimately connected with notions of individual strength and prepotence, to abdicate one's independence, even to a person of power who is not a member of the community, is an act of renunciation of some significance. The patron in accepting the dependence of his client, who thus admits, implicitly, the inferiority of his status, himself recognizes moral obligations towards the client. The dependence of the client draws attention to the power of his patron, while the protection of the patron suggests that the client is a man of some standing and respectability in his own community. The first consideration protects the patron from the accusation of weakness or foolishness which he would otherwise face if he casually assisted a man of lower status with whom he had no particular relations of kinship, friendship, or patronage: the second represents for the client honourable grounds for the admission of an inferior status which in other circumstances would betray the honour of his community and his own manliness. The social reputations of the two men are now linked. If a patron cannot effectively protect his clients his prestige is diminished; and in his own community the client, too, suffers for the incapacity of his patron, since the potential of his strength from this source is seen to be less than was supposed. But when the protection is effective, both patron and client gain prestige from the relationship. The colleagues of the patron envy him the power which his control of a body of clients assures for him; other families in the client's community envy him his cleverness in winning powerful patrons. But the Sarakatsan client will not share with others the vicarious influence which patronage brings him, unless they are kinsmen or affines. For he believes that if he shares his advantage, he loses it. And this is a further reason why relationships across the boundaries of the community with persons of influence are exclusive and particular connexions established by the individual family.

We see that while the organization of administration stretches down, as it were, from the central Government towards the village community but loses power and the ability to take decisions the farther it extends from its point of origin, the structure of the system of patronage, which is based on social relationships between clients seeking for a man with the ability and friendship connexions to protect them and a patron who accepts these duties in return for political allegiance, grows upwards and through lawyers, other persons of influence, and Members of Parliament, is linked to the legislative assembly. Thus the organization of government and the structure of patronage are parallel hierarchies related through ties of friendship. The shepherd or villager is excluded from the Government hierarchy, but through the structure of patronage he may be able vicariously to submit his case before a senior official in the public service.

Patronage is the means through which the local community is linked to the wider national society. And it is significant that the group which seeks this connexion is the individual family and not the community. This is clearly the case amongst the Sarakatsani, but even villagers do not cooperate in seeking Government favour except where the interests of the whole village as such are attached. If the President of a village is able to help a village friend by his influence in the town, he does so in the role of friend or patron, not as President and leader of the village. And in personal affairs a villager or shepherd may often go directly to his patron[1] in the town. The importance of this is that the community is integrated piecemeal with the wider society along lines of personal obligation and not through membership of a large corporate group capable of attempting an infinitely stronger resistance to the authority of the State.

More generally, patronage links persons of different social status introducing into their social relations a common area of shared values which would otherwise not exist. In the context of the Zagori village it links the shepherds to the more important villagers, enabling the former

to come to terms with the villagers' hostile attitude and the latter to mobilize the voting power of the shepherds in their own support. Since different shepherd families support different village personalities, it ensures that the latter continue to hold office and power even in villages where shepherds considerably outnumber villagers on the electoral roll.

Similarly, the patron-client relation between the lawyer and the villager or shepherd relates members of local village and shepherd communities to the professional classes in the small towns and larger provincial centres. It gives political power and prestige to the patron. It brings prestige to the client also but above all it means that he is never entirely helpless in the face of the impersonal indifference of Government action which threatens the precarious balance of his economy. Patronage relations produce a certain equity in the distribution of facilities and privileges and place some check on the victimizing of individuals. It achieves this by relating the universal franchise to the personal, social, and political aspiration of individuals competing for power and honour; or to put it more briefly, by relating natural rights to personal prestige.

Finally, the bond of debt and the qualified patronage of the merchant and the town shopkeeper brings the shepherd into a permanent association with some of the leaders of town commerce. It provides the merchant with an assured source for his raw material and the shopkeeper with a stable clientele. It gives the shepherd vicarious access to the metropolitan market and to the credit facilities of the national banking system. Without these facilities it is fair to say that he could not continue to lead his traditional way of life.

NOTES

1 In the case of a villager the 'protector' is very often a kinsman. See Ernestine Friedl, 'The Role of Kinship in the Transmission of National Culture to Rural Villages in Mainland Greece', *American Anthropologist*, 1959, vol. lxi, pp. 30-38.

THE LEGITIMACY OF A CACIQUE
PAUL FRIEDRICH

THE IDEA OF LEGITIMACY has fascinated and puzzled the political scientist just as the phenomenon of the *cacique* has often characterized Mexican political life; an integrated understanding of the idea and of the phenomenon can only be achieved by coordinating the sister disciplines of political theory and political ethnography. By the former I refer primarily to the insights and questions in the corpus of ideas on politics and government that leads from Easton and Weber back to Hobbes and to Aristotle. By political ethnography I refer to the descriptive analysis, both historical and structural, of such phenomena as leaders, factionalism, and political ritual and ideology, within the relatively circumscribed arena of the village, the local lineage, or the tribe. The mutual relevance of the sister disciplines is clear: political theory is relevant to political ethnography insofar as its insights and discriminations help illuminate new field data, and the reverse is true insofar as the ethnography suggests interesting qualifications or raises novel conceptual questions. The present article attempts to accomplish both these goals of relevance by interrelating the complex notion of legitimacy (one of the cornerstones of political theory), to the life history and role description of one type of local leader: the Mexican agrarian cacique.

LEGITIMACY THEORY

Let us agree to refer to control over men and resources as "power," and to the patterns by which men cooperate and compete for such power as "politics." Politics is largely public (as contrasted with relations within family and household) and is concerned with the capacity for making decisions that will affect the community.

Political power may be differentiated in terms of its functions. At one extreme, simple or naked power is based on little more than economic coercion or physical violence, as when a cacique contrives the assassination of a rival. Contrasting with such naked force is the power based on a partly rational or reasoned or at least explicit appeal to the values or principles of a community, and in particular to the political (and governmental and legal) values which might be called its "political culture." In the degree to which the villagers think, believe, or feel

that a leader's rule is right, and that he is acting on the basis of their ideal political culture, we may speak of "legitimacy." Legitimate rule is validated by a persuasive and convincing relation to the political tradition, and to the ideals and positive norms of the political culture.

Of such legitimacy there is variation along at least two significant dimensions: (1) the logicality of the relation between power and norm, and (2) the acceptability or popularity of the norms themselves. At one extreme, the actions of a leader may be related to the norms and values in a way that is susceptible of reasonable, logical, and convincing elaboration and justification (C. Friedrich, 1963, p. 216); granted primogeniture and patrilineal succession, Prince Harry was the legitimate heir to Henry IV. On the other hand, power may be rationalized in a way that is weak, ambiguous, or illogical, or is based on unpopular or intolerable premises. Many and perhaps most leaders stand somewhere between the various extreme types of legitimacy.

The revolutionary caciques of Mexican agrarian revolt were genuinely legitimate in that some of their actions were logically related to accepted values and goals: many peasants saw them as the agents of needed reform and the protectors of their communities against the predations of landlords. Yet their anti-clericalism was partly alien, and their often autocratic rule ran counter both to their claims of altruism and to the traditional norms of government in many villages. Such leaders sought to legitimize their rule, and this process of legitimation was often more apparent than their state of imperfect and impermanent legitimacy. Much essentially scholastic debate could be obviated if legitimacy were thought of as a matter of process and flux rather than a static thing with fixed and proper attributes.

The analysis in the following paragraphs concerns some of the component or constituent notions that underlie the usage of "legitimacy" and related terms and does not purport to set forth the "one and only" set of attributes of legitimate rule, nor the "one and only" set of meanings of legitimacy. I intend, rather to review briefly about a dozen of the widely cited criteria for legitimacy in order to provide a tentative conceptual scaffolding for a subsequent analysis that is highly empirical and concerned with the field data on one particular leader. The scaffolding draws on the following four levels of theory: (1) the traits of a cross-cultural sample, (2) the microsystemic analysis of single systems, (3) sociological "ideal types," and (4) some postulates of classical political theory. These sources yield a broad spectrum of notions that have proven relevant to the interpretation of ethnographic data on a cacique.

In the first place, statistically oriented, cross-cultural discussions of politics may cite relatively simple rules of legitimacy that have been found to be axiomatic in particular political cultures, and these simple rules may be adduced without any elaboration of the underlying premises or axioms that make up the cultural system; for example, election by majority, or birth into a royal lineage, or "performance"—as when an African king must make rain, or when agrarian caciques and other overseers of modernization legitimize their rule by citing "progress" improvements in the standard of living and the like. Because such traits in the surface structures of political cultures appear to be governed by a limitation of possibilities, in the sense that a small number recur independently all over the world, it is in fact fruitful to handle them statistically in terms of the cross-cultural models being developed by Murdock, Ember, and others. Moreover, trait lists of criteria that occur at least sporadically are invaluable because they suggest questions about what may be obscure or unknown in a particular situation and culture.

Of a different phenomenological order are the criteria for legitimacy that are worked out with reference to a more or less adequate analysis of the institutions, such as economics (e.g., premises about land use), or the social stratification, or the religion of one particular culture; above all, how do the criteria for legitimacy fit into the larger network of principles of politics, government, and law? Examples of the structural or microsystemic approach are the numerous analyses of the religious and legal bases of African despotism, which show that the values underlying legitimacy can be handled objectively if the analyst limits himself to verifiable inferences drawn from observed behavior and recorded discourse. The present article illustrates the microsystemic analysis of a case of problematical legitimacy in one political culture.

Legitimacy has also been treated in "free-flowing" discussions that use a personal but more or less global sample in order to infer or construct heuristically simplified and abstract types. For example, in Weber's scheme the basic contrast is between non-individually and individually based legitimacy. Individually based or "charismatic" legitimacy depends on extraordinary personal qualities, usually military or religious, which may be regularly rewarded within an established cultural system or in revolutionary or otherwise disorganized or rapidly changing situations. The second or "non-individual" legitimacy again subdivides into two kinds: (1) "traditional legitimacy" accrues to leaders to whom is ascribed a relatively fixed status by the mores and jural norms of a "patrimonial society," whereas (2) "rational legitimacy" may be achieved within the legal or quasi-legal framework of a bureaucracy or some other explicit structure of administration or government. Clearly, Weber's charismatic, traditional, and rational bases of legitimacy are neither logically coordinate nor entirely, mutually exclusive, but they effectively label and tentatively explicate three aspects of the phenomenon that loom large in world history—and, indeed, even in the data of the village discussed below.

Useful notions of legitimacy also have emerged from attempts to deduce prescriptive theories of the functions and ends of government. Thomas Hobbes, for example, developed a theory of natural law from psychological postulates in which "rational self-preservation" made necessary and right what he called "a fictitious corporation"—"covenants of the sword" and "fear of coercive power" naturally played an important role (Sabine, 1950, pp. 459-69). There are many interesting relations between Hobbes' ideas and the political behavior and the notions of legitimacy set forth in conversation and speeches by the autocratic but progressive caciques of agrarian villages in Mexico: the political importance of the dyadic personal relations that radiate out from any one individual would seem an ethnographic comment on "the atomistic nature of man"; the struggle to death, flight, or exile of opposed village factions often exemplifies Hobbes' "war for survival"; the revolutionary caciques, defending the peasant against the "priests, landlords, and other exploiters," and the middleman functions of their modern descendants are a Mexican variation of "the ruler as protector"; finally, the caciques' agency in expropriating and administering land under the agrarian laws and their attempts to simulate conformity to the Agrarian Code suggest the Hobbesian equation of the legal and the legitimate. Thus, although we may reject the old philosopher's strategy and personal motivation, his specific arguments do raise questions about the ethnography of legitimacy that a political ethnographer can avoid only at his intellectual peril.

Despite the indubitable value of the subtleties of legitimacy theory, the primary personal experience that motivates this study is the incontrovertible and literally prima facie ethnographic fact of a concern with legitimacy among the Mexican Indian peasants of the Pazacu valley. To some extent this concern was registered or marked by the veering of conversations in neighboring villages toward criticism of the autocratic rule in Durazno. To some extent it was registered by a plethora of labels for what might be called "the man in the cacial slot": *el elemento, el jefe del pueblo, el hombre fuerte, el principal, el meromero, el lider, el cacique*—each term expressive of a nuance or connotation in a speaker's attitude. Finally, the concern was indicated by the singularly strong contrast between the public care to avoid mentioning or naming a cacique as such and the extreme intensity with which his status ("cacique"), his behavior, and his power and legitimacy cropped up in private or household dialogue and in the whispered conversations of intrigue. In this singular dialectic between the public and the private, and the overt and the covert, the phenomena of *caciquismo* resembled witchcraft, at least in one Tarascan town.[1]

THE CACICAL STATUS

The word "cacique" (pronounced *kah-see-ke*) comes ultimately from the Arawak Indian language (Alegria, 1952) but is now used throughout the Spanish-speaking world, including Spain itself. Consonant with the size of this universe and the diversity of social conditions, the meaning of the word varies enormously—from the militaristic boss of a national state, to a conservative, upper-class, and paternalistic landlord, to the chief of a small band of South American hunters and gatherers, to the religious leader of a Zuni pueblo. But these and most other referents share at least several component or constituent meanings: strong individual power over a territorial group held together by some socioeconomic or cultural system. Moreover, most although certainly not all of the referents of "cacique" imply detachment or freedom from the normative, formal, and duly instituted system of government.

In Mexico the term and the phenomenon of cacique are centuries old, deeply and perhaps ineradicably built into the traditions and the way of life and the idioms of Mexican Spanish. With particular reference to Mexico, this article defines a cacique as a strong and autocratic leader in local and regional politics whose characteristically informal, personalistic, and often arbitrary rule is buttressed by a core of relatives, "fighters," and dependents, and is marked by the diagnostic threat and practice of violence. These caciques bridge, however, imperfectly, the gap between peasant villagers and the law, politics, and government of the state and nation, and are therefore varieties of the so-called "political middleman" (Wolf, 1956).

The patterns of cacical recruitment and succession in rural Mexico vary greatly. Although stereotypically there is one sole cacique, one also finds two main alternatives: (1) two or three co-caciques, who may be functionally differentiated (for example, one for local leadership, one for outside office and contacts, and one to manage the violence of the "fighters"), and (2) one dominant cacique and his second-in-command and heir apparent, who is usually a cousin, a brother, or (like Pedro) a nephew. In other words, succession to the status of cacique normally transpires through a "political family" of persons who are loosely related by marriage and bilateral descent. While a line of caciques or the members of a cacical family often share the same patronymic, they may also be linked to each other primarily through women—as in the special case of the descendants of the twelve daughters of Pedro's great-grandfather. In any case, the "family" encapsulates a smaller group of five to fifteen politically active, ambitious, or committed men who share the same last name either as patronymic or as matronymic, or who are closely related by marriage (e.g., brothers-in-law), or by ritual coparenthood of baptism (*el compadrazgo de bautismo*). From within this core group the most able, ambitious, and powerful man will be selected by consensus and other informal means to replace a dead cacique. In many caciazgos the cacical "family" will split about every decade or two and the resulting new faction (*partido, banda, grupo*) will either replace an expelled or debilitated one or hazard its luck as a "third party." The above are mainly descriptive generalizations and do not correspond so much to explicit norms as to pragmatic rules (Bailey, 1966, p. 212). The ethnography of cacical success in rural Mexico remains unknown, and a fascinating and fruitful topic for some future field worker with a flair for travel and rapid discovery procedures.

In Mexico the cacique is a historically egregious phenomenon and is widely regarded as a serious economic and legal problem. The term and its associated concept contrast with several other term-concepts of approximately equal political significance: (1) *luchador* or *pistolero*, the favorable and pejorative epithets, respectively, for the armed fighters and bodyguards that typically protect the cacique; (2) *lider*, a relatively neutral term for a leader; (3) *representante (del pueblo)*, the laudatory expression for a man who more or less genuinely represents his community, and also for the elected or informally agreed-upon official who represents the village at the municipal level (there is great variation in the usage of this term in Michoacan) (4) *caudillo*, the label for political bosses and quasimilitary dictators at the state, provincial, and national levels; and, finally, (5) *jefe*, with various modifiers, is used for the heads of political units from the family, the household, the faction, the *barrio*, the village, the province, the state, the party, and also for the *jefe maximo*—the president of the Mexican nation.

Of the above and other types of political status I am primarily concerned with a variety of cacique that arose during the Mexican Revolution. They are called "agrarian" because they have been instrumental in carrying out local land reform (usually by expropriating landlords or small farmers) and in establishing and maintaining the communalistic *ejidos*. I have also taken some account of the agitators and charismatic figures who initiate reform, but my main concern is with the caciques of the last twenty years who have been operating as peasant leaders, party men, and part-time bureaucrats in areas where agrarian reform and ejidos have become familiar and unavoidable facts of life.

Agrarian caciques are informally recognized by the peasants and by the government, possess local power, and use violence consistently. These quintessentially political leaders may also have de facto rights to make decisions for their villagers and vague obligations to maintain "control," to observe agrarian legislation, and to protect their citizens against outside "exploiters"—particularly priests and credit institutions such as the national bank and usurous money lenders. On the other hand, compared to other leaders with a similar degree of great power, it is striking how little the cacique is hedged about with explicit and generally accepted rights and obligations. The informality and implicitness and covertness of the cacique's role is congruous with his freedom of action and the enormous individual and idiosyncratic variation. Precisely this personal freedom from the legal and governmental system implies a lack of support by that system, and throws into sharp relief the question of the legitimacy of the cacique himself; while agrarian caciques do not fully illustrate the possibility that "there may be political conditions under which legitimacy is not possible" (C. Friedrich, 1963, p. 239), they do closely enough approximate that possibility to raise interesting and perhaps novel questions.

ETHNOLOGICAL BACKGROUND

The political ethnographer seeks to relate the range of variation in political culture to the ideas and methods of the social sciences, particularly of political science. It follows that his explicitness about his point of view should be matched by a reasonably detailed sketch or characterization of the behavioral, historical, and cultural context—of the relevant ethnographic facts and patterns without which his "bit of data" and his particular analysis cannot be evaluated by the reader.

The Tarascans are a population of some 70,000 Indian peasants who dwell in 66 villages high in the cool, green mountains of the state of Michoacan in southwestern Mexico. The Tarascan language is still exclusively spoken in many communities, although today there is 50 to 100 per cent bilingualism in a large minority, and some, such as the one to be discussed, are definitely shifting to Spanish (West, 1946, pp. 18-19). The Tarascan diet, although based on the indigenous maize, beans, chili, and squash, is supplemented by a large number of introduced or imported foods (such as beef and oranges); the men wear the familiar combination of straw sombreros with colored tassel, *huarache* sandals, colored woolen serapes, and white manta or blue denim. The areal economy is extremely diversified, with a complicated system of village specialization, internal markets, and many exports to the outside world—notably pottery, musical instruments, and fish. Most of the Indians live in immediate or moderately expanded families within compact villages, usually of a grid pattern around a central plaza. The "real political constitutions" vary from religiously conservative gerontocracies to democratic and representative government by informal consensus (e.g., San José), to left-wing cacicazgos in Tanaquillo and the village to be discussed below. Much time and energy is required by the ritual and organization of the annual fiesta cycle of the Tarascan variety of folk Catholicism.

On the north-central edge of the Tarascan sierra is located the Pazacu region, in an environment that has always been distinctive. First, a huge, marshy lake provided most of the inhabitants with their livelihood, but in the 1890s this was drained by Spanish entrepreneurs (backed by the Diaz dictatorship), and converted into an extraordinarily productive maize bowl; the struggle for these fertile acres has been the main theme of politics ever since. The southern part of the Pazacu region contains the mestizo *municipio* or county seat (its growth since 1940 from a population of 4,000 to more than 25,000 has created unusual pressures toward changing the political structure of the municipio and its constituent villages, pressures which the agrarian caciques have often failed to resist).

To the east of the county seat lie three large Tarascan villages, technically "agrarian communities" and *tenencias*. All three engage almost exclusively in using mattocks and ox-drawn plows to cultivate maize, largely as a cash crop. All are organized as *ejidos*, the land being administered and harvested by the community while its usufruct is enjoyed inalienably by the ejidal families, who plow, seed, and cultivate their distinct plots. Two of the villages have a considerable amount of land that is owned on a relatively private, individualistic basis.[2]

One of the three villages—for which the pseudonym of *Durazno* will be used—has a population of about 1,500 divided into about 300 families, all but 60 of which work an ejido plot of five acres, or some private land, or both. The typical family income is over 2,000 pesos, plus maize for subsistence. On the other hand, about a third of the *ejidatarios* are heavily indebted to village moneylenders and corn-buyers, and about thirty ejido families receive only their yearly allotment of maize at harvest time. Since the 1930s the material life of the village has been markedly altered by the introduction of limited electrification, of pumped water, of corn mills, and of the paved east-west highway. By 1955 about 54 children were studying in schools and colleges in the state and national capitals, and about thirty ex-villagers were working as teachers, engineers, and technicians in various parts of Mexico.

Like its economy, village social and religious organization also reflects a peculiar mingling of twentieth-century innovations and the "indigenous" synthesis of Mexican Indian and Spanish Colonial elements. Durazno was felt to be Indian on the grounds of race and local custom, but about 10 per cent of the adults are married to outsiders. Children are brought up mainly by their parents and other close relatives, but the compulsory four years of primary school has

made over half the population functionally literate, and another (overlapping) half incapable of speaking Tarascan. During adolescence marriage is initiated by a romantic courtship followed by elopement or by bride-capture. Most young couples eventually set up a new household, but by one mechanism or another the majority of villagers live in somewhat expanded families or household groups, which include at least two adult men and women: a father and his married son, two married brothers, and the like; in addition, de facto matrilocal units arise for special reasons. Descent is reckoned bilaterally.

Political alliances and groups are heavily influenced by personal ties. Loyalty is virtually axiomatic between brothers and uterine half-brothers, but the bond between cousins, uncles, and nephews varies enormously. The average man has what might be called a "political kindred" of ten to twenty or more relatives by blood and marriage who will support him to some extent. The familiar and informal tie of "intimate friendship" and the highly institutionalized and etiquette-laden bond of ritual co-parenthood account for an additional five to seven or more fairly close associates on whom a man can depend for economic and political support. In my opinion, the vitality of these dyadic relationships has been quickened by the factionalism and blood vengeance of the last forty years (P. Friedrich, 1966a).

Minor personal conflicts and violence that is largely political are handled by informal arbitration within the village, but some delinquents are brought to the county seat, especially in cases of theft of livestock or sexual offenses. Local government is divided between two arms, each with its own set of officers: (1) the ejidal administration, and (2) the civil government, which is concerned with taxation, keeping the peace, and the like. Finally, although the priest is admitted only once a month, and although anti-clericalism has weakened or eliminated numerous fiestas (P. Friedrich, 1966b), there is a cycle of communal rituals, secural and religious. The Christmas season and the fiesta to the patron saint ("Our Father Jesus") are enthusiastically celebrated.

In sum, Durazno is a Tarascan community that, largely because of *agrarista* politics, has moved about halfway to a superficially mestizo way of life. Economically, socially, religiously, and politically, however, an extraordinary degree of local autonomy persists. Village autonomy is one of the most deeply held values in Tarascan culture (Aguirre Beltran, 1953, p.

179), and casts an aura of legitimacy around the mediating and middleman functions of the cacique.

In 1955 Pedro Caso looked and could play his part of a wealthy, powerful cacique from an agrarian Indian village. Avoiding mestizo suits and the black felt hat, he dressed more like a peasant on holidays: cheap pointed shoes, pressed khaki trousers, clean white shirt, and a Michoacan sombrero with its small colored tassel. When in the county seat he usually carried a .45 pistol over his right hip, hidden by the bottom of his athletic jacket. He had largely forgotten to speak Tarascan, but usually understood obscene jokes, could get the drift of extended discourse, and made quite a point of explaining the etymology of Tarascan place names to mestizo politicians. Of medium stature, agile, swarthy, and with flashing dark brown eyes, he was felt by both villagers and outsiders to appear "very Indian, because of the skin, and the face."

Pedro was born out of wedlock in 1911 to a niece of Durazno's leading agrarian agitator. Pedro's father, a young, landless Tarascan, was strongly affected by Emiliano Zapata's "Plan of Ayala" (1911), early joined one of the agrarian armies, and was killed in action four years later. Much of Pedro's childhood, which coincided with the Mexican Revolution (1911-20), was spent on the sugar plantations of the southern coast of Michoacan, where his mother, who "had very few plumes," accompanied her younger brother and made tortillas for the laborers. Because of the vicissitudes and economic insecurity of the times she set up a joint matrilocal household with her mother, her brother, and several sisters and female cousins and their children. By this time Durazno and the two neighboring Tarascan communities had established local committees to litigate for the last lands. In 1919, Pedro's great-uncle, the agrarian agitator, was assassinated by agents of the Pazacu valley landlords, riddled with bullets while he slept under a tree. This great-uncle, a lawyer and enlightened liberal, has remained for Pedro a vague ideal which he could invoke, but whom he could never realistically hope to equal.

One year later, another of Pedro's uncles, named Primo Tapia, returned from the United States, where he had been living as a migrant laborer and anarchist agitator. Assisted by six cousins and other relatives and friends, he soon integrated the several agrarian movements in the valley, and set up strong local militias. Pedro, the favored nephew, carried messages by night and performed minor services, such as holding his uncle's stirrup when the latter was mounting. For four years he witnessed the intermittent violence of the agrarian struggle, including the assassination (with ox goads) of the second-most "valiant fighter" and the epic battle (with his mother at the forefront) for the first fruits of the newly won ejido lands. From 1925 to 1928 he studied in an agriculture school and participated in a Communist cell in the state capital. Then, for a decade, he taught primary school in various parts of Michoacan, including the southern "hot country," while also learning about state politics as the assistant of one of his mother's cousins—Pablo Perez, by then a successful orator and party strongman in the state capital. To paraphrase Eric Wolf (1960, pp. 239, 244), Pedro acquired some of the etiquette of mestizo communication and became sure of foot along the often shadowy or hidden passageways of state politics.

In 1938 Pedro returned to a village rent by internecine strife between two leaders, both of them his uncles: one was Pablo Perez de las Casas, and the other was his mother's brother, whom he often even addressed as father; the latter eventually achieved a precarious dominance in Durazno, largely because of the support of five nephews, including Pedro, who had been reared under him in the joint household mentioned above. Pedro, more agile and energetic than most peasants, began to till ever-larger tracts of land. He also served as president of the important Regional Committee, usually referred to as the Durazno Committee, and became full-fledged in the violence of Pazacu county—"the slaughterhouse (el rastro) of Michoacan." Like his relatives, Pedro was known as "a killer." In 1951 he was "elected" alternate to one of the two state senators, an important politician from a liberal family who has since become state governor. By the time of my field work (1955-56), Pedro was widely known to regional leaders, was serving as county treasurer, and had emerged as the second "principal element" in Durazno. In the scheme of Brandenburg (1964, p. 158), Pedro, as an occasional party man, municipal official, and local cacique elect, stood on the tenth of the twelve rungs in the ladder of political prestige.

Petro played many roles in his village, particularly in its economy. He had learned agricultural skills as a boy and had spent some thirteen years working the soil like a peasant, but during the early 1950s, partly because of a back injury, he shifted gradually to illegal share-cropping (i.e., renting ejido plots from men too lazy or drunk to cultivate them), to usurous moneylending, and to buying standing maize before the harvest (his second wife eventually became one of the village's four outstanding moneylenders and maize-buyers). As the appointed local representative of the national Ejido Bank and as the accomplice of the local capitalists, Pedro was instrumental in excluding most outside credit, which in a sense could be interpreted as protecting the community against the fixed rates of interest and the inexorability of collection on loans made by "outside exploiters." By 1956 his total income from these capitalistic enterprises, from his 40-odd acres (owned, rented, and ejidal), and from his official jobs, probably totaled well over 50,000 pesos a year, making him the third-wealthiest person in the pueblo (his mother's brother was first and his mother was fifth). Nevertheless, his adobe house, though comparatively well-appointed inside (with concrete floor and a gas oven), did not look materially different from the others strung along the street. His main "luxury" was a scorn of tortillas and a subsistence mainly on dairy products and meat. Most of his surplus income went into the education of his seven children in schools in the state and national capitals, and into outside political investments in the state chapter of the Masons, and the doffers of the huge national Party of Institutional Revolution (PRI), which is financed primarily by 3 to 5 per cent of its membership, including—in Scott's terminology—"the ambitious officers of farm groups" (1959, p. 154).

Pedro's political, legal, and governmental functions were also diverse. He spoke relatively well in public but, like his uncle, did so only on rare occasions, such as the visit of a government inspector or during a crisis of political support. His specialty was relating the provisions of the national agrarian legislation, particularly about twenty key sections of the *Codigo Agrario*, to the partly illegal and politically muddied realities of the local ejido. As covert arbiter, Pedro—within his home—settled minor squabbles, judged cases of violence that were often technically criminal under law, and acted as matchmaker after elopement and bride-capture (he was one of the two men in Durazno who knew by heart the lengthy Tarascan speech requesting reconciliation). In this ritually demanding jural role, his main objectives were to settle and judge in accordance with local mores,

to distribute compensations and punishments over as wide a field as possible, and to protect his fellow villagers from prosecution under state and federal law—with the attendant court expenses, fines, and jail sentences. The extreme informality and usual effectiveness of his arbitration certainly reduced public questioning of his legitimacy, although it came nowhere close to eliminating it.

His personal relations were divergent but congruent with his political activities. He had only one "intimate friend" and only one "real" and publicly acknowledged ritual co-parent or *compadre* (aside from the main usuress's son, who played both roles). Otherwise, Pedro was the compadre of many poor or immigrant peasants, who treated him as a patron. His active and natural kinship was limited to two half-brothers, a first cousin, and his mother's brother, although two of these linked him indirectly to a much larger number of villagers. Pedro's pattern of personal relations was matched by those of his mother's brother, and by those of the two caciques of the fallen faction, all of whom were also isolated within the pueblo, while having many proclaimed "friends" and politically useful compadres in many other parts of the state. Pedro's dearth of close ties was taken as proof of his "arrogance" and alienation vis-à-vis fellow villagers.

Pedro's marital and sexual history resembled those of the other caciques in my limited sample. He had been married twice, both his wives were mestiza outsiders, and both weddings were secular; for personal and political reasons, he eschewed the expense and traditional dances of the ecclesiastical and folk religious wedding, which is certainly the major ritual of passage in Durazno. Otherwise, his first wife was several years his senior, and about 1935 became deranged by home life (i.e., coexistence in the extended household), and ran off to Mexico City. The second wife, also somewhat older, had had children by a previous marriage and, with advancing age and obesity, came to be resented and disliked by Pedro. Pedro had numerous and sometimes ostentatious affairs with wives and widows in Durazno,, and with other women (such as his Pazacu secretary). In quite Mexican fashion, his sexual history was felt by the villagers to be connected with his political ambition, and both were taken to demonstrate his "egoism."

THE FACTIONAL CONTEXT

"The faction is the political group *par excellence* within the pueblo, and even in the region and state it is the factions within the formally instituted parties . . . that provide the framework (for) the power struggle. Unlike the higher levels, however, the faction within Durazno is a primary, face-to-face group, governed by informal discussion, mutual observation, and long-standing, many-sided familiarity" (P. Friedrich, 1965a, p. 198). At least since the 1880s the number of factions in Durazno has always been two, except for a year of temporary cohesion following the agrarian revolt (1925-26), and a few months of near unity after the expulsion of the Rocas (1936-37), and two short intervals with "third parties" (1945 and 1952-54). For over thirty years the dominant faction has selected local officials, including those for the lucrative and prestigious ejido government. Factionalism in Durazno has been determined to an extraordinary degree by personal ambition and small-arms violence, has long been linked to the left-wing state politics of Lazaro Cardenas, and ranks with caciquismo itself as a political phenomenon of great theoretical interest.

The rules of the game are pragmatic and often implicit. The faction has an active core of five to ten men, a larger membership of twenty to thirty, and a still more numerous penumbra of inactive, indifferent, or even involuntary followers. The only persons a cacique can be said to represent are the second ring of about two dozen men, particularly its core, and many of the latter are his relatives. The patent contradiction between his "real" constituency as against his claim to speak for a "united community" raises in an acute form the question of his legitimacy. By the same token, a review of the factional background of Durazno reveals much about the legitimacy of its cacique.

Durazno factions have regrouped ten times in forty years. During the Mexican Revolution the village was divided between two factions that were diametrically opposed. One was led by two mestizo families and supported by a considerable minority of the wealthier or more conservative peasants; for obvious reasons, its members sided with the clergy and the intrusive Spanish landlords. The second faction, to which young Pedro and most of his relatives adhered, consisted for the most part of landless families and the relatively educated grandchildren of the venerated patriarch who had led the village in the 1870s. The leaders of both factions could and did legitimize their actions by highly explicit criteria of law and economics; for example, the traditional village lands had been alienated, but ownership by the Spaniards had been

legalized, and the lands themselves, though needed by the villagers for subsistence, also had been greatly improved by the Spaniards through drainage and cultivation. Such pros and cons were learned early by the boy Pedro. The first stage of agrarian factionalism terminated approximately in 1919 with the leading agitator's assassination, which, like so much of Durazno's violence, was connected with an impending gubernatorial struggle.

During the second stage of factionalism (1920-26) the agrarian committees were activated, enlarged, and joined to those of the neighboring villages under the inspired leadership of one of Pedro's uncles, Primo Tapia. This man had been a student of the Flores Magon brothers (Mexican anarchists and ideological precursors of the Mexican Revolution), and had agitated and organized for the "Wobblies" (Industrial Workers of the World) for several years in Nebraska and Colorado. He introduced an explicit if simple-minded anarcho-syndicalist ideology whereby his faction of "exploited Indians" was waging rightful battle against the "abbots, capitalists, Iberian exploiters," and so forth. By 1924-25 the exploited indigenes had won huge grants of land in accordance with the Agrarian Regulatory Law of 1922. Most of the "reactionaries" were killed, driven out, or persuaded to change their views. But in 1926, Primo Tapia, by then an important areal leader (k'er juRamiti), and accused of being a Communist, was captured by government agents and assassinated by direct order of the national president. Through subsequent years he continued to grow as a symbol of legitimate agrarian aspirations in Michoacan, and to be used by Pedro and other Caso relatives to legitimize the Durazno cacicazgo.

The victorious agrarian faction split in half. The "true revolutionaries" or "Reds," led by a Caso cousin of Tapia, were closely bound to the incipient state machine of Cardenas, and favored a perpetuation of the completely communalistic land use that had been instituted by Tapis (i.e., seeding, cultivation, and harvesting by brigades, and distribution of the harvest on the basis of need and days worked). Against them was pitted the new opposition faction led by a half dozen members of the large Roca political family (including a Roca de las Casas), and committed to breaking up the ejido into inalienable family plots and to not sharing any of the land with the mestizo families, most of them former peons of the landlords. In sum, the two new factions were still divided by substantive and more or less rational issues of policy and ideology—involving, in this case, questions of economic equity and the political autocracy of the Caso caciques. On the other hand, the contest now was between villagers and not against an outside enemy. The first two years of this third stage (1926-28) witnessed the unusual situation whereby the factional standoff resulted in a truly open election, with two ballots and different factions winning control of the civil and ejidal governments. Both kinship loyalty and radicalism of ideology made Pedro an activist within the Caso faction.

In 1928 the new Caso cacique, a distant uncle of Pedro, was assassinated by the Rocas, who, during their temporary subsequent dominance, managed two subdivisions of the ejido in accordance with the Law of Ejidal Patrimony of 1925; by 1932 the Durazno ejido had been split into 218 inalienable family plots. But Roca rule terminated with the election of Cardenas as national president and the sudden death of the upstart governor to whose statewide faction they had belonged. The Casos acquired full "legal guarantees," that is, a relatively free hand in expropriating land and retaliating against enemies. Almost all of the Roca political family and most of its additional adherents left Durazno forever (about 150 men, women, and children).

After about a year of fragile unity, the fourth stage was precipitated by a so-called "question of skirts," a public altercation over 34 pesos between the wives of the two co-caciques, both uncles of Pedro. These two first cousins were similar in personality and political orientation but differed profoundly in other ways. Pablo Perez had fought through the regional agrarian reform and had then become a fairly prominent state leader (he served for three years as head of Cardenas statewide *Confederacion Michoacana de Trabajo*). Oton had returned only in 1926, a few months before the death of the agrarian hero, Primo Tapia, but had since become the dominant leader within the community of Durazno. The new factions were no longer motivated by substantive ideological issues but by the ambition and "pure egoism" of the caciques. Yet the leaders of both factions proclaimed the now orthodox agrarista ideology and, even in 1956, Pedro and Oton persisted in categorizing their internecine schism together with the agrarian revolt as parts of "the struggle" (*la lucha*). Between 1937 and 1939 about 21 politically motivated homicides occurred, with the Caso faction under Oton eventually gaining a precarious dominance because of the latter's ability to elicit the support of the best "fighters" (*luchadores*) and of politicians and army men in other parts of the state. The results were tested in the presidential campaign of 1939-40, "one of the bloodiest in Mexican history" (Brandenburg, 1964, p. 93). Eight of the "original agrarians" had their ejido plots expropriated.

The fifth stage of factionalism lasted one year (1945-46), as the second cacique in the fallen faction organized a short-lived "third party" devoted to a revitalization of the agrarian principles of Primo Tapia and to the restitution of the eight ejido plots. Several men perished; even Oton was nearly assassinated, but managed to regain power after the election of the new Cardenista governor. The ringleader of the opposition and several others left town.

From 1946 to 1952, after a long period of *relative* tranquility, a second "third party" arose under a leading "fighter" (and a cousin of Pedro), who advocated a return to "the spirit of Primo Tapia," greater freedom for the clergy, and a series of material improvements (a short road, and a bridge in the ejido, were constructed). By this time factionalism was being determined by a new factor: the resentment of many villagers and about two-thirds of the leaders against the so-called "interminable caciazgo" of Pedro's uncle, Oton. On the other hand, many in the new faction were of shaky loyalty, and several of its leaders embezzled funds and engaged in other irregularities. Within two years the ringleader had been wounded in ambush, and public meetings had been forcibly dispersed by Pedro and other nephews of Oton. The followers and fighters in the broken faction redistributed themselves among the existing Caso and Perez factions.

By 1956 Pedro was regularly cited with Oton as "one of the principal elements" who dictated to the pueblo and was a source of its troubles. It was generally believed, however, and actually true, that the two men "could hardly stand each other" (*casi no se llevan*). In 1959-60, after several homicides—including that of Oton—a third neutralist and vaguely conservative faction emerged with leaders and a following that was strongly opposed to the established cacicazgo qua cacicazgo. Pedro and his halfbrothers and several other men left town for varying periods of time. But in 1963 the man who had been senator during Pedro's term as alternate was elected governor. Within Durazno the rebellious faction was dispersed, and Pedro, now sole leader of the Casos, returned "to direct the destinies of his pueblo."[3]

This history suggests important qualifications to the currently developing theories of factionalism (Nicholas, 1965). For example, the Durazno factions did have many of the defining features of corporate groups, such as a structure of authority, perpetuity through time, and a large measure of control over a territory (the ejido); but the most striking fact of all is that for more than half a century these factions have been unambiguously and indeed obviously ideological—in the sense of disagreeing about economic and legal premises (1911-20), about economic, social, and religious matters (1920-26), and about the specifics of ejidal repartition and local government (1926-35). Since 1937 the Caso and Perez factions have vied with each other in the fervid espousal of radical agrarian socialism, or *cardenismo*, while a series of "third parties" have struggled for economic equity, or a mitigation of anti-clericalism, or "a return to the principles of Primo Tapia." The fact of gradual homogenization, of a gradual shift from logically and diametrically opposed positions (1911-24) to essentially identical positions (1937 to 1957), has not mitigated the degree to which factional leaders is obviously related to the less salient preoccupation of the caciques with their own legitimacy and to the concern of the villagers with the many illegitimate features of the same caciques.

THE LEGITIMACY OF A CACIQUE: NEGATIVE FEATURES

The case of Pedro raises questions about legitimacy precisely because he is clearly illegitimate in many ways. To begin with, one is not elected cacique, nor does a cacicazgo depend on instituted, public, or democratic selection. Indeed, as the leaders of an ideologically extremist faction in the minority, with commitments to violence, Pedro and the three uncles who preceded him could never have won a free election, and the expedient informality of Pedro's local cacicazgo contradicts the notion of "a mandate from the people." This failure verifiably to represent his community flies in the face of the model precedent set by his uncle, Primo Tapia, the charismatic revolutionary who on several occasions was delegated to perform major tasks and was elected as "the representative" by public assemblies of the Durazno community or by large contingents of agrarians from the Pazacu Tarascan towns.

The fact that Pedro was not elected and that his rule is temporally unrestricted also contradicts the higher ideal of the Mexican Revolution and the Mexican notion that the succession of chiefs in a community should be orderly, regular, and solemnized through a public process of election and institution. (For example, all official documents close with the exhortation: "No Re-election! Effective Suffrage!") It is true that Pedro, in a manner of speaking, was elected president of the regional committee for thirteen years, and that he went through the ritual of nomination and election as alternate (*suplente*) to the national senator, but these were personal achievements and hardly affected the non-representative character of his rule within Durazno.

In the second place, Pedro's status as a cacique is not legitimized or enhanced by charisma in either of its two most usual senses: the religious and the personalistic. He lacks the persuasive idiom, the magnetic personality, the ideological fervor, and the other less apparent qualities that rally followers to a strong faction or a revolutionary movement. Most villagers acknowledge his learned skills and acquired contacts, but I doubt that even a large minority submits to him because of a firm belief in his extraordinary powers as a person (Weber, 1915 (1958), p. 295). The position in which he has matured has called forth and cultivated a set of personal traits that—if not always antithetical—at least differ sharply from those of Primo Tapia, whose rude but eloquent phrase and bold vision of an anarchist-agrarian future "touched the sensitive parts" of a restless and landless peasantry.

Pedro tries to legitimize his status through the progressive ideology of the national party and speaks—albeit vaguely—of material progress, agrarian reform, and public education. This attempted legitimation, nevertheless, blatantly contradicts his own behavior, which has been effective in cutting down the local teaching staff, in excluding capital investment from without, and in the illegal reallocation of almost two dozen plots of ejido land from usufruct by "original agrarian fighters" who struggled with Tapia, to younger relatives and dependents of the dominant faction of which Pedro is now cacique.

RELIGION

Pedro's status and corresponding roles conspicuously lack legitimacy in terms of religion. Ever since the return of Primo Tapia and agrarian movement in the village has been anchored to the radical socialism of the Michoacan left, and committed ideologically to an explicit and sometimes militant anticlericalism. Today Pedro subscribes to the principles of the liberal Masonic Order, of which he is a high-ranking member. Also beginning with Tapia, the agrarian caciques have either excluded or drastically curtailed the activities of the clergy (Pedro would accept an invitation from Durazno's leading Catholic lady to sup with the priest, but also would make sure that the latter came to Durazno only once a month). As for religious ritual, since Tapia's death the caciques have suppressed or weakened the annual cycle of communal fiestas, eventually reducing many of them to a shabby relic; in 1956, Pedro held himself aloof and only looked on at "Tacari," Tiger Day, and a few other festivities. Finally, the agrarian caciques have always striven for a deemphasis of baptisms, weddings, and wakes, partly on anti-clerical principles and partly from a practical realization that they were a most opportune entree for the clergy. Under Pablo's part-time rule villagers were publicly denounced and actually punished for baptizing their children. Oton and Pedro followed this tradition in public (while secretly baptizing their children to please their wives). Moreover, Pedro has partly replaced the priest as the peacemaker and matchmaker after the elopements and bride-capture. In other words, many local caciques have somehow paralleled or followed the national government in working out a practical compromise between agrarian social ism and Mexican Catholicism. Although statistics were not obtained, two leaders and several older persons told me that the poorest and most ignorant villagers—especially the women—believed that Pedro and Oton were endowed with supernatural power—by virtue of the test that two decades of black magic called against them had failed to work! This, however, did not mitigate what remains the salient negative feature of their legitimacy: opposition to religious ritual, and refraining from seeking the support of the Catholic clergy and the supernatural sanctions of the Christian religion.

POSITIVE FEATURES: FAMILY

In a metaphorical and not too realistic sense, Pedro is a modern successor to the prehistoric princes of Tarasco. As a sort of joke, he and the younger agrarian leaders refer to themselves as "the princes" (los principes) in order to heighten the contrast with the respected elders who make the decisions in many communities and who are called "the principal ones" (los principales). In addition, Pedro is partly legitimized by virtue of occupying a sort of semantic and social slot—that of cacique—to which most villagers are resigned and, despite envy and malevolence, expect to be filled.

In point of historical fact, Pedro has succeeded to a line of no less than six clearly remembered and well-known local leaders, one of them an "ancestor" and the rest various kinds of "uncle" (tio): the venerated "representante" of the village in the 1870s, then the liberal lawyer and "original" agrarian agitator who was assassinated in 1919, then Primo Tapia, the flamboyant revolutionary and regional leader of the 1920s, then the able but short-lived distant uncle Tomas (assassinated in 1928), and finally, the two uncles whose internecine struggle for power has dominated Durazno factionalism for over twenty years. The village has been controlled with little respite by the members of one "political family," a loosely knit name group that is called the "casos" but also includes many de las Casas, and others, affiliated by blood or marriage.

This continuity in power, this effective rule by one or two of the most able and ambitious within a half-fictive kinship group, has reached the point where the Casos declare it a right and natural state of affairs; and many villagers either agree or have resigned themselves. As Pedro's half-brother said: "Only the Casos are fit to rule in Durazno." Pedro's subscription to the familial criterion is demonstrated by the fact that he switched the order of his patronymic and matronymic, "so that my children would be Casos." The tradition of Caso rule, despite its recency, had considerable strength, and by 1955-56 approximated the colloquial sense of rule by hereditary right. Although standing at a low moral level, the Caso dynasty illustrated what one political philosopher has called "the normative power of the factual."

ABILITY

Although cynical about political homicide and an egoist in the pursuit of women and land, Pedro also has considerably enhanced his legitimacy through his demonstrated performances and aptitudes. To a limited extent, he has been implicated in public works, such as the agrarian reform and the introduction of electrification, pumped water, and the national highway; but he has often been accused of indifference, insincerity, or procrastination. To some extent, also, he brings arbitration, official "pull," or quasi-technical advice to the ignorant and needy peasants, and Pedro himself boasts about this. First and foremost, however, the performances that legitimize his status are those that demonstrate his aptitudes or personal superiority—as a relatively lucid speaker with a certain dexterity in handling the Agrarian Code, as a sophisticated arbiter of personal conflicts, as a tough and resolute competitor but also relatively tempered in the use of assassination, and as an efficient bureaucrat and a small-time politician with many useful contacts. Pedro's performance is not legitimizing because of moral goodness or even benefits to his public; rather, it satisfies a set of "hard-nosed" and essentially amoral questions about his ability to lead and his effectiveness in knowing how to give orders and control the community.

TRADITIONAL NORMS

If legitimacy means the validation of power in moral and jural terms, then normative contradictions within an agrarian community must raise disturbing questions about its cacique. For example, Pedro and his uncle are not legitimate within the pre-revolutionary framework, partly because they are not venerated *principales* who have served at personal expense in the annual cycle and have sharply curtailed ecclesiastical influence. Also, their enormous incomes and egregious power contradict the mores of economic equality and leveling that derive from Indian tradition and anarchist-tinged agrarian reform. On the other hand, the vitality of these norms is demonstrated by Pedro and Oton's modest dress, by their adobe houses, and their own emphasis that they are "Indian peasants."

Even radical agrarians share certain archaic norms, notably of "peace" and "the unity of the pueblo." Within the obviously narrow limits of reason, Pedro and his uncle strive to legitimize their rule by depicting themselves and their faction as maintaining harmony and being "with the pueblo," and trying to foil the opposite faction in its attempts at schism. Within their implicitly Hobbesian theory, the villagers are molecular sheep—stupid, docile, and lazy—who can be unified only under one man—the cacique (Hobbes, 1651 (1951), chap. 16).

HIGHER LEVELS

Unlike the elders and chiefs of many pre-revolutionary villages, whose legitimacy could be defined almost exclusively in terms of local values, the agrarian cacique has always conspicuously attempted to validate his power by appeals to higher political and governmental levels of leaders, institutions, and ideas. Pedro tries to legitimize his role by describing his friendship with politically powerful persons: compadres in nearby county seats, and "very good friends" such as the former state senator, A. Madariaga Rios. Both Pedro and Oton seek to demonstrate

their affinity to authoritative institutions and officials such as *gobernacion* (the national executive center in Mexico City), and the Department of Agrarian Affairs, and the National Peasant Confederation; in 1956 the secretary-general of the latter (*la Campesina*) was persuaded to speak at the local "Primo Tapia Day" (one of the secular fiestas which the agrarian caciques actively observe (P. Friedrich, 1966b)).

Both caciques try to perpetuate the dying fires of agrarian ideology through invoking the dimly remembered charisma of its heroes. They appeal to semi-legends such as Emiliano Zapata, and exaggerate their roles in the "struggle," and their subscription to the socialistic dogmas of "the Center" in Mexico City. Both men exploit every opportunity to underscore their personal friendship with the man who still enjoys the greatest charisma in Michoacan, and perhaps in Mexico: the former president, Lazaro Cardenas. The charisma of the great agrarian caciques and caudillos, past or distant or both, casts a spotty reflection of legitimacy on the bureaucrats and minor party officials of fully institutionalized agrarianism. And inasmuch as Durazno is an agrarian community, it is primarily the Caso and Perez leaders who—if only occasionally—articulate its new ideals in public assemblies, in discussions before the town hall, and in private homes.

Leaders such as Pedro and Oton legitimize their rule in two directions. Just as they demonstrate to the local peasants their connections with higher levels, so they present themselves before state politicos and higher administrators as indigenous revolutionaries, grass-roots agrarians, and the like. To create this image as "Indian revolutionaries" they exploit to the limit their knowledge of Tarascan, their participation in the revolt, their de facto "control" of Durazno and contiguous pueblos, and the incontrovertible fact that both men have resided almost continuously in their indigenous community (with the obvious exception of Pedro's thirteen years as a student and teacher); in contrast, a damning charge against Pedro's uncle, Perez, that dates from the 1930s, is that he moved to the state capital and "disacknowledged his own people." The ideological leverage of such posturing is enormous in a state political machine whose radicalism—perhaps the most extreme and articulate in Mexico—consists to a large degree of championing the lowly Indian and forcing through massive expropriations of land for the benefit of the (Indian) peasant. Thus Pedro can persuasively claim to represent his Indians, although actually rather unresponsive to their needs; he is primarily responsible to the Cardenas machine in his activities, his beliefs, his personal alliances, and his political combinations. In terms of the logic of legitimacy, his position depends on decomposing and realigning the constituent meanings of responsibility and representation (C. Friedrich, 1963, p. 302).

LEGALITY

Durazno is a "typical" agrarian community in that ever since the sanguinary revolt and reform of the 1920s its leaders have broken and flouted the criminal law on assault and homicide. Tapia ordered many assassinations; Oton personally shot down five villagers with his pistol; and Pedro both planned and committed political killings. Yet by a singular dialectic the legitimacy of such caciques is argued mainly in terms of laws that have been enacted formally and are "on the books." The reason for this seeming paradox in agrarian politics is that statutory law itself is sharply divided into, first, the criminal and civil codes of the state and nation and, second, the large corpus of national legislation and executive decrees that affect agrarian reform and the administration of the ejidos. This agrarian legal corpus was thought out and formalized by jurists and agrarian experts before its "tumultuary and giddy" introduction into peasant villages. Even early and initiatory caciques such as Primo Tapia created considerable authority through their "reasoned elaboration" of the premises and mandates of major national laws, notably the Agrarian Law of 1915, Article 27 of the Constitution of 1917, and the Agrarian Regulatory Law of 1922. Agrarista villagers depended on Tapia's familiarity with the welter of often conflicting statutes and the state-level rules of procedure for agrarian expropriation. The solitary Roca leader with some legal training served a similar function during the enforcement of the Law of Ejidal Patrimony of 1925, as did Pedro and one of his cousins during the Cardenas presidency, when Durazno—equipped with telephones and typewriters—was a regional headquarters for agrarian litigation. For forty years the Durazno caciques have vehemently and logically insisted that, by effectuating a reform and supervising an ejidal economy, they have been not only obeying but actively executing the law of the land. Their arguments are often legalistic in the pejorative sense of strutting the letter of the law or in manipulating its wording for contrary ends.

By 1956 Pedro was Durazno's most expert interpreter and defender (and perverter) of the two score or so most relevant sections of the total of 1,063 sections in the Agrarian Code. Al-though in part weakened by misinterpretation, the provisions of the code did seriously affect land use by laying down rules for the administration of the ejido and the selection of its officers, and by explicitly stating many of the principles by which the village had been living for over thirty years. For example, during a tense and dramatically ironic session of the ejido, Pedro quoted verbatim Article 165, according to which peasants acquired rights in any plot by working it for two years—although everyone in the meeting knew that for the two-year minimum the original ejidatarios had been prevented by force from tilling their plots.

Despite such partial and occasional perversions, the Durazno ejido operated largely in accordance with the intent of the agrarian reform. The primary of ejidal economics, and the political awareness of many of its peasants, had made infringements of the Agrarian Code a delicate and sometimes explosive matter. Covert infractions were denounced vigorously by the opposition, attracting the attention and the inspectors of the national government. Caciques such as Oton and Pedro contravened agrarian laws often enough, but they also limited and often disguised their actions because these selfsame laws were a main source of their legitimacy. The two men, like their agrarian predecessors, were in the quasi-Hobbesian position of equating or confusing the legitimate with the legal, and of justifying, validating, and falsely rationalizing their rule because of its logical relations to the agrarian law of the land.

CONCLUSIONS

The legitimacy of an agrarian cacique is precarious, is subject to questions, and arises from a dialectic between forces and arguments that hang in near balance.

Let us review the negative features. The status is not elective, or representative in any public or institutional sense, which contradicts strong sentiments both in the national government and in many Indian villages against local bosses who depend on outside support. Second, small-arms violence; both in objective extent and in the public attitudes toward it, has become an integral component—a sort of diagnostic trait—of the politics in agrarian cacicazgos. In part, this violence is congruous with the traditions of the revolution and with the local mores of the vendetta, and of murder because of political envy and romantic jealousy. But the sheer quantity of politically motivated homicide, like its extreme politicization, runs counter to many villages' attitudes (P. Friedrich, 1962, p. 326), and blatantly infringes many state and national laws. Pedro's rule is technically illegal and undermines the criminal law of the land. Moreover, agrarian politics lacks supernatural support and has always been anti-clerical; its leaders have done much to debilitate the communal rituals that were formerly concatenated with the politico-governmental system. Last, many of the early revolutionary leaders had extraordinary personal power and aptitudes, but most of today's agrarian caciques lack such charisma, and many are personally disliked or even deprecated by many or most of their villagers. In sum, the weak or negative legitimacy of today's agrarian cacique arises from a combination of his non-representative quality, the illegality of his acts, and from the fact that he disorganized and partly destroyed the established economic, sociopolitical, and religious order.

The positive features of the agrarian cacique's legitimacy include, first of all, that he is normally heir to rule by virtue of an informal intrafactional or intrafamilial consensus, that he is "next in line" to succeed in a strong familial tradition of local control and even autocracy. Also, the revolutionary caciques aroused a sense of moral outrage and resentment against economic injustice that was in turn translated into a legitimation of their status as protectors of the peasant village against landlords and other predatory aliens. The caciques of today—while demonstrably dispensable for the running of the ejido—continue enviously to guard its external relations with the priests, the outside creditors, and "other exploiters." Similarly, these "political middlemen" do as a matter of practical fact relate several political publics, particularly the demands and supplies of their peasant communities to the demands and supplies of the state and national politico-governmental systems; they must present themselves effectively to their peasant inferiors as cogs in the cardenista leadership, and to that higher echelon or elite as "indigenous peasants and revolutionaries"; their posture has powerful leverage in a state still controlled by the Cardenas block, and among the many state and national leaders who are emotionally and ideologically committed to "indigenism" and "the agrarian revolution." Finally, the agrarian caciques in Durazno were skilled and motivated, and it is probably true that the local reform would not have been realized, or even initiated, without their leadership. Since the 1920s it has been the agrarian caciques who understood and explained the details of the agrarian legislation by which the ejidos are governed. Their legitimacy is arguably based on the fact that they implemented agrarian law and pub-

lically discussed its provisions and principles. To sum up, the status of an agrarian cacique, such as Pedro Caso, rests on a (quasi-) hereditary right of succession, and on a Hobbesian combination of de facto power to make decisions for the community, of "protecting" the community and brokering many of its external relations, and finally, of equating the legitimate with the legal, or articulating and claiming to represent the agrarian laws of Mexico.

In addition to discussing the cacique in terms of legitimacy theory, I also proposed that the data of political ethnography is "relevant" insofar as it "raises novel conceptual questions." Specifically, just how is Pedro Caso more than just material for another case study, more than another felicitous congruity between field data and orthodox theory? Just how is he not only intrinsically interesting, but perhaps relevant to some reformulation or invigoration of contemporary legitimacy theory?

Theories of legitimacy and similar phenomena share one feature: they are largely or entirely limited to a special and rare kind of leader —the one who is "on top," who is relatively or completely sovereign and whose legitimacy is consequently a matter of relations downwards to followers, subjects, and other inferiors within the body politic. For example, Hobbes is clearly preoccupied with the legitimacy of the monarch, of the sovereign ruler over a strong national state. Kings, state dictators, and presidents continue to enjoy a perhaps undue priority in the thinking of sociologists and philosophers with an interest in the purely theoretical aspects of politics and government.

In fact, the overwhelming mass of political leaders and of leadership phenomena concern, not the sovereign pinnacle, but the interstitial (or "intercalary") levels, the "political middlemen" who link and articulate diverse publics and political cultures. The political middleman is a leader largely by virtue of presenting and representing the communications of his multiple publics to each other, and I have tried to demonstrate in the case of Pedro Caso that a number of illegitimate features can be balanced or offset by the middlemanship which intervenes between the village and local landlords, state politics, and national agrarian law. Since the middleman's publics are often structurally complex, and since the ideologies which he links—particularly the ideas on legitimacy—are often even more complicated, the legitimacy of the middleman will of necessity include conflicts and contradictions of interest, motivation, and various types and levels of knowledge. The legitimacy of peasant leaders in larger politics thus is largely a question of a nexus or intersection between forces, directions, and currents. By following out the interplay between these forces or directions, we can come closer to understanding the legitimacy of an agrarian cacique and, by extrapolation, the nature of the legitimacy (and of similar phenomena such as power and authority) of any other sort of middleman—from the head of the union local to the chairman of an anthropology department. The agrarian cacique such as Pedro Caso, precisely because he is as "intrinsically interesting" as a Machiavellian prince, but also because he is so unambiguously a non-sovereign middleman, leads us to consider and perhaps properly evaluate the relational attributes of leadership and the relational aspects of the component notions of legitimacy.

APPENDIX

The present study is the partial result of eighteen months of field work conducted in Mexico between February, 1955, and August, 1956 (about fourteen of them *in situ* in Durazno and Tiripendo), under the auspices of the Wenner-Gren Foundation and the Mexican government (the latter through the Buenos Aires Convention Fellowship Program).

My field methods included general ethnography, participant observation, a year of political functions, genealogical and sociometric description of the kinship and friendship in both factions, a study of legal records in the county, state, and national capitals, and the detailed, written records of two local chroniclers. I also interviewed most of the leaders in the fallen faction—one was my most accurate informant, but got only two hours with Pablo Perez because he was evasive and often away. I was on good terms with Pedro's mother, his two half-brothers, and his first cousin and "real" compadre. My interviewing, like most political communication in Durazno, was in Spanish, although Tarascan was used for trivial conversation. I would emphasize that my statements here refer to the situation up to 1956 (except in a few cases where personal letters have made possible a more up-to-date remark). As a rather vague postscript, I would add that the assassination of Oton and the enormous growth of the Pazacu industrial and commercial complex and the governorship of Madariaga have all contributed to a drastic change in the politics of Durazno. Insofar as I could judge during a short visit in 1967, a cacique had not emerged to replace the deceased Pedro, and control was shared by many families and individuals.

Durazno should not be taken as in any sense "typically Tarascan": few Tarascan towns have had comparable histories of violence and agrarian reform, and of the seven Tarascan towns in which I have done field work of at least two weeks, Durazno was the only one with a true cacicazgo (although two others had had one in the past, and one had a quite different type with five contending "caciques").

My interaction with Pedro ranged through diverse contexts: local fiestas and assemblies, meals with him, his relatives, and his enemies, formal interviews with him on his life and politics, and finally, a Rorschach exam (Xeroxed responses available on request). Pedro's personal attitude ranged from formal but aloof for the first six months, to friendly and hospitable for the next six (while I was getting the most on politics), to renewed coolness during the last months of my sojourn.

The first sketch of this article is one of nine life histories in Chapter VI of my Ph.D. thesis. The pseudonyms in this article correspond to those in the *Ethnology* article (1965), and in "An Agrarian 'Fighter,'" where Pedro is referred to as "the cacique's eldest nephew," or "one of the caciques." *The* cacique was Oton.

I gratefully acknowledge the helpful suggestions of Catherine Ives and Julian Pitt-Rivers, and of the "Conference on Inter-face Relations in Mesoamerica" (Chicago, May, 1966, organized by Robert Hunt). The following persons read the present version and gave valuable comments: Margaret Hardin Friedrich, Melford Spiro, T. N. Pandey, Carl Friedrich, Waud Kracke, and Ralph Nicholas.

REFERENCES

Aguirre Beltran, Gonzalo 1953 *Formas de gobierno indigena.* Mexico: Imprenta Universitaria.

Alegria, Ricardo E. 1952 Origin and diffusion of the term "cacique." In Sol Tax (ed.), *Selected papers of the XXIX International Congress of Americanists.* Chicago: University of Chicago Press.

Bailey, Fred G. 1966 Parapolitical systems. This volume.

Bradenburg, Frank 1964 *The making of modern Mexico.* Englewood Cliffs, N.J.: Prentice-Hall.

Codigo Agrario y Ley de Colonizacion y Disposiciones Relacionadas

—— 1955 *Editorial Olimpo*. Mexico

Degraziz, Sebastian 1959 *What authority is not. The American Political Science Review*, 53: 321-31.

Deutsch, Karl W. 1963 *The nerves of government*. New York: The Free Press.

Easton, David 1965 *A framework for political analysis*. Englewood Cliffs, N.J.: Prentice-Hall.

Fallers, Lloyd 1955 The predicament of a modern African chief: an instance from Uganda. *American Anthropologist*, 57: 290-305.

Friedrich, Carl 1961 Political leadership and the problem of charismatic power. *Journal of Politics*, 3-24.

—— 1963 *Man and his government*. New York: mcGraw-Hill.

Friedrich, Paul 1957 Cacique: the recent history and present structure of politics in a Tarascan village. Unpublished doctoral dissertation, Yale University.

—— 1962 Assumptions underlying the Tarascan political homicide. *Psychiatry*, 25(4): 315-27.

NOTES

1 A Harvard graduate student, when he left Durazno after three months of field work (1959), had never heard of Pedro Caso, Durazno's cacique. Until I began boring into politics during my fourth month in the field in 1955, Pedro was only a familiar face.

2 The ejido is a preconquest form of communalistic land usufruct that was revived, amplified, and system- ized in accord with modern socialistic theory, and made the frame for Mexico's sweeping program of agrarian reform. The best scholarly reference is still Simpson (1937), particularly because one of the chapters is a case study of Tarejapu.

3 He continued in this role until his death from a heart attack three years later.

FACTIONS, PARTIES, AND POLITICS IN A MALTESE VILLAGE[1]

JEREMY BOISSEVAIN

I. INTRODUCTION

THE OBJECT OF this paper is to give more precision to the term *faction* and in so doing to further our understanding of a useful analytical category. This will be done by examining various divisions in a Maltese village against the existing theoretical background on the subject of factions. In spite of the fact that almost 30 years ago Linton (1936:229) suggested that the study of factions presented "an interesting and still almost unexplored field," relatively little work has been done on the subject. Though Siegel and Beals recently treated factionalism at considerable length in two interesting papers (1960a and b), they said little about factions, for their primary interest was the study of conflict, not factions. But regardless of where it is classified in the conflict continuum, factionalism is conflict between factions. It would thus seem that a more profitable approach to the study of factionalism would be to begin by examining the groups among which there is conflict.

The term faction is often employed loosely to designate groups of very different levels of structural complexity, whose only characteristics in common seem to be that they are in con- flict with other like groups. The use of specific terms in the analysis of social organization assumes comparisons and ultimately leads to the formulation of comparable problems (cf. Barth 1961:13). Yet it is obvious that comparison is meaningless if the things being compared are not of the same order. For example, the term faction is used by Murdock (1949:90) to designate competing regional districts, tribal moieties and enduring village political divisions; by Lewis (1954) for rival kinship groups with important social, economic and ceremonial functions; and by Mayer (1961:122ff.) for temporary groups recruited over particular disputes. But are all these various groups factions in the conventionally accepted sense?

Harold Lasswell defined a faction as "any constituent group of a larger unit which works for the advancement of particular persons or policies." He also noted that "the term itself drops out of usage when certain lines of cleavage have become rather permanent features of the political life of a group; these divisions are accepted as parties" (Lasswell 1931:49). Many years later, Raymond Firth, in summing up the findings of a symposium on factions in Indian and overseas Indian societies (Firth *et al*. 1957), pointed out that they are loosely ordered groups; that their bases of recruitment are structurally diverse; and that they tend to become activated on specific occasions and not as a regularly recurring feature. He also drew attention to the fact that regular structural units of a sub-society may be regarded as factions by the society at large (Firth 1957:292). This referred specifically to a matter stressed by H. S. Morris, one of the contributors to the symposium, who noted that though Europeans and Africans in Uganda regard the caste and sectarian groups of the Indian Community as factions, they are actually permanent corporate groups for which the term faction is inappropriate. He observed that the term might have been appropriate at an earlier stage of history before these groups "solidified into permanent elements of the structure of Indian society" (Morris 1957:316).

A faction is thus seen as a loosely ordered group in conflict with a similar group over a particular issue. It is not a corporate group, though at a certain point in time it may undergo a change and become a group of a higher order for which the term faction is no longer appropriate. This apparently takes place when a faction solidifies and assumes a certain permanence. But we are not told very much about the criteria used to judge the relative solidness and permanence of factions. This is a matter to which I shall give some attention.

With these preliminary remarks in mind, we can now look more closely at the conflicting groups whose members tried to get me to commit myself to their particular causes during the period I lived among them. In describing these groups I avoid the term faction. Which groups may and which may not be appropriately called factions is a matter with which I deal at the end.

II. THE SETTING

The 330,000 inhabitants of the former British colony of Malta are crowded on to three small islands with a total area of 122 square miles. Malta's history has been determined by its small size and strategic location in the center of the Mediterranean; for centuries it has been run as an island fortress. All government services are administered from Valletta, the capital, by Maltese civil servants; there are no mayors, headmen, or councillors who represent or administer the individual villages (exceptions are the village councillors of the Civic Council established in July 1961 on Gozo, Malta's small sister island). In the absence of secular authorities at the village level, the Parish Priests have emerged as the traditional spokesmen in both religious and secular affairs for the fervently Roman Catholic population. Though Malta has a long history of limited self government, when I carried out my field work the islands were under Governor's rule. The colony became an independent nation on September 21, 1964.

Farrug (not its real name), the village with which this paper deals, is a small, compact parish of about 1,400 inhabitants, who are chiefly dependent upon wage labor for their livelihood. Most work for the Malta Government or the British Armed Services stationed on the island. Though it is somewhat smaller than most Maltese villages, the central structural features of Farrug are much the same as those of its larger neighbors. Authority is distributed between the Parish Priest, the police, and a host of elected and appointed office holders representing the interests of the many formal and informal associations and groups in the community. Of these, only the Parish priest and the police are able to back up their commands with sanctions which compel respect, if not obedience. The current Parish Priest is the sixth to be assigned to the village since the end of the war. Most of the others were transferred after running afoul of the village's many conflicting groups.

The people of Farrug occasionally remark that there are too many clubs and societies for the size of the village. There are two brass band clubs, a football club, and an active Labour Party committee. There are also two sections of Catholic Action, a male branch of an ascetic lay society (MUSEUM) and three confraternities, or devotional brotherhoods, dedicated to the Blessed Sacrament, the Holy Rosary, and St. Roque. The only time the village meets as a group is in some religious context. That is, for worship, devotional processions and certain feasts. In each village, the most important of these is the annual *festa* of the patron saint. These *festas* provide the chief public entertainment of the countryside, and the good name of a village depends upon its ability to celebrate a lavish feast. Thus most of the issues and decisions which affect the village as a group have to do with religious matters.

III. PATTERNS OF CONFLICT

Although Farrug tries to present a tightly united front to outsiders, cleavages cut across it at various levels. Some of these divisions are temporary, others have become permanent; but regardless of their duration, all inhabitants are painfully aware of them, for persons made vulnerable through their network of personal relations are often obliged to support a particular division. In doing this they are forced to become the opponents of neighbors and relatives in other divisions. This is a characteristic of all small communities, but it is particularly true of a village such as Farrug, in which the inhabitants are closely related through kinship and affinity. Ninety percent of the inhabitants were born in the village; the remainder have married into it.

The Maltese call conflicting groups within a village *partiti*, singular *partit*. A partit is a group which supports a person or policy in competition with a rival group supporting a different person or policy. A partit can thus be either a faction or a party in Lasswell's sense. Partiti are said to have *pika* between them. Pika denotes relations of competition, ill-feeling, or hostility. Villagers consider partiti to be a bad thing, for they disrupt the harmony of the village and make it more difficult to project the ideal image of village unity to the outside world.

The oldest division in Farrug is that between the followers, or partit, of St. Martin, the patron saint of the village, and the partit which supports St. Roque. The latter is a secondary saint as regards his official position in the parish, but one who has come to assume an importance almost equal to that of the titular saint in the social life of the community. A more recent cleavage is that between the supporters of the Malta Labour Party and those who support the Archbishop in his fight against it. Within these two major divisions, and within the village's formal associations, cleavages sometimes occur over temporary issues and disputes. Less frequently disputes unrelated to these major divisions cut across the village. We may now examine these divisions in some detail.

IV. FESTA PARTITI

In terms of structure, origin, social composition and disputes, all the festa partiti in the country resemble each other very much.[2] Each of the two partiti in Farrug has its own band club, the officers of which are the leaders of the partit. These band clubs each have elaborate premises, and arrange the organizational aspects of the external feast of their patron saint. They are the nuclei of the partiti. The religious confraternities are also aligned with the partiti: the older confraternities of the Blessed Sacrament and the Holy Rosary support St. Martin, while that of St. Roque celebrates the feast of its namesake. Several of the partiti leaders are also officers of their respective confraternities. In addition to the formal members of its band club and confraternities, each festa partit has a rank and file of men, women, and children who are not members of either, but who still support the partit against its rival.

The festa partiti compete with each other over almost every aspect of their festas, from the decoration of the streets and the adornment of the statue to the number of guest bands and the quantity and quality of fireworks. Even the exact number of communicants, the number and size of candles on the altars and the amount of light bulbs illuminating the facade of the church enter into the competition. During the year I spent in the village, for example, St. Martin's supporters spent over $3,700 on the centenary celebration of their patron, while their rivals spent almost $1,700 on the annual festa of St. Roque.[3] Most of the money was spent on illuminating the streets and the church, on guest bands and on the raw materials for the fireworks which were made in the village by the partisans.

The origin of these partiti was related to me by the president of the St. Roque band club. I have checked the story and believe it to be substantially correct. It is in many respects similar to the accounts which I collected about the origins of the festa partiti in other villages. This is the story as he told it to me:

A new parish priest who had a strong personal devotion to St. Roque came to the village in 1877. Because he wanted to inject some more life into this rural parish he asked for and received permission from the Archbishop to establish a confraternity dedicated to St. Roque. The first feast in honor St. Roque marking the establishment of the confraternity was celebrated in October 1878. The feast was simple, but during the next few years it grew in scale. In 1886 some persons began to grumble about having to pay for another feast. There was a feeling of "You collect for your feast and we'll collect for ours." In 1888 the parish priest had a quarrel with some villagers about his alleged misuse of parish funds to buy street decorations for the feast of St. Roque. These accusations made him furious. From that day onward he threw his support behind the feast of St. Roque. Full scale partiti came into being about 1890, and each partit opened a social club soon after.

St. Martin partisans maintain that their club was founded about 1880 and that the founders of the St. Roque club broke away from theirs around 1900. Thus they claim their club has considerable seniority. St. Roque supporters do not admit this. Since there are no written records to support either claim, the clubs are usually deadlocked over the seniority issue and refuse to allow their bands to play on the rare occasions when they are supposed to take part in a ceremony together.

The members of the partiti no longer change sides, although this occurred in the generation following their establishment. Today a person is either born into a partit, or he marries into it. Children support the feast of their parents, and an outsider marrying into the village generally supports that of his spouse. Marriages between members of rival partiti are regarded as undesirable, although they occasionally do take place. Thus 72% of the marriages contracted within the village took place within the same partit. Children of mixed marriages support the feast of their favorite parent: boys normally follow their fathers and girls their mothers.

Though each partit claims that it is larger than its opponent, the band clubs each have a membership of about 80 men, and I found that the village was fairly evenly divided between the two. Forty-eight per cent of the men and women supported St. Martin, 42% St. Roque, and 10% were uncommitted. Of those uncommitted, 63% were outsiders who had married into the village.

But if there is not a significant difference in the size of the partiti, there is in their social composition. The supporters of St. Martin, on the whole, belong to a higher occupational class than their rivals. I found that 83% of the white collar workers support St. Martin, while only 38% of the farmers, the lowest occupational class, do so. Considering the way membership is now inherited, it would appear that the social position of the members of the founding generation influenced their choice of partit. Apart from this class division, I found no evidence in Farrug, or in any other village so divided, of other pre-existing cleavages out of which these festa partiti might have grown. Finally we may note that there is no territorial division between the partiti. There is a tendency, however, for more St. Martin supporters to live in the better residential area near the church, and for St. Roque supporters to live in the less desirable sections of the village. This is a reflection of their occupational class. Social mobility does not involve a change of partit though it is often linked to a change of residence.

Disputes between the partiti concern matters which affect their precedence and ability to display devotion to their saints. The course which such disputes take is highly formalized. They usually begin when the St. Roque partit petitions the Parish Priest for a new privilege. St. Martin leaders then try to check their rivals by threatening to cancel their feast. At this point the Parish Priest passes the dispute up to the Archbishop's Curia for judgment. Both sides then use all the influence they can in order to obtain a decision favorable to them. If the decision is favorable to St. Martin, the dispute usually ends quickly, for St. Roque's partisans cannot threaten to cancel their feast for fear that the Church might suppress it forever. This has occurred in some villages. But if the decision is favorable to St. Roque and his followers, St. Martin's partisans refuse to hold their feast for a year or so, or until they can wring some concession from the Parish Priest or the Archbishop. After that a new dispute arises over some other issue, and the process starts over again.

But let us look at some of the major skirmishes during the last ten years. From 1952 to 1954 there was trouble over the right of the St. Roque religious rights. When the Parish Priest backed St. Roque, St. Martin followers not only refused to celebrate their feast, but they also exploded a huge home-made paper bomb under the unfortunate cleric's house. Relations were restored when the Archbishop transferred the priest (at the latter's urgent request) and modified the St. Roque procession route. In 1956 the St. Martin band club refused to celebrate its festa because the St. Roque confraternity had been given permission to renew two of the bunches of artificial flowers which stand on the secondary saint's altar. The following year the St. Roque band refused to play at the installation ceremony of the new Parish Priest because the Archbishop had denied the St. Roque confraternity permission to hang a new picture over the altar of its saint. In 1960 the Parish Priest infuriated St. Roque followers when he did not allow the partit to participate in the centenary festa for St. Martin. (The poor man's hands were tied, for St. Martin supporters refused to have anything to do with the festa if their rivals took part in it.) And while I was in the village, there was a sharp dispute over which band was to have precedence at the installation ceremony of the new Parish Priest. They could not agree, so neither played.

So far I have discussed only the more important clashes between the partiti. During the course of a year, numerous fund raising fairs run by the band clubs are also occasions on which the village divides along festa partit lines. While supporters of the partit running the fair flock to it, their rivals either stage their own fair or, and this is more usual, they hire several buses and leave the village for a picnic or a pilgrimage to some shrine of their saint. Rivalry runs highest, of course, during the festas. Then 40 or more policemen are often required to keep the jeering and abusive rivals—men, women, and children—from coming to blows.

V. POLITICAL RIVALRY

The open conflict between the followers of the Malta Labour Party, on the one hand, and the Archbishop, on the other, has divided Malta into two bitterly opposed groups. This division is reflected in Farrug, where we find that national political issues have cut deeply across the division of the festa partiti. The Parish Priest is the leader of the persons who support the Archbishop. His most enthusiastic followers are the members of MUSEUM and Catholic Action. The lay leaders of the latter society are for the most part also officers of the St. Martin club, as are the other important persons who help the Parish Priest.

The Labour supporters look to the members of the village MLP committee for leadership. These are also mostly prominent members of the St. Martin partit. Most are skilled workers and technicians employed with the government or the dockyard. This committee was elected while I was in Farrug; previously there had been no active formal officers. Now the Labour group in Farrug is tightly linked to the national Party structure.

In general, the Labour Party recruits its support from skilled and unskilled laborers who work outside the village in the dockyard area and in the industrial departments of the Government. They are opposed, speaking again in very general terms, by the professional and salaried classes and the farmers, who support the church. The Labour Party secured a good measure of support outside these rough lines during the three years it was in office. It did this by helping the farmers, establishing social assistance and health schemes, building many new schools and other public works, and by officially transferring the hiring of casual government laborers from the hands of patronage conscious politicians to the government Labour Office.

But the increasingly anti-clerical policy of the Labour Party and the heavy sanctions the church began to impose on it have alienated many Labour supporters. During 1961 the church took firm steps to make people choose between it and the Labour Party. The Archbishop interdicted most of the Labour Party leaders. He also instructed confessors to deny absolution to those persons who read, contribute to, print, or sell the Labour newspaper. Individual priests now also refuse absolution to those who attend MLP

meetings or show sympathy for it in other ways. They portray Dom Mintoff, the Labour Party leader, as a socialist devil working to give the Islands over to Communism in the manner of Cuba's Castro.

About 70% of Farrug supports the Labour Party,[4] though considerably less than half that number are dues-paying members. Both festa partiti reflect this division. There are, however, relatively few occasions when all the supporters of either the MLP or the church face each other as groups at the village level. The few times I saw this occur were during national rallies. May Day provided such an occasion. In the morning the Labour supporters, mostly men, went to take part in the big Labour Parade in Valletta. The same afternoon their opponents from the village, mostly women and children, went to the Archbishop's rally just outside Valletta. While the groups were each gathered in the village, there was a good bit of name calling and singing of appropriate songs: the Catholic Action girls sang the Papal Hymn; and some of the Labour enthusiasts sang their own words to the same melody.

During the year there were also a number of incidents in the village that were directly related to this political tension. Slogans appeared on the walls; the Parish Priest had to tell a young Labour supporter to leave the church for being rude; unknown persons destroyed some decorations of the MUSEUM; and someone set fire to the front door of a shop belonging to one of the Labour leaders.

VI. CONFLICT WITHIN ASSOCIATIONS

In looking at the village as a whole, we have seen how two important principles of organization—loyalty to a certain saint and loyalty to a political ideology—have divided the people of Farrug into various opposing groups. Virtually every person in the village is committed to supporting one of the festa partiti and has taken a position for or against the Labour Party. These principles, in turn, form potential lines of cleavage in the formal village associations that are not aligned with a political party or festa partit.

The two band clubs are exclusive units with regard to the festa rivalry. The boy's Catholic Action is, in effect, also an exclusive group, for after the Parish Priest chased out the sons of Labour supporters, only about eight young men remained. All of these are St. Martin supporters. Although the MUSEUM members are mixed, their important issues concern spiritual matters, and they have divorced themselves from the festa activity. The Labour committee is also mixed with regard to festa rivalry. But thus far this has not been a source of conflict within the group, possibly because the Labour leaders are also important members of the St. Martin band club. The members of the girl's Catholic Action and the Football Club include some of the most vocal partisans of St. Martin and St. Roque. This results occasionally in the division of the associations along festa partit lines. For example, the Football Club was almost deserted during the two months preceding the St. Martin centenary, when rivalry between the festa partiti was running very high. Both societies try to avoid division by taking no formal part in the celebration of the two festas.

The situation with regard to political loyalty is somewhat different. The Labour Party committee and the church societies are exclusive groups. In practice the Football Club is as well, for all its active members are Labour supporters. That leaves only the band clubs with politically mixed membership. Open conflict between rival political partisans has not yet occurred in the St. Roque Club, although the lines of potential cleavage are present. This is chiefly because the leaders of the club have made it a matter of principle to suppress their personal political feelings in order to preserve the unity of the club. They feel that only as long as they are tightly united can they survive as a partit in the face of the church's determination to put an end to festa rivalry by reducing secondary feasts and eliminating the secondary partiti.

In contrast, the continued existence of the St. Martin partit is not threatened by the church. Indeed the church's policy is to build up titular festas at the expense of secondary celebrations. It thus does not have the same functional need to remain united as does its rival. This has made it more vulnerable to internal dissensions. Moreover we have also observed that both the MLP supporters as well as their opponents are led by persons who are at the same time leaders of the St. Martin club. At club committee meetings these persons continue to oppose each other over many issues of club policy. This division amongst the club leaders causes the rank and file to take up sides. If the dispute is resolved rapidly it has no effect on the unity of the group. But if the conflict remains unsettled for some time all members may be asked to align themselves. At this point the continued existence of the club as a united corporate body is seriously threatened by the possibility of one of the groups leaving the club. This physical division is usually avoided by the activity of peace makers who

place the unity of the club over partisan loyalties. For example, during the recent centenary celebration, the St. Martin band club was divided over whether to fire the traditional salute of firecrackers for the Archbishop when he came to take part in the festa. The Labour element won, and the club voted against the salute, but there was bitter feeling over the matter. This, however, disappeared when the Archbishop announced that he could not come. The opposing elements in the club then united and celebrated a rousing feast, much to the chagrin of their rivals. But in 1930 the club actually split in two over a similar crisis between the supporters of Lord Strickland, on the one hand, and the Archbishop, who opposed him, on the other. The two clubs eventually reunited, but not until the political conflict at the national level began to subside following the suspension of the constitution in 1933. When I left Malta the St. Martin club seemed to be facing such a crisis again. The young Labour members had just successfully boycotted the festa of their Patron Saint in retaliation for the attacks of the church on their political party. Older members of both political colors, who remembered the bitterness of the 1930 split, were trying to bring the opponents together to avoid an open breach in club unity.

VII. OTHER ISSUES

Occasionally the village is divided by incidents totally unrelated to either festa partiti or national politics. These incidents are rare, for there are relatively few matters unrelated to politics or festas in which the community has a collective interest. But such an event occurred in Farrug. It concerned one of the few pieces of common property that a village possesses, namely their parish church. The inhabitants of Farrug are very possessive about their parish church, as are all villagers in Malta and Gozo. For them, the parish church is more than just a central place of worship: it is the repository of the village's collective wealth. Generations of inhabitants have spent huge sums to decorate it, and they show it with pride to all visitors. It is, in a very real sense, physical proof of their piety. For this reason any alteration to it is a matter of concern to all the members of the village, irrespective of whether they support St. Martin, or St. Roque, or the Labour leader or the Archbishop.

A number of years ago the Parish Priest proposed to redecorate part of the church. The villagers welcomed this interest in their church and contributed generously. But when the scaffolding was removed they discovered, to their horror, that besides regilding the ceiling, he had placed his personal coat-of-arms high over the chancel. He was the first priest to have done such a thing, and he had done so without consulting the village! There was much grumbling, but in time the priest was promoted to a larger parish, and the matter appeared to be forgotten. Then one morning, two months after he had left, the village was startled by the news that persons unknown had sneaked into the church in the dead of night and hacked off the offending coat-of-arms. In its place gleamed the freshly painted emblem of the village. To add insult to injury, the nocturnal painters telephoned the priest to announce that he would find something interesting the next time he visited Farrug. Though the offended priest called in the police, they did not find the culprits. The village has a good idea who the guilty ones are, but no one speaks, for most are quite pleased that the arms have been removed.

The incident divided the village, in general, and the St. Martin partit, in particular, for about a month. Most of the members of the St. Roque partit were extremely pleased at this humiliation of a person whom they had regarded as their enemy. And most of the members of the St. Martin partit, though they had looked on the priest as their friend, were also secretly pleased that the coat-of-arms had been removed. But a few members of the St. Roque partit, and three of the leaders of the St. Martin club objected to the insulting way a priest had been humiliated. The three leaders of the St. Martin club, all of whom had continued to maintain important personal relations with the ex-Parish Priest, proposed that their club apologize to him and hang his picture in the sacristy of the church. Though they worked hard in their partit to mobilize support for this apology, they met with very little success. Their proposal was defeated when it came to a formal vote in the club, and though the three officers resigned in protest, the issue died with the defeat of their motion.

VIII. CONCLUSION

In this paper I have tried to isolate several sets of conflicting groups and present them so that their essential structural features could be observed. At the level at which the village is seen as a group we distinguished the festa partit, the political divisions, and the loose groups which came into existence over the coat-of-arms. At a lower level we observed that many of the village's constituent groups and associations were

divided from time to time by specific issues which affected their members.

In terms of structure and organization, these groups differ considerably. Each festa partit has a wide base of members, some of whom are members of the partit club, whose elected officers are leaders of the partit. Each partit meets as a group fairly often and each owns property. The partiti have existed for 70 years and the people regard them as permanent groups. Membership in a partit is inherited. The two rival political groups in the village are also each composed of many supporters, some of whom are members of formal associations whose elected and appointed officers are looked to as leaders of the whole group. Each meets occasionally, but the members own no property in common. Though this political division has existed for about 11 years, the people do not look upon it as permanent. Membership is voluntary and not inherited. The divisions which arose over the coat-of-arms issue did not have associations at their center, nor, at the village level, did they have formal leaders, though in the St. Martin partit they did have informal leaders or spokesmen. The temporary rival groups which formed within the village associations over such issues as the fire-cracker salute were structurally similar to the opposing coat-of-arms groups in the St. Martin partit, though they recruited support along political lines.

For which of these groups, if any, is the term faction appropriate? I suggest that the only groups which are clearly factions, in the sense that Lasswell and Firth used the term, are those of the order of the fire-cracker and coat-of-arms groups within the St. Martin partit. These were temporary groups which arose over specific issues and, except for leaders, they had none of the corporate characteristics of the kind that Maine and Radcliffe-Brown pointed to (Maine 1890; Radcliffe-Brown 1950:41). We can thus speak of the Labour or the anti-Labour factions in the band clubs, or of the festa factions in the Football Club or Catholic Action. These were groups which recruited support along lines of cleavage which had their origin outside the groups in which they arose. In this they differed somewhat from the opposing groups which arose within the St. Martin partit over the removal of the coat-of-arms. Here recruitment was not based upon pre-existing external cleavages: in the case of its leaders, membership of the dissident group within the partit was based upon friendship with the offended priest, or to be more precise, upon clientship with an influential patron, and in the case of those whom they rallied to their cause, it was based upon kinship. But these various sets of opposing groups, regardless of their basis of recruitment, were factions, for they were temporary groups recruited over particular disputes.

In contrast, the festa partiti are units of a higher structural order. Though they began as factions, they now exhibit a full range of corporate characteristics (permanence, common property, frequent meetings, elected leaders, etc.). They are clearly not *factions* but *parties* in the sense that Lasswell used the term. The political divisions, on the other hand, are not clearly the one or the other. Two years ago I think the term faction would have been appropriate. Then, the members did not meet regularly in opposition to each other and, in the case of the Labour group, did not have formal leaders at the village level. But in the last year they have become corporate groups, though their members still don't regard them as permanent and membership is voluntary and not inherited. Thus they are no longer true factions.

But what of the division which arose at the village level over the removal of coat-of-arms? I would suggest that it is not appropriate to regard as factions persons holding opposing views on a particular issue, unless they can be seen to have some sort of unity and leadership. As it so happened, these persons were not forced to state their position openly and align themselves against each other. If they had been asked to express their opinion by concrete action—such as contributions for the picture to be hung in the sacristy—it is likely that the division would have cut deeply enough to force those holding similar opinions to enter into contact with each other to defend their point of view. At this stage it would have been possible to speak of opposing factions at the village level. But the dispute was resolved before this deeper division occurred, and thus factions did not arise.

It would appear then that the factors which are critical in determining whether competing groups of a larger unit are factions are their corporate structural characteristics and the way the members themselves regard their permanence. Where a group exhibits a full range of corporate characteristics and its members regard it permanent, the term faction is not appropriate. Neither is it appropriate to the division between persons who hold opposing opinions on a particular issue if they have not been forced to align themselves openly to defend their point of view against their rivals. A faction is thus a group located between divided public opinion, on the one hand, and competing structural units, on the other.

In closing I must point to one other attribute of factions. It will be evident from the foregoing that in examining factions I have been looking at political groups of the lowest order. That is, they are groups which compete to influence the outcome of disputes and policy in accordance with their own interests (Mair 1962:10; Smith 1960:17). As such they provide the movement, the dynamic aspect of any structure. Often characterized as disruptive, they are in effect the means by which community decisions are achieved and changes effected within a social system. I would suggest that factions are found in every society, and that it is therefore of great importance to pay attention to their composition, recruitment, and operation in the analysis of political processes.

REFERENCES

Barth, Fredrik
   1961 Comment on Jack Goody, the classification of double descent systems. Current Anthropology 2:3-25.
Firth, Raymond et al.
   1957 Factions in Indian and overseas Indian societies. British Journal of Sociology 8:291-342.
   1957 Introduction. In R. Firth et al., Factions in Indian and overseas Indian societies. British Journal of Sociology 8:291-342.
Lasswell, Harold D.
   1931 Faction. In Encyclopedia of Social Sciences. New York, The Macmillan Company.
Lewis, Oscar
   1954 Group dynamics in a North Indian Village—a study of factions. Delhi, Programme Evaluation Organization of the Government of Indian Planning Commission.
Linton, Ralph
   1936 The study of man. New York, D. Appleton-Century Company.
Maine, Sir Henry S.
   1890 Ancient law. London, John Murry.
Mair, Lucy P.
   1962 Primitive government. London, Pelican Book A542.
Mayer, Adrian C.
   1961 Peasants in the Pacific: a study of Fiji Indian rural society. London, Routledge & Kegan Paul.
Morris, H. S.
   1957 Communal rivalry among Indians in Uganda. In R. Firth et al., Factions in Indian and overseas Indian societies.
Murdock, George P.

1949 Social structure. New York, The Macmillan
Company.
Radcliffe-Brown, A. R.
1950 Introduction. *In* African systems of kinship
and marriage. A. R. Radcliffe-Brown and Daryll
Forde, eds. London, Oxford University Press for the
International African Institute.
Siegel, Bernard J. and Alan R. Beals

1906a Pervasive factionalism. American Anthropologist 62:395-417.
1960b Conflict and factionalist dispute. Journal of
the Royal Anthropological Institute 90:107-117.
Smith, M. G.
1960 Government in Zazzau: 1800-1950. London,
Oxford University Press for the International African
Institute.

NOTES

1 The field-work on which this paper is based was carried out between July 1960 and September 1961 in Malta under a grant from the Colonial Social Sciences Research Council, for which I am most grateful. I should also like to thank those who commented upon earlier versions of this paper read at the London School of Economics' Seminar on Comparative Social Institutions in 1962, and at the 1962 meeting of the American Anthropological Association in Chicago.

2 Twelve of Malta's 29 rural villages and towns are divided by this type of rivalry. Two others have rival band clubs not related to the cult of saints.

3 This disparity in expenses can be explained by

the fact that in 1935 the Church in Malta severely restricted the celebrations of secondary saints in an attempt to control the rivalry between festa partiti and to keep the secondary celebrations from surpassing the titular festas. Thus St. Roque supporters were not allowed to decorate streets remote from the church, and were permitted to hold only two brass band programs, although their rivals held nine.

4 Exact figures are not available, as I was not able to gather systematic data on this subject owing to the pitch of political and religious fervor prevailing at the time.

THE HINDU JAJMANI SYSTEM:
A Case of Economic Particularism

HAROLD A. GOULD

THIS PAPER DEALS with the system of traditional economic relationships, called the jajmani system, which is a widespread feature of the peasant-village culture of India. The analysis is based partly on field work which I undertook in the north Indian village of Sherupur (a pseudonym) in 1954-55 and partly on secondary sources. Although by no means capable of illuminating all of the important aspects and implications of non-pecuniary patterns of economic interaction in rural Indian life, it is hoped that what follows will add to the reader's understanding of such patterns.

I

The precise character of economic relationships in the villages of India is determined by the complex division of labor that exists there and by the particular set of religious attitudes which underlie and perpetuate that division of labor. Up to a point, Indian villages are not unlike the peasant-agricultural communities one finds anywhere in the world.[1] That is, they contain a

group of families, usually compound in structure, residentially centralized in the midst of their agricultural lands. Technology is simple and productivity low; poverty is extensive and life centers around the quest for subsistence. The pursuit of material self-sufficiency is associated with a general centripetal orientation to life in both the family and the community. But in India, although all villages are primarily dependent upon subsistence agricultural production, all families do not practice agriculture directly. Only a certain proportion do so while the rest specialize in various craft and menial occupations. In exchange for these various services the cultivators pay a systematically determined share of their produce to those providing them.

At the heart of rural India's complex division of labor is caste. Compound patrifamilies are the loci of rural productivity and these are ritually subdivided into endogamous clusters in accordance with the moral valuation which the Hindu religion places upon their occupational activities. The criterion of ritual evaluation is whether or not the caste occupation, or perhaps more accurately *the configuration of caste functions*, does or does not subject its practitioners to ritual contamination. Roughly, those clusters of patrifamilies whose work activities put them in continuous contact with "blood, death, and dirt,"[2] singly or in combination, are regarded as "unclean" castes and must avoid connubial, commensal, and many other forms of social contacts with those clusters of patrifamilies who are "clean." The latter are called Twice Born castes because their males may experience the second, or spiritual, birth of initiation into the sacrosanct community of ritually pure Hindus. Basically, the distinction is between the landowning, cultivating castes, on the one hand, who dominate the social order and the landless craft and menial castes, on the other, who are subordinate within it. Hinduism elaborately rationalizes and congeals this fundamental distinction.

What must not be overlooked as one views this caste system, however, which Kingsley Davis[3] regards as the most thoroughgoing attempt of all time to make "absolute inequality" the basis of social relationships, is that the unclean occupations are just as necessary to the Hindu's concept of community life as are the clean ones. In other words, castes who remove dead animals are Untouchable on that account but they are also intrinsically essential to the Hindu social system because the Twice Born are ritually prevented from performing this unclean occupation. By the same token, *all* unclean occupations are at once degrading to their practitioners yet essential to the appropriate organization of any orthodox Hindu community. Ritual purity for some can be maintained only at the expense of defilement for others where, as in India, the criteria of ritual status are the fundamental occupational functions required to enable the community to operate.

Villages like Sherupur, therefore, must face and resolve a social structural dilemma towards which the Hindu social system predisposes Indian community life. Such centripetal principles as the corporate or joint family, caste endogamy, face-to-face interpersonal relations, distrust of the impersonal, "outside," etc., make avoidance-orientations a pervasive aspect of the peasant's life. The wrong contact, the wrong deed, can lead to ritual contamination, outcasting, and expulsion from the ancestral community. On the other hand, these very social structural features which give such power to avoidance-orientations are the same ones which make interfamilial, intercaste, and intervillage contacts inescapable. For since the sources of contamination are also the sources for the Twice Born castes of essential goods and services which they may not provide for themselves, systematic ways of modifying the divisive potentialities of caste, while at the same time preserving the institution itself, must exist if the community is to survive in a manner which preserves its Hindu moral premises.

We may put the issue this way: Contacts with "outsiders" (non-kin, other castes, other villagers, etc.) who may be ritually defiling are feared yet recognized as essential for a number of purposes; which in turn necessitates the establishment of formal social mechanisms capable of reconciling the urge to avoid social intercourse for religious reasons with the need to establish and maintain it for instrumental reasons. Social structures like the *Gaon Panchayat* (Council of Elders) achieve this reconciliation at the political level in rural India; the so-called jajmani system does so at the economic level.

Declares Wiser:

A social organization such as the Hindu caste system, which gives each occupational group a fixed standing within the community, must of necessity have certain patterns of behavior which enable each caste to maintain its own status and satisfactorily engage in relationships with others. Among these behavior patterns are marriage, social intercourse in matters of eating, drinking, and smoking, conventions of untouchability and unapproachability, and service (jajmani) relationships.[4]

II

The world of the Indian peasant is heavily laden with kinship values. Much of his life is spent within the ambit of the corporate family and its extensions which is in turn bound to its traditional (ancestral) village. Most of the people who supervise the peasant's activities and whose activities he in turn supervises are kin of varying degrees and are ordinarily members of the common household. Movement beyond the confines of the village is often predetermined by the location of affinal and consanguineal kin whom one has elsewhere. Within the village, interfamilial interaction takes place among families who have ordinarily been in continuous association for generations. In short, the kinship system constitutes the framework within which the peasant carries on those relationships which from his standpoint possess the highest measure of trustworthiness, durability, and meaningfulness.

When, therefore, a person must venture outside the confines of his own kinship unit, he tends wherever possible to establish with whomever he encounters ties which approximate as nearly as possible those customary between genuine kin. This is an expression of the idea implicit in the peasant's mind that the most stable relationships in one's life are those based on kinship.

When villagers must deal with strangers (says Marriott) they have the choice of including the stranger either in a family or in an intercaste type of relationship. If strangers are thrown together anonymously as in a bus or in an urban shop and if their common activities are casual ones, then they may classify each other by relative age as pseudokinsmen. Ultimately they may trace more specific connections through villages with which they share real family relationships.[5]

These are the premises which underlie the kind of ties which get established among participants in the jajmani system. Faced with the necessity of bringing families of different castes and, therefore, of different ritual status, into stable economic interaction, without at the same time contaminating each other, certain principles of kinship organization are brought into operation. The manner in which this is done represents the culture's answer to the need for extrafamilial and extravillage interaction for the attainment of economic ends consistent with the Hindu moral order.

Naturally, all possible components of kin relationships are not projected into the organization of the jajmani system. Only those which have relevance to its particular problems and aims have been selected. They pertain (a) to the patterning of superordinate-subordinate relations between *jajmans* (patrons) and their *purjans* or *kam karnewalas* (workers, suppliers of services, etc.), (b) to the range of commitments between participants, and (c) to the temporal continuity of the relationships established.

Families of the clean castes (Twice Born) are the patrons, the *jajmans*, while the unclean castes (Sudra and Untouchable) are the *purjans*, the providers of services. In short, it is a matter of land-owning, wealth- and power-controlling high castes providing a structurally fixed share of their agricultural produce, along with numerous "considerations," in exchange for craft and menial services rendered by the mainly landless, impoverished, politically weak lower castes. The latter thereby absorb the onus of ritual contamination associated with the tasks they perform and facilitate the ritual purity and consequent moral apotheosis of the former. They are at once outside the ritual pale yet essential to the functional pale of Hindu society.

This superordinate-subordinate dimension of the jajmani system is primarily paternalistic and only remotely pecuniary in its basis. It is a matter of a particular *jajman* engaging the services of a particular *purjan* who thereby obligates himself to maintain this tie in perpetuity as long as both discharge their diffuse set of responsibilities to each other. Sons of each family are expected to continue the relationship into the succeeding generation, as are son's sons, etc., while preserving intact all of its power, ritual, and material implications. A *purjan* must defer to, respect, and defend his *jajman* (ideally, of course), as well as serve him, in a way strongly analogous to the manner in which a son of a corporate family is expected to orient himself to the father. Put briefly, a *purjan* is to his *jajman* as a son is to his father, at least in the formal respects which have been enumerated above.

The term "considerations" is Wiser's and refers to those features of the jajmani system which in his view lie at its heart and explain the peasant's preference for it over more rationalized economic relations. This may be, and we will examine the nature of these "considerations" in a moment, but no doubt of equal importance is the fact that these "considerations" symbolize the fact that the jajmani tie is personal, face-to-face; that it involves not merely a carefully accounted exchange between a buyer and a seller, but also a plethora of explicit and implicit commitments *between two families* very like, in comprehensiveness and affect, the commitments which kin make to each other *within families*. Furthermore, like kin relationships, community pressures can reinforce the jajmani tie and thereby help assure its preservation.

Taken together, these kin-like properties of the jajmani system maximize the probabilities that the division of labor necessary to the ritual continuity of the Twice Born castes and the functional integration of the village community can be preserved. All parties concerned both give to the system and derive from it a host of crucial benefits on a diffuse, face-to-face basis which reproduces the solidarities and securities afforded by the kinship system; this renders the jajmani system as meaningful as it can be from the villagers' point of view.

III

Against the background of the foregoing, let us examine some of the structural features of the jajmani system as revealed in the data from Sherupur.

Regarding the "considerations" which are to Wiser of such fundamental importance, seventeen are listed in his book.[6] I reproduce them here because they correspond with my own findings in Sherupur and because they help to illustrate the highly particularistic nature of jajmani ties:

1. Free residence site
2. Free food for family
3. Free clothing
4. Free food for animals
5. Free timber
6. Free dung
7. Rent-free land
8. Credit facilities
9. Opportunity for supplementary employment
10. Free use of tools, implements and draft animals
11. Free use of raw materials
12. Free hides
13. Free funeral pyre lot
14. Casual leave
15. Aid in litigation
16. Variety in diet
17. Healthful location

In addition to the above there are the formal rates which *jajmans* (patrons) establish with their *kam karnewalas*. These involve agreements by *jajmans* to provide a certain quantity of their grain every six months to their respective *purjans* in accordance with some relevant criterion of amount of service rendered. The following rates were found to be operative in Sherupur:

1. Washerman (*dhobi*) 8 pounds of grain per woman in the household per six months.
2. Blacksmith (*lohar*) 16 pounds of grain per plow owned by *jajman* per six months.
3. Barber (*nai*) 16 pounds of grain per nuclear unit with child in joint-family per six months.
4. Potter (*kumhar*) 16 pounds of grain per family per six months.
5. Plowman (*kori*) 28 pounds of grain per six months plus $2 per month per *jajman*.
6. Priest (*Brahman*) 28 pounds of grain per family at plowing time to compensate for organisms killed by the plow.

There are other avenues of distribution besides the formal reimbursements and the "considerations." High caste families give extra amounts of grain or other crops, like peas, plus balls of molasses (*gur*) and sweetmeats, etc., to their *purjans* at times of marital or funerary rites or after a bountiful harvest. There is no formal

rate that can be calculated for these emoluments, however. Cast-off clothing may be given to *purjans* and the head of a Rajput (Kshatriya) landed family in Sherupur indicated the following forms of largesse as being regularly received by the Brahman priest:

1. Fourteen sears (28 lbs.) of grain at plowing time as recompense for the killing of organisms by one's plow.
2. Ten percent of the dowry of any marriage which he helps arrange.
3. Twelve free meals annually (one each month) after there has been a death in the family.
4. One dhoti, one blouse, and one pair of chappals when a woman of the family dies.
5. One dhoti, one shirt, and one pair of chappals when a man in the family dies.
6. One pice to three annas each time an astrological reading is solicited.

A *jajman* and his *purjans* tend to comprise a closed system of socio-economic interaction in many respects. The barber who cuts his Kshatriya patron's hair may also cut the hair of some of his fellow *purjans* and in exchange receive the services which they are qualified to render. In factional rivalries in villages the inter-caste lines that get drawn will often reflect *jajman-purjan* networks. But there are important respects in which *jajmani* relationships are not closed systems of interaction. *Purjans* usually have several Twice Born "clients" and their circuits among their *jajmans* constitute avenues of interfactional communication through which marital negotiations can be conducted and through which ameliorative gestures can be made if rivalries have disrupted pathways of direct approach between families, etc.

Take the case of the barber who was a *purjan* of Sherupur's leading Rajput family. It may be seen in Table 1 that this man serves four villages and a total of fifteen joint-families.

These fifteen joint-families contain twenty-five nuclear units with children, which is the barber's rate-standard, with the result that his yearly grain income from his various *jajmans* is

TABLE 1.

The Grain Income from the Jajmani Ties of a Barber Serving Sherupur

Village	Joint-families	Nuclear units with children	Amount of grain per year
A	2	3	96
B	3	6	192
C	6	11	176
D	4	5	160
Totals	15	25	624

in excess of six hundred pounds. The kind of grain is never stipulated in these arrangements but depends upon the individual agreements arrived at between the parties. The barber's functions and reimbursements do not end here. He cuts hair on a commercial basis besides and averages about thirty dollars a month from this source. He performs a number of additional non-economic services for his patrons. As Opler and Singh[7] put it, "one of his major functions is to groom the living and the dead, and that grooming has special meaning for Hindu ceremonial life, especially in the rites of birth, marriage, and death." In marriage negotiations the *nai* (barber) is often responsible for garnering information about the status and resources of a potential bride's family. In other words, his interfactional mobility is employed for "marital reconnaissance."

After a bride joins her husband it is frequently the *nai's* wife who is brought in to aid the young woman in her difficult adjustment to her affinal household. Both Opler and Singh and I found barber's wives performing this role.

Thus, on the whole, the barber is as indispensable in his way to an orthodox Hindu home as is a son. Relations are close, essential, and enduring. To varying degrees, but always to an important degree, this is true of all *jajman-purjan* ties. They involve, as has been said, projections of kinship values into economic relationships which thereby make the latter seem to be "real," i.e. dependable. The villager neither understands nor trusts the "professional" relationship characteristic of the urban-secular society. To him the man who avoids assuming a host of diffuse obligations along with the specific one for which two people have come together at any given moment, i.e. the man who declines to put himself under the obligational structure customary between kin, is thought to be dishonest, capable of feeling no moral compunction to fulfill his side of a bargain. As Marriott declares:

The people of Kishan Garhi thus recognize three great social realms—that of kinship and family, which is an area controlled by limitless demands and mutual trust; that of the village and caste, which is an area in part controlled by particular obligations and formal respect; and that of the outside world, of government and the market place, which is an area controllable only by money and power—things which the villager scarcely possesses.[8]

IV

The question of the full amount of goods and services which get circulated by a complete network of *jajman-purjan* ties cannot be answered with the degree of precision possible where pecuniary standards of measurement exist. However, some idea of the volume of grain disseminated by *jajmans* to their *purjans* on the basis of the formal commitments made between them for the village of Sherupur is obtainable. This is simply a matter of calculating the number of service ties of each category known to exist for Sherupur and multiplying by the appropriate rate of reimbursement in each case. The figures thus obtained are naturally somewhat idealized inasmuch as they do not take cognizance of "considerations" and of innumerable other "intangibles" which are the added hallmarks of this particularistic system of relationships. But they do suggest the magnitude of the economic interaction involved. Table 2 summarizes this aspect of the analysis.

TABLE 2

Distributions of Grain to Purjans by their Jajmans in Sherupur, Per Annum

Purjans	Units of reimbursement	Amount of grain exchanged (lbs.)
Barber (nai)	23	368
Washerman (dhobi)	43	688
Blacksmith (lohar)	18	606
Plowman (kori)	11	616
Potter (kumhar)	18	576
Priest (pundit)	11	616
Carpenter (barhai)	19	608
Totals	143	4078

It will be seen that a turn-over of more than two tons of grain a year is attained by the formal jajmani commitments alone in Sherupur. This takes place in a community numbering forty-three families, with a total of two hundred twenty-eight people, of which only nineteen families function as *jajmans* in any meaningful sense, i.e. as patrons who receive services and disburse grain.

On the other hand, no village is ordinarily self-contained with respect to jajmani relationships. The unit of self-sufficiency is the "local culture." This encompasses the radius of ten or twelve miles within which the bulk of a village's affinal ties are found (village exogamy is obligatory in northern India). Sherupur contains families of blacksmiths, plowmen, tailors, and leather-workers to serve its nineteen cultivating families. It also has a single resident Brahman priest. But barbers, carpenters, washermen, potters and others come from neighboring communities within the "local culture."

Thus the "local culture" is not only interlaced with affinal connections but also with caste and jajmani ties. It is a kinship of villages founded upon real and quasi-kinship ties among its residents made necessary by the counterpressures of corporate family life, occupational differentiation, ritual avoidance, on the one hand, and the requirements of functional integration of community life, on the other.

BIBLIOGRAPHY

Davis, Kingsley 1951 *The Population of India and Pakistan* (Princeton: Princeton University Press).

Embree, John 1946 *Suye Mura: a Japanses Village* (London: Kegan Paul).

Firth, Raymond 1946 *Malay Fishing Village* (London: Kegan Paul). 1952 *Elements of Social Organization* (London: Watts and Co.).

Lewis, Oscar 1951 *Life in a Mexican Village: Tepoztlan Restudied* (Urbana: University of Illinois Press).

Marriott, McKim 1955 "Western Medicine in Northern India" (in Benjamin D. Paul, ed., *Health, Culture and Community*, pp. 239-268, New York: Russell Sage Foundation).

Opler, Morris, and Rudra Datt Singh 1948 "The Division of Labor in an Indian Village" (in Carelton S. Coon, ed., *A Reader in General Anthropology*, pp. 464-496, New York: Henry Holt).

Passin, Herbert 1955 *Untouchability in the Far East* (Monumenta Nipponica, vol. 11, pp. 27-47).

Redfield, Robert 1930 *Tepoztlan* (Chicago: University of Chicago Press). 1941 *The Folk Culture of Yucatan* (Chicago: University of Chicago Press). 1950 *Chan Kom Revisited* (Chicago: University of Chicago Press). 1955 *The Little Community* (Chicago: University of Chicago Press). 1956 *Peasant Society and Culture* (Chicago: University of Chicago Press).

Wiser, William 1936 *The Hindu Jajmani System* (Lucknow: Lucknow Publishing House).

NOTES

1 Cf. Redfield, 1930, 1941, 1950, 1955, 1956; Firth, 1946, 1952; Lewis, 1951; Embree, 1946, etc.
2 Passin, 1955.
3 Davis, 1951.
4 Wiser, 1936, p. 8.

5 Marriott, 1955, p. 248.
6 Wiser, 1936, pp. 10-11.
7 Opler and Singh, 1948, p. 480.
8 Marriott, 1955, p. 249. Kishan Garhi is the name of the village which Marriott studied.

PART V

Application: Clientelism – Middle-Level Perspectives (Brokerage)

PATRONAGE AND COMMUNITY-NATION RELATIONSHIPS IN CENTRAL ITALY[1]

SYDEL F. SILVERMAN

ONE OF THE most strategic yet formidable problems in the anthropological study of complex societies is the relationship of the parts to the whole of such societies. Most attempts to tackle this problem have been concerned primarily with those parts which are localized social systems, or communities,[2] interdependent with though analytically separable from the whole, a national social system. The community and national levels of sociocultural integration of Steward (1955: 43-63), the discussion of tensions between pueblo and state by Pitt-Rivers (1954: 202-210), the community-oriented groups and nation-oriented groups of Wolf (1956), and the local roles and national roles of Pitkin (1959) are only a few examples of this recurring contrast, the social analogue of the great-tradition/little-tradition approach to complex cultures. Such a model immediately sets the task of formulating the interaction between the two systems.

One of the more promising efforts to describe this interaction has been the concept of the "mediator," an individual or group that acts as a link between local and national social systems. Wolf introduced the idea of the cultural "broker" in a discussion of data from Mexico, defining as "brokers" the "groups of people, who mediate between community-oriented groups in communities and nation-oriented groups which operate through national institutions" (Wolf 1956: 1075). The mediating functions which Wolf emphasizes are economic and political, and he traces a succession of three phases in the post-Columbian history of Mexico during which these functions were carried out by different groups in the society. In his review of peasant-society research published the same year, Redfield (1956) observed that a recurrent phenomenon in many societies is the existence of a "hinge" group, administrative and cultural intermediaries who form a link between the local life of a peasant community and the state of which it is a part. The concept of the mediator is relevant to many studies of "part-societies" which exist within a larger encompassing whole. It describes the pivotal chiefs within colonial nations, whose positions derive from earlier periods of tribal autonomy, as well as the elites looked up to by peasants, deriving from a historical balance between two stable classes; the formal agents of national institutions, who penetrate into communities from distant capitals, as well as the upwardly mobile villagers who move into positions in national institutions.

In the analysis of material collected during

field work in a Central Italian community, the concept of the mediator proved to be most pertinent for understanding the relationship of the community to the larger society during a particular period. However, it was found that if this relationship is followed over time, not only are there changes with regard to the groups which perform mediation functions, as Wolf (1956) showed for Mexico, and the roles through which mediation is effected, as Geertz (1960) showed for Java, but there are fundamental changes in the structuring of links between community and nation. These changes suggest that the concept of the mediator is most useful if defined narrowly and thus restricted to a particular form of part-whole relationship.

The concept refers to a status which functions as a link between a local system and a national system. In interactional terms, the mediator may be seen as one to whom action is originated from the national system and who in turn originates action to the local system; to some extent, the direction is reversible, the mediator still being the middle element. However, if the mediator were to be defined merely as anyone who acts as a means of contact between the systems, it would include such a wide range of phenomena as to become virtually meaningless. Moreover, such a definition would obscure the important differences between various kinds of contacts which may exist.

Wolf (1956: 1075) referred to the "brokers" as persons who "stand guard over the critical junctures or synapses of relationships which connect the local system to the larger whole." By taking Wolf's terms in their full implications, it is possible to arrive at a more precise definition. First of all, the functions which those who are defined as mediators are concerned with must be "critical," of direct importance to the basic structures of either or both systems. For example, a person who brings awareness of a new fashion in clothing from the national into the local system would not by virtue of this function alone be considered a mediator, even though he does act as a communicational intermediary. Second, the mediators "guard" these functions, i.e., they have near-exclusivity in performing them; exclusivity means that if the link is to be made at all between the two systems with respect to the particular function, it must be made through the mediators. As a result, the number of mediator statuses is always limited. To the extent that alternative links become available, so that the mediators lose their exclusive control of the junctures, they cease to be mediators. These two criteria, critical functions and exclusivity, limit the extension of the concept.

Persons who provide contact between the two systems but who do not necessarily fulfill both criteria will be referred to here as "intermediaries." While the terminology is clumsy, it is felt that there is an important distinction which needs to be made between the broader category, "intermediary," and the special kind of intermediary, the "mediator."

It seems to be general that there is a rank difference between the mediator and the other persons in the local system who are involved in the mediated interaction. The mediators may take on their function because of previous possession of a higher rank, or they may achieve a higher rank as a result of assuming the mediator role. In either case, the relationship between the local and the national system assumes a "vertical" form.

The concept of the mediator was developed out of the study of particular kinds of societies, those to which anthropologists first turned when they began to move beyond the primitives, namely complex societies which still retain a strong "folk" element. That it is within such societies that the concept finds its widest applicability suggests the possibility that it may represent a form of part-whole relationship peculiar to the preindustrial state society. It is obvious that in a society at a pre-state level of integration there would be little necessity for mediators. On the other hand, the existence of mediators implies that the local units are separate from each other and from the larger society to the extent that a limited group can have exclusive control over the connections between part and whole—a situation associated with preindustrial societies. However, if the mediator is characteristic of this sociocultural level, it may be expected to be replaced by other kinds of community-nation interaction with further integration of the national society.

The present discussion explores this possibility. It examines the traditional mediators in the community of Colleverde, a patron group, and traces the impact of contemporary national development upon them. It attempts to show that "mediators" can best be understood as elements of a particular form of part-whole relationship, one which exists at a particular level of development of complex societies but which is superseded with further development.

THE COMMUNITY

Colleverde (a pseudonym) is an Umbrian *comune* near the geographical center of Italy, about 50 kilometers from the provincial capital, Perugia, and approximately 150 kilometers north of Rome. The medieval castle-village which is the functional center of the community is situated on a hilltop overlooking the valley of the Tiber. The countryside of the *comune* covers a wide range of environmental variation, from a strip of level plain along the banks of the Tiber (about 150 meters above sea level), through a region of low and medium hills, to the woods, meadows, and wasteland of a high-hill zone (up to 650 meters). In 1960, Colleverde parish (one of two parishes in the *comune*, each of which may be considered a separate community) had a population of 1,885 in 465 households. About one-fifth of the inhabitants live in the village, the remainder on dispersed farms in the surrounding countryside.

About 80 per cent of the active population are agriculturalists. The majority work self-contained farmsteads, most of which comprise between two and fifteen hectares. Except for minor variations due to altitude, each farm produces the entire range of local crops and animals: wheat, olives, wine grapes, maize, a variety of minor crops grown for human and animal subsistence and for renewal of the land, meat calves (which since the advent of tractors after World War II have been rapidly eliminating the work oxen which were formerly raised), pigs, a few sheep, and barnyard fowl. In addition, industrial crops (tobacco, sugar beet, and tomato) have been introduced on a small scale in the irrigated tracts of the plain. Of these products, only the wheat, calves, and industrial crops are raised primarily or exclusively for sale. At least two-thirds of the land is cultivated under the *mezzadria* system of share-farming, while the remainder is worked by peasant proprietors, tenant farmers, and a few wage-laborers.

The *mezzadria* system is based on a contractual association between a landowner, who furnishes the farm (including cleared land, farmhouse, out-buildings, and livestock) and advances all working capital as needed, and a peasant family who provide labor and the minor equipment. All other expenses and the income of the enterprise are divided between them, theoretically half and half; in 1948 the peasant's share of the income was raised by law to 53 per cent. As compared with other sharecropping systems, the *mezzadria* is distinguished by three elements: the integrated farm, the family labor unit, and the active participation in investments and operation of the enterprise on the part of both owner and cultivators.

The integrity of the farm and the major dependence upon a family for its labor requirements imply a recurrent imbalance between the number of working hands and the size of the farm. Adjustment is made primarily by a movement of families among farms as major changes in family size occur. Partly because large households traditionally were advantageous to the *mezzadri* (enabling them to work a larger farm),[3] the ideal household consisted of a patrilocal extended family, in which all sons brought their brides to live in their father's household and in which authority and economic control were vested in the family head. Although during the past few decades the largest households have been breaking up, more than half the *mezzadria* families still have at least one married son residing in the parental household. In the community as a whole, however, only a third of the households consist of extended families, and the predominant form is the nuclear family.

The community is economically and socially heterogeneous. The fundamental principle of settlement pattern, the segregation of village center and countryside, demarcates the most pervasive social division, the people of "inside" and those of "outside." This cleavage is occupational: those who do not work the land (landowners and administrators of agricultural properties, professionals, clerks, merchants, artisans, and laborers) as against those who do. It is the major correlate of social-class differentiation: the *signori* (the local upper class) and a middle group consisting of the working people of families resident in the village for generations, as against the great lower class. It describes, in general, political party alignments within the community: the Right and Center as against the Left. To some extent it parallels a difference in the spirit of religious participation: the "cynical" (in the view of the Colleverdesi) as against the devout. It is also a cultural division, for the village is regarded as the seat of civilization surrounded by rusticity, bringing *civilta* (that which is "civilized," in the sense of "citified") to the countryside and bestowing the aura of *civilta* on the whole community.

PATRONAGE

Until the recent postwar period, the mediation of relations between Colleverde and the larger society was the function of a patronage system. Before discussing this function, it will be helpful to describe the general features of traditional patronage in the community. Patronage patterns are familiar to all the older contemporary Colleverdesi, whose recollections (supplemented by local historical documents) were the basis for the following reconstruction. However, only vestiges of them remain today.

Patronage as a cross-cultural pattern may be

defined as an informal contractual relationship between persons of unequal status and power, which imposes reciprocal obligations of a different kind on each of the parties. As a minimum, what is owed is protection and favor on the one side and loyalty on the other. The relationship is on a personal, face-to-face basis, and it is a continuing one.

As is the case in other cultures where a patron-client relationship receives explicit recognition, patronage in Central Italy is not coterminous with all the meanings of the term for "patron" (cf. Kenny 1960: 14-15; Foster 1963: 1282). In Colleverde, the term *padrone* is applied to: (1) the legal owner of something, for example a house or a dog; (2) one who controls something, such as the mistress of a household, or one who has self-control; (3) an employer, when reference is made to him by or to an employee; (4) the grantor of a *mezzadria* farm, whether or not he is actually the landowner and whether or not there is anything more than minimal contact with the cultivators; (5) a guardian deity; and (6) a patron in a patron-client relationship.[4] However, all of these usages which refer to one person as the *padrone* of another describe potential bases for the formation of a patron-client relationship.

The most important patron-client relationship in Colleverde was that between the parties to the *mezzadria* arrangement. The relationship developed informally, by extension of the formal terms of the contract. A peasant might approach the landlord to ask a favor, perhaps a loan of money or help in some trouble with the law, or the landlord might offer his aid knowing of a problem. If the favor were granted or accepted, further favors were likely to be asked or offered at some later time. The peasant would reciprocate—at a time and in a context different from that of the acceptance of the favor, in order to de-emphasize the material self-interest of the reciprocative action—by bringing the landlord especially choice offerings from the farm produce, by sending some member of the peasant family to perform services in the landlord's home, by refraining from cheating the landlord, or merely by speaking well of him in public and professing devotion to him.[5] Or the peasant might be the first to offer his "favors," in anticipation of those he would later have to ask of the landlord. Whether or not a true patronage relationship developed from the *mezzadria* association depended upon the landlord's inclination, his need of support, and his place of residence (or the length of an absentee owner's yearly sojourn in Colleverde).

The *mezzadria* association was particularly conducive to the development of a patronage relationship, for the institution had the effect of bringing landlord and peasant into long and personal contact with each other. The minimum duration of the contract is one year, but typically it persists for several years, and traditionally it was common for a farm to be occupied by the same family for many decades and even for generations. The landowner's role as director of the enterprise requires his continuing interest and his physical presence much of the time. Some proprietors employ managers (*fattori*), who range from unskilled foremen and commercial agents to highly trained agricultural technicians, but traditionally even when this was the case the landlords maintained close contact with their farms. In contrast to the typical situation in southern Italy, the landowning class throughout the *mezzadria* area has a strong tradition of active interest in agriculture; for example, many receiver higher education in fields which equip them for the management of their property. There is, in fact, a marked tendency to glorify their attachment to their land and "their" peasants.

Until recent years, the owners of Colleverde's land were the nucleus of the village population, constituting a local upper class. In other communities of the area, those proprietors who did not reside in the rural centers lived in the nearby towns and small cities and often retained part-time residences near their land. Thus the landlords were accessible. Moreover, close and continuing contact between landlord and peasant was encouraged not only by the necessary interaction related to the operations of the farm but also by the cultural definition of the *mezzadria* relationship. The association was ideally a personal and affectionate tie ranging far beyond the formal contract covering the enterprise, a tie between two families, one the protector and benefactor and the other the loyal dependent. To the peasant, the landlord was the most immediately available person to turn to for economic aid or for knowledge about the world outside. To the landlord, a patronage relationship was at the least a great convenience. It provided a check against being taken advantage of, a check that was cheaper, more reliable, and in any case a useful supplement to supervision by *fattori*. It facilitated contacts with the peasant and contributed to the day-to-day efficiency of the enterprise. Finally, it was a means of controlling potentially disruptive influences from the outside. It is significant that the paternalism of the *mezzadria* landlords has often been pointed to as a factor in delaying the spread of labor agitation to the Central Italian hill region for several decades after its onset in many agricultural areas of the nation about 1870 (Bandini 1957: 77-78).

A peasant whose own landlord was unavailable or who was unable or unwilling to dispense favors occasionally turned to other landowners. More common was the formation of a patron-client relationship between lower-class persons who were not *mezzadri* and a local landlord or other local person of high status and power. The potential client would approach one of the *signori* with a request, or he might attempt to establish the relationship first by presenting him with some small gift or by making himself available to run errands or help out in various ways. Such relationships, although they did not center about common participation in an agricultural enterprise, resembled and may be said to have been patterned after the landlord-peasant relationship.

The patron-client relationships in Colleverde differed from those which Foster observed in Mexico in one important respect. An essential aspect of such relationships in Tzintzuntzan is that they are dyadic; they can exist only between two individuals: "Ego conceptualizes his obligations and expectations as a two-way street, he at one end and a single partner at the other end" (Foster 1963: 1281). In Colleverde, however, the dyad was not the only or even the most frequent form. When the relationship was formed between *mezzadria* landlord and peasant, the landlord became patron not to an individual but to an entire household. His obligations automatically extended to all members of the peasant family, unless some member specifically rejected his own obligations as client. On the other hand, the wife of the landlord became *la padrona*, and she was expected to adopt the role of patroness, especially toward the women of the peasant family. To a lesser extent, other members of the landlord's family were also treated as patrons and sometimes accepted the obligations of patronage. These extensions of the patron and client roles to whole households were not the result of independently established contracts; they were more or less automatic, although the other persons were not strictly bound to accept the role.

Furthermore, there was in Colleverde the concept of an individual (or a married couple or family) becoming patron to a group made up of unrelated persons. Traditionally, there were several community associations and organized projects (an important example was the 40-member band) which were initiated and/or maintained by local *signori*, who were considered their patrons. Such persons gave economic support and political protection to these groups (not to their members as individuals). Similarly, certain *signori* regarded themselves and were generally regarded by others as patrons of the community, with the responsibility to provide benefits for the community as a whole. One way in which this was done was by leaving a will providing that part of their patrimony be used in specific ways by the community. Such endowments were a major source of public funds and community charities.

THE PATRON AS MEDIATOR

The descriptions of patronage systems in various cultural settings suggest that one of the most important aspects of the patron's role is to relate the client to the world outside the local community. Pitt-Rivers (1954: 141) emphasized this point in his analysis of an Andalusian village: "It is, above all, (the patron's) relationship to the powers outside the pueblo which gives him value." In Andalusia, a structure of patronage links the authority of the state to the network of neighborly relations and balances "the tension between the state and the community" (Pitt-Rivers 1954: 154-155). Kenny (1960: 17-18), writing about Castile, observed that the patrons are validly described as "gatekeepers," for "they largely dominate the paths linking the local infrastructure of the village to the superstructure of the outside urban world." In general, the patrons described from recent times in Spain and Latin America, and those of traditional Central Italy, are mediators in the full sense of the definition adopted here. Their functions are critical ones, for they have an essential part in the basic economic and political structures of the society. Moreover, persons become patrons precisely because their capacity to perform these functions is virtually exclusive.

It would appear, in fact, that patrons are particularly well adapted to performing the function of mediation between the local and the national system. The patron usually has a distinctly defined status in both systems and operates effectively in both. Furthermore, the relationship between patron and client is stable and durable. As Foster has pointed out, continuance of the relationship is assured by never permitting a balance to be achieved between the obligations of the parties; the account is never settled, but rather each constantly wins new credits which will be redeemed at a future time or incurs new debts which must later be paid. Stability of the patron-client tie is reinforced by its patterning after a kin relationship, the patron becoming "like a father" in obligations to and respect due from the client (as the close connection between "patronage" and "paternalism" suggests). Personalized terms of address are used, there generally are affective overtones to the relationship, and frequently there is a denial of utilitarian motives and an insistence instead upon the non-priced demands of "loyalty," "friendship," or being "almost like one of the family." (One Colleverdese woman explained her economically advantageous relationship with her patroness with the statement, "We are old friends, so we always ask each other for favors.") In societies where social mobility is limited and where kinship therefore cannot function as a link between the local and the national system (cf. Friedl 1959), patronage provides a close, highly sanctioned, and self-perpetuating relationship between different social strata as a link between the systems.

Nevertheless, the data from Colleverde suggest that this aspect of patronage is a fairly recent acquisition. Until the unification of Italy in 1860, mediation of the client's dealings with the outside was only a minor aspect of the patron's role. The patronage system had its basis in the peasants' dependence upon the landlords, who historically were the peasants' sole recourse to physical protection and economic aid. However, under the domain of the States of the Church, the community had only tangential relations with the larger political unit, and for most Colleverdesi the sphere of social interaction extended no farther than the nearby market towns and a radius of neighboring communities within which there were cycles of fairs and religious festivals. Certainly for the lower classes extralocal contact was minimal, and there was little necessity for mediation.

After 1860, however, the new nation began the task of knitting together the separate regions and communities. The degree of contact between the national and the local system increased steadily, and more and more the nation encroached into the lives of Colleverdesi of all classes. The governmental bureaucracy entered the community, bringing to the peasants the bewildering demands of official papers and legal codes and occasionally offering equally bewildering economic benefits. New roads and railroads brought outsiders into the community and took Colleverdesi out. Obligatory military service and temporary labor opportunities in other areas took men to distant parts of the nation. To some the developing national institutions meant potential jobs, both within the community and outside it. In order to deal with their expanding

world, the lower-class Colleverdesi needed help. The peasants turned to those who had always aided them. Persons who had no landlord, or whose landlord was unwilling or unable to help, sought other sources.

Of the functions performed by the patrons during the period from 1860 to 1945, some represent a continuity with the earlier role of the landlord: lending money or guaranteeing loans, giving employment, helping to provide dowries for the daughters of the client families, providing medicines and helping to obtain medical services. However, to these were added many new functions, involving the mediation of contacts with the world outside the community. The patron filled out the papers which were required at every significant step in the individual's life, and he spoke to bureaucrats on his client's behalf. As government benefits were introduced, the patron was needed to obtain them. For example, Sra. M., whose husband was killed during World War I, tried in vain for months to collect a government pension for war widows, and only after her patron spoke of her case to the appropriate officials did she succeed in getting it. The patron interpreted the law to his client and offered advice. If there were trouble with the authorities, the patron would intervene. Many cases could be cited of persons who were arrested by the *carabinieri* and released after intervention of the patron, and of others who were sentenced to prison and for whom the patron obtained pardons.

If a client had to go out of the community for any purpose, the patron would recommend him to some acquaintance at the destination. In fact, all dealings with institutions or persons outside the local system required personal recommendations from a mediator.[6] When M.'s grandfather tried to get the local tobacco concession, when R. applied to a military specialists' school, when F. took his deaf sister to a physician in Rome, when P. as a young man went periodically to the coastal plain to seek work, when T. took his bride to Perugia to choose a coral necklace—all would have considered it foolhardy to do so without a recommendation from a respected contact, and to get a recommendation a patron was needed. As jobs in the national institutions expanded, access to them was also a matter of recommendations, and this remained no less true even after adoption of the *concorso* system, an open competition for available jobs based on examinations.

In the patronage patterns of traditional Colleverde which were vividly recalled by older informants, the mediation functions were, in fact, the major importance of the patron. For example, the most valuable patron was neither the wealthiest nor the most generous, but the one with the best connections. Yet this aspect of the patron's role was elaborated only in the late nineteenth and early twentieth centuries. It was only after the community became incorporated into a complex nation, a nation which made demands upon and offered opportunities to individuals and which required extensive contact between the local and the national system, that the dominant features of "traditional" Colleverdesi patronage emerged.

In general, the patrons of Colleverde in the 1860-1945 years can be characterized as a small group of local *signori*, no more than a dozen heads of households at any given time. Most were *mezzadria* landlords, owning as little as two or three small farms or as much as several hundred hectares of land. Some of the landlords also occupied professional or administrative positions of authority in the community, as schoolteachers, pharmacists, physicians, tax collectors, priests, and elected administrators. In addition, some of these positions were held by non-landed members of local landowning families, who also formed part of the patron group. The non-landowning patrons also included a few bureaucrats and professions (the *comune* secretaries, two of the pharmacists, a physician, and some of the priests), who came to Colleverde from other towns in Umbria.

The patrons were not an aristocratic group, although a few landowning families traced remote kinship ties to Umbrian nobility. New members were recruited from the commercial class of the towns and cities of the region, for it was this class that throughout Umbria was taking over the holdings of the traditional landowners and educating its sons for the burgeoning bureaucracy and the professions. There was little mobility into the patron group from the lower classes of Colleverde, for the sons of the prosperous peasants and artisans who were able to purchase land, even those who acquired substantial holdings, were not accepted as "true" *signori*, nor were they likely to possess the connections with *signori* in other communities which were an important foundation of patronage power. Despite their ties and sometimes their origins outside the community, the patrons were fully a local group. They lived in Colleverde, and their identification with it was strong.

Each patron performed a wide range of mediation functions, the same individual often being for his clients at once the economic, political, social, and ideological link to the larger society. As a group, the patrons controlled virtually all the critical junctures between the local and the national systems. Colleverde's economic relationships with the rest of the nation were for the most part the concern only of the major landlords. This follows from the duality of the traditional *mezzadria* economy: only the landowners sold produce on the market, while the peasants' share was consumed for their own subsistence. Direct participation in the political life of the nation was limited to the patrons. The mayor and the administrative council of the community were selected from this group; they were elected, but until well into the twentieth century few persons other than the *signori* were eligible to vote. Moreover, it was primarily members of this group who acted as local representatives of the state, for local jobs in the bureaucracy were passed from one member of the elite to another. Even the religious ties of the community to the Universal Church were to a large extent in the hands of the patrons. Not only were the priests of Colleverde themselves often part of the patron group (as major landlords holding the several Church-owned *mezzadria* farms and usually as members of landowning families), but the patrons constituted the lay leadership of the local Church, and many had kin connections with Church officials throughout Umbria and in the Vatican.

The patrons had numerous social relationships based on kinship and friendship extending beyond the community, and they practiced frequent inter-community visiting. The peasants, in contrast, maintained only rare ties of closest kinship outside the immediate area. Finally, because the patrons were long the only literate persons in Colleverde, they were the carriers of the national culture, and values and ideas filtered down through them to the rest of the community. In sum, this group were mediators precisely because they had, almost exclusively, direct access to the nation and because they occupied those formal positions which were the links between the local and national systems. In turn, this control of the mediation functions was the primary source of their power to exert patronage.

Looking outward from the community, the mediators' relationships with the national system were of two kinds. First, the local patrons had extensive ties with near and distant kinsmen, friends, and business associates—social and power equals to themselves—in other village centers, in towns, and in cities of the region. These were continuing relationships based on reciprocal, equivalent obligations. Second, the Colleverdesi patrons, as well as their equal numbers in other communities, were themselves clients to more powerful, higher-status patrons.

These higher patrons did not function at the village level but belonged to the spheres of town and city. Thus, through a hierarchy of patronage (cf. Kenny 1960: 22-23; Gillin 1962: 37), Colleverde was linked to the higher units of organization within the nation.

The structure of the traditional relationship between Colleverde and the larger society may now be summarized. A small group of local upper-class families, the nucleus of which were the major landowners of the community, functioned as mediators. Although they considered themselves as Colleverdesi and were active in community life, they were also participants in the national society. Within the local context they acted out the national culture, creating—of a village of only 300 inhabitants—an urban-like, "civilized" center in the rustic countryside. Interaction between the mediators and those in the community for whom they mediated was based on a continuing and intimate patron-client relationship, which was an extension of the landlord-peasant relationship defined by the land-tenure system. Because of the nature of this relationship and the constant presence of the patrons, the clients were strongly aware of a wider social sphere without direct participation in it. Thus, the countryside was linked to the village (and the village lower class to its upper class) by the vertical bond of patronage, while the village was in turn linked to the outside through the patrons' participation in two kinds of networks: horizontal ties with equivalent members of other communities and vertical ties through hierarchies of patrons operating at progressively higher levels of national integration.

This description is an example of only one form that a part-whole relationship through mediators can take. Such a relationship varies significantly in at least five different ways. First, there is the tie between the mediators and those in the local system for whom they mediate, which need not be one of patronage. Not only are there other mechanisms by which the connection with a mediator may be established (such as kinship, ritual kinship, employment, or political appointment) and other cultural rationales for maintaining the connection, but the mutual rights and obligations and the kind of interaction involved may be different. The relationship may be limited to specific areas rather than as wide-ranging as the patron-client tie; the interaction may be sporadic rather than fairly continuous; and the quality of the relationship may be more or less emotionally intense than that between patron and client in Colleverde.

Second, the nature of the mediators themselves may vary greatly—their history, their traditions, and the manner in which they are recruited and replaced. For example, a mediating group recruited from economically successful peasants would be quite different from the patrons of Colleverde, a landowning class with quasi-aristocratic traditions.

Third, there is variation in the particular functions which the mediators perform and in the way in which these functions are combined. A political functionary whose main business is the collection of taxes is a mediator of a very different kind from the Colleverdesi patrons, whose functions touched every aspect of life. In the case of Colleverde, all mediating functions were combined and performed by the same group, but at the opposite extreme there might be a separate mediator for each function.

Fourth, the size of the mediating group may vary, determining a smaller or larger number of channels into the local system. In Colleverde there were multiple channels, intermediate between the extreme possibilities of a single individual as mediator and a situation in which each household has its own links to the national system.

A fifth dimension of variation is the kind of relationship of the mediators to the local system and the degree of their integration into it. The patrons of Colleverde were fully a part of the local system and locally resident. However, mediators may also be part of the local system yet not reside in the community, they may reside locally but remain detached from the local system, or they may be outsiders with only tangential relationships to the local system.

THE ELIMINATION OF MEDIATORS

In the period since World War II there have been fundamental changes in the relationship between the Central Italian rural community and the larger society. The patrons of Colleverde, the traditional mediators between the local and the national system, have been pushed out of the strategic link positions. However, they have not simply been replaced by other emerging groups. Rather, it may be said that there has been change in the nature of the links between community and nation.

In contemporary Colleverde there is no longer a patron group. In part this is the result of the economic decline of the families which formed the nucleus of this group. A century ago, all but a minor part of the landed property in the community was concentrated in their hands. With time, however, there has been a continuing increase both in the total number of landowners and in the proportion of land owned by persons of non-local or lower-class origin. These changes began with the inheritance provisions of the Civil Code of 1865, which required that a large portion of the patrimony be divided equally among all children. A high birth rate and a declining mortality rate among the landowning families during the late nineteenth century contributed to the subdivision of inheritances. By the turn of the century some of the landlords had fallen into debt, and mortgaged land gradually passed to members of the urban commercial class and to estate agents who were able to exploit their employers' indebtedness. At the same time, and particularly in the years during and after World War I, a number of local peasants and other landless individuals were able to acquire small amounts of land, through profits from agriculture or through wage labor or commercial ventures. After World War II this trend was intensified; it was accelerated by laws encouraging peasant proprietorship, but mainly it was the result of the rising values of livestock, the expansion of cash crops, and wage-labor opportunities in a nearby tobacco factory and in the industries of northern Italy, Germany, and France.

The present distribution of land ownership indicates an absence of any substantial holdings in the hands of either local descendants of the traditional patron families or other local residents who might have taken over the role of the patrons. The contemporary holdings fall into three general categories, according to size. The major landlords, four individuals with holdings of about 100 hectares each, are all outsiders— absentee owners, none of whom was raised or lived for any length of time in Colleverde, and whose relations to their peasants and the community in general are impersonal. Four landlords have what may be considered medium-sized holdings (about 35 to 50 hectares). All are Colleverdesi by birth and residence, but none is of a traditional landowning family, and none thinks of his role as properly one of patronage or is regarded in this way by others in the community (they are scornfully referred to as "*signori* merely through money," as opposed to the "true *signori*, thorough birth and mentality"). Among the owners of small holdings are many of the descendants of the old patron group, some of whom still live in Colleverde, frugally, and some of whom have moved into bureaucratic and professional positions in larger centers, returning to the community for summer holidays and for retirement in their old age.

Thus the economic decline of the traditional patrons has not been accompanied by the emergence of any new group to assume an analogous role, for there is no longer any local concentration of wealth sufficient to provide the foundation of a patron group. Moreover, of the most prosperous persons in the community today, none either belongs to the tradition of patronage or has the social status to which the patron role is appropriate.

In the absence of a patron group, what has become of the traditional functions of the patrons? Many of the functions of economic assistance have been taken over by the state. Instead of the favors of a patron, there are governmental credit institutions, a national health plan, an official charitable organization supported by land set aside for this purpose by the government, assistance for infants and nursing mothers, sickness and disability benefits, old-age pensions, and special allotments during agricultural crises and other times of special need. Other institutions which will be mentioned below (political parties, syndicalist organizations, and the Church) also offer assistance on a limited scale.

The primary concern here, however, is with the mediation functions formerly performed by the patrons. Some of these have been eliminated entirely in the postwar period, as persons of all classes and categories have been brought into direct participation in the national system. The partial incorporation of the *mezzadri* into the market economy (the last occupational category to be so affected), the movement of political activity into the piazzas and bars of the community consequent upon universal suffrage, the emphasis upon individual membership in a Universal Church at the expense of community-wide, locally oriented religious activity—these are all manifestations of the general process of the integration of separate communities into a national unit, which implies an increasing degree of nonmediated participation in national life. The most important specific developments in Colleverde which have facilitated this increase in non-mediated participation have been inexpensive means of transportation (particularly local bus service and the motorcycle), the expansion of literacy and elementary education which provide the basic skills of participation, and radio and television which bring knowledge of the larger society even to the immobile and illiterate.

Nevertheless, the individual Colleverdesi continues to be related to the national system through a number of indirect links as well. These indirect links, corresponding to the formal positions and informal roles through which the patrons acted as mediators, have been taken over by other groups, both from within and outside Colleverde.

The elective administrative positions of the

community have been held since the first free elections after World War II primarily by *mezzadria* peasants, as a result of the consistent victories of the Communist-Socialist coalition ticket. The only group which has any possibility of succeeding to local political control, the members of the organized political opposition, consists mainly of the upwardly mobile sons of peasant proprietors, artisans, and merchants.

The local bureaucratic positions are filled today through the *concorso* system, the effect of which is to recruit more and more personnel from the lower classes and to distribute them over an ever expanding geographic range. Thus many of the jobs in Colleverde which are subject to the *concorso* are occupied by non-local persons. The *comune* secretary (an administrative position second in importance only to the elected mayor), the civil police officer, the head of the post office, the tax collector, several of the schoolteachers, the doctor, the veterinarian, the midwife, and (as everywhere in Italy) the *carabinieri* are outsiders. All these positions, with the exception of the *carabinieri*, were traditionally held by members of the local landowning families. Other bureaucratic functionaries in Colleverde—clerks in the town hall, the postal clerk, and the excise-tax official—are local persons, the educated sons of lower-class families. Only the pharmacist, who is a woman, and some of the teachers are descendants of the traditional patron group.

In addition to occupying these formal positions which are links between the local and the national systems, the patrons also acted as informal intermediaries for individual clients. Today there are several organizations which perform this function in Colleverde, assisting individuals to deal with the world outside the community, providing advice and, to a lesser extent, recommendations and intervention. Since the establishment of free elections, various political party groups have attempted to outdo each other in offering conspicuous services, and intervention with the higher powers is the most potent of these. Labor unions and other syndicalist organizations, which act to protect the interests of their members, have also re-emerged since the war.

Although most of the twenty or more national and regional organizations which have some formal representation in Colleverde exist there by name only, three or four are regularly resorted to for help by Colleverdesi. Among these groups, one sponsored by the Church is of particular importance. The local Church has been a vigorous partisan in the postwar political conflict in the community, and in its bid for popular support it has been an innovator of various services and projects. In order to counteract the drawing power of the favors offered by the Leftist organizations, the priest organized a local chapter of A.C.L.I., the national Catholic labor organization. Today an official of the provincial A.C.L.I. comes to Colleverde once a week to offer advice of any kind to any member, such as aid in claiming a pension or guidance to men seeking temporary work abroad.

There are still in Colleverde some vestiges of personal, informal patronage by local individuals rather than by institutions. Occasionally a landlord in relation to a peasant, or an employer to an employee, will take on special obligations as intermediary or protector. However, even in the rare cases where such a relationship persists over a period of several years, the patronage functions actually performed are restricted to particular areas and limited by the usually slight power of the patron. Much more characteristic of landowner-*mezzadro* relationships today is the merely superficial observance of command and deference behaviors; in fact, the use of the term *padrone* often becomes almost sarcastic, reflecting the landlord's failure to fulfill the functional obligations of a patron.

In general, two kinds of personal patrons may be distinguished in the community today. In the first place, there are a few individuals who consider themselves patrons and who have deliberately tried to take on patronage roles in the traditional form. One, the wife of a prosperous merchant (who like his wife is of lower-class parentage) has several clients to whom she gives gifts of food and loans of money and for whom she helps to obtain employment; however, she is dependent for these gifts and loans upon whatever she can set aside while managing her husband's store, over which she has no formal control. Another, a retired public official descended from an old landowning family, is for several people a source of advice on matters relating to law and government. Similarly, the pharmacist is sought for advice by a number of lower-class persons, but like the retired official her role is restricted to specific areas. Each of these individuals is limited by his actual power. Having little to offer the clients and little more than personal satisfaction to receive, none has succeeded in more than simulating the role of the traditional patron.

In addition, there are some persons who have the power to perform important patronage functions. Personal intermediaries are still required in dealing with the national government and other powers outside the community. It is through recommendations that most jobs are obtained, official matters settled, and so on. For example, since the rapid increase in the number of persons qualified for white-collar and professional work has greatly intensified competition in the *concorso* system, the selection is determined largely by recommendations, performance on the examinations being only a minimal qualification. The most valuable local sources of recommendations are the political party secretaries and the priest. As in the traditional patron-client relationship, these new intermediaries exchange favors for loyalty, namely political support. However, unlike the traditional patronage forms, these relationships are functionally specific and of brief duration. Alignments shift frequently as favors are bestowed where most profitable in return for temporary support (ultimately, votes).

It has been seen that new groups have moved into positions which enable them to act as intermediaries. Can the change, therefore, be best understood as a shift from one kind of mediator to other kinds? If "mediators" are defined as persons who have exclusive control over the functionally important junctures between the local and the national systems, the answer to this question must be negative. Instead of a small patron group who alone have direct access to the national system and thus control all connections with it, there are today separate ties for each functionally distinct aspect of the interaction between local and national systems, and with regard to each aspect there are many different ties which are alternative links. The clerk whom one sees about collecting government insurance benefits is not the same person as the official agent to whom one sells surplus wheat. Moreover, if the clerk's response is unsatisfactory one can go to an official of the union of *mezzadri* or to the A.C.L.I. center in the Church; similarly, if one prefers, the wheat may be sold to an independent merchant or to the landlord instead of to the official agent. The number and diversity of indirect links to the larger society, and particularly the existence of alternative possibilities, preclude the presence of mediators.

In addition to the increase in indirect links, there has also been a qualitative change. Today, a large proportion of the indirect links are structurally horizontal, relating persons of equivalent rank and social category. Ties between persons of particular occupational groups in various communities throughout the region and nation have been strengthened and institutionalized in the syndicalist organizations. Politically, the major identification of individual Colleverdesi

is as members of social and economic interest groups which cut across communities. The political intermediaries—the elected administrative officials, the bureaucrats, and the grantors of favors—are drawn from all social strata and to an increasing degree from the lower rungs. Outwardly extended social relationships based on kinship and friendship are no longer restricted to one class in Colleverde but are maintained at least to some extent by all segments of the population. This trend has been intensified by the postwar outmigration of many Colleverdesi families (most of whom moved to towns and cities in Central Italy), which has meant to their relatives and close friends still in Colleverde numerous new ties with other centers—ties which it was possible and pleasurable to maintain through visiting back and forth on holidays. Thus, from the point of view of the Colleverdesi peasant of today, the national society is known and participated in not primarily through an upper-class landlord, but through the mayor who is also a peasant, the labor union confined to *Mezzadri*, other formal organizations composed of lower-class persons, and relatives and friends who live in other towns.

In sum, the traditional mediators have not simply been succeeded by new groups in the society taking control of the "critical junctures," nor has such control simply passed to persons occupying different roles from that of the traditional mediators. New groups have become intermediaries and new roles have appeared through which persons may act as intermediaries, but there has also been occurring a fundamental shift in the form of relationship between the local and the national systems. The junctures can no longer be "guarded" by any group. Direct participation by individuals in the national system, alternative links between the systems, and structurally horizontal links are basic elements in the emerging form.

CONCLUSION

Twice in the recent history of Colleverde there has been an intensification of contacts between the community and the larger society. The first time, in the years following the unification of Italy, the interclass bond of patronage became the basis of the linkage between the local and the national systems. Mediators guarded the junctures between part and whole, at once facilitating contacts between community and nation and limiting the access of local persons to the larger society. The second time, in the period after the Second World War, a new part-whole relationship developed. Horizontal, outward ties were strengthened at the expense of vertical, local ties. Diverse competing intermediaries, as well as an increasing degree of non-mediated participation in the national society, replaced the mediators. The kind of change which can be observed in Central Italy is undoubtedly occurring in many industrializing nations. It may be that the mediator represents a general form of community-nation relationship characteristic of an early phase of development of nation-states, a form which regularly gives way as the process of integration of the total society advances.

BIBLIOGRAPHY

Bandidi, M. 1957 Cento anni di storia agraria italiana. Roma.

Foster, G. M. 1963 The Dyadic Contract in Tzintzuntzan, II: Patron-Client Relationship. American Anthropologist 65: 1280-1294.

Friedl, E. 1959 The Role of Kinship in the Transmission of National Culture to Rural Villages in Mainland Greece. American Anthropologist 61: 30-38.

Geertz, C. 1960 The Changing Role of Cultural Broker: The Javanese *Kijaji*. Comparative Studies in Society and History 2: 228-249.

Gillin, J. P. 1962 Some Signposts for Policy. Social Change in Latin America Today, pp. 14-62. New York.

Istituto Nazionale di Economia Agraria. 1956 La distribuzione della proprietà fondiaria in Italia, v. I: relazione generale, a cura di Giuseppe Medici. Roma.

Kenny, M. 1960 Patterns of Patronage in Spain. Anthropological Quarterly 33: 14-23.

Pitkin, D. S. 1959 The Intermediate Society: A Study in Articulation. Intermediate Societies, Social Mobility, and Communication, ed. V. F. Ray, pp. 14-19. Proceedings of the 1959 Spring Meeting of the American Ethnological Society. Seattle.

Pitt-Rivers, J. A. 1954 The People of the Sierra. London.

Redfield, R. 1956 Peasant Society and Culture. Chicago.

Silverman, S. F. 1963 Landlord and Peasant in an Umbrian Community. Unpublished Ph.D. dissertation, Columbia University.

Steward, J. H. 1955 Theory of Culture Change. Urbana.

Wolf, E. R. 1956 Aspects of Group Relations in a Complex Society: Mexico. American Anthropologist 58: 1065-1078.

NOTES

1 The field work on which this paper is based was carried out in a rural community of Central Italy from August, 1960, to September, 1961. The project was supported by a predoctoral fellowship (MF-11, 068) and grant (M-3720) from the National Institute of Mental Health, United States Public Health Service. A more detailed description of the community is given in my doctoral dissertation (Silverman 1963).

The term "Central Italy," following the agricultural-economic definition adopted by the National Institute of Agrarian Economics (Italy), designates the large area extending over the sub-Appenine hills of Emilia-Romagna and the hills and plains (but not the mountains) of Tuscany, Umbria, the Marches, Latium, and Abruzzi-Molise north of the province of Campobasso (Istituto Nazionale di Economia Agraria 1956: facing 108).

2 The boundaries of the local system are not precisely coextensive with the community, since a local system may include regular relationships between members of different communities and since any community in a complex society has within it some representation of the national system. However, this paper will follow the common practice of using the term "community" interchangeably with "local system."

3 The upper limit of household size was about twenty members. The average size, based on estimates from a population register covering the period 1881-1907, was seven or eight. Today, the average mezzadria household consists of about six members.

4 In the third, fourth, and sixth instances, the term may also be used for address. Alternatively, the *padrone* may be addressed in the respectful form of using the given name preceded by *Sor* or *Signora* (rarely, *Sora*). In Colleverde, as in Foster's community, there is no specific term for "client."

5 Until the reforms of recent years, the *mezzadria* contract required a number of "extra" obligations of the peasant to the landlord, including gifts of fowl and eggs in specific quantities at different times of the year and various forms of unreimbursed labor in the landlord's household. Thus it is not always apparent whether a peasant's offering was the fulfillment of the formal *mezzadria* contract or part of a voluntary patron-client relationship. However, the essence of the latter was that the quantity or value of the goods and services given exceeded the formal requirements.

6 The recommendation, the importance of which has diminished only slightly though the channels have changed, is a request for a personal favor to the recommender, and it is not at all concerned with the qualifications of the person on whose behalf it is made. The value of a recommendation depends first upon the status of the recommender, second upon the closeness of his connection to the addressee, and third upon the closeness of the connection between the recommender and the recommended.

THE TRANSFORMATION OF CLIENTELISM
IN RURAL COLOMBIA*

STEFFEN W. SCHMIDT

THE RECENT GROWTH of studies using clientelism (patron-broker-client relations) as a framework for analysis clearly attests to its vitality as an explanatory vehicle.[1] According to one scholar,

A focus on political clientage, despite the tentative character of much preliminary evidence, seems to satisfy, some of the requirements put forth by comparative scholars in their current mood of self-assessment. Joseph LaPalombara has argued for the development of partial or middle range theories and Roy Macridis has appealed for a return to the study of institutions and political elites. Political Clientelism seems to meet the requirements of both. Moreover, because of its apparent generic character, political clientelism emphasizes the artificiality of the usual criteria of political development-secularization and differentiation. More important, the recognition of political clientelism and interpersonal relationships as a fruitful arena of inquiry should indirectly challenge some of the assumptions on which the contemporary study of comparative politics is based.[2]

By emphasizing informal and personal relationships in the political process, clientelist analysis overcomes the difficulty of analyzing and describing polities where the study of interest groups, political parties, voting patterns and ideology fails to account for political behavior. Or it may help to explain particular political phenomena in polities which have been successfully studied using the traditional reference points, for example, cases of so-called political corruption or behavior motivated by personal loyalty, benefit, friendship, etc.[3]

The patron-client relationship has been described by Scott as " . . . an exchange relationship between roles . . ." involving an individual of higher status (patron) and a person of lower status (client). The former provides the latter with protection and benefits while the client reciprocates by giving the patron support and loyalty.[4] John Powell indicates that the relationship involves *proximity* in that the participants must be able to interact face-to-face frequently, *reciprocity* since the relationship is largely voluntary and is nourished by the mutually beneficial pay-offs which both patron and client find in it and *unequal status* since this guarantees the contribution of differing types of resources by each actor, resources which the other needs and wants but doesn't have.[5]

While these elements of clientelism stress the two person nature of it (the dyadic relationship), students of the process are quick to point out that it is the quasi-group or network characteristics of clientelism which have more significant political meaning.[6] Moreover the stacking up of clientelist networks creates, in addition to the patron and client a third, but not necessarily distinct role type, namely the political broker.[7] To illustrate let's assume that Mr. Alvarez (Mr. A) is a peasant living near and working for a cattle ranch owned by Mr. Bueno (Mr. B). Mr. Alvarez chose Mr. Bueno as godfather to his children,[8] his wife helps out occasionally with housework at the ranch, Mr. Alvarez also brings token produce or a chicken to Mr. Bueno and he always votes for the National Party of which Mr. Bueno is the local leader. Mr. Bueno feels obligated to help Mr. Alvarez in critical situations, such as taking his daughter to the doctor in town when she was very ill. He also provides transportation and a new shirt, pants, shoes and hat for Mr. Alvarez twice a year for elections, hosts a feast of roasted meat, potatoes, liquor and sweets and featuring a big fireworks display; he also provides Mr. Alvarez with the symbolic friendship with an "important" person which is very important both psychologically by giving a sense of belonging and for practical reasons (for example, when Mr. Alvarez's boy was arrested and accused of stealing, Mr. Bueno intervened on the boy's behalf with the authorities and had him released).

In this example, Mr. Alvarez is of course the client and Mr. Bueno the patron. The relationship is dyadic, has proximity, is reciprocal, is between unequals and in addition, the relationship is multiplex—covering a wide range of situations. It is likely that Mr. Alvarez only has one patron and it is also likely that Mr. Bueno has several or many clients. Thus to schematically represent the relationship we would find it to look thus:

PATRON-CLIENT
NETWORK PYRAMID

Mr. Bueno (patron)

Mr. Alvarez (client)

(other clients)

305

Rather than being simply a dyad, this structure actually is "multi-dyad." Moreover, it is quite likely that in the region where Mr. Alvarez and Mr. Bueno live other individuals may have clientelist relationships, and it is possible that in political terms there are other individuals who support the National Party. In concluding the hypothetical picture we might indicate that Mr. Bueno who is an important local leader of the National Party relates to Mr. Caseres (Mr. C) who is the provincial leader of the party. Let's illustrate schematically once more:

PATRON-BROKER-CLIENT NETWORK PYRAMID

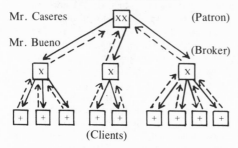

Mr. Caseres   (Patron)

Mr. Bueno   (Broker)

(Clients)

These patron-client networks in Scott's terminology, look like a pyramid.[9] If we were to continue the ideal type model suggested here and if we were to estimate only its political dimensions we could say that Mr. Bueno is a political "broker" who mediates between Mr. Caseres who is a regional patron and Mr. Alvarez and other clients. Mr. Caseres in turn relates to several people like Mr. Bueno. If we were to speak only about the two person relations between Mr. Bueno and Mr. Caseres we might say that Mr. Bueno is the client and Mr. Caseres is the patron. Thus the patron-broker-client network pyramid is created by the stacking up and combining of many dyadic patron-client networks.

We have used for illustrative purposes the most classic case of clientelist relations, the landowner/peasant roles,[10] however, the literature suggests that similar relationships exist in urban areas[11] (not the least of which perhaps was the classic case of urban bosses relating to immigrant neighborhoods in large North American cities). Moreover while the illustration and indeed this paper as a whole places the setting in Latin America, clientelist relations are by no means limited to that area and one can find an increasing literature on the subject for all types of political systems.

One entrapping element in clientelist studies, however, is its place on the continuum of polit-

ical development. If we accept the conventional divisions Traditional, Charismatic and Rational-Legal as the grossest distinction of political leadership types, clientelism appears to fall more into traditional and charismatic rather than rational-legal situations.[12] While this is a rather unexplored area of discussion one ought to point out that the recent discoveries in North American politics generically referred to as the Watergate process, suggests a very rich soil for patron-broker-client analysis. One ought to also point out that the political system in which these events took place, would generally be said to have a rational-legal type leadership style, although these two concepts hardly seem appropriate in light of the revelations.[13] Moreover, in the face of "modernization" variously defined there is at least the implicit assumption that clientelist relations will break down and either be transformed or disappear and be replaced by other styles of interaction (for instance, bureaucratic type relationships).[14]

This "breakdown" of clientelism is explained for a variety of reasons.[15] First, clientelist relationships to begin with are more likely in situations of resource scarcity, inequality of access to services and unequal influence. Secondly, the sheer size of changing (growing) communities, their increasing complexity and differentiation of roles and functions ought to also make it more difficult to maintain intimate and multiplex relationships. Finally, in the case of Latin America the demand for greater bureaucratization in the face of commercial and industrial growth, the impressive expansion of relationships with other societies could be cited as pressures for the breakdown of the "traditional" and "personalistic," "Latin" qualities of clientelism.

Counter arguments, however, could be made for the viability of clientelism in "modern" situations. For example, one might say that scarcity is a relative matter. For an upper middle class North American there may be many things which are difficult to obtain—a $50,000 a year income being inadequate to satisfy $85,000 expectations. Thus the things that drive a peasant or a big city immigrant to seek a patron to satisfy his or her needs might also drive a $50,000 a year real estate speculator or Agriculture Department bureaucrat with $85,000 expectations to seek a patron.[16] In turn one might argue that the needs of Mr. Bueno are replicated in different form but with similar consequences in North American or Western European businessmen or politicians. For example, the need for loyal followers/

supporters/subordinates, the reassurance of personal and, therefore, semi-permanent networks of people on which to depend, might be as great in the president of the United States or a powerful building contractor in Chicago as it is for a cattleman or city politician in Latin America. Larger and more complex communities in turn do not necessarily make clientelism more difficult (much less impossible) to function. Chicago, New York, Boston are hardly small and uncomplicated and yet they spawned the most written about studies of Bosses. One might argue that the elasticity of clientelism lies in that it aggregates people at the micro-level (ranch, village, city neighborhood or even city block) and stacks these dyads and dyadic networks like building blocks, into complex and often very large structures. Finally, it could be shown that even bureaucrats may find the need to establish personal relationships in order to expedite policies. In another context, patronage and the bureaucracy in connection with favoritism, corruption and personal gain are of course two terms often used together. In the last analysis it is hardly conclusive that large, modern institutions (and societies) operate on "impersonal" criteria in the first place. Close friendships between the directors of large corporations (oil companies, for example) and the possibility of clearly patron-client relationships for instance between such actors as the defense related industry (patron) and the Defense Department (client) ought to probably be included in the literature on clientelism. Thus there are many extremely intriguing and important questions being raised by the students of clientelism. In some instances asking the right question itself may be a valuable contribution to the literature.

What we propose to do in the following pages is to analyze and describe clientelist relationships between leaders and followers in a Colombian village (pseudonym—*Salado)* and the surrounding rural areas in the same district (called *veredas* or rural neighborhoods in Colombia).[17] We feel that this micro-analysis will shed some light on the questions asked earlier and will illustrate how the transformation of clientelism has taken place and for what reasons in one community. It should be clearly understood that the specific permutations of clientelist networks not only in different societies but in Colombia itself are very great. Thus *Salado* which is a coffee growing community, has had inter-party conflict including periods of great violence between the Liberals and Conservatives, a small village of the sort that have existed in Colombia for 200 years, is different from communities where there is a single, overwhelming family or estate which controls the life of the area, from towns dominated by one of the two parties and where violence was kept low, or from larger towns and cities which have emerged in Colombia since 1930. However, we feel that the *processes* at work in this specific setting may have universal undercurrents and that for this reason Salado is an important example of how clientelism manifests itself and changes over time.

TRADITIONAL LEADERSHIP

Until recently, the late 1950s, Salado seems to have been characterized by a very concentrated Patronalism in the form of Monseignor Jose Maria Soto. *Monseñor* as he was called, came to Salado as village priest in the late 20s. His family was landowning and coffee producing, a distinguished name in the neighboring Department of Antioquia. Monseñor was a "man of great passion who loved everyone in town as if they were his own," as a retired school teacher put it. This devotion was expressed in *Monseñor's* almost total control over the development of the town and *Municipio*— something which no one else had been able to or wanted to undertake. In the process he spent a considerable part of his family wealth on the town and died penniless. In his extraordinarily energetic lifetime *Monseñor* brought into being most of the major community institutions and services which are found there today. He founded a health center and worked to build it into a hospital; he started a school which became Salado's high school and today bears his name and is among rural high schools one of the better ones in the country; he spent 30 years building the municipal cemetery, organizing Sunday work groups to construct it and then had "honorary" children's brigades which were charged with the responsibility of keeping the grounds weed free, the walls whitewashed, the brass cross on the gate polished; as Salado grew, *Monseñor* saw the need for more educational facilities and he corresponded for years with religious orders, finally finding one interested in starting a private girls' school which functioned in the town until the early 1960s when attendance fell and it was converted into a night school. *Monseñor's* greatest project was converting the "old" church, partly collapsed from earthquakes and the ravages of rain and wind, into a rather impressive structure which included two magnificent spires, a parrish house, and a city block of houses surrounding the church, which are rented, thus becoming a constant source of income for social and religious projects.

Monseñor also founded the local chapter of the Sociedad de San Vicente de Paul, a layman's order which undertakes charitable projects. *Monseñor* purchased half a city block, built a clean, modern compound of houses which to this day are an important subsidized housing source for indigent families. Finally, it was through his search and extended correspondence (in French as people were quick to add), with European companies, that Salado came to have an aqueduct made with "the best Belgian pipes made" as a source of water which still supplies the town. Pictures in family scrapbooks and stories of the volunteer labor, townspeople working Sundays, of the arrival and blessing of the pipes, of the first rush of water through the completed water work, are still told.

Thus, one is deeply impressed with the virtual hegemony which this energetic man had in Salado. There was very little disagreement that *Monsenõr* had been for the last 50 years the single most important man in the community. There was also a surprising degree of acceptance of his role. Almost everyone liked him or agreed that he was vitally important in bringing the community from backwardness to respectability.

Politically, *Monseñor* was "neutral." However, this seems to have meant more that he did not aggressively identify himself with politics. Still some Liberals who suffered from the political violence of the 1950s said they couldn't understand why *Monseñor* allowed them to be persecuted[18]—age was the greatest culprit because they indicated that he had in the past always "protected us from people who tried to exploit this town." Another reason mentioned was that *Monseñor* withdrew from church activity to devote his time to building the high school up and improving its curriculum and an acting village priest was appointed who sided unambiguously with the Conservatives. Whether it is a myth among some of the Liberals or whether it was based on fact, it was said that the new priest would always ask when someone was dying and needed his presence, "Is he a Conservative or Liberal?" He was said, depending on his mood to occasionally suggest that a Liberal should "be happy that we will bury him in our cemetery."

With *Monseñor's* senility and later death, a community landmark disappeared. No one has replaced him. Perhaps no one can because he was a "period" leader; a man who came to an isolated town, overwhelmed it with his energy, devoted his life and fortune to its development and became irreplaceable. Unfortunately, the town's municipal and parrish archive are both in an unusable condition and unfortunately there is very little written history. However, from the foregoing description and the sharp transition which followed his death, one can suggest that an important change in leadership style has taken place. *Monseñor* was largely a traditional hegemonic broker who linked the community to the outside world and in no small measure brought it into the modern world. Yet he was also protective—he "protected us from people who tried to exploit this town." Moreover, his dominance was so smothering that some of his projects (most notably the cemetery) have suffered from neglect and are decaying. No one was prepared to assume his leadership.

However, despite his selfless intentions and constant devotions to Saldo, *Monseñor* died at a time when the *Municipio* required new undertakings especially in agricultural modernization and community development at the *vereda* (rural neighborhood) and marginal urban *barrio* (urban neighborhood) level. These were not undertaken by any central figure but rather seem to have become the domains of a larger number of individuals who are not as easily identified by people in the community as *Monseñor*.

It is extremely difficult to determine the extent to which this larger universe of people were also important during *Monseñor's* time. Nevertheless, it seems that they have come to assume a much more prominent place in recent times.

Finally, there is evidence that the role of technical bureaucrats is becoming more important and that to an as yet undetermined extent the bureaucrat may sometimes come into conflict with the brokers. Under *Monseñor* Soto a hegemonic patronal system developed which facilitated a controlled development of the community with relatively passive inputs from the people themselves. *Monseñor's* death diffused the leadership roles and seems to have given opportunities to people who had personal characteristics which led them to take initiatives on behalf of themselves and clients. It may well be that these individuals were already active in the latter years of *Monseñor's* efforts. It is reported elsewhere that the present "leaders" (especially for example, brokers in *veredas*, presidents of *Juntas de Accion Comunal* (*JAC*—Community Development Committees) had always been "helpful," "well connected," etc.

These brokers, however, in some sense are

faced with a rapidly growing national bureaucracy which is extending services and personnel into the rural areas. Whether the broker will serve as an intermediary between the "new" bureaucracy and "his" community or whether he will be competing with the increasingly more directly accessible government services and personnel is a question which requires further investigation. It suffices here to underline the transitional process of brokerage in Salado which has given over a period of time a diverse complexion to its function.

It was my intention as I approached the investigation of clientelism in this community to ask the question "Can one identify political brokers in the community, if so, what functions do these perform and to what extent are their characteristics similar to those described by social scientists in the general literature and by Colombian historians and recent commentators in particular?"

This paper, therefore, describes leader-follower relationships in Salado, analyzes public images of leadership, and tries to identify several patterns of brokerage.

An effort is made here to identify the sorts of broker relations which one might expect would differentiate leadership clusters in a community. In looking over the literature on patron-client relations it seems that a significant distinction between leadership perception in clients might be those serving the dyadic tie and those serving the pyramid or networks of clients. That is to say a difference between leadership in which the payoffs are personal and that in which they are to a community (not necessarily the whole community but a functionally defined cluster). Another assumption made, and borne out by the findings, was that certain leadership *roles* themselves (rather than the individuals holding them) would have become institutionalized.

I have called these three types respectively *particularistic brokers*, *community brokers* and *positional brokers*.

It was found that urban and rural residential identity are important factors which differentiate broker status in the *municipio* studied. Urban residents can more readily identify *Positional Leaders* as being important to them while rural residents tend to lean more toward *Particularistic Brokers'* more immediate and informal roles. *Community Brokers* grow out of the neglect of groups by the public sector and the need of these people for essential resources and services. *Community Broker* types are identified as encompassing comprehensive functions which benefit an entire group; *Particularistic Brokers* are mentioned in the context of two-person payoff; *Positional Brokers* appear to perform both functions but there is greater ambiguity in their role.

Brokers were found to play a vital role in this community linking together individuals, and clusters of individuals, providing a sense of participation and some flow of resources to the clients. It was also found that brokers are perceived by people as having characteristics different from ordinary people and in some demand in the community. Finally brokers and clients share to a large extent their political party affiliation.

The distinction between village and clusters of houses in the surrounding countryside (Salado vs. *vereda*) is an important factor in Colombian rural society. Not surprisingly it was found that people living in the municipality studied could also be divided between those living in town (and municipal political-administrative seat) proper and those living in one of the many scattered clusters of small farms on the outlying areas.

The identification and attachment to the *vereda* is based often on family ties, on the sentimental perception of the land and on the social networks which develop among people of each vicinity.[19]

LEADERSHIP ROLES

These affective ties should, if they are strong enough, be reflected in definitions of political interest, for example leadership roles. Within the framework of the greatest latitude and opportunity to self-identity a question was asked, which might shed some light on one area of defining leadership; namely, the reputational aspect. Table H reflects the answers arranged by actual place of residence of respondent.

The columns above identify the following[20] (1) *Positional*—these were responses in which the position rather than any given individual occupying it were given (i.e. the mayor, the president of the *Concejo*); (2) *Individual*—indicates the cases in which a name was given (i.e. Don Jose Tobares); (3) *No Answer*.

The obvious significant fact is that village residents were more conscious of the established political roles and tended more to define the question by pointing to some highly visible and institutionalized political position. Of these positions the mayor, being the highest executive authority in the village, obtained the largest number of responses. The following breakdown indicates the positional roles identified.

Table H
(% of Total by Residence)

Question: "Who is the most important person around here politically?"

	% Positional	% Individual	% No Answer	% Total
Salado (Village)	68.0 (N 196)	22.5 (N 65)	9.5 (N 28)	100 (N 289)
Vereda (Country-side)	14.0 (N 14)	82.0 (N 82)	4.0 (N 4)	100 (N 100)
Out of Salado	72.7 (N 8)		27.3 (N 3)	100 (N 11)

Table I
Response of Village Residents

Question: "Who is the most important person around here politically?"

Positions Named	Number Responding
Mayor	*(N 62)*
Personero (Public Works Director)	*(N 31)*
Tesorero (Treasurer)	*(N 15)*
Pres. Consejo (Councilman)	*(N 18)*
Priest	*(N 2)*
Pres. Comite de Cafeteros (coffee growers)	*(N 34)*
Leader of Party	*(N 30)*
Others	*(N 4)*
Total	(N 196) Universe (N 289)

This response was surprising since the most reasonable hypothesis based on descriptions of other communities in Latin America suggests that institutionalized roles are secondary to the more personalist definition of political power (and general influence as well), perhaps growing out of patron-client dyads or other intimate interpersonal links. Moreover, the responses seemed extraordinary in that they focused on the mayor as the most frequently described role, when in the process of interviewing and in observing the functions of that office it so clearly occupied a ceremonial place rather than an active and visibly power oriented one. The other roles identified on the other hand included a number that were associated with financial power, or with the ability to allocate budgetary resources; these are the *personero* (the director of municipal public works projects) and the treasurer. There appeared a likelihood that this association in the public mind stimulated the connection with political importance. A second question immediately following that in Table H was asked. Table J indicates the question and responses.

Table J

Question: "If you have a problem which can be solved by someone with political influence here, who would you go see?"

	% Position Named	% Individual person named	% No Answer	% Total
Salado (Village)	54.0 (N 156)	36.0 (N 104)	10.0 (N 29)	100 (N 289)
Vereda (Country side)	11.0 (N 11)	84.0 (N 84)	5.0 (N 5)	100 (N 100)
Out of Salado	45.5 (N 5)	27.3 (N 3)	27.3 (N 3)	100 (N 11)

Here a shift occurred and many people identified an individual rather than a role as being personally useful to them, even though over half of the village residents (54%) continue to identify a role rather than an individual. The following table (K) indicates the individuals named by town residents as important. Table M indicates those named by *vereda* residents.

The mayor (Aristeto), *personero* (Don Eustebio) and president of the *comite de cafeteros*[21] (Don Eliseo) were all named as positional roles of importance as well as being designated by name. The difference in responses can be explained by the fact that people giving individual names rather than institutional roles (i.e. Don Aristeto instead of the "mayor") are relating empirical experiences; are making reference to some concrete instance in which they witnessed that individual's political influence.

There were 29 people unable to identify politically relevant leadership. These included 23 marginal household heads (mostly female), three students who "hadn't thought about it ever before because I'm not interested in political questions" as one put it, one lady and two men who also had no apparent conception of politics.

These responses by 289 village residents of Salado indicate a rather dispersed definition of political influence both by institutional roles and by individuals considered politically relevant. The *role dispersal* covered eleven separate positions including political parties, local government, the church, the *Banco Cafetero*, the coffee growers committee, and educational leadership, while eighteen *individuals* were identified as being politically important.

Interesting factors that must be pointed out are the characteristics of Don Nacho and Don Gibardo. Both are *concejales* (members of the city council), the former is also the local leader of the new third party ANAPO while the latter is an active Conservative. However, it is their common characteristic of being presidents of *Juntas de Accion Comunal* (JAC) that is interesting. Of the people naming Don Nacho (who is president of the JAC *Barrio* Bolivar) nineteen were residents of that *barrio* and of the seventeen people identifying Don Gibardo all were residents of *Mil Ochenta* of which Don Gibardo is the JAC president. The residence of the individuals making this response is not duplicated in the case of any of the other people named.[22] However, of the fifteen naming Don Eliseo, eight had coffee farms or grew coffee and four seemed to express a strong partisan Liberal identity, two interesting facts given Don Eliseo's influence as president of the *comite de cafeteros* and leadership of the Liberal party in Salado. Of the twelve naming Don Toraso, two were school teachers which is interesting since he is instrumental in determining the appointment of instructors and six had children in high school which may also have influenced their awareness of Don Toraso as rector of that institution. One of the latter, in fact, said, "Don Toraso is a very good man, he got my daughter Alicia a scholarship to continue her studies in Sucre. He knows a lot of important people there." In none of the other cases were there any distinguishing characteristics to the respondents which might explain their selection other than the brother of the *personero* choosing his brother (rumor had it that the latter got a town job thanks to his brother's influence in the public works projects).

In attempting to explain the attachment of respondents to individuals, it became *most clearly* evident that two of the people named had a functional constituency and were named because

Table K

People Named by Salado (Village) Residents as Important:

Individual	Number Identifying	Occupation & Positions of Person Named
Don Nacho	22	ANAPO Leader/Councilman JAC
Don Eliseo	15	Liberal Leader/Pres. Coffee growers Assn., store owner
Don Toraso	12	Rector of High School/Ed. Inspector, store owner
Don Arturo	8	Councilman
Don Gibardo	17	Councilman/JAC
Don Eustebio	7	Personero
Don Aristeto	6	Mayor
Others	17	
	(N 104)	Universe (N 289)

they seemed to fulfill the constituencies, rather than personal expectation.

Don Nacho is a wonderful man who works very hard to make our life better. He is the only one who has made us progress; the rest never cared and most people here in the barrio are not educated enough to be leaders.

From five in the morning you can see Don Gibardo running through town looking for help; money for some bricks here, a few meters of pipe there, a pledge to help us buy Eternit for the *castea* roof somewhere else, to the mayor's office to fight with him to have one of our boys let out of jail. Mil Ochenta is going to progress because Don Gibardo just won't give up.

These two quotations are characteristic of the reasons given for selecting the man. Both *Mil Ochenta* and *Barrio Bolivar* are low income areas of Salado, by the description of their inhabitants and by an inspection and comparison of facilities with other parts of the community, neglected and left up to their own devices. Both have only recently established *Juntas de Accion Comunal* and in both of them community projects initiated and propelled by the JAC president were under way or in the case of a small school, a *caseta*[23] and an access road in the *Barrio Bolivar*, already finished. These projects were carried out primarily by the use of volunteer work (*convite*) by its inhabitants.

From village residents responses a threefold classification of leadership seems possible.[24]

(1) *Community positional roles*—These are selected because they are rather permanent and visible, because a high degree of symbolic prestige is associated with them (the mayor and priest for instance), because they reflect a connection with other indicators of power (money in the case of the *personero* and treasurer, political power in the case of party leaders), or because they are a socio-economic factor in the ethos of Salado (the *Comite de Cafeteros* which has a club, the school director who epitomizes "culture" and educational power).

(2) *Particularistic payoff*—In these cases the identification of an individual as politically influential is a function of a personal experience, almost inevitably one in which the respondent had "gotten something done;" getting a scholarship for a daughter, a loan from the *comite de cafeteros* (either cash, seeds, fertilizer, tools), a son out of jail through the intervention of the mayor, or the road in front of his house fixed by going to talk to the *personero*. In these cases a very strongly dyadic relationship of necessarily any great permanence, nevertheless the responses suggest a two-person connection as the critical factor in understanding the prominence of the individual identified as important.

(3) *Community brokerage*—In two cases the evidence strongly suggests that these individuals conform to the notion of a multi-functional role played by individuals; played within the context of a geographically contained constituency. That is to say these individuals, through an institutional framework (the *Juntas de Accion Comunal*) represented channels of access for the inhabitants of two neighborhoods to a wide range of potential necessities. Moreover these individuals appear as more than instrumental leaders; they are "forces," "makers of progress," mobilizers and as shall be suggested further on, opinion and political leaders.

In turning to the responses given by rural residents of Salado, that is to say those living in *veredas*, we find first of all that a significant majority conceived of political importance in individual rather than positional-role terms. The positional roles identified were the following:

Table L
Positional Roles Identified as Important – Vereda Residents:

President Comite de Cafeteros	(N 6)
Mayor	(N 3)
Government Agronomist	(N 2)
Leader of Party	(N 1)
Personero	(N 1)
President JAC	(N 1)
Total	(N 14) Universe (N 100)

These answers correspond quite closely to those given by village residents with the exception of the naming of the government agronomist (an extension agent from the state capital who works for the *Instituto Colombiano Agro-* pecuario (ICA), and provides directly and through his staff, agricultural advice and aid)[25] and the selection of the president of the *Junta de Accion Comunal* generically.

Table M
People Named by Vereda Residents as Important:

Individual	Number Identifying	Occupation & Positions of Person Named
Don Franco	(N 12)	JAC/coffee grower
Don Chepe	(N 12)	JAC/coffee grower
Don Moreno	(N 11)	JAC/coffee grower/*tienda* owner
Don Addfo	(N 10)	coffee agent
Don Ciliano	(N 9)	JAC/store owner
Don Eliseo	(N 8)	LIBERAL Leader/Pres. *granero*/coffee grower
Don Anastacio	(N 6)	Police chief
Don Lino	(N 5)	JAC
Don Eustebio	(N 5)	Personero
Don Geronimo	(N 3)	School teacher
Don Toraso	(N 2)	High school rector/Ed. inspector *granero*
Don Aristeto	(N 1)	Mayor
Total	(N 84)	

Two important differences emerge in comparing village and *vereda* responses. First there is such a marked difference in the number of community positional roles identified vis-à-vis the other two kinds suggested, the particularistic payoff and the community brokerage. The rural resident thus appears to define his political universe more narrowly and less symbolically or ceremonially. Secondly there is an important shift from a predominance of particularistic reasons given for naming individuals, (i.e. "he helped me get a scholarship for my son" or "when we had the *invierno* (winter or the rainy season) I couldn't get in to my farm so Don Eustebio had a load of gravel brought in and dumped on the road for me") in the town of Salado, toward a more community oriented definition ("he is the only one who cares about our *vereda* and is working to make life better here for us").[26] Of the 84 responses identifying individuals in Table J, 47 (50.5%) can be classified as community brokerage oriented ones. In the urban context it was 41 out of 104 (39.4%).[27]

This seems to be caused primarily by a greater dependence of *vereda* dwellers on immediate leadership, their vulnerability to weather or crop pests, and the relative absence of public services to which they can have automatic access.[28] It is most significant that the identification of leadership was most strongly related to leadership in the local *Junta de Accion Comunal* (JAC). This institution seems to have more to serve as a locus of community affairs. It is furthermore important to indicate that when respondents were asked if the individual named "has been important for a long time," the answers overwhelmingly suggested that the person was considered

to have been important for many years. This means that these people have preceded the founding of *Juntas de Accion Comunal* (most of which came into being in the late 1960s) a visible forces in the *vereda*. An interesting insight was provided by one response.

Don Lino has always been a very good man wit me and my family. I remember when my hou collapsed in '56 he lent me three hundred pes to buy *guadua* (a special building bamboo) an the other things we needed to rebuilt it. Now is still helping but it's much better with the Jur (de Accion Comunal) because we can defe ourselves. People are always taking advanta of the humble people, but since Don Lino is spected and knows important people we are n all better off.

Similar comments made in various vere suggest that there may be a dynamic connect between particularistic payoff and commu oriented brokerage. In the case of Don L (named by five people in the *vereda* of Ocan there seems to be a transition from his role a good man with me and my family" to a slig different role as head of the Ocampo JA which his effectiveness is perceived as his ity to "defend" the inhabitants of the ve against all kinds of outside threats. What cisely these are was very difficult to ascer One concludes, in fact, that the "threats" more the consequence of a general feelir vulnerability toward many things, express a slightly paranoic fear of outsiders.

Generally speaking, in both the villag *veredas* the individuals named by respor obtain influence and are recognized as beir litically important because of one or more

following characteristics:

(A) Financial or economic resources
(B) Education, ability to speak well
(C) Connections with many people
(D) A "dynamic" personality. Drive, energy
(E) Willingness to use force, toughness.[29]

A young man said:

Don Moreno is the toughest guy in El Plano (*es el tipo mas berraco*). In '52 some people appeared on his *finca*. They were armed and he's pretty sure they were after him for political reasons. He slipped out of the house and as they came close to the front door he fired both barrels of his shotgun at them from a coffee bush ten meters away. They managed to drag themselves away; there were four. His shotgun was damaged by the blast but Don Moreno never even blinked.

Don Moreno thus can be characterized by his toughness and his willingness to use force. In this particular case that characteristic dominated the descriptions although in addition he was also identified as a "man who will always let you buy some rice and some sugar on credit" or a "real friend who serves *aguardiente* with a generous hand" both of the latter factors stemming from Don Moreno's ownership of a small *tienda*. If we accept the assumption that *vereda* residents look with some distrust at "the outsiders," this gentleman appears to satisfy the conception of a defender who can be relied upon to protect the community, who will not yield to anyone.

The combination of the five factors in any given individual seem to vary greatly. Don Eliseo, for instance, was variously described as:

(1) "A man who helps us very much because as president of the *comite* (de cafeteros) he has seen to it that we will get electricity after so many years."
(2) "Don Eliseo is respected by everyone because he is generous and cultured (*culto*)."
(3) "He is probably the best connected person I know. As *diputado* to the assembly he made connections in Sucre and all these people are useful if things are going to be done."

Thus it should be noted that these "facts" about an individual are the basis for people's reactions to him. They serve as the primary point of legitimacy for his influence. Don Moreno never blasted four people with a double barreled shotgun; as best as the story could be restructured he fired a 38 revolver through the bathroom window at two armed men who were approaching the house one late afternoon in 1952. However, the fact that people told the story of the shotgun blast (and a number of versions at that), and the apparent fact that people wanted to believe the story, made it as important in understanding their relationship to Don Moreno as if the story had been totally accurate. In other words, they would probably not have related to him any differently if in reconstructing it we had found it to be true. Finally, it should be observed that the larger, in a sense symbolic story *was* based on an actual incident and, therefore, his "image" is rooted in a whole chain of real events which linked together his legitimacy as a tough he-man.

Therefore, it is felt that the five characteristics of leadership suggested earlier are important to the leader-follower relationship in Salado precisely because they are the aggregate perception

Table N

Question: *"If you have a problem which can be solved by someone with political influence here, who would you go see?"*

People Named by Salado-Village Residents as Important:

	Political Party of Respondent		
Individual Named	Liberal	Conservative	ANAPO
Don Nacho (ANAPO)	(N 1)	(N 3)	(N 18)
Don Eliseo (Liberal)	(N 12)	(N 2)	(N 1)
Don Toraso (Conservative)	(N 4)	(N 6)	(N 2)
Don Arturo (Liberal)	(N 7)	(N 1)	
Don Gibardo (Conservative)	(N 1)	(N 16)	
Don Eustebio (Conservative)		(N 7)	
Don Aristeto (Conservative)	(N 1)	(N 4)	(N 1)
Others (N 17)			

Total (N 104)

Table O

People Named by Vereda *Residents as Important:*

	Political Party of Respondent		
Individual Named	Liberal	Conservative	ANAPO
Don Franco (Liberal)	(N 10)	(N 2)	
Don Chepe (Conservative)	(N 1)	(N 9)	(N 2)
Don Moreno (Conservative)		(N 11)	
Don Adolfo (Liberal)	(N 8)	(N 2)	
Don Cicliano (Liberal)	(N 9)		
Don Eliseo (Liberal)	(N 6)	(N 1)	(N 1)
Don Anastacio (Conservative)		(N 6)	
Don Lino (Conservative)		(N 5)	
Don Eustebio (Conservative)		(N 3)	
Don Geronimo (Liberal)	(N 3)		
Don Toraso (Conservative)		(N 2)	
Don Aristeto (Conservative)	(N 1)		

Total (N 84)

first of all of what a leader should be characterized by and secondly, because there are individuals who fulfill one or usually a combination of these factors, and these individuals are listed by name when one asks questions like, "Who is the most important person around here politically?" or "If you have a problem which can be solved by someone with political influence here, who would you go see?"

Finally, if we look at the responses in Tables K and M (people named by village and rural residents) by party affiliation of the respondents and compare that with the affiliation of the individual named, we find a close congruence (Tables N and O).

This is an interesting fact because it confirms the idea that brokers tend to aggregate a political party following and act as local mobilizers for national political parties.

Two additional cases which could not be closely investigated but which were widely commented on were those of Toño "Campana" (Tony "bell") because he was a railroad station master) and the "Restrepo Clan." Toño "Campana" had worked for many years as Station-Master in a *vereda* through which the railroad ran. He had become politically active in the early 1960s and finally became a member of ANAPO in 1969. The *vereda* in which he was station master (Estación Caldas) had been in everyone's memory slightly more Conservative than Liberal. However, in the 1970 election it shifted very sharply toward ANAPO.[30]

Don Toño had over the years appointed a large number of people in *Estación Caldas* to maintenance crews and other railroad connected local jobs. Apparently when he decided to shift to ANAPO the people who were obliged to him felt they should do the same. There was no mention of any resistance to this, of pressure put on them to vote ANAPO. The people who knew and worked with, for or lived near Don Toño simply felt they should do this.

The second case involved a three family clan dominated by the Restrepos who constituted a traditional enclave in one of the *veredas*. This clan exercised tight influence over its households. Not only were they wary of outsiders coming into this *vereda* but they in fact often prohibited it completely. The Restrepos were in-bred, and had developed a lilting accent which people took delight in imitating. They ran their own school which apparently was totally inadequate; the Restrepos were known to be illiterate and uncultured. Politically the whole clan was Conservative. One young Liberal who had worked hard on the 1970 election campaign said he had tried to go into the *vereda* to campaign and was told to either leave or they would carry him out in a coffin. The Restrepo men were known to be "good fighters." "Arcesio Restrepo knows all 65 movements with the peinilla"[31] as one respondent put it.

Several years ago Arcesio was coming into town when a Liberal jumped out of the bushes outside town and said he was going to kill Arcesio. Arcesio is said to have unsheathed his *machete*, said, *"Apurate pues que voy pa' misa,"* ("Make it snappy then. I'm going to mass."), made short shrift of the assailant, leaving him to bleed to death on the path, and making it into town in time for noon mass.

Political characteristics thus *are* an important factor in strengthening clientelist ties.[32]

CONCLUSION

Like most Colombians, Saladeños identify very closely with the immediate place in which they live with village residents and those living in *veredas* the two most visible groups. These two population clusters differentiate themselves in responses to questions asking that they identify political influentials. The urban resident tends more frequently to point out positions or roles (i.e. the mayor, the priest) while the *vereda* resident more often names a person (i.e. Don Lino, Don Eliseo).

Community positional roles are almost self-evident since they represent the obvious and the visible positions in the community. The tendency for urban dwellers to focus on these somewhat more than on individual influentials lies first of all in that it is more obvious that these positions (the mayor, for instance) reflect the nexus between the community and other communities. The ceremonial function of a number of these roles is apparent. Second, the urban dweller is more comfortable and familiar with the duties of official positions and can more realistically be expected to resort to these in his search for solutions to problems. To the *vereda* inhabitant who comes into town once a week at the most, who often feels somewhat awkward in that setting, who is removed from what little "pomp and circumstance" surrounds official positions; to him the official positions are not that meaningful.

The second characteristic of leadership which is called here particularistic payoff is common to both urban and rural dweller. It represents the immediate gratification which an individual gets from asking a favor or getting advice. It results almost exclusively from dyadic ties, short or over a long period of time between individuals.[33]

Finally leaders who can be called community brokers were identified. These appeared to be two urban leaders who preside over *Juntas de Accion Comunal* in two marginal *barrios*, and they also are "leaders" of *veredas*; individuals who represent some coherent political vehicle for people clustered around most commonly again a *Junta de Accion Comunal*. These leaders are significantly different from the other two types in that they are defined first of all by a functional, proximate constituency, and secondly, they are distinct because they are described in responses as somehow embodying the future prosperity and well-being of the community with which they identify. Both these seem on the surface to describe someone like the

mayor of Salado as much as they describe Don Nacho of the *barrio* Bolivar or Don Moreno of El Plano. However, it should be pointed out that in the case of the mayor, he was last on the list of people identified in Table K as being a person one would approach to solve a political problem while Don Nacho was first in that same ranking even though the position he occupies (Pres. JAC, *Consejal*, leader of ANAPO) were in the first two cases not mentioned as positionally important roles and only his position as a party leader was indicated as significant.[34]

Another interesting observation was made regarding community brokers in *veredas*; many of them were identified as having been important for a number of years ante-dating the institutional position they now occupied (JAC pres., for instance). It seemed that in many of these cases, leaders had changed from serving particularistic functions for *Bolivar* was built, thanks to ICCE,[35] a *barrio* television set was a gift from the ministry of education, etc. Don Gonzalo was no less active in searching outside sources for assistance.

On the basis of the descriptions of leaders and of observing their actual and psychological function five characteristics; wealth, education, connections, personality and aggressiveness were identified as the most important leadership qualities.[36]

One might summarize these factors by suggesting that an important distinction between role identification and name identification of leaders lies in the visibility of the institutional positions. However, even more importantly one must conclude that community brokers appear to serve an important function when clusters of people are deprived of direct access to services and cannot assume individual initiatives to contact bureaucracies for help with their problems. The brokers in this case are not necessarily characteristic of only traditional or marginal segments of the community. It was found that sometimes the growing complexity and incomprehensibleness of state or national bureaucratic agencies virtually required a broker who could "interpret" or translate difficult procedural matters into a form suitable for community decision-making.[37] Don Nacho resigned from the JAC *barrio* Bolivar because he said in an evening meeting of that group, "People are spreading rumors that I am a dictator and that I want to run this place. Here I resign and that's all." He was unanimously reinstated ten minutes later. As one resident put it, "He's the only one who knows how to write those letters and fill out the forms we need in order to get something. He's the only one who cares about our people here in the *barrio* instead of himself or instead of wanting to become a national politician. If Don Nacho quits, everything will go back to misery and loneliness, as it has always been."

We have shown in the preceding pages that the transformation of brokerage in the community studied involved several processes. First of all, with the demise of the most prominent patron of Salado, Monseñor, a more complex brokerage situation developed. Rather than declining or vanishing altogether, clientelism in Salado took on a more functionally and role specific characteristic.[38] As the last comment from a member of the Junta de Accion Comunal in the barrio Bolivar suggests, even when outside resources become available to people (such as bureaucratic services flowing in from the national government and no longer subject to a patron's good will) people may need the "special" talents of a broker to interpret or solicit the newly available funds and services.

We have only briefly touched upon the role of bureaucrats themselves and how they are connected to the clientelist networks of the community. Before the National Front bi-partisan coalition which provides for equal sharing in all political as well as bureaucratic positions, competition for these jobs was keen and generally sharply divided by party lines. Loyalty to the party, hard work for it in elections or local leadership in organizing party members was most frequently rewarded with public jobs. Since the majority of public positions in Colombia are appointive rather than elected (including the mayor who is appointed by the state governor who is appointed by the president of the republic) the extent of politicization in this area has been extremely high. Clientelist relationships thus were quite crucial for obtaining preferments of all sorts stemming from the public sector.

With a bi-partisan arrangement, which has dominated politics from 1957 to 1974 when it is officially phased out, one might have assumed that the bureaucracy could become more "a-political" and provide services on a community wide basis. Even if this were true, and there is evidence that the bureaucracy during this period became more "technical," the relevance of clientelist type linkages and relationships may not entirely disappear. As I have extensively argued elsewhere,[39] modern bureaucrats may find it necessary to establish clientelist links with the people of communities they are trying to serve, before these people are willing to accept new methods, new programs or bureaucratic advice. The bureaucrat himself may object to and resist

going beyond his official functions when he deals with people, however, it is the people's initiative itself which often forces him (or her) to establish more multiplex relationships.

Thus a third transformation of clientelism may very well be under way, one in which government bureaucrats become the patrons or brokers and in which they may eventually develop political as well as technical interests in their roles. The dilemma is most clearly evident where bureaucrats want to achieve changes which are resisted by local traditional notables (land reform for instance) and where they may feel a need to mobilize people behind a technical program in order to insure its success. One could argue that this process, in a system where clientelist bonds become rather strong, could lead to far reaching political as well as program oriented connections between bureaucrats and clients.

What lies at the bottom of this succession of changes in clientelistic roles is the expectation on the part of people in Salado and other rural communities in Colombia, that they must draw the individual into personal, complex and semi-permanent relationships with themselves in order to assure a predictable connection between themselves, the individual to whom they want to be tied and the preferments which will flow from that relationship. If this is the case, clientelism ought not to be viewed as a passing phenomenon characteristic of tradition, backwardness, or marginality and subject to replacement by more impersonal styles of interaction. Rather it might be viewed as a viable and deeply institutionalized perception of role interaction, one which surely can survive many structural and ecological changes. It should not be forgotten in the last analysis, and this is true in most systems where clientelism has been found to dominate interpersonal relations, that the rural peoples we have described in Salado migrate to cities and take with them their understanding of how best to relate to other people. Thus it is reasonable to assume that clientelist links in political, social and economic relations survive and flourish in the cities.[40]

Future investigations of clientelism in cross national research ought to therefor concentrate among other things on three specific areas. First, one should establish the historical roots of inter-personal relations in the system under investigation—"How have people of different socio-economic status related to each other in the past and with what political consequences?" Second, it should be determined whether changes in roles and political relationships have qualitatively changed the basis of interpersonal relations—"Has clientelism broken down, disappeared, or remained but adapted to new realities?" Finally, a very serious effort must be made to estimate the impact of urbanization, migration and bureaucratization on clientelism— "Have these forces weakened clientelism, do they promise to destroy patron-broker-client relations, or can it flourish in spite of these processes?"

These questions are important because they will generate some answers for the theoretically most intriguing problems political scientists face. Since clientelism is a vertical relationship, that is to say a process whereby people of different socio-economic status relate to each other, its breakdown could produce greater horizontal identities and links (i.e. class based political competition). Thus the transformation of clientelism is a crucial weathervane for understanding political competition, conflict, and change.

APPENDIX I: *Characteristics of Three Broker Types in Colombia*

	Positional	Particularistic	Community

Payoff	symbolic
	—
	coextensive with
	  larger community
	  (i.e. *municipio*)
		personal
		  preferments
			group betterment
			—
			procuring barrio
			  or vereda services
			—
			sub-group in
			  municipality

Role
occupants
	Mayor
	Priest
		Gamonal
		friend with
		  connections
		coffee buyer
		store owner
		creditor
		landowner
			President of Junta
			  de Accion Comunal
			—
			modern or "rebel"
			  Priest
			—
			"modern" bureaucrat

Political
factor
	political order
	—
	administration of
	  Governor's program
	—
	faith
		individual voting
		  loyalty
		—
		party or leader
		  loyalty
			group political
			  following
			—
			social change
			  "revolution"
			—
			carrying out
			  development projects

Causal
factor
	inaccessibility
	  of role
	  of visibility
	ceremonial value
		dyadic
		—
		proximity of
		  participants
		—
		absence of aggre-
		  gating and articu-
		  lating instruments
		—
		personal needs
		
		absence of public
		  service
			defined boundaries
			—
			aggregating and
			  articulating
			  institutional dyadic
			  network
			group need
			—
			group consciousness

NOTES

*This paper was presented at the 1974 annual meeting of the American Political Science Association, Palmer House Hotel, Chicago, Illinois, August 29 - September 2, 1974. Copyright 1974, the American Political Science Association.

The author wishes to thank the National Science Foundation and Iowa State University, in particular Daniel Zaffarano and Wallace Russell for partial support in carrying out this research. Douglas Chalmers and Lambros Comitas of Columbia University were helpful in their comments on earlier parts of this project. The analysis and conclusions are, of course, the author's alone.

1 A good review of the underpinnings of clientelist analysis is A. Heath, "Exchange Theory," *British Journal of Political Science*, (1) (January 1971), pp. 91-120.

Several interesting general explorations of the subject include: Robert Kaufman, "The Patron-Client Concept and Macro-Politics: Prospects and Problems," paper delivered at the 1972 annual meeting of the APSA; Rene Lemarchand and Keith Legg, "Political Clientelism and Development," *Comparative Politics*, Vol. 4, #4 (January 1972), pp. 149-179. More specifically focused to one area are Rene Lemarchand, "Political Clientelism and Ethnicity in Tropical Africa: Competing Solidarities in Nation-Building," pp. 68-90 and James C. Scott, "Patron Client Politics and Political Change in Southeast Asia," pp. 91-113 in *The American Political Science Review*, Vol. LXVI, #1 (March 1972).

The most useful and provocative discussion of aspects of clientelism in Latin America is Douglas Chalmer's "Parties and Society in Latin America," *Studies in Comparative International Development*, VII, #2 (Summer 1972), pp. 102-128.

2 Keith Legg, "Interpersonal Relationships and Comparative Politics: Political Clientelism in Industrial Society," *Politics* (Sydney), Vol. 7, #1, May 1972, pp. 1-11. p. 11.

3 See for instance J. A. Barnes "Networks and Political Process" in Marc Swartz, ed., *Local-Level Politics: Social and Cultural Perspectives* (Chicago: Aldine, 1968), pp. 107-130 and Carl Landé, *Leaders, Factions and Parties: The Structure of Philippine Politics*, monograph #6, (New Haven: Yale University - Southeast Asian Studies, 1964).

4 Scott, op. cit., p. 92.

5 John D. Powell, "Peasant Society and Clientelist Politics," *American Political Science Review*, LXIV, #2 (June 1970), pp. 411-425.

6 The classic reference for this is Adrian Mayer, "The Significance of Quasi-Groups in The Study of Complex Studies," in Michael Banton, ed., *The Social Anthropology of Complex Societies*, (London: Tavistock, 1966). This is also stressed in Carl Landé's "Networks and Groups in Southeast Asia: Some Observations on The Group Theory of Politics," *The American Political Science Review*, Vol. LXVII, #1, (March 1973), pp. 103-127.

7 For an excellent discussion of this see Alex Weingrod, "Patrons, Patronage, and Political Parties," *Comparative Studies in Society and History*, X (July 1969), pp. 376-400.

8 Godparenthood as an important element in clientelist ties is especially prominent in the literature on Latin America, although it is not a necessary ingredient in the establishment of ties. See for example William T. Stuart, "The Explanation of Patron-Client Systems: Some Structural and Ecological Perspectives," in Arnold Strickon and Sidney M. Greenfield (eds.), *Structure and Process in Latin America: Patronage, Clientage and Power Systems*, (Albuquerque: University of New Mexico Press, 1972), pp. 19-42.

9 Scott, op. cit. p. 96.

10 See Powell, op. cit., Benno Galjart, "Class and 'Following' in Rural Brazil," *America Latina* (July-September 1964), pp. 3-24. The classic study for Colombia remains Orlando fals Borda, *Peasant Society in the Colombian Andes* (Gainesville: University of Florida Press, 1962). Charles B. Loomis in *Turrialba: Social Systems and the Introduction of Change*, (Glencoe: The Free Press, 1953), also describes the landowner peasant as the basis of the rural political process.

11 Junichi Kyagoku and Nobutaka Ike discuss this in *Urban-Rural Differences in Voting Behavior in Postwar Japan*, (Stanford University Political Science Series, #66). See also Wayne A. Cornelius, "Local-Level Political Leadership in Latin American Urban Environments: A Structural Analysis of Urban Caciquismo in Mexico," Annual meeting, APSA, 1971.

12 It is also assumed that clientelism is characteristic of traditional or transitional societies a notion which is brilliantly critiqued by Keith Legg, "Interpersonal Relationships . . ." op. cit. especially p. 3 and 4.

13 The United States is, of course, also a "modern" society. What is fascinating about the Watergate affair is the personal loyalty to Richard Nixon which in the testimony before the Senate investigating committee was said to have been the reason for corrupt and covert behavior. This, according to the admission of many people involved. Beyond Watergate, American politics is full of incidents of personal motivations, corruption, voting frauds, extortion (for instance, Senator Gurney's alleged extortion of Florida builders) and so forth all of these at least components of clientelist behavior.

14 Legg says, "Certainly no one would argue that face-to-face relationships are impossible or unimportant in modern society." (p. 3) He continues "there is no difficulty in assuming a condition of widespread scarcity, and consequently, the impetus for patron-client exchange in transitional society. But in modern society a broader notion of survival. Some goods and services—top positions, access to information to name a few—are every bit as crucial for given individuals" (p. 4). He then observes that " . . . at the elite level, everyone is in a way a broker, because

connections themselves are major resources. It is through connections, through the maintenance of acquaintance networks, that access and information can be exchanged. These resources are particularly crucial not only for career building with a single organization, for jumping from one hierarchy to another, but also for maintaining and extending organizational goals, with which individual careers may be inextricably linked." (p. 10), Legg, op. cit.

15 For an interesting discussion of one aspect of this see James Scott and Benedict Kerkvliet, "How Rural Patrons Lose Legitimacy: A Theory with Special Reference to Lowland Southeast Asia," *Comparative Studies in Society and History*, 16, #1 (1974).

16 We have already indicated that Legg op. cit. argues that clientelist needs (scarcity for example) may be relative in each given situation. Landé in speaking about the desirability of dyadic ties for individuals seeking high offices (he gives as an example presidential advisors), indicates that even in modern democracies, dyadic structures flourish. Landé "Networks and Groups . . ." op. cit. p. 127.

17 Salado with an urban population of approximately 6,000 and a rural population of 14,000 was studied by the author in 1971. Four hundred people were interviewed. The district is primarily a coffee growing area, there is no obviously dominant family or enterprise and there were not spectacular cleavages in the socio-economic status of residents in the district.

It should be noted here that the effort to pinpoint leadership by the decisional method proved to be interesting but inconclusive. It seemed important to determine who was actually involved in decisions made, especially those which affected community life (that is to say "major" public decisions). Two individuals, the inspector of schools, owner of a general store and principal of the high school and another man who was said to be "always in charge of those things" were the two principal (I am tempted to say if my universe of community decisions were larger, ubiquitous) actors in major public decisions. Both were intensely disliked precisely for their ever-present role at the head of municipal commissions. However, they also appeared to have developed a sort of institutionalized neutrality—they were in charge because undesirable as it was for them to run major public undertakings, they were the lesser of evils. Being "in charge" does not, of course, tell us what the broader universe of participants was, and this proved to be a problematic undertaking. Larger decisions such as building a new permanent *mercado* (community or farmer's market place), the canalization to alleviate periodic severe flooding and erosion, the expansion of rural electrification, street pavement plans and the planning of a direct-dial telephone system which would extend into some rural parts, appear to have included almost everyone of importance in the community.

This seemed patently impossible until I discovered that the planning of these projects took place as do most other aspects in the community on an informal, and extensive basis. The market place project, for example, appears to have taken two and a half years to plan because every step of the way new objections were raised, new problems discovered, and additional individuals with "a stake" in the decision, unearthed.

I found great disagreement over whether or not the making of decisions in this way (which as described above is a consensus system) is better compared with how these matters were approached in other times. Some felt that it was more "fair" that everyone who wants to is consulted and then a major project is undertaken or is abandoned. Others indicated that in the end some come out ahead and others lose anyway and that, therefore, even if it does take longer the results are still the same. It should be made clear that there was widespread agreement on the fact that in the past decisions were made by "those in control" which almost inevitably was the political party "in control" with Monseñor being the chief organizer. As indicated in the survey, the members of the opposition party ANAPO feel very strongly that "those in control" (the Frente Nacional Liberals and Conservatives) very much discriminate against Anapistas in making public decisions today. This is thought to be true even though the leader of ANAPO is found to be actively present in the major decisions to which reference was made earlier.

There is aside from "major" decisions a virtually unlimited universe of "minor" decisions in which the decision-making participation is of limited interest in which the government bureaucracy assumes a prominent role. In these decisions which often affect "their" constituencies, brokers play an important role.

18 Salado as so much of rural Colombia was ravaged by decades of violence between partisans of the traditional Liberal (1930-1946) and Conservative (1946-1953) parties. After the short dictatorship of Gen. Rojas Pinilla (1953-1957) the leadership of the two parties arranged a National Front, a coalition with parity between the parties in all elected and appointed positions.

19 Fals Borda in his study of Saucio indicates that people's attachment to the *vereda* is almost as if it were a part of their extended family. op. cit. p. 43.

20 The definition of community leadership is subject to controversy. At least four approaches to measuring "community power" can be found in the American literature. (1) The "Decision-making" approach, as defined for instance, Robert Dahl *Who Governs?* (New Haven: Yale University Press, 1961). (2) "Social Participation" studies have also been used to pinpoint leadership. Donald W. Olmsted "Organizational Leadership and Social Structure in a Small City," *American Sociological Review* (June 1954), 273-281, is an example of this approach. The assumption underlying this method is that membership and intensity of activity in voluntary associations is a useful indicator of leadership and intensity of activity in voluntary associations is a useful indicator of leadership (i.e. membership and intensity of activity=community leadership). (3) The Positional method is probably the most widely used since to some extent it has been the original focus of Political Science. It consists of defining formal authority positions (usually the "top" positions) in institutions and organizations and identifying the individuals holding these positions. (4) Fi-

nally one finds the reputational approach whose most prominent advocate has been Floyd Hunter who applied it in the classic study *Community Power Structure* (Chapel Hill: University of North Carolina Press, 1953). In this approach reliable and well-informed informants are asked to name the top community leaders and the covergence of a sample of these responses used as the measure for identifying leaders.

Recent approaches have combined the four methods. As Linton C. Freeman in *Patterns of Local Community Leadership* (New York: Bobbs-Merrill, 1968) says " . . . the differing approaches to the study of community leadership seem to uncover different types of leaders. Studies of reputation, position and organizational participation all seem to get at the *institutional* leaders. Studies of participation in decision-making, on the other hand, uncover the *effectors* of community actions. And studies of social activities seem to seek out the *activists* who gain entry by dint of sheer commitment, time and energy." (italics mine) p. 42.

The applicability of U.S. community study approaches to Colombia will be discussed further on. I am simply interested in making the reader aware of the avenues to defining leadership which were considered prior to this study.

The "positional" in this study differs from the use of the word described in #3 above. It identifies the cases where a formal position (rather than the name of a person) was given in responses.

21 The *comité de cafeteros* is a local branch of the National Coffee Growers Association (Federacion National de Cafeteros) which is one of the most influential organizations in Colombia. The local *comités* are found in coffee growing areas and form a vital part of the agrarian economy. They have access to technical aid, credit; the *comité* promotes crop yield improvement, rural electrification, education. It is in other words a rather comprehensive entity which is especially effective because of its influential national committee and, therefore, its quasi-official capacity.

22 The residential distinction in both cases was that the only two Juntas de Accion Comunal in the town of Salado. Both are in *barrios* that have been rather badly neglected in respect to public services.

23 *Caseta*—A structure made usually of a concrete floor, bamboo walls and tin or eternit roofing which is used as a meeting and entertainment center for the members of the *Junta de Accion Comunal*.

24 The clusters are arbitrarily defined by the nature of the spontaneous responses of interviewees. Thus they are as recorded here mutually exclusive. On the basis of the response it was decided into which of the three it should fall.

25 I spent six consecutive hours in conversation with Dr. Carlos Armendariz Castro, ICA extension director for the state. His comments on the relationship of the agronomy bureaucracy to farmers provides some invaluable perspectives on *vereda* life. For instance he indicated that the loss of a good extension agent would set his work back sometimes two years. "these guys establish deep relationships of trust with the *campesinos*. The hardest thing to overcome initially is the opposition of the *gamonales* who are really afraid, probably for good reason because some of my

boys really without wanting to, come to almost dominate the districts where they work. You know people come to them for just about anything. They probably only spend half their time helping the district in agricultural problems."

26 F. G. Bailey has discussed these personal demands on congress party leaders in India saying "In Orissa, party politicians used to complain about the diversity of demands made by their own constituents ('He wanted me to find a bride for his son') . . ." F. G. Bailey "The Peasant View of the Bad Life," in Theodor Shanin (ed.) *Peasants and Peasant Society*, (Harmondsworth, England: Penguin Books, 1971), p. 309f.

27 However, there is also a correspondingly high non-political characteristic associated with most individuals (see comments above) such as owning a store or being a coffee agent (buyer) which may be extremely important in allowing the individual named to play an important role in the instrumental dyadic payoff situation as well.

28 The hospital, two secondary schools, a fire department, a dentist, the cemetery, church, post office, telephone exchange, general stores, bank, drug stores, agricultural services offices, *comite de cafeteros* center all are located exclusively in the urban section of the *municipio*.

29 It's interesting to point out that there is a general similarity in the characteristics of leadership qualities found by Freeman and associates in their study of Syracuse and the five general ones listed here. For example, in his category, *Activists* help shape the future of their community" . . . by sheer commitment of time and effort to community affairs." *Op. cit.*, p. 42. This seems to correspond to group (D). *Effectors* are " . . . Government personnel and professional participants, and the others are the employees of the large private corporations directed by the institutional leaders." p. 41. In their case, connection-group, (C) seems to be a similar element. Finally *Institutional* leaders " . . . are frequently the same individuals who are the heads of the largest and most actively participating business, industrial, governmental, political professional, educational, labor and religious organizations in Syracuse." p. 41. The similarity here with the "community positional roles" described earlier is striking.

30 The rise of a third party ANAPO under the leadership of former dictator Gen. Gustavo Rojas Pinilla is an important case for students of clientelism. I argued elsewhere that with the sharing of power by the Liberals and Conservatives between 1957 and 1974 half of the politically active leadership and patronage personnel of both parties found itself on the outside. ANAPO thus probably represented an opportunity for individuals whose importance to the parties was "devalued" by the National Front, to plug into a potential alternative clientelist network. *Political Clientelism in Colombia*, unpublished Ph.D. dissertation, Columbia University, New York, 1973. See especially Chapter V and VI.

31 The machete or *peinilla* is used by rural people in Colombia very much like a sword.

32 I have shown elsewhere that the clientelist con-

nections between political leaders in Salado and state or national leaders was crucial during periods of violence. Food, arms, money and even new jobs or homes, relocation in some other part of the country were thus secured. *"La Violencia* Revisited: The Clientelist Bases of Political Violence in Colombia," *Journal of Latin American Studies*, VI, #1, 1974 pp. 97-111.

33 Of interest in this connection is Barbara Ward's description of the importance of credit in the formation of brokerage relations. She suggests that small shopkeepers in great numbers are found in non-Western villages because these operate not as competitive enterprises but rather as creditors. Cash advances are often needed by a subsistence farmer who may need credit until his harvest comes in. Cash credit farmers quite clearly need it because they have to buy almost all of their foodstuffs and cash crops in most cases are seasonal. Barbara E. Ward, "Cash or Credit Crops? An examination of some Implications of Peasant Commercial Production with Special Reference to the Multiplicity of Traders and Middlemen," pp. 148-163 in *Economic Development and Cultural Change*, Vol. VIII, #2, (January, 1960). In Salado the small store owner is quite actively engaged in lending money and selling on credit. I would suggest that this resource is a very important one in the establishment of particularistic payoff dyads. It must be remembered that coffee growing (a cash crop activity) is the most wide-spread agricultural activity.

34 The contrast between the mayor in this community and the role defined by Mark Kesselman in the case of French mayors is quite interesting. In the case of France, Kesselman suggests that the mayor, " . . . opposes political divisions in the commune and . . . stresses instead the value of community harmony. The mayor's own efforts to unite the commune help confirm his belief that the commune is naturally united." p. 8. This is caused in France by a political culture, he suggests, which " . . . rejects political controversy; the practice is one of paternal leadership by an indispensable man." p. 161. *The Ambiguous Consensus* (N.Y.; A. Knopf, 1967)

The French mayor is a stable community leader who is elected for a six year term. Kesselman points out that mayors of the larger towns and of the fifty smallest communes had extremely long periods of office (in the latter case an average of 20.8 years), (p. 35). Both the premium on consensus and harmony and the local, stable nature of the office differ greatly from the Colombian case. First of all, the mayor is appointed for a one-year term which is sometimes but not often renewed. Second, and most important, the national political norm is one which has always encouraged conflict and division because the Colombian parties have been power rather than policy or ideology oriented. For a brief discussion of power, policy and ideology orientation in political parties see Karl Deutsch, *Politics and Government* (Boston: Houghton Mifflin, 1970), pp. 56-65.

35 The land for the school, interestingly, was given to the *barrio* by Don Seno who is Don Nacho's father. Don Seno is also the treasurer of the JAC and since no

better place could be found, a large unused room in Don Seno's house serves as the television viewing room for the set obtained from the government, thus there is a very deep and personal tie between the community efforts and the role of Don Nepo and Don Seno in that context.

36 These can be contrasted with the descriptions of French local leaders who as Wylie indicates, are supposed to " . . . mind their own business and seem indifferent to the affairs of other people." Laurence Wylie, *Village in the Vaucluse* (New York: Harper and Row, 1964), p. 6. Quoted in Kesselman, *op. cit.*, p. 39. Kesselman, however, also indicates that some mayors describe themselves as "the father of a communal family" while others consider their job to be similar to that of the manager of a business, pp. 43-52. The "business-mayor" role conforms to the type of leadership found in the larger Colombian *municipios*; for example, the dynamic former mayor of Bogota, Virgilio Barco, was a city planner—a technocrat whose job it was to rebuild the city; the mayor of Cali undertook the job of transforming that city for the 1971 Pan American games.

37 It is interesting to note that in a little known study, Douglas St. Angelo suggested that in Dubois County, Indiana, local political leaders perform a similar role; "the 'broker role' of local party officials and leaders is extensive in the county investigated for this report. The local party core often served as a link between citizens, local government units and formal organizations in the area, and national administrators." "The 'Broker Role' of Local Political Parties and Federal Administration," *Research Reports in Social Science*, (Talahassee: Florida State University, August 1965), p. 24.

38 One student of clientelism has said "While traditional patron-client relationships appear to be breaking down in many peasant societies, other types of dyadic structures and techniques will continue to play a part in politics as long as political actors seek and are able to advance their interests particularistically." Landé, "Networks and Groups . . ." *op. cit.* p. 127. Scott in one paper discusses the breakdown of patron-client bonds in Southeast Asia partly as a result of the shift in "outside" resources which become available to the patron (for instance, when Colonial authority penetrates the system). This makes it less attractive for the individual to continue the rather costly and time consuming clientelist relations with his client. James C. Scott, "The Erosion of Patron-Client Bonds and Social Change in Rural Southeast Asia," paper delivered at the 1972, annual meeting of the APSA.

39 "Bureaucrats as Modernizing Brokers? Clientelism in Colombia," *Comparative Politics*, Vol. 6, #3 (April 1974), pp. 425-450. The historical roots and processes of Colombian clientelism have been discussed in "Patrons, Brokers and Clients: Party Linkages in the Colombian System" manuscript.

40 For an interesting discussion of this in a new residential area of Bogota see A. Eugene Havens and William L. Flinn, "The Power Structure in a Shanty Town," in A. Eugene Havens and William L. Flinn (eds.) *Internal Colonialism and Structural Change in*

Colombia (New York: Praeger Publishers, 1970). Havens and Flinn also show that large numbers of people in the shanty town they studied are not tied into relationships with the leaders of the community nor are even informed about community affairs. In this paper we concentrated on the factors creating and characterizing clientelism and underemphasized the weakness of clientelist links in cases where people essentially rely on it for no more than credit at the local general store. Therefore, an area of crucial importance, and one for which methodological strategies might be devised, is measuring the *depth* and *intensity* of the patron-client bond in specific dyads.

The functioning of clientelism in a non-competitive political setting is quite instructive since it places significant strains on the mechanisms which are crucial to clientelism. For a discussion of this in the Colombian National Front period see my paper "Politics Without Breakdown; Political Clientelism and the Colombian Party System in the National Front" prepared for delivery at the Annual Meeting of the Southwestern Political Science Association, Hilton Palacio del Rio Hotel, San Antonio, Texas, March 27-29, 1975. Copyright 1975, The Southwestern Political Science Association.

PATRONS, PATRONAGE, AND POLITICAL PARTIES*

ALEX WEINGROD

I

WHAT IS MEANT BY "patronage"? The term appears with increased frequency in anthropological analysis. Indeed, it has become a major concept in the study of peasant societies, somewhat analogous to the concept of the "big man" in certain kinds of chiefdoms, or "fission and fusion" in lineage-type societies. There is, however, considerable ambiguity in the meaning given to the term. Consider, as examples, the following three excerpts from recent anthropological studies:

Patronage is founded on the reciprocal relations between patrons and clients. By patron I mean a person who uses his influence to assist and protect some other person, who then becomes his "client", and in return provides certain services for his patron . . . Patronage is thus the complex of relations between those who use their influence, social position or some other attribute to assist and protect others, and those whom they so help and protect.[1]
. . . The structure of the system of patronage, which is based on social relationships between clients seeking for a man with the ability and friendship connections to protect them and a patron who accepts these duties in return for political allegiance, grown upwards and through lawyers, other persons of influence, and Members of Parliament, is linked to the legislative assembly. Thus the organization of government and the structure of patronage are parallel hierarchies.[2]
In patronage, the transactor (patron) has the power to give some benefit which the respon-

dent (client) desires . . . Examples of this would be the improvement of a road near the respondent's house, or the employment of the respondent (or his relative) in an office over which the (patron) has control. The number and extent of such benefits naturally vary with the power of the (patron); but even the most influential is unlikely to please everyone who comes to him . . . He must therefore husband these direct patronage transactions so that they produce linkages with key people who can bring followers with them.[3]

Looked at in one way, these quotations seem to focus upon the same issue: the three authors assume that patronage relations can be successfully identified, all stress the inequality in power between patrons and clients, and each also emphasizes the reciprocal character of the social ties that are formed. One might see, in addition, a descending order of abstraction in the three statements. Boissevain writes generally about "influence", Campbell restricts this somewhat to relations of "political allegiance", while Mayer is more concerned with highly specific "benefits". This range in abstraction could perhaps be seen to give meaningful limits to the term. More to the point, however, this range of meaning indicates that "patronage" is used to designate quite different situations: the same term is being used, but different meanings are given to it.

To be more specific, in the previous quotations patronage is used in both the *anthropological and the political science sense*. It is hardly surprising to find both of these views represented: just as patronage has acquired a certain meaning for anthropologists, so too political scientists have for some time been studying "patronage systems". The perspectives of the two disciplines are, however, exceedingly different ones. It is therefore important to be clear about these distinctions and to explore their implications.

What have anthropologists meant by patronage? Patronage in anthropological usage has a special, or technical, meaning—it is meant to designate a particular kind of interpersonal relationship. In this sense patronage could be classed with terms such as "joking relations" or "kinship behavior"; that is, the term has reference to a particular pattern of social interaction. This use of the term goes back at least as far as Fustel de Coulanges' *The Ancient City*: for de Coulanges' patronage referred to a condition of legal inequality between patrons, who held political and ritual rights, and clients, who lacked such rights and could therefore only act through the mediation of their patron.[4] Although contemporary usage has frequently obscured this original meaning (the term is now typically applied to relationships between persons in different class positions, rather than to ties between the "free" and "unfree" as de Coulanges intended), anthropologists writing about patronage continue to stress the inequality aspect of patronage relations. Foster, for example, writes that "patron-client contracts are phrased vertically".[5] In this regard landowners are the classic instance of the "patron", while the peasants who rent their land are the typical anthropological "client". Although the landowner is powerful, and the peasant weak, each needs the other —their relations are "reciprocal". Thus Wolf writes that the patron provides "economic aid and protection against both the legal and illegal exactions of authority", while the client responds with "demonstrations of esteem", "information on the machinations of others", and the "promise of political support".[6] In addition to inequality and reciprocity, the personal, enduring character of these relationships is frequently emphasized: indeed, Pitt-Rivers takes patronage to be a kind of "lopsided friendship".[7]

Patronage in this sense is not usually thought of as being within a formal system of government or authority. Quite the contrary, it is an informal hierarchy—a kind of friendship network focused upon influence. As in Campbell's example, the network may extend to include "lawyers, Members of Parliament" and "other persons of influence". Thus, to summarize briefly, the study of patronage as phrased by anthropologists is the analysis of how persons of unequal authority, yet linked through ties of interest and friendship, manipulate their relationships in order to attain their ends.

What do political scientists have in mind when they write about patronage? Unlike the special sense in which anthropologists use the term, patronage in the vocabulary of political science has a kind of "folk" meaning. That is, patronage refers to the ways in which party politicians distribute public jobs or special favors in exchange for electoral support. The political party—a formally organized group—is the major unit in this use of the term. For example, V. O. Key writes that patronage may be considered "as the response of government to the demands of an interest group—the party machinery—that desires a particular policy in the distribution of public jobs".[8] Writing in a more general vein, Sorauf concludes that

patronage is best thought of as an incentive system—a political currency with which to purchase political activity and political responses. The chief functions of patronage are: maintaining an active party organization . . . Promoting intraparty cohesion . . . Attracting voters and supporters . . . Financing the party and its candidates . . . Procuring favorable government action . . . Creating party discipline in policy making.[9]

The "political response" that Sorauf writes of is, of course, voting—the political parties exchange jobs and favors in their quest for support at election time. In political science studies of patronage the key terms are "bosses" and "political machines", or merit versus political appointments. Patronage from this perspective is therefore largely the study of how political party leaders seek to turn public institutions and public resources to their own ends, and how favors of various kinds are exchanged for votes.

The contrasts between the anthropologists' and the political scientists' meanings are clear enough. To the anthropologist patronage refers to a type of social relationship, while to the political scientist patronage is a feature of government. The anthropologist who studies patronage considers "dyadic contracts", while the political scientist studies a formal organization. Patronage for anthropologists is an enduring relationship, while in the political science sense patronage is most clearly enunciated during election campaigns. There are, to be sure, areas of overlap: "patron-client" ties may be said to characterize certain relationships within a political-party directed patronage system (for instance, between "boss" and "worker"). Yet a patronage system cannot be simply reduced to a series of "patron-client" ties; a political party is much more than a set of "dyadic contracts". In brief, these two meanings of the term are so divergent that it is surely important to specify which type of "patronage" is being considered.

Such specificity is required not merely for reasons of clarity, but also since defining patronage in one way or the other determines how issues are posed. Several examples may help to illustrate this point. Patronage in the political science sense is a major topic in F. G. Bailey's *Politics and Social Change*. Bailey, a social anthropologist, is interested in examining how Indian villagers relate to state bureaucratic institutions, and how state-level political machines operate in the village context. Given his interest Bailey considers such issues as how politicians put together "vote banks", the reasons why villagers vote as they do, how the regional political machines are controlled, and so forth. Even though Bailey's data are not fully complete his study is a pioneering attempt to relate "peasants" to "patronage". Sydel Silverman's recent study of a central Italian village provides an interesting counterpoint to Bailey's analysis. Entitled "Patronage and Community-Nation Relations in Central Italy", Silverman's excellent study traces the demise of a local patron group. The patrons described in this study are the major village landowners, local bureaucrats and professionals. In the pre-World War II period this group is described as holding great power since it could control relationships between the village and the state; following World War II, however, land became fragmented, and many of the local bureaucrats and professionals were civil service appointees only temporarily stationed in the community. Since the "economic decline of the traditional patrons has not been accompanied by the emergence of any new group to assume an analogous role", Silverman concludes that "in contemporary Colleverde there is no longer a patron group".[10] Silverman uses the term "patron" in the anthropological sense, and in this regard her conclusions are undoubtedly sound. Yet while she indicates how and why this relationship has disappeared, Silverman does not show clearly enough how community members may be systematically linked to the *new political party patronage system*. Landowners may no longer be patrons, but, as she herself shows, the villagers do use political party and other connections as they seek for favors and assistance in dealing with various governmental bureaus.

What one means by patronage thus *does* make a difference: with another view of patronage Silverman would no doubt have explored a different set of issues, or interpreted her data in a different manner. Her general conclusions regarding the passing of patron-client ties are, however, extremely relevant. That is, patronage in the anthropologists' sense appears increasingly to be a historical phenomenon, while patronage in the political science sense becomes more relevant to contemporary issues. "Lopsided friendships" do, of course, recur in contemporary village communities, but they no longer have the significance they once held. Traditional relationships between "patrons" and "clients" (landlord and tenant) become less critical, while relations between political party leaders or agents and their supporters become more significant. Elected officials and party-linked administrators now play major roles, so that anthropologists studying at the village level will wish to rule some aspects of party politics and government agencies into their analysis. It seems clear that the impact of universal suffrage, mass political parties and, more generally, mass society, has been to transform the political conditions of many rural societies.

II

Distinguishing between the meanings of patronage is a necessary first step. Additional questions need to be raised, however. How can patronage, in either the anthropological or the political sense, be interpreted? Why are patron-client ties prevalent in certain types of societies, and why are these relationships frequently superseded by political-party directed patronage?

Responding to these questions leads in two closely related directions: first, to a consideration of the political organization of the state, and second, to an analysis of the relationships between the different segments that compose the state.[11] Put in these terms, *patron-client ties can be seen to arise within a state structure in which authority is dispersed and state activity limited in scope, and in which considerable separation exists between the levels of village, city and state. Party-directed patronage, on the other hand, is associated with the expanding scope and general proliferation of state activities, and also with the growing integration of village, city and state.* The major distinctions, then, are between a state which regulates and a state which reforms, and between "segmentation" and "integration". Silverman has stated this distinction succinctly: the patron-client tie, she writes, "represents a general form community-nation relationship characteristic of an early phase of development of nation-states, a form which regularly gives way as the process of integration of the total society advances".[12]

Lattimore's model of the "cellular structure" of the classic Chinese state is a useful way to conceptualize the type of state within which patron-client ties may emerge.[13] By introducing the model of "cellular structure" Lattimore draws attention to two important features of certain states: first, the various communities or regions that compose the state are only loosely tied to one another; and second, the political structure of the state is centered in the capital and the great cities, and reaches out into the countryside only to preserve order and to collect revenues. The state does not take as its task to transform the countryside; quite the contrary, officials make only infrequent sojourns to the hinterland, although state power is represented there by police detachments, various clerks, courts, tax and land registries, and so forth. The state officials are, moreover, typically recruited from small, comparatively restricted groups. What is important for our purposes is that various "gaps" occur within this cellular structure: there are, for example, gaps between regions, between communities, and between villager and city-based officials. It is within this context of relative segmentation that a category of "mediators" arise who may act to bridge the different regions or levels. Such mediators—lawyers, landowners, merchants, politicians—are, of course, precisely those persons who are usually labelled as "patrons." Indeed, that patron-client ties serve as a kind of mediating mechanism is abundantly documented in the anthropological literature.[14] The classic landlord-peasant relationship well illustrates the crucial dealings with state officials; since the peasants have little information about and even less influence with these officials, they appeal to their landlord-patron to intervene for them. The landlord as patron has a wide range of contacts outside the village—ties with such members of the regional or national elite as bankers, administrators, or politicians—and therefore he may use his influence on behalf of his peasant-client. As Kenny observes, patrons "largely dominate the paths linking the local infrastructure of the village to the superstructure of the outside world," and they are therefore able to play the mediator role.[15]

The need for mediators arises from the "gaps" between the levels: why then are there gaps? The segmentation, or isolation, of regions and communities can be traced to a number of different factors. A primitive transportation system, the absence or poor development of regional and national markets, laws against migration, a rigidly enforced endogamous marriage rule, a high degree of linguistic diversity—these are among the factors that lead to a kind of local isolation. A closed system of social stratification also results in "gaps" in the system. In addition, as Bendix and Eisenstadt have recently emphasized, the political authority of the state may not reach effectively into the hinterland since the state lacks sufficient force; the inability of the "center" to control the peripheral areas is a principal cause of segmentation.[16] Then too, since the mediators themselves thrive upon the gaps in the system they have an interest in preserving local isolation. Under these circumstances the various local or regional units might be sufficiently separate from one another for them to be described as being "isolated". Social ties would mainly become concentrated within and limited to community or family members, and as a consequence most persons would rarely enter into regular relationships with persons in other status positions or in other locales. It is this gap between levels or locales which leads "clients" to search for "patrons", and which places such power in the hands of mediators.

Just as patron-client ties arise within a state which regulates, so too the emergence of political-party directed patronage is closely associated with a different type of state. Party patronage is closely associated with a different type of state. Party patronage becomes of great importance as state power expands throughout the society, and as the political parties themselves become ever more closely linked within the state structure. In this type of state, officials no longer restrict their activity merely to maintaining order and collecting revenues; they rather seek to transform the conditions of the countryside. Studies of development, for examples, have over and again stressed the vastly expanded role of government agencies and political parties.[17] Development implies the establishment of new national or regional organizations, the initiation of new agricultural and industrial programs, the recruitment of cadres of workers, the commitment of huge capital funds, etc. These new resources of jobs and funds are typically administered or controlled by political party members or by persons designated by the parties: since the parties are seen as the "spearhead" of development, the party hierarchy and rank and file are likely to be closely associated with the major development agencies. Myron Weiner's comment regarding contemporary India is an excellent case in point:

Since the Congress Party controls not only the state and national governments, but most of the local governments and new quasi-governmental bodies (such as cooperatives) as well, the Party has been able to establish extensive control over patronage. Through the use of patronage, the party leaders serve as a link between the villager and the complex administrative and governmental machinery.[18]

This close association of party with government opens new possibilities for patronage; once having gained control of these resources the parties use them to serve their own electoral ends. The "politics of development" is thus a central cause of the expansion of party patronage.

Moreover, these conditions also serve to magnify the importance of political party leaders in contrast with other potential elite groups. The local party secretary, rather than the landlord, provides access to the resources of persons that the villager wishes to reach and to influence. It is the party functionary who provides information regarding loan programs, who can contact the government's tax collector on the villagers' behalf, or who can help the villager send his son on to high school. The new men of influence are thus likely to be the political men, and it is their ability to deal effectively with the wider system that gives them their power. Patron-client relations may continue under these circumstances, but it is more likely that political-party directed patronage becomes increasingly significant: the party-boss and his workers—the professionals—control ever wider resources, and they are likely to better provide for their "constituents" than can the patron for his "clients".

The expanding economic and social role of the state can thus be seen to underlie the spread of patronage. It should be emphasized, however, that these changes are symptomatic of an even more profound transformation: namely, the movement of change from "traditional" to "mass" society. That is, the distinctions of status and culture that long characterized the countryside have increasingly less validity and force, whereas new egalitarian values and institutions have a much wider relevance. To use Shils' phrase, what is involved here is that "the mass of the population has become incorporated into society".[19] Mass society implies, among other attributes, the universalization of suffrage, a greater concern for the welfare of each citizen, a wide expansion of the activities of government, as well as spreading "the culture which was once confined to a narrow circle at the center over a far greater radius".[20] New groups enter into political activity, and society itself becomes more uniformly politicized. Ranging throughout the society, the political parties are

arenas for new contacts, new types of association, as well as important networks of communication and information. As national groups the parties may serve to bridge the gaps between one locale and the next; by recruiting new groups into activity they may also overcome status distinctions that traditionally separated one class or ethnic group from the next. Thus, in brief, the parties serve a "bridging" or "mediation" function, and act to break down social isolation and to develop a kind of regional or national "integration". This is not to say that the rural areas of developing societies have lost their isolation and are now meaningfully integrated within larger systems; yet surely the parties have played a major role in whatever integration has taken place.[21]

III

In the remaining sections of this article I want to briefly illustrate several of the ideas discussed earlier. The data to be presented are based upon studies of Sardinia, and more particularly, the analysis of a single Sardinian zone. Sardinia is an especially relevant case since it is a part of a classic Mediterranean "patron-client" area, and also since it has recently witnessed widespread programs of social and economic development. My purpose in this section is not to present an ethnographic review of rural Sardinia; it is rather to outline a transition from a political system based upon patron-client ties, to a system in which political party patronage has become predominant.

When the Sards, or for that matter Italians in general, speak of patronage they use the term *clientela*. *Clientela* is a word that one hears and reads with great frequency; indeed, when local politics is described by the Sards it appears as if *clientela* is the core of the political system. Some present-day instances of *clientela* include, for example, how the local manager of a national bank approves loans as favors to persons whose support he can count upon at the next municipal election; how a village nursery school is established after a group of village nuns intervenes with a government official, while the local village council who are not members of the party in power are unable to enlist support for the village school; how the head of a large public agency uses government employees to canvass vote support during a national election campaign; how landowners who belong to the parties in power receive loans administered by government agencies, while other landowners are not made aware of the loan programs; how an elected member of the regional assembly obtains tobacco and wine licenses for several families of his supporters; how an internationally-sponsored local development project failed since its key personnel could not be fitted into the party-directed administrative system.

This list could be expanded at great length. I cite these instances to indicate, in a preliminary way, the kinds of situations that are classed by Sards under the heading of *clientela*. As brief as these examples are, a number of conclusions can be drawn from them. First, *clientela* does not have the meaning of "clientship", but rather refers to a leader and his band of supporters: *clientela* can be literally translated to mean "connexion", and what is implied are relations between those who have influence and others who wish to benefit from its use. *Lui fa una clientela*, "he is drumming up support", is a common way of describing how an ambitious man distributes favors as a means of enlisting supporters. Second, in the instances cited, favors are distributed by political party agents to the party's supporters: *clientela* thus relates to political-party directed patronage, rather than to patron-client ties. Third, what is being described is largely the intervention of power-holders as they seek benefits for themselves or for their supporters. *Clientela* therefore involves a kind of favoritism—it is based upon highly personal ties rather than upon universalistic criteria. (It is for this reason that *clientela* is looked down upon with disfavor; *clientela*, emphasizing personal motives and greed, is contrasted with politics of an ideological kind or with public-spirited administration in which "connexions" are made irrelevant.) Fourth, the interventions described are mainly in areas of administrative responsibility, so that favoritism is to be found within bureaucratically structured, large-scale organizations. Finally, although voting is part of the "currency" of *clientela*, patronage is not restricted to election campaigns. There is a deferred payment aspect —a kind of "promissory note"—so that while voting and elections are crucial, an analysis of the system must take into account debts that are built up over considerable periods of time.

Bellieni, in his discussion of nineteenth-century Sard politics, makes the point that "public activity was never a debate of ideas. The parties were nothing more than a *clientela* of minor leaders."[22] What Bellieni means by *clientela*, however, differs in important ways from the present-day political organization; that is, the scope and character of the political parties has changed greatly in the century since Italian

unity. In order to understand these changes it is necessary to outline the evolving structure of government and parties in Sardinia and, equally important, to indicate the social and economic contexts within which the parties develop. Two stages in rural Sardinian political organization will be sketched out: in the first stage a kind of fragmentation between communities and regions prevailed, and in that phase patron-client ties were a major means of political organization, while the second stage is characterized by a more general social integration, and in that stage party-directed patronage became increasingly significant.

Stage I (1870-1922). The French geographer Le Lannou begins his classic study of Sardinia by stressing the island's "isolation" (l'isolemente): "The various districts", he writes, "have for a very long time been isolated from one another. ... Since the middle of the last century certain areas have been difficult to enter and therefore have lived a separate life".[23] Le Lannou's emphasis upon the island's internal fragmentation is extremely perceptive: although small in size and population (Sardinia measures roughly 140 miles by 40 miles, and has a present-day population of nearly a million and a half: it is the least densely populated area of Italy), Sardinia has throughout its history been divided into a series of comparatively insulated, separate zones. Geographic factors are one principal cause of regionalism: the interior of the island is mountainous and arid, while the coastal zones lack any substantial agricultural hinterland. Moreover, the towns along the coast historically were linked more to Spain, Italy or France than to the interior: Sassari, the major northern town, was commercially oriented towards France and northern Italy, while Cagliari, the largest city on the south coast, faced more to Rome and the Italian south. The high incidence of malaria in the south and southwest of the islands seems also to have inhibited travel and contacts between regions. Political and historical factors also contributed to the island's fragmentation. Far from the political center, Sardinia was poorly administered, and as a consequence road and rail connections were few and poorly maintained. Indeed, Le Lannou writes that "the difficulties of interior travel . . . is the most potent factor in the island's (internal) isolation".[24] Recurrent unsettled political conditions, and in particular the bandit tradition in the interior, also contributed to a lack of contact between segments of the island. Moreover, since throughout its history sections of the island fell under the influence of different invading groups, the Sard language exhibits considerable linguistic diversity. There are at least six different regional dialects, and this broad linguistic diversity must also have been a barrier to island-wide contact. In brief, Sardinia as a whole can be seen to have been a checkerboard of separate geographic, political and linguistic regions, each region only loosely articulating with others.

In addition to this regionalism, there has also been a striking degree of separation between local communities: until recent times social relationships appear to have been concentrated at the village level, rather than between villages or regions. There is considerable evidence of a kind of "community isolation"—most villagers established and maintained social ties within their own community, rather than developing networks of contact between locales. That isolation was characteristic of the countryside, and that it has recently given way to a greater integration between communities, can be seen in the following tables. Tables I and II summarize data regarding marriage and godparent choice. The data were collected in Surughu (the name is fictitious), of Oristano. Since accurate records were kept in the *commune* and the church registry it is possible to gauge some key aspects of population movement over a lengthy period of time.

TABLE 1

Marriages by Place of Residence of Bride and Groom, 1866-1965 (in per cent)

Year	Between Villagers	Between Villagers and Residents in Six Adjoining Villages	Between Villagers and All Others
1866-75	93.7	4.4	1.9
1876-85	91.9	3.6	4.5
1886-95	88.5	8.9	2.6
1896-05	85.0	5.7	9.3
1906-15	88.6	7.9	3.5
1916-25	93.8	4.0	2.2
1926-35	81.4	4.8	13.8
1936-45	80.1	5.9	14.0
1946-55	72.6	15.3	12.1
1956-65	50.8	11.1	38.1
	N=1,160	N=111	N=141

The data summarized in these tables indicate important ways in which social relationships were concentrated at the local level. Marriage is a key index: a tendency towards village exogamy might, for example, have proliferated ties in a wide range of locales and there provided channels of contact and information within a region and between regions. However, as Table I indicates, marriage did not link villagers to members of other communities, but served rather to isolate the village socially. Taking the number of villagers who intermarried together

with those who married persons in the six adjoining villages (these six villages border on Surughu, and they are from four to eight miles from the village center), the incidence of local level endogamy amounts to ninety-two per cent. It is only in the post-World War II period that village endogamy declines, and this change has become significant only in the past decade. It is important to note, however, that while in general marriage has not been a "bridging mechanism", differences are evidence between social classes: genealogies collected from among the more professionally oriented, wealthy villagers show that village exogamy has been more prevalent among the "upper strata" of village society. For these few families marriage may have been a means of linking the village elite to regional and island-wide networks.

TABLE 2

Choice of Godparents, by Year (in per cent)

Period	Villager Chosen Godparent	Other Chosen Godparent
1917-1927	92.7	7.2 N=375
1956-1965	66.6	33.4 N=392

An emphasis upon village-level ties is also apparent in the selection of godparents: Table II indicates that villagers selected godparents from within the community, rather than from among other locales. A change in this pattern during recent times is also indicated: as with marriage choice, so too in the last decade godparents are increasingly chosen from outside the village. In general, however, godparenthood, a tradition which is said to develop ties of "quasi-kinship", has developed these ties primarily at the local level.[25]

TABLE 3

Land Ownership (in hectares)

Hectares	Percentage
0-1	15.4
1-5	39.0
6-10	22.3
11-15	10.1
16-20	5.2
21-25	3.2
26-30	1.2
31-35	1.2
36-40	0.0
41-45	0.4
46-50	0.8
51-70	0.0
71-75	0.4
76-80	0.0
81-85	0.0
86-90	0.4
	99.6 N=246

This same emphasis upon local-level ties can also be seen in the village's economic, ritual and governmental organization. Two points need to be emphasized regarding the village's economy: first, nearly all villagers owned comparatively small parcels of land, and no single family or group of families monopolized landholdings. This pattern of land distribution is summarized in Table III; while the range in holdings varies from less than one to 88 hectares, it is clear that no single holding is dominant. According to the villagers this general pattern has not changed substantially in the past half-century (the data in Table III are based on 1962); although individual holdings may have grown or diminished in size, these variations have been within the pattern of comparatively small-scale landholdings. Second, until recent times village markets were near at hand, so that economic exchanges did not extend far beyond the village context. Agricultural production was mainly in grain, olives and animals (cattle, sheep and goats). These commodities were partially consumed within the household, with the surplus sold to town-based cheese merchants. The sheep or cows were normally pastured on village lands, although occasionally pasture was rented from neighboring villages. Animal markets were held in towns from fifteen to 25 kilometers from the village; the villager who marketed his animals in town might also purchase various manufactured goods (cloth, arms, small tools, etc.). What should be stressed is that the village economy did not necessitate social relationships beyond the level of village or regional town; market activities did not significantly affect the concentration of ties at the local level.

Similarly, the organization of ritual was also primarily at the village level. Each village has its patron-saints, and every village celebrates the *feste* of their *santi*. At Surughu, for example, three local festivals were celebrated. The *feste* were organized by local committees, and, although outside entertainers might be invited, the participants were mainly villagers and their relatives or friends from the immediately surrounding area. Since each village celebrated its own round of festivals, the villagers at Surughu also attended *feste* in the adjoining villages. In addition to these purely local concentrations, some villagers also attended the religious procession and fair held yearly in Oristano, and some attended the spring *carnivale*. Both the fair and *carnivale* drew persons from throughout the Oristano area. In brief, the yearly round of religious festivals was local or regional in scope, and did not bring villagers into contact with persons from more distant areas of the island. Indeed, there are no paramount religious sites or occasions which may draw together persons from widely scattered locales.

Although ritual organization was local in scale, religious organization did of course link the village to the Catholic Church hierarchy. Surughu was in the domain of the Archbishop of Oristano; like all other villages in the island it was part of a major network of social and political contact. Oristano was a major church center, and there the village priests had access to church officials at various levels of authority. This link to an island-wide organization of considerable power is important in understanding the structure of political relationships.

The structure of government during the first quarter of this century is of major interest. The main point to emphasize is that while various administrative and judicial organs of the state functioned to maintain order at the local level, government did not take as its task to intervene or to regulate most social or economic affairs. To be sure, taxes were collected, import and export regulations set, roads built and maintained, different administrative arrangements experimented with; yet the scope and purpose of government was limited to maintaining order; it was not to initiate change or transform existing structures. For the villagers at Surughu the state was represented by a small number of local officials, a small post of *carabinieri*, and by judicial and administrative officers centered in the nearby town. The local posts were those of mayor (*sindaco*), counsellor (*consigliero*) and secretary (*segretario*). Mayor and counsellors were selected by the villagers at periodic elections, while the secretary, who represented central government in the village, held an appointive post. The *sindaco* and his fellow counsellors were empowered to set and to administer certain local policies; for example, they administered the sale or rental of communal lands, levied village taxes, proposed various village public works and organized local festivities. The mayor's signature was required on various personal and communal documents, he met and negotiated with higher level state functionaries, and he also spent considerable time in meetings or in discussing public affairs. The *segretario*, who was under the direction of the prefect appointed by the interior ministry, acted as a kind of "monitor" over local affairs: expert in administrative regulations, the secretary saw to it that the council's decisions were within the administrative code. His daily tasks were to keep a record of vital statistics, oversee the work of the *municipio* office, and to prepare the various permits and certificates that were frequently required.

The law courts, as well as higher level state administrative offices, were located in the nearby town. The offices of the *prefetura*, for example, were centered there, as was the *catasta*, the registry of land deeds. Although a law suit or a question of tax might bring a villager to town, most villagers had only infrequent need to deal with the town or city based authorities.

This analysis has thus far stressed the various ways in which social ties were concentrated at the local level. With the exception of several of the more wealthy families and the local priests, there is considerable evidence for a kind of local "segmentation" or "isolation". It is within this context that patron-client ties emerged as the dominant mode of local political organization: the "gaps" in the system—gaps between village and town, and between the villager and the governing elite—gave rise to a category of "mediators" or patrons. Patron-client ties were of principal importance since, to use Wolf's phrase (and to change the metaphor), a small number of persons were able to "guard the synapses" that bind the local to the regional and national levels.[26]

Who were the patrons, and how did the political system operate? At Surughu the influential men included several of the larger landowners, two families of lawyers, the village priest, and preeminently, the village *sindaco*. Although their holdings were comparatively small, some landowners did employ other villagers as shepherds (*servopastore*) or in a system of sharecropping (*mezzadria*). The economically advantageous position held by the larger landowners was frequently translated into political influence; at times they served as *consiglieri*, but, more typically, they formed close ties of mutual benefit with village political leaders. To some extent the landowners did act as "patrons": they intervened with the mayor or secretary on behalf of their *mezzadria* client, or they might act as spokesmen for their *servopastore* when they fell afoul of the law. The record of godparent choice during this period shows that several of the larger landowners were frequently chosen as *padrino* and *madrina*. Although they might be classed as men of influence, none of the landowners was economically powerful enough to assert a major influence in village affairs. Indeed, they themselves typically acted through the *sindaco*. The two families of lawyers, the Poddu's and Cubeddu's (the names are fictitious) did have lines of contact outside the vil-

lage, and they were frequently turned to for assistance; in the case of the Poddu's, marriage had aligned them with other professional families in other sections of the island. As will later be made clear, the importance of these two families rose dramatically during the Fascist period. The village priest, in addition, took an active part in local affairs, and frequently used his channels of information and contact to assist his parishioners. These transactions were not linked within a political party system; the church network provided an excellent source of regional and island-wide ties independent of political party or other formal organizations.

While landowner, lawyer and priest were all "influentials", and frequently played the role of "patron", the *sindaco* was the major political force in the village. Re-elected to office in the period between 1911 and 1919, the *sindaco*, Antonio Serra, dominated village affairs throughout this period. In alliance with several of the landowners, in league with the local *segretario*, with the tacit and sometimes active assistance of the priest, Serra emerged as the local "boss" of the village. By controlling the affairs of the *commune* Serra was able to grant favors and to mobilize a *clientela*; for example, communal lands were rented or in some cases sold to his allies, he intervened in his friends' behalf before the state administrative officers, his supporters' requests for prompt dispatch of their documents were granted, and so forth. (It is commonly alleged among the villagers, for example, that he was able to gain deferment from military conscription for the sons of his friends during World War I.) Even though his activities were monitored by the *prefetura*, the *sindaco* was able to assert very great power in the village; his cleverness was admired, yet Serra also seems to have been feared.

Serra was a member of the Republican party, and during national election campaigns he supported the Republican candidates. Since some government posts were controlled by the parties, his party affiliation gave him access to higher level administrative personnel. The parties, however, were not coordinated, permanent organizations; they were loose assemblages of local leaders—such as Serra—who concerted efforts only during election periods. As one observer put it, "these small groups come under the wings of the major parties, from whom they receive in exchange protection and help in local contests, and in particular protection for personal favors".[27] A local "boss" such as Serra therefore had great local autonomy. Moreover, the party itself had only limited favors that it could bestow. Since, as was pointed out earlier, the functions of government were comparatively limited ones, the parties did not control rich or considerable resources. This is an extremely important point: Serra was a "patron", he was able to develop and to control a "*clientela*", but his power was not significantly magnified by his party affiliation. To put it simply, he was a "local boss", and not a "party boss".

Stage II (1923—to the present). Fascist rule brought, of course, very important changes in the organization of the state. Whereas previously "government" and "party" were in theory separate systems (although in fact some positions were allotted to the parties), according to the fascist theory of the "corporate state" the two became fused; the party leaders, with Mussolini at their head, assumed total control of the state. Moreover, while formerly state activities were comparatively limited in scope, under Fascist rule they were greatly expanded. Although Sardinia was far from the political center, fascist control was accompanied by important changes. To briefly list some of these: an intensified program of road and rail construction was begun throughout the island; the state assumed control over trade unions and cooperatives, and in addition also organized a complete spectrum of state-directed enterprises; a variety of women's, children's and youth groups began activities; the previously competitive party-system was done away with, and the older political parties were either incorporated within the Fascist party or eliminated; in Sardinia an intensive repressive campaign was launched against the bandits. The members of the Fascist party were, of course, especially active in the many state activities. Through its control of the state machinery the party could allocate crucial resources of jobs, funds for various projects, as well as personal favors and privileges; to quote Carl Schmidt, "the Party's monopoly of thousands of jobs, and the special privileges given to loyal Fascists in securing posts and winning promotions" meant that the party had become the major dispenser of political patronage.[28] With these resources in its grasp, the party also became an increasingly coordinated structure: if local party organization had formerly been weak, and the parties little more than an agglomeration of local leaders and their *clientela*, the Fascists achieved a much greater degree of nation-wide coordination and control.

What effect did these changes have at Surughu? In a variety of ways the village became more closely linked to regional and island-wide social, economic and political networks. For example, new roads were constructed between Surughu and other villages in the zone and Oristano. An island-wide bus service was begun, so that the villagers could travel more quickly and easily to other centers. The market orientation of the local economy also grew in scale; a number of local shops were opened, production of cheese and meat for the market grew, and so too did the use of mass consumption goods. A local cheese producers' cooperative was organized as part of a general project to further develop the cheese industry. Although some villagers became members of the Fascist party, and others participated in various social and athletic events, these activities were never sustained; the "movement" as such did not deeply touch the lives of most of the villagers. On the other hand, the active Fascist party members did occasionally participate in regional party activities. Indeed, party membership and activity represented a new focus of local solidarity.

According to the Fascist scheme of local government, election for office was done away with, and an appointed official was instead charged with the daily operation of village public affairs. The village head, or *podesta*, was of course nominated from the party cadres; for example, for a number of years the *podesta* at Surughu was an active Fascist from a nearby village. The responsibilities of a *podesta* were in most ways similar to those of the previous *sindaco*; that is, they were minor administrative responsibilities. As *sindaco* Antonio Serra had earlier established himself as a kind of local "boss." None of the village officials during Fascist rule assumed analogous positions. Greater influence was frequently held by the local Fascist party secretary, who, as a member of the island-wide system of political control, had access to various centers of power. More important, several local figures reached higher positions of influence: two young lawyers, Mario Poddu and Paolo Cubeddu, attained strategic island-wide and even national posts, and their positions of prominence were important in the restructuring of local political relations.

Both Poddu and Cubeddu had earlier been active in the Partito Sardo d'Azione, the Sardinian nationalist party whose program stressed autonomy for the island. With the rise of fascism, however, both joined the movement and rose rapidly to high posts. Poddu became a leading figure in Sardinian affairs, and in the early 1920s was given responsibility for agricultural development throughout the island. It was during his tenure, for example, that a series of cheese cooperatives was formed; the cooperative at Surughu was formed at that time. In addition to their economic functions, these cooperatives gave Poddu an opportunity to develop a wider political following; the local cooperative directors were chosen from among his friends and supporters, and with this base of support he could further extend his political ambitions. In short, Poddu was able to use his position in the party and government to build a *clientela*. Paolo Cubeddu also rose to a position of eminence; indeed, in the 1930s he became an undersecretary in the Mussolini regime. Although both men had left the village (Poddu lived in Oristano, Cubeddu in Rome), they were frequently in touch with local matters; friends and family members turned to them for advice, they both engaged in various economic transactions in the region, their local allies frequently received various benefits, and so forth. Each was thus a kind of "grand patron" in regard to the village" from their positions of influence in party and government they were able to bestow patronage benefits to their supporters and friends.

To have had two of its "sons" in such high positions was certainly a rarity: in none of the surrounding villages were there persons of comparable political stature. There is no evidence, though, that this special relationship brought spectacular benefits to the village; the cheese cooperative is still referred to as "Poddu's", but such cooperatives are to be found in numerous villages. The significance of these two men as "grand patrons" lies elsewhere; namely in the magnified role of the political party as the central mechanism in the economic and political life of the village. Under Fascism Sardinian society became increasingly politicized—party affairs became increasingly significant since the party was extraordinarily powerful. The villagers therefore searched for links to the party hierarchy as they pursued their own interests, or for that matter, the interests of the village. In this regard the villagers at Surughu were fortunate—but their behavior was in no way different from that of persons in other villages. To be a "local boss"—to develop a village *clientela* —was no longer sufficient. The key decisions were made within the party, and one's influence in regional and island-wide party circles had become the measure of political power.

Political democracy returned to Italy, of course, following the Second World War. The Fascists were both legally and socially repudiated, and in place of the "corporate state" Italy moved to a republican "welfare state" type of regime in which political-party patronage, *clientela*, continues to be a major mode of political organization.

Once again, how are these trends reflected at the village level? Those processes which can be thought of as further integrating Surughu with the region, with Sardinia as a whole, and in principle, with the Italian nation, have been further magnified in the past two decades. Bus and rail connections between the village and the various centers of the island are now excellent; Oristano is a mere thirty minutes away by bus, and six times a day the bus takes villagers to and from the town. Since 1947 a considerable number of villagers have migrated to Oristano, so that most villagers now have kinsmen or friends in the town. An even larger wave of migration has taken many young men and women to Italy, and in some cases to Switzerland, Germany and Australia; upwards of 150 Surughese now work as domestics in Rome or Milan, or in factories in Turin and Hamburg. The economy of the village is in no small measure now a "remittance economy", and each month money is funneled into local hands. The male migrants frequently return home for extended visits, and several have also returned to take up residence; they return often with private cars, or with other luxury consumption goods.

As shown in Tables I and II, since 1950 a growing proportion of marriages and godparent choices have been between villagers and persons resident in other locales. This shift may be taken as an index of the increasingly wide networks of contact that typify the past two decades. In addition, a large number of village youngsters now attend the various secondary training schools at Oristano, and more than thirty young people attend university classes at Cagliari and Sassari. Then, too, very few traces remain of a "self-sufficient" rural economy: although itinerant merchants may sell their wares each week in a kind of local market, and some produce is consumed in the village, the Surughese now purchase mass-consumption goods in local stores or in Oristano, and they market their cheese, animals, and olive oil to a number of fairly large-scale firms. The local bars feature television, and nearly every home has a radio; the youngsters, both male and female, attend summer dances held at nearby night spots, and styles of fashion quickly follow the lead of Roman "high couture". To summarize briefly: the social and also cultural "gaps" between the village system and the region and nation have become increasingly narrowed, and in a number of important ways the villagers are now participants in the "mass society" and "mass culture" of contemporary Italy.

Just as the economic and social ties of the villagers now extend far beyond the village level, so too village political organization has become coordinated with various regional and national organizations. What is essentially the pre-Fascist form of local government has been reconstituted; that is, the village *sindaco* and *consiglieri* are once again elected in periodic balloting between competing party groups, and the familiar *segretario* and *carabinieri* are assigned to the village by central state authorities. Local offices therefore have a certain simplicity. At the same time, however, the issues that local government must be concerned with are considerably enlarged. For one thing, the "welfare-state" orientation of the state has broadened the scope of governmental activity. There are now problems of pensions, assistance to the indigent, public health, schooling, regional planning, that become the concern of village officers. Moreover, large-scale programs of rural development have been initiated, most notably, by the *Cassa per il Mezzogiorno*, the Fund for the South, which has sought to bring about a transformation in the countryside. In addition to national Italian programs such as the Cassa, since Sardinia enjoys regional autonomy within the Italian state, the Sardinian *Regione* also sponsors a broad spectrum of development activities. There are, in brief, an entire series of development and assistance programs, all of them a governmental or quasi-governmental kind, and each administered in typical bureaucratic fashion. What this means, of course, is that both individual villagers and the village officers themselves have increasingly frequent dealings with state officials.

Government and party in contemporary Italy are, in theory, meant to be separate; in fact, as is widely recognized, they are closely intertwined. The Christian Democratic Party (DC) has formed the government after each national election, and it has also been able to control many of the state organs. This close association between state and party is not limited to the DC: all of the coalition parties have been able to delegate some state resources to party members, and the parties outside of the coalition have also developed powerful economic institutions (such as the trade unions). La Palombara's comment regarding the *Cassa per il Mezzogiorno* has relevance to bureaucracy and administration more generally:

A representative of the I.R.I. notes that the Cassa per il Mezzogiorno . . . has become a gigantic patronage organization which employs people and awards developmental contracts strictly on the basis of political considerations.

While he is aware that this sort of behavior occurs in any society, he asserts that in Italy the Christian Democrats and the Catholics have managed to raise it to colossal scale.[29]

In Sardinia, both the national organs of state and also the Autonomous Regional government have been closely linked to the political parties: funds, jobs, favors of various kinds are sensitive to party calculations and manipulation.

In contrast with the turn of the century, when Antonio Serra was a "local boss", or equally in contrast with the Fascist period during which Poddu and Cubeddu served as "grand patrons", since the establishment of the Republic no single figure has dominated the politics of Surughu. Rather than a single line of authority, there now exist multiple lines and competing systems. As is obvious, these lines focus around the various political parties: since state activities are so numerous and of such import, and since the parties are so closely associated with the state, it follows naturally that the parties have become major lines of contact and communication. At Surughu, as in nearly all Sardinian villages, each of the parties has a local party secretary and a number of party supporters. During election campaigns party members become exceedingly active; between elections, organized activity is typically dormant. More to the point, however, the parties and their agents continuously seek to serve their supporters by assisting them in their frequent dealings with the state bureaucracies. Here the parties play a very critical role: the local secretary knows a clerk in some office—a fellow party member—and so he writes a letter of introduction for his friend. In Surughu the local secretary of the Communist Party, and the local priest, are continuously occupied with helping the villagers in their dealings with the bureaucracies. That the local priest is deeply involved in such matters is hardly surprising; while under Fascism the political influence of the Church was sharply limited, the present-day alliance of the Church with the DC is an elementary fact of Italian political life. At Surughu there is a kind of enactment of the "Don Camillo" tales: priest and Communist compete for support—they develop a kind of *clientela*—by writing letters, giving advice, communicating with their friends at higher levels, and so forth.

Finally, party-patronage is significant not only for individuals, but also for the community as a whole. Whether or not, and at what speed, a request from the village officers will be acted upon by higher level authorities depends upon who is asking, and to whom the question is addressed. When the local administration is composed of the same party as the regional administration—if they are both DC, for example—, there is a strong possibility that the community's requests will be acted upon; not so if they are competing parties. Moreover, even within a single party there are frequently rival groups competing for power: the regional party leaders themselves seek to build a *clientela*, so that how a village's requests are dealt with is influenced by the ties of support between local and regional party leaders. It is therefore clear that *clientela*—political-party directed patronage—is a vital aspect of political relations at the local level.

IV

This brief analysis of *clientela* in Sardinia indicates one theme that the study of patronage may follow. There are, of course, numbers of other themes. In general, it seems likely that the anthropological study of patronage will proceed in three closely related directions: first, to a consideration of how patronage networks may be related to other networks of social interaction; second, to an examination of party-patronage in the context of "development"; and third, to the analysis of patronage networks as a kind of "intervening mechanism" between the local community and the nation. What are the goals and problems of these studies?

The question of how patronage networks are linked to other social networks forms one promising perspective. Adrian Mayer's recent work in an Indian town is a good illustration of this kind of analysis. Mayer shows that patronage forms one basis of association between persons; for example, during an election campaign "patrons" and "brokers" establish various ties with their supporters.[30] Mayer terms such associations "action sets" and "quasi-groups", and seeks to show how they are composed and how they may intertwine with other groups. A principal aim of this kind of study is to show how these associations affect the basic social processes of the community; for example, Mayer indicates that by studying action-sets and quasi-groups one may "build up a picture of the developmental cycle of factions" within the town.[31]

The model that informs this perspective is a kind of "structural analysis": the units are "quasi-groups" rather than lineages or age sets, but it is clear that the principles of analysis stem from the "structural" view that has characterized much of recent social anthropology. What Mayer and others are seeking to do is to accommodate the kind of analysis anthropologists

have worked out for "pre-literate" societies to a new range of more complex societies. If, as in Mayer's case, the units are towns (or villages), and if emphasis is placed upon political organization, then patronage is certain to form one interesting focus: how patronage resources are used to mobilize support, how the political machines are organized and led, or how competitive politics may lead to shifting allegiances, are among the topics that may be profitably examined. One important problem here is to draw "proper" boundaries around "the system": which interactions must one rule into his analysis in order to satisfactorily study social process in a town? Is it useful to imagine that a town is a "closed system"—or is it necessary to rule in features of the regional or national political and economic systems?[32]

The relationships between "patronage" and "development" form a second, and in many ways parallel, interest. Two general kinds of studies, the first ethnographic, the second evaluative may be indicated. Although there have been many studies of the "politics of developing areas", there has as yet been little detailed ethnography of political behavior. What the local political party branches in an African or an Asian state in fact do, what it means to be a local "party secretary", how local issues or interest become articulated, or how patronage resources are in fact dispersed—all of this and a great deal more require closer study. Since patronage is so closely enmeshed within the party organization of the developing countries, and ethnography of political behavior will detail the ways in which the patronage system works. Such studies may also serve to link more closely the work of political scientists and social anthropologists; the political scientist typically begins in the capital cities and then "works down", while the anthropologist begins in the countryside and "works up". Studies of patronage may be an area in which the two meet.[33]

In addition to these descriptive tasks, the problem of whether party patronage represents an "obstacle" to development, or whether it in fact serves development needs, also needs further clarification. On the one hand, the ability to award patronage resources can be seen to open new avenues for political mobility, and to stimulate political talents at the various levels; in this sense patronage can be seen as an instance of what Spiro calls the "development of politics" in the new states.[34] At the same time, it is at best unclear whether these activities also contribute to "political development", or in fact retard social and political transformation. To cite an example from Sardinia: party patronage has surely brought new groups into the political arenas, yet frequently the development of projects that have been initiated serve the party needs better than they do the economic needs of the island. A more proper evaluation of the relationships between "patronage" and "development" clearly needs a considerable time span for proper analysis: what over the short-run appears as "involution" may in the long-run have "evolutionary" consequences.

Finally, patronage studies may also move beyond the community-level of analysis to focus more clearly upon those institutions that encompass a number of different "levels". Patronage needs to be explored not only in a community context, but also as a kind of association, a network of communication, and a means of political organization and control that operates throughout a society. F. G. Bailey's analysis of Indian political machines is a good example of such a study.[35] To cite another instance from Sardinia: how *clientela* operates at the local level can usefully be interpreted in the larger context of political party leaders, the economic and political elites, as well as the party cadres and the local "influentials". Policies and decisions at the state level need to be explored on their own terms, as well as in regard to how they are reflected at other levels. What is called for, then, are broad studies which will locate patronage within the general forms of social, economic and political stratification.

NOTES

*The research upon which this article is based was sponsored by a grant from the National Science Foundation (GS-1125). Field work was carried out in Sardinia between June and December, 1966. An earlier version of this paper was presented to the Anthropology Colloquium of Brandeis University; the many useful suggestions of the colloquium members are gratefully acknowledged. Professors M. S. Robinson and David Kaplan were also kind enough to comment upon the paper.

1 Jeremy Boissevain, "Patronage in Sicily", *Man*, Vol. 1, Number 1 (1966), p. 18.

2 J. Campbell, *Honour, Family and Patronage* (Oxford, Clarendon Press, 1964), p. 260.

3 Adrian Mayer, "Quasi-Groups in the Study of Complex Societies", in M. Banton, Editor, *The Social Anthropology of Complex Societies* (New York, Frederick A. Praeger, 1966), pp. 113-114.

4 Fustel de Coulanges, *The Ancient City* (New York, Doubleday Anchor Books, no date), p. 255.

5 George Foster, "The Dyadic Contract: A Model for the Social Structure of a Mexican Peasant Village", *American Anthropologist*, Vol. 63 (1969), p. 1281.

6 Eric Wolf, "Kinship, Friendship, and Patron-Client Relations", in M. Banton, Editor, *op. cit.*, p. 17.

7 J. Pitt-Rivers, *The People of the Sierra* (London, Weidenfield and Nicholson, 1954), p. 140.

8 V. O. Key, *Politics, Parties and Pressure Groups* (New York, Thomas Y. Crowell, 1964), p. 348.

9 F. Sorauf, "The Silent Revolution in Patronage", in E. Banfield, Editor, *Urban Government* (New York, The Free Press, 1961), pp. 309-310.

10 Sydel Silverman, "Patronage and Community-Nation Relationships in Central Italy", *Ethnology*, Vol. IV (1965), pp. 183-184.

11 The analysis presented here follows along "structural lines". Patronage has also been interpreted in terms of "values" and "value orientations". For recent examples of patronage examined in terms of values, see G. Foster, "The Dyadic Contract in Tzintzuntzan, II: Patron-Client Relations", *American Anthropologist*, Vol. 65 (1963), pp. 1280-1294; and J. Boissevain, *op. cit.*

12 S. Silverman, *op. cit.*, p. 188. Several of the ideas presented in this article follow from "leads" in Silverman's work.

13 Owen Lattimore, *Inner Asian Frontiers of China* (Boston, Beacon Press, 1962), p. 284.

14 For example, see Boissevain, *op. cit.*; Campbell, *op. cit.*; M. Kenny, "Patterns of Patronage in Spain", *Anthropological Quarterly*, Vol. 33 (1960), pp. 14-23; Pitt-Rivers, *op. cit.*; and Wolf, *Peasants* (New York, Prentice Hall, 1966).

15 M. Kenny, *op. cit.*, pp. 17-18.

16 For example, see R. Bendix, "Social Stratification and the Political Community", *Archives Européennes de Sociologie*, Vol. 1, No. 2 (1960), pp. 181-212; and S. N. Eisenstadt, "The Causes of Disintegration and Fall of Empires", *Diogenes*, Number 34 (1961), pp. 82-107.

17 Several recent examples include: D. Apter, *The Politics of Modernization* (Chicago, University of Chicago Press, 1966); and A. Zolberg, *Creating Political Order* (Chicago, Rand, McNally, 1966). See also C. Geertz, *The Social History of an Indonesian Town* (Cambridge, MIT Press, 1966).

18 M. Weiner, "India's Two Political Cultures" (Mimeo), 1964, p. 21.

19 E. Shils, "Mass Society and Its Culture", *Daedalus*, Vol. 89 (1960), p. 288.

20 E. Shils, "The Theory of Mass Society", *Diogenes*, No. 39 (1962), p. 50.

21 An interesting "dialogue" regarding political parties and political "integration" can be seen in the contrasting views of Zolberg and Apter. See D. Apter, *Ghana in Transition* (New York, Atheneium, 1963); and A. Zolberg, *op. cit.*

22 From Giuseppe Fiori, *Vita di Antonio Gramsci* (Bari, Editori Laterza, 1966), p. 13.

23 M. Le Lannou, *Patres et Paysans de la Sardaigne* (Tours, Arraults, 1941), p. 13.

24 *Ibid.*, p. 13.

25 For an analysis of "ritual kinship", see S. Mintz and E. Wolf, "An Analysis of Ritual Co-parenthood (*Compadrazgo*)", *Southwestern Journal of Anthropology*, Vol. 6 (1950), pp. 341-368.

26 E. Wolf, "Aspects of Group Relations in a Complex Society: Mexico", *American Anthropologist*, Vol. 58 (1956), p. 1075.

27 G. Fiori, *op. cit.*, p. 13.

28 Carl Schmidt, *The Corporate State in Action*: *Italy Under Fascism* (New York, Oxford University Press, 1929), p. 37.

29 J. LaPalombara, *Interest Groups in Italian Politics* (Princeton, Princeton University Press, 1964), p. 344.

30 Adrian Mayer, *op. cit.*, especially pages 102-114.

31 *Ibid.*, p. 116.

32 This general problem is usefully considered in *Closed Systems and Open Minds*: *The Limits of Naivety in Social Anthropology*, edited by Max Gluckman (Edinburgh and London, Oliver and Boyd, 1964).

33 The general question of the relationships between political and social anthropological studies is discussed in my article, "Social Anthropology, Political Sociology and the Study of New Nations", *British Journal of Sociology*, Vol. XVIII, June 1967, pp. 121-134.

34 H. Spiro, "The Primacy of Political Development", in H. Spiro, Editor, *Africa. The Primacy of Politics* (New York, Random House, 1960), p. 153.

35 F. G. Bailey, *Politics and Social Change*: *Orissa in 1959* (Los Angeles, University of California Press, 1963).

LEADERS, FOLLOWERS, AND OFFICIAL PATRONS IN URBAN MEXICO*

WAYNE A. CORNELIUS

MY STUDY of six predominantly low-income neighborhoods *(colonias proletaris)* on the periphery of the Mexico City metropolitan area, as well as briefer observation of more than 50 additional *colonias* scattered throughout the city, led me to the conclusion that wherever strong local leaders existed, they were likely to exhibit those characteristics of leadership traditionally associated with the rural *cacique* in Mexico.[1]

In Spanish-speaking countries the term *cacique* is often applied to any individual who is thought to exert an excessive influence on local politics. Friedrich (1968: 247) has defined a *cacique* as a "strong and autocratic leader in local and/or regional politics whose characteristically informal, personalistic, and often arbitrary rule is buttressed by a core of relatives, 'fighters,' and dependents, and is marked by the diagnostic threat and practice of violence." He also notes that the existence of a *cacicazgo* (i.e., a concrete instance of caciquismo) has always implied "strong individual power over a territorial group held together by some socioeconomic or cultural system" and a certain degree of "detachment or freedom from the normative, formal, and duly instituted system of government" (Friedrich, 1968: 247).[2] Ugalde who, like Friedrich, has studied Mexican *caciquismo* in a small rural community, offers a similar but less inclusive definition:

We would define *cacique* as the leader who (1) has total or near total political, economic, and social control of a geographic area; (2) has in his power the potential use of physical violence to make his wishes become the law of his territory; and (3) is acknowledged and implicitly legitimized as the only leader of his realm by outside higher political leaders. (Ugalde, 1973: 124).

Although my fieldwork suggests that *caciques* operating in an urban setting may not share all of the traits listed in these definitions, their behavior seems to approximate the traditional model of *caciquismo* quite closely in most respects. The major departures from this model will be discussed below.

In Mexico as in much of Latin America as a whole, *caciquismo* has been an historically ubiquitous phenomenon, and it is still an important, if largely covert, feature of the political landscape in rural areas.[3] During the past thirty years in much of Latin America, as large numbers of *caudillos* and *caciques* in the countryside have either disappeared or have lost their influence in state and national politics,[4] there has been an increasing tendency to refer to *caciquismo* as a phenomenon confined to the more backward rural areas, where it is closely tied to the isolation and strong tradition of local political control by a single family or extended family often characteristic of the rural closed community (González Casanova, 1970: 33; Drake, 1970: 407; Lambert, 1967: 154). Similarly, Padgett (1966: 83) has observed that "the more remote the rural area and the farther it is from ready accessibility to a large city, the easier it is for the *cacique* to establish and maintain himself in power" and implies that the reduction in the number of old-style *caciques* remaining in power in Mexico today can be attributed largely to the "growing urban character of the country."

More recent research indicates that such statements and explanations about the decline of *caciquismo* are incorrect. A large-scale field study by researchers at the National University of Mexico has found so many *caciques* still operating in rural areas that its principal investigator has estimated that one exists in practically every small locality in the country (Paré, 1972; Paré, quoted in *El Día,* 23 May 1973: 2). And my own observations in Mexico City, as well as those of researchers in other Latin American cities, suggest that there are highly significant manifestations of *caciquismo* in urban contexts. Ray (1969: 59) found that many low-income neighborhoods of Venezuelan cities are dominated by *caciques* who "represent the supreme, and almost absolute, authority in their barrios. They sanction, regulate, or prohibit all group activities and exercise a strong influence over any decisions that might affect their communities." Other instances of urban *caciquismo* have been observed in Venezuela (Bamberger, 1968), Nicaragua (Toness, 1967: 38), and Chile (Equipo de Estudios Poblacionales del CIDU, 1972b: 68); and there even appear to be analogues of the phenomenon in some small and medium-sized cities in Africa (see Barrows, 1974: 290-293). Thus it would appear that urbanism *per se* does not inhibit the emergence of *caciquismo* as a pattern of leadership among low-income people. In fact, as I will argue below, the formation of squatter settlements on the periphery of most large cities in Latin America may provide important new opportunities for this type of leader.

In both urban and rural contexts, the *cacique* is recognized by both the residents of the community in which he operates and supra-local authorities of the government and the official party as being the most powerful person in the local political arena. Public officials invariably deal with him to the exclusion of other potential leaders in all matters affecting the community. The *cacique* also possesses de facto authority to make decisions binding upon the community under his control, as well as informal police powers and powers of taxation (usually described as "taking up a collection" to finance a given project, service, or activity). Thus in some respects the traditional *cacicazgo* represents a sort of informal government-within-a-government, controlled by a single dominant individual who is not *formally* accountable either to those residing in the community under his control or to external political and governmental authorities. As the *cacique* of Colonia Nueva bluntly put it, "Aquí no hay más ley que yo" (Here there is no law but me).[5]

The *cacique* usually gains power through self-imposition, with the acquiescence (and occasionally the active support) of a majority of community residents. Since he (or she) holds no elective post and is not dependent on supra-local officials for appointment, he may remain in power until he voluntarily renounces his leadership role or is removed by force. As Friedrich (1968: 258-259) has pointed out, the fact that the *cacique's* rule is temporally unrestricted is one of the most important distinguishing characteristics of his status in Mexican politics. In the Mexican system, local *caciques* are virtually the only officially recognized political leaders whose tenure is not necessarily affected by the sexennial, constitutionally-mandated changes of the national administration or the triennial replacement of municipal governments. In one squatter settlement included in my study, a single *cacique* had held power continuously from 1959 until the time of the study; in another, the *cacicazgo* established upon invasion of the land in 1952 endured until 1964. In rural areas *cacicazgos* have been found whose origins antedate the Revolution of 1910 (see Reyes Heroles, 1972).

The *cacique* is a truly indigenous leader who emerges from the same community over which he exerts his influence, and whose followership is confined to the residents of that locality. Moreover, his political activity is oriented primarily to local issues and concerns. Thus the *cacique* must be distinguished from local leaders who are simply "imposed" on a community by supra-local forces. Similarly, he must be contrasted with individuals who function only as local agents or representatives of the government, political parties, labor unions, or other organizations of the national political system whose activity is oriented in some degree toward the local community but whose primary concerns are clearly supra-local in nature.[6]

The *cacique's* relationship to his followers

tends to have a far more utilitarian character than that of other types of local leaders in the *colonias proletarias*, whose influence derives largely from the esteem in which they are held by their followers. Because of this lack of affective underpinnings, the *cacique's* relationship with his followers can be quickly undermined by particularly flagrant financial indiscretions and abuses of authority or, as noted below, by failure to meet certain standards of performance over an extended period of time. Thus the *cacique* must strive continually to legitimize his claim to leadership status through every means at his command. At any given point, this process of legitimation may be incomplete and subject to reversal.[7]

The *cacique* may be heartily disliked and distrusted by many of his followers, who correctly suspect him of using his leadership position to advance his own financial interests. Like the old-style *caudillos* whose code of behavior he frequently emulates, the *cacique's* primary aim is to increase his personal wealth.[8] He loses few opportunities to enrich himself and his principal aides; and despite the poverty of most of its inhabitants, the community which he controls usually offers a rich harvest of such opportunities. In all three of the squatter settlements included in my study, *caciques* had been deeply involved in a variety of illicit moneymaking activities, including trafficking in lots or permits to occupy land within the settlement, fraudulent collection of money for personal use, commercial exploitation of local mineral resources, and the charging of special fees for access to basic urban services such as electricity. To the economic returns from activities such as these, the *cacique* may add the income derived from property owned within the community, often including small businesses, houses, and land.

While illicit land deals are by far the most important source of income for *caciques* in many communities, the frequent collection of donations ("*cuotas*" or "*cooperaciones*") from the residents may be equally lucrative. The *cacique* usually justifies his requests for such payments in very general terms by reference to his ongoing negotiations with government officials to secure land titles, basic urban services, and other improvements for the community. The money is ostensibly used to cover costs of transportation for the *cacique* and his assistants, bribes or gifts for presentation to public officials, letter-writer's fees, and other expenses incurred in negotiations. The residents of one squatter settlement included in my study were even persuaded to provide full financial support for the local *cacique*, his wife and six children, to free them for full-time attention to negotiations with the government and other community affairs. Each family in the *colonia* contributed five to ten pesos each week (a total of U.S. $100 - $200) for this purpose. Individual *cuotas* were determined by the *cacique* on the basis of income, and he maintained a complete register of household heads and their estimated weekly income. In addition to the regular weekly donations for the *cacique's* living expenses, he also collected special *cuotas* from time to time, including one assessment of 100 pesos (U.S. $8) per family to purchase an automobile for his personal use. (He subsequently demolished it in a traffic accident.) *Cuotas* collected by *caciques* in other communities included in the study were usually tied to a specific community project or need, such as installing a provisional water supply system, repairing the community meeting hall, or grading the main street; but it was evident that the sums collected were far in excess of the amounts actually spent by the *caciques* for these purposes.

The barely concealed economic motivation of some *caciques* in assuming their position and maintaining themselves in power often leads to charges of fraudulent collection and handling of community funds on the part of dissident residents. Some excerpts from my interviews are typical of these complaints.[9] A small merchant, Colonia Texcoco: Why would someone want to become a political leader? To make money fast, like Sr. González (the local cacique), who came here poor and now has two buildings and a lot of money. A street vendor, Colonia Periférico: Sra. Moreno (the local cacique) asked each family for 1040 pesos (U.S. $83.20) to pay for the *trámites* (bureaucratic procedures) needed to legalize our plots of land. This made me mad, because it was not true that all that money was needed. A factory worker, Colonia Nueva: There are too many people living in the *colonia* now. This is due to Sra. Ortiz and her husband (the local *cacique*), who made it possible for them to settle here. In exchange for a certain amount of money, they give permission to move into the *colonia* . . . One man refused to give her a cent, so they had his house torn down and later threw him out of the *colonia* . . . They are getting rich from all that money, with which they are building their house there below and are farming their land in their *pueblo* (home town).

BASES OF THE CACIQUE'S INFLUENCE

What factors help to explain the influence exerted by the urban *cacique* over the affairs of the community which he rules? What is it which induces others in such a community to follow his leadership, in the face of clear evidence of personal profiteering and other abuses of authority? To answer questions such as these we must examine the set of resources which the *cacique* brings to his leadership position, and which serve to consolidate and legitimize his control over the community.

Personally Controlled Resources

Some of these resources take the form of personal skills or aptitudes which are viewed by the residents as equipping the *cacique* for his leadership role. For example, the *cacique's* skill at organizing and unifying the community is highly valued by its residents, who firmly believe that a high degree of unity and organization improves the community's position in negotiations with government officials for urban services, official recognition of land tenure rights, and other types of benefits. Thus to the extent that the *cacique* can represent himself as effective in maintaining a high degree of unity and organization within the area under his control, he gains in influence and legitimacy. Moreover, the capacity to mobilize and organize people, both for internally-oriented purposes and for participation in political activity outside the settlement, helps to impress external political actors and to enhance the *cacique's* bargaining position in dealing with them.

A well-developed capacity for effective self-expression is another useful skill which the *cacique* usually brings to his leadership role. Since he is entrusted with the task of seeking external assistance in the development of the settlement, the ability to articulate with eloquence and conviction the needs and aspirations of the residents is regarded as very important in dealing with public officials as well as mass media representatives who may be willing to publicize the settlement's needs and petitions for assistance. The oratorical skills of the *caciques* in both Colonia Nueva and Colonia Periférico were frequently displayed before the residents at public meetings, during which the *caciques* did virtually all of the talking and often read from the petitions which they had drafted for presentation to government officials.

Patronage resources also help the *cacique* to consolidate his grip on the community. He normally enlists the services of several close aides who assist in mobilizing and organizing settlement residents, collecting money from them, and generally communicating and enforcing his will. In return, these individuals receive a share of the economic rewards flowing from the *cacicazgo*. The *cacique* usually adds to his *comitiva* (or retinue of closest subordinates) a number of individuals serving as nominal representatives of the city government or official party in the settlement, whose appointments he has engineered through contacts with higher authorities. The *cacique* may also appoint members of this group as officers in the community's improvement association (*junta de mejoras*) or governing council (*mesa directiva*). The members of the *cacique's* entourage are often bound to him not only through patronage rewards but ties of fictive kinship (*compadrazgo*) as well, which strengthens their personal loyalty and responsiveness to his commands. They form a highly cohesive "political family" which supports, protects, and insulates the *cacique* against harassment by dissatisfied residents or predatory outsiders.

The *cacique* relies to some extent on coercive resources to compel financial cooperation and general obedience among his followers. He generally has exclusive control over the actions of city police within the community and makes effective use of this police power to coerce and intimidate dissidents and potential rivals. Like his rural counterpart, the urban *cacique* is characteristically accompanied by one or more armed supporters used both as personal bodyguards and for "enforcement" purposes within the community; and they may also stand guard conspicuously outside his house. In Colonia Nueva and Colonia Periférico, overt coercion by *caciques* occasionally took the form of breaking up meetings of suspected opposition groups. On at least one occasion, the *cacique* of Colonia Nueva incited a mob to expel a recalcitrant family from the community by demolishing their house. Yet one does not observe the kind of consistent and highly visible application of physical force, including extensive small-arms violence and politically motivated homicide, which apparently constitute an integral component of community life in agrarian *cacicazgos* (Friedrich, 1965: 205-206, 1968: 265; Simpson, 1967: 341-342).

One possible explanation for the lesser reliance of the urban *cacique* on physical force lies in the fact that he is under relatively close scrutiny by higher political and governmental authorities. A more convincing explanation, however, is suggested by the greater diversity of coercive tactics available to the urban *cacique*, which may be liberally employed to intimidate and enforce "discipline" while avoiding the political costs generally associated with the application of physical force. Most of these alternative forms of pressure are economic in nature. For example, in a squatter settlement a *cacique* may possess nearly absolute control over the allocation of land within the settlement, initially through the illicit sale of credentials or permits to occupy land in the area and later during the process of "lotificatión"—surveying and subdivision of the land occupied by the settlement into individual parcels—which follows government recognition or legalization of the settlement. This control over land distribution enables the *cacique* to build a followership composed of families personally indebted to him for landholding opportunities (Cf. Ray, 1969: 59).

The *cacique's* control over land distribution can also be employed in coercive fashion. As a squatter settlement matures and virtually all land within it becomes occupied, the *cacique* may reallocate parcels of land from the original occupants to more recent arrivals, particularly relatives and close subordinates of the *cacique* himself. Some plots may be reallocated several times, and families refusing to submit willingly to displacement may be relocated by the *cacique* on the least desirable land in the settlement or simply expelled from the settlement.

Residents of Colonia Nueva and Colonia Periférico, both squatter settlements with well-established *cacicazgos*, showed extreme sensitivity to the ability of the *cacique* in their community to restrict access to settlement within the community and to evict current occupants of the land should their behavior fail to meet the *cacique's* expectations. The mere suggestion that one's plot of land might be reallocated to some other resident, or even an outsider, was usually sufficient to compel obedience.

Derivative Power

Still other kinds of resources explaining the influence of a *cacique* within his domain are external to the community and not subject to his personal control. Most important of these external resources are the *cacique's* relationships with supra-local political and governmental officials, professionals such as lawyers, doctors, architects, and engineers, and other high-status individuals possessing skills or resources relevant to the satisfaction of community needs. Such contacts are highly valued by residents of low-income neighborhoods (Cf. Peattie, 1968: 88-89; Maruska, 1972: 67-68). They are viewed as enabling the *cacique* to deal effectively with external actors and secure benefits for the community which would be beyond the reach of some-

one lacking regularized channels of access to higher levels of authority. And, in fact, numerous studies of both rural and urban communities in Mexico show that personal linkages between local leaders and higher authorities represent the key to success in negotiations for government benefits.[10] Thus the *cacique* strives continually to impress his followers with the range and importance of the contacts he has succeeded in establishing, depicting himself as enjoying the exclusive support and recognition of various high-ranking officials in the city and even federal governments and stressing the usefulness of such contacts in his negotiations on behalf of the community.

In a broader sense, the *cacique's* relationships with external political actors are extremely important to understanding the influence he exerts within the community. "Derivative power" flowing from sources outside the *cacique's* domain can be used effectively to consolidate his position within the community and discourage challenges to his authority.[11] The *cacique* attempts to extend his contact with politicians and bureaucrats as widely as possible within the government-official party apparatus, thereby increasing the number of potential sources of derived power to which he has access. He must strive also to demonstrate to his followers as often and as conspicuously as possible—preferably by congratulatory messages and even personal visits to the community by high-ranking officials—that he does in fact enjoy their favor.

Excessive dependence on external support may prove costly, however, in the event that such support is withdrawn. To actually fall into disgrace with supra-local officials, and to have this loss of support or recognition become widely known among residents of the community, may seriously undermine the *cacique's* position in the community. In fact, the most effective tactic of dissatisfied residents seeking to depose a given *cacique* is to work diligently at discrediting him in the eyes of outside authorities and, if successful, to inform as many settlement residents as possible of the *cacique's* loss of official support. Once it becomes widely known that the *cacique* has fallen into official disfavor, residents may consider his usefulness to the community to be at an end and may be highly receptive to opposition efforts aimed at displacing him. This tactic was successful in securing the removal of the long-time *cacique* in Colonia Militar, one of the squatter settlements included in my study, and it greatly reduced the influence of the *cacique* in Colonia Nueva. In the latter community, the effort by dissident residents to discourage further external support for the local *cacique* was launched by the following petition, addressed to the President of the Republic, for whom the *colonia* had originally been named:[12]

Subject: Protest against illegal acts of dispossession, *caciquismo*, anarchy, terror, and fraudulent sale of lots in Colonia Nueva

C. Presidente de los Estados Unidos Mexicanos
Los Pinos
México, D.F.

Subject: Protest against
illegal acts of
dispossession,
caciquismo, anarchy,
terror, and fraudulent sale
of lots in Colonia Nueva

A large group residing in the *colonia* which proudly bears your name, we have gathered to send to you our most energetic protest against acts of dispossession, *caciquismo*, anarchy, terror, and fraudulent sale of lots in our *colonia*, because, on being informed of the founding of our *colonia* you honorably and unconditionally granted us your highly valued support, with the firm intention, as has always been your way, that this land would be made available exclusively to humble persons like ourselves, of few economic resources. But now it seems that the graded (levelled) and regularized lots have been given by the leaders not only to a small group of residents of Colonia Nueva, but also to numerous persons alien to us and unknown to all, who are almost certainly persons who have given money to the leaders, Sr. Guillermo Ortiz and his wife, Juana Ramírez de Ortiz, in exchange for these lots . . . In addition, we accuse these leaders of asking elevated *cuotas* to maintain themselves and for projects that are never carried out, as well as demanding money in order for persons to be taken into account when the lots are distributed. It might be mentioned that Sr. Ortiz asked the residents to buy him an automobile for his personal use, which was acquired for him by means of an additional *cuota* of one hundred pesos per family, without taking into consideration that the majority of us who live in this *colonia* are persons of limited resources, but it was necessary to give this money or face the consequences, since the threat remained that he who gave no money might be left without the lot to which he was legally entitled.

We might mention for your information that the *colonia* has always cooperated well to defray the personal expenses of the leaders: we have paid for surgical operations and costs of illnesses of Sr. Ortiz, births and costs of illnesses of his wife. Since Sr. Ortiz has no permanent employment, we almost always cooperate with

them with two or three *pesos* daily for the maintenance of their home, in addition to which each week they require of us a sum which varies from five to ten and fifteen *pesos* for the improvement of the *colonia*. We want you to know that the reason why we have decided to send you our most energetic protest is that before they will turn the lots over to us a *cuota* of 150 *pesos* is required from each us for a gift to Sra. Ramírez de Ortiz. Since there are many of us who cannot pay this amount, we have been threatened with not being taken into account when the lots are distributed.

We earnestly beg you to send instructions to open an investigation of this matter, so that as quickly as possible an end can be brought to the exploitation of which we are victims and, in this manner, to protect your honorable name deservedly given to our *colonia*. We ask you not to mention any knowledge of this message to our leaders, so that the investigation can have positive and sure results.

Finally, and as our duty to you, we should explain that we abstain from signing and identifying the persons who fully support our message, because on prior occasions there have been various protests such as this one, but which have never succeeded because minor employees of official agencies have prevented these denunciations from reaching the hands of honest persons who, like you, would grant without delay a just solution to our problems. Instead, the denouncers, unmasked in the end, have been ridiculed by the leaders and branded as traitors.

We must make clear that the protests which were sent previously to you . . . and to other officials have nothing to do with our protest. Those were denunciations or protests made with a single motive: that (the petitioners) be given a lot on which to live, and that's all. Ours is the same, but with the variation that we ask in addition to this *that new leaders or representatives be given to us* who are honest persons and strictly supervised by you or by the offices whose duty it is, to prevent in the future the vicious circle we now lament.

With full confidence in you, since we have called you our benefactor, we ask in the name of many humble Mexican homes, your energetic intervention with the object of ending the unbearable situation of imposition, injustice, and abandonment in which we find ourselves, with the firm promise on our part that we will repay with our acts, for whatever they are worth, the attention which you doubtless will grant us.

A GROUP OF RESIDENTS
OF COLONIA NUEVA

While this petition and subsequent follow-up visits of groups of dissident residents to various government offices did not elicit direct government intervention to impose new leaders in Colonia Nueva, a government engineer was sent to take charge of the distribution of lots to community residents. This deprived the local *cacique* of one of his principal instruments of control and self-enrichment.

Standards of Performance

Although initially the *cacique* is simply self-appointed to his leadership role, it is achievement-related criteria which usually determine whether he is able to consolidate and legitimize his position. Demonstrated performance in securing benefits for the community is particularly important in this respect. In the eyes of most of his followers, the *cacique's* effectiveness as a leader is measured primarily by his success in maintaining a constant flow of concrete, material benefits to the community as a whole as well as to individual residents. Assistance provided by a *cacique* on an individual basis may include recommendations to prospective employers, introductions to public officials, procuring of small business permits, licenses, and other types of legal documents, legal advice, help in securing medical treatment, help in getting children enrolled in already overcrowded schools, and other favors. As long as it appears that the individual and collective interests of community residents are being advanced as a result of the *cacique's* leadership, his exploitative behavior will be tolerated by most of his followers. In Colonia Militar, for example, the *cacique* who organized the land invasion through which the settlement was established enriched himself for many years by illegally extracting mineral deposits from the *colonia;* but it was only after a group of dissident residents

proved that he had sabotaged the *colonia's* negotiations for official recognition of land tenure rights that he was deposed.

The strongly instrumental nature of the ties which bind the *cacique* to his followers requires him to be a highly visible actor in the community. His house must be a center of constant movement and activity. He must be present at the scene of any major misfortune or community development project. In a broader sense he must actively seek to be identified personally with any and all public works, services, and other improvements introduced into the area under his control—whether or not he himself was actually responsible in some way for securing these benefits. In many instances the *cacique* may claim full credit for an improvement for which he was in no way responsible and may actually have opposed covertly in his dealings with political and governmental agencies.

The success of the *caciques* operating in Colonia Nueva and Colonia Periférico in cultivating the image of the "doer" in community affairs is amply demonstrated by the survey data reported in Table 1. Residents of these *colonias* are far more likely than those of other communities included in the study to be aware of the existence and activities of local leaders; and in Colonia Nueva and Colonia Periférico, virtually all respondents who were able to identify one or more community influentials mentioned the incumbent *cacique* and his closest associates. When asked why these individuals had the most influence in the community, a majority mentioned past or ongoing service to the community, exemplified by success in securing land titles

TABLE 1

Orientations Toward Community Leaders, by Community[a]

	Colonia Nueva	Colonia Periférico	Colonia Texcoco	Colonia E. Propio	Unidad Popular	Colonia Militar	ALL
Can identify at least one community leader[b]	98.5%	93.4%	59.8%	84.2%	49.1%	63.2%	76.2%
Have high awareness of community leadership[c]	98.5	87.2	25.4	45.0	18.9	31.1	52.6
Perceive "service to community" as primary basis of leader's influence[d]	41.1	60.1	12.0	27.2	15.1	8.9	27.5
Evaluate community leadership positively[e]	90.3	77.4	34.4	53.3	32.1	48.8	57.3

[a]Inter-community differences on all orientations are statistically significant, by Chi-square test, at the .001 level. The maximum and minimum N's for each community are as follows: Colonia Nueva, 130-125; Colonia Periférico, 101-94; Colonia Texcoco, 124-105; Colonia Esfuerzo Propio, 131-117; Unidad Popular, 77-69; Colonia Militar, 116-110.

[b]Question: "In your opinion, who are the three persons who have the most influence in (respondent's community of residence)?—That is, the persons who are most successful in getting their own way and getting things done?"

[c]Measured by a summative index constructed from several questionnaire items. See Cornelius (1975: Appendix C) for item content. Index scores were dichotomized into low and high categories with the cutting point located as close as possible to the total sample median, computed on the basis of all respondents in the weighted sample.

[d]Question: "Why do these people (community leader(s) identified by respondent) have more influence in this *colonia* than others?"

[e]Measured by a summative index.

or urban services, obtaining benefits and doing personal favors for individual residents, and other types of service-oriented activities. Note that the proportion of respondents who view community service as the primary basis of leader influence falls off sharply in the communities lacking fully dominant *caciques* at the time of the study (Texcoco, Esfuerzo Propio, Unidad Popular, Militar). Finally, when asked a series of questions requiring them to evaluate the accomplishments, responsiveness and overall competence of local leaders, residents of the *cacique*-dominated communities were much more positive in their evaluations than those of other communities. Although the survey data from Colonia Nueva were gathered prior to the erosion of the *cacique's* influence in the community due to a partial withdrawal of support by outside authorities, my informal interviews during the latter period revealed no tendency to devalue the *cacique's* previous contributions to community development.

In dealing with certain problems, such as the legalization of land tenure within the community, the *cacique* may be confronted with a painful dilemma: The residents expect him to make a certain amount of progress toward resolving such a problem over a given period of time; yet the fixation of land tenure arrangements by governmental action may sharply diminish the *cacique's* own opportunities for extracting personal economic gain through control of land use within the community. So he may engage in a considerable amount of footdragging in his actual efforts to secure official action to deal with the tenure problem. In this and other problem areas, it is often in the personal economic interest of a *cacique* to act against the interest of his followers. Accordingly, he may choose to press for short-term ameliorative action by the government rather than seek permanent, comprehensive solutions to the settlement's developmental problems. He may even carry out elaborate deceptions of his followers regarding the progress of his negotiations for governmental action on these basic problems. In the long run, however, the *cacique* must clearly "produce" on such salient concerns as reducing insecurity of land tenure within the community. If he fails to do so, he will find it increasingly difficult to maintain the allegiance of his followers and forestall potential challenges to his leadership.

Leadership Style

The overall style of leadership employed by the *cacique* is also important to an understanding of his influence within the community. Leader-ship style includes the manner in which the *cacique* makes his influence felt among community residents, his approach to handling conflict and dissent, and his way of involving residents in community decision-making. Like the leadership style of his rural counterpart, the urban *cacique's* style could be characterized as highly personalistic, pragmatic, informal, and autocratic (Cf. Friedrich, 1968: 246-248). However, his manner of dealing with community residents either individually or collectively need not be overly abrasive or domineering. He prefers to assert his influence in subtle ways, relying upon the threat posed by the negative sanctions at his disposal to compel obedience, and resorting to strong-arm tactics only against the most uncooperative and openly rebellious residents of the community (Cf. Ray, 1969: 61).

Open conflict with recalcitrant individuals and opposition groups within the community is avoided if at all possible. To allow overt confrontations to develop would detract from the *cacique's* image as an essential unifier and harmonizer in the community, both in the eyes of his followers and of external authorities. The same rule applies in presiding over meetings of the community improvement association or other types of public assemblages. Open cleavages are not allowed to emerge in public; formal votes on community issues are hardly ever taken, "consensual" decision making being the accepted practice. Thus in a well-functioning urban *cacicazgo*, the overt political factionalism and vicious interpersonal feuding characteristic of many rural communities in Mexico, as well as some low-income communities in urban areas, are seldom in evidence.[13] Public meetings are handled (or more precisely, orchestrated) by the *cacique* in such a manner as to give the illusion of meaningful rank-and-file participation, making it appear that the *cacique's* role is confined to one of providing needed information or "orientation". In reality, of course, the *cacique* makes all important decisions affecting the community according to his own judgment, with no more than ritualistic consultation of the residents. He demonstrates a certain degree of sensitivity to public opinion, but only to the extent necessary to forestall potential coups and avoid overt group conflicts within the community. The *cacique's* responsiveness to the preferences of his followers seems to vary directly with their ability to perceive alternatives to the *cacique's* leadership as a means of satisfying their needs for security and essential services.

In sum, the *cacique's* influence within his domain is based on a set of demonstrated achievements, aptitudes, sanctions, and resident perceptions which, taken together, enable him to compel obedience if not affection on the part of his followers. He is regarded with a mixture of respect, cynicism, and fear. He is expected to use his power to line his own pockets whenever possible, but self-enrichment is overlooked as long as certain standards of performance are met. Most community residents support the *cacique* for the same reason expressed most vividly in the informal campaign sloagn of a notoriously corrupt Brazilian politician: "He steals, but he gets things done."[14]

Leadership Roles

The kinds of roles performed by the *cacique* within the political and social life of the community and its relationships with the external environment relate closely to the various bases of influence discussed above. The *cacique* gains in legitimacy to the extent that his followers perceive him as fulfilling widely shared expectations associated with the performance of these leadership roles. The most important of these roles are formal organization leader, informal opinion leader, political mobilizer, and political broker or middleman.

In his role as formal organization leader, the *cacique* usually heads the community's improvement association (*junta de mejoras*) and customarily identifies himself to outsiders as president of this body. Depending on how seriously he regards the *junta* as a community institution and not just as an instrument of personal rule, the *cacique* may have an important and positive impact on the vitality of such an organization over time (Cf. Ray, 1969: 46, 54, 61). As head of the improvement association the *cacique* has wide authority to establish priorities for community development. In a very real sense he is responsible for defining the community's objectives and organizing them into an agenda for negotiation with external authorities. The *cacique's* performance of this leadership role also helps to legitimize his control over the allocation of many of the benefits secured from external political and governmental sources among community residents.

The performance of community leaders as informal opinion leaders may have significant consequences for the development and internalization of community norms, value orientations, and traditions. Among the communities included in this study, opinion leadership by local leaders was most sustained and effective in the communities recently dominated by *caciques*,

Colonia Nueva and Colonia Periférico. The *cacique* of Colonia Nueva was particularly adept at this kind of leadership. One of his principal aims was to create a sense of community solidarity and unanimity by fostering collective perceptions of "external threat" to the community's survival and developmental chances. Specifically he sought to exploit the residents' insecurity regarding land tenure by exaggerating the threat to continued occupancy of the land posed by the legal and political maneuvers of the landowners whose property was invaded to form the settlement, long past the period during which such maneuvers were likely to be effective. Such tactics had the effect of enhancing the *cacique's* reputation as a unifier and harmonizer of interests, while also strengthening his image as the community's foremost protector and defender against powerful forces bent on its destruction.

Of equal importance in terms of opinion leadership are the *cacique's* efforts to shape his followers' images of the supra-local political system. Through overblown descriptions of his personal relationships with external political actors and overly generous accounts of his negotiations with such actors to secure benefits for the community, the *cacique* may create highly positive (and often unrealistic) perceptions of the accessibility of high-ranking officials to citizen influence attempts. The *cacique* also finds it politically expedient to cultivate a collective sense of dependence upon the government—and indirectly, upon himself—for help in the development of the community. Pursuant to this objective, he may even work at undermining the confidence of his followers in the efficacy and desirability of self-help efforts. The incidence of self-help community development activity was low in all of the communities included in this study, despite the existence of a variety of needs which might have been met at least provisionally through this kind of activity. A lack of initiative on the part of community leaders is partly to blame.

The *cacique* may also have a highly significant impact on the process of political learning among his followers in his role as political mobilizer. Through frequent public meetings to discuss community affairs, visits to the offices of politicans and government functionaries, voter registration drives, and other kinds of group activity, the *cacique* mobilizes resident participation in politically relevant activities. In doing so, he increases awareness of the relevance of politics and political participation to the satisfaction of individual and community needs. Especially

TABLE 2

"Mobilized" Participation in Community Affairs, Among Residents of Colonia Nueva[a]

Form of participation	%
Participation in *comisiones*, during past year[b]	
None	26.7
Participated on 1-2 occasions	8.5
Participated on 3-9 occasions	17.3
Participated on 10-19 occasions	10.5
Participated on 20-49 occasions	13.7
Participated on 50 or more occasions	9.2
Participated very often, almost always, but can't recall number of occasions	14.0
Attendance at community meetings[c]	
None	17.2
Attended 1-2 meetings	3.3
Attended 3-9 meetings	12.2
Attended 10-19 meetings	4.9
Attended 20-49 meetings	27.1
Attended 50 or more meetings	18.7
Attended very often, almost always, but can't recall number of meetings	16.6
Participation in security patrols[d]	
None	18.1
Participated on 1-2 occasions	0.0
Participated on 3-9 occasions	4.8
Participated on 10-19 occasions	7.1
Participated on 20-49 occasions	22.5
Participated on 50 or more occasions	34.9
Participated very often, almost always, but can't recall number of occasions	2.5

[a]N's range from 131 to 134.
[b]Question: "Do you ever go on *comisiones* with other residents of this colonia? (If Yes:) During the past year — that is, from June of 1969 to May of this year — in how many *comisiones* did you participate?"
[c]Question: "Do you ever attend meetings *(juntas)* of the colonia? (If Yes:) During the past year — that is, from June of 1969 to May of this year — how many *juntas* did you attend?"
[d]Question: "Do you ever participate in the *vigilancia* (protection, security/arrangements) for the colonia? (If Yes:) During the past year — that is, from June of 1969 to May of this year — in how many *guardias* or *veladas* (security patrols) did you participate?"

if participation in activities organized by the *cacique* is necessary to prevent the imposition of negative sanctions by him, extraordinarily high levels of resident participation may be achieved.

Thus the success of some *caciques* in sustaining participation in both regime-supportive and collective demand-making activity can be explained by their success in solving what has been termed the "public goods dilemma" of community organizers:

The benefits of collective neighborhood organization efforts are nondivisible public goods, and if there is no way to coerce all the members of the aggregate into paying their share of the costs of these goods—that is, in organizational participation—or unless there is some way to *exclude the noncontributor from the benefits of the collective goods*, there is very little incentive for the rational self-interested person to make a purely voluntary contribution to such efforts.

(O'Brien, 1974: 236-237)

In all three of the squatter settlements included in the present study, *caciques* had used their control over land occupancy within the community to make it known that "noncontributors"

to collective political action would be excluded from any benefits resulting from such action.

This kind of negative incentive structure had been developed most fully in Colonia Nueva, whose *cacique* kept meticulous records of each household head's participation in the *"comisiones,"* community meetings, and security patrols which he organized. *"Comisión"* was the term applied by the *cacique* to a variety of group activities, including attendance at public appearances of the President of the Republic and other high-ranking officials, ground breaking or inauguration ceremonies for innumerable public works in many different parts of the city, and government or PRI-sponsored meetings and rallies. Still other *comisiones* took the form of visits by delegations of community residents, led by the *cacique* and his wife, to the offices of government functionaries with whom the *cacique* was negotiating for assistance to the community.

As shown in Table 2, migrants living in Colonia Nueva participated frequently in *comisiones* and other group activities organized by the local *cacique*, despite the fact that most *comisiones* occurred on week days when male heads of family would normally be at work outside the community.[15] While much of the participation in these activities was no doubt in response to pressures exerted by the *cacique* and his assistants, data from the sample survey as well as participant observation suggest that those involved also perceived their behavior as an instrumental act aimed at influencing government decision making. When asked why they had participated in *comisiones*, for example, more than 80 per cent of the respondents replied that this kind of activity "helps the *colonia*." When asked to specify in what ways this kind of activity helped the *colonia*, four out of five respondents said that it increased official awareness of the needs and. problems of the *colonia*, or otherwise improved the *colonia's* chances of receiving government assistance.

In the role of political broker or middleman, the *cacique* mediates in a number of ways between his followers and higher levels of authority.[16] He represents the community under his control before supra-local officials and has primary responsibility for articulating the demands and grievances of his followers to such officials. In doing so the *cacique* helps to bridge the gap between community residents—many of them of recent rural origin and having little or no detailed knowledge of the organization and functioning of the city and national political systems —and the institutions of the larger society (Cf. Friedrich, 1968: 247). He serves as their protector against arbitrary governmental action, and transmits to them the information that flows out of the official party-government apparatus. He is primarily responsible for informing community residents of governmental programs or actions which affect them individually and collectively. In sum, a *cacique* performing the role of political broker or middleman "stands guard over the crucial junctures or synapses of relationships which connect the local system to the larger whole" (Wolf, 1965: 97).

The *cacique* seeks to monopolize all links between the community under his control and political and bureaucratic structures in the external environment. He will take pains to portray himself as the only officially recognized intermediary between community residents and these structures—the only person who is in a position to work productively with the government for the betterment of the community. And he will actively strive to minimize the contact of individual residents with outside officials, except for contact which is mediated by his own actions as broker or political mobilizer. The *cacique* is thus able to increase the residents' sense of dependence on him for the performance of political brokerage.

RELATIONS WITH OFFICIAL PATRONS

The *Cacique* is usually linked as a client to one or more patrons in the government-official party apparatus, usually upper-echelon functionaries in the various offices of the city government or official party having responsibility for dealing with the problems of low-income sections of the city. The friendship and good will of these persons are cultivated assiduously by the *cacique* through a variety of means.[17] Like all such clientage arrangements, the relationships between the *cacique* and his external patrons are based on the "reciprocal exchange of mutually valued goods and services" (Powell, 1970: 412). As well as granting him a large measure of autonomy in the running of local affairs and the allocation of government benefits within his community, the *cacique's* patrons represent a source of derivative power which, as indicated above, may have an extremely important bearing upon his overall influence in the community. The *cacique* also relies upon his patrons to expedite administrative actions favorable to the community and maintain an acceptable flow of material benefits to the area.

In return, the *cacique* can be counted upon to mobilize large numbers of people within the area under his control to attend PRI meetings and rallies, public appearances of the President and other high-ranking officials, public works inaugurations, ceremonies held to commemorate the legalization of squatter settlements, and other civic events. Since the patron is usually in competition with other ambitious *políticos* to demonstrate to higher authorities a capacity to "move people" and otherwise turn out grassroots support for the regime, the *cacique's* "available masses" take on special importance. The *cacique* is also expected to maintain "control" of his settlement—to keep order, avoid scandals and public demonstrations embarrassing to the government, and head off any other types of occurrences which might disrupt social tranquility or undermine confidence in the regime. He also has obligations to "orient" his followers politically (i.e., propagandize on behalf of the regime and strengthen local identification with it) and to organize the participation of his followers in elections, voter registration campaigns, and other forms of officially prescribed political activity. Finally, the *cacique* is expected to assist the regime in minimizing demands for expensive, broad-scope benefits which might "load" the political system beyond its responsive capabilities. He does this by encouraging his followers to view the community as an entity isolated from other *colonias proletarias* in the city, with problems and solutions particular to that community. By defining the problems confronting the community in such parochial terms, the *cacique* helps to insure that demand making by community residents will be focused upon short-term, community-specific needs. Flagrant violation of any of these basic terms of the informal contract between the *cacique* and his patron may be punished by a withdrawal of the patron's support and recognition, with all the negative consequences which that may entail.[18]

The fact that the *cacique* maintains close relationships with non-local politicians and government bureaucrats does not mean that he is totally subservient to them. The *cacique* does not function simply as an appendage of the government-official party apparatus, although he performs useful services for it and cooperates with his official patrons to the greatest extent possible. He retains considerable freedom of action in managing the internal affairs of the community under his control, and it is clear that his position is not entirely dependent upon derivative power from external sources. The best evidence of this relative autonomy is provided by those *caciques* who have succeeded in remaining in power after one or more complete turnovers of officials at the end of each presidential term. Such turnovers have the effect of cutting off, at least for a time, the *cacique's* most important source of external support.

Origins and Durability of Urban Caciquismo

What factors help to explain the emergence and persistence of *caciquismo* as a pattern of local leadership in the urban setting? Ray (1969: 63) has argued that in the Venezuelan context "what determines a barrio's choice of leadership is the economic, social, and political character, as it had developed in the post-war period, of the city in which the barrio is located." He goes on to assert that *caciques* are more likely to emerge in those cities "which have remained relatively unaffected by the forces of modernization" and whose occupational structure lacks a strong, modern, industrial sector. But the diversity of leadership patterns observed *within* many large cities in Latin America—including Mexico City—suggests that the most important variables in this regard may be those relating to the character of the urban neighborhood itself.[19]

In Mexico City the settlement which has originated through illegal land invasion (either organized or accretitive) appears to be a social context particularly conducive to the emergence of caciquismo. *Caciques* have also emerged frequently in the numerous illegal subdivisions or *fraccionamientos clandestinos* formed on the periphery of the city by land speculators lacking government authorization to subdivide and often clear title to the land as well. Both types of settlements suffer initially from extreme service deprivation and insecurity of land tenure, and often become the object of negative sanctions or threats by the government or private landowners. The emergence of *caciquismo* in such areas may be related both to the illegality of their origins and the magnitude of the developmental needs and problems which they must confront. Since prior to granting official recognition to such a settlement the government assumes no responsibility for its governance or improvement, there is greater latitude for individual strong men to assume control and deal with their followers in an arbitrary and autocratic manner. The lack of a governmental "presence" combines with the severity of problems confronting such settlements to create a situation in which people may feel a greater need to enter into a dependency relationship with a local *cacique*.

If this is true, we might hypothesize that, as a community's most acute needs for urban services and security of land tenure are satisfied, the *cacique* presiding over it will find it increasingly difficult to maintain his position.[20] Official recognition of land tenure rights and subdivision of the land into individual parcels may be especially damaging to the *cacique's* influence in the community, for such acts simultaneously deprive him of important coercive resources (i.e., those deriving from control over the allocation of land within the community) and satisfies the single most deeply felt need of his followers. The *cacicazgos* in both Colonia Nueva and Colonia Periférico were substantially weakened by government "legalization" of these squatter settlements.

The emergence of *caciques* in certain communities could also be related to the composition of their population in terms of rural-urban origins. Since a majority of the people in the squatter settlements included in this study are of rural origin, it might be argued that the leadership phenomena observed in these areas represent just another manifestation of what has been termed "residual ruralism"—i.e., the "transference from the rural areas of institutions, values, and behavior patterns and their persistence or adaptation to the specific requirements of the urban setting" (Germani, 1967: 179; Cf. Cornelius, 1971: 111-112). Thus it might be hypothesized that the migrant's support for a *cacique* represents a simple transference of leadership role expectations from his place of origin to the urban *colonia proletaria*.[21] Moreover, peasants as well as rural migrants to the city are believed to have a strong predisposition toward authoritarianism and defer readily to any kind of authority figure. We might expect the stability of a *cacicazgo* to be threatened by changes in the distribution of these "supportive" predispositions or attitudinal orientations among the population of the community, as the first generation of migrants internalizes new "urban" norms and the second generation—with no rural socialization —comes to maturity. Yet the survey data from Colonia Nueva and Colonia Periférico, the two communities still dominated by *caciques* at the time of the survey, lend little support to these hypotheses. They show that migrants do, in fact, exhibit stronger predispositions toward authoritarianism and deference to authority than native-born city dwellers; but they are no more likely than the natives in these communities to evaluate local leadership positively. Nor are there any significant differences between migrants and their eldest Mexico City-born sons in terms of leader evaluations.

Perhaps the most fundamental threat to the durability of an urban *cacicazgo*—especially one situated in a squatter settlement—arises as the local community begins to develop a more complex set of social, economic, and political relationships to its external environment, and becomes more fully integrated into the physical structure of the city. The influence of the *cacique* in his key role as broker between his followers and the institutions of the external environment may be substantially reduced through such evolutionary change.[22] As urban incorporation proceeds and individual residents become more familiar with the contours of the larger urban society and political system, an increasing amount of direct, *non-mediated* contact will occur. The *cacique* may also be faced with increasing competition from non-resident brokers or middlemen who encroach upon his domain. Eventually he may be displaced as *cacique* by one of these competitors; or more likely, the *cacicazgo* may simply dissolve, giving way to some form of externally imposed leadership, a set of competing factions with no clearly dominant individual leader, or perhaps no discernible leadership structure at all. Thus it might be most accurate to conceive of urban *caciquismo* as a transitory, if often temporally extended, phenomenon restricted to a particular phase in the evolution of a low-income community and the political learning of its inhabitants.

Caciquismo and "Political Reform"

The existence of widespread *caciquismo* in both rural and urban Mexico has become an increasingly controversial issue in recent years. It has been acknowledged and condemned repeatedly by high-ranking officials including the President of the Republic and the head of the official political party (PRI).[23] The party chief pointedly warned that "it would be inconsistent to be against rural *caciquismo*—a residue of the old prerevolutionary regime—while ignoring the threat of urban *caciquismo*" (*El Día*, 24 June 1972: 1). The topic arose in the context of President Luis Echeverría's efforts to introduce some limited democratizing reforms into official party structure and practices, in the hope of arresting or even reversing the recent trend toward higher levels of electoral abstentionism (see Segovia, 1974). The argument made by Echeverría, his party chairman, and other top officials is simply that the regime no longer needs *caciques* to turn out the vote for its candidates, and that continued reliance upon them will contribute to rising abstentionism and political alienation among the masses. These concerns were clearly articulated by the PRI chairman in a much-publicized speech to party workers (Reyes Heroles, 1972):

There are comrades (PRI militants) who in good faith—at least I think it is—tell us that it is an error to fight *caciquismo*; that the *caciques* constitute part of the power of our Party . . . that we are breaking the backbone of the Party. I sincerely don't believe it. No ruler can base his support on *cacicazgos*. If he believes it, it's a mistake; it is he who supports the *caciques*. If it is arguable that *caciquismo* fulfilled a function (for the Party), it is, on the other hand, completely unarguable that it should disappear in our time. In the brief experience which we have had in this struggle, we see that the people, when we fight *caciques*, have voted with enthusiasm, have stopped abstaining; because they know that in voting they are deciding their destiny and are conquering something (*caciquismo*) which holds back their locality. In contrast to this situation, we see how abstentionism grows in those localities in which the Party, due to the internal play of forces and to deliberate resistance to change, has not been able to run candidates who would guarantee the elimination of the *cacicazgo* . . . In these cases abstentionism grows, the people don't decide their own affairs, they resign themselves, only, perhaps, to explode later.

Not surprisingly, lower-ranking party politicians and government functionaries tend to have a much different view of the *cacique's* role in the political system. They are expected by their superiors to maintain social and political control of those segments of the population falling within their jurisdictions, as well as to secure high turnouts of PRI voters and participants in other forms of regime-supportive political activity. *Caciques* have found it so easy to gain and hold power in small communities, both rural and urban, because they make it so much easier for the ambitious, lower-echelon official to do his job (see Paré, 1972). Such officials tend to discount the argument that autocratic, exploitative *caciques* acting as ward heelers for the PRI are contributing to alienation and abstentionism among the poor. Eliminating the *caciques* would require lower-level officials to invest more time and energy in grassroots political organizing, in social contexts with which they are largely unfamiliar. As presently structured,

The PRI . . . can work with selected individuals who are strategically placed in the (social) structure, with the knowledge that they will deliver the support of their followers to the Party . . . The Party thus does not always require a separate organizational structure; it can use personal contacts to work through other organizations and institutions.
(Purcell and Purcell, 1973: 13)

National-level leaders also must weigh the advantages of political control and mobilization through dependable, local *caciques* against the uncertainties and potential divisiveness of grassroots organizing by outsiders; but they seem to have concluded that at least a strong rhetorical commitment to the eradication of *caciquismo* is essential to the drive for party reform.

From the standpoint of the rural and urban poor, too, the costs and benefits of *caciquismo* as a form of local-level leadership are quite mixed. In the urban context, the economic costs of this form of leadership to individual residents of a low-income neighborhood can be fearsomely high. Yet the residents of such communities, especially more recently formed squatter settlements, know that they confront a number of key developmental problems which must be resolved if their community is to survive and mature into a dwelling environment that satisfies their needs for security of land tenure, basic urban services, schools, markets, paved streets, recreational facilities, and other improvements. The evidence from Mexico City suggests that strong leadership—whether provided by a *cacique* or some other type of local leader—*can* significantly increase the capacity of a low-income community to manipulate the political system in order to secure government assistance in community development.

NOTES

*Abridged from Wayne A. Cornelius, *Politics and the Migrant Poor in Mexico City* (Stanford, Calif.: Stanford University Press, 1975), chapter 6, by the author. Reprinted by permission of Stanford University Press.

1 The findings reported in this paper derive from 14 months of field research conducted in Mexico City during the 1970-1972 period. Data were gathered through unstructured, in-depth interviewing, participant observation, sample surveys, and documentary research. For a full description of the study design and methodology, see Cornelius (1975: Chap. 1 and Appendix D). The fieldwork and data analysis were supported by the Danforth Foundation, the Foreign Area Fellowship Program of the American Council of Learned Societies and the Social Science Research Council, the National Science Foundation (grant GS-2738), the Center for Research in International Studies at Stanford University, the Center for International Affairs at Harvard University, and the Ford and Rockefeller Foundations' Program in Support of Social Science Research on Population Policy (grant RF-73070).

2 Friedrich's pioneering ethnographic work on Mexican *caciquismo* is reported most fully in a doctoral dissertation (Friedrich, 1957) and in a more recent monograph (Friedrich, 1970). See also Friedrich (1966).

3 For a general survey of the phenomenon of *caciquismo*, both historical and contemporary, in Latin American countries, see Kern, ed. (1973). Additional discussions of *caciquismo* in the Mexican context are provided in Instituto de Investigaciones Sociales (1975), Días Días (1972), and R. Scott (1964: 102-104).

4 The term *caudillo* is usually applied to political strongmen who made their influence felt on the regional or national level. As Wolf and Hansen (1967) have pointed out, there is much in the code of *caudillo* behavior—particularly its emphasis on personalized loyalties, frequent recourse to violence, and an arbitrary, autocratic style of governance—which is also characteristic of many local *caciques*, especially in rural areas.

5 As I shall note below, however, the urban *cacique's* actions are influenced to some extent by supra-local political actors, and he is informally accountable to them for the performance of certain political services.

6 The *cacique's* relationship to his followers approximates in certain respects a patron-client relationship; yet as we shall see, the *cacique* does not operate exclusively with personally controlled local resources (as does the patron in a true clientage relationship), and the mutual rights and obligations and the types of interaction involved are usually different as well.

7 Friedrich (1968: 244) has argued convincingly that the legitimacy of a *cacique* should be viewed "as a matter of process and flux rather than a static, fixed attribute of his leadership status."

8 Undoubtedly there are certain psychological satisfactions which accrue from exercising a leadership role in a social setting like a squatter settlement; but it is clear that the *cacique's* primary motive for acquiring and retaining power is economic in nature.

9 Pseudonyms are used here and elsewhere in this chapter to identify the research communities and their leaders.

10 This is a principal conclusion of the review of Mexican community studies by Purcell and Purcell (1973). See also Grindell (1975: chap. 7); Ronfeldt (1972), and Cornelius (1975: chap. 7).

11 The concept of "derivative power" employed here is elaborated in Adams (1967: 40, 250 ff). The dependence of local leadership in low-income neighborhoods of Latin American cities upon derivative power has been noted by several investigators (Vaughan, 1968; Toness, 1967: 59, 68-70; Ray, 1969: 56, 61-62; Roberts, 1973: 306-330). It has also been characteristic of some *caciques* in rural Mexico (see Friedrich, 1965: 199, 203; Friedrich, 1968: 262-263; Ugalde, 1973: 133-134).

12 Translated from a copy of the petition provided by informants in the community.

13 For descriptions of such faction-ridden communities, see Friedrich (1965), Torres Trueba (1969), Butterworth (1973: 223-228), Ugalde (1973: 128-133), and Ugalde, *et al*. (1974).

14 The slogan was that of Ademar de Barros, who served as mayor of the city of São Paulo, governor of São Paulo state, and was a perennial candidate for President during the 1950s and early 1960s. He garnered a substantial portion of his electoral support from *favelados* (squatter settlement residents) and other elements of the urban poor.

15 It was possible to collect such detailed data on resident participation through survey interviews because the *cacique* had provided each adult resident of the *colonia* with a printed form for each type of activity (*comisiones, juntas, guardias*), upon which the dates of all instances of participation were carefully stamped by the *colonia* secretary.

16 The concept of political brokerage has been developed principally by anthropologists concerned with relationships between the nation and the traditional rural community (see Wolf, 1965; Silverman, 1965; Betley, 1971; Rollwagen, 1974). But it has also been employed in the context of linkages between traditional and modern sectors within the urban setting (Hanna and Hanna, 1967, 1969, 1971; Kurtz, 1966; Ugalde, 1970: 173-175; Bartolome, 1971; Snyder, 1972). Numerous investigators have characterized local leaders in Latin American squatter settlements

as political middlemen, brokering the relations of politicians with their followers in the urban electoral arena. See especially Bourricaud (1970), Giusti (1971: 83), E. Leeds (1972: 24-29), Lopes (1970: 164-165), Rios (1960), Toness (1967: 58-59), and Vaughan (1968). For a general discussion of the importance of political brokerage activity by local-level leaders in Latin America, see Chalmers (1972: 110-111).

17 These officials are, in turn, linked through informal clientage relationships to politicians and bureaucrats at higher levels of authority. This pattern has been referred to as an "extended patron-client relationship" or "clientele system" (Powell, 1970; Nowak and Snyder, 1970). The Mexican political system can be usefully conceived in terms of tiers of patron-client linkages operative at all levels of the system (see Fagen and Tuohy, 1972: chap. 2; Tuohy, 1973; Grindle, 1975).

18 The following summary of an interview with a PRI leader reflects considerable sensitivity to the problems created by *caciques* who abuse their power excessively: The party leader "admitted that there are *caciques* in the *colonias* (*proletarias*), but (contended) that they have to behave: 'If the *cacique* has power he is recognized, but demands are made of him.' From the conversation it was clear that these demands do not include just loyalty to the Party but also a measure of honest behavior. Otherwise another leader will be helped to take over. To my question about how they can do it when the powerful *cacique* is present, the informant answered, 'We put him in jail for awhile; when he comes out there is already another group in charge'" (Schers, 1972: 93).

19 For descriptions of *non*-cacical leaders in low-income neighborhoods of Mexico City, see Eckstein (1972) and Ornelas (1973).

20 For highly suggestive discussions of the relationship between satisfaction of basic needs and changes in local leader-follower relations, in both rural and urban contexts, see Silverman (1965: 183-184 ff.), González Casanova (1970: 35), J. Scott (1969: 1155-1157), and Wolf (1965: 98).

21 Cooper (1959) has investigated the relationship between leadership role expectations and degree of orientation to urban-industrial life, in the context of work situations studied in a rural village, a medium-sized town, and a large city in Mexico. He found that as one moves from the traditional rural community along a continuum toward the modern urban-industrial environment of Mexico City, attitudes toward what constitutes "good" and "bad" leadership exhibit considerable change.

22 Rogler (1974) has documented the negative consequences of urban assimilation for the influence of the local political boss in a Puerto Rican migrant community in the United States.

23 The "struggle against *caciquismo*," in both rural and urban settings, has been a persistent theme in Presidential rhetoric since 1972. See especially the speeches of Luis Echeverría reprinted in *El Día* (Mexico City), 3 October 1972: 1; 22 May 1974: 3; 24 May 1974: 8; 6 March 1975: 12; *Excélsior* (Mexico City), 10 April 1975: 1A, 9A; 11 April 1975: 22A.

REFERENCES

Adams, Richard N. 1967 *The Second Sowing: Power and Secondary Development in Latin America*. San Francisco: Chandler.

Bamberger, Michael 1968 "A Problem of Political Integration in Latin America: The *Barrios* of Venezuela," *International Affairs*, Vol. 44, No. 4: 709-719.

Barrows, Walter L. 1974 "Comparative Grassroots Politics in Africa," *World Politics*, Vol. 26, No. 2 (January): 283-297.

Bartolomé, L. J. 1971 "Política y redes sociales en una comunidad urbana de indígenas Toba: un análisis de liderazgo y 'brokerage'," *Anuario Indigenista*, Vol. 31: 77-98.

Betley, Brian J. 1971 "Otomí Juez: An Analysis of a Political Middleman," *Human Organization*, Vol. 30, No. 1: 57-63.

Bourricaud, Francois 1970 *Power and Society in Contemporary Peru*. New York: Praeger.

Butterworth, Douglas 1973 "Squatters or Suburbanites?—The Growth of Shantytowns in Oaxaca, Mexico," pp. 208-232 in Robert E. Scott (ed.), *Latin American Modernization Problems*. Urbana-Champaign: University of Illinois Press.

Chalmers, Douglas A. 1972 "Parties and Society in Latin America," *Studies in Comparative International Development*, Vol. 7, No. 2 (Summer): 102-128.

Cooper, Kenneth 1959 "Leadership Role Expectations in Mexican Rural and Urban Environments." Unpublished Ph.D. dissertation, Stanford University.

Cornelius, Wayne A. 1971 "The Political Sociology of Cityward Migration in Latin America: Toward Empirical Theory," pp. 95-147 in Francine F. Rabinovitz and Felicity M. Trueblood (eds.), *Latin American Urban Research, Vol. 1*. Beverly Hills, Calif.: Sage Publications.

——— 1975 *Politics and the Migrant Poor in Mexico City*. Stanford, Calif.: Stanford University Press.

Díaz Díaz, Fernando 1972 *Caudillos y caciques*. México, D. F.: El Colegio de México.

Drake, Paul W. 1970 "Mexican Regionalism Reconsidered," *Journal of Inter-American Studies*, Vol. 12, No. 3 (July).

Eckstein, Susan 1972 "The Poverty of Revolution: a study of Social, Economic, and Political Inequality in a Central City Area, A Squatter Settlement, and a Low Cost Housing Project in Mexico City." Unpublished Ph.D. dissertation, Columbia University.

Equipo de Estudios Poblacionales del CIDU 1972 "Reivindicación urbana y lucha política: los campamentos de pobladores en Santiago de Chile," *Revista Latinoamericana de Estudios Urbano Regionales*, Vol. 2, No. 6 (November): 55-82.

Fagen, Richard R., and William S. Tuohy 1972 *Politics and Privilege in a Mexican City*. Stanford, Calif.: Stanford University Press.

Friedrich, Paul 1957 "Cacique: The Recent History and Present Structure of Politics in a Tarascan Village." Unpublished Ph.D. dissertation, Yale University.

——— 1965 "A Mexican *Cacicazgo*," *Ethnology*, Vol. 4, No. 2: 190-209.

——— 1966 "Revolutionary Politics and Communal Ritual," pp. 191-220 in Marc J. Swartz, Victor W. Turner, and Arthur Tuden (eds.), *Political Anthropology*. Chicago: Aldine.

——— 1968 "The legitimacy of a *Cacique*," pp. 243-269 in Marc J. Swartz (ed.), *Local-Level Politics: Social and Cultural Perspectives*. Chicago: Aldine.

——— 1970 *Agrarian Revolt in a Mexican Village*. Englewood Cliffs, N.J.: Prentice-Hall.

Germani, Gino 1967 "The City as an Integrating Mechanism: The Concept of Social Integration," pp. 175-189 in Glenn H. Beyer (ed.), *The Urban Explosion in Latin America*. Ithaca, N.Y.: Cornell University Press.

Giusti, Jorge 1971 "Organizational Characteristics of the Latin American Urban Marginal Settler," *International Journal of Politics*, Vol. 1, No. 1 (Spring): 54-89.

González Casanova, Pablo 1970 *Democracy in Mexico*. London and New York: Oxford University Press.

Grindell, Merilee S. 1975 "Exchange Processes and Public Policy in Mexico." Unpublished Ph.D. dissertation, Massachusetts Institute of Technology.

Hanna, William J., and Judith L. Hanna 1967 "The Integrative Role of Urban Africa's Middleplaces and Middlemen," *Civilisations*, Vol. 17, No. 1-2; 12-29. 1969 "Influence and Influentials in Two Urban-Centered African Communities," *Comparative Politics*, Vol. 2, No. 1: 17-40. 1971 *Urban Dynamics in Black Africa: A Guide to Research and Theory*. Chicago: Aldine.

Instituto de Investigaciones Sociales, Universidad Nacional Autónoma de México 1975 *Caciquismo y el poder político en el México rural*. México, D. f.; siglo Veintiuno.

Kern, Robert, Ed. 1973 *The Caciques: Oligarchical Politics and the System of Caciquismo in the Luso-Hispanic World*. Albuquerque: University of New Mexico Press.

Kurtz, Norman R. 1966 "Gatekeepers in the Process of Acculturation." Unpublished Ph.D. dissertation, University of Colorado, Boulder.

Lambert, Jacques 1967 *Latin America: Social Structures and Political Institutions*. Berkeley: University of California Press.

Leeds, Elizabeth R. 1972 "Forms of 'Squatment' Political Organization: The Politics of Control in Brazil." Unpublished M.A. thesis, University of Texas, Austin.

Lopes, Juárez Rubens Brandao 1970 "Some Basic Developments in Brazilian Politics and Society," pp. 162-166 in Richard R. Fagen and Wayne A. Cornelius (eds.), *Political Power in Latin America: Seven Confrontations*. Englewood Cliffs, N.J.: Prentice-Hall.

Maruska, Donald L. 1972 "Government Policy and Neighborhood Organizations in the Squatter Settlements of Lima." Unpublished Honors Thesis, Dept. of Government, Harvard University.

Nowak, Thomas and Kay Snyder 1970 "Urbanization and Clientelist Systems in the Philippines," *Philippine Journal of Public Administration*, Vol. 14, No. 3: 259-275.

O'Brien, David J. 1974 "The Public Goods Dilemma and the 'Apathy' of the Poor toward Neighborhood Organization," *Social Service Review*, Vol. 48, No. 2 (June): 229-244.

Ornelas, Charles 1973 "Land Tenure, Sanctions, and Politicization in Mexico, D.F." Unpublished Ph.D. dissertation, University of California, Riverside.

Padgett, L. Vincent 1966 *The Mexican Political System*. Boston: Houghton Mifflin.

Paré, Luisa 1972 "Diseño teórico para el estudio del caciquismo actual en México," Revista Mexicana de Sociología, Vol. 34, No. 2 (April-June), 335-354.

Peattie, Lisa R. 1968 *The View from the Barrio*. Ann Arbor: University of Michigan Press.

Powell, John D. 1970 "Peasant Society and Clientelist Politics," *American Political Science Review*, Vol. 64, No. 2: 411-425.

Purcell, Susan K., and John F. H. Purcell 1973 "Community Power and Benefits from the Nation: the Case of Mexico," pp. 49-76 in Francine F. Rabinovitz and Felicity M. Trueblood (eds.), *Latin American Urban Research*, Vol. III. Beverly Hills, Calif.: Sage Publications.

Ray Talton F. 1969 *The Politics of the Barrios of Venezuela*. Berkeley: University of California Press.

Reyes Heroles, Jesús 1972 "Cuando se combaten los cacicazgos, el pueblo vota con entusiasmo: texto íntegro del discurso del Presidente del PRI pronunciado en Aguascalientes," *El Día* (Mexico City), Dec. 7, p. 9.

Ríos, José Arthur 1960 "El pueblo y el político," Política (Caracas), No. 6: 11-36.

Roberts, Bryan R. 1973 *Organizing Strangers: Poor Families in Guatemala City*. Austin: University of Texas Press.

Rogler, Lloyd 1974 "The Changing Role of a Political Boss in a Puerto Rican Migrant Community," *American Sociological Review*, Vol. 39, No. 1:57-67.

Rollwagen, Jack R. 1974 "Mediation and Rural-Urban Migration in Mexico: A Proposal and a Case Study," pp. 47-63 in Wayne A. Cornelius and F. M. Trueblood (eds.), *Anthropological Perspectives on Latin American Urbanization: Latin American Urban Research*, Vol. IV. Beverly Hills, Calif.: Sage Publications.

Ronfeldt, David 1972 *Atencingo: The Politics of Agrarian Struggle in a Mexican Ejido*. Stanford, Calif.: Stanford University Press.

Schers, David 1972 *The Popular Sector of the Partido Revolucionario Institucional in Mexico*. Tel Aviv: the David Horowitz Institute for the Research of

Developing Countries, Tel Aviv University. Research Report No. 1. (Submitted as a Ph.D. dissertation in Political Science, University of New Mexico, 1972.)

Scott, James C. 1969 "Corruption, Machine Politics, and Political Change," *American Political Science Review*, Vol. 63, No. 4: 1142-1158.

Scott, Robert E. 1964 *Mexican Government in Transition*. 2nd ed., Urbana: University of Illinois Press.

Segovia, Rafael 1974 "La reforma política: el ejecutivo federal, el PRI, y las elecciones de 1973," *Foro Internacional* (México), Vol. 14, No. 3: 51-67.

Silverman, Sydel F. 1965 "Patronage and Community-Nation Relationships in Central Italy," *Ethnology*, Vol. 4, No. 2: 172-189.

Simpson, Lesley Byrd 1967 *Many Mexicos*. 4th ed. Berkeley: University of California Press.

Snyder, Peter Z. 1972 "Indigenous Neighborhood Gatekeepers in the Process of Urban Adaptation." Paper presented at the Annual Meeting of the American Anthropological Association, Toronto, Nov.-Dec.

Toness, Odin A., Jr. 1967 "Power Relations of a Central American Slum." Unpublished M.A. thesis, University of Texas, Austin.

Torres Trueba, Henry E. 1969 "Factionalism in a Mexican Municipio," *Sociologus* (Berlin), N.S. vol. 19, No. 2: 134-152.

Tuohy, William S. 1973 "Centralism and Political Elite Behavior in Mexico," pp. 260-280 in Clarence E. Thurber and Lawrence S. Graham (eds.), *Development Administration in Latin America*. Durham, N.C.: Duke University Press.

Ugalde, Antonio 1970 *Power and Conflict in a Mexican Community*. Albuquerque: University of New Mexico Press. 1973 "Contemporary Mexico: From Hacienda to PRI, Political Leadership in a Zapotec Village," pp. 119-134 in Robert Kern (ed.), *The Caciques*. Albuquerque: University of New Mexico Press.

Ugalde, Antonio, Leslie Olson, David Schers, and Miguel Von Hoegen 1974 *The Urbanization Process of a Poor Mexican Neighborhood: The Case of San Felipe del Real Adicional, Juárez*. Austin: Institute of Latin American Studies, University of Texas.

Vaughan, Denton R. 1968 "Links Between Peripheral Lower-Income Residential Areas and Political Parties in a Latin American City." Unpublished paper, Dept. of Anthropology, University of Texas, Austin.

Wolf, Eric R. 1965 "Aspects of Group Relations in a Complex Society: Mexico," pp. 85-101 in Dwight B. Heath and Richard N. Adams (eds.), *Contemporary Cultures and Societies of Latin America*. New York: Random House.

Wolf, Eric R., and Edward C. Hansen 1967 "Caudillo Politics: A Structural Analysis," *Comparative Studies in Society and History*, Vol. 9: 168-179.

PART VI

Application: Clientelism – National Perspectives

PATTERNS OF PATRONAGE IN SPAIN

MICHAEL KENNY

IT IS MY INTENTION here to define the terms patron and client as they shall be used in this article; to review the bases for the patronage system as it is found in Spain; to trace certain of its patterns; to sketch some of its outward expressions; and finally to describe some of the rules that regulate structural relationships at all status levels whereon patronage operates. My remarks are confined to Spain and, in particular, to the two provinces of Castile—the Old and the New.

When we think of the word "patron" in English we tend to dwell on the idea of sponsorship; of someone (or some organisation perhaps) who is a benefactor; of one who supports by his influence and power a "client" who stands in need of help or protection. Perhaps we drift back in time and think of struggling poets and playwrights seeking the support of a patron who could open the gate to success. Modern colloquial American has an apt term for a special form of this in the world of entertainment, namely the patron who is known as an "angel". We are all familiar with the great ecclesiastical patronage to artists of old and, some of us, now, are more conscious of equally powerful political patronage. All of us have at one time or another

patronised particular stores, inns or businesses and it is not without significance that the higher we ascend the social scale in certain contexts so we become clients instead of patrons. We are clients to our lawyers who become for us our advocates—in a sense, the champions of our cause. We also become patrons, too, at times, as our own power and influence increases.

Preoccupied as we are with our modern secularism, we perhaps forget that an obsolete use of the word "patron" was reserved for reference to a tutelary god. We perhaps forget, too, that the patron in Roman times was not only a man of distinction but, under the law, was also a master who had freed his slave yet retained certain reciprocal rights over his client; the client, or ex-slave, was familiarly called by the name of his master/patron.

All these meanings, except (now) the last, are comprehended by the use of the word *patrón* in Spanish. But one must stress the widespread use in the religious sense particularly to mean a guardian saint of a town or village and to designate that holy figure who is reputed to have special powers in a given field. Moreover, a landlord, the proprietor of an inn or restaurant, the master or coxswain of a boat—all are *patrones*. Finally, *patrón* is employed in the sense of a pattern, a model to follow and copy.

Closely linked to the word *patrón* is its ally *padrino** variously significant as a godfather, a second who assists at a duel, a protector, and, when in special reference to the marriage ceremony, a "best man" or groom's man. The *padrino* acts, or is expected to act in most instances, as a surrogate *patrón*.

As a working tool, therefore, I define *patrón* as ". . . someone who is regarded (and who regards himself) at once as a protector, a guide, a model to copy, and an intermediary to deal with someone else or something else more powerful than oneself, whether or not such power is imaginary or real in a single context or in all, and whether or not the advantages to be gained from his patronage are material or intangible". Likewise, a client is ". . . someone who avails himself of a patron's services and who maintains a reciprocally beneficial relationship with him". These relationships I see functioning in a system conveniently viewed in pyramidal form.

With this definition in mind we may ask what are the theoretical bases on which the patronage system rests. Without doubt the most important of these is a sense of kinship, either real or fictive. The values of the family and its unity whether in nuclear or extended form are still paramount in Spain. Godparenthood provides an exterior stimulus to these values by setting up a cherished spiritual relationship which has very real practical advantages as well. Furthermore, the model of the ideal Spanish family is still largely that of the Christian Holy Family. The most accessible member of the latter family, in terms of intercession or mediation with God, is the Virgin Mary; hence the ubiquitous recourse to her powers for she occupies a special category of her own—not only saint and Immaculate Virgin but also Mother of God.

The charismatic emanation and dispersion from those nearest God is, in part, extended to those in authority in general; to those, in fact, whose ideal role is a parental, a protective and an intermediary one. And herein lies a paradox since, although this role by definition should embrace care for the whole range of society, the fear of this charismatic quality becoming too thinly dispersed automatically restricts the growth of each patronage group and gives it an exclusiveness all its own.

With this singular regard for authority must be associated the emotional satisfaction derived from giving and receiving protection and support as well as that of special treatment in the arranging of difficult matters. This paternalistic satisfaction has peculiar force when the patron and client are closely allied by reciprocal economic ties, for example the landlord-tenant relationship, such as is the case in the so-called *jajmani* relationship in India. But its potency is more understandable among a people whose stoic consideration of this transient life comes perilously close to fatalism, whose traditional class structure of the many poor and few rich is changing but slowly, and whose dependence on moral and material support in this largely barren land of the ,mystics is an almost instinctive "just-in-case" type of insurance.

Hence the element of chance becomes a social force in Spain, startlingly apparent in all walks of life and expressed in one form at least by a wholesale recourse to decision by lot. Ranging from the division of the pine tree common patrimony in a Castilian village and the national selection of young men for the military draft to the fervid playing of the national lottery and the choice of subjects for examining oneself in the central school for diplomats— the results depend on the casting of lots. Luck is fickle; God's ways are mysterious. Patronage, therefore, provides one at least down-to-earth insurance policy.

Closely weaved into these other bases is a real sense of the obligations to give, to receive, and to return. There is no servility in the idea of service yet, one must add, the "do-gooder" is conspicuously absent from this society. The love of the grant gesture, the display, the courtesy formulas, the show of generosity go hand in glove with a disdain for life and an arrogant individuality—two constantly recurrent themes in the literature. They set up a complicated web of obligations which, once entered into, are difficult to throw off. Generosity becomes a point of honour, and to receive the gesture and return it in equal or greater kind is important not only as a rather negative means of saving face but also as a positive way of achieving higher status.

These bases on which the patronage system rests provide at once a framework to build on and a pattern to copy. In line with the definition given, one may see that the patronage system embraces all figures in the authoritarian structure, both spiritual and temporal. God is the final patron and the ultimate source of all patronage; bracketed with the Father are the other two members of the Trinity. Yet, the patronage system, depending as it does on essentially personal relationships, naturally favours the completely human figures of the Virgin and the saints who are thought to intercede with the utterly spiritual trinity of authority.

So too with the ecclesiastical authorities who are thought to be next closest to the Godhead and therefore competent through their monopoly of spiritual powers to dispense indulgences. Moreover, since prelates in general are automatically associated in the popular mind with administrative and judicial officials as part of the authoritarian structure on earth, their assistance at some point in the total patronage system is considered essential.

Since the sixteenth century Spain has been ruled by a bureaucratic absolutism. Many bureaucrats (if not all) themselves owe their present positions to either direct nepotism or to conscious use of a patronage group. They thus tend to perpetuate a procedure to which they originally resorted and to which they are committed and indebted. Each official, major or minor, weaves himself a web of influence and support with the object of absorbing the maximum possible power into his own hands. The concept of *mando personal*—personal command—is not peculiar to the present regime. Everyone wants and strives to be a "chief", to be a power unto himself, "responsible only to God and to history".

Similar observations could be made of the power elites (a relative term) in the political and economic spheres, themselves duplicated in miniature at progressively lower levels in society. The smallest political unit in community terms is the pueblo wherein the power elite effectively controls patronage on a social as well as on a political and economic plane. In other contexts, this elite has been referred to as "gatekeepers" in that they largely dominate the paths linking the local infrastructure of the village to the superstructure of the outside urban world. The mayor, the priest, the Civil Guard sergeant, the doctor, the rich landlord are well-known leaders or "chiefs" who play, as the mood moves them, an innovating or controlling role in local affairs. Their friendship, their interest, their influence, their benevolence and indeed their services must be courted in case of need or difficulty. They in turn are linked to the towns through more powerful urban patrons as clients themselves.

Spain has been called the land of the *patria chica* because of the strength of municipal feeling and the desire to live in compact communities. Here is an urban-minded people living, in the main, under harsh rural-type conditions. Consumed with a passionate envy due to an inordinate individualism, obsessed by an exaggerated sense of honour and a dread of shame,

plagued by a peevish fear of public opinion and a preoccupation with the temporality of this earthly existence, the Castilian takes refuge behind the solid walls of his family group. Yet, only by extending these walls through the artifices of godparenthood and the patronage system can his kin's interests be safeguarded outside the family.

Only a few of the outward expressions of the patronage system can be stated here. It is increasingly the case that godparents for a child are chosen from outside the effective kin circle, where available kin fail to provide a secure source of influence. This is particularly true in urban areas where an employer or an influential friend is selected because he belongs to a more powerful patronage group. He is expected to sponsor the child when it grows up and, incidentally, to aid the family in the meantime. The godfather, whose responsibilities to the child begin on a spiritual plane, gradually acquires social responsibilities to the family as a whole. The spiritual and social welfare of the child become fused by present-giving at Baptism, Confirmation and First Communion ceremonies; by care and guidance during school; by assistance on entering a career, on marriage, and even at death—in fact, at the crises in life. Should the child be left parentless, the godparent is expected to bring him up.

At the village level, the Mayor and *cacique* (the local prototype of the political "boss") consciously trade patronage for political and material support. It is a common thing for the sixth or seventh son of a poor family to be sent to the seminary and trained for the priesthood through the good graces and sponsorship of a local patron. The father, for his part, will extend his services as a voter and also as a shepherd or harvest worker to the patron of his son. The son/priest in turn will ensure his patron's spiritual welfare by prayer and special Masses said for his benefit.

In the towns and cities, the "arranging" of affairs with officialdom becomes the concern of the patronage system. Certificates are required for mere vicinage, social benefits, all kinds of trading activity, voting, and even migration—for a man may be returned to his pueblo unless he can prove that he will live with relatives or has a house to go to. Entry to certain schools may depend on presentation of a certificate of Baptism and perhaps First Communion as well. Most applications for certificates are usually made in triplicate and must be countersigned elsewhere. It is not surprising that many agencies now offer to deal with the whole procedure of official applications for a small fee. Otherwise, the man claiming sickness benefits or seeking a housing permit or the like must lose many mornings' work waiting at government offices. Where his personal presence is not necessary his wife may go in his stead taking her sewing and a sandwich especially if she has to wait for hours at the window-counter marked "URGENT". Once made, the application takes months to clear and its success is always in doubt.

At a higher level in the urban setting where power is more closely associated with wealth, lobbying for the highly prized and exclusive concessions such as import and export licenses reveals a specially intimate type of patronage "pyramid". It is not a question here of considering that one may be entitled to these things by right, for between what is one's right and what is possible lie a thousand indifferent shrugs of the shoulder.

The process of circumventing these obstacles thrown up by authority can only be eased by having an *amigo*—a friend—in the right places. To have *enchufe* (literally meaning "plug") is to be able to make contact with the right people at a judicious moment. It is the new equivalent of the old friend at Court. It is a short cut through the maze of authority which balances the tension between State and community. It is the rule of *amigocracy*.

The sheer impersonality of officialdom places the bureaucrat at a social distance from the ordinary citizen and, in a sense, gives him added power. The diversity of urban life and regulation by specialized agencies whose equivalent function in the village would be on an informal level throw up complicated strata of power and authority which can only be dealt with by cultivated friendship and patronage. The enormous bulk of documentation required at every turn induces a procrastination increased by the supineness of poorly-paid officials which is said to breed corruption at the upper strata and to occasion letters of recommendation by the hundred to the humblest office manager.

To embark with any reasonable chance of rapid success on any venture involving a brush with the authorities, one must be armed with a battery of recommendations. These usually take the form of visiting cards which are now rarely used as such by the actual owner of the card. Rather, a patron will give to his client a card covered with phrases indicating that he "has great interest" in the bearer and signed with protestations of friendship to his contact— usually a patron of similar status in an influen-tial position. It has the magical quality of a passport which opens many doors to success.

Obligation to kin overrides all other obligation and onto the kin circle widened by ritual god-parenthood is welded the *amigocracy* or friendship pattern. But friendship has never been disinterested and its obligations and rights, like those of the family, are based on a reciprocity of services which are more important than mere duty to employer or State. One may be drawn into aiding a friend of a friend of a cousin one has never seen. This sort of extension is often a cause of annoyance to many. Yet it is the logical outcome of the system and it may be considered as the "throwing stick" of the extended family unit which gives it more power and range when dealing with the excesses or defects of authority. If, for example, the so-called black market operates freely in public it does so because it is sanctioned by the community. It cannot therefore have the same sinister connotation that it has acquired in English. Where the State fails the people will take over and it does so by adapting its normal kin and friendship patterns to the needs of the situation. Thus, when something is highly desirable and in short supply, helping a friend or relative (whose name is lower down on the priority list than a mere stranger's name) is considered only right and proper; and this even though the favour has not been solicited and the action strictly illegal.

It is not, therefore, mere caprice which governs favouritism in, for example, the granting of awards, titles, contracts or concessions, or, more important still, the provision of sinecures and jobs with security of tenure and care. The final commander of the Armada, the Duke of Medina-Sidonia, was not a naval man and was prone to seasickness, but he was a favourite for whom a post had to be procured.[1] The lament of those days . . . "so many men without posts; so many posts without men" . . . had a double edge for it is not so much a question of the right man for the job as of having (or even creating) a job for the right man. The "right" man, in terms of patronage, should not be confused with the "best" man, in terms of efficiency.

Nevertheless, the patron/client relationship is not a one-way affair only, with the client being a passive recipient of the patron's favours. It is the client's bounden duty not only to promise loyalty and support to his patron but actively to fulfil that promise and voice it abroad. By doing so he not only obeys a fundamental rule of the patronage system, i.e., that of constantly stimulating loyalty channels, but he also creates good will, adds to the name and fame of his patron and thus ensures him a species of immortality.

This is quite evident in the case of religious patrons of whom there are many and various. Apart from one's own namesake (a patron/protector from the moment of birth), there are patron saints for every association from bullfighters to bootblacks, for almost every part of the body, for finding or keeping a fiancé, for reaping a good harvest—for almost every situation of need one may imagine. The clients who seek favours through the patronage of the Virgin or a patron saint make "promises". It should be noted here that such promises are to be carried out only if and when the favour is granted. The outward symbols of these promises can be seen in the mauve shirts or dresses worn publicly for set periods; in the penances such as walking barefoot (trailing chains by the ankle) or carrying heavy crosses in Holy Week processions; in pilgrimges to designated shrines; in the donation lists of good causes; or in the simple placing of specially carved candles before an image of the Virgin or patron saint. In many country churches, as also in the smaller urban churches found in the twisting side streets, the walls are covered with *ex-votos*—miniature facsimiles in wax of a person or part of the body that has been cured. These outward signs are the client's accepted way of repaying the services of his religious patron. They are a mute and proud public testimony of the power and influence of a patron who spreads his favours widely.

Clients may of course have a number of patrons, for it is always wise to cover oneself. Yet, in stressing the reciprocity rule—equally valid for the patron/patron relationship—one sees that at the back of the material advantages involved there lie a striving to level out great inequalities, a fight against growing anonymity (especially in the urban setting), and a seeking out of the primary personal relationship. For the client, of course, there is as well the material benefit gained: for the patron there is his "investment" in supporters—his clients; between patrons themselves there is a comfortable cementing of relationships. The success or failure of these motivating factors is clearly revealed only in a crisis when protestations of loyalty and support significantly show the alignment of forces and the delineation of patronage "pyramids." Spanish political life has been marked by the manoeuvering of such groups until a "strong man" emerges around whom spheres of patronage newly orbit. To a lesser degree, they are evident also in the rival cults of the Virgin and saints when, as patrons of villages or parishes or organizations, they are at times used as symbols of hostility between groups.

In short, the patronage system, working in one particular context at a fixed point in time, may be visualized diagramatically as a pyramidal structure. At the top, is the supreme patron—God—Who, in the last resort, has no need of favours (or support) from anyone. In descending order of size, I see, enclosed by the whole pyramidal structure, separate autonomous pyramids of influence. At the top of each reigns a patron, and the sides and base of the pyramid are composed of clients who are themselves patrons to subordinate groups of clients. Circling the peaks of patronage pyramids are groups composed of patrons of more or less equal power who communicate with each other on behalf of their respective clients. At the base of the whole pyramidal structure are the disconnected clients at the lowest level who are never patrons unless they climb the sides of the pyramid.

One should point out here that a diagram is an abstraction, a tool, not to be reified, for then it loses its value as a guide. There can of course be movements up and down the pyramid of patronage, for, let there be no mistake, as soon as a patron becomes weak and is unable to fulfil his role, another will be sought who is more effective. In this sense the client/patron reationship at least is ruthless.

Only clients at the base, and God will have no circle of equals in the patron to patron reationship since the one is forever a client and the other is forever a patron. With these exeptions, everyone is at some time or another (in one role or another) both patron and client. I conclude, therefore, that there are three basic functional types of structural relationship in the patronage system: (a) the patron/client, (b) the patron/patron and (c) the client/patron. There can, by definition, never be a client/ client reationship because, at the moment the one offers the other some service under the patronage system he ceases to be a client in that context.

I have attempted to portray the essence of the patronage system as I see it operating in Spain today. There are many refinements to such a system not included here. They must form the basis of a further study at greater length to be made in the future.

NOTES

*So for that matter is the word *compadre* ("co-parent"); but the relationship between *compadres*—theoretically based on equality—is not specifically pertinent here.

[1]Even though he did not relish the task. There are times when unsolicited "favours" by a patron can prove embarrassing, even dangerous. This is a case in point.

PATRON-CLIENT RELATIONSHIPS IN SOUTHERN ITALY*

LUIGI GRAZIANO

ABSTRACT

POLITICAL CLIENTELISM in Southern Italy has shown great persistence and capacity for conditioning the entire Italiam political development. Accounting for these characteristics, clientelism is better understood as the product of the incomplete capitalistic rationalization of the Southern economy. Throughout the 19th century in Sicily, the *feudo* remained the basis of the economic and social structure, while in the continental South the feudal system disintegrated more quickly and widely. The resulting different models of social relationships within the *Mezzogiorno*, make it meaningful for our purposes to distinguish between two types of clientele, which may be termed *clientela mafiosa* and *Neopolitan clientele*.

The second part of the article is concerned with the dynamics of the clientelistic system in post-1945 Southern Italy and more generally with the relationship between clientelism and political development. The transition from the clientelism of the notables to political party-directed patronage is studied both at the local level and in the context of the whole South. It is then argued that clientelism is a very poor tool for political development since it has two effects on the social structure and the political process: these effects will be called *disorganic integration* and *exclusivism*.

INTRODUCTION

By studying the clientelistic system in Southern Italy, one is able to verify some hypotheses about the dynamics of patron-client ties and, more generally, about the relationship between clientelism and political development. One of the most striking characteristics of that system has been its persistence and its capacity to condition the entire Italian political development. The "Southern question", of which clientelism is a specific and fundamental political aspect, originated in the course of the development of the modern Italian state and today it is widely recognized as the most urgent national problem. Similarly, the clientelistic system in the South, instead of disappearing under the impact of modernizing forces such as the state and the market, has contributed to fashion an "indigenous" model of political development in which the clientelistic element is the single most important aspect.

A subtle *meridionalista* of the last century, who was very attentive to the social bases of the Southern political system, had already clearly perceived its capacity for expansion. Commenting on the effects of newly-established local elective institutions on the Mezzogiorno, Pasquale Turiello wrote in 1882:

It is easier to predict that with the process of time the local clientelistic system (a structure which alone can progress as a result of such institutions in the midst of individual and private interests) will spread from the South to the North, rather than a collective and objective consciousness to the Southern elective administrations[1].

Set in this wider context the understanding of the clientelistic system in the Mezzogiorno will help us to understand the "premodern" characteristics of the present Italian political system. All of these characteristics—be they a question of the pattern of bureaucratic intervention which La Palombara terms *"parentela"*[2] or the "premodern" type of political participation discussed by Di Palma[3]—can be traced to one fundamental aspect of Italian politics: its particularism[4]. The patron-client tie and its contemporary version, party-directed patronage[5], can be considered as the paradigmatic form of such particularism, both from the structural and cultural viewpoints.

What accounts for the persistence of Southern clientelism and the particular configuration of Italian political development, a development in which the state-created "wider" institutions finally looked "more like networks of intermediaries than the other way around"?[6] I think that to begin to answer this question we cannot simply look at the culture of the country and the role of the state.[7] The culture is always grounded in the economic and social structure of society, as Sydel F. Silverman has demonstrated with specific reference to "amoral familism".[8] On the other hand, the Italian historical experience after 1860 indicates that the expanding role of the state can have very different effects on the nature and diffusion of clientelism depending upon the stage of capitalistic development in a given society.

My argument will be that the persistence and specificity of Southern clientelism is best understood if we regard it as the product of the incomplete capitalistic rationalization of the Southern economy. The impact of the modern Italian state and its elective institutions on a semi-feudal Mezzogiorno has enormously developed local clientele and generated political clientele centered around the member of parliament. Ultimately, the incompleteness of the Italian revolution on the economic and social plane has meant that the state has less "rationalized" the South than the South has "meridionalized" the Italian state. *Le mort saisit le vif.*

A second, more general question we want to raise is: What is the potential of clientelism for political development? I think that such a potential has been overestimated if not completely misunderstood. In reading some of the literature on patronage in the new nations, it is obvious that clientelistic bargaining is seen as a sort of apprenticeship to the "adjustive bargaining ethos" underlying pluralist democracy.[9] Similarly, Weingrod's distinction between patron-client ties and party-directed patronage takes up its true "evolutionary" meaning if one considers that the transition from the first to the second species of patronage parallels the change from "traditional" to mass society.

According to Weingrod (and many others) mass society implies some kind of vaguely defined social and geographic "integration"; we will have to ask ourselves which sort of integration clientelism brings about. Furthermore, mass society must imply new types of associations capable of articulating and aggregating interests and demands in a more efficient way

than the clientelistic system does. (I will elaborate on this point later in the paper.) Again we will have to ask: Can such a type of social relationship (clientelism) which is by definition hierarchical, dyadic and informally organized, allow the emergence of conditions necessary for the development of less particularistic, more categorical groups?[10]

In the light of the Italian experience, my answer and my thesis is no. Clientelism seems to be a very poor tool for political development because it has two distinctive effects on the social structure and on the political process: these effects may be labelled *disorganic integration* and *exclusivism*. That is, when clientelism integrates people in the social and political systems, it does so in a (dyadic) way which prevents the restructuring of society along associational lines. Clientelism is the product of a disorganic society and tends to preserve social fragmentation and disorganization. Secondly, clientelism integrates but very selectively, the other side of particularism being exclusivism. This becomes clear if instead of looking at the pyramidal structure of a clientelistic society as M. Kenny does,[11] we consider the system from the viewpoint of participation. From the latter perspective we can say that in a particularistic society and polity, participation is a very rare "currency" (Di Palma) and that the logic of the system imples that such a "currency" remains rare.

In the first part of this paper we will explore some of the structural conditions of Italian Southern clientelism and try to distinguish between a *Sicilian pattern* (*clientela mafiosa*) and a *Neapolitan pattern* of clientelism; we will furthermore consider the role of the state after 1860. In the second part, which is partially based on fieldwork done in a community of the Salerno area, we will deal with the dynamics of clientelism in post-1945 Italy and the relationship between clientelism and political development.

THE STRUCTURAL FOUNDATIONS OF CLIENTELISM
IN SOUTHERN ITALY

*The Impact of the Market on
the Southern Clientelistic System*

Analytically and to a large extent practically, modern politics is categorical politics: the political bargaining and the political struggle take place essentially between voluntary groups (associational groups or social classes) which are based upon, and represent, shared interests.[12] In order for this kind of interest and group to emerge, particularistic ties of personal-concrete dependence must cease to be predominant. Theoretically as well as historically, the capitalistic market is the most powerful agent in the dissolution of such ties. Market relations are anonymous, general and abstract: they depersonalize all human relations.[13] Thus by considering the process and the degree of capitalistic rationalization of an economy, we may learn something about the survival of conditions which account for the persistence of clientelistic relationships as well as other species of dyadic relationships.

After 1860, the first task of the Italian bourgeoisie was to create a national market. This was an urgent task, given the low degree of commercialization then prevailing within and among Italian regions, particularly in the South. The creation of a national market requires two processes: (a) expansion of the communication network to facilitate the circulation of goods; and (b) social division of labor (separation of industry from agriculture and industrial specialization), without which there is no need to exchange. In its turn, process (b) implies the transformation both of feudal land property and of feudal methods of agricultural management. The latter double transformation occurred in the Mezzogiorno in a very incomplete way.[14] Let us see why.

The birth of the Southern landed middle class is connected with the laws which abolished feudal property and rights. In the continental Mezzogiorno, the law of 1806 and successive laws divided the feudal lands in two parts: one part was left as free property to the barons and the rest was given to the communes as *demanio comunale*.[15] *The demanio comunale* was meant to be assigned in small plots to landless peasants as a compensation for the communal rights (*usi civici*) previously exercised by the population on the baronial lands.

It is well known that the division of *demanio comunale* originated the most enduring, widespread and fiercest social struggles in the whole history of the South. The claims on these lands played a major role in the *brigantaggio*, the peasant war which erupted in 1860, as well as in all the successive peasant riots.[16] In general, the dominant groups in each commune tried to procrastinate the assignment of these lands in order to usurp them;[17] when the peasants did receive small plots, they were unable to keep them for lack of capital or as a result of usury. Thus a law meant to create peasant property actually increased the land monopoly of the middle and large landowners.[18] Hence the double characteristic of land property in the South:

(a) Parasitic attitude of landowners more inclined to increase their land by force than to improve it; and

(b) Uncertain legal status and illegitimacy (particularly in the eyes of the peasants) of most of the land property.[19]

A crucial and complementary aspect of bourgeois and middle class land property in the South is the following: such property was *not* created at the expense of free baronial land. Even after 1860, when the Northern ruling class wanted to compensate the *galantuomini* (southern middle class) for their role in the process of national unification, the land they received did not encroach on semifeudal property; it came essentially from the commercialization of *manomorta* (state and communal *demanio*, land of the Church and religious charitable institutions).[20] Baronial lands were spared because too many bourgeois and *galantuomini* "by way of purchase or usurpation took the place of the old counts and barons".[21] Secondly, this process of wealth formation strengthened the only element of unity of an otherwise fragmented ruling class: its anti-clericalism.[22]

This origin of the landed middle class and bourgeoisie and the survival of a very extensive baronial property had two fundamental effects: it prevented the birth of a class of landed peasants and "powerfully contributed to preserve the backward and semi-feudal character of all social and agrarian relationships in the Mezzogiorno".[23] Although this was a general characteristic of the South, one might expect that social relationships were not uniformly "semifeudal". We must now consider local variations which may be relevant for a typology of patron-client ties *within* the Mezzogiorno.

I would suggest that it is possible and meaningful for our purposes to distinguish between two prevailing patterns of social relationships, which we may call the *Sicilian pattern* and the *Neapolitan pattern*. I shall illustrate these and sketch two corresponding types of clientelistic politics: the *clientela mafiosa* and the *Neapolitan clientele*.

Sicily did not experience the "modernizing" impact of direct French rule as did the continental Mezzogiorno between 1805 and 1815. The first law against feudal property and rights was enacted in 1812 under strong British pressure, but legally feudalism was not completely abolished until 1838. Still in 1860 ex-baronial property in Sicily, which accounted for nine-tenths of all Sicilian land, remained largely undivided.[24]

The economy of the *feudo*, as the latifundium

continued significantly to be called, gave Sicilian social structure an organization and a cohesion lacking elsewhere in the South. The continental Mezzogiorno may be defined in Gramscian terms as "a great social disgregation": in Sicily "one could not talk in general of social disgregation but the elements of organization and cohesion remained essentially those of the feudal epoch".[25] Since the *feudo* played such a fundamental role in Sicilian society, it is important to consider its economic and social structure.

The land of the *feudo* was generally divided in two parts. The landowner (or the tenant) dedicated himself to cattle breeding and to some specialized cultivations (typically olives and grapes). The wheat-growing section of the *feudo* was rented out in small plots and for periods of 2-3 years to peasants (*borgesi*) who cultivated the land with their own, necessarily primitive instruments. Hence the two predominant characteristics of the *feudo* economy were: a very low productivity and very limited entrepreneurial role of the landowner. The latter obtained from the *feudo* both a capitalistic profit and above all, a rent in kind, in money and in personal services from the *borgesi*.

Increasingly after 1860, the landowner rented out the whole *feudo* to a tenant, called *gabellotto*. The *gabellotto* was a capitalist to a greater degree than the landowner: he generally paid a cash rent to the proprietor and often he cultivated a larger extent of the land by employing wage earners. At the same time, the *gabellotto* lived on extortion: he took advantage of his strategic position between the peasant and the absentee landlord and built his fortune by exploiting both of them. He is the symbol of the kind of feudal entrepreneurship which epitomizes Sicily's encounter with capitalism.

It is surely of great significance that the *gabellotto*, who was the main agent of capitalism in the Sicilian countryside, was also the central element of the new middle-class Mafia; that is, of a structure which embodied a feudal (violent, arbitrary, personal) concept of power. After 1860 the Mafia ceased to be an organization at the service of the feudal lords and increasingly became the instrument of a middle class *in fieri*. While the *gabellotto* represented the rural Mafia, a parallel city Mafia developed and performed the mediating functions which proliferated as a result of the bureaucratic complexity of the modern Italian state. More often than not, the *mafioso* of the city was the educated son of a *gabellotto*.[26]

To complete the picture of the *feudo*, let us consider finally the plight of the peasant. The *feudo* was structured in a rigidly hierarchical fashion. *Gabellotti*, *soprastanti* (supervisors) and *campieri* (armed guards) ensured, often by force, that the *borgese* honored his contractual and customary obligations. Not only did the contractual obligations favor the *padrone* to an exorbitant extent,[27] but above all they were indeterminate and variable; as such they lent themselves to all kinds of abuses, naturally to the peasants' detriment.

It is important to note that it is the very imprecision of *all* peasants' obligations which allows the margin of incertitude necessary for a precapitalistic ruling class to pursue its parasitic role. Thus, the semi-feudal character of the South is among other things reflected in the fact that until recently (and to a degree still today) the Mezzogiorno could be considered a precontractual society.

Finally the peasants were subject to customary obligations of feudal origin called *angherie*.[28] Here again, it was not only the heaviness of the burden which was resented by the peasant, but "the incertitude, variety and continuous mutability of these rights"—in a word, the arbitrary way of their imposition. The peasants felt at the mercy of other people's whims, of an abundant or a bad harvest, of a good or ferocious *gabellotto* and *campiere* and so on. We must add that the very cyclical nature of the *feudo* economy contributed to making a serf of the *borgese*. The wheat was harvested once a year, and in order to live he *had* to borrow money from the usurer or wheat from the *padrone*. In the latter case—the least onerous—the rate of interest often amounted to 25%.[29]

In this kind of society, where there seems to be no notion of common good and violence is the fundamental rule of the game, ties of dependence tend to be very personal and highly "moral": ties of loyalty, solidarity, *omertá*. There is no contradiction between the violence which permeates Sicilian clientelism and the accentuated paternalism which characterizes it. Simply, when the power differential is so great and the client is socially isolated, a highly affective relationship is the best strategy to soften the terms of an unequal exchange.[30] Such deference can become, with the process of time, a cultural compensatory mechanism which preserves this very inequality of reciprocity.[31] The fundamental resource base of patronage[32] is in Sicily the direct control of land. The new intermediaries in the cities came from the landed middle class. For the latter kind of patrons, their professional knowledge and skill became increasingly important as the incorporation of the island into the bureaucratic framework of the new state proceeded. As for the resource base of clientage, the client provided labor and other personal services, and occasionally the physical assistance needed in inter-faction feuds. Finally, the relationship appears to be a relatively stable one.

With respect to the organization of the clientelistic system, a patron-client network needed not to be specifically organized in Sicily; such a system was, so to speak, "spontaneously" suggested by the social and economic structure and by a culture which expressed strong regional antagonism to the national state. Turiello remarked that the first instinct of the Neapolitan is to *abuse* the law, while the Sicilian rather *despises* a law which he does not recognize as his own. In the continental South, such impulse to turn the law to one's personal advantage "creates the need for special ties," *camorre* among the most subordinate elements in society, *clientele* among the people who have enough connections to use the law for particularistic purposes;[33] in Sicily the Mafia provides both the moral code and the social organization necessary to sustain a network of patron-client ties. In other words, the Mafia appears to be the specific form of traditional Sicilian clientele.

If we turn to the continental Mezzogiorno, the picture varies considerably. Generally speaking, the disintegration of the feudal system there proceeded much more quickly than in Sicily. The division of *demanio comunale*, purchases of Church land and a greater erosion of ex-baronial property on the part of a rising middle class, had created a greater degree of commercialization of the economy and a far greater social stratification. The peasant presented himself much more frequently on the market, the *feudo* itself was not such a self-sufficient unit as in Sicily, rents were more often paid in cash, and the propensity to invest was far more widespread.

As a result, the continental Mezzogiorno was characterized by a social stratification much different from the Sicilian pattern. Besides the ex-feudal landlords, one finds a sizeable class of wealthy bourgeois landowners; then a class of rich peasants (*massari*) who cultivated large estates, used wage labor and often practised usury on the poor peasants. As Sereni remarks, usury in cash (as opposed to the usury in kind practised by *gabellotti* and proprietors in Sicily) has been "one of the most powerful agents of disgregation and differentiation of the peasant mass" in the continental South.[34] The middle class was both more numerous and socially

important than in Sicily; often its members were instrumental in allowing the landowners to usurp the land of *demanio comunale* and received some land in return. Such a class, mainly constituted by professional people, often controlled the municipal administrations and charitable institutions and played as such, as we shall see in a moment, a crucial political role. Finally the mass of peasants were tied to the land by a variety of contracts but were lacking any internal cohesion.

Compared with Sicily, the continental clientelistic system appeared less as a "survival system" than as a device meant to mitigate the extreme lack of associational life in the South. As indicated before, some of the basic problems of the continental South stemmed from the "disgregation" of its society. Turiello refers again and again to the "excessive isolation (*scioltezza*) of individuals" who feel no moral bond outside the family, and views the clientele as the specific remedy for a disjointed society. The clientele, he wrote, are "the only associations which actually show real operative energy in a civil society which has been divided within itself for centuries" and in which people unite not on the basis of mutual trust but only when forced by necessity.[35]

In the continental South, the mediating function is essentially performed by the intellectual bourgeoisie, whose power derives, as we noted, from the control of municipal resources. Its knowledge and skill are used to mediate between the town and the national community. As opposed to Sicily, patron-client relationships are more shifting and more instrumental, and coercion plays a lesser role. The resource base of clientage is represented by the labor services and the economic support given by the peasants to the landlord, as well as by the political services they rendered to the municipal administrators.

The overall social function of the mediation performed by the intellectual bourgeoisie has been described by Gramsci in the following terms:[36]

The southern peasant is tied to the big landowners through the activity of the intellectual. The peasant movements, in so far as they are not expressed in at least formally autonomous and independent mass organizations (i.e. organizations capable of selecting peasant cadres of peasant origin and of reflecting the differentiations and progress achieved in the movement) always end up by losing themselves in the ordinary forms of the State apparatus—Communes, Provinces, Chamber of Deputies—through the combinations and breaking up of local parties which consist of intellectuals but are controlled by the big property owners. . . .

The Impact of the State on the Development of Clientele

Given the totalitarian concept of power which is typical of a semifeudal society, it is not difficult to imagine the devastating effects that the introduction of elective procedures and local self-government had on the political life in the South. The commune was given important prerogatives in a variety of administrative areas (communal roads, schools, charitable institutions, demanio comunale, credit, etc.). The power which was previously dispersed among local notables and royal functionaries was concentrated in the hands of the mayor. As a result, the stakes in the fight for municipal power were greatly heightened.

Within the communes, the absolute power of the middle class and the bourgeoisie was wielded on the premise that the state would not and could not exercise its regulatory function. The prefects were busy more with electoral politics than with good administration of the communes; because they were dependent on the influence of the local notables for the election of deputies acceptable to the government, the activities of the local administrations went largely unchecked. In these conditions it is not surprising that the commune became the center of all sorts of abuses ranging from completely iniquitous systems of taxation to usurpation of demanio pubblico and abuse of charitable institutions.[37] More specifically, the introduction in the communal political arena of new resources had two effects on the local clientelistic system.

The first effect was to greatly intensify the struggle for the conquest of municipal power. Such power was no longer sought as a means to establish a feudal superiority, but as a means of enrichment for a rising middle class.[38] In the absence of any notion of the commune as an institution established for the collective good, and in the absence of any concept of common advantage shared by organized groups of the small ruling class, the struggle necessarily took place between competing clientelistic factions. The prevailing totalitarian concept of power, which resulted in the exclusivist exercise of local authority, meant that the alternative to joining a clientele was to be totally powerless.

The second, apparently contradictory effect was, I believe, a restriction of the clientelistic network. Even if it is difficult to gather specific evidence on this point, I think this happened for two reasons. On one hand the balance of strength

between the galantuomini and peasants changed so radically after 1860 to the advantage of the former that probably not much reciprocity was left in their relationships. The introduction of an electoral suffrage restricted to a tiny minority also contributed to upset the balance. On the other hand, the new power of the middle class had very limited legitimacy in the eyes of many peasants, who now could impute directly to the municipal administrators the old and new abuses imposed on them. The hate they harbored previously for a distant central authority, a hate somewhat mitigated by the paternalism of the Bourbon kings, was now concentrated against the new local ruling class.[39]

Indirect evidence of this phenomenon of expulsion from the clientelistic network may be seen in the fact that increasingly the peasants had recourse to other less peaceful methods of bargaining and struggle: camorra, brigantaggio and other forms of anomic behavior (burning of communal woodlands and archives, assaults on town halls, etc.). Not only in the South clientele, mafia, comorra and brigantaggio all seem to stem from the same basic reality, namely a lack of discipline of private interests[40] but they may be considered as functionally alternative ways adopted by the subordinate classes to mitigate their plight.

The same conditions which brought about the totalitarian kind of politics that we have observed at the local level, produce a certain image of the national government and of its role. Franchetti observed in this connection that "everybody instinctively and sincerely considers the public aurhority in all its manifestations as a brutal force allied or inimical to this or that person for whatever purpose he may have, good or bad".[41] In the same vein, Turiello wrote about a "barbarian intolerance" felt in the South for the impersnal and legal power of the state. Thus it is not surprising that the Southern ruling classes asked from the state the same kind of partial, violent, arbitrary protection as the one asked from the Mafia. Such a conception of the state explains the tendency of the local clientele to transform themselves into political clientele and "privatize" the state after their fashion.[42]

This was successfully done in 1876. The parliamentary and electoral victory of the so-called Sinistra was in fact the victory of clientele over the political parties, a sort of "revenge" of a disorganic South on a socially more structured North.[43] Sociologically speaking, the Sinistra did not represent different interests from the Destra, but a desire for change of the Southern elite until then excluded from governmental power. After a few years, this very lack of social differentiation between the two parties and the ideological nature of the power of the *Sinistra* in the South, led to the triumph of *trasformismo*, the parliamentary counterpart of clientelism.

Graphically the clientelistic structure of the Italian parliamentary regime after 1876 may be represented as follows:

GOVERNMENT

Deputy
Prov. Deputy

CENTRAL
BUREAUCRACY

Mayor
Great Electors   PREFECTS
Electors

The great electors may be divided in three categories:[44] (1) the prefects; (2) individual great electors (landowners and big tenants; professional men, capitalists, and wealthy people in the cities); and (3) political associations. The latter groups were constituted mainly in the cities by people who had a "certain electoral value" (Mosca) but not enough to act individually as great electors. They were internally structured in a very hierarchical fashion and often were composed of workers who would exchange their votes for some benefits procured by the leaders of such groups. At the same time, the difficulties met in organizing associations in the South, the obvious advantages derived in such a milieu by anybody who could put together one hundred votes, and finally the strength of already existing closely knit traditional associations, meant that in the Mezzogiorno such groups were often infiltrated by *mafia* and *camorra*.[45]

The provincial deputies were a very important link in the clientelistic system. The *deputzaioni provinciali* were specifically charged with the supervision of communes and charitable institutions; furthermore, they controlled vast funds for public works and as such acted as very important centers of patronage. Generally, in each province there was a patron who could control the provincial network of clientele.

The national deputy, whose powers became increasingly independent of party discipline, was the central element in the whole system; the various patron-client pyramids constituting such a system culminated in the single deputy who would represent interests and claims to other, more powerful deputies.

The parliament could thus be pictured as being constituted by deputies who had access to the government in varying degrees and who tended to gravitate around the most powerful of their colleagues. The latter, among whom the ministers were chosen, compensated the client-deputy by providing benefits which were always of a particularistic nature; this was so because the deputy did not aggregate the claims of many electors, but essentially represented the demands of his great electors. These in turn were only responsive to services they could use to increase their personal influence and grateful only for those benefits which could be directly imputed to the intervention of a deputy. In other words, in the absence of any notion of collective interests, the provision of collective goods is unproductive in terms of political influence.

The particularistic nature of the incentives which kept the system going required that the minister had to dispose of rewards and sanctions of an equally particularistic nature; that is, he had to be as free as possible from bureaucratic norms of conduct. Such a functional requirement of the system is confirmed by the enormous discretion legally and practically recognized among the ministers in the organization and in the functioning of the bureaucracy. Mosca remarked that "the minister is the absolute arbiter of anything which a little state functionary may hope for, or may fear".[46] On the other hand, the administration of the state became a gigantic spoils system for the benefit of political clientele.[47]

As a means to putting a limit to the deputies' power, the government had recourse to the prefects as great electors. The fundamental role of the Italian prefects in the manipulation of elections is too well known to be elaborated on here.[48] As such, they played an essential role in the re-establishment of some sort of balance of power between the deputies and the government. The deputies create the government on which they impose more often than not their will; the government reacts by creating a certain number of faithful deputies.[49]

Such a role played by the prefect in the functioning of the Italian parliamentary regime may be considered the symbol of a particularistic and arbitrary system of government which tends to perpetuate itself. One is not confronted with a system which produces stability in a context of dynamic change, but with a system which produces stability in a context of immobilism. Of such a system, Mosca underlined its "inertia"[50] and Turiello its "administrative immobility" due to the play of conflicting influences of people whose only common interest is the preservation of their own power.[51]

Clientelism of the Notables

Soon after 1945, the community I investigated still bore traces of very backward social relationships. Economically, the community was still predominantly agricultural with just under 50% of the active population engaged in primary activities.[52] The land was generally leased in plots of varying size. When land was used for pasture, the contract typically included some restrictive clauses imposed by the landowner.

One recurrent clause established the maximum amount of land which the tenant was allowed to till. Such imposition was due to the fact that the leased land was normally endowed with livestock which had to be returned to the proprietor at the expiration of the lease. Given the absence of fertilizers, selected seeds and other resources of modern cattle-breeding technique, and the very bad conditions of the roads, the cattle could be fed only with fodder produced on the farm. Hence the necessity to reserve a portion of its surface for cattle feeding. One may say that the technical backwardness of agriculture, a poor communication network and the Salerno plain still partially infested by malaria were all conditions not conducive to an active exchange economy.[53]

A second clause concerned the granting of credits to the tenant. Typically the landowner would advance money to the tenant to provide him with the capital necessary for the cultivation of the land. The anticipo greatly accentuated the dependence of the tenant on his landlord. The granting of an anticipo was also practised by the local industrialist vis-a-vis his suppliers (of milk, tomatoes, etc.). The industrialist would commit himself to buying a fixed amount of produce yearly; the farmers would accept his offer as a guarantee against the hazard of a limited market. Generally the credits were granted at such rates of interest as to cause the permanent indebtedness of the farmers.[54]

With the development of industrial cultivations, particularly tobacco and tomatoes, a kind of sharecropping prevailed—the so-called compartecipazione stagionale. By this contract, a peasant family would take a small plot on lease specifically for a particular cultivation. The lease was usually for a year, since for their peculiar technical characteristics, such cultivations could not be repeated on the same plot for two successive years. Hence the precariousness of this kind of contract. The proprietor, or the tenant who sublet part or all of his farm, would provide most of the capital (for ploughing, equipment, irrigation, fertilizers, etc.), while other minor expenses were shared with the peasant.

In the area I studied, the traditional method of recruiting farm labor is the caporalato. The seasonal character of the cultivations prevailing in the Sele plain determines a recurrent need for seasonal manpower. The caporale is the middleman who goes into the hilly towns of the hinterland and hires the required number of day laborers, thus performing an important function for the farmer. His strategic position vis-a-vis the laborers stems from his recruiting power in a land of widespread unemployment and from his control of the means of transportation (busses). We may say that he literally provides an essential linkage between the peasants of the interior and the economic activities of the coastal plain.[55]

Such a mediating role, which has been important for the capitalistic development of the Sele plain,[56] contains however some pre-capitalistic elements. Until quite recently, the laborer was not paid directly by his employer, but through the caporale who would retain the price of his recruiting service plus transportation fees. Above all, the caporale tends to monopolize the relations of the peasant with the external world and penalize those who do not respect that monopoly. That is why trade-unionism and caporalato tend to exclude each other. The caporale occasionally does provide special services for some of the laborers (some of them may bribe him to obtain better work), but as long as the caporalato prevails, the relationship of the peasant with the external world cannot but be dyadic and hierarchical. In other words, an intermediary may bridge social and geographical gaps only to preserve them indefinitely.

A widespread anti-mercantile mentality, very limited entrepreneurial spirit and lack of individual autonomy of the peasants demonstrate how superficial had been the penetration of capitalism in these rural areas. For instance, the impersonality of price was not easily accepted: to sell at a lower price a product of inferior quality was considered a loss of prestige. The merchants preferred to maintain prices more or less at the same level and differentiate them through discounts granted to the single client and by adjusting the computation of the tare to the quality of the goods (a higher tare for cheap goods, a lower tare for better ones). The entrepreneurial spirit, which also in the Salerno area had not been encouraged by the process of formation of the landed middle class,[57] suffered further as a result of: (1) the massive emigration of the most enterprising peasants; and (2) the old propensity of the middle class and the bourgeoisie for careers in the state bureaucracy and in the professions. Finally the subordination of the peasants and their state of cultural estrangement from the world of the *padroni* prevented them from giving an autonomous contribution to the productive process.[58]

From the political viewpoint, the town I studied was not less stagnant. Landowners and professional men were the "great electors"; significantly, one of the notables talked of "second degree election" to qualify the role played by his peers in "orienting" the peasants' vote.[59] Such a political stagnation was not shaken, as was the case in the North, by the *Resistenza*. Thus, the first two-post fascist elections (1943, 1946) took place *without any political competition*, an occurrence which even by Southern Italian standards was exceptional. In the 1946 institutional referendum, the republic obtained 40 votes in the town (which at the time had 12,000 inhabitants).

The only electoral list presented in 1943 and 1946 was a royalist list formed by the liberal notable (a lawyer and a landowner) who had been the first mayor of the town in 1911.[60] In both elections this man persuaded younger and less conservative citizens to join his list instead of creating others. According to the son of this notable, one of the reasons why the most important people in town wanted one list only was their repugnance at being judged by the population.

Against this economic and political background, it is not surprising that local power was exercized through a network of patron-client relationships. The fundamental difference with the pre-fascist period was the concentration of economic power in the hands of a new class of industrial entrepreneurs. Starting from about 1920, some important industries developed locally, mainly in the branches of tobacco and tomatoes.[61] While the former was the jumping-board for the parliamentary career of a man who presented himself as a royalist candidate in 1946 and as a Christian Democrat candidate in 1948, the tomato industry was concentrated in the hands of a family which wielded undisputed power in the town until 1952. Between 1945 and 1952, and again from 1954 until 1959, the mayor of the town belonged to this family.

The power base of this family, which I shall call Amabile, was perhaps more financial than industrial. The family had great influence on the tomato producers who generally addressed themselves to the industrialist for their financial needs; credit was granted to them on the understanding that they would sell their goods to Amabile at prices generally fixed by the latter. In 1946, at a time of expanding export to the United States, Amabile took the initiative of having a bank office established in the town, which previously had none. When I add that Amabile also had a lot to say about the policy of the two largest banks in Salerno, the picture of his financial strength is completed.

The cultural counterpart of this position of economic power lay in the "natural respect" most of the town people felt for such a successful industrialist. The older Amabile, mayor of the town from 1954 until 1959, is still remembered as a man who would cause a stir each time he decided to take a walk along main street. The deference was greatest among his workers and generally the working masses, while patronage was used in his relations with the petty bourgeoisie (in terms of employment, granting of commercial and building licenses by the town hall, etc.) and economic intimidation of local producers. When "natural" deference and economic pressure were not sufficient as means of political control, Amabile would have recourse to corruption, as he did in 1952 when he unsuccessfully tried to prevent the formation of rival electoral lists, or to the threat of violence.

We may try now to present in a more systematic way the conditions and the instruments of political control which typically accompany the clientelism of the notables. In doing so, I shall contrast this kind of patronage with what Weingrod terms party-directed patronage and with a non-clientelistic type of politics. The addition of a non-clientelistic model of politics to Weingrod's typology of patronage seems to me a logical necessity since it is impossible to define clientelistic politics without trying to specify what clientelism is not. The typology which follows will serve as an introduction to party-directed patronage which I shall deal with in the next section:

Stages of development	Traditional society	Transitional society	Mobilized society
Prevailing economic, political, and cultural conditions	—Semi-feudal economic relationships. —Concentration of economic strength in the hands of a few notables. —Lack of political competition among organized groups. —Highly deferential culture.	—Growing commercialization of the economy. —New private economic activities and heavy public investments. —Organized political parties and electoral competition. —Disappearance of deferential culture and lack of legitimacy of the new party bosses.	—Capitalistic market. —Policy of planned economic development. —Hegemonic role of a mass party. —Ideological and political legitimacy of the hegemonic party.
Instruments of local political control.	—Party of notables. —Economic power of the notables. —Traditional legitimacy. —Corruption. —Violence or threat of it.	—Bureaucratic party of patronage. —Mass patronage based on public resources. —External party connections. —Use of unions for particularistic services. —Corruption. —Violence or threat threat of it.	—Centralized mass party. —Political and ideological mobilization of the masses. —General trade union services. —Violence or threat of it against "class enemies."
Types of relationship: leaders-followers.	—Exchange in part contractual and in part based on cultural prescriptions.	—Contractual relationships.	—Contractual and ideological relationships.

Party-Directed Patronage and Political Development

Around 1954, a profound change occurred in the political system of the Mezzogiorno—the transition from clientelism of the notables to party-directed patronage. I shall examine this transition by considering first the rising to power of a local boss,[62] and secondly by situating such a transition in the change of strategy of the leading Italian party (Democrazia Cristiana) throughout the South.

In the case I studied, the passage from traditional clientelism to party-directed patronage was more of a break than a slow transition. In 1952, the socialist party (PSI), which previously was hardly present in the town, obtained 40%

of the votes and together with the Communists the majority of the municipal seats. There seems to be three possible factors which contributed to such an "electoral revolution," as the change is locally termed: (1) the land struggles which reached a peak in 1949/50 (an intensive mobilization took place in the Sele plain where the town I studied is situated); (2) a revolt against the power of the Amabile family (at the 1952 elections, the industrialist and his brother were respectively leading the royalist and the Christian Democrat electoral lists, thus monopolizing the two most important local parties); and (3) a sort of revolt of the hilly section of the town, from where the leading Socialist exponent came, against the expanding economic role of the plain section.

While this electoral phenomenon is anything but clear, its consequences were obvious and important: political and electoral competition entered the town. This happened concurrently with, and partly as a result of, the appearance of a new type of political leader. The DC politician who arrived in town around 1952 was the first politician with extensive party connections at the provincial level to take part in the local political struggle. Until 1944, this man had been director of one of the tobacco plants owned by the big industrialist and DC MP mentioned above; in such a position he could establish contacts which, as we shall see, proved invaluable later on. Since that time, he had been one of the leaders of the party in Salerno; as a party man, he was in a position to fully appreciate the precariousness of the old paternalistic system in a period of rapid electoral mobilization and economic change.

At the beginning of his local political career, one finds two skillful alliances. First, with the help of the secretary of the commune (who was still the bureaucrat appointed by the fascist mayor), he was able to find out administrative irregularities committed by the socialist administrators and obtain from the prefect the termination of their mandate. The second alliance was with the industrialist Amabile. Still a newcomer in the town, the party boss was far too weak to battle on two fronts, socialists on one hand, and the well-established paternalistic power of Amabile on the other. In view of the fact that the latter still commanded a sizeable electoral following, the party boss struck a bargain with him.

The 1954 administrative elections, which followed the fall of the left-wing administration, were a great success for the DC list, headed by Amabile (the party boss being the second in such a list). These elections, as well as the whole electoral record of the town and in fact of the South, confirmed the large shifting of votes which regularly follows an influential man's change of party affiliation.[63] Deprived of the patronage of the industrialist, the monarchist party lost more than two-thirds of its previous electoral strength, while the DC more than doubled its own electoral following.

The industrialist Amabile was elected mayor through pressure he applied on many DC councillors who were economically dependent on him, but the real strong man of the new administration (1954-59) and the rising star of town politics was Rota, as we shall call the party

boss. He did not enjoy the traditional legitimacy derived from wealth and moral leadership; thus he had to build up his power from scratch. While for Amabile his political-administrative role was simply a corollary to his economic supremacy, Rota used his political-administrative powers both to legitimize his role as a leader and to consolidate his economic position as a building constructor. From 1954 to 1959 he was in fact town councillor in charge of public works and urban planning; in such a capacity he controlled the office which in a period of intensive urbanization and urban renewal was to become the center of local political struggle.

A second crucial resource was also available to Rota for political patronage. At the beginning of the fifties three of the four tobacco factories of the town were bought by a state-controlled agency. The party boss, as previously remarked, knew most of the directors of the factories and it was therefore easy for him to influence the placement policy of the industry; he claims that between 1954 and 1959 he placed more than 600 workers in those factories.[64]

Rota could finally have recourse to a third fundamental resource, namely his Rome party connections. He was and presumably still is a friend of one of the national leaders of the DC. He claims, for instance, that he obtained the funds for a new elementary school directly from Mr. Emilio Colombo. In general, his connections allowed him to intervene in all sorts of informal arrangements whereby local people could obtain through his mediation the intervention of powerful political figures in Rome for the solution of their personal problems.

The party boss used these resources to buy votes. In contrast to the industrialist who as a notable enjoyed a more or less "spontaneous" support, he was a politician who had to build electoral backing in an increasingly competitive political setting. It seems to me that the sort of transformation in the outlook of simple people described by F. G. Bailey with reference to Orissa electors[65] has occurred in our town.

The elector feels that he need not ask simply for mercy as was the case when political competition was non-existent, but that he has now an electoral power he may use to establish predominantly contractual relations with the boss. The latter in his turn has perfectly adapted his political style to the new competitive situation. The industrialist used to receive homage from a population which had largely internalized a deferential attitude; the party boss on the contrary toured the different quarters of the town and almost literally lived in the streets, ready to help out the poor worker who had an ill daughter, the unemployed with huge families, and needy people in general, for whom he used to organize impressive Christmas banquets to which the Bishop was invited. He thus created around him a network of people whom he could help and of course blackmail at the right time—as was, and still is, the case for many DC town councillors who are financially dependent on him.

To establish himself, Rota needed an instrument which in 1954 was almost unknown in the town, namely the political party. He needed it because as a newcomer he could not fight the leadership of Amabile on a man-to-man basis. He had to balance the latter's economic power and traditional legitimacy with a new organized political power capable of giving him a modern legitimacy. The town people had to understand, he told the interviewer, that what was being done was possible because he, the party boss, was the local representative of a powerful national organization. On the other hand, it was precisely in the context of the party that Rota, relying on his superior capacities and connections, was able to politically liquidate his ally-opponent, Amabile. By 1959 he was powerful enough to lead alone the DC to a remarkable electoral success and become mayor.

By 1960 his municipal power was unchallenged, but such a power rested on the precarious basis of an extensive patronage. As the party boss himself admits, by that time the town hall had become a sort of "charity institution." He decided then to "depersonalize the function of mayor" essentially by sending the postulants to the Catholic trade union. The result was that the same conception of politics was transferred from the mayoralty to at least one of the unions which, being directed at the time by a man very sensitive to this particularistic approach to politics, became part of the clientelistic machine. It is known for instance that this union leader used to impose a fee for the services rendered by the union, an illegal practice he shared with other local union leaders.

The party boss's rise to power in the town I studied was the local version of a process of change of leadership which took place throughout the South. Let us examine why and how this change came about.[66] In the process of formation of the present Italian political and economic systems (1948-1952), the Christian Democrats were subject to two fundamental and interdependent limiting conditions: (1) political and economic integration in the international system of the West; and (2) "freezing" of the internal left-wing opposition (socialists and communists).

The dramatic worsening of the international situation in 1947-48 meant that the building of the new political and economic systems had to be done as quickly and with as little trauma as possible. In the South, where a politically characterized Catholic subculture never existed, the DC had to establish its power from nothing. Thus lacking the time, and probably also the political will, to build new bases of power in the South, the DC relied on the already existing network of traditional clientele. In a sense, the tobacco entrepreneur we met before, a man whose power was rooted in "industrial paternalism"[67] and who was royalist in 1946 before becoming a Christian Democrat in 1948, well represents the process of absorption of influential people practised by the DC in the South.

In 1954 the then political secretary of the DC Fanfani launched the idea of the DC as a mass party. Fanfani's design was meant to free the DC from some very powerful pressure groups (Church, Italian Confederation of Industry, etc.) which could weigh heavily on the party in a period of ministerial instability (such as the one which followed the 1953 political elections). In the South this plan implied that the party be freed from local notables. Be it noted that many of the latter were already disenchanted with the DC for its policy of agrarian reform.[68] The financial means necessary to realize such a design of party autonomy were provided by the great expansion of state economic intervention in the South after 1950.

A mass party implies the capacity for the party leadership to directly reach the "base" of the organization and to mobilize it. In order to bypass the old notables, Fanfani created the Office for the Political and Organizational Development of the Depressed Areas (known as *Ufficio Z.D.*). The aim of the Office was, in Fanfani's words, to transform the party members "from passive recipients of more or less appreciated favors into people who selfconsciously seek projects that will lift them out of their extraordinary depression".[69]

Fanfani succeeded in defeating the old clientele but the DC became less of a mass party than a party of mass patronage. Why? Fanfani sent functionaries from the *Ufficio Z.D.* all over the South to create antinotable factions. The party bureaucracy was amply renovated, particularly in the secretariats of the provincial federations. There was an obvious danger in such a development: that in the process of eliminating an old network of intermediaries, a new network would come into being. The danger was not small when one considers that most of the new local DC personnel was tied up with, or was originally involved in the state developmental projects and could therefore influence the allocation of important public resources.

Such a danger could be avoided only by mobilizing the members of the party, that is by devising a *political* and not a purely *organizational* strategy. In the historical conditions of the South, this meant the adoption of a series of economic and social reforms capable of putting an end to the emargination of the Southern rural masses. The DC chose otherwise. At least starting from 1955, the party addressed itself less and less to the workers and the peasants and increasingly to the middle class. In that year, Fanfani said that the DC must give the middle class of the South "a new force to assume willingly the function of pilot of Southern Italian society".[70] Such a political option, together with the organizational developments made necessary by the anti-notable campaign, had a profound influence both on the nature of the new DC and on the Southern political system.

The new peripheral leadership of the DC, which was supposed to have been disciplined by a centralized mass party, became on the contrary increasingly autonomous in the performance of its mediating function between the central state power and the middle class. This mediation could not but be clientelistic once any "project" of social transformation of the South had been abandoned. Such a development towards party-directed patronage was inevitable since, "as political power shifts from prestigious individuals to party organizations without a corresponding rise in political ideology, patronage must take the place of personal loyalty as the basis of affiliation".[71] Not only the power structure of the DC remained dispersed and decentralized; by the very option made in favor of the middle class as the main social basis for that structure, the DC acquired a political interest in the expansion of "paleo-capitalistic" activities which would give such a class a chance to develop.[72]

What then is the structure of the new clientele? As Tarrow has observed, its fundamental and specific characteristic is the following one: the role of great electors is now essentially performed by secondary associations which the party has been able to "capture".[73] The role of the notable has not disappeared, but the politicians of the party in power rely above all on such organizations as trade unions, youth movements, professional groups and the like. Tarrow refers to the new clienteles as "horizontal clienteles". I will devote the concluding remarks of this arti-cle to the impact which the clientelistic system has on the functioning and structure of such associations.

In many cases, the "capture" of the voluntary groups by the party implies for the former the abandonment of their institutional aims. This is particularly the case for those organizations which represent interests potentially antagonistic to the interests of the party, such as the trade unions and other workers' associations. Following are some examples drawn from Tarrow's work. An informant is reported to have said that "In the South, where the new working class is emerging, the ACLI, constituted to aid in the formation of a working class conscience, operates mainly as a center of patronage". Another informant deems that "the CISL in the South is essentially a clientele system dependent upon state industry".[74]

Such cases are important not only in themselves, but because they illustrate a general point which applies to *all* secondary associations operating in a clientelistic context: *any clientelistic system undermines the autonomy of social groups and their organizations and tends to absorb them in a political game directed by the groups in power.* We must understand why and how this happens. The need to "capture" the organized social forces derives from the necessity to control conflict in societies where conflicts are potentially explosive. Whenever a new actor appears in the political market of the South and is provided with a sufficiently threatening bargaining power, the ruling party has the instinctive reaction of a monopolist: first it tries to intimidate the newcomer and if unsuccessful to corrupt him.[75] The possibility of a free confrontation is something which is foreign to the culture of a "particularistic" leader and which is above all too threatening for his totalitarian power.

How does the absorption occur? In a particularistic culture and organization of power it occurs through dyadic contacts established between the various group leaders on one hand and the power holders on the other. Typically a "captured" trade union leader instead of waging social struggles on behalf of the union members operates through his personal contacts with other leaders; as a result he provides his associates with services of a particularistic rather than a categorical nature. Hence the structuring of the relationships within the trade union in a hierarchical, dyadic way with the leader in the traditional position of "gatekeeper". The secondary group is formally categorical, but everybody is aware that what matters are special connections with the group leader.

In a society where non-particularistic attitudes are difficult to conceive and where men of power have always been seen as engaged in a common conspiracy against the subordinate, the new clientele system has surely destructive effects. I witnessed myself the *enormous distrust* felt by the workers towards their union leaders in the town I studied. Collective action which has always been supremely difficult in the South, is not made any easier. In brief, lack of effective organized action discourages the emergence of categorical groups; people who share an objective interest and may even be conscious of it, feel forced to act through the age-old channels of dyadic communications.

From a comparative perspective, we may say that the problem of political communication and organization we witness in Southern Italy is not very different from the one studied by F. G. Bailey in Orissa.[76] We are confronted with two kinds of particularism: individualistic in the case of Italy, corporative in India. In either case particularism makes the communication between the elite and the masses extremely difficult. In Orissa relations with people from outside the village have not yet acquired "legitimacy". The link must be made by a "man of the world", but a "man of the world" loses *ipso facto* the confidence of the villagers. In the South, politics is understood as a process free of violence, intimidation and corruption, lacks "credibility" for the good reason that it has never been practised. The development of the Southern society has indeed made some forms of collective action indispensable, but the clientelistic context forces the group to pursue such an action through leaders—brokers who, by their particularistic behavior, undermine the trust of the group members.

Furthermore, secondary associations "captured" by powerful patrons perform the interest articulation function quite inefficiently. We may say that these associations perform such a function in the same way as non-associational interest groups (in Almond's terms). This is so because such associations: (1) do not explicitly represent categorical interests, but only unprocessed particularistic claims of single people; (2) there are no "orderly procedures for the formulation of interest and demands", but rather competition among informal groups which try

to "push through" their claims; and (3) these claims are transmitted in not aggregate form to single deputies, bureaucrats, etc., rather than to the bureaucratic structures they belong to.[77]

It follows from Almond's scheme that in clientelistic politics the boundary maintenance between the polity and the society is rather poor. We may qualify this statement by adding that such a boundary is very unevenly maintained: the totalitarian nature of clientelistic politics implies that while many people are excluded from the political system, others reach into it directly. This is so because the rule of the game is what the Spanish call *enchufe* and the Southern Italian peasants in a more graphic way *la maniglia* (the *handle* to open powerful doors). In a particularistic system, participation is, as Di Palma says, a very rare and valuable currency. The whole system hinges on the preservation of "gatekeepers" roles and in fact implies a necessary crystallization of these roles.

Such a system has to exclude large numbers of people not only for its "organizational" logics, but because it implies a very expensive method of mobilization. James C. Scott[78] among others has underlined its *inflationary* consequences. This in turn derives from the fact that in clientelism, as well as in machine politics, the "machine element" prevails over the "movement element".[79] Everybody expects to obtain material rewards and after a while, the market runs out of goods.

The parallel between clientelism and machine politics suggests a final remark. A process of bargaining which may have worked, if it has worked, in a more consensual society and in the context of an expanding economy, may be highly destructive where these conditions do not prevail. In the first case the bargaining may integrate new groups in the social and political systems without undermining their autonomy. In Italy, the clienteles have persisted for so long, have been so exclusivistic in the exercise of their power and have relied so much on the protection of the state, that the resulting bargaining has caused a further devitalization of society. Politically, they have served less as an introduction to pluralist democracy than as a means of fostering a system of government fundamentally opposed to the democratic process.

NOTES

*This is a revised version of a paper delivered at the 1972 Annual Meeting of the American Political Science Association, Washington, D. C., September 5-9. Copyright 1972 A.P.S.A.

1 Pasquale, Turiello, *Governo e governati in Italia*. Vol. 1. Bologna: Zanichelli, 1882, p. 97 (my translation).

2 Cf. Joseph La Palombara, *Interest Groups in*

Italian Politics. Princeton University Press, 1964, ch. IX. As defined by La Palombara, *parentela* involves a "relatively close and integral relationship between certain associational interest groups and the politically dominant party", La Palombara, p. 306. Such a relationship makes possible a highly partisan and effective interest group intervention in the bureaucracy and influences the very structure of that bureaucracy.

3 Giuseppe Di Palma, *Apathy and Participation. Mass Politics in Western Societies*. New York: The Free Press, 1970. Di Palma relates the *instrumental* and *sporadic* character of political participation prevailing in Italy to the particularism of Italian politics. He writes that in Italy "persons may participate because they want a personal benefit or need to maintain positions of privilege or administrative protection, not because they feel committed to politics as citizens participating with other citizens". In "modern societies" participation implies a general "act of allegiance to the polity"; in Italy participation is a "very valuable currency" used by relatively few people to ensure that an unpredictable and ineffective polity delivers the goods they want. Di Palma, pp. 202, 13.

4 A policy (law, administrative act, political platform) may be said to be particularistic "when it advocates treatment for specific subjects that does not fall within the general rules established for the category to which the subjects belong". Di Palma, p. 13. The contrary of particularistic is categorical.

5 On the distinction between patron-client tie and party-directed patronage, cf. Alex Weingrod: "Patrons, Patronage and Political Parties", *Comparative Studies in Society and History* (July 1968). A definition of the patron-client relationship mainly based on the anthropological literature is: James C. Scott; "Patron-Client Politics and Political Change in Southeast Asia." *American Political Science Review* (March 1972). Scott writes: "The patron-client relationship—an exchange relationship between roles—may be defined as a special case of dyadic (two person) ties involving a largely instrumental friendship in which an individual of higher socio-economic status (patron) uses his own influence and resources to provide protection and/or benefits for a person of lower status (client) who, for his part, reciprocates by offering general support and assistance, including personal services, to the patron".

For a discussion of the dyadic model of social interaction see G. Foster, "The Dyadic Contract in Tzintzuntzan: Patron-Client Relations", *American Anthropologist* 65 (1963), 1280-1294.

6 Jane C. Schneider, "Patron and Client in the Italian Political System". Ph.D. dissertation, University of Michigan, 1965 (microfilm). Jane C. Schneider writes that in the South "even in the presence of state-created wider, modern institutions . . . an 'upward circulation' of patterns of social relations" has prevailed over the "rationalizing 'downward circulation' due to the influence of the State". She adds that the same concept of 'upward circulation' can be aptly applied to the entire Italian political development, which Schneider considers as "the outcome of a 'plug in'

configuration in which the 'wider institutions' began to look more like networks of intermediaries than the other way around".

7 So far in the literature on clientelism, anthropologists have mainly focussed on the social structure and above all, on *culture*, political scientists on variables linked to the political system. For instance, Michael Kenny in his macro-sociological study on the Castiles, indicates four "theoretical bases" of the clientelistic system: (1) "a sense of kinship, either real or fictive" (the "most important" basis); (2) the religious element; (3) the emotional satisfaction derived from giving and receiving support; and (4) the real sense of the obligation to give, receive and return. M. Kenny, "Patterns of patronage in Spain", *The Anthropological Quarterly* 33 (January 1960).

Eric R. Wolf focuses on two factors favoring the development of dyadic relationships: (1) relative freedom of the individual from ties of corporative solidarity (family, village) and sufficient openness of kinship and friendship relationships; and (2) "weak formal institutional structure of society and its capacity to deliver a sufficiently steady supply of goods and services, especially to the lower levels of the social order". Eric R. Wolf, "Kinship, Friendship, and Patron-Client Relations". In Michael Banton, ed., *The Social Anthropology of Complex Societies*. New York: F. A. Praeger 1966.

J. Boissevain characteristically concludes his study of patronage in Sicily writing: "Patronage is to a very large extent a self-perpetuating system of belief and action grounded in the society's value system". Jeremy Boissevain, "Patronage in Sicily", *Man* 1 (March 1966).

All the anthropologists who have studied patronage in Catholic countries or among Catholic minorities (for instance the Italian-Americans studied by W. Foote Whyte) insist on the legitimizing role of religion (the Virgin as "the closest relative of the Big Boss", saints as patrons, etc.).

Among the political scientists, A. Weingrod (1968) focuses on the social and economic role of the state and the "bridging" function of political parties. James C. Scott indicates four conditions favorable to patronage in the new nations: (1) heterogeneous composition of political parties and (2) of the population; (3) lack of government legitimacy; and (4) size of governmental economic role. James C. Scott, "Corruption, Machine Politics and Political Change", *APSR* (December 1969). Among the few scholars who have concentrated on the economic structure of society, I would mention: Sydel F. Silverman, "Patronage and Community—Nation Relationships in Central Italy", *Ethnology* IV (1965); and "Exploitation in Rural Central Italy: Structure and Ideology in Stratification Study", *Comparative Studies in Society and History* 12: 3(July 1970).

The latter article focuses on the crisis of the complex social relationship linking *mezzadri* to landowners during a stage of greater penetration of the national market and growing influence of the state. On the impact of the capitalistic market on a society characterized by an enclave economy, absence of effective bureaucratic and legal control and lack of interpersonal trust, see Peter T. Schneider, "Friends of Friends: Coalition Formation and Colonialism in Western Sicily", unpublished paper.

8 Sydel F. Silverman. "Agricultural Organization, Social Structure and Values in Italy: Amoral Familism Reconsidered", *American Anthropologist* 70 (February 1968).

9 See for instance Myron Weiner, *The Politics of Scarcity*. Chicago: University of Chicago Press, 1962, particularly Almond's preface.

10 In contrasting particularistic and categorical types of groups, we refer to analytical constructs which are polar opposites. For a systematic treatment of dyadic vs. pressure group politics see Carl H. Landé, "Networks and Groups in Southeast Asia: Some Observations on the Group Theory of Politics". Paper delivered at the 1971 Annual Meeting of the APSA, Chicago, Sept.

Empirically, particularistic and categorical types of attitudes are always mixed, as G. A. Almond has pointed out. G. A. Almond, "A Functional Approach to Comparative Politics". In G. A. Almond and J. A. Coleman, eds., *The Politics of the Developing Areas*. Princeton University Press, 1970(pbk edition). See particularly the section on the culturally mixed character of political systems, pp. 20-25.

11 Kenny, 1960.

12 In the Bentleyan school of thought, the concept of interest has a purely subjective status, while in Marxian analysis interest has a subjective as well as an objective dimension. Isaac D. Balbus, "The Concept of Interest in Pluralist and Marxian Analysis", *Politics and Society* 1:2 (February 1971), 151-177. Balbus convincingly demonstrates the heuristic and normative advantage of the Marxian concept of interest, especially for understanding social change.

13 On all these points see: Schlomo Avineri, *The Social and Political Thought of Karl Marx*. Cambridge University Press, 1970, particularly pp. 162-174 (The Universality of Capitalism). Marx wrote in the Manifesto: "The bourgeoisie, wherever it has got the upper hand, has put an end to all feudal, patriarchal, idyllic relations. It has pitilessly torn asunder the motley feudal ties that bound man to his 'natural superiors', and has left remaining no other nexus between man and man than naked self-interest, than callous 'cash payment' " (quoted by Avineri, p. 162).

14 The most extensive study on capitalism in the South is Emilio Sereni, *Il capitalismo nelle campagne*, Einaudi: Torino, 1947 (pbk edition 1968). In this section, we will draw heavily on Sereni. All references are from the 1968 edition.

15 The text of the Neopolitan law of 1806 is to be found in G. de Rosa and A. Cestaro, eds., *La questione meridionale. Antologia di scritti de documenti*. Napoli: Ferraro, 1970, pp. 119-122. In Sicily the formal abolition of feudalism occurred in 1812. In both cases, the change was brought about by foreign agents, by Giuseppe Bonaparte and Gioacchino Murat in Naples, under pressure from the British government in Sicily.

16 The classical study on the *questione demaniale*

is by Giustino Fortunato, "La questione de maniale nell' Italia meridionale" (1879), reprinted in de Rosa and Cestaro, pp. 157-174. Cf. Sereni, *passim*.

17 According to Sereni, in 1860, out of 600,000 hectares of ex-baronial land until then attributed to the communes, only 205,000 ha. had been assigned. For a detailed study of the methods of usurpation and the endless legal disputes originated by the division of *demanio communale*, see Leopoldo Cassese, "Una lega di resistenza di contadini nel 1860 e la questione demaniale in un comune del Salernitano". In L. Cassesse, *Scritti di storia meridionale*. Salerno: Laveglia Editore, 1970, pp. 303-355.

18 Fortunato, p. 167.

19 Turiello, pp. 311-312. Rosario Villari has remarked that the Italian South is possibly the only area in Western Europe where bourgeois and middle class property has never been accepted as an "accomplished and definitive fact". Hence the "anachronistic" character of land struggles in the South. Rosario Villari, *Il sud nella storia d'Italia*, Bari: Laterza, 1966, vol. 1, p. 161.

20 The land of *manomorta* represented great wealth; Sereni calculates that around 1860-1870, at least one-sixth of all Italian land belonged to *manomorta*. Sereni, p. 136.

21 The changes in land ownership which occurred in the South can be exemplified by the changes which took place in the Roman countryside:

	1870	About 1900
Property of nobles	55%	53%
Manomorta	30%	7%
Bourgeois and middle class property	15%	40%

These figures are considered by Sereni as "fairly representative for all Southern Italy". Sereni, p. 144.

22 On anti-clericalism as the only unifying element of the Southern ruling class cf. Luigi Sturzo, "Il Mezzogiorno e la politica italiana". In de Rosa and Cestaro, *La questione meridionale*, pp. 235-291.

23 Sereni, p. 145.

24 Sereni, pp. 148-149.

25 Sereni, pp. 148-149.

26 On the close relationship between Mafia and the middle class, see Francesco Saverio Romano, *Storia della mafia*. Verona: Mondadori, 1966, and Leopoldo Franchetti, *La Scicilia nel 1876, condizioni politiche e amministrative*. Firenze: G. Barbera, 1877.

On Mafia as a popular and national (Sicilian) movement which radically changed character under the impact of capitalistic relationships, see Eric J. Hobsbawn, *Primitive Rebels: Studies in Archaic Forms of Social Movements in the 19th and 20th Centuries*. New York: Praeger, 1959.

On the Sicilian middle class, see Gaetano Mosca, *Partiti e sindacati nella crisi del regime parlamentare*. Bari: Laterza, 1949 (particularly the section *Uomini e cose di Sicilia*).

27 Within the Sicilian *feudo*, the two typical contracts were *terratico* and *metateria*. In both cases the

rent was paid in kind, generally in wheat; the quantity of wheat depended on the amount of land cultivated (*terratico*), or was in proportion to the harvest (two-thirds in the *metateria*).

28 Examples of *diritti angarici* imposed on the peasants are: *diritto di messa* (a tax paid to the priest who went to the *feudo* to celebrate mass); *diritto di cuccia e del maccherone* (the right of the *campiere* to be housed and nourished by the peasant); and *jus primae noctis*.

29 See Pasquale Villari, *La Sicilia e il socialismo*. Milano: Treves, 1896, p. 69. An even worse kind of usury was practised in the sulphur mines. Villari, pp. 13-54.

On usury, Turiello wrote: "Usury may be called the natural industry of a man inclined to fight against another man, while on the contrary true industry requires a disposition . . . to trust and cooperate among many". Turiello, p. 223.

30 For similar attitudes of the Orissa peasant in India, see F. G. Bailey, "The Peasant View of a Bad Life", *The Advancement of Science* 23 (December 1966).

In a very different context, Michel Crozier has remarked that when the exercise of power is unrestrained by some notion of a collective interest, bargaining becomes too destructive for the system. In such cases, "La négotiation est niée au profit de la morale. . . . A travers la discussion morale, s'exercent pressions et contre-pressions; on parle de juste salaire et de nécessaires prerogatives du chef". Michel Crozier, La societé bloquée. Paris: Editions du Seuil, 1970, p. 41.

31 On the notion of inequality of reciprocity see Alvin Gouldner, "The Norm of Reciprocity: A Preliminary Statement", *American Sociological Review* 25:6 (1960) Gouldner sees reciprocity as an exchange of benefits which are in principle quantitatively measurable.

On the possibility of giving an objective definition of exploitation see Barrington Moore, Jr. *Social Origins of Dictatorship and Democracy*. Boston: Beacon Press, 1966, ch. IX.

32 For a useful conceptualization of the dimensions of variation in patron-client ties, see Scott, "Patron-Client Politics and Political Change in Southeast Asia".

33 Turiello, pp. 244-245.

34 Sereni, p. 163.

35 Turiello, p. 148.

36 Antonio Gramsci, "Alcuni temi della quistione meridionale". In A. Gramsci, *La quistione meridionale*. Roma: Editori Riuniti, 1970, p. 152. English translation in A. Gramsci, *The Modern Prince*. New York: International Publishers, 1958, pp. 28-51. (The English version of the quoted passage is from the latter book, p. 44.)

37 A detailed account of the abuses committed by local administrators is in Turiello, *passim* and Franchetti, *passim*.

38 Turiello, p. 355.

39 It is reasonable to suppose that many subordinate people felt like the peasant who reportedly said: "Under Franceschiello (the last Bourbon king) poor people were better off. The new (king) came and was called Re Galantuomo because the *galantuomini* chose him as a king for themselves. Now the Commune is theirs: they rent the (communal) woodlands among themselves, while before all of us could use them freely and now watch out if you sneak a bit of wood". Quoted by Turiello, p. 362.

40 On *brigantaggio*, *camorra*, *mafia* and *clientela* as "different forms of the same phenomenon"—namely the lack of discipline of private interests—see Turiello, p. 181.

41 Franchetti, *passim*.

42 The dependence of local clientele on governmental power accounts for the link between Southern political clientelism and authoritarianism. In moments of crises, the first instinct of the Southern ruling class has been to ask for a strong national government. This was the case for instance in 1898-1900 as well as in 1920-1922. See Villari, particularly pp. 312-313. On the close link between the Southern question and the centralized structure of the Italian State, see Ernesto Ragionieri, *Politica e amministrazione nella storia dell' Italia unita*. Bari: Laterza, 1967; and Roberto Ruffilli, *La questione regionale*. Milano: Giuffre, 1971.

43 Turiello, p. 237 onward.

44 Gaetano Mosca, *Teorica dei governi e governo parlamentare*. Milano: Istituto Editoriale Scientifico, 1925, pp. 252-256.

45 Mosca, p. 256.

46 Mosca, p. 178. Mosca underlines the "bureaucratic irresponsibility" of the functionaries who were "pure instruments" in the hands of their ministers (pp. 168-189).

47 Mosca remarks that thousands of jobs in the public administration, the distribution of public works, the terms of public contracts, the granting of honors, etc., became part of a gigantic market. Ultimately *all* the functions of the state were performed in a discriminatory way, including the administration of justice, taxation and the national service (Mosca, pp. 164-165).

48 The classical study on the manipulation of elections by the executive power is Gaetano Salvemini, *Il ministro della mala vita*. Originally published in 1911 and reprinted in G. Salvemini, *Il ministro della mala vita* (E. Apih, ed.), Milano: Feltrinelli 1962.

See also Mosca, pp. 196-198. Mosca considered the electoral role of the prefect beneficial. Since in his opinion the deputy was imposed at any rate by a small minority, it was better that "such imposition comes from the central authority rather than from a local clique, which often may be composed by a small number of *camorristi*" (p. 197).

49 Mosca, p. 252.

50 Mosca, p. 252.

51 Turiello, p. 304.

52 The occupational structure of the community I investigated evolved in the following way:

Branches of activity	1951	1961
Agriculture	48.5*	37
Industry	31.0	37
Tertiary activities	20.5	26

*As a percentage of the active population aged 10 or older. The figures are drawn from the nationwide censuses held in 1951 and 1961. The figures of the 1971 census were not yet known at the time of writing.

53 Leopoldo Cassese underlines the impact of such a geographical fragmentation of the Salerno province on the mutual estrangement of peasants (*cafoni*) and city-dwellers. L. Cassese, "Contadini e operai del Salernitarno nei moti del Quarantotto". In L. Cassese, *Scritti di storia meridionale*, pp. 189-269. Cassese is the best historian of the peasants of the Salerno area and this study of his is a very good analysis of the social structure of the Salernitano in the nineteenth century.

54 Interview, Paestum, April 23, 1972.

55 In order to preserve his monopolistic position as an intermediary, the busses provided by the *caporali* would often take different roads to get to work in order to confuse the laborer so that he could not get in touch directly with a prospective employer.

56 On the relation between *caporalato* and the capitalistic development of agriculture, see G. Accardi, G. Mottura and E. Pugliese, "Braccianti, sindacato e mercato del lavoro agricolo", *Rassegna Italiana di Sociologia* 12:1(1971).

57 The division of *demanio comunale* seems to have followed (in the Salerno area) the pattern we have delineated. For instance, Fortunato (p. 169) remarked that the division of the very large *demanio* of Eboli, an important town of the Sele plain, had resulted in the creation of "two or three of the biggest owners of latifundia of the Salerno plain". Cassese writes that the bourgeois' attitude towards the countryside was "absenteeistic and aristocratic", while he considered industry as the "field of activity for reckless people". Cassese also underlines the subordinate position of the local bourgeoisie *vis-à-vis* the foreign (mainly Swiss) capitalists who created the bases of the Salerno industry in the 1830's. See Leopoldo Cassese, "Contadini e operai del Salernitano nei moti del Quarantotto", pp. 196-197.
On the link between traditional social relationships in the South and entrepreneurship, see Svimez, *Sviluppo industriale e imprenditori locali*. Giuffré: Roma, 1962. This work results from a research conducted by Alessandro Pizzorno and Salvatore Cafiero.

58 The point can be illustrated by the following episode. An agricultural entrepreneur asked his peasants: Which of the cows of the farm are in your opinion the best ones? *They are all yours*, was their answer. Interview, Paestum, April 23, 1972.

59 Same interview.

60 The Sele plain began to be freed from malaria only in the second half of the nineteenth century. This explains the very recent creation of the town I studied as an autonomous commune.

61 The tomato and tobacco industries have this in common—they are both seasonal. In the former industry, for instance, the average ratio between full-time and seasonal workers is 1 to 20. The resulting weakness of the occupational structure in the town allowed ample space for clientelistic pressures on the workers.

62 I use the term 'boss' in the sense specified by James C. Scott; that is, as a local leader who "is the most powerful man in the arena" and whose power "rests more on the inducements and sanctions at his disposal than on affection or status". The boss must rely on palpable inducements and threats because he lacks the traditional legitimacy of the notable. See Scott, "Patron-Client Politics and Political Change in Southeast Asia".

63 This is equally true of the Socialist Party (PSI). In 1962, when the Center-Left coalition government became a concrete possibility at the national level, the local socialist leader refused to follow his party's directives, arguing that an alliance with such a hated man as the local DC boss would have been suicidal. At the administrative elections which took place in 1962, the PSI lost 2,000 votes, while the independent list formed and headed by the dissident leader obtained 2,400 votes.

64 Interview, Pontecagnano, 13 and 18 November 1970.

65 Bailey, "The Peasant View of a Bad Life".

66 In the analysis which follows, I draw heavily on a talk given by Prof. Alessandro Pizzorno at the Casa della Cultura in Milan, March 18, 1972.

67 On "Industrial paternalism" see John W. Bennett, "Paternalism" in *International Encyclopedia of the Social Sciences*.

68 See Sidney Tarrow, *Peasant Communism in Southern Italy*. New Haven: Yale University Press, 1967, pp. 306-307.

69 Quoted by Tarrow, p. 309.

70 Tarrow, p. 311.

71 Tarrow, p. 325.

72 Pizzorno in the cited talk.

73 Tarrow, p. 332 onward.

74 Tarrow, p. 332 onward.

75 This is what happened to the Communist lawyer sent by the PCI to organize the party to the town I studied. The DC boss first tried to persuade him to give it up by threatening the clients who would have recourse to his legal services; then, the Communist leader was offered an attractive bank job in Salerno. According to this leader, the amount of pressure put on an opposition politician in the South is such that it makes it very difficult for a professional man to resist. As a result, he underlines the necessity for professionalizing the politician in order to allow him some political autonomy. In the particular case, the lawyer was able to stand the sudden decrease in the number of his professional clients by becoming a legal consultant to the Communist-dominated trade union in Salerno. Interview, Pontecagnano, 9 December 1970.

76 F. G. Bailey, *Politics and Social Change: Orissa in 1959*. Los Angeles: University of California Press, 1963.

77 Almond and Coleman, *The Politics of the Developing Areas*, pp. 34-35.

78 Scott, "Corruption, Machine Politics and Political Change".
See also on the inflationary consequences of party-directed patronage: Francine R. Frankel, "Democracy and Political Development: Perspectives from India", *World Politics* 21:3 (April 1969); and Martin

Kilson, *Political Change in a West African State*. Cambridge, Mass.: Harvard University Press, 1967.

In delineating a "reciprocity model of African politics", Kilson links the "bankruptcy determined by the implementation of the "reciprocity principle" to the "authoritarianism" of African leaders who increasingly have recourse to "administrative graft" for their political needs.

On the cost of the politics of patronage practised by the Congress Party in Calcutta see Myron Weiner, *Party Building in a New Nation: the Indian National Congress* (University of Chicago Press, 1967), pp. 368-370.

For an interesting discussion of some of the dysfunctional consequences of clientelism on development cf. René Lemarchand and Keith Legg, "Political Clientelism and Development: A Preliminary Analysis", *Comparative Politics* 4:2 (January 1972).

79 On movements and machines see Bailey, *Politics and Social Change*.

JAPANESE POLITICAL CULTURE
AND DEMOCRACY

NOBUTAKA IKE

MOST OF THE TIME, politics involves collective action on the part of numerous individuals. What makes such collective action possible is political culture, which Sidney Verba has defined as "the system of empirical beliefs, expressive symbols and values which defines the situation in which political action takes place."[1] Stated in another way, political culture has to do with psychological variables, that is, with the attitudes and orientations of individuals toward politics. These attitudes and orientations are widely shared because they are learned through transmission from one generation to another, through the family, schools, the mass media—in short, through the socialization process. Since these attitudes are shared, individuals, when stimulated by political symbols, personalities or events, are led to participate in joint or reciprocal action.

One would expect that in stable societies the political culture would change rather slowly. By contrast, in revolutionary situations, there are likely to be drastic transformations in political culture that will often be purposefully induced by the ruling elite. In the case of Japan we do not have, of course, a revolutionary situation, but still there has been a certain amount of discontinuity occasioned by the innovations, particularly in the institutional structure (see Chapter 3), imposed by the Occupation forces after 1945. The main thrust of Occupation policy was to encourage more individualistic beliefs and behavior. While it cannot be denied that the Occupation did leave its mark and that more recent social change has also helped to modify Japanese political culture, the surprising thing is that the magnitude of change has remained remarkably small. As we have suggested in the previous chapter, in political culture as in many other areas, modernity has not swept away tradition.

TRADITION VS. MODERNITY

What do we mean by tradition and by modernity in political culture? In the present context, tradition refers to social values that have been handed down from the past. Specifically, it is the expectation that the individual will be subordinated to the group, whether it be the family, village, work gang, business firm, or club. Subordination implies that an individual's norms will be congruent with those of the group, that he will work for the good of his group, and that he will be loyal to it. By contrast, modernity suggests a more autonomous person. This does not mean that he is antisocial, but rather that he thinks for himself, that he makes "rational" choices among alternative courses of social action, that he is not compulsively submissive to political authority.

Some empirical data on Japanese attitudes related to tradition and modernity are available. One important source is the nationwide survey on national character carried out by the Institute of Mathematical Statistics in Tokyo at five-year intervals beginning in 1953. These surveys contained a battery of questions designed to get at the problem of tradition versus modernity. The findings indicate that over the years there has been a gradual but nevertheless persistent shift in attitudes in the direction of modernity. But although there were a number of questions that elicited agreement from the majority of respondents, relatively few individuals (a little more than 10 percent) agreed consistently with all these questions. That is, on some questions indi-

TABLE 1

Reply		U.S.	Japan
1. Help select a possible mate and serve as a go-between		2%	6%
2. Offer personal advice to the worker if requested		29%	70%
3. Merely present a small gift from the company		9%	19%
4. Not be involved in such a personal matter		60%	5%

Source: Arthur Whitehill, Jr., and Shin-ichi Takezawa, *The Other Worker* (Honolulu: East-West Center Press, 1968), p. 171. Reprinted by permission of the publisher.

viduals belonged with the majority, but on others they did not. Stated another way, there were certain attitudes that may be considered to be typically Japanese, but there were only a small percentage of typically Japanese individuals. This suggests the likelihood that relatively few individuals are consistently traditional or modern in their attitudes; rather, each person represents a varying mixture of traditional and modern views.

It is, however, possible to generalize as to who is likely to be more modern. Education appears to exert a powerful influence. That this should be so is not altogether surprising; education usually makes people more skeptical, critical, and independent. Educated people are less likely to submit themselves to the pull of social conformity. But even education has not succeeded in removing the traditional penchant for paternalism and the dependency it implies. One of the questions asked in the survey had to do with attitudes toward one's work supervisor.

Let us assume that there are two types of section chiefs; if you were to work under one of them, which one (of the following) would you prefer?
1. He does not make unreasonable demands that violate work rules, but he does not look after you in matters that do not pertain to your work.
2. Sometimes he makes unreasonable demands that violate work rules, but he looks after you even in matters that have nothing to do with your work.

More than 70 percent of those questioned preferred the supervisor who, although a hard taskmaster, was willing to look after one's personal and other non-work-related needs. Moreover, response to this question has varied little over the fifteen-year span covered by the surveys. Equally interesting, the response is remarkably uniform, whether the person giving the answer is young or old, uneducated or educated, worker or professional. In short, age, education, and occupation, which are important variables when it comes to other questions, appear to have little effect.

Table 1 shows the results of another study that probed attitudes of both American and Japanese industrial workers. The question was: "When a worker wishes to marry, I think his (her) superior should _____." As can be seen, the majority of American workers in the sample did not wish their supervisors to be involved in their personal lives, whereas the majority of Japanese workers did. The evidence again suggests that many Japanese prefer paternalistic, diffuse, all-embracing relationships—in other words, patron-client relationships.

ATTITUDES TOWARD AUTHORITY

What effect, if any, does preference for paternalism have on attitudes toward politics? Here it is not possible to give a simple, clear-cut answer. A logical extension of patron-client relationships into the larger political setting would be rule by a strong man, a kind of benevolent dictator. But it is evident that the Japanese have avoided rule by a strong man and have preferred to operate through groups. The national character surveys cited above have tried to measure sentiment toward one-man rule. They have asked this question: "There is this view: Let us say we want to make Japan a better country, and if an outstanding political leader appeared, it would be better to leave everything up to him rather than for the people to debate among themselves." The percentage of those approving this statement has declined from 43 percent in 1953 to 30 percent in 1968, while the number of those disapproving it has risen from 38 percent in 1953 to 51 percent in 1968.[2]

There would appear to be a fundamental consensus that the government in power must periodically appeal to the electorate for confirmation of its privilege to continue in office. There are numerous examples of countries in the so-called Third World in which the leader will declare that he intends to keep his office for life, or in which tanks roll in the streets to signal a change in government. This sort of thing has not occurred in Japan since 1945, and it is hard to imagine it happening—an observation that seems to attest to the existence of a consensus in favor of democratic rules of the game. Moreover, the longer that these rules are followed, the more firmly established they will become. Democracy, like good whiskey, improves with age.

Yet it is curious that despite this commitment to democracy, those who manage to get into office via the democratic method enjoy so little public esteem. Robert Ward has noted that "politics and politicians in the abstract are not usually regarded as being particularly trustworthy."[3] This negative view also extends to political parties, which consist for the most part of an organized group of politicians. One interpretation of this phenomenon advanced by a Japanese political scientist, Jun-ichi Kyogoku, is that the Japanese people believe government authority should be fair and impartial; when they see politicians behaving in a partisan manner and sometimes involved in corrupt practices, they feel great disappointment and moral indignation.[4] So far, this lack of trust in politicians has not become severe enough to seriously undermine support for the democratic system.

Another phenomenon related to aversion to partisanship is an unwillingness to accept the notion of majority rule. A basic premise of Western democratic thought is that when unanimity does not exist, decisions should be in accordance with the wishes of the majority. There is a further understanding that the rights of the minority are to be respected and that the minority has the privilege of trying in the future to become a majority. Institutional devices are sometimes provided to protect a minority from the majority; for example, the filibuster in the American Congress. Still, as a practical method of getting work done, the idea of majority rule is widely followed. In Japan (and this is also true in many other parts of Asia), the time-honored method of arriving at decisions is through consensus. This method rests on the premise that members of a group—say, a village council—should continue to talk, bargain, make concessions, and so on until finally a consensus emerges. The result is that the group remains unified, and does not split into a majority and a minority. Despite the spread of democratic norms, this tradition of rule by consensus still has its appeal and sometimes leads to cries against the "tyranny of the majority"—for example, when the ruling party with its majority pushes through legislation over the strong protests of the opposition.

So far we have been concerned with who should govern and in what manner; now we turn to the issue of what the government should do One of the important purposes of government is to solve problems that arise through collective action. A striking characteristic of twentieth-century developments in many parts of the world is the increasing tendency to turn to government when difficulties arise, for the increasing differentiation and complexity in modern societies make it difficult—if not impossible—for individuals to find solutions. Some obvious current examples are pollution of the environment and the decay of large cities. The frequency with which governments are implored to help solve problems, however, varies from country to country, and appears to be related to the political culture—that is, to the attitudes people have about what government ought and ought not to do. As David Easton has written: "The cultural norms, transmitted across the generations, dictate and regulate which wants a member is expected to solve for himself or in cooperation with others, and which it is acceptable in the society for the members to seek to fulfill through political action."[5] To take one example, in modern societies the problem of social welfare for the individual buffeted by economic adversity, illness, or old age demands attention; yet a Japanese commentator is critical of the Western European view that the state should be responsible. So far as he is concerned, in Japan there are three instruments for coping with such problems: the family, life insurance companies, and the employer. Only those individuals who do not have access to these instruments should rely on the state.[6]

It would appear then that in many instances cultural norms inhibit people from seeking to satisfy their wants and needs through organized political action. One practical consequence of such inhibitions is that the danger of countless demands overloading the political systems is very much lessened. The burden of political leadership is made that much lighter, and the possibilities of continued stability are enhanced.

A MODEL OF PATRON-CLIENT DEMOCRACY

The preceding comments on Japanese political culture, brief as they are, have already suggested that Japanese democracy is somewhat different from the Western systems with which we are more familiar. In order to better understand this type of democracy, let us compare it with different "models" of democratic systems.

1. The Rational Choice Model—The expectation here is that all citizens are both well informed about political issues and problems and

highly interested. Moreover, these citizens, on the basis of their information and interest, participate regularly and actively in politics. They not only vote, but also discuss politics with their friends and neighbors, join political organizations, and make their wishes known to their legislative representatives. In addition, they have a clear understanding of the feasible alternative courses of political action, and are capable of choosing one of these on the basis of enlightened self-interest. Clearly, this is an idealized picture of democracy, one that is rarely achieved in practice.

2. *The Civic Culture Model*—This is a more elitist model of democracy. It presupposes that the body of citizens would contain various kinds of individuals, ranging from those who are apathetic to those who are active in political affairs. Political participation, however, will be intermittent rather than continuous and will ordinarily be mediated by voluntary associations of one kind or another. Most of the time, citizens will be willing to leave the job of government to the political elite. They feel confident that if the need arises, they will be able to interpose themselves into the political system and thus influence political outcomes. The British political system can be taken as a typical example of this kind of model.

3. *The Pluralistic Democracy Model*—This model postulates the existence of not one but a number of power centers. Power will therefore be dispersed, and for that reason, limited. Even the ability of the majority to have its way will be circumscribed by the veto power of the minority or minorities. The effect is to limit coercion and to encourage constant negotiation among the power centers, thus enhancing the ability to maximize consent and the resolution of conflict through peaceful means. Perhaps the most conspicuous example of this model would be the American political system.

The model suggested for Japan is different from all of these, yet combines elements from each.

4. *The Patron-Client Model*—Like the civic culture model, this is essentially an elitist type. Given the predominance of vertical relationships between patrons and clients, voluntary associations, which depend on horizontal ties, are developed in only a rudimentary way. Individuals therefore tend to relate to the political system through their patrons, who typically are local notables, political bosses, union leaders, local politicians, and leaders of local organizations. Those who are not involved in patron-client relationships are likely to be apathetic; if they participate in politics at all, they do so haphazardly and intermittently.

In this model, voters tend to trade their ballots for anticipated benefits that are particularistic in character—that is, for jobs and favors for themselves or their relatives; schools, roads, hospitals, and other public works projects for the community. Political issues and questions of ideology are relatively unimportant. Under these circumstances, inputs in the form of demands for broadly conceived public policy are negligible.

This type of democracy will work reasonably well provided two conditions are met: (1) There exists some source within the political system that originates inputs calling for public policy outputs. (2) The demands for particularistic pork-barrel projects do not escalate to the extent that they overload the capacity of the system to meet them. In the case of Japan, the two conditions appear to be met, but we will defer further discussion of this point to Chapters 7 and 11.

NOTES

1 Sidney Verba, "Comparative Political Culture," in Lucian W. Pye and Sidney Verba (eds.), *Political Culture and Political Development* (Princeton, N.J.: Princeton University Press, 1969), p. 513.

2 Tokeisuri Kenkyujo, *Kokumin-sei no Kenkyu* (Study of National Character) (Tokyo, 1968), p. 126.

3 Robert E. Ward, "Japan: The Continuity of Modernization," in Pye and Verba, *op. cit.*, p. 71.

4 Jun-ichi Kyogoku, "Changes in Political Image and Behavior," *Journal of Social and Political Ideas In Japan*, II, 3 (December 1964), 122.

5 David Easton, *A Systems Analysis of Political Life* (New York: Wiley, 1965), p. 103.

6 Jiro Sakamoto, "Nihon-teki Fukushi Kokka no Koso" (Conception of a Japanese-style Welfare State), *Chuo Koron*, 79, 12 (December 1964), 70.

A FACTIONALISM MODEL FOR CCP POLITICS

ANDREW J. NATHAN

UNTIL THE CULTURAL Revolution, the predominant western view of contemporary Chinese elite conflict was that it consisted of "discussion" (t'ao-lun) within a basically consensual Politburo among shifting "opinion groups" with no "organized force" behind them.[1] The purges and accusations which began in 1965 and apparently still continue, have shaken this interpretation, and a number of scholars have advanced new analyses—sometimes explicit, sometimes implicit, sometimes of general application, sometimes applied only to a particular time span or segment of the political system. Of these new views, perhaps the most systematic—and at the same time the one which represents the least change from the pre-Cultural Revolution "opinion group" model— is the "policy making under Mao" interpretation, which sees conflict as essentially a bureaucratic decision-making process dominated by Mao.[2] A similar but less explicit "Mao-in-command" model sees Mao as "testing" his colleagues' political loyalty and sometimes decisively beating back efforts to challenge his pre-eminence.[3] Deviating further from the "unorganized opinion group" model are interpretations which explain political alignments and policy advocacy in terms of leaders' attachments to various bureaucratic "interest groups" —whether these be Field Armies, "commissars" vs. "commanders," "the Party" vs. "the gun," "the legal specialists" vs. "the new cadres," or whatever.[4] Other models and variants could be listed.

The purpose of this paper is to delineate and argue for the applicability of a "factionalism" model of Chinese Communist Party (CCP) elite politics.[5] The reader's indulgence is asked as I turn the everyday term "faction" to a special purpose. Model-building of the sort attempted here requires as a first step the isolation of a rigorously defined type of political structure—in this case, a political structure based upon a particular type of leader-follower relationship. I have appropriated the term "faction" for the special type of structure described below partly for lack of a better term, and partly because I think that the definition I am giving the term falls somewhere near its core meaning, especially as used in the anthropological literature.

Several other caveats must also be entered. First, the model is not intended to explain "everything" about CCP elite politics. Like the other models mentioned above, it seeks to clarify how the Chinese leaders organize themselves to carry out conflict, how they mobilize resources (and what resources) for the struggle, under what formal or informal rules the conflict is carried out, what sanctions are visited upon the losers, and so forth. Like the other models, it is consistent with various interpretations about the ultimate motives for conflict, which at various times may have encompassed disagreements about the nature of man,[6] the state of the world,[7] the role of the Party[8] or the means to economic development,[9] personal concern about the fate of the revolution,[10] or personality clashes.[11] Furthermore, the model deals only with what might broadly be called organizational constraints on political behaviour, and not with the other sets of constraints—e.g., ideological and cultural—which provide additional "rules of the game." Third, it has to be accepted at the outset that the available data on CCP elite conflict will not be adequate to accept or reject the model decisively—if they were, we could develop a presumably more suitable model directly from the data.[12] Indeed, the utility of the model is precisely that, if it passes an initial test of fitting existing data, it suggests ways of understanding and interpreting the situation that the data are too slim to suggest by themselves, and thus fills gaps in our knowledge, on a tentative and speculative basis, through a species of reasoning through analogy. In the following pages I will, first, present the model as an abstract proposition; then, try to show that the available data on politics at the central level are consistent, as far as they go, with the model; next, suggest how Chinese Communist politics, especially since the late 1950's, might be interpreted in a way consistent with the model; and finally, discuss some further implications and problems.

THE STRUCTURE OF FACTIONS

The starting point is a kind of human behavior which I shall call the "clientelist tie."[13] A clientelist tie is a non-ascriptive two-person relationship founded on exchange, in which well-understood rights and obligations are established between the two parties. The hallmarks of a clientelist tie are as follows:

(i) It is a relationship between two people;

(ii) It is a relationship especially selected for cultivation by the members from their total social networks;

(iii) It is cultivated essentially by the constant exchange of gifts or services. (This does not imply that the subjective content of the relationship is cynical or unfriendly: the contrary is normally the case);

(iv) Since the exchange involves the provision by each partner of goods or services the other wants, the parties to the tie are dissimilar; very often they are unequal in status, wealth, or power;

(v) The tie sets up well-understood, although seldom explicit, rights and obligations between the partners;

(vi) It can be abrogated by either member at will; and

(vii) It is not exclusive; either member is free to establish other simultaneous ties (so long as they do not involve contradictory obligations).

Such ties include patron-client relations, godfather-parent relations, some types of trader-customer relations, and so forth. Corporate ties, such as lineage relations, co-membership in an association, or co-membership in a group of blood brothers exceeding two in number, are not clientelist ties, although shared corporate membership often provides an initial contact which leads to the establishment of clientelist tie as defined here.

The clientelist tie must be clearly distinguished from two other kinds of relationship with which it is readily confused, the power relationship and the (generic) exchange relationship. To take the second problem first, the clientelist tie is founded on exchange. But, according to Peter M. Blau, all social processes except those that are irrational or non-goal-oriented or expressive—in other words, all social processes in which people interact with other people in order to elicit behaviour from them instrumental to some goal—can profitably be analyzed in terms of exchange.[14] And according to Marshal Sahlins, any kind of reciprocity, including the "negative reciprocity" of an eye for an eye, can be usefully classified as exchange.[15] Blau and Sahlins are persuasive on the utility of their respective analytical systems, but it is essential to be clear that the clientelist tie as defined here is an exchange relationship of a limited and specific kind. Embedded in different cultures it takes somewhat different forms and is more or less explicitly recognized, spelled out, legitimated, and reinforced. But, in any case, it is relatively stable and persistent, involves well-understood rights and obligations, and is purposely culti-

vated by the participants. If nearly all of social life is to be regarded as exchange, then clientelist ties should be regarded as a special, quasi-contractual sub-type of exchange relationship.

At the other extreme, the clientelist tie must be distinguished from the power relationship of "imperative coordination."[16] If for some reason the subordinate has no real choice but obedience, the consequences for political behaviour of the superior-subordinate relationship will be quite different from what they would be if the real possibility of abrogating the tie existed. Since the consequences are so different the distinction is analytically necessary. It may be objected that, in many cases, the right of abrogation formally exists but in fact cannot be exercised, as in the relationship between landlord and tenant on some Latin American haciendas, or between lord and vassal in feudal Europe. These relationships, I would argue, should be regarded as relationships of imperative co-ordination rather than as clientelistic relations. Of course it is often difficult to tell the difference. There is a grey area, e.g., as the hold of the landlord begins to weaken but before it is effectively challenged by that of a local political machine. The analytic boundary lies somewhere within that grey area.

Clientelist ties in a given society articulate to form complex networks which serve many functions, including social insurance,[17] trade,[18] and the mobilization and wielding of influence (i.e., political conflict). It is with this latter function that I am concerned here. What happens when political conflict is organized primarily through clientelist ties rather than through formal organizations, corporate lineage units, or mass or class movements? I would argue that there are three possibilities.

First, the individual seeking to engage in political conflict may do so by cashing in on his personal ties to operate as a power broker, without directly and explicitly involving his partners in any common or sustained endeavour. Examples include influence-peddling by lawyers who specialize in arranging access to particular bureaucracies, mediation of political disputes by middlemen, and the bridging of government/ village gaps by local "linkage figures."[19] The second possibility, which occurs in a setting of genuine electoral competition, has been called the "clientelist party," "vertical group," or "machine"—a mass political organization which buys electoral support with particularistic rewards distributed through a leader-follower network of clientelist ties.[20]

The third possibility occurs in an oligarchic

FIGURE 1

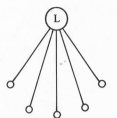

Simple faction

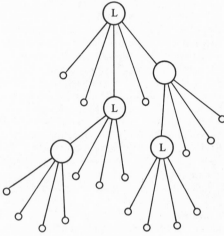

Complex faction

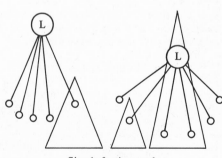

Simple factions and
support structures

a few layers.[22] I call such a structure—one mobilized on the basis of clientelist ties to engage in politics and consisting of a few, rather than a great many, layers of personnel—a faction.[23] Such configurations include what may be called simple or complex factions, and may control from within or without one or more "support structure" or power bases, such as clubs, parties, mobs, newspapers, banks, ministries, armies, and the like. To save space, I simply indicate some of these possibilities in Figure 1, and forgo formal definitions and systematic comparative analysis. What all these configurations share in common is the one-to-one, rather than corporate, pattern of relationships between leaders (or subleaders) and followers. Structurally, the faction is articulated through one or more nodes; and it is recruited and co-ordinated on the basis of the personal exchange relationships I have called clientelist ties.

THE STRUCTURAL CHARACTERISTICS OF FACTIONS

To proceed from this conception to the behavioural characteristics it implies, I must elaborate some of the structural characteristics of factions.[24]

Because it is based upon personal exchange ties rather than authority relations, a faction does not become corporatized after recruitment but remains structured along the lines of the original ties which formed the bases of recruitment.[25] Upward and downward communications therefore tend to follow the lines of recruitment. This lends the faction considerable flexibility: the leader sees the opportunity for political gain, separately recruits each member into the faction,[26] and directs the activities of each member for the overall good of the faction. The members need never meet, although they may do so. The members' activities in disparate locations and institutions can be co-ordinated through individual communications with the leader.[27] Indeed, in routine political situations, regularized co-ordination can be dispensed with entirely, since the faction as a whole can rely on the members' loyalty to the leader to insure that each member works to the faction's benefit. Thus, the faction is capable of the greatest flexibility in seizing political opportunities and in engaging in a general political strategy on the basis of scattered positions throughout a political system or an organization.

On the other hand, such a communications pattern involves certain liabilities. Upward and downward communications are not delivered directly to the recipient (in the case of complex

or relatively small-scale setting when an individual leader mobilizes some portion of his network of primary, secondary, tertiary ties, and so on,[21] for the purpose of engaging in politics. A machine or clientelist party consists of a great many layers of personnel, but this third type of clientelist political structure consists of only one or factions) but flow through a series of nodes (sub-leaders). The more steps through which the information flows, the more time it takes and the more distorted it is likely to become.[28] This is one of several structural characteristics which tend to set limits to the number of levels to which the faction can extend without becoming corporatized[29] and to the degree to which large factions can engage in finely co-ordinated activities. The faction, in short, is highly flexible but self-limiting in its extensiveness.

Since it is founded upon exchange relationships, a faction depends for its growth and continuity upon the ability of the leader to secure and distribute rewards to his followers. It tends to expand and contract with success or failure, and may even be dissolved when removed from power. But it can always be reconstituted when it regains the capability to reward its members. The faction is thus capable of intermittent but persistent functioning. It takes form out of the general network in response to an opportunity for political gain, and when it becomes necessary to retire from politics, as during the dominance of the political arena by an enemy, it can become relatively dormant. Its political activities temporarily cease, especially if the members have scattered; or the activities may continue at a low level of occasional contact with other opposition groups to scheme for a return to power. When the enemy is overthrown, the faction may return to full activity unchanged in form and flexibility.

It also follows that a faction cannot survive its leader. The members may continue in political activity after the leader's death or retirement; several members may associate for a time and continue to be known by the original name of the faction. Members may also join other factions as temporary allies or they may seek to found their own faction. But since the set of clientelist ties on which it is founded forms a unique configuration centered on the leader, the faction can never be taken over as a whole by a successor. The unique combination of personnel and strategic political positions held by the faction cannot be completely reconstructed once the leader is lost.

The more extended the complex faction becomes, the greater the number of subordinate leaders it contains and the farther removed they are from the primary leader. The leader of each simple faction within the complex faction is primarily responsible to his own followers for political spoils. The possibility exists that this responsibility may come into contradiction with the loyalty he owes his own leader—who is pursuing the interests of a different set of persons. This creates the tendency for the leaders of lower segments to betray the interests of the faction as a whole in order to secure greater rewards for the segments below them, which are capable of operating as distinct factions if they free themselves from the larger faction.[30]

Because of this tendency towards breakdown, complex factions are most likely to develop, and are likely to develop to the largest size, within bureaucratic formal organization. In formal organizations, first, the personal loyalty of faction leaders at lower levels to leaders at higher levels is reinforced by hierarchical authority patterns. Second, the faction has the benefit of the intra-organizational communications network to aid in coordinating its activities. Third, the effort to gain control of the organization or to influence its policies requires the co-operation of the sub-leaders at the various levels and tends to bring their interests into harmony. In short, the hierarchy and established communications and authority flow of the existing organization provides a kind of trellis upon which the complex faction is able to extend its own informal, personal loyalties and relations.

There is a tendency for vertical cleavages to develop within the complex faction, running up to the level directly under the highest leader. Vertical cleavages also develop at each lower level, but remain latent while they are submerged within the greater rivalry between the two major segments. (Because the struggle is for access to and influence over the leader, there is a tendency for these cleavages to be limited to two.) The conflict between the two major entities become two new complex factions.

Internal cleavage tends to be increased by the fruits of victory. First, the path to victory inevitably involves reaching opportunistic alliances with factional leaders who are incorporated as allies within the faction but are not reliable. Second, the increases scale and numerical force of the faction as it grows enhances the tendency mentioned earlier for divergent interests to emerge among component sub-leaders and sub-factions. Even if loyalty prevents an open revolt against the leader, it permits political clashes and struggles among his subordinates. Third, if the faction comes near to or achieves victory in a conflict arena as a whole, the unifying factor of a common enemy ceases to exist, while divisive factors such as struggle over spoils and efforts by smaller, enemy factions to buy over component units increase in salience. Fourth, the growth of the faction tends to deprive the leader himself of direct control over component units, weakens his position *vis-à-vis* subordinates, and thus hastens his political retirement and the consequent open split of the faction. In short, division and decline is the almost inevitable result of success. The only way to avoid such disintegration is to refuse to expand beyond the borders of an internally unified and easily defended factional base.

Finally, it follows from all the above that the faction is limited in the amount and kinds of power it can wield and generate. A faction is limited in size, follower commitment, and stability by the principles of its own organization. Certain other types of conflict structure, for example highly organized political parties or armies, can, by virtue of their complex, functionally specialized organization, their clear boundaries, and their high degree of control over participants, engage in feats of mobilization, indoctrination, and co-ordination which are beyond the capacities of factions.[31] A faction of course is limited in power only so long as it remains a faction; there is nothing inherent in the existence of a faction to prevent the members, if they need more power, from organizing themselves in some other way. However, the fact is that people often do not organize themselves in another way, but in factions. Why they choose to do so, and what conditions may cause them to shift to another form of organization, are important questions beyond the scope of the model.

THE CHARACTERISTICS OF FACTIONAL POLITICS

For simplicity, I limit the following discussion to an ideal-typical political system which is primarily organized by factions. Presumably factions will behave somewhat differently when they are competing against other structures which are not factions (for example, clans or political parties), but the easiest case to deal with is the "pure case" of an all-factional system. This section completes the model of factional politics by attempting to show what modes of conflict will be typical of factions operating in an environment consisting primarily of rival factions.[32]

A first set of propositions is based upon the power limitations typical of factions. Factions, I have argued, enjoy less power capability than formal organizations because of the limitations on their extent, co-ordination, and control of followers implied by their basis in the clientelist tie, their one-to-one communications structure, and their tendency towards breakdown. It follows from this that the several factions in a given factional arena will tend, over time, to enjoy relative power equality; for no faction will be able to achieve and maintain overwhelmingly superior power. One faction may for the moment enjoy somewhat greater power than rival factions, but this power will not be so much greater that the victorious faction is capable of expunging its rivals and assuring permanent dominance.[33] This is the more so because the flexibility of the weaker factions and their capability for intermittent functioning enhance their ability to evade and survive repression. A faction engaging in conflict with other factions must therefore operate on the assumption that it will not be able decisively and finally to eliminate its rivals. The faction which holds power today can expect to be out of power and vulnerable tomorrow. Politicians in a factional system are "condemned to live together."[34] This enables us to posit that the following modes of conflict will be typical of factional systems.

1. Since the impulse to crush one's rivals decisively is stymied by the limited nature of power, a code of civility arises which circumscribes the nature of political conflict.[35] Factions relatively seldom kill, jail or even confiscate the property of their opponents within the system (the killing and jailing of persons felt to present a threat to the system in another matter; see point 12). Indeed, factional systems require punctiliously polite face-to-face conduct between politicians. As Leites has written with respect to the French Assembly of the Third and Fourth Republics, "the vicissitudes of political life exacerbate one's feelings, but it is imperative that rage be channelled into entirely appropriate expressions so as not to endanger one's career."[36]

2. Since factions are incapable of building sufficient power to rid the political system of rival factions, they have little incentive to try to do so. For any given faction, the most important and usually most immediate concern is to protect its own base of power while opposing accretions of power to rival factions, while initiatives to increase its own power and position are of secondary importance. Defensive political strategies therefore predominate over political initiatives in frequency and importance.

3. When a faction does take a political initiative (which it does only on those rare occasions when it feels that its power base is secure and its rivals are relatively off balance), it relies upon secret preparation and surprise offensive. This minimizes the ability of rivals to prepare their defensive moves in advance and provides the aggressive faction a momentum which carries it further than would otherwise be the case before the defensive moves of rivals stop its progress.

4. In the face of such an initiative, the defensive orientation of the other factions in the system tends to encourage them to unite against the initiative. Thus factional political systems tend to block the emergence of strong leaders. The strong leader constitutes a threat to the other factions' opportunities for power, and they band together long enough to topple him from power. (In many political systems this leads to governmental instability. In France under the Third and Fourth Republics, for example, where the Government was dependent for its office upon an alignment of parliamentary factions, the very fact that a politician was able to organize a Cabinet set in motion the jealousy and opposition that soon led to its fall. Where the titular government leader is supra-factional and enjoys little power, however, the formal governmental leadership of a factional system may remain stable for long periods.)

5. Since the political life of a factional system consists of occasional initiatives by constituent factions, followed by defensive alliances against the initiator, any given faction is obliged to enter into a series of constantly shifting defensive alliances. Factional alliances cannot remain stable. Today's enemy may have to be tomorrow's ally.

6. It is therefore impossible for factions to make ideological agreement a primary condition for alliance with other factions. As I argue below, factions operate within a broad ideological consensus (point 13) while exaggerating the small differences that remain among them (point 10). The struggle for office and influence is unremitting, immediate, and never decisively resolved. In order to stay in the game, factions must often co-operate with those with whom they have recently disagreed. Although factional alignments do not cross major ideological boundaries, within those boundaries they are not determined by doctrinal differences.[37]

7. When decisions (resolutions of conflict, policy decisions) are made by the factional system as a whole, they are made by consensus among the factions. To attempt to take action without first achieving such a consensus would take the ruling coalition beyond the limits of its power: the decision could never be enforced. Furthermore, the effort to enforce a decision would hasten the formation of an opposition coalition to topple the ruling group from power. Decision by consensus also has the advantage that action is taken in the company of one's rivals, so that responsibility cannot be pinned on any single faction.[38]

8. There is a typical cycle of consensus formation and decline which characterizes factional systems. The cycle begins with a political crisis.

As the factions contemplate the crisis, "the limits of what every party (or every clique or individual) may be capable of attaining" becomes clear to all, and after a lapse of time the crisis becomes "ripe." "Imperious necessity . . . make(s) the . . . groups disregard their positions of principle" which had blocked consensus, and action becomes possible.[39]

As a result of the consensus among the factions on the need for action, a faction or factional alliance achieves office and receives a mandate to act. The victorious faction takes culturally appropriate actions to test and solidify the support the other factions have been obliged to give it. The leader may refuse to take office until the other factions have publicly committed themselves to him; he may try to associate the leaders of other factions in the action he proposes to take; he may allow, or encourage, the crisis to worsen. Ultimately, however, he acts.

The third phase is the decline of the factional consensus. The actions taken by the faction in power inevitably have implications for the relative strength of all the factions in the system. While the actions carry the system through the crisis which had produced the consensus, they benefit some factions—usually the one in power and its allies—more than others. The other factions act to block the effort of the leading faction to strengthen itself, and the factional consensus deteriorates. The factions return to mutual squabbling.

The period of factional conflict often lasts a long while as the factions manoeuvre for political resources, alliances, and a favourable moment and pretext for precipitating a new crisis. Eventually a faction feels it is in a good position to take a political initiative, to precipitate a test of strength with its major opponent. In many factional systems, this takes the form of asking the most obstructive opposition factions to form a government in the expectation that they will fail.[40] Whatever its form, the test of strength initiates a new crisis which begins another cycle. cal resources, alliances, and a favourable manoeuvre for political resources, alliances, and a favourable moment and pretext for precipitating a new crisis. Eventually a faction feels it is in a good position to take a political initiative, to precipitate a test of strength with its major opponent. In many factional systems, this takes the form of asking the most obstructive opposition factions to form a government in the expectation that they will fail.[40] Whatever its form, the test of strength initiates a new crisis which begins another cycle.

A second set of propositions is based upon the fact that factions consist of a series of clientelist ties. The resources with which the faction carries out political conflict are not corporate, shared resources, but the personal resources of the individual members—their personal prestige, official positions, and their own further clientelist ties.

9. To weaken their rivals, factions try to discredit opposition faction members, dislodge them from their posts, and buy away their allies. This leads to a politics of personality in which rumour, character assassination, bribery and deception are used. Passions of jealousy and revenge are aroused, opportunism and corruption are fostered, and urgent short-term political goals require the compromise of principles. These, in short, are the "comic opera" politics or "pure politics" so characteristic of factional systems.[41]

10. A further characteristic of factional political conflict may be called doctrinalism, i.e., the couching of factional struggle for power in terms of abstract issues of ideology, honour, and face.[42] Factions adopt rigid and minutely defined ideological positions, exaggerate small differences on abstract questions, and stress the purity of their own motives. Yet the issues which arouse such fierce and elaborate debate appear upon close examination to be those with strategic implications for factional power.[43] Although the real distance between cliques in ideology and programme is small (points 12 and 13), and although no faction is likely to be able to carry out an innovative political programme, grand policies and sweeping programmes are articulated and debated, with small points attracting the most passionate and lengthy discussion.

Such debate serves several purposes. First, it distinguishes one faction from another,[44] providing a rationale for the continued struggle among such otherwise similar entities. Second, it provides an opportunity to discredit other politicians and to justify oneself on abstract or ideological grounds. Third, the broad programmes often include inconspicuous provisions of true strategic political importance. The struggle which is couched in abstract terms is really over the advantages of a policy to one side or the other.

A third set of propositions concerns the size and shape of the factional system as a whole and the way it relates to its political environment.

11. Any factional arena is composed of a limited and not very large number of factions. This is so because in an arena with a very great number of factions, it will be in the interests of the factions to amalgamate, in order to defend against other factions doing the same thing. The incentives to amalgamate cease to be stronger than those to engage in conflict only when the total number of factions has been reduced to the point where most of the constituent factions enjoy enough strength to launch political initiatives and defend themselves, while further amalgamation would simply bring in more followers to share the rewards of the faction without decisively affecting its ability to survive. It is doubtful whether more than a score or two of factions can exist in a given factional system or arena. (The limitations on the number of members in a faction, and on the number of factions in a system, form a logical circle with the initial assumption of an oligarchic or small-scale arena.)

12. I have already established that the members of the small factional elite act within a code of civility which limits the severity of the sanctions they employ, and under tactical constraints that require alliances with former enemies and opposition to former allies.[45] This closely knit elite is further united by one overriding shared interest: that the resources over which they are struggling should be allocated among themselves and in accordance with the rules of conflict they are following, rather than to some force from outside the system which pays no attention to those rules and whose victory would end the political existence of the factions. The result is a sharp difference between the modes of intra-elite conflict described in points 1 to 10 and the drastic steps which may be taken by the united factional elite to resist external enemies or to destroy counter-elites who challenge the legitimacy of the factional system.[46] When, for example, foreign conquest, rebellion, or a military *coup* threatens to overthrow a factional regime, the factions unite behind a suitable leader long enough to preserve the system, before returning to politics as usual.[47] If the threat to the system comes from within, from a factional leader attempting to break the rules, the efforts of the other factions are directed towards defeating that attempt and re-establishing the stability of the system.

13. Within the factional elite, it is taboo to question the principle of legitimacy upon which the factions base their claim to a role in the larger society. Thus, for example, a factional parliament, regime, or party may play the role, in the larger society, of a central or local government, on the basis of a constitutional or charismatic claim to legitimacy. No matter how much the vicissitudes of struggle oblige the factions to trample in fact upon constitutional principles, or to disobey in fact their symbolic leader, these must never be openly questioned

or flouted since that would encourage other forces in the larger society to "throw the rascals out."[48] Thus politicians in factional systems compete in expressions of fealty to the constitution or leader and rationalize every action and every position in terms of their fidelity to it or him. Care is taken to assure the constitutional or charismatic continuity of the regime.

14. Issues which arise within the elite are resolved only slowly and with difficulty. The consensus which is necessary for action is difficult to achieve because every decision is more advantageous to some factions than to others. Only the cycle of crisis and consensus brings action, but it is short-term action to meet the immediate emergency, and may in any case be followed by contradictory decisions after the next cycle of conflict. The resulting failure of policy to move clearly in any one direction is what was called, in the French Third and Fourth Republics, *immobilisme*.

15. The immobilism of factional systems, the lack of extreme sanctions employed in their struggles, and their tendency to defend their existence against rival elites or external threats mean that they are in a certain sense extremely stable. It does not seem to be true, as some observers have suggested, that factional systems have an inherent tendency to break down.[49] In the absence of outside pressures (in which I include those from social forces within the society), no force within the factional system is capable of amassing enough power to overthrow it. Thus, only continued factionalism can be predicted on the basis of the fact that a system is already factional.

There will, of course, be other causes acting upon a factional system which also affect the outcome. Personal, cultural and technical resources for more complex organizations may be present to a greater or lesser degree; so may leaders' political vision and the will to move beyond the factional form of organization; and so may the challenge of changing social conditions. Members of factional systems may abandon factions for other forms of organization (often clientelist political parties). But if they do so, it will not be because of any dynamic of the factional system itself. More often than not, factional systems under challenge from within or without respond by trying to reassert their equilibrium rather than by changing their internal structure.

DOES CHINA HAVE FACTIONAL POLITICS?

To the extent that this model is applicable to China, one would expect to find either direct evidence of the existence of factions, such as descriptions of the organization and membership of specific factions, or circumstantial evidence of their existence, such as incidents which display the modes of conflict I have described. On the other hand, we would have to abandon the model as an explanation for Chinese political behaviour where we found evidence of other conflict structures or of modes of conflict not consistent with the model. The Cultural Revolution period is a good place to begin the search because of the relative openness of political conflict at all levels. The available evidence, I will argue, permits the view that Chinese politics at the central government level has been structured largely by factions, especially if the Cultural Revolution is regarded not as a first outbreak of factionalism but as an episode in which a long-standing factional system attempted to defend its existence against an attack based on outside social forces; that political conflict at the intermediate (regional and provincial) levels has been non-factional or, at most, intermittently factional; and that the local-level mass movements of the Cultural Revolution were essentially non-factional.

The centre is an ill-defined elite of several hundred high officials of the party, army and state bureaucracies. All the members of this elite have devoted their lives to the revolutionary movement, are Party members and have served extensively with the PLA. Despite differing current affiliations, therefore, it is a single elite whose political ties and concerns cross institutional boundaries.[50] While Central Committee membership is prestigious, it does not define the central elite, whose composition shifts more rapidly than Central Committees can be reconstituted.[51] Informal organs such as the work conference,[52] with flexible membership, are the locus of political conflict within this central elite.

There is some direct evidence of the existence of personal factions in this top elite. Scholars have been able to identify certain figures as followers of, among others, T'ao Chu,[53] Lin Piao,[54] Liu Shao-ch'i,[55] and, of course, Mao. Analyses of the backgrounds of purged leaders have suggested that certain shared experiences may have led to the formation of personal ties which help to explain who was purged during the Cultural Revolution.[56] Many purged leaders have been charged with crimes like "fostering personal forces, establishing their personal authority, winning over defectors and renegades, forming private parties. . . ."[57] However, none of this evidence is really conclusive and it remains impossible to delineate with any confidence who the major factional leaders have been, much less their followers.

Turning to circumstantial evidence, the central political arena quite clearly displayed most of the characteristic modes of conflict of factional systems during the Cultural Revolution. Almost all commentators noted the absence of extreme sanctions against defeated politicians.[58] Most defeated leaders were punished only by re-education, while even the most severely sanctioned political leaders suffered only the humiliation of mass denunciations; few, if any, were executed. At the time of writing some purged leaders are even returning to office.[59] Also noteworthy was the effort to provide some legal validation, however flimsy, for the deposition of leaders like Liu Shao-ch'i and P'eng Chen, suggesting a concern for the constitutional continuity of the regime.

Defensive tactics predominated during the Cultural Revolution. One thinks of P'eng Chen's efforts through his 12 February directive to turn the brunt of Mao's attack onto the "academic authorities"; the counter-mobilization of loyalist Red Guards or revolutionary rebels by local officials under attack; the disregarding or distortion of directives from the centre; the "sham" confessions which were actually self-justifications.[60] By contrast, political initiatives such as Yao Wen-yuan's attack on Wu Han, or the launching of the Red Guards, were relatively rare, and were apparently prepared in secret and sprung by surprise. Opposition to the emergence of a strong leader was shown by the resistance of other leaders to the accretion of power in Mao's hands. The shifting of factional alliances is reflected in the rise and fall of various propaganda directors, chiefs of staff, and the like; in the purging by 1969 of three-fifths of the pre-Cultural Revolution Central Committee; in the fall of 23 of 28 provincial leaders, of four out of five members of the original Group of Five directing the Cultural Revolution and of 13 of 18 members of the Central Cultural Revolution Group.[61] The irrelevance of doctrine in determining factional alliances is suggested by the fact that many attacked as anti-Mao during this period had records which were utterly pro-Mao,[62] while Chou En-lai, for example, who has not always been particularly pro-Mao, has so far managed to retain the title of a Maoist. The purges of Ch'en Po-ta and Lin Piao in 1971 gave further validation of this point.

That decision-making within the central elite was made by consensus and compromise is suggested by the contradictory orders which were often issued simultaneously or even within the same document, such as the famous Sixteen Points; and by the oscillations noted by many analysts between radical and moderate policies emanating from the centre.[63] A closer look at these oscillations suggests that they followed the typical factional cycle in which a crisis leads to a policy decision, which itself becomes the focus of renewed conflict leading ultimately to another crisis. For example, the events of July-September 1967 began with a crisis, the Wuhan incident, which temporarily unified the factions at the centre against rule-breaking violence by local military commanders against central officials. The call was issued to "pluck out a small handful" in the Army. During August, the Red Guards responded by stealing weapons and attacking the PLA. Thus, the July decision which originally represented the joint interests of all the factions at the centre in suppressing armed action by military dissidents began to redound too strongly to the political advantage of the pro-Red Guard factions at the centre. This led to renewed policy debate at the centre and presumably to a showdown which issued in a new decision—this time repudiating the concept of attacking a handful in the Army, and purging three members of the Central Cultural Revolution Group.[64]

The "comic opera" conflict of personal vilification and imaginative attack was certainly a feature of the Cultural Revolution, and, as I have shown, such tactics are serious and meaningful in factional systems, where the personal prestige, position and contacts of the politician are his prime resources. Equally evident was doctrinalism, as seen, for example, in the practice of "waving the Red Flag to oppose the Red Flag."

Of the 15 characteristics of factional politics, then, 10 are visible in, or consistent with, the events of the Cultural Revolution. The eleventh —the relatively small number of factions in the system—cannot be confirmed or denied on the basis of our present inadequate information. It is perhaps too early to reach a judgment with respect to two further characteristics, immobilism and stability, although one could certainly argue that no matter how much the Chinese political system seemed to be breaking down during the Cultural Revolution, it did not actually break down; and no matter how much it seemed to be making definite policy decisions, it did not opt for any single consistent foreign policy, development strategy, defense policy, policy on the role of intellectuals, or the like, but wavered between contradictory poles very much like a system composed of constantly shifting factional alliances.[65]

This leaves two features to look for—a taboo on discussion of the principle of legitimacy, and solidarity of the factions in the face of outside threats. The episode of the Red Guards would seem to contradict these predictions, since members of the elite went outside the elite itself to mobilize a social force, the students (which had previously threatened many elites in modern Chinese history), and encouraged this force to attack the leaders of the Party itself. This contradiction can be resolved by arguing that the politics of the central elite was already factional in the early 1960s and that Mao, for reasons discussed below, decided to break the rules of factional politics and directly mobilize a social force to destroy the factional system; that the non-Maoist members of the factional elite responded, as the model predicts, with solidarity against the student threat and took steps to demobilize the Red Guards; and that in doing so, they scrupulously avoided criticizing Mao, since they had in recent years increasingly based the legitimacy of the regime upon Mao's personal charisma rather than on the claimed historical mission of the Party as an institution. I will expand upon this interpretation of the Cultural Revolution, after surveying the evidence on intermediate and local-level conflict.

Data on political conflict at the intermediate levels of the Chinese political system have been scarce. Perhaps the most confident assertion we can make is that relatively independent political sub-systems ("independent kingdoms") have existed in the Chinese political system. These include provinces—two famous examples being Inner Mongolia under Ulanfu and Szechwan under Li Ching-ch'üan[66]—and bureaucracies such as the five Field Army systems of the PLA[67] and the state bureaucracy under Chou En-lai.

There was political conflict within many or all of these "independent kingdoms" during the Cultural Revolution. There were struggles in every province and region over the composition of the Revolutionary Committees,[68] and conflict was reported in such bureaucratic units as the PLA Air Force[69] and the Ministry of Foreign Affairs.[70] Although such episodes often displayed earmarks of factional conflict—they were long, complex, and indecisive, with a succession of contradictory policy outputs; there seemed to be limits on sanctions imposed on defeated leaders; they were characterized by personal vituperation and by "waving the Red Flag to oppose the Red Flag"—we know too little about events in most of these arenas to characterize them with confidence.

Even if we tentatively conclude that the Cultural Revolution witnessed factional conflict in many of the intermediate-level arenas of the Chinese political system, a number of important points remain obscure. Was political conflict factional in these arenas in the years before the Cultural Revolution, or did the Cultural Revolution bring out factions by causing the disintegration of institutions like Party committees and PLA hierarchies? How did intermediate-level factions during the Cultural Revolution relate to factions at the centre? Perhaps the most satisfactory guess is that before the Cultural Revolution such "independent kingdoms" were institutional power bases dominated by factions whose leaders were participants at the central level. Factions within these local arenas were merely latent, and intra-province or intra-bureaucracy conflict was primarily "institutional" (resolved by authoritative institutional decisions arrived at by following legitimate, regular procedures of decision-making). The Cultural Revolution, initiated at the centre and necessarily involving the fates of the "independent kings" around the country, weakened these institutions and gave intermediate-level factions the chance to emerge and fight for power.

As for the local levels, the evidence for factionalism there seems, at first glance, to be unambiguous. Beginning in January 1967, the Chinese press periodically launched attacks on "factionalism, anarchism, and sectarianism" at the local level. But on closer inspection, it appears that what the Chinese press called factionalism is not what is specified in our model. In the first place, the Red Guard units did not behave like factions in the sense as defined here. They engaged in violent clashes, sometimes killing their enemies, and seemed to stress aggressive initiatives rather than defensive tactics. Rather than entering shifting alliances to block the emergence of strong leadership, Red Guard units tended to amalgamate in each city into two large armed camps, each under a strong leader. While it is often unclear why a Red Guard unit chose to ally with one camp rather than another, there is no evidence that pre-existing clientelist ties structured the choice of association; rather, shared class background and ideological position appear to have been the determining factors. Instead of cycles of consensus and conflict, Red Guard organizations seem to have engaged in a downward spiral of increasingly violent confrontation.[71]

Indeed, the few concrete studies of the Red Guards and other units of "mass factionalism" show that these units were not structured as factions.[72] The most detailed study, that of Bennett and Montaperto, shows that the Red Guards in one Canton school at first organized as an elite formal organization consisting of "five-red" students, structured along the same lines as the school itself, so that the lowest unit in the Red Guard organizational hierarchy was a group of students selected from a given class (*pan*).[73] As this structure crumbled, the movement took on the loose structure of a mass of "friendship groups," each of which was apparently a corporate unit rather than a faction.[74] The Red Guard units then sorted themselves out into two stable alliance systems.[75]

The structure and political behaviour of Red Guard and other "mass factions" bear more resemblance to those of certain loosely structured mass social movements[76] than to those of factions in our definition. The coherence of these "mass factions" of the Cultural Revolution was based not upon the mobilization of exchange-based clientelist ties for the pursuit of political gain, but upon the mobilization of social tensions and resentments which arose because of the differential access to rewards enjoyed by different social categories. People allied themselves with those whom they perceived as belonging to the same category, as disadvantaged in the same way and as seeking the same type of reparation. The difference between the Cultural Revolution "mass factions" and most other mass movements was that they were highly responsive to signals from "the centre" and thus lent themselves to manipulation as somewhat clumsy instruments in the factional struggle being waged there.[77]

This does not mean that there was not also factionalism in our sense in villages and enterprises. It seems probably that the launching of the Red Guards into factories and suburban areas weakened institutional control and led in at least some places to the mobilization of factions to pay off old scores or otherwise take advantage of the opportunity presented. But although this sort of thing very probably happened, we lack the evidence to prove that it did.

CCP POLITICAL HISTORY INTERPRETED IN
TERMS OF THE FACTIONALISM MODEL

This preliminary survey of the evidence suggests that we are justified in delving further into the implications of the model for Chinese politics. Let us accept as a working hypothesis that during the Cultural Revolution the politics of "the centre" were structured largely by factions, that the politics of the Red Guards were non-factional, and that the intermediate-level "independent kingdoms" were at first internally

organized as stable institutions, but suffered outbreaks of factionalism. At this point, let us also take the leap of assuming that if factionalism was present in the Cultural Revolution it had also been present in earlier periods. It would be tedious to defend this assumption for each stage of party history, and unnecessary in an article whose purpose is to establish the plausibility and not the necessary correctness of a line of analysis. Although the factionalism argument is easiest to make for the 1959-72 period—which is indeed stressed in what follows—our exploratory purpose is best served by sketching the interpretation that would flow from the maximum assumption: factionalism since the earliest days of the party.

Let us begin with two well-established facts: that the Chinese Communist Party and its Army have formed throughout their history a single institutional system with a single elite performing simultaneously the functions of political and military leadership[78]; and that while the institution as a whole was striving towards power in the Chinese revolution, its elite was from the beginning frequently racked with internal conflict.[79] Studies of intra-Party conflict have focused heavily on the explicit content of the ideological and policy issues under debate and have not analysed the way in which the Party/Army elite organized itself for intra-Party conflict or the way in which such conflict was carried out. The doctrinalism of these debates, the lack of extreme intra-Party sanctions, the inability of Mao to exclude his opponents and their views from the Party, all hint at the operation of factions; this suspicion is encouraged by the charges aired during the Cultural Revolution that Mao's enemies had built personal followings and opposed him throughout the history of the Party. As the Party/Army grew, I would argue, each major leader played upon his personal network of clientelist ties to cultivate a personal faction, seeding his followers in important Party and Army posts[80] and using them and their resources of office, prestige, and personal connections to further his own standing in the movement and the adoption of the policies he thought it should follow. As it happened, the organization of intra-Party debate by factions boded better for the future of the movement than would some other types of intra-Party dissension. Through its limitation of sanctions and its shifting alliances, factionalism bound the movement together and prevented its fragmentation into permanently hostile rival movements.[81] Since the CCP as a whole existed in a condition of strong threat from the Kuomin-tang and the

Japanese, it could not have survived if it had not limited its internal rivalries to factional forms.

With liberation in 1949, the organizational sub-structure beneath the elite increased in size and complexity, and the resources of power available for control by elite factions increased. However, the central elite itself, I would hypothesize, remained factional in its internal divisions. I am not able to identify the factional leaders, but the obvious starting points for further research are such names as Mao Tse-tung, Teng Hsiao-p'ing, Liu Shao-ch'i, Lin Piao, P'eng Chen, P'eng Teh-huai, and Kao Kang. Factionalism would have been superseded (i) if intra-elite conflict had ceased, which it clearly did not; (ii) if a member of the elite had mobilized the institutional means (as did Stalin) or the personal charisma to earn the sole power to resolve conflict, which also clearly did not occur; (iii) if the Party had split into permanently hostile segments which moved beyond the rules and resources of factional conflict towards the goal of mutual extirpation, which obviously did not occur, or (iv) if the Party had established procedural rules (e.g., voting in the Central Committee) which all its elite members accepted as the sole legitimate way to resolve controversy, and whose decisions were accepted as binding by all. This final alternative—the institutionalization of the Party as a conflict-resolving mechanism—may have seemed for a time to have occurred, but as the 1950s wore on the evidence accumulated that, on the contrary, factionalism continued.

The factional conflicts were for the most part deeply hidden. Only occasionally, as in the Kao-Jao purge of 1954 and the P'eng Teh-huai purge of 1959, did factionalism erupt into public view.[82] But the 1950s and early 1960s were full of circumstantial evidence of factional conflict. This evidence included the regularly shifting policy lines (the alternation of radical and moderate policies in agriculture, foreign policy, cultural affairs and the like),[83] the often simultaneous issuing of contradictory policy signals, and the resulting failure of the system to move consistently in any single policy direction after the initial establishment of order and the destruction of the landlord class and other opposition elements. If, despite factional conflict, the allocation of most of the top posts in the polity remained essentially stable for most of the period, it was perhaps because many positions, such as Central Committee seats, were more honorary than substantive. Real power shifted more rapidly than formal position. Moreover, the struggle for position in the first decade or so after

liberation probably centred on control of newly liberated regional and provincial "independent kingdoms."[84] It was a phase in which factional efforts were heavily directed at competing to consolidate power within the broad polity. The process which William Whitson has discerned in the PLA, in which each Field Army became the consolidated power base of one or more factions, while "observers" from other factions were present in each Field Army (also serving as "hostages"),[85] was probably widely repeated in other institutions throughout the system. As control of these bases became stabilized, the struggle shifted to new posts higher up in the system.

There is no reason to suppose that Liu Shao-ch'i and Mao were consistently on opposite sides of the issues during these years; quite possibly in the shifting alliances of elite factions they sometimes found themselves on the same side of an issue. But in 1959 in the aftermath of the Great Leap they found themselves opposing one another. Factional rivalries perhaps at this point reached a new stage of intensity, with the "independent kingdoms" stabilized under factional control and conflict now focused on positions at the very top of the system. Most factional leaders were unified in the wish to subtract from Mao's too dominant power. The bargain which was struck called for greater power to pass into the hands of Liu Shao-ch'i and his followers and allies, and for Mao to move into a weaker position.

The period of 1959-62 was one of contradictory developments of the sort to be expected in the aftermath of such a factional consensus. Mao's actual power was weak, and within the small world of the elite he was subjected to persistent, damaging attack by followers of one of his rivals, P'eng Chen. At the same time, his charisma was exploited by the regime to strengthen ts legitimacy, harmed by the Great Leap; the cult of Mao was launched even while —and perhaps all the more willingly because— Mao was himself in eclipse. The new Minister of Defense, Lin Piao, in an effort to solidify the control over the PLA of his own faction, initiated a programme to study the thoughts of Mao within the Army.[86] Whether he was already then allied with Mao or simply turned to the Mao-study campaign as a convenient means of consolidating his personal influence against rival factions in the PLA is unclear. In any case, the campaign made Lin a natural ally for Mao in the latter's counterattack on his rivals which began in 1962.

Mao's counterattack of 1962-4, carried out

with the help of Lin Piao, was still within the rules of factional strife. It included the socialist education campaign, the learn-from-the-PLA campaign, the extension of PLA influence throughout the country, the escalation of the cult of Mao, and the pressure for attacks on intellectual cadres in the Party.[87] Mao's strategy was to use his national prestige, which his opponents had been obliged to enhance for the sake of the regime itself, and his alliance with Lin Piao, to undermine the personal power of his rivals, founded in the Party and cultural apparatuses. The rivals responded in typical factional fashion by stymying, blocking, and evading Mao's initiatives.[88]

If Mao had continued to attack his rivals in the factional tradition of the Party, he would eventually have precipitated another of the periodic elite crises, a realignment of factions and a redistribution of power which might have improved his position. But Mao decided to break the rules, to mobilize new sources of power from outside the elite. We may speculate that his goal was no longer merely an improved position for his faction in the elite, but an end to factionalism and its associated policy oscillations, and an institutionalization of the Party as an instrument of Maoist will, capable of outliving Mao himself. Perhaps a sense of impending death aroused at this moment a new sense of urgency.[89] Lacking the organized intra-Party power base of Stalin, Mao prepared to mobilize student power to drive his rivals out of office. The students were an attractive choice because of their historical role as official-topplers in modern China, because of Mao's faith in the revolutionary qualities of youth, and because of their suppressed tensions which were capable of exploding into a passionate political movement upon orders from a respected authority. "Perhaps for the first time in the history of a Communist state," as John W. Lewis has written, "a leadership faction (was to go) outside the party for its main support."[90]

If the essence of the Cultural Revolution was, as I have argued, a student-based Maoist attack on the factional Party elite, then its decisive period was the year in which the battle was fought over mobilizing versus demobilizing the students. This year (August 1966 to September 1967), saw a series of efforts by the factional elite to resist Mao's extra-Party offensive, demobilize the Red Guards, and restore the factional conflict system, if not the factional alignments, of the first 15 years of the regime. The ultimate reason for the victory of Mao's rivals was that Mao had no direct organizational link to the Red Guards, and was obliged to employ means under the control of the Party centre (the authority of the Party centre, the hierarchy of Party committees, the official press) to call the Red Guards into existence and to direct their activities. Even as he reached outside the factional system for his instrument of power, he remained dependent upon the Party for the means of wielding the instrument. In order to achieve his aims, Mao would have had to retain a shifting majority within the Party centre as he isolated his enemies one by one for attack by the students. This ultimately proved impossible. His efforts to achieve this shifting majority account for the rapid series of typical factional cycles of consensus, conflict, and crisis, each finding its response in the alternately rabid and restrained behaviour of the Red Guards, which characterized the central year of the Cultural Revolution. Although the shifting alignments within the Party centre are invisible to us, the rhythms of the struggle can be perceived.

The first cycle began with the launching of the Red Guards in August 1966, under a compromise document, the Sixteen Points, which ordered the Red Guards to be both radical and restrained; proceeded through the counter-mobilization of loyalist student and worker-peasant groups by party officials; and moved to a crisis of disorder in September which caused the factions at the centre to agree on the Red Guards' returning home and on the focusing of attacks on a small number of high Party officials who had already suffered factional reverses in the preceding months. In the second cycle, the Maoists launched new attacks centred in Peking and Shanghai on officials in government organs, and denunciations were published of some high non-Maoist officers of the PLA; a crisis of disorder in factories, docks and railways caused a new decision from the centre in January 1967, for the intervention of PLA units to restore order. In the third cycle, factions resisting Mao seized the initiative and, in the "February adverse current," took a number of steps further restricting the Red Guard movement; the Maoists countered by publishing new attacks on the "top Party person," signalling a revival of Red Guard activism throughout the country; the resulting disorder finally reached such serious proportions that the centre once again reached a decision in late April or early May 1967, for the re-imposition of order by the PLA on the local scene. In the fourth cycle, the Wuhan incident (July 1967) provided the Maoists with a pretext for demanding an attack on non-Maoist officers in the PLA; the resulting upsurge of the

Red Guards led to the stealing of weapons and the outbreak of serious fighting; in response, the centre reached the decision once again to clamp down on the masses; in September Chiang Ch'ing gave a speech attacking mass factionalism and three Maoist members of the Central Cultural Revolution Group were purged.

The defeat of the fourth launching of the Red Guards, I would argue, settled the fate of Mao's effort to end factionalism at the Party centre. Key factions at the centre—perhaps an example was the faction of Chou En-lai—had supported Mao long enough to enable him to launch the successive Red Guard outbursts; we may speculate that such factions advanced their own positions as members of other factions became discredited by Red Guard attacks. Now such swing factions feared further Red Guard activism, either because they were ready to consolidate their own positions or because they felt that future attacks would be directed at them. Mao could no longer garner the support he needed within the central elite to give him access to the tools necessary to direct the Red Guards. He could no longer divide and conquer in the Party centre; on this issue, the other factions of the centre were now united against him and his allies. Although the Cultural Revolution was to continue in name and with occasional outbreaks of violence, and although the press was to carry word of struggles between the left and the right until 1969, after September, 1967 there was no longer any hope of using the Red Guards to cleanse the Party centre of factionalism.

But this did not mean that disorder came to a halt. Conflicts at the intermediate and local levels of the system had been called into being by the factional struggle at the top. They now had a momentum of their own. At the mass organization level, there was the problem of putting a stop to the downward spiral of vengeance, resentment and violence, and of channelling aroused student activism into some controllable organizational framework. At the intermediate levels, many of the formerly secure "independent kingdoms" had seen outbreaks of internal conflict, possibly of a factional nature, and most of these struggles were still under way. Thus the period from the autumn of 1967 to the autumn of 1968 was spent in trying to organize the masses in "great alliances" and the provincial and regional officials in revolutionary committees. The job of resolving local controversies and restoring order must have been rendered all the more complex by the fact that the interests of the factions of the Party centre were intimately bound up in each decision made. The

shape of the future would be determined by the allocation of power in the regional and provincial revolutionary committees. These would be the new "independent kingdoms" upon which future factions would base their power.

The decision on who would control the contested intermediate levels of 1968 was not solely in the hands of the Party centre (as it had been in the 1950s), but also depended upon the balance of strength of the locally contending groups (whether factions or not). The support of a central faction was not adequate to assure the dominance of an otherwise weak local figure over the revolutionary committee, while a strong figure without central backing could bargain for such legitimation with central factions. The implications of this fact for the personnel makeup of the factional centre of the Party was enormous. Many of the old factional leaders had already been humiliated and pushed from power. Now leaders on the regional and provincial levels found themselves in a position to bargain with the remaining factions of the centre for exchanges of support. The result has been called an expansion of the central-level arena of conflict[91] to include the intermediate-level leaders; I would interpret it as a partial changing of the guard in which a new generation of factional leaders[92] was drawn into the central elite to replace those of the old elite who had fallen during the preceding two years. The system of factional conflict, however, remained unchanged.

Since 1968 there have been conflicts over whether the Cultural Revolution was good or bad, conflicts over the role of students and conflicts over the constitution of the Party. These conflicts have been carried out with many echoes of the Cultural Revolution—attacks on Liu Shao-ch'i "and other political swindlers," exhortations to rebel, occasional outbreaks of local violence. There have also continued to be changes in personnel at the higher levels of the system—e.g., the purges of Yang Ch'eng-wu, Ch'en Po-ta, Lin Piao and his followers. But I would argue that, although these conflicts have been intricate and significant, they indicate not that the Cultural Revolution remains unsettled, but that China remains in the pre-Cultural Revolution pattern of factional conflict at the centre.

SOME PROBLEMS AND IMPLICATIONS
OF THE MODEL

The style of argument I have adopted—development of an abstract model, and its speculative application to a concrete case—has advantages and drawbacks. Two of the advantages seem especially important. First, since the Cultural

Revolution, our analysis of Chinese politics has been undergoing a re-evaluation; various explicit and implicit models are being advanced, and it would be useful if these could be discussed and compared more systematically than has so far been the case. Second, since data on Chinese elite politics are scarce, an explicit model has the heuristic and exploratory function of suggesting one reconstruction of what the unknown facts may be.

The drawbacks must not be minimized. A model's ability to provide hypothetical bridges across gaps in the data is earned at the price of rigorous assumptions that may be only imperfectly fulfilled in complex reality. The factionalism model posited here assumes a situation where politicians rely exclusively upon clientelist ties to structure political action—a condition which must be set if a relatively coherent and comprehensible model is to be constructed, but which is not likely to be fully satisfied by many actual cases. A given political system is more likely to be a mixed than a pure type, both at a given moment in time, and, even more emphatically, through time, as forms of political organization change. Systems are usually mixed, but models are pure: the correspondence is seldom perfect. A model remains useful to the extent that it provides a relatively accurate diagram of the predominant dynamics of a system at a given point in time.

The model simplifies, too, by considering only one of the many sets of constraints that mould behaviour. It explains the effects of political behaviour of a given organizational framework, but it does not explain why men adopt that framework, how long they will stick to it, or indeed, why they insist on disagreeing with one another at all; it leaves unanswered such questions as why a certain government office is important for a certain faction to control, why a certain constitutional or charismatic legitimation is accepted, and why some revelations discredit a politician and others do not. A more complete explanation of behaviour in any political system would have to take into account not only what might be called the "organizational-structure" constraints on behaviour which have been discussed in this paper, but also cultural constraints, institutional constraints, and ideological constraints.

Particularly important in any fuller explanation of CCP elite politics would be the interplay between organizational and ideological constraints. There is certainly no contradiction between commitment to Maoist ideology and participation in factions. Although "faction" as such is deplored, factions may simply be conceived as ways of co-ordinating the efforts of like-minded colleagues to achieve goals in which they believe. As the model argues, factional struggle occurs within the context of a broad ideological consensus on goals and methods. It would therefore be a mistake to identify the factionalism model with a crude power struggle theory, if the latter assumes that leaders are cynical in their ideological statements. But it would be equally foolish to believe that in China alone men's perspectives on ideological and policy issues are not influenced by their individual political vantage points. The occasional impression that this is so may be the result of our knowing so much more about the issues than about the vantage points.

NOTES

*I am grateful to Norman Fainstein, Frederic J. Fleron, Jr., Ellen Frost, Mark Kesselman, Donald W. Klein, Steven I. Levine, Sharon G. Nathan, Michel C. Oksenberg, Robert H. Silin, Tang Tsou and Ezra F. Vogel for valuable comments, and to participants in various seminars and colloquia at which the ideas were tried out. An earlier version was prepared during a research associateship at the Center for Chinese Studies, University of Michigan, and was presented at the 1971 annual meeting of the American Political Science Association.

1 Franz Schurmann, *Ideology and Organization in Communist China* (Berkeley: University of California Press, 1966), pp. 55-7. Opinion groups twice solidified into "factions" ("organized opinion groups"), Schurmann notes, in the Kao-Jao and P'eng Teh-huai affairs. But these were quickly rooted out.

Schurmann's conception seems to include the possibility that certain leaders will take consistent positions in these debates, ending up sometimes in the majority and sometimes in the minority. We may thus regard as variants of his model those interpretations which classify leaders as "radicals" or "moderates," "dogmatists" or "pragmatists," etc., and view the Chinese political process as a debate among them.

2 Michel C. Oksenberg, "Policy making under Mao, 1949-1968: an overview," in John M. H. Lindbeck, ed., *China: Management of a Revolutionary Society* (Seattle: University of Washington Press, 1971), pp. 79-115.

3 See Philip Bridgham's three articles on the course of the Cultural Revolution: "Mao's 'Cultural Revolution': origin and development," *The China Quarterly* (*CQ*) 29 (January-March 1971), pp. 1-35; "Mao's Cultural Revolution in 1967; the struggle to seize power," *CQ* 34 (April-June 1968), pp. 6-37:

and "Mao's Cultural Revolution: the struggle to consolidate power," *CQ* 41 (January-March 1970), pp. 1-25. See also his "Factionalism in the central committee," in John Wilson Lewis, ed., *Party Leadership and Revolutionary Power in China* (Cambridge: Cambridge University Press, 1970), pp. 203-35. The term "Mao-in-command" is my own.

4 On Field Armies, see William Whitson, "The Field Army in Chinese Communist military politics," *CQ* 37 (January-March 1969), pp. 1-30. On commissars versus commanders, see William Whitson, "The military: their role in the policy process," in Frank N. Trager and William Henderson, eds., *Communist China, 1949-1969: A Twenty Year Appraisal* (N.Y.: The New York University Press, 1970), pp. 95-122; and Ellis Joffe, *Party and Army: Professionalism and Political Control in the Chinese Officer Corps, 1949-1964* (Cambridge, Mass.: Harvard University, East Asian Research Center, 1965), and "The Chinese Army under Lin Piao: prelude to political intervention," in Lindbeck, ed., *China*, pp. 343-74. On the Party and the gun, see, among others, Ralph L. Powell, "The Party, the government and the gun," *Asian Survey (AS)* X:6 (June 1970), pp. 441-71. On legal specialists versus new cadres, see Victor H. Li, "The evolution and development of the Chinese legal system," in Lindbeck, ed., *China*, pp. 221-255. For further discussion of the "interest group" and "Mao-in-command" models see my "Models of conflict in Chinese politics," *Problems of Communism*, Vol. XXI, No. 3 (May-June 1972), pp. 80-3. The "policy making under Mao" and "interest group" models could nicely be combined, but so far as I am aware no one has yet done so in print.

5 That is, politics in the upper level of the CCP from 1921 to 1949, and at the "central level" (see below) of the CPR since 1949.

6 See, for example, Richard M. Pfeffer, "The pursuit of purity," *Problems of Communism*, Vol. XVIII, No. 6 (November-December 1969), pp. 12-25; Frederick C. Teiwes, "A review article: The evolution of leadership purges in Communist China," *CQ* 41 (January-March 1970), pp. 122-35.

7 See, for example, Franz Schurmann, "The attack of the Cultural Revolution on ideology and organization," in Ping-ti Ho and Tang Tsou, eds., *China in Crisis*, Vol. 1, *China's Heritage and the Communist Political System*, Bk. Two (Chicago: The University of Chicago Press, 1968), pp. 558-60.

8 See, for example, Leonard Schapiro and John Wilson Lewis, "The roles of the monolithic party under the totalitarian leader," in John Wilson Lewis, ed., *Party Leadership*, pp. 114-45; Benjamin I. Schwartz, "The reign of virtue: some broad perspectives on leader and Party in the Cultural Revolution," *Ibid.* pp. 149-69; and Stuart R. Schram, "The Party in Chinese Communist ideology," *Ibid.* pp. 170-202.

9 See, for example, Jack Gray, "Mao's economic thoughts," *Far Eastern Economic Review*, Vol. LXVII, No. 3 (15 January 1970), p. 16.

10 See, for example, Robert Jay Lifton, *Revolutionary Immortality: Mao Tse-tung and the Chinese Cultural Revolution* (New York: Vintage Books, 1968).

11 For example, those interpretations which stress Chiang Ch'ing's jealousy of Wang Kuang-mei (Mrs. Liu Shao-ch'i or Mao's resentment of insults suffered at the hands of Liu Shao-ch'i.

12 The model was first developed to explain political factionalism in early Republican China in my Ph.D. dissertation, "Factionalism in early republican China: the politics of the Peking government, 1918-1920," Department of Government, Harvard University, 1970. It has gone through various revisions in response to the criticisms of colleagues and to my own reading on both Chinese and non-Chinese politics. The logical status I would claim for the model, as distinct from the conditions of its development, is that of an internally consistent description of what political conflict would be like under certain assumptions.

13 In recent years studies of the political and other functions of clientelist ties have proliferated. Terminology varies ("dyadic contract," "dyadic alliance," "patron-client tie," etc.) but there is little question that various authors are referring to the same quite clearly defined phenomenon. Among the many discussions of the clientelist ties or their political uses are George M. Foster, "The dyadic contract: a model for the social structure of a Mexican peasant village," in Jack M. Potter, May N. Diaz and George M. Foster, eds., *Peasant Society: A Reader* (Boston: Little, Brown, 1967), pp. 213-30; James C. Scott, "Patron-client politics and political change in Southeast Asia," *American Political Science Review (APSR)* LXVI: 1 (March 1972), pp. 91-113; and Carl H. Landé, "Networks and groups in Southeast Asia: some observations on the group theory of politics," paper prepared for delivery at the 1971 annual meeting of the American Political Science Association, forthcoming in *APSR*.

Clientelist ties have been highly developed, and have played important roles, in China, where they have been embedded in and reinforced by a cultural stress on the mutual rights and obligations involved in social roles. See especially Benjamin I. Schwartz, "On attitudes toward law in China," reprinted in Jerome Alan Cohen, *The Criminal Process in the People's Republic of China, 1949-1963: An Introduction* (Cambridge, Mass.: Harvard University Press, 1968), pp. 62-70; and Lien-sheng Yang, "The concept of *pao* as a basis for social relations in China," in John K. Fairbank, ed., *Chinese Thought and Institutions* (Chicago: University of Chicago Press, 1957), pp. 291-309. In this article I must beg a number of important questions: what are the specific forms and functions of clientelist ties in Chinese life and how have these ties changed in the revolutionary process in China? Some thoughts on these matters are contained in my paper, " 'Connections' in Chinese politics: political recruitment and *kuan-hsi* in late Ch'ing and early republican China," prepared for delivery at the 1972 annual meeting of the American Historical Association.

14 Peter M. Blau, *Exchange and Power in Social Life* (New York: John Wiley and Sons, 1964), p. 5 and *passim*.

15 Marshal D. Sahlins, "On the sociology of primitive exchange," in Michael Banton, ed., *The*

Relevance of Models for Social Anthropology (London: Tavistock, 1965), p. 144 and *passim*.

16 Max Weber, *The Theory of Social and Economic Organization*, A. M. Henderson and Talcott Parsons, trans. (New York: Free Press, 1964), pp. 152-3.

17 *Cf.* Foster, "The dyadic contract."

18 For suggestive studies of clientelist ties in operation in non-political contexts, see, among others, James N. Anderson, "Buy-and-sell and economic personalism: foundations for Philippine entrepreneurship," *AS* IX:9 (September 1969), pp. 641-68; Mary R. Hollnsteiner, "Social structure and power in a Philippine municipality," in Potter, *et al.*, eds., *Peasant Society: A Reader*, pp. 200-12; Sidney W. Mintz, "Pratik: Haitian personal economic relationships," *Ibid.* pp. 54-63; and Robert H. Silin, "Marketing and credit in a Hong Kong wholesale market," in W. E. Willmott, ed., *Economic Organization in Chinese Society* (Stanford: Stanford University Press, 1972), pp. 327-52.

19 See, for example, Karl D. Jackson, "Communication and national integration in Sudanese villages: implications for communications strategy," paper prepared for presentation at a meeting of the SEADAG Indonesia Seminar in New York City on 30 March-1 April 1972; Martin and Susan Tolchin, *To the Victor . . . Political Patronage from the Clubhouse to the White House* (New York: Vintage, 1972); William Foote Whyte, *Street Corner Society: The Social Structure of an Italian Slum*, Enl. ed. (Chicago: University of Chicago, 1955), Pt. II.

20 Distinctions can probably fruitfully be made between "clientelist parties," defined as integrating all levels of the political system through clientelist ties, and "machines," defined as operating strictly on the local level. Among the major theoretically-oriented studies of such organizations are James C. Scott, *Comparative Political Corruption* (Englewood Cliffs, N.J.: Prentice-Hall, 1972), chs. 6-9; and John Duncan Powell, "Peasant society and clientelist politics," *APSR* LXIV:2 (June 1970), pp. 411-25.

Scott has gone furthest in specifying the conditions under which clientelist parties or machines can develop (*Corruption*, esp. pp. 104-22, and 151-7). The problem of the conditions of machine development becomes especially important when, as here, one is dealing with a mass participation system that nonetheless has oligarchic factions. Obviously a key difference between contemporary China and those political systems in which clientelist parties or machines have developed is that in China there is no real electoral competition for power. Among the case studies of political systems organized by clientelist parties are Robert H. Dix, *Colombia: The Political Dimensions of Change* (New Haven: Yale University Press, 1967), esp. chs. 8 and 9; Keith R. Legg, *Politics in Modern Greece* (Stanford: Stanford University Press, 1969), esp. chs. 6-8; Myron Weiner, *Party Building in a New Nation: The Indian National Congress* (Chicago: The University of Chicago Press, 1967); and William Foote Whyte, *Street Corner Society*, esp. ch. VI. I am grateful to Michael Bucuvalas and Pedro Cabán for bringing Legg and Dix to my attention.

21 For ways of conceptualizing a network from the standpoint of an individual ego, see: J. A. Barnes, "Networks and political process," in Marc J. Swartz, ed., *Local-Level Politics: Social and Cultural Perspectives* (Chicago: Aldine, 1968), pp. 107-30; and Adrian C. Mayer, "The significance of quasi-groups in the study of complex societies," in Michael Banton, ed., *The Social Anthropology of Complex Societies*, A.S.A. Monograph 4 (London: Tavistock, 1966), pp. 97-122.

22 It seems unnecessary to specify an exact size boundary between factions and machines since the difference between the two is so large. The difference, of course, is not just one of size; as a consequence of their different sizes and different degrees of selectivity in recruitment, as well as of the different natures of their respective arenas, machines and factions behave in thoroughly distinguishable ways.

23 This conception of a faction is similar to that offered by Ralph Nicholas, "Factions: a comparative analysis," in Michael Banton, ed., *Political Systems and the Distribution of Power*, A.S.A. Monograph 2 (London: Tavistock, 1965), pp. 27-9, and to Landé's concept of the "dyadic following" in his "Networks and groups." Let me stress again that I have defined "faction" in a technical sense. By faction I do not mean an "organized opinion group" (*cf.* Schurmann, *Ideology and Organization*, p. 56) contending warlords, or Red Guards. Nor should the word faction as used here be regarded as a translation of the Chinese terms *p'ai, hsi, tang,* or *hui*. Whether any of these things can be called a faction by the present definition can only be determined upon close structural analysis. Although restrictive, the definition advanced here seems to fit a wide range of configurations found in political systems and sub-systems including governments, parties, bureaucracies, parliaments, courts and villages in a number of different geographical areas and historical periods. Some examples are cited in my dissertation, pp. 373-85.

24 Each structural characteristic discussed is not necessarily unique to factions (for example, guerrilla bands may be equally flexible, and for some of the same reasons), but none of them is universal and the combination of characteristics is distinctive.

25 If a faction becomes corporatized the clientelist relations and the structure ceases to be a faction in this sense. What might encourage or discourage corporatization of a faction is a question that cannot be investigated here. For the concept of "corporate" used here, see Weber, *Theory of Social and Economic Organization*, pp. 145-8.

26 The follower may in turn recruit others as his own followers.

27 For a suggestive exploration of the advantages of this sort of communications pattern, see Alex Bavelas, "Communications patterns in task-oriented groups," in Daniel Lerner and Harold D. Lasswell, eds., *The Policy Sciences* (Stanford: Stanford University Press, 1951), pp. 193-202.

28 See Barry E. Collins and Bertram H. Raven, "Group structure: attraction, coalitions, communications, and power," in Gardner Lindzey and Elliot Aronson, eds., *The Handbook of Social Psychology*, 2nd

ed. (Reading, Mass.: Addison-Wesley, 1969), Vol. IV, pp. 137-55.

29 It may be asked why communications patterns and other structural features to be discussed below limit the size of factions but not of "clientelist parties." For one thing, although a clientelist party is founded on patronage dispensed through clientelist ties, it also takes on elements of formal organization (party label, headquarters, officers, rules) to enable it to administer its mass electoral base. It is in this sense not a "pure type" of clientelist structure. Even more fundamentally, each type of political structure ideal-typically stands in an adaptive relationship to its political environment. The clientelist party is adapted to, and tends to maintain, a mass electoral political system. The faction is adapted to and tends to maintain an oligarchic or small-scale system. Although I argue that certain elements of factional structure limit factional size, I could just as well build the argument in reverse: a political setting which involves relatively few people makes it possible for men to organize themselves in ways that would not be suited to large organizations.

30 Cf. The "size principle" as enunciated by William H. Riker, *The Theory of Political Coalitions* (New Haven: Yale University Press, 1962), pp. 32-3.

31 Cf. Amitai Etzioni, *Modern Organizations* (Englewood Cliffs, N.J.: Prentice-Hall, Inc., 1964), *passim*.

32 As was the case with the structural characteristics of factions, the claim is not made that the modes of conflict characteristic of factions are each unique to factional systems, merely that none of them is universal to all political systems and that the combination of all of them is found only in factional systems.

33 A major reason for differences in the power of factions is the differing power of their support structures (regional and/or institutional power bases). But opposing power bases cannot be entirely eliminated, nor, given the tendency of large, victorious factions to split, can they be taken over.

34 Nathan Leites, *On the Game of Politics in France* (Stanford: Stanford University Press, 1959), pp. 23 and 45.

35 Cf. F. G. Bailey, "Parapolitical systems," in Swartz, ed., *Local-Level Politics*, p. 282; Bernard Gallin, "Political factionalism and its impact on Chinese village school organization in Taiwan," *Ibid.* p. 390; and Melford E. Spiro, "Factionalism and politics in village Burma," *Ibid.* pp. 410-12.

36 Leites, *On the Game*, p. 117.

37 In the Chinese context, for example, factional alignments did not cross the ideological boundaries between the late Ch'ing conservatives on the one hand and the constitutionalists and revolutionaries on the other, or between the Kuomintang and the CCP. But within each major ideological current factional alignments were not (how could they be?) determined by pure, *a priori* ideological compatibilities. Ideological stands were developed and revised in the course of politics. For a case study of the process by which ideological standpoint becomes defined in the course of political conflict, as rivals force one another to delineate and clarify their positions, see Benjamin I.

Schwartz, *Chinese Communism and the Rise of Mao* (Cambridge, Mass.: Harvard University Press, 1952).

38 Cf. Leites, *On the Game*, pp. 48-9.

39 *Ibid.* Ch. 4, esp. pp. 97-8.

40 Cf. *Ibid.* pp. 82-3.

41 Cf. James L. Payne, *Patterns of Conflict in Colombia* (New Haven, Yale University Press, 1968), pp. 3-24. Payne attempts to explain factionalism in Colombian politics on the basis of the prevalence of "status," rather than "programme," incentives among Colombian politicians. However, if our model is correct, factionalism can occur in the presence of either type of incentive. Politicians in factional systems will tend to act as if they were motivated by status incentives because of the importance of personal prestige and personal connexions as political resources in factional systems. It is immaterial to the model how high-minded the ultimate motives for conflict are.

42 Cf. Leites, *On the Game*, pp. 7-34.

43 Cf. Payne, *Patterns of Conflict*, pp. 249-50.

44 Myron Weiner, *Party Politics in India: The Development of a Multi-Party System* (Princeton: Princeton University Press, 1957), pp. 237-40. See also Lewis A. Coser, *The Functions of Social Conflict* (New York: The Free Press, 1964), pp. 33-8.

45 On the unifying effects of conflict, see further Coser, *Functions, passim*; and George Simmel, *Conflict and the Web of Group-Affiliations*, Kurt H. Wolff and Reinhard Bendix, trans. (New York: The Free Press, 1955), pp. 13-123.

46 The same distinction holds if, as I shall argue was the case with the CCP until 1949, the group of factions is itself the counter-elite and its enemies are the ruling elite.

47 Of course, they do not always succeed in preserving the regime. If the social context of the regime has been changing so that, *e.g.*, new problems demand solutions or new groups demand access to the system, immobilism (see below) may prevent the regime from responding successfully. The consequent loss of legitimacy may make it an easy target for a strong rival. An example is the crumbling of the Peking Government before the Kuomintang advance in 1928.

The Clemenceau and Poincaré ministries in France are well-known instances of resistance by a factional system to external threat. See Philip M. Williams, *Crisis and Compromise: Politics in the Fourth Republic*, paperback ed. (Garden City, N.Y.: Anchor Books, 1966), p. 11.

48 Cf. Simmel, *Conflict*, p. 41.

49 Bernard J. Siegel and Alan R. Beals, "Pervasive factionalism," *American Anthropologist*, 62 (1960), pp. 394-417. For a critique, see Nicholas, "Factions," pp. 56-7.

50 Cf. in particular Stuart R. Schram, "The Party," p. 171; Howard L. Boorman, "Teng Hsiaop'ing: a political profile," *CQ* 21 (January-March 1965), p. 119; Whitson, "The Field Army," *passim*.

51 "In fact, CC membership has been in recent years a badge of recognition or a reward for things done." Donald W. Klein and Lois B. Hager, "The ninth Central Committee," *CQ* 45 (January-March 1971), p. 37.

52 Parris H. Chang, "Research notes on the changing loci of decision in the Chinese Communist party," *CQ* 44 (October-December 1970), pp. 170-3.

53 Ezra F. Vogel, *Canton under Communism: Programs and Politics in a Provincial Capital, 1949-1968* (Cambridge, Mass.: Harvard University Press, 1969), p. 325; Michel Oksenberg, "Occupational groups in Chinese society and the Cultural Revolution," in *The Cultural Revolution: 1967 in Review*, Michigan Papers in Chinese Studies, No. 2 (Ann Arbor, Mich., 1968), p. 26.

54 "Lin Piao: a historical profile," *Current Scene*, Vol. VII, No. 5 (10 March 1969), p. 3; Bridgham, "Mao's Cultural Revolution: the struggle to consolidate power," p. 16; Ralph L. Powell, "The increasing power of Lin Piao and the Party-soldiers, 1959-1966," *CQ* 34 (April-June 1968), pp. 62-3.

55 Schapiro and Lewis, "The roles of the monolithic Party," p. 131.

56 Parris H. Chang, "Mao's Great Purge: a political balance sheet," *Problems of Communism*, Vol. XVIII, No. 2 (March-April 1969), p. 8; Whitson, "The Field Army," pp. 13-21.

57 Cited from *Hung-ch'i (Red Flag)*, No. 12, 1967, in "Quarterly chronicle and documentation," *CQ* 32 (October-December 1967), p. 198.

58 *E.g.*, see Charles Neuhauser, "The Chinese Communist Party in the 1960s: prelude to the Cultural Revolution," *CQ* 32 (October-December 1967), p. 3.

59 Among these most prominent so far are Chao Tzu-yang and Ch'en Tsai-tao, but many less prominent cadres are also said to have been reinstated.

60 *Cf.* Ezra F. Vogel, "The structure of conflict: China in 1967," in *The Cultural Revolution: 1967 in Review*, pp. 106-7.

61 See Richard Baum, "China: year of the mangoes," *AS* IX:1 (January 1969), pp. 3-4; Gordon A. Bennet, "China's continuing revolution: will it be permanent?" *AS* X:1 (January 1970), p. 3.

62 *Cf.* Merle Goldman, "The fall of Chou Yang," *CQ* 27 (July-September 1966), pp. 132-148.

63 For example, see Bridgman's three articles cited above, note 3. Also *cf.* Baum, "China: year of the mangoes," pp. 4-5.

64 See "Quarterly chronicle and documentation," *CQ* 32 (October-December 1967), pp. 184-221.

65 Of course at any given moment there seemed to be a definite policy line, but the question is whether the line was consistently sustained or whether it gave way to a contradictory line.

66 On Ulanfu, see Paul Hyer and William Heaton, "The Cultural Revolution in Inner Mongolia," *CQ* 36 (October-December 1968), pp. 114-28; on Li Ching-ch'üan, see "Stalemate in Szechuan," *Current Scene*, Vol. VI, No. 11 (1 July 1968), pp. 1-13. Frederick Teiwes, in his *Provincial Party Personnel in Mainland China, 1955-1966* (New York: East Asian Institute, Columbia University, 1967), has shown that provincial leadership was mainly stable during the 1956-66 period (p. 62), which seems consistent with the "independent kingdoms" view advanced here, although Teiwes himself concludes that the data do not

support the idea of provincial-level factions (pp. 27-8).

67 Whitson, "The Field Army."

68 *Cf.* Jürgen Domes, "The role of the military in the formation of revolutionary committees 1967-68," *CQ* 44 (October-December 1970), pp. 112-45.

69 "Quarterly chronicle and documentation." *CQ* 32 (October-December, 1967), p. 196.

70 Melvin Gurtov, "The foreign ministry and foreign affairs during the Cultural Revolution," *CQ* 40 (October-December 1969), pp. 65-102.

71 This analysis is based on Vogel, *Canton*, pp. 323-35; Gordon A. Bennett and Ronald N. Montaperto, *Red Guard: The Political Biography of Dai Hsiao-ai* (Garden City, N.Y.: Doubleday, 1971); and John Israel, "The Red Guards in historical perspective: continuity and change in the Chinese youth movement," *CQ* 30 (April-June 1967), pp. 1-32.

72 See, *e.g.*, "Mass factionalism in Communist China," *Current Scene*, Vol. VI, No. 8 (15 May 1968), pp. 1-13.

73 Bennett and Montaperto, *Red Guard*, pp. 72-7.

74 *Ibid.* p. 142.

75 *Ibid.* p. 186; Vogel, *Canton*, pp. 329-30.

76 See Ralph H. Turner, "Collective Behavior," in Robert E. L. Faris, ed., *Handbook of Modern Sociology* (Chicago: Rand McNally, 1964), pp. 382-425; and Lewis M. Killian, "Social movements," *Ibid.* pp. 426-55.

77 *Cf.* Israel, "The Red Guards," p. 19.

78 Schram, "The Party"; Whitson, "The Field Army."

79 See, for example, Schwartz, *Chinese Communism and the Rise of Mao*; John E. Rue, *Mao Tse-tung in Opposition, 1927-1935* (Stanford: Stanford University Press, 1966).

80 *Cf.* Whitson, "The Field Army," pp. 3-8 and 21-6.

81 This generalization applies best to the history of the Party after about 1938. Before that time were several incidents of intra-Party military conflict and of permanent splits.

82 On the Kao purge, see Bridgham, "Factionalism in the central committee," pp. 205-211; Teiwes, "A review article," pp. 122-6. On the P'eng Teh-huai purge, see both of these articles and David A. Charles, "The dismissal of Marshal P'eng Teh-huai," in Roderick MacFarquhar, ed., *China Under Mao: Politics Takes Command, A Selection of Articles from The China Quarterly* (Cambridge, Mass.; The M.I.T. Press, 1966), pp. 20-33. What is known about these episodes is consistent with the view that they represent instances of factional conflict.

83 The phenomenon of policy oscillation in the CPR has been noted by many analysts, and various efforts have been made to explain it. What is striking about many—not all—of these analyses is that they are non-political, avoiding any hint that elite conflicts might underlie the oscillations. For some noteworthy attempts to deal with this problem, see Schurmann, *Ideology and Organization*, pp. 73-104; Shinkichi Et, "Communist China: moderation and radicalism in the Chinese revolution," in James B. Crowley, ed.,

Modern East Asia: Essays in Interpretation (N.Y.: Harcourt, Brace and World, Inc., 1970), pp. 337-73; G. William Skinner and Edwin A. Winckler, "Compliance succession in rural Communist China: a cyclical theory," in Amitai Etzioni, ed. *A Sociological Reader in Complex Organizations*, 2nd ed. (N.Y.: Holt, Rinehart and Winston, 1969), pp. 410-38; and Alexander Eckstein, "Economic fluctuations in Communist China's domestic development," in Ho and Tsou, eds., *China in Crisis*, Vol. I, Bk. 2, pp. 691-729.

84 *Cf.* Vogel, *Canton,* chs. 2 and 3.

85 Whitson, "The Field Army," pp. 15, 23-4.

86 The developments of this period are reviewed in Bridgham, "Mao's Cultural Revolution" origin and development," pp. 2-7. Also see Powell, "The Increasing Power," pp. 45-6 and 62—; Joffe, "The Chinese Army under Lin Piao," in Lindbeck, ed., *China*; and Merle Goldman, "Party policies toward the intellectuals: the unique blooming and contending of 1961-2" in Lewis, ed., *Party Leadership*, pp. 268-303.

87 Bridgham, "Mao's 'Cultural Revolution': origin and development," pp. 8-12.

88 Neuhauser, "The Chinese Communist Party," pp. 19-25.

89 As Robert Jay Lifton has argued, in *Revolutionary Immortality*.

90 John W. Lewis, "Leader, commissar, and bureaucrat: the Chinese political system in the last days of the revolution," in Ho and Tsou, eds., *China in Crisis*, Vol. 1, Bk. Two, p. 474. Note that if one views the Cultural Revolution not as a factional attack on Mao, but as a Maoist attack on factions, one disposes of most of the objections to a factional interpretation raised by Teiwes, "A review article," pp. 126-35.

91 Chang, "Research notes," p. 177.

92 *Cf.* Klein and Hager, "The ninth Central Committee," pp. 55-6. This is a "new generation" in the sense that these men had not previously been operating at the central level. Most or all of them had previously been high officials of the Party or the Army or both. They had been followers in factions, we assume, but now they emerged as leaders in their own right, in the aftermath of the deterioration of many of the pre-Cultural Revolution factions.

PARTIES AND SOCIETY IN LATIN AMERICA

DOUGLAS A. CHALMERS

STUDENTS OF LATIN American politics have often observed that party behavior and roles are confused and contradictory. However, confusion, like beauty, lies in the eyes of the beholder. Without the appropriate lens (of concepts and questions) the landscape is bound to look puzzling. Finding such a lens is no easy task. Methodological sophistication may help, and occasionally a serendipitous computer may uncover an illuminating scale or correlation. First, however, one has to find the proper focus for these new instruments.

The efforts being made to systematize comparisons of parties through the compilation of increasingly complex dimensions of party structure and activity (e.g., Janda, 1968) may provide some valuable insights, but only if they are related to variations in the political systems in which the parties are found. Contrasts among parties or party systems, once exposed, inevitably lead to the query, "so what?" Functionalists tell us of many functions (e.g., integration, stability, enhanced capability and democratization) that may result from the roles played by parties (e.g., articulation, aggregation, socialization). Many imply that differently structured parties

or party systems have varying consequences for the political system. This proposition is irrefutable and meaningless unless a specific relationship between structures and functions is suggested. Even suggesting hypotheses has been hazardous and unsatisfying, in part because there is an intervening variable that overwhelms the relationship. That intervening variable is the character of the other structures in the socio-political system.

Political scientists have several ways of describing this intervening variable, but the most prevalent ones are not adequate. A common one is the democratic-dictatorial dimension. Similar parties have different consequences at either end of the scale. This dimension also contributes to explaining why parties are structured differently, since some types of parties are more common in democratic systems than in dictatorial ones. (This latter kind of argument is always in danger of becoming tautological since the operational test of democracy is often the character of the party system involved.)

The inadequacy of the democratic-dictatorial variable is all too clear when applied to Latin America. Dictatorial episodes have certainly altered the role of, or suppressed, parties, but there is a strong continuity to be explained, since they reappear after the fall of the dictator, either with no change, or simply changes in name, and, perhaps, some rearrangement of the elite groups. For example, it is not hard to find continuity in Brazilian parties beginning with the Old Republic and going through the first Vargas dictatorship, the New Republic, and finally even under the present military regime.

Recently the most popular key to solving the riddle of "so what?" (and "why?") has been the protean notion of development. Since parties are relatively modern phenomena, and since there has been an apparently systematic evolution of parties (in Europe, at least), it has become common to suggest that certain types of parties are characteristic of specific levels of development (e.g., as development increases, parties become increasingly mass-oriented and articulated). With respect to functions, similar parties have different functions at different levels of development, e.g., strongly articulated mass parties may be integrative in a transitional phase, and disintegrative at a more advanced stage.[1]

Levels of development also seems inadequate as an intervening or explanatory variable with regard to Latin America. Parties have certainly evolved, but their evolution never matches the expectations of outside observers. Despite assertions that Latin American parties are "growing up," or that modern parties are emerging,[2] most inquiries that set out to find in Latin America parties with the characteristics which were present in Europe and the United States at similar stages of development result in negative or unconvincing conclusions. Part of the difficulty lies in the fact that many characteristics of Latin American parties and party systems (e.g., personalism, instability, multiplication of small parties, splintering of major parties, relative lack of programmatic content) seem to remain relatively constant, whatever their level of development.

As an intervening variable conditioning the functions of parties, the notion of levels of development also gets little beyond highly abstract argumentation. To say, as some have,[3] that Latin America needs some form of mobilizing, national-integrating party does not get far when such parties do not exist. Finally, the utility of the concept of development levels is also questionable because the personalist and programmatically fluid Latin American parties do not seem to change their functions in vary-

ing stages of the developmental process.

It is possible to argue that some basic fault in the system, e.g., the peculiar political culture, or a tendency for military and business elites to establish private governments, prevents the emergence of functional parties. There is strong reason to doubt that at any level of development, the kinds of parties felt to be national-integrating and mass-mobilizing in other parts of the world (i.e., parties with a strong charismatic leader, a "political religion" and a strongly articulated organization) would in fact accomplish those functions in Latin America. They are not only unlikely, but could only be successful after an extremely costly destruction of existing social and political patterns.[4]

The line of argument so far leads to the conclusion that some other set of intervening and explanatory variables is necessary to understand and interpret political parties, particularly, but not only, in Latin America. This paper takes the view that such a set of variables can be found in aspects of the distinctive sociopolitical structure common to Latin America. Using four dimensions, the following pages will describe what I call the Latin America type of sociopolitical structure, and discuss the manner in which it shapes parties and the opportunities they have for performing important functions in Latin American political systems. I will assert the universality of this Latin American type of sociopolitical structure within the area, and its distinctiveness compared with other parts of the world.[5]

The reader may well throw up his hands at this point—to have been led by such a complex route to such a conventional end point. Discussions of the distinctiveness of Latin America can be found in all sorts of literature.[6] To some extent, what follows is merely a synthesis of such discussions, but with somewhat different purposes. The objective is not to show the impossibility of comparing Latin America with other areas, as some studies do, but to lay the groundwork for meaningful comparison. Further, much discussion of Latin America's distinctiveness is intended to show or explain the backwardness of the area, and is thus linked to its level of development. I am interested in aspects that appear to be relatively permanent, and therefore are independent of the level of development. One might think of the Latin American type of structure as describing aspects of Latin America's distinctive *path* of development.

The prima facie reasons for assuming that a distinctive path of development common to all Latin American countries exists have been spelled out often enough. Geographic and racial characteristics were long considered central, but more immediate have been the area's common culture and enduring peripherality to a more developed world.

Because of her colonial experience, Latin America's Iberian-based culture is astonishingly dominant throughout the area. Although Latin Americans can easily cite differences between Argentines, Brazilians and Mexicans, the more important fact is that despite the distances and the weakness of inter-American contacts, the culture of Latin American nations remains profoundly uniform. Further, despite the massive presence of indigenous populations, the vast importations of slaves and the waves of European migration, opposing subcultures have in very large part been transformed, exterminated or completely subordinated. The content of the culture, its relative uniformity throughout the area and its dominance in each country are major determinants of the area's distinctive socio-political structure.

The other factor contributing to Latin America's distinctive path of development is its dependence on, and orientation towards, the more economically developed, technology-producing and politically powerful nations. Neither colonies nor satellites for the last century-and-a-half, Latin America remains dependent on the European-North American center, and highly receptive to influences emanating from it. This is in part because of Latin America's European cultural background, and in part because the area is penetrated by many groups of influential foreigners and "linkage groups."[7]

The distinctive sociopolitical structures resulting from this common culture and peripheral status deserve a name, and the temptation to provide one is strong. Terms that come close would be "authoritarian," "corporate," or perhaps Apter's (1965, ch. 1 and passim) "neomercantilist." Jaguaribe (1967: 145 ff.) refers to "neo-Bismarckian" and "colonial-fascist" variations. "Fascist" is a term that often lurks in the writings about Latin America, and has some credibility if only because the three European regimes often linked with that term—Spain, Portugal and Italy—have clearly been important influences in Latin America.[8] All these terms have severe limitations, however, either because of their partial applicability, their emotional overtones, or their opacity. Resisting the temptation to add yet another, I will content myself with the unenlightening "Latin American" to characterize the structural type, and proceed to a description of four of its characteristics.

These four characteristics are: (1) the diffuse vertical character of its social structure (or negatively, the absence of either polarizing conflicts or pluralistic, autonomous group formation); (2) the intertwining of the social structures with political ones; (3) the confrontations and fluidity of alliances among elites who have disparate power capabilities; and (4) the prominence of a technician-centered decision-making style. Separately, all these characteristics can be found in other systems. Together they form a pattern distinctive to Latin America.

(1) The Diffuse Vertical Character of the Social Structure

All reasonably integrated societies establish numerous hierarchies of social interaction, which, however specialized, provide systems of authority relationships, social status rankings, channels of mobility and a sense of identity for their participants. As modernization proceeds, these hierarchies become more specialized, more bureaucratized and more numerous. They are vertical, in the sense that they link upper and lower statuses and establish superior-subordinate relationships. In some societies, as in much of Europe, this verticality is destroyed when conflict between upper and lower statuses, because of cultural differences or class conflicts, creates some form of polarization. In other societies, such as the United States, the weakness of the upper strata and dispersion of the population made possible another alternative, in which modernization weakened the vertical links between local notables and higher authorities, and myriad groups and associations were formed on a relatively autonomous basis, producing the oft-noted pluralist pattern (cf. Hays, 1967: 152). In Latin America, the verticality has not been broken by conflict, nor have groups and associations been strong enough to resist subordination to upper strata.

In later stages of development, the breaks in the vertical structures of even polarized societies are repaired (or new links are forged), as in the supercession of class polarities in

Europe. The bewildering variety of autonomous groups in countries such as the United States also slowly becomes more and more involved with, and controlled by, upper level (chiefly governmental) institutions. The distinctiveness of the Latin American pattern is that it began with strongly elite-centered vertical social structures and has by and large avoided any break in the continuity. The path has been different, although the end points appear to be converging.

The result of this continuity in Latin America is that the vertical ties have not been destroyed, the hierarchies continue to represent diffuse interests, and, from the point of view of the individual member, his ties to the hierarchy (and particularly to the communities found at its base) remain strong and exclusive. The following explanation may clarify these points.

The continuing verticality of relationships means that society is structured according to numerous pyramids of status and authority, in which lower-level elites are oriented towards, and dependent upon, upper elites. Each pyramid is in fact a hierarchically arranged set of smaller pyramids. The traditional pyramid, or hierarchy, has small town or village communities at the base, and a chain of regional and national elites above them. Newer hierarchies may be based on trade unions, reformed agrarian units, and the like, but have the same hierarchy of regional and national elites above them, within, perhaps, an official syndicalist structure. This latter type I will call the "bureaucratic-corporatist" hierarchy.

Since these hierarchies are not the result of class or cultural conflicts, their structures do not represent clearly defined and specific interests, other than that of their own preservation and prosperity. Their goals and interests are thus diffuse. The hierarchies encompass many social and economic strata, many occupations and activities, and remain, in political terms, more like cliques and factions (with their followings and subordinates) than class or interest groups.[9]

From the point of view of the individual, his basic identification and orientation is towards the community for most aspects of his social, religious and occupational life. The community involved is usually geographically defined (e.g., a town, an hacienda, an urban neighborhood). In more modern circumstances, for example in major cities and larger provincial towns, there may be considerable division of labor and specialization, and a variety of secondary associations for economic, health, educational, cultural and social activities. However, the community is not weakened, because these secondary associations limit their links with similar secondary associations in other localities, and serve primarily as intermediaries between the individual and the community leaders.

In the modern urban setting an individual may live in one place and work in another. Ties to the work place are often exceedingly limited. The union is seen as essentially a remote grouping to the individual, whose primary loyalties even for occupational questions are to his local community. The union becomes important either when it becomes another community-oriented structure (and thus deemphasizes its ties with national union structures), or when the worker becomes completely involved in the union as a sort of community in itself. The latter may happen in strongly working-class neighborhoods, mining towns and the like. When the latter occurs, the basis for the bureaucratic-corporatist structure is established. This suggests, perhaps as a basic cultural trait, the propensity towards a single comprehensive group identification among most Latin Americans.

An indication of the extent of an individual's ties to a community is the emphasis on the complex and extended chain of face-to-face and personal relationships (often reinforced by family ties) that link him with other members of the community in varied and diverse occupations. Given the diffuse and vertical nature of the structures, these face-to-face ties are also important in relating subordinates (individuals and subleaders) to upper levels of the particular hierarchy of which they are a part.

A brief historical sketch of the development and change in these diffuse vertical structures will make this characteristic of the Latin American structure more concrete. The traditional pattern of social organization in colonial and early nineteenth-century Latin America was clearly hierarchical. Some would call it feudal because of the concentration of power in the hands of the landlord; others would call it bureaucratic, because of the importance of the civil, military and clerical bureaucracy in limiting the power of the "lords." Two aspects of the social organization stand out. First is the very sharp stratification, with its attendant gross inequality of wealth, status and power. Second is the dependence of the local elites on, and their orientation towards, the national elites. This dependence was subject to considerable variations due to the inability of minimally effective national elites to maintain control, especially over outlying areas. In periods of severe weakening of the national elites, particularly in the immediate post-Independence period, this dependence was at a minimum. The autonomy of the local power holder was probably at a maximum among the almost subsistence-oriented hacienda owners. The heads of export-oriented landholdings, and the elites in the often overlooked provincial towns were also powerful, but not because they were free from control by the center, as were the subsistence hacienda owners, but rather because of their "bargain" with the center. In return for their unlimited support of the central elites, they received a monopoly of the benefits that came down from above.[10]

Change came about not by disturbing the essential vertical links, but by creating new ones. This seems to have been so because the opportunities, the stimuli and the resources for change generally came from outside or from the top down, and involved the exploitation of new resources, rather than the redirection of old ones. The elites built a new vertical structure, usually without having to sharpen tensions within the older structures by squeezing new capital or energies out of the work force at their base.[11]

The most striking case of this pattern is the agricultural and raw material exploitation in the period of expanding international trade beginning in the mid-nineteenth century. The stimulus was outside demands and technology, and the resources were usually unused land or untapped mineral deposits. The labor was often immigrant (as in Argentina and southern Brazil) or apparently "excess" rural populations. Notable exceptions to this pattern, which were in addition revolutionary, occurred in Mexico at the turn of the century, and more recently in the northeast of Brazil. Although in these latter cases initiatives came from the top, the available resources involved exploitation of a labor force which produced a change for the worse in its traditional relationships. There may well be other unanalyzed exceptions which did not become revolutionary, but the prevailing pattern at the turn of the century seems to have been *new* chains of authority and status built on *new* resources (e.g., mines, coffee and banana plantations). The situation becomes more complicated, although not fundamentally different, with the rise of cities. Since the reasons for the continuity are intimately linked with the central importance of national political institutions, I shall now turn to the next characteristic, which

deals with that aspect, before continuing the historical sketch.

(2) The Intertwining of Social and Political Structures

The cause and consequence of the persistence of diffuse vertical structures in Latin American society has been the importance of governmental institutions in the creation of wealth, status and other value-producing activities of society. This does not imply that government touches all of the population, since clearly there are many "parochials," but they are concentrated in the rural, provincial, subsistence economies and in some segments of the marginal urban population. If an activity pays well, is socially important, and involves high levels of intellectual or technical competence, it is likely to depend on official institutions for licensing, concessions, the right to cross borders with goods, money, persons or knowledge, or even for the initiative on which many Latin American entrepreneurs seem to depend.

By emphasizing the importance of official institutions, I am not alleging the power of those institutions. The structural characteristic refers to "intertwining" and not "dominance." The situation is somewhat like that analyzed by Neustadt (1960) in discussing the U.S. presidency. The fact that everyone depends on government action logically only entails the government becoming a "chief clerk." Whether the government is powerful depends on whether *it leads* its complex constituencies or is manipulated by them. The latter is often the case. Latin America is known for the importance of the private sector in its development. This describes not autonomous entrepreneurs, but entrepreneurs powerful or clever enough to control the government. It is not, therefore, the power of government over the society that we are discussing. There is a fairly broad consensus among observers that Latin American governments are weak.

The intertwining of the social and political structures is, like the diffuse vertical character of the social structures, not a modern or traditional characteristic but one which has existed throughout Latin American history. The background is the "bureaucratic-patrimonialism" of the Spanish Empire summed up by Sarfatti (1966). The omnipresence of the bureaucracy has produced a legacy of legalism and red tape, which has by no means disappeared. The power of this bureaucracy has not been so great as to create a dominant mandarin class, and its procedures have not been so rigid as to have made it some sort of "meritocracy." Rather, its imposing facades are often penetrated by people intent on circumventing established procedures. The Latin American language is full of terms to describe both the act and the person performing it.[12]

One index of the pervasive involvement of the bureaucracy is the importance of public office as a sign of social status, as a means of social mobility and as a payoff for political support. In some rural areas, in provincial towns as well as in the hacienda communities, the blending of political and social status seems to have been almost complete, with the result that social and political roles become completely undifferentiated. The most obvious example is the all-powerful social-political-economic rural or urban paternalistic boss (*patrón*). Although in the larger towns the boss is becoming extinct, the blending of the various functional elites is great. There is much lateral movement among them, and intensive face-to-face relationships link them closely. The presence of a power elite or of an oligarchy is unquestionable, although its autonomous power is diminished by (a) factional conflicts among the oligarchs, (b) a considerable degree of mobility—because ascriptive criteria are not rigidly enforced for entry into the elite, and (c) the fact that these oligarchs have to deal with a chain of middlemen or brokers, producing a pattern closer to what Samuel Eldersveld referred to as a "stratarchy," rather than a centralized hierarchy.[13]

Explanations for the persistence of this intertwining of social with political structures often center on the "patronal" cultural traits emphasized in the literature on the Latin American character.[14] The government is seen as an overarching sort of boss. More explanation is needed, however, as to why the government in particular becomes the object of this expectation, especially among the relatively high-status figures who stand at the head of the various social hierarchies.

At least part of the answer lies in the fact that the resources for productive activity not only enter the society from the top, but in a fashion that assigns an important role to official institutions. The need and opportunity for governments to regulate exports and imports is the most dramatic example. Governments sometimes merely used the opportunity to enrich the office holders, but many engaged in aggressive campaigns to secure credits, technical assistance and build the necessary infrastructure. In the process of industrialization, the government's role was crucial, too, at a minimum in providing some form of tariff protection or subsidy. Whether encouraging foreign penetration, or seeking to control it, the government necessarily assumed a crucial position.

More recently, the factors underlying government involvement in social structures have been more subtle. Throughout the twentieth century, there has been considerable agitation in most major countries for measures to alleviate the poverty and alienation of workers and peasants, or, from another point of view, to avoid the social conflicts rocking Europe and the United States. This agitation grew in intensity and reached a peak in the 1930s. Although the agitation varied from country to country, it had three elements in common. First, the agitation came chiefly from intellectuals and very small groups of workers (e.g., the miners in Chile and Bolivia). Second, both the elites hoping for change and those hoping to avoid it agreed on the need for government action. Third, the models for the solution of the social problems, whether deriving from the Soviet Union or the United States, involved activist governmental intervention. The reaction was (1) the passage of labor codes; (2) a high degree of government intervention in labor disputes; (3) the adoption of welfare programs; and (4) the stimulation, either by the government or by government-related parties, of officially protected and controlled labor unions. Much of this was done in the absence of significant labor agitation or organization, and in some cases when the industrial labor force was still very small.[15]

Although the relationship of the government to the peasants is more complex because of the latter's greater number, dispersion and diversity, the trend appears to involve the same government-related vertical hierarchies, such as community development programs, officially sponsored rural unions, and relatively bureaucratized land reform programs. Therefore, although the expansion of the scope of national politics has increasingly encompassed people of lower socio-economic strata, it has done so by creating still relatively diffuse, vertical hierarchies, which are dependent on, or intertwined with, the national political structures.

Some Consequences of Diffuse, Vertical Structuring and Intertwining—The two characteristics of the distinctive Latin American structure so far discussed account for some notable socio-political features of the area. First, they explain the persistent importance of the local community as a basis of political organization, despite the much cited fact that local governments are notably short on resources and functions.[16] The local community is in many ways the microcosm of the kind of social organization that I have been describing. If not dominated by a single all-powerful patrón, it is likely to be divided into factional groupings which constitute small-scale diffuse hierarchies. The links of these factions with upper-level elites or their temporary alliances with factions in other communities do not destroy the sense of community in the way that pluralistic specialization or class conflict might. Leaders must deal with the community as a whole (favoring, of course, their particular supporters). The basic unit of society, and of politics, is not the specialized group—as, for example, U.S. "group theorists" would suggest—but rather the community.

Even in larger cities, where one would expect considerably more specialization and differentiation, there are signs of something similar to the more traditional communities. This seems most obvious among the inhabitants of the shanty-towns and squatter settlements. They may not be the rural slums within the city that Bonilla (1961) suggested, since the inhabitants make considerable changes in their occupations, norms and values on moving to the city; however, the people do appear to become structured essentially around the neighborhood, to develop their own factional structures and bosses, and to present themselves as a community unit to higher authorities (see Mangin, 1967).

Even when the traditional vertical hierarchy is replaced by a more bureaucratized and corporatist framework, such as official unions, the *ejidal* system in Mexico, or the networks of relations linking the rank-and-file public servants, the comprehensiveness of the community and the relations between leaders and followers remains essentially the same. The membership itself may be more functionally differentiated, but the ties among members and between leaders and members are not confined to the concerns associated with the differentiating characteristic. The leaders are still something like the "all-purpose" patrones of the traditional pattern. For example, the members of an ejido in Mexico are differentiated from other members of Mexican society by their concern with agriculture; but the ejido is concerned with functions beyond the purely agricultural, and the ejido leader must deal with health, educational, financial and even religious matters as well. This local

comprehensive community is the basic building block of social and political organization, even in what might appear to be highly differentiated structures.

The second major consequence of the diffuse vertical structuring of society and the intertwining of social and political structures is the importance of the brokerage role. In either the older traditional local-regional-national hierarchies, or in the newer bureaucratic-corporatist ones, there must emerge individuals who can interpret the diffuse needs of the communities of which they are a part, as well as secure and distribute the benefits that come from above. The demands of the community are in part those of that community as a whole—for example, in a small town the demand for a new public center or a road connection to a larger town. More often, perhaps, the broker needs to be able to interpret and rank the varied personal needs of the members of his community which are highly particularistic (i.e., demands for personal favors, jobs, concessions or special dispensations). This is not an inconsiderable task because the needs cover so many concerns and interests. If the group involved were highly specialized, the broker would be less important, since the demands might be more readily inferred by higher authorities on the basis of the occupational, cultural, religious or social character of the group. A diffuse comprehensive community requires someone "close to the ground." Looked at from below, the broker is important, too, since he constitutes the indispensable personal link with the leadership above. These brokers, which are omnipresent in Latin America, do not exist only at the local level, but rather are ordered in pyramidal chains, constituting the essential links of the diffuse vertical structures.

The last consequence to be mentioned is the importance of status as a political motivation. Several observers have noted that politicians seem more interested in achieving recognition as socially prominent people than in forwarding ideologies, programs or policies (e.g., Payne 1968; Leff, 1968: 99). The reasons for this lie partly in the fact that since political and social roles are blurred, it is sometimes impossible to distinguish the drive for power from the drive for status. More fundamentally, however, status *is* power, since in a system of brokers of the kind described, the ability to deliver the goods depends on establishing firm, but flexible connections with those at the top. The connections must be diffuse and affective (i.e., friendship and loyalty), and such friendships are strongest when status is equal.

(3) Confrontations and Fluid Alliances Among Elites with Disparate Power Capabilities

Latin American systems diverge most from the authoritarian and corporatist models because of the existence of diverse elites whose alliances are changeable enough to result in Latin America's well-known instability: coups d'état, continual cabinet changes, military ultimatums, dramatic resignations, and so forth. It is difficult to call a system authoritarian when there is no secure basis of authority, or corporatist when the center into which groups are incorporated is not fixed.

That Latin American systems have many elites is hardly distinctive. The distinctiveness lies in the fact that the power bases of the elites are so disparate that they cannot resolve their conflicts through some relatively simple process such as voting in general elections or in parliament, or institutionalized collective bargaining. These stable processes and procedures, which can either be the result of custom or written law, I shall call "constitutional technologies." In Latin America, available and accepted constitutional technologies have not been sufficient to institutionalize the management of conflict.

The model which sums up many of the characteristics of the situation among Latin American elites is that provided by Anderson (1967, ch. 4). He pictures the various elites, which he calls "power contenders," as possessing radically different resources for influencing politics ("power capabilities"). Because of the disparity among these capabilities, the elites interact not by any fixed rules which would compare their power and award positions of authority to one of them, or to a coalition of several, but rather by a system of direct confrontations. The results of these confrontations are tentative alliances among groups of elites which are always subject to change in the event of a new power demonstration and a new confrontation. Elections and parliamentary maneuvering are thus not definitive resolutions of conflicts, but only one way of demonstrating power in confrontations with other elites who may or may not be participating in elections or in the parliamentary process.

As Anderson portrays it, there are some rules to this game. First, power is usually demonstrated, and rarely directly employed. Since a premium is placed on the *demonstration*, extra weight is given to those elites who are capable of rapid and impressive shows of power—such as the military, the students and the capital-city urban groups in general. Further, since the proc-

ess is one of demonstrating rather than using power, elites are rarely eliminated—with the exception of revolutionary situations—[17]and Latin American systems are what Anderson calls "living museums" of old and new elites. Finally, new contenders are not rigidly excluded for long, since rules for inclusion and exclusion are not rigid, and a new group capable of demonstrating its power may enter the game.

The confrontations that result are somewhat different from the political conflicts in Europe between the wars, and the contemporary pattern of confrontation politics in the United States, which involves peace advocates, blacks and students. In Latin America, the conflicts are between elites at the apex of the diffuse vertical hierarchies such as the military, the traditional hierarchies and the new bureaucratic-corporatist ones. In the European and U.S. patterns, the conflicts have been based more on class and ideology. The difference is not absolute, since one finds military interventions in Europe and class and ideological outbursts in Latin America— e.g., in early labor agitation, some peasant revolts and student demonstrations. These latter, however, have been minor in Latin America, unless they have served to trigger conflict among the more powerful hierarchies. Although the emergence of class and ideological conflicts has been considered imminent in Latin America, these projections appear to be based more on extrapolations from European experience than on hard data. Given Latin America's vertical structures and the *increasing* emphasis on initiatives flowing from the top—which reinforces these structures—there seems to be little reason to believe that the pattern of conflict will change dramatically in the future.

Anderson's model underplays the ways in which most potential conflicts are resolved and the level of direct confrontations is kept within manageable proportions, short of instability. Four factors stand out. The first is the extraordinarily complex network of face-to-face relationships among members of the various elites, which not only facilitates inter-elite communication, but also blurs the edges among the various elites. Not only, for example, is a businessman likely to have friends or relatives among the landed elite, but he may well have been or aspire to become, a landowner himself.

A second factor involves cooptive techniques. Many presidents avoid excessive conflicts through cooption of elite members into various sorts of advisory councils, up to and including the cabinet. The proliferation of ad hoc and permanent commissions, new agencies (useful for changing representation without disturbing past arrangements), independent regulatory groups and the like is evidence of the use of such strategies.

A third factor is the existence of an overarching consensus, such as was provided by the Mexican Revolution. The consensus gives increased legitimacy to the government in its endeavors to secure revolutionary goals, and limits power demonstrations on the part of elites which might be interpreted as threats to the government, and, by extension, to the efforts it has been making to secure these goals.

A final factor in explaining how potential conflicts are resolved and the level of direct confrontations is kept manageable is the purposeful weakening by the government of certain elites. The success of the Calles regime in the late 1920s and early 1930s in Mexico in weakening the military and the church is a relevant example (cf. the analysis of this process by Lieuwen, 1961: 101 ff.).

The existence of these conflict-mitigating mechanisms, the last two of which depend on exceptional circumstances, does not make the Anderson model less valid. They may make the confrontations less violent or less public, and the system more outwardly stable, but they do not necessarily change its basic character. Fluid alliances and confrontations are still the dominant characteristics.

In order to explain these characteristics we must focus on the nature of both the power capabilities and the available constitutional technologies. With respect to the first, there are two sets of actors in Latin American systems whose primary resources for exerting influence are extraordinarily difficult to compare by any known constitutional technology. The first is obviously the military and its capability for physical coercion. In the caudillo period, when many factions made use of weapons which, compared to the present, were less developed, the confrontations involved the use of force on the part of all contenders. As military professionalism increased, as it did beginning with the growth of national armies trained by foreign experts, and as progressively more successful efforts were made to purify electoral procedures by eliminating direct coercion of the voter, violence has become a power capability concentrated only in the military, which sharpened the disparities among elites. This is ironic, since many observers have considered professionalism and purified electoral procedures ways of eliminating the military as a political force. As the military's continued presence indicates, such has not been the case,

and the proposition could easily be defended that the military has become more, instead of less, disruptive or potentially disruptive. In the conventional literature, the intervention of the military is explained by a circular argument. The military intervenes because of weak constitutional processes, and the constitutional processes are weak because the military intervenes. The cycle can be broken only if the military is deprived of any political motivation, which is exceedingly difficult in a situation of sociopolitical change in which various groups—e.g., the middle class, as Nun (1967) suggests—have close enough links with the military and sufficient cause to influence the military in a political direction. The cycle might also be broken if someone were to invent a means of measuring and assessing the power of the military vis-à-vis other powers in society. At present, the only evident device for avoiding conflicts involving the military is to make high military officers close advisors of the president—the stop-gap cooptive mechanism described above.

The foreigner—in the form of diplomatic representatives, foreign businessmen, aid missions, technical assistance groups, the CIA, Soviet and Castroite agents—are a second group of elites whose power capabilities are exceedingly difficult to measure and take account of in a systematic institutionalized fashion. In an earlier, less complex era, ambassadors and businessmen could participate in the electoral and parliamentary processes rather openly. With the rise of nationalist feeling, supported by the universally proclaimed principles of self-determination and nonintervention, such open intervention became increasingly difficult. The power of these groups has not diminished, but it tends to be demonstrated publicly only through very diffuse propaganda (appeals to cooperation and "alliances for progress"), or through covert means, such as under-the-counter subventions of politicians. Basically, however, the power capabilities of the foreigner consist of his control over flows of resources from abroad—including weaponry, skills and money. Such control is not amenable to systematic measurement by available constitutional technology.

The ad hoc means of limiting conflicts consist of regular face-to-face contacts and cooption, at least for those foreigners with accepted status within the system. It is also conceivable that there are institutionalized means, now being evolved, for systematically managing potential conflicts with the foreigner, e.g., the procedures of international or joint commissions. On the surface, there appears to be no stable basis for institutionalization of the foreigner other than his complete elimination, which is advocated by extreme nationalists, or the complete colonial subjection of Latin America to him, which is no longer acceptable to either group.

Looking at the problem from the point of view of the constitutional technology itself, it may be that the pattern of fluid alliances and confrontations in Latin American politics can be explained by the unfortunate fact that with independence, Latin America adopted a set of constitutional (liberal-democratic) procedures which were popular in the United States and Europe at the time. They are still emotionally defended, but they have never been appropriate to the particular sorts of power capabilities which exist in Latin America. Whether or not Latin America would have done better to have adopted some other model, or evolved its own is beside the point. Perhaps in the long run it will find its own, but for the present the lack of fit between the available means for managing conflict and the kinds of power capabilities that need to be managed is a fact.

(4) The Technician-Centered Decision-Making Style

Many recent analyses of Latin American politics emphasize the importance of the experts or technicians. These are specialists of one sort or another who, being close to the president, important ministries, central banks, development corporations and the like, often play a decisive role in decision-making (cf. Vernon, 1963). The presence of experts is hardly unique to Latin America, and their increasing importance in political decisions in the United States has received considerable attention. However, a broader look into Latin American politics suggests that this is not purely a modern characteristic, but that it has existed for a long time.

Today's *técnicos* (technicians) are yesterday's *científicos* (scientists), *bachareis* and *licenciados*. The cientificos were a prominent group during the Porfirio Diaz regime in Mexico. Bachareis and licenciados are literally persons with university degrees. The words can be used to describe people in and out of government, but the terms also have a somewhat more narrow meaning. Bacharelismo, for example, was the tendency to grant some people, whose status in part came from their degrees, substantial deference and latitude in policy-making. In analyses of Brazil, the bachareis have been seen as replacing the older, less sophisticated coronel or political boss as the principal decision-making figure. As is probably true in other systems in which bureaucracies have long been central to social and political processes, Latin America

appears to have been marked for a long time by the presence of a substantial and politically important set of advisors and experts who play a significant role in decision-making. For convenience, I shall use the modern term, technicians, to refer to this group in all of its many historical manifestations.

The technicians have always been more or less independent of any particular interest and of the social structures I have been describing above, although not, of course, immune to their influences. Essentially the reference group of the technician has been the intellectual community, centered around journals, newspapers, universities, literary clubs, and sometimes around government agencies.[18] Perhaps the technicians' most salient feature is their awareness of and concern with ideologies, technologies and intellectual currents abroad.

What is important about the technicians is not only their presence. It is the fact that many important decisions seem to be made by them, operating as a fairly small elite group, on the basis of their estimates of the situation, their ideological perspectives and the (at times) scant information they have at their disposal about the realities of their own country.[19]

The technician-centered decision-making process has several distinctive characteristics. First, an apparently very large number of the major issues in Latin American politics are placed on the political agenda by events or individuals which have little to do with the activity of interest groups. Policies—notably welfare policies, labor legislation and the like—are often initiated, promulgated and implemented without significant agitation by those concerned. Participation comes, if at all, only in later stages of implementation and revision. Where agenda-setting stimuli do come from is uncertain, given the relatively few case studies of decision-making available. The signal may be a small but violent demonstration, the slump of an economic index, or the success of an opposition politician in mobilizing support behind an issue. An international crisis may provide the signal, as when the Cuban Revolution triggered concern with agrarian reform. Alternatively, a new president may be looking for something spectacular—such as Kubitschek and Brasilia—to establish his reputation. Whatever the sources—and it would be worthwhile to discover systematically what they are—the decisions often do not arise from demands, and there is typically a great deal of uncertainty as to just how groups in the society will be affected or will react. As a result, the relation between the technicians and the organized groups in society tends to be one in which the latter play a defensive and opportunistic role. The representatives of various groups seek to find out what the government is doing, avoid possible threats to the prosperity and status of the group, and, if possible, get a part of the "action" in the form of contracts, concessions and appointments.

Other characteristics of this technician-centered decision-making process are that the decisions have a strong element of abstractness (sometimes an ideological quality), are often invested with high emotional content (they are said to be *the* conclusive answer to the problem at hand), and frequently contain elements imitative of experience in other countries (see the analysis of the Latin American decision-making style in Hirschman, 1963, ch. 4). Cynics and critics are prone to point out, for example, that the decisions are (1) often badly adapted to the society to which they must be applied, since they are based on foreign experience; (2) highly legalistic, involving extremely detailed provisions without much attention to the possibility of their implementation; and (3) often unenforced. Progressive constitutional provisions that remain unenforced for decades are cited as evidence of the latter point.

Although it is true that the legislative, and even constitutional act—which North Americans are used to thinking of as definitive—is often highly tentative, it may be much more influential than is sometimes thought, as Hirschman (1963: 111) has pointed out. Although there is reason to doubt the efficacy of many laws, the problem in analyzing them lies as much in the perspectives and expectations of the observer as in the decision-making process itself.

The technician-centered decision-making style described above is often explained by recourse to a crudely defined political culture. Latin American legalism, the tendency to grant status to "doctors," and patronalismo are norms which support this style. However, also important is the fact that Latin America evolved on the periphery of the main intellectual, technological, educational and ideological centers of the world. Latin Americans, long oriented toward these centers, have adapted to this peripherality by developing roles and techniques—which don't always work—to make use of the ideas, programs and plans which have been available to them. Further, the example of social and political conflicts in other parts of the world has stimulated government action to avoid these conflicts, as noted above. This has placed a high premium on the intellectuals, who are required to interpret the foreign situation, analyze the domestic situation, and provide plans to avoid possible catastrophes. Although the prescriptions of intellectuals and technicians may simply produce new problems in their efforts to solve old ones, this does not seem to create a crisis of confidence in the technician-centered decision process. A new set of experts, or perhaps even the same ones who created the new problems, are often called upon to solve them.

PARTY ROLES IN LATIN AMERICA

The roles which political parties play in Latin America are shaped and limited by the Latin American sociopolitical structure.[20] The structure produces no single role for all parties, since one clearly finds many variations among the parties in the area, but it makes some types of parties extremely unlikely and causes the major parties to share certain characteristics. It is not always easy to specify the roles of parties, because the blending of an individual's social and political roles, which is characteristic of the Latin American structure, often makes it difficult to determine whether he is acting out a party role or some other one. For example, determining whether a president is acting as a party leader or in some other capacity is not purely a methodological problem, since the blurring of the lines between his roles is part of the system.[21] At a lower level, it is difficult to ascertain whether some brokers—e.g., a local boss—should be considered as part of the party.

The most important effects of the Latin American sociopolitical structure on the role of parties are the following: (1) the parties represent diffuse vertical hierarchies rather than specifically defined interests; (2) the parties cannot represent all of the diffuse vertical hierarchies (i.e., their representative role is limited); (3) the parties do not deal directly with the masses, but rather work with brokers, which serves to make certain types of resources and symbols more important to the parties than others; and (4) the parties' role in decision-making is limited and specialized, and not particularly dominant.

REPRESENTATION

Let us turn now to the effect of the sociopolitical structure on the parties' representative role (numbers (1) and (2) above). Many of the ideas regarding the representative role of political parties in competitive systems are only partially relevant to Latin America because most theories are based on the assumption that parties are either *the* political organizations of a specific stratum (e.g., working-class parties, regional-culture parties, etc.) as in Continental Europe, or that parties are a kind of professional aggregating institution for a variety of specialized interest groups, as is sometimes alleged concerning Anglo-Saxon parties.[22] With variations produced by overlapping bases, degrees of consensus, false consciousness (such as working-class tories), these two models dominate the literature concerning the relationships between parties and social groups.[23]

In Latin America, the absence of sharp polarizing cleavages or pluralistic, autonomous group formation means that the model of parties is quite different. Their social bases are the vertical diffuse structures discussed above. National parties are collections of subhierarchies, linked at the top, which parallel and are blended with the diffuse, vertical sociopolitical hierarchies. In some cases the hierarchies to which a party is connected are all of the same type, e.g., all the party hierarchies of the same party are tied to traditional sociopolitical hierarchies. A concrete example would be the PSD in Brazil, which was primarily composed of a large number of factional hierarchies within the various states. In other cases, a national party is tied with more than one type of sociopolitical hierarchy, e.g., some of the party subhierarchies parallel traditional factional hierarchies, while others within the same party parallel corporatist ones. A concrete example from the same country, Brazil, would be the PTB which brought together both state factional groupings and much of the official trade-union structure. The ideological parties common in the area and the ad hoc personalist parties are a kind of incomplete version of the Latin American political party, for their structures (if any) parallel no sociopolitical hierarchy nor constitute available leadership for them. The ideological and ad hoc personalist parties, in this sense, can be considered as free-floating.

Historically speaking, the typical kinds of parties that have emerged are the following: first came the cliques of the elites that stood at the head of the traditional hierarchies. Then came the so-called middle-class parties such as the Argentine and Chilean radicals. These were not formed to represent new specific interests but rather to reduce the oligarchical quality of the traditional hierarchies (through such means as emphasizing liberal-democratic constitutional procedures) and open up some lines of mobility to positions at the top of the traditional hierarchies to new people. Then came what Di Tella calls the "populist" parties. These created new power bases by establishing new bureaucratic-

corporatist hierarchies, or sought to build themselves into ones that had been created by innovative leaders such as Getulio Vargas in Brazil, or Perón in Argentina. All these types of parties have in common the fact that they are not tied to a particular class or specialized interest group in spite of contrary appearances at times.

Apparent class ties emerge, for example, because the older parties are linked with an oligarchy that commands a network of local and regional bosses. The parties appear to be simply parties of the oligarchy. However, appearances are misleading, since these traditional networks encompass a wide range of socioeconomic statuses, and the degree of upward mobility or paternalistic concern for provincial middle classes and peasants is often much higher than commonly assumed.[24]

The populist parties, which mobilize mass support among the working class also appear to be class based. However, only under certain conditions are parties forced to build upon a relatively solid class organization. When class enclaves exist, the party in the area will tend to be class based. Examples are some of the Communist and Left-wing parties based in primarily mining communities. Parties also tend to emphasize and develop their class base in certain situations in which they are in opposition. Democratic Action in Venezuela and the APRA party in Peru utilized class symbolism when they were in opposition. If such an opposition succeeds in its quest for power, the rhetoric of class orientation may be retained, although the party is by then tied to an emerging or existing corporate structure of official or officially influenced institutions within which one finds all classes and statuses. The PRI in Mexico and Democratic Action in Venezuela are examples of this type of party.

The small groupings of intellectuals with ideological reasons for asserting a class identification—e.g., the smaller Communist, Socialist, *fidelista*, Fascist, Falangist and Christian Democratic parties—also may give the impression of being class based. The significant fact about these parties, however, is that they have very little social base at all, and generally receive few votes, although they may nonetheless play an important role in the decision-making process. Their importance is derived from the fact that decisions are often shaped by foreign ideologies which influence the technicians, many of whom come from these small parties.

A second consequence for party roles in Latin America deriving from the distinctive sociopolitical structure is that the parties cannot and do not represent *all* of the diffuse vertical hierarchies in the system. Parties in Latin America have often been criticized for not representing the interests of the lower classes or the people, i.e., the less powerful. True as this may be, the more important influence shaping their role is that they can only indirectly, if at all, represent some of the most powerful groups in society. For roughly the same reasons that the military and the foreigner cannot be institutionalized by the existing constitutional technology, these two elites cannot be built into a system of party representation. Parties, in Latin America as elsewhere, depend on the open and public interplay of opinions and the mobilization of prestige and financial resources to win votes and support. In the present situation, it is exceedingly difficult to turn the physical coercive power of the military, or the foreign-based financial and technical power capabilities of the foreigner into public symbols or votes. Parties may establish alliances with either the military or the foreigner—as for example Democratic Action in Venezuela—but it is always a tentative arrangement. Parties cannot accept for long periods of time the direct use of these groups' power capabilities, both because it compromises the parties in the eyes of their electorate, and also because they are likely to be overwhelmed by such power. More obviously, the military and the foreigner do not accept the sharp discounting of their real power which exclusive reliance on parties would entail.

The result is that parties represent constituencies that do not include all the real power contenders. As a consequence, parties tend to have an antimilitarist (or civilian-government-supporting) point of view, and, with respect to the foreigner, a nationalist one. In neither case, but particularly with respect to the military, can this be a hard-line opposition, because the chances of decisively defeating either the military or the foreigner are, to say the least, remote, and the parties must keep open the possibility of future alliances with these elites. Only if some form of constitutional technology is created through which relations with them can be institutionalized, *and* only if—as has historically been the case with electoral and parliamentary institutions—parties can somehow establish a legitimate claim to dominate those institutions, will parties be able to assume a comprehensive representative role. The prospects for either development seem dim.[25]

BROKERS AND PARTY RESOURCES

The third effect of the Latin American sociopolitical structure on the roles of parties is that party leaders do not deal directly with the masses, but rather work with brokers (who may or may not be nominal party members) located in the diffuse vertical hierarchies. This means that the crucial payoff is not made by the party to the rank-and-file but to the broker. The party does not have to deliver substantial benefits to the workers, the peasants, the inhabitants of the urban squatter settlements, or the middle class as a unit. The necessary payoffs are of a different sort, as are the political symbols employed by the parties.

Dealing with brokers means first of all providing those individuals—a local boss, a labor leader, a head of a peasant organization, a functionary in a civil service employees' organization—with personal benefits, ranging from opportunities for wealth to access to better-paying and more prestigious jobs. Winning the allegiance of the brokers also means providing them with the where-withal to ensure support from their own followers. As noted above, enhancing the broker's status is one way of doing so, since it gives the broker greater opportunities to get concessions. The broker must also be provided with patronage and public-works types of projects that can be distributed to his faithful.

Some of the resources needed to make the above types of payoffs can be provided directly by the party. Party financial resources can be used to cover some of the costs, and the status and position of the party leaders can be lent to the broker by means of prominent and public association of the party leader with the broker. Many of the benefits a party distributes to its brokers ultimately depend on favors secured from the government. The party's most important resource, therefore, is often its contacts with people who are closer to the centers of decision-making.

The top party leader frequently enters into what appears to be direct contact with the rank-and-file. Visits are made or time is regularly set aside in which individuals can come and make personal petitions for jobs and the like. Such direct contact, which is reminiscent of the traditional boss style, is often not spontaneous but rather arranged by the party leader and the broker to gain more popular support. Such contact may also serve the purpose of enabling the party leader to check up on the subordinate broker and is thus a kind of control mechanism used to keep brokers in line.

The small-scale particularistic and even individual benefits which Latin American parties distribute are very much like the benefits distributed in U.S. politics in the heyday of the urban machines and by the modern congressman in his so-called "errand running." All party systems have some elements of these particularistic patronage and public works mechanisms for support-building. The distinctiveness of Latin America comes from the predominance of this type of benefit over more universalistic or class benefits.

The other interaction which takes place between leaders and followers is focussed upon symbols rather than concrete benefits. Although the ties that bind the party leader and the broker are essentially highly pragmatic and concrete, the party leader needs a method of identifying himself to the rank-and-file, say, in a polling booth. The chains of particularistic ties make this more necessary because of the remoteness of the leader from the mass of followers. In party systems based on class or interest groups, such symbols may be provided by the party name, flag, greeting or schematized program. In an aggregating party system, the symbols are essentially those which demonstrate the control of the parties over decision-making, the legitimacy of the parties and their skills in providing meaningful compromise solutions. The symbols might involve the identification of the parties with decision-making centers—such as the cabinet or parliament.

These types of symbols are not absent in Latin America, but others, tied to social position and capacity to deliver the particularistic benefits are more important. The leaders of parties closely tied with existing social hierarchies may use their titles, formal positions, or prominent family names. Leaders without such a direct tie to an existing institution indicate their capabilities to their followers by means of symbolic demonstrations of their accessibility. The classic case of symbolic accessibility was President Cárdenas of Mexico who opened the telegraph lines on a regular basis for individual petitions. Another technique is to exploit the openings of schools, roads, water works and showcase buildings to demonstrate what the leader has to give. Symbols of personal prowess, from military to sexual, or even sharp dealing (for example, the unofficial slogan of an ex-governor of Sao Paulo that "he steals, but he gets it done") reinforce the image of a man who can deliver if followed and supported.[26]

The final effect of the sociopolitical structure on Latin American parties is to make their role in decision-making a limited and specialized one. Their role is not dominant because they do not represent all the powerful groups and because their resources for influencing decision-making are limited. The resources in their possession include information they can provide to decision-makers, their ability to stage mass demonstrations in the game of confrontation politics and votes.

With regard to the first of these resources, the information that party leaders can provide is influenced by the fact that they represent the diffuse interests of vertical structures rather than specific interests. Information about demands and attitudes is thus likely to be very particularistic (e.g., community X wants a school) or very vague (e.g., the public mood is against too much accommodation with foreigners). The party leaders are not likely to provide very good information about the demands and the priorities of, say, the capital goods producers, or all those affected by a proposed water resources project, or all those subject to proposed new income or excise taxes, in short, information about the categories of persons who are likely to be dealt with directly in legislation and policy-making. An exception to this might be the relatively few cases where a policy treats a whole hierarchy, as seems to be the case with minimum wage policies and the parties closely tied to the corporatist labor union structure. On the whole, the diffuseness of the interests of the structures to which parties are tied makes the information they have at their disposal only partially useful to the policy-makers.

The information which the small, free-floating ideological parties are able to provide constitutes a partial qualification of the above. These parties often formulate intellectual evaluations of programs or interpret government policies according to a relatively coherent ideological point of view. Such information may be useful and impressive to the technicians, although the political weakness of the ideological parties in terms of mass support means that their role in decision-making is also limited, although in a different way.

Another resource that parties have at their disposal for influencing or supporting decisions is their ability to mobilize masses of people for rallies and marches. Such a resource may be very useful in the politics of confrontation. These mass demonstrations are often organized by parties in support of a government. The PRI in Mexico, for example, frequently organizes such demonstrations through its contacts in the labor, peasant and (particularly important) public employee organizational networks. The demonstrations are designed to show that the government has overwhelming popular support and serve as a warning to potential opponents. Another example would be the rallies organized by Joao Goulart, through the labor-union-related PTB, to indicate support of his government.

The parties' ability to organize dramatic demonstrations is a resource that can also be used to oppose, rather than support, the government. Given the dependence of the parties on other vertical structures and the government itself, it is not surprising that parties, per se, have rarely been able to maintain a high level of direct confrontation with the authorities by means of mass demonstrations. The Peronists have done so in Argentina, but this has been more the result of union activity than party activity. Democratic Action of Venezuela, when it had built a fairly strong organization for itself while in opposition, was unusually successful in mobilizing a massive demonstration at the time of the fall of Pérez Jiménez, but as noted before, this was an atypical situation. It has been argued that in Peru, the tactics of the opposition party APRA have involved the systematic use of mass demonstrations to pose a threat to public order, but once again, this seems to have been more dependent on the unions than on the party itself (cf. Payne, 1965).

The fact that political parties have not been notable for mounting effective demonstrations of physical power in the opposition may account for the trend in the last decade among revolutionaries to increasingly downplay the significance of parties as instruments for major change. The tacticians on the fidelista Left appear to be concerned with building a guerilla military force and avoiding the "inevitably compromised" political parties (e.g., Debray, 1967).

Votes are the most obvious resource which Latin American parties have at their disposal for influencing decision-makers, since virtually all countries have adopted a formal liberal-democratic framework, despite periodic lapses from the norm. Votes are crucial to party leaders because they are their distinctive power demonstration. At the same time, given the fluidity of interactions among the elites and the tentativeness of elections, they are clearly not sufficient.

A party obtains votes in several ways. First there is the support which results from voter identification with a very prominent individual who is also in the party. The mechanism involved is two-staged. First, loyalties are established between the community members and the local brokers, and then between the local brokers and the party leaders in the community. Whether or not stable party identification results

depends on the stability of the relationship between the parties and the upper levels of the hierarchies of which the communities form the base. In Colombia, for example, party identification seems very strong because of the continuity of the attachment of Conservatives and Liberals with traditional hierarchies in that country. In Brazil, on the other hand, where the intensity of loyalty to the local leaders is just as strong, party identification is relatively weak because the discontinuities in party existence have made the links between the brokers and particular parties much weaker. The same kind of variations can be seen with respect to more modern corporatist hierarchies. In Mexico the party identification is very strong because of the continuity of the party's tie with the corporatist hierarchies created in the 1930s. In Argentina, despite an overarching loyalty to Perón and the strong loyalties of the Peronist voters to the labor unions, there is a very weak identification with particular parties because (partly through military intervention) the parties were not able to attach themselves strongly to the corporatist network of unions.

LOCATION OF PARTIES IN THE DECISION-MAKING PROCESS

Since parties are not dominant in the decision-making process, the problem for the analyst is to specify what sort of specialized roles they do play. From the above analysis one can conclude that parties are likely to be more prominent on certain kinds of issues, namely "distributive" ones (see the useful, if partial, classification of issues in Lowi, 1964) in which choices are made concerning how major public works programs in roads, housing and the like are to be distributed among the many particularistic claimants. They may play some role in major redistributive issues, but it is usually confined to a symbolic level, such as the issuing of vague declarations about the need to redistribute income, carry out agrarian reform, or (very commonly) limit foreign control.

Another way of looking at the role of the party in the decision-making process is to ask at what stage in the process the party becomes involved. This is in contrast to analyzing the involvement of parties on particular sorts of issues discussed above. Parties may raise issues and put them on the agenda—e.g., when a party on the rise raises the necessity of some form of reformist program. Parties are more likely to play a role in later stages of decision-making, acting in defense of the existing networks of vertical relationships. Defense in this context means not simply preservation of the status quo, but basically reaction to, rather than initiation of, policy. Parties or individual party leaders may be the agents of landholders (e.g., to delay a land reform program being proposed by the technicians), but it is more likely that the parties will try to get the best deal for their clients, including particular advantages for individuals and groups among them in the form of contracts or concessions. As has often been noted, some landholders can make a handsome profit out of a land distribution program, even if the landowners as a whole are hurt by it.

THE FUNCTIONS OF LATIN AMERICAN PARTIES FOR DEVELOPMENT

Given the limited role that Latin American parties play, many of the dramatic and decisive functions attributed to parties in other parts of the world are inappropriate with regard to Latin American parties.[27] Parties are simply not strong enough to single-handedly transform the political culture, provide totally new bases of authority, develop and impose a dramatic and revolutionary program of social change, or stabilize and democratize a system in rapid change.

Parties by themselves rarely do any of these things and the task of analysts of any party system is to discover what specific sorts of contributions to development parties do make. The Latin American sociopolitical structure makes some kinds of contributions much more likely than others.[28]

One factor that shapes the potential functions of parties (along with all other institutions) is the fact that Latin America faces certain developmental problems or crises and not others. For example, Latin American parties play no role in the establishment of national territorial identity, since with minor exceptions Latin American boundaries have been stable for a long time. The problem of integrating diverse cultures is present in latent fashion, as observers of the still evident contrasts between Indian and European cultures have pointed out. However this has not been a politically relevant problem of the kind found in Asia and Africa since the social institutions for subordination and gradual assimilation of the Indians were established during the colonial period.

The developmental problems have been of a more conventional nature, speaking from the North American and European point of view. That is, the problems have focussed upon the need to integrate new groups into the political process, provide more fluid and productive channels for recruitment of new elites, and increase the capabilities of national governments.

It is the way in which these problems are posed and the roles and resources of the parties which determine potential party functions.

INTEGRATION OF NEW GROUPS

One of the functions which Latin American parties have performed is that of increasing the integration of new groups into the political process, and making the regimes responsive to these groups. The European and U.S. parties performed these functions by presenting the people with the opportunity to make a direct influential choice of leaders or policies, and/or by forming specifically lower-class parties. In contrast, Latin American parties have contributed by helping to modify the old diffuse vertical structures, and by stimulating the creation of new ones more attuned to the masses.

Old hierarchies, such as the traditional rural ones linked with the PSD in Brazil, have been forced, at least in part by the electoral needs of the party, to support somewhat more populist policies than one might expect, as shown by their endorsement of the developmental programs of Jusecelino Kubitschek. According to the description of the Mexican political system by Padgett, PRI can act to modify the corporatist structures in that country by constituting a channel through which complaints about local bosses unresponsive to rank-and-file demands may be made and corrective action taken.[29] Whether or not the net result of party action in either of these two cases has been to increase the significance and the participation of the lower status groups is debatable and needs further research, but it is clear that the potential is there.

More obviously functional for participation has been some parties' role in stimulating the creation of new vertical hierarchies, chiefly of the bureaucratic corporatist kind. In Venezuela, Democratic Action organized peasant and worker groups first as party affiliates and then delivered them into corporate structures in the government once the party assumed power. In Argentina, Mexico and Brazil, the sequence was a bit different, in that the respective parties became one instrument through which an incumbent president furthered or consolidated the formation of a corporate structure with industrial workers at the base, and in the case of Mexico with the peasants as well.

RECRUITMENT OF NEW ELITES

The recruitment of elites has not usually been thought of as an important developmental function, but given the importance of mobility and status in Latin American parties it deserves special treatment. As structures parallel to the diffuse vertical hierarchies in Latin America, the parties contribute to the recruitment of new elites. That is, in addition to the recruitment and training of standard types of political leaders to replenish existing roles, the parties have made room for new sorts of leaders. The placing of new kinds of leaders into the existing roles has served to modify and modernize the character of those roles.

Although the parties in general cannot be considered to have played a dominant role in the recruiting of new and innovative technicians, some of the smaller, ideologically inclined parties have done so. For example, the small Christian Democratic Party in Peru, in alliance with the rising populist Popular Action party of Belaúnde, managed to place some of its members in positions of responsibility when the latter attained power. The successful evolution of an out-of-power party of intellectuals into a governing one, as in the case of the Christian Democrats in Chile, has also stimulated an influx of new technicians into the governmental apparatus. Since not much is known as to where the technicians in Latin America come from, it is not possible to indicate more fully the contribution of parties in this regard.

The diffuseness of party goals—deriving from the kinds of groups they represent—has also facilitated the cooption of new, more specifically political talent. The Colombian and the Mexican party systems have been remarkably successful in coopting those who show some talent for mobilizing political support. One of the chief strategies for advancement in these, and probably other, systems is to "make trouble" in the form of localized activity in opposition to the existing parties. If one is skillful enough, the strategy may result in an invitation to take a prominent and responsible place in the existing parties.

Cooption is often portrayed as a way of avoiding change, since the coopted leader is assumed to have sold out his principles for personal benefits. With the diffuse sets of goals and commitments that parties have in Latin America, the loyalty required of the coopted leader does not necessarily mean that he gives up his principles, but only his disruptive means of expressing them. Although cooption is not likely to produce revolutionary changes in leadership, we do not really know enough about the consequences of cooption to say whether the result is the imposition of a conservative conformity, or a change, albeit subtle, in the orientation of the structures which absorb these new elites. The potential for a positive function is thus present.

SUPPORT FOR NEW GOVERNMENT POLICIES

The most obvious developmental function of parties is to provide support for decision-makers who are attempting to carry out new and innovative policies. Given the limited role of parties in Latin America they are hardly ever in a position to guarantee such support, but their functions are important nevertheless.

One must distinguish between the initial period, when new departures are being explored, and the later institutionalization of new policies. In the initial phase, as in the Cárdenas period in Mexico, the early years of the Frei administration in Chile, and the first phase of the Betancourt regime in Venezuela, parties have an important and conventional function of articulating and justifying the need for expanded governmental operations and of demonstrating electoral or other forms of mass support for these changes. In the later phases their functions change. Because of the gap between the party constituencies (which exclude the military and the foreigner, for example) and the real distribution of power with which party leaders are faced upon assuming power, the party leaders usually discover that the implementation of many of the party's most cherished goals is not feasible. A crisis period ensues, during which the more idealistic party members must be made to come to terms with the new situation. Democratic Action in Venezuela after 1959 and Frei's Christian Democratic Party at the present time are examples of parties in such crises.

A solution—perhaps being followed in Chile—is to reduce the radicals within the party to something like the "base-less" parties of intellectuals, and to convert the party organization itself into something closer to the patronage and public-works distribution system by linking it with the corporatist hierarchies. Thus, the party's function of providing support for decision-makers in the second phase depends on its ability to build and control a new system of particularistic payoffs, such as the Mexican PRI seems to have done with consummate skill.

The reader will no doubt be somewhat shocked at the notion that parties serve a positive function by transforming the idealistic and principled initiatives of a new group of leaders into a traditional machine which builds new paternalistic structures, coopts potential trouble-makers, and pursues the old game of payoffs and personal favors. Ideally, parties might be expected to do more—to not only secure support, but to somehow force the wielders of power to be (or continue to be) democratic, progressive or development-minded. To the extent that the parties make the hierarchies pay attention to the masses, the parties may contribute to keeping the policy-makers alert and responsive. In general, the contribution of parties to the institutionalization of new policy departures is the more limited, although often crucial one of constructing, managing and representing the new corporatist structures which new policy departures almost inevitably will need.

This partial list of potential functions for Latin American parties may reinforce the feeling that parties are not positive factors for development in Latin America. It is true, of course, that the net consequences of their activity may be negative. But the analyst must be careful to arrive at such a judgement after evaluating the actions of parties in areas where they *can* be positive, and not on the basis of assumptions that parties ought to be able to do other things which they may have done in other parts of the world.

CONCLUSION

It is not inevitable that the so-called developing countries will in fact develop, or that if they do, they will do so without protracted and painful crises. If they do move forward with minimum costs, it will be in part because men have found institutions and structures which not only provide the impetus for change, but do so with maximum adaptation to the existing values and structures of society.

Latin American parties do not seem destined to provide the magic key for painless (or even painful) development. They are likely to play an important part—either negative or positive—in such development as does take place. The parties are the products of their environment, and their opportunities are conditioned by the social and political structures which exist in each country. The distinctive Latin American structure provides some clues as to what may be expected of Latin American parties.

Exploring these clues leads to some moderately surprising conclusions which challenge the explicit and implicit assumptions of many analyses of Latin American parties. The aspects of parties often identified as faults—absence of a solid, independent organization network, presence of personalistic leadership, weakness of ideological or programmatic content, rapid rise and fall of ad hoc parties, lack of sharp identification with class or other specific interests—are clearly the product of the Latin American sociopolitical structure. More important is the fact that it is these characteristics which make parties functional within that structure. It is their diffuse

and status-oriented goals which make them capable of penetrating and possibly reforming the diffuse vertical structures in the system and absorbing new nonconformist elites. It is the fluidity and flexibility of their ties with specific interests which make it possible for them to act as critics and reformers of the entrenched elites. For the small ideological parties, it is their lack of organization which makes possible their direct access to the technicians and administrative decision-makers, without being compromised by having to service their own structures with demands for patronage and payoffs. It is not certain that these advantages will result in contributions to development, but only through them is any positive result likely.

It is impossible to empirically refute the belief that the "whole system is rotten" and that it must be revolutionized and destroyed before real progress can be made. It *is* possible to argue, however, that such a transformation of Latin America's historically entrenched patterns of behavior is highly unlikely. It is not likely first because the existing patterns are built in and reinforced by a well-established culture and the continuing impact of Latin America's peripheral position vis-à-vis the economically more developed world centers. It is also unlikely because there are many elements of this Latin American sociopolitical structure that parallel those of the most modern societies we know. This is obvious with respect to the technician-centered decision-making process, which, although of longer standing in Latin America, is broadly similar to the present importance of technicians and experts in modern systems such as the United States and the Soviet Union. The diffuse vertical structures of Latin American societies are not fundamentally dissimilar to the emerging corporatist networks among industrial labor in the United States, Europe and the Soviet Union. The efforts to create a sense of community among the inhabitants of U.S. cities in general, or among the black population specifically—assuming that black separatist tendencies do not dominate—can also be considered efforts to create diffuse vertical hierarchies. The intertwining of government and society in modern societies is too obvious to require comment, and the fluidity of alliances among elites with disparate power bases is, at least, always a possibility. The increase in confrontation politics in the United States and Europe may indicate that pride in the efficacy of their constitutional technologies may be exaggerated or misplaced.

I am not arguing that there is necessarily a complete reconvergence of structural characteristics between Latin America and the more economically developed world, since I suspect that the paths of development will always be distinct. However, the similarities do suggest that the Latin American structure cannot be automatically considered out-of-date and doomed to destruction in the process of change. If it is destroyed, something not so very different would have to be created in its place.

Whatever the situation in the future, comparative analyses of parties and party systems within Latin America, and between Latin America and other parts of the world, will have to systematically take into account the sociopolitical structure and the conditions and opportunities it establishes for parties.

NOTES

1 The notion of crisis offers an as yet unsuccessfully elaborated addition to theories of development which might prove most useful for the analyses of institutions such as parties. Much more flexibility is promised by the concept that nations have different sequences of crises, different crisis loads and therefore different needs. If it is to become such a tool, the term "crisis" will have to become more sharply related to *historical* situations, rather than overall problems of development. For a treatment which seems to be content with the latter "problem approach," see Lapalombara and Weiner (1966). For an interesting attempt to make the crisis notion historical, see Rustow (1968, chs. 1, 4).

2 Alexander (1964: 101) states that "Latin America is growing up politically." See also Martz (1966).

3 Cf. Scott (1966: 333) where the author says, "precisely because Latin American countries are involved in fast-moving and basic change they are faced with the concerted pressures of development crises which call for the kind of unity and widely based representation in the political process that mass parties of national integration can offer."

4 Cuba is the one case where something close to the desirable form of national-integrating party seems to have evolved. It was a costly process, and there also is some doubt as to just how important a role the party per se has played.

5 The Latin American sociopolitical structure described here could be considered an ideal type. Alternatively, one could think of it as one position on a matrix of 16 generated by dichotomizing and crossing the four variables discussed below.

6 The reason for believing in the existence of a distinctive Latin American type is not simply the fact that much literature on the area treats it as such. Several recent studies have concluded that there is something distinctive about Latin America, without having set out to do so. See for example Russett (1964) and Tanter and Midlarsky (1967). There are many other analyses which arrive at a classification of Latin America as a type by not quite so rigorous techniques (e.g., Black, 1966).

7 For the term "linkage groups" see Deutsch (1966). Deutsch defines linkage groups as those groups which have domestic ties, but which are also a part of an international system. A "penetrated" political system is defined by Rosenau (1966: 65) as "one in which non-members of a national society participate directly and authoritatively through actions taken jointly with the society's members, in either the allocation of values or the mobilization of support on behalf of its goals." See my suggestions of effects of these patterns in Chalmers (1971).

8 It is interesting that of the models developed by Moore (1966) the one that most closely approximates the Latin American historical pattern is that which he often identifies with the term "fascist," although the fit is clearly not perfect.

9 It has been argued that every one of the most radical and presumably class-oriented political movements in Latin America—that led by Francisco Juliao in the Brazilian northeast—was a "following" of a boss (Juliao), rather than a class movement. Cf. Galjart (1964). For some of the rejoinders and arguments, which seem not so much to disagree with Galjart as to assert the desirability of forming class-consciousness among the peasantry, see *América Latina* (1965) and Obregón (1967: 301).

10 See for example Leal (1948). In this classic analysis of the Brazilian *coronel*, the author describes the bargain between private and public power made by this rural boss. An analysis of the historical evolution of the relations between the peasant and the government in Mexico of great relevance here is that of Wolf (1956).

11 This analysis owes much to the arguments in Moore's (1966) work.

12 The best known, perhaps, is the Brazilian term *jeito* (know-how).

13 Cf. Eldersveld (1964, ch. 1). He describes the "stratarchy" as being not a "centralized 'unity of command' or a general dilution of power throughout the structure," but a system of "strata commands" which "operate with a varying, but considerable degree of independence."

14 In Almond and Verba's (1963) terms, the culture is "subject" rather than "participant" oriented.

15 This observation recurs in studies of decision-making and elite studies in Latin America. See for example Hirschman (1963).

16 For Brazil, see for example Donald (1960). A fascinating parallel phenomenon is that of the Brazilian states, which are resource poor, but which are the political base of the very powerful governors, who have played a key role in making and breaking presidents in that country.

17 As Anderson himself notes, the rule of no exclusion was broken in the Latin American revolutions, with regard to the older class of landowners in Mexico, and much of the professional and upper classes in Cuba.

18 The support of intellectuals by government agencies seems to have been a particularly common Brazilian pattern. See for example Bonilla's (1963) discussion of ISEB.

19 This technician-centered decision-making pattern is clearly much more characteristic of some kinds of decisions (e.g., monetary, foreign exchange, national investment planning) than others (e.g., public works programs). It is also more characteristic of an issue in some time periods than in others (e.g., it was more characteristic of labor policy decisions in the 1930s than it is in the same decisions today).

20 In this paper, "role" refers to the location and activities of parties within the sociopolitical structure. "Function" refers to the consequences for the system of such a role. Some functions will be discussed in the next section. The terms are confused in the literature. My use of "role" is roughly parallel to what Almond calls "transformation functions," and my "function" is closer to his "system-maintaining" and "output" functions. Cf. Almond and Powell (1966, ch. 2).

21 The blurring of roles often brings about rather confused debates on the importance of parties. See for example the apparent dispute between Scott (1958) and Brandenburg (1964) concerning the importance of the Mexican PRI. A good deal of the dispute is an argument about who is acting as a party leader, and when.

22 These two models parallel the distinction made by Almond (1960, Introd.) between the "articulating" and "aggregating" roles. The argument here is that parties in Latin America do neither. Also note the assumptions made in the excellent analysis by Lipset and Rokkan (1967, introd.) in which cleavages between specific interests are assumed to be exactly reflected and even measured by their party representation, limited only by the thresholds which limit in varying degrees the entry of parties into the system. They do not consider the situations in which parties are not basically representative of interest groups or classes.

23 Extreme polarization of society would be represented by the sharpness with which the various groups are divided and the hostility that exists among them. Lipset and Rokkan (1967: 15 ff.) call attention to a stable form of extreme separation in society (with parties at the head of each grouping) in the Dutch phenomenon called *Verzuiling* (from the Dutch word for "column").

24 The argument is merely that one cannot assume a priori whose interests are represented. It is significant that identifying an oligarchy in terms of interests and backgrounds is not an easy task. See Payne's (1968: 439) comments on the problem.

25 The inability of parties to represent powerful elites produces a circular reinforcement of the pattern. Domestic business elites, for example, who do not have as incomparable a power capability as the military or foreigner, limit their identification with parties because of the latter's weakness, as well as because of the normal fear of too close an identification with potential losers.

26 These sorts of resources for party leaders are more like those in the United States than elsewhere in the world. This suggests the inapplicability of the aggregation model of parties to the United States. There is a difference between the United States and Latin America, however, in that the parties in the United States seem to constitute not party hierarchies intertwined with vertical structures as in Latin America, but relatively independent alternative lines to the top.

27 For the distinction between "role" and "function" see footnote 20. Of the many possible kinds of functions, I shall only be concerned here with ones related to development, and not system-maintenance ones.

28 To the revolutionary minded, the functions in the present system will be irrelevant, and only those of destroying the existing structure and building a new one will be of interest. Although I doubt that such destruction is likely, and do not discuss the revolutionary functions of parties, it is relevant to note that in Latin America's two revolutions, the Mexican and the Cuban, parties played reduced roles. In Mexico, parties were unimportant until long after the Revolution, and in Cuba, the guerilla movement was far more important than parties. Even after the Revolution, the party has developed much more slowly, and with apparently more limited functions than, say, in the U.S.S.R.

29 Padgett (1966: 1 ff.). Note that Padgett, in summing up the functions of the party (pp. 60 ff.), emphasizes not developmental functions but system-maintaining ones. The modification of the corporatist structure seems, on the basis of his analysis, to be potentially an important development function.

REFERENCES

Alexander, Robert J. 1964 "The Emergence of Modern Political Parties in Latin America." In J. Maier and R. W. Weatherhead (eds.), Politics of Change in Latin America. New York: Praeger.

Almond, Gabriel A. 1960 The Politics of the Developing Areas. Princeton: Princeton University Press.

Almond, Gabriel A., and G. B. Powell, Jr. 1966 Comparative Politics. Boston: Little, Brown.

Almond, Gabriel A., and Sidney Verba 1963 The Civic Culture. Princeton: Princeton University Press.

Anderson, Charles W. 1967 Politics and Economic Change in Latin America. Princeton: Van Nostrand.

Apter, David 1965 The Politics of Modernization. Chicago: Chicago University Press.

Black, C. E. 1966 The Dynamics of Modernization.

New York: Harper & Row.

Bonilla, Frank 1961 "Rio's *Favelas*: The Rural Slum within the City." New York: American Universities Field Staff Reports.

———, 1963 "A National Ideology for Development: Brazil." In Kalman H. Silvert (ed.), Expectant Peoples. New York: American Universities Field Staff Reports.

Brandenburg, Frank 1964 The Making of Modern Mexico. Englewood Cliffs: Prentice-Hall.

Chalmers, Douglas A. 1971 "Developing on the Periphery: External Factors in Latin American Politics." In James N. Rosenau (ed.), Linkage Politics. New York: Free Press.

Debray, Regis 1967 Revolution in the Revolution? New York: Monthly Review Press.

Deutsch, Karl W. 1966 "External Influences on the Internal Behavior of States." In Barry Farrell (ed.), Approaches to Comparative and International Politics. Evanston: Northwestern University Press.

Donald, Carr 1960 "Brazilian Local Self-Government: Myth or Reality?" Western Political Quarterly (December).

Eldersveld, Samuel J. 1964 Political Parties: A Behavioral Analysis. Chicago: Rand, McNally.

Galjart, Benno 1964 "Class and 'Following' in Rural Brazil." América Latina (July-September).

Hays, Samuel 1967 "Political Parties and the Community-Society Continuum." In W. N. Chambers and W. D. Burnham (eds.), The American Party Systems. New York: Oxford University Press.

Hirschman, Albert O. 1963 Journeys Toward Progress. New York: Twentieth Century Fund.

Jaguaribe, Helio 1967 Problemas do Desenvolvimento Latino-Americano. Rio de Janeiro: Civilizacao Brasileira.

Janda, Kenneth 1968 "Retrieving Information for a Comparative Study of Political Parties." In William J. Crotty (ed.), Approaches to the Study of Party Organization. Boston: Allyn & Bacon.

Lapalombara, Joseph, and M. Weiner (eds.) 1966 Political Parties and Political Development. Princeton: Princeton University Press.

Leal, Victor Nunes 1948 Coronelismo, Enxada e Voto. Rio de Janeiro.

Leff, Nathaniel 1968 Economic Policy-Making and Development in Brazil, 1947-1964. New York: Wiley.

Lieuwen, Edwin 1961 Arms and Politics in Latin America. New York: Praeger.

Lipset, Seymour M., and S. Rokkan 1967 Party Systems and Voter Alignments. New York: Free Press.

Lowi, Theodore 1964 "American Business, Public Policy, Case Studies and Political Theory." World Politics (July).

Mangin, William 1967 "Latin America's Squatter Settlements: A Problem and a Solution." Latin American Research Review (Summer).

Martz, John D. 1966 Acción Democrática: The Evolution of a Modern Political Party in Venezuela. Princeton: Princeton University Press.

Moore, Barrington, Jr. 1966 Social Origins of Dictatorship and Democracy. Boston: Beacon.

Neustadt, Richard 1960 Presidential Power. New York: Wiley.

Nun, Jose 1967 "The Middle Class Military Coup." In Claudio Véliz (ed.), The Politics of Conformity in Latin America. New York: Oxford University Press.

Obregon, Anibal Quijano 1967 "Contemporary Peasant Movements." In Seymour M. Lipset and Aldo Solari (eds.), Elites in Latin America. New York: Oxford University Press.

Padgett, L. Vincent 1966 The Mexican Political System. Boston: Houghton-Mifflin.

Payne, James 1965 Labor and Politics in Peru. New Haven: Yale University Press.

——— 1968a "The Oligarchy Muddle." World Politics (April).

——— 1968b Patterns of Conflict in Colombia. New Haven: Yale University Press.

Rosenau, James N. 1966 "Pre-theories and Theories of Foreign Policy." In Barry Farrell (ed.), Approaches to Comparative and International Politics. Evanston: Northwestern University Press.

Russett, Bruce 1964 "The Problem of Identifying Regions." Buenos Aires: Instituto Torcuato Di Tella (working paper).

Rustow, Dankwart A. 1968 A World of Nations. Washington, D.C.: Brookings.

Sarfatti, Magali 1966 Spanish Bureaucratic-Patrimonialism in America. Berkeley: Institute of International Studies.

Scott, Robert E. 1958 Mexican Government in Transition. Urbana: University of Illinois Press.

——— 1966 "Political Parties and Policy-Making in Latin America." In Joseph Lapalombara and M. Weiner (eds.), Political Parties and Political Development. Princeton: Princeton University Press.

Tanter, Raymond, and Manus Midlarsky 1967 "A theory of Revolution." The Journal of Conflict Resolution (September).

Vernon, Raymond 1963 The Dilemma of Mexico's Development. Cambridge: Harvard University Press.

Wolf, Eric R. 1956 "Aspects of Group Relations in a Complex Society: Mexico." American Anthropologist 58: 1065-78.

I want to thank Susan Kaufman for help in clarifying the concepts discussed here, along with Arturo Valenzuela and Charles MacCormack. I would also like to thank the Social Science Research Council for supporting me for a year in Brazil. The intellectual frustration of studying Brazilian parties led me to the belief in the necessity of the type of analysis done here. This paper constitutes the framework for a project in which I will compare the party systems of Argentina, Brazil, Chile, Colombia, Venezuela and Mexico.

PERU: CLIENTELISM AND INTERNAL CONTROL

LAURA GUASTI

I. THEORETICAL BASES OF DEPENDENCY
AND INTERNAL CONTROL

The importance of internal limitations to the development of misdeveloped[1] societies has been indicated by several contemporary theorists of economic dependency, or imperialism. Brown argues that direct economic limitations, resulting from external penetration of misdeveloped societies, have not been the most important factors inhibiting these societies' development. The primary inhibitory factors of development have been the political and economic effects *within* misdeveloped societies of external penetration. Brown briefly indicates that "semi-feudal" landownership patterns, and the power of merchant, or "comprador" capital within a misdeveloped society are the factors which hold back the industrial development of the society. Both are encouraged by external actors and external economic relationships.[2] Baran argues that the effects of the "feudal-mercantilist order" within a misdeveloped society (which is a political and social coalition of wealthy "compradors," powerful native industrial monopolists, and "feudal" large landowners) are to stifle economic and social development, suppress popular movements, and maintain the domestic market as a dependent appendage of Western capitalism's "internal market." The internal control within a misdeveloped society of the "comprador administrators" makes possible continued foreign exploitation of the misdeveloped society and its domination by imperialist powers.[3]

Both Brown and Baran do little more than distinguish "feudal" from other types of relationships within misdeveloped societies. Frank discusses in more depth the presence of "feudal" relationships within misdeveloped capitalist societies. He argues that these relationships are, in fact, not feudal but commercial, because they are based on a monopoly of agricultural resources by large landowners, and are an integral part of the mercantilist capitalist system within misdeveloped societies. He further argues that the mercantilist capitalist system within these societies is initiated and maintained by direct or indirect imperialist penetration. Frank indicates that the Spanish conquest of Latin America and transfer of a mercantilist system from Spain to the continent initiated a process which continues to create inequality and an increasing concentration of economic resources, political power, and social prestige within Latin America's misdeveloped societies.[4]

Brown, Baran and Frank's arguments about the internal consequences of imperialist penetration do not adequately examine the specific internal mechanism which maintains the misdevelopment, inequality, and dependency of penetrated societies vis-à-vis external actors and their home governments. This paper attempts an analysis of the internal mechanism of control within misdeveloped societies. The basic argument may be stated as follows:

1) clientelism is the mechanism of internal control in misdeveloped societies, and its functioning is congruent with the international structure and dynamics of political dependency.

2) ongoing modifications in the structure and dynamics of clientelism are the result of changes in the international structure and dynamics of dependency; specifically, the internal "corporatist"[5] structure and dynamics which are becoming visible in various misdeveloped societies are clientelism modified to make internal control in these societies congruent with the ongoing major change in the international capitalist market— the rise and growth of the multinational corporation.

This paper will argue that the clientelistic structure is the basic structure of misdeveloped, dependent societies. Where the structure existed to some extent before external penetration, it was maintained, modified, and strengthened by that penetration. Where it did not exist before external penetration, it was created as a result of external penetration. The unequal, dependent position of misdeveloped societies within the international capitalist market either maintains or develops the internal clientelistic structure. The structure itself functions to carry inequality and dependency to all levels of the societies, to maintain these characteristics within the societies over time, and to cause the failure of these societies to direct resources to their own basic industrial development.

The paper will also argue that corporatism is not a new internal structure in misdeveloped societies, but a modification of the existing clientelistic structure and dynamics. It attempts to maximize centralization of the structure, funnel domestic surplus to the highest levels of the structure, and focus strong control over the society and its resources in the national level of the government. The cause of this modification in the clientelistic structure is the changing pattern of capital movement within the international market, and of foreign investment within misdeveloped countries; specifically, the increasing power of multinational corporations, and their movement to centralize control of international resources and capitalist production. Thus the modification of the clientelistic structure into a corporatist structure in misdeveloped societies is fundamentally a movement to modify the internal mechanism of control in misdeveloped societies to function more suitably for the interests of the current dominant actors in the international capitalist market, the multinational corporations.

To focus these arguments, the paper will examine the clientelistic structure and dynamics in one misdeveloped society—Peru—and discuss clientelism's presence, basic characteristics, past and current changes in these characteristics, and their consequences for different classes of the society.

Before beginning the discussion, one definitional modification needs to be made. Brown defines imperialism as an economic relationship of dependency. I suggest a more useful, inclusive definition of imperialism is a political relationship of dependency, with politics defined as the activity of acquiring and distributing tangible and intangible resources within a group, and of resolving conflicts that develop among members of the group over the pattern of distribution. Using this definition it becomes more apparent that, at a basic level, "politics" and "economics" as currently defined, are different means for carrying out the activity.[6]

II. CLIENTELISM AS THE INTERNAL STRUCTURE OF CONTROL

The clientelistic structure is a political structure whose basis is a highly unequal distribution of resources within a society, and whose functioning serves to maintain the dependency of each class on those above it. Fundamentally, it is characterized by the patron-client relationship (whose prototype is the landlord-peasant relationship, continually mislabelled as a "feudal" relationship) which, besides being based on an unequal holding of resources, is dyadic, or face-to-face, and flexibly diffuse in the types of resources that can be exchanges between the pa-

tron and client. The patron-client relationship is thus an unequal exchange of resources across class lines on an individualized basis. The relationship tends to maintain the lower class client in his dependent position vis-`a-vis the higher class patron because the client is more in need of the resources the patron monopolizes than the patron is in need of the resources the client offers. The client therefore can afford much less to terminate the exchange than the patron can. However, the commercial value of the resources given by all the clients of one patron to that patron is greater than the commercial value of the resources given by the patron to all his clients, and so the clientelistic, patron-centered group serves to funnel clients' surplus to the patron. (Surplus has often meant anything in excess of minimum survival, or occasionally, less than minimum survival.)

Within the larger society, the patron-centered group is expanded into patron-client networks. Patrons exist at different levels of the society (national, regional, local) and lower-level patrons are the clients of higher-level patrons who have access to greater amounts and types of resources. The lower-level patrons enter into these relationships to gain access to the greater resources so that they can increase their own client base (because they will have more resources to distribute) and concomittantly, their own wealth and prestige. When lower-level patrons gain access to resources they do not directly control in order to distribute them to their clients, they act as brokers between their clients and higher level patrons.

Patrons who have control over, or access to approximately equal quantities of different types of resources often establish what have been called "friendship" relationships[7] with each other to exchange non-comparable resources, doing so for their personal benefit and to distribute to their clients. These relationships also expand the patrons' access to resource and help to maintain their positions as patrons. The highest level patrons within the society depend, for both their access to and control over important resources in the society, on their unequal relationships with foreign capitalists, who control or have influence over the use of greater resources than do the highest level patrons of the misdeveloped society. The patrons also depend on the maintenance of the disadvantaged international market position of their society, from which these relationships derive. The entire system of clientelistic networks within a society rests on the existence of unequal concentrations and control of resources. These occur from the lowest level of the misdeveloped society to the international market, where the society holds a disadvantaged position because international resource concentrations and control are held within the dominant capitalist societies.

Both patron-client and friendship relationships are often formalized through ritual kinship relationships, in Latin America called compadrazgo.[8] These increase the personalism and thus, the security of patron-client relationships, because they reduce their arbitrariness especially for the lower class client, in part by ensuring that channels of access to resource will persist over time. The use of ritual kinship implies that exchange relationships among family members are considered more reliable, and family relationships of exchange often are important within the clientelistic structure. They appear to increase in importance at higher levels of the society, where control over and access to greater quantities and types of resources occurs. Thus, family relationships seem to be used as a means to consolidate and maintain control over larger quantities and types of internal resources within the clientelistic structure.

The clientelistic structure, then, extends from local to national levels of a society, and from lower to upper classes. Within the structure, the pattern of cross-level and cross-class relationships established within networks is flexible and variable. The clientelistic structure is a political structure because all types of material and nonmaterial resources needed and desired by the members of a society are acquired and distributed, and conflicts over distribution resolved through the dynamics of the structure. The clientelistic structure includes both the government and commercial sectors of the society, and therefore is the basic political structure of the society.

III. INTERNAL CONTROL DURING THE
COLONIAL PERIOD

The following five sections will take up the first point of the paper, that clientelism is the internal mechanism of control in misdeveloped societies, and examine the situation of Peru to see: (1) whether or not a clientelistic structure existed, and continues to exist within the society from the time of Spanish colonization, when Peru first entered into the international commercial market; (2) to what extent the structure served as an internal mechanism of control, congruent with the needs of foreign capital, maintaining inequality and dependency within the society. These sections will examine data on the colonial period, then shift to an examination of

the characteristics and dynamics of the classes that have become visible in the post-independence period—upper, middle, working and peasant classes.[9]

The presence of a clientelistic structure in Peruvian society is discernible from the time of the Spanish colonization of the area, which occurred within the context of commercial goals.[10] The Spaniards created a dependent, mercantilist capitalist market within the former empire of the Incas, and acquired a monopoly over important resources. During the colonial period land, minerals, and labor were most important.[11] Peru and the other Spanish colonies were producers of raw materials, supplying various European markets directly or indirectly. The colonial commercial market was dominated by its dynamic centers, mining and export agriculture, and these centers responded to the needs of the colonial metropolis.[12] In the colonies the Spaniards became mining entrepreneurs, producers of commercial crops, and merchants.[13]

The Quechuan population, in what became Peru, was converted into a dependent labor force for mining and agricultural production. By the creation of ecomiendas, which were royal concessions of a group of Quechuans (usually an entire community) to an individual Spaniard, large numbers of the Quechuan people became directly dependent on an individual encomendero, to whom they had to pay tribute and provide labor services.[14] The encomienda was a commercial enterprise which enabled the encomenderos to collect sufficient wealth through tributes and services to create the basis for several types of commercial activities.[15] In the 18th century, the encomiendas were superseded by private ownership of land, which usually was organized as haciendas. These lands were either bought or seized from the Quechuans, who were forced to remain on them as colonos, or nonwage laborers. The haciendas were also commercial enterprises producing for local and regional markets.[16]

The great number of Quechuans who were incorporated into the encomiendas, and later, the haciendas, became directly dependent for acquisition of survival resources on the encomenderos and hacendados, with whom patron-client exchanges occurred. The extent of the Quechuans' dependence was considerable. Within the haciendas, the colonos were given small plots of land for subsistence farming. Sometimes the hacendado supplied housing, tools and credit (in kind, e.g., seeds). In return, the colonos were required to work the hacendado's land for a specific number of days per week or month, planting and harvesting the hacendado's cash crops. They also had to provide personal services in the hacienda house for a specific number of days per week or month, as well as give a certain number of their best animals to the hacendado each year.[17]

The hacendado, acting as a patron, was the final judge of disputes that arose within the hacienda.[18] In commercial activities, the hacendado acted as a broker for the hacienda colonos by controlling the marketing of all goods produced on the hacienda and the purchase of all goods from the market. The hacendado therefore was the single source of all survival resources for the colonos. He also acted as a broker between the colonos and government officials, mediating between them to help the colonos when they were in trouble with the police or other officials.

In addition to physical services and animals, the colonos individually gave the hacendado what was expected to be unquestioning loyalty in all disputes with other hacendados or with government officials. When necessary, the colonos were required to serve in the hacendado's private militia.[19] The inequality in resource control and exchange between colono and hacendado during the colonial period was great. The colono's dependency in resource exchange was maximized because the hacendado monopolized channels of access to all survival resources, and to resource relationships outside the hacienda.

The Quechuan communities that were not absorbed by the encomiendas and haciendas were in unequal but relatively less dependent positions vis-a-vis the Spaniards than were the communities that were incorporated. The former were labelled "independent" communities by the Spanish Crown, and were permitted to retain control over their communally-held lands. This allowed them to retain their separate internal political structure, based on a relatively egalitarian communal holding of land. The "independent" communities were oriented to non-commercial subsistence farming until at least the middle of the 19th century. The people within these communities often served as a reserve labor force for the surrounding haciendas, as a consequence of the continual encroachment of neighboring haciendas on communal lands that left the communities with insufficient land to maintain a subsistence existence. Community members often depended on seasonal work on the haciendas to supplement their farming and provide the extra margin of resources needed for survival. In order to obtain guaranteed seasonal work, they found it necessary to enter into patron-client relationships with the neighboring hacendados.

During the colonial period clientelistic networks expanded from local to regional to national levels. The networks included mine owners, priests, police, and officials at various levels of the government,[20] and were the means by which the hacendados of an area controlled the resources within their area.[21]

IV. POST-INDEPENDENCE CHANGE IN THE STRUCTURE AND RESOURCE BASE OF THE UPPER CLASS

In the post-Independence period, Peru has continued to be in a dependent position within the international capitalist market. Foreign capital has dominated the domestic commercial sector, especially the most dynamic commercial sub-sectors. During the 19th century, Peru's financial and commercial interests were dominated by British capital. After World War I, existing agricultural, mining and financial interests were dominated by United States' capital. More recently created industrial and financial interests have also been dominated by North American capital.[22]

After independence was achieved in the early 19th century, the Spanish upper class merged with a growing upper class group whose monopolistic resource base was created as a result of the growth of a profitable international market for cotton, phosphate, and especially, guano. During the latter part of the century, foreign investment in Peru and changes in the international market led to the growth of export agriculture on the coast, and to the concomittant rise of a second upper class group, whose resource strength was founded in the control of coastal cash crop plantations.[23] The power of this small group, which organized the resources it controlled as family holdings, was based primarily on the monopolized control of cotton and sugar exports. This control was achieved in conjunction with two foreign companies operating in this sub-sector. The other important export sub-sector in Peruvian society was the extraction of oil and minerals which, from its initiation in the latter part of the 19th century until 1968, was under complete foreign control.[24]

During the 20th century, the second export-based upper class group (based on cash crop exports) expanded its resource base into banking and light manufacture industries. Its almost exclusive domestic dominance over important societal resources began to be challenged during the post-World War I period by another new upper class group whose resource strength came from the rapid growth of intermediate manufacturing industries. The rise and growth of light and intermediate manufacturing industries were controlled by foreign capital, particularly North American capital.

Three important patterns may be discerned. First, the rise and growth of upper class groups were directly connected to the changing demands of the international market, that is, the power of upper class groups was based on externally important resources. Second, the power of upper class groups was derived from domestic monopolies of externally important resources. Third, though upper class groups held domestic monopolies of resources within their respective sub-sectors, control over externally important resources was often shared with foreign capital. Where this happened, foreign capital was almost always in the dominant, and the upper class groups in the dependent, position in controlling resource development and use.

Despite challenges to its dominance, the agricultural export upper class retained domestic control over a strong concentration and variety of resources. In the mid 1960s eight plantations, controlled by five families and one North American corporation, accounted for almost the entire sugar crop, while one hundred and forty-five families controlled about 80% of the cotton crop. Among them, these families controlled 45% of the best coastal farming land and generated 25% of total exports, 36% of domestically controlled exports and 6% of the GNP.

Although the importance of agricultural exports for Peru's position in the international market has decreased, this group has not become inconsequential, because it has augmented its resource holdings in banking and credit, insurance, real estate in the larger, faster growing cities, and manufacturing, mining and oil enterprises. In the mid 1960s, forty-five families or family-controlled corporations were represented on the board of the Sociedad Nacional Agraria, the most important agrarian interest group in the society up to 1970. Fifty-six per cent of these families were also important shareholders in banking and finance companies, 53% were important shareholders in major insurance companies, and 75% were owners of real estate agencies. Fifty-six per cent held shares in commercial enterprises, 64% held large shares in industrial enterprises, 20% had shares in mining concerns and 12% had shares in one or more oil companies.[25] Most important for its retention

of power was this upper class group's acquisition of a dominant domestic position in the distribution of credit,[26] which was largely under foreign control until 1970. Bank board directorships were mostly shared between members of this upper class group and foreign capitalists. By virtue of its position in the credit system, this group also controlled a substantial part of import activities. This upper class group has maintained its position since the 19th century, as well as its close connections with foreign capital, and until the mid 1960s, it was the more powerful upper class group.

During the 19th century, the agricultural upper class group merged with older upper class groups through intermarriage and "friendship" relationships. These two types of relationships have continued to characterize upper class interactions as a new manufacturing-based upper class has arisen. The members of the agricultural export group have been described as playing the role of brokers in domestic-international resource exchanges and old-new upper class resource exchanges.

The upper class as a whole has been described as a "network of families with their clienteles." Family ties and "close personal alliances" have been the means to continue and expand resource control for upper class groups through family members or clients acquiring important positions in different commercial areas.[27] Family resources have been controlled by the head of each family so that, within families, control over resources has been monopolistic and thus unequal. The family heads have been described as "patrons" because of their position within the families, which allows them to own and control various enterprises without having to personally manage them. Hired managers, not the owners, engage in direct exchange relationships with workers, and therefore act as brokers in the resource exchanges that occur between owners and workers. Managers in upper class-controlled enterprises have usually been middle class persons. Their positions have been described as resulting from the "graciousness" of the owners, who retain basic control over resource exchanges.[28]

This very general evidence indicates that the position and characteristics of the Peruvian upper class are those of the highest level patrons in a clientelistic structure: (1) control over heavily concentrated resource holdings; (2) familial, friendship, brokerage and patronal ties between themselves, foreign capitalists, and managerial employees. New upper class groups arising in various periods have entered the upper class networks through these same ties and have exhibited the same characteristics. The evidence also indicates that the power and domestic dominance of the upper class have been directly connected to the resource demands of the international market and that upper class groups within their own sub-sectors have often been in dependent positions vis-à-vis foreign capital.

The sierra hacendados control considerably fewer resources than do the export and manufacturing-based upper class groups, and have been less definable over the past one hundred years as part of the upper class. Until approximately the middle of this century, they maintained some social or kinship ties with the coastal upper class, and maintained their position as regional patrons much as the colonial hacendados did. The gamonal, or regional patron, controlled the appointment of local government officials and judges, and could prevent the enactment or enforcement of government actions he opposed. His power rested fundamentally on his control of land. The regional clientelistic networks which the gamonales developed enabled them to gain sufficient votes to elect themselves or one of their clients to the national legislature. The sierra departments were over-represented in the legislature, and therefore legislative positions helped the gamonales maintain control over their regional resources by undermining national government control at the local level.[29]

The patronal position of the gamonales has been weakened and undermined by two factors. First, the relative importance of sierra regional land holdings as a resource has progressively decreased during the last century as the importance of the resource base of the coastal upper class has increased. As indicated earlier, the latter has been a direct effect of international market demands. Second, the national government has progressively increased its ability to control regional resources. The decreasing power of the sierra hacendados can be seen as an effect of the centralization of the political structure of the society (which is discussed further below) and the concentration of power in groups in direct contact with, and most dependent on the international market and foreign capital.

Relationships between members of the upper class and government officials, as well as the type of access the upper class has had to public sector resources appear clientelistic in character. In the early 19th century, military men held the presidency and many high level government posts. Upper class members and the military

(whose internal characteristics at this time were also those of a clientelistic network; see below) interacted on favorable terms, and upper class individuals also held high government positions.[30] After the rise of the agricultural export upper class, this new elite was increasingly able to staff national government positions with their people. The class as a whole gained dominating influence over factions and leaders of political parties,[31] and this influence continued to an important degree until 1962. To guarantee the retention of its resource base, the upper class relied heavily on favorable national economic policies and, until recently, no government administration has adopted measures directly contrary to upper class interests. The government personnel who established alliances with upper class members acted as brokers for the latter in preventing the success of any major domestic threat to upper class control.

Until the consolidation of two large and more permanent parties in the late 1950s, there were generally two kinds of elected personnel in the government sector: local or regional level patrons, and the clients of important national government leaders. Upper class members acquired government brokers from these two groups. Since the turnover of elected personnel was rapid until the consolidation of the two parties, the upper class had to reconstruct its "networks of allies" before and after each election.[32] These "networks" were characterized by personalism and patronage.[33]

From this limited data it appears that the interactions of upper class members with people who held government posts were clientelistic, and served to maintain upper class control over resources.

V. MIDDLE CLASS DEPENDENCY AND BROKERAGE

The rise of a Peruvian middle class was the result of bureaucratic expansion, caused by an increase in Peruvian exports into the international market and a concommitant growth in domestic, national-level government activity.[34] Two middle class groups exist. The "old" middle class consists of doctors, lawyers, and bureaucrats. Members of the "new" middle class are the "technicians" holding jobs in commercial and government bureaucracies. Some studies have indicated the recent rise of a third group, a rural agricultural and commercial petite bourgeoisie whose growth has been caused by the expansion of the commercial market into rural areas.[35]

The middle class has consistently been described as "dependent," failing to develop a "value system" separate from the upper class[36] because its members participate in the "politics of clientele,"[37] and see themselves as individual "servants or customers of a given patron or class." Individual members seek "alliances" with upper class individuals, with "powerful patrons or cliques," to ensure middle class acquisition of stable employment and successful careers. All middle class groups have been described as performing brokerage roles.

In the mid 1960s the government sector gained greater central control of "development" resources, as a result of pressure from the United States, through the Alliance for Progress, to carry out certain changes within the society. An increased number of loans for "developmental" purposes from the United States and international lending agencies, and direct AID grants led to a proliferation of new "developmental" agencies and government bureaucratic personnel. This considerably increased the size of the "new technocratic" middle class. Members of this group have been described as having achievement (versus ascriptive) values, and as seeing themselves as developmental planners oriented toward demonstrating competence and skill in job performance.[38] This group, however, as other middle class groups, operates within commercial or government bureaucracies, which have consistently been described as being clientelistic substructures. " . . . At all levels, the 'new technicians' are faced with the importance of personal connections and with unequal competition based on recommendation and ascribed privileges . . ."[39] The government civil service has been described as affected at all levels by "political patronage."[40] As a whole, the government bureaucracy has used "patrimonial hiring practices." Relatively recent efforts to "modernize" the recruitment and organization of the bureaucracy because of the new "developmental" focus have also been pervaded by "patrimonialism." Although efforts were made in a restricted number of areas to hire technicians and professionals rather than untrained people, individuals still tended to be hired "because of their political and/or social affiliations than for any specialized knowledge." A recent discussion of the government bureaucracy described it as a "vast clientele of powerful interests and pressure groups" which functions as a "service market" for these interest groups and for those which emerge within the bureaucracy itself.[41]

Two conclusions follow from these descriptions. First, the bureaucracy and the middle class are involved in cross-class clientelistic networks as brokers. Second, new networks have grown within the bureaucracy itself, founded primarily on control of, or direct access to "developmental" resources obtained directly from external sources. The middle class, since its rise in the 19th century, has thus participated in a clientelistic structure, primarily as brokers within networks whose highest level patrons have been members of the upper class. More recently, it has participated in new networks organized around the control of new "development" resources from abroad.

VI. GROWTH OF THE WORKING CLASS AND ITS INCLUSION IN CLIENTELISTIC NETWORKS

The rise of the working class began at least as early as the end of the 19th century, during the period of rapid growth in coastal export agriculture. At this time, the clientelistic colono-hacendado exchanges of the coastal haciendas changed to include cash wage payments. What could be called a rural proletariat became increasingly visible as these relationships in the coastal areas became more and more commercialized. However, non-cash exchanges also continued on some coastal plantations.

Until the expropriation of the sugar plantations in 1970, permanent plantation workers were given housing, medical care, food rations, soap, cloth and low cash wages in exchange for their labor. On some coastal rice plantations the old hacienda labor exchanges continue in part. In exchange for their labor on plantation lands, workers are given a plot of land to farm, though occasionally they are also remunerated by low cash wages. There is variation in whether or not the workers are required to sell their plot-grown crops to the plantation, whose managers market them, or are allowed to sell directly to merchants outside the plantations.[42] Inequality and flexibility in resource exchange continue in coastal worker-manager relationships, as does the dyadic nature of the relationships, because the workers usually deal directly and individually with foremen and managers. To varying degrees, the workers establish compadrazgo relationships with them also. Managers and foremen sometimes serve as judges to settle disputes among workers, much as the colonial hacendados did. Thus, coastal plantation worker-manager relationships retain clientelistic characteristics.

The urban working class grew in the early part of this century in Lima and other coastal cities. It has always been relatively small. By the 1920s textile workers, as well as miners and sugar plantation workers, were organizing into unions. After the rise of APRA (Alianza Popular Revolucionaria Americana) in the late 1920s, which has been the most long-lived political party in Peru, these unions and their leaders became closely involved and affiliated with APRA leaders. APRA began as an ideological party whose membership and appeal were primarily middle and working class (and whose early statements also included peasant interests) against the upper class' monopolistic control of domestic resources. Its political position became decreasingly radical, and in 1958 it formed an alliance with a political party organized to support Manuel Prado, an upper class member, for the presidency. Prado won the election because of APRA support. The working class unions, largely as a result of the changes in APRA's orientation to the upper class and to the government, became increasingly dependent on government personnel, especially the Minister of Labor and the President, to personally act as brokers in manager-worker disputes over resources. Protective social legislation was enacted nationally in the early 1920s but it was less a response to the embryonic strike capacity of the unions than an effort to anticipate and deflect overt class conflict. This legislation has been described as having been "paternalistically" provided by the president at that time because its passage through the national legislature was assured by the mobilization of the president's clientelistic relationships with legislators, and because it was in part an attempt to avoid a threat to the president's personal power.

The large majority of the working class has remained non-unionized. The small portion that has organized has remained in a weak position vis-à-vis government personnel. As indicated earlier, the latter acquire and/or distribute resources through participation in clientelistic networks. Working class unions are directly dependent on them for the enactment and favorable application of labor legislation and for the settlement of resource conflicts with managers and owners. Thus, working class organization leaders also have to participate in clientelistic networks to get resources. No information seems available on the extent to which individual relationships between union leaders and APRA party leaders, government personnel and commercial managers were dyadic or diffusely flexible, but recent literature indicates that "paternalistic" relationships between employers or managers and workers has continued and that the hiring of manual labor in union organized enterprises is clientelistic. The hiring system in these enterprises is tied to a "network" by which personal recommendations of upper class individuals, or job applications filled out by friends or relatives establishes a "working clientele and market of services between the union bureaucracy and the bosses."[43] Thus, although working class organizations exist, clientelistic relationships have persisted between workers and employers or managers, and clientelistic networks have expanded to include union leaders and government bureaucrats as brokers between workers and employers.

VII. THE PEASANTRY AND CHANGE IN THE DYNAMICS OF INTERNAL CONTROL

We may summarize the salient features of Peruvian political life visible so far. An underlying political structure with clientelistic characteristics and dynamics is apparent. The structure has a heavy concentration of resources at the upper class level. The control of resources is organized through familial and friendship relationships at that level. These relationships form the upper level of clientelistic networks which cut across the middle and working classes on a dyadic, flexibly diffuse and unequal basis. Middle class members are usually in broker positions between upper and lower class members in these networks, through their positions as clients of upper class individuals. Middle class brokerage is performed primarily within commercial and government bureaucracies. Acquisition of the resources on which clientele networks are based is often directly dependent on the international market or the actions of dominant capitalist governments and international lending agencies. The most powerful patrons are dependent on external resources. The one patronal group whose primary resource has not been dependent on external sources has been progressively losing power and influence.

It is within the literature on the peasant class that the clientelistic structure and its dynamics are most visible, not only across classes, but across regions of the country. Changes which have occurred in the clientelistic structure, particularly within this century, and the consequences of these changes are also most visible within the literature on the peasantry.

For the colonos on sierra haciendas, the impact of the regional clientelistic structure and its dynamics, established primarily by hacendados during the colonial period, remained largely unchanged from that time until the beginning of the

20th century. However, the "independent" or indigenous communities experienced a slightly greater penetration of the clientelistic structure into their communal life. After Independence and the formal centralization of the government, appointed representatives of the national government were placed within the communities. These appointments were controlled by the communities' neighboring hacendados. The impact of this penetration of the clientelistic structure on the communal political structure was not large at this time for two reasons. First, the national government had little or no control over regional and local resources. Second, individual peasants (campesinos) had already been included at the lowest level of local and regional clientelistic networks outside the communities since the colonial period.

In the early part of the 20th century, the campesinos of the indigenous communities began to experience changes both in the control they held over their limited quantity of resources and in the characteristics of their relationships with patrons from outside the communities. These changes increased in magnitude during the 20th century, and their causes can be traced to changes occurring simultaneously in the pattern of private and governmental foreign investment in Peru.

A growth in foreign capital investment, and shift from agricultural export and raw material extraction to consumer manufacturing industries producing for the domestic market began before World War I, and increased considerably after the War. As stated earlier, at that time North American capital became the dominant source of foreign investment in Peru and has remained so. The shift in foreign investment fostered the rise and growth of manufacturing industries, which have remained under foreign capital control. There have been several long term effects on Peruvian society of this growth of manufacturing for the domestic market. The primary effect, coming from the need to expand the domestic market to absorb new and increased production, has been the slow but persistent extension of the commercial market from Lima to the rural regions. This expansion first affected the regions surrounding Lima, and only recently has become noticeable in the farthest sierra regions.

A second effect of the expansion of the domestic market was the growth of a transportation and communication infrastructure to facilitate commerce. This was carried out by the national government, which received capital assistance from international lending agencies.[44] This change had important consequences for the government's clientelistic structure. The direct acquisition of external resources by the government made access to this sector through existing clientelistic networks increasingly important for gaining access to or control over the new resources. Within the government, new patrons were created who controlled these new resources and new patronage networks were fostered which focused on these patrons rather than on upper class families or groups. Simultaneously, the growth of transportation and communication facilities enabled the national government to begin acquiring control over regional and local resources. Thus, one important consequence of the growth and shift in foreign investment in Peru was to increase the magnitude and importance of the resources controlled by government-based patrons.

Commercial market expansion also led to the expansion of clientelistic networks within the commercial sector. New networks centered on individuals who could gain access to some of the new foreign capital through investment and participation in manufacturing industries. These individuals constituted a new upper class group. Monopolistic upper class control of domestic resources was maintained with this market expansion, and as the commercial market increasingly reached the sierra regions these also became included within commercial sector clientelistic networks which have centered in Lima and the coast. Thus, a second important consequence of the growth and shift in foreign investment was the expansion within the commercial sector of coastal control over rural resources and the increasing centralization of this control in the coastal upper class.

After World War II, and particularly in the 1960s, consumer manufacturing began a period of rapid growth, as did intermediate-level industry. Both areas continue to be of increasing importance. The impetus for this new growth also came primarily from North American capital. During this period, multinational corporation subsidiaries became important within the domestic commercial sector. The subsidiaries are primarily engaged in raw material extraction (mining and oil), but a small percentage of North American and Western European multinational subsidiaries are in capital goods producing industries.[45]

This new commercial growth has increased the magnitude of commercial market expansion into the rural areas, those farthest from the coast being increasingly affected, and has had an increasing impact on the society. Concentration of resources within the commercial and government sectors, and the focusing of resource control in the coast, especially in Lima, has become more pronounced. In the late 1960s, 67% of all investment in domestic industrial enterprises was located in Lima, as was the largest amount of foreign investment in these enterprises.[46]

At the same time, the United States' creation of the Alliance for Progress in the early 1960s placed a new importance on "development" within misdeveloped societies and led to AID and international lending agency loans to the Peruvian government. The result has again been growth of the transportation and communication infrastructure, as well as proliferation of the government bureaucracy to distribute the new resources. Much of the emphasis of the Alliance for Progress, and specifically of AID grants for Peru, was on the growth of domestic agricultural production in the rural regions. Therefore government bureaucratic expansion reached particularly into the rural areas. The results of the increase in resources controlled by the government sector again were to expand the clientelistic networks within the sector, develop new networks based on directly acquired external resources, particularly within the bureaucracy, and centralize the clientelistic structure, by concentrating resources in the national government, and by expanding this sector's clientelistic networks to local rural levels.

Thus, the new period of growth and industrialization, resulting from new patterns of foreign investment, has magnified the effects of earlier changes to foreign investment patterns. These effects have been: (1) the expansion of the clientelistic structure within both the government and commercial sectors; (2) the increased concentration of resources at the highest level of these sectors; (3) the increased centralization of control over domestic resources from local to national level in the government sector and from lower to upper class in the commercial sector; and (4) the continued growth in importance of government sector resources vis-à-vis commercial sector resources.

The effects of these shifts in the pattern of foreign investment in Peru have led to other significant changes within the clientelistic structure and its dynamics. Changes in the types and importance of resources exchanged within the structure as a whole, and a decrease in the diffuseness and personalism of clientelistic relationships have occurred. The presence and effects of these two changes can best be seen in the experiences of the peasant class, and particularly of the campesinos in the indigenous communities.

The expansion of the commercial market had the following consequences for the indigenous communities: privatization of communally held lands; increased migration to the coast for temporary or permanent work; and direct participation of the campesinos in the domestic commercial market.[47] The cumulative result of these three changes was to break down the non-clientelistic communal political structure, and to expand government and commercial sector clientelistic networks directly into the communities. Community leaders increasingly were those who gained wealth, familiarity with the commercial market, and a speaking knowledge of Spanish through migration or direct local participation in commercial activites. These individuals became patrons to poorer community members, and brokers for them in resource exchanges with patrons outside the community. Thus, for the first time, clientelistic exchanges were occurring among indigenous community members, and these exchanges were connected into the larger clientelistic networks existing outside the communities.

The campesinos' need for clientelistic connections progressively increased as a result of the continuing effects of market expansion. In addition to the effects discussed above, a further impact stemmed from the considerable disadvantage experienced by campesinos trying to sell crops produced with subsistence farming techniques and poor quality seed and land. The primary source of agricultural aid—seed, fertilizer, credit, and technical knowledge—was the national government and its "developmental" agencies, as a result of the Alliance for Progress and AID program in Peru. Therefore the campesinos found it increasingly important to establish clientelistic relationships with bureaucrats in the "developmental" agencies in order to get these very important resources. They did so directly or through the new brokers within their communities.

One consequence of new campesino links to markets and the government, and the increased extensiveness of the clientelistic structure as a whole has been a decrease in the diffuseness and personalism of patron-client relations. Where before a campesino client was able to go to one patron to negotiate for all or most of his needed resources, the client now must go to several patrons, each controlling or with access to a single important resource, to get all the resources he needs.[48] This is particularly the case with resources controlled by bureaucratic patrons or brokers.

Earlier, too, patron and client often lived in

the same location and interacted regularly or frequently. The dyadic character of the clientelistic relationship still remains, but the personalism and familiarity that existed between patron and client have decreased or disappeared in many relationships.[49] This is again particularly true of exchanges with bureaucratic personnel. The exchange position of the campesino has worsened, as he has few resources to offer. It has meant the loss of the magnanimity and "noblesse oblige" of the patron. The patron's protectiveness and limitedly magnanimous exchanges with his clients, whom he knew and with whom he interacted often, decreased the level of arbitrariness and vulnerability which the relationship could hold for the client. Equally important, two of the limited number of resources a campesino client could offer a patron were loyalty and increased prestige. These important negotiating resources for the campesino client have lost their value with the increase in impersonalism in the clientelistic relationship.

Thus, four more changes have been visible within the clientelistic structure: (1) a variable decrease in personalism; (2) decreased diffuseness; (3) change in the importance of resources and the locus of their control; and (4) increased extensiveness and centralization of the clientelistic structure. For the individual campesino these changes have signified weakened bargaining power with patrons, and therefore, a more pervasive position of dependency.

For the society as a whole, the cumulative effects of these changes have been to increase the dependency positions of clients, particularly lower class clients; and to increase the capability of elite patrons to control resource acquisition and distribution within the society. The ultimate consequences of these changes and, fundamentally, of the changes in the pattern of foreign investment in Peru, have been: (1) to increase the capability of the clientelistic structure to funnel surplus within the society to the highest level of the structure; and (2) to increase the concentration of domestic resources in the hands of class groups whose position is dependent on foreign private and government capital investment, and on the pattern of international capital movement.

VIII. POST-INDEPENDENCE CHANGES IN THE MILITARY
AND THE CURRENT REVOLUTIONARY GOVERNMENT

The remaining sections will examine the development of "corporatist" clientelism as the internal mechanism of control in misdeveloped societies which makes these societies' structure and dynamics congruent with the needs of the multinational corporations within the international capitalist market. The sections will briefly discuss the structure and changes in the Peruvian military since Independence, and then examine the effects of the current military junta's "revolutionary" policies, which have been consistently defined as leading to national development. We will analyze whether or not the junta's policies are working to break down the clientelistic structure of Peruvian society, which has been the fundamental domestic obstacle to development, and, if not, what the structural consequences of these policies have been for Peruvian development.

The Peruvian military began as clientelistic networks organized around individual caudillos, who were patrons controlling a variety of resources distributed among their followers.[50] In the early years of the Republic, different caudillos held the presidency through the support of their groups. The caudillo groups did not seriously compete with upper class groups for control of resources, but operated within a modus vivendi with upper class families that included having upper class members in higher level government positions.

Near the end of the 19th century, the agricultural export upper class group took direct control of the presidency and the government sector. "Professionalization" of the military began during this period, but the military continued to operate in clientelistic networks that persisted both within the military and between officers and upper and middle class civilians in Lima and department capitals. Until 1956, the military men who ousted elected presidents organized their coups and ensuing administrations through "personal followings."

In the 1950s the United States government began its program of military aid to Peru and to other Latin American countries. The program involved joint military missions, grants to buy equipment and develop training schools, and training programs that included study in the United States. As a result of this program, the Peruvian military gained control of new sources of power from abroad. Military training became increasingly "professionalized" and included training in technical skills, and studying Peruvian economic and political problems with a "developmental" and nationalistic focus. The military officers who received this wider as well as more specialized education were increasingly antagonized by the actions of the agricultural export upper class, APRA, and the inability of the government sector to carry out developmental policies. The antagonism increased in the 1960s and resulted in the 1962 and 1968 coups, led by officers who had studied in the United States.[51]

The military government that was created after the 1968 coup has remained in power.

In 1970 the current military junta decreed an agrarian reform law whose partial enactment resulted in the most extensive agrarian reform to occur in Peru. The junta denounced foreign capital involvement in agricultural export activities and domestic control over these activities by the agricultural export upper class. The reform was meant to end the monopolistic resource control of the agricultural upper class and connected foreign interests which had caused agricultural stagnation and been, in the junta's view, the major obstacle to domestic development.[52] The reform also was intended to encourage redistribution of investment capital from agriculture to industry.

The coastal sugar plantations and an unknown but fairly large number of sierra haciendas, beginning with those that had experienced serious colono-hacendado conflicts over land rights, were expropriated. The owners were allowed to keep medium sized holdings whose size was regulated by the reform law. The law's provisions for owner compensation were structured to encourage a shift of landowners' capital from agricultural to industrial investment.

The goal of the reform was to develop the primary sector and encourage small and medium sized farm holders through governmental provision of agricultural credit, equipment, seed, fertilizer and technical training. Governmental help was also to go to cooperatives newly established on lands where division might otherwise decrease productivity. Indigenous communities were to be organized into campesino cooperatives; lands previously held communally were to be reinstated and worked communally to counter the severe productive problems of minifundization.

The implementation of the agrarian reform neither weakened the control of foreign capital nor the clientelistic structure of the society. Nor did it seriously undercut the resource power of the coastal agricultural upper class. The actual land holdings of the coastal plantation owners were expropriated. However, the other agricultural export interests of this upper class group and of foreign capitalists involved in this area were not affected. The manufacturing industries based on plantation products which had been set up by both groups were left untouched.[53] By 1968, in any case, the coastal agrarian elite depended less on land and more on control of banking and financing, a control shared with foreign capital. Its control in this area has not been reduced. Therefore the monopolistic control over domestic resources of this group has not been

significantly diminished by the agrarian reform.

There are several examples of the continuation of clientelism in agricultural activities despite the reorganization of landholdings and new formal structure specified by the reform law. On some of the sierra haciendas converted into cooperatives former managers of the haciendas have been retained to continue directing agricultural production. Before expropriation, the colonos on these haciendas had been involved in patron-client relationships with the managers. The failure to change personnel has resulted in the absence of structural change within the new cooperatives, and the continuation of clientelistic relationships between campesinos and administrators.[54]

On other expropriated haciendas managers were replaced by bureaucratic technicians from the reform agencies. However, the colonos who had been brokers for other hacienda colonos before expropriation continue to perform their brokerage roles and to control more resources than the other colonos did or do control. Further, I suspect that the replacement of managers by bureaucratic personnel to administer the lands also has not changed the clientelistic character of the relationships the colonos had with the administrators of the lands. One reason is that bureaucratic personnel had acted as brokers for colonos within the larger clientelistic structure before 1968. A second reason is that there is evidence from other types of agricultural holdings that the agrarian reform bureaucrats continue to be involved in clientelistic relationships with peasants and higher level bureaucrats.

In indigenous communities where reorganization into campesino cooperatives has been attempted, there are examples of community leaders maintaining clientelistic connections with bureaucrats in the agrarian reform agencies, especially with those bureaucrats involved in the implementation of the reform within the communities. The community leaders use these relationships to mobilize higher level bureaucratic support for their continuation as leaders.[55]

Thus, despite the junta's agrarian reform actions and their efforts to reorganize the political structure in rural areas, clientelistic relationships and networks continue to exist and to characterize rural exchanges. Particularly at the local rural level, the junta's actions have not begun to break down clientelism.

IX. THE MOVEMENT TOWARDS CORPORATISM

Neither the junta's agrarian reform efforts nor other actions it has taken have worked to decrease the high degree of foreign capital control over domestic commercial activities, with which the existence and functioning of the clientelistic structure are intimately tied. Rather, the junta's actions have worked to increase this control.

Within a year after the 1968 coup, the junta took several actions that appeared to directly challenge North American capital interests, which were the strongest controlling foreign interests in Peru. Six days after the coup, most of the assets of the International Petroleum Corporation, a wholly owned subsidiary of Standard Oil of New Jersey, were confiscated, and a few months later all its holdings were expropriated. A few months after taking power, the junta also pressed Peru's 200 mile water rights claim, and captured North American fishing boats found within the 200 mile limit. In 1969 the agricultural holdings of the Cerro de Pasco Corporation were expropriated. However, these actions were the only occasions of direct challenge to North American capital interests, and now do not appear to have seriously jeopardized continued North American and other foreign capital investment in Peru.

The agrarian reform law did not distinguish between domestic and foreign capital when it provided an opportunity to convert agricultural investment into industrial investment. Therefore the reform also allowed foreign enterprises to shift their capital into industrial activity, and created the possibility of increased foreign control of industrial production.

Except for the IPC expropriation, foreign capital investment in oil production has not been attacked. The junta established requirements that the oil companies in Peru (which are all foreign controlled, save one) sell the greater part of their crude oil to Petroperu, the government-controlled oil enterprise, at prices fixed by Petroperu. Simultaneously, however, the junta has encouraged greater foreign investment in oil production. The proportion of North American capital investment in oil since the IPC expropriation has been almost equal to the level of investment before the expropriation.[56] The junta has not attempted to control or limit foreign investment in mining activities either. Instead, it has cooperated in the initiation of a considerably expanded copper mining project made possible by new foreign investment.

More importantly, the junta's measures to encourage industrialization have directly encouraged increased foreign capital investment in domestic industries. The junta has explicitly stated that foreign capital investment is essential for increased and expanded industrialization.[57] The junta's measures explicitly encourage multinational investment, and monopolization of resources in industry. One significant legislative decree has given tax exemption and benefits to companies existing or to be created in Peru which provide multinational services and whose capital resources are entirely foreign.

The junta's monetary and credit policy has rather rigidly conformed to the International Monetary Fund's policy of drastically reducing public expenditures, curbing inflation, and maintaining currency stability. This rigid adherence results from the junta's desire for and success in getting new IMF loans for "development."[58] The domestic effects of this policy have been to increase mergers among the largest and most important industrial enterprises, and to cause the decline or failure of middle-sized industrial enterprises. The industrial enterprises which have reduced production or gone bankrupt because of the junta's recessionary policy are those with a weaker financial base and less developed technology, and they are the enterprises controlled by domestic capital. The impact of the junta's credit policy, therefore, has been to debilitate that sector of industry where domestic capital had not been under foreign capital control. Thus, there have been four consequences of the junta's "development" policies: (1) to decrease industrial competition within Peruvian society; (2) to increase the concentration of capital within the largest industries; (3) to increase foreign capital, and especially multinational, control of domestic industries and raw material extraction; and (4) to increase the dependence of domestic capital on foreign capital.

Therefore, the junta's policies do not appear to be challenging, or functioning to break down the clientelistic structure of the society, or its dependent position vis-`a-vis foreign capital. Rather, the policies seem to operate to modify the distribution of resources *within* the clientelistic structure in the direction of increased concentration of resources and multinational penetration.

What the junta seems to be attempting is the creation of a corporatist structure within the society. Its measures to ensure middle, working and campesino class participation function to control the formal structure established for participation. These measures, combined with the junta's commercial sector policies, work to facilitate control of domestic resource exchanges within the commercial sector by the national government, with the relatively passive acceptance of government decisions by workers, and particularly by peasants.[59] I have argued at greater length in another paper that corporatism in a misdeveloped society (as, for example, in Brazil) is a modification of the clientelistic structure of the society.[60] I suggest that the corporatism which the junta seems to be trying to establish in Peru is an effort to more tightly structure and to centralize clientelistic networks within important commercial areas of the society, and to place the commercial sector of the clientelistic structure under the control of the government sector. The purpose of this is to maximize the centralization of the clientelistic structure and the funneling of domestic surplus to the highest levels of the structure. The highest level at which domestic resource *control* would be located is the national government. This modification of the clientelistic structure would be compatible with, and continue, the changes in the clientelistic structure discussed earlier, which had been occurring before the 1968 coup, and which were fundamentally the result of the changing pattern of foreign investment within Peruvian society and the changing pattern of international capital movement. I suggest that the corporatist modification of the clientelistic structure is also the result of the changing pattern of foreign investment in Peru and capital movement within the international market, particularly the greater and increasing importance of multinational corporations within both markets and their efforts to centralize international control of resources and capitalist production within themselves. Thus I would suggest that the effort to modify the domestic clientelistic structure into a corporatist structure is fundamentally a movement to modify the internal mechanism of control of a misdeveloped society to function more suitably for the interests of the current dominant actors in the international capitalist market, the multinational corporations.

This paper argues for two linkages: (1) that between the domestic clientelistic structure and dynamics of a misdeveloped society, and the structure and dynamics of the international capitalist market; and (2) the connection between the direction of change in the clientelistic structure and dynamics of a misdeveloped society, and the direction of change in contemporary imperialism. There is a reasonable amount of evidence to support the argument that the basic political structure of one misdeveloped society, Peru, is clientelistic and that the dynamics of the structure are closely connected to the dynamics of the society's dependent position within the international capitalist market. The second argument obviously follows from the first. Though it is more speculative, because there is much less evidence available now to substantiate or to negate it, it is also more important to attempt to understand the significance of current changes and the possibilities of positive development in Peru and other misdeveloped societies.

NOTES

1 Misdeveloped is a more honest word to use to describe Third World societies. The various connotations of "underdeveloped" or "developing" are either pejorative, or wrong, or both. Third World societies are in fact neither *under*developed nor in the process of developing positively. These societies have "developed," but in ways that have been advantageous to the economies of North American and European societies rather than to their own. Further, the structure and dynamics of this "development" have prevented, and continue to prevent internal economic, social and political growth which is beneficial to Third World societies. The past and present internal structures and dynamics in Third World societies which have caused these consequences have been created by the societies' external penetration by North American and European economies. Therefore Third World societies have *mis*developed, connoting that beneficial development has been externally interfered with and replaced by pejorative development. I would like to thank Professor Maurice Zeitlin for introducing me to the word, which succinctly connotes what has long been apparent.

2 Michael Barratt Brown, *After Imperialsim*, London, William Heinemann, Ltd., 1970, p. 401.

3 Paul Baran, *The Political Economy of Growth*, New York, Monthly Review Press, 1957, pp. 174, 196.

4 Andre Gunder Frank, *Capitalism and Underdevelopment in Latin America*, New York, Monthly Review Press, 1967, pp. 243-244.

5 Phillipe Schmitter describes corporatism as follows: " . . . These traits relate to a world view that stresses a hierarchical and harmonious structure of distinct social groups. The social groups are linked vertically to the upper strata or at least the governing authorities, who in turn have a special asymmetrical responsibility for the well-being of those below them. I have therefore called the aggregate of these traits corporatism . . . Corporatism is a belief in and acceptance of a natural hierarchy of social groups, each with its ordained place and its own set of perquisites and responsibilities. These 'orders' have and accept voluntary restrictions on their autonomy and horizontal interaction. They are seen as linked by vertical lines of subordination directly to higher social institutions, which are conceded the right and the duty to intervene in intergroup conflicts for the sake of social peace. Al-

though corporatism stresses the immutability of the social and political order, it by no means precludes individual mobility or the participation of newly formed interest associations, provided such associations accept certain limitations on their autonomy and patterns of interaction . . ." Phillippe C. Schmitter, *Interest Conflict and Political Change in Brazil* (Stanford University Press, 1971), pp. 95, 98-99.

6 For a long time I have found the rigid distinction between, and separation of "politics" and "economics" useless, if not outright misleading, for understanding less complex societies, peasant "politics," and misdeveloped societies. The academic separation of "economics" and "politics" makes as much sense as if, to use a very simplistic example, the study of car driving and bus riding were made into distinct disciplines, with separate methodological tools, paradigms, and theories (of course, with each almost never being allowed to refer to the other), while refusing to recognize that the fundamental characteristic of both is that they are *means*—in this case, of transportation. I use the word politics rather than economics to include both means because I have found that people can more readily recognize that politics involves economics than recognize that economics involves politics.

7 See Luigi Graziano, "Patron-client Relationships in Southern Italy," Paper presented at the American Political Science Association meeting, Washington, D.C., September, 1972.

8 For a detailed discussion of compadrazgo, see Eric Wolf and Sidney Mintz, "An Analysis of Ritual Co-Parenthood (Compadrazgo)," in Jack Potter, et al., *Peasant Society*, Boston, Little Brown & Co., 1967, pp. 185-199.

9 The data available for this examination is sometimes vague or incomplete, and much that is needed to rigorously test my argument is lacking now.

10 Rodolfo Stavenhagen, "Seven Fallacies About Latin America," in James Petras and Maurice Zeitlin, eds., *Latin America: Reform or Revolution?*, Greenwich, Fawcett Publications Inc., 1968, p. 17.

11 Frank, p. 243.

12 Stavenhagen, p. 18.

13 Eric Wolf in Frank, pp. 124-125.

14 Magali Larson Sarfati and Arlene Bergman, *Social Stratification in Peru*, Berkeley, Institute of International Studies, 1969, p. 30.

15 Frank, p. 127.

16 Larson and Bergman, p. 31.

17 Julio Cotler, "La Mecánica de la Dominación Interna y del Cambio Social en el Perú," in *El Perú Actual*, Mexico, Instituto de Investigaciones Sociales, 1970, p. 57.

18 Carlos Astiz, *Pressure Groups and Power Elites in Peruvian Politics*, Ithaca, Cornell University Press, 1969, p. 85.

19 F. LaMond Tullis, *Lord and Peasant in Peru*, Cambridge, Harvard University Press, 1970, p. 90.

20 José Matos Mar and Fernando Fuenzalida, "El Proceso de la Sociedad Rural," in José Matos Mar, ed., *El Campesino*, Lima, Moncloa-Campodónico, 1970, p. 115.

21 Cotler, p. 68.

22 Aníbal Quijano Obregón, *Nationalism and Capitalism in Peru: A Study in Neo-Imperialism*, New York, Monthly Review Press, 1971, p. 3.

23 Larson and Bergman, p. 12.

24 Aníbal Quijano Obregón, "Tendencies in Peruvian Development and in the Class Structure," in Petras and Zeitlin, p. 293.

25 Larson and Bergman, pp. 262, 265-266.

26 François Bourricaud, "Structure and Function of the Peruvian Oligarchy," 1966, p. 24.

27 Larson and Bergman, pp. 261-263, 267, 270, 271.

28 Bourricaud, p. 22.

29 Astiz, p. 291.

30 Bourricaud, p. 25.

31 Astiz, pp. 37, 192.

32 Larson and Bergman, pp. 271, 282-283.

33 Astiz, p. 90.

34 Larson and Bergman, p. 260.

35 Quijano, 1968, p. 311.

36 Bourricaud, p. 26.

37 Astiz, p. 69.

38 Bourricaud, pp. 26-27.

39 Larson and Bergman, p. 288.

40 Kenneth Benton, "Peru's Revolution from Above," *Conflict Studies, #2*, January, 1970, p. 5.

41 Quijano, 1968, p. 319.

42 Delbert Fitchett, *Agricultural Land Tenure Arrangements on the Northern Coast of Peru*, Santa Monica, Rand Corporation, 1966, pp. 11-15.

43 Quijano, 1968, pp. 317-318.

44 James Carey, *Peru and the United States 1900-1962*, Notre Dame, University of Notre Dame Press, 1964, p. 7, and Robert Weigand, "The United States, Latin American Regional Integration, and Peru," Working paper prepared for Peru Policy Project, May 1970, pp. 3, 7.

45 Fritz Wils, *Industrialization and Industrialists in Lima-Callao*, The Hague, Institute of Social Studies, p. 15.

46 Quijano, 1971, p. 16.

47 For a more detailed analysis of these changes and their consequences, see my paper "Campesinos, Cargos and Patrones: Clientelism and the Indigenous Peasant Communities of Peru," December, 1973, MS.

48 Charles Kleymeyer, *Social Interaction Between Quechua Campesinos and Criollos*, Ph.D. dissertation, Madison, University of Wisconsin, 1973, pp. 111.

49 William Stein, *Hualcan: Life in the Highlands of Peru*, Ithaca, Cornell University Press, 1961, p. 42.

50 For a detailed discussion of the Peruvian military in the early years of the Republic, see Liisa North, *Civil-Military Relations in Argentina, Chile and Peru*, Berkeley, Institute of International Studies, 1966, pp. 8-10, 21-25.

51 Luigi Einaudi, "U.S. Relations with the Peruvian Military," in Daniel Sharp, ed., *U.S. Foreign Policy and Peru*, Austin, University of Texas Press, 1972, pp. 37-48.

52 Julio Cotler, "Political Crisis and Military

Populism in Peru," *Studies in Comparative International Development*, VI, #5, 1970-1971, p. 108.

53 Quijano, 1971, p. 53.

54 Normal Gall, "Peru: The Master is Dead," *Dissent*, 17, #3, June 1971, p. 289.

55 David Palmer and Kevin Middlebrook, *Corporativist Participation under Military Rule in Peru*, MS, pp. 24-30.

56 Quijano, 1971, pp. 21-22.

57 Cotler, 1970-1971, pp. 112.

58 Quijano, 1971, pp. 28, 39.

59 Passive acceptance is what appears to be aimed for, not what has been achieved.

60 See my paper "Corporatist Brazil and Clientelism," June 1972, MS.

REFERENCES

Astiz, Carlos, *Pressure Groups and Power Elites in Peruvian Politics*, Ithaca, Cornell University Press, 1969.

Baran, Paul, *The Political Economy of Growth*, New York, Monthly Review Press, 1957.

Brown, Michael Barratt, *After Imperialism*, London, William Heinemann, Ltd., 1970.

Benton, Kenneth, "Peru's Revolution from Above," *Conflict Studies, #2*, January 1970.

Bourricaud, François, *Power and Society in Contemporary Peru*, New York, Praeger, 1970.

———, "Structure and Function of the Peruvian Oligarchy," 1966, pp. 17-31, (no indication of the journal).

Bradfield, Stillman, *Mutual Obligations Between Management and Workers in Peru*, Technical Report #5, Advanced Research Projects Agency, 1968.

Bravo Bresani, Jorge, "Mito y Realidad en la Oligarquia Peruana," in *La Oligarquia Peruana*, Colección - Perú - Problemas 2, Lima, Instituto de Estudios Peruanos, Moncloa-Campodónico, 1970, pp. 55-89.

Burgess, Eugene, and Frederick Harbison, *United States Business Performance Abroad: Casa Grace in Peru*, National Planning Association, 1954.

Calderon, Paul, *Foreign Investment and the Problem of Development in Peru*, Peru Study Group, ASIIA, University of Chicago.

Carey, James, *Peru and the United States 1900-1962*, Notre Dame, University of Notre Dame Press, 1964.

Chaplin, David, "Industrialization and the Distribution of Wealth in Peru," 1967-1968, (no indication of the journal).

———, "Peru's Postponed Revolution," *World Politics*, XX, #2, April 1968, pp. 393-420.

———, *Political Stratification and Mobilization - Revolution and Developmental Process*, September 1967, MS.

Craig, Wesley, "Peru: The Peasant Movement of La Convención," in Henry Landsberger, *Latin American Peasant Movements*, Ithaca, Cornell University Press, 1969, pp. 274-296.

———, "Systematic Power Relations and Social Change in Rural Peru: A Non-Marxian View," Paper presented at the annual meeting of the Rocky Mountain Social Science Association, May 1973.

Cotler, Julio, "La Mecánica de la Dominación Interna y del Cambio Social en el Perú," in *El Perú*

Actual, Mexico, Instituto de Investigaciones Sociales, 1970, pp. 47-87.

———, "Political Crisis and Military Populism in Peru," *Studies in Comparative International Development*, VI, #5, 1970-1971, pp. 95-113.

Cotler, Julio and Felipe Portocarrero, "Peru: Peasant Organizations," in Henry Landsberger, ed., *Latin American Peasant Movements*, Ithaca, Cornell University Press, 1969, pp. 297-322.

Einaudi, Luigi, "U.S. Relations with the Peruvian Military," in Daniel Sharp, ed., *U.S. Foreign Policy and Peru*, Austin, University of Texas Press, 1972, pp. 15-56.

Fitchett, Delbert, *Agricultural Land Tenure Arrangements in the Northern Coast of Peru*, Santa Monica, Rand Corporation, 1966.

Frank, Andre Gunder, *Capitalism and Underdevelopment in Latin America*, New York, Monthly Review Press, 1967.

Fuenzalida, Fernando, "La Estructura de la Comunidad de Indigenas Tradicional," in *La Hacienda, La Comunidad y El Campesino en el Perú*, Lima, Moncloa-Campodónico, 1970, pp. 61-104.

———, et al., *Modernidad y Tradición Local en Una Comunidad de Indigenas del Valle de Chancay*, Lima, Instituto de Estudios Peruanos, 1967.

Gall, Norman, "Peru: The Master is Dead," *Dissent*, 17, #3, June 1971, pp. 281-320.

Goodsell, Charles, "Diplomatic Protection of U.S. Business in Peru," in Daniel Sharp, ed., *U.S. Foreign Policy and Peru*, Austin, University of Texas Press, 1972, pp. 237-257.

Graziano, Luigi, "Patron-client Relationships in Southern Italy," Paper presented at the American Political Science Association meeting, Washington, D.C., September 1972.

Guasti, Laura, "Campesinos, Cargos and Patrones: clientelism and the Indigenous Communities of Peru," December 1973, MS.

———, "Corporatist Brazil and Clientelism," June 1972, MS.

Handelman, Howard, *Struggle in the Andes: Peasant Politics and Mobilization in Peru*, Ph.D. dissertation, Madison, University of Wisconsin, 1971.

Hunt, Shane, *Distribution, Growth and Government Economic Behavior in Peru*, Development Research Project, Discussion paper #7, Princeton, Princeton University, 1969.

Kleymeyer, Charles, *Social Interaction Between Quechua Campesinos and Criollos*, Ph.D. dissertation,

Madison, University of Wisconsin, 1973.

Lalone, Daniel, *Cholification and the Nationalization of Peruvian Society: A Crisis in Peruvian National Development*, Los Angeles, California State College, MS.

Larson Sarfati, Magali and Arlene Bergman, *Social Stratification in Peru*, Berkeley, Institute of International Studies, 1969.

Matos Mar, José and Fernando Fuenzalida, "El Proceso de la Sociedad Rural," in José Matos Mar, ed., *El Campesino*, Lima, Moncloa-Campodónico, 1970, pp. 105-134.

North, Liisa, *Civil-Military Relations in Argentina, Chile and Peru*, Berkeley, Institute of International Studies, 1966.

Palmer, David and Kevin Middlebrook, *Corporativist Participation under Military Rule in Peru*, MS.

Payne, James, *Labor and Politics in Peru*, New Haven, Yale University Press, 1965.

Peru Desk, United States Department of State, "U.S. Aid to Peru Under the Alliance for Progress," in Daniel Sharp, ed., *U.S. Foreign Policy and Peru*, Austin, University of Texas Press, 1972, p. 423-438.

Powelson, John, "United States Policy Toward Peru - The International Lending Agencies," Working paper for the Peru Study Group, May 1970.

Quijano, Obregón, Aníbal, *Nationalism and Capitalism in Peru: A Study in Neo-Imperialism*, New York, Monthly Review Press, 1971.

————, "Tendencies in Peruvian Development and in the Class Structure," in James Petras and Maurice Zeitlin, eds., *Latin America: Reform or Revolution?*, Greenwich, Fawcett Publications Inc., 1968, pp. 289-328.

Rodriguez, R. F., *Market for U.S. Products in Peru*, Washington, D.C., United States Department of Commerce, 1961.

Stavenhagen, Rodolfo, "Seven Fallacies About Latin America," in James Petras and Maurice Zeitlin, eds., *Latin America: Reform or Revolution?*, Greenwich, Fawcett Publications Inc., 1968, pp. 13-31.

Stein, William, *Hualcan: Life in the Highlands of Peru*, Ithaca, Cornell University Press, 1961.

Strasma, John, "The U.S. and Agrarian Reform in Peru," in Daniel Sharp, ed., *U.S. Foreign Policy and Peru*, Austin, University of Texas Press, 1972, pp. 156-205.

Tullis, F. LaMond, *Lord and Peasant in Peru*, Cambridge, Harvard University Press, 1970.

United States Agency for International Development, *U.S. aid to Peru Under the Alliance for Progress*.

Weigand, Robert, "The United States, Latin American Regional Integration, and Peru," Working paper prepared for the Peru Policy Project, May 1970.

Wils, Fritz, *Industrialization and Industrialists in Lima - Callao*, The Hague, Institute of Social Studies.

Wolf, Eric, and Sidney Mintz, "An Analysis of Ritual Co-Parenthood (Compadrazgo)," in Jack Potter, et al., eds., *Peasant Society*, Boston, Little Brown & Co., 1967, pp. 185-199.

PART VII

Clientelism Theory and Development

HOW TRADITIONAL RURAL PATRONS LOSE LEGITIMACY:
A Theory with Special Reference to Southeast Asia

JAMES C. SCOTT · BENEDICT J. KERKVLIET

I. INTRODUCTION[1]

THE FRENCH counter-revolutionary peasants of the Vendee, who marched with local cures and shouted "Vive la Noblesse", "Vive le Roi", were no less active politically than revolutionary peasants who murdered nobles and sacked chateaux and abbeys. Filipino tenant farmers in Central Luzon who canvass votes for their landlords are no less active than tenants who canvass votes for advocates of land reform. The crucial question, therefore, is not so much whether peasants act or not, but rather whose side they are on—whether they are mustered out in the faction of some local notable or whether they act, in some sense, on behalf of more strictly peasant interests as opposed to those of agrarian elites. As long as the peasant sees his relation to agrarian elites as one of legitimate dependence—as long as he feels himself part of a vertical community—peasant "class-conscious-ness" is unlikely. Accounting for the rupture of these vertical ties, where they existed, is thus an integral part of any explanation for the sustained appearance of the peasantry qua peasantry on the historical stage.

This paper attempts to understand the process by which the vertical social bonds which often linked peasants to an oligarchic political order

have, in certain portions of Southeast Asia, weakened or broken completely. The interpretation of agrarian class relations developed here has both a general and a particular aim. First, it presents a general analytical framework that tries to distinguish between what peasants regard as unjust dependence and what they see as legitimate dependence. Second, we believe the argument is applicable to changes in rural class relations in much of Central Luzon (the Philippines), the Mekong Delta (Viet-nam), and Lower Burma. Without undertaking a detailed application of the framework to these areas, we provide a brief empirical illustration from Central Luzon and outline schematically the broad effects of colonial structural change in Southeast Asia on peasant-elite relations.[2]

In terms of theory, the general question addressed here is, "What is the basis of patron-client structures of deference and how do they lose their moral force?" An answer to this question can provide only *one* segment of an analytical bridge between rural patron-client politics and more "class-based" forms of peasant action. Although older patron-client bonds may lose legitimacy, new vertical links may join peasants to politicians, office-holders, or rural bosses and provide many of the essential services of the older relationship. Where alternative

bonds between a high-status landlord and each of his tenants in a *traditional* agrarian economy —relationships that serve, in a sense, as the prototypes of patron-client ties.

First, patron and client are not equals. The basis of exchange between them both arises from and reflects the disparity in their relative wealth, power, and status. A patron is most often in a position to supply goods and services unilaterally which the potential client and his family need for their survival and well-being.[9] A locally dominant lord, for example, may be the major source of protection, security, employment, of access to arable land or to education, and to food in bad times. Such services could hardly be more vital and hence the demand for them tends to be highly inelastic; that is, an increase in their effective cost will not diminish demand proportionately. Being a monopolist or at least an oligopolist for critical needs, the patron is in an ideal position to demand compliance from those who wish to share in these scarce commodities.

While a client is hardly on an equal footing with his patron, neither is he entirely a pawn in a one-way relationship. If the patron could simply issue commands, he would have no reason to cultivate a clientele in the first place. His need for a personal following which can be mobilized on his behalf requires some level of reciprocity. Thus, patron-client exchange falls somewhere on the continuum between personal bonds joining equals and purely coercive bonds. Determining exactly where between these two poles a particular patron-client system should be placed, or in which direction it is moving, becomes an important empirical question in any attempt to gauge its legitimacy.

The inequality of patron and client quite often includes a status dimension as well as wealth and power dimensions. As a member of a more exalted stratum, the patron, unlike his client, is as much part of the great tradition as part of the little community—a representative of the center at the periphery. In fact, an essential part of his local power may come by virtue of the literacy, education, military functions, office-holding, or ritual privileges that are directly connected to his status. As the social apex of a local community, a patron often acts as a broker for his clients with outside officials—much as the patron saint in folk Catholicism is expected to help his devotees while also acting as their broker with the Lord.[10]

The status dimension of patronage, where it is pronounced, is a double-edged sword. On the one hand, it reinforces the patron's claim to position and authority with the sanctions and values of a wider culture. On the other hand, it also imposes certain normative standards of service and performance upon the local patron classes which serve as an ethical basis for judging their behavior. The lower clergy often exemplifies this duality. In the normal course of events, religious values accept and justify both the local stratification and elite behavior. At other times, however, when tax, rent, tribute, or conscription claims jeopardize local security and subsistence, it is the lower clergy—Thomas Munzer in Germany, pongyis and ulamas in the Buddhist and Islamic countries of Southeast Asia—who can often be found at the head of local peasantry as defenders of their rights.

The second distinguishing feature of patron-client dyads is their diffuse, face-to-face, personal character as opposed to the explicit quality of impersonal contracts or of formal relations of authority. As Marc Bloch has shown for the traditional feudal bond, its diffuseness was more an indication of its sweeping strength than of its imprecision. " 'To serve' or . . . 'to aid', and 'to protect'—it was in those simple terms that the oldest texts summed up the mutual obligation of the armed retainer and the lord. Never was the bond felt to be stronger in the period when its effects were thus stated in the vaguest and, consequently, most comprehensive fashion. When we define something, do we not always impose limitations on it?"[11] It is this diffuseness and wide range of reciprocity that is perhaps the most strongly traditional quality of patron-client bonds. Not only is the patron a single comprehensive focus for many of his clients' basic needs but their dependence on him is *personal*. Unlike purely formal authority whose relations with subordinates is regulated by impersonal controls or explicit contractual ties which specify the nature of reciprocal services owed, the patron and client share an open-ended set of obligations to one another. Such a strong "multiplex" relation, as Max Gluckman terms it, covers a wide range of potential exchanges. The patron may very well ask the client's help in preparing a wedding, in cultivating his fields, winning an election campaign, or finding out what his local rivals are up to; the client may approach the patron for help in paying his son's tuition. In filling out government forms, or for food or medicine when he falls on bad times. The link is a very flexible one in which the needs and resources of the partners, and, hence, the goods and services exchanged, may vary widely over time.

These central features of the patron-client tie

distinguish it from other veritcal dyadic ties with which it is often confused. It differs in several important respects, for example, from the link joining the "cacique", the bandit leader, or a local "boss" to his men.[12] While such power figures are also personal leaders with private followings, they generally are *nouveaux arrives* with little claim to higher status, their role is less institutionalized—less culturally sanctioned— than the role of a patron, and their relationship to their men is less diffuse and relies more heavily on coercion and/or material rewards. Patron-client reciprocity must also be distinguished from the kinds of exchange that normally occur between, say, moneylenders and borrowers, officials and citizens, employers and employees. As the functionally specific role categories suggest, such exchange is typically restricted to a single category of reciprocity, it is less durable over time, and the terms of the exchange are governed in large part by impersonal regulations and legal contracts. An employer *may*, of course, also be the patron of his employee, but then the scope and nature of the exchange go far beyond what the categories "employer" and "employee" connote.

As a social mechanism the patron-client bond is neither modern nor wholly traditional. In one sense, to be sure, the style of the patron-client link, regardless of its context, is distinctively traditional. It is particularistic where (following Parsons) modern links are universal; it is diffuse and informal where modern ties are specific and contractual; and it produces vertically-integrated groups with shifting interests rather than horizontally-integrated groups with durable interests. Despite their traditional style, however, patron-client networks both serve as a formula for bringing together individuals who are not kinsmen and as building-blocks for elaborate chains of vertical integration. They cannot be merely dismissed as vestigial remains of old structures but must be analyzed as a type of social bond that may be dominant under some conditions and marginal under others.

Although we cannot elaborate here on the structural conditions which promote patron-client networks, three should be mentioned: (1) the persistence of marked inequalities in wealth, status, and power which are accorded some legitimacy; (2) the relative absence (or collapse) of effective, impersonal guarantees such as public law for physical security, property, and position—often accompanied by the growth of semi-autonomous local centers of personal power; and (3) the inability of either kinship units or the traditional village

to serve as effective vehicles of personal security or advancement.[13]

Elements of Exchange

As a diffuse pattern of reciprocity, the goods and services exchanged by patron and client reflect the evolving needs and resources of each. Some elements of exchange are easily quantifiable while others are not. Any realistic assessment of the balance of exchange must consider both. Although no enumeration of services can do justice to this diversity, what follows is simply an attempt to describe the major categories of exchange in a way that illustrates the scope of reciprocity found in traditional patron-client exchange and, at the same time, the particular exchanges that were often a part of landlord-tenant relations in Southeast Asia early in the twentieth century.

Patron to Client Flows

1. *Basic Means of Subsistence*—This is the central core of the classical patron-client bond. In many agrarian settings this service boils down to the granting of access to land for cultivation and it may include the provision of seed equipment, marketing services, technical advice, and so forth. In the case of office-based patronage, it may mean the provision of steady employment or opportunities for gain, thereby guaranteeing subsistence.

2. *Subsistence Crisis Insurance*—Typically, the patron is expected to be a friend in need. One of his most valued services is his willingness — and obligation—to give loans in time of economic distress, to help in case of sickness or accident, or to carry his client through the year following a poor harvest. As a generalized relief agency of first resort, the patron often guarantees a subsistence "floor" for his clients by absorbing losses (in agriculture or income) which might otherwise jeopardize their livelihood.

3. *Protection*—The need for physical security was a central feature of the feudal bond in Europe. It is especially prominent in office-based patronage but common in land-based patronage as well. Protection may mean building fortifications and maintaining an armed band or the promise to take revenge on the client's behalf. It means shielding the client both from private dangers (banditry, personal enemies) and from public dangers (soldiers, outside officials, courts, tax collectors).

4. *Brokerage and Influence*—If the patron protects his clients from outside depredations, he also uses his power and influence to extract rewards from the outside for the benefit of his

clients. Protection is his defensive role vis-à-vis the outside; brokerage is his aggressive role. In the case of the warrior-patron the relationship with the outside is as often one of plundering as of bargaining. The interests of patron and client coincide in relations with the outside since it is not a question of distribution of resources within the network but of wresting resources from the outside which increase the pool available for distribution among the following—and perhaps expanding the clientele.

Collective Patron Service—Patrons as a group may perform services for the community as a whole which are counted valuable benefits but are not easily divisible into dyadic exchanges. In the same way that an individual patron subsumes his clients and "represents" them, so the group from whom patrons are recruited often represent the community itself.

Internally, patrons are often responsible for many *collective economic functions* of the village. They may subsidize local charity and relief, donate land for communal use, support local public services (such as schools, small roads, and community buildings), host visiting officials, and sponsor village festivals and celebrations. Quite apart from providing tangible resources to the community, patrons in most stratified villages are seen to supply much of its *organization and leadership*. That is, they may not only subsidize celebrations, small public works, and village marketing arrangements, but they also furnish the initiative and mobilizing potential for these activites. Finally, the patrons collectively may be valued also for their capacity to mediate disputes and preserve local order.

In dealing with the outside world, patrons may do together for the village what a particular patron is expected to do for his client. That is, they may *protect the community* from outside forces—whether the state or private marauders—and they *advance the community's* interests by securing works and services, administrative favor, community loans, agricultural assistance, and so on.

Client to Patron Flows

Flows of goods and services from client to patron are particularly hard to characterize because a client is usually his patron's "man"—and his services consist in lending his labor and talents to his patron's designs, whatever they might be. Some typical elements of this overall compliance include:

1. *Basic Labor Service*—An employer-employee relationship, though not at all of the impersonal contract kind, is at the core of the dependence nexus in most strong and durable patron-client bonds. The client contributes his labor and other specialized skills to the farm, office, or enterprise. Such services range all the way from bearing arms as a member of the patron's band to daily manual labor in the patron's fields.

2. *Supplementary Labor and Goods*—Clients commonly provide several subsidiary services to their patron which become an anticipated part of the exchange. These may include supplying water and firewood to the patron's household, personal domestic services, food offerings, and so forth. Some of these services are substantial, some are mainly of symbolic value as expressions of deference, and in more commercialized settings, some have been discontinued in lieu of cash equivalents.

3. *Promoting the Patron's Interests*—This catch-all category signifies the client's membership in his patron's faction and the contribution he is expected to make to the success of his leader and, indirectly, his own prosperity. A typical client protects his superior's reputation, acts as his eyes and ears, campaigns for him if he should stand for office, and generally uses his skills and resources to advance his patron over other patrons.

III. DEPENDENCE AND LEGITIMACY

A crucial question for rural class relations in patron-client systems is whether the relationship of dependence is seen by clients as primarily collaborative and legitimate or as primarily exploitative. Here the issues of compliance and legitimacy are analytically distinct.[14] By virtue of his control over critical goods and services which peasants need, the patron is often in a position to require compliance with many of his demands. Whether that compliance is accompanied with approval or disapproval, with legitimacy or simply with resignation, however, depends on the client's subjective evaluation of the relationship.

Accepting Barrington Moore's interpretation of exploitation as a more or less objective phenomenon, it is possible, in a given agrarian context, to view changes in the legitimacy or approval given a class of patrons as largely a function of changes in the objective balance of goods and services changed individually and collectively between the strata.[15] The notion of balance is somewhat complex because we are dealing here with a balance within a context of unequal exchanges. The question, however, is not whether the exchange is lopsided, but rather *how* lopsided it is.[16]

For the client, the key element of evaluation is the ratio of services he receives to the services he provides. The greater the value of what he receives from his patron compared with the cost of what he must reciprocate, the more likely he is to see the bond as legitimate. For the patron, on the other hand, the level of satisfaction with the bond depends on the ratio of the value of his client's services to the costs of retaining him. The two ratios are not mirror images and the patron's gain is thus not necessarily the client's loss. For example, the opening of a new school may make it easier (less costly) for the patron to help his client's children get an education while not necessarily reducing the value of that service to clients. The patron's position is improved and the client's is not worsened. Under other circumstances, though, patron and client *are* at loggerheads; a landlord who previously took 50% of the harvest and now takes 60% is gaining at the direct expense of his client.

The concept of balance employed here is not directly quantifiable, but both the direction and approximate magnitude of change can often be ascertained. Once the kinds of services and their frequency or volume are specified in both directions, we have a rough picture of the existing balance. If the patron discontinues a service and the client's services remain unchanged, we know the balance has become less favorable for the client. If patrons demand more services from clients without doing more for the clients, we also know that clients are now worse off than before.[17]

Beyond changes in the nature and number of reciprocal services themselves, the cost of a given service may shift. In an era when wage labor opportunities are opening up, a patron's demand for free labor service from his clients may seem more onerous (costly) than before and hence affect the balance. The balance may be similarly altered by a change in the value of a given service. Thus, the value of physical protection was especially high in the chaos of the early feudal period in Western Europe but declined later as banditry and invasions subsided. Variations in the cost or value of a service can, in such cases, lead to a shift in the legitimacy of the exchange while the content of the exchange remains constant.

This conceptualization of reciprocity runs into difficulty, of course, when we want to know *how much* of a shift has taken place and not merely its direction, and also when we try to gauge the net effect of changes which push the balance in different directions. Precise calibration is out of the question, but we can detect gross differences. When a patron, for example, ceases to give subsistence loans prior to harvest, we may be able to infer roughly how large an effect this will have on the balance of exchange from our appreciation of the scarcity of food at that season and from other historical evidence— including protest, banditry, and even starvation. With a series of changes it may similarly be possible to estimate both their net direction and something of their extent. Some cases may prove impossible to judge but in other instances the evidence points clearly one way. In areas such as Central Luzon, the Mekong Delta, and Lower Burma, the unmistakable shift in the balance of exchange against the peasants from 1910-1935 make the calculations hardly necessary.

The *relational* quality of exchange requires emphasis. An analysis of changes in the legitimacy of agrarian elites thus necessarily focuses on changes in the exchange relationship and not on the position of the peasantry taken alone. Although shifts in the relationship and shifts in the peasantry's material well-being may often coincide, they may occasionally diverge as well. It is possible for peasants to experience an improvement in their standard of living—perhaps due to state assistance, high market prices, etc. —while, at the same time, their position in the balance of exchange with landowners is deteriorating as rentier owners revoke past services. A crisis in agrarian class relations may, in such instances, accompany an advance in peasant welfare. The opposite case, in which peasants are materially worse off but enjoy improved terms of trade with landowners is also conceivable.[18] The test, then, is not the level of welfare but the terms of exchange and how they are shifting.

Any assessment of the balance of exchange must also consider, as peasants themselves do, the entire pattern of reciprocity. The more precommercial the context, the more likely the exchange will involve a great variety of reciprocal services beyond the arrangements for cultivation and crop division. A patron's crisis help, influence, and protection may be more valuable in the peasant's estimation than a five or ten per cent increase in the share of the crop he may retain. The disappearance of such services may thus jeopardize the legitimacy of agrarian elites even though landowners take less of the crop and peasant labor requirements are reduced.

The exchange approach to rural class relations helps cast the problems of "false-consciousness" and the role of "outside agitators" in a new perspective. Inasmuch as peasants have a sharp appreciation of their relations with rural elites, they have no difficulty in recognizing when more and more is required of them and less and less is given in return. Peasants are thus not much subject to "mystification" about changes in objective class relations; they do not need outsiders or a new ideology to help them recognize a pattern of growing exploitation which they experience daily. This does not mean outsiders are inconsequential. On the contrary, they are often critical to peasant movements, not because they convince peasants that they may provide the outside power, assistance, and supra-local organization that helps peasants act.[19] It is thus at the level of collective action that the typically small scale of peasant social life constitutes a disability, not at the level of assessing class relations.

Some Complications and Realities

If the legitimacy of the patron for the client were simply a direct linear function of the balance of exchange, our task would be deceptively simple. The multiplicity of human identifications and the discontinuous character of human needs, however, makes such an easy formula inconceivable. Four basic qualifications—or modifications—seem necessary to create a tool for analysis which, while it may become more unwieldy, begins to reflect more fully the complex relationship it addresses. In particular, the simpler model overlooks (1) the relation of patron and client roles to other social categories; (2) the effect of tradition on legitimacy; (3) the effect of sudden changes in the balance of reciprocity on the legitimacy of patrons; and (4) the existence of physical and cultural thresholds beyond which effects are discontinuous.

Patron-Client and Other Roles—It is important to know whether patron-client roles coincide with, or cut across, other salient social roles. Taking first the case of cross-cutting cleavages, patrons and clients may well share certain social identities—such as kinship, ethnicity, religion, community, region, rural residence—which place them in the same camp along some dimensions of potential social conflict. This is likely to have two major results. First, to the extent that such shared identifications signify moral communities, they may work to guarantee minimum benefits to the client. A landowner may give more consideration to the claims of a tenant who is a co-religionist of the same race than to a tenant with whom he does not share these identities. This consideration is not merely a question of moral obligation but

also a *strategic recognition* that he may need to call on racial or religious solidarity in other arenas of conflict. Second, to the degree that other shared interests are salient, they reduce the social significance of the patron-client balance.

Cleavages that coincide with the patron-client division work in precisely the opposite fashion. A client who is of a different race and religion from his patron cannot rely on many claims of a shared community to buttress his claim to consideration. In addition, coinciding cleavages both exacerbate and compound the potential for hostility in patron-client relations. The animosity between Indian landlords and Burmese tenants and laborers in the Irawaddy Delta was simultaneously a patron-client conflict *and* a cultural conflict.[20] Each dimension of the conflict served to magnify the other.

In practice, then coinciding cleavages tend to intensify the dissatisfaction with any given balance of patron-client exchange by infusing it with additional areas of conflict while cross-cutting cleavages tend to reduce the dissatisfaction of any particular balance by creating other shared social interests which diminish its social significance.

Tradition and Stable Exchange—From the standpoint of the client there is obviously a difference between a stable, traditional patron-client relationship and one that is more impermanent and formless. Given similar balances of exchange, the traditional exchange is likely to be viewed as more legitimate. Its greater legitimacy seems to flow *not* simply from its antiquity but rather because its age represents, in effect, a higher probability that the implicit terms will be observed and that the flow of services will continue into the future. The client assumes that his patron will conform to at least the minimal traditions of service if he can and that local opinion and institutions will help to guarantee the observance of traditional terms. If the client then considers a traditional patron-client contract preferable to less traditional arrangements, his choice has some rational basis. Tradition represents legitimacy because it generally promises a higher level of performance according to expectations, durability, and cultural sanction than less institutionalized forms of security.

Breaches of Stable Exchange—In stable agrarian settings, the power relationships between peasants and elites may have produced a norm of reciprocity—a standard package of reciprocal rights and obligations—that acquires a moral force of its own. The resulting norms, so long as they provide basic protection and security to clients, will be jealously defended against breaches which threaten the peasants' existing level of benefits. Sudden efforts to reset these norms will be seen as a violation of traditional obligations which patrons have historically assumed—a violation that serves as the moral rationale for peasant outrage. Thus any balance of exchange above a certain minimum is likely to take on legitimacy over time and *even small movements* away from the balance that reduce peasant benefits is likely to encounter a fierce resistance that invokes tradition on its behalf.

The peasants' defence of traditional exchange in such cases is no mindless reflex. It is motivated, of course, by the fear that a readjusted balance would work against them. A classic example of this situation is the English agricultural uprising in the 1830s when farm workers, whose bargaining position had weakened, invoked traditional local customs of hiring and employment against the commercial innovations of landowners.[21] If, on the other hand, the patron class should feel that *its* bargaining power with peasant clients has deteriorated as, for example, the position of the French rural aristocracy vis-à-vis a commercializing peasantry in the 18th century, it is they rather than the peasants who will be found defending tradition. It is because the commercialization of agriculture so frequently works *against* the interests of most peasants that one generally finds the peasantry cast in the role of defending traditional rights and obligations against erosion and demanding the restoration of the *status quo ante*.

Fundamental Social Rights—For the client, the basic purpose of the patron-client contract, and therefore the cornerstone of its legitimacy, is the provision of basic social guarantees of subsistence and security. If and when the terms of trade deteriorate sufficiently to threaten these social rights which were the original basis for attachment and deference, one can anticipate that the bond will quickly lose its legitimacy. The patron may still be able to extract services from the client but clients will increasingly consider the relationship unjust and exploitative. Legitimacy, then, is not a linear function of the balance of exchange. Instead, there are certain thresholds for the client below which the loss of legitimacy is swift and often complete. No doubt these thresholds have a cultural dimension since they depend on what is necessary for the satisfaction of minimum cultural decencies—e.g., caring for elderly parents, celebrating crucial rituals—but they also have an objective dimension—e.g., enough land to feed the family, subsistence help in case of sickness or accident,

minimum physical protection against outsiders. A relationship of dependence that supplies these minimal guarantees will retain a core of legitimacy, one that abrogates them transgresses nearly universal standards of obligation.

The claim to basic social rights which might be termed the "right to subsistence" or even the "right to a living" is so widespread in traditional society that it all but constitutes the fundamental social morality of traditional, pre-capitalist society. Where peasants have lived in largely unstratified communities, it can be seen as the implicit principle behind the social mechanisms of redistribution and reciprocity which tend to guarantee all villagers a livelihood. In more stratified peasant communities it finds expression in a set of shared norms and social pressures which prescribe a minimum level of performance for local patrons.

Many customary obligations of the traditional patron-client contract were considered subordinate to the basic claims of subsistence and protection. Thus during periods of crop failure or plague in feudal Europe the lord (and the ruler of the kingdom as well) was expected to forego a portion of his normal claims to dues and grain if payment would jeopardize his clients' rights to subsistence. A failure to make these allowances, either wilfully or inadvertently, put tremendous strains on the legitimacy of patron demands.[22] That the peasants' subsistence claim received wide social recognition is shown convincingly in Karl Polanyi's moving account of the traditional elite's support for the futile Speenhamland relief system in England, a system constructed to guarantee a minimum food ration to the poor in the face of commercial pressures which had overwhelmed traditional parish relief practices.[23] The Leveller and Digger movements drew their great moral force precisely by appealing to traditional subsistence principles under which the elite must guarantee work and a basic livelihood to all.[24] Again and again, the popular paternalist view that the social order should guarantee a man and his family a subsistence is the key to many riots and uprisings in 18th and 19th century Europe—outbreaks which were legitimized in the popular mind by the failure of the ruling class to meet its fundamental obligation of providing for the minimum well-being of their subjects.

In traditional societies where most of the peasantry and lower class are not expected and do not expect to be part of the politically relevant public, the unwritten expectation that preserves these boundaries is that the elite, political class will assure a minimum level of subsistence and protection to the non-participant lower classes. At the center of the system of patron-client reciprocity then, is the exchange of deference and compliance by the client in return for the patron's provision of *minimal social rights*. When these guarantees break down, the structure of exclusion loses a key element of its legitimacy.

So long as the aggregate structure of patronage remains intact, the failure of a single patron does not call into question the domination of the patron class. Structural changes in the economy or state which bring about a widespread collapse of the social guarantees of patronage, however, may threaten the claim to ascendency of the entire patron class. As the peasantry experiences a collective failure of the elite to meet what are seen as the social obligation of its position, its claim to that position will be increasingly unjustified.[24a] The consequence, barring repression, may be a burst of peasant activity that simply aims at restoring the old balance of exchange or taking what is needed for subsistence, or it may be a more fundamental attack on the social hierarchy itself.

In understanding the peasant's view of the patron-client relationship, we do well to avoid seeing the peasant as either a fickle, cost-conscious bourgeois, with but fewer alternatives, or as a serf whose loyalty knows no bounds. We do far better to view the peasant as a cultivator who faces a set of continuing existential dilemmas over his economic and physical security which he is often poorly equipped to solve by himself or with other peasants. To the extent that someone of higher status is willing to assist and protect him, and providing the cost is not prohibitive, a relationship of deference may develop that grows in its resilience and closeness as expectations about mutuality and assistance are met. The patron validates his friendship by helping the peasant at times of crisis. It is on that basis that trust and confidence grow; friendship and favor are, for the client, synonymous. When a relationship of patronage fails to protect the peasant, it not only leaves him worse off but it also represents a betrayal of the trust he had placed in a powerful friend.[25] Pitt-Rivers noted, in this context, how the system of patronage in Andalusia rested on performance. "Patronage is good when the patron is good, but like friendship upon which it is based it has two faces. It can either confirm the superiority of the *senorito* or it can be exploited by the rich man in order to obtain a nefarious advantage over poor people. It covers a range of relationships from noble protection of dependents in accordance with the moral solidarity of the pueblo to the scurrilous coercions of the later period of *caciquismo*. The system is, clearly, only to be judged good insofar as it ensures that people do not go hungry, that injustice is not done. Where the majority of the community can look to the patron in time of need, such a system reinforces the integration of the pueblo as a whole. Where those who enjoy the advantages of patronage are a minority, then they and their patrons are likely to be resented by the remainder."[26]

The reverence in which the institution of patronage is held thus ultimately depends upon how well it helps peasants survive the recurrent crises of food supply, defence, and brokerage which mark their life. Its failure as an institution to serve these basic human needs must inevitably tarnish the claim to deference of those patrons who sit astride it.

Relative Bargaining Positions

A particular balance of exchange in patron-client relations reflects the relative bargaining positions of the two parties. One way of assessing the comparative bargaining strength of patron and client is to consider the client as both a buyer of scarce services and a seller of his favor and compliance, and then to ask what his market position is in terms of (1) his demand for the services of the patron and (2) his ability to pay (reciprocate) the supplier. As the discussion below indicates, the aggregate bargaining position of clients depends largely on structural factors such as the concentration of landholding, population growth, and the spread of state power.

Demand—The effective demand for patron services rests in part on whether there are alternative sources for such services. If there is unclaimed arable land, if the peasant can fall back on his kin group for protection and upon professional moneylenders for loans, the peasant's dependence on patrons is somewhat diminished. The more effective and numerous such alternative mechanisms are, the more they serve to establish a baseline below which the terms of patron-client exchange cannot sink. The patron class as a whole thus competes against other social mechanisms for the provision of important needs.[27] For patron-controlled services, client demand will hinge primarily on how *vital* and *scarce* these services are. A man who can distribute jobs amidst widespread unemployment can drive a harder bargain with his clients than he could if jobs were plentiful.

Ability to Reciprocate—A particular client with special religious, military, or agricultural skills may find himself in a better bargaining position than most. Collectively, however, the average position of clients vis-à-vis patrons depends on structural factors that either enhance or diminish the importance of creating personal following. A few of the major factors which have historically augmented the value of building a clientele are the need to assure a permanent and reliable labor force where cash wages are inadequate to the task, the need for a substantial supply of manpower to help defend the patron's domain, and the need for an electoral following to win control of local resources. In such circumstances, clients may anticipate a somewhat more favorable balance of exchange.

Assuming that a following is valuable, a shortage of potential clients will also benefit peasants. In feudal Europe as in traditional Southeast Asia, arable land, to which clients could flee, was plentiful while labor was not. Local elites thus measured their wealth and power by the number of people settled within their domain, not the extent of land they held. But as population grew and land became scarce, the client's bargaining position weakened.

Coercion and the Balance of Exchange

The discussion of patron and client bargaining strength has thus far been carried on in terms of market terminology and has ignored the role of coercion. Many patrons, by virtue of their local power, are potentially able to resort to coercion to improve their bargaining power—to require more and give less. One service, however, cannot be extracted at a greater rate by coercion, and that is the client's active loyalty as opposed to his dependence. Reliance on force can increase the client's dependence and even obedience, up to a point, but only at a cost in legitimacy and active loyalty.[28]

Here legitimacy could be viewed as a service the client can potentially give the patron. The more the patron needs the active loyalty of his clients, the more likely he will avoid using force. Other factors such as collective military tasks, meticulous labor requirements (e.g., viniculture) and, in modern times, elections, may enhance the value of legitimacy for patrons and hence their reluctance to use coercion.

Perhaps the best guarantee, however, that a patron will observe terms of exchange that foster his legitimacy among clients is for his power base to rest upon them rather than outside them. If he can depend on outside backing by police, courts, or military to guarantee his domination of local resources, he will be able to use coercion locally at little cost. If, on the other hand, his base of power is local—if he needs a loyal personal following to protect and validate his local domination of patronage resources—he has vested interests in maintaining legitimacy

among his local retainers. The growth of central states and colonial regimes, inasmuch as they provided local elites with outside legal and coercive backing, thus greatly strengthened the hand of local patrons.

Signs of Coercive Exchange—The use of the patron's coercive advantage not only makes it possible for him to squeeze more from the peasant, but it also effects the kinds of services he provides. To the extent that he relies on coercion, more of the patron's "services" will be of a negative kind. That is, he will extract compliance from the peasant in return for *not* seizing his land, for *not* jailing him, and so forth. The distinction is essentially between a patron who actually protects his clients from outside dangers and one who organizes essentially a "protection racket" in which clients comply in order to be protected against their "patron". Clients can easily distinguish between real protection and extortion; the test for them is whether they would be better off without the patron's services. If such negative services outweigh any real benefits, the relationship is less a patron-client bond than a forced dependence which inspires no legitimacy.

Reliance on coercion by the patron is likely to have another effect on the services he offers clients. If we take the patron-client network (a patron together with his clients) as a unit, we can distinguish roughly between the resources the patron either creates or brings from the outside on the one hand, and the resources he monopolizes within the network on the other. Does the patron merely monopolize the available land and its produce or does he organize the clearing of new land, assist with marketing, and otherwise help during the farming cycle? The distinction here is between the patron who makes an obvious and substantial contribution[29] to maintenance and expansion of the network's resources and one who extracts a surplus without making any such contribution. In this case, too, clients recognize that the more extractive a patron, the better off they would likely be without him.

IV. DETERIORATING BALANCE OF EXCHANGE
IN SOUTHEAST ASIA

The political and economic transformations which accompanied colonial rule in Southeast Asia tended to systematically erode the bargaining position of the peasant/client and to enhance the control of an ascendent landowning/office-holding class. In directly ruled lowland areas—particularly those which were settled comparatively recently, such as Cochin China and Lower Burma—the transformation was most rapid and traumatic. In peripheral highland areas under indirect rule the same tendencies, while noticeable, were far less pronounced. Where the peasant's position substantially deteriorated, networks of fairly stable and voluntary clientage gave way increasingly to systems of precarious and involuntary dependence. The brief examples of changing agrarian conditions which follow will provide an appropriate background for a brief examination later of the broad structural factors responsible for the deterioration of legitimate dependence.

The Tinio Rice Hacienda

The social history of a Nueva Ecija (Central Luzon) rice hacienda from 1900 to 1946 reveals in rich detail the declining position of the peasantry.[30] The transformation is strikingly evident in the contrasts between the hacienda management of Manuel Tinio from about 1905 till 1924 and that of his son, Manolo, from 1924 until 1940.

Manuel Tinio attracted tenants to his hacienda land by offering each of them two to four hectares and a house lot. In terms of the elements of exchange described earlier, Tinio provided the *means of subsistence* to his tenants in the form of land, capital improvements such as irrigation, the price of seed and transplanting costs, and occasionally the free use of a buffalo. For this he received one half the crop under the *kasama* system of tenancy. Beyond the basic tenancy arrangement, however, Tinio supplied his tenants with a more or less comprehensive *subsistence crisis insurance*. He provided *rasyons* (rice from his granary) at no interest while the land was being cleared and between harvests. He gave cash loans (at interest) and would carry tenant debts beyond one year, especially after a poor harvest. At times of birth, baptism, marriage, or death in a tenant family, or when illness struck, Tinio could be expected to make a personal contribution to the family. Finally, the landlord permitted gleaning after the harvest. *Protection* services were less significant although the hacienda provided some security from bandits and Tinio would probably vouch for a tenant who ran afoul of the law. Tinio's *brokerage and influence* was important in finding work for the children of tenants who left the hacienda and in assisting those who needed official papers or licenses. As the single dominant landlord in the area, Tinio himself provided services to the community as a whole which ranged from organizing and contributing to local charities, public works, and festivals, settling local disputes, and acting as the representative of local interests with outside authority.[31]

The tenant-client in this arrangement furnished *basic labor services* in the form of clearing the land (also a capital improvement), harrowing, plowing, and harvesting. He also added to the farm's capital equipment by furnishing farm implements and usually a buffalo as well. Expenses for thrashing and irrigation maintenance were shared equally with the *hacendera*. Beyond these labor services, the tenant supplied *supplementary goods and services*. He contributed his and his family's labor to the repair and maintenance of the landlord's house and equipment and to various domestic chores whenever asked. Periodic small gifts of eggs, cakes, and so on, were also common. Finally, Manuel Tinio's tenants *promoted their patron's interests* by their loyalty, their personal concern for his property and reputation, and their willingness to be mobilized as voters on his behalf.

The key fact about this exchange relationship is that it was regarded as legitimate—in retrospect at least—by tenants. Those old enough to remember him describe Manuel Tinio, for example, as their benefactor and protector.

Manolo Tinio, who succeeded his father, fundamentally altered the balance of exchange. He moved to the provincial capital and managed the hacienda largely through *katiwala* (overseers). The personal attention and intervention that had characterized his father all but disappeared, and tenant families celebrating marriages or baptisms, or struck by death, illness, or other personal disasters were unlikely to receive any assistance. The practice of free chickenfeed was stopped and gleaning was restricted and closely supervised. For the tenants, the most drastic step was the withholding of *rasyons* between harvests. Manolo Tinio had better uses for his capital, since such loans carried no interest, and his tenants were forced to borrow from professional moneylenders from whom they could expect little mercy. As an impersonal absentee landlord, Manolo provided fewer protective services to his tenants, was less likely to use his influence or contacts on their behalf, and, of course, made fewer contributions as a leader or financial backer of community-wide projects. By any standard there had been a substantial cutback in the goods and services to tenants by the landowner and while tenants may have owed fewer personal labor services to the owner, this could not begin to compensate them for what they had lost.

What they had lost, quite clearly, was the basic economic security that the crisis subsistence guarantee of the traditional hacienda system had provided. The tenants of Manuel Tinio knew that if the crop failed, if their family faced ruin, or if they needed the influence of a powerful man, they could generally rely upon him to help an investment they were prepared to make to ensure a continued link with a powerful protector.

Manuel Tinio did not furnish these services from an excess of sentiment. He gained a great deal by having his land cleared at little cost, by securing a loyal clientele of tenants at a time when local power was important, and by creating a stable labor force at a time when land was not yet scarce. The tenants of his son Manolo, however, were in a considerably weaker position. The population had grown, creating a surplus of potential tenants and agrarian laborers, while land was increasingly scarce. The colonial state could more effectively guarantee claims to landed property, and the commercialization of the economy meant that tenants who looked elsewhere found increasingly uniform conditions of tenancy.

It was this change in relative bargaining positions that allowed Manolo to "rationalize" his hacienda and revoke much of the subsistence crisis insurance and personal assistance his father's tenants had enjoyed. The previous ties binding the paternalistic relationship were gradually cut until the only strand remaining was the economic one. Yet even that grew weaker because increasingly the economic relationship was insufficient to meet the peasants' minimum needs. The loss of such vital patron services exposed tenants to the impact of market insecurities and resulted in a radical deterioration of landlord-tenant relations. Discontent took a variety of forms depending on local circumstances but it was almost always directed against the landlords, their agents, or their property.

The history of changing terms of tenancy on the Tinio estate in the 20th century is the history of much of Central Luzon. Within central Luzon the most heavily commercialized areas such as Pampanga, Nueva Ecija, and parts of Bulacan experienced the most traumatic changes while in provinces such as Pangasinan, Tarlac, or Bataan, the tenant's position did not deteriorate so quickly or so completely and in the Bisayan and Bicol regions it deteriorated hardly at all. As late as 1960 it was possible to distinguish between the "tenancy system found in most of Pangasinan" in which "a tenant is allowed to enjoy some measure of self-respect" and the absentee system found in "areas of extreme and insecure tenancy like Nueva Ecija and Pampanga" in which "he is not."[32] These variations should not, however, obscure the central tendency. Small holders have fallen increas-

ingly into the tenant or labor class while traditional cacique owners have been replaced by an absentee rentier class who hold land for its security and income and who offer little of the protection or material assistance given by their predecessors. Landlord-tenant relations have tended to become "very impersonal and usually limited to economic aspects only."[33]

Sufficiency and the Distribution of Risk

The growing power of landowners to dictate the terms of exchange was reflected both in what they demanded from tenants (and laborers) and what they gave. Tenants typically had to assume more of the costs of cultivation, the crop division often shifted in the landlord's favor, and prospective tenants increasingly had to pay "key money" to rent a plot.

Most of the landlord's growing bargaining strength, however, was manifested in his ability to refuse services that once had been part of tenant's expectations. The accounts or agrarian history which note that the relations between landlords and tenants have become more "rational", "businesslike", "impersonal", "purely financial", and "less feudal" often reflect the disappearance of personal services and material assistance on the part of the landholder.[34] While a marginal loss of these services might not have had dramatic effects on the legitimacy of the landlord, the revocation of *rasyons*, loans, and personal brokerage eliminated services that were crucial for the peasantry. However difficult traditional dependence had been, it normally included minimal *social rights* in the form of an elite obligation to provide for their dependents' subsistence. The central basis of the client's attachment was the patron's reliable promise of assistance. As the set of personal services that embodied this social guarantee were eliminated, the client thus lost what was, from his point of view, a service that played a key role in legitimizing his dependence.

The transformation described here can be viewed as a shift in the distribution of risk in agriculture. In effect, the traditional landlord-tenant exchange entitled the landlord to the surplus product only after he had made provision for his tenants' subsistence requirements. This arrangement placed a floor under the real income of peasants and shielded them from the most severe fluctuations in production or prices. With the commercialization of agriculture, an increasing share of the risk is pushed on to the tenant who, being close to the subsistence margin, is least able to absorb these fluctuations. "Agriculture is always the kind of enterprise with which God has a lot to do. With the commercialization of agriculture, the enterprise is further subject to fluctuation in the gross income from its produce. Rentiers, especially if they are capitalists investing in land rather than aristocrats receiving incomes from a feudal patrimony, shift as much of the risk of failure as possible to the tenant. Whether the rent is share or cash, the variability of the income of the peasantry is almost never less, and is often more than the variability of the rentier's income. This makes the income of the peasantry highly variable, contributing to their political sensitization."[35]

Nowhere is the loss of the subsistence guarantee more apparent than in Robert Sansom's account of the agrarian economy of the Mekong Delta in the 20th century.[36] Prior to 1930 it appears that some of the elements of personal crisis assistance were present in landlord-tenant relations as this description by an elderly landlord indicates. "In the past, the relationship between the landlord and his tenants was paternalistic. The landlord considered the tenant as an inferior member of his extended family. When the tenant's father died, it was the duty of the landlord to give money to the tenant for the funeral; if his wife was pregnant, the landlord gave money for the birth; if he was in financial ruin the landlord gave assistance; therefore the tenant had to behave as an inferior member of the extended family".[37] While this statement was probably intended to be self-serving, there is little doubt that the incidence of such practices declined dramatically in the 1930s as the demand for land to farm increased and as the concentration of ownership grew. Rents shifted from a share of the crop to a fixed rent in kind established on the basis of what the land would produce in a good year. The tenant thus assumed the burden of risk from crop yields while the landowner's income was stabilized. Owners increasingly rented only to tenants who would cultivate larger parcels and were solvent, so as to minimize demands for loans and assistance. "Tolerance", the practice of reducing the rent after a poor harvest, became more infrequent since landlords could insist on high rents even in a bad year as the price of renewing a tenancy. Finally, the security of tenure itself declined as landlords dismissed tenants and replaced them with others who would pay more. The most striking demonstration of landlord power, and its human costs, came during the 1930s when, in spite of a large decline in the export price of rice, the volume of exports was maintained at the cost of the subsistence needs of an expanding peasantry. Paddy available for internal consumption in the 1935-1937 period was equivalent only to 127 kg per capita (as compared with 240 kg as a fair subsistence figure) while the real wage of agrarian laborers also declined precipitously.[38] Far from protecting the peasantry, the landlords were now, as the aggregate figures show, able to cushion the fluctuation in their own income from the pool of peasant subsistence needs.

Lower Burma was another variant of the same theme. The "customary" 10-15 per cent (circa 1900) share of the harvest due owners had reached 40-50 per cent by 1920 in much of the Delta. "The refusal of many landlords to grant remissions when flooding or insect pests reduced their tenants' outturn was another expression of the growing strength of the landlord class. Remissions had been a fairly widely accepted feature of landlord-tenant relations in the first phase of development but, in the decades of transition, many landlords did not allow them no matter how desperate their tenant's situation".[39] Tenants were less secure, landlords demanded more services from them (e.g., carting, provision of seed), and even extorted a further fee from those who wished to cultivate the same plot the next year.

The Transformation of Exchange Relationship

For the peasantry of Lower Burma, Cochin China, and Central Luzon, the momentous social changes accompanying the rise of a permanent central state and the commercialization of the agrarian economy, telescoped into a century or less, a process that took three centuries in Western Europe. The penetration of colonial rule tended to reduce the political autonomy of the village by destroying the relative autarchy of subsistence agriculture. The impact of these changes on the situation of the peasantry must form the core of any social history of that class and also the key to most of the dramatic changes in rural class relations.

A history of agrarian class relations in Southeast Asia has yet to be written and is probably not even conceivable until after a much greater accretion of local and provincial social histories provides the raw material. It is possible, however, to suggest how some of the major structural changes in colonial Southeast Asia shifted the conditions of dependency against the peasantry and thereby undermined the legitimacy of agrarian elites.

The effects of colonialism on relations of personal dependency must be gauged against pre-colonial forms of the patron-client bond. Any thorough account of pre-colonial dependency would, at a minimum, have to distinguish between inland, seacoast, and highland kingdoms, between areas close to the center of a kingdom and areas at the periphery, and between periods of growing central authority and periods of declining central authority. For our purposes, however, the crucial fact about traditional patron-client relationships in the region is that the bargaining resources of clients generally prevented the balance of exchange from moving radically in favor of the patron.

At least three factors buttressed the client's position. First, the kin group often functioned as a main unit of vengeance thus offering the peasant some primary backing and, more important, village residence gave him some claim on the subsistence resources available to the community if he fell on hard times. The minimal guarantees of kinship and village seldom eliminated the need for patron-client bonds altogether. They did, however, help set sharp limits to the bargaining strength of would-be patrons. As alternative, primary social networks they operated, especially in relatively autonomous communities of subsistence agriculturists, to provide some of the same services of protection and security that a patron might offer and thereby restrict not only the degree of imbalance in individual patron-client exchanges but also the social significance of clientage in the community as a whole.

Second, the fact that the client could often flee to unoccupied arable land meant that control of manpower was more important than control of land and that the building of a following required more services than simply the provision of land. Although moving from an existing community to new land was hardly without costs to the client—especially in wet-rice areas—the existence of unoccupied land was the bedrock of what freedom the peasant enjoyed in pre-colonial Southeast Asia.

The final feature of pre-colonial Southeast Asia which reinforced the client's bargaining position was the *localization of power* which denied patrons access to outside support. What this meant was simply that a local leader in a peasant village could seldom rely on outside force or law to protect him; instead his wealth and position were ultimately validated by the legitimacy he acquired in the local community. Unless a local leader could persuade much of the community that his dominance was no threat or could win enough personal allies to sustain his position, he was in danger.[40] The frailty of the state forced local leaders to create a loyal local following large enough to sustain their position and made it prudent for them to honor local norms.

The impact of colonial change on patron-client relationships can be described under three somewhat artifical headings: (1) the process of social differentiation, (2) the growth of a permanent state apparatus, and, most important (3) the commercialization of agriculture and the concentration of landownership.

Social Differentiation

The process of social differentiation has perhaps not changed the degree of personal dependence so much as the *distribution* or *concentration* of that dependence; it tends to replace one or a few strands of comprehensive exchange and dependency with multiple dependencies—each of less intensity and comprehensiveness.[41] This transformation is aptly summarized by Schumpeter's contrast of traditional nobility and new commercial elites. "The Feudal master class was once—and the bourgeoisie was never—the supreme pinnacle of a uniformly constructed social pyramid. The feudal nobility was once lord and master in every sphere of life—which constitutes a difference in prestige that can never be made up".[42] What had been a more diffuse, whole-person relationship became increasingly a series of separate and more narrow ties. The peasant dealt with one person to rent land, another to adjust his head tax, another for slack season employment, and perhaps still another for loans in time of need. In general, each new patron's effectiveness tended to be specialized to that area of the diversifying social structure in which he had a foothold. Where they did not actually become contractual, the growing narrowness of scope and fragility of such patron-client ties lent them an increasingly contingent and secular tone.

The Growth of the Colonial State—As the colonial state expanded and increasingly breached the administrative isolation of the village, it also created in its wake a host of new patronage roles. Government touched more and more routine local activities, thus increasing the need for peasants to cultivate the favor of officials, or, failing that, friends of officials. The structure of patronage aligned itself with the new structural realities in the village as peasants tried to protect their interests in matters of taxation, land titles, licenses, court litigation, and so forth.

The major effect of colonial rule on local officials, in this context, was to completely transform their relationship to the local community. Since most local officials prior to colonialism had little reliable outside backing, they maintained their local standing by cultivating a substantial local following by observing essential community norms and by minimizing outside claims on community resources. But colonialism decisively broke their dependence on the village. Instead of being largely a creature of the locality who dealt with the center, they became increasingly creatures of the center who dealt with the local community.[43] In terms of the balance of exchange between local officials and peasants, therefore, the relative power of the patron was vastly inflated, his need for clients was reduced, and the incentive to serve the community by protecting it against the larger state was broken.[44]

The Commercialization of Agriculture—With the penetration of the cash economy into the countryside, the bargaining power of elites vis-à-vis peasant clients was greatly enhanced. The legal order of the liberal economy as applied to Southeast Asia fostered the growth of a new elite stratum of landowners, whose power rested in their ownership of the very means of subsistence, and a growing subordinate class of tenants and laborers, whose day-to-day livelihood was dependent on the land or work it could get from members of this elite. The dependence entailed in securing access to land was further exacerbated by the fact that the would-be tenant competed with a growing agrarian population for this privilege.[45] Exposed now to the effects of volatile market prices for crops and necessities, the possibilities for security outside such networks of dependence were small. Finally, of course, the colonial state guaranteed the concentration of landed property which provided the essential foundation for more onerous forms of dependence.[46]

The peasantry in pre-colonial Southeast Asia was often spared the most exploitive forms of personal dependence by the availability of cultivable land, pasturage, fuel, and other subsistence resources that were either free or communally supplied. A combination of growing population pressure, increasing private ownership of what had been essentially public resources, and colonial restrictions on land and forest use worked to narrow this margin of freedom or to eliminate it altogether. This reduction in the peasant's independence and mobility further reduced his capacity to escape more exploitive dependence relations.

The traditional moral economy of the village generated redistributive pressures which worked against the development of large differences in wealth and tended to ensure all villagers a minimum livelihood, insofar as local resources permitted.[47] Social changes under colonialism did not completely destroy such local redistributive norms. Their effectiveness—their protective capacity for the resident peasantry—was, however, seriously undermined by: (a) the ability of externally-backed elites to ignore local opinion, (b) the fact that local property and wealth were increasingly controlled by outsiders who were less subject to village levelling pressurers, and (c) demographic pressures which simply overwhelmed local absorbitative capacity.

Colonial economic policy prompted a crystallization of dependency relations. The peasant's objective of an assured subsistence could increasingly be achieved, if at all, through a position of dependence as the tenant, debtor, or tied laborer of a member of the landowning, money-lending class. The commercialization of agriculture also transformed the class composition of the countryside. Smallholders tended to be squeezed out and to fall into the tenant class; secure tenancy tended to give way to insecure tenancy; insecure tenants tended to fall into the laboring class which was itself increasingly made up of shifting day laborers who were unprotected by any social arrangements and exposed to the full effects of fluctuating commodity prices and labor demand. There were three facts to this process. First, the effects of colonial administration and economics had created the elements of a patron class whose services were more desperately needed by the peasantry; rural stratification was increasingly polarized between the independent and the dependent.[48] Second, as the bargaining position of the peasant worsened, the conditions of his dependence grew more and more onerous as landholders provided fewer services less reliably and/or exacted a growing social and economic price for their assistance. Finally for many who fell to the bottom, particularly agrarian wage laborers, relations of dependence broke down altogether and the subsistence guarantee disappeared. The process of "restratification" did not occur gradually or smoothly; cycles of boom and bust intensified both instability of the rural class structure in general and the size and composition of the agrarian proletariat in particular.

Rentier tenancy, the most extreme form of imbalance—which developed particularly in portions of Lower Burma, Cochin China, and Central Luzon—meant the elimination of virtually all landowner services save the provision of land—and that at a high and often invariable rent. Gone is the crucial subsistence insurance for the subordinate peasantry; gone is the personal assistance and brokerage of the landowner; gone is any palpable contribution to cultivation itself. Left is a peasant who shoulders almost all the tasks and risks of farming and a landowner who does nothing at all except to collect rents. The owner's monopoly of land can still call forth dependence but not legitimacy, since he contributes nothing to justify his claim to half or more of the crop in the eyes of the peasant. If the owners were to disappear tomorrow, the major, if not the sole, effect their absence would have would be to relieve the peasantry of the necessity of paying rents. It is no wonder, when every other strand of a once diffuse relationship has disintegrated except for the collection of rent, that the class of absentee owners should appear exploitive.

Rural class relations that had once rested, in part, on consent became, under the forces of commercialization and colonial government, increasingly characterized by coercion and exploitation. If the peasant believed himself exploited by landlords, there is no need to resort to theories of "rising expectations" or "outside agitators" to explain this perception. The growth of agrarian unrest followed a real deterioration in the peasant's terms of exchange and the areas most affected were those in which the commercial and political impact of colonial rule had most undermined the peasant's bargaining position. Relations of dependence were no longer meeting basic subsistence needs. This situation provided both the basis for a sense of exploitation and the moral basis for action. The default of the elite-centered, vertical community of dependence was the necessary, though hardly sufficient, condition for new forms of peasant class consciousness, class organization, and class action. Cast adrift in the liberal agrarian economy of colonialism, the peasantry was faced with the alternatives of acting to restore the traditional balance of exchange or of seeking (or creating) new social mechanisms of protection.

NOTES

1 We are grateful to the National Institute of Mental Health and the Psychology and Politics Program at Yale University for supporting this research. The argument has benefited greatly from the criticisms of Ed Friedman, Fred Hayward, Frank Weinstein, Lewis Austin, Marvin Rogers, Ricard Merelman, Murray Edelman, Francine Frankel, and Howard Leichter.

2 A companion paper by James C. Scott entitled *The Erosion of Patron-Client Bonds and Social Change in Rural Southeast Asia*, is theoretically less elaborate but deals more fully with Southeast Asia (*Journal of Asian Studies*, Nov., 1972).

3 There is an extensive literature, mostly anthropological, dealing with patron-client bonds which we have relied on in constructing this definition. Some of the most useful include: George M. Foster, *The Dyadic Contract in Tzintzuntzan: Patron-Client Relationship*, American Anthropologist, 65, 1963, p. 1280-1294; Eric Wolf, *Kinship, Friendship, and Patron-Client Relations*, in M. Banton, ed., *The Social Anthropology of Complex Societies*, New York, Praeger, 1966; J. Campbell, *Honour, Family, and Patronage*, Oxford, Clarendon Press, 1964; John Duncan Powell, *Peasant Society and Clientelist Politics*, American Political Science Review, LXIV, 2, June, 1970; Carl Landé, *Leaders, Factions and Parties. The Structure of Philippine Politics*, (Monograph No. 6), New Haven, Yale University-Southeast Asian Studies, 1964; and Alex Weingrod, *Patrons, Patronage, and Political Parties*, Comparative Studies in Society and History, 19, July, 1968, p. 1142-1158. See also James C. Scott's *Patron-Client Politics and Political Change in Southeast Asia*, American Political Science Review, LXVI, March, 1972, 91-113.

4 If clients occasionally switch patrons, they still remain the retainers of higher status figures.

5 Carl Landé, the first to explicitly apply the patron-client model to Southeast Asian politics, found it an indispensable tool in explaining the alliances between "big people" and "little people" and the absence of class-based voting which characterize Philippine politics. Cfr Landé, *op. cit.* A careful study of village politics in Upper Burma by Manning Nash concludes that a villager's basic political decision was one of affiliating with a well-to-do patron who could protect him and advance his interests. Cfr *The Golden Road to Modernity. Village Life in Contemporary Burma*, New York, Wiley, 1965. Local politics in Malaysia and Thailand has been explained in comparable terms. Cfr M.G. Swift, *Malay Peasant Society in Jelebu*, London, Athlone Press, 1965 and Herbert Phillips, *Thai Peasant Personality*, Berkeley, University of California Press, 1965. Even in rural Java where party labels might suggest a class based ideological polarization, one major interpretation has emphasized the factional nature of *santri-abangan* cleavages, in which parties are commonly led by rich peasants who bring along their kin, neighbors, and clients. Cfr Robert R. Jay, *Religion and Politics in Rural Central Java*, (Cultural Report Series), New Haven, Yale University-Southeast Asian Studies, 1963, p. 98-99. On this point also see Donald Hindley, *The Communist Party of Indonesia 1951-1963*, Berkeley, University of California, 1966, Ch. 14; Rex Mortimer, *Class, Social Cleavage, and Indonesian Communism*, Indonesia, 8, Oct., 1969, p. 1-20; and W.F. Wertheim, *From Aliran to Class Struggle in the Countryside of Java*, Pacific Viewpoints, 10, 2, Sept. 1969, p. 1-17.

6 J.S. Furnivall has provided probably the best analysis to date linking criminality to agrarian change

in Upper and Lower Burma. See his *Colonial Policy and Practice*, New York, New York University Press, 1956, 2nd ed., p. 131-141.

7 We are indebted to Barrington Moore, Jr.'s persuasive argument that exploitation is, for the most part, an objective relationship in which feelings of exploitation bear a relationship to the services an elite offers the peasantry in return for the surplus it extracts. *Social Origins of Dictatorship and Democracy*, Boston, Beacon Press, 1966, p. 453-483. His argument was advanced considerably by its successful application to Central Italy by Sydel F. Silverman in which the categories of exchange are carefully analyzed. *"Exploitation" in Rural Central Italy. Structure and Ideology in Stratification Study*, Comparative Studies in Society and History, 12, 1970, p. 327-339. It is from Moore and Silverman, from Peter Blau's theoretical work on exchange theory, *Exchange and Power in Social Life*, New York, Wiley, 1964, and from observation in Central Luzon that our conceptualization of agrarian relations is drawn. See also Arthur Stinchcombe's fine essay on rural class relations in *Agricultural Enterprise and Rural Class Relations*, American Journal of Sociology, 67, 1961-62, particularly the portion on family-sized tenancy.

8 The term is that of E.P. Thompson who applies it in a similar fashion to the early English working class and their attitude toward the price of bread. See his classic *The Making of the English Working Class*, New York, Vintage, 1966, p. 203.

9 Blau, *op. cit.* Blau's discussion of unbalanced exchange, p. 21-25 *et seq.*, and the disparities in power and deference that such imbalance fosters is directly relevant to the basis of patron-client dyads.

10 George M. Foster, *The Dyadic Contract in Tzintzuntzan, II, Patron-Client Relationship*, American Anthropologist, 65, 1963, p. 1173-1192.

11 Marc Bloch, *Feudal Society*, London, Routledge, Kegan Paul, Ltd., 1961, p. 129, translated by L. A. Manyon.

12 We are grateful to Clifford Geertz for convincingly arguing the importance of these distinctions.

13 Bloch, *Feudal Society*, p. 148, cites comparable circumstances for the Merovingian period in explaining the growth of the distinctive ties of personal dependence characteristic of French feudalism.

14 Empirically, of course, disapproving submission may be difficult to distinguish from approving submission if there are no means for the expression of discontent.

15 This is not to deny that norms of equity in the balance of exchange do not vary from culture to culture. They most certainly do. For this reason it would be dangerous, in the absence of gross differences, to draw conclusions about the relative legitimacy of agrarian elites in two different cultural and historical settings on the basis of the comparative balance of exchange between elites and peasants in each setting. Within a *particular* cultural and historical context, however, *shifts* in the balance of exchange are likely to be reflected in shifts in the legitimacy with which subordination is viewed.

16 This remains the case so long as the clientele is linked individually to the patron. While his following as a *whole* may be important to the patron, any particular client is generally expendable. If the clientele dealt with the patron as a unit, of course, the situation would change.

17 These models, in fact, correspond roughly to two processes of agrarian change. The former is characteristic of a commercializing landowner class which reduces or terminates most services performed by the traditional aristocracy while continuing to squeeze the peasants. The latter resembles the efforts of a declining rural aristocracy to survive by exacting each and every feudal privilege while being unable to maintain, let alone raise, their services for their retainers.

18 Empirically this might occur in traditional settings when landowners provide rations to their peasant clients following a serious crop failure. Here a slight decline in material welfare might accompany improved class relations.

19 "Outsiders" may often encourage local action merely by winning a victory that destroys the miasma of elite power that had previously served to check peasant power.

20 Cfr Michael Adas, *Agrarian Development in Lower Burma and the Plural Society*, University of Wisconsin, Ph.D. Thesis, 1971.

21 E.J. Hobsbawm & George Rude, *Captain Swing*, New York, Pantheon, 1968. In many respects this account is instructive for an understanding of the peasant relations to breaches of exchange brought about by the "green revolution" in the past decade. Cfr Francine Frankel, *India's Green Revolution*, Princeton, Princeton University Press, 1971.

22 Roland Mousnier, *Peasant Uprisings in Seventeenth-Century France, Russia, and China*, New York, Harper & Row, 1970, p. 305-348, translated by Brian Pearce.

23 Karl Polanyi, *The Great Transformation*, New York, Farrar & Rinehart, 1944.

24 Harold J. Laski, *The Rise of European Liberalism*, London, Allen & Unwin, 1936, 1947, p. 113, 2nd ed.

24a There may be a further progression in consciousness here. The failure of a single patron undermines his claim to position but not that of the patron class. The failure of the patron class undermines its claim to position but, not necessarily, the peasantry's faith in other potential patron classes (e.g. party bosses) who might perform according to expectations. Perhaps it is only the repeated failure of patronage as a system that saps the legitimacy of vertical patronage *per se* rather than the legitimacy of a particular patron class.

25 The amount of anger and moral indignation generated by such a failure probably depends upon how critical the services were and what alternatives the client has.

26 J.A. Pitt-Rivers, *The People of the Sierra*, Chicago, Phoenix Books, University of Chicago Press, 1961, p. 204.

27 The vertical patron-client tie is but one of several social mechanisms that can provide important guarantees for peasants. One way of determining how

significant patron-client structures are in a given context is to ask what proportion of the rural populace is tied to patrons. In practice, however, a peasant may rely simultaneously on his neighbors, his kin, village custom, a patron, and perhaps even the law for assistance and protection, and it is thus a matter of gauging the *relative* importance of patron-client ties. The social weight of rural patron-client bonds is, then, a function both of the proportion of the population that is covered by them and their relative importance in satisfying social needs for those who are covered.

28 The resort to coercion by the patron(s) is limited both by the effectiveness of the coercive force at his disposal (often quite limited in fragmented political systems) and the counterbalancing effect of a tradition and capacity for rebellion by the peasantry. Hobsbawm shows convincingly how even unsuccessful peasant uprisings can bring about, for a time, an improvement in the balance of exchange. The agricultural uprisings of the 1830s in Southern England did not sweep away the landowning gentry but they did retard the introduction of thrashing machines for more than a decade. *Captain Swing*, Ch. 15.

29 These are the tests Moore uses for the legitimacy of agrarian elites, though he does not distinguish between external and internal resources, *op. cit.*, p. 471. Knowing how to treat services such as leadership (as distinct from subsidies) in organizing local charity and public works is more of a problem. In the absence of peasant experience in these activities, they are likely to be considered a tangible service. But once peasants have developed an organizational capacity for such tasks, their value is undercut.

30 For a more complete account of peasant reaction to these changes see Ben Kerkvliet, *Peasant Society and Unrest Prior to the Huk Revolution in the Philippines*, Asian Studies (Manila), 9, Aug., 1971, p. 164-213.

31 At one point Tinio was governor of the province. For another account of collective landlord services in Central Luzon, see John A. Larkin, *The Evolution of Pampanga Society*, New York University, Ph.D. Dissertation, 1966, p. 126-128.

32 J.N. Anderson, *Some Aspects of Land and Society in a Pangasinan Community*, Philippine Sociological Review, 10, 1 and 2, Jan.-Apr. 1962, p. 56.

33 Akira Takahashi, *Land and Peasants in Central Luzon*, Honolulu, East-West Center Press, 1969, p. 117-118. As Takahasi points out, the terms of tenancy, even in the Bulacan Village he studies, are not as severe as in many other rural areas of Asia. As late as 1950, for example, almost one-third of the tenant class was related to the owner of the land they rented. (Robert T. McMillan, *Land Tenure in the Philippines*, Rural Sociology, 20, 1, 1955, p. 27.) Although that may have made little difference in the formal conditions of tenancy, it probably improved the security of tenure and the possibility of loans for those concerned. Perhaps the tradition of rebellion and popular elections—which, in a sense, restore local redistributive pressures by requiring officeholders to have a sizeable local following—have also prevented even more extreme conditions from developing.

34 For example, H. Ten Dam, *Cooperation and Social Structure in the Village of Chibodas*, In Vol. 6, *Indonesian Economics. The Concept of Dualism in Theory and Policy, of Selected Studies of Indonesia by Dutch Scholars*, The Hague, V. van Hoeve, 1969, p. 367, and Larkin, *op. cit.*, p. 173.

35 Stinchcombe, *op. cit.*, p. 186.

36 Robert L. Sansom, *The Economics of Insurgency in the Mekong Delta of Vietnam*, Cambridge, Mass., M.I.T. Press, 1970, ch. 2, p. 18-56.

37 *Ibid.*, p. 29. Ngo Vinh Long, *The Colonial Peasants of Viet-Nam, 1900-1945*, p. 10, suggests that this quote overstates the paternalism of landlords in the early 20th century. (forthcoming)

38 Sansom, *op. cit.*, p. 35-37. This figure assumes an equal distribution of rice and thus understates the gravity of the situation. It should be added that the internal shortage of rice resulted less in actual starvation than in a shift to less desirable food sources such as cassava and sweet potatoes.

39 Michael Adas, *Agrarian Development in Lower Burma, op. cit.*, p. 411.

40 This is true both in settled communities where the requirements of legitimate leadership were culturally fixed and in *djago* (bandit) areas where a leader must share out enough of the loot to retain the loyalty of his gang. Leaders who fail to establish their legitimacy and generosity and have no outside backing are likely to find their clientele switching to other leaders or simply striking out on their own.

41 Godfrey and Monica Wilson, *The Analysis of Social Change: Based on Observations in Central Africa*, Cambridge, Cambridge University Press, 1945, p. 28, 40.

42 Joseph Schumpeter, *Social Classes in an Ethnically Homogeneous Society*, New York, Meridan, 1955, p. 101-168. In areas like Central Luzon, Lower Burma and Cochin China, the structural pressures tending to narrow the scope of personal dependence were reinforced by the cultural distance (in terms of language, ethnicity, social background) between much of the landlord class and the peasantry. The situation was different in areas like Tonkin or Java.

43 See, for example, Harry J. Benda, *The Structure of Southeast Asian History: Some Preliminary Observations*, Journal of Southeast Asian History, 3, 1, March, 1962, p. 126, and Sartono Kartodirdjo, *The Peasants' Revolt of Banten in 1888*, 's-Gravenhague, Martinus Nijhoff, 1966, Ch. 3.

44 The degree of this shift in the balance of exchange and the speed with which it occurred varied widely. On balance, its impact was most pronounced where colonial authority was strongest and where local authorities were outsiders appointed and paid from above. Its impact was slower and less pronounced where colonial power was less firmly established and where local officials were from the community and chosen locally.

45 Eric Wolf, in the final chapter of his *Peasant Wars of the Twentieth Century*, New York, Harper & Row, 1968, p. 277-286, has a fine discussion of how the commercialization of agriculture created new demographic pressures and allowed landlords to rely on

the state to enforce their terms on the peasantry. We have both, it appears, found Karl Polanyi's analysis of the effects of the market economy on traditional society to be seminal.

46 It clearly makes a difference whether the pattern of landownership becomes one of a few locally dominant landholders as in the Mekong Delta, parts of Central Luzon, and Lower Burma or one of predominantly small holdings as in the Tonkin Delta and in East and Central Java. A pattern of largeholdings tended to more quickly develop into commercial or rentier forms of land exploitation which eliminated most of the links of personal service between patron and client. Smallholdings tended to create more modest and fragmented forms of patronage in which the personal links between the landowner and tenant or laborer were likely to last longer.

47 Such norms were, of course, least in evidence in the comparatively new, atomized directly-ruled settlements of Cochin China and Lower Burma, and most apparent in older, more cohesive settlements such as Tonkin and Java.

48 "It will thus be seen that agriculture in Indo-China has gradually evolved into a position in which there are two very distinct elements: on the one hand the large and medium-sized landowners . . . who exercise their influence through the authority of the mandarins, the local councils and chambers of agriculture, etc., their associations, the press and the credit system; on the other hand, the working masses: smallholders, tenant-farmers, share farmers, wage earners, all more or less subject to the other group". Jean Goudal, *Labour Conditions in Indo-China*, Geneva, International Labour Organization, 1938, p. 193, quoted in Sansom, *op. cit.*, p. 28.

FROM ALIRAN TOWARDS CLASS STRUGGLE IN THE COUNTRYSIDE OF JAVA[1]

W. F. WERTHEIM

BEFORE THE SECOND World War, the structure of native Javanese society had been mostly referred to in terms of social stratification. In Van Vollenhoven's work on *Adat Law*, the distinction between the *prijaji*-aristocracy and the commoners appeared as a basic element in the overall structure of Javanese society.[2] Similarly, the main distinction within Javanese village society was based, in pre-war literature, on social status: the nuclear villagers, as fully qualified members of the village community on the basis of their descent from the mythical founder of the village entitled to a share in the irrigated farm land (*sawah*) of the village, were to be distinguished from those villagers who belonged to the newcomers' families and, consequently, could possess only dry land (mostly a compound with the house they had built upon it) and worked as sharecroppers on the land of the former.[3]

When Javanese society was studied, for the first time, shortly after the war, by a team of American sociologists and cultural anthropologists, they found it useful to introduce a new structural principle for understanding Javanese society as it functioned at the time of their field research. Clifford Geertz coined the term *aliran* to characterise the newly discovered structural principle. The way *aliran*—which literally means "stream", but should rather be translated as "ideological orientation"—functions in Javanese society, has been analysed by Geertz most extensively in his *Social History of an Indonesian Town*.[4] Robert Jay, also a member of the M.I.T. team that studied *Modjokuto*, an anonymous middle-sized town in the western part of the province of East Java, has stressed the same structural principle—although without using the term *aliran*—in his study of Javanese rural society.[5]

The core of Geertz's thesis is, that Javanese society is vertically divided according to ideological orientations, and that these orientations are structurally expressed in organizational affiliations. In "Modjokuto" he found society divided according to the ideological orientations professed by the four main parties dominating the political life of Indonesia. The main watershed is the one between the *santri*—the pious Moslems—and the non-*santri*, who are nominally Moslem but are in fact adhering rather to a syncretistic type of religion in which many remnants of Hinduism, Buddhism and of Havanese folk religion are to be encountered.

Geertz associates the ideology of the Javanese *prijaji* aristocracy with the Indonesian Nationalist Party, the *PNI*, whereas the ideology of the village commoners, the *abangan* (the red ones) finds expression in the Indonesian Communist Party, the *PKI*. The *santri* (literally: students of religion; in the past the term *putihan*, the white ones, was also sometimes used), again can be divided into orthodox and modernists, the former being associated with the *Nahdatul Ulama*, the association of Islamic Scholars, whereas the latter were politically organized within *Masjumi*, the Council of Indonesian Moslem Associations.

Geertz's main point is, however, that the division according to ideology is not restricted to political orientations but pervades the entire Javanese society. Since independence a host of functional organisations have been set up, such as women's associations, youth organizations, boy scouts, sports clubs, charitable societies, labour and peasant unions, art groups—and all of them are in some way affiliated with a definite ideological cluster.

Moreover, as both Geertz and Jay have argued, political factionalism is not restricted to urban society. Since the preparations for nationwide elections in the early fifties called for proselytizing in the countryside, national parties started to extend their appeal to the villagers. In such a way, the traditional distinction between two types of Moslems, the *santri* and the *abangan*, developed into a true cleavage pervading the whole Javanese society from top to bottom.

Two sociologists from the University of Amsterdam, Dr. Basuki Gunawan and O. D. van den Muijzenberg[6], have attempted to reduce the *aliran* phenomenon to a broader sociological model. They suggest that the phenomenon basically coincides with the well-known one called in Dutch society "verzuiling" (pillarisation). As those familiar with Dutch society know, it has been characterised throughout the twentieth century by a division of all types of social activities according to the different ideological "pillars" of Dutch society: Protestantism, Catholicism and a-religious Humanism. Dutch sociologists have generally associated the "pillarisation" phenomenon, which also pervades the whole range of organizational activities, with the struggle for "emancipation" of the Catholic minority that had been at a serious disadvantage, both educationally and politically, at the start of the nineteenth century, owing to the suppression of the Catholic religion during the period of the Dutch United Republic.[7]

Similarly, the two authors relate "pillarisation" in Java with the urge for "emancipation" among the *santri*-oriented traders' middle class, who suffered from discrimination and from the middle of the nineteenth century onwards developed a value system well-distinguished from both the traditional Javanese *prijaji* values of the aristocracy and those of the westernising intelligentsia. As an expression of the new cultural values the rising Moslem middle class created their own organizational apparatus. In their turn, other ideological groups, such as the Marxists, called a counter-movement into life which, again, expressed itself organizationally not only in a strong political party but in a host of unions covering different sectors of social life.

The structural principle as elaborated by Geertz and, with a different terminology, by Gunawan and Van den Muijzenberg, is opposed to the principle of social stratification as a conceptual frame. The vertical alignments cross-cut the social hierarchy and, by their existence alone, form an impediment to the birth of a solidarity on a class basis. In a society where vertical alignments predominate, organisational ties are slow in arising between peers of different ideological orientation and, on the other hand, a common ideology does not necessarily imply a similar class background.

The relevance of this point is clearly indicated in some of the data reported by Robert Jay from a village he studied not far from Modjokuto. Though one would expect, that the *santri* aligned with Nahdatul Ulama or Masjumi should largely constitute the richer peasantry, whereas the PKI would draw its following mainly from the poor peasantry and the landless proletariat, earning their living either as sharecroppers or as land labourers, social reality was less simple than that. The leaders of both factions belonged to the rich peasantry; both of them found a broad following among the poorer peasantry. In both cases poor peasants, of course, formed the large majority. In either case, therefore, landowners and labour force were quite often combined within one single faction. The division between the two factions in several cases conformed to the residential pattern, some boroughs being fully *santri*, while others were completely PKI-oriented, and still others were mixed.[8]

If the phenomenon reported by Jay should be considered representative of the general situation in the countryside of Central and the western part of East Java—the areas to which Geertz's analysis in terms of *aliran* society refers—this would have a great significance for our understanding of the developments in the Javanese countryside since the revolution. However, Jay's information, though not essentially wrong, should be qualified—which does not detract from its basic importance but on the contrary may add a temporal dimension, in addition to the structural one implied in the analysis by

Jay and others, to our understanding of what really happened, both before and after the Untung coup of 30 September, 1965.

Jay's observation is significant inasfar as the case of the village studied by him is not an isolated phenomenon.[9] When I crossed the Javanese countryside with groups of students from the Agricultural Faculty in Bogor, in 1956 and 1957, I was more than once struck by the fact that one could find PKI-insignia in the home of a wealthy peasant. Yet, this remained an exception rather than a common occurrence. The great majority of rich peasants, as well as village chiefs (*lurah*) or aldermen (*kamitua*) had a different political orientation.

Moreover, the national election results of 1955 and the regional ones of 1957 made clear, that political affiliations were to some extent related to the general level of prosperity of an area. I remember a curious sally that a colleague, a forestry expert (from the Agricultural Faculty in Bogor (West Java)) made during the electioneering period: "Formerly, when we wanted to assess the fertility of different soils in Java, we looked at the soil itself and took samples. Now we have discovered a much easier method: we have to look only a few feet above the soil. Wherever we find a majority of PKI-signs, we know the soil is poorest, where PNI prevails, soild are somewhat better; where NU predominates, soils are good; in Masjumi areas they are first rate, and in a few extremely fertile areas near large towns, where the population is specialising on vegetable growing, PSI-signs are abundant." It was no surprise to him, that the PSI, the Indonesian Socialist Party, made a very poor showing at the 1955 elections.

There are indications that by 1964 the situation had not basically changed. Lance Castles, in his study of the Islamic School at Gontor, in the Ponorogo area in East Java not far from "modjokuto", tells us something about the class composition of the students who were getting a modernised *santri* education: the entrance fee was Rp. 5,000 a month, which means that the pupils, the *santris*, must have come from richer village families. An informant told Castles "that lots of his ex-pupils were farmers and many too had more than the statutory maximum of land". A large number of pupils came from Djember (East Java) or Klaten (Central Java), both of which "are districts with many rich peasants, growing in both cases the rather 'capitalist' crop of tobacco". There were no pupils from distinctly poor rural regencies in Central Java, as specified by Castles.[10]

Gunawan, in his recent study of the sociological sources of the Untung-coup, also relates the different "pillars" of Javanese society with various socio-economic groupings: "the reformist-islamic pillar mainly rests upon the urban traders and the cultivators of commercial crops, the nationalist pillar upon the officials and those mainly relying upon the bureaucratic elite as the leading element within society. The Orthodox-Islamic pillar still found its main following among the rice-growing *santri*, whereas the communist one found its support among the labourers in industrial enterprises and plantations, as well as among poor *abangan* peasants."[11] Further on, Gunawan states that the rural *santri* mostly are landowners who do not work their own land but employ sharecroppers; in addition they act as money-lenders for the poorer peasants.[12] Evidently, neither he nor van den Muijzenberg consider a situation as encountered by Jay in the village he had studied typical of the Javanese countryside.

It is clear that the statistical correlations between social and economic class and ideological orientation in pre-coup Java should be studied more thoroughly—as far as the basic materials are available—before we could try correctly to evaluate the quantitative significance of the phenomenon related by Jay. Even in the absence of more concrete data, however, it is possible to elaborate its sociological implications at greater depth.

As we have seen, Gunawan and van den Muijzenberg have already tried to fit the *aliran* principle within a broader sociological frame: the "pillarisation" phenomenon. However, it seems to me that it is dangerous to draw sociological parallels between a pre-industrial and a highly industrialised society. Therefore, I have attempted to fit the *aliran* phenomenon with its concomitant tendency towards vertical organization, into a different conceptual frame typical of many pre-industrial societies. This conceptual frame is the patronage phenomenon.

Patronage relationships are to be found in many societies where a clear-cut system of social stratification has developed and an aristocratic order prevails. Some cultural anthropologists give the impression that the patronage-clientele relationship should be viewed as a phenomenon restricted to certain cultural areas, for example the Roman Catholic or Greek-Orthodox ones where spiritual kinship called into life by godfather arrangements plays an essential role. It is much more probable, however, that patronage is a phenomenon structurally related with an aristocratic order and liable to be observed in some form or other in any aristocratic society, as a personal network linking definite aristocratic families with a segment of the common people. It is this clientele relationship which provides, for many members of the poorer peasantry, a measure of security in a society where personal rule prevails and a public administration according to objectively accepted norms is all but unknown.

At any rate, there are many indications that patronage was not absent from traditional Javanese society, though the phenomenon has to my knowledge never been specifically studied. This is remarkable, since for other areas of Indonesia, such as South Sulawesi and Bali, it has been described in some detail.[13]

The significance of the patronage-clientele relationship in the context of Javanese social structure dawned upon me when I was confronted, in December 1956, with the migrants' society of Sukohardjo, South Sumatra. The village had been established, in 1939, by colonists from Java as a result of the so-called "colonization of intellectuals," a project promoted by the nationalist organization Parindra as a means of combating unemployment during the world crisis. "Intellectuals" was a term to be taken in a very broad sense indeed: some of the colonists had not got much farther in the colonial educational system than the final diploma of the six years' Dutch native primary school (H.I.S.), where instruction was provided in Dutch instead of in the vernacular. In the pre-war colonial situation, however, this achievement was enough, in the eyes of native society, to mark a person off from the common people as an "intellectual."

The significant point about this "colonisation scheme" for intellectuals was, that each colonist was entitled to take five *magersari* along to the Lampung resettlement area. These *magersari* would form a kind of following for the "intellectual", and they were expected to help the patron with the heavy work of land reclamation. The final arrangement in the newly opened Sukohardjo area would be that the "intellectual" was entitled to five hectares, where as the *magersari* could only claim one hectare each.[14]

Mohammad Hatta has seriously criticised the basic inequality transferred, in this manner, from traditional Javanese rural society into the new territories which, in his view, should have reflected the egalitarian ideals of a new democratic Indonesia.[15] But what matters in the context of our argument, is that the arrangement clearly reflects an engrained pattern of social

relationships between *prijaji* and non-*prijaji* typical of traditional Java. In trying to find more particulars on the *magersari* institution, however, I could only find the term as a Javanese equivalent for *penumpang* or *numpang*, a land labourer or sharecropper living on the compound of his master.[16]

There are, however, other indications for the significance of the patron-client relationship in Java. Most striking is the role played by the *panakawan*, the clownesque servants of the divine hero in the traditional *wayang* play. The hero cannot move without his followers, who more or less represent the common people and who, despite their caprioles, provide him with the strength or astuteness to succeed.

The specific relationship between master and land labourer has been described in some detail by the Dutch rural sociologist H. ten Dam, though not for Central Java but for a mountainous area of West Java.[17] Ten Dam provides us with a profound analysis of the various ways of life of the different layers of Sundanese village society. He shows that the Indonesian state has no meaning whatever for them: it does not provide for any welfare measures for those underdogs and is a *pemerintah jang melarang melulu* (a government that does nothing but forbid). The land labourers only mind their material living for today—tomorrow will take care of itself. Though they do not really trust their master-landowner, he is the only security they possess, which means that in all political issues they will follow his lead.[18] Apparently, the bond between land labourer and master, as described by ten Dam, is a patron-client relationship, probably not unlike the *magersari* relationship in other parts of Java. Developing a close solidarity with their peers is a luxury they, in normal circumstances, cannot afford in their actual social and economic situation. From the course of events witnessed by ten Dam and myself, one can deduce that even in abnormal times the way towards greater freedom is mostly blocked.

Ten Dam describes, in his report published in 1951, an attempt by some of the landless people to settle as independent peasants in the forest clearings high up the mountains where the Republican insurgents withdrew during the revolutionary struggle against the Dutch. Their reliance upon their own strength, however, involved a heavy risk: as soon as the Republic had established its authority their claim upon the newly cleared lands was challenged by the Forestry Service that gradually had to start reafforestation of the mountain slopes. This implied that, after some years, the peasants would have to return to their former position as labourers on the village land of the larger landowners. Quite a number of them refused to return to the traditional bondage and applied for "transmigration" to South Sumatra. Unfortunately, when I visited ten Dam's village in 1957, the resettlement scheme seemed to have failed. Something had gone wrong, no transport was available, and the applicants who had sold their belongings, had to withdraw from the list. It was difficult for me to establish whose fault this was. I was not sure whether it was not due to a kind of connivance between the authorities in charge and the large landowners who hated the idea of losing their cheap labour force. Again the threat was there of a renewed bondage.

Patron-client relationships are generally characterised not only by social inequality and consequently by a cluster of asymmetrical obligations, but by their informal nature. These relationships, however, undergo a certain change in the newly independent states.

The transformation of informal into more formalised patron-client relationships has been well established for the Philippines. In traditional society, the patron-client relationships certainly existed. Within rural society each of the local leading families was able to muster a following. A local leader with his clientele generally formed one of the factions into which village society was split.

When politics entered the local communities in the course of this century and the national political parties had to compete for the rural vote, the vertical split tended to permeate the whole Filipino society. The representatives of the political parties at the intermediary levels jockeyed for power in the countryside and attempted to attract the most powerful faction within each village. In the process the informal type of patron-client relationship was gradually replaced by formal organisations which vertically split the whole of Filipino society. But generally the factions were easily interchangeable. For the faction leaders it was not so much the professed ideology of a political party that mattered—the ideological difference between the two being hardly greater than in the United States—but political power.[19]

What happened in Indonesia was rather similar—but the striking difference was that in large parts of Java—(the typical area of Javanese culture) ideology mattered decidedly more. This was due to the fact, that the factions in rural Java had been strongly influenced, for over a century,

by the *santri-abangan* split which was related to the religious issue.

From Jay's study one could gain the impression that factions are a recent phenomenon in Javanese society, produced by the spread of party politics, as related to the different ideological *alirans*, over large parts of rural Java. The evidence for Jay's picture of the past, is, however, slender and even highly debatable.[20] The picture is exclusively based on the life story of an older Javanese from a village which Jay does not appear to have studied in a direct way. His spokesman gives the impression of having eulogised the harmony of rural life in the past—though he did not deny that there used to be some inter-village hostility—at the time when he was still a youngster, and contrasted it with present society disturbed by ideological rifts and cleavages.

Without an attempt to substantiate this picture from the past with analyses made by contemporaries I would not dare to rely upon such an isolated judgment by an individual who gives the impression of being, as so many elders, a *laudator temporis acti*. Unfortunately, before the Second World War the type of profound sociological research which could have brought to light the existence of factionalism within Javanese village society, had not yet been developed by Dutch or Indonesian students of *adat* law. The picture of a coherent, harmonious Javanese *desa* was readily accepted by both the Dutch civil service and *adat* experts, in accordance with the well-known adagium of the Minister of Colonies J. C. Baud, in the mid-nineteenth century, that the *desa* was the palladium of peace in Java.

Since a patronage system generally appears in the combination with factional divisions, it is highly probable that the picture of an idyllic rural Java in the past could not be upheld any more than Gandhi's picture of a rustic and idyllic village society, a kind of Paradise Lost, in India.[21]

However, it is also highly probable that, not unlike Indian village society, the cleavages in Java's rural society have been, if not created, then at least much hardened and systematised by the intrusion of external party politics. The difference between the informal patronage-client structure of traditional aristocratic society and the post-independence type of patron-client networks rests upon the formal organisational structure of the latter and upon the spreading of the initial factions on a nation-wide scale.

The new structural principle also affects the social stratification system. Henceforth, it is no longer birth or achievement that exclusively determine one's status. Collective organisations increasingly dominate social life, and one's position or that of one's family, to a large extent, depends upon the question whether one belongs to the *ins* or *outs*.[22] Certain *alirans* are ascendant in a given political situation and this definitely affects the chances both of members and non-members of the ascendant *aliran* for a good job or, in extreme cases, even for bare survival. For in a society, where the living standard for the large majority is hardly above subsistence level, patronage by a well-to-do and better educated person still provides the only available security for the destitute. But instead of being based on purely informal and personalised relationships, the network now tends to follow the new organisational pattern, and the local *aliran* leaders assume the function of patrons for their following.

I would suggest, that it is at this point that the structural pattern in a pre-industrial society, even in its Javanese *aliran* garb, diverges from the "pillarised" society in an industrial country like the Netherlands. In the latter country, social security and livelihood are largely provided for by the basic governmental or legal institutions which, as a rule, function in an objective and impersonal manner. Where the pillars have a seemingly autonomous function, as for example in the educational and medical field, they are still subject in their activities to norms set by the official authorities. It is true, that in addition, the pillars regulate social and recreational activities, and may provide for individual members of their group a strong support, both in the economic and political field. Patronage relationships are definitely not absent from this type of vertical organisation, wherever preference is being given to coreligionists both in appointments and in customer relationships. But these patronage arrangements are marginal rather than central both in relation to government administration and in providing for a livelihood, which distinguishes them sharply from the much more pervasive type of vertical organisation in pre-industrial "new states".

The most intriguing problem is, however, to assess, to what extent the ideological content of an *aliran* affects the vertical patronage-like relationship. This issue becomes crucial for political parties professing a patently leftist and egalitarian ideology.

This issue has given rise to a highly interesting discussion between two Dutch rural sociologists in relationship with the activities of the peasant unions, the *Ligas Camponesas*, in Brazil.[23] Benno Galjart stated that the Ligas, despite their leftist ideological orientation, functioned in the traditional patron-client pattern. Juliao, the father and chairman of the Ligas, was himself a typical patron, belonging to the educated class and with a distinct urban background. In order to attract a following, he did not wage a class struggle, says Galjart, but attempted to obtain from the authorities, in the specific traditional way, all kinds of privileges in particular for the members of his unions. Other organisations, some of them under Catholic leadership, competed with Juliao's unions for a following and should be considered, according to Galjart, as rival factions of a similar structure.

Gerrit Huizer, though agreeing with Galjart's analysis in many points, still accorded much more weight to the signs, in the Ligas Camponesas, of an incipient class consciousness and class struggle. By reducing all the activities and achievements to traditional patron-client relationships, Galjart discards several aspects which, in Huizer's view, can only be understood in terms of a rising class solidarity among the poor peasantry of the Brazilian Nordeste. Huizer reminds the reader of a 500 to 1,000 per cent wage increase obtained, as Galjart himself had stated, by peasant labour organisations, the syndicates organised by Catholic priests, through "a successful two day strike which tied up the entire sugar area of Pernambuco", accomplished by 200,000 agricultural workers. He also points to the invasions of large landholdings organised by peasants, though under non-peasant leadership, as described by Galjart himself. According to Huizer "the organisational discipline of these invasions which showed itself in the fact that hardly any violent action was involved, proves an increasing class-consciousness".[24]

Therefore, Huizer's argument with which I agree, amounts to an attempt at refining Galjart's thesis by asserting that the Brazilian peasant unions combined the two aspects: though conforming, in certain respects, to the familiar pattern of patron-client relationships, the unions manifested at the same time several traits which could not be understood except as signs of an incipient solidarity on a class basis.

In Galjart's view the ease with which the Branco administration suppressed the Ligas is a proof of their weakness as a class organisation, as soon as the leaders are no longer recognised by the authorities as patrons to be acknowledged and respected as such, nor enabled to bestow favours upon their following.

In my opinion, the April 1964 military coup, which to a large extent was a reaction against the activities of the Ligas and the land reforms enacted by the Goulart administration, should be viewed, in accordance with Huizer's analysis, as a symptom of the alarm caused among the richer landowners and the military and bureaucratic circles allied with them by the incipient rural class struggle. The suppression of the Ligas, far from proving that they were not class organisations at all, proved rather how effective they were, under a government that was prepared to leave them a certain scope for social and political activity. Only by brute repression, that is to say by abandoning the patron-client relationship and by taking a clear-cut class position over against the rural proletariat, could the larger landowners temporarily suppress the peasant movements. The vertical organisations combining both landowners and land labourers were no longer viable under the Branco regime.

It appears to me, that what happened in Java shows striking parallels with recent developments in Brazil. Geertz's analysis of Javanese society during the fifties in terms of vertically divided *alirans* is certainly, to a large extent, valid. In his recent book Gunawan has rightly demonstrated, that the PKI has stressed quantity instead of quality, and attempted to build up a large following, without paying enough attention both to ideological training and to class composition of members and following. Whereas its great competitor for political power, the military leadership, shifted from quantity to quality, that is to say transformed a people's army, that had fought the Independence War, into one on a professional basis, the PKI sought its strength mainly in numbers.[25] As a consequence, in several villages leaders were courted who, on the basis of their traditional prestige, were expected to bring a broad mass of followers along. In Bali, the party even attracted a few rajas as popular leaders.

In the long run, these tactics and the ensuing blurred class composition of the party would prove a basic weakness. On the other hand, however, the stress upon class solidarity and class appeal was never completely absent from PKI-strategy. The party and its rural accessory, the Indonesian Peasant Union (BTI) has repeatedly attempted to analyse village society in class terms, and to devise its tactics accordingly.[26]

The element of class struggle was much reinforced by developments in the early sixties. Geertz has clearly demonstrated that increasing agrarian over-population in Java has produced a process which he has called "involution"—the reverse of evolution.[27] Poverty among the peasantry was on the increase, and there seemed to be no outlook for an improvement in the living standard, despite Sukarno's slogans about self-sufficiency in food and clothing. The intrusion of native capitalism in the countryside called into life a class of landlords, not a few of them absentees living as officials in the cities; it also diminished the modest measure of security for the destitute embodied in traditional patronage relationships. The peasantry became more restive, and consequently, if the BTI and PKI wanted to retain their following, they had to take the lead in this rural unrest.

As a consequence of the prevailing rural unrest, and in order to placate the *kom* component of the uneasy NASAKOM alliance which was a device to reconcile the different *alirans* at the top level, in 1960 President Sukarno had to introduce relatively radical land reform laws which, in turn, increased the restiveness among the poor peasantry who expected a fair and speedy implementation of the new legislation.

Consequently, in the early sixties a true rural class struggle developed which the PKI, willy nilly, was forced to support. It is this pressure from below which is not given due recognition in Gunawan's otherwise lucid and instructive analysis in the chapter entitled "From coalition between pillars towards class struggle" of his recent book *Kudetà*. Gunawan does not make sufficiently clear, why the PKI, in the early sixties, suddenly reversed its policy towards its NASAKOM partners by adopting a class strategy which previously had been largely absent from its overall internal policy. Dissatisfaction about the slow and reluctant implementation of the land reforms provoked the so-called "one-sided actions" by poor peasants which, after a short hesitation, were endorsed by the PKI leadership. In so doing, however, the PKI came in serious conflict with its allies in the NASAKOM coalition. Soon a bitter discussion between communists and nationalists raged in the party newspapers.[28] The struggle with the N.U., mainly in East Java, even took on the character of regular physical clashes.

The bitterness was probably enhanced precisely by the lack of a clear class basis in the BTI and PKI tactics. There were accusations—the correctness of which has still to be proved—that the one-sided actions were not aimed at those landlords or rich peasants who were members or sympathisers of the PKI or BTI. On the other hand, according to these accusations, land belonging to non-PKI peasants was often distributed even if, according to the norms concerning size of landholdings, they should have been left untouched. It is certain, that there were instructions of the PKI not to discriminate between PKI and non-PKI and strictly to keep to the text of the Agrarian Law. But in view of the non-class composition of the party there is a good chance, that in several areas the accusations were not completely unfounded.

At any rate, one of the consequences of the class struggle waged by the peasantry under PKI leadership was that the ruling strata and the richer landowners became seriously alarmed, as they did in Brazil about the same time. The precarious balance between the different *alirans*, kept by Sukarno under the NASAKOM structure, began to crumble. Whereas the PKI-leadership, unaware that the time for compromises with other vertical organisations was definitely over, tried to keep the precarious balance at the top intact, the army leadership, in collaboration with the village gentry and the *santri* rich peasantry, profited from the abortive Untung-coup in which some PKI-leaders appear to have been more or less actively involved, to crash down upon the PKI-cadres and following in the countryside. Whereas what happened in the cities rather looked like a continuation of the pre-coup struggle, on an *aliran* basis, between competing elites, the countryside, especially in Central and East Java, where the PKI and BTI had been influential and where the one-sided actions had been more or less successful, became the theatre of a murderous repression and reaction against the peasantry that had taken part in those actions. Only by taking account of the class struggle character of the tensions in the countryside can the size and brutality of the mass murders be understood. On the other hand, in some regions, where the slaughtering was not done mainly by the shock troops (RPKAD), the *santri* and PNI-landowners still could muster a significant section of the village youth to commit the murders. This can be attributed to the patronage pattern of social relationships: for example, the followers of the rich *santri*, many of them poor sharecroppers, will have obeyed their patron rather than acting on a basis of class solidarity. Otherwise the massacre of the PKI and BTI peasantry could never have assumed such a massive character, nor would it have found the leftists as defenceless as it actually did.[29]

Though much more research on what really happened in the countryside before and after the coup is needed, it seems evident that it was, fundamentally, a repetition of the occurrences in Brazil after April 1964. Land reforms appear to have been put, by the Suharto regime, into the ice-box.[30] The rich landowners have regained their lands, and the military leaders are practising a sharp repression against those who tend to resurrect agrarian unrest. Non-commissioned officers appear to have been appointed on a large scale as village heads. Whereas the incipient class struggle of the poor peasantry failed for the time being, it is the large landowners, supported by the rule of the military authorities, who are, thus, openly waging their own brand of class struggle. The poor peasants, bereft of the modest security they enjoyed under the traditional patronage system, will have to look for new organisational forms to bring a true class solidarity into play; those new forms will certainly maintain some elements of the traditional patronage, as for example an urban leadership by those who have enjoyed a better education. But it is clear that their chances for future success will depend heavily on the extent to which they will be able to organise on a much more outspoken class basis, instead of having their class composition blurred by a misguided quest for a nominal rather than real, mass following.

In the foregoing analysis, parallels have been drawn with Brazil. It seems to me, that with all the cautiousness that is required in drawing historical parallels, another comparison would be to the point: with what happened, after 1927, in China. There, as in Indonesia in 1965, the military established an authoritarian rule, and turned against the communists, with whom, earlier, an uneasy coalition had been maintained. There are strong indications[31] that rural unrest, which had alarmed the gentry and many urban intellectuals with landed interests, was at the root of the *volte-face* of the Kuomintang.

Though rural unrest gained in strength under the leadership of the underground Communist Party, it was only after the defeat of the Japanese, that the final battle between Communists and Kuomintang could be won by the former. The recent book by William Hinton, *Fanshen*,[32] makes clear how the communists managed to bring the large majority of the peasantry on their side. During the Japanese occupation, the gentry was forced into collaboration with the brutal occupation forces, which removed the already seriously weakened patronage function the gentry had been able to fulfil in previous times for part of the poor peasants.[33] At first, the communists reacted, after the Japanese defeat, according to a kind of *aliran* pattern: those who had collaborated with the Japanese, whatever their class position, were made the target of the revenge taken by the communist cadres and their following; on the other hand, a good record during the occupation saved even rich peasants from suffering under land redistribution. But at the end of 1947, the strategy of the communists was put on a clear class basis; and, according to Hinton's analysis, only then could the rural uprising under communist leadership become successful.[34]

The Chinese experience appears, therefore, basic for an understanding of how difficult it is to transform the agrarian unrest prevalent in many parts of the world from a patronage pattern into a true class struggle. On the other hand, for a historian it is not only important to study revolutions that succeed; it is at least as important to study why revolutions fail to come about—or why they misfire.

REFERENCES

Aidit, D. N., 1964, *Kaum tani mengganjan setan² desa; Laporan singkat tentang hasil riset mengenai keadaan kaum tani dan gerakan tani Djawa Barat, Djakarta.*

Asmu, 1960, "Msalah Landreform", in *Bintang Merah*, January.

Castles, Lance, 1966, "Notes on the Islamic School at Gontor", *Indonesia*, 1.

Chabot, H. Th., 1950, *Verwantschap, stand en sexe in Zuid-Celebes*, Groningen/Djakarta.

———, 1967, "Bontoramba: A Village of Goa, South Sulawesi", in Koentjaraningrat (ed.), *Villages in Indoneisa*, Ithaca, N.Y.

Djojodigoeno, M.M. and Tirtawinata, 1940, *Het adatprivaatrecht van Middel-Java*, Batavia.

Fried, Morton H., 1956, *Fabric of Chinese Society*, London.

Galjart, Benno, 1964, "Class and 'Following' in Rural Brazil", *America Latina*, 7, 3.

———, 1965, "A Further Note on 'Followings'", *America Latina*, 8, 3.

Geertz, Clifford, 1963a, *Peddlers and Princes: Social Development and Economic Change in Two Indonesian Towns*, Chicago/London.

———, 1963b, *Agricultural Involution; The Processes of Ecological Change in Indonesia*, Berkeley/Los Angeles.

———, 1965, *The Social History of an Indonesian Town*, Cambridge, Mass.

Gunawan, Basuki, 1968, *Kudetà; staatsgreep in Djakarta*, Meppel.

———, and van den Muijzenberg, O. D., 1967, "Verzuilingstendenties en sociale stratificatie in Indonesie", *Sociologische Gids*, 14.

Han Suyin, 1966, *A Mortal Flower: China, Autobiography, History*, London.

Hatta, Mohammad, 1945, *Beberapa Fasal Ekonomi: Djalan Keekonomi dan Kooperasi*, 1 Djakarta.

Hinton, William, 1956, *Fanshen: A Documentary of Revolution in a Chinese Village*, London.

Hollnsteiner, Mary, 1963, *The Dynamics of Power in a Philippine Municipality*, Quezon City.

Huizer, Gerrit, 1965, "Some Notes on Community Development and Rural Social Research", *America Latina*, 8, 3.

Jay, Robert R., 1963, *Religion and Politics in Rural Central Java*, New Haven.

Kruijt, J. P. and Goddijn, Walter O. F. M., 1962, "Verzuiling en ontzuiling als sociologisch proces", In A.N.J. den Hollander c.s. (ed.), *Drift en Koers: een halve eeuw sociale verandering in Nederland*, Assen.

Lande, Carl H., 1965, *Leaders, Factions and Parties: the Structure of Philippine Politics*, New Haven.

Lewis, O., 1958, *Village Life in Northern India*, Urbana.

Rutgers, S. J., 1929, *Het boerenvraagstuk in Sovjet-Rusland, Europa, Amerika, Indië, China*, Rotterdam.

Singh, Baljit, 1961, *Next Step in Village India*, London.

Slamet, Ina E., 1963, *Pokok² Pembangunan Masjarakat Desa: Sebuah Pandangan Anthropologi Budaja*, Djakarta.

ten Dam, H., 1951, *Desa Tjibodas*, a stencilled report of the Lembaga Penjelidikan Masjarakat Desa dan Usaha Tani, Bogor.

———, 1962, "Cooperation and Social Structure in the Village of Chibodas", in *Indonesian Economics: The Concept of Dualism in Theory and Policy*, The Hague.

ter Haar, B., 1948, *Adat Law in Indonesia*, New York.

Utomo, Kampto, 1957, *Masjarakat Transmigran Spontan Didaerah W. Sekampung (Lampung)*, Bogor.

Utrecht, Ernst, 1967, "Massamoord in het Paradijs", *De Groene Amsterdammer*, 7-1-67.

———, 1968, "Kleine boer niet in tel De landhervormingen in Indonesie", *De Nieuwe Linie*, 24-2-68.

van Vollenhoven, C., 1918, *Het Adarecht van Nederlandsch-Indië* 1, Leiden.

Wertheim, W. F., 1964, *Indonesian Society in Transition: A Study of Social Change*, The Hague/Bandung.

———, 1966, "Indonesia Before and After the Untung Coup", *Pacific Affairs*, 39.

NOTES

1 Paper read at the International Conference on Asian History at Kuala Lumpur, August 1968.

2 van Vollenhoven (1918): 524.

3 van Vollenhoven (1918): 525; ter Haar (1948): 71 ff.

4 Geertz (1965): 127 ff.

5 Jay (1963).

6 Gunawan and van den Muijzenberg (1967); 146 ff; see also Gunawan (1968): 25 ff.

7 Kruijt and Goddijn (1962): 227 ff.

8 Jay (1963): 90 ff, more in particular 94-100.

9 Jay (1963) himself claims that the *desa* studied by him was not all exceptional in this respect (p. 99).

10 Castles (1966): 30 ff.

11 Gunawan (1968): 38.

12 Gunawan (1968): 39.

13 Chabot (1950): 101 ff; and (1967); 204 ff; and Geertz (1963a): 99ff.

14 See for a description of the initial arrangements and of the way Japanese occupation and its aftermath, the Indonesian revolution, disturbed them, Kampto Utomo's brilliant doctoral thesis, (1957): 40 ff. From his data it becomes clear, however, that the "intellectual" colonists, as far as they had stayed, had achieved on the average a certain prominence; whereas from the original *magersari* group only one had achieved a certain affluence as a landowner.

15 Hatta (1945): 83 ff; see also Utomo (1957): 70 ff.

16 ter Haar (1948): 126 n., 8. Neither van Vollenhoven (1918) nor Djojodigoeno and Tirtawinata (1940) mention the term.

17 ten Dam (1962): 350 ff.

18 ten Dam (1951).

19 For a discussion of patronage in the Philippines see Landé (1965); Hollnsteiner (1963).

20 Jay (1963): 31 ff. ("Kebonsari: The Traditional Synthesis").

21 See, for example, Lewis (1958): 147 ff; Singh (1961): 1-15.

22 Wertheim (1964): 165 ff.

23 Galjart (1964); Huizer (1965).

24 Huizer (1965): 139.

25 Gunawan (1967).

26 See for example Asmu (1960) as discussed in Slamet (1963): 24 ff; Aidit (1964).

27 Geertz (1963b).

28 *Polemik Merdeka—Harian Rakjat* (n.p., n.y., but reproducing a dispute from 1964).

29 Frank Palmos in the Australian newspaper *The Sun*, 5th August 1966, anonymously reprinted in *The Economist*, 20th August 1966. The agrarian issue as a main source of the mass murders has been stressed in Wertheim (1966): 115 ff. Utrecht (1967) confirms my thesis, expounded in an earlier issue of the same weekly, that in large parts of East and Central Java the mass murders were mostly directed at landless peasants, though in a few instances his interpretation of the facts is somewhat different from mine, and in a few others Professor Utrecht provides important additional information.

30 Utrecht (1968); Wertheim (1966): 124.

31 See for an analysis by a contemporary Rutgers (1929): 125-126; Han Suyin (1966): 66, 103 ff. I also drew a parallel between present-day Indonesia and China during the late twenties in (1966): 126-127.

32 Hinton ((1956).

33 See Fried (1956): 103 ff. on the *kan-ch'ing* relationships; Hinton (1956): 58-68, 80 ff. on the patronage role of the Catholic Church that was lost as a consequence of the Japanese occupation.

34 Hinton (1956): 7 ff.

MODERNIZATION AND DEVELOPMENT:
The Role of Regional Elites and Noncorporate Groups in the European Mediterranean*

PETER SCHNEIDER · JANE SCHNEIDER · EDWARD HANSEN

THIS PAPER is about social change in underdeveloped areas. It is based on field work in the European Mediterranean between 1965 and 1967. Hansen worked in the wine and champagne district of Villafranca del Panadés, roughly 30 miles from Barcelona, in Catalonia. The Schneiders were in the wheat and pastoral latifundium zone of Western Sicily. The two regions exhibit quite different patterns of land use and tenure, social stratification and settlement. We were struck, however, by two characteristics which they shared. First, we found a plethora of noncorporate social structures (for the most part coalitions) which organized *fundamental* economic and political activities of a quite modern sort. In rural Catalonia, coalitions of businessmen, skilled workers and government functionaries are formed within the context of an emergent bar culture, centered in major towns like Villafranca. In Western Sicily, until quite recently, the locus of similar coalitions was the latifundium. As yet, no clearly defined urban tradition has replaced this predominantly rural one. In both the Spanish and the Sicilian examples, the celebration of friendship, especially at banquets and feasts, provides ideological support to coalition formation, generating relations of trust critical to economic and political activities.

Second, both regions have experienced significant modernizing changes, in the absence of any fundamental alteration in the organization of production. Both regions are thoroughly caught up in the integration of their respective nations, Spain and Italy, underway since the 1930s. There have been marked improvements in the standard of living since World War II, and patterns of consumption are now similar in many ways to those of advanced metropolitan centers. Yet, in Catalonia and Western Sicily, these developments are not associated with the emergence of primary industry or the transformation of agriculture. In both places there is much talk of the 'failure' of various attempts at industrial or agrarian reform. These 'failures' have occurred more often and with greater impact in Western Sicily, the poorer and more backward of the two regions. Western Sicily also shows a higher rate of emigration to external industrial centers, and a much greater dependence on emigration remittances to finance local economic activity. Even so, much of Catalan economic growth since World War II depends upon the financing and initiative of 'foreign' industrial centers. The region itself has no preeminent claim to its own resources, human or material.

We would like to develop a model of economic and political growth which will explain both the similarities and the differences which we observed in these two regions. We found that this could not be accomplished with the once popular unilineal model of social, economic and political evolution implicit in the 'traditional-modern' continuum, according to which all societies are either traditional, or modern, or 'transitional'. In terms of this model, the coalitions and associated ideologies which we found in Catalonia and Western Sicily would indicate transitional status: coalitions do modern things in a traditional 'face-to-face' way. The virtual absence of indigenous industry and agricultural

transformation in Western Sicily, and the presence of considerable light industry and rationalization of viticulture in Catalonia, would suggest that the latter region has gone somewhat further in the transition from traditional to modern. The model would insist, however, that it is only a matter of time before both places arrive at their urban-industrial destination.

Without belaboring the point let us mention two reasons why we find the model inappropriate. (It has already been subject to penetrating criticism in this journal, among other places. See, for example, Bendix, 1967.) First, it does not do justice to our coalitions—to their complex structure, their ideological components, and their longevity as a form of social organization. The coalition is a social form which predates the Industrial Revolution and persists to the present day, always as a device for the organization of critical economic and political activities. It is therefore a remarkably stable 'transitional' form; the end of the transitional period is not in sight; and the word 'transitional' is stretched beyond recognition. Second, we are reluctant to accept the optimism of the unilineal model. That all societies will become industrial in their own right is unlikely, at least so long as coal and oil are the predominant sources of energy. Increasingly one sees the world as a system in which some areas control the means of industrial production (regardless of where they are located) while most areas have access to these means only in restricted measure, or not at all.

The elaboration of an alternative model must, we think, move in the following directions. First, we see the need for a revision of the community—nation matrix. Research on growth and change should define a local region as the primary unit of analysis, in order to deal effectively with social structures which transcend community boundaries. It should place this region in its international as well as its national setting, in order to deal with some of the tremendous economic and political forces which clearly do not respect national political boundaries. Among other things, this means studying the region as the source, or the object, of imperialist pressures.

Second, we suggest a distinction between 'corporate' and 'noncorporate' groups (to be defined below), which contains no *a priori* developmental assumptions. All societies exhibit various elements of corporate and noncorporate organization; whether one or the other is present in critical sectors at any given time is *not* necessarily a function of level of complexity, or general evolutionary advance.

Finally, the concept 'modern' strikes us as overloaded when it implies, as it usually does, urban and industrial. We are currently working with the hypothesis that modernization and industrial development are not only different processes, but that they are, in some important ways, antithetical processes. Thus, modernization may preclude development, and development may well inhibit or delay modernization.

We hope that the following elaboration of these ideas will provoke discussion and critical response. We recognize that, for many, the unilineal approach has already been superseded by a theory of growth based on 'late development effect' (Bendix, 1967; Dore, 1969; Moore, 1966), which insists that change cannot be the same for postwar Nigeria as it was for seventeenth-century England (Dore, 1969). This approach is limited only by its continued assumption of eventual development for all societies. We would like to recognize the possibility that many societies may not develop, however much they may change in response to new inputs from already developed centers. This attitude is very close to Geertz's analysis (1968) of 'agricultural involution' and to recent reassessments of Latin American political and economic history. Andre Gunder Frank's case studies of Chile and Brazil argue that 'economic development and under-development are the opposite sides of the same coin' (1969:9). In his work as well as that of Stein and Stein (1970) we find, in common with our own effort, an emphasis on the reciprocal effects of dominance and subordination in the relationships between metropolitan centers and underdeveloped satellites. Indeed, in our rudimentary typology of developmental careers, Latin America and the Western Mediterranean would be grouped together, for reasons which will be suggested in the following pages.

I. UNITS OF ANALYSIS:
THE REGION AND ITS INTERNATIONAL SETTING

Anthropologists and political sociologists have long recognized the limitations of the community study, and have rectified these limitations by focusing on the relationship between the community and the nation state. Following Redfield, they have seen the community as the repository of little traditions and taken the state as the source of a contrasting great tradition. The meeting of great and little traditions, and eventual disappearance of the latter as community resources and leaders are mobilized by national elites and state institutions penetrate the local arena—this is said to be the essential process of political modernization (Etzioni, 1963; Nettl, 1967). It is quite possible, of course, that the process is reversible, that modernization creates (among other things) the diffusion of little traditions upward into metropolitan culture. In any case, the focus on community and nation-state is still incomplete, if the effective political actors are *regional* elites which relate to extranational as well as national metropolitan centers.

Regions have been defined by their ecology, mode of production, patterns of land use and tenure, social structure, cultural tradition, custom and sometimes by ethnicity as well (Wagley, 1964). Juan J. Linz and Amando de Miguel (1966) for example, delineate, not one, but eight Spains, and Charles Wagley (1964) can distinguish six Brazils. For our purposes, the region becomes a political unit with an indigenous elite and hierarchy when it participates as such in a struggle for domain. The political elite may then represent a specific economic interest, often but not necessarily vested in a single crop. In the Mediterranean, a culture area whose involvement with international markets is uniquely long and intimate, there are no nations (except possibly Andorra) that are not divisible into regions of political and economic significance.

Where regions are politically organized, they are children of political ecology, rather than products of 'cultural continuity' or historical tradition, or even of geography. As such they may thwart attempts at national integration, erecting barriers between the community and the nation. Long ago the Spanish philosopher, Ortega y Gassett (1928) argued that the regions of Spain were the principal threat to the development of that country as a modern nation, because each was self-contained, 'hermetically' sealed against the others. This is not to say that regional elites are necessarily less 'modern' than their national counterparts; their experience with the great traditions of cosmopolitan centers may equal if not surpass that of national leaders. This is certainly true of the Catalan haute bourgeoisie, dominant in that region for the last 150 years. In Sicily, the *latifondisti*, the landed aristocracy of the past, lived almost exclusively in the regional capital, Palermo, or in cities abroad. Their style of life was that of the foreign city, especially Paris (Mack Smith, 1968:284-94; Pitré, 1944; Ponteiri, 1933).

We can think of two reasons why a region might resist the consolidation of a national domain. If it has a long history of autonomy, it might organize itself politically to resist encroachment on its territory, resources and people. Berbers of the High Atlas demonstrated this kind of regionalism by resisting the hegemony of successive states with force (Wolf, 1969; 238-9). That they occupied an ecological niche in which the arm of the state was easily severed from the body, that they pursued a way of life in which tactical mobility and the skilled use of violence were paramount, undoubtedly contributed to the efficacy of their resistance. Most would-be autonomous regions have fared less well.

The other basis for a region's resistance to national consolidation might be its foreign connections. Many regions supply critical commodities to world markets, and are thus more intimately involved in an international commercial orbit than they are in national affairs. Such a condition gives political as well as economic leverage to the region. Never fully autonomous, never approaching nationhood itself, it can nonetheless play off one external center against another, maximizing its relationship with one to resist the hegemony of the other. If demand for a regional resource runs high on international markets, and the nation state seeks to control the export of that resource, a black market materializes and thrives. When demand falls off, regional elites then turn to the state for support, having amassed enough power and wealth in international trade to name their own price. The state, in exchange for the region's loyalty, is forced to make certain concessions: it will promise not to tax or otherwise control the region's exports or, better still, it will underwrite the profitability of its major crops or mineral wealth with protective tariffs. The state will promise not to interfere in regional affairs, that is, not to consolidate national authority at the expense of the regional elite. On the contrary, it may reserve seats for members of that elite in the national government.

The power of a region *vis-à-vis* its nation is, of course, an empirical question, and subject to variation over time. In the Middle Ages Catalonia was virtually a nation itself, and much larger than it is today. Its subsequent resistance to the hegemony of the Spanish state was expressed in the idiom of Catalan nationalism. Sicily was colony to a long succession of foreign powers, including the Catalans in the fourteenth and fifteenth centuries. Its historical resistance to the state takes the form not of nationalism but of 'separatism' in which regional forces occasionally seek to exchange dependence upon one foreign power for dependence upon another. In the words of one historian, Sicily,

With her commerce in the hands of foreigners . . . without a long enough period of organic development of her productive forces . . . remained divided from within . . . She was not strong enough to emancipate herself, and render herself independent, but neither was she weak enough to be definitely absorbed into the unity of another nation. Somehow she (that is, her elite) always got away with specific 'liberties' or 'privileges' under different foreign governments (Romano, 1964:235-6).

An emblem of the postwar Sicilian separatist movement depicts two soldiers of the separatist army, severing with machine guns the chain that bound Sicily to Rome, while replacing it with another chain that would link the island to America as its forty-ninth state. The Allied occupation, not to mention the prewar migrations, had nurtured that hope.

It is our contention that regions with a substantial historical experience at playing off one set of forces against another will exhibit characteristics not pronounced elsewhere. In particular they will have elites whose power and sophistication qualify them for national arenas, even though the regions in question are economically backward, preindustrial and agrarian. How else to explain the power of the South in the American national government, post-Civil War, than in terms of its historic link to the British Empire and English cotton markets? Furthermore, many of these regions will sustain a clandestine circulation of commodities on such a scale, and for such long periods of time, that social structures and entrepreneurial styles will be formed by the experience. Capital accumulation under such conditions means 'living by one's wits' in an organizational context that places a premium on *ad hoc*, temporary arrangements. This type of capitalism is hardly prototypical of Weber's legal-rational bureaucracy (P. Schneider, 1972; Wolf and Hansen, 1967).

Some societies exhibit in much greater degree than others the consequences of internationally connected and politically organized regionalism. It is our impression that these consequences are most pronounced in areas long involved with the international commercial networks. Many regions in the early colonies of Spain and Portugal became involved in these kinds of cross-pressures as early as the sixteenth and seventeenth centuries. Such pressures were especially characteristic of the eighteenth century, when England aggressively undermined the Spanish Empire through piracy and smuggling (Stein and Stein, 1970:85-123). The significance of this early involvement was twofold: it preceded the era in which economic growth and change necessitated massive government involvement, planned economies and socialism. That is, it fell within the epoch when primitive capital accumulation through private entrepreneurship was still possible.

Second, by preceding the Industrial Revolution, and the late nineteenth-century era of industrially backed imperialism, early colonization allowed maximum scope for the consolidation of regional domains. Undercapitalized and ineffectual means of transportation and communication; having to rely upon indigenous powerholders and *mestizos* for the organization of colonial dominance; the inability of the metropolis to control the adventurers and settlers who migrated abroad—all these encouraged the rise of regional elites and regional power structures which were separate from, if not independent of, the colonial apparatus. Timing seems a critical variable in the imperial drama.

II. LEVELS OF COMPLEXITY AND
TYPES OF ORGANIZATION

The timing of colonial dominance would also seem to be relevant to the emergence of noncorporate groups such as patron-client chains and coalitions, these being critical to the origin of capitalist institutions in pre-nineteenth-century colonies. For our purposes, organization has to do with power, not just 'who gets what, when and how', but in more general terms, power defined as the distribution of energy in a social system. Both corporate and noncorporate organization provide means of regulating power relationships, defining access to resources, stratifying and controlling people. A corporate group has legal status, i.e., it is chartered, and controls property which is vested in the group *per se*. Furthermore, the corporate group has a life of its own: it may well antedate and survive any particular set of members.

A noncorporate group is not chartered, although there may well be an ideology, a common mentality, or behavioral grammar which defines the routes of entrance into the group and regulates the conduct of its members. Most important, the assets of a noncorporate group are not vested in the group, *per se*. They remain the property of its individual members.[1] In short, the noncorporate group may be a coalition, clique or patron-client chain, in which individuals pool resources and skills.[2]

It is our hypothesis that noncorporate groups occur where the distribution of power in a system has not been routinized, structured by more stable corporate institutions. By way of contrast, corporate power is a function of consolidated political systems in which large segments of the population are irrelevant to the power field.

Where the distribution of power has not been routinized individuals become decision-makers with a variety of possible tactics at their disposal; where it has been structured within a system, an individual's decisions are bound by the limits of his status in that system.

Given that both corporate and noncorporate groups organize power in society, both are equally relevant to social structure, and both are culturally determined. Indeed, as our Mediterranean examples indicate, coalition formation can be highly institutionalized, drawing heavily on cultural codes, traditions, ideologies and organizational models. It does not help us to refer to such structures as 'informal' organizations (which, after all, is a contradiction in terms), since the concept 'informal' usually connotes an activity which is ancillary, secondary, or interstitial, and we are talking about social groups that organize critical economic and political functions. We suggest that where social groups celebrate the ideology of friendship, fictive kinship, or patronage, they have transcended informality and are oriented towards the organization of power. The concept 'informal' usually overlooks power. Even where the sociology of complex organization recognizes the network of friendship ties as a matrix for collective action, the resulting structural consequences are not fully appreciated. Rather, they are relegated to 'bureaucracy's other face' (Page, 1946).

Social science has also misled us on formal organization, having been taken in, perhaps, by what bureaucracy says about itself (and by Weber's romance with the ideal of bureaucracy). The charter of a 'formal organization' is also ideology, through which is advertised how fair, impersonal and universally applicable are its rules of operation. It is in contrast to this message that other bases for decision-making appear not to count, or to count much less. Just as corporate kin groups falsify genealogies in order to legitimate exceptions to the rule (Sahlins, 1968:55), so bureaucrats couch decisions in terms which are consistent with the manual, regardless of how these decisions are motivated. In both cases, the true purpose of the charter, the articles of incorporation, the manual, is not alone to set down rules which serve as guides to action, but to control people and resources, curtail individual initiative, help people to endure their lot without rancor and resentment, and without wrecking the organization or punishing anyone but themselves.

The distinction between corporate and noncorporate departs in another important way from the 'formal-informal' dichotomy. It makes no evolutionary assumptions. We do not associate noncorporate organization with *Gemeinschaft* societies, nor do we associate corporate organization with modern, ration, bureaucratic, industrial and urban societies. A price-fixing cartel in the North American electronics industry is a noncorporate group, while a Mae Enga lineage and a Chinese *tsu* are corporate. All societies have sectors which are corporately organized and other sectors where power is found in different, but overlapping domains.

In the United States, for instance, one would expect to find noncorporate structures prevalent at the top of the social order (among upper and middle-level management personnel in a large corporation, for example), where the allocation of power is uncertain. But below that level rational-bureaucratic rules impede the emergence of fragmented power fields, just as does the centralization of productive resources which occurs inexorably with the progress of technology. Thus it is largely at or near the top that the power field is fluid, while corporate structures are the instruments of those who wield power at this level. In effect, the upper echelon creates a buffer between itself and the underlying population. The higher one goes in a bureaucracy, we suggest, the more likely one is to encounter cliques, factions, patron-clients chains and coalitions organizing critical activities. Further down the hierarchy, noncorporate structures based on dyadic ties may well exist—love affairs, softball teams and coffee-break cliques are ubiquitous—but they are mostly irrelevant to the political life of the organization.[3]

In the regions of the Western Mediterranean under discussion, the fragmentation of power extends, by and large, throughout the social system. Everywhere power seems to be in different, but overlapping domains. This is an area in which individuals at all levels are politicians: they calculate, wheel and deal, and intrude themselves into widely divergent spheres of action. They are celebrated for their initiative and drive, notorious for their capacity to store information about political and social debits and credits, and remarkably skilled at interpersonal relations. The would-be entrepreneur in this context is always alive to the opportunities for forming coalitions with others, in order that resources and skills might be pooled on a temporary basis to accomplish specific ends.

In other words, in the Western Mediterranean, every man can be his own sovereign. To be sure, the lower down the social scale we go, the less the probability of his resounding success. But even in the poorest towns of a latifundist region, there are wide varieties of resources and

talents that are not tied down in corporate structures, that are available if only a person can make the right connections (Davis, 1969; J. Schneider, 1969). It is not surprising that the picaresque novel is a Mediterranean genre, or that Lazarillo de Tormes is a literary figure with whom Spaniards can still identify. Similarly, the Mediterranean genius of statecraft was Machiavelli and not Colbert, while its political scientist was Pareto instead of Max Weber. In our minds, the social structure of the Western Mediterranean is most clearly understood from the perspective of network analysis, and least comprehensible if approached through traditional sociological categories alone.

Good reasons underly these generalizations. First, the fragmented power field is, like political regionalism (itself an example of fragmentation), a consequence of the *early* penetration of capitalist markets. As we have seen, prior to the Industrial Revolution the administration and political organization of colonial dominance was problematic, with the result that control by the central power over tax collectors and judges, civil servants and landlords was intermittent and incomplete. For example, the Spanish Empire in Sicily, while influenced by experiments with salaried bureaucracies in the republics of Northern Italy, was in fact based on the less centralizing principle of prebendal domain (see Wolf, 1966:51-2). When such a system coincides with an expanding market economy, it breeds widespread corruption as offices become capital assets on which to make profits. Judges in sixteenth- and seventeenth-century Sicily were not paid salaries but received fees, called 'candles'. It was said that a case would be won by the litigant who lit the most candles for the judge to see by (Koenigsberger, 1969:91). The central authorities, operating from far-off Madrid, could attempt to control such situations only through a system of checks and balances, that is, by encouraging factionalism and espionage, and hence exposure, all the way down the line (Koenigsberger, 1969:97-104). Competition for advantages in a fluid power domain was characteristic of the private sector too. For landlords no more had the means to administer their estates than the state had the means to administer the landlords. Instead, brokers of various kinds did this work, not for salary but for profit. A guard on the latifundium, for example, had as capital assets his gun, horse, a small piece of land, and his position of authority. He capitalized on these assets by entering conspiracies to rustle the landlord's animals (Alongi, 1886; Franchetti, 1925; Mack Smith, 1968:367-8).

Here too, power was more fragmented in fact than on paper.

The fragmentation and fluidity of power characteristic of a region colonized prior to the Industrial Revolution had a lasting impact on its social structure. Such conditions discouraged the emergence of centralized control and coordination based on a hierarchy of settlements in which clearly defined centers maintained political, economic and social hegemony over satellite towns and villages. In less urbanized regions, where production was almost exclusively geared to export, these conditions even discouraged the rise of market towns (Morse, 1962; P. Schneider, 1972). The same fragmentation of power and decentralization of control encouraged the elaboration of complex cultural codes governing the accumulation and deployment of resources by noncorporate groups responding to market pressures and opportunities in the absence of legal guarantees and secular controls. These groups, and their associated cultural codes, lived on to provide the framework within which modern (but nonindustrial) capitalism evolved. They are the functional equivalent of the joint stock association in Western Europe.

As we have seen, noncorporate coalitions are less stable than corporate groups. Indeed, their very instability constitutes an adaptive advantage in the form of spontaneity and flexibility. Perhaps the most important source of the coalition's instability (adaptability) is the fact that its members retain control over the assets they contribute to the collective effort, and are likely to make only a partial commitment to that effort (one never puts all one's eggs in a single basket). This means that new members, with new resources, can be added with relative ease to accommodate changing circumstances. It also means, however, that individuals can withdraw not only themselves, but their assets too, unilaterally and without warning. It is to prevent this kind of sabotage, as well as to build a climate of trust in which future coalitions can readily be assembled, that banqueting, impromptu feasts, and other celebrations of friendship, patronage, kinship and fictive kinship are common. Both the noncorporate group and its ceremonial supports thus reflect the inability of entrepreneurs to count on the state to guarantee their interests. The state may have been an important source of wealth, in the form of government contracts, licenses, loans and so on; but in distributing this patronage it took little or no initiative to help its clients organize among themselves. If anything, it intensified competition among them as a means of surveillance and local control. This could only intensify the pressure on regional entrepreneurs to create local and independent organizational strategies for relating to world markets.

We would guess that these patterns existed not only in the European Mediterranean, but in most early colonies, where entrepreneurial elites, most of them operating in regional domains, invented special means of creating and reinforcing noncorporate groups. Support for this hypothesis can be found in Anthony Leed's masterful description of the Brazilian *panelinhas* (1964) and in Hollnsteiner's (1963:123-9) study of a Philippine community. In each of these examples we see how noncorporate organization is given continuity and form by codes drawn from regional tradition and experience. Similarly, culturally specific variation is evident in our own material. In the case of Catalonia, a region characterized by long-term indigenous urbanization, Catalan nationalism was a predominant these celebrated by regional elites, especially during periods of extreme conflict with Madrid. By emphasizing its Catalan origins and identitiy, the Barcelona bourgeoisie held itself together, regulated competition and consolidated its resources more effectively than its class equivalents in other regions. In periods of maximal regional autonomy the Catalan bourgeoisie even managed to create state-like corporate institutions on a regional basis (Vicens Vives, 1959).

By contrast, Western Sicily, less urban from the start and once, as we noted earlier, a Catalan colony, hever had a comparable urban and nationalist elite. Its entrepreneurs originated in the countryside, in the ranching and pastoral sector of the economy. The pastoral themes of honor and shame, and the threat or exercise of violence were important to the process of coalition formation there; coalitions moreover rarely become corporate groups.

It seems to us that the distinguishing feature of the early colonies is the protracted period during which trust and regulation required ideological reinforcement. It is as if Freemasonry—also a parallel phenomenon—had ended up as the organizational matrix of European capitalism, rather than as an extra-curricular activity, albeit of significance to small businessmen. Entrepreneurs in the early colonies spent a longer time and more energy creating noncorporate structures with which to respond to market forces. These structures have continuity for this reason. They also have continuity because the effects of the Industrial Revolution have come only slowly and piecemeal to these regions, and only from without. We shall pursue this factor in the following section.

The Western Mediterranean was subject to the very early expansion of capitalist markets; indeed, capitalism was invented there. As such it shares an experience with other parts of the world similarly affected by the individualizing forces of the market coupled with a slow and tortuous consolidation of the state. As a culture area, however, it is also unique for having been part of a cradle of expanding empires since the Bronze Age; in this it shares a tradition with all regions bordering on the Mediterranean Sea. In many regions of the Mediterranean (Catalonia less so than Sicily), imperial expansion brought agriculture into confrontation with pastoralism in such a way that resources and social structures were highly fragmented in both sectors, again without compensatory reconsolidation by state institutions (J. Schneider, 1971). In these terms we think we can account for the familism and individualism which are much noted in Mediterranean ethnographies. (For example, Banfield, 1958; Campbell, 1964; Peristiany, 1965.) In most Mediterranean societies power is fragmented, not only at the top and bottom of the social order, but throughout it. Noncorporate organization flourishes at every level, although not always in so dramatic a way as among entrepreneurial elites.

III. MODERNIZATION AND DEVELOPMENT

If the early preindustrial expansion of international markets helps us to understand noncorporate organization in the Western Mediterranean, what explains the persistence of these forms in the clearly postindustrial twentieth century? In a word, the persistence, indeed the further consolidation, of international patterns of dominance and dependence. In Western Europe, capitalism became industrial. In most of the Mediterranean, capitalist institutions have expanded in the relative absence of indigenous industrialization. We would argue that the industrialization of Western Europe, and the failure of the Mediterranean to industrialize are related events. To understand the nature of this relationship, we find it necessary to distinguish between modernization and development, proposing that these terms are not synonymous, and might usefully stand for two mutually exclusive processes.

Modernization refers to the process by which an underdeveloped region changes in response to inputs (ideologies, behavioral codes, commodities and institutional models) from already established industrial centers; a process which is based on that region's continued dependence upon the urban-industrial metropolis. Development refers to the process by which an underdeveloped region attempts to acquire an autonomous and diversified industrial economy on its own terms. We assume that contemporary economic and political relations between 'advanced' and 'backward' regions are asymmetrical; such that industrial metropolitan centers dominate markets and claim resources in farflung hinterlands. If this be so, then a contemporary underdeveloped region cannot attempt to industrialize, or even transform its agricultural technology, without withdrawing from the influence of established centers of dominance. Thus, whereas modernization emphasizes intense and continuing contact with established industrial societies, development requires that an underdeveloped society withdraw from such influence, at least partially and temporarily. It should be noted that withdrawal may involve heavy sacrifice and, when compared with modernization, result in a slower rise in such indices of growth as standard of living and percentage of population in nonagricultural pursuits. On the other hand, extensive modernization might preclude development. In many societies the two alternatives coexist and are represented by conflicting social forces, further evidence of the extent to which they may be antithetical.

The dominant feature of postwar economic growth in regions such as Catalonia and Western Sicily has been modernization in the absence of significant development. There has been a rise in incomes and a decline in the proportion of population engaged in agriculture; consumer products are more readily available, more young people have access to educational institutions, information is more widely diffused through the media of mass communications, and in some regions mass political parties have penetrated into the rural hinterlands. All of this, however, is a consequence of close contact with industrial centers, not of withdrawal from them, and has not been accompanied by significant expansion in the productive capacities of the regions involved. As a result, most of what is consumed in these regions—the furniture, TV sets, bathroom fixtures, cosmetics, and so on—is produced elsewhere.

Even when production facilities are located in a backward region, as they occasionally are, they are usually not indigenous to that place, but rather are transplanted from established industrial centers. Capital, technologies of production, often raw materials and management personnel come from without, and the originating establishments remain in firm control of the productive process and of the ultimate distribution of profits. Because Fiat assembles automobiles in Spain and Sicily does not mean that those places are capable of automobile manufacture on any large scale.[4] It does mean that Fiat, like other manufacturers foreign to the underdeveloped region, is more than willing to take advantage of inexpensive land, government subsidies, tax benefits, low-cost labor (relatively unimportant when new factories are highly automated) and new consumer markets. The profits which accrue to these operations are not concentrated and reinvested *in situ*.

One would think that certain kinds of light industry would be a likely prospect for economic development in backward areas, inasmuch as they may require a minimum of technical know-how, a modest amount of capital, and produce commodities which enjoy great market demand. But even here the foreign producer often gains the upper hand, making it virtually impossible for local initiatives to succeed. Nestled in the vineyards of the Alto Panadés were the spanking new factories of Krupp (West Germany, cement), Purina Chows (U.S.A., chicken feeds), and Cinzano (Italy, vermouth). Local entrepreneurs attempting to manufacture the same products with undercapitalized, older and smaller plants were at a serious disadvantage in local markets.

In any event, the rapid diffusion of a great variety of new products and services has changed the rhythm of life in many backward regions, and this is certainly modernization. But where is the money coming from to underwrite the new purchasing power of these populations, if not from indigenous industrial development? There are, it seems to us, three primary sources, one or more of which might be important in any given region. First, there is what Franklin calls 'welfaristic capital investment' in the form of price subsidies, grants and loans for the purchase of agricultural machinery, land reform programs, unemployment and retirement benefits, medical care and medical insurance, most of which are administered by the national governments of the countries in which backward regions are located (Franklin, 1969:174). Rarely do such investment programs significantly alter the productive capacities of these regions, although they may certainly improve the standard of living of those who are the most direct beneficiaries. (It is in this sense that they are welfaristic.) Land reform in Southern Italy, for exam-

ple, seems geared to distributing parcels of land to as many landless or smallholding peasants as possible, without substantially changing the mode of production in that area. This certainly resolves the 'land question' among these peasants, but it does not increase their yield per hectare (Franklin, 1969; Tarrow, 1969). Even where agricultural machinery is employed, there is little change in productivity. If land tenure is not reorganized, and new crops are not introduced, if there is no infrastructure for marketing these crops efficiently, then these 'improvements' simply amount to labor-replacing devices.

A second major source of purchasing power in the backward regions of the European Mediterranean is the cash which Mediterranean migrants remit to their home towns from salaries which are earned elsewhere. In Sicily alone, during the decade 1951-61, more than 400,000 men left the island in search of employment in the industrial centers of Western Europe (based on figures provided by Renda 1963:99-125; *Unitá*, 1966). Unlike the earlier migrations to the New World, the postwar pattern has involved predominantly temporary and 'nomadic' movement from hometown to industrial center and back again, by men who leave their families behind, and have every intention of investing their earnings in a better life at home. In fact, the receiving countries (West Germany, Switzerland, France, Holland, England) make it exceedingly difficult for the emigrant to settle permanently there, even if he should desire to do so. In effect, Italy is exporting labor (not persons) to the more advanced regions. In Italy, emigration remittances for the year 1966 amounted to approximately $815 million, and accounted for all of that country's surplus in the international balance of payments (*New York Times*, 1967). This fact alone suggests that emigration does have a considerable impact on the economies of the regions and nations involved.

A third source of new wealth is tourism. Nearly all of the Mediterranean governments have, with considerable success, mounted intense campaigns to woo the citizen of the developed country to spend a vacation on some lovely Riviera. Spain, for example, has for the past decade followed a policy designed to attract tourist dollars, and tourism has become its principle source of foreign exchange (Tamames, 1965).[5] Like emigration, tourism has the dual function of attracting foreign currency and employing peasants (as well as urban proletarians) who have been forced off the land by the introduction of 'labor-saving' machines and the decline in value of agricultural products on world markets.

A final source of increased purchasing power is derived from the preceding three, all of which give rise to secondary and tertiary economic activities, all more or less parasitic in terms of development: (1) the unbridled expansion of bureaucratic agencies and offices which are ostensibly created to administer welfaristic reforms, including tourism, but which also function to distribute civil service sinecures to members of a rapidly growing middle class which cannot find employment in industry or advanced agriculture because the latter do not exist; (2) the boom in housing construction and public works contingent on emigration, tourism and welfaristic investment; and (3) the rapid multiplication of commercial establishments and activities, also contingent on the three primary sources of rising incomes.

This paper is not the place to discuss all of the significant consequences of modernization as we have described it above. We would, however, like to point out several of these consequences which bear on the distinction between modernization and development. First, modernization often means the incorporation of distorted metropolitan life styles by dependent regions. In contrast we would expect that developing regions would make a conscious and deliberate attempt to isolate themselves from such influences, at least temporarily, and to impose such isolation on other regions they control. The outcome for modernizing societies is not the simple diffusion of metropolitan ways and things. The American tourist in Spain is clearly not a model for the American middle-class way of life in Detroit, nor are the TV images of Italian middle-class life in Milan the real thing. The Sicilian migrant laborer who lives with hundreds of other Sicilians in a company barracks near a Swiss industrial plant is hardly being exposed to a very complete picture of the Swiss way of life. Yet, the impact of such culture contact, although distorted, may be pronounced. In Villafranca del Panadés, for example, all of the young people participated in the resort life of the nearby coast, quickly equating the behavior and possessions of German, French, British, American and Scandinavian youths with all that was modern and desirable. Soon the trappings of what Sukarno once called cultural imperialism appeared everywhere, on the local scene in Villafranca as well as at the resort towns. Coca-cola and Scotch became prestigious drinks, juke boxes in glossy new bars blared hard rock music, and the sexual standards of local maidens were threatened by comparison with the reported conduct of foreign girls on the coast. This too is modernization.

Secondly and more seriously, welfaristic investment, tourism and emigration are ways of strengthening the dependence of the region in question on metropolitan centers without a radical reordering of either society. All of these create a redistribution of wealth, from developed to undeveloped regions, and back again, a redistribution which does not threaten, indeed it supports, the basic modes of production and commerce in both places. All of them create new markets for commodities produced in the metropolis, while at the same time neutralizing the 'peasant problem' in the dependent regions. In Catalonia, for example, peasants forced off the land by mechanization can find, at least as long as tourism grows, employment in hotels and restaurants, as well as in the construction of those facilities. In other words, tourism helps vitiate the political and economic problem of an otherwise 'irrelevant' once agrarian population. Similarly, emigration has long been recognized as a 'safety-valve' (*valvola di sicurezza*) for the political pressures that build up in Southern Italy. The fact that Sicilian migrants now return to Italy with their hard-earned savings to purchase some elements of an urban middle-class life style is simply an added bonus for the industrial producers of the North.

Finally, the modernization of dependent regions is an inherently unstable process. An economic recession or depression in the United States and Western Europe will have a considerable impact on the backward places as tourists stay home, the job market in Western Europe dries up, capital welfare funds are curtailed, and a variety of ancillary activities are affected. (In the Sicilian town of Villamaura, where the Schneiders did their field work, the mere rumor of a cutback in hiring at the factories of West Germany and Switzerland was sufficient to cause a virtual halt in local house construction as migrants decided to conserve their savings in view of the possibility of bad days ahead.)

Because it is unstable, modernization creates a middle class which has the power to consume but not to create new sources of capital. It is a class without autonomy or leverage. Typical of the new bourgeois type is his understandable tendency to invest in sectors of rapid, but short-range profit; to speculate at the expense of planning and to eschew industrial or agrarian enterprises which would require heavy capitalization. The predominant economic activities of such a type include real estate speculation, commerce appropriate to the new consumer markets which modernization engenders, and perhaps agricultural or light industrial production, cautiously capitalized because of its vulnerability to fluctuations on world markets. Such activities lend themselves well to organization by flexible, shifting and temporary noncorporate groups, which explains the persistence of these structures in the European Mediterranean. Excluded is capital accumulation. If anything, modernization implies either the fragmentation and dispersal of money, or its waste. After the war the newly created Sicilian regional government received from the state some 215 billion lire in 'reparations'. The money is an important source of capital for four or five Sicilian banks in whose custody it rests. None of it has been allocated or spent for anything by the state. At the same time, the West Sicilian countryside is dotted with the evidence of bogus schemes for growth: we have seen factories and first-category hotels, built under government subsidy, which never opened because the subsidies ran out before equipment could be installed and personnel hired to run them.

IV. CONCLUSION: TOWARDS A TYPOLOGY OF
PROCESSES AND OUTCOMES

The processes of modernization and development are associated with two basic elite types. On the one hand there are elites which depend upon the continuity of imperial domination; on the other hand are elites organized explicitly to weaken or sever ties of dependency. *We will call these two types of elite 'dependence' and 'development' elites, respectively*. Within each type there are many degrees of potency and efficacy as well as a variety of organizational patterns and codes. There are, however, a few variables in terms of which the two are consistently distinguished. Development elites stress the role of the state in economic planning, they tend to be utopian, in Mannheim's (1936) sense of this word; they have plans and visions according to which they seek to mobilize national resources and people for national aims; finally, in attacking dependence elites with strong external ties, they incorporate and use certain segments of the masses, in turn important participants in the drama of change. Leaders of the French Revolution constituted one unusually forceful example of a development elite; the Bolsheviks were another. Less forceful examples would be the nationalist leaders in control of many societies in the last quarter of the nineteenth century. A dependence elite is ideological rather than utopian

(in Mannheim's sense); it is reactive, quick to rationalize its class interests, but not to take the initiative. In keeping with this, it places more emphasis on markets than on the state and responds to the pressure of the masses in piecemeal fashion when it becomes necessary to do so. The masses are a source of wealth or trouble; they are not an instrument of policy.

Since we so often hear the phrase 'developing nation' or 'underdeveloped nation', we tend to associate development with the nation-state, and a national elite. Consonant with our earlier argument that the subnational region may be a useful unit of analysis, we would argue that regions may generate development or dependence elites; although we would not expect a regional development elite to remain viable in the long run, if it were subordinate to an elite at the national level and could not command resources and markets in a larger and more varied domain. A good example of a regional development elite in the Western Mediterranean is the Catalan *haute bourgeoisie* of the nineteenth and early twentieth century. This social class, which consisted of about thirty large families, attempted to create a Catalan industrial revolution, with some initial success particularly in Barcelona. It met, however, with fierce opposition from the Spanish state, dominated by agrarian interests from the South and center of the nation. These interests acted in concert with England to dampen the fires of development, not only in Catalonia, but in the Basque country as well (Vicens Vives, 1959). The battle with the state focused on free trade, with the state supporting this policy and the Catalans arguing for protective tariffs. Failing to gain an advantage over foreign importers, the Catalan bourgeoisie began to politicize the struggle by fomenting an ideology of nationalism in its own region, holding out the possibility of an autonomous Catalonia to the Catalans, all of whom suffered in one way or another from the excesses of the Spanish state—taxes, loss of markets through idiotic government policies, conscription to fight unpopular wars, and so on (Brenan, 1964; Trueta Raspall, 1946; Vicens Vives, 1959). In many ways, the Spanish Civil War, which found the catalans on the side of the republic, represented a conflict between modernizing dependence elites, ensconced in the South and Center, and development elites in the North.

The Civil War in Spain ended in the dominance of another kind of development elite, one which has had to compromise at many points with the utopia of complete withdrawal from the West, but one which has nonetheless launched a modest industrial advance in Spain. As this elite is based in Madrid, not Catalonia, it is not surprising that we note change in the Catalan bourgeoisie since the war. It no longer seeks autonomy from the central government. In fact, it encourages quite the opposite relationship. Members of this elite now receive credit from the government, but they do not set the terms of this credit, and have some difficulty even in lobbying effectively for these benefits. The bourgeoisie has abandoned its utopian developmental goals of the past century, and has lost all real initiative. Once the originator of separatist and nationalist ideals, it is now notoriously apolitical. Catalan nationalism is now the political province of the regional *petit bourgeoisie* (Hansen, 1969).

In Western Sicily's history there is no development elite comparable to the *haute bourgeoisie* of Catalonia; this is consistent with the less urban and less autonomous past of the region. In the past, a dependence elite of *latifondisti* wielded enormous power and survived virtually unchallenged until, in the nineteenth century, Sicilian wheat began declining on world markets. In the nineteenth and early twentieth century when Catalonia was developing, Sicilian industries entered a period of marked decline, except when they were salvaged by foreign capital. Many small industries were ruined after the unification of Italy in 1860 which paved the way for the industrial development of the North (Mack Smith, 1968:445-53; Rochefort, 1961:224-39). During the first phase of that development, in the last quarter of the nineteenth century, there were significant changes in the South and Sicily, noticeable especially in the rise of a new class of rural-based entrepreneurs, strong enough to acquire landed estates, infiltrate (but not overthrow) the aristocracy, and control the interior towns. In the mid-1970's, this class gave its support to the Italian state in exchange for a protective tariff on wheat and began investing capital in a transformation of the milling process. The new steam and gas powered mills were, however, owned in part by North Italian interests (Ciaccio, 1900:93-4), and the new class, as committed as the aristocracy to the latifundium, functioned strictly as a dependence elite, subordinate to North Italian metropolitan expansion. In a society so heavily dominated by dependence elites, development elites did not form, unless one can count a tiny urban intelligentsia, coopted by those who owned or controlled land and who alone could 'make' elections, or an even smaller nucleus of socialists, definitively repressed in the 1890s for organizing strikes.

In the postwar period, there has been no tariff protecting a Sicilian product nor, with the possible exception of citrus fruits, have foreign markets sought the island's resources with much consistency. (Migrant labor is an exception of a peculiar kind.) As a result, the island now has no single clearly identifiable elite. The dominant strata include landowners and professionals as before but these groups have widened substantially to include functionaries of all political parties and a rapidly expanding category of paraprofessionals from artisan and peasant background. Again we note a contrast with Catalonia, a region with resources and products still in demand, and in which it is possible to delinate clearly the outlines of the regional elite.

Our brief sketches of Catalonia and Sicily suggest the basis for a typology of growth processes and possible outcomes which could, eventually, encompass a wide range of societies. This basis focuses on elite structures. First there are societies—the United States, Western Europe, Japan and the Soviet Union—have in common a sufficiently autonomous past so that dependence elites never enjoyed the monopoly on power which was enjoyed, for example, by Sicilian *latifondisti*. As Gunder Frank points out, none was deeply colonized by an industrial power (1969:56). The growth careers of these societies are, however, quite different, and a good typology would want to clarify why development in one case required 'socialism in one country', in another case facism and war, in a third a national mobilization considerably less 'total'. We think the critical variables here are timing, and internal strength and locus of dependence elites, although to explore these variables is beyond our present purpose.

With advances in industrial technology, with the increased consolidation of world markets in a world commercial system, and with the rise of multinational corporations, development becomes ever more difficult to achieve. Many societies today, most of them ex-colonies of the postindustrial period, have supported the rise of articulate development elites. Often these societies do not have viable dependence elites. Neither of these situations, however, guarantees development. The necessity in late development for a rapid accumulation of substantial capital resources makes it extremely difficult for contemporary backward nations to escape the webs of dominance surrounding both eastern and western centers of industrial and commercial power. Third World governments whose nationalist leaders have promulgated policies of withdrawal in the interest of development have in many instances been forced to reverse themselves, denationalizing existing industrial establishments, and inviting foreign capital to return. Their elites (would-be development elites) are in a losing race with time as the population they govern finds it increasingly unattractive, and perhaps intolerable, to support the sacrifices required for development. Under these conditions the alternative of modernization becomes increasingly more attractive. Popular demand continues to grow for the ever more familiar consumer goods which are peddled by the West. Imposing a 'Stalinist phase' becomes logistically, organizationally and perhaps morally less feasible with every passing year (Keyfitz, 1965).

A third possibility, represented in some growth phases of the societies in group one, but also in certain other societies which have not developed, is that dependence and development elites are nearly equipotential; neither gains undisputed hegemony. It occurs to us that fascism and military dictatorships may express a high level of contradiction, within a society, between the modernizing and developing alternatives. This contradiction seems especially pronounced in regions peripheral to, but not remote from, the original industrial core—regions penetrated by expanding markets well before the nineteenth century.

Finally, there are societies in which modernization is the dominant mode of change, and though there may be a succession of elites, they are all dependence elites, competing for power which originates elsewhere. These elites may be more or less clearly defined, depending on what the region has to offer external power holders. In regions such as Western Sicily and Catalonia a rapid increase in purchasing power has resulted in an equally rapid extension of entrepreneurial activities. At the same time, however, it has channeled the energies and resources of the most dynamic elements of the bourgeoisie into nonproductive (albeit profitable) ventures, thus diminishing the prospect of long-term substructural growth and eventual autonomy. One might, therefore, suggest that under conditions of modernization, the more entrepreneurs there are, the lower the likelihood of development. Furthermore, the same conditions which give rise to feverish entrepreneurial activity also generate noncorporate groups which play a critical role in political and economic organization. We would argue that noncorporate organization in these societies represents an 'outcome' and not a stage in the 'development' of bureaucracy and industry.

At this point we can offer no very complete taxonomy of growth careers and outcomes to replace the bankrupt 'traditional to modern' continuum. The industrial revolution will ultimately 'touch' all parts of the now underdeveloped world, bringing with it all sorts of 'modernizing' influences and many attempts at withdrawal and development; but only the most naive optimist can assume that substructural development is ineluctable in these places. The dominance of American and Soviet military, economic and political forces over most of the Third World creates forbidding obstacles to withdrawal and development. Yet the process of modernization is threatened by economic depression at the center as industrial metropolises overextend their hegemony in competition with each other. In other words, we cannot be sanguine about the prospects for either modernization or development, barring some very significant rearrangements in the relations which currently exist between rich and poor parts of the world.

BIBLIOGRAPHY

Alongi, G. (1886), *La Maffia, Studio sulle Classi Pericolose Della Sicilia*. Firenze: Fratelli Bocca.

Banfield, E. C. (1958), *The Moral Basis of a Backward Society*. Glencoe: The Free Press.

Barnes, J. A. (1968), 'Networks and Political Processes'. Pp. 107-30 in Marc J. Swartz (ed.), *Local Level Politics*. Chicago: Aldine.

Bendix, R. (1967), 'Tradition and Modernity Reconsidered'. *Comparative Studies in Society and History*, 9:292-347.

Boissevain, Jeremy (1968), *Networks, Brokers and Quasi-groups: Some Thoughts on the Place of Nongroups in the Social Sciences*. Unpublished mimeograph.

Brenan, G. (1964), *The Spanish Laybrinth*. Boston: Cambridge University Press.

Campbell, J. K. (1964), *Honour, Family and Patronage: A Study of Institutions and Moral Values in a Greek Mountain Community*. Oxford: Clarendon Press.

Ciaccio, Can. Mario (1900), *Sciacca: Notizie Storich e Documenti*. (*Volume Primo*.) Sciacca: Tipografia Bondoniana (dei Fratelli Bojuso).

Davis, J. (1969), 'Honour and Politics in Pisticci'. Pp. 69-81 in *Proceedings of the Royal Anthropological Institute of Great Britain and Ireland, 1969*.

Dore, Ronald P. (1969), 'Making Sense of History', *European Journal of Sociology*, 10:295-305.

Etzioni, Amitai (1963), *The Active Society*. New York: The Free Press.

Franchetti, L. (1925), *Condizioni Politiche e Amministrative della Sicilia*. Firenze: Vallecchi Editore.

PART VIII

Appendix

POLITICAL CLIENTELISM:
A Bibliographical Essay

JAMES C. SCOTT

As THIS VOLUME attests, the study of clientelism has been the product of anthropologists, historians, sociologists, and political scientists who, notwithstanding their collective achievements, have often worked in ignorance of one another. The purpose of this bibliographical essay is to help put them back in touch. In particular, it should acquaint area specialists with the theoretical underpinnings of clientelism and with comparable work undertaken elsewhere.

Given the geometrical growth rate of relevant literature, we make no effort to be comprehensive or to suit all tastes. Four major considerations have guided our selection of material. First, we have included, to our knowledge, all the major conceptual analyses of clientelism and patron-client relations as well as the seminal case studies in which the concept was first elaborated. Second, we have tried to take note of the most important contributions to analytical fields such as exchange theory, network analysis, and game theory which might provide the basis for the theoretical development of clientelsim. Beyond clientelism *per se*, we have included a fair sampling of the literature dealing with such closely allied topics as factionalism, machine politics, feudalism, corruption, populism, fic-

tive kinship, and brokerage. As a final consideration, we have noted a large number of case studies of clientelist forms and dynamics in different world regions. Some regions, such as Latin America, Southeast Asia, and Southern Europe, will seem heavily overrepresented here owing both to the prevalence of patron-client structures in these areas and to the vagaries of ethnographic research.

I. CLIENTELISM AS A STRUCTURE AND CONCEPT

Aside from the selections in Part II of this reader, there are a number of notable attempts to define and develop the concept of clientelism. A brief introduction to the term and its usage is Anthony Hall, "Patron-Client Relations," *Journal of Peasant Studies*, I:4 (1974), also reprinted in this volume. For five notable attempts to define and clarify patron-client analysis, see: Robert R. Kaufman, "The Patron-Client Concept and Macro-Politics," *Comparative Studies in Society and History*, 16:3 (June, 1974); René Lemarchand and Keith Legg, "Political Clientelism and Development: A Preliminary Analysis," *Comparative Politics*, 4:2 (January,

1972); Jeremy Boissevain, "Patrons as Brokers," *Sociologische Gids*, 16:6 (November-December, 1969); Andrew J. Nathan, "Clientelism in Politics," a paper prepared for the Columbia University Seminar on the State, October 30, 1972; and, particularly, Luigi Graziano, "A Conceptual Framework for the Study of Clientelism," to appear in Graziano, ed., *Il Clientismo Politico* (Milan, 1975).

Much of the conceptual development of clientelism can also be traced in a series of ethnographic case studies. Among the best known are the community studies by Eric R. Wolf and Sidney Mintz in Julian Steward, *et al.*, *The People of Puerto Rico* (Urbana, Illinois, 1956); and a simultaneous article by Eric Wolf, "Aspects of Group Relations in a Complex Society: Mexico," *American Anthropologist*, 58 (1956). The function and dynamics of patron-client relations are also carefully depicted in F. G. Bailey's study of an Indian state, *Politics and Social Change in Orissa in 1959* (Berkeley, 1963) and in Michael Kenny's "Patterns of Patronage in Spain," *Anthropological Quarterly*, 33 (January, 1960). Two fine studies of patronage in Sicily, the *locus classicus* of personal followings, are Alex Weingrod's "Patrons, Patronage, and Political Parties," *Comparative Studies in Society and History*, 19 (July, 1968), and Jeremy Boissevain's "Patronage in Sicily," *Man*, 1:1 (March, 1966). See also Boissevain's more recent valuable discussion of patronage and related concepts in his *Friends of Friends: Networks, Manipulators, and Coalitions* (Oxford, 1974). Finally, the relationship between forms of clientelism and systems of land tenure and labor organization is perceptively analyzed in Adrian C. Mayer, "Patrons and Brokers: Rural Leadership in Four Overseas Indian Communities," in Maurice Freedman, ed., *Social Organization: Essays Presented to Raymond Firth* (London, 1967).

Clientelism is distinguished from other forms of leadership and social structure in two excellent general studies by well-known anthropologists. F. G. Bailey's *Stratagems and Spoils* (New York, 1969) emphasizes the various reward structures that hold "teams" of political actors together while Frederik Barth, "Models of Social Organization," Royal Anthropological Institute, Occasional Paper No. 2 (1966) focuses on the distribution of power, status, and economic resources.

A valuable collection of articles on clientelism in Latin America is Arnold Strickon and Sidney M. Greenfield, eds., *Structure and Process in Latin America: Patronage, Client-*

age and Power Systems (Albuquerque, 1972). It includes articles on Argentina, Brazil, Bolivia, Colombia, Dominican Republic and deals with both clientelism between states and the absence of clientelism. The editors' introduction is a useful guide to the literature and the bibliography is extensive. For those interested in the transformation of clientelist relations in the past few decades, a forthcoming collection of original articles edited by Ernest Gellner and John Waterbury entitled *Changing Forms of Patronage in the Mediterranean* should be particularly valuable. Despite its regional focus, it provides a guide to the growing importance of the state in distributing resources and organizing clienteles. Marc J. Swartz, ed., *Local-Level Politics* (Chicago, 1968), although not explicitly focused on patron-client relations, contains much of the best analytical and case material on the subject by anthropologists.

As a distinctive structure of action, patron-client networks are often compared to corporate or categorical groups. Carl Landé's article in Part II of this volume helps to systematize this comparison. Mancur Olson Jr.'s *The Logic of Collective Action* (Cambridge, Massachusetts, 1965) is an outstanding analysis of how non-clientelist interest groups also provide reward structures which make participation rational.

The term "patrimonialism" as used by Max Weber to denote traditional forms of authority with full *personal* powers, is closely associated with patron-client relations. For Weber's discussion of patrimonial authority, see Talcott Parsons, ed., *Max Weber, The Theory of Social and Economic Organization* (New York, 1947), pp. 347 *et seq*. Suggestive applications of the term to politics in the third world may be found in Guenther Roth's "Personal Rulership, Patrimonialism and Empire-Building in the New States," *World Politics*, XX:2 (1968), and Gerald A. Heeger, *The Politics of Underdevelopment* (New York, 1974), especially chapters 2 and 3.

At least one enterprising attempt has been made to apply patron-client analysis to politics in advanced industrial nations: see Keith Legg, "Interpersonal Relationships and Comparative Politics: Political Clientelism in Industrial Society," *Politics* (Sidney), 7 (May, 1972).

Notable Case Studies

Case studies of clientelist structures abound. A number of those studies, however, merit special mention because of their theoretical or methodological contribution to the analysis of clientelism or because of their rich and suggestive detail. A classic ethnographic study is Frederik Barth's *Political Leadership Among the Swat Pathans*, London School of Economics Monographs in Social Anthropology, No. 19 (London, 1965) which analyzes the dynamics of leadership among landowners and "saints" in a mountainous area of what is now Pakistan.

For Northern Europe, Sir Lewis Namier's *The Structure of Politics at the Accession of George III* (New York, 1957) is a detailed, standard study of family-based factional alliances in eighteenth-century England which should be read in conjunction with Robert Walcott, Jr.'s *English Politics in the Early Eighteenth Century* (Cambridge, Massachusetts, 1956). The analysis by Mart Bax, *Harpstrings and Confessions: An Anthropological Study of Politics in Northern Ireland* (Oxford, 1974) is a fine study of clientele-building in contemporary politics. In addition to the literature on feudal France, Charles Tilly's study of the counterrevolution in *The Vendée* (Cambridge, Massachusetts, 1964) makes excellent use of sociological and economic data to analyze the patronly leadership of the Vendée peasantry by the local clergy.

The case material on Southern Europe is especially rich. Three studies of rural Spain merit particular mention: Michael Kenny, *A Spanish Tapestry: Town and Country in Castile* (Bloomington, 1961); J. A. Pitt-Rivers, *The People of the Sierra* (Chicago, 1961); and Edward Malefakis, *Agrarian Reform and Peasant Revolution in Spain* (New Haven, 1970). The last two are especially valuable in explaining changes in forms of patronage and in relating clientelism to economic structure. Sidney Tarrow's brilliant study of how clientelist patterns have infused the Communist Party in Southern Italy, *Peasant Communism in Southern Italy* (New Haven, 1967), is also a valuable analysis of modern forms of political clientelism.

Specialists on Africa should consult Lloyd Fallers, *Bantu Bureaucracy* (Cambridge, 1958), for a useful discussion of the shift from kinship to clientelism in rural Ugandan politics. René Lemarchand's *Rwanda and Burundi* (London, 1970) contains the best analysis of the breakdown of feudal clientelism among the Tutsi and the Hutu. For electoral clientelism in post-independence Africa, Colin Leys, *Politicians and Policies: An Essay on Politics in Acholi, Uganda, 1962-1965* (Nairobi, 1967), and Aristide R. Zolberg, *One-Party Government in the Ivory Coast* (Princeton, 1969), are perhaps the most valuable.

Two notable ethnographies of tribal groups in Southeast Asia, E. R. Leach, *Political Systems of Highland Burma: A Study of Kachin Social Structure* (Boston, 1965), and Roy Franklin Barton, *The Kalingas: Their Institutions and Custom Law* (Chicago, 1949), contain excellent discussions of the nature of personal followings in stateless societies. Akin Rabibhadana's *The Organization of Thai Society in the Early Bangkok Period: 1782-1872* (Ithaca, 1969) is the best description of institutionalized clientelism in a traditional Southeast Asian kingdom.

The role of personal alliances in post-independence Southeast Asian politics has been the subject of a number of fine monographs: David Wilson's *Politics in Thailand* (Ithaca, 1962) is an analysis of clientelist patterns among Thai civilian and military elites while Fred W. Riggs, in *Thailand: The Modernization of a Bureaucratic Polity* (Honolulu, 1966), attempts a more detailed empirical analysis of clique structures and factional alignments among the political and commercial elites. The best overall description and analysis of Philippine electoral politics in clientelist terms is Carl Landé's *Leaders, Factions, and Parties: The Structure of Philippine Politics* (New Haven, 1964). For a sophisticated account of the relationship between cultural cleavage and the pattern of personal followings, see Clifford Geertz, *The Social History of an Indonesian Town* (Cambridge, Mass., 1965).

Anthropological Studies of Leadership and Peasant Society

A number of general works on social organization an leadership by anthropologists are useful guides to the pattern of personal alliances found in small scale societies and their relation to both culture and economic life. See especially, Georges Balandier, *Political Anthropology*, translated by A. M. Sheridan Smith (New York, 1970), for an insightful discussion of reciprocity and leadership in traditional society. Valuable social analyses of personal followings are found as well in Frederik Barth, "Models of Social Organization," Royal Anthropological Institute, Occasional Paper No. 2 (1966), and Raymond Firth, *Elements of Social Organization* (Boston, 1963). Herbert Lewis' *Leaders and Followers: Some Anthropological Perspectives*, Addison-Wesley Modules in Anthropology (Reading, Mass., 1974), contains a thoughtful discussion of the field of leadership in anthropological theory as well as an excellent bibliography. Finally, Frederick G. Bailey's *Stratagems and Spoils* (New York, 1969) and Jeremy Boissevain's *Friends of Friends* (Oxford, 1974) should be mentioned again in this context for their analyses of leadership structures and rewards.

Understanding the origin and nature of clientelism as well as alternative models of social organization in rural areas requires a basic knowledge of rural sociology. The most elaborate collection on this subject, which brings together classic work in a host of related fields is Pitrim A. Sorokin, *et al.*, *A Systematic Source Book in Rural Sociology*, Volumes I and II (Minneapolis, 1930). Charles Loomis and J. Allen Beegle, *Rural Social Systems* (New York, 1950), provide a network analysis of rural communities while Gerhard E. Lenski, *Power and Privilege: A Theory of Social Stratification* (New York, 1966), develops a theory of distribution and class structure as it applies to peasant societies.

A great deal of both the theoretical work and case material on clientelism and agrarian social organization may be found in two excellent collections: Jack M. Potter, May N. Diaz, and George M. Foster, *Peasant Society: A Reader* (Boston, 1967), and Marc J. Swartz, *Local-Level Politics* (Chicago, 1968). An impressive effort to synthesize existing knowledge is Eric Wolf's *Peasants* (Englewood Cliffs, N.J., 1966).

The development of clientelism cannot be understood apart from the major changes in peasant society arising from modernization, the commercialization of agriculture, and the growth of the state. The analysis of the changing relationship of the peasant to the wider society in George Dalton, "Peasantries in Anthropology and History," *Current Anthropology*, 13: 3, 4 (June-October, 1972), raises most of the relevant issues. Everett M. Rogers, *Modernization among Peasants: The Impact of Communication* (New York, 1969), deals with many of the same issues though it is very much tied to psychological theories of modernization.

The role of agrarian commercialization is particularly important in accounting for the deterioration of patron-client bonds and peasant mobilization. Two outstanding attempts to understand peasant revolutions in these terms are Barrington Moore, Jr., *The Social Basis of Dictatorship and Democracy: Lord and Peasant in the Making of the Modern World* (Boston, 1966), and Eric R. Wolf, *Peasant Wars of the Twentieth Century* (New York, 1969). Each develops a theory of revolutionary potential which is applied to a series of cases and the bibliographies are excellent guides to the literature. Useful discussions of structural change and peasant mobilization may also be found in Joel M. Halpern,

The Changing Village Community (Englewood Cliffs, N.J., 1967), and Joel Migdal, *Peasants in a Shrinking World: The Socio-Economic Basis of Political Change* (Princeton, forthcoming). Henry Landsberger, in *Latin American Peasant Movements* (Ithaca, 1969), develops a series of hypotheses to explain the emergence and form of peasant mobilization which is followed by a number of excellent case studies. An impressionistic but rich account of an individual peasant's participation in the Mexican Revolution is Oscar Lewis' classic, *Pedro Martinez: A Mexican Peasant and His Family* (New York, 1964), especially Part II.

II. THEORETICAL APPROACHES TO CLIENTELISM

Exchange Theory and Reciprocity

Clientelism may be seen as a special form of exchange relationship between individuals, one relatively more powerful than the other, which serves as the basis for networks of alliance. Long ago, Thomas Hobbes in *Leviathan*, Ch. 10, noted how the provision of scarce services created personal followings and structures of authority. More recently, theories of exchange relations have been developed, largely by sociologists, to explain group formation, cohesion, and leadership. The progenitor of much of this work was Georg Simmel. His analysis of exchange, dominance, reciprocity, and conflict may be found in two volumes: Georg Simmel, *On Individuality and Its Social Forms* (Chicago, 1971), especially pp. 43-140, and Kurt Wolff, *The Sociology of Georg Simmel* (Glencoe, Ill., 1950).

The development of exchange theory as the basic building block of social organization of any kind is largely the work of George Homans and Peter Blau. Their works are enormously helpful in understanding the theoretical underpinnings of clientelism. A brief statement of the notion of exchange and its relation to social theory may be found in George C. Homans, "Social Behavior as Exchange," *American Journal of Sociology*, 63 (1957-58). Homans' major work on the subject is *Social Behavior: Its Elementary Forms* (New York, 1961). Perhaps the most elaborate deductive theory of exchange is Peter Blau's classic, *Exchange and Power in Social Life* (New York, 1964), in which the subjects of reciprocity, power, and legitimacy are treated at great length. The theories of both men are explained and evaluated in an excellent review by D. Heath, "Exchange Theory," *British Journal of Political Science*,

1:1 (January, 1971). Inevitably, the notion of exchange is connected to the moral idea of reciprocity. By far the best analysis of how reciprocity provides the normative basis for exchange and leadership and the maintenance of social systems is Alvin W. Gouldner's "The Norm of Reciprocity: A Preliminary Statement," *American Journal of Sociology*, 25:2 (April, 1960), which is reprinted in this volume. Gouldner has further developed his theory of reciprocity to account for stable patterns of interaction which functional theory alone cannot explain in "Reciprocity and Autonomy in Functional Theory," in *Symposium on Sociological Theory* (Evanston, Illinois, 1959). For an analysis of balance and imbalance in exchange and the distribution between legitimate authority and exploitation, one should consult Richard M. Emerson, "Power-Dependence Relations," *American Journal of Sociology*, 27:1 (February, 1967). John W. Thibaut and Harold H. Kelley, *The Social Psychology of Groups* (New York, 1959), deal at greater length with dyadic structures of reciprocity as the constituent elements of groups and also attempt to show how the norm of reciprocity may be used to distinguish legitimate dependence from exploitation. See also, in this connection, Murray Glanzer and Robert Glaser, "Techniques for the Study of Group Structure and Behavior," *Psychology Bulletin*, 58 (1961).

There have been at least three major efforts to develop and apply exchange theory beyond the original insights of Blau and Homans: Peter Newman, *The Theory of Exchange* (Englewood Cliffs, N.J., 1965), which deals largely with exchange in economics; R. L. Curry, Jr., and L. L. Wade, *A Theory of Political Exchange* (Englewood Cliffs, N.J., 1968); and Sidney Waldman, *Foundations of Political Analysis* (Englewood Cliffs, N.J., 1972). A good guide to the current debate on the value of exchange theory and its relationship to structural-functionalism in particular is provided by a recent issue of *Sociological Inquiry*, 42:3 and 4 (1972). See especially, Sidney R. Waldman, "Exchange Theory and Political Analysis," pp. 101-128; David Easton, "Some Limits of Exchange Theory in Politics," pp. 129-148; and Terry N. Clark, "Structural-Functionalism, Exchange Theory, and the New Political Economy: Institutionalization as a Theoretical Linkage," pp. 275-298. More specifically, the application of exchange theory to the structure and dynamics of political interest groups in Robert H. Salisbury, "An Exchange Theory of Interest Groups," *Midwest Journal of Political Science*, 13:1 (February, 1969), and Mancur Olson, Jr., *The Logic of Collective Action* (Cambridge, Mass., 1965), offer many insights into reward structures and social cohesion.

Aside from the value of sociological theories of exchange for the analysis of patron-client networks, the notion of exchange as used by economists may also contribute to our understanding of how patronage resources are mobilized, traded, and deployed. The most elaborate and suggestive effort to develop a framework of political analysis along these lines is Warren Ilchman and Norman Uphoff, *The Political Economy of Change* (Berkeley, 1969). As a sequel to their highly regarded book, the same authors have collected a large number of policy-oriented articles which demonstrate the value of such metaphors from economics as political investment, savings, rates of exchange, and capital-output ratios. See Ilchman and Uphoff, eds., *The Political Economy of Development* (Berkeley, 1972). Finally, there is a recent enterprising attempt to apply exchange theory to the process of revolution by Jeffrey Race, "Toward an Exchange Theory of Revolution: Southern Viet Nam and Northern Thailand," ms. (1973).

The concept of reciprocity as the underlying principle of social behavior and social structure in traditional societies extends back at least as far as Bronislaw Malinowski's *Argonauts of the Western Pacific* (London, 1922), and his subsequent *Crime and Custom* (London, 1926), which described Triobrland society in terms of "well-balanced chains of reciprocal services." The classic application of exchange to kinship structures is Claude Levi-Strauss' description of the exchange of women in *Les Structures élémentaires de la parenté* (Paris, 1949), English translation, Boston, 1969. A seminal anthropological analysis of generosity and reciprocal gift-giving that is of great value in understanding the patterns of cooperation and rewards in patron-client networks is Marcel Mauss, "Essai sur de don," *Année sociologique*, seconde série, 1 (1923-24) and translated by I. Cunnison as *The Gift: Forms and Functions of Exchange in Archaic Societies* (Glencoe, Ill., 1954).

Perhaps the best recent effort to synthesize the existing literature on reciprocity and exchange in traditional settings is Marshall Sahlins' "On the Sociology of Primitive Exchange," in M. Banton, ed., *The Relevance of Models for Social Anthropology* (New York, 1965). Sahlins examines such issues as how forms of reciprocity vary with kinship connections, physical proximity, and status differences as well as providing a superb bibliography of field work bearing on this topic. A summary of this analysis written for nonspecialists may be found in Ch. 4 of Sahlins' *Tribesmen* (Englewood Cliffs, N.J., 1968). A valuable discussion of the differences between traditional exchange and reciprocity on the one hand and impersonal market forms of exchange on the other may be found in Cyril S. Belshaw, *Traditional Exchange and Modern Markets* (Englewood Cliffs, N.J., 1965). The finer-grained anthropological analysis of reciprocity is necessary to distinguish its various forms and content from what is called generally the "norm of reciprocity." Mary N. Hollnsteiner's description of reciprocity patterns among Filipinos, "Reciprocity in the Lowland Philippines," *Philippine Studies*, 9:3 (July, 1961), though only a case study, is probably applicable to many other peasant societies as well.

Bilateral Descent and Social Networks

Much of the early conceptual work on dyadic alliance and clientelism in anthropology grew from the analysis of bilateral descent. Unlike patrilineal or matrilineal societies which tend to structure local society into mutually exclusive clans and lineages, bilateral descent does not create such sharp social boundaries but rather a series of overlapping kindreds which are specific to each individual. The kindred is less of a structural given than a pattern of hand-fashioned dyadic alliances quite similar to patron-client networks. One of the earliest attempts to specify the operating principles of bilateral kindreds was Robert N. Pehrson, "The Bilateral Network of Social Relationships in Könkämä District," *Slavic and Eastern European Series*, Vol. 6 (Bloomington, Ind., 1957). The distinctive social organization of kindreds in Southeast Asia is examined in several important articles collected by George Peter Murdock, *Social Structure in Southeast Asia* (Chicago, 1960).

The student of clientelism and dyadic alliance structures in Latin America, Europe, and Southeast Asia will find the analytical material on personal kindreds a valuable place to begin. Many of the principles at work in structuring the personal kindred seem applicable to strategies of alliance and reciprocity generally in these societies. See, in particular, William Davenport, "Non-unilinear Descent and Descent Groups," *American Anthropologist*, 64:4 (1959); J. D. Freeman, "On the Concept of the Kindred," *Journal of the Royal Anthropological Institute of Great Britain and Northern Ireland*, 91:2 (1961); and W. E. Mitchell, "Theoretical Problems in the Concept of Kindred," *American Anthropologist*, 65 (1963). Despite the fact that bi-

lateral kinship seems to offer a wider scope of choice in social alliances, a number of well-known anthropologists have emphasized the role of rewards and personal choice in structuring active kinship alliances generally. For example, see Rodney Needam, *Structure and Sentiment* (Chicago, 1962); Louis Dumont, "Descent, Filiation, and Affinity," *Man*, 61:11 (1961); E. R. Leach, *Political Systems of Highland Burma* (Boston, 1965); and Raymond Firth, *Elements of Social Organization* (London, 1951), Chs. 1 and 2. For a suggestive comparative analysis of kinship groups and personal alliances in Africa and Southeast Asia, see Carl H. Landé, "Kinship and Politics in Pre-modern and Non-Western Societies," in John .T. McAlister, Jr., *Southeast Asia: The Politics of National Integration* (New York, 1973).

The analysis of kindreds as networks of personal allliances may be expanded to cover networks of alliance among non-kin. One of the clearest formulations of network analysis and the dynamics of personal followings in terms of what are called "action sets" is J. A. Barnes, "Networks and Political Process," in J. C. Mitchell, ed., *Social Networks in Urban Situations* (Manchester, 1969). Barnes's "Class and Committees in a Norwegian Island Parish," *Human Relations*, 7 (1954), distinguishes the close-knit "action-sets" typical of traditional society with the more atomized personal networks of industrial society. The principles of network formation and action are also analyzed in Otto Blehr, "Action Groups in a Society with Bilateral Kinship: A Case Study of the Faroe Islands," *Ethnology*, 3:3 (July, 1963).

Both anthropologists and sociologists have sought to develop the analysis of personal networks in directions that are applicable to the study of clientelism. A special issue of the *Canadian Review of Sociology and Anthropology* (1970) is devoted to this topic. Other valuable theoretical discussions are Edward J. Jay, "The Concepts of 'Field' and 'Network' in Anthropological Research," *Man*, 64:177 (1964), which contains a cogent review of the literature; Lawrence W. Crissman, "On Networks," *Cornell Journal of Social Relations*, 4:1 (1969); and Norman E. Whitten, Jr., "Network Analysis in Equador and Nova Scotia: Some Critical Remarks," *Canadian Journal of Sociology and Anthropology* (1974).

Network analysis has proven a valuable tool for understanding the informal personal alliances that structure the social environment of urban populations, particularly the urban poor. In this context, see E. Bott's Pine study, *Family and Social Network* (London, 1957), and the collection assembled by J. Clyde Mitchell, ed., *Social Networks in Urban Situations* (Manchester, 1969). The classic analysis of leadership among urban gangs in America is William Foote Whyte's *Street Corner Society: The Social Structure of an Italian Slum* (Chicago, 1955), Part II. Whyte emphasizes the dyadic bonds of mutual favors as the structural principle of gang formation and cohesion.

Any dynamic model of clientelism must necessarily address the issue of how the forms of personal alliances shift under the impact of large scale social and economic changes. Godfrey and Monica Wilson's early study of East Africa, *An Analysis of Social Change* (Cambridge, 1945), employs network analysis to account for the expansion of the scale of social relations in the colonial period. Their analysis is highly suggestive for any dynamic theory of social dependence. Other applications of network analysis to urban, African social structure include: A. L. Epstein, "The Network and Urban Social Organization," *Rhodes-Livingston Journal,* 29 (1961); P. C. W. Gutkind, "Network Analysis and Urbanism in Africa: The Use of Micro and Macro Analysis," *Canadian Review of Sociology and Anthropology*, 2:3 (1965); Gutkind, "African Urbanism: Mobility and Social Network," *International Journal of Comparative Sociology*, 6:1 (1965); and David Parkin, *Neighbors and Nationals in an African City Ward* (Berkeley, 1969) which compares social networks by ethnic group and over time.

The concept of social network has been employed by anthropologists of Indian civilization to explain social and cultural linkages between the village community and the outside world. Such links are often of a personal and clientelist character and underscore how patron-client networks follow the lines of economic and political power. Two excellent articles on the subject are: Bernard Cohen and Mck. Mariott, "Networks and Centers in the Integration of Indian Civilization," *Journal of Social Research*, 1:1-9 (1958) and Morris Opler, "The Extensions of an Indian Village," *Journal of Asian Studies*, 16:1 (1956). M. N. Srinivas and André Béteille have attempted to explain much of Indian social organization in similar terms in their "Networks in Indian Social Structure," *Man*, 64:212 (1964). For an expressly political application of network to local Indian politics, see Adrian C. Mayer, "System and Network: An Approach to the Study of Political Process in Dewas," in Trilok Madan and Gapala Sarana, eds., *Indian Anthropology* (Bombay, 1962).

G. William Skinner's seminal article, "Marketing and Social Structure in Rural China," Part I, *Journal of Asian Studies*, 24:1 (November, 1964), is a careful and ambitious theoretical attempt to show how hierarchical marketing networks structure the outward linkages of alliances in peasant society. The structural principle of extra-local social ties elaborated for rural China are probably applicable in most peasant societies and form the geographical basis for the integration of patron-client networks.

The sociometry required in mapping out personal alliance systems and patron-client networks is enormously complicated. Mathematical graph theory has been proposed as a possible mapping procedure which will uncover power configurations. Oysten Ore, *The Theory of Graphs* (Providence, 1962) is a general introduction to this methodology. Its possible application to the study of power relations is explained by John R. P. French, Jr., "A Formal Theory of Social Power," *The Psychological Review*, 63 (May, 1956). Finally, A. Bavelas presents a formal mathematical analysis of reciprocity and "power balancing" that is applicable to clientelism in his "A Mathematical Model for Group Structure," *Applied Anthropology*, 7 (Summer, 1948).

Game Theory

The nature of the bargaining and exchange between partners in a dyadic alliance may be analyzed in terms of game theory as well. A fine introduction to the conceptual basis of game theory is Anatol Rapoport, *Two-Person Games* (Ann Arbor, 1966). For specifically political applications of game theory to coalition formation and factional competition in elections, see William Riker, *The Theory of Political Coalitions* (New Haven, 1962).

Traditional Economies

A central issue in economic anthropology concerns the extent to which the concepts of capitalist economic analysis, e.g., price, supply, demand, marginal costs, are applicable to traditional economic relations. Those who argue that the operation of traditional economies are *sui generis* and cannot be understood in modern market terms stress the importance of reciprocity, kinship, status, and custom in determining production, price, and exchange. For exponents of this analytic tradition, economic exchange cannot be understood apart from networks of personal alliances. Inasmuch as clientelism involves the exchange of goods and services between dyadic partners, the economic analysis of reciprocity and distribution in traditional societies provides potential theoretical basis for the analysis of dyadic coalitions. The pioneer in this field is Karl Polanyi whose book, *The Great Transformation* (Boston, 1957) represents a brilliant analysis of the contrasts between the pre-capitalist market and the "instituted" market as developed in nineteenth-century England. This theme is pursued in a stimulating series of essays on the nature of markets in traditional states in Karl Polanyi, Conrad Arensberg, and Harry Pearson, eds., *Trade and Market in the Early Empires* (Glencoe, Ill., 1957). The leading heir of this tradition is George Dalton who has collected and edited Polanyi's major writings in *Primitive, Archaic, and Modern Economies: Essays of Karl Polanyi* (Boston, 1971). See also Dalton's *Economic Anthropology and Development: Essays on Tribal and Peasant Economies* (New York, 1971), and his edited collection of articles, *Tribal and Peasant Economies: Readings in Economic Anthropology* (Garden City, N.Y., 1967), both of which are valuable for the economic analysis of clientelism. An excellent collection which brings together the early applications of "economizing" to traditional society, the "substantivist" positions of Polanyi and others, and the "formalist" critiques of the substantivist view is Edward E. LeClair, Jr., and Harold K. Schneider, eds., *Economic Anthropology: Readings in Theory and Analysis* (New York, 1968).

The substantivist position of traditional economic exchange is also supported by the work of Marcel Mauss, *The Gift*, translated by I. Cunnison (Glencoe, Ill., 1954), and Marshall Sahlins, "On the Sociology of Primitive Exchange," in Michael Benton, ed., *The Relevance of Models for Social Anthropology* (London, 1965), both cited earlier. For two arguments which take a middle position on this issue, see Melville J. Herskovits, *Economic Anthropology: The Economic Life of Primitive Peoples* (New York, 1965), first published in 1940, especially Part III and Raymond Firth and B. S. Yamey, eds., *Capital, Saving, and Credit in Peasant Societies* (London, 1964).

Finally, there are a number of studies of small scale trade in the Third World which emphasize the role of personal dyadic alliances in structuring the relationships between buyers and sellers. Two of the best are Sidney W. Mintz, "Pratik: Haitian Personal Economic Relationships," *Proceedings of the 1961 Annual Spring Meeting of the American Ethnological Society* (Seattle, 1961), and James N. Anderson, "Buy-and-Sell and Economic Personalism: Foundations for Philippine Entrepreneurship," *Asian Survey*, 9:9 (September, 1969).

III. RELATED CONCEPTUAL FIELDS

Fictive Kinship

In many societies the bond between a patron and his client may take the form of ritualized kinship thereby reinforcing their mutual obligations. This is particularly the case in the Catholic areas of Southern Europe and Latin America where the role of the godfather is institutionalized. For two general discussions of fictive kinship together with valuable bibliographies, see Julian Pitt-Rivers, "Pseudo-kinship," *Encyclopaedia of the Social Sciences*, Vol. 8, pp. 408-413, and S. N. Eisenstadt, "Ritualized Personal Relations," *Man*, 56 (1956). An excellent analysis of the forms and functions of ritual kinship historically and their relationship to forms of land tenure may be found in Sidney W. Mintz and Eric R. Wolf, "An Analysis of Ritual Co-Parenthood (Compadrazgo), *Southwestern Journal of Anthropology*, 6 (Winter, 1950). This discussion provides a valuable guide to historical and case-study material on the subject. The relationship between ritual kinship and religious groups within the Hispanic tradition is insightfully explored by George Foster, "Confradia and Compradrazgo in Spain and South America," *Southwestern Journal of Anthropology*, 9 (1953).

It would be impossible to list the many variants of this institution in other cultural milieus, but a few such case studies deserve mention. For the *oyabun-kobun* variant in Japan, see Iwao Ishino, "The Oyabun-Kobun: A Japanese Ritual Kinship Institution," *American Anthropologist*, 55 (1953), and Nobutaka Ike, *Japanese Politics: An Introductory Survey* (New York, 1957), especially Ch. 2. For comparable patterns in India, see Stanley H. Freed, "Fictive Kinship in a North Indian Village," *Ethnology*, 2 (1963).

Feudalism

The tie between lord and vassal or between nobles and serfs is, for Western sociologists, the historical prototype of patron-client relations. Students of contemporary forms of clientelism will find the rich scholarly literature on feudalism of great value for understanding the origin, principles, and dynamics of patron-client structures. As one might suspect, Karl Marx had a great deal to say about feudalism as a form of economic organization. *Capital*, Vol. I, translated by Eden and Cedar Paul (New York, 1930), pp. 43-59, contains an insightful discussion of feudal reciprocity as does *Pre-Capitalist Economic Formations*, translated by Jack Cohen with an introduction by E. Hobsbawm (London, 1964). Three other fundamental sources for the study of feudal social organization are Max Weber's discussion of patrimonialism in *The Theory of Social and Economic Organization*, Talcott Parsons, ed. (Glencoe, Ill., 1947); Joseph Schumpeter, *Social Classes in an Ethnically Homogeneous Environment*, translated by Heinz Norden (New York, 1955), pp. 101-168; and Karl Polanyi, *The Great Transformation* (Boston, 1957).

An important comparative study of feudal institutions in Western Europe, Japan, India, China, Russia, and ancient Mesopotamia, Iran, Egypt, and Byzantium is Rushton Coulborn, ed., *Feudalism in History* (Princeton, 1956). For Western Europe, one can not do better than Marc Bloch's magnificent *Feudal Society*, 2 vols., translated by L. A. Manyon (Chicago, 1971), which traces the development of feudalism and analyzes the forms of personal dependence it created. The relationship between feudal society and the growth of the state is examined in Roland Mousnier's controversial *Peasant Uprisings in Seventeenth Century France, Russia, and China*, translated by Brian Pearce (New York, 1970). Finally, the role of the social obligations of elites as implied by the feudal ethos is perceptively explained by E. P. Thompson in "The Moral Economy of the English Crowd in the Eighteenth Century," *Past and Present*, No. 50 (February, 1971).

There is an excellent and growing literature on African forms of feudalism. In particular, the feudal organization of the Tutsi lords and Hutu serfs in Rwanda has been analyzed in some detail by Jacques J. Maquet, *The Premise of Inequality in Rwanda* (London, 1961); René Lemarchand, "Les Relations de clientèle comme moyen de contestation: le cas du Rwanda," *Civilisations*, 28:4 (1968); and Lemarchand *Rwanda and Burundi* (London, 1970). For an attempt to explain African feudal systems on the basis of the level of economic activity and cultural integration, see Jacques J. Maquet, "Une hypothèse pour l'étude des féodalités africaines," *Cahiers d'études africaines*, 6 (1961).

Three additional noteworthy studies of African feudal structures are M. G. Smith's study of the Hausa kingdoms of Northern Nigeria, *Government in Zazzau* (London, 1960); Jacques Lombard, "La Vie politique dans une ancienne société de type féodal: Les Bariba du Dahom-

ey," *Cahiers d'études africaines*, 1:5 (1960); and Edward I. Steinhart, "Vassal and Fief in Three Interlacustrine Kingdoms," *Cahiers d'études africaines*, 7:4 (1967).

Religious Clientelsim

The relationship between a "saint," prophet, or religious teacher and his followers may often be viewed as a patron-client relationship despite the fact that grace and divine inspiration supplement the material resources of the patron. In some societies, networks of religious patronage may constitute a "shadow" social structure in potential conflict with secular forms of authority. In others, religious clientelism may become the predominant mode of authority. Perhaps the best study of religious patronage and its relation to secular authority is Frederik Barth, *Political Leadership Among the Swat Pathans* (London, 1965).

The unique and independent role of religious teachers in the Islamic tradition appears to particularly favor the growth of religious clientelism in the Muslim world. For two studies of the Senegalese Islamic brotherhoods, see Donald Cruise O'Brien, *The Murids of Senegal: The Socioeconomic Structure of an Islamic Order*, Ph.D. (University of London, 1969), and Lucy Behrman, *Muslim Brotherhoods and Politics in Senegal* (Cambridge, Mass., 1970). The role of *tarekats*, or brotherhoods, in the rebellion in West Java in Indonesia near the turn of the century is perceptively examined by Sartono Kartodirdjo in *The Peasants' Revolt of Banten in 1888* (The Hague, 1966). More recently, the importance of patron-client bonds in a modern Indonesian Islamic revolt has been carefully analyzed by Carl D. Jackson, *Traditional Authority and National Integration: The Dar'ul Islam Rebellion in West Java*, Ph.D. (Massachusetts Institute of Technology, 1971). Clifford Geertz has provided a more general assessment of the religious teacher in Javanese culture in "The Changing Role of a Cultural Broker: The Javanese Kijaji," *Comparative Studies in Society and History*, 2 (1960).

Religious patronage in non-Islamic settings is occasionally significant as well, though followings created seem to flow as much from the secular power of the patrons as from their grace. Jeremy Boissevain has traced the growth of clerical and anticlerical factions along these lines in Malta in *Saints and Fireworks: Religion and Politics in Rural Malta* (New York, 1965). The patronage-based authority of the syncretic sects in South Viet Nam, the Hoa Hao and Cao Dai, is described in Frances Hill, "Millenarian Machines in South Vietnam," *Comparative Studies in Society and History*, 13:3 (July, 1971).

Factionalism

It is difficult to separate the literature on factionalism *per se* from the general literature on clientelism for the simple reason that many factions are not much more than loose alliances among patron-client networks. Thus, many of the general works on clienteles cited early in this essay contain valuable discussions of factions. In addition, much of the rich literature on electoral factionalism is listed later in this essay under the heading "elections and clientelism."

A working definition of the term faction—"a conflict group recruited by a leader along diverse principles"—and an analysis of factional shifts in Indian village politics may be found in Ralph Nicholas, "Factions: A Comparative Analysis," in M. Banton, ed., *Political Systems and the Distribution of Power* (London, 1965). F. G. Bailey's "Parapolitical Systems," in Marc Swartz, ed., *Local-Level Politics* (Chicago, 1968), is also a good introduction to the subject in which the rise of factions is seen as evidence that traditional forms of social control are weakening. For another analytical perspective on factions see Norman K. Nicholson, "The Factional Model and the Study of Politics," *Comparative Political Studies*, 5 (Fall, 1972). William Riker's use of game theory to determine the nature of coalition formation and the size of winning coalitions in *The Theory of Political Coalitions* (New Haven, 1955) is also a suggestive methodological approach to factional conflict.

With the exception of Riker, the studies cited above come from students of Indian politics where much of the best work on factionalism has been carried out. Bernard J. Siegel and Alan R. Beals, using Indian village data, have co-authoried two articles which attempt to explain both the origins and development of local factionalism: "Conflict and Factionalist Dispute," *Journal of the Royal Anthropological Society*, 90 (1960), and "Pervasive Factionalism," *American Anthropologist*, 62 (June, 1960). A complementary study by D. F. Miller, "Factions in Indian Village Politics," *Pacific Affairs*, 38:1 (Spring, 1965), analyzes the shift from traditional factions to "machine" factions based more on mobility and material rewards.

One of the finest overall studies of clienteles and factions in Indian politics is Myron Weiner, *Party-Building in a New Nation* (Chicago, 1967) which has several detailed district case studies. At the provincial level there have been

two excellent full-length studies of factionalism: Paul R. Brass, *Factional Politics in an Indian State: The Congress Party in Uttar Pradesh* (Berkeley, 1965), which relates both the form and dynamics of local clientelism to the social and economic ecology of the locality and Mary C. Carras, *The Dynamics of Indian Political Factions: A Study of District Councils in the State of Maharashtra* (Cambridge, 1972), a methodologically sophisticated study of factional development and shifts that emphasizes the role of rational economic calculation. For an explanation of province-wide factionalism linked to a dominant, oligarchic order with few class cleavages, see B. D. Graham, "The Succession of Factional Systems in the Uttar Pradesh Congress Party," in Marc Swartz, ed., *Local-Level Politics* (Chicago, 1968). Two additional theoretically valuable case studies are D. Pocock, "The Basis of Factions in Gujerat," *British Journal of Sociology*, 8 (1957), and Ralph W. Nicholas, "Village Factions and Political Parties in Rural West Bengal," *Journal of Commonwealth Studies*, 2:1 (November, 1963). Finally, a unique comparative study of factional patterns among Indians, both in India and abroad, which focuses especially on plantation workers, is Raymond Firth, "Factions in India and Overseas Dependencies," *British Journal of Sociology*, 8 (1957).

There are a number of case studies of factionalism elsewhere in the world which are particularly noteworthy, either for their rich empirical detail or for their analytical suggestiveness. For village-level politics, see Bernard Gallin, "Political Factionalism and Its Impact on Village Social Organization in Taiwan," in Marc Swartz, ed., *Local-Level Politics* (Chicago, 1968). Gallin is particularly instructive on the impact of new institutions that cut across lineage lines and promote clientelistic competition. Melford E. Spiro, "Factionalism and Politics in Village Burma," in Marc Swartz, ed., *Local-Level Politics* (Chicago, 1968), and Norman B. Schwartz, "Goal Attainment through Factionalism: A Guatemalan Case," *American Anthropologist*, 71:6 (December, 1969) are also particularly valuable. For factionalism among political elites in Italy, Alan Zuckerman's "On the Institutionalization of Political Clienteles: Party Factions and Cabinet Coalitions in Italy," paper presented to the 1973 annual meeting of the American Political Science Association, New Orleans, is an intriguing analysis of the underlying stability of party factions amidst shifting cabinet alignments. For a factional view of the Japan Socialist Party and foreign policy issues, see Chae-jin Lee, "Factional Politics in the

Japan Socialist Party: The Chinese Cultural Revolution Case," *Asian Survey*, 10:3 (March, 1970). The only study, to my knowledge, which analyzes the factional structure of the army in a Third World nation is Ann Gregory, "Factionalism and the Indonesian Army: The New Order," *Journal of Comparative Administration*, 2:3 (November, 1970). Gregory's analysis of the historical and contemporary bases of factionalism in the military is a valuable approach that might be applied to the ruling institution in many Third World countries, not to mention Greece, Portugal, and Spain.

Electoral Clientelism and Machine Politics

There is little doubt that the institution of competitive elections may create new structures of patronage. Where class or ethnic divisions do not dominate the political process, this is especially likely to be the case. Even where ethnic or class cleavage is pronounced, clientelism may nonetheless permeate the formation of coalitions both within and between communal or class formations. In much of Europe, as in the Third World, electoral systems have promoted the growth of new classes of public patrons and brokers, influenced the pattern of public policy, and integrated local clienteles into larger vote-producing coalitions. The structure of parties, shifts in political alignment, and the distribution of political rewards can, in a great many electoral systems, only be explained by reference to clientelism.

Perhaps the best place to begin the study of electoral clientelism is historically, with the development of electoral politics in Western Europe. Two excellent analyses of political clienteles in eighteenth-century England, when suffrage was still sharply limited, are Sir Lewis Namier, *The Structure of Politics at the Accession of George III* (New York, 1957), and Robert Walcott, Jr., *English Politics in the Early Eighteenth Century* (Cambridge, Mass., 1956). The transformation of clienteles and the growing use of material incentives to build political followings in nineteenth-century post-Reform Law England may be followed in William B. Gwyn's admirable *Democracy and the Cost of Politics in Britain* (London, 1962). French politics in the nineteenth century may be understood in comparable terms, although the weight of the central government was, if anything, more pronounced. See, for example, Theodore Zeldin's discussion of the role of prefectural patronage under the Second Empire in *The Political System of Napoleon III* (London, 1958), and André Siegfried's fine *Tableau politique de la France*

de l'ouest sous la troisième république (Paris, 1913).

The development of political parties in the United States can, of course, hardly be understood apart from the major role of state and national patronage structures. An excellent historical view of American party structure may be found in William Nisbet Chambers and Walter Deane Burnham, eds., *The American Party System: Stages of Political Development* (New York, 1967), and particularly Burnham's article in that collection, "Party Systems and the Political Process." The importance of material incentives in creating the Republican Party from a congerie of local factions is demonstrated in Harry J. Carmen and Richard J. Luthin, *Lincoln and the Patronage* (New York, 1943).

"Machine politics" represent a particular form of electoral clientelism which received its prototypical expression in urban America around the turn of the last century. By virtue of the political coordination of favors, patronage, and public contracts such parties created formidable electoral majorities which repeatedly swept into power. The analysis of their origin, dynamics, and eventual demise offers important insights into the electoral impact on forms of patronage. Much of the theoretical work in this area has come from Edward Banfield and James Wilson. Banfield's *Political Influence: A New Theory of Urban Politics* (New York, 1965) elaborates a general theory of influence which is then used to explain the pattern of machine politics. See also James Q. Wilson, "The Economy of Patronage," *Journal of Political Economy*, 69:4 (August, 1961), and Edward Banfield and James Q. Wilson, *City Politics* (Cambridge, Mass., 1965). Much of the finest material on machine politics, including Robert Merton's classic analysis, "The Latent Functions of the Machine," is available in Edward Banfield, ed., *Urban Government: A Reader on Administration and Politics* (New York, 1969).

Case studies of particular urban machines abound. The best analysis of early urban machines which emphasizes the role of spoils in concentrating power in an otherwise segmented political system is Seymour Mandelbaum, *Boss Tweed's New York* (New York, 1965). The most careful effort to relate the socio-economic characteristics of urban population to the strategy of the machine is Harold F. Gosnell, *Machine Politics: Chicago Model*, second edition (Chicago, 1968). For the classic insider's view of how the "benign" machine coordinates favors, payoffs, and votes, see William L. Riorden's entertaining *Plunkitt of Tammany Hall* (New York, 1963). City machines in the United

States have generally been viewed positively as integrators of the poor and providers of social welfare services to immigrant populations. An important and persuasive argument that the machine has represented, above all, the interests of commercial elites is Alan Rosenbaum, "Machine Politics, Class Interest, and the Urban Poor," *Politics and Society* (forthcoming, 1974).

Electoral politics in Southern Italy, especially since World War II, have been explained in terms of patronage and clientelist networks. Luigi Graziano has attempted to account for the pattern of co-optation based on the economic power of the state which has successfully resisted demands for structural change in "Patron-Client Relationships in Southern Italy," *European Journal of Political Research*, 1 (1973). See also in this context Joseph LaPalombara's discussion of Christian Democrat patronage in the south in his *Interest Groups in Italian Politics* (Princeton, 1964). The Communist Party in Southern Italy has also not been immune to the pervasive structures of clientelism. Sidney Tarrow's *Peasant Communism in Southern Italy* (New Haven, 1967) is an important attempt to show how clientelism has deradicalized the Communist Party in this region.

Many students of electoral politics in less developed nations have found the machine model of clientelism a productive analytical tool. For an argument that attempts to show how the conditions for machine politics were replicated in many new nations, see James C. Scott, "Corruption, Machine Politics, and Political Change," *American Political Science Review*, 63 (December, 1969).

During the first decade of political independence in Africa, a number of dominant parties mobilized their electoral followings along clientelist lines with the help of public patronage and employment. Perhaps the finest general study of such parties is Aristide R. Zolberg, *Creating Political Order: The Party-States of West Africa* (Chicago, 1966) which minimizes their ideological and unitary qualities and instead emphasizes their machine characteristics. A later analysis by the same author, "The Structure of Political Conflict in the New States of Tropical Africa," *American Political Science Review*, 62:1 (March, 1968) shows how the process of "demand inflation" coupled with the contraction of state resources undermined the legitimacy of these parties. The case for the "machine model" in Africa is also examined by Henry Bienen, "Political Machines in Africa," in Michael Lofchie, ed., *The State of Nations: Con-*

straints on Development in Tropical Africa (Berkeley, 1970). Two valuable general surveys of the structure of electoral politics in West Africa during the same period are: W. Arthur Lewis, *Politics in West Africa* (Toronto, 1965), and D. C. Lloyd, *Africa in Social Change: West African Societies in Transition* (New York, 1968). There are also a number of excellent case studies of West African politics which trace the growth of patronage politics. For Ghana, see Dennis Austin, *Politics in Ghana* (London, 1964); for the Ivory Coast, Aristide R. Zolberg, *One-Party Government in the Ivory Coast* (Princeton, 1969); and for Nigeria, John P. Mackintosh, *Nigerian Government and Politics* (London, 1966). A superb local case study from Nigeria which describes the economic and political links between the cattle-landlords of Ibadan and their Hausa clientele may be found in Abner Cohen, *Custom and Politics in Urban Africa* (Berkeley, 1969).

Although Tanzania most closely resembles the unitary, ideological, socialist party state which failed to develop in West Africa, the role of patronage and clientelism is nonetheless important. The particular mixture of material incentives and structural change promoted by TANU is examined in Henry Bienen, *Tanzania: Party Transformation and Economic Development* (Princeton, 1970) and in Norman N. Miller, "The Rural African Party: Political Participation in Tanzania," *American Political Science Review*, 64:2 (June, 1970). Elsewhere in East Africa, students of clientelism should consult Colin Leys's insightful provincial case study of the linkages between public policy and local party cleavages in pre-Amin Uganda: *Politics and Policies: An Essay on Politics in Acholi, Uganda, 1962-1965* (Nairobi, 1967).

Much of the best literature on electoral patronage in Asia is to be found in the discussions of Indian politics already cited under "factionalism." Myron Weiner's *Party-Building in a New Nation: The Indian National Congress* (Chicago, 1967) is perhaps the best discussion although it seems far too sanguine about the structural consequences of clientelistic politics in a nation like India. The nature of urban boss-rule in India is examined in Marcos Franda's analysis of Calcutta politics, "The Political Indians of Atulya Gosh," *Asian Survey*, 4 (August, 1966).

Elsewhere in Asia, studies of electoral politics seldom fail to emphasize the patron-client networks and the particularistic rewards that so often characterize the operation of parties. A few such studies are especially noteworthy. For an analysis of the most durable parliamentary system in Asia, see Calvin Woodward, *The Growth of a Party System in Ceylon* (Providence, 1969). Studies of elections *per se* are particularly useful in the analysis of clientelism for they often expose latent patterns of dependence which may be mobilized to win votes. Herbert Feith's analysis of Indonesia's first national elections is exemplary in this respect: *The Indonesian Elections of 1955*, Interim Report Series, Modern Indonesian Project (Ithaca, N.Y., 1958). For electoral mobilization in a more traditional, bureaucracy dominated system, see Herbert P. Phillips, "The Election Ritual in a Thai Village," *Journal of Social Issues*, 14 (December, 1958). Party mobilization in Burma before the military takeover is analyzed along explicitly clientelist lines in Manning Nash, "Party Building in Upper Burma," *Asian Survey*, 3:4 (April, 1963) and in his larger work, *The Golden Road to Modernity* (New York, 1965). For the Philippines prior to martial law, see Carl Landé, *Leaders, Factions, and Parties: The Structure of Philippine Politics* (New Haven, 1964) and David Wurfel, "The Philippines," in Arnold Heidenheimer and Richard Rose, eds., "Comparative Studies in Political Finance: A Symposium," *Journal of Politics*, 25:4 (November, 1963).

Populism in Latin America, though it arose in opposition to oligarchic traditions, has often mobilized the vote of poor migrants along clientelist lines. A general discussion of the populist phenomenon in Latin America which stresses the role of dependency relationships and patronage is Alistair Hennessy, "Latin America," in Ghita Ionescu and Ernest Gellner, eds., *Populism: Its Meaning and National Characteristics* (London, 1969). Victor Nuñez-Leal's *Coronelismo: Enxada y Voto* (Rio de Janiero, 1948) is one of the earliest analyses of clientelist electoral politics in Brazil. Studies of urban electoral patronage may be found in the Cornelius essay reprinted in this volume and in Richard Fagen and William S. Tuohy, *Politics and Privilege in a Mexican City* (Stanford, 1972). For an excellent discussion of patterns of rural clientelism within the Acción Democrática in Venezuela, see John D. Powell, *Political Mobilization of the Venezuelan Peasantry* (Cambridge, Mass., 1971).

Corruption

Inasmuch as patron-client politics often involves payoffs to patrons, brokers, and clients which violate formal laws, the study of clientelism is illuminated by the study of corruption.

The literature on machine politics, cited above under "electoral clientelism and machine politics" includes inevitably the analysis of corruption. One of the first comparative analyses of corruption covering nineteenth-century England and West Africa is Ronald Wraith and Edgar Simkins, *Corruption in Developing Countries* (London, 1963). M. G. Smith's "Historical and Cultural Conditions of Political Corruption among the Hausa," *Comparative Studies in Society and History*, 6 (January, 1964) and J. David Greenstone's "Corruption and Self-interest in Kampala and Nairobi," *Comparative Studies in Society and History*, 8 (January, 1966) contain valuable discussions of the relation between traditional structures of loyalty and the growth of corruption. Most of the best analytical material on corruption has been assembled by Arnold Heidenheimer in *Political Corruption: Readings in Comparative Analysis* (New York, 1970). See especially Heidenheimer's introductory analysis, and the articles on the Third World. An analysis of both electoral and non-electoral forms of corruption which makes use of clientelism is James Scott, *Comparative Political Corruption* (Englewood Cliffs, 1971). For extensive bibliographies on the subject of corruption see Heidenheimer's *Political Corruption* cited just above and James Scott, "Corruption in Underdeveloped Countries: A Bibliography," *Cultures et Developpment*, 5:1 (1973).

Bureaucracy and Clientelism

The works already listed under "electoral clientelism" necessarily contain a good deal of material on clientelism both within the bureaucracy and between the bureaucracy and other institutions. In addition to this rich material, those interested in administrative clientelism should consult the essays in Joseph LaPalombara, ed., *Bureaucracy and Political Development* (Princeton, 1963), sponsored by the Committee on Comparative Politics of the Social Science Research Council. In particular the articles by LaPalombara, S. N. Eisenstadt, and Fred W. Riggs comprise a useful introduction to bureaucratic politics and its relation to political change. Essays on Nigeria by J. Donald Kingsley, on Viet Nam by John T. Dorsey, Jr., and on Pakistan by Ralph Braibanti in the same volume examine the origin and development of bureaucratic clienteles. A Latin American case study of bureaucratic clientelism which also develops some hypotheses about the brokerage role of the bureaucracy is Steffen Schmidt's "Bureaucrats as Modernizing Brokers," *Comparative Politics*, 6:3 (1974).

Much of the theoretical work on reciprocity and administrative clientelism in the Third World has come from the prolific pen of Fred Riggs. The most elaborate statement of his approach to bureaucratic politics is *Administration in Developing Countries: The Theory of Prismatic Society* (Boston, 1964). Riggs sets out a structural-functional model of administrative behavior based on the "transitional" nature of underdeveloped nations. His suggestive but controversial approach is further developed in a later case study: *Thailand: The Modernization of a Bureaucratic Polity* (Honolulu, 1966). Riggs's discussion of clique structures, policy making, and commercial-administrative clientelism in Thailand is both empirically and methodologically valuable. A more historically oriented study of the Thai bureaucracy which also emphasizes the social values of deference and clientelism is William J. Siffin, *The Thai Bureaucracy: Institutional Change and Development* (Honolulu, 1966).

IV. CLASS, EXPLOITATION, AND CLIENTELISM

Is clientelism to be seen simply as a social vestige of feudal economic and political structures? If so, under what conditions does it persist or disappear? When are vertical structures of deference legitimate and when are they viewed as exploitative? How does the transition from patron-client structures of loyalty to class-based organization take place? Questions of this kind have assumed a growing importance for students of clientelism as recognition of clientelist forms of politics has become more firmly established. While a good deal is now understood about how clientelism operates, relatively less is understood about its historical or analytical relationship to other forms of social organization.

The classical Marxist view linking clientelism to the social order of feudalism is best elaborated in Marx, *Pre-Capitalist Economic Formations*, translated by Jack Cohen (London, 1964) which has been extracted from the larger *Grundrisse* and, of course, volume 1 of *Capital*. Two excellent analyses of the social and economic basis of feudal structures are Joseph Schumpeter, *Social Classes* (New York, 1955) and Gerhard E. Lenski, *Power and Privilege: A Theory of Social Stratification* (New York, 1966). The best collection of theoretical material on stratification which addresses the questions of the social relations between strata is J. A. Jackson, ed., *Social Stratification* (Cambridge, 1968). See especially the following articles: "Deference" by Edward Shils; "Prestige, Participation and Strata Formation" by S. H.

Eisenstadt; and "Class, Status, and Power" by W. G. Runciman.

It is by no means clear that clientelism implies a complete absence of class consciousness even under the classical forms of feudalism. Marc Bloch's *Feudalism*, translated by L. Manyon (Chicago, 1971), clearly shows the sharp sense of natural and contractual rights held by the serfs on feudal manors. The question of class consciousness is, however, an important one in clientelism. Aside from Marx himself, two of the most valuable discussions of class consciousness and social structure are Stanislaw Ossowski, *Class Structure in the Social Consciousness*, translated by Sheila Patterson (New York, 1963) and the classic Georg Lukács, *History and Class Consciousness: Studies in Marxist Dialectics*, translated by Rodney Livingstone (Cambridge, Mass., 1970), especially pp. 46-222. A recent collection on this subject with an important essay by Eric Hobsbawm entitled "Class Consciousness in History," is Istvan Meszaros, ed., *Aspects of History and Class Consciousness* (London, 1971).

The issue of class consciousness is, of course, related to how legitimate or illegitimate the patron-class's control over scarce values is perceived to be by subordinate classes. One analytical tradition, linked with exchange theory, holds that the legitimacy of the patron is directly related to the balance of reciprocity between client and patron. An early exponent of this approach is Emile Durkheim, *Professional Ethics and Civic Morals* (London, 1957), pp. 208-214. This view is developed by George Homans, *Social Behavior: Its Elementary Forms* (New York, 1961); Peter Blau, *Exchange and Power in Social Life* (New York, 1964); and Alvin Gouldner, "The Norm of Reciprocity: A Preliminary Statement," *American Journal of Sociology*, 25:2 (April, 1960). Some experimental evidence for the moral norm of equal exchange is reported by J. S. Adams, "Inequality in Social Exchange," in Leonard Berkowitz, ed., *Advances in Experimental Social Psychology*, Vol. 2 (New York, 1965).

Most discussions of class and clientelism implicitly treat each as mutually exclusive forms of social solidarity. There is some evidence, however, that class formation and clientelism are not incompatible but may coexist and overlap. For a very suggestive argument along these lines, see Hamza Alavi, "Peasant Classes and Primordial Loyalties," *Journal of Peasant Studies*, 1:1 (October, 1973). Claude Rivière, "Les classes sociales en pays sous-développés," *Cultures et Développment*, 5:3 (1973), is one of the best current discussions of class analysis and its relationship to clientelism. Arnold Strickon has suggested that class consciousness and clientelism may coexist and be situationally cued: "Class and Kinship in Argentina," *Ethnology*, 1 (1962) and "Folk Models of Stratification, Political Ideology, and Socio-Cultural Systems," *The Sociological Review Monographs*, No. 11 (1967).

The relationship between class and clientelism is illuminated in a series of studies of left-wing movements which are clientelistically organized. For clientelism in Southern Italy, see Sidney Tarrow, *Peasant Communism in Southern Italy* (New Haven, 1967) and Luigi Graziano, "Patron-Client Relationships in Southern Italy," *European Journal of Political Research*, 1 (1973), reprinted in this volume. Much of this analysis is in the tradition established by the great Italian communist A. Gramsci in *The Modern Prince* (New York, 1958). Studies of the "radical" peasant leagues in Northeast Brazil have also emphasized the vertical links of patronage and deference which undercut their capacity for class representation. In this context, see Anthony Leeds, "Brazil and the Myth of Francisco Juliao," in Joseph Maier and Richard W. Weatherhead, eds., *The Politics of Change in Latin America* (New York, 1964); Benno Galjart, "A Further Note on Followings," *America Latina*, 8:3 (July-September, 1965). The social structure of the Indonesian Communist Party in Java prior to 1965 provides some striking parallels with Southern Italian communism. Clientelism within the PKI is analyzed in Rex Mortimer, "Class, Social Cleavage and Indonesian Communism," *Indonesia*, 8 (October, 1969); W. F. Wertheim, "Patronage, Vertical Organization and Populism," in B. Endo, H. Hoshi, and S. Hazuda, eds., *Proceedings 8th International Congress of Anthropological and Ethnological Sciences*, II (Tokyo-Kyoto, 1968). See also Wertheim's analysis of the transition from patronage to class struggle in this volume.

The question of how vertical structures of loyalty and patronage break down is a critical one for both historical analysis and the theory of clientelism. The most elaborate theory available is Barrington Moore Jr.'s theory of exploitation and the decline of feudalism in *Social Origins of Dictatorship and Democracy: Lord and Peasant in the Making of the Modern World* (Boston, 1966). Sydel Silverman's article and that of Kerkvliet and Scott reprinted here, develop and apply Moore's analysis to Central Italy and Southeast Asia. Another analysis of the same issue that is very suggestive is G. Alberti, "The Breakdown of Provincial Urban Power Structure and the Rise of Peasant Movements," *Sociologica Ruralis*, 12:3 and 4 (1972). Students of clientelism should also consult a number of case studies which single out such factors as population growth, the commercialization of agriculture, technical change, and the growth of the state which make for more exploitative and hence less legitimate patron-client ties. For India, see E. Kathleen Gough, "The Social Structure of a Tanjore Village," in McKim Marriott, ed., *Village India* (Chicago, 1955) and Francine Frankel, *India's Green Revolution: Economic Gains and Political Costs* (Princeton, 1971). For Indonesia, see H. ten Dam, "Cooperation and Social Structure in the Village of Chibodas," Vol. 6, *Indonesian Economics: The Concept of Dualism in Theory and Practice of Selected Studies of Indonesia by Dutch Scholars* (The Hague, 1971). Two excellent studies of the Philippines which address this subject are: Akira Takahashi, *Land and Peasants in Central Luzon* (Honolulu, 1969), and Benedict J. Kerkvliet, "Peasant Society and Unrest Prior to the Huk Revolution in the Philippines," *Asian Studies* (Manila, 1972). Some of the same forces undermining traditional forms of clientelism appear to be at work in Malaysian society and are examined in M. G. Swift, "Economic Concentration and Malay Peasant Society," in Maurice Freedman, ed., *Social Organization: Essays Presented to Raymond Firth* (London, 1967); in Clive Kessler, "Muslim Identity and Political Behavior in Kelantan," in William Roff, ed., *Essays on Kelantan* (New York, 1973); and in Masuo Kuchiba and Yoshihiro Tsubouchi, "Paddy Farming and Social Structure in a Malay Village," *The Developing Economies* (1972). Finally, there is the interesting case of directed social change designed to destroy old patterns of social submission in Peru, described in a series of articles: "The Vicos Case: Peasant Society in Transition," *American Behavioral Scientist* (entire issue), 8:7 (March, 1965).

A related issue in the class vs. clientelism controversy concerns the role of economic imperialism in fostering the continuation of internal networks of dependency. Laura Guasti's essay in this volume is devoted to this question as is Peter Flynn's article, "Class, Clientelism, and Coercion: Some Mechanisms of Internal Dependency and Control," MS (1973).

REGIONAL LITERATURE

In the course of this analytical bibliography, many of the outstanding case studies from particular regions have already been noted. Below we have tried to compile, by region, more of the material on clientelism which has come to our attention. Although this listing is hardly exhaustive, we hope that it includes a fair sampling of what is available to area specialists.

AFRICA

Achebe, Chinua. *A Man of the People*. New York, 1966.

Apter, David. *The Gold Coast in Transition*. Princeton, 1955.

——. "The Role of Traditionalism in the Political Modernization of Ghana and Uganda," *World Politics*, 13 (1960).

Ayida, A. A. "The Contribution of Politicians and Administrators to Nigeria's National Economic Planning," in A. Adedeji, ed., *Nigerian Administration and Its Economic Setting*. Ibadan, 1968.

Balandier, Georges. *Political Anthropology*. New York, 1970.

Barker, Jonathan S. "The Paradox of Development: Reflections on a Study of Local-Central Political Relations in Senegal," in Michael Lofchie, ed., *The State of the Nations: Constraints on Development in Independent Africa*. Berkeley, 1970.

Bates, Robert H. *Unions, Parties, and Political Development: A Study of Mineworkers in Zambia*. New Haven, 1970.

Behrman, Lucy. *Muslim Brotherhoods*. Cambridge, Mass., 1970.

Bienen, Henry. "Political Machines in Africa," in Michael Lofchie, ed., *The State of the Nations: Constraints on Development in Independent Africa*. Berkeley, 1970.

——. *Tanzania: Party Transformations and Economic Development*. Princeton, 1970.

——. *Kenya: The Politics of Participation and Control*. Princeton, 1974.

Buxton, Jean. "Clientship Among the Mandari of the Southern Sudan," in Ronald Cohen and John Middleton, eds., *Comparative Political Systems: Studies on the Politics of Pre-industrial Societies*. New York, 1967.

Cohen, Abner. *Custom and Politics in Urban Africa*. Berkeley, 1969.

——. "The Social Organization of Credit in a West African Cattle Market," *Africa*, 35 (1965).

Colson, Elizabeth. "Competence and Incompetence in the Context of Independence," *Current Anthropology*, 8 (February-April, 1967).

Coquery-Vidrovich, L. "Recherches sur un mode de production africaine," *La Pensée*, 164 (1969).

Dorjahn, V. R. and Fyfe, Christopher. "Landlord and Stranger: Change in Tenancy Relations in Sierra Leone," *Journal of African History*, 3:3 (1962).

Douglas, Mary. "Blood-debts and Clientship Among the Lele," *Man*, 90 (1960).

Dudley, B. J. *Parties and Politics in Northern Nigeria*. London, 1968.

Epstein, A. L. "The Network and Urban Social Organization," *Rhodes-Livingston Journal*, 29 (1961).

Fallers, Lloyd. *Bantu Bureaucracy*. Cambridge, 1958.

——, ed. *The King's Men: Leadership and Status in Buganda on the Eve of Independence*. London, 1964.

Fitch, Bob and Oppenheimer, Mary. *Ghana: The End of an Illusion*. New York, 1966.

Gluckman, Max. "Tribalism in Modern British Central Africa," *Cahiers d'Etudes Africaines*, 1:3 (1960).

Greenstone, J. David. "Corruption and Self-Interest in Kampala and Nairobi," *Comparative Studies in Society and History*, 8:2 (January, 1966).

Gutkind, P. C. W. "Network Analysis and Urbanism in Africa: The Use of Micro and Macro Analysis," *Canadian Journal of Sociology and Anthropology*, 2:3 (1965).

——. "African Urbanism: Mobility and Social Network," *International Journal of Comparative Sociology*, 6:1 (1965).

Hess, Robert L. *Ethiopia: The Modernization of Autocracy*. Ithaca, 1970.

deHeusch, Luc. "Mythe et société féodale: le culte du kubandwa dans le Rwanda traditionnel," *Archives de Sociologie des Religions*, 18 (1964).

Hill, Polly. "Landlords and Brokers," *Cahiers d'Etudes Africaines*, 6:23 (1966).

Hopkins, Raymond. *Political Roles in a New State*. New Haven, 1971.

Jackson, Robert H. "Social Structure and Political Change in Ethiopia and Liberia," *Comparative Political Studies*, 3:3 (April, 1970).

Kilson, Martin. *Political Change in a West African State*. Cambridge, Mass., 1966.

Landé, Carl. "Kinship and Politics in Pre-modern and Non-western Societies," in John T. McAlister, Jr., ed., *Southeast Asia: The Politics of National Integration*. New York, 1973.

Lemarchand, René. "Les Relations de clientèle comme moyen de contestation: le cas du Rwanda," *Civilisations*, 28:4 (1964).

——. *Rwanda and Burundi*. London, 1970.

——. "Political Exchange, Clientelism, and Development in Tropical Africa," *Cultures et Developpment* (1971).

—— and Legg, Keith. "Political Exchange, Clientelism, and Development in Tropical Africa: A Preliminary Analysis," *Comparative Politics*, 4:2 (January, 1972).

Levine, Donald. *Wax and Gold: Tradition and Innovation in Ethiopian Culture*. Chicago, 1965.

Lewis, I. M. *A Pastoral Democracy: A Study of Pastoralism and Politics Among the Northern Somali*. Oxford, 1961.

Lewis, W. Arthur. *Politics in West Africa*. Toronto, 1965.

Leys, Colin. *Politicians and Policies: An Essay on Politics in Acholi, Uganda, 1962-1965*. Nairobi, 1967.

——. "Politics in Kenya: The Development of

Post-peasant Society," *British Journal of Political Science*, 1:3 (1971).

Liebenow, Gus. *Liberia: The Evolution of Privilege*. Ithaca, 1969.

Lloyd, P. C. "The Traditional Political System of the Yoruba," *Southwestern Journal of Anthropology*, 10 (1954).

———. *Africa in Social Change: West African Societies in Transition*. New York, 1968.

Lombard, L. "La vie politique dans une ancienne société de type féodale: les Bariba du Dahomey," *Cahiers d'Etudes Africaines*, 1:5 (1960).

Luckham, Robin. *The Nigerian Military*. Cambridge, 1974.

Mackintosh, J. P. *Nigerian Government and Politics*. London, 1966.

Mair, Lucy. "Clientship in East Africa." *Cahiers d'Etudes Africaines*, 2:6 (1961).

Mannoni, O. *Prospero and Caliban: The Psychology of Colonization*, translated by Pamela Powesland. New York, 1956.

Maquet, Jacques. "Une hypothèse pour l'étude des féodalites africaines," *Cahiers d'Etudes Africaines*, 6 (1961).

———. *The Premise of Inequality in Rwanda*. London, 1961.

——— and d'Hertefeld, M. *Elections en société féodale*. Bruxelles, 1959.

Marris, Peter. *Family and Social Change in an African City*. Evanston, Ill., 1962.

——— and Somerset, Anthony. *African Businessmen*. London, 1969.

Meillesoux, Claude. *Anthropologie économique des Gouro de Côte d'Ivoire*. Paris, 1964.

Melson, Robert and Wolpe, Howard. *Nigeria: Modernization and the Politics of Communalism*. East Lansing, 1971.

Miller, Norman N. "The Rural African Party: Political Participation in Tanzania," *American Political Science Review*, 54:2 (1970).

Morganthau, R. *Political Parties in French-speaking West Africa*. Oxford, 1964.

Nadel, S. F. *A Black Byzantium: The Kingdom of the Nupe in Nigeria*. London, 1942.

O'Brien, Donal Cruise. *The Murids of Senegal: The Socio-economic Structure of an Islamic Order*. London, 1972.

Parkin, David. *Neighbors and Nationals in an African City Ward*. Berkeley, 1969.

Post, K. W. J. and Vickers, Michael. *Structure and Conflict in Nigeria 1960-1965*. Madison, Wis., 1973.

Rivière, Claude. "Les Classes sociales en pays sous developpés," *Cultures et Developpment*, 5:3 (1973).

Samoff, Joel. *Tanzania: Local Politics and the Structure of Power*. Madison, Wis., 1974.

Sandbrook, Richard. "Patrons, Clients, and Factions: New Dimensions of Conflict Analysis in Africa," *Canadian Journal of Political Science*, 5:1 (1972).

———. "Patrons, Clients, and Unions: The Labour Movement and Political Conflict in Kenya," *Journal of Commonwealth Political Studies*, 9 (March, 1972).

Sklar, Richard. *Nigerian Political Parties*. Princeton, 1963.

———. "Political Science and National Integration," *Journal of Modern African Studies*, 5:1 (May, 1967).

Smith, M. G. *Government in Zazzau*. London, 1960.

———. "Historical and Cultural Conditions of Political Corruption Among the Hausa," *Comparative Studies in Society and History*, 6 (January, 1964).

Smock, A. *Cultural and Political Aspects of Rural Transformation: A Case Study of Eastern Nigeria*. New York, 1972.

Southall, Aiden. *Alur Society*. Cambridge, 1956.

———. *Social Change in Modern Africa*. London, 1962.

Steinhart, Edward I. "Vassal and Fief in Three Interlacustrine Kingdoms," *Cahiers d'Etudes Africaines*, 7:4 (1967).

Terray, E. *Le Marxisme devant les sociétés primitives*. Paris, 1969. Translated by Mary Klopper as *Marxism and Primitive Societies: Two Studies*. New York, 1972.

Tuden, Arthur. "Ila Property Relations and Political Processes," in Marc Swartz, ed., *Local-Level Politics*. Chicago, 1968.

Vincent, Joan. *African Elite: The Big Men of a Small Town*. New York, 1971.

Watson, William. *Tribal Change in a Money Economy: A Study of the Mambwe People of Northern Rhodesia*. Manchester, 1958.

Whitaker, S. "Three Perspectives on Hierarchy: Political Thought and Leadership in Northern Nigeria," *Journal of Commonwealth Political Studies*, 3:1 (March, 1965).

———. *The Politics of Tradition: Continuity and Change in Northern Nigeria, 1946-1966*. Princeton, 1970.

Willaume, J. C. *Patrimonialism and Political Change in the Congo*. Stanford, 1972.

Wilson, Godfrey and Wilson, Monica. *An Analysis of Social Change*. Cambridge, 1945.

Wraith, Ronald and Simkins, Edgar. *Corruption and Developing Countries*. London, 1963.

Young, M. Crawford. *Politics in the Congo*. Princeton, 1966.

Zolberg, Aristide. *Creating Political Order: The Party-States of West Africa*. Chicago, 1966.

———. "The Structure of Political Conflict in the New States of Tropical Africa," *American Political Science Review*, 62:1 (March, 1968).

———. *One-Party Government in the Ivory Coast*. Princeton, 1969.

EAST ASIA

Abegglen, James C. *The Japanese Factory*. Glencoe, Ill., 1958.

Beardsley, Richard K., Hall, John W., and Ward, Robert E. *Village Japan*. Chicago, 1959.

Befu, Harumi. "Network and Corporate Structure:

A structural Approach to Community Interrelationships in Japan," *Studies in Asia* (1963).

Bennett, J. W. "Economic Aspects of a Boss-henchman System in the Japanese Forestry Industry," *Economic Development and Cultural Change*, 7 (1958).

———— and Ishino, Iwao. *Paternalism in the Japanese Economy*. Minneapolis, 1963.

Curtis, Gerald L. *Election Campaigning, Japanese Style*. New York, 1971.

Fei, Hsiao-t'ung. *China's Gentry: Essays in Rural-Urban Relations*. Chicago, 1960.

Freedman, Maurice. *Lineage Organization in Southeastern China*. London School of Economics Monographs in Social Anthropology, No. 18. London, 1958.

Fried, Morton H. *The Fabric of Chinese Society: The Study of Social Life of a Chinese County Seat*. New York, 1953.

Gallin, Bernard. *Hsin Hsing: A Chinese Village in Change*. Berkeley, 1966.

Ike, Nobutoke. *Japanese Politics: Patron Client Democracy*. New York, 1972.

Ishino, Iwao. "The Oyabun-Kobun: A Japanese Ritual Kinship Institution," *American Anthropologist*, 55 (1953).

Leiserson, Michael. "Factions and Coalitions in One-Party Japan: An Interpretation Based on the Theory of Games," *American Political Science Review*, 62:3 (1968).

Maruyama, Masao. *Thought and Behavior in Modern Japanese Politics*. London, 1963.

Michael, Franz. *The Origin of Manchu Rule in China*. Baltimore, 1942.

Nakane, Chie. *Japanese Society*. London, 1970.

Nathan, Andrew J. "A Factionalism Model for CCP Politics," *The China Quarterly* (January-March, 1973).

Pye, Lucian W. *Warlord Politics: Conflict and Coalition in the Modernization of Republican China*. New York, 1971.

Reischauer, Edwin O. "Japanese Feudalism," in Rushton H. Coulborn, ed., *Feudalism in History*. Princeton, 1956.

Skinner, G. William. "Marketing and Social Structure in Rural China," Parts I, II, III, *Journal of Asian Studies*, 24:1, 2, 3 (1964-1965).

Thayer, Nathaniel B. *How the Conservatives Rule Japan*. Princeton, 1969.

Totman, Conrad. *Politics in the Tokugawa Bakufu*. Cambridge, 1967.

Yanaga, Chitoshi. *Big Business in Japanese Politics*. New Haven, 1968.

LATIN AMERICA

Amado, Jorge. *Violent Land*. New York, 1965.

Bolton, Ralph. "El Fuete y el sello: Patrones cambiantes de liderazgo y autoridad en pueblos peruanos," *America Indigena*, 30:4 (October, 1970).

Buve, R. Th. "Patronaje en las zonas rurales de México," *Boletín de Estudios Latinoamericanos y del Caribe* (Amsterdam), 16 (June, 1974).

Casagrande, Joseph B. and Piper, Arthur R. "La transformación estructural de una parroquia rural en las tierras altas del Ecuador," *America Indigena*, (October, 1969).

Chalmers, Douglas. "Political Groups and Authority in Brazil," manuscript.

————. "Parties and Society in Latin America," *Studies in Comparative International Development*, 7:2 (Summer, 1972).

Cochran, Thomas C. and Reina, Ruben. *Entrepreneurship in Argentine Culture*. Pittsburgh, 1962.

Cotler, Julio. "La Mecánica de la dominación interna y del cambio social en el Peru," in Instituto de Investigaciones Sociales, *El Peru Actual*. Mexico City, 1970.

Eul Soo Pang. "The Politics of Coronelismo in Brazil: The Case of Bahia, 1889-1930." Ph.D. thesis, University of California, Berkeley, 1970.

Fagen, Richard R. and Ruohy, William S. *Politics and Privilege in a Mexican City*. Stanford, 1972.

Fals Borda, Orlando, *et al. La Violencia en Colombia*, Vols. I and II. Bogota, 1962, 1964.

————. *Peasant Society in the Colombian Andes*. Gainesville, Florida, 1962.

Feder, Ernest. *The Rape of the Peasantry*. New York, 1971.

Flynn, Peter. "Class, Clientelism and Coercion: Some Mechanisms of Internal Dependency," manuscript. Glasgow, 1973.

Foster, George M. "Confradio and Compadrazgo in Spain and South America," *Southwestern Journal of Anthropology*, 9 (1953).

————. "The Dyadic-Contract: A Model for the Social Structure of a Mexican Peasant Village," *American Anthropologist*, 63:6 (December, 1961).

————. "The Dyadic Contract in Tzintzuntzan, II: Patron-Client Relationship," *American Anthropologist*, 65:6 (December, 1963).

Freyre, Gilberto. The Masters and the Slaves. New York, 1956.

————. "The Patriarchal Basis of Brazilian Society," in Joseph Maier and Richard Weatherhead, eds., *Politics of Change in Latin America*. New York, 1964.

Friedrich, Paul. "A Mexican Cacicazgo," *Ethnology*, 4:2 (1965).

————. "The Legitimacy of a Cacique," in Marc Swartz, ed., *Local-Level Politics*. Chicago, 1968.

Galjart, Benno. "Class and Following in Rural Brazil," *America Latina*, 7:3 (July-September, 1965).

————. "A Further Note on Followings," *America Latina*, 8:3 (July-September, 1965).

Greenfield, Sidney. "Patronage Networks, Factions, Political Parties and National Integration in Contemporary Brazilian Society," Discussion Paper No. 12, Latin American Center. University of Wisconsin, Milwaukee, 1970.

Guasti, Laura. "Peru: Clientelism and Internal Control," see this volume.

Gunder-Frank, André. *Capitalism and Underdevelopment in Latin America*. New York, 1967.

Hall, M. "Social and Economic Obstacles to Agrarian Reform in Northeast Brazil." M. Phil. Thesis, Glasgow, 1970.

Harris, M. *Town and Country in Brazil*. New York, 1956.

Havens, A. Eugene and Flinn, William L., eds. *Internal Colonialism and Structural Change in Colombia*. New York, 1970.

Heath, Dwight B. "New Patrons for Old: Changing Patron-Client Relationships in the Bolivian Yungas," *Ethnology*, 12:1 (January, 1973).

Hennessy, Alistair. "Latin America," in Ghita Ionescu and Ernest Gellner, eds., *Populism: Its Meaning and National Characteristics*. New York, 1969.

Hobsbawm, E. J. "Peasants and Rural Migrants in Politics," in Claudio Veliz, ed., *Obstacles to Change in Latin America*. London, 1965.

Horowitz, Irving Lewis, ed. *Masses in Latin America*. New York, 1970.

Hutchinson, H. *Village and Plantation Life in Northeast Brazil*. Seattle, 1957.

Hutchinson, B. "The Patron-Dependent Relationship in Brazil: A Preliminary Analysis," *Sociologica Ruralis*, 6:1 (1966).

Jaquaribe, Hélio. *Economic and Political Development: A Theoretical Approach and a Brazilian Case Study*. Cambridge, Mass., 1968.

Kaufman, Robert R. "The Patron-Client Concept and Macro-Politics: Prospects and Problems," *Comparative Studies in Society and History*, 15:1 (1973).

————. "Corporativism, Clientelism and Partisan Conflict in Latin America: A Comparative Study of Argentina, Brazil, Chile, Colombia, Mexico, Venezuela and Uruguay," manuscript (1973).

Kern, Robert, ed. *The Caciques: Oligarchical Politics and the System of Caciquismo in the Luso-Hispanic World*. Albuquerque, 1972.

Klein, Emilio. "Tipos de dependencia y obreros agrícolas en Chile," *Boletín de Estudios Latinoamericanos y del Caribe*, 16 (June, 1974).

Landsberger, Henry. *Latin American Peasant Movements*. Ithaca, 1969.

Leeds, Anthony. "Brazil and the Myth of Francisco Juliao," in Joseph Maier and Richard W. Weatherhead, eds., *Politics of Change in Latin America*. New York, 1964.

————. "Brazilian Careers and Social Structures," *American Anthropologist*, 66 (1964).

Lewis, Oscar. *Pedro Martinez: A Mexican Peasant and His Family*. New York, 1964.

Mintz, Sidney W. "Pratik: Haitian Personal Economic Relationships," *Proceedings of the 1961 Annual Meeting of the American Ethnological Society*, pp. 54-63.

Nuñez-Leal, Victor. *Coronelismo: Enxada y Voto*. Rio de Janiero, 1948.

Paulson, Belden H. "Local Political Patterns in Northeast Brazil: A Community Case Study," Land Tenure Center Paper No. 12. Madison, 1964.

Payne, James L. *Patterns of Conflict in Colombia*. New Haven, 1968.

Powell, J. D. "Peasant Society and Clientelist Politics," *American Political Science Review*, 64:2 (1970).

Roy, Talton F. *The Politics of the Barrios of Venezuela*. Berkeley, 1969.

Schmidt, Steffen. "Political Clientelism and Civil-Military Relations: Colombia," in Steffen Schmidt and G. Dorfman, eds., *Soldiers in Politics*. Los Altos, California, 1974.

————. "Bureaucrats as Modernizing Brokers," *Comparative Politics*, 6:3 (1974).

————. "La Violencia Revisited: The Clientelist Basis of Political Violence in Colombia," *Journal of Latin American Studies*, 6:1 (1974).

————. "The Transformation of Clientelism in Rural Colombia," Paper presented at the 1974 Annual Meeting of the American Political Science Association. Chicago, September, 1974.

Schmitter, Philippe C. *Interest Conflict and Political Change in Brazil*. Stanford, 1971.

Schwartz, Norman B. "Goal Attainment Through Factionalism: A Guatemalan Case," *American Anthropologist*, 71:6 (December, 1969).

Stavenhagen, R. "Seven Fallacies about Latin America," in J. Petras and M. Zeitlin, eds., *Latin America: Reform or Revolution*. New York, 1968.

————, ed. *Agrarian Problems and Peasant Movements in Latin America*. New York, 1970.

Steward, Julian, *et al. The People of Puerto Rico*. Champaign-Urbana, 1956.

Strickon, Arnold and Greenfield, Sidney. "The Analysis of Patron-Client Relationships: An Introduction," in Strickon and Greenfield, eds., *Structure and Process in Latin America: Patronage, Clientage and Power Systems* Albuquerque, 1972. See case studies in this volume as well.

Strickon, Arnold. "Folk Models of Stratification, Political Ideology, and Sociocultural Systems," *Sociological Review Monographs*, No. 11 (1967).

Torres-Truela, Henry E. "Faccionalismo en un municipio mexicano," *America Indigena*, 30:3 (July, 1970).

Traven, B. *Government*. New York, 1968.

————. *The Carreta*. New York, 1970.

"The Vicos Case: Peasant Society in Transition," *American Behavioral Scientist*, 8:7 (March, 1965).

Wagley, Charles. "Luso-Brazilian Kinship Patterns: the Persistence of a Cultural Tradition," in Joseph Maier and Richard W. Weatherhead, eds., *Politics of Change in Latin America*. New York, 1964.

Whitten, Norman E., Jr. *Class, Kinship, and Power in an Ecuadorian Town*. Stanford, 1965.

————. "Network Analysis in Ecuador and Nova Scotia: Some Critical Remarks," *Canadian Journal of Sociology and Anthropology* (1974).

Wolf, Eric R. "Aspects of Group Relations in a Complex Society: Mexico," *American Anthropologist*, 58 (1956).

———— and Hansen, Edward C. "Caudillo Politics: A Structural Analysis," *Comparative Studies in Society and History*, 9 (1966-1967).

MEDITERRANEAN

Blok, Anton. *The Mafia of a Sicilian Village: 1860-1960*. Oxford, 1974.

Boissevain, Jeremy. "Factions, Parties, and Politics in a Maltese Village," *American Anthropologist*, 66:6 (December, 1964).

———. *Saints and Firewords: Religion and Politics in Rural Malta*. London School of Economics Monographs in Social Anthropology, No. 30. New York, 1965.

———. "Patronage in Sicily," *Man*, 1:1 (March, 1966).

———. "The Place of Non-groups in the Social Sciences," *Man*, 3:4 (December, 1968).

———. *Friends of Friends: Networks, Manipulators, and Coalitions*. Oxford, 1974.

Brenan, Gerald. *The Spanish Labyrinth*. Cambridge, 1964.

Campbell, J. K. *Honour, Family and Patronage: A Study of Institutions and Moral Values in a Greek Mountain Community*. Oxford, 1964.

Friedl, Ernestine K. *Vasilika: A Village in Modern Greece*. New York, 1962.

Gellner, Ernest. *Saints of the Atlas*. London, 1969.

——— and Micaud, Charles, eds. *Arabs and Berbers: From Tribe to Nation in North Africa*. London, 1973.

——— and Waterbury, John. *Changing Forms of Patronage in the Mediterranean*, forthcoming.

Graziano, Luigi. "Patron-Client Relationships in Southern Italy," *European Journal of Political Research*, 1 (1973).

Hess, H. *Mafia: zentrale Herrschaft und lokale Gegenmacht*. Tübingen, 1970.

Holtinger, Arnold. "Zuama in Historical Perspective," in Leonard Binder, ed., *Politics in Lebanon*. New York, 1966.

Kenny, Michael. "Patterns of Patronage in Spain," *Anthropological Quarterly*, 33 (January, 1960).

———. *A Spanish Tapestry: Town and Country in Castile*. Bloomington, 1961.

LaPalombara, Joseph. *Interest Groups in Italian Politics*. Princeton, 1964.

Lapidus, Ira M. *Muslim Cities in the Later Middle Ages*. Cambridge, Mass., 1967.

Legg, Keith R. "Regime Change and Public Policy in a Clientelist Polity: The Cases of Greece and Italy." Paper presented at 1972 Annual Meeting of American Political Science Association. Washington, D.C., September, 1972.

———. *Politics in Modern Greece*. Stanford, 1969.

Malefakis, Edward. *Agrarian Reform and Peasant Revolution in Spain*. New Haven, 1970.

Pitt-Rivers, J. A. *The People of the Sierra*. Chicago, 1961.

———, ed. *Mediterranean Countrymen: Essays in the Social Anthropology of the Mediterranean*. Paris, The Hague, 1963.

Riegelhaupt, Joyce F. "Peasants and Politics in Portugal." Paper presented at the 1972 Annual Meeting of the American Political Science Association. Washington, D.C., September, 1972.

Schneider, Jane. "Family Patrimonies and Economic Behavior in Western Sicily," *Anthropological Quarterly*, 42 (July, 1969).

———. "Of Vigilance and Virgins: Honor, Shame, and Access to Resources in Mediterranean Societies," *Ethnology*, 10:1 (January, 1971).

Schneider, Peter, Schneider, Jane and Hansen, Edward. "Modernization and Development: The Role of Regional Elites and Non-corporate Groups in the European Mediterranean," *Comparative Studies in Society and History*, 14:3 (June, 1972).

Schneider, Peter. "Friends of Friends: Coalition Formation and Colonialism in Western Sicily." manuscript.

Silverman, Sydel. "Patronage and Community-Nation Relationships in Central Italy," *Ethnology*, 4:2 (April, 1965).

———. "Exploitation in Rural Central Italy: Structure and Ideology in Stratification Study," *Comparative Studies in Society and History*, 12 (1970).

Tarrow, Sidney. *Peasant Communism in Southern Italy*. New Haven, 1967.

Taylor, Lilly Ross. *Party Politics in the Age of Caesar*. Berkeley, 1961.

Waterbury, John. *Commander of the Faithful* (Morocco). New York, 1970.

Weingrod, Alex. "Patrons, Patronage, and Political Parties," *Comparative Studies in Society and History*, 19 (July, 1968).

Zuckerman, Alan. "On the Institutionalization of Political Clienteles: Party Factions and Cabinet Coalitions in Italy." Paper presented at the 1973 Annual Meeting of the American Political Science Association. New Orleans, La., September, 1973.

NORTH AMERICA

Burnham, Walter Deane. "Party Systems and the Political Process," in William Nisbet Chambers and Walter Deane Burnham, eds., *The American Party System: Stages of Political Development*. New York, 1967.

Banfield, Edward C. and Wilson, James Q. *City Politics*. Cambridge, Mass., 1965.

Banfield, Edward C. *Urban Government: A Reader on Administration and Politics*. New York, 1969.

Carman, Harry J. and Luthin, Richard H. *Lincoln and the Patronage*. New York, 1943.

Fried, Marc. "Functions of the Working-class Community in Modern Urban Society: Implications for Forced Relocation," *Journal of the American Institute of Planners*, 33 (1967).

Gosnell, Harold F. *Machine Politics: Chicago Model*, 2nd ed. Chicago, 1968.

Mandelbaum, Seymour. *Boss Tweed's New York*. New York, 1965.

Riorden, William L. *Plunkitt of Tammany Hall*. New York, 1963.

Rosenbaum, Alan. "Machine Politics, Class Interest, and the Urban Poor," manuscript.

St. Angelo, Douglas. "The 'Broker Role' of Local Political Parties and Federal Administration," *Research Report in Social Science*. Tallahassee, 1965.

Scott, James C. "Corruption, Machine Politics, and Political Change," *American Political Science Review*, 63 (December, 1969).

Sorauf, Frank J. "Patronage and Party," *Midwest*

Journal of Political Science, 3:2 (May, 1959).
Tolchin, Martin and Tolchin, Susan. *To the Victor: Political Patronage from the Clubhouse to the White House*. New York, 1971.
Whyte, William Foote. *Street Corner Society: The Social Structure of an Italian Slum*. Chicago, 1955.

NORTHERN EUROPE

Bloch, Marc. *Feudal Society*, Vols. I and II. Translated by L. A. Manyon. Chicago, 1961.
Bott, E. *Family and Social Network*. London, 1957.
Barnes, J. A. "Class and Committees in a Norwegian Island Parish," *Human Relations*, 7 (1954).
———. "Networks and Political Process," in Marc Swartz, ed., *Local-Level Politics*. Chicago, 1968.
Bax, Mart. *Harpstrings and Confessions: An Anthropological Study of Politics in Northern Ireland*. Oxford, 1974.
Coulborn, Rushton, ed. *Feudalism in History*. Princeton, 1956.
Gwyn, William B. *Democracy and the Cost of Politics in Britain*.
Hobsbawm, E. J. and Rudé, George. *Captain Swing*. New York, 1968.
Kane, Eileen. "Man and Kin in Donegal: A Study of Kinship Functions in a Rural Irish and an Irish-American Community," *Ethnology*, 7:3 (1968).
Mingay, G. E. *English Landed Society in the Eighteenth Century*. London, 1963.
Mousnier, Roland. *Peasant Uprisings in Seventeenth Century France, Russia, and China*. Translated by Brian Pearce. New York, 1970.
Namier, Sir Lewis. *The Structure of Politics at the Accession of George III*. New York, 1957.
Pehrson, Robert H. *The Bilateral Network of Social Relationships in Könkämä Lapp District*. Slavic and Eastern European Series, Volume 6. Bloomington, 1957.
Richards, Peter G. *Patronage in British Government*. London, 1963.
Siegfried, André. *Tableau politique de la France de l'ouest sous la troisième république*. Paris, 1913.
Thompson, E. P. "The Moral Economy of the English Crowd in the Eighteenth Century," *Past and Present*, No. 50 (February, 1971).
Thompson, F. M. L. *English Landed Society in the Nineteenth Century*. London, 1963.
Tilly, Charles. *The Vendée*. Cambridge, Mass., 1964.
Walcott, Robert Jr. *English Politics in the Early Eighteenth Century*. Cambridge, Mass., 1956.
Zeldin, Theodore. *The Political System of Napoleon III*. London, 1958.

SOUTH ASIA

Aiyappan, A. *Social Revolution in a Kerala Village: A study of Culture Change*. Bombay, 1965.
Bailey, Frederick G. *Politics and Social Change in Orissa in 1959*. Berkeley, 1963.
Barth, Frederik. *Political Leadership Among the Swat Pathans*. London School of Economics Monographs in Social Anthropology, No. 19. London, 1965.
Bayly, C. A. "Patrons and Politics in Northern India," *Modern Asian Studies*, 7:3 (July, 1973).
Beidelman, Th. O. *A Comparative Analysis of the Jajmani System*. New York, 1959.
Beteille, A. *Caste, Class, and Power*. Berkeley, 1965.
Brass, Paul R. *Factional Politics in an Indian State: The Congress Party in Uttar Pradesh*. Berkeley, 1965.
Breman, Jan. *Patronage and Exploitation: Changing Agrarian Relations in South Gujerat, India*. Berkeley, 1974.
Carras, Mary C. *The Dynamics of Indian Political Factions: A Study of District Councils in the State of Maharashtra*. Cambridge, 1972.
Cohn, B. and Marriott, McKim. "Networks and Centers in the Integration of Indian Civilization," *Journal of Social Research*, 1:1-9 (1958).
Elder, Joseph. "Change in the Jajmani System of an Uttar Pradesh Village," in K. Ishwaran, ed., *Change and Continuity in India's Villages*. New York, 1970.
Firth, Raymond. "Factions in India and Overseas Dependencies," *British Sociology*, 8 (1957).
Fox, R. G. *Kin, Clan, Raja, and Rule: State-hinterland Relations in Preindustrial India*. Berkeley, 1971.
Franda, Marcus. "The Political Idioms of Atulya Gosh," *Asian Survey*, 6 (August, 1966).
Frankel, Francine. *India's Green Revolution: Economic Gains and Political Costs*. Princeton, 1971.
Freed, Stanley A. "Fictive Kinship in a North Indian Village," *Ethnology*, 2 (1963).
Gough, E. Kathleen. "The Social Structure of a Tanjore Village," in McKim Marriott, ed., *Village India*. Chicago, 1955.
Gould, H. A. "The Hindu Jajmani System: A Case of Economic Particularism," *Southwestern Journal of Anthropology*, 14 (1958).
Graham, B. D. "The Succession of Factional Systems in the Uttar Pradesh Congress Party," in Marc Swartz, ed., *Local-Level Politics*. Chicago, 1968.
Kolenda, P. M. "Toward a Model of the Hindu Jajmani System," *Human Organization*, 22 (1963).
Lewis, Oascar and Barnouw, Victor. "Caste and the Jajmani System in a North Indian Village," *Scientific Monthly*, 83:2 (August, 1956).
Lewis, Oscar. "Group Dynamics in a North Indian Village: A Study in Factions," *Economic Weekly*, 6 (1954), pp. 423-425, 445-451, 477-482, 501-506.
Mayer, Adrian C. "Patrons and Brokers' Rural Leadership in Four Overseas Indian Communities," in Maurice Freedman, ed., *Social Organization: Essays Presented to Raymond Firth*. London, 1967.
Miller, D. F. "Factions in Indian Village Politics," *Pacific Affairs*, 35:1 (Spring, 1965).
Nicholas, Ralph W. "Village Factions and Political Parties in Rural West Bengal," *Journal of Commonwealth Studies*, 2:1 (November, 1963).
———. "Factions: A Comparative Analysis," in M.

Banton, ed., *Political Systems and the Distribution of Power*. London, 1965.

———. "Structures of Politics in the Villages of Southern Asia," in D. G. Mandelbaum, ed., *Society in India*. Berkeley, 1970.

Opler, Morris. "The Extensions of an Indian Village," *Journal of Asian Studies*, 16:1 (November, 1956).

Pocock, D. "The Basis of Factions in Gujerat," *British Journal of Sociology*, 7 (1957).

Rao, K. R. and Norman, Rupert T. "Poverty, Politics, and Participation in Kanpur, India," paper presented to the 1972 Annual Meeting of the American Political Science Association. Washington, D.C., September, 1972.

Srinivas, M. H. and Béteille, A. "Networks in Indian Social Structure," *Man*, 64:212 (1964).

Weiner, Myron. *Party-Building in a New Nation*. Chicago, 1967.

Wiser, W. H.*The Hindu Jajmani System*. Lucknow, 1936.

Woodward, Calvin. *The Growth of a Party System in Ceylon*. Providence, 1969.

SOUTHEAST ASIA

Agpalo, Remigio E. *The Political Elite and the People: A Study of Politics in Occidental Mindoro*. Manila, 1972.

Anderson, James N. "Some Aspects of Land and Society in a Pangasinan Community," *Philippine Sociological Review*, 10:1 and 2 (January-April, 1962).

———. "Buy-and-Sell and Economic Personalism: Foundations for Philippine Entrepreneurship," *Asian Survey*, 9:9 (1969).

Barton, Roy Franklin. *The Kalingas: Their Institutions and Custom Law*. Chicago, 1949.

Brochieux, Pierre. Grands proprietaires et fermiers dans l'ouest de la Cochinchine pendant la periode coloniale," *Révue Historique*, 246:no. 499 (1971).

Dozier, Edward P. *Mountain Arbiters: The Changing Life of a Philippine Hill People*. Tucson, 1966.

Feith, Herbert. *The Indonesian Elections of 1955*. Interim Report Series, Modern Indonesia Project, Cornell University. Ithaca, 1958.

———. *The Decline of Constitutional Democracy in Indonesia*. Ithaca, 1962.

Firth, Raymond. *Malay Fishermen: Their Peasant Economy*, 2nd ed. London, 1966.

Geertz, Clifford. "The Changing Role of a Cultural Broker: The Javanese Kijaji," *Comparative Studies in Society and History*, 2 (1960).

———. *The Social History of an Indonesian Town*. Cambridge, Mass., 1965.

Gregory, Ann. "Factionalism and the Indonesian Army: The New Order," *Journal of Comparative Administration*, 2:3 (1970).

Grossholtz, Jean. *Politics in the Philippines*. Boston, 1966.

Gullick, J. M. *Indigenous Political Systems of Western Malaya*. London School of Economics, Monographs in Social Anthropology, No. 17. London, 1958.

Hanks, Lucien M. Jr. "Merit and Power in the Thai Social Order," *American Anthropologist*, 64:6 (December, 1962).

———. "The Corporation and the Entourage: A Comparison of Thai and American Social Organization," *Catalyst* (Summer, 1966).

———. "Entourage and Circle in Burma," *Bennington Review*, 2:1 (1968).

———. *Rice and Man*. Chicago, 1972.

Hill, Frances R. "Millenarian Machines in South Vietnam," *Comparative Studies in Society and History*, 13:3 (July, 1971).

Hollnsteiner, Mary R. "Reciprocity in the Lowland Philippines," *Philippine Studies*, 9:3 (July, 1961).

———. *The Dynamics of Power in a Philippine Municipality*. Manila, 1963.

Huizer, Gerritt. "Peasant Mobilization and Land Reform in Indonesia." Institute of Social Studies, Occasional Paper No. 18. The Hague, 1972.

Husin, Ali, S. "Patterns of Rural Leadership in Malaya," *Journal of the Malaysian Branch of the Royal Asiatic Society*, 41:Part 1 (July, 1968).

Jackson, Karl. "Traditional Authority and National Integration: The Dar'ul Islam Rebellion in West Java." Ph.D. thesis, Massachusetts Institute of Technology, 1971.

Jackson, Karl and Moeliono, Johannes. "Communication and National Integration in Sudanese Villages," East West Communications Institute. Honolulu, 1972.

Jay, Robert R. *Religion and Politics in Rural Central Java*. New Haven, 1963.

Kaufman, Howard Keva. *Banghaud: A Community Study in Thailand*. Monographs of the Association of Asian Studies, No. 10. Locust Valley, N.Y., 1960.

Kerkvliet, Benedict J. "Peasant Society and Unrest Prior to the Huk Revolution in the Philippines," *Asian Studies* (Manila, 1972).

——— and Scott, James C. "How Traditional Rural Patrons Lose Legitimacy: A Theory with Special Reference to Southeast Asia," *Cultures et Developpment*, 5:3 (1973).

Kessler, Clive. "Muslim Identity and Political Behavior in Kelantan," in William Roff, ed., *Essays on Kelantan*. New York, 1973.

Kiefer, Thomas M. "Institutional Friendship and Warfare Among the Tausug of Jolo," *Ethnology*, 7:3 (1968).

———. *The Tausug: Violence and Law in a Philippine Moslem Society*. New York, 1972.

———. The Tausug Polity and the Sultanate of Sulu: A segmentary State in the Southern Philippines," *Sulu Studies*, 1 (1972).

Koentjariningrat. "Javanese Data on the Unresolved Problems of the Kindred," *Ethnology*, 7:1 (January, 1968).

———. "Some Social-anthropological Observations on Gotong Rojong Practices in Two Villages of Central Java." Monograph Series, Modern Indonesia Project, Cornell University. Ithaca, 1961.

Landé, Carl. *Leaders, Factions, and Parties: The Structure of Philippine Politics*. Monograph No. 6, Yale University Southeast Asian Studies. New Haven, 1964.

———. "Networks and Groups in Southeast Asia: Some Observations on the Group Theory of Politics," *American Political Science Review*, 62:1 (1973).

Larkin, John A. *The Pempangans*. Berkeley, 1972.

Leach, E. R. *Political Systems of Highland Burma: A study of Kachin Social Structure*. Boston, 1965.

Lehman, F. K. *The Structure of Chin Society: A Tribal People of Burma Adapted to a Non-Western Civilization*. Urbana, 1963.

Lewis, Henry T. *Ilocano Rice Farmers: A Comparative Study of Philippine Barrios*. Honolulu, 1971.

Machado, K. G. "From Traditional Faction to Machine: Changing Patterns of Political Leadership and Organization in the Rural Philippines," *Journal of Asian Studies*, 33:4 (August, 1974).

McCoy, Alfred W. "The Politics of the Poppy in Indochina: A Comparative Study of Patron-Client Relations under French and American Administration," a paper presented to the 1973 Annual Meeting of the Association of Asian Studies. Chicago, 1973.

Milne, R. S. "Patrons, Clients, and Ethnicity: The Case of Sabah and Sarawak in Malaysia," *Asian Survey*, 13 (October, 1973).

Moerman, Michael. *Agricultural Change and Peasant Choice in a Northern Thai Village*. Berkeley, 1968.

———. "A Thai Village Headman as a Synaptic Leader," *Journal of Asian Studies*, 28:3 (May, 1969).

Mortimer, Rex. "Class, Social Cleavage and Indonesian Communism," *Indonesia*, No. 8 (1969).

Murdock, George Peter. *Social Structure in Southeast Asia*. Chicago, 1960.

Nash, Manning. "Party-building in Upper Burma," *Asian Survey*, 3:4 (April, 1963).

———. *The Golden Road to Modernity*. New York, 1965.

Nowak, Thomas and Snyder, Kay A. "Urbanization and Clientelist Systems in the Philippines," *Philippine Journal of Public Administration* (July, 1970).

———. "Clientelist Politics in the Philippines: Integration or Instability?," *American Political Science Review*, 68:3 (September, 1974).

Nurge, Ethel. *Life in a Leyte Village*. Seattle, 1965.

Phillips, Herbert P. "The Election Ritual in a Thai Village," *Journal of Social Issues*, 14 (December, 1958).

———. *Thai Peasant Personality*. Berkeley, 1965.

Piker, Steven. "The Post Peasant Village in Central Plain Thai Society," manuscript.

Quaritch-Wales, H. G. *Ancient Siamese Government*. London, 1934.

Race, Jeffrey. "Toward an Exchange Theory of Revolution: The Cases of South Vietnam and Northern Thailand," manuscript.

Rabibhadana, Akin. *The Organization of Thai Society in the Early Bangkok Period, 1782-1873*. Interim Report Series, No. 12, Cornell Thailand Project. Ithaca, July, 1969.

Riggs, Fred W. *Thailand: The Modernization of a Bureaucratic Polity*. Honolulu, 1966.

Selosomardjan. *Social Change in Jogjakarta*. Ithaca, 1962.

Skinner, G. W. *Leadership and Power in the Chinese Community of Thailand*. Ithaca, 1958.

Spiro, Melford E. "Factionalism and Politics in Village Burma," in Marc Swartz, ed., *Local-Level Politics*. Chicago, 1968.

Swift, M. G. *Malay Peasant Society in Jelebu*. London School of Economics, Monographs on Social Anthropology, No. 29. London, 1965.

———. "Economic Concentration and Malay Peasant Society," in Maurice Freedman, ed., *Social Organization: Essays Presented to Raymond Firth*. London, 1967.

Takahashi, Akira. *Land and Peasants in Central Luzon*. Honolulu, 1969.

ten Dam, H. "Cooperation and Social Structure in the Village of Chibodas," in Vol. 6, *Indonesian Economics: The Concept of Dualism in Theory and Policy of Selected Studies of Indonesia by Dutch Scholars*. The Hague, 1961.

Wertheim, W. F. "Patronage, Vertical Organization, and Populism," in B. Endo, H. Hoshi, and S. Hazuda, eds., *Proceedings 8th International Congress of Anthropological and Ethnological Sciences*, II (Tokyo-Kyoto, 1968).

———. "From Aliran Towards Class Struggle in the Countryside of Java," *Pacific Viewpoint*, 10 (1969).

Wilson, David. *Politics in Thailand*. Ithaca, 1962.

Wurfel, David. "The Philippines," in Arnold Heidenheimer and Richard Rose, eds., "Comparative Studies in Political Finance: A Symposium," *Journal of Politics*, 25:4 (November, 1963).

GROUP POLITICS AND DYADIC POLITICS:
Notes for a Theory

CARL H. LANDÉ

ONE OF THE MAJOR assumptions in the building of "models" of political systems has been the group basis of politics. The theory in this regard rests upon the evidence that in the United States and in most other modern Western countries, as well as in a good many non-Western ones, individuals act in politics as members of discrete groups. As Robert A. Dahl has pointed out (*Who Governs?* Yale, 1961, p. 5), the disposition to work through groups stems from the experience of ordinary men that "an individual . . . is politically rather helpless, but a group unites the resources of individuals into an effective force." Groups may be of different kinds. There are the primary groups familiar to anthropologists—lineages, clans, and castes. There are organized voluntary associations. And there are groups which are nothing more than categories, that is to say, unorganized groups consisting of all individuals who have some particular characteristic in common.

The group basis of politics is assumed in the analysis of a wide variety of modern political systems. Marxist theoreticians take classes to be the important categorical groups: one class rules and exploits, using the state as its instrument for this purpose; another class is ruled and exploited. The theorists of the fascist corporate state also assume the group basis of politics, though they express it in organismic terms: each occupational group, like the organs of a living body, performs its specialized function for the body politic and should be represented through an appropriate corporation. Democratic theorists, too, view the state as a large group containing many subgroups. However, in democratic theory the tendency is to stress that the member of the larger group may belong to many different groups at one and the same time. Nor do democratic theorists insist on subordinating these groups to the state to the extent that the fascist theorists do.

In all of these models—Marxist, fascist, democratic—categorical or primary groups may be transformed into formally organized associations in order to increase their political effectiveness. For example, the proletariat, having become class-conscious, joins the Communist party. The occupational groups of the fascist state are organized into corporations. The dairy farmers, manufacturers, or the advocates of civil rights in the democratic state, once aware of common interests or objectives, create organized interest groups in order to be more effective in politics. The detribalized natives of Africa, living in the polyglot city, create mutual-aid associations and even political parties composed of members of the same clan or tribe. Members of rival subcastes in parts of India throw their support to opposing political parties.

Let us look in somewhat greater detail at the group-based model of the modern democratic state. The model is familiar to all students of American politics as well as to most ordinary American citizens. But it will be somewhat less familiar, because less relevant, to Filipino readers and therefore to avoid any confusion we shall outline the model here before passing to an alternative model.

The group model of politics assumes first that there is a comprehensive collectivity, the nation, all of whose parts share a common national interest. Within it are to be found numerous distinctive categories of people, many of whose members have formed themselves into associations. The members of some of these categories have in common nothing but geographic propinquity, i.e. their identification with particular states, counties, cities, and towns. Other categories are based upon specialized economic interests or distinctive points of view, and people so oriented form themselves into a wide variety of voluntary associations. Some of the functions of these subgroups within the nation are of interest only to their own members. Thus, states and cities limit their governmental activities to the area within their own boundaries, much of the activity of professional associations concerns the internal life of the profession, and churches direct the practice of religion for their own communicants only. But other functions of subgroups have an effect upon the larger body politic and thus affect the members of other subgroups. For example, the people of a locality may want the federal government to build public works there and this comes at the expense of the nation as a whole. A demand by labor for a higher minimum wage affects not only the consuming public in general but employers in particular. In the model of a political system based upon groups, individual citizens satisfy their private needs by joining others with similar needs to seek general legislation designed to satisfy all citizens with such needs. Thus the individual's particular objectives are attained as he fights for the categorical objectives of the group. The local government of an individual town joins the governments of other towns to lobby for the adoption of broad national programs designed to help all local governments. An individual working man, wishing to increase his own wages, joins other working men to pressure Congress to raise the minimum wage for all working men. Individual members of organized and unorganized groups resort to this cumbersome method of advancing their private interests by working for the interests of countless others not solely because of fellow-feeling for other members of their group, but also because they have no alternative but to do so. This is due to a further attribute of the model of group-based politics. The expectation, based upon past experience, that laws will be enforced rigidly and impersonally, that the individual will benefit only through laws which provide for similar benefits for all others in the same category of persons, and that no one in his category will be forbidden to do anything not forbidden to the others. In short, the model assumes the rule of general laws. Further, the model assumes that the ordinary citizen knows the various categories to which he belongs and will recognize fellow members of these categories, enabling him to join in collective efforts to seek laws in their common interest. It also assumes that the ordinary citizen knows the categories whose interests clash with his own and will recognize and respond unfavorably to attempts from any quarter to advance such interests at the expense of those of his own categories. It follows, in this model, that groups of politicians banded together into political parties must choose between those categories to whose demands they will give priority and those whose demands they must neglect. It follows that each party will make a somewhat different choice of priorities in order to take advantage of the dissatisfaction of the categories neglected by other parties. It follows, finally, that the ordinary citizen will know which party does the most for the bulk of the categories to which he belongs and will give that party his political support.

As for the structure and direction of groups, the model of group-based politics prescribes that the loyalties that bind the individual to the major

groups to which he belongs be strong and stable, that the collective interests of each group take precedence over the personal interests of its head, and that though such a head may exercise considerable authority in the name and the interest of the group his position as an officeholder remain dependent upon the group's belief that he is faithful and effective servant of these interests.

The second model, the model of a political system whose basic structural unit is not the group but the dyad, will be less familiar to Western readers than the preceding one. But it is more familiar, because more relevant, to Filipinos. Some of the characteristics of dyad-based politics have been alluded to in connection with the description of the Philippine party system found earlier in this monograph. It may be helpful at this point to bring together these characteristics by describing a model of a system structured entirely by dyads. It must be stressed that insofar as the student of political science is concerned the model presented here is but a theoretical one since it is unlikely that there is any advanced political system whose structure is purely dyadic. The basic structural unit of the model, the dyad, is a relationship of mutual aid between two individuals. If the relationship arises out of primary ties, as between two close kinsmen, the choice of dyadic partners may involve little discretion. Where no such primary tie exists, the individual has considerable freedom in his choice of dyadic partners, in the number of such partners, and in the intensity and endurance with which he will maintain each dyadic relationship. For this reason, and because only two persons are involved in each dyadic relationship, certain other principles follow:

1) Property is shared rather than pooled, each partner lending or giving property to the other, but with possession or ownership at any instant in time remaining in one individual.

2) The sharing of property and the giving of other aid is based upon strict reciprocity.

3) Because the intensity of interation may differ from dyad to dyad, graded favoritism in the treatment accorded different dyadic partners as well as nonpartners is made explicit.

4) Because dyads are fragile, their maintenance requires continued cultivation through the exchange of favors. Dyadic relationships, being systems of exchange or barter, must be between individuals who are unlike. Each gives to the other something the latter cannot provide for himself. The dissimilarity of the two partners may be temporal or categorical. In the first instance two individuals who in other respects are

alike have a surplus or shortage of the same commodity at different times: A lends to B when B is in need and B returns the favor when A finds himself in short supply. In the second instance individuals who are categorically distinct supply each other what neither can supply for himself: an extreme example is the *Jajmani* system found in parts of India under which two individuals of different castes provide each other with services which, because of ritual prohibitions, they cannot perform for themselves (e.g. a higher caste Hindu might perform religious ceremonies for his lower caste partner who serves as his barber).

5) Because a dyad consists of but two persons, and because their dissimilarity is often of a categorical sort, the benefits obtained through dyadic relationships are particular rather than categorical. The shoemaker makes shoes for the butcher and the butcher supplies meat to the shoemaker, but the shoemaker is not likely to be asked to interest himself in the welfare of the butchering trade as a whole, nor the butcher to support legislation designed to help the shoe industry.

Because dyadic relationships are between unalikes, a great many of them bind together persons of unequal social status, wealth, or power. Of particular interest to the student of politics are relationships in the last of these categories. This brings us to the model of a dyadically structured political system of leadership and followership, which may be described as follows:

1) The system rests on the single leader with his random collection of followers, some of whom are bound to their leader by primary ties, others not.

2) In genesis and in structure the system is leader-centered rather than group-centered, with the leader creating his group rather than the reverse. A man decides to become a leader and proceeds to build up a following by seeking the voluntary adherence of individual followers one by one.

3) The bonds that tie the system together are vertical and dyadic. There is a strong bond of patronship and clientship between the leader and each of his followers, but there is little sense of corporateness, little group solidarity among the latter. Such group spirit as exists stems from the fact that various individuals have chosen to follow the same man.

4) The interests that unite the leader and his followers are particular rather than categorical: the purpose is not the attainment of a common general objective but the advancement of the leader's and his followers' complementary private interests.

5) These interests differ in accordance with the status of those concerned. The leader seeks power and prestige, each follower seeks protection and largess. To achieve his ends the leader needs followers, to achieve theirs the followers need a leader. It is a symbiotic relationship.

6) As in other dyadic arrangements the ties between the leader and each follower rest on reciprocity. As both adherence to a leader and the willingness to take on a follower are voluntary actions rather than prescribed obligations, each must take pains to make the arrangement worth the other's while. The leader must exert himself to obtain benefits for his followers, and each of these must take care to prove his worth to his leader. If either finds the returns not commensurate with his investment, he can be expected to withdraw from the arrangement. The follower may abandon his leader and seek another one. The leader may cease to supply benefits to a worthless follower.

7) Dyadic leadership-followership systems are both dynamic and unstable. A leader's following will expand quickly as he wins access to new sources of largess but, as his position depends upon the continued adherence of followers, he can also lose his following rather easily. The leader will not be deposed. Instead, his followers simply melt away as his ability to continue to supply benefits becomes doubtful. This is the reason why in leadership-followership systems of the dyadic type the personal attributes of the leader, including his wealth, are of great importance in determining the size and the loyalty of his following. Upon the leader's death one of his lieutenants may manage to salvage a part of the following. Or the following may simply dissolve, for most followers will have networks of alternative personal connections and among these there may be a potential leader to whom they can attach themselves.

8) Finally, large leadership-followership systems of the dyadic type are likely to consist of several tiers of followings. Each of the principal leader's immediate followers has personal followers of his own and these in turn are leaders in their own right. The system is made up of chains of vertical dyads which link the topmost leaders to those at the bottom of the pyramid indirectly through a series of subleaders. The multitiered structure of large leadership-followership systems stems from the fact that dyadic systems depend upon close face-to-face relation-

ships between the two dyadic partners. An individual will not follow a leader who is so remote that he cannot be approached and reminded of his obligation to his client. The tiered character of large leadership-followership systems makes them quite unstable. If a subleader falls out with a higher leader he can break away and attach himself to a different one, taking most of his own following with him.

The model of a group-based political system, outlined earlier, corresponds rather closely to the actual political systems of present-day Western Europe and North America. But there is no modern state that can be adequately described solely in terms of our dyadic model. The only self-contained political systems that can be so described are found in simple bilateral societies such as those of the Kalingas (Barton 1949) and of early Northern European tribes in the time of Tacitus. But these cannot properly be described as "states." There are, however, genuine nation-states whose political systems contain substantial elements of dyadic structure mixed in varying degrees with elements of a group structure. In fact, it is probable that both types of structure may be discerned in almost every political system. Dyadic structure principles were present to a relatively high degree in the systems of royal succession, aristocracy, and administration of the premodern monarchies of Southeast Asia. By contrast, the political systems of present-day Western Europe and North America contain a relatively small proportion of dyadic structure. The philippine political system as it has been described in this monograph contains substantial elements of both types of structure. The "formal" institutions are based largely upon the group principle: the institutions of government established by the Constitution and by law are either offices or entities having the character of discrete groups; political parties as they are described in their own rules are discrete groups and so are the numerous voluntary associations whose lobbyists appear in Congress. Yet when one looks at the informal structures devised by Filipinos who operate these formal institutions one finds that political parties are far from the tight-knit groups that their rules suggest. Within and between the parties one finds a large and active network of dyadic relationships which undermine party unity. The real structure of each of the two parties reveals itself as a multitiered system of personal followings clustered together by their shared enmities at the municipal and provincial levels into competing factions and arranged, for electoral purposes, under the flimsy umbrellas of two party denominations. Looking behind the formal organization of interest groups, one finds that the really effective ones draw their strength from the aggressive leadership and the personal connections of their organizers rather than from their members' sense of group solidarity. Less effective interest groups often are little more than vehicles for the promotion of the personal careers of their leaders. When one looks at the reality of public administration in the Philippines, one finds the legally prescribed line of authority within the departments or agencies overlaid by complex networks of dyadic alliances and patron-client relationships, many having their upper termini not within a department itself but with influential politicians outside them, a situation that can seriously undermine the ability of responsible heads of the departments to control their subordinates and to carry out efficiently the duties of their departments. Similarly, the nation's system of justice, which calls for the rigid and impersonal enforcement of the law, too often is undermined by the demands for favoritism and leniency emanating from friends and allies of both the accused and the agents of the law, which the latter may find extremely hard to resist.

Few political systems remain unchanged over long stretches of time, and rapid structural change is particularly characteristic of former colonies as they seek an adjustment between their foreign-imposed constitutions and their native ways of organization. It seems reasonable to suppose that the mixture of group and dyadic structure is one of the changeable features of the political systems of these former colonies. But a change in the mixture need not be in the same direction everywhere. In many of the new states of Africa there seems to be a shift from group-structured politics based upon loyalty to lineage, clan, or tribe to a more flexible dyadic pattern of political organization founded upon essentially personal loyalties to new leaders which cut across the traditional divisions of these segmentary societies. In the Philippines the shift, though not exclusively unidirectional, seems preponderantly and in the long run to be in the opposite direction. Though in certain spheres, notably in that of public administration, the erosion of the American-imposed civil service system since independence has led to a proliferation of dyadic structure in this sphere, the increasing number and effectiveness of organized interest groups suggests that pressure group politics will gradually replace a politics of personal connections. This development could force each political party to respond to the irreconcilable categorical demands of opposing interest groups by establishing more or less regular alliances with certain of these groups and leaving the other groups to the other party. But that this will produce a system of markedly contrasting parties each appealing to a different social class, or that

this will happen very soon, is rather unlikely. For such a change would require an almost total transformation of the structural basis of the existing parties.

PATRON-CLIENT RELATIONS:
Concepts and Terms
ANTHONY HALL

DEFINITION

THE TERM 'PATRON' is derived from the Spanish *patrón*, meaning a person of power, status, authority and influence. It may signify an employer, a ceremonial sponsor or even a protecting saint, but is only relevant in relation to a less powerful person or 'client' whom he can help or protect (Foster, 1963). The patron grants favours in return for goods, loyalty, political allegiance and other services from his dependent clients. Such reciprocal relationships may be expressed in terms of formal contracts with institutionalised rights and obligations for each party, as amongst certain East African tribes (Mair, 1961), to the less formal, more flexible relationships found in Mediterranean areas and in Latin America. In general, the relationship between individual patron and his client is biased against the latter who is, by definition, economically and politically far weaker, although the patron may be dependent on the collective support of his various clients in critical situations such as in promoting electoral fraud or in disputes with neighbouring landowners.

ORIGINS

Although patron-client relations can be traced far back in history, it was only with the growth of feudalism in Western Europe and Japan that relationships of personal protection and subordination between lord and peasant came to form a basis for social, economic and political organization (Bloch, 1961). Under feudalism ties of patron-clientage formed a basic part of the system of land tenure and agricultural production, and they persisted in rural areas such as the Iberian Peninsula and Southern Italy until long after the decay of 'pure' feudalism. The usefulness of the system for maintaining a cheap and sub-

servient labour force was recognized by the Spanish and Portuguese colonizers who set out to exploit the resources of Latin America and Southeast Asia. Thus, the encouragement of patron-clientage or 'feudalistic' relations on estates and plantations reduced costs of production in what was essentially capitalistic enterprise linked to the world mercantilist system (Stavenhagen, 1968).

CHARACTERISTICS

Patron-client relations have developed in rural areas where land ownership is heavily concentrated in the hands of a relatively small and powerful group able to monopolize wealth, political power, education and the means of communication with the world external to the rural community. Communities in which landholdings are fairly evenly distributed tend to develop very few linkages of patron-clientage but are characterised, rather, by instrumental and reciprocal exchange relationships amongst equals, or what have been called 'colleague contracts' (Foster, 1961). Both types originate in situations of economic hardship and insecurity, to offer protection which neither the State nor the family can provide. Patron-clientage usually persists when rural communities are isolated by poor communications and avenues of upward social mobility for peasants are non-existent within the rigid class structure based on land ownership, as for example in pre-Unification Italy (Silverman, 1967), in Andean and Mexican rural communities (Foster, 1963) or in the sugar, cocoa and coffee plantations of Brazil. Whether share-cropping or a system of wage payments is in operation, the peasant is forced into debt with the landowner in order to alleviate severe economic hardship. In areas of highly concentrated rural population where landowners hold a monopsony over the labour market, such as the sugar producing region of Northeast Brazil, wage rates are forced down to well below the legal minimum by employers who are able to break the law with little fear of prosecution. With no effective union movement to push up earnings, poor wages thus reinforce debt dependency and perpetuate the need for a system of patronage which ensures servile obedience from workers in exchange for favours and loans (Hutchinson, 1957 and Hall, 1970).

In Mediterranean countries and in Latin America the spread of popular Catholicism has helped to reinforce patron-clientage by preaching the natural helplessness of mankind and the need for protectors and benefactors, both human and divine. God, Jesus Christ, the Virgin Mary and the many 'patron saints' are seen as givers of favours and protection against daily uncertainties and crises, to whom gifts, prayers and penances are offered in return (Foster, 1963 and Boissevain, 1966).

TYPES OF PATRON-CLIENTAGE

The rather diffuse nature of patron-client relations makes them difficult to categorize, but it does seem possible to draw a broad distinction between those based on overt acceptance of traditional values by the subordinate (patrimonial) and those based increasingly on more obvious forms of repression by the powerful because their legitimacy is slowly decreasing (repressive). (i) *Patrimonial*: Northeast Brazil provides one of the best examples of the closed, patrimonial system where the crude physical coercion, typical of North American slave plantations for example, was moderated during the period of slavery by a brand of paternalism which has continued to play an important role in labour relations from the colonial period to the present day. This paternalism was brought to Brazil by the Portuguese and was a function of the extended family, in which the head of the household was responsible for the welfare of all those under his authority including his family, slaves and free workers (Freyre, 1956 and Hutchinson, 1966). In a situation of weak central government and self-contained, isolated rural plantation communities, this type of patron-clientage was thus a solution for the weak and unprotected who could shelter under the wing of a powerful patron, and for the strong who could, in this way, gain economic support and political followings. Essentially, it was under slavery, and still is today, based to a large extent on general accept-

ance by the rural mass of the prevailing socio-economic system and value structure which allowed them to be exploited; as long as the system of patronage provided them with a living they returned their loyalty to the master. (ii) *Repressive*: Cruder forms of repression seem, however, to be playing an increasingly important part in landowners' attempts to resist erosion of the traditional rural class structure and value system, in the face of cultural, political and market pressures. In Northeast Brazil studies have revealed how rural patrons (plantation and sugar refinery owners) have been forced to resort to far more overt, cruder forms of social control. Threats, violence and even murder were common in the early 1960s as landowners attempted to stem protest by rural workers at the inadequacy of the system of production and patronage in meeting subsistence needs. The formerly unquestioned respect of worker towards patron typical of the colonial era when patrimonialism flourished has, in many instances, been changed into resentful and begrudging obedience by the pressure of economic vicissitudes and the beginnings of social change. In Southeast Asia comparable evidence suggests that factors such as monopoly of land by a new class of landowners combined with the exposure of peasants to the volatile pressures of commercialized agriculture, have destroyed the legitimacy traditionally enjoyed by rural patrons, leading to a sense of exploitation and causing agrarian unrest (Scott and Kerkvliet, 1973).

Whether such unrest is viewed in terms of Marxist class conflict or simply as momentary 'followings' of opportunistic, paternalistic leaders (Galjart, 1964), the important fact is the inherently *coercive* nature of patron-clientage. Coercion here does not refer solely to physical force, but, more importantly, to less obvious factors which trap the weak and poor in a vicious circle of poverty that allows them no alternative means of earning a living, and which perpetuates the values which legitimize the power structure. Supports of the system such as the provision of employment and the means of subsistence, plus limited communication with the outside world, tended to isolate the rural structure from social change. When these supports become weakened fundamental relationships such as those of patron-clientage are also affected, thus revealing in the increasingly repressive measures adopted by rural patrons (debt dependency, credit systems, threats, etc.) to counteract the effects of these pressures, the fundamentally coercive nature of patron-client relations. Much analysis of patron-client relations